Foundations of National Power

Also by Harold and Margaret Sprout:

THE RISE OF AMERICAN NAVAL POWER, 1776-1918

TOWARD A NEW ORDER OF SEA POWER: AMERICAN NAVAL POLICY AND THE WORLD SCENE, 1918-1922

Foundations of National Power

Readings on World Politics and American Security

Edited with Introductions and Other Original Text by

Harold & Margaret Sprout

Published by Princeton University Press

Princeton, New Jersey, 1945

Sales Agent

D. VAN NOSTRAND COMPANY, Inc.
250 Fourth Avenue, New York

COPYRIGHT, 1945, BY PRINCETON UNIVERSITY PRESS
MANUFACTURED IN THE UNITED STATES OF AMERICA

Contents

INTRODUCTION	vi
PART I: BASES OF INTERNATIONAL POLITICS	1
1. The Ways of International Politics	3
2. Why Some Nations Are Strong and Others Weak	28
3. The World Stage of International Politics	63
4. The Pattern of World Politics	81
PART II: THE EUROPEAN REALM OF THE GREAT POWERS	121
5. The European Realm	122
6. Great Britain	148
7. France	211
8. Mediterranean and Middle East	264
9. Germany	311
10. Eastern and Southeastern Europe	373
11. The Soviet Union	384
PART III: THE AFRO-ASIAN REALM OF RIVAL IMPERIALISMS	457
12. The Afro-Asian Realm	458
13. Japan	495
14. China: Past, Present, and Future	546
PART IV: THE AMERICAN REALM BETWEEN EUROPE AND ASIA	603
15. The American Realm	604
16. The United States	642
PART V: FOUNDATIONS OF PEACE AND A NEW WORLD ORDER	691
17. The Terms of Peace	692
18. Security for the United States: How Can We Achieve It?	731
INDEX	769

Introduction

THE SECOND WORLD WAR has altered profoundly the relations of the United States with other nations. Venerable foreign policies—such as neutrality toward European wars and avoidance of military alliances with foreign powers—require fresh appraisal in the light of changing conditions. We may court disasters more terrible than those which have befallen Germany and Japan if, as in 1919, we turn our backs on the Old World and try to go about our business as if the war had never occurred.

This is so in part because of the revolutionary character of developments in science and technology. We now have bombing planes capable of carrying several tons of high explosive or incendiary missiles to targets 1,500 miles or more from their base of operations. We are told that robot rocket bombs hurtling down from the stratosphere are but grim harbingers of more deadly weapons "just around the corner." A world-renowned physicist is reported to have said recently: "It is as if we had uncorked a bottle from which some violent genie has escaped; we cannot get it back into the bottle again."

Fortunately for us, the Second World War is drawing to a close before the new weapons can be turned against the United States, as they probably would have been had the war continued, and as they almost certainly would be in any future war. We thus have a chance—our last chance in the opinion of qualified observers—to evolve new national policies to shield us from such a fate. The urgency of this task cannot be exaggerated. It provides a compelling incentive for re-inventory and appraisal of the changing world situation in which we find ourselves as a result of the shattering events of the Second World War.

It is now generally accepted that progress toward a more durable world order is possible only within the framework of the existing multi-state system, usually called the family or society of nations. Mobilization for war and the waging of war have everywhere tightened the hold of the state on the individual. The compelling necessity for team-work and the sacrifices of war have simultaneously strengthened the citizen's loyalty to his own country. For better or for worse, the great struggle seems to have pushed far into the background any possibility of creating a super-national world-state, at least in our time. The Dumbarton Oaks and San Francisco conferences have been directed to the task of framing a charter for an international security organization, not a federal union of the victorious nations.

While the basic principles of the multi-state system have survived more or less intact, the war has wrought profound changes in the structure of the society of nations. The global struggle has wrecked some nations, weakened others, strengthened a few, and altered the relations of each and all—our own included. Any random sampling of events emphasizes the sweeping changes that have taken place and are still taking place in the political pattern of our world.

One has only to think of the destruction of the Nazi state which as recently as 1942 held sway from the Atlantic to the Volga. Or the narrow margin by which Great Britain and the whole Allied cause escaped irreparable disaster after the fall of France in 1940. Or the phenomenal rise of Soviet prestige and influence, resulting from the epic defense and victories of the Red Army. Or the tragic change that has come over the fortunes of France, only a generation ago the leading military power in Europe. Or the total break-up of the old European order—economic and political. Or the comparable break-up in the Far East in consequence of the sensational advance and equally sensational defeats of Japan.

The first step—for the ordinary citizen as for the statesman, staff officer, or foreign-office official—is to achieve a clear and realistic view of the current world situation, and of the major trends in sight. We want answers to such questions as: How has the war altered the international position of Great Britain and the British outlook on the world? Can France recover her former standing and influence among the nations? Can the German people play a constructive role in a new world order or must they be subjected indefinitely to international controls? What changes are taking place in eastern and southeastern Europe, in the Mediterranean, and in the Near and Middle East? Will China be rent by civil war or will the Chinese emerge from their long struggle with Japan politically united and prepared to play a large role in world affairs? Can a disarmed and demilitarized Japan still be a menace to security in the Pacific? How strong is the Soviet Union? What do the Russians want—in Europe, in the Middle East, in the Far East? Do Soviet aims conflict seriously with our own? What is the measure of American strength? How has the war affected our national position in the world? Why should Americans concern themselves with the strength, the aims, and the policies of Great Britain, France, the Soviet Union, China, or other nations?

No single person, no single field of knowledge, has the answers to all these and many similar questions which are the active concern of us all. In most instances no conclusive answer is possible. But events will not wait. Our statesmen and their advisers cannot postpone decisions, and they need the support of an aroused and educated public opinion.

It is hoped that *Foundations of National Power* will be of some service in helping Americans to frame a strategy of peace that meets the requirements of national security and fits the facts of the developing world situation. The book offers no panaceas, no cut-and-dried solutions. It has no doctrine other than the conviction of the editors that broad and comprehensive knowledge of the strength, the aims, and the policies of nations is basic to understanding the problem of security in a dynamic world.

The contents of the book are drawn from many sources representing many specialized fields of knowledge. A roster of the authorities quoted would include eminent statesmen, political scientists, historians, economists, demographers, geologists, geographers, physical scientists, engineers, journalists, military experts, and other specialists. Each of these specialties can make its own contribution to an understanding and to the solution of the international problems of our time. The function of the editors has been to fit these specialties together into a pattern or mosaic that is both readily comprehensible and faithful to the realities of our world and to the trends of our age.

The readings selected are not the only ones that could have been chosen. Every topic could be enriched by the inclusion of additional items. Only the inexorable limitation of space has prevented a broader and richer treatment of every country and every subject. At the same time, the editors have tried to make their choices as representative as possible of the best thought on the subjects and areas covered.

The general plan of the book is simple. It is divided into five parts or sections. Part I deals with certain fundamental conditions and factors which have shaped the course of international relations through the centuries. Parts II, III, and IV present the pattern of international rela-

INTRODUCTION

tions and the major political forces at work in each of three great geographical regions or realms. Part V deals with two specific problems of the day—the terms of peace for the enemy states and the bases of a workable international organization to keep the peace and provide security, and a sense of security, for all nations.

The order of treatment, indeed the whole book, is the product of experience gained with a course on world affairs developed in the Navy's college training program. This course was introduced at the personal initiative of the Honorable James Forrestal, Secretary of the Navy. It was given experimentally for several terms in the Navy V-12 Program at six universities, and is now a regular feature of the curriculum of the Naval Reserve Officer Training Program.

During the experimental period the course was given at the University of California at Berkeley by Professor Robert J. Kerner; at the University of North Carolina by Professor Samuel T. Emory; at Northwestern University by Mr. William A. Bryan; at the University of Pennsylvania by Professor Robert Strausz-Hupé; at Princeton University by Professor Harold Sprout, Professor John Schroth, and Dr. William Fletcher; and at Yale University by Professor Arnold Wolfers. Under the general editorship of Harold Sprout, but with active assistance and advice from all the men associated with the course, a body of readings was prepared and revised from term to term. These materials constituted the foundation upon which the editors have built the present volume.

Certain strategical ideas incorporated in the chapter introductions and other pieces of original text by the editors were previously presented in the texts originally prepared by Harold Sprout for: (1) *A War Atlas for Americans*. Published in 1944 by Simon & Schuster, Inc., New York, for the Council on Books in Wartime; and (2) Part II of *Geographical Foundations of National Power*. Army Service Forces Manual, M-103. Government Printing Office, Washington, 1944.

Many besides those previously named have contributed generously. Professor Edward Mead Earle of the Institute for Advanced Study at Princeton has been actively associated with the enterprise from the beginning. Both he and Professor Wolfers of Yale, read and criticized the chapter introductions and other pieces of original text prepared by the editors. In one form or another we have benefited from the advice and criticism of many others, including Dr. Isaiah Bowman, President of the Johns Hopkins University; Professor Grayson Kirk of Columbia University; Professor David Rowe of Yale University, and Professors Frank Notestein and Taylor Thom of Princeton. Mr. Datus Smith, director of the Princeton University Press, has been not only an efficient publisher but also a helpful and constructive counselor at every stage of the work.

Acknowledgment for permission to use copyrighted materials is made in each instance at the place in the book where the item appears. A more general word of appreciation, however, is due at this point. Without the cooperation of the many copyright owners represented in this volume, the undertaking could not possibly have been completed.

Finally, a word of appreciation to the Secretary of the Navy and to the officers of the Training Activity of the Bureau of Naval Personnel. They have steadfastly supported the educators to whom they entrusted the development of this experiment. Their enthusiasm and encouragement has been a big factor in bringing this volume to completion.

While the editors have thus received help and advice from many sources, we alone are responsible for the final selection of readings and for the views expressed in the chapter introductions and other pieces of original text which appear from place to place throughout the book.

Princeton, September 1, 1945　　　　　　　　　　　　　　　　H. S.
　　　　　　　　　　　　　　　　　　　　　　　　　　　　　　M. S.

Part I

Bases of International Politics

Chapter 1
The Ways of International Politics

THE ways of international politics in our time are the ways of the multi-state system. The day may come when most or all of mankind lives under one rule. A single nation, for example, might conquer all the rest and extend its sway over the globe, as Hitler's Germany aspired to do. Or the different peoples of the earth might unite more or less voluntarily into a super-national world federation. Neither eventuality is in prospect today. The war has altered considerably the structure of the multi-state system. Some nations face utter ruin. Many have been frightfully devastated. A few have grown relatively much stronger. But the multi-state system itself, with its emphasis upon national sovereignty, has survived virtually intact.

In certain respects, indeed, the war has even strengthened the system. In many countries the struggle for survival has measurably tightened the moral as well as the physical hold of the state on the individual. For most men the highest loyalty is more than ever loyalty to country. There is little disposition anywhere to put all one's eggs in the basket of unproved internationalism. Such facts have not escaped the attention of practical statesmen. For them as for most of their constituents, the existing multi-state system still constitutes the framework of international politics, into which must be fitted new institutions and new modes of action for safeguarding peace in the future.

One salient feature of the multi-state system is the all but universal disparity between legal rights and status on the one hand, and actual power, influence, and responsibility on the other. As everyone knows, mankind is divided into separate political communities, differing greatly in composition, structure, strength, and external relations. Those occupying a legal status of recognized independence are variously called nations, states, or powers. The strongest of these are called Great Powers. Communities whose recognized status is something less than full sovereignty are called dominions, protectorates, or colonies, depending upon the degree to which they are legally subject to external authority. Such designations, however, often have little practical significance.

There may be much or little correlation between legal status and actual strength and influence. The voice of Canada, a member of the British Commonwealth and legally subject to the British Crown, carries far more weight in international councils than does, for example, the voice of Liberia, Ethiopia, or many another nominally sovereign but actually weak or backward state.

In the absence of a super-national world government to serve as arbiter of human relations which reach beyond the confines of one community, the aims and policies of the various members of the society of nations, backed up by their own force and persuasion, set the pattern of international politics. This has been so for several centuries. It is so today; and there is little evidence that it will not continue to be so for a considerable time to come.

For this reason, the role of national power is basic to any discussion of international politics. That is not to say that power is the only factor, or that power is wholly military. The techniques of exerting influence over one's neighbors are many and varied. They include not only the crude display or use of armed force, but also economic inducements, ideological appeals, and numerous other modes of persuasion. A nation's way of life, its ideals, its philanthropies, its intellectual achievements, its wealth and economic productivity, the qualities of its statecraft, the spirit of its culture, and many other factors all have a bearing upon its relations with other nations and upon its place in the world. But non-military sources of influence can be enormously strengthened or gravely weakened by the presence or absence of military power. The possibility of violence, however remote, is a factor in every international equation, just as it is in most political situations within a single country. The very expression "Great Power," used to designate the strongest nations, is an admission of the widespread recognition that influence tends to become a function of power in the practice of diplomacy as well as in the waging of war.

No one will deny that international relations under our multi-state system fall far short of the ideal of a world state and a universal brotherhood of man. No equilibrium or balance of power among sovereign states of unequal and ever-changing strength, it must be admitted, can hope to have the comparative stability of a national government wielding supreme power over, and commanding the allegiance of, its constituents. There is always danger that those nations which possess superior power will abuse it. No wholly effective means has yet been found to curb nations seeking to advance their aims by resort to violence.

To admit the imperfections of our world, while doubting the possibility of achieving utopia in one fell swoop, is not (as is so often charged) a counsel of defeatism and despair. There is real hope for a better world, provided the custodians of greatest power can carry over into the peace the united front forged in the heat of battle, and provided further that they will accept the moral restraints as well as the positive responsibilities necessary to win the confidence of the smaller or weaker countries. Later on we shall give some attention to the problem of rebuilding a more durable world order within the framework of the multi-state system. Discussion of that problem, however, should be grounded upon a clear understanding of the elements and practical workings of the multi-state system. A first step in this direction is to explore the nature and role of power, and that is the common focus of the readings selected for this chapter on the "ways of international politics."

INTERNATIONAL RELATIONS UNDER THE MULTI-STATE SYSTEM

By Brooks Emeny

From *Mainsprings of World Politics*, by Brooks Emeny. Headline Series, No. 42. Copyright 1942 by Foreign Policy Association, New York; reproduced by permission. Dr. Emeny is author of *The Strategy of Raw Materials;* and co-author, with the late Frank Simonds, of *The Great Powers in World Politics*.

THE history of the modern world has been marked by four great peace settlements: Westphalia, 1648, which brought to a close the Thirty Years War; Utrecht, 1713, which ended the War of the Spanish Succession; Vienna, 1815, which followed the defeat of Napoleon; and Versailles, 1919, which terminated World War I.

Of these four settlements the Peace of Westphalia was historically the most significant in several respects. In the first place, it brought to a close a long succession of bloody religious conflicts and settled the principle that Europe could remain half Catholic and half Protestant. But even more important, it established the idea of the nation as a sovereign independent unit, and defined the modern state system.

Europe at that time marked the limits of western civilization, except for certain colonial areas. The other regions of the earth were either unexplored or comprised the peoples of Oriental and Mohammedan culture, to whom the concept of the sovereign independent state was completely foreign.

Since that time the world has become

universally organized along the lines of the European state system. As western civilization has spread and embraced the entire surface of the earth, all peoples have accepted the idea of the territorially defined sovereign independent state. Under this system no nation owes allegiance to a higher sovereign authority nor brooks any interference with its internal or external affairs, unless by its own choice or through forced submission to the superior power of another state or coalition.

It is in these respects that the peace settlements of Utrecht, Vienna and Versailles are historically of great interest. Each marked the reconstruction of the state system following a tremendous upheaval which arose from the attempt of a single nation or coalition to destroy that system by conquest. Thus the idea of Louis XIV and of Napoleon that France should dominate the Continent and thereby upset "the balance of power" between the nations of Europe, was as intolerable to British sovereign interests as to the other nations, victims of French conquests. The similar ambitions of Germany under Wilhelm II and Hitler have been productive of identical reactions, though on a tremendous world-wide scale.

Wars have existed from earliest times between groups of mankind. They are not, therefore, peculiar to the nation-state system. In fact the western world has known but two periods of relative peace. The first of these periods existed during the single sovereignty of the Roman Empire. . . . The second period prevailed during the medieval Papacy, under whose temporal powers some moderating influence over the conflicting ambitions of ruling princes was exercised. In neither instance, however, did the sovereign independent state, as we understand it, exist.

With the development of the nation-state system, the nature of wars has varied from century to century. Between the Peace of Westphalia and the French Revolution, conflicts between nations were primarily dynastic struggles. The rivalry of the sovereign princes for possession of larger territories and colonial holdings typified this period. But since Europe was composed of sovereign independent states, the attempt of any one or combination of them to gain sufficient power to threaten the security of the others, served to upset the existing equilibrium. Thus the balance-of-power system became the natural by-product of the nation-state system. The wars of Louis XIV, of Napoleon, of Kaiser Wilhelm II and of Nazi Germany have each in turn challenged that system with identical reactions on the part of nations whose security was thereby threatened.

But if the wars of the seventeenth and eighteenth centuries were largely dynastic, those of the nineteenth and twentieth have become primarily nationalistic. It was the French Revolution that introduced a new phase in the conflict of states by giving rise in Europe and the rest of the world to a strong spirit of nationalism. During most of the nineteenth century this generally took the form of irredentist or ethnic struggles, motivated by the desire of groups of people with like background and customs, or speaking the same language, to unite under a single sovereignty. The unification of Italy, through the efforts of Mazzini and Garibaldi, and of Germany under Bismarck, were both an expression of this desire and resulted in the creation of two Great Powers.

World War I gave impetus to another force with explosive potentialities, i.e. economic nationalism. This came as a natural result of the ever-tightening squeeze of competition between nations unequal one to another, and territorially limited in many cases both as to the means of livelihood and of power.

But while wars have become more extended and devastating, there have likewise been considerable developments with respect to the peaceful settlement of disputes and the techniques of international organization. Since the writings of Grotius some three hundred years ago there has evolved a large body of public and international law. The conduct of nations among themselves has become more regularized in certain respects through universally accepted treaty engagements. But, unlike domestic law, this vast body of rules of conduct has not received the necessary sanction of police power. Its only sanction has been the voluntary acceptance and good will of the sovereign states themselves.

Similarly in the realm of international government, a signal growth in administrative technique and arbitration has taken place. The nineteenth and early twentieth centuries witnessed frequent convenings of important world assemblies, devoted not only to peace arrangements following war but likewise to the adjustment of causes of conflict.

This long-established practice of international conference received recognition of permanent need under the Covenant of the League of Nations after 1919. All elements of national government—legislative, executive, administrative and judicial—were to be discovered in the League in the form of the Assembly, the Council, the Secretariat and the World Court. But adequate authority for these bodies was lacking in case of serious disagreement between the nations party to the Covenant, except for a degree of moral force.

Despite the unprecedented expansion of machinery for preserving peace which has taken place during the twentieth century, wars have increased rather than decreased in extent and devastation. For no nation, and particularly no Great Power, has been willing to accede to the jurisdiction of the League, or to any other international body, in matters affecting vital national interests. And modern technology has placed armaments in the hands of nations with a destructive power beyond anything known to human history.

Since states have remained faithful to the doctrine of national sovereignty they have refused to conform their policies in essential matters to the dictates of public international interest. Similarly, in resisting the sanction of international law, the creation of an international police force, and the exercise of super-state authority, they have continued to interpret attempts at regional or world jurisdiction in their own affairs as a direct challenge to their sovereign rights and interests.

Under these conditions the pledge of the nations, signatories to the Kellogg Pact in 1928, to "renounce war as an instrument of national policy" was nothing more than an absurdity. No nation renounced thereby its right to proceed according to its own interpretation of its national interests. Nor did the signatories pledge the use of their armed forces either unilaterally or collectively to punish violators of the Pact.

Since states have been unwilling to subject their vital national interests to the restraints of international authority, it has followed naturally that they have sought to clothe their policies with force. Armaments, in fact, have always been the most familiar prerogative of sovereignty. But in the modern Age of Industrialism, only those nations which possessed the natural resources for the establishment of heavy industries could create the sinews of power necessary to maintain their individual sovereign rights against all challenging authority. Thus a premium has been placed upon the possession or availability of the industrial raw materials and agricultural resources of the world, since a nation's ability to defend its rights depends upon its own strength in relation to its neighbors'.

Fundamentally, then, the central dilemma of international relations derives from the fact that the absence of superstate authority imposes upon each country ultimate dependence upon its own resources in the defense of its security. While ordinarily the ends of national policy will be achieved by peaceful means, once the gathering forces of recrimination, fear and greed become overwhelming, there remains no arbitrament but that of force.

POLITICS: DOMESTIC AND INTERNATIONAL

By Nicholas J. Spykman

From chap. 1 of *America's Strategy in World Politics*, by N. J. Spykman. Copyright 1942 by Harcourt, Brace & Co., New York; reproduced by permission. The late Dr. Spykman was Sterling professor of international relations at Yale University and formerly director of the Yale Institute of International Studies, which sponsored the publication of the book quoted.

Human beings have invented a great variety of techniques designed to win friends and influence people. These different methods can be classified under four broad headings: persuasion, purchase, barter, and coercion, although this does not mean that every endeavor to make others do our bidding can be neatly pigeonholed into one of these categories. On the contrary it will be found that most successful policies are a judicious mixture of all four. The relative amount of each of the ingredients differs from case to case, from individual to individual, from community to community, and it is the community which defines what is acceptable and what is condemned. Where freedom and individual dignity are cherished, persuasion is more acceptable than coercion and the use of the latter is usually restricted as between individuals. The state alone, not the citizen, can legally coerce by means of the night stick, tear gas bomb, and sub-machine gun.

From an ethical point of view power can be considered only as a means to an end. It is, therefore, important that the use which is made of it should be constantly subjected to moral judgments, but to hope for a world that will operate without coercion and to decry man's desire to obtain power is an attempt to escape from reality into a world of dreams. Man creates society through cooperation, accommodation, and conflict, and all three are essential and integral parts of social life. He works together with others for common ends and creates the instruments of government for that very purpose. He accommodates himself to his fellows by shaping his conduct in conformity to common values and by accepting the normative pressure of custom and the rules of law. But he also accepts conflict for personal gain or impersonal ideal. Strife is one of the basic aspects of life and, as such, an element of all relations between individuals, groups, and states. A world without struggle would be a world in which life had ceased to exist. An orderly world is not a world in which there is no conflict, but one in which strife and struggle are led into political and legal channels away from the clash of arms; are transferred from the battlefield to the council chamber and the courtroom.

For groups as for individuals there are two forms of approach to desired objectives in case of opposition and conflict, direct action and "political action." The first means that the group acts directly upon the individuals whose cooperation is necessary to achieve the desired result. The second means that the group tries to achieve success through the use of the coercive power of the state. A great deal of modern economic life involves group struggle in the form of direct action: sharecroppers against landowners, farmers against milk distributors, industrial unions against trade unions, labor unions against employers, and industrial corporations among themselves. Many a western railroad and pipeline owes its present right-of-way not to a court decision but to the successful outcome of a bloody battle at strategic points between the forces of opposing companies.

An industrial dispute may start with a negotiation between an employer and a labor union. If negotiation fails, the parties may attempt mediation or accept arbitration. They may, on the other hand, refuse the peaceful solution and declare war in the form of a strike or a lockout. In that case the opponents will have tried all the possible methods of influencing each other's behavior, including persuasion, purchase, barter, and coercion. The strength of the group will obviously influence its choice of method, but it would be a mistake to assume that power is important only in the case of coercion. On the contrary, the fact that the labor union is powerful may make a test of strength unnecessary and successful negotiation that much easier.

The union and every other group is, therefore, forced to devote itself not merely to the pursuit of its objectives but also to the constant improvement of its strength. Any association, however simple its purpose, which depends for the realization of its objectives on the actions of other men or groups becomes involved in the struggle for power and must make not only self-preservation but also improvement of its power position a primary objective of both internal and external policy.

Labor unions, like all groups operating within the state, have an alternative method to their objective. If the direct approach is too difficult, they can try an indirect route through the legislature and attempt to obtain the use of the law-making power of the state. It is sometimes possible to achieve rewards for labor through legislative definitions of minimum standards which cannot possibly be obtained by direct action on employers. The Woman's Christian Temperance Union may act directly through persuasion and the picketing of saloons, or it can act indirectly through the Eighteenth Amendment. It is to this technique in the national sphere that the term "political activity" is applied, the struggle for control of the government for the purpose of serving individual or group interest.

To the extent that private groups intend to work through government agencies they must add to their broad power objective the specific task of increasing political strength. For one particular kind of group, the political party, political power is the main object and *raison d'être*. It exists for the purpose of influencing public policy, and it can achieve its aim only by winning elections in competition with other political parties. The struggle for power is here so near the surface that it is easily visible, and everybody is, therefore, willing to agree that for the political party the improvement of its relative power position must be a constant endeavor. When the war chest is depleted more quickly than filled, when loyalty weakens, when organization and discipline deteriorate, the party will be on its way out, to be replaced by one of its competitors.

There are a great many instances when political action in the form of indirect pressure through the legislature is not possible. The group may be without political power because sex or property qualifications have disfranchised its members. The issue may be one in which the government cannot act because of constitutional restrictions, budget limitation, or lack of administrative agencies. In that case the group will have to choose between direct action and political activity of a special kind aimed at constitutional amendments, the extension of government power, changes in the distribution of authority, and the creation of new agencies. Political activity is then directed not at the use of the existing instruments of government but at their modification and the creation of new ones.

Groups which must operate within the power organization called the state must conduct their external policy within the limits of the permissible methods. In theory the state reserves to itself the legal monopoly of physical force, and only those forms of coercion which are free from physical violence are permitted. There are obviously wide differences in the ability or willingness of different states to enforce this principle and great variations in the same state at different times, running all the way from "perfect order" to "complete anarchy." . . .

In international society, as in other social groupings, there are observable the three basic processes of cooperation, accommodation, and opposition. Not only individuals and groups but also states maintain the three types of social relations. They have cooperated for common ends and created the instruments of international administration in the fields of communication and transportation without which modern international intercourse would be impossible. They have, through acceptance of common values, developed modes of accommodation by building out of custom and precedent a body of rules called international law. States have often obeyed these rules voluntarily and have been willing to adopt peaceful procedures for the settlement of disputes. But they have also accepted conflict and used coercion including war for the achievement of their national objectives.

The situation which characterizes the relations of groups within a state only in periods of crisis and breakdown of central authority is normal for the relations of states within the international society. It is the so-called sovereign independence of states, the absence of higher authority, and the freedom from external restraints that give to interstate relations their peculiar character of anarchy.

This historical state system consisting of sovereign independent units has been subject to two processes, conquest and confederation, which, if successful, might have changed its basic character. But neither process could ever achieve more than partial success. There have been strong and vigorous states which conquered their neighbors and enslaved the weak, but not even the gigantic empires of antiquity managed to absorb the states beyond their regional control and integrate them into simple hegemonic systems. Equally unsuccessful has been the process of the delegation of power from below. There have been confederations in all historical periods, but they were always partial and limited, partial in the sense that they included only a small number of states and limited in the sense that the interstate organizations were formed for specific and usually administrative purposes. Illustrations of international cooperation and limited confederation are many, but there has never been a case of the actual transfer of military power and political authority from individual states to the organs of an international community.

The essential difference between the international community and the national community as conditioning environments for group behavior is, therefore, the absence in the former of a governmental organization capable of preserving order and enforcing law. The international community has never, in fact, guaranteed the member states either life, liberty, property, or the pursuit of happiness, whatever the paper provisions of international conventions may have stipulated. Each individual state has continued to depend for its very existence, as much as for the enjoyment of its rights and the protection of its interests, primarily on its own strength or that of its protectors.

Self-preservation used in connection with states has a special meaning. Because territory is an inherent part of a state, self-preservation means defending its control over territory; and, because independence is of the essence of the state, self-preservation also means fighting for independent status. This explains why the basic objective of the foreign policy of all states is the preservation of territorial integrity and political independence.

In addition to the primary task of survival, the foreign policy of states is directed at a great many specific objectives which can be classified in different ways. They are geographic, demographic, racial, ethnic, economic, social, and ideological in nature and include such items as: the acquisition of naval bases, the limitation of immigration, the assimilation of minorities, the search for access to raw materials, markets, and investment opportunities, the protection of the social order against disruptive alien forces, the encouragement of cultural relations, and the restriction of the trade in dangerous drugs.

The same two methods which are used in the national sphere for promoting group interests are used in the international sphere for promoting state interests. States may use the direct method, acting immediately upon other states; they may use such international organizations as exist; or they may devote their foreign policy to the creation of new instruments. The relative importance of each of these methods is, however, very different from that which prevails in the national sphere. The character of international society today makes direct power over other states far more useful than ability to influence international organizations.

At the time of the founding of the League of Nations and during its early history when it was still expected that the new organization might develop into an important agency of international government, there were many struggles for control between the large and the small powers and competition between individual states for seats on the council and the important committees. It looked for a while as if the struggle for power on the battlefield might really be transformed into a struggle for power in the council room. But when it became clear that the council room was merely a place for deliberation and the League only a forum for debate, interest lagged. It was futile to try to control a government that had no power. The foreign ministers sent their assistant secretaries and finally even these stayed home. The edifice that was to house the parliament of nations became an expensive symbol of a forlorn hope.

Direct action from state to state has remained the normal and most prevalent form of approach. It represents the most characteristic expression of foreign policy. Absence of international government is responsible not only for the significance of direct action but for the fact that there is no community restraint on the methods used. In international society . . . the struggle for power is identical with the struggle for survival, and the improvement of the relative power position becomes the primary objective of the internal and the external policy of states. . . .

Because power is in the last instance the power to wage war, states have always devoted considerable effort to the building of military establishments. But the relative power of states depends not only on military forces but on many other factors—size of territory, nature of frontiers, size of population, absence or presence of raw materials, economic and technological development, financial strength, ethnic homogeneity, effective social integration, political stability, and national spirit. In the struggle for power these items become important secondary objectives. They have value in themselves, and they are means to power.

The power position of a state, however, depends not only on its own military strength but also on that of its potential enemies. This means that there is a second approach to power apart from the enlargement of one's own war equipment. Its purpose is to influence directly the power position of other states, to weaken some, to strengthen others. To achieve this aim, states are willing to use their military power not only for the protection of their own territory but also for the protection of the territory of others, not for any altruistic reasons but because the continued existence of the third state contributes to their own security.

. . . But willingness to support other states has not been motivated solely by a desire for the security of a frontier or a zone of special strategic significance, but also by a desire to stop the expansion of some great state which after further growth might become a menace. The policy is then directed at the prevention of hegemony, a power position which would permit the domination of all within its reach.

. . . Experience has shown that there is more safety in balanced power than in a declaration of good intention. To preserve the balance requires action not only against the neighbor that becomes too powerful but also against distant states. As a matter of fact, the best period for the application of this policy is before continued expansion makes the growing state a neighbor. . . .

It is obvious that a balance-of-power policy is in the first place a policy for the Great Powers. The small states, unless they can successfully combine together, can only be weights in a balance used by others. But although they are stakes rather than players, their interest in the outcome of the game is none the less great. A small state is a vacuum in a political high pressure area. It does not live because of its own strength but because nobody wants its territory or because its preservation as a buffer state or as a weight in the balance of power is of interest to a stronger nation. When the balance disappears, the small states usually disappear with it.

Since the Renaissance and the Reformation, the balance of power has been a favorite topic of speculation among the political philosophers of Europe. After Emperor and Pope had lost their function as keystones in the European political order, a search began for a new integrating principle. It was found in the "balance of power," which became the subject of learned discourses. . . . If all states were held in check, no state could win a war; and, if no state could win a war, then no state would start a war or threaten war. Equilibrium is balanced power, and balanced power is neutralized power. A society in political equilibrium is a society in which force is useless and in which men will, therefore, live happily by the reign of law and devote themselves to the arts and graces.

To the men of learning it seemed obvious that states ought to pursue a balance-of-power policy; that the law of nature and Christian ethics both demand such a policy. States ought to direct their diplomacy not merely at counterbalancing specific threats to themselves but at establishing a balanced system for the whole of the international society. They ought to pursue a balance-of-power policy not merely to preserve their own relative power position but to preserve peace.

Statesmen have always been eager to accept from the theologian and the philosopher the correct formulation of the ethical precepts that should guide foreign policy, and since the seventeenth century all power politics has, therefore, been presented not as a crude attempt to survive in a tough world but as a noble endeavor aimed at the establishment of political equilibrium and the preservation of order.

Formulated in those terms the success has not been overwhelming. We might search for an explanation in the fact that the process is not guaranteed and that not all statesmen are good technicians, but it is perhaps safer to explain the result on the theory that they were not really interested in achieving a balance. There are not many instances in history which show great and powerful states creating alliances and organizations to limit their own strength. States are always engaged in curbing the force of some other state. The truth of the matter is that states are interested only in a balance which is in their favor. Not an equilibrium, but a generous margin is their objective. There is no real security in being just as strong as a potential enemy; there is security only in being a little stronger. There is no possibility of action if one's strength is fully checked; there is a chance for a positive foreign policy only if there is a margin of force which can be freely used. Whatever the theory and the rationalization, the practical objective is the constant improvement of the state's own relative power position. The balance desired is the one which neutralizes other states, leaving the home state free to be the deciding force and the deciding voice.

It would seem that this objective does not require quite the accuracy in measuring which the search for a perfect equilibrium would require, but, even so, the task is full of difficulties. It is easy to balance mechanical forces because they can be measured, but there is no measuring stick for political power. Are two states balanced, is their power equal, is the relationship between the two sets of alliances in equilibrium? On that question there is usually profound disagreement. The relative power remains a purely subjective judgment. Each state always feels that the other one needs balancing. In so far as the power concerned is in the last instance a power to wage war, it might be assumed that the military men would know the answer, but theirs is an opinion equally subjective, even if a little more expert. The most learned generals have disagreed as often as the statesmen. The only objective test of relative strength is to fight the war and see who wins, but this is hardly a helpful guide to the state that wants to decide whether to fight or not.

The second difficulty lies in the fact that the elements contributing to strength are not static but dynamic; they do not stay put. A new economic development, a new raw material, a new weapon, a new martial spirit may produce the most profound inequality between states that only a few years before had been approximately equal. Besides, in a world of states of equal strength, what is there to prevent the combination of two of them against a third?

Another problem which sometimes appears is the discovery that the state selected to be the ally in the opposition to the growing power has already made a deal with the opponent, and the chance for a balance has been missed. Similar unfortunate results may flow from the fact that statesmen occasionally believe in the innocence of other statesmen. This permits some of them to achieve enormous expansion by the accretion of small additions of territory. The state of Lusitania announces that it has only one very limited aim, the incorporation of a little territory of the state of Mauritania after which the true balance will have been established, and it will never aspire to another square foot of land. The demand is so small, the request so modest that it is obviously not worth fighting for. It will, of course, be discovered afterwards that there is still no perfect balance, that there is still need for an additional piece of territory. This even smaller piece is likewise not worth fighting for. It lies perhaps in a region outside the immediate interest of the state which must decide how to act, and so its annexation goes unopposed. It is by this process of gradual conquest that most of the successful hegemonies have been established.

An actual balance-of-power policy operates along several lines, boundary-making, compensation, the creation of alliances, and varying degrees of intervention in wars, grading all the way from slight deviations from neutrality to full participation as an ally. Boundary-making is important at the end of a war, and historically the Great Powers have always demanded to be heard at the peace settlement even if they had not participated in the conflict. Under the theory of compensation, states have permitted other states to grow provided they themselves obtained an equal accretion of strength and prestige. It was under this principle of compensation and in the name of the balance of power that the Treaty of Westphalia parceled out the small German principalities among Austria, Bavaria, Brandenburg and Sweden; that Poland was divided four times; that Africa was carved up; and that plans were laid for the partition of China.

In addition to boundary-making and compensation, nations have used systems of alliances to check the growth of a dynamic power. The least expensive and, therefore, the most preferable method would be for a state to encourage an alliance between third parties strong enough to ward off the danger. But this is seldom possible, and the state must be prepared to make its own positive contribution and become part of the alliance. The alliance may stipulate merely a limited contribution in the form of a fixed sum of money, a specific number of ships, or a defined number of soldiers. There is, however, little protection in such limitation. If the survival and continued independence of the ally is really important for the state's own security, its assistance may have to go far beyond the original promises. It will, in fact, have to be increased to whatever is necessary to assure victory and security.

The purpose of the alliance, like the purpose of all power politics, is to achieve the necessary margin of safety in the field of action. But the margin of security for one is the margin of danger for the other and alliance must, therefore, be met by counter-alliance and armament by counter-armament in an eternal competitive struggle for power. Thus it has been in all periods of history. One state successfully conquers adjacent territory and makes each new conquest the steppingstone for further expansion, each accretion of power the means for further enlargement. Power tends to grow and diffuse through wider areas, and the states in the vicinity have the choice between collective defense and ultimate absorption.

The weak states of the Tigris-Euphrates Valley allied themselves against their stronger rivals and preserved their independence for centuries, until Hammurabi finally established the Babylonian Empire. A new and inconclusive struggle for power then emerged over a much wider area between the Egyptians, the Assyrians, the Hittites, and the Persians with the smaller states in the region being used as buffers and weights. The Greek city-states maintained a precarious balance by means of the Delian and Peloponnesian Leagues under the leadership of Athens and Sparta, but they failed to combine against the menace of Macedonia. Rome, the victorious, found no league to stem her vast expansion, and defeated her enemies one by one. Had they known how to combine, Carthage, Egypt, and Macedonia might have preserved their independence far longer and confined Rome within the boundaries of Europe.

Modern European history begins with the struggle for power among the Italian city-states which was later transferred to the national states over an ever-widening area eventually including the whole world. When the House of Hapsburg under Charles V attained such vast domains that it threatened to become a menace to other states, these states combined to check its ascendancy. Similar was the fate of the hegemonic aspirations of Spain under Philip II, France under Louis XIV and Napoleon, and Germany under Kaiser Wilhelm II. The fate of Germany's new bid for European domination depended on the outcome of the Second World War.

In this endless story of struggling states, there have been short periods in which an approximation to balanced power prevailed, not because anybody wanted it or tried to achieve it, but because two states or two sets of states were trying to upset it in different directions. Such a situation is inherently unstable because all parties are constantly attempting to destroy it, but while it lasts it brings mankind important benefits as the philosophers had promised. In an international society in which states are intent on preserving their independence, both against world conquest and against world government through federation, balanced power is the only approximation to order. . . .

Although it is quite possible to conceive of a great variety of forms of political organization for the international community, there are in reality only a few basic types of power distribution. International society might disappear as such and the individual states might become incorporated into a single world state, or the world might be ruled through the hegemony of one or two large empires. On the other hand, the international community might continue to operate through an unstable equilibrium of a number of large powers. . . .

Plans for far-reaching changes in the character of international society are an intellectual by-product of all great wars, but, when the fighting ceases, the actual peace structure usually represents a return to balanced power. . . .

ENDS AND MEANS IN INTERNATIONAL POLITICS

By Walter Lippmann

From chaps. 2 and 6 of *U.S. Foreign Policy, Shield of the Republic*, by Walter Lippmann. Copyright 1943 by Walter Lippmann; Little, Brown & Co. and Atlantic Monthly Press; reproduced by permission. The author is the well known American interpreter of world affairs.

A FOREIGN policy consists in bringing into balance, with a comfortable surplus of power in reserve, the nation's commitments and the nation's power. The constant preoccupation of the true statesman is to achieve and maintain this balance. Having determined the foreign commitments which are vitally necessary to his people, he will never rest until he has mustered the force to cover them. In assaying ideals, interests, and ambitions which are to be asserted abroad, his measure of their validity will be the force he can muster at home combined with the support he can find abroad among other nations which have similar ideals, interests, and ambitions.

For nations, as for families, the level may vary at which a solvent balance is struck. If its expenditures are safely within its assured means, a family is solvent when it is poor, or is well-to-do, or is rich. The same principle holds true of nations. The statesman of a strong country may balance its commitments at a high level or at a low. But whether he is conducting the affairs of Germany, which has had dynamic ambitions, or the affairs of Switzerland which seeks only to hold what it already has, or of the United States, he must still bring his ends and means into balance. If he does not, he will follow a course that leads to disaster. . . .

The fundamental subject of foreign policy is how a nation stands in relation to the principal military powers. For only the Great Powers can wage great wars. Only a Great Power can resist a Great Power. Only a Great Power can defeat a Great Power. And therefore the relationship of his nation with the other Great Powers is the paramount—not by any means the sole, but the paramount—concern of the maker of foreign policy. Unless this relationship is such that the combination against him is not stronger than the combination to which he belongs, his foreign policy is not solvent: his commitments exceed his means, and he is leading his people into grave trouble.

Therefore, no Great Power can be indifferent to any of the other Great Powers. It must take a position in regard to all of them. No Great Power can stand alone against all the others. For none can be great enough for that. If its object is to win a war it has chosen to wage, or not to lose a war imposed upon it, a Great Power must have allies among the Great Powers. And if its object is, as ours must be, to preserve the peace, then it must form a combination of indisputably preponderant power with other great states which also desire peace.

Thus the statesman who means to maintain peace can no more ignore the order of power than an engineer can ignore the mechanics of physical force. He should not, to be sure, frivolously "play power politics." But he must with cold calculation organize and regulate the politics of power. If he does not do that, and do it correctly, the result must be a cycle of disastrous wars followed by peace settlements which breed more wars.

For a hundred years between Waterloo and the invasion of Belgium there existed in the world an order of power which was good enough to prevent a great war. There were localized, limited, short wars, but there was no general and total war. Over this order Great Britain presided by means of her unchallenged command of the seas. Within this order Germany, Japan, and the United States developed into Great Powers. But this order of the nineteenth century was unique in modern history and the very fact that it favored the rise of new powers meant that the order was certain to be transitional.

By the turn of the century the old order no longer corresponded with the true distribution of power in the world, and—since men were not wise enough and good enough to construct a new order of power—there began the cycle of twentieth century wars. During this period none of the great states has been able to form a workable foreign policy. One and all they have misjudged the forces with them and the forces against them, and until they construct an order of power which fits the realities of power, they must continue in the cycle of disaster.

In 1914 Germany, with no ally except the rapidly decomposing former Great Power, Austria-Hungary, went to war with a combination of Great Powers which finally included all the Great Powers. This ensured her defeat. Germany realized her error, and in 1939 she thought she had corrected it. She had made alliances with Italy and Japan, two of her former enemies, and a pact with a third, Russia; and she carefully cultivated the isolationism of the fourth, America. Thus she inaugurated her second war under auspicious circumstances, and won rapid, spectacular, and cheap victories. But then she fell into the error she had sought to avoid. Instead of wooing the vanquished, she infuriated them. Instead of placating the neutrals, she menaced them: Russia by invading her, America by threatening South America and by promoting the alliance with Japan. This brought into being the great coalition which destroy[ed] Germany's power.

The foreign policy of Japan during this same period consisted in antagonizing all her neighbors—Russia, China, Britain, the Netherlands, and the United States. The only ally she made was Germany, which was not a Far Eastern power. Therefore, the Japanese policy was a sheer gamble on the hope that Germany would engage all the Great Powers so as to give her a free hand. The gamble was correct in the year 1942. But only for that year. For Japan had risked everything to win everything in a war which, as regards the final alignment of power, was being decided on the other side of the world.

The foreign policy of the other states was in this period no less misguided and very nearly as disastrous. At the Armistice of 1918 they constituted a combination so strong that they had within their reach the means to construct a new order of power. But they did not do this. On the contrary they dissolved the combination. First, they ostracized Russia, being more concerned with the passing danger of an ideology than with the permanent order of power. Then they isolated Japan. Then they isolated themselves one from the other—America from Britain, and Britain from France, and France from Italy. When the victorious combination of 1918 had been completely dissolved, the new combination of the aggressor states was formed without opposition. By 1936 it existed, and its first important action was to prevent the British, the French, and the Russians from recreating their own alliance. At Munich in 1938 Hitler compelled Great Britain and France to separate themselves from Russia. The United States had in the meantime persuaded itself, by passing the Neutrality Act, that it must be separated from

Britain and France while it became increasingly embroiled with Japan.

The common error in the foreign policy of all the Great Powers is that they did not take the precaution to become members of an indisputably powerful combination. The aggressor combination was not powerful enough to win: it was powerful enough only to plunge the world into war. The combination of the defenders was not formed until they were on the edge of catastrophe.

Thus we must conclude that in the order of power—in the relationship among the states which are Great Powers because they can raise great forces and can arm them—the object of each state must be to form a combination which isolates its enemy. From 1935 to 1940 it was Hitler's object to isolate Great Britain. He did not succeed and therefore he must lose the war. [After] 1941 it [was] the object of the United Nations to separate Germany and Japan and then defeat each of them separately. Every state, whether it is bent on aggression or on pacification, can achieve its purpose only if it avoids being isolated by a combination of the other great states.

To be isolated is for any state the worst of all predicaments. To be the member of a combination which can be depended upon to act together, and, when challenged, to fight together, is to have achieved the highest degree of security which is attainable in a world where there are many sovereign national states.

The world we live in is a world of many sovereign national states, and for the purposes of practical action this condition is given and is unalterable. A Roman Peace, in which one state absorbs and governs all the others, is so completely impossible in our time that we need not stop to argue whether it would be inferno or utopia. If there is to be peace in our time, it will have to be peace among sovereign national states, and the makers of foreign policy can be concerned with no other kind of peace.

Since the first concern of the makers of foreign policy in a sovereign national state must be to achieve the greatest possible security, their object must be to avoid isolation by becoming members of an adequate combination. If they are entirely successful, the adequate alliance to which they belong will either be unchallenged, and they will have peace without fighting for it, or it will be invincible and they will have peace after a victorious war. To be one against the many is the danger, to be among the many against the one is security.

It follows that when the alliance is inadequate because there is an opposing alliance of approximately equal strength, the stage is set for a world war. For then the balance of power is so nearly even that no state is secure. It cannot know whether it would win or lose the war which it knows is probable. Therefore, it is confronted with the need to calculate the risks of striking first and seizing the advantage of the initiative, or of waiting to be attacked in the hope, usually vain, that it will become too strong to be attacked.

Europe from 1900 to 1914 was in this condition of unstable balance. There was no certain preponderance of force with the Triple Entente or with the Central Powers. The question was put to the test of battle, and it was not until the weight of America was drawn in from the outside that a decision was reached and the war could come to an end. From the rise of Hitler to Munich Europe was again in this condition. No one knew, not Hitler, not Stalin, not Chamberlain or Daladier, the relative strength of the Axis and of the opposing combination. Only when Hitler succeeded at Munich in separating the Franco-British allies from Russia, had he so altered the balance of power in his favor that a war for the conquest of Europe was from his point of view a good risk.

If, then, the object is not only to provide for security against being defeated in war but also to organize a peace which prevents war, the alliance to be adequate must be so dependable and so overwhelmingly powerful that there is no way of challenging it. The combination must be so strong that war against it is not a calculated risk, in which much might be won at a great price, but is instead an obvious impossibility because there would be no chance whatever of winning it.

To form such an overwhelming combination and maintain it is not easy. That is why peace has never yet been made universal, and why, when it has been achieved, it has not lasted. The combinations have tended to dissolve under the pressure of special interests within their member states. Old powers decline and new powers emerge. And never yet have statesmen been equal to the task of passing from one order of power to another without gigantic and prolonged wars. The cycle of these wars continues until by the survival of the strongest in the struggle for existence the new order of power is formed by a preponderant combination. . . .

CAN POWER POLITICS BE ABOLISHED?

By Carl Becker

From chap. 4 of *How New Will the Better World Be?* by Carl Becker. Copyright 1944 by Alfred A. Knopf, Inc., New York; reproduced by permission. The late Dr. Becker was professor of history at Cornell University.

For good or evil, words often have great influence in their own right, apart from the things they represent. Like actors on the stage, they have their entrances and their exits, play an important role for a time, and then lose favor. They may, like men, be born free and equal, but like men they have their ups and downs. Certain words in particular suddenly acquire greater prestige than they deserve, and then after a time, from too much use or because the things they refer to have become sinister or merely ridiculous, they lose their popularity and either cease to be used at all or are used only to distort what they originally represented. . . .

Something of this sort has happened to such good old words as "politics," "power," "empire," and "imperial." The term "politics" has taken on a certain unsavory meaning, as when we say "playing politics," or "it's only politics." In international relations playing politics, otherwise known as "the diplomatic game," has recently become a little more unsavory, or even sinister, by being described as "power politics." . . .

During recent years the terms "power politics" and "imperialism" have come to be more than terms of reproach; they have come to denote something wholly evil. The reason is that we identify them with the philosophy and practice of Hitler and the rulers of Japan. We are all convinced, and rightly so, that the kind of power politics which they practice and approve of is wholly evil, and that the kind of imperial domination which they aim to achieve is no less evil. And so all power politics and all imperialism seem to us wholly evil—something which we are not guilty of, something which we are fighting to destroy. It is chiefly for this reason that many people find it possible to think and say that after the war is over "power politics must be abandoned." . . .

It will be worth while to trace the history of these terms, and to examine the things which they refer to, in order to see whether the things referred to are in themselves wholly evil and whether in any case they can be easily ignored or got rid of.

Something more than three thousand years ago the famous Greek philosopher Aristotle wrote a book, or left notes which were made into a book, entitled *Politics*. For Aristotle, and for the Greeks and Romans and the people of the Middle Ages, the term "politics" referred to the institutions, laws, customs, and moral and religious ideas by which men managed to live together in a community. Its meaning was not limited to the form of government and the making of laws, but included the economic activities and moral ideas of the community as well. But in the sixteenth century Machiavelli discussed the art of government without reference to morality and ethics; and in the next two centuries certain writers dealt with the activities by which men make a living and acquire wealth as a separate subject, which was called "political economy" or "economics." Since that time the term "politics" has been commonly understood to refer to the form of government and laws and activities by which the people are governed.

In the eighteenth century, when people were mostly governed by absolute kings, there were of course no elections and no political parties; but there were influential noble families, and industrial "guilds," and financial corporations— all representing certain interests, and all seeking to get the favor of the king. The head of a powerful noble family, for example, might for various reasons have great influence with the king (or with the king's minister, or the king's mistress), which of course he would use for getting what he wanted for his family or his friends. When he did this he was "playing politics," but that isn't what it was called at that time. It was said that he "had the ear of the king," or that he was "making use of his interest through the minister."

Then kings mostly lost their power, and in the nineteenth century in most European countries laws were made, as they are in the United States, by assemblies composed of representatives elected by the people. For getting the representatives elected and for advocating certain measures, political parties were formed; and those who made a business of managing the parties or getting elected to office were called "politicians." The term "politics" came then to have a double meaning. In general it referred to the form of government and the making of laws; but it also referred to the activities of politicians in winning elections and getting laws passed that would be agreeable to the people who supported their candidates. In an ideal democracy people are supposed to forget about their personal and private interests and to support measures that will serve the common interests of the nation. Many people do this all of the time, and most people do it some of the time. But it is not always, or often, easy to know what the common interest is, whereas it is always easy to know what is for the immediate interest of the individual or the group to which he belongs. In the United States there are many such groups—farmers, laborers, big business, commerce, the South, the industrial Northeast, the Middle West, and so on. It is no longer great families but these groups and sections that have a powerful "interest." They have not "the ear of the king," but they have the ear of their representatives in the House and Senate, and through them they have great influence in getting the laws passed that will be, or that they think will be, beneficial for them. They exert great "pressure," and this competitive struggle of the groups and sections for getting what they want whether it is for the common good or not is called "pressure politics." Since the groups have political power, it would be equally correct to call it "power politics."

The term "pressure politics" doesn't sound quite so bad as "power politics," and that may be why the one term is used for domestic politics whereas the other is reserved for international politics. But still, to those who are thinking of some ideal democracy, even the term "pressure politics" doesn't sound any too good. However it sounds, we all know that it expresses the way in which democracy actually works, and after all it is inevitable that it should work that way. By and large, men pursue their own interests, and where the interest of a group is clearly discernible and can be promoted or injured by legislation, it is inevitable that the group should try to promote or protect it by legislation. The practical justification for doing so is that democratic government rests on the will of the people, and the will of the people can be determined only by majority vote; and in practice the majority vote is determined by the competitive pressure of the various groups. The groups that at any time get what they want, by pressure on congressmen, log-rolling bargains, or otherwise, may be said to represent for that purpose and that time the will of the nation.

The trouble with this is that all people have many interests, some of which can be promoted by certain laws only at the expense of the others. Farmers and laborers are both "producers" and "consumers." As producers they want higher prices for what they sell; but as consumers they want lower prices for what they buy. Their interest as producers is more apparent to them, and more easily promoted by legislation, than their interest as consumers. Besides, everybody is a consumer and all consumers have, as consumers, the same interest; but the class of "everybody" which makes up the consumers is not organized, and therefore cannot easily exert "pressure" on legislation. We feel, therefore, that the term "pressure politics" doesn't sound quite right because pressure politics benefits only those who are organized to promote their private interests at the expense of the others. In such an emergency as the present war the term sounds worse than in times of peace. It is perfectly obvious that "playing politics" and "pressure politics" promote the private interest of some but interfere with the interest of the nation as a whole, which is to win the war and not to raise prices for farmers, or increase wages for industrial laborers, or secure fat profits for war contractors. We see this, and so with one accord, or almost with one accord, we say: "Playing politics and pressure politics are out for the duration." We do not say that pressure politics "must be abandoned after the war is over." We are not quite so naïve or befuddled as to believe that. We just say that it must be out for the duration. And even that is a little naïve, because obviously it isn't entirely out even for the duration.

The technique of politics in international affairs is much the same as in national affairs, but this fact is obscured because the conditions are somewhat different and we use different terms to describe it. We speak of "international relations" instead of international "politics," of "playing the diplomatic game" instead of "playing politics," of "power politics" instead of "pressure politics." In international politics the interests involved are independent states instead of groups or sections within the state; the interests are promoted by exerting "power" rather than "pressure"; and the conflict of interests is resolved, not by a legislative body enacting laws that can be enforced by judicial process, but by treaties or agreements voluntarily subscribed to by the states involved. If the interests are regarded as vital and cannot be reconciled by agreement, the only way out in international politics is war. In national politics the conflict of interests between groups or sections may also become irreconcilable by peaceful means, although in strongly united nation-states this is less likely to happen; but when it does happen the way out is the same as in international politics—civil war, which is sometimes called revolution.

There is, however, one very important difference between national and international politics. The conditions which separate nations are ordinarily more deep-seated and permanent than those which separate groups within the nation. An English-speaking farmer in Iowa is, after all, not a "foreigner" to an English-speaking (or even a German-speaking) laborer in Detroit in the same sense, or to the same degree, that an Italian in Rome is a foreigner to an Englishman in London. For this reason the common interests of the various groups in the United States are more apparent, even if in the long run they are not more real, than the common interests of the various nations of Europe or of the world. And therefore the conflicts of interest more easily appear to be, even if they are not in fact, irreconcilable by peaceful means. And since there is no international government by which agreements can be enforced, any state which has sufficient power is in a position to use its power without any restraint except that which is self-imposed—the restraint which is imposed by its own sense of decency and justice. When the rulers of a powerful state, unrestrained by any sense of decency or justice because they have none, frankly adopt the doctrine that might makes right and ruthlessly act upon it, then "power politics" becomes the entirely evil thing that the present German government has made of it. But to suppose that power politics is always wholly evil because Hitler and his humorless, bleak-faced Nazi supporters have made a wholly evil use of it is only to obscure and distort the political realities of the world in which we live.

It obscures and distorts the political realities at the present moment by leading us to suppose that the United States is not, never has been, and never will be engaged in the game of "power politics" or concerned in anything so futile as the attempt to maintain peace by adjusting the "balance of power." The effect that can be produced by a slight shift in the use of words is indeed astonishing. We call attention every day to our great political power, to our mounting naval and military power, and to the certainty that this power will be sufficient to crush the power of Germany and Japan. Yet no one will admit that we are engaged in the nefarious business of power politics or that we are fighting for a restoration of the old balance of power. These are words that we associate with Germany and Japan. The things they represent must therefore be wholly evil. And so we easily delude ourselves by the notion that when Germany and Japan are crushed by our superior power, power politics will be abandoned and no one will be concerned to maintain a balance of power.

But if we regard things instead of words, it is clear that the term "power politics" is what the grammarians call a "redundancy." The simple fact is that politics is inseparable from power.

States and governments exist to exert power, for the maintenance of order, the administration of justice, the defense of the community against aggression—in theory always and solely for these good ends. But the power, much or little, is always there, and will be used for some end, good, bad, or indifferent. In any country the government may be strong or weak. In the world at large there are Great Powers and minor powers. In each country and in the world at large there is either a stable balance of power, an unstable balance of power, or no balance of power at all. But there is always power. "Power," as Lionel Gerber says in his book *Peace by Power*, "never vanishes. If you do not wish to retain or wield it, somebody else will. You may feel the effects of power as a passive recipient; you may deal with it as an active agent. There is no escape, no immunity." Political power exists in the world and will be used by those who have it—for good ends we hope, but at all events for some ends. . . .

After the war is over, there will still be power politics, and no doubt there will be evils connected with it; but it need not be, and we have good reason to suppose that it will not be, the wholly evil thing it has been in the hands of Germany and Japan. There will also be a balance of power, but that does not mean that we must or should return to the old balance-of-power *policy*. Hitler has indeed demonstrated, as Napoleon did before him, that the balance of power is not, like an electric clock, a self-regulating mechanism which needs only to be set up in order to keep the peace without further attention. That happy idea was born in the eighteenth century when there were, in Europe, six Great Powers about equally strong. The idea was that if each Great Power looked after its own interests without any regard to the others, any threatened domination by any one or two of them would automatically give rise to counteralliances sufficiently strong to redress the balance. Except for the smashing conquests of Napoleon, this idea worked well enough for two centuries, if not to prevent wars, at least to prevent any one power from destroying the political independence of any of the others. But this idea of a self-regulating balance will no longer serve any good purpose. The experience of the present war has shown that if each country looks after its own interests without regard to the others, the result is likely to be, not a stable balance of power, but a balance wholly in favor of aggressor states, and totally disastrous to the political and cultural independence of the others. . . .

Even those who deplore great political power because it is inherently dangerous (or most of them—there are always Gandhi and his followers) recognize that a "new and better world" cannot be made without it. They say, and everybody says, that there can be no new and better world unless Great Britain, Russia, and the United States take a leading part in making it. But why these countries especially? Precisely because they have very great political power, precisely because they have sufficient power, if they work together, to determine what shall and shall not be done in the world and to see that it is or is not done. . . .

POWER AND RESPONSIBILITY IN AN ORDERED WORLD

By W. T. R. Fox

From chap. 1 of *The Super-Powers, The United States, Britain, and the Soviet Union—Their Responsibility for Peace*, by W. T. R. Fox. Copyright 1944 by Harcourt, Brace & Co., New York; reproduced by permission. The author is research associate in the Institute of International Studies at Yale University which sponsored publication of the book quoted.

THE western state system has always been dominated by a few great states. Out of the chaos of the Thirty Years' War there emerged a Europe whose political life was ordered by a select coterie of the more powerful who recognized each other as "The Great Powers." It is altogether likely that man must, in the future as in the past, guard against the menace of arbitrary power. Because some states have great power and others have much less, there will always be the danger that the government of some Great Power will see in that difference an opportunity for cheap and profitable aggression. But power can be used to protect as well as to enslave. In the world we are going to have to live in, differences in power do and will exist. Our problem is to discover the conditions of security in that world. . . .

When men in their daily conversation refer to states as "Great Powers" or as "small powers," they testify to the importance of the possession of power. Trends in the distribution of power among nations largely determine the evolution of the pattern of international relationships, because the possibility of the resort to violence is never excluded. The relations of states in such a world community will in this book be called "power politics." It is a peculiarly American notion to assume that problems in a world of power politics can be solved by creating a world of no-power politics. This belief was not, however, shared by Hamilton, Jefferson, and many other early statesmen of the Republic. Their writings reveal a keen insight into the relation between American security and European power politics. Hamilton understood that with a modest naval establishment the United States would "be able to incline the balance of European competitions in this part of the world as our interest may dictate."

The century of comparative peace in Europe after Waterloo obscured the vital connection between America's security and Europe's struggles. Theodore Roosevelt was perhaps the first modern American in high public office to base foreign policy on a frank recognition of the necessity for constantly calculating military-power relationships. This was no doubt what Walter Lippmann had in mind when he recently wrote that "Theodore Roosevelt had . . . the elements of a genuine foreign policy." . . .

Even the austere Henry Adams confessed to being fascinated by [Secretary of State] John Hay's efforts to construct about the American nucleus a power combination which would include Britain, Germany, and finally Russia. Hay, he thought, was attempting at the international level to do what the titans of industry were doing at home, to form a trust which would substitute monopoly for competition. The game, he felt, was less sordid when played in foreign affairs since the participant was a person acting not in his own private interest but in that of his country. For Adams too, foreign affairs was an intriguing game to be won for one's country if possible.

The American people certainly felt a pleasurable sensation because of their country's new status as a Great Power. It was natural for them to give willing support to their enthusiastic President in his bold adventures in world politics. Later in two world wars they discovered that power politics was not merely a game, that some governments played "for keeps," and that playing the game meant that sons and brothers and fathers had to give up their lives. They can hardly be blamed for wanting to have the United States withdraw from the game. Some advocated the "isolationist" way out of the game, which meant simply refusing to play. Others advocated the "internationalist" way out, by calling for a revision of the rules according to which units of military power would no longer be the counters of victory and defeat. Neither group exhibited the sophisticated understanding of power politics essential to providing a foreign policy for the United States in the world as it really is. Those who continued to favor America's playing the game as a game were called imperialists.

If power politics were a game, power itself would be merely a scoring device; and attainment of great power would be a relatively innocuous consequence of great wealth, great population, and a favorable geographic position. Since power politics is not a game but a central feature of the organized political life of the twentieth century, it makes the most enormous difference in whose hands predominant power rests. Those few who soberly pointed out that power politics is more than a game, that power really exists, that it is the highest task of statesmanship to harmonize conflicting power groups and to canalize armed power so that it may perform its legitimate, protective role in international affairs were called by the isolationists, "interventionists."

Americans, surrounded by visual evidence that in many ways the new is better than the old, have frequently assumed that the same is true in international politics. To many, the "Old World" system of power politics appears absolutely bad. They have therefore concentrated their attention upon discovering some totally new principle by which inter-state relations should be regulated. Americans occasionally assert that they have discovered such a principle in the "Good Neighborly" relations that characterize New World politics. They may instead have demonstrated how, by moderation and tact, a Great Power can make its preponderant position generally palatable to its less powerful neighbors. This is no mean achievement; it does not, however, provide an escape from power politics. It may be valid totally to reject the old way, but it is invalid to do so until one understands what one is rejecting. It is especially important to understand which parts of the old system cannot be rejected because they cannot be changed. If, for example, there will be in the future as in the past a small number of Great Powers, each incapable of being coerced except by combinations including other Great Powers, a "plan" for avoiding future war which is built on a different assumption has little to contribute to the urgent task of preventing war in our time.

We have said that military power itself is neither good nor bad; it is ethically neutral. It is good or bad only as it is used for good or bad purposes. We need not pause for the moment to inquire what constitutes a "good" use of power. It is enough to point out that mankind generally, outside the Axis countries, finds it good that the power position of the Soviet Union, the United States, and the British Commonwealth has improved and that these powers rather than their opponents will shortly be the custodians of preponderant power.

Fifty years from now or five hundred years from now men may have discovered a substitute for armed force in world politics. It is not too soon to start planning for that day. To understand the international relations of the next generation, however, one needs to know the precise location of preponderant military power. This power will lie either in the hands of the victorious Great Powers or in some supra-national authority itself controlling directly a police force of world-wide jurisdiction. As a possibility for producing general security in our own time, the second alternative is of only theoretical importance. For it to materialize, the Great Powers would have to permit the creation of a supra-national police force strong enough to coerce any one of them and constitutionally able to do so. The Soviet Union is not, however, likely to feel that its physical security would be enhanced by permitting a supra-national agency in which it might be outvoted to possess a land army capable of defeating the Red Army. Nor will Great Britain and the United States be anxious to see a supra-national naval force brought into existence which could cut the North Atlantic life line essential to the security of both. Only if all the surviving Great Powers were simultaneously and collectively prepared to entrust their security to a supra-national agency with preponderant force at its command could the necessary transfer of authority take place without still another world war. Something called an international police force may or may not be created; but it may safely be predicted that there will still be American, British and Russian armies, navies, and air forces after the present war.

The task of the peacemaker is not, therefore, to emasculate the surviving Great Powers. It is rather to seek a definition of the national interest of each in such terms that each will find it possible to collaborate with the others to maintain a stable and just post-war order. If one or more of the surviving Great Powers develops a policy of unlimited expansion or of "power for the sake of domination," the quest for all-round security will necessarily fail. What are the conditions under which this eventuality may be avoided?

In periods of peace, great power and great responsibility have always gone hand in hand. In the words of Pascal, "justice without force is impotent. Force without justice is tyrannical. We must therefore combine justice with force." When for short intervals the powerful have proved irresponsible or the responsible impotent, world order and world peace have both been the losers. Responsible but impotent France and powerful but irresponsible Germany were in the 1930's equally dangerous. America's irresponsible isolationism and League of Nations impotence also demonstrate how the sundering of power and responsibility set the stage for a second world war. Since a reincarnated League can hardly be made powerful enough in its own right, some other way must be found which responsibility and power can be firmly joined.

If the leaders of each of the great states should come to believe that it "pays"—in terms of the values pursued by each—to use power in a moderate and responsible fashion, the prospects for continuing peace would be good. Today's student of power politics has a clear responsibility; he must discover the conditions under which such a development might occur.

One further word needs to be said. . . . It is possible to write about power without assuming either that power is an end in itself or that territorial expansion is the chief preoccupation of statesmen. The struggle for power, under those assumptions, could never, even theoretically, come to an end except through successful conquest of the world, and even then the possibility of world-wide civil war could not be excluded. Power in international politics is power *over*; it is a relational concept. It is therefore perfectly obvious that not every state can simultaneously become more powerful. One state's gain is necessarily another's loss, and a loss which the loser will not view with equanimity.

If, however, power is regarded as a means to the attainment of security, the picture need not be quite so black. There are times when nations have refrained from building up their armed forces in particular directions because they would not thereby increase their security. The agreement to keep the long Canadian-American border unfortified must rank as among the major steps in rendering the United States' continental homeland secure. It has permitted the formation of a North American "security union" to the immense advantage of both Canada and the United States. Britain's security has come to depend so largely on America's power (and vice versa) that an improvement in the power position of one no longer induces a sense of insecurity in the other. Americans have not yet made up their minds as to whether the spectacular improvement in the power position of Soviet Russia bodes ill in the long run, although they can hardly be in doubt as to its short-run beneficial effects. For the moment, it is sufficient to point out that the quest for security and the quest for power are not necessarily identical. One state's security is not necessarily every other state's insecurity. Greater security, like greater prosperity but unlike dominant power, is an objective toward which it is at least conceivable that all states can move simultaneously. If "security" is a more accurate word than "domination" to describe the power objectives of leaders of the great states, then there is at least a possibility that in our time the Great Powers can collaborate in a system of general security. It is only necessary to reiterate that participation in this general security system must seem to offer greater security to *each* of the Great Powers than non-participation....

Chapter 2

Why Some Nations Are Strong and Others Weak

A LONDON weekly, *The Economist,* observed recently: "There is much talk, in current discussion, of the Great Powers and of the role that they will have to play in the postwar world. . . . But there has been very little attempt to define what a Great Power is."

What makes some nations strong and others weak? Why, for example, do the United States, the Soviet Union, and Great Britain constitute the "Big Three" of the United Nations? Why do we speak of China as a "potentially" Great Power? Why has Italy, long an aspirant to Great-Power status, never quite been able to stay in the "major league"? Why are there such disparities of strength between Britain and India, between the United States and Brazil, or between the Soviet Union and China? What, in short, makes a nation a Great Power? And what standard of comparison, what yardstick, will show one nation's strength in relation to other nations?

One criterion of national strength is obviously the standing armaments which each nation maintains ready for action in time of peace. In some cases, peacetime armaments give a fair indication of a nation's total strength and its relative position. During the 1930's, for example, such a yardstick, judiciously used, would have thrown great light upon the over-all power position of the Soviet Union. In other cases, comparison of standing armaments would have led to absurd results. It would have given Italy a higher rating than Great Britain, higher even than the United States. Nevertheless, peacetime armies, navies, and air forces are an important element of national power. They may become more so in the future as a result of advances in war technology which make surprise attacks more deadly and shorten the time in which a country can mobilize its resources for defense. In 1939 it mattered little what forces Poland could have mobilized if given the time to do so, for Poland did not have time.

But military power in being is by no means all that matters, even in this era of mechanized Blitzkrieg. For most countries, especially those with large area and consequent depth for retreat if necessary, the human and material resources that can be converted into military power also count heavily. Likewise important are a nation's economic power and its capacity for political leadership.

In making an over-all estimate of a nation's international position, one logical starting point is population. Without people there would be no power and no politics. The number of people, their age distribution, their health and literacy levels, and other qualities, all have a bearing upon a country's position. But population by itself does not spell power. China, for example, has more people than the Soviet Union and the United States combined. The question then becomes: What else is necessary to give a people political standing and influence with other nations?

For one thing, economic resources. Without food people starve. Without raw materials they cannot build shelter and transport, or fashion weapons with which to fight and to defend themselves. But economic resources alone do not give people power. Czarist Russia possessed the same forests, the same farm lands, and the same mineral wealth as the Soviet Union does today. Czarist Russia, like the Soviet Union, had more manpower than any other European state. Yet Russia under the Romanoffs was a pitifully weak country compared with the Soviet Union in this war. Manpower and economic resources are essential, but tools, skills, and organization are required to transmute them into political power and influence.

Economic development is a factor of the greatest importance. Advanced and efficient methods of production, an adequate and smoothly running transportation system, scientific research and a progressive technology, all play a vital role in determining a country's international position. The Soviet Union has greater manpower than the United States, and comparable economic resources. But the United States has a long lead in economic development, and this advantage in industrial tools and skills is reflected in the vastly greater American production of weapons and other equipment required to wage war in the machine age. But mass production of the latest equipment itself depends upon organization which becomes still another factor in the equation of national strength and international prestige and influence.

Organization consists of regulations and other means for securing cooperative disciplined work toward a desired end. Organization involves all sorts of working relationships among individual persons, corporations, and government itself. Genius for organization has frequently been cited as one of the keys to Germany's achievements in science, in economic production, and in war. Organization is the key to American economic production. Organization is the very basis of military achievement.

State structure and internal organization vary greatly from country to country. Differences in the pattern of national life are indicated by such terms as democracy, totalitarianism, capitalism, fascism, national socialism, state capitalism, and communism. Among the most controversial questions are those relating to the comparative ability of states differently constituted to frame a foreign policy, to carry on diplomacy, to plan a national defense, to mobilize for war, and to wage war successfully.

Closely related to questions of state structure and organization are other questions of equal importance bearing on the moral qualities of a people. What is their moral stamina, their ability to pull together, their discipline, their susceptibility to alien propaganda, ideologies, and a fifth column in their midst?

We now have the principal factors for making an estimate of a nation's power potential, or the power which it might mobilize within its own frontiers if given the necessary time to do so. Such an estimate can be expressed in the form of a crude equation thus: manpower plus economic resources plus tools and skills plus organization plus morale equals power potential which, given time, can be transmuted into power in being.

What a state can do with its power depends upon still other factors. It is a political axiom that power is local. That is to say, a state can never bring more than a portion of its total power to bear in a given place under any set of conditions. The portion of its power that a state can bring to bear diminishes progressively the further away from home it is exercised. Also the size and shape of a country's boundaries, the nature and length of its frontiers, the location of allies and possible enemies, and the over-all political situation in the world, all have a bearing on the extent to which a state's power can be concentrated or must be dispersed over a wide area.

One word of caution. A nation's strength and political influence cannot be measured with mathematical exactness. The estimation of national power is not a science. It seems unlikely ever to become one. There are too many variables and human intangibles.

But judgments respecting the present and prospective strength of nations need not rest upon pure guesswork. Methods have been devised, and are constantly being improved, for measuring the tangible elements of national power, and for crowding into an ever shrinking space the factors not yet susceptible of more exact measurement.

The following readings indicate the general character of these methods of analysis and how they can be used to answer the question raised in this chapter: what makes a nation a Great Power?

THE FORMS OF POLITICAL POWER

BY E. H. CARR

From chap. 8 of *The Twenty Years' Crisis, 1919-1939*, by E. H. Carr. Macmillan & Co., London; reproduced by permission. The author, for many years a member of the British diplomatic service, is professor of international politics in the University College of Wales.

POLITICAL power in the international sphere may be divided, for purposes of discussion, into three categories: (a) military power, (b) economic power, (c) power over opinion. We shall find, however, that these categories are closely interdependent; and though they are theoretically separable, it is difficult in practice to imagine a country for any length of time possessing one kind of power in isolation from the others. In its essence, power is an indivisible whole. . . .

Military Power. The supreme importance of the military instrument lies in the fact that the *ultima ratio* of power in international relations is war. Every act of the state, in its power aspect, is directed to war, not as a desirable weapon, but as a weapon which it may require in the last resort to use. . . .

War lurks in the background of international politics just as revolution lurks in the background of domestic politics. There are few European countries where, at some time during the past thirty years, potential revolution has not been an important factor in politics; and the international community has in this respect the closest analogy to those states where the possibility of revolution is most frequently and most conspicuously present to the mind.

Potential war being thus a dominant factor in international politics, military strength becomes a recognized standard of political values. Every great civilization of the past has enjoyed in its day a superiority of military power. The Greek city-state rose to greatness when its hoplite armies proved more than a match for the Persian hordes. In the modern world, powers (the word itself is significant enough) are graded according to the quantity and the supposed efficiency of the military equipment, including manpower, at their disposal. Recognition as a Great Power is normally the reward of fighting a successful large-scale war. Germany after the Franco-Prussian War, the United States after the war with Spain, and Japan after the Russo-Japanese War are familiar recent instances.... Any symptom of military inefficiency or unpreparedness in a Great Power is promptly reflected in its political status. The naval mutiny at Invergordon in September 1931 was the final blow to British prestige which compelled Great Britain to devalue her currency. The execution of the leading Soviet generals for alleged treason in June 1937 was thought to reveal so much weakness in the Soviet military machine that the influence of Soviet Russia suffered a sudden and severe slump....

These facts point the moral that foreign policy never can, or never should, be divorced from strategy. The foreign policy of a country is limited not only by its aims, but also by its military strength or, more accurately, by the ratio of its military strength to that of other countries. The most serious problem involved in the democratic control of foreign policy is that no government can afford to divulge full and frank information about its own military strength, or all the knowledge it possesses about the military strength of other countries. Public discussions of foreign policy are therefore conducted in partial or total ignorance of one of the factors which must be decisive in determining it.... Many contemporary books and speeches about international politics are reminiscent of those ingenious mathematical problems which the student is invited to solve by ignoring the weight of the elephant. The solutions proposed are neat and accurate on the abstract plane, but are obtained by leaving out of account the vital strategic factor.... If every prospective writer on international affairs in the last twenty years had taken a compulsory course in elementary strategy, reams of nonsense would have remained unwritten.

Economic Power. Economic strength has always been an instrument of political power, if only through its association with the military instrument. Only the most primitive kinds of warfare are altogether independent of the economic factor.... The whole progress of civilization has been so closely bound up with economic development that we are not surprised to trace, throughout modern history, an increasingly intimate association between military and economic power.... The rise of modern nations has everywhere been marked by the emergence of a new middle class economically based on industry and trade. Trade and finance were the foundation of the short-lived political supremacy of the Italian cities of the Renaissance and later of the Dutch. The principal international wars of the period from the Renaissance to the middle of the eighteenth century were trade wars (some of them were actually so named). Throughout this period, it was universally held that, since wealth is a source of political power, the state should seek actively to promote the acquisition of wealth; and it was believed that the right way to make a country powerful was to stimulate production at home, to buy as little as possible from abroad, and to accumulate wealth in the convenient form of precious metals. Those who argued in this way afterwards came to be known as mercantilists. Mercantilism was a system of economic policy based on the hitherto unquestioned assumption that to promote the acquisition of wealth was part of the normal function of the state.

The *laissez-faire* doctrine of the classical economists made a frontal attack on this assumption.... The classical economists conceived a natural economic order with laws of its own, independent of politics and functioning to the greatest profit of all concerned when political authority interfered least in its automatic operation. This doctrine dominated the economic thought, and to some extent the economic practice (though far more in Great Britain than elsewhere), of the nineteenth century. The theory of the nineteenth century liberal state presupposed the existence side by side of two separate systems. The political system, which was the sphere of government, was concerned with the maintenance of law and order and the provision of certain essential services, and was thought of mainly as a necessary evil. The economic system, which was the preserve of private enterprise, catered for the material wants and, in doing so, organized the everyday lives of the great mass of the citizens. . . .

Even before 1900, a more penetrating analysis might have shown that the illusion of a divorce between politics and economics was fast breaking down. It is still open to debate whether late nineteenth century imperialism should be regarded as an economic movement using political weapons, or as a political movement using economic weapons. But that economics and politics marched hand in hand toward the same objective is clear enough. . . . The War [of 1914-1918], by overtly reuniting economics and politics, in both domestic and foreign policy, hastened a development which was already on the way. It was now revealed that the nineteenth century, while purporting to take economics altogether out of the political sphere, had in fact forged economic weapons of unparalleled strength for use in the interests of national policy. . . . In no previous war had the economic life of belligerent nations been so completely and ruthlessly organized by the political authority. In the age-long alliance between the military and the economic arm, the economic arm for the first time was an equal, if not a superior, partner. To cripple the economic system of an enemy power was as much a war aim as to defeat his armies and fleets. "Planned economy," which means the control by the state for political purposes of the economic life of the nation, is mainly a product of the War. "War potential" has become another name for economic power.

. . . We may divide into two broad categories the methods in which economic power is pressed into the service of national policy. The first will contain those measures whose purpose is defined by the convenient word autarky; the second, economic measures directly designed to strengthen the national influence over other countries.

Autarky is . . . an instrument of political power. . . . The principle of autarky received its classic definition from the pen of Alexander Hamilton, who in 1791, being then Secretary of the United States Treasury, made a report to the House of Representatives which enunciates, in words which might have been written today, the whole modern doctrine of autarky. Hamilton had been instructed to advise on "the means of promoting such [manufactures] as will tend to render the United States independent of foreign nations for military and other essential supplies." One short passage may be quoted from the report:

"Not only the wealth but the independence and security of a country appear to be materially connected with the prosperity of manufactures. Every nation, with a view to these great objects, ought to endeavour to possess within itself all the essentials of national supply. . . . The extreme embarrassments of the United States during the late war, from an incapacity of supplying themselves, are still a matter of keen recollection; a future war might be expected to exemplify the mischief and dangers of a situation to which that incapacity is still, in too great a degree, applicable, unless changed by timely and vigorous action."

And Hamilton went on to examine in turn all the methods by which the desired result might be attained—duties, prohibitions, bounties and premiums. In Germany, just fifty years later, [the economist] List argued that "on the development of the German protective system depend the existence, the independence and the future of the German nationality"; and in the latter half of the nineteenth century successive Prussian victories drove home the intimate connection between a highly developed industrial system and military power.

Throughout this period Great Britain, in virtue of her industrial supremacy, enjoyed virtually complete autarky in all industrial products, though not in the raw materials required to produce them. In food supplies, she ceased to be self-supporting about 1830. But this defect was in large part remedied by her naval power, the maintenance of which became one of her chief preoccupations. . . . Complete reliance was placed on the capacity of the navy to protect the ordinary channels of trade, and thereby make up for the inevitable absence of sufficient supplies at home. . . .

The impulse which [the First World War] gave to the pursuit of autarky was immediate and powerful. . . .

The development of synthetic materials by Germany and the accumulation by Great Britain of stocks of foodstuffs and essential raw materials are two of many significant symptoms. Autarky, like other elements of power, is expensive. It may cost a country as much to make itself self-supporting in some important commodity as to build a battleship. The expenditure may turn out to be wasteful, and the acquisition not worth the cost. But to deny that autarky is an element of power, and as such desirable, is to obscure the issue.

Economic Power. The second use of the economic weapon as an instrument of national policy, i.e. its use to acquire power and influence abroad, has been so fully recognized and freely discussed that the briefest summary will suffice here. It takes two principal forms: (a) the export of capital, and (b) the control of foreign markets.

(a) The export of capital has in recent times been a familiar practice of powerful states. The political supremacy of Great Britain throughout the nineteenth century was closely associated with London's position as the financial center of the world. . . . The attainment of political objectives by direct government investment has occurred in such cases as the purchase by the British Government of shares in the Suez Canal Company and the Anglo-Iranian Oil Company, or the construction of the Chinese Eastern Railway with Russian government capital. More often, governments used their power to stimulate investments by banks and private individuals in the interests of national policy. . . .

In the first post-war years, France strengthened her influence over Poland and the Little Entente by abundant loans and credits, public and private, to these countries. Several governments granted or guaranteed loans to Austria for the political purpose of maintaining Austria's independence; and in 1931 French financial pressure obliged Austria to abandon the project of a customs union between Austria and Germany. The rapid decline of French influence in Central Europe since 1931 has been closely connected with the fact that France, since the crisis, has been unable to continue her policy of financial assistance to these countries. When in December 1938 it was announced that the French Schneider-Creusot group had sold its interest in the Skoda works to a Czechoslovak group representing the Czechoslovak Government, a correspondent of *The Times* [of London] commented that "this transaction is another indication of France's retreat from Central Europe, and puts an end to a chapter of French political expansion." . . .

(b) The struggle to control foreign markets provides a further illustration of the interaction of politics and economics; for it is often impossible to decide whether political power is being used to acquire markets for the sake of their economic value, or whether markets are being sought in order to establish and strengthen political power. . . . An admirable example of the intertwining of political and economic power may be found in the British position in Egypt. British economic penetration in Egypt in the last two decades of the nineteenth century resulted from British military occupation, which was designed to protect British interests in the Suez Canal, which had been acquired to protect British trade routes and strategic lines of communication. . . .

The most characteristic contemporary method of acquiring markets and the political power which goes with them is . . . the return to a system of thinly disguised barter. Thus British purchases of meat and cereals in the Argentine and of bacon and butter in Denmark and the Baltic States have secured markets in those countries for British coal and British manufactures. The Ottawa Agreements are a slightly more complicated variation on the same theme. In the Central European and Balkan countries Germany, by purchasing local products (mainly cereals and tobacco) for which no other lucrative outlet could be found, has secured not only a market for German goods, but a sphere of political influence. One of the symptoms of the artificial character of French political influence in this region after the [First World] War was her failure to secure for herself any substantial share in its trade. Purchasing power has become an international asset. . . . A new power has thus been placed in the hands of countries with a large population and a high standard of living. But it is a wasting asset which, if used to excess, tends to destroy itself.

Power over Opinion. Power over opinion is the third form of power. . . . Power over opinion is . . . not less essential for political purposes than military and economic power, and has always been closely associated with them. The art of persuasion has always been a necessary part of the equipment of a political leader. . . . But the popular view which regards propaganda as a distinctively modern weapon is, none the less, substantially correct.

The most obvious reason for the increasing prominence attached to power over opinion in recent times is the broadening of the basis of politics, which has vastly increased the number of those whose opinion is politically important. . . .

Contemporary politics are vitally dependent on the opinion of large masses of more or less politically conscious people, of whom the most vocal, the most influential and the most accessible to propaganda are those who live in and around great cities. The problem is one which no modern government ignores. In appearance, the attitude adopted toward it by democracies and by totalitarian states is diametrically opposed. Democracies purport to follow mass opinion; totalitarian states set a standard and enforce conformity to it.

In practice, the contrast is less clear cut. Totalitarian states, in determining their policy, profess to express the will of the masses; and the profession is not wholly vain. Democracies, or the groups which control them, are not altogether innocent of the arts of molding and directing mass opinion. . . . There remains a solid substratum of difference between the attitude of democracies and totalitarian states toward mass opinion, which may prove a decisive factor in times of crisis. But both agree in recognizing its paramount importance.

The same economic and social conditions which have made mass opinion supremely important in politics have also created instruments of unparalleled range and efficiency for molding and directing it. The oldest, and still perhaps the most powerful, of these instruments is universal popular education. The state which provides the education necessarily determines its content. No state will allow its future citizens to imbibe in its schools teaching subversive of the principles on which it is based. In democracies, the child is taught to prize the liberties of democracy; in totalitarian states, to admire the strength and discipline of totalitarianism. In both, he is taught to respect the traditions and creeds and institutions of his own country, and to think it better than any other. . . .

But when we speak of propaganda today, we think mainly of those other instruments whose use popular education has made possible: the radio, the film and the popular press. The radio, the film and the press share to the fullest extent the characteristic attribute of modern industry, i.e. that mass-production, quasi-monopoly and standardization are a condition of economical and efficient working. Their management has, in the natural course of development, become concentrated in fewer and fewer hands; and this concentration facilitates and makes inevitable the centralized control of opinion. The mass-production of opinion is the corollary of the mass-production of goods. Just as the nineteenth century conception of political freedom was rendered illusory for large masses of the population by the growth and concentration of economic power, so the nineteenth century conception of freedom of thought is being fundamentally modified by the development of these new and extremely powerful instruments of power over opinion. . . . The issue is no longer whether men shall be politically free to express their opinions, but whether freedom of opinion has, for large masses of people, any meaning but subjection to the influence of innumerable forms of propaganda directed by vested interests of one kind or another. Some control by the state of this power over opinion has become necessary if the community is to survive. In the totalitarian countries, radio, press and film are state industries absolutely controlled by governments. In democratic countries, conditions vary, but are everywhere tending in the direction of centralized control.

The organized use of power over opinion as a regular instrument of foreign policy is a modern development. Prior to 1914, cases occurred of the use of propaganda by governments in international relations. . . . But the field of propaganda was limited; and the only people who exploited it at all intensively were the revolutionaries. . . .

It did not take long for the belligerents of 1914-1918 to realize that "psychological war must accompany economic war and military war." It was a condition of success on the military and economic fronts that the "morale" of one's own side should be maintained, and that of the other side sapped and destroyed. Propaganda was the instrument by which both these ends were pursued. . . . The new conditions of warfare nullified, in this as in so many other respects, the distinction between combatant and civilian; and the morale of the civilian population became for the first time a military objective. . . .

The demoralization of the civilian population [during the First World War] was the primary objective not only of many air raids but of the German long-range bombardment of Paris by "Big Bertha"; and the work of the bomb and the shell was reinforced, especially during the last months of the war, by an intense output of printed propaganda. Throughout the war, the close interdependence between the three forms of power was constantly demonstrated. The success of propaganda on both sides, both at home and in neutral and enemy countries, rose and fell with the varying fortunes of the military and economic struggle. When at length the Allied blockade and Allied victories in the field crippled German resources, Allied propaganda became enormously effective and played a considerable part in the final collapse. The victory of 1918 was achieved by a skillful combination of military power, economic power, and power over opinion.

Notwithstanding the general recognition of the importance of propaganda in the later stages of war, it was still regarded by almost everyone as a weapon specifically appropriate to a period of hostilities. . . . Yet within twenty years of the Armistice, many governments were conducting propaganda with an intensity unsurpassed in the war period; and new official or semi-official agencies for the influencing of opinion at home and abroad were springing up in every country. This new development has been rendered possible and inevitable by the popularization of international politics and by the growing efficiency of propaganda methods. Since both these processes are likely to continue, its permanence seems assured. The ever increasing use of propaganda as a regular instrument of foreign policy has been one of the factors contributing to recent international tension. Recognition of power over opinion as a normal instrument of policy will tend to deprive it of the disturbing influence which it at present exercises. . . .

Most political ideas which have strongly influenced mankind have been based on professedly universal principles and have therefore had, at any rate in theory, an international character. The ideas of the French Revolution, free trade, Communism in its original form of 1848 or in its reincarnation of 1917, Zionism, the idea of the League of Nations, are all at first sight (as they were in intention) examples of international opinion divorced from power and fostered by international propaganda. But reflection will correct this first impression. How far were any of these ideas politically effective until they took on a national color and were supported by national power? . . . The military power of Napoleon was notoriously the most potent factor in the propagation throughout Europe of the ideas of 1789. The political influence of the idea of free trade dated from its adoption by Great Britain as the basis of British policy. The revolutionaries of 1848 failed everywhere to achieve political power; and the ideas of 1848 remained barren. Neither the First nor the Second International attained any real authority. As 1914 showed, there were national labor movements, but there was no international labor movement. The Third or Communist International enjoyed little influence until the power of the Russian state was placed behind it. . . . Propaganda is ineffective as a political force until it acquires a national home and becomes linked with military and economic power.

. . . When we set power over opinion side by side with military and economic power, we have none the less to remember that we are dealing no longer with purely material factors, but with the thoughts and feelings of human beings.

Absolute power over opinion is limited in two ways. In the first place, it is limited by the necessity of some measure of conformity with fact. . . . Good advertising may persuade the public that a face cream made of inferior materials is the best. But the most expert advertiser could not sell a face cream made of vitriol. . . . Education, which is one of the strongest instruments of this power, tends at the same time to promote a spirit of independent inquiry which is also one of the strongest antidotes against it. In so far as it strains and interprets facts for a specific purpose, propaganda always contains within itself this potentially self-defeating element.

Secondly, power over opinion is limited—and perhaps even more effectively —by the inherent utopianism of human nature. Propaganda, harnessed to military and economic power, always tends to reach a point where it defeats its own end by inciting the mind to revolt against that power. It is a basic fact about human nature that human beings do in the long run reject the doctrine that might makes right. . . . This vital fact gives us another clue to the truth that politics cannot be defined solely in terms of power. Power over opinion, which is a necessary part of all power, can never be absolute. International politics are always power politics; for it is impossible to eliminate power from them. But that is only part of the story. The fact that national propaganda everywhere so eagerly cloaks itself in ideologies of a professedly international character proves the existence of an international stock of common ideas, however limited and however weakly held, to which appeal can be made, and of a belief that these common ideas stand somehow in the scale of values above national interests. . . .

POPULATION AS AN ELEMENT OF NATIONAL POWER

"Wars are fought by men," writes Horst Mendershausen (*The Economics of War*, rev. ed., copyright 1943 by Prentice-Hall, Inc., New York). "Machines and raw materials are dead matter if they are not put to use by human beings."

Mere numbers, however, are by no means a reliable index of a nation's military potential. This point was emphatically stated in *The Problems of a Changing Population* (National Resources Committee, Government Printing Office, Washington, 1938). "Wealth, technical skill, organization, and morale are probably more important in all military affairs than mere numerical strength today. This is obviously so in aerial and naval operations. It may be true to such an extent that a population policy aimed purely at increasing the general level of well-being would be most advantageous from the standpoint of increasing military resources."

The more numerous populations of China or in India represent only a fraction of the military potential of the United States or Soviet Union. On the other hand, the Low Countries of Europe, despite high per-capita wealth, tools, and skills, lacked the numbers to resist the German invasion of 1940.

Thus, estimates of a country's military potential must take into account both *size* and *quality* of its population.

This theme is developed briefly in *Introduction to War Economics,* by a group of Brown University Economists (Richard D. Irwin, Inc., Chicago, 1942):

"A large population is a distinct asset in wartime both as a source of workers for industry and as a reservoir of manpower for the armed forces, provided sufficient resources are available to support such a population at a high level of efficiency. . . .

"Population estimates are at best almost meaningless as a measure of manpower potential for either industrial or military service. There is no 'standard' man, any more than there is an 'economic' man. . . .

"If war were carried on by soldiers equipped with but rudimentary weapons fighting only in such numbers that they could live on the country in which they fought, then counting heads would be of more significance. In a modern war, however, mere numbers is no standard for judging war-making capacity for a number of reasons. Population potential for war purposes will depend greatly upon what we may call the general economic standard of living. A country with a high general standard enjoys a great many advantages in mustering its population for war. Consumption can be cut very drastically without impinging upon the minimum standard for health, and thus large numbers of people can be freed for war production or for fighting. A high standard is usually accompanied by relatively short hours of labor, a considerable leisure class, a relatively high school-leaving age for young people, a large class of retired workers, and a great number of non-working women supported entirely by husbands or families. All of these factors are enormously important as a source of labor power and fighting power in wartime.

"Another consideration which must not be overlooked is the raw materials position of a country. If a nation has cheap and abundant sources of raw materials, it need not in wartime divert workers to the production of substitutes and will therefore enjoy an advantage over countries less richly endowed. The Axis countries must experience a considerable strain upon their labor force because of the necessity of producing synthetic *ersatz* materials such as rubber and oil.

"Still another very important factor is the average productivity of the worker in all lines of production. This depends upon the techniques of production employed, the amount of capital used per worker, and the general standard of education and skill. Output per worker in the United States will be found to be higher on the average than output per worker in the Axis countries, and enormously higher than average worker output in the Asiatic countries. Our interest in population, after all, is not in the biological aspects of the human race but in the economic aspects, especially productivity. Mere counting of heads reflects a biological rather than economic point of view.

"Finally, even in the military forces the soldier of one nation is obviously not equal to the soldier of another. Quite apart from courage and stamina, the well-armed, well-equipped, and well-supplied soldier is worth several soldiers not so well endowed as himself. A Chinese army vastly outnumbering the Japanese has for several years been unable to drive the invader from China, and the well-equipped and skillfully directed British armies were able to overcome the Axis forces in Libya in the fall of 1940 although greatly outnumbered on the actual field of battle."

FOODSTUFFS AND RAW MATERIALS AS ELEMENTS OF NATIONAL POWER

By Karl Brandt

From chap. 5, an essay by Karl Brandt in *War in Our Time*, edited by H. Speier and A. Kahler. Copyright 1939 by W. W. Norton & Co., New York; reproduced by permission. Dr. Brandt is professor of economics and a member of the Food Research Institute at Stanford University.

THE question of raw materials with reference to peace and war leads straight into a confusing jungle of problems in international relations and political economics.

The maze begins with the very conception of what constitutes a raw material. It is true that superficially we pretend to know what this group name covers. The large catalogue of raw materials contains commodities of vegetable and animal origin as well as minerals. It includes the sources of man's food, clothing, shelter, of the feed for his animals, of heat, light and power, and of all sorts of industrial goods. Thus raw materials embrace, first, vegetable and animal products carrying carbohydrates, proteins, fats and vitamins; second, wood, vegetable and animal fibers, rubber, hides and skins; third, stored fuels like peat, lignite, coal, oil and natural gas; fourth, other ferrous and non-ferrous minerals. The activities they entail are equally various: collecting, fishing and hunting, mining, forestry, agriculture, horticulture and synthetic production.

The situation becomes even more complex if we search for characteristics that would determine whether a specific commodity is a raw material, or that determine whether it is an essential, an optional or merely a luxury good. We soon discover that we can do no more than simply list those commodities which, often enough for heterogeneous reasons, are considered somewhere as raw materials, adding perhaps one or several question marks in the column denoting the necessity of their use. There are no objective measurements of necessity. It is an evaluation, determined ultimately by manifold social, technological and economic standards as they are followed by a specific civilization or social group at a specific time. While 80 million Japanese will point today to the necessity for large supplies of gasoline and crude oil, the present 80 million Javanese may easily get along without them. While Eskimos will insist on fish as the essential component of their diet, the Hindus may not care to have any, and vice versa with rice. The majority of the world's population lives on a more or less vegetarian diet; if all peoples should prefer to obtain a large part of their nutritional energies from animal products, as the leading occidental nations do now, the world would be faced with an insoluble maldistribution of food. Fortunately peoples have developed their diets through the ages in conformity with their environment and their ability to secure supplies. And yet their habits and thereby their demands are changing as time passes.

The determination of what is and what is not a necessary raw material is even more functional with reference to fibers, fuels and other minerals. During the sixteenth and seventeenth centuries wood was almost the only fuel used in industry. In the beginning of the nineteenth century oil did not mean much; nor was the significance of waterpower sites or lignite deposits recognized, because the hydroturbine, the steam turbine and the electric generator had not been invented. In 1850 Chilean saltpeter as fertilizer was practically worthless; in 1900 it was an invaluable treasure of international importance; by 1920 it was on its way to oblivion. In 1880 the "manmade" metal aluminum was not known for technical use, while in 1930 it ranked as one of the first-grade metals for general application in industry and the household. Its substitute, magnesium, also "invented" and man-made, was of no importance in 1920, whereas today it is a serious competitor. Such examples could be multiplied.

Human wants are continuously shaped and reshaped by civilization, its technical and social standards and its progress. Some of man's greatest achievements lie in his successful adaptation to the available raw materials, in his rendering more of them accessible and with his genius discovering new ones.

Except for wild fruits and the products of hunting and fishing, raw materials are not readily available. What really exist and are potentially available in abundance or scarcity, either near by or in the distance, are the so-called "natural resources." And again we face an ambiguous term with many meanings, tempting those who use it to many fallacies of assumption and interpretation. In public discussion and in a good deal of contemporary literature on applied economics and government, "natural resources" are spoken of as if they represented accessible stores of raw materials open to exploitation by anyone ruthless enough to grab the values offered by nature. The wholesome and well-meant emphasis on conservation of natural resources has persuaded vast numbers of the people in this country to believe that up to a generation ago certain rugged individualists maliciously destroyed the beautiful treasure of timber, thereby stealing what had been bestowed by Providence upon this continent and future generations. A similar belief is held with reference to the oil fields today. But in point of fact the American pioneers deserve the gratitude of their heirs for performing the truly gigantic and most necessary task of clearing, with ax, saw and fire, 300,000,000 acres of land from virgin forest, thereby conquering the inimical wilderness and rendering it livable. Those who blame them would not be able to offer any other realistic advice than plain repetition if they were the responsible advisers to the Brazilian government today. If some lumber companies continue in these days cutting practices which were justified in the pioneer period this is an entirely different case; but even there the fault is that of the forest-tax authorities.

This example is given only in order to show that natural resources are at first little more than an opportunity for man to derive raw materials from them. Ordinarily the resources, because of their very origin, are not readily realizable. To make them accessible and to conquer them man must—as in all his production—apply intelligence and inventiveness, management, labor and capital. If these factors are not present and, if man has not conceived the idea of using the opportunity offered by nature for the satisfaction of his wants, the environmental condition has not yet become a natural resource. It may be nothing more than a nuisance or a pest. In the 'sixties of the last century the State of Pennsylvania passed laws against the pollution of creeks and rivers with gasoline, which was then a useless waste product; only kerosene counted, which is today itself a byproduct.

Whether a certain situation in the environment is considered as a "natural resource" depends on a multiplicity of conditions: on whether the specific society has already developed a demand for the raw material that may be made available; on whether a sufficient standard of technology and skill has been built up to launch the attack upon the resource; on the availability of sufficient skilled labor and on the presence of sufficient capital, if only in the form of equipment and food supplies for the labor force. And yet with all these conditions fulfilled it may be found that the efforts to exploit the resource are comparatively too great. In this case it may relapse into a potential reserve or may be discarded and forgotten as such.

If the exploitation should prove profitable from the standpoint of the social group as a whole, the yield in raw materials may be exceedingly different under the application of different principles. How long the resource will continue to yield depends partly on the speed of exploitation, but even more on its intensity and efficiency. Petroleum, for instance, can be mined by drilling a well in which natural gas pressure spits the oil above the surface. When the gas is exhausted the well stops producing, and may then be abandoned. The oil of the gusher can be made available for use in the crude manner of skimming off the small percentage of gasoline, leaving the rest of the oil to be used instead of coal as a fuel. With an advanced technique the yielding capacity of the same well may be multiplied by more efficient drilling, by maintaining or recreating the gas pressure, by proceeding later on with pumping out the oil, and especially by fractional distillation, cracking and refining. Similarly the duration of the resource may be prolonged by thrift and greater efficiency in consumption. This example is typical for practically every one of the known resources. At the same time it illustrates a logical historical sequence of increasing intensity in production and utilization.

Enough has been said to indicate how relative is the whole question of raw materials and natural resources. There is no objective measurement by which we can ascertain, for a particular country, the potential necessity of known resources or even the existence of resources we are yet unaware of; and in regard to international relations we are equally at a loss if we try to form an absolute judgment on the distribution or maldistribution of "natural resources."

It appears utterly impossible to measure political phenomena which are described by such misconceived concepts as "population pressure" or "resource-man ratio." With these suggestive terms it is often attempted to interpret a complex situation in simplified pseudo-physical terms. The most popular form of this fallacy is the specifically American idea that this country's relatively high standard of living depends on its favorable "land-man ratio." If that were correct the Argentine ought to have the highest standard of living and the greatest wealth per capita among the nations; and, if the land-man ratio referred to minerals as well as land, Mexico would probably have the title to the most luxurious economic status, while Belgium and Switzerland would rank among the poorest countries in the world.

The assumptions that a specific piece of land as such has a certain "absorptive power" for population, and that land as such can be classified as profitable or "submarginal," are modern fancies which cause more harm than the notion that the machine impoverishes human society. Land, like all natural resources, is no more than an opportunity for man to apply his inventiveness, management, labor and capital. Each of these factors may contribute in varying degree to the yield. Consequently poor land may yield highly, while rich land may yield nothing or carry the most impoverished farm population. Ten thousand acres of land may not be worth a penny, in spite of sufficient rainfall and a high content of plant nutrients. Its "absorptive power for population" may be zero. It begins to have a social value only when it is cleared of woods or brush, developed with roads and public utilities, drained or irrigated, tilled and planted either in part or as a whole— in short, when it is developed by men, animals and machines. It may be farmed by one man with the aid of ten laborers or sharecroppers and provide him and his crew with so small an output that all of them are condemned to poverty. Or it may be farmed by fifty or a hundred families and offer a satisfactory livelihood to several hundred people. It all depends on the use of capital and skill. Land which is thus useless and may nevertheless be given a value is to be found in every country, even in those with the supposedly highest "population pressure," though in smaller amounts than in thinly populated areas.

In attempts to appraise natural resources we face the dilemma that every possible measuring rod involves imponderable philosophical or ethical axioms like justice or duty. Shall we measure the natural resources of a country by geologists' estimates of total deposits, or by the capacity of the existing industry, or by the actual output? Shall a nation be considered to have the moral duty to invent devices for the full utilization of its own resources, or shall it be considered to have a claim on those of its neighbors?

In 1914 Germany as a highly industrialized country produced 75 per cent of her food at home. As a consequence of the [First] World War she lost fertile surplus-producing agrarian provinces in the East. At present [1939] she has attained a domestic food production of 87 per cent of her needs, and it is quite conceivable that within a decade or two she might be entirely self-supporting in spite of her growing population. The use of minerals as fertilizers, taken from the underground and from the air, as well as improvements on the land and better farming methods, combined with a shift of consumption toward synthetic substances, are working toward that end. Denmark has increased her exclusively domestic agricultural production (excluding conversion of foreign raw materials) by 200 per cent within fifty years. It may well be that a certain portion of the German farm output is produced at higher costs than those on the world market, but the Danish increase of production has been achieved under a regime of free trade.

In discussing the international distribution of natural resources it is often admitted that a particular "have-not" nation has, indeed, the resource in question but that it is "sub-marginal." Sub-marginality is an appraisal of the profitability of exploiting a natural resource at a specific time on a specific soil, with consideration of all the factors affecting net profits. Hence such a term is inappropriate in discussing the international problems of natural resources. According to prevailing American ideas about farming, three-fourths of all European agriculture must be operating on "sub-marginal" land. At the same time, hundreds of thousands of American farmers live on fertile land the life of rural proletarians. The complexity of the cost structure for the total production of a commodity within a national economic system, and the lack of any international basis of comparison for the items involved, render the whole discussion of international cost comparisons highly academic.

This preliminary reconnaissance of some of the problems underlying the question of raw materials and natural resources makes it possible to draw several conclusions.

First, the utmost caution should be observed in applying to this subject concepts and measuring rods which are either too ambiguous to mean much or, worse than that, basically deceptive. "Population pressure," "density of population per square mile," "sub-marginality of existing resources," are such terms. International raw material problems should be approached not with the static assumptions of any *status quo* or with moral postulates but with expert knowledge and with awareness of contemporary trends in economic and technical development.

Second, man has considerably more freedom of action in adapting himself and adjusting the particular civilization of his society to a given environment than an uncritical survey suggests or than certain propagandists would have us believe. Technical progress and science have made it more possible for man to substitute for non-available raw materials and resources those that are accessible, thus making him less dependent on specific resources. For the commonwealth of nations as a whole the earlier scarcity of raw materials has changed more and more into an abundance which, significantly enough, is often called from the point of view of price a "surplus" situation.

Third, the raw material problem of nations cannot be solved permanently within their narrow political boundaries, because the conception of what constitutes an essential raw material changes continuously with technical progress in the pursuit of peace and national defense.

Fourth, the use of crude gauges for measuring the adequacy of a nation's natural resources or domestic supply of raw materials leads to calling the most inventive and industrious nations saturated and the skimming exploiters and rugged primitives the "have-nots."

It is within man's capacity to make adjustments and to invent new solutions. For a more adequate production of foodstuffs it is possible to intensify agriculture and horticulture; for power and fuel it is possible to shift from "deposit resources" to "flow resources" and harness the latent energies of lakes, rivers and tidal sites; for metals synthetic products can be substituted; and in general consumption it is possible to promote thrift and an intensified utilization of available materials. Thus nothing can be more misleading than to assume that there is something like a natural law which by the force of economic gravitation makes nations inevitably dependent on foreign raw materials. It all depends on a large number of factors, many of which are subject to modification by man, and no generalization is permissible.

FOODSTUFFS AND RAW MATERIALS

By the Editors of A.S.F. Manual M-103

From chap. 1 of *Geographical Foundations of National Power*. Army Service Forces Manual M-103-1, Government Printing Office, Washington, 1944.

Raw materials fall into two main categories: (1) those derived from vegetable and animal sources—the products of agriculture, forestry, and fisheries; and (2) those derived from mineral resources.

Agriculture, Forestry, and Fisheries. The products of agricultural, pastoral, and forest lands are conditioned by climate, soil, land forms, and drainage and, in the cases of pastoral and forest land, by natural vegetation. Agricultural and pastoral lands yield primarily food, but also the textile fibers for clothing, and a few weapons and tools. Every nation bases its economy in the first instance upon agriculture, including the rearing of animals. In the aggregate, agricultural products bulk the largest and have the greatest total value of all classes of products required by a nation.

Forests, natural or planted, are being used in an increasing variety of ways as modern technology converts them into building materials, paper, plastics, clothing, and many other products. Rubber, derived originally from forest trees but now primarily from plantations, is vital to modern highway transport.

Oceans yield food and a number of other products, such as whale oil and fertilizers. Because of differences in salinity and water temperature, certain parts of the ocean are far more productive than others, and nations like Norway and Japan derive an important part of their national income from neighboring fishing grounds. In general, however, ocean products make only a relatively minor contribution to the sum total of a nation's resources.

Mineral Resources. A nation otherwise well endowed by nature may lack vital minerals. Mineral resources are the prime ingredient of weapons, tools, and of much other equipment, including building materials, and constitute, next to agricultural products, the most critical element in national self-sufficiency, especially in wartime.

Coal, iron ore, and petroleum are the first requisites. The total world production of these in 1938 was about 1½ billion metric tons, 162 million metric tons, and 2 billion barrels, respectively. Such astronomical figures mean little to the reader. However, if we express the world production of mineral products in terms of percentages of the world production of iron ore, comparisons may be made. On this basis in 1938 the world production of coal was 907 per cent and that of petroleum was 315 per cent (assuming 4 barrels to the metric ton).

Coal is used primarily as a fuel. In the United States about three-quarters of the coal consumed is for heat and steam power, one-tenth for the production of electricity, and the remaining 15 per cent for making coke and its by-products. Coke, of course, is the form of coal used in the manufacture of steel.

Steel far outranks all other products derived from mineral resources in general utility, and is produced in greater bulk than any but building materials. Not only are most tools and weapons forged from steel, but also the machinery for making and transporting them. Iron is the principal ingredient of steel. About 2 tons of iron ore are required to make 1 ton of steel, but approximately a third of the world's steel is made not from iron prepared especially for the purpose, but from scrap iron. Steel is an alloy of iron with other metals, among which manganese is usually essential. Only a small quantity of manganese (about 14 pounds to the ton) is required in relation to the quantity of iron that goes into steel, and the world production of manganese ore in 1938 was only 3.15 per cent of that of iron ore. About half a dozen other metals are indispensable in the various kinds of steels used in modern warfare, notably chromium (0.7), nickel (0.07), tungsten (0.02), molybdenum, and vanadium. Though these are strategic minerals of prime importance, the world production of the ore of each of them, as the figures indicate, is considerably less than 1 per cent of that of iron ore.

Among other mineral products essential in modern technology, and of which the world production (1938) exceeded 1 per cent of that of iron ore, are petroleum (315), potash (12.4), bauxite (2.37), sulphur (1.73), copper (1.28), and lead (1.05). Petroleum has been called the lifeblood of a nation. In terms of weight, roughly three times as much petroleum is produced as iron ore, but only about a third as much petroleum as coal. Petroleum supplies the motive power for airplanes, submarines, tanks, and the majority of ships. Upon petroleum and rubber are dependent the advances of the past few decades in highway transportation throughout the world. Aluminum, which is made from bauxite, has rendered the airplane possible. Potash is used primarily for fertilizers. Copper is the means of transmitting electric current. Lead is a principal ingredient in paint. Sulphur "is perhaps the most important chemical mineral."

SELF-SUFFICIENCY IN RAW MATERIALS

By the Editors of A.S.F. Manual M-103

From chap. 1 of *Geographical Foundations of National Power*. Army Service Forces Manual M-103-1, Government Printing Office, Washington, 1944.

SELF-SUFFICIENCY, as respects a nation's total economic needs, may be described as the nation's ability to sustain itself at any given level of consumption without access to outside sources of supply. The level of consumption frequently used as a yardstick is the normal peacetime standard of living. This varies from nation to nation. At one extreme is the high plateau of the American standard; at the other is the Chinese standard, with the great majority of the people living below the level of bare subsistence. Between those two extremes there are as many levels as there are nations. Few of them can boast a standard necessary for the maintenance of good health and proper physical development.

A second variant arises in the definition of the expression "access to outside sources of supply." Great Britain, cut off by blockade from access to her dominions and oversea colonies, could not survive long the onset of a more powerful nation controlling the sea and air approaches to the British Isles. Conversely, free communications within the British Commonwealth of Nations make her a formidable opponent for any nation.

War introduces the third variant. It superimposes upon normal peacetime demands of the civilian population the military requirements of the armed forces and their auxiliaries, such as transport and communications and the special needs of civilian defense. Not only is the total output required to meet the demands of modern mechanized war far greater than that needed for peacetime consumption, but the emphasis shifts sharply into certain specific fields. Basic foodstuffs and textile fibers, iron and the steel alloys, various non-ferrous metals, and the mineral fuels are the commodities in greatest demand.

From the above it is clear that no clean-cut objective definition of national self-sufficiency can be written. Even if the field is limited to wartime conditions where its application may measure the difference between victory and defeat, the life or death of a people, the concept remains somewhat nebulous. In common military acceptance, as followed in this text, the expression is taken to mean a nation's capacity to sustain itself economically in time of war. In such application, due consideration must be given to the effectiveness of the executive control maintained over all phases of the national economy. The records of the First World War, for example, show clearly that Germany got far more utility out of every kilowatt, foot-pound, and calorie produced than did any of her opponents. Lastly, it must be remembered that the self-sufficiency yardstick is never static in point of time. The depletion of natural reserves, the discoveries of the laboratory leading to the development of substitute materials, and the introduction of new techniques on the battlefield are all quickly reflected in the changing demands on the nations' raw material resources.

Notwithstanding all the imponderables involved, it is nevertheless practicable to estimate with a fair degree of accuracy to what extent a nation can sustain a full-scale war effort. After calculating its own shortages, a forehanded people can then build up in advance stockpiles of reserve raw materials to compensate for its basic deficiencies. Goering's "guns before butter" campaign produced not merely guns. The butter and other goods sold abroad returned to Germany in the form of Canada's nickel, America's copper and petroleum, Malaysia's tin. Such stockpiling represented a substantial part of the Axis' import trade. Germany's potential opponents, less forehanded, did not fail to estimate the extent of such stockpiles. In general, it was agreed that Germany had made ready for a war of several years' duration.

The studies initiated by various military agencies in the United States shortly after the close of the First World War led in time to certain refinements of analysis and classification. To begin with, all commodities deemed necessary for the maintenance of a normal peacetime economy plus those needed for the prosecution of war were classed as the *great essentials*. When it is noted that raw materials from more than 60 countries entered into the production of a 1938-model American automobile, it is evident that the list of *essentials* is long. Necessarily, domestic substitutes for a large percentage of those 60 commodities could be found. Similar substitutions could be made in the production of other manufactured goods. And the pinch of necessity promptly transfers many peacetime "essentials" to the luxury class. The final result is a list of items deemed indispensable to: (1) the maintenance of a standard of living acceptable to the American people; (2) the production of war matériel and supplies under a schedule of amounts, types, and time called for by war plans.

A very substantial proportion of the commodities needed by the United States can be obtained within the continental domain. Indeed no other power enjoys a comparable degree of self-sufficiency. Nevertheless there is a more or less acute need of many commodities obtainable only in part or not at all within the United States proper. These items are listed in two general categories, *strategic* and *critical*, the former being procurable in whole or in substantial quantities only from outside the continental limits of the United States and the latter presenting less difficult problems of procurement.

It is clear that no two nations would set up the same tables of strategic and critical materials. For example, manganese is a first-priority strategic commodity in the United States, whereas in Soviet Russia its abundance reduces it to the class of an essential. Even as to essentials, we find variations, due largely to variations in living standards. Wheat and wheat flour are so classed in the United States; in Germany, accustomed to a black-bread diet, the per-capita consumption is far lower.

National self-sufficiency, the unattainable goal of every empire-builder of the past and the declared objective of both the European and Asiatic leaders of the Axis, is not subject to accurate measure. Even if it were possible to calculate the absolute needs of a people for its proper sustenance and the added volume of output for the prosecution of war, human appetites and desires would tend to raise the sum, human endurance in time of stress would tend to lower it. The figures are affected even more by swift and unpredictable changes in the tactics and techniques of war. Any person predicting as recently as 1939 the current consumption rate of aluminum and other light metals resulting from the emphasis on air power would have been thought mad. At best, the measure of national self-sufficiency is crude and must be regarded as flexible. Actually it is simpler and safer to take note of marked deficiencies in the major commodities. . . . The sum of such deficiencies, after allowances have been made for stockpiles of reserves built up in prewar days, can then be expressed in terms of their effect on a nation's long-range military potential.

TECHNOLOGY AND NATIONAL POWER

By Ralph Turner

From "Technology and Geo-Politics," by Ralph Turner in *Military Affairs,* Spring issue, 1943. Copyright 1943 by American Military Institute; reproduced by permission. The author is professor of history at Yale University.

It is the purpose of these remarks to examine briefly . . . technology as a factor in the power situations of states. . . .

When the chief weapon was a chipped stone ax, warfare and its economic support were not complex. Both the raw materials and the operations in shaping them were simple. However, those men with the easiest access to flint and sinew or rawhide were not necessarily the best armed, for superiority depended upon skill in fashioning them into weapons. At one point in the archeological record it appears that an invention—a finely chipped point that served as an arrowhead or a spearhead —made possible a deep invasion of lands held by men armed mainly with chipped stone hand-axes and knives. It is easily guessed that this invention altered greatly the methods of combat.

With the invention of metallurgy the geographical, economic, and technological basis of military action became widely organized both in space and in institutions. Workable deposits of copper were eagerly sought after. Transportation brought the ore or metal to the seat of the skills required for its shaping into weapons. A wider range of skills, resting on a larger body of knowledge, was required than for the production of stone weapons. This complex of actions was first organized in the ancient urban cultures which, in turn, rested on a capacity to produce an amount of food sufficient to permit some part of a population to devote its energies to activities other than those of agriculture.

On the one hand urban cultures embodied in the institution of slavery the control over workers that the scarce metal weapons gave to a few men. On the other hand urban cultures organized controls over extended geographical areas, thereby giving rise to empires. The seats of urban cultures and their empires were originally in geographical areas favorable to the agricultural production that supported the differentiation of a ruling class, not practicing agriculture, from a peasantry. . . . It appears, therefore, that the state and its development internally as a class structure and externally as an empire rested upon the technological advances that created an economic surplus and differentiated a power-wielding class. Geographical factors were significant in this development only as they affected the actions which these technological advances made possible.

After the invention of metallurgy each technological achievement that increased the capacity to produce wealth, facilitated the transport of men and supplies, intensified social intercourse among peoples, and altered the types and designs of weapons affected the organization and development of urban cultures. Among these achievements, those which improved the mining of ores and the manufacture of metals were especially important for they reacted ultimately upon the production of wealth, the relation of social classes, the organization of the state, and the form of effective power.

The use of the horse for military purposes—the armed knight shortly after 2000 B.C., followed about two hundred years later by the charioteer—gave those who possessed metals and horses a distinct advantage over those who lacked them. The scarcity of tin and copper—the ingredients of bronze—limited the size of well-armed forces, a fact which quickly gave rise to new military classes. The first extended empires were organized by peoples ruled by these classes.

The arming and armoring of infantrymen capable of defeating armed horsemen and charioteers became possible about 1000 B.C. when iron-working was first widely developed. The first shift in power occasioned by this technological advance was organized in the Assyrian Empire. One Assyrian emperor is credited with having possessed as much as two hundred tons of iron.

Greece, Macedonia, the Hellenistic Kingdoms, and Rome achieved different military results as the techniques of iron-working and of transport advanced and as the designs of iron weapons improved. The engineers of the Hellenistic Kingdoms worked out the defensive and offensive potentialities of the then-existing knowledge of mechanics, setting the practices of siege warfare until the introduction of gunpowder. Rome owed an advantage in the Punic Wars to an iron-working industry which made possible the supplying of weapons to the other enemies of Carthage. In the second century of the empire, Rome's central military power weakened because ship design did not advance sufficiently to allow the transfer of adequate quantities of bulky goods from the distant provinces to Italy.

Some time before A.D. 500 an advance in iron-working, probably in India, reached Europe by way of Persia, Syria, Egypt, and North Africa; it again made possible the arming and armoring of the horseman so that he could prevail against infantrymen. Both the Sassanian Persian Empire and the late Roman Empire displaced light-armed cavalry and mobile infantry with a heavily-armed cavalry. The cost of the new equipment was a decisive factor in limiting the size of armies and the strength of military classes. This development, together with the siege practices of the Hellenistic engineers, set the pattern of medieval warfare. Toward the end of the Middle Ages innovations in metal-working which contributed to the improvement of the crossbow tended to decrease the supremacy of the armored knight over the infantryman.

When gunpowder, invented in China about 100 B.C., was adapted to military uses in Europe some time after A.D. 1200, developments now casually familiar to most students of economic and military history got under way. A note on the evolution of firepower will suggest the trend of these developments in so far as they are significant in the present discussion.

Gunpowder was originally more important for breaching defensive works than for combat; in fact, it was not until the last half of the seventeenth century that firearms finally displaced late medieval weapons. At this time the smooth-bore, muzzle-loading musket which fired a heavy ball came into general use. It was effective about two out of five times at one hundred yards; at two hundred yards it had no accuracy at all. This was the technological basis of eighteenth century warfare. The volley was the leading device for achieving a maximum firepower. Close-order movement of highly disciplined troops was necessary in order to concentrate this firepower. For this reason maneuvering became an essential element of generalship. To offset these offensive methods defensive masonry and earthworks were highly developed. Both the cost of weapons and the difficulty of supplying an army kept the armies small.

Napoleon took advantage of a development of artillery. His smooth-bore, muzzle-loading cannon which fired "case shot" had an effective range of four hundred yards; for this reason, his batteries, remaining out of range of the musket, could destroy the closed ranks of the old-style infantry. The English open-square, as well as the loose ranks introduced in the French armies, was an answer to this method of concentrating firepower. It was finally overcome by the development of the rifle that fired the conical bullet; against men armed with this weapon, which had an effective range of six hundred and fifty yards, the men of the old-style batteries had no chance.

The rifled gun barrel, invented in England, first came into common use in the English colonies of the Atlantic seaboard where its accuracy at a range of two hundred yards was especially useful to the woodsmen for whom it was both an economic implement and a weapon. Difficulties of manufacture prevented its wide adoption for military purposes.

The present relation of rifles to field pieces and heavy guns was established after 1850 when improved rifling and breech-loading devices were added to each. With trajectory-firing the range of field pieces was extended to over two thousand yards and as a result the infantry and the artillery entered into a new combat organization which was first clearly worked out in the American Civil War. Advances in metalworking which permitted a high accuracy—to the forty-thousandth of an inch—supported these innovations in armaments. At the same time the other developments, summarized by the phrase "The Industrial Revolution," altered the conditions of manufacturing and transport having significance for military action.

In the twentieth century the combination of the internal combustion engine and the gun has made a revolution in both sea and land warfare. Both the tank and the airplane stem from this combination. But their forms are also due to developments in chemistry and metallurgy which have produced new explosives and the lighter and harder metals, as well as having made easier the production and the shaping of ever greater quantities of all metals.

Today mere numbers of men, or the possession of raw materials, or the holding of strategic positions is not the essential source of power. Only those nations having scientists, engineers, and skilled workers who are masters of the knowledge and the skills required for devising and operating intricate machines and chemical processes can adequately equip armed forces. Armed forces are now the cutting edges of a vast social machine organized to achieve the maximum power which contemporary technology makes it possible to produce: thus total war. The present global war differs from the World War 1914-1918 in its economics, politics, tactics, and strategy, largely because of the transformation of the base and the form of power this fact suggests.

When conceived in general terms the role of technology in warfare can be stated as follows: The determining factor in warfare is the capacity to put metal in motion in the largest amount and with the greatest speed and maneuverability so that it will most effectively limit and reduce an enemy's capacity to accomplish the same ends. Every action from finding minerals in the earth and extracting them from it, through every process of manufacturing metals and shaping them, to all movements of metals to and upon the area of combat form a grand technological sequence. The organization and maintenance of this sequence is the central problem of waging total war. Subsidiary actions of all kinds must support this sequence and facilitate its operation. . . .

The grand technological sequence is established by (a) the means of production, (b) the means of transport, (c) the means of communication, and (d) the means of violence. The means of production affects the output of raw materials and finished goods in each of its phases. The means of transport determines the rate of movement of raw materials and finished goods from place to place within the geographical area from which raw materials are obtained and where combat occurs. The means of communication permits the organization of complex cooperative efforts extending throughout the grand technological sequence and over the geographical area it occupies. The means of violence determines the kinds of war matériel necessary for combat and, consequently, affects the organization and movement of the grand technological sequence at every point.

If this sequence is conceived in terms of industries, such as the electric power, the steel-making, or the oil-refining, or the meat-packing, several classes of vulnerabilities can be recognized. In waging total war these vulnerabilities become points of attack for an enemy; the maintenance of efficient operation in spite of these vulnerabilities is the fundamental problem of organizing an effective war effort.

1. A well defined set of raw materials is required by an industry. Some of these materials (basic) are required in large amounts if production is to be adequate. Others (critical) are required in small amounts if the output is to have high quality. To lessen the supply of any of these commodities in any way is an effective act of war. When a people is known to lack certain raw materials, interference with their obtaining them, however accomplished, is an effective act of war.

2. Technological "bottlenecks" exist in an industry. In an industry there are points at which operations can be interfered with more easily than at others (a) because they are very complex, (b) because they may be concentrated in one or a few plants, (c) because they may require some rare raw material or an apparatus difficult to obtain and maintain, and (d) because they may require highly specialized labor. Since these technological "bottlenecks" may

give rise to conditions greatly limiting output, to interfere with operations at such points is an effective act of war. Sabotage is most likely at these points.

3. An industry has a geographical extension. The raw materials of an industry are obtained from certain places. Transportation follows certain routes. Plants are located at certain points. Enemy interference at various points in this geographical extension may be possible, but its effects at different points will be different depending on aspects (such as technological "bottlenecks," labor supply, and transport concentration) of the industry other than mere location.

4. An industry requires a specialized labor force. This specialized labor force consists of both occupational and degree-of-skill groups which, of course, have a proportional relation to one another. These groups must be available at certain points in the technological sequence of an industry and, consequently, at certain geographical locations. A deficiency in any one of these groups will seriously disturb the operation of the grand technological sequence.

5. An industry operates under a system of controls originating partly with government, partly with owners, and partly with laborers. The efficient operation of an industry depends upon the organization and direction of effort made possible by this system of controls. Controversies among the various groups sharing power in an industry are likely to decrease its efficiency. Foreign influence among owners (cartel agreements, for example) and among workers (propaganda of various kinds) is almost certain to prevent an industry from contributing fully to a war effort. Sabotage is likely to have origin in discontent or disloyalty among these groups.

6. An industry depends on some industries and, in turn, supports others. The raw materials and equipment of an industry are derived from other industries, and its products in turn become the means of carrying on other industries. A nation at war requires an integration of many industries in a continuous service to its war effort. Full mobilization requires that this integration work smoothly at top speed and at maximum output. In some industries interference with the supply of a raw material, or the operation of a production process, or transport, or labor supply, or management may seriously disturb the production of primary war matériel or, in some others, may cause a deterioration of over-all productive capacity.

To deliver a full war effort a nation must operate the grand technological sequence efficiently from beginning to end. Its vulnerabilities must be protected against both internal and external interference. Its managerial and labor forces must achieve a high degree of cooperation. One industry must not be out of balance with others. Military and civilian needs must be met according to the availability of raw materials and the demands of the military situation, not according to a civilian standard of living. The limit to the decrease of a standard of living should be set not by the morale of the people but by the energy required to operate the grand technological sequence at the required level of efficiency for success in war. Military organization and direction in combat areas affects the final utilization of the power which a nation can produce through the sequence.

When viewed in its geographical extension the grand technological sequence of a nation may be seen as forming at least three classes of critical economic areas, that is, regions in which interference with its operations will affect adversely the nation's war effort: (a) critical raw material areas, (b) critical transportation areas, and (c) critical production areas. A critical raw material area has a high concentration of the facilities of production of basic and/or essential raw materials. A critical transportation area has a high concentration of the transportation facilities required for moving raw materials, finished goods, and war matériel through the grand technological sequence. Logistics is only the final aspect of this movement. A critical production area has a high concentration of the facilities of production of war machines, munitions, and other supplies required by armed forces.

When the organization and activities of a nation at war are analyzed in the foregoing terms, the ways in which technology conditions its entire effort may be summarized as follows:

1. Technology gives usefulness to a raw material, establishes the proportions of it required for use in combinations with other raw materials in the production of various commodities, and, consequently, fixes the amount of it that is needed for a given war effort.

2. Technology makes possible the development of substitutes for raw materials that are in short supply. Usually these substitutes are more costly in labor and less efficient in action than the materials they replace. To force a nation to resort to the use of substitute raw materials means increasing its difficulties in carrying on a war.

3. Technology gives importance to geographical regions accordingly as they supply raw materials or a combination of raw materials required for a given war effort or as they domicile the facilities, including the labor supply, required for the production of war matériel.

4. Technology establishes the means of transport and, thereby, determines the routes over which raw materials, war matériel, and other supplies required for a given war effort, are shipped. It fixes, therefore, the amounts of these commodities that can be concentrated at any given point.

5. Technology fixes the kinds and amounts of labor required for a given war effort. It sets, therefore, the problem of allocating a nation's population at the various tasks that constitute this effort. In these terms the armed forces a nation can organize and maintain are discovered to be relative to the efficient operation of its grand technological sequence.

6. Technology determines the forms, fixes the qualities, and limits the quantities of war matériel a nation can produce and place in combat areas. Above all it establishes technological differentials in war machines and munitions, thereby giving advantages to the armed forces of the nation possessing the most advanced application of science in the production of arms and armament. Today differentials in the maneuverability and firepower of airplanes, in the muzzle velocities of guns, in the toughness of armor plate, in the designs of warships, in the volatility of gasoline (along with hundreds of other technological items) enter into the making of a nation's war potential. The widespread interest in "secret weapons," as well as the intensive research in the scientific aspects of war, indicate the dependence of military effort upon technology.

7. Technology conditions military tactics and enters deeply into the determination of military strategy. The German Blitzkrieg was a utilization of the new method of offensive warfare. New tactics were devised for the units using these weapons and for the units cooperating with them. New tactics have been introduced steadily as the present war has progressed. In so far as

the war is a struggle between the "have-not" and the "have" nations, its strategy has been influenced by the need of the "have-not" nations to obtain new sources of raw material supplies. Japan's campaign in Southeast Asia and the East Indies was determined partly by her need for certain raw materials and partly by a desire to deprive Great Britain and the United States of the sources of certain raw materials. The important point in this connection is that strategy is affected quite as much by the means of military action possessed by a nation as by the geographical situation in which the action must be organized.

THE POWER OF IDEAS

By Bertrand Russell

From chap. 10 of *Power: A New Social Analysis*, by Bertrand Russell. Copyright 1938 by W. W. Norton & Co., New York; reproduced by permission. Earl Russell is a distinguished British scholar and an authority in many fields ranging from mathematics to politics.

THE power of a community depends not only upon its numbers and its economic resources and its technical capacity, but also upon its beliefs. A fanatical creed, held by all the members of a community, often greatly increases its power; sometimes, however, it diminishes it. As fanatical creeds are much more in the fashion than they were during the nineteenth century, the question of their effect on power is one of great practical importance. One of the arguments against democracy is that a nation of united fanatics has more chance of success in war than a nation containing a large proportion of sane men. Let us examine this argument in the light of history.

It should be observed, to begin with, that the cases in which fanaticism has led to success are naturally better known than those in which it has led to failure, since the cases of failure have remained comparatively obscure. Thus a too-rapid survey is apt to be misleading; but if we are aware of this possible source of error, it is not difficult to avoid.

The classic example of power through fanaticism is the rise of Islam. Mohammed added nothing to the knowledge or to the material resources of the Arabs, and yet, within a few years of his death, they had acquired a large empire by defeating their most powerful neighbors. Undoubtedly, the religion founded by the Prophet was an essential element in the success of his nation.... Fanaticism, while Mohammed lived, and for a few years after his death, united the Arab nation, gave it confidence in battle, and promoted courage by the promise of Paradise to those who fell fighting the infidel.

But although fanaticism inspired the first attempts of the Arabs, it was to other causes that they owed their prolonged career of victory. The Byzantine and Persian Empires were both weakened by long and indecisive wars; and Roman armies, at all times, were weak against cavalry. The Arab horsemen were incredibly mobile, and were inured to hardships which their more luxurious neighbors found intolerable. These circumstances were essential to the first successes of the Moslem.

Very soon—sooner than in the beginning of any other great religion—fanaticism was dethroned from the government. Ali, the Prophet's son-in-law, kept alive the original enthusiasm among a section of the faithful, but he was defeated in civil war, and finally assassinated. He was succeeded in the Caliphate by the family of Ommiyah, who had been Mohammed's bitterest opponents, and had never yielded more than a political assent to his religion. . . . From that moment onwards, for a long time, the Caliphate was distinguished by free-thinking latitudinarianism, while the Christians remained fanatical. From the first, the Mohammedans showed themselves tolerant in their dealings with conquered Christians, and to this toleration—which was in strong contrast to the persecuting zeal of the Catholic Church—the ease of their conquest and the stability of their empire were mainly due.

Another case of the apparent success of fanaticism is the victory of the Independents under Cromwell. But it may be questioned how much fanaticism had to do with Cromwell's achievements. In the contest with the King, Parliament won mainly because it held London and the eastern counties; both its manpower and its economic resources far exceeded those of the King. . . .

On a larger scale, the history of the French Revolution is analogous to that of the Commonwealth in England: fanaticism, victory, despotism, collapse, and reaction. Even in these two most favorable instances, the success of the fanatics was short-lived.

The cases in which fanaticism has brought nothing but disaster are much more numerous than those in which it has brought even temporary success. It ruined Jerusalem in the time of Titus, and Constantinople in 1453, when the West was rebuffed on account of the minute doctrinal differences between the Eastern and Western Churches. It brought about the decay of Spain, first through the expulsion of the Jews and Moors, and then by causing rebellion in the Netherlands and the long exhaustion of the Wars of Religion. On the other hand, the most successful nations, throughout modern times, have been those least addicted to the persecution of heretics.

Nevertheless, there is now a widespread belief that doctrinal uniformity is essential to national strength. . . .

The question I am asking is not the broad one: Should freedom of thought be encouraged, or at least tolerated? I am asking a narrower question: To what extent is a uniform creed, whether spontaneous or imposed by authority, a source of power? And to what extent, on the other hand, is freedom of thought a source of power?

When a British military expedition invaded Tibet in 1905, the Tibetans at first advanced boldly, because the Lamas had given them magic charms against bullets. When they nevertheless had casualties, the Lamas observed that the bullets were nickel-pointed, and explained that their charms were only effective against lead. After this, the Tibetan armies showed less valor. When Béla Kun and Kurt Eisner made Communist revolutions [in Hungary and Germany after the First World War], they were confident that Dialectical Materialism was fighting for them. I forget what explanation of their failure was offered by the Lamas of the Comintern. In these two instances, uniformity of creed did not lead to victory.

To arrive at the truth in this matter, it is necessary to find a compromise between two opposite truisms. The first of these is: men who agree in their beliefs can cooperate more wholeheartedly than men who disagree. The second is: men whose beliefs are in accordance with fact are more likely to succeed than men whose beliefs are mistaken. Let us examine each of these truisms.

That agreement is a help in cooperation is obvious. In the civil war in Spain, cooperation has been difficult between Anarchists, Communists, and Basque Nationalists, though all equally desired the defeat of Franco. In the same manner, though in a less degree, on the other side, cooperation has been difficult between Carlists and modern-style Fascists. There is need of agreement as to immediate ends, and also of a certain temperamental congeniality; but where these exist, great differences of opinion may become harmless. . . .

The uniformity which is needed to give power to a nation, a religion, or a party, is a uniformity in practice, depending upon sentiment and habit. Where this exists, intellectual convictions can be ignored. It exists in Great Britain at the present day, but it did not exist until after 1745. It did not exist in France in 1792, or in Russia during the [First World War] and the subsequent civil war. . . . It is not difficult for a government to concede freedom of thought when it can rely upon loyalty in action; but when it cannot, the matter is more difficult. It is obvious that freedom of propaganda is impossible during a civil war; and when there is an imminent danger of civil war, the argument for restricting propaganda is only slightly less overwhelming. In dangerous situations, therefore, there is a strong case for an imposed uniformity.

Let us now take up our second truism: that it is advantageous to have beliefs which are in accordance with fact. So far as *direct* advantages are concerned, this is only true of a limited class of beliefs: first, technical matters, such as the properties of high explosives and poison gases; secondly, matters concerning the relative strengths of the opposing forces. Even as regards these matters, it may be said, only those who decide policy and military operations need have correct views: it is desirable that the populace should feel sure of victory, and should underrate the dangers of attack from the air. Only the government, the military chiefs, and their technical staffs need know the facts; among all others, blind confidence and blind obedience are what is most to be desired.

If human affairs were as calculable as chess, and politicians and generals as clever as good chess players, there might be some truth in this view. The advantages of successful war are doubtful, but the disadvantages of unsuccessful war are certain. If, therefore, the super men at the head of affairs could foresee who was going to win, there would be no wars. But in fact there are wars, and in every war the government on one side, if not on both, must have miscalculated its chances. For this there are many reasons: of pride and vanity, of ignorance, and of contagious excitement. When the populace is kept ignorantly confident, its confidence and its bellicose sentiment may easily be communicated to the rulers, who can hardly attach the same weight to unpleasant facts which they know but conceal as to the pleasant facts that are being proclaimed in every newspaper and in every conversation. Hysteria and megalomania are catching, and governments have no immunity.

When war comes, the policy of concealment may produce effects exactly opposite to those intended. Some, at least, of the unpleasant facts which had been kept dark are likely to become patent to all, and the more men have been made to live in a fool's paradise, the more they will be horrified and discouraged by the reality. Revolution or sudden collapse is much more probable in such circumstances than when free discussion has prepared the public mind for painful events.

. . . In a community in which men have to accept, at least outwardly, some obviously absurd doctrine, the best men must become either stupid or disaffected. There will be, in consequence, a lowering of the intellectual level, which must, before long, interfere with technical progress. This is especially true when the official creed is one which few intelligent men can honestly accept. The Nazis have exiled most of the ablest Germans, and this must, sooner or later, have disastrous effects upon their military technique. It is impossible for technique to remain long progressive without science, or for science to flourish where there is no freedom of thought. Consequently, insistence on doctrinal uniformity, even in matters quite remote from war, is ultimately fatal to military efficiency in a scientific age.

We may now arrive at the practical synthesis of our two truisms. Social cohesion demands a creed, or a code of behavior, or a prevailing sentiment, or, best, some combination of all three; without something of the kind, a community disintegrates, and becomes subject to a tyrant or a foreign conqueror. But if this means of cohesion is to be effective, it must be very deeply felt; it may be imposed by force upon a small minority, provided they are not specially important through exceptional intelligence or character, but it must be genuine and spontaneous in the great majority. Loyalty to a leader, national pride, and religious fervor have proved, historically, the best means of securing cohesion. . . .

To sum up: A creed or sentiment of some kind is essential to social cohesion, but if it is to be a source of strength it must be genuinely and deeply felt by the great majority of the population, including a considerable percentage of those upon whom technical efficiency depends. Where these conditions are absent, governments may seek to produce them by censorship and persecution; but censorship and persecution, if they are severe, cause men to become out of touch with reality, and ignorant or oblivious of facts which it is important to know. Since the holders of power are biased by their power-impulses, the amount of interference with freedom that conduces most to national power will always be less than governments are inclined to believe; therefore a diffused sentiment against interference, provided it does not go so far as to lead to anarchy, is likely to add to the national strength. But it is impossible to go beyond these generalities except in relation to particular cases. . . .

DEMOCRACY: VULNERABILITY AND STRENGTH

By Albert T. Lauterbach

From chap. 1 of *Economics in Uniform*, by A. T. Lauterbach. Copyright 1943 by Princeton University Press. Dr. Lauterbach has been a member of the Military and Foreign Affairs Seminar in the Institute for Advanced Study at Princeton.

Until recently, the democratic nations believed ardently, and perhaps almost superstitiously, in an inherent superiority of the democracies over totalitarianism which would operate automatically to check successful aggression. Their conviction was that the oppressed populations would offer resistance, even to the extent of active revolt, against any attempt of their governments to involve them in a prolonged war, and that lack of democratic control as well as crude compulsion must necessarily result in hampering red tape and decreased efficiency of labor. Few people were able to distinguish between dictatorships on the old model, such as those of the late Marshal Pilsudski in Poland or Primo de Rivera in Spain, and up-to-date totalitarianism, based on modern technology and industry, supported by considerable sections of the population, and concentrating sooner or later upon the preparation of aggressive wars. This blind belief, the belief "that unplanned, uncoordinated industry, wasting half its time and money in domestic warfare, can build a national defense capable of defeating the aggression of a nation completely organized to equip and sustain its armed forces in ruthless execution of a definite plan of world domination," brought disaster to France.

Historical factors had led many sincere democrats to believe that only a weak democracy could be a safe democracy, that the amount of governmental organization and executive powers of all kinds should be kept at the lowest possible level, and that the initiative of the individual, not merely in the economic field but in any field, was bound under all circumstances to be superior to state interventionism and controls.

It is not proposed here to go into the question of to what extent such general assumptions were ever correct, either in the United States or elsewhere. As far as the recent period is concerned, the experience of France and of other countries appears to be evidence of potential weaknesses of the democracies of an opposite character. . . .

Voluntary cooperation is superior to autocratic regimentation, but only if it is accompanied by two indispensable conditions. First, individual incentives . . . must not be allowed to lead to industrial anarchy, or to interfere with efficient social coordination—which presupposes sufficient executive power. Secondly, there must be enough time to permit voluntary collaboration to operate. If either of these conditions is lacking, as happens in times of acute emergency, then reliance upon voluntary factors may mean national suicide.

In the initial phase of American rearmament, the Administration was unable to prevent delays which in the aggregate threatened to assume vital proportions. Gradually, however, the conviction spread that should the international war end in an Axis victory, with subsequent Nazi domination of the world, American business had more to lose than high profits, and American labor more than high wages. Originally, each group's main concern was to maintain and increase its share both of the national income and of social influence, although under the tacit assumption that the framework of the existing society and international order was to remain unchallenged.

It became clear that the menace of totalitarian aggression could be met only by an equal or superior coordination of the economic, political, military, and propaganda activities on the part of the democratic nations. To the problem of what the general policy of the United States should be in a period of emergency there was added the ancillary question of what political or social forces were to be in charge of this coordination, and therefore, of American preparedness. Part of the basic philosophy of this country had consisted of the practically unqualified identification of the interests of business with those of the nation as a whole. Private initiative, guided by profit considerations, was regarded as the natural, and perhaps the only possible, basis of national policy under any conditions. . . .

In so far as businessmen were at the same time technical or administrative experts in their respective fields, their active influence upon defense preparation met with almost general approval. There remained the problem of how far beyond this special capacity they were better qualified than other people to lead a military economy that was bound to become increasingly dissimilar to the competitive market system in which they had successfully carried on their business activities, and to what extent the profit incentive to which they were accustomed was still applicable to a national economy reorganized on a war basis.

Both the *Industrial Mobilization Plan*—an official blueprint for possible war emergency policies, first adopted in 1931 and reshaped in 1939—and the prevailing concept of preparedness in this country had originally been based upon the assumption of "business as usual," or on the idea of rearmament being superimposed upon normal business rather than replacing it. Moreover, if the national interest was fundamentally identical with that of private business, and if the latter knew best how to run the country in good or bad times, then the logical course of action was evidently to reduce disturbing intervention, especially in critical periods, to the very minimum. The *Industrial Mobilization Plan* was not of course put into effect, and the actual industrial mobilization of the United States has taken place along different lines. The original desire to supply at least the illusion of competition to a field which by its very nature is hardly consistent with genuine competition, had to be abandoned in the process of achieving national large-scale rearmament. . . .

The reliance upon latent economic resources, which turned out to be fatal for France and was at the root of many of the British difficulties, has been a factor of decreasing importance in the United States, but the decisive role of the time factor in dealing with a totalitarian aggressor has been recognized in this country, as elsewhere, only reluctantly. Public opinion has been slow to realize that great resources, economic and otherwise, may be a liability rather than an asset unless they are actually developed and available for use, because otherwise they encourage complacency.

Finally, the experiences of Europe have taught America that a purely technical concept of preparedness can be equally dangerous. Political blunders can outweigh almost any quantity of physical armaments. The Munich Pact, which in the opinion of observers like Sir Nevile Henderson . . . gave Britain and France an indispensable breathing space for rearmament, in fact destroyed Czechoslovakia and with it forty well-trained pro-Ally divisions and many airports near the heart of Germany. Moreover, it gave Hitler the huge Skoda and Witkowitz armament works, and above all, contributed substantially toward the demoralization of all the potential allies of the Western Powers in Europe, throwing Soviet Russia into Hitler's arms in the decisive summer of 1939. Can it be seriously claimed that this was offset by the production of a few thousand British airplanes or French tanks in the following year of "breathing space"—before the defeat of France?

Or, consider the long-term results of British non-intervention during the Italo-German invasion of Spain with the consequent establishment of the Franco regime. Here again it is very doubtful whether the cruisers and destroyers that Britain constructed subsequently were enough to meet the naval problems resulting directly or indirectly from this course of foreign policy. Physical rearmament is simply large-scale waste of national resources unless it is based on a sound general policy. The fate of the Maginot Line, which may serve as a further example, is so well known that it need only be mentioned here.

It is a widespread opinion that one of the basic differences between democracy and totalitarianism is that the former is essentially peaceful, while the latter necessarily aims at war. The historical truth of both propositions, the first in particular, is open to question. But in any case, there is nothing against which the aversion of the American people has been stronger in recent years than a "preventive war." The aggression which it appears to involve has been considered by many as incompatible with the spirit of democracy. . . .

Recent developments have demonstrated for America the importance of long-term preparation and coordination, and of the initial advantage, in modern warfare, which need by no means be identical with a policy of aggressive militarism. It has been increasingly realized that if and when a nation finds that her existence is incompatible with that of certain totalitarian enemies, and if she decides upon a policy of resistance rather than capitulation, then it may be suicidal for her to go on leaving the initiative to the enemy. . . .

For many years it was only with great reluctance that the democratic countries asked themselves whether totalitarian and democratic states can coexist, because of the obvious consequences of a negative answer. As for National Socialism, it had never left any doubt of its aim to extinguish democracy as an institution. The possibility of peaceful coexistence of the Axis regimes side by side with the democratic systems remained to be proved by the latter, for the former did not even pretend to seek it.

The logical alternative, which most democrats, first in Europe and then in the United States, were reluctant to admit, would obviously have been the preventive destruction of National Socialism and its international system. There is some probability that this might have been accomplished some years ago without the necessity of military action. There is no general agreement as to whether the remilitarization of the Rhineland, or the Spanish War, or the *Anschluss*, or the Munich crisis, or any other moment would have been the most suitable or the final one, but there is virtual unanimity of opinion that there was such a moment. This opportunity was missed, but even so, for several years afterwards, military action remained only one among several possible methods, and its effective coordination with economic, diplomatic, and propaganda methods was just as important as the amount of military equipment available.

Any preventive action against the Nazi regime was, from the long-term viewpoint, bound to be defensive. . . .

The Second World War has also clarified for the American people the real relationship between peace and democracy. The Italian and German experiences have taught that peace in itself, however desirable, does not guarantee democracy as long as other factors of social disturbance, such as periodical depressions, prevail. British experience, on the other hand, has shown that even total war does not necessarily mean dictatorship, serious as the inevitable wartime regimentation may be. In wartime as in the post-war period to come, there is only one dependable guarantee for a survival or revival of democracy: the democratic spirit of the people themselves, coupled with an active determination to make this spirit prevail in society and government.

CHALLENGE TO DEMOCRACY

By D. W. Brogan

From "A Political Scientist and World Problems," by D. W. Brogan in *The Annals of the American Academy of Political and Social Science*, July 1942. Copyright 1942 by the American Academy of Political and Social Science, Philadelphia; reproduced by permission. The author is professor of political science at Cambridge University.

In time of formal peace a free state not only is, but must and should be, less efficient in its military organization than a tyranny. This may not have always been so. When tactics reach a point which makes the independence of the rank and file, their ability and will to fight on their own, of primary importance, a free state produces better soldiers than a tyranny. Prussian discipline was fantastically rigid because the Prussian soldier's normal state of mind was that of a would-be deserter. The freer discipline of the French revolutionary armies was possible because the French soldier could be trusted to turn up on the battlefield, even if he had plundered and straggled the day before.

As far as the old tyrannies were technically backward because they feared the apparent political implications of general education, they could not have as good artillery or engineer corps as freer peoples. This was abundantly illustrated in the history of the old Russian Army. But we have discovered that there is no necessary connection, in the short run, between the technological virtues and the liberal virtues. A master of the art of the chemical engineer may be a political idiot or a servile servant of an anti-intellectual state. The tyrannical states have found it possible to produce enough airmen and tank gunners for the exploitation of their technical superiority in preparing war in time of peace. That superiority was *given*; nothing that any conceivable French or British government could have done to prepare for war could have produced armaments equal to those of Germany. Much more could and should have been done than was done, but our best would have been inadequate.

Nor is the reason hard to find. In order to exploit to its utmost the industrial potential of a modern nation for armaments, it is necessary to prevent that industrial potential from producing its normal results in consumers' goods, in leisure, in power to think, to grumble, to be idle. An anecdote of Hitler's Germany before the declaration of war illustrates my point—in reverse. A worker employed in a baby-carriage factory was puzzled by the character of his work. So, being an intellectually curious man, he smuggled out all the different parts and tried to assemble a baby carriage for his child's use. But, as he explained to his wife in complete bewilderment, "Whatever I do, it always turns out to be a machine gun." That story is true of the free state, in reverse. Whatever we do in peacetime, we cannot help turning out baby carriages, radios, books, goods which people want because they want them, instead of the goods that it takes all the persuasive power of press, radio, pulpit, school monopoly, plus castor oil and rubber truncheons, to make people at least pretend to want.

A free society exists, has its claim on loyalty, because it exists for something more and (as we think) better than its own power. Its own power is an essential condition of its attaining its higher aims, but it is not an end in itself. The very liberty of prophesying, that is part of our view of the good life, prevents that almost monomaniacal preoccupation with the instruments of military power that makes the preparation of the totalitarian state for total war so effective. That state is always at war; for that it exists and has its being. It would be strange indeed if a state existing for other ends could incidentally reach the militarist end too. It is the essential feature of modern war, with its overwhelming emphasis on technical equipment, that you must choose between guns and butter. And in a sense neither state has any real choice. Hitler must choose guns, and we must, in peacetime, choose butter.

One consequence is that the totalitarian powers will always be able to beat the gun; they will be able to organize espionage, sabotage, all kinds of military surprises, in a fashion impossible to us. And I hope that I may be permitted to suggest that one phrase of the last war bears revival. We must make the world safe for democracy; that is even more evident now than it was in 1917 and 1918. . . .

The baseless optimism of recent years has been expensive enough to justify some critical acerbity. But the whole picture is not black. It is worth noting that the totalitarian successes have their price, as well. For if the totalitarian powers gain by their refusal to allow consumers' choice now, they are forced to promise it for the future. The people's car may be pie in the sky, but it is significant that Hitler was forced to promise pie in the sky, and disillusionment with the postponement may be an important factor in the weakening of German morale. Nor is this material disappointment the only or the most important one.

The totalitarian leaders have been forced to purloin and pervert the language, or, if you like, the jargon, of the older, humanistic, liberal order. The new connotations, given to words like "liberty" and "justice" may completely alter their meaning; but that the words are still used shows that they have an emotive power that no dictatorial regime has managed to destroy. . . .

And even in the material field, it must be remembered that the very reasons that make truly adequate preparation for modern war impossible in free states make any calculation of their wartime possibilities which is based on their peacetime performance very dangerous indeed. War means the release of *new* energies for a peaceful state; it makes little difference to a permanently warlike state. So there are reserves of moral and physical power in the free nations which, with time, can be developed into the instruments of the defeat of the Axis; but only if we remember always that, as Paul Reynaud said, time is on no one's side—it is a neutral.

. . . It is true that only our mistakes can defeat us, but we shall make fewer mistakes and none which will be fatal, only if we get into the habit of acting on the knowledge that there is nothing predestined in our victory, and yet do not allow that knowledge to frighten us out of necessary confidence in our power to endure and triumph. A democracy is based on a view of the role of the people's will in government. If we *will* victory (which means wish it with a knowledge of the price and a willingness to pay it), we shall have our will. If we merely *want* victory, making no great effort to find the price or disputing the bill, we go the way of admirable societies which died because they were politically inadequate to the cruel necessities of the times in which their fate was decided.

Chapter 3

The World Stage of International Politics

THE world is the stage upon which mankind enacts the drama of international politics. This stage, as everyone knows, is a globe roughly 8,000 miles in diameter, 25,000 miles in circumference. It is covered by an intricate pattern of land and water, oceans and narrow seas, continents and islands, mountains and plains, rivers and inland seas, climatic zones, forests and grasslands, soil and mineral resources.

These earth facts constitute the bedrock—sometimes the shifting sands—of international politics. That is not to say that geography alone can explain the political history of mankind, or forecast the political future. But without geographic knowledge there can be no real understanding of the rise and fall of nations, of the unfolding global pattern of political relations, or of man's repeated attempts to establish a more stable political order upon the earth.

"The geographical position of a nation," once declared Jules Cambon, famous French diplomat, "is the principal factor conditioning its foreign policy—the principal reason why it must have a foreign policy at all."

A German statesman, Richard von Kühlmann, put the thought into its larger political context when he observed that "geographical position and historical developments are so largely determining factors of foreign policy that, regardless of changes in the form of government, the foreign policy of a country has a natural tendency to return again and again to the same general and fundamental alignment."

Or, in the words of Sir Halford Mackinder, dean of British geographers, "the great wars of history are the outcome, direct or indirect, of the unequal growth of nations, and that unequal growth is not wholly due to the greater genius and energy of some nations as compared with others; in large degree it is the result of the uneven distribution of fertility and strategical opportunity upon the face of the globe."

To bring the earth, its larger surface features, and their positional relationships, within the range of human perception, men have devised tools in the form of scale models of our terrestrial globe and maps drawn upon a flat surface. Because of the bulk, weight, and cost of large model globes, people depend chiefly for their geographical information upon flat maps such as hang on our walls, fill our atlases, and grace our newspapers and magazines.

Flat maps are constructed in various ways. None are, or can be, faithful replicas of the earth's features as these appear upon a globe. Each type of flat map has its own unique distortions. Broadly speaking, the larger the area represented, the greater is the distortion. Each projection, or type of map, has its special uses. Undiscriminating use of "any old map," without regard to its particular qualities, has been a common source of geographical misconceptions which in turn are responsible for many popular delusions regarding the relations of nations.

In short, maps are indispensable but tricky tools for the study of world politics. Used with discrimination and with knowledge of their limitations, maps can illuminate almost every international problem. Without them the statesman, the military strategist, and the ordinary citizen in private life are as helpless as a navigator without chart and compass. But as already emphasized, the map must fit the job, or at least be used with awareness of its limitations. Hence the very great importance of entering upon the study of world affairs with knowledge of the qualities of maps most frequently encountered, as well as with a clear picture of the geographical pattern of our world.

MAPS, STRATEGY, AND WORLD POLITICS

By Richard Edes Harrison
and Robert Strausz-Hupé

From "Maps, Strategy, and World Politics," by Richard Edes Harrison and Robert Strausz-Hupé, in *The Smithsonian Institution Report for 1943*. Adapted from an article first published in *The Infantry Journal*, November, 1942; reproduced by permission. Mr. Harrison is the well-known cartographer. Mr. Strausz-Hupé, author of *Geopolitics, The Struggle for Space and Power*, is professor of political science at the University of Pennsylvania.

If the earth were flat as a table top, there would be few problems in map-making. Each item of geographical interest could be shown in true relationship to any other item since the map, like a table top, is a plane and, hence, two-dimensional. The earth, unfortunately, is a round solid. Map-making is mainly concerned with the problem of representing three dimensions on a two-dimensional piece of paper. Consider a globe—it represents the world in all respects, distances, areas, directions, shapes; this it does because it is a three-dimensional scale model. If a globe had a skin, it would be impossible to peel it off and flatten it into any single shape without splitting or stretching it. How to perform this operation is the dilemma of map-making. The greater the extent of the sphere's surface depicted by the map the greater is the distortion, and the smaller the extent of the surface the smaller the distortion. In large-scale tactical maps it shrinks almost to the vanishing point but it is present, nevertheless. In an area large enough to show a perceptible curvature of the earth, the distortion becomes an appreciable factor. It reaches a maximum when we attempt to depict the whole earth on one map.

This difficult art of trying to represent the impossible is called cartography, and the devices by which cartographers attempt to show a round surface on a flat and generally rectangular piece of paper are called projections. Map-making through the ages has necessarily limited itself to controlling distortion, so that one of the four properties—distance, direction, shape, or area—is shown correctly at the expense of the others, or to achieve the best compromise among them without any one being mathematically true. For example, a map on which all areas are shown in true relative size (called equal area) is bound to have distortions in shape, distance, and direction. In some, two properties can be satisfactorily combined, as for example in the azimuthal equidistant map. This is so constructed that from its central point direction and distance are true to any other point, but a nonradial distance is more or less seriously out of scale. (The term "azimuthal" is typical of the obscure terminology of cartography. In the case of maps it simply means radial, or as the spoke of a wheel.) The well-known Mercator map has the remarkable property of showing both true compass directions (but not the great circle directions) and true shape. The size of areas and distances, however, are highly misleading.

Perhaps the question most frequently asked of cartographers is, "What is the best world map?" The question goes to the heart of the cartographer's problem, for the answer is "There is no such thing as the perfect map." One can pick out a "best" map for a given purpose, but that map will not satisfy other requirements. For example, the density of population is measured by the number of people inhabiting a specific area and should be shown on an equal area map, for to show it on a map where unit areas differ would introduce another variable making the study of relative density valueless. Where true compass direction between points is required (as in navigation), we must use Mercator; where great circles (the shortest distance between two points on the globe) is the object of study, we must use the gnomonic projection which is unfortunately limited in scope to less than a hemisphere. To measure distances accurately we must have recourse to the globe or use cumbersome methods for translating these distances from different projections. In fact, all these questions can best be studied on a scale model of the earth. Only a scale model is proportionately accurate in all respects—provided it is accurately made. Unfortunately the globe has disadvantages too. One can see less than half of it at a given moment; it is bulky; it is expensive. A fine collection of good detailed maps or a first-class atlas can be purchased for the price of an 18-inch globe. But a globe is the one and only corrective for the distortion present in all maps. . . .

The search for a compromise solution has led to many ingenious projections. . . . One way of approximating true geographic relationship is to decide what part of the global area is of least interest and select a projection which tends to lump the distortion in that area. Thus the "center of remoteness" from the war and its connecting lines is at or very near the South Pole. In fact, from the South Pole to the thirtieth parallel south of the Equator is an enormous area, nearly one-third the earth's surface, in which no engagement of importance has been fought and which supply lines touch only peripherally. To banish the distortion into the "inactive" area, we center the map on the opposite, or North Pole, and make linear scale true along radii from its pole along the meridians. This is called —in the semantics of cartography—the North Polar azimuthal equidistant projection and is, in spite of its name, a pretty good map for global strategy. . . .

From the Pole to within 20° of the Equator there is remarkably little distortion on this map. This area contains all the major world powers. . . . The Mercator projection which for centuries has had an iron grip on the naval, military, and teaching professions, divides its distortions equally between the North and South Polar regions, and is true on the Equator only. Owing to the construction of the Mercator projection, the regions immediately adjacent to the Poles cannot be shown at all, since they fade into infinity. Yet, because of the Mercator's usefulness in navigation, most seafaring men have come to think of intercontinental relations mainly in terms of Mercator. Mercator's world is the world of sea power.

Politically ours is a Northern Hemisphere world. For 93 per cent of the world's population and about 75 per cent of the world's habitable land lie in northern latitudes. Modern history has been made in the northern latitudes. The power centers of the world are situated 40° or more north of the Equator. London, Berlin, Tokyo, and Moscow lie from 900 to 1,500 miles closer to the North Pole than to the Equator. Obviously a map whose maximum accuracy is at the Equator (like Mercator) cannot be expected to show the interrelation of the centers of power in North America, Europe, and Asia. This relationship can be rendered most successfully on one of the polar projections.

The map reader need not be misled by the distortions of a particular map; it is only necessary to note the specific distortion and make the proper visual correction. The main pitfall to avoid is the continual use of one map, for the mind is inexorably conditioned to its shapes. It begins to look "right" and all others "wrong." There are some examples of how this conditioning has produced false notions of geography. Example number one is provided by the Pacific war area. The Pacific is so large that any map of the entire ocean must have considerable distortion, but for generations we have depended almost exclusively on the Mercator projection. Similarly, the interrupted homolosine projection, devised by the late Chicago professor, Paul Goode, sacrifices the polar regions to distortion. Its greatest accuracy lies in the zones of the world's great shipping lanes and hence, in the areas of naval strategy as conceived in the nineteenth century. Now both the United States and Japan lie on the fringe of Mercator's and Goode's area of reasonable accuracy, and the shortest line between them goes far above this area from Seattle across the Alaska Peninsula and curves above 55° N. before swinging southwestward along the Kurile Islands to metropolitan Japan. A few miles south of this line lies that too-long neglected bastion of North American defense, Dutch Harbor, while 2,300 miles south of that is Pearl Harbor.

Pearl Harbor, in fact, lies on a line between San Francisco and Australia, and could only be called a flank defense by one familiar with the globe. Alaska, on the other hand, offers a jumping-off place for all the shortest routes from the United States to Asia, Japan, Siberia, China, India. For example, from the Mid-Western industrial center of the United States to Chungking, as flown by our ferry command across the South Atlantic to Lagos to Khartoum to Karachi, and so on, is more than 12,000 miles; by way of Fairbanks and Siberia about 8,000 miles. On Mercator the 12,000-mile jaunt looks reasonable enough. But the direct air route New York-Chungking (which passes close to the North Pole) is difficult to trace on the Mercator projection, as on this map it would go vertically off the top of the map near western Greenland, reappear above the central coast of Siberia and drop directly south to Chungking.

Example number two is provided by the Atlantic theater of war. Both New York and London lie in the area of sharply increasing distortion on Mercator. The great circle route between them reaches the fifty-third parallel. Hence the earlier perplexities of Anglo-American relations. Hence also the widely held misconceptions of the Arctic, which is not a stagnant, impassable waste, but a fluid, practicable pathway of the Atlantic. In fact, the Mercator mind blankly abandons the Arctic to infinity while it faithfully records the true proportions of the jungles of equatorial Africa, Amazonian rain forests, and the deserts of the Arabian peninsula. The Arctic is not only a branch of the Atlantic but provides a back-alley access to the Pacific. To be sure, ice blocks it for half of the year, but the savings in time and distance mark it still as a potential traffic lane. For example, the distance from North Atlantic naval bases to the Bering Sea by way of the Northwest Passage is less than half what it is by way of the Panama Canal.

The importance of Iceland has been long recognized by the British and American commands. A glance at an Arctic map reveals the Norwegian coast as the only Axis frontage on the Arctic basin. The importance of a northern all-year route is shown by the figures: New York-Moscow via Murmansk, 5,300 miles; New York-Moscow via the Persian Gulf, 14,400 miles. This is not to suggest that the southern route be abandoned, for this route has the great advantage that supplies delivered at the head of the Persian Gulf can be distributed on comparatively short notice to several different fronts, the Russian, Egyptian, Syrian, and Indian.

Example number three of thought conditioning by maps we can find on our home continent. [During the war with Germany] our eastern and western seaboards [were] far more conscious of danger from Axis bombing, yet Toledo, Detroit, Duluth, and Winnipeg [were] as close to Nazi-held Norway as Norfolk, Va.

Salt Lake City, all of Montana and Idaho, part of North Dakota and Winnipeg [were in 1942] as close to Japanese air bases as Los Angeles. If [some future enemy] were to establish advance bases in Greenland or Alaska, most of the Middle West would be in as great danger as the seaboards. Here again are facts not revealed on most of the maps in common use.

We have pointed out that all maps must be misleading in themselves, but use of a map even with knowledge of its limitations can also produce misleading conceptions of geography. Continual use of a given map in a fixed position results in dulling of perception. For example, the Mercator projection shows us with perfect accuracy the north-south geographical relation, yet most people are skeptical when told that all of South America lies to the east of Savannah, Ga. By looking at a Mercator wall map with the aid of a mirror, the true relation is made plain. The shapes on the map, of course, have not changed, they are merely reversed, and in the reflected image the immense eastward sweep of the coast from Brownsville to

Natal is startlingly revealed. It is useful to turn maps upside down, or point them in a direction which might represent the point of view of an individual or a nation, as for example a Briton's view of the continent, or Hitler's view of the Middle East. This practice is recommended in defiance of the rooted conviction of the cartographer that north must always be at the top of the page. The globe has no "top."

The assault on map traditionalism has been led mainly by American magazines and newspapers in their search for visual aids to reports from the theater of war. ... Many college geographers now realize that the United States has been lagging far behind other nations—the British and notably the Germans—who not only produce large quantities of maps but pound away at geography and all its lessons, political, economic, and military, throughout all grades of schooling. American cartography is now meeting this challenge with boldness and ingenuity—particularly as regards the representation of large areas. German map-making—profuse in detail and meticulous in execution—has largely stuck to conventional projections, and Mercator's hold on German cartography may account for some German misconceptions as regards the strategic position of the United States and the Soviet Union. By contrast, American cartography now leads in the imaginative use of those projections which show large areas and true distances, and thus are best suited for teaching the new geography of international air communications.

The psychological isolationism of the United States, be it said in conclusion, can be in large measure traced to our failures in map-making and the teaching of geography—the prerequisites of education in international relations. The world is round. By the skillful presentation of its "roundness" strategic realities are made clear.

MAPPING THE WORLD

By Nicholas J. Spykman

From chap. 2 of The Geography of the Peace, *by N. J. Spykman. Copyright 1944, by Harcourt, Brace & Co., New York. Reproduced by permission. The late Dr. Spykman was Sterling professor of international relations at Yale University and formerly director of the Yale Institute of International Studies, which sponsored the publication of the book quoted.*

THERE are three general classes of grids which may be conveniently identified in terms of the manner in which, theoretically, the globe is projected onto the surface of a cone, a plane, or a cylinder. Not every projection will fit into this classification and, actually, most of them were not developed in this simple manner. The use of the geometric figures, however, serves to make the construction of the various grids in general use more easily understood.

Conic Projections. When a cone is wrapped around the earth so that it touches the surface along one parallel, called the tangent parallel, the meridians and parallels can be presumed to be projected from the globe onto the cone which can then be opened out to present a flat map. The parallels will be represented by concentric circles and the meridians will radiate out from a central point which is the pole. Such a map would be accurate in scale at the tangent parallel, but would be more and more inaccurate the farther the map was extended beyond that line. So great, indeed, would be the distortion north and south of the standard parallel that it would be impossible to draw the whole world on the projection.

Fig. 1. Principle of the Conic Projection.

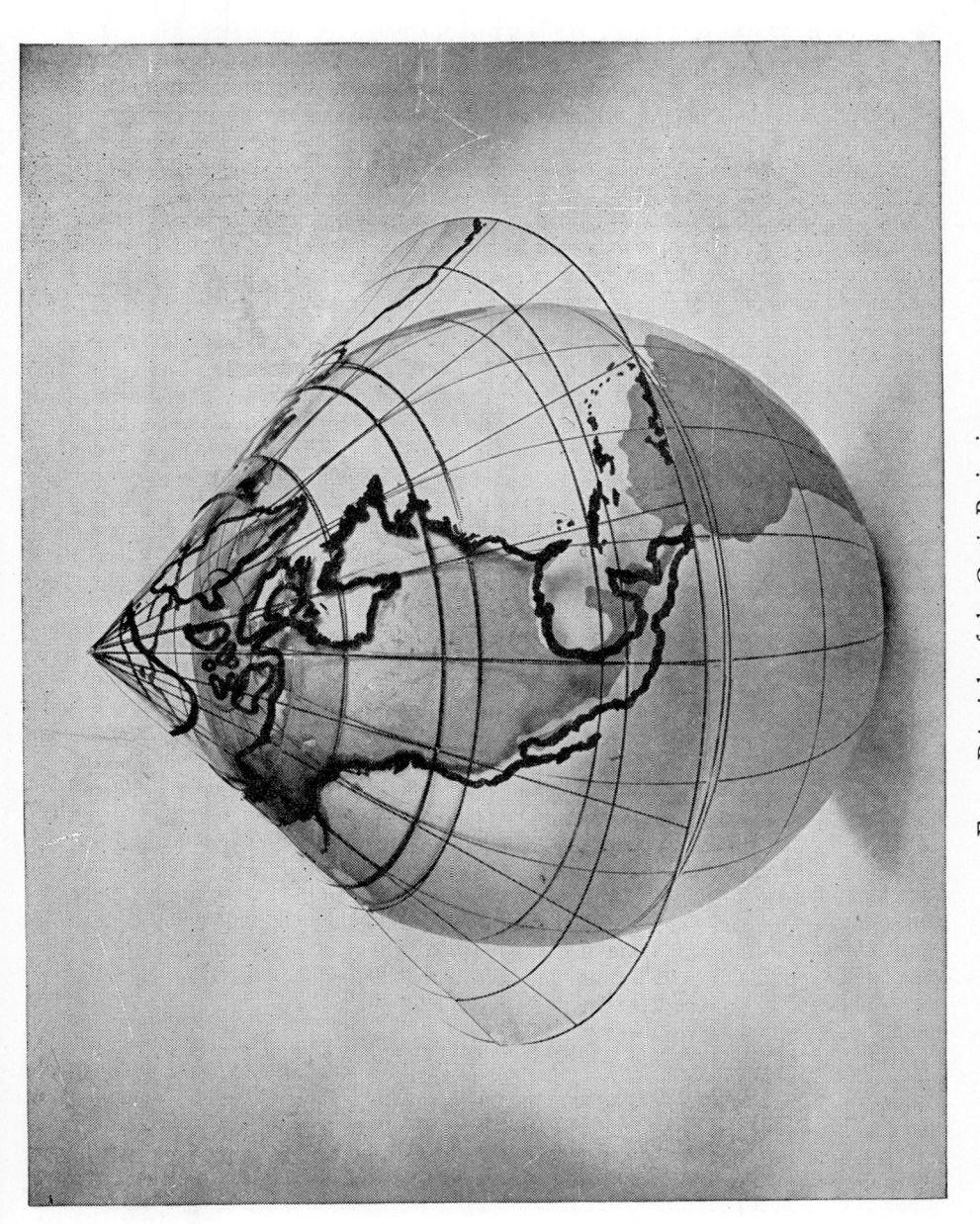

Courtesy Herbert Gehr, *Life* Magazine. Models by Norman Bel Geddes. Copyright 1942 by Time, Inc.

Mathematical variations in the construction of this grid do permit the use of two tangent parallels so that we are given two areas of accuracy. It is also possible to vary the spaces between the parallels so that any given part of the chart will bear the same relation to the area it represents as the whole map bears to the whole area. This property of equal-area representation is an important quality of many different projections which are used when it is necessary to plot accurately the distribution of products in different countries. A further variation of the conic group is possible which will space the concentric parallels in such a manner that every small quadrangle on the chart will have the same proportions as the corresponding section on the globe. This quality of conformality, which means that the shape of small areas is correct, is also characteristic of other projections and makes them extremely useful for navigators and engineers. Various kinds of special equal-area and conformal maps have been developed and would have to be considered in any complete exposition of the field of cartography. In this brief summary, we can only mention their existence.

It is clear, however, that none of the conic projections is adapted for use in world maps. They are excellent for the mapping of individual countries, but none of them is adaptable for presenting the whole face of the earth on a continuous sheet and they can therefore be of little direct use in geopolitical studies.

Azimuthal Projections. The recent emphasis on global geography and particularly on "maps for the air world" has brought one particular group of projections to the attention of the public. This is the type known as "azimuthal" or "zenithal" and may be thought of as developed by projecting the surface of the globe upon a plane from some eye point, which is presumed to be either within the globe or at some specific spot outside it. The main reason for their popularity today is that they have the quality of making all great circles which pass through the center of the projection appear on the chart as straight lines. All points on the globe equally distant from the center of the projection are represented as equally distant on these maps.

Since air routes can often follow great circle courses on the globe and are largely concerned with the shortest distance between two points, the value of this class of charts is evident. Their limitations are, however, great when the real factors of global politics are considered. Air line distances are not the sole determining factor either in war or in peace. Location of states with relation to other states as defined by land and sea transportation is still of more vital concern to the well-being and power of a country. It must also be noted that these projections are limited to the mapping of less than a hemisphere with any degree of accuracy. Indeed, three of the class, the gnomonic, orthographic, and stereographic, are never able to show a complete sphere. It is thus difficult to get a clear picture of all the land masses at one time. In an age of global politics, this is definitely a drawback.

Theoretically, the network of meridians and parallels in the azimuthal projections is developed by projecting the surface of the globe upon a plane from some eye point considered to be either within the globe, on its surface, or at some point outside it. The so-called gnomonic projection presumes the eye point to be at the center of the globe and all great circles are thus drawn as straight lines on a plane which is assumed to touch the globe at the selected central point of the map. Here, any

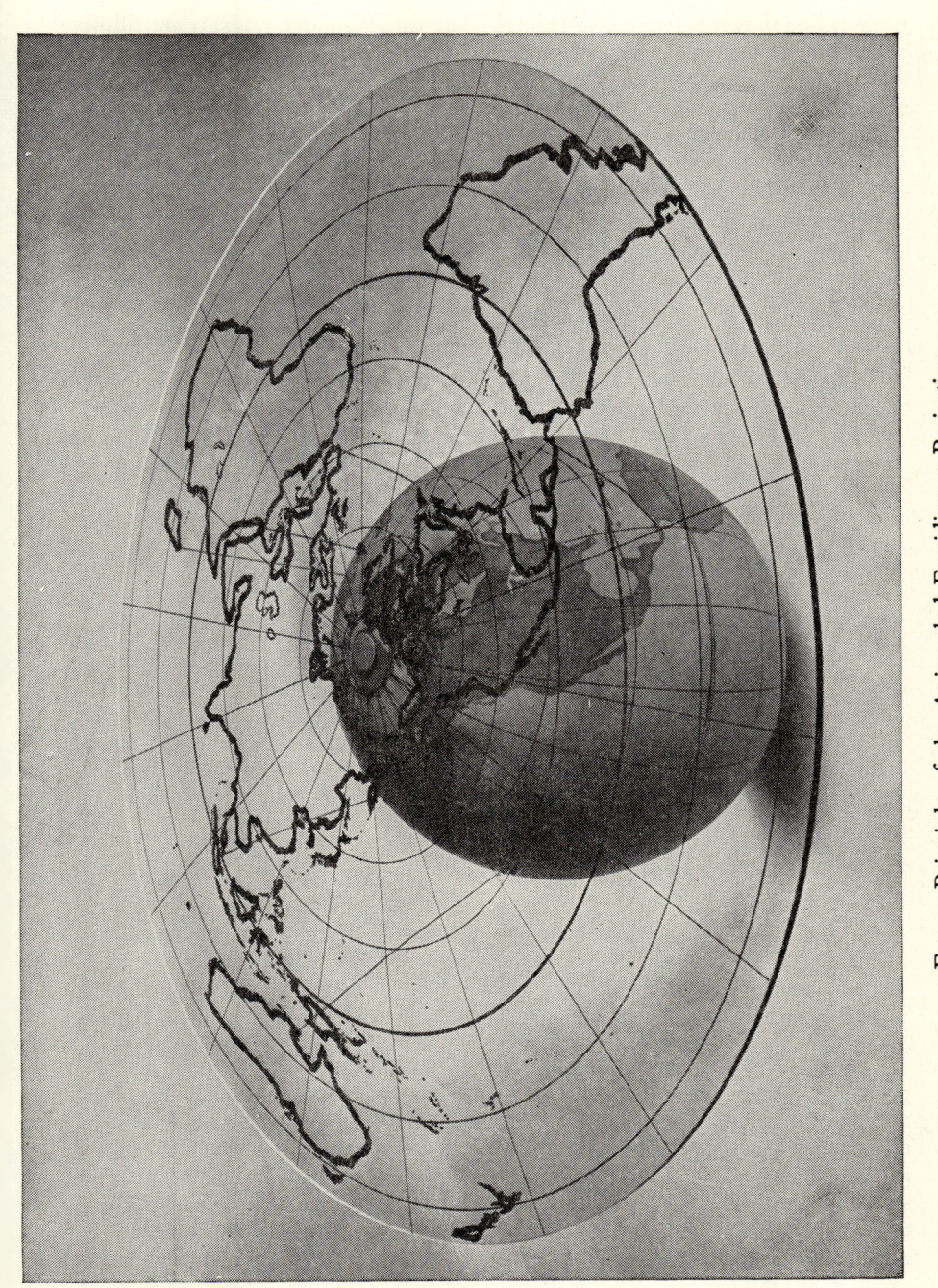

FIG. 2. Principle of the Azimuthal Equidistant Projection.

Courtesy Herbert Gehr, *Life* Magazine. Models by Norman Bel Geddes. Copyright 1942 by Time, Inc.

straight line drawn between two points represents a great circle and is thus the shortest route between the points. The grid can therefore be of great assistance in the study of air routes, but its usefulness for a general geopolitical analysis of the world is limited because of the The parallels and meridians are ellipses except when the pole is at the center, in which case the meridians are straight lines or when the center is a point on the Equator, in which case the parallels become straight lines. The projection is neither equal-area nor conformal and

Fig. 3. Orthographic Projection.

From R. E. Harrison and R. Strausz-Hupé, "Maps, Strategy, and World Politics," in *The Smithsonian Institution Report for 1943*.

great distortion near the boundaries of the map and because it can only be used to plot an area less than a hemisphere in extent.

The most visual of all projections is the orthographic which is really a picture of the globe taken from a point situated an infinite distance away so that a whole hemisphere can be shown. the distortion at the peripheries is large. Because of these great variations in scale, the grid cannot be used for very exact work. Its main value is in giving people a general impression of the surface of the earth on one hemisphere.

The stereographic projection is much like the orthographic in appearance and, like it, is limited to the portrayal of a hemisphere. It is developed by presuming that the eye is at a point on the surface of the globe looking directly through it to the opposite side which is the center of the projection. The meridians and parallels are thus closer together near the center rather than farther apart as is the case on the orthographic. The projection is conformal but the variation in scale between the center and the edge is extremely large.

The most useful of the azimuthal grids for radio and air communications is the azimuthal equidistant projection because correct distances and accurate directions can be measured from the center of the map to any point on the earth and it can be extended to show the whole surface of the globe on one map. It can be drawn with any point in the world as its center and a series could be constructed with all the major cities as centers so that air-line distances from all of them could be accurately measured. The greatest drawback is that the distortion of shape and area is very great beyond the hemisphere line.

World Maps with Horizontal Parallels. The last group to be considered is one in which the grids are usually drawn with horizontal straight lines for the parallels and the east-west relationship is correctly shown. This makes them adaptable for simple, diagrammatic maps even though they involve a certain amount of distortion in the higher latitudes. They can all be easily drawn on a world scale and must thus be considered very helpful in problems of world analysis.

... In order to get a clear picture of the interrelations of the large land masses on the earth's surface, it is sometimes very desirable to be able to continue the map in either or both horizontal directions.

The only class of projections which does permit the representation of the world more than once on the same map, is the cylindrical group. These may all be considered to be derived from the projection of the global surface onto a cylinder wrapped around it and then spread out as a plane surface. Since the meridians are equally spaced on the Equator and are vertical lines while the parallels are horizontal lines, the continents can be repeated indefinitely in an easterly or westerly direction.

The most familiar example of this type is the Mercator which has the parallels so placed that the scale along the meridians and parallels is the same for any small area as it is on the globe. This makes it a conformal projection with all compass directions represented as straight lines. Because of the variation in scale toward the North and South Poles, the shape of the large areas in the northern and southern latitudes is distorted. This disadvantage has been overcome to a certain extent in variations of the Mercator grid. Gall's stereographic projection assumes that the cylinder cuts the globe at the parallels of 45° N. and 45° S. Since only these two parallels are true to scale, the equatorial regions are reduced and the polar regions are exaggerated, but the polar distortion is not so great as it is in the Mercator. A very recent modification developed by O. M. Miller of the American Geographical Society is identical with the Mercator projection between the 45° parallels north and south and materially lessens the distortion in the higher latitudes.

Choosing A World Map. The chart which has been used traditionally to indicate the political relationships of the states of the world on a global scale is a cylindrical map, usually on the Mercator projection, with the center along the north-south axis at 0°, that is, the longitude of Greenwich. This places Europe in the center with the rest of

Fig. 4. Principle of the Mercator Projection.

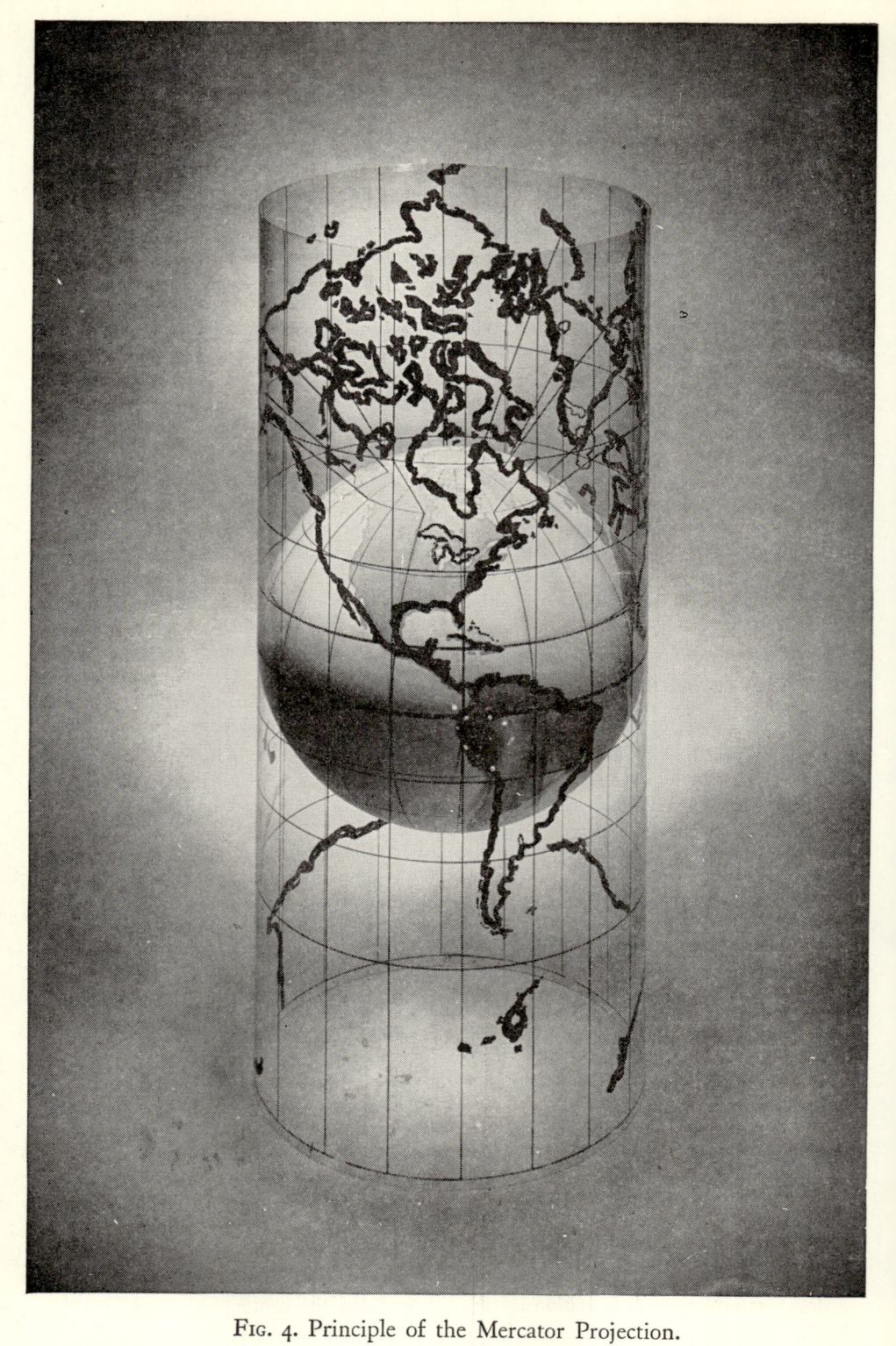

Courtesy Herbert Gehr, *Life* Magazine. Models by Norman Bel Geddes. Copyright 1942 by Time, Inc.

the world grouped around it. During the age of maritime power when Europe was expanding her control over all the world, such a centralization of the map was entirely correct. It was from Europe that political domination spread over the world, and it was the frame of reference is a map of the world with Europe in the center. Even though other projections came to be used to correct the distortions of the Mercator, it was still true that the central meridian chosen was almost always in the neighborhood of Greenwich.

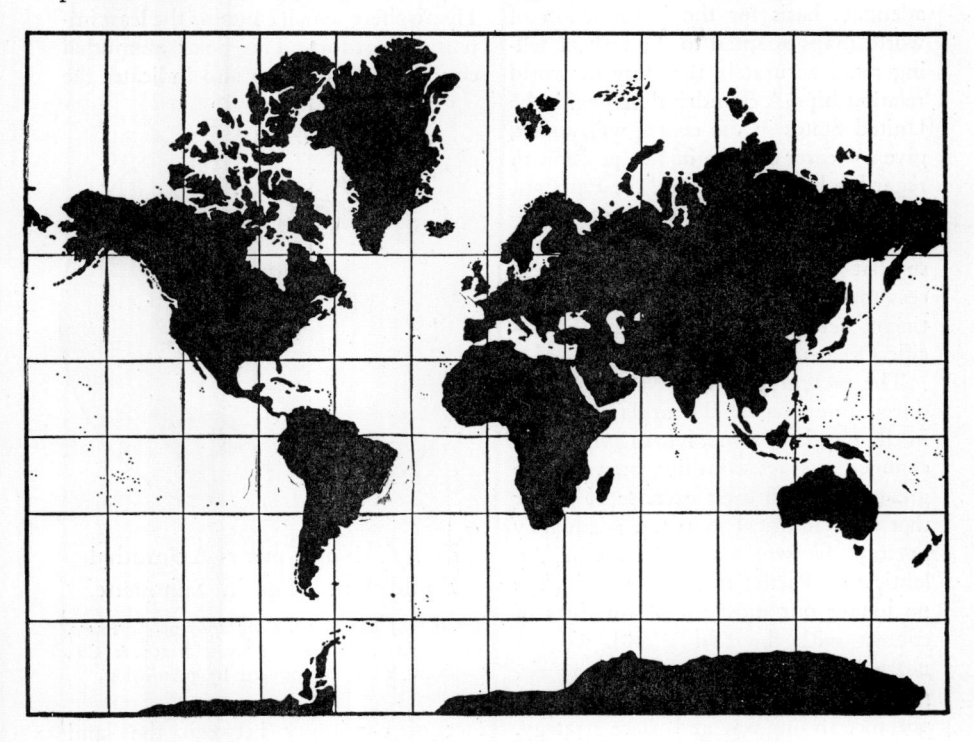

FIG. 5. Europe-centered Mercator World Map in Silhouette.

From N. J. Spykman, *Geography of the Peace*. Copyright 1944 by Harcourt, Brace & Co., New York; reproduced by permission.

condition of balance or unbalance of forces in Europe that largely determined the power position of states everywhere else.

It was in terms of such a Europe-centered world that the great regions of the earth received their names. The Western Hemisphere, the Near East, the Far East—all these with their connotations in terms of directions are logical only if it is remembered that the

So long as the center of the world power was in Europe and the principal states struggling for world dominion were European while the rest of the world represented a colonial or quasi-colonial world, this Europe-centered map was entirely satisfactory. With the opening of the twentieth century, however, independent sources of power emerged to challenge her position as sole determinant of world politics. In the Western Hemisphere and in the Far East powerful states became more and more independent of European domination and began to look at the world from their own point of view.

Such a radical alteration in the distribution of power in the world was an adequate basis for the introduction of world maps adapted to the task of telling more accurately the story of world relationships. A cylindrical map with the United States in the center will, today, give a clearer picture of her position in regard to both Europe and the Far East. She is now a continental country, unified by railroads and the Panama Canal, so that both her shores have easy access to both sides of the Eurasian Continent, across the Atlantic and the Pacific Oceans.

The present war, however, has introduced a new factor, the airplane, which, in the minds of some, has so completely changed the relationships between the great states and their exercise of power that no cylindrical map can adequately portray the world of today. Our Atlantic and Pacific fronts, it is said, are no longer our most important lines of contact with the Old World. To the north lies a third front which the airplane will dominate and which, in importance to our war and peace strategy, will quickly dwarf all other fronts, if it has not already done so. Since the northern front is the one which brings us closest in terms of air power to the Eurasian centers of power, it is inevitable, so the argument goes, that any accurate map for war strategy must concentrate on that front.

The map which performs this function most adequately is a polar azimuthal equidistant projection. Not only does it emphasize and show truthfully the distances, directions, and relationships across the North Pole, but it also presents more accurately than any other map the land masses of the Northern Hemisphere from the Pole to within 20° of the Equator. It is this area of the globe which is most important both economically and politically and it is, therefore, good to have the necessary distortions grouped in the Southern Hemisphere which contains the least important territory. This polar azimuthal equidistant projection also indicates the

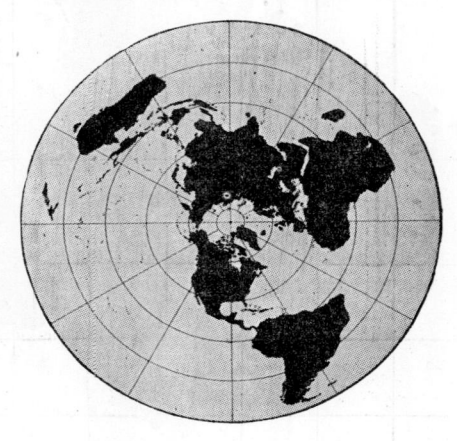

FIG. 6. North-polar Azimuthal Equidistant Map in Silhouette.

From N. J. Spykman, *Geography of the Peace.* Copyright 1944 by Harcourt, Brace & Co., New York; reproduced by permission.

fact of continuity between the land masses around the Arctic Ocean, whereas the traditional cylindrical projections emphasize the oceanic discontinuity and place the Western Hemisphere in a peripheral position which fails to bring out her importance and integral relationship to Eurasia. On such a chart, also, the global nature of the world is emphasized and kept before the eye. To those who are promoting the so-called "new geography," the sins of the Mercator projection are infinite and warrant its complete scrapping by all who presume to deal with global warfare. Since the northern latitudes are of such importance in the world of today, the distortions which this chart makes manifest in these latitudes must be overcome.

The importance of air power can certainly not be denied or even questioned. It is well, nonetheless, to look carefully at the actual meaning of that importance in terms of the geography which conditions all exercise of power. The Atlantic, Pacific, and Polar sections of the maritime front between the Old and the New Worlds have always had and will continue to have a very different geopolitical significance. For three hundred years, the Atlantic has been the great highway between Europe and the Americas, and the Pacific has, for almost the same length of time, offered a wide road to the Far East. The Arctic Ocean, on the other hand, has functioned primarily as a barrier to communication between the two hemispheres. The search for the northwest passage has inspired heroic deeds of exploration and endurance in the polar regions of the globe, but climate and the limits of technology have, until recently, kept that area one of the most insurmountable obstacles to man's conquest of the earth's surface. Next to the Antarctic Continent and the Sahara Desert, the littoral of the Arctic Ocean has remained the most extensive wasteland on earth.

The airplane has given us a new weapon in the fight against the inhospitable nature of the north and we are finding it possible to cross the area on long-distance flights that link together tenuously the North American and Eurasian Continents. The near future, however, will scarcely see much of a change in the relative importance of the three maritime zones. The one hundred freighters and thirteen ice-breakers that pushed their way through the cold waters of the Arctic Ocean during the one hundred days of the navigating season of 1940 carried a maximum of 160,000 tons of goods. These ships plus the planes which, now and then, carry important passengers and a few tons of precious freight across the polar regions will not for a long time take the place of the thousands of ships and hundreds of planes that dot the Atlantic and Pacific water and sky. In a fairly normal year of trade, 1937, Atlantic ports of the United States imported 10,461,136 tons and exported 20,456,934 tons of material, while Pacific ports imported 4,075,080 tons and exported 11,746,962 tons. It will be many years before the Arctic lines of communication in the air are able to compete on equal terms with the sea-borne commerce of the Atlantic and Pacific Oceans.

It is true that the shortest distance between a number of cities in the Northern Hemisphere would follow a great circle across the North Pole. It is also true that, with the approach of stratosphere flying, climatic conditions in that region are not much more severe than in stratosphere flying over other parts of the world. The factor of climate remains, nevertheless, a powerful obstacle to the development of the auxiliary land and sea routes that are necessary to the establishment of large-scale air transport over long distances. To the extent that the former can be developed, they will keep the air routes away from the Pole and near to the open water. It is asking too much of the imagination to expect that the traffic across the Arctic Ocean will ever be more than an infinitesimal fraction of that which will continue to span the oceans either in war or in peace. This being the case, there is no advantage in presenting the position of the United States in the world on a map which emphasizes the least important section of the maritime front and focuses attention on the largest uninhabited region of the globe.

Asking us to look at polar maps has been a useful way of reminding us that the world is round also in a northerly direction, although some writers have been so delighted with their new discovery that they have talked as if their flat polar maps were somehow rounder than other flat maps. They may have been useful in inspiring our militarists to speculate about new and daring strategic possibilities. But the fact remains that the polar projection is of strictly limited help in understanding the problems of the United States in total war. The significant fact about the position of North America in the world is not that the icy wastes of northern Canada and Russian Siberia are the littoral of a mediterranean sea and that the Mackenzie and the Lena Rivers flow into the same ice-covered ocean. It is the fact that our continent lies between the European and Asiatic power centers of the Old World and is separated from them by oceanic distances.

OUTLINES OF WORLD GEOGRAPHY

By Brooks Emeny

From *Mainsprings of World Politics*, by Brooks Emeny. Headline Series No. 42. Copyright 1943 by Foreign Policy Association, New York; reproduced by permission. Dr. Emeny is author of *The Strategy of Raw Materials*, and co-author with the late Frank Simonds of *The Great Powers in World Politics*.

HUMAN relations are profoundly influenced by the impact of land and sea upon mankind. If all regions of the earth were equally endowed with natural resources and favorable climate, the problems of human relations might be greatly simplified. This is a world of extremes, however, in which riches and poverty are on every side and man's unfulfilled desires are without limit.

Today there are no unclaimed lands. The world of unknown frontiers has gone forever. Through the long process of history the earth has become completely divided between peoples of different races and cultures, who live under separate political units known as nation-states. All states differ as to size of territory and population and as to the extent of their endowment in natural resources. The artificial political boundaries between them, moreover, restrict the freedom of their people to come and go about the world as they choose, or to exploit the natural resources of neighboring lands.

But barriers against migration and freedom of trade do not reduce the desirability of the other fellows' territory. This is one of the reasons why the fruits of conquest have always been a lure and justification for war in the never ending struggle for survival and power. Today, each nation possesses what it has, not by divine right, but by virtue of the chances and hazards of historic conquests and events.

The earth's surface is approximately 196 million square miles. Of this, 139 million square miles is sea, leaving 57 million square miles of land, or a little over one-fourth of the globe, upon which over two billion human beings seek their livelihood. There are many peculiarities about the land areas of the earth which account not only for overcrowding in some sections and sparseness of habitation in others, but which also influence profoundly the pattern of present-day international relations.

Ours is essentially a Northern Hemisphere world. Eighty-five per cent of the land areas of the earth lie north of the Equator. In contrast to those of the Southern Hemisphere, they are richly endowed with the basic essentials of in-

WATER   MOUNTAINS   DESERTS   ICE

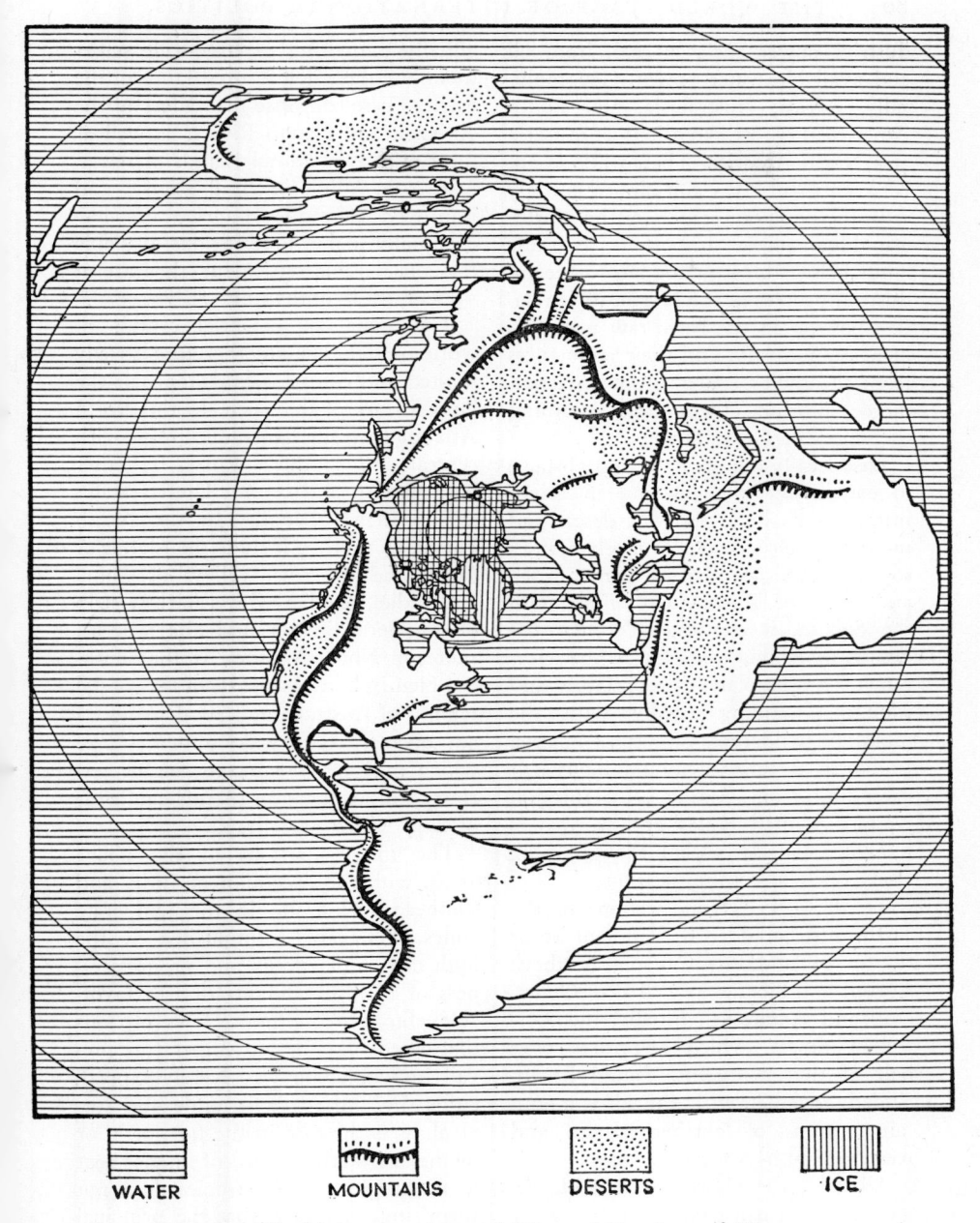

Fig. 7. World Geography and Natural Barriers of Water, Mountains, Deserts, and Ice.

From Brooks Emeny, *Mainsprings of World Politics*. Copyright 1943 by Foreign Policy Association, New York; reproduced by permission.

dustrial power such as coal, iron, oil and available water power. Geographically, Africa, Australasia, and South America serve as extensions of Eurasia and North America. Their trade is not between themselves, but almost entirely with the populous centers of the Northern Hemisphere. Important as these lands below the Equator are to the industrial peoples of the North, their relative poverty in the basic raw materials of heavy industry, and their remoteness from the major centers of world commerce, preclude them from attaining the status of Great Powers. . . .

Historically the greatest land obstacle to extensive settlement and intercommunication . . . is the vast desert and mountain belt which completely divides southern Africa and Asia from Europe and most of Russia. Beginning with the Sahara, it continues through the deserts of Arabia and Iran to the enormous barren plateaus of Tibet and Mongolia, ending finally with the mountain wilderness of eastern Siberia. In North America a mountainous belt extending from Alaska . . . through western United States and Mexico is likewise sparsely settled though more easily open to communication.

To these forbidding sections of the earth must be added the lands of ice or tundra of northern Canada, northern Europe and Siberia, as well as of Greenland and Antarctica. Finally, the Australian desert, which comprises over half of that continent, should be included, together with the lofty mountain regions of northern India and western South America.

All told, the above inhospitable regions of the earth comprise over 40 per cent of its land surface. In these areas live . . . less than one-sixtieth of the world's population.

In an entirely different category from the above, though in many respects equally uninviting to large-scale settlement, are the tropical forest lands of the earth. These comprise the valleys of the Amazon and Congo Rivers, as well as most of the equatorial islands of southeast Asia. While medical science and improved technique in agriculture may eventually make these regions available for considerable settlement, they are at present most uninviting. . . .

The actual or potential centers of world population are therefore strictly limited and comprise less than half the land surface of the earth. In the North Atlantic basin they include Europe with central and southern Russia, together with eastern and central United States and southern Canada. In the North Pacific world they include the islands of Japan and the river valleys of China and India, together with a narrow strip of southern Siberia and the western shores of North America. In the Southern Hemisphere only parts of the coastal regions of Australia and South America are open to large-scale settlement, to which may be added considerable territory still available in the plateau areas of east Africa and Brazil.

The major portions of the above areas, with the exception of India and southern China, lie in the temperate zones. They are distinguished by the high degree of energy and progressiveness of their inhabitants due to favorable climatic conditions. It is obvious that where extremes of temperature prevail human energy is severely sapped, either by the mere struggle for survival, as is the case in the far north, or by the debilitating effects of intense heat in the tropics and sub-tropics. It is not surprising, therefore, that the principal centers of world power today have sprung from those regions which provide seasonal climatic changes which are productive of more vigorous and intense human effort.

Chapter 4
The Pattern of World Politics

THE earth is the stage but man selects the play. Man can move the scenery around a little, but only a little. In the main he has to take the stage pretty much as he finds it and shape the play accordingly. Even so, he has considerable range of choice, a choice that is ever in flux as he creates new weapons, perfects new means of communication and transport, and makes other advances in technology.

As just stated, man can alter within narrow limits the physical properties of the stage upon which he plays out successive acts in the drama of world politics. He has dug canals, changed the course of rivers, used up irreplaceable minerals, cut down forests and planted new ones, worn out the soil and sometimes restored its fertility, tunnelled through mountains, built harbors, and otherwise altered the earth's surface structure.

In certain instances, such man-made changes have profoundly modified the pattern of world politics. Take, for example, the opening of the Suez Canal. That engineering feat radically altered the political and military situation of every European state fronting on the Mediterranean. This short-cut to the Indian Ocean transformed the military geography of the British Empire, and affected Britain's political relations with every country around the globe. Many other examples could be cited, in which some man-made change in the earth's surface has altered the pattern of international relations.

More frequent and usually more unsettling have been changes in the pattern of world relations resulting from mechanical inventions which have given new meaning to fixed geographic facts. Man has advanced with giant strides in his conquest of time and space. The same is true of the mechanics of waging war. Advances in the technology of weapons, transport, and communications, as well as parallel advances in sanitary engineering, medicine, dietetics, climatology, weather forecasting, and other technical fields, have widened or narrowed the range of choice open to the statesman and the military strategist. The military and political meaning of geographic facts must therefore be continuously reexamined in the light of an ever advancing technology.

Innumerable illustrations could be cited. Take, for example, the strategical properties of oceanic space. They have fluctuated with every advance in navigation and naval technology. Sailing ships could remain at sea for weeks or months at a time. But they were dependent for movement upon the direction and strength of the wind. Steam power has given fleets greater tactical mobility. But fuel requirements have set rigid limits on their strategical radius of action. Invention of steel hulls, rifled ordnance, armor plate, mines, automotive torpedoes, submarines, and other naval equipment have repeatedly altered not only the methods of naval combat but also the radius of naval power, the protective value of the oceans, the use of narrow seas, and the potentialities of sea power in general.

A single invention may start a long chain of technical developments which eventually transform the political and military pattern of the globe. One such invention was the internal combustion engine. This invention, together with thousands of other inventions which preceded and followed it, has given us tanks, submarines, planes, motor vehicles of all kinds, and other paraphernalia of modern war and present-day communications. Directly or indirectly, the internal combustion engine has undermined the position of certain countries. To others it has opened up strategical opportunities formerly beyond reach. The ramifications of this invention have penetrated to the ends of the earth.

As previously described (see chapter 2 above), political power today rests upon a broad base of industrial plant, organization and infinitely complex manufacturing processes. Coal and iron ore must be brought together in immense quantities to make the incredible amounts of steel required by modern civilization. Iron must be supplemented by other metals and non-metallic raw materials. Battles can be won or lost in the laboratories where scientists labor to produce better fuels, stronger alloys, substitutes for missing materials, precision instruments, and other components of national power.

Under these conditions, significant military power is a virtual monopoly of a few great states. The tendency is for the strong to grow stronger while the weak become relatively weaker. This strategical revolution has world-shaking ramifications. The Second World War has unsettled military doctrines and political relationships which only yesterday seemed as solid and enduring as the Rock of Gibraltar itself. Space, location, distance, climate, minerals, and other earth features are taking on new political meanings and values.

Against this background of changing strategical values and changing political relationships, we turn now to a survey of the political and military structure of our world, and to a preliminary inquiry into the changes which are being hammered out upon the anvil of the Second World War.

FROM MAHAN TO MACKINDER

By the Editors

Two names stand out in the literature of international politics during the past half-century. These are Alfred Thayer Mahan and Sir Halford J. Mackinder. The former was an American naval officer; the latter, a British geographer.

Mahan interpreted world history largely as a continuing struggle for control of the seas. Mainly from intensive study of the seventeenth, eighteenth, and nineteenth centuries, the golden age of sea power, he reached the conclusion that control of the pathways of seaborne commerce was, and would continue to be, the key to world power.

Mackinder interpreted history as a struggle between sea power and land power. There was no assurance in his view that the contemporary predominance of the maritime nations was more than a passing phase in that historic struggle. On the contrary, he held that the "grouping of lands and seas, and of fertility and natural pathways is such as to lend itself to the growth of empires, and in the end of a single world empire" which would combine dominant sea and land power under one rule and extend its invincible sway over all the lands and seas of the globe.

Mahan emerged from the anonymity of a routine naval career with the publication in 1890 of his book, *The Influence of Sea Power upon History, 1660-1783*. Almost overnight he became internationally famous. No other single person has so directly and profoundly influenced the naval doctrines and the national policies of so many nations. In one way or another his writings influenced the statecraft of the United States, Great Britain, Germany, France, Italy, Russia, Japan, and many lesser powers.

Mahan was not a systematic thinker. His writings consisted of rambling histories of naval warfare and magazine articles on current affairs. His philosophy of history and his ideas on world power are scattered hit-or-miss through these writings. One cannot read them without gaining a general sense of Mahan's larger conceptions of history. But it is impossible to single out any one passage, or group of passages, in which these are concisely summarized. Mahan's interpretations of history and his views on the future of sea power have, therefore, to be pieced together from fragments plucked from books and articles published through more than two decades of voluminous writing.

The key to Mahan's firm belief in the continued predominance of sea power over land power can be found in numerous early passages. In 1893, for example, in "Hawaii and our Future Sea Power," in *The Forum:*

"The sea, until it approaches the land, realizes the ideal of a vast plain unbroken by obstacles. . . . But upon a plain, however flat and monotonous, causes, possibly slight, determine the concentration of population into towns and villages, and the necessary communications between the centers create roads. Where the latter converge, or cross, tenure confers command, depending for importance upon the number of routes thus meeting and upon their individual value. It is just so at sea. While in itself the ocean opposes no obstacle to a vessel taking any one of the numerous routes that can be traced upon the surface of the globe between two points, conditions of distance or convenience, of traffic or of wind, do prescribe certain usual courses. Where these pass near an ocean position [i.e., a land position fronting upon the ocean], still more where they use it, it has an influence over them, and where several routes cross nearby that influence becomes very great—is commanding. . . ."

This concept of the sea as a vast plain, crossed and criss-crossed by unmarked but heavily traveled highways, was associated in Mahan's mind with the conviction that overland transport could never compete, either commercially or strategically, with movement by sea. In a typical statement, in "The Isthmus and Sea Power," in the *Atlantic Monthly,* he said in 1893:

"For more than four hundred years the mind of man has been possessed with a great idea, which, although by its wide diffusion and prophetic nature resembling one of those fundamental instincts, whose very existence points to a necessary fulfillment, first quickened into life in the thought of Christopher Columbus. To him the vision, dimly seen through the scanty and inaccurate knowledge of his age, imaged a close and facile communication, by means of the sea, that great bond of nations, between two ancient and diverse civilizations, which centered, the one around the Mediterranean, the birthplace of European commerce, refinement, and culture, the other upon the shores of that distant Eastern Ocean which lapped the dominions of the Great Khan, and held upon its breast the rich island of Zipangu. Hitherto an envious waste of land, entailing years of toilsome and hazardous journey, had barred them asunder. A rare traveller now and again might penetrate from one to the other, but it was impossible to maintain by land the constant exchange of influence and benefit which, though on a contracted scale, had constituted the advantage and promoted the development of the Mediterranean peoples. The microcosm of the land-girt sea [i.e., the Mediterranean] typified then that future greater family of nations, which one by one have been bound since into a common tie of interest by the broad enfolding ocean, that severs only to knit them more closely together. . . ." (Both Mahan quotations are from *The Interest of America in Sea Power,* courtesy Little, Brown & Co.)

The rise and exploits of British naval power were, in Mahan's eyes, proof of the paramount importance of control of the "broad enfolding ocean." In a later chapter [see pp. 166ff. below], his analysis of Britain's global sea power will be summarized and evaluated.

Mahan doubted whether Great Britain could permanently keep the trident so hardly won and so firmly held in the nineteenth century. He looked forward with growing confidence to a day when the United States would succeed Britain as the leading maritime power. It was inconceivable to Mahan that one of the continental powers of Europe or Asia could ever challenge successfully the maritime position of the Anglo-American peoples. Again and again he expressed the conviction that no nation with strong neighbors across its land frontiers could ever seize the trident of global sea power. The necessity of diverting large resources to maintaining the land armaments necessary to defend even one exposed land frontier would constitute a fatal handicap. No such nation could compete successfully with insular Britain or continentally insular America for command of the seas.

That was Mahan's reading of history and of the conditions and circumstances of his own era. And to that view he stuck to his death in 1914, although with some misgivings in his last years as he watched Germany forge ahead to become the strongest land power in Europe and a sea power second only to Great Britain.

Sir Halford Mackinder, as previously noted, challenged the conclusions reached by Mahan. In Edward Mead Earle's introduction to the 1942 printing of Mackinder's best known book, *Democratic Ideals and Reality*, the issue is put as follows:

". . . Forty years ago—when Mahan's theories concerning the supremacy of sea power were at the height of their prestige—Mackinder told his fellow-countrymen that Britain had no 'indefeasible title to maritime supremacy,' that sea power could be outflanked by land power, that the rise of great industrial states in Europe (nourished by protectionism) could undermine the foundations of British economic and strategic security, that it was no longer possible for England to pursue a policy of limited liabilities. Futhermore, he warned that, should Britain once surrender the long lead which she then held over her competitors, she probably would have lost for all time both her naval supremacy and her position as a Great Power.

"He saw that Germany and Russia were so situated on the continent of Europe that, should they combine or should either acquire control of the other, they would rule the world. He understood that modern transportation was reducing continents to islands. Europe, Asia, and Africa constituted not three continents but one—the 'World-Island.' This World Island is the true center of gravity of world power, the Western Hemisphere being only an island of lesser proportions, lesser manpower, and lesser natural resources. The 'Heartland' of this World Island is . . . so situated geographically and strategically that it could dominate the World Island as a whole. Hence his classic warning:

Who rules East Europe commands the Heartland;
Who rules the Heartland commands the World-Island;
Who rules the World-Island commands the World."

The following selections from Mackinder's book, *Democratic Ideals and Reality*, should be read in the light of its time and context. This book was addressed primarily to British statesmen charged with negotiating terms of peace with the defeated Central Powers. The book was written in the winter of 1918-1919. Its preface is dated February 1, 1919. At that moment the Peace Conference in Paris was just getting down to business.

Against this background, the purpose of Mackinder's book becomes clear. It was primarily a warning. The Allies had won a military victory. But in the winter of 1918-1919, they had yet to win the peace. Mackinder foresaw the danger that Germany might recover from military defeat and attempt to build another empire. He feared and warned his countrymen against the danger of German military and managerial genius integrating under one rule the huge manpower and vast material resources of the great Eurasian plain, or "Heartland," reaching from Central Europe deep into Asia.

On the second page of this prophetic book, Mackinder introduced this warning note which runs through every succeeding chapter. "Unless I wholly misread the facts of geography," he wrote, "the grouping of lands and seas, and of fertility and natural pathways, is such as to lend itself to the growth of empires, and in the end of a single world-empire. If we are to realize our ideal of a League of Nations which shall prevent war in the future, we must recognize these geographical realities and take steps to counter their influence."

Mackinder's solution for this threatening problem was to build a solid tier of buffer states from the Baltic to the Black Sea. In this manner he would keep Germany and Russia apart, and prevent the former from gaining control of the incomparable resources of the Heartland.

In retrospect it seems clear that Mackinder's remedy left much to be desired. The buffer states were created, but they proved an illusory barrier against the hammer blows of the Wehrmacht which the Nazis forged in defiance of the peace treaty of 1919. One can also pick flaws with Mackinder's oversimplified analysis of the historic struggles between sea power and land power. And one cannot escape the conclusion that he seriously underestimated the military potential of the New World in general, and of the United States in particular.

On the other hand, Mackinder did understand, more clearly than most of his contemporaries, that railways, motor vehicles, airplanes, and other technical developments in transport and in military mobility, were making possible the political integration of larger and larger land areas. He grasped the resulting peril to the political and military position of Great Britain, and to the future security of the British Empire. In *Democratic Ideals and Reality*, Mackinder strove to arouse his countrymen to the danger ahead, and to find a way to meet it.

Though written as a tract for the times, this book, as Dr. Earle has said elsewhere in his introduction, "has the rare quality of timelessness. . . . There is no better statement anywhere of the facts of geography which condition the destiny of our world. There is nowhere else so realistic an appraisal of the relative strength of sea power and land power and the manner in which the balance between them may be upset by inventions such as railways, motor transport, submarines, and aviation. . . . It is a measure of Mackinder's stature to say that his work is more important today than the writings of Admiral Mahan for those who would understand the political dynamics of our world."

SEA POWER vs. LAND POWER
By Sir Halford J. Mackinder

From chaps. 3 and 4 of *Democratic Ideals and Reality*, by Sir Halford J. Mackinder. Copyright 1919, by Henry Holt & Co., New York; reprinted 1942 with an introduction by Edward Mead Earle; reproduced by permission.

THE physical facts of geography have remained substantially the same during the fifty or sixty centuries of recorded human history. Forests have been cut down, marshes have been drained, and deserts may have broadened, but the outlines of land and water, and the lie of mountains and rivers have not altered except in detail. The influence of geographical conditions upon human activities has depended, however, not merely on the realities as we now know them to be and to have been, but in even greater degree on what men imagined in regard to them. . . .

To this day, our view of the geographical realities is colored for practical purposes by our preconceptions from the past. . . . In order, therefore, to appreciate where we now stand, it will be worth while to consider shortly the stages by which we have arrived. Let us begin with the succeeding phases of the seaman's outlook.

Imagine a vast tawny desert, raised a few hundred feet above the sea level. Imagine a valley with precipitous rocky slopes trenched into this desert plateau, and the floor of the valley carpeted with a strip of black soil, through the midst of which winds northward for five hundred miles a silvery navigable river. That river is the Nile flowing from where the granite rocks of Assouan break its navigability at the first cataract to where its waters divide at the head of the Delta. From desert edge to desert edge across the valley is a crow-fly distance of some ten or twenty miles. . . . Egypt, in this long sunken belt, was anciently civilized because all the essential physical advantages were here combined for men to work upon. On the one hand were a rich soil, abundant water, and a powerful sunshine; hence fertility for the support of a population in affluence. On the other hand was a smooth waterway within half a dozen miles or less of every field in the country. There was also motive power for shipping, since the river current carried vessels northward, and the Etesian winds—known on the ocean as the trade winds—brought them southward again. Fertility and a line of communications—manpower and facilities for its organization; there are the essential ingredients for a kingdom.

We are asked to picture the early condition of Egypt as that of a valley held by a chain of tribes, who fought with one another in fleets of great war canoes, . . . Some one of these tribes, having defeated its neighbors, gained possession of a longer section of the valley, a more extensive material basis for its manpower, and on that basis organized further conquests. At last the whole length of the valley was brought under a single rule, and the kings of all Egypt established their palace at Thebes. Northward and southward, by boat on the Nile, traveled their administrators— their messengers and their magistrates. Eastward and westward lay the strong defense of the deserts, and at the northern limit, against the sea pirates, a belt of marsh round the shore of the Delta.

Now carry your mind to the Mediterranean. You have there essentially the same physical ingredients as in Egypt but on a larger scale. . . . From the Phoenician coast for two thousand miles westward lies the broad waterway to its mouth at Gibraltar, and on either hand are fertile shorelands with winter rains and harvest sunshine. But there is a distinction to be made between the dwellers along the Nile banks and those along the Mediterranean shores. The conditions of human activity are relatively uniform in all parts of Egypt; each of the constituent tribes would have its farmers and its boatmen. But the races round the Mediterranean became specialized; some were content to till their fields and navigate their rivers at home, but others gave most of their energy to seamanship and foreign commerce. Side by side, for instance, dwelt the home-staying, corn-growing Egyptians and the adventurous Phoenicians. A longer and more sustained effort of organization was therefore needed to weld all the kingdoms of the Mediterranean into a single political unit.

Modern research has made it plain that the leading seafaring race of antiquity came at all times from that square of water between Europe and Asia which is known alternatively as the Aegean Sea and the Archipelago. ... It is of deepest interest for our present purpose to note that the center of civilization in the pre-Greek world of the Aegean, according both to the indications of mythology and the recent excavations, was in the island of Crete. Was that the first base of sea power? From that home did the seamen fare who, sailing northward, saw the coast of the rising sun to their right hand, and of the setting sun to their left hand, and named the one Asia and the other Europe? ... There are so many islands in the Archipelago that the name has become, like the Delta of Egypt, one of the common descriptive terms of geography. But Crete is the largest and most fruitful of them. Have we here a first instance of the importance of the larger base for sea power? The manpower of the sea must be nourished by land fertility somewhere, and other things being equal—such as security of the home and energy of the people—that power will control the sea which is based on the greater resources.

The next phase of Aegean development teaches apparently the same lesson. Horse-riding tribes of Hellenic speech came down from the north into the peninsula which now forms the mainland of Greece, and settled, Hellenizing the early inhabitants. These Hellenes advanced into the terminal limb of the peninsula, the Peloponnese, slenderly attached to the continent by the isthmus of Corinth. Thence, organizing sea power on their relatively considerable peninsular base, one of the Hellenic tribes, the Dorians, conquered Crete, a smaller though completely insular base.

Some centuries passed, during which the Greeks sailed round the southern headlands of the Peloponnese into the Ionian Sea, and colonized along the shores of that sea also. So the peninsula came to be a citadel in the midst of the Greek sea-world. Along the outer shores of the twin waters, Aegean and Ionian, the Greek colonists were but a fringe exposed to attack from behind. Only in the central peninsula were they relatively, although as the sequel shows not absolutely, safe.

To the eastern, outer shore of the Aegean the Persians came down from the interior against the Greek cities by the sea, and the Athenian fleet carried aid from the peninsular citadel to the threatened kinfolk over the water, and issue was joined between sea power and land power. A Persian sea raid was defeated at Marathon, and the Persians then resorted to the obvious strategy of baffled land power; under King Xerxes they marched round, throwing a bridge of boats over the Dardanelles, and entered the peninsula from the north, with the idea of destroying the nest whence the wasps emerged which stung them and flew elusively away. The Persian effort failed, and it was reserved for the half-Greek, half-barbaric Macedonians, established in the root of the Greek Peninsula itself, to end the first cycle of sea power by conquering to the south of them the Greek sea base, and then marching into Asia, and through Syria into Egypt, and on the way destroying Tyre of the Phoenicians. Thus they made a "closed sea" of the Eastern Mediterranean by depriving both the Greeks and the Phoenicians of their bases. That done, the Macedonian king, Alexander, could advance lightheartedly into Upper Asia. We may talk of the mobility of ships and of the long arm of the fleet, but after all, sea power is fundamentally a matter of appropriate bases, productive and secure. Greek sea power passed through the same phases as Egyptian river power. The end of both was the same; without the protection of a navy, commerce moved securely over a waterway because all the shores were held by one and the same land power.

Now we go to the western Mediterranean. Rome there began as a fortified town on a hill, at the foot of which was a bridge and a river-wharf. This hill-bridge-port-town was the citadel and market of a small nation of farmers, who tilled Latium, the "broad land" or plain, between the Apennines and the sea. "Father" Tiber was for shipping purposes merely a creek, navigable for the small sea-craft of those days, which entered thus from the coast a few miles into the midst of the plain, but that was enough to give Rome the advantage over her rivals, the towns crowning the Alban and Etruscan hills of the neighborhood. Rome had the bridge and the inmost port just as had London.

Based on the productivity of Latium, the Romans issued from the Tiber to traffic round the shores of the Western Mediterranean. Soon they came into competition with the Carthaginians, who were based on the fertility of the Mejerdeh Valley in the opposite promontory of Africa. The First Punic War ensued, and the Romans victoriously held the sea. They then proceeded to widen their base by annexing all the peninsular part of Italy as far as the Rubicon River.

In the Second Punic War, the Carthaginian general, Hannibal, endeavored to outflank the Roman sea power by marching round it, as Xerxes and Alexander had done in regard to the sea powers opposed to them. He carried his army over the western narrows from Africa into Spain, and then advanced through Southern Gaul into Italy. He was defeated, and Rome annexed the Mediterranean coasts of Gaul and Spain. By taking Carthage itself in the Third Punic War, she made a "closed sea" of the Western Mediterranean, for all the shores were held by one and the same land power.

There remained the task of uniting the controls of the western and eastern basins of the Mediterranean, connected by the Sicilian Strait and the Strait of Messina. The Roman legions passed over into Macedonia and thence into Asia, but the distinction between Latin West and Greek East remained, as was evident when civil war came to be waged between the Roman governors of the West and the East, Caesar and Antony. At the sea-fight of Actium, one of the decisive battles of the world's history, the Western fleet of Caesar destroyed the Eastern fleet of Antony. Thenceforth for five centuries the entire Mediterranean was a "closed sea"; and we think in consequence of the Roman Empire as chiefly a land power. No fleet was needed, save a few police vessels, to maintain as complete a command of the arterial seaway of the Mediterranean as ever the kings of Egypt exercised over their Nile-way. Once more land power terminated a cycle of competition upon the water by depriving sea power of its bases. True that there had been the culminating sea battle of Actium, and that Caesar's fleet had won the reward of all finally successful fleets, the command over all the sea. But that command was not afterwards maintained upon the sea, but upon the land by holding the coasts.

When Rome had completed the organization of her power round the Mediterranean, there followed a long transitional epoch, during which the oceanic development of Western civilization was gradually preparing. The transition began with the Roman road system, constructed for the greater mobility of the marching legions.

After the close of the Punic Wars four Latin-speaking provinces encircled the western Mediterranean—Italy, Southern Gaul, Eastern and Southern Spain, and Carthaginian Africa. The outer boundary of the African province was protected by the Sahara Desert, and Italy had in rear the Adriatic moat, but in Gaul and Spain Rome found herself the uncomfortable neighbor of independent Celtic tribes. Thus the familiar dilemma of empire presented itself; to advance and end the menace, or to entrench and shut it out, but leave it in being. A still virile people chose the former course, and the frontier and the roads were carried through to the ocean along a thousand miles of frontage between Cape St. Vincent and the mouths of the Rhine. As a consequence the Latin portion of the Empire came to be based on two features of physical geography: on the one hand was the Latin Sea, the western Mediterranean; and on the other hand was the Latin Peninsula, between the Mediterranean and the ocean.

Julius Caesar penetrated to the Bay of Biscay, and built a fleet wherewith he defeated the fleet of the Veneti of Brittany. Then, because the Celts of Britain were giving help to their Gallic kinsmen, he crossed the Channel and smote them in their island base. A hundred years later the Romans conquered all the lower and more fruitful portion of Britain, and so eliminated the risk of the rise of a sea power off the Gallic coast. In this way the Channel also became a "closed sea," controlled by land power.

After four centuries the land power of Rome waned, and the seas on either side of the Latin Peninsula then soon ceased to be "closed." The Norsemen raided over the North Sea from their fiords, and through the Channel, and through the Straits of Gibraltar, even into the recesses of the Mediterranean, enveloping with their sea power the whole great peninsula. They seized forward bases in the islands of Britain and Sicily, and even nibbled at the mainland edges in Normandy and Southern Italy.

At the same time the Saracen camelmen came down from Arabia and took Carthage, Egypt, and Syria from the Empire—the provinces, that is to say, south of the Mediterranean. Then they launched their fleets on the water, and seized part of Sicily and part of Spain for overseas bases. Thus the Mediterranean ceased to be the arterial way of an empire, and became the frontier moat dividing Christendom from Islam. But the greater sea power of the Saracen enabled them to hold Spain, though north of the water, just as at an earlier time the greater sea power of Rome had enabled her to hold Carthage, though south of the water.

For a thousand years Latin Christendom was thus imprisoned in the Latin Peninsula and its appendant island of Britain. Fifteen hundred miles northeastward, measured in a straight line, trends the oceanic coast from the Sacred Promontory of the ancients to the Straits of Copenhagen, and fifteen hundred miles eastward, measured in the same way, lies the sinuous Mediterranean coast from the Sacred Promontory to the Straits at Constantinople. A lesser peninsula advances toward the main peninsula of each strait, Scandinavia on the one hand, and Asia Minor on the other; and behind the land bars so formed are two land-girt basins, the Baltic and Black Seas. If Britain be considered as balancing Italy, the symmetry of the distal end of the main peninsula is such that you might lay a

Latin cross upon it with the head in Germany, the arms in Britain and Italy, the feet in Spain, and the center in France, thus typifying that ecclesiastical empire of the five nations which, though shifted northward, was the medieval heir of the Roman Caesars. Toward the east, however, where the Baltic and Black Seas first begin to define the peninsular character of Europe, the outline is less shapely, for the Balkan Peninsula protrudes southward, only tapering finally into the historic little peninsula of Greece.

Is it not tempting to speculate on what might have happened had Rome not refused to conquer eastward of the Rhine? Who can say that a single mighty sea power, wholly Latinized as far as the Black and Baltic Seas, would not have commanded the world from its peninsular base? But classical Rome was primarily a Mediterranean and not a peninsular power, and the Rhine-Danube frontier must be regarded as demarking a penetration from the Mediterranean coast rather than as the incomplete achievement of a peninsular policy.

It was the "opening" again of the seas on either hand which first compacted Europe in the peninsular sense. Reaction had to be organized, or the pressures from north and south would have obliterated Christendom. So Charlemagne erected an empire astride of the Rhine, half Latin and half German by speech, but wholly Latin ecclesiastically. With this empire as base the Crusades were afterwards undertaken. Seen in large perspective at this distance of time, and from the seaman's point of view, the Crusades, if successful, would have had for their main effect the "closing" once more of the Mediterranean Sea. The long series of these wars, extending over two centuries, took two courses. On the one hand, fleets were sent out from Venice and Genoa to Jaffa and Acre on the Syrian coast; on the other hand, armies marched through Hungary, along the famous "corridor" of the Morava and Maritza Valleys, and through Constantinople and Asia Minor into Syria. The comparison is obvious between these campaigns of the Crusaders by land, from a German base round to the back of the Mediterranean Sea, and the similar campaign of Alexander from his Macedonian base. A good many parallels might, indeed, be drawn between the half-Greek Macedonians and the half-Latin Germans. . . . But his position in the broad root of the Greek Peninsula enabled the Macedonian to conquer the Greek sea base, as the position of the German in the broad root of the greater Latin Peninsula has always made him dangerous to the Latin sea bases beyond the Rhine and the Alps.

The peoples of the Latin civilization were thus hardened by a winter of centuries, called the Dark Ages, during which they were besieged in their homeland by the Mohammedans, and failed to break out by their Crusading sorties. Only in the fifteenth century did time ripen for the great adventure on the ocean which was to make the world European. It is worth pausing for a moment to consider further the unique environment in which the Western strain of our human breed developed the enterprise and tenacity which have given it the lead in the modern world. Europe is but a small corner of the great island which also contains Asia and Africa, but the cradle land of the Europeans was only a half of Europe—the Latin Peninsula and the subsidiary peninsulas and islands clustered around it. Broad deserts lay to the south, which could be crossed only in some three months on camel back, so that the black men were fended off from the white men. The trackless ocean lay to the west, and to the north the frozen ocean. To the northeast were interminable pine forests, and rivers flowing either to ice-choked mouths in the Arctic Sea or to inland waters, such as the Caspian Sea, detached from the ocean. Only to the southeast were there practicable oasis routes leading to the outer world, but these were closed, more or less completely, from the seventh to the nineteenth century, by the Arabs and the Turks.

In any case, however, the European system of waterways was detached by the Isthmus of Suez from the Indian Ocean. Therefore from the seaman's point of view Europe was a quite definite conception, even though the landsman might think of it as merging with Asia. It was a world apart, but within that world was ample fertility, and in its water-paths a natural provision for the intimacy of a family of nations. Water-paths they were, with branchings and crossings, for the boatmen, not venturing out on to the high seas, still sailed between the coasts and the horizon, just as they threaded their way between the two banks of the rivers. In the relatively roadless days, moreover, which followed on the decay of the Roman road system, the boatmen frequented many of the headwaters of the rivers, which we have now abandoned as no longer worth navigating.

There were two fortunate circumstances in regard to the medieval siege of Europe. On the one hand, the Infidels had not command of inexhaustible manpower, for they were based on arid and sub-arid deserts and steppes, and on comparatively small oasis lands; on the other hand, the Latin Peninsula was not seriously threatened along its oceanic border, for the Norsemen . . . were based on fiord valleys even less extensive and less fruitful than the oases, and wherever they settled—in England, Normandy, Sicily, or Russia—their small numbers were soon absorbed into the older populations. Thus the whole defensive strength of Europe could be thrown against the southeastern danger. But as the European civilization gained momentum, there was energy to spare upon the ocean frontage. . . .

After the essays, without practical result, of the Norsemen to force their way through the northern ice of Greenland, the Portuguese undertook to find a seaway to the Indies round the coast of Africa. They were inspired to the venture by the lead of Prince Henry, "the Navigator," half Englishman and half Portuguese. At first sight it seems strange that pilots like Columbus, who had spent their lives on coasting voyages, often going from Venice to Britain, should so long have delayed an exploration southward as they issued from the Straits of Gibraltar. Still more strange does it appear that when at last they had set themselves to discover the outline of Africa, it took them two generations of almost annual voyaging before Da Gama led the way into the Indian Ocean. The cause of their difficulties was physical. For a thousand miles, from the latitude of the Canary Islands to that of Cape Verde, the African coast is a torrid desert, because the dry trade wind there blows off the land without ceasing. It might be a relatively easy matter to sail southward on that steady breeze, but how was the voyage back to be accomplished by ships which could not sail near the wind like a modern clipper, and yet dared neither sail out onto the broad ocean across the wind, nor yet tediously tack their way home off a coast with no supplies of fresh food and water, in a time when the plague of scurvy had not yet been mastered?

Once the Portuguese had found the ocean-way into the Indian seas, they soon disposed of the opposition of the Arab dhows. Europe had taken its foes in rear; it had sailed round to the rear of the land, just as Xerxes, Alexander, Hannibal, and the Crusaders had marched round to the rear of the sea.

From that time until the opening of the Suez Canal in 1869, the seamen of Europe continued in ever-increasing number to round the Cape, and to sail northward on the eastern ocean as far as China and Japan. . . . From the point of view of the traffic to the Indies, the world was a vast cape, standing out southward from between Britain and Japan. This world promontory was enveloped by sea power, as had been the Greek and Latin promontories beforehand: all its coasts were open to ship-borne trade or to attack from the sea. The seamen naturally chose for the local bases of their trading or warfare small islands off the continental coast, such as Mombasa, Bombay, Singapore, and Hongkong, or small peninsulas, such as the Cape of Good Hope and Aden, since those positions offered shelter for their ships and security for their depots. When grown bolder and stronger they put their commercial cities, such as Calcutta and Shanghai, near the entry of great river-ways into productive and populous marketlands. The seamen of Europe, owing to their greater mobility, have thus had superiority for some four centuries over the landsmen of Africa and Asia.

The passing of the imminent danger to Christendom, because of the relative weakening of Islam, was, no doubt, one of the reasons for the break-up of medieval Europe at the close of the Middle Ages. . . . As a result of this break-up, there arose five competing oceanic powers—Portuguese, Spanish, French, Dutch, and English—in the place of the one power which would, no doubt, have been the ideal of the Crusaders.

Thus the outcome of a thousand years of transition, from the ancient to the modern conditions of sea power, is such as to prompt a comparison between the Greek and Latin Peninsulas, each with its offset island. Peninsular Greece and insular Crete anticipated in their relations the Latin Peninsula and the island of Britain. Under the Dorians the greater resources of the peninsular mainland were utilized for the conquest of Crete, but at a later time the rivalry of Sparta and Athens prevented a full exploitation of the peninsula as a sea base. So in the case of the greater peninsula and greater island, Britain was conquered and held by Rome from the peninsular mainland; but when the Middle Ages were closing, several rival sea bases occupied the Latin Peninsula, each of them open to attack from the land behind, as Athens and Sparta had been open to the Macedonian invasion. Of these Latin sea bases, one, Venice, fronted toward Islam, while the others contended with internecine feuds for the command of the ocean, so that in the end the lesser British insular base, faced by no united peninsular base, became the home of a power which enveloped and contained the greater peninsula.

. . . From Norman days, until the growth of the modern industries upon the coal-fields, the English nation was almost uniquely simple in its structure. It is that which makes English history the epic story that it is, until the histories of Scotland and Ireland come to confuse their currents with it. One fertile plain between the mountains of the west and north and the narrow seas to the east and south, a people of farmers, a single king, a single parliament, a tidal river, a single great city for central market and port—those are the elements on which the England was built whose warning beacons blazed on the hilltops from Plymouth to Berwick-on-Tweed, in that night of Elizabeth's reign when the Spanish Armada had entered the Channel. . . . The real base historically of British sea power was our English plain —fertile and detached; coal and iron from round the borders of the plain have been added in later times. . . .

Every characteristic of sea power may be studied in British history during the last three centuries, but the home base, productive and secure, is the one thing essential to which all things else have been added. . . .

Four times in the past three centuries was it attempted to overthrow British sea power from frontages on the peninsular coast opposite—from Spain, from Holland, and twice from France. At last, after Trafalgar, British sea power definitively enveloped the Latin Peninsula, having subsidiary bases at Gibraltar, Malta, and Heligoland. . . .

When the Napoleonic War was over, British sea power encompassed, almost without competition, that great world-promontory which stands forward to the Cape of Good Hope from between Britain and Japan. British merchant ships on the sea were a part of the British Empire; British capital ventured abroad in foreign countries was a part of British resources, controlled from the City of London and available for the maintenance of power on and over the seas. It was a proud and lucrative position, and seemed so secure that the mid-Victorian folk thought it almost in the natural order of things that insular Britain should rule the seas. . . .

Perhaps the most remarkable outcome of British sea power was the position in the Indian Ocean during the generation before the war [of 1914-1918]. The British "Raj" in India depended on support from the sea, yet on all the waters between the Cape of Good Hope, India, and Australia, there was habitually no British battleship or even first-class cruiser. In effect, the Indian Ocean was a "closed sea." Britain owned or "protected" most of the coastlines, and the remaining frontages were either on islands, as the Dutch East Indies, or on territories such as Portuguese Mozambique and German East Africa, which, although continental, were inaccessible under existing conditions by land-way from Europe. Save in the Persian Gulf, there could be no rival base for sea power which combined security with the needful resources, and Britain made it a declared principle of her policy that no sea base should be established on either the Persian or Turkish shores of the Persian Gulf. . . .

. . . Owing to the continuity of the ocean and the mobility of ships, a decisive battle at sea has immediate and far-reaching results. Caesar beat Antony at Actium, and Caesar's orders were enforceable forthwith on every shore of the Mediterranean. Britain won her culminating victory at Trafalgar, and could deny all the ocean to the fleets of her enemies, could transport her armies to whatsoever coast she would and remove them again, could carry supplies home from foreign sources, could exert pressure in negotiation on whatsoever offending state had a sea-front. Our concern here has been rather in regard to the bases of sea power and the relation to these of land power. In the long run, that is the fundamental question. There were fleets of war canoes on the Nile, and the Nile was closed to their contention by a single land power controlling their fertile bases through all the length of Egypt. A Cretan insular base was conquered from a larger Greek peninsular base. Macedonian land power closed the Eastern Mediterranean to the warships both of Greeks and Phoenicians by depriving them impartially of their bases. Hannibal struck overland at the peninsular base of Roman sea power, and that base was saved by victory on land. Caesar won the mastery of the Mediterranean by victory on the water, and Rome then retained control of it by the defense of land frontiers. In the Middle Ages Latin Christendom defended itself on the sea from its peninsular base, but in modern times, because competing states grew up within that peninsula, and there were several bases of sea power upon it, all open to attack from the land, the mastery of the seas passed to a power which was less broadly based, but on an island—fortunately a fertile and coal-bearing island. On sea power, thus based, British adventurers have founded an overseas empire of colonies, plantations, depots, and protectorates, and have established, by means of sea-borne armies, local land powers in India and Egypt. So impressive have been the results of British sea power that there has perhaps been a tendency to neglect the warnings of history and to regard sea power in general as inevitably having, because of the unity of the ocean, the last word in the rivalry with land power. . . .

The Great War [of 1914] began in the old style, and it was not until 1917 that the new aspects of reality became evident. In the very first days of the struggle the British fleet had already taken command of the ocean, enveloping, with the assistance of the French fleet, the whole peninsular theater of the war on land. The German troops in the German colonies were isolated, German merchant shipping was driven off the seas, the British expeditionary force was transported across the Channel without the loss of a man or a horse, and British and French supplies from over the ocean were safely brought in. In a word, the territories of Britain and France were made one for the purpose of the war, and their joint boundary was advanced to within gunshot range of the German coast—no small offset for the temporary, though deeply regretted, loss of certain French departments. After the Battle of the Marne the true war map of Europe would have shown a Franco-British frontier following the Norwegian, Danish, German, Dutch, and Belgian coasts—at a distance of three miles in the case of the neutral coasts—and then running as a sinuous line through Belgium and France to the Jura border of Switzerland. West of that boundary whether by land or sea, the two powers could make ready their defense against the enemy. Nine months later Italy dared to join the Allies, mainly because her ports were kept open by the Allied sea power.

On the Eastern Front, also, the old style of war held. Land power was there divided into two contending forces, and the outer of the two, notwithstanding its incongruous Czardom, was allied with the sea power of the democratic West. In short, the disposition of forces repeated in a general way that of a century earlier, when British sea power supported the Portuguese and Spaniards in "the Peninsula," and was allied with the autocracies of the eastern land powers. Napoleon fought on two fronts, which in terms of today we should describe as Western and Eastern.

In 1917, however, came a great change, due to the entry of the United States into the war, the fall of the Russian Czardom, and the subsequent collapse of the Russian fighting strength. The world strategy of the contest was entirely altered. . . . We have been fighting lately, in the close of the war [of 1914-1918] a straight duel between land power and sea power, and sea power has been laying siege to land power. We have conquered, but had

Germany conquered she would have established her sea power on a wider base than any in history, and in fact on the widest possible base. The joint continent of Europe, Asia, and Africa, is now effectively, and not merely theoretically, an island. Now and again, lest we forget, let us call it the World Island in what follows.

One reason why the seamen did not long ago rise to the generalization implied in the expression "World Island," is that they could not make the round voyage of it. An ice-cap, two thousand miles across, floats on the polar sea, with one edge aground on the shoals off the north of Asia. For the common purposes of navigation, therefore, the continent is not an island. The seamen of the last four centuries have treated it as a vast promontory stretching southward from a vague north, as a mountain peak may rise out of the clouds from hidden foundations. Even in the last century, since the opening of the Suez Canal, the eastward voyage has still been round a promontory, though with the point at Singapore instead of Cape Town.

This fact and its vastness have made men think of the Continent as though it differed from the other islands in more than size. We speak of its parts as Europe, Asia, and Africa in precisely the same way that we speak of the parts of the ocean as Atlantic, Pacific, and Indian. . . .

Let us consider for a moment the proportions and relations of this newly realized Great Island. It is set, as it were, on the shoulder of the earth with reference to the North Pole. Measuring from Pole to Pole along the central meridian of Asia, we have first a thousand miles of ice-clad sea as far as the northern shore of Siberia, then five thousand miles of land to the southern point of India, and then seven thousand miles of sea to the Antarctic cap of ice-clad land. But measured along the meridian of the Bay of Bengal or of the Arabian Sea, Asia is only some three thousand five hundred miles across. From Paris to Vladivostok is six thousand miles, and from Paris to the Cape of Good Hope is a similar distance; but these measurements are on a globe twenty-six thousand miles round. Were it not for the ice impediment to its circumnavigation, practical seamen would long ago have spoken of the Great Island by some such name, for it is only a little more than one-fifth as large as their ocean.

The World Island ends in points northeastward and southeastward. On a clear day you can see from the northeastern headland across Bering Strait to the beginning of the long pair of peninsulas, each measuring about one twenty-sixth of the globe, which we call the Americas. Superficially there is no doubt a certain resemblance of symmetry in the Old and New Worlds; each consists of two peninsulas, Africa and Euro-Asia in the one case, and North and South America in the other. But there is no real likeness between them. The northern and northeastern shores of Africa for nearly four thousand miles are so intimately related with the opposite shores of Europe and Asia that the Sahara constitutes a far more effective break in social continuity than does the Mediterranean. In the days of air navigation which are coming, sea power will use the waterway of the Mediterranean and Red Seas only by the sufferance of land power, a new amphibious cavalry, when the contest with sea power is in question.

But North and South America, slenderly connected at Panama, are for practical purposes insular rather than peninsular in regard to one another. South America lies not merely to south, but also in the main to east of North

America; the two lands are in echelon, as soldiers would say, and thus the broad ocean encircles South America, except for a minute proportion of its outline. A like fact is true of North America with reference to Asia, for it stretches out into the ocean from Bering Strait so that, as may be seen upon a globe, the shortest way from Pekin to New York is across Bering Strait, a circumstance which may some day have importance for the traveler by railway or air. The third of the new continents, Australia, lies a thousand miles from the southeastern point of Asia, and measures only one sixty-fifth of the surface of the globe.

Thus the three so-called new continents are in point of area merely satellites of the old continent. There is one ocean covering nine-twelfths of the globe; there is one continent—the World Island—covering two-twelfths of the globe; and there are many smaller islands, whereof North America and South America are, for effective purposes, two, which together cover the remaining one-twelfth. The term "New World" implies, now that we can see the realities and not merely historic appearances, a wrong perspective.

The truth, seen with a broad vision, is that in the great world-promontory, extending southward to the Cape of Good Hope, and in the North American sea base we have, on a vast scale, yet a third contrast of peninsula and island to be set beside the Greek Peninsula and the island of Crete, and the Latin Peninsula and the British Island. But there is this vital difference, that the world-promontory, when united by modern overland communications, is in fact the World Island, possessed potentially of the advantages both of insularity and of incomparably great resources.

Leading Americans have for some time appreciated the fact that their country is no longer a world apart.... But North America is no longer even a continent; in this twentieth century it is shrinking to be an island. Americans used to think of their three millions of square miles as the equivalent of all Europe.... Now, though they may not all have realized it, they must no longer think of Europe apart from Asia and Africa. The Old World has become ... a unit, incomparably the largest geographical unit on our globe....

What if the Great Continent, the whole World Island or a large part of it, were at some future time to become a single and united base of sea power? Would not the other insular bases be outbuilt as regards ships and outmanned as regards seamen? Their fleets would no doubt fight with all the heroism begotten of their histories, but the end would be fated. Even in the present war [1914-1918] insular America has had to come to the aid of insular Britain, not because the British fleet could not have held the seas for the time being, but lest such a building and manning base were to be assured to Germany at the Peace, or rather Truce, that Britain would inevitably be outbuilt and outmanned a few years later.

The surrender of the German fleet in the Firth of Forth is a dazzling event, but in all soberness, if we would take the long view, must we not still reckon with the possibility that a large part of the Great Continent might some day be united under a single sway, and that an invincible sea power might be based upon it? May we not have headed off that danger in this war, and yet leave by our settlement the opening for a fresh attempt in the future? Ought we not to recognize that that is the great ultimate threat to the world's liberty so far as strategy is concerned, and to provide against it in our new political system?

Let us look at the matter from the landsman's point of view.

LAND POWER VS. SEA POWER

FOUR centuries ago the whole outlook of mankind was changed in a single generation by the voyages of the great pioneers, Columbus, Da Gama, and Magellan. The idea of the unity of the ocean, beforehand merely inferred from the likeness of the tides in the Atlantic and Indian waters, suddenly became a part of the mental equipment of practical men. A similar revolution is in progress in the present generation in the rapid realization of the unity of the Continent owing to modern methods of communication by land and air. . . .

The northern edge of Asia is the inaccessible coast, beset with ice except for a narrow water lane which opens here and there along the shore in the brief summer owing to the melting of the local ice formed in the winter between the grounded floes and the land. It so happens that three of the largest rivers in the world, the Lena, Yenisei, and Obi, stream northward through Siberia to this coast, and are therefore detached for practical purposes from the general system of the ocean and river navigations. South of Siberia are other regions at least as large, drained into salt lakes having no outlet to the ocean; such are the basins of the Volga and Ural Rivers flowing to the Caspian Sea, and of the Oxus and Jaxartes to the Sea of Aral. Geographers usually describe these inward basins as "Continental." Taken together, the regions of Arctic and continental drainage measure nearly a half of Asia and a quarter of Europe, and form a great continuous patch in the north and center of the Continent. That whole patch, extending right across from the icy, flat shore of Siberia to the torrid, steep coasts of Baluchistan and Persia, has been inaccessible to navigation from the ocean. The opening of it by railways—for it was practically roadless beforehand—and by airplane routes in the near future, constitutes a revolution in the relations of men to the larger geographical realities of the world. Let us call this great region the Heartland of the Continent.

The north, center, and west of the Heartland are a plain, rising only a few hundred feet at most above sea level. In that greatest lowland on the globe are included Western Siberia, Turkestan, and the Volga basin of Europe, for the Ural Mountains, though a long range, are not of important height, and terminate some three hundred miles north of the Caspian, leaving a broad gateway from Siberia into Europe. Let us speak of this vast plain as the Great Lowland.

Southward the Great Lowland ends along the foot of a tableland, whose average elevation is about half a mile, with mountain ridges rising to a mile and a half. This tableland bears upon its broad back the three countries of Persia, Afghanistan, and Baluchistan; for convenience we may describe the whole of it as the Iranian Upland. The Heartland, in the sense of the region of Arctic and Continental drainage, includes most of the Great Lowland and most of the Iranian Upland; it extends therefore to the long, high, curving brink of the Persian Mountains, beyond which is the depression occupied by the Euphrates Valley and the Persian Gulf.

Now let us travel in imagination to the west of Africa. There, between the latitudes of the Canary and Cape Verde Islands, is a desert coast: it was the character of that coast, it will be remembered, which so long baffled the efforts of the medieval sailors to make the southward voyage round Africa. With a breadth of a thousand miles the

Sahara spreads thence across the north of Africa from the Atlantic Ocean to the Valley of the Nile. . . . The Sahara is the most unbroken natural boundary in the world; throughout history it has been a barrier between the white and the black men.

Between the Sahara and the Heartland there is a broad gap which is occupied by Arabia. . . . Arabia may be regarded as spreading for eight hundred miles from the Nile to beyond the Euphrates. From the foot of the Taurus Mountains, north of Aleppo, to the Gulf of Aden, it measures no less than eighteen hundred miles. As to one half, Arabia is desert, and as to the other half mainly dry steppes; although it lies in the same latitudes as the Sahara, it is more productive and carries a more considerable population of wandering Bedouin. Moreover, it has larger oases, and therefore larger cities. What, however, most distinguishes Arabia both from the Heartland and the Sahara is the fact that it is traversed by three great waterways in connection with the ocean—the Nile, the Red Sea, and the Euphrates and Persian Gulf. None of these three ways, however, affords naturally a complete passage across the arid belt. The Nile was navigable from the Mediterranean only to the first cataract, midway across the desert, though locks have now been constructed at Assouan which give access as far as the second cataract; and the navigation of the Euphrates ascends only to a point a hundred miles from the Mediterranean. Today it is true that the Suez Canal unites the Mediterranean to the Red Sea, but it was not only the isthmus which formerly impeded through traffic by this route; persistent north winds of the trade-wind current blow down the northern end of the Red Sea, which is beset with rocks, and sailing ships do not willingly attempt the northward voyage to the Canal, which would therefore have been relatively useless but for steam navigation. . . .

It follows from the foregoing description that the Heartland, Arabia, and the Sahara together constitute a broad, curving belt inaccessible to seafaring people, except by the three Arabian waterways. This belt extends completely across the Great Continent from the Arctic to the Atlantic shores. In Arabia it touches the Indian Ocean, and as a consequence, divides the remainder of the Continent into three separate regions whose rivers flow to the ice-free ocean. These regions are the Pacific and Indian slopes of Asia; the peninsulas and islands of Europe and the Mediterranean; and the great promontory of Africa south of the Sahara. The last-named differs from the other two regions in a very important respect. Its larger rivers, the Niger, Zambesi, and Congo, and also its smaller rivers, such as the Orange and Limpopo, flow across the tableland of the interior, and fall steeply over its edge to relatively short seaward reaches in the narrow coastal lowlands. The long upland courses of these rivers are navigable for several thousand miles, but are for practical purposes as completely detached from the ocean as the rivers of Siberia. The same, of course, is true of the Nile above the cataracts. We may, therefore, regard the interior of Africa south of the Sahara as a second Heartland. Let us speak of it as the Southern Heartland, in contradistinction to the Northern Heartland of Asia and Europe. . . .

Outside Arabia, the Sahara, and the two Heartlands, there remain in the World Island only two comparatively small regions, but those two regions are the most important on the globe. Around the Mediterranean, and in the European peninsulas and islands, there dwell four hundred million people, and in the southern and eastern coastlands of Asia, there dwell eight hundred million people. In these two regions, therefore, are three-quarters of the people of the world. From our present point of view the most pertinent way of stating this great fact is to say that four-fifths of the population of the Great Continent, the World Island, live in two regions which together measure only one-fifth of its area.

These two regions resemble one another in certain other very important respects. In the first place, their rivers are for the most part navigable continuously from the ocean. . . .

The similarity of these two Coastlands is not limited to the navigability of their rivers. . . . The monsoon winds of the summer carry the moisture of the ocean from the southwest on to India and from the southeast on to China; the west winds from the Atlantic bring rain at all seasons upon Europe, and in the wintertime upon the Mediterranean. Both Coastlands are therefore rich with tillage, and for that reason nourish their great populations. . . .

[In a long passage omitted for lack of space, Mackinder develops the theme that the Coastlands of Europe and of southeastern Asia, but especially of Europe, have from earliest times been repeatedly attacked and sometimes overrun, by the inhabitants of the Heartland. In modern times, he continues, the Heartland, in a strategical, as distinguished from a strictly geographical sense, has come to include all land and water dominated by land power—"the region to which, under modern conditions, sea power can be refused access, though the western part of it lies without the region of Arctic and continental drainage." He thus draws the strategical boundaries of the modern Heartland to include, "the Baltic Sea, the navigable Middle and Lower Danube, the Black Sea, Asia Minor, Armenia, Persia, Tibet, and Mongolia."]

When the Russian Cossacks first policed the steppes at the close of the Middle Ages, a great revolution was effected, for the Tartars, like the Arabs, had lacked the necessary manpower upon which to found a lasting empire, but behind the Cossacks were the Russian plowmen, who have today grown to be a people of a hundred millions on the fertile plains between the Black and Baltic Seas. During the nineteenth century, the Russian Czardom loomed large within the great Heartland, and seemed to threaten all the marginal lands of Asia and Europe. Toward the end of the century, however, the Germans of Prussia and Austria determined to subdue the Slavs and to exploit them for the occupation of the Heartland, through which run the land-ways into China, India, Arabia, and the African Heartland. The German military colonies of Kiauchau and East Africa were established as termini of the projected overland routes.

Today armies have at their disposal not only the Transcontinental Railway but also the motorcar. They have, too, the airplane, which is of a boomerang nature, a weapon of land power as against sea power. Modern artillery, moreover, is very formidable against ships. In short, a great military power in possession of the Heartland and of Arabia could take easy possession of the crossways of the world at Suez. Sea power would have found it very difficult to hold the Canal if a fleet of submarines had been based from the beginning of the war on the Black Sea. We have defeated the danger on this occasion [by the Allied victory in the First World War], but the facts of geography remain, and offer ever-increasing strategical opportunities to land power as against sea power.

THE POLITICAL MAP OF EURASIA

By Nicholas J. Spykman

From chap. 4 of *The Geography of the Peace*. Copyright 1944 by Harcourt, Brace & Co., New York; reproduced by permission. The late Dr. Spykman was Sterling professor of international relations at Yale University and formerly director of the Yale Institute of International Studies, which sponsored the publication of the book quoted.

The fundamental fact which is responsible for the conditions of this age of world politics is the development of ocean navigation and the discovery of sea routes to India and America. . . . Formerly, history had given us the pattern of great land powers based on the control of contiguous land masses such as the Roman, Chinese, and Russian Empires. Now the sea has become a great artery of communication and we have been given a new structure of great power and enormous extent. The British, French, and Japanese empires and the sea power of the United States have all contributed to the development of a modern world which is a single field for the interplay of political forces. It is sea power which has made it possible to conceive of the Eurasian Continent as a unit and it is sea power which governs the relationships between the Old and the New Worlds.

This important change in the organization of power was first comprehensively recognized and analyzed in 1890 by Alfred Thayer Mahan in his book *The Influence of Sea Power upon History, 1660-1783*. It was, however, the British geographer Sir Halford Mackinder who, in 1904, first studied in detail the relations between land and sea power on a truly global scale. He used a map centered on Siberia as the basic tool for his analysis and treated Europe, not as the center of the world, but as one of the many peninsulas of the Eurasian land mass. The Western World was confronted with a new view of the face of the earth which its preoccupation with Europe as the center of the universe had obscured. In his best-known work, *Democratic Ideals and Reality*, published in 1919, Mackinder asked again for a global view of world politics and developed more extensively his analysis of the Eurasian Continent. . . .

Mackinder's World. The Mackinder analysis began with the idea of the Heartland. The vast expanse of Siberia was considered as a unit in terms of internal drainage and access to the sea. This enormous area can be treated as a unit because all its rivers drain into the Arctic Ocean or the inland waters of the Caspian and Aral Seas and no part of it touches the open ocean at any point. The nomadic tribes who have always inhabited this region have been intermittently engaged in trying to reach the sea and have, consequently, exerted a tremendous military pressure on the states that have at various times occupied the coastal regions. This latter territory Mackinder calls the Inner Crescent and includes within its boundaries all those continental states which had direct access to the sea and thus exercised both maritime and land power. Beyond lie the islands and off-shore continents of the Outer Crescent while the fringes of the oceans are occupied by the overseas continents of the Western Hemisphere.

From this point of view, the continuity of the land masses of the Western Hemisphere is broken up because the Siberia-centered map shows the Atlantic seaboard of the North and South American Continents facing Europe, while the Pacific seaboard faces the Far East. At the time Mackinder first published his map, in 1904, it was prophetic rather than true to the realities of the day for it was not until the Panama Canal was completed that the full power potential of the United States was made available in the Western Pacific. Today, however, a map with the Eurasian Continent in the center has a definite validity because the Western Hemisphere has a vital interest in and connection with both the European and Far Eastern sections of the Old World.

The constellation of power in the Eastern Hemisphere was defined by Mackinder in terms of the relation between the land power of the Heartland and the sea power of Great Britain. Security for the British Empire depended on the preservation of a power equilibrium between the maritime and continental states of the World Island. If either of the two gained the ascendancy, the whole Continent would be dominated and the pivot area controlled by a single power. With this vast land mass as a base, a sea power could be developed which could defeat Great Britain with ease. It was, therefore, the task of British foreign policy to prevent any integration of power on the continent of Europe and, particularly, to see that nothing would lead to an effective military alliance between Germany and Russia.

This analysis has a very basic validity in terms of the topography of the Eurasian land mass. As we have already pointed out, there is a definite central lowland plain surrounded by a ring of mountains stretching almost continuously from Scandinavia to the Chukchi Peninsula in Siberia and effectively barring the approach of people from the inland area to the ocean. Beyond this mountain barrier lie the lowland coastal regions of Europe, the Middle East, India, and China.

... The central continental plain can continue to be called the Heartland but we may note that it is, in effect, to be equated with the political extent of the Union of Soviet Socialist Republics. Beyond the mountain barrier, the coastland region, which is called by Mackinder the Inner Crescent, may more effectively be referred to as the Rimland, a name which defines its character accurately. The surrounding string of marginal and mediterranean seas which separates the Continent from the oceans constitutes a circumferential maritime highway which links the whole area together in terms of sea power. Beyond lie the off-shore islands and continents of Great Britain, Japan, Africa, and Australia which compose the Outer Crescent. The term "off-shore" describes so well their essential relationship to the central land mass that we shall use this terminology rather than that of Mackinder. The Oceanic Belt and the transoceanic New World complete the picture in terms of purely geographical factors.

On the basis of this over-all picture of the Old World, we can now take up in detail the specific regions into which we have divided it and analyze their meaning in terms of power potential and the politics of global security. We must evaluate the role which each zone has in the past played in international society, for only in such a context will it be possible to understand the course of the Second World War and the possibilities of the peace.

The Heartland. The importance of the Heartland region was first suggested to Mackinder by his conception of the value of a central position with interior lines of communication made powerful and unified by the development of land transportation to a point where it could begin to compete with sea communication. He also envisaged the transformation of the steppe land from an area of low economic potential to one of high economic potential.

The actual facts of the Russian economy and geography make it not at all clear that the Heartland is or will be in the very near future a world center of communication, mobility, and power potential. First of all, the distribution of climate in the world makes it certain that, in the absence of revolutionary developments in agricultural technique, the center of agrarian productivity will remain in western Russia rather than in the central Siberian region. . . . Although the Russian state covers an area far larger than Canada, the United States, or Brazil, the actual extent of arable land is only a very small part of the total area. We must avoid the mistake of identifying all of Russia, or the Heartland, as a region of great potential agrarian productivity.

Looking again at the geographic distribution of coal and iron deposits in the world as well as the oil fields and water power, we note that these essential elements of industrial power are located largely west of the Ural Mountains. It is true that there are reserves of coal and iron in Siberia, the exact extent of which are unknown but which undoubtedly constitute a sizable quantity. Some reports say, also, that there are reserves of oil which can be important if developed. Certainly, the Soviet government has made and will continue to make constant and strenuous endeavors to shift the center of industrial production eastward. So far it has undoubtedly succeeded in developing factories and mines to an extent which has made it possible for Russia to provide herself with a large proportion of her vast wartime needs. The figures on the industrial production of the great area between the Urals and Novosibirsk remain vague and inaccurate and it is difficult to arrive at a complete estimate of the actual and potential importance of this region. It is, nevertheless, certain that it already supplements to an important extent the more fertile region to the west and southwest, although it must be remembered that it is not capable of supporting a large population from the produce of the land.

The railroad, the motor road, and the airplane have certainly created a new mobility in the center of the Eurasian land mass. It cannot, however, be ignored that this area is ringed to the north, east, south, and southwest by some of the greatest obstacles to transportation in the world. Ice and freezing temperatures for a large part of the year, and towering mountains pierced by only a few difficult passes, form its borders. A large part of the Rimland areas which touch the Heartland have even poorer transportation facilities. Afghanistan, Tibet, Sinkiang, and Mongolia are regions with no railroads, practically no motor roads, and only a few tortuous caravan routes of the most primitive sort. The law of the inverse ratio of power to distance remains valid within the same political unit as well as between political units. Within the immediate future, Central Asia will undoubtedly remain a region with a fairly low power potential.

The significance of this region was also defined by Mackinder in terms of position. The fact that the core of the Heartland lies in the center of the Eurasian land mass gives it the advantage of interior communication with the lands of the Inner Crescent. It is obvious that the problems of an army which is working along the diameters of a circle of territory will be less difficult than those of forces which have to function along the circumference of that same region. In comparison with the exterior lines of British naval power running from Great Britain through the circumferential highway around the Eurasian Rimlands, Russia has interior lines of communication. The transportation lines between Russian Turkestan and northwest India are certainly interior as compared with the sea route from Southampton to Karachi.

It must be pointed out, however, that interior lines function in terms of two points of reference rather than one. The relations between the center and the circumference may easily be changed if a point on the circumference becomes in turn the center of another circle of communication. Thus, the strategic implications of the position of the Heartland in relation to the British Empire have meaning only if the military strength to be applied at the Indian frontier originates in Great Britain. The moment the defense of that frontier or the Persian frontier or the Chinese frontier rests on a locally developed war potential, the whole concept of interior and exterior lines is changed. What is true for India and China if they have to be defended by British sea power is no longer true if their military strength can be made a by-product of their own industrial development. In this case, unless the raw materials of power in the central Asiatic regions of Russia turn out to be great enough to balance those of the Rimland regions, Soviet strength will remain west of the Urals and it will not be exerted overpoweringly against the coastlands to the east, south, and southwest.

The Rimland. In Mackinder's conception, the Inner Crescent of amphibian states surrounding the Heartland consists of three sections: the European coastland, the Arabian-Middle Eastern desert land, and the Asiatic monsoon land. The first two regions are clearly defined as geographical areas but the third is a unit only from the special historical point of view represented by Great Britain. To the seaman, the Asiatic monsoon land looks like a single region. The similarities of climate and the easy accessibility of the area to sea power contribute to this impression. This territory is also well protected from the Heartland by a string of barriers from the Himalayas and Tibet to the vast desert and mountain regions of Sinkiang and Mongolia. These mountains do not, however, make the monsoon lands behind them a single unit. The ranges of Burma and Indo-China extend down to the sea and interpose a great obstacle to contacts between the two great states. The fact that Buddhism reached China from India by way of Sinkiang and Thailand points to the difficulty of maintaining direct relations. Throughout their history, these two centers of oriental culture have remained fairly isolated from each other and their only contacts have been of a cultural and intellectual nature.

India and the Indian Ocean littoral, then, fall into a different geopolitical category from China, and it is scarcely accurate to classify them together as the Asiatic monsoon lands. The future will probably see the power of the two regions expressed as two distinct units connected only across the lower part of the Indo-China Peninsula by land or air power and around Singapore in terms of sea power. If this is true, then the Asiatic Mediterranean will continue to have great significance for the political strategy of the independent Asiatic world even as it has been of vital importance in the era of western sea power encirclement.

The Rimland of the Eurasian land mass must be viewed as an intermediate region, situated as it is between the Heartland and the marginal seas. It functions as a vast buffer zone of conflict between sea power and land power. Looking in both directions, it must function amphibiously and defend itself on land and sea. In the past, it has had to fight against the land power of the Heartland and against the sea power of the off-shore islands of Great Britain and Japan. Its amphibious nature lies at the basis of its security problems.

The Off-Shore Continents. Off the southeastern and southwestern shores of the Old World lie the two mediterranean seas beyond which stretch the continents of Australia and Africa. The position of these two off-shore continents is determined largely by the state which controls the European and Asiatic Mediterranean Seas. The Mackinder analysis defines the great desert region of Africa as a continental area inaccessible to sea power and therefore a Southern Heartland comparable to the northern one. This concept was perhaps of some value in understanding the political history of Africa before the penetration of that continent by the white man. It also had a certain validity in terms of British-Russian opposition as long as the circumferential envelopment of the Old World went by way of the Cape of Good Hope.

Since the completion of the Suez Canal, this interpretation has lost all practical significance. There is no sense using a term which connotes that an area is impenetrable to sea power when that area has actually been transformed by sea power penetration.... Notwithstanding any geographic similarity that can be suggested between the two regions, the Southern Heartland differs in one basic and fundamental respect from the Northern Heartland. It contains no political power and has no power potential of its own. It is not and never has been the seat of outward pressure toward the crescent. It does not, therefore, function in the total global picture in any manner similar to the Northern Heartland.

The significance of both these off-shore continents in world politics is limited by climatic conditions which restrict their productive capacity and, consequently, their power potential. The greatest proportion of Africa lies in the tropical zone and is either extremely dry or extremely humid. In either case the continent does not contain, except at the extreme southern tip, the resources necessary for the building up of political units capable of exerting an important influence on the rest of the world. In the same way, the desert regions of Australia are so extensive that the remaining territory is left without the size and resources required for the formation of a power of the first rank.

The Dynamic Pattern of Eurasian Politics. The general pattern of political action on the Eurasian Continent has been defined by Mackinder in terms of the pressure of nomadic peoples in the Heartland outward against the states of the Rimland. When the nomads who roamed the grasslands of the central lowland were replaced by the organized power of the Russian state, the same pattern was continued. The empire sought access to the sea and found its road blocked in the nineteenth century by British sea power which had expanded across the Eurasian littoral. The British imperial position rested on a maritime encirclement of the Eurasian land mass which was maintained by the predominance of her naval power along the circumferential maritime highway. This position could be threatened by the emergence of a competing sea power on the littoral of the Continent, or by the penetration of Russian land power to the coast.

So convinced was Mackinder of the fact that any conflict in Europe must follow the pattern of land power-sea power opposition that he declared, in 1919, that the true character of the war which had just been concluded was not visible until after Russia had been defeated. British sea power could then be considered to be fighting against a land power which dominated the Heartland. This interpretation would seem to be a little hard on the role of France as a land power, and it is strange to ignore the three years of Russian resistance on the eastern front.

... The Mackinder study represented a picture of the constellation of forces which existed at a particular time and within a particular frame of reference. It was first elaborated in 1904 before the conclusion of the British-Russian Entente of 1907 and was strongly influenced by the previous century of conflict between Russia and Great Britain. When, in 1919, his book *Democratic Ideals and Reality* was published, the conception of an inevitable historical opposition between Russian land power and British sea power was reemphasized. The fallacy of this blanket application of a theory of history is seen when we realize that the opposition between these two states has never, in fact, been inevitable. Actually, in the three great world wars of the nineteenth and twentieth centuries, the Napoleonic Wars, the First World War, and the Second World War, the British and Russian Empires have lined up together against an intervening Rimland power as led by Napoleon, Wilhelm II, and Hitler.

In other words, there has never really been a simple land power-sea power opposition. The historical alignment has always been in terms of some members of the Rimland with Great Britain against some members of the Rimland with Russia, or Great Britain and Russia together against a dominating Rimland power. The Mackinder dictum "Who controls eastern Europe rules the Heartland; who rules the Heartland rules the World Island; and who rules the World Island rules the World" is false. If there is to be a slogan for the power politics of the Old World, it must be "Who controls the Rimland rules Eurasia; who rules Eurasia controls the destinies of the world."

POPULATION AND POWER IN THE POST-WAR WORLD

By Dudley Kirk

From "Population Changes and the Post-War World," by Dudley Kirk, in *The American Sociological Review*, February 1944; reproduced by permission. Mr. Kirk is research associate in the Office of Population Research at Princeton University.

Great changes have occurred and are occurring in the size and distribution of the world's population. These changes are among the more fundamental and predictable determinants of the future. In their larger aspects population trends have shown a great deal of stability ... and it seems reasonable to suppose that they will continue to do so. ...

A generation ago, behind every discussion of population problems there loomed the gloomy figure of Malthus. The writings of demography were filled with the dangers of overpopulation. These dangers have not disappeared; in most of the world there is still a heavy pressure of population on developed resources, and the Malthusian controls of famine, disease, and war are still the major checks to population growth. But a different interpretation of population phenomena has become more popular, partly owing to obvious changes in population trends, partly because of a reevaluation of the relationship between population growth and economic development in the modern world.

Population Trends as a Function of "Progress." The dismal outlook of never-ending pressure of population on the food supply was dispelled in Western civilization by the achievements of the agricultural and industrial revolutions, and to a lesser extent by the exploitation of new lands and of old peoples. These have combined to provide the economic basis for both rising levels of living and extraordinarily rapid population growth. In the past three centuries the population of European race has increased sevenfold: from 100 millions in 1650 to 700 millions at the present time. In the same period it has increased from less than a fifth of the world's total to more than a third. But accompanying the achievement of higher levels of living, both as cause and consequence, has been the spread of the empirical outlook on life conducive to the restriction of family size and the termination of population growth. As is well known, the indefinite continuation of inter-war trends would ultimately lead to the depopulation of Western Europe and of Europe overseas.

Rapid population growth and the subsequent slowing of growth arising from control of family size are intrinsic elements in the nexus of cultural traits that are valued as "progress." Their development has not been haphazard. Within Europe, for instance, there has been a clear pattern of cultural diffusion from the initial locus of development in Northwestern and Central Europe. Modern education, improved health conditions, and economic advance are parts of the same cultural complex, indigenous to the West and for many decades past in the process of spreading across the Continent. Progress flows along the lines of communication, is assisted by the presence of natural resources appropriate to industrialization, and is checked by natural and cultural barriers, but in general the level of material achievement of any given area in Europe is a function of its distance from the centers of diffusion in the West. Generally speaking, to go eastward in Europe is to go backward in time. The mode of life in some of the remote corners of Europe, as in the mountain districts of Yugoslavia, in Bessarabia, or in the Caucasus, has many points of resemblance to that existing in Western Europe several generations ago. Intermediate areas tend to blend toward one extreme or the other depending upon their geographical location and cultural associations. In these terms Europe is a cultural unit, all in the same stream of development, but with differences in the level of attainment growing from differences in the time at which the transition began from a peasant, self-sufficient society to an urban, industrial society.

Outside of Europe technological civilization has made progress likewise in relation to the accessibility, both cultural and geographical, to the centers of its development. It has now gained a solid foothold even among non-European peoples. . . . The spread of industry and the growth of cities have been well-nigh universal phenomena of recent times. Though in many countries these exist now only in embryonic form, it is questionable if there is a single country in the world that has not experienced some increase in industrial output and in modern urban influences during the twentieth century.

Demographic trends have shown an almost equal, and closely related, consistency in the direction of their development. Every country in the world with sufficiently good vital statistics to permit a judgment of trends displayed declining mortality rates in the inter-war period (1919-1939). With few exceptions in the world, and none in the sphere of Western civilization, the birth rates likewise were lower at the end than at the beginning of the period.

The Continuum of Demographic Development. In regard to demographic matters the different countries of the world may be considered as on a single continuum of development, a continuum having both spatial and temporal significance. It is spatial in that the degree of development is related to the cultural and geographical accessibility to the most advanced countries. It is temporal in that each country in its development is following a general historical pattern common to all. In areas relatively untouched by Western influences, the typical demographic situation today is one of high birth rates and high death rates, with a low value placed on human life both in its inception and in its destruction. Of course this was also the demographic position of Europe at an earlier period. In normal years such areas have a substantial margin of natural increase, which is periodically checked by disasters of one sort or another. As modern influences increase, the beginnings of police control, better transportation, and the application of elementary public health measures all ameliorate the effects of these disasters. Before the war, the British in India, the Dutch in Java, the Japanese in Korea, we ourselves in the Philippines and Puerto Rico, had softened the impact of calamity, and had made effective the normally high rate of natural increase. This is the typical "colonial" situation today, characteristic of most of the Far East, the Mohammedan world, and much of Africa and Latin America. It was the condition of roughly half the population of the globe before the war.

In more developed countries further application of relatively elementary principles in the saving of lives had brought about further declines in the death rates. Later, the advance of modern influences, in the form of urban ways of life and the values which have accompanied this way of life in Western civilization, has resulted in the spread of the small-family pattern, first among the upper classes and then among all the urban elements of the population. Such developments have yielded the beginnings of the decline of the birth rate, with clear indication that it would continue if unimpeded by a return to earlier values or by the inauguration of repressive population policies. In Southern and Eastern Europe, in the more progressive countries of Latin America, and in Japan, the decline of the death rate in the inter-war period was accompanied by a declining birth rate. In these countries the pattern of fertility decline was established. However, the momentum of past growth, as reflected in the youth of their populations and the inevitable lag in the decline of fertility from its present levels posit substantial future growth of population in these areas for some years to come.

The countries nearer the centers of Western civilization have progressed further in the transition than those less fully caught up in the rising tide of material values. In the core of Western civilization in Northwestern Europe demographic evolution before the war had proceeded to the point where the birth rate was overtaking the death rate in its decline. The list of countries facing the likelihood of future population decline is a roster of the nations that have led the world in material progress.

The continuum of population development may be divided into three significant segments, each with its peculiar problems in the post-war world. About half the population of the world is in the first stage, the stage of great potential growth. Western influences have made possible a reduction in the death rate without compensating declines in the birth rate. In a relatively stable postwar world these areas will experience tremendous population growth, comparable in amount though probably not in rate, to that experienced by the Western world at an earlier period of its history. A second, and transitional, stage has been achieved by those nations now caught up in the tide of industrialization and urbanization, but formerly, at least, on the peripheries of Western civilization. In these countries birth and death rates have both been declining, but the birth rates are still sufficiently high to support population growth for some time to come. Finally, there are those countries that face the prospect of depopulation if the net fertility declines of the inter-war period are continued.

... Perhaps what is most significant to us now, with the problems of planning a peace a public issue, is the political implications of the differing demographic trends, first, within Europe, and second, in the relationships between the Western peoples and the rest of the world.

Power Implications of Population Trends: Within Europe. ... Within Europe, economic development and population change have gone hand in hand. Both have undoubtedly been elements in the changing distribution of political power.

The predominant position of France on the Continent of Europe two or three centuries ago was partly a function of the fact that she was the wealthiest and in many respects the most advanced country in Europe. It is also undoubtedly associated with the fact that she was probably at the same time the most populous nation of the Continent, not even excluding Russia, which now has four times her population. The economic and political position of France in relation to the remainder of Europe has changed enormously since 1800, and this change is probably not entirely unrelated to the fact that she now stands fifth rather than first among European nations in regard to population size.

The rise of Germany likewise has demographic foundations. In the Napoleonic period, Germans lived in a Europe dominated not only politically, but also numerically by the French. As the result of the economic development of Germany and the population increase made possible by this development, since the middle of the last century Germans have become much the most numerous of the European peoples aside from the Russians. As the largest single group, occupying a central position in Europe, it is natural that the Germans should have sought to bring the balance of political power into line with their growing numerical and industrial importance. That this could have been achieved more effectively through peaceful rather than through warlike means is now unfortunately beside the point.

By virtue of its more rapid natural increase and the Nazi annexation of German-speaking areas, Germany in 1939 had twice the population of France and a considerably larger population than that of Britain. However, from the demographic point of view, Germany had already passed the crest of the wave. The last war had serious consequences. But these were overshadowed by the effects of fertility declines. The population of the old Reich in 1939 was perhaps 6 million less because of World War I. It was 13 million less as the result of the decline of the birth rate since 1910. Prior to Hitler's accession to power the net reproduction rate had fallen to a lower level than that of

France, the classic country of depopulation. The Nazi population policies, though moderately successful in their objective of increasing the number of births, nevertheless fell very far short of reestablishing 1910 fertility. The eastward wave of population increase has come and gone in Germany, and she is on the receding side of the tide in company with her Western neighbors. Demographically, Germany is in substantially the same position as England, France, and Scandinavia, all of which face the prospect of stationary or declining populations. War may speed the approach of population decline; post-war population policies may retard it. But the underlying demographic situation will probably not be altered. Aside from an unforeseen volume of immigration the era of rapid population growth in these countries is past.

The populations of Eastern Europe grew much faster than those of Western European countries in the inter-war period despite political disorder and the more severe effects of World War I in the East. At an earlier period the large population growth of this region was made possible by the fact that large areas were then in the process of initial agricultural settlement, or, put in other terms, in transition from a pastoral to a settled farm economy. In Russia there was new settlement not unlike that of our own frontier. This agricultural settlement represented a superior form of land utilization, and made possible the support of a far denser population than had formerly existed. More recently the wave of material progress represented by industrialization and an urban way of life has reached Eastern Europe from its centers of origin in the West. In Russia the contrast of the old and the new resulted in such severe stress on the old social order that it was swept away and the new technical civilization was ushered in with an impetus previously unexampled in history. These developments have made possible rapid population increase such as existed in Western Europe at an earlier period. Despite war and revolution, which apparently cost Russia a total population deficit of 26 millions, including both deaths and loss of births, since 1900 the population of the territory of the Soviet Union has grown more rapidly than that of Western Europe. Its present age structure and fertility levels suggest that the present war will not have a serious retarding influence on her future rapid growth. The youth of the Russian population is suggested by the fact that the median age is under 23 years, as contrasted with 32 in Northwestern and Central Europe now and with a median age of 40 in that region by 1970 on a projection of inter-war vital trends. The reported birth rate in the U.S.S.R. for 1938 was 38.3 per thousand population or over twice that of the United States in the same year.

Ignoring the war and assuming fertility declines comparable to those experienced in Western Europe at the same level of fertility, the population of the Soviet Union in 1970 would exceed 250 millions. The war will reduce the growth potential, but barring a demographic catastrophe greatly exceeding that of World War I and the Russian Revolution, the U.S.S.R. gives every promise of growing more rapidly than the remainder of Europe. In 1939 the U.S.S.R. had twice the 80 millions living in the area of Greater Germany. In 1970 it will probably have three times as large a population, and there will probably be no Greater Germany. What these differences can mean in terms of military potential may be indicated from the trends of manpower. On the assumptions of growth suggested, the U.S.S.R. by 1970 would have more men of prime military age, 20-34, than its six closest rivals in Europe combined. The increase in the number of men of this military age by 1970 would alone be as large as the total German military manpower of that age today, or that to be expected from any reasonable demographic trends to 1970.

As long as the Russians were poor, illiterate, and thinly scattered over an enormous area, their numbers were not very effective against the industrialized nations of the West except in terms of resistance through sheer inertia of size. Even in the present war, distance and weight of numbers have been an important element in the Russian successes. But the Soviet Union is moving into a position in which it will be able to make its people as effective economically, person for person, as those of Western Europe in general and Germany in particular. Since the Russian manpower of a generation hence will almost certainly be greater proportionately than it is today, a future German challenge to Russia and the world along the lines of 1914 and 1939 seems improbable. Demographic trends alone suggest that this conflict is Germany's last chance for European and world domination.

To say that Russia will be powerful is, of course, not equivalent to saying that she will be a threat. Large population growth in Russia does not involve the serious difficulties that it would, for instance, in Germany. In the Soviet Union rapid growth for some time to come is probably necessary for the maximum development of large available resources in relation to existing population. It should present no greater problem than it did in the United States after the Civil War. Russia has ample resources, ample territory, and a great need for labor to develop unexploited areas in Asia and in the Arctic. The problem is not one of resources or of territory. It is rather that of converting a population only two or three generations from serfdom into a literate, physically healthy, technically competent, urban people. At least that is the job as seen by the Russians themselves according to many reports, and it is a job certainly appropriate to the predominant values of our own world.

Power Implications of Population Trends: Europe and Asia. A less certain, but ultimately equally significant development is the eastward movement of power, not only in Europe, but in the world. As long as Western European civilization was able to maintain an effective monopoly on the industrial techniques that give power in the modern world, numbers were relatively unimportant in the relations between Western countries and the densely populated Orient. Numbers are an element of power in any social group. But to be effective they must be implemented with resources and skills, and cemented by social cohesion and unity of purpose. Clearly, numbers are of little importance when two civilizations of very different values meet. The domination of India by a handful of Englishmen is an obvious case in point. The British had at their command a great technical superiority of weapons and a social organization directed at the achievement of material ends. The British and the Indians simply were not interested in the same things: the goals and values of their respective societies were almost diametrically opposed. To most Indians the assumption of political control by the British was a matter of complete indifference.

This is no longer the case. Whether through the success of our own efforts at indoctrination, or through frank admiration for our achievements, oriental and other colored peoples are absorbing important elements of our civilization. Thus the Japanese have clearly demonstrated, first, that a non-European people can establish an astonishingly strong industrial civilization, almost entirely on its own initiative, and, further, that a poor but industrious folk can accomplish this with a poverty of natural resources that would seem hopeless by Western standards. But in terms of a reasonable evaluation of its economic and political potential Japan seems no more formidable in relation to Asia as a whole than would England, shorn of its empire, in relation to a united Europe. And China, at least, seems on the way to achieving a unity that Europe was never able to accomplish.

It is commonly assumed that overpopulation in China, as indicated by the prevailing poverty of the people, will prove a great barrier to the economic progress of the country and hence to its rise as a world power. However, it needs to be pointed out that China is not so hopelessly overpopulated as is commonly supposed and that this condition does not represent an insuperable obstacle to industrialization. It is perhaps surprising to note that the over-all density of population in China is only half that of Europe west of Russia though her total population is roughly comparable in size. Even in China proper, population density is much less than in Western Europe. Overpopulation in China, as elsewhere, is indicated by a high ratio of population to developed resources. It has reality only in relation to a given stage of technological development. In other areas technical changes have obviously brought about enormous changes in the carrying capacity of the land. Four hundred years ago the present area of continental United States supported only 200 or 300 thousand Indians living on the margin of subsistence. With our present technological development, the same area readily supports 130 million or several hundred times as many people, and at a much higher standard of living. In existing circumstances the level of living in a country is much more closely related to its degree of technological development than it is to the absolute numbers of its population. Overpopulation is not a matter of too many people any more than it is a matter of too little economic production.

Considered in this light the problems of the densely populated countries of the Far East take on a much more hopeful aspect than has commonly been attributed to them. Given its present economic structure, it is undeniable that China is overcrowded. But it does not appear fanciful to suppose that at the level of technical efficiency now prevailing in Europe the present population of China could be maintained at something approximating Europe's levels of living. This would assume a potential resource base somewhat comparable to that of Europe west of Russia in an area more than twice as large.

It is obvious that the Chinese population does not now have either the capital or the trained personnel to achieve the present per capita production of Europe in the near future. However, there are compelling precedents in recent history demonstrating that neither of these is an insuperable obstacle. In Russia a backward and illiterate peasantry is being converted almost in a single generation into a literate, forward-looking proletariat rapidly acquiring the skills necessary for efficient industrial production. And on the other side of China is the convincing example of Japan, which has constructed an industrial economy with a paucity of natural resources that would be appalling to any Western people.

In China herself something of the

possibilities both for industrialization and for higher per capita output in agriculture have been demonstrated in these war years. In this period China has built up an army of some 10 million men, chiefly taken from the peasantry and consequently withdrawn from agricultural production. At the same time agricultural production in western China has apparently remained at least as high as before the war, partly because the men withdrawn from agriculture were inefficiently used in agriculture anyway, and partly because even in the space of five years some progress has been made, especially in the use of better seed. These factors combined are sufficient to free 10 million men as industrial workers in this area after the war. Furthermore, the army was provided with small arms, i.e. rifles and light machine guns, and the appropriate ammunition, almost entirely from domestic production. When it is considered that most of China's prewar industries were located in the coastal cities now occupied by the Japanese, such an accomplishment must be considered a remarkable one. The capital for this achievement was naturally obtained at great sacrifice. But the means of industrialization can be wrung from a people living as close to the margin of subsistence as the Chinese if there is a central government with the necessary will and unity. . . .

Whether Asia will follow the course set by Western Europe in the decline of the birth rate is obviously a crucial question. Where birth control runs counter to the prevailing values, as in India, its diffusion may be slow. However, the influences operating against the acceptance of birth control probably also operate against economic development and against further declines in the death rates. The only Asiatic country to have undergone sufficient industrialization and urbanization to offer a test case is Japan. In that country birth control had apparently established itself before the war. In Japanese cities, where birth control would most likely first achieve general use, the prewar fertility seems to have been only about five-eighths that in the rural areas. In the country as a whole the age distribution and vital trends in the inter-war period were similar to those of England between 1880 and 1900, and indicate a stage of demographic evolution comparable to that of England in that period. The Japanese case is not conclusive, but it is illuminating; it suggests that the barriers between the Western and Eastern worlds are not too great to prevent the diffusion of the birth control pattern.

The decline of the birth rate in Asia is eminently desirable as long as the continent faces elementary difficulties in feeding its huge population. Emigration is no real solution for the future. There are no longer empty countries either willing or able to welcome the surplus populations on a scale sufficient to afford relief. The economic problems are serious. And yet it seems probable that given a modicum of political stability, the oriental countries will be enabled to experience both a rising level of living and rapid population increase for a time. It is true that they have less of a margin above subsistence than the Western countries had at a comparable stage of economic development. But it is also true that they have the experience of the West to draw upon in the solution of their difficulties.

Asia as a whole appears to be on the verge of a great awakening. This awakening may take many generations and undoubtedly will not occur evenly throughout the continent. But the tempo of change has been so increased that it seems possible that this awakening will occur with tremendous explosive force, and much sooner than is commonly supposed. If the modernization of Asia follows the course that it took in Europe it will be accompanied by large population increase. Increase of population, and the very mass of the Asiatic population itself, could be ignored in the past as unimportant in the balance of world power. But with the prospect that the Asiatic masses will ultimately learn to forge the tools that will give them power, the differential population trends may become of very great importance. Population increase has been part and parcel of the spread of European populations over much of the globe. In the past European populations have been growing very rapidly in a relatively slowly growing world. The present outlook is for relatively stationary or declining populations among Western European peoples in a rapidly growing world. Western European peoples will almost certainly become a smaller part of the total population of the world. To the extent that numbers are a factor in the distribution of economic and political power, there will be some redistribution of power from old to new centers. . . .

THE EMERGING PATTERN OF WORLD POLITICS

By William T. R. Fox

From chap. 2 of The Super Powers: The United States, Britain, and The Soviet Union—Their Responsibility for Peace, by W. T. R. Fox. Copyright 1944 by Harcourt, Brace & Co., New York; reproduced by permission. Dr. Fox is research associate in the Institute of International Studies at Yale University which sponsored publication of the book quoted.

Until the twentieth century the Great Powers were all European powers. Today, none of the three greatest powers is strictly European; nor are any of the three main centers of power located in continental Western Europe. . . . Today Europe is an arena whose internal struggles periodically involve the whole civilized world in organized bloodshed, and whose struggles end only with the intervention of powers outside the Continent. The transition from the old, world-dominating Europe to the new "problem-Europe" is a central fact in the international politics of our time. . . .

The first of the existing world powers was Britain. Her domination of the whole maritime world in the nineteenth century gave her a unique position in relation to the other European powers. Britain's head start in the Industrial Revolution would have guaranteed her a position of primacy in any case. But in an era of water transportation, when overland movement of goods and men was costly and slow, and when the discovery of the New World and the rise of north European trading centers had reoriented Europe toward the Atlantic Ocean, her earlier marginal position became central. She had "the finest site on the Main Street of the world." As an island near the European continent, she could with her mighty navy effectively control the narrow seas through which the men and goods of other powers must pass. Whether by design or by good fortune, acquisition of defensible bases at Gibraltar, Malta, Suez, Aden, Singapore, Cape Town, and the Falkland Islands—defensible because they could be supplied most efficiently by the very sea routes whose security their possession ensured—reinforced and perfected the British position. From a communications point of view that country thus controlled both the "main four-corners" of Europe and all its seaward approaches.

In the nineteenth century, however, forces were at work which were to destroy in large part Britain's unique advantages. Her industrial techniques were adopted first across the Atlantic in the United States and then with surprising rapidity in the island empire of Japan.

The United States emerged from its Civil War a nation whose place among the Great Powers could not long be denied. In terms of its capacity to make war it demonstrated its coming of age by putting into the field in the 1860's armies which were tremendous in size and in striking power. The United States was not for a generation after the Civil War an important naval power, but this was at least partly through choice. Its incomparably bountiful West was a far richer prize than any European power could win by military or naval conquest. That the young giant of the Western Hemisphere was strong enough to repel any European intruder, the ever-scheming Napoleon III came to understand after his fiasco in Mexico, when he tried without success to keep the Archduke Maximilian upon the Mexican throne.

Japan, too, experienced large-scale industrialization in the nineteenth century. Although her country lacked rich mineral resources, her statesmen were determined by a total mobilization of her human and mineral resources to make up for this deficiency. Having learned the ways of the Occident, she promptly used her new knowledge to protect herself against the powers of Europe and to assure primacy in the Orient.

With the opening of the twentieth century, therefore, two non-European powers claimed admission to the inner circle of the Great Powers. By Britain's withdrawal from the Caribbean in the 1890's, symbolized by her reluctant acquiescence in the statement of Secretary of State Olney that "Today the United States is practically sovereign on this continent, and its fiat is law upon the subjects to which it confines its interposition," and by her alliance with Japan in 1902, she acknowledged that the *Pax Britannica* no longer ran to the ends of the earth. Britain was still the only true world power. She had admitted the regional dominance of the United States and Japan; but without a globe-encircling series of bases these powers were still only regional powers, no matter how big their fleets of capital ships. "Such regional dominance might very well be the most effective means of insuring certain countries—the United States, for example—against blockade or invasion. But . . . no local command of the sea could endow the United States or any other country . . . with a leverage on world politics even approaching that which British statesmen had long derived from their naval ascendancy in Europe's narrow seas." With the formal acceptance of the transoceanic regional powers into the inner circle of the Great Powers, the first stage in the outward migration of power from Europe was reached.

These moves were certainly hastened by a trend of events within Europe that was equally unfavorable to the maintenance of British maritime supremacy. Brandenburg-Prussia, in the early eighteenth century "Europe's biggest little sand-box," had grown until by 1900 Germany under Kaiser Wilhelm II had won her place as the leading land power of Europe. With the development of the railroad, the strategic position of a centrally located country with an efficient transportation network improved enormously. Bismarck's quick victories against Denmark, Austria, and France gave proof of the new efficiency of overland transport. For Britain this meant a loosening of her former vise-like grip on the main channels of intra-

European communication; there were now alternative and speedier routes.

During the mid-nineteenth century, when the Russian bear was the bête noire of the British Foreign Office, the further consolidation of North German power under Prussian leadership was watched with friendly interest. But Germany overreached herself. In the words of Sir Eyre Crowe, "Germany had won her place as one of the leading, if not, in fact, the foremost power on the European continent. But over and beyond the European Great Powers there seemed to stand the 'World Powers.' It was at once clear that Germany must become a 'World Power.'"

This Great Britain was not prepared to admit. Once the German determination to become a world power, by building up a strong fleet, became clear, Britain was necessarily so heavily preoccupied with Europe that her days of unchallenged leadership elsewhere were over. To maintain her physical security at home she was forced to make concessions in America and Asia and to form alliances on the continent of Europe. Her strength after 1900 was still sufficient to make her a valued partner in the alliance system. By forming with France and Russia the Triple Entente the prospects of preserving an equilibrium against the Triple Alliance of the three Central Powers in European politics were somewhat improved, but Britain's days of splendid isolation were over. She was still a power, but only one power in a family of eight. Of these, five were European; two were non-European; and one, Britain, controlled the sea routes between Europe and the outer world.

The First World War saw the complete disintegration of the Austro-Hungarian Empire so that the number of potential candidates for Great Power status was permanently reduced by one. Another, Russia, was torn by internal revolution, and, strong or weak, would have been blackballed by the "respectable" powers if her Bolshevik rulers had sought a place for her in the inner circle. A third, Germany, was temporarily so completely disarmed that some of her smaller neighbors, notably Poland, sometimes played a "Great Power" role in their relations with her. A fourth, Italy, had at Caporetto and elsewhere made a very poor showing for a power that claimed to be a Great Power. However, since Italy was on the side of the victors, for the moment no voice was raised to exclude her from the ranks of the powers, with the return of peace there were therefore only four—or, with Italy, five—functioning Great Powers.

It was the application of the United States' military strength that broke the stalemate in the European War of 1914-1918. The United States could no longer, therefore, be classified merely as a regional Great Power. The second stage in the outward migration of power had now been reached, for a non-European power inclined this balance in Europe as it chose.

The United States had now become in every sense of the word a world power. Her dominant role in the Washington Conference of 1922 showed that she was quite as influential in the Pacific as in Europe. There were, therefore, two World Powers after 1919, the United States and Great Britain. The third Great Power, France, was essentially a European power; and the fourth, Japan, was exclusively an Asiatic power. The first three dominated the Peace Conference of Paris which established the new order in Europe, while the first, second, and fourth dominated the Washington Conference of 1922 which set the pattern of power politics in the Pacific throughout the inter-war period.

The twenty-year "long armistice" saw the revival of German power and the reentry of Russia into the European alliance system. With Italy, which was shortly to reveal its true weakness, there were on the eve of the Second World War seven Great Powers. . . . The conclusion of the war will see only three of the original seven still functioning as states of the first rank. The final stage in the outward migration of power from Western Europe will then be reached. No Great Power will remain in non-Russian continental Europe.

The three survivors—Great Britain, the Soviet Union, and the United States—are all world rather than European powers. The demonstrated military efficiency of the Soviet Union in Europe leaves no doubt that it could give a good account of itself in the Far Eastern conflict zone. It, like Britain and the United States, must be classified as a world power.

The states of continental Western Europe will not, however, be mere pawns in a game of international politics played by outsiders. The rapidity with which De Gaullist France has arisen from the ruins of the Third Republic is a reminder that Europe's political power will be by no means negligible. Complete military defeat is no guarantee against the ultimate reconstruction of the armed force of a defeated state, as the world learned from Germany's spectacular military rebirth in the 1930's. As a member of the winning team, the French National Committee is pressing France's claim for reentry into the circle of Great Powers. Germany, too, will some day reassert its claim to Great Power status. Perhaps with less success, so may Italy.

In Asia, there are two candidates for recognition as first-rank powers. China's adherence to the Moscow Declaration and Chiang Kai-shek's participation in a conference at Cairo with Roosevelt and Churchill have been interpreted by many as signifying that the Big Three has already become a Big Four. Since the Japanese will be disinclined to regard their country as a "third-rate power" no matter how complete their defeat in the present war, Japan also will be a candidate.

How many of the five states here mentioned will join the United States, Britain, and the Soviet Union as powers of the first rank after there has been opportunity for recovery from the wounds left by the Second World War? Is a state ever "entitled" to be included in the inner circle? Arguments of a military and of a moral character are frequently intertwined; but one must at the outset distinguish between the "right" to sit in the inner councils of the decision-makers and the "strength" to assume great responsibilities in the post-war world. . . .

After the final Axis defeat, reconstructed France and victorious China will, in their respective spheres of interest, demand a full share in development of the post-war political order. But France is essentially a European and Mediterranean power; even with Indo-China restored she would not really be a Great Power in the Far East. China is exclusively an Asiatic power; no one would expect her to assume responsibilities for the enforcement of security in Europe. Both may be rated as "great" powers in the general international organization which may be set up after the war, but in contrast with the Big Three, they are only regional powers.

It is not merely the geographically restricted interests of France and China which distinguish them from the Big Three. The artificial character of French hegemony on the continent of

Europe in the 1920's was demonstrated by its rapid disintegration during the 1930's. Without support from some or all of the Big Three, her long quest for *sécurité* must remain unsatisfied. Only as a regional partner of the powers with global interests and global resources could she achieve this goal. She will be a valued partner because her European territory could constitute a gigantic bridgehead for military operations against a renewed German aggression, and because her North African territory will in an air age be essential to the maintenance of communications between the eastern and western Mediterranean. Her trump card in bidding for support from Great Britain or Russia is the alternative possibility of collaborating very closely with the other. Her chief reliance in demanding help from the Big Three acting in concert will be their interest in preventing her collapse before or her collaboration with a resurgent Germany. France will soon be strong again, but her strength will not be comparable to that of Soviet Russia and the United States, and she lacks the far-flung bases of Britain.

China's position will on the other hand be more favorable than before the war with respect to her near neighbors. With more than 400,000,000 people in a continental area greater than that of the United States, she possesses two of the necessary qualifications. China, however, is not a power which can undertake great international responsibilities beyond her own borders. She has no armed power available for export. Instead, internal political issues are being decided by external intervention. Chiang Kai-shek's primacy at home depends in large measure on his capacity to attract foreign support. With political and social integration achieved, China will become a most important regional power, but her military might is clearly not of the same order as that of Russia, Britain, or America.

The time and circumstances under which Germany or Japan might be permitted to reenter the circle of Great Powers depend on the extent to which the present war coalition coheres in the post-war world; but Germany and Japan too will be at most regional powers, and they may not be powers at all. As for Italy, she should never have been rated as more than the least of the Great Powers. Her performance in two world wars does not suggest an active role for Italy in the high politics of the post-war world.

There will be no fewer than three and no more than seven Great Powers. Within this group, there will be "world powers" and "regional powers." These world powers we shall call "super-powers," in order to distinguish them from the other powers which may enjoy the formal and ceremonial prestige of Great Power status but whose interests and influence are great in only a single theater of power conflict. With bases both in the East and in the West and with communications assured between East and West, the bulk of the super-powers' armed force is highly mobile. It can, as in the present emergency, be thrown into whichever of the major theaters of war grand strategy dictates.

The three aggregations of power which qualify for status as super-powers on the basis of their world-wide influence would also qualify as super-powers on the basis of military potential greater than that of the other four powers. "Great power plus great mobility of power" describes the super-power. Acting in coalition, the Big Three can bring preponderant power to bear wherever desired. In conflict, they would confront each other on many and widely scattered fronts.

The distribution of armed power in the new world of the super-powers will vary in another significant respect from that of the past. The major centers of industrial power will be widely separated from each other and peripheral with respect to both the European and the East Asian conflict zones. This contrasts with the situation prevailing when a majority of the powers of first rank were located within continental Europe. Especially after the development of the European railway network between 1850 and 1870, high-speed mobilization of land armies made Blitzkrieg against an adjoining Great Power practicable. . . .

The statesmen of the super-powers must remember, however, that military power, like hydroelectric power, can be transmitted to distant points only with much diminished efficiency. The grossly inadequate force with which General MacArthur had to conduct war in the Southwest Pacific in 1942 and 1943 is evidence in point. The gigantic convoys which had to be organized to support the Anglo-American campaign in the Mediterranean and the comparatively small number of front-line divisions which this tremendous effort supported are further proof. Completely adequate communications and supply lines require a substantial diversion of men and matériel from the fighting front. The tanker which carries oil, itself burns oil. The troopship has a permanent crew which will never be part of an invading land force. The steel in the freighter's hull and superstructure will never be available for tanks and guns. The longer the supply line the smaller the proportion of the total military effort which can be applied in actual combat. It is clear, therefore, that, since the centers of greatest power are more widely separated than heretofore, the new military situation makes it enormously difficult for one super-power to defeat another. Wars between the powers of first rank will necessarily be protracted, far-flung, and indecisive. All ought therefore to be anxious to avoid such a conflict.

Under the old system the proximity of the powers to each other heightened the tension under which the European state system operated. Demands of one Great Power upon another or upon some small power could not be accepted or rejected by reference to some generally accepted standard called "justice." Since relatively small variations in military power could spell victory or defeat in a war whose imminence it was difficult to judge, concessions were rarely made simply because they were just. In the new situation, on the other hand, relatively small variations in military power will not jeopardize the military security of any of the super-powers. The possibility of settling disputes by compromise or by reference to the merits of the dispute ought correspondingly to be enlarged.

The prospects for a stable and just peace would, therefore, on the basis of this very brief sketch of the world of the super-powers seem to be somewhat improved. . . .

Part II
The European Realm of the Great Powers

Chapter 5

The European Realm

Down to the closing years of the nineteenth century Europe was the world's political dynamo. That small continent was the center from which ideas and influence radiated to the farthest corners of the globe. Directly or indirectly most of the world paid tribute to Europe. All the Great Powers were European states. One of these—Great Britain—wielded a power and a stabilizing influence so immense as to earn the title *Pax Britannica*. No other region approached Europe in wealth, productivity, and power. Europe was the dominant force in the nineteenth century society of nations.

The geographical base of the European Realm was somewhat larger than the so-called continent of Europe which is but a huge irregular peninsula reaching westward from Asia. The European Realm included, of course, the off-shore islands of Great Britain; also the coastal margin of North Africa, the Near East, part of the Middle East, and the vast interior plain that stretches eastward beyond the Ural Mountains. The European Realm embraced, in short, most of the lands and narrow seas lying north and northwest of the great desert-mountain barrier which reaches from the western bulge of Africa almost to the northeast coast of Siberia.

Within this European Realm is the birthplace of western civilization. The history of western civilization is the record of the development and spread of culture from its earliest seats in the eastern Mediterranean to the more remote lands of northwestern Europe and thence to lands beyond the seas.

The peoples of Europe set the political pattern of our world. From them sprang the multi-state system with its political fragmentation of the world and repudiation of any political loyalty higher than that to the national state. From them came the Industrial Revolution, the early impetus to scientific and technical progress, the growth and spread of large-scale inter-regional commerce, modern concepts of imperialism, the accelerating development of military power, and a long series of wars culminating in the global struggles of our time.

The fourth quarter of the nineteenth century witnessed the beginnings of political developments which were eventually to end Europe's political primacy among the continents. One of these developments was the rapid rise of United States power following the great Civil War in America. Another was the hot-house industrialization and militarization of Japan which got under way about the same time. A third was the political unification of the Germanic peoples, Germany's bid for European hegemony, and the resulting wars which have devastated Europe in our time. Still a fourth fundamental development, accelerated by the struggles for power in Europe and in the Far East, has been Russia's phenomenal rise to a position of political primacy in Eurasia, accompanied by large-scale migrations of population and industries to the Urals and beyond.

These and other developments have shaken Europe to its foundations and profoundly altered the relations of the European peoples with the rest of the world. Europe no longer enjoys a virtual monopoly of political power and world leadership. Today the three greatest powers are all peripheral to that continent. The United States lies completely outside the European Realm. Great Britain, always peripheral in a sense because of its off-shore insular position, is coming to depend increasingly upon the human and material resources of its commonwealth partners overseas. The Soviet Union is increasingly a Eurasian, rather than a strictly European, power as the result of its deliberate and forced development of new industrial centers beyond the Urals.

Western and Central Europe has lost, probably irrevocably, its historic dominance and world leadership. But there is wide disagreement as to the role which the European peoples can or will play in the world of tomorrow.

There is the view, on the one hand, that Europe has become "an arena whose internal struggles periodically involve the whole civilized world in organized bloodshed, and whose struggles end only with the intervention of powers outside the continent." To the advocates of this view, "the transition of the old, world-dominating Europe to the new, 'problem-Europe' is a central fact in the international politics of our time." (*The Super Powers,* by W. T. R. Fox. Copyright 1944 by Harcourt, Brace & Co., New York.)

Against this view many voices have been raised in protest. Europe, it is argued, still has nearly 400 million people, representing the greatest accumulation of skills and talents on the globe and a long tradition of leadership, the world's most stimulating climates, vast mineral wealth, huge tracts of rich farmland and forest. "Regardless of what people in other global spheres may think, the Europeans will not consider themselves as mere pawns in the hands of world powers. They do not want to see their continent become the playground of non-European power politics." ("The Future of Europe," by Friedrich Baerwald, in *Thought,* Fordham University Quarterly, September 1944.)

To test these conflicting views, it will be necessary to study the situation and prospects, the aims and the resources, of the principal European nations one by one. But it will facilitate such a study to begin with an over-all survey of the Continent as a whole.

THE DOMINANCE OF EUROPE: A PRE-WAR VIEW

By Samuel Van Valkenburg and Ellsworth Huntington

From chap. 1 of *Europe,* by S. Van Valkenburg and E. Huntington. Copyright 1935 by Samuel Van Valkenburg and Ellsworth Huntington. John Wiley & Sons, New York; reproduced by permission. The authors are well known geographers. Dr. Van Valkenburg is a recognized authority on political geography. Dr. Huntington's specialty is the influence of climate upon civilization.

Civilization today is European. The people of the United States, Canada, and Australia all rightly claim to be European in blood and culture. Those of Latin America make the same claim, although with less truth. Japan, China, India, and even Africa are trying to Europeanize themselves as fast as possible, or at least to follow the modified European culture of America. This universal tendency to admire and imitate Europe provides strong evidence that Europe is still supreme among the continents. . . .

Location. One of the most widely recognized reasons for the dominance of Europe is its location. Just as every human being, by reason of his egoistic nature, is disposed to think of himself as the center of the sphere in which he moves, so every country and continent tends to see itself as the center, with the rest of the world grouped around it. Old maps of the time of Ptolemy are centered around Egypt; Rome in its ancient glory looked upon itself as the heart of the universe. For outstanding countries like these, this view was essentially sound, because at the time in question they were really dominant. This dominance was partly a matter of favorable location in respect to other active people and to the geographic conditions which at that time were most conducive to the progress of civilization. Thus Egypt was located near the line of contact between the parts of Africa and Asia where progress was then most rapid. At a later date Rome was for centuries the geographical center of the Mediterranean world around which civilization had then spread. In the same way, during the nineteenth century, Europe, surrounded by its political and economic vassals, looked upon itself as the center of the world. This is the natural result of historical development, but from the earliest times this development has been influenced by Europe's peculiar location. The importance of this location depends partly on the accessibility of the continent to other continents and to ficiently mild to melt the glaciers which had covered northern Europe, an almost empty continent was ready for human occupation. Asia was the chief source of immigrants, although the anthropological relics discovered in Europe also display marked African traces. In later times, when the Continent was

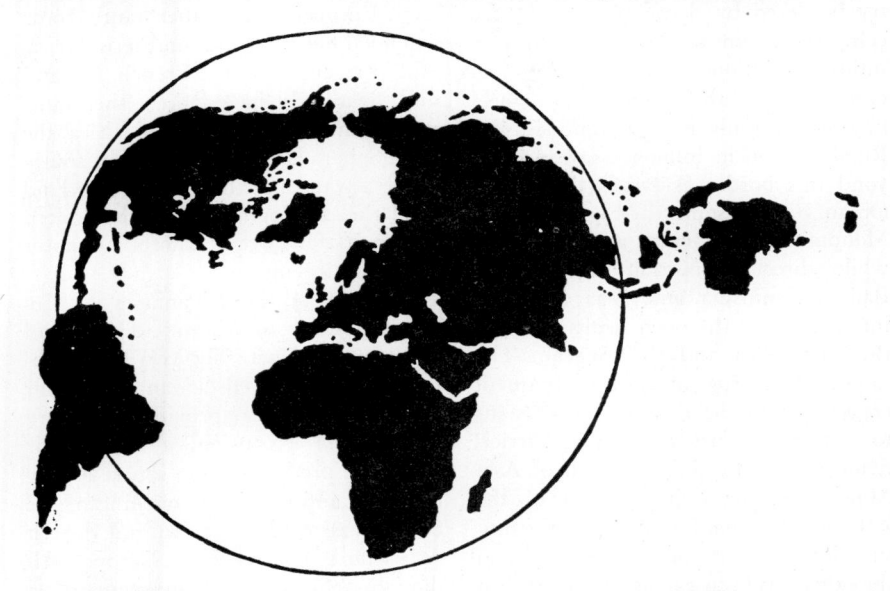

FIG. 8. Europe's Central Location. Western Europe lies at the center of the so-called land-hemisphere, the hemisphere so drawn as to include the greatest possible land area. This land hemisphere, it should be noted, contains all of the Great Powers.

From C. B. Fawcett, *A Political Geography of the British Empire.*
Ginn & Co., London and Boston; reproduced by permission of University of London Press.

the oceans. Even more important is the combined climatic effect of the Continent's position in respect to latitude, ocean currents, winds, and storms. . . .

Location in Respect to Asia and Africa. Leaving the climate for later study, let us look at Europe's location. The early population of Europe came mainly from Asia and Africa, and the proximity of these continents has always been highly important. After the Ice Age, when the climate became suf- well populated, and when the main lines of present race divisions had been established, the connection with Asia and Africa saved Europe from the disadvantages of isolation which hampered the Americas, and especially Australia. New migrations brought vigorous, fresh inhabitants among whom the weaklings had perished. Even more important, perhaps, is the fact that the cultural and intellectual contributions of these two great continents spread into Europe, thus stimulating its civilization.

The association with Asia and Africa, however, is not so close as to prevent the individual development of Europe. The long zone where Europe joins Asia north of the Caspian Sea is partly a desert, and partly a mountainous country bordered by dense forests and the cold Arctic tundra. Hence constant or intimate relations were long precluded except under the impetus of world migrations. Only in later centuries did Russia extend its influence eastward beyond this border as far as the Pacific Ocean. Farther south the high Caucasus Mountains offer only a few passes, while direct connection between the Balkan Peninsula and Asia Minor is interrupted by the open straits between the Black Sea and the Aegean. The famous Bosporus, in spite of frequent crossing from the time of the Persians to that of the Turks, remains a barrier, made greater by the dry basin of Asia Minor and the difficult relief of the Balkan peninsula. Nevertheless, the mutual influence of each continent upon the other has been extensive; the eastern Roman Empire was partly European, and partly Asiatic; the Greeks populated the coast of Asia Minor until they were forced out a few years ago; the Turks still occupy the European shores of the Bosporus—relics of an empire which might have made Europe subservient to Asia if communication had been easier. Nevertheless, Europe is so separated from Asia that cultural influences have spread more easily than people. "Ideas," as Miss Ellen C. Semple has well said, "are light baggage."

A similar situation prevails even more strongly in respect to Africa. The Straits at Gibraltar and south of Sicily have never been great impediments to mutual influence. Sicily was often under African rulers from the great days of Carthage to the period of the Saracens. The Carthaginians conquered Spain, and Hannibal marched from there to Italy by way of France and the Maritime Alps. In later days the Moors inhabited the Iberian peninsula for centuries, but the wall of the Pyrenees set a limit to their expansion. Outward from Europe, on the other hand, Rome extended her sway into northern Africa, and in recent times the French, Italians, and Spaniards have taken this same region under control. But in Africa, the great Sahara Desert prevented the southward advance of Europeans overland until the development of such modern means of transport as caterpillar motor cars and airplanes.

Even today the advantages of Europe's position in relation to Asia and Africa are distinct. The two great continents have served as an outlet for European energy by providing territory for colonial expansion, a market for European products, and a source of raw materials and food. The opening of the Suez Canal made southern and eastern Asia more accessible to Europe. Although Asia now shows signs of a nationalistic awakening with anti-European tendencies, Africa is still essentially a possession of Europe. The commercial and political expansion of western Europe was due in part to Asia and Africa. The difficulties of modern Europe arise partly because it must now share its export markets in India and China with other countries.

Location in Respect to America. Europe is also advantageously located in relation to the Americas. Western Europe faces the economic heart of the United States. The value of this situation has been enhanced by the shortening of the time of transit between Europe and America to four or five days by water and far less by air. Yet the distance is such that it has permitted independent development of the lands oversea. The breakdown of Spain's former colonial empire, the total loss of what is now the United States by Great Britain, and the establishment of only very loose political connections between Great Britain and Canada indicate that the economic and political leadership of Europe in North America has passed. But this does not lessen the value of a location in western Europe opposite the most active part of North America.

In relation to South America the location of western Europe is as good as that of any other highly advanced region. The distance to Argentina and Brazil from western Europe is not much longer than from New York. Hence the commercial interests of Europe and the United States meet there on an equal footing. Air lines from the United States southward over the West Indies, and from Europe to Brazil by way of northwest Africa, now bring both regions nearer to South America. They intensify the rivalry in the South American market, but do not give either of the northern continents any new advantage of location. In earlier times the distance of South America from the colonizing countries of Europe was a fundamental factor in the loss of colonial control.

Today Europe retains all the advantages of its world location and is ready to use them in the battle to preserve its dominance. . . .

Size and Shape. The size and shape of Europe also help to make it the dominant continent. In comparison with gigantic Asia, Europe is almost too small to be accounted a separate continent. A man from Mars would certainly call Europe merely a great peninsula jutting westward from Asia. We call it a continent only because the idea of Europe and Asia as separate land masses became fixed long ago among people who knew only of the separation caused by the Aegean and Black Seas and had no idea of the plain which joins the two north of the Caspian Sea. Nevertheless, Europe is so divided from Asia by deserts and mountains, and its character and history have been so diverse, that it is very convenient to call it a continent.

The small size of Europe presents decided advantages. In conjunction with the relatively slight breadth from north to south it gives Europe a high degree of unity. Contrast this unity with the diversity of the other continents. In Asia the different centers of civilization have been too far apart to become closely connected; they influenced one another, but remained separate. In Africa the same conditions prevailed. Deserts cut off the center of the continent from the extreme north and south. In the center, dense equatorial forests interpose an almost impassable barrier except by way of the Nile and the eastern upland. Hence North and South Africa have always been greatly separated, and the south remained isolated until Europeans reached it by sea.

In Europe, on the contrary, the small size, as well as the relief and climate, are favorable to unity through the interchange of people and ideas. Despite the great variety of its political and economic units, as well as of its races and culture, most of Europe has a certain quality which is definitely recognized as European. . . .

In shape, as well as size, Europe finds an advantage over the other continents. Nowhere else do interior seas, having open connections with the ocean, invade the land so deeply without dissecting it into disconnected islands. Not only do the arms of the sea enter the Continent, but nearly everywhere the coastline is bordered by small islands which favor the establishment of settlements and the development of shipping. All around the Continent the sea penetrates the land, creating the irregular coastline which offers so many economic advantages.

The Baltic Sea and the North Sea, for example, provide seacoast advantages for all of northern Europe. The medieval Hanseatic League, the beginning of modern commercial Europe, found its reason for existence in these seas. It included seaports near the Baltic and North Seas, and inland cities as far as Cologne. Its later growth was due largely to the possibilities of sharing directly in world trade by way of these arms of the sea.

England, separated from Europe only by the English Channel, reaps all the advantages of these waterways. It gets still other advantages because it not only faces the most productive European countries, but has an advanced position in Europe in the direction of North America. . . .

The climatic effect of the shape of Western Europe is even greater than its effect on transportation. The long northeastern trend of the coast from Portugal to northern Norway enables the westerly winds to send a constant flow of warm water along this coast. Thus the winters of western Europe are kept mild, and frequent storms are produced which give rain at all seasons. . . . These advantages are increased by the fact that the North Sea and the Baltic, like the Mediterranean and Black Seas, carry the oceanic conditions far inland.

The Mediterranean and Black Seas, which originally caused Europe to be counted as a continent, bring coastal advantages to all of southern Europe. By way of the Suez Canal they also lead to southern and eastern Asia. Without these seas Europe would have no identity for it would be a mere fraction of a combined Asia and Africa. Their warm waters were the basis of the ancient Mediterranean civilizations expressed in the rise of Phoenicia, Greece, Carthage, and Rome. Today they provide the background of the Mediterranean development of France and Italy. They do this not only by affording easy means of transportation, but still more by their effect on climate. Without the Mediterranean and Black Seas the whole region from Spain to southern Russia would be desert or steppe. As it is, the so-called Mediterranean type of climate, with its rainy winters and dry summers, penetrates far eastward, even to western Persia and the south side of the Crimean Peninsula. The densely populated and fertile Mediterranean coastal plains, with their subtropical vegetation, their thousands of coastal settlements, their great modern harbors exporting products of the hinterland, and their numerous islands with fishing settlements—all these are the result of a great downfold in the earth's crust which led the Atlantic Ocean so far inland as nearly to connect it with the Indian Ocean. To Europe the Mediterranean is a gift of the gods. This intimate penetration of the sea both north and south of Europe prevents any part of the continent except Russia from being far from oceanic influences. It tends strongly to produce unity by reducing the contrasts of climate. The nature of the climate in turn has much to do with that of the soil. Thus climate, soil, transportation, and many other conditions are all greatly influenced by the shape of the Continent and the intrusion of arms of the sea. . . .

EUROPE: TERRAIN, RESOURCES, AND REGIONS

By R. H. Whitbeck and V. C. Finch

From chap. 22 of *Economic Geography*, by R. H. Whitbeck and V. C. Finch. Revised edition. Copyright 1941 by R. H. Whitbeck and V. C. Finch; McGraw-Hill Book Co., New York; reproduced by permission. The late Dr. Whitbeck was professor of geography at the University of Wisconsin where Dr. Finch holds a similar position.

The land surface of Europe is one of great diversity. Mountains, hill lands, nearly enclosed basins, and broad plains are interwoven in a manner that produces great diversity within relatively small areas. This is much more true of Western Europe than of Eastern, and it is one of the reasons why travel in Western Europe has been so much enjoyed. Although the distribution of these features may seem the result of mere chance, a study of them shows that in geological age, type, and arrangement they have an order or system the major features of which are readily understood. Briefly these features include three systems of highlands: north, middle, and south. Between them are two types of lowlands, very unequal in extent.

In the northwest are ancient rocks, comparable with those of Laurentian Canada. The western margins of these are broadly uplifted and carved by erosion into the highlands of Norway, Scotland, and northern Ireland. Eastward in Sweden and Finland the same kind of rocks are worn down to a low level. Both high and low, these hard rocks have been heavily ice-scoured by continental glaciation, with results similar to those in Canada—disturbed drainage and innumerable lakes, thin soils, boulder-strewn surfaces, and areas of bare and polished rock.

Midway in Europe between north and south are isolated hill lands, also of ancient rocks but less extensive than those of the north. They, too, are a part of the foundation structure of the continent. These appear in southern Ireland, Wales and Cornwall, Brittany, central France, and the hill regions of central Germany, such as the Black Forest and the mountains of Bohemia. They were not overridden by the continental glaciers. A great block of land in western Spain and Portugal belongs in this same category. It is mainly a tableland, or plateau, traversed by mountain ridges.

Southern Europe is characterized by rugged mountains. These trend in a generally east-west direction and include the Pyrenees, Alps, Apennines, Carpathians, and Caucasus. They are so young in age that they appear to be still in a process of growth. Occasional displacements of the rocks by internal forces jar the region in the severe earthquakes that visit the Mediterranean border. Such have occurred in southern Italy many times, and the disastrous Turkish earthquakes of December 1939 were of the same origin. The active volcanoes of Italy may be thought of as a related phenomenon.

Between the northern highland and the central hill region is the North European Plain. This begins in southern France and extends north and east, including eastern England, Belgium, the Netherlands, Denmark and the Baltic plain of Germany and Poland. At that point it expands greatly, both north and south, and includes most of Russia from the Black Sea and the Caucasus Mountains to the Arctic Ocean. It terminates in the east against the low ridges of the Ural Mountains. This plain is one of rolling surface and has underlying rocks much like those of the central plain of North America.

Fringing the Alpine mountain chains are the lesser plains of southern Europe. They include basin lands in southern France, the Po Valley of Italy, and the Danubian plains of Hungary, Yugoslavia, Rumania, and Bulgaria.

... The central plain in particular, from England to central Russia, is the most used are the Thames, the Rhine, the Danube, and the Volga. But the Vistula, the Oder, the Elbe, the lower courses of the Seine and Scheldt, and many of the rivers of Russia besides the Volga also carry a large traffic.

In northwestern Europe the sinking of the land relative to sea level deepened

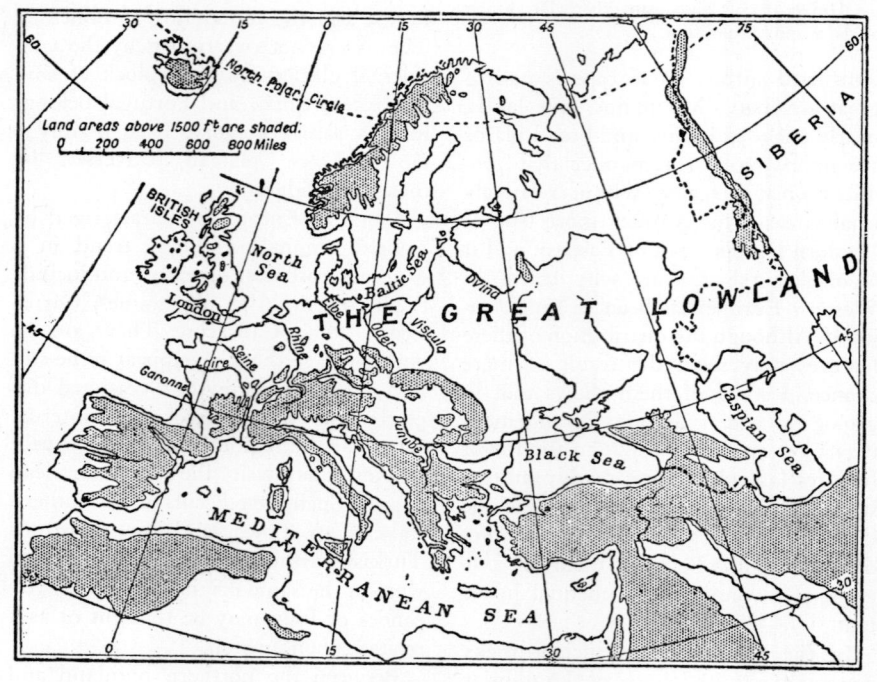

FIG. 9. Europe: Mountain and Plain.

From C. B. Fawcett, *A Political Geography of the British Empire.*
Ginn & Co., London and Boston; reproduced by permission of University of London Press.

focus of industrial and commercial activity. Tillable lands, sources of industrial power, and highly developed communications enable it to support the larger part of the total population of the continent.

The River Systems of Europe. The rivers of Europe include several of sufficient size to serve as navigable waterways, and these have played a large part, and still do, in commerce. Those the lower courses of several of the rivers and converted them into estuaries that admit ocean vessels for considerable distances. On these estuaries, most of the great ports are located—London, Liverpool, Hull, Antwerp, Hamburg, Bremen, and many others.

The Climates of Europe have played an important part in the development of its resources, civilization, and industries. The essential conditions that have shaped its climates are two: (1) position in the middle latitudes on the eastern side of one of the great oceans and (2) the nature and arrangement of the surface features. In Europe, in contrast with both North and South America, an open and deeply indented coastline is presented to the westerly winds, and mainly it is the ends rather than the bold and continuous fronts of the mountains that face the sea. Under these conditions mild and moist winds penetrate far inland along the North Sea, the Baltic, and the Mediterranean. One of the results of this is that Europe is the only continent that has no arid desert, unless a small area in southeastern Russia bordering the Caspian Sea be rated as such. . . .

Forest Resources. Northwestern Europe has large forest resources. Sweden, Finland, and northern Russia in the zone of subarctic climate have coniferous forests that are comparable with the better forest districts of eastern Canada. Eastward they grade off toward the taiga of the Ural district and Siberia. Southern Germany and the Carpathian and Balkan regions have mixed forests more like those of the Great Lakes region. England, Belgium, the Netherlands, and France had such forests originally, but they have been more largely cleared to make place for farm lands and pastures even on many of the hilly areas of types that in central Europe have been kept in forests. In the Mediterranean lands, with their scant summer rainfall, the original forests were thinner and consisted largely of oak. They have suffered much from grazing animals and lack of attention and are now generally sparse. In most of Europe the timber has been largely removed from lands capable of cultivation, but this is less true in central Russia than elsewhere. Southeastern Russia, on the other hand, was not originally forested but was prairie grassland or even short-grass steppe.

Soil Zones in Europe. The soil zones of Europe have developed as a consequence of climatic conditions, the character of the natural vegetation that occupied the land in prehistoric times, and the nature of the surface and its geologic history. There are several broad zones in which the soils are of contrasting types. Those of the north are of the light-colored, leached podsolic type, like those of the Canadian forest region. In most of the North European Plain the prevailing soils are of the brown, forest type like those of southern Michigan or Ohio, fertile if properly managed. In southern Europe types of subtropical red soils of only moderate fertility prevail. The old grasslands of southern Russia, however, yielded soils of dark color and high fertility. These are comparable with the soils of the Dakotas or Nebraska. Near the Caspian Sea are alkaline desert soils. The fact that some of the soils of Western Europe are actually more productive of crops than the naturally rich lands of southern Russia is more a tribute to the greater and more dependable rainfall of that region and to the skill of the farmers than an expression of the natural productiveness of the soils themselves.

Mineral Resources. Europe is rich in some of the vital industrial mineral resources but poor in others. Her production of gold, silver, copper, and tin are small, and only in southeastern Russia and in Rumania are there considerable supplies of petroleum. Of coal, iron, manganese, bauxite, and potash, however, the resources are large, but these are very unequally distributed. The coal is confined almost entirely to the sedimentary rocks of the northern plain. Deposits are found in England, northern France and Belgium, Germany, and central and southern Russia. In contrast, the ancient rocks of Scandinavia and the complicated structures of the Mediterranean lands are almost without this essential fuel. Iron ore is found most abundantly in the older rocks of central Europe, as in northern Spain, northern England, northeastern France, the mountains of Bohemia, southern Russia, and the Ural region. Some is found also in North Africa, and ores of the highest grade are mined in the far north of Sweden. It appears therefore that the countries that occupy the North European lowland are best equipped with coal and are well supplied with iron, the prime mineral essentials of modern industrialism. This same region has also the principal deposits of zinc, lead, potash, and several other minor minerals.

The mineral resources of Europe as a whole are highly utilized. The Continent has far less than half the known coal and iron ore of the world, yet normally it mines as much as all the rest of the world. Europe and Anglo-America together produce more than 95 per cent of the world's coal and iron both. This expression of the high industrial development of these regions, more than anything else, shows why the North Atlantic Ocean is the greatest highway of international trade.

Waterpower. Since the potential waterpower of a continent depends upon the area of the continent, as well as upon the rainfall and runoff and the relief of the land, Europe could hardly rank high in total potential waterpower. . . . Europe ranks highest among the continents in *developed* waterpower, exceeding North America. In both these continents about a third of the potential power has been brought into use. In Europe two regions yield a large part of the total. They are (1) the glaciated highland of Scandinavia and (2) the Alpine region of France, Italy, Germany, and Switzerland. It cannot be said that the use of waterpower has yet assumed large importance in the industries of Europe as compared with coal, although it is increasing rapidly.

The North Sea Countries. It already has been pointed out that the Atlantic Ocean exerts a profound influence upon the climate of Western Europe. . . . The British Isles, the Scandinavian countries, Belgium, Holland, most of Germany, and a part of France are north of the 49th parallel of north latitude, which is the northernmost latitude of any of the states of the United States. Even the northern boundary of Minnesota and North Dakota is several degrees farther south than London or Berlin. The North Sea countries lie between the parallels of 50° and 60° N. latitude, but they have winter temperatures resembling those of our eastern states that lie nearly 1,000 miles farther south, for example, Virginia and Maryland. These countries have ample rain for agriculture, little snow except on the mountains, mild winters, temperate summers, and ever changing weather.

The western edge of the real continental block of Europe is out in the Atlantic well to the west of Ireland. The British Isles are a part of the actual continent, and the North and Baltic Seas are shallow parts of the ocean which now cover portions of the North European Plain. A moderate sinking of the land in the recent geologic past cut the British Isles off from the rest of the Continent. Sinking coasts are usually irregular coasts, with offshore islands and broad river mouths which make good harbors. The North Sea countries have such a coast—an excellent coast for the purposes of ocean commerce. Of 12 leading ports of the world, 6 are on the borders of the North Sea—London, Antwerp, Rotterdam, Amsterdam, Hamburg, and Bremen. In normal times more overseas commerce is handled by the North Sea ports than by all the other ports of Europe.

The shallow waters that border the coast of Western Europe are ideal breeding grounds for fish, and one of the most productive sea-fishing regions of the world is there. Many people in all the West European coast regions are engaged in fisheries, especially in the North Sea and off the coast of Norway.... The ocean fisheries have been one of the most effective of all agencies in making the North Sea peoples seagoing and sea-loving . . . the invariable first steps in the making of maritime nations. . . .

With the unimportant exceptions of a short strip of the Norwegian coast and the Scottish coast, the North Sea is bordered by plains. This, of course, is to be expected when it is recalled that the North and Baltic Seas are merely drowned portions of the North European Plain. The absence of mountain barriers in this part of Europe, the ease with which the rivers can be used for navigation, and the general utility of the land for agriculture have been favorable to the economic development of the North Sea countries. This condition is quite in contrast with the mountainous lands around the Mediterranean Sea; and the relative decline in the commercial importance of the Mediterranean countries and the rise of the North Sea countries is, in no small part, due to the surface features of these two regions.

[The lands around the North Sea were] highly important commercially even before the rise of steam-driven machinery, notably during the period of the Hanseatic League, a league of commercial cities that flourished between the fourteenth and seventeenth centuries in the region around the North and Baltic Seas. The greatest expansion of the commerce of Western Europe, however, has taken place in the last century —the century of coal and iron. Most of the great coal deposits and iron deposits of Europe are in the lands that surround the North Sea, and practically half the factory manufacturing of the world is done in these same lands— England, northern France, Belgium, and Germany, especially.

The Mediterranean Region. Early European civilization grew up on the shores of this sea, and during the long period when Rome was mistress of the world the Mediterranean bound together nearly all the known world. It was small enough and had islands and peninsulas at sufficiently frequent intervals to permit the small vessels of that period to navigate its waters. But with the discovery of the New World and of the routes around the southern end of Africa and of South America, a new era of navigation began. The Atlantic grew in importance, and the Mediterranean suffered a relative decline. After the opening of the Suez Canal (1869) the Mediterranean again increased in importance as a route of commerce and is now one of the chief ocean trade routes of the world.

Unlike the North Sea, the Mediterranean is almost everywhere bordered on the north by mountains and on the south by mountains or deserts. Here there are no broad, fertile plains traversed by navigable rivers. Entrance to the interior of the Continent is somewhat difficult, the Rhone Valley in France being the principal open gateway to the north. The mountainous character of southern Europe, its less abundant mineral resources, and its dry summers are reasons for the lower industrial development of the Mediterranean lands and the general poverty of the people, the majority of whom seek to obtain a living from the scanty soil.

The distinctive features of Mediterranean climate as well as frontage upon an almost enclosed sea tend to draw together the fortunes of all Mediterranean lands in both Europe and northern Africa. In this region mild and moderately rainy winters alternate with hot and very dry summers. Under these conditions agriculture acquires a distinctive character. Its outstanding features include (1) cereal crops, especially wheat, which are able to grow during the cool, moist season and come to maturity before the summer drought is established; (2) perennial crops, such as the olive and the grapevine, which are able to endure drought or send their roots deep for subterranean water supplies; (3) intensive horticultural crops, such as citrus fruits and vegetables, which depend upon irrigation; and (4) animal industries, especially sheep and goats, which are able to make efficient use of the hilly, non-agricultural lands and the sparse, dry pastures of the summer season. So general are these types of agriculture that in one form or another they are to be found from Spain and Algeria on the west to Palestine and Turkey on the east, in spite of the differences in race and religion and the contrasts in cultural history among the peoples who inhabit the various portions of the Mediterranean borders.

Eastern Europe. The three outstanding characteristics of eastern Europe are ... (1) it is occupied almost wholly by Slavs; (2) it is mainly (but not wholly) a region of plains; (3) it is dominantly agricultural, with manufacturing developed to any large extent only in restricted areas, especially those which touch the highly industrialized districts of Western Europe.

The vast plains of Eastern Europe extend through many degrees of latitude from the Black Sea borders northward to the shores of the Arctic Ocean. They include wide variations in climate, vegetation, and soils, and corresponding differences in agriculture and land utilization. Their inhabitants are predominantly agricultural peasants who dwell in rural villages and live by the tillage of the soil or the exploitation of forests and other natural resources. However, recent decades have seen the rise of manufactures and manufacturing centers, a trend that is making rapid progress under the present Russian political regime.

EUROPE BEFORE 1914

By J. M. Keynes

From chap. 2 of *The Economic Consequences of the Peace*, by J. M. Keynes. Copyright 1920 by Harcourt, Brace & Co., New York; reproduced by permission. The author is a distinguished British economist.

Before 1870 different parts of the small continent of Europe had specialized in their own products; but, taken as a whole, it was substantially self-subsistent. And its population was adjusted to this state of affairs.

After 1870 there was developed on a large scale an unprecedented situation, and the economic condition of Europe became during the next fifty years unstable and peculiar. The pressure of population on food, which had already been balanced by the accessibility of supplies from America, became for the first time in recorded history definitely reversed. As numbers increased, food was actually easier to secure. Larger proportional returns from an increasing scale of production became true of agriculture as well as industry. With the growth of the European population there were more emigrants on the one hand to till the soil of the new countries, and, on the other, more workmen were available in Europe to prepare the industrial products and capital goods which were to maintain the emigrant populations in their new homes, and to build the railways and ships which were to make accessible to Europe food and raw products from distant sources. Up to about 1900 a unit of labor applied to industry yielded year by year a purchasing power over an increasing quantity of food. It is possible that about the year 1900 this process began to be reversed, and a diminishing yield of nature to man's effort was beginning to reassert itself. But the tendency of cereals to rise in real cost was balanced by other improvements; and—one of many novelties—the resources of tropical Africa then for the first time came into large employ, and a great traffic in oil-seeds began to bring to the table of Europe in a new and cheaper form one of the essential foodstuffs of mankind....

What an extraordinary episode in the economic progress of man that age was which came to an end in August 1914! The greater part of the population, it is true, worked hard and lived at a low standard of comfort, yet were, to all appearances, reasonably contented with this lot. But escape was possible, for any man of capacity or character at all exceeding the average, into the middle and upper classes, for whom life offered, at a low cost and with the least trouble, conveniences, comforts, and amenities beyond the compass of the richest and most powerful monarchs of other ages. The inhabitant of London could order by telephone, sipping his morning tea in bed, the various products of the whole earth, in such quantity as he might see fit, and reasonably expect their early delivery upon his doorstep; he could at the same moment and by the same means adventure his wealth in the natural resources and new enterprises of any quarter of the world, and share, without exertion or even trouble, in their prospective fruits and advantages; or he could decide to couple the security of his fortunes with the good faith of the townspeople of any substantial municipality in any continent that fancy or information might recommend. He could secure forthwith, if he wished it, cheap and comfortable means of transit to any country or climate without passport or other formality, could dispatch his servant to the neighboring office of a bank for such supply of the precious metals as might seem convenient, and could then proceed abroad to foreign quarters, without knowledge of their religion, language, or customs, bearing coined wealth upon his person, and would consider himself greatly aggrieved and much surprised at the least interference. But, most important of all, he regarded this state of affairs as normal, certain, and permanent, except in the direction of further improvement, and any deviation from it as aberrant, scandalous, and avoidable. The projects and politics of militarism and imperialism, of racial and cultural rivalries, of monopolies, restrictions, and exclusion, which were to play the serpent to this paradise, were little more than the amusements of his daily newspaper, and appeared to exercise almost no influence at all on the ordinary course of social and economic life, the internationalization of which was nearly complete in practice....

Population. In 1870 Germany had a population of about 40,000,000. By 1892 this figure had risen to 50,000,000, and by June 30, 1914, to about 68,000,000. In the years immediately preceding the war the annual increase was about 850,000, of whom an insignificant proportion emigrated. This great increase was only rendered possible by a far-reaching transformation of the economic structure of the country. From being agricultural and mainly self-supporting, Germany transformed herself into a vast and complicated industrial machine, dependent for its working on the equipoise of many factors outside Germany as well as within. Only by operating this machine continuously and at full blast, could she find occupation at home for her increasing population and the means of purchasing their subsistence from abroad. The German machine was like a top which to maintain its equilibrium must spin ever faster and faster.

In the Austro-Hungarian Empire, which grew from about 40,000,000 in 1890 to at least 50,000,000 at the outbreak of war, the same tendency was present in a less degree, the annual excess of births over deaths being about half a million, out of which, however, there was an annual emigration of some quarter of a million persons.

To understand the present situation, we must apprehend with vividness what an extraordinary center of population the development of the Germanic system had enabled Central Europe to become. Before the war the population of Germany and Austria-Hungary together not only substantially exceeded that of the United States, but was about equal to that of the whole of North America. In these numbers, situated within a compact territory, lay the military strength of the Central Powers. But these same numbers—for even the war has not appreciably diminished them—if deprived of the means of life, remain a hardly less danger to European order.

European Russia increased her population in a degree even greater than Germany—from less than 100,000,000 in 1890 to about 150,000,000 at the outbreak of war; and in the year immediately preceding 1914 the excess of births over deaths in Russia as a whole was at the prodigious rate of two millions per annum. This inordinate growth in the population of Russia, which has not been widely noticed in England, has been nevertheless one of the most significant facts of recent years.

The great events of history are often due to secular changes in the growth of population and other fundamental economic causes, which, escaping by their gradual character the notice of contemporary observers, are attributed to the follies of statesmen or the fanaticism of atheists. Thus the extraordinary occurrences of the past two years in Russia, that vast upheaval of society, which has overturned what seemed most stable—religion, the basis of property, the ownership of land, as well as forms of government and the hierarchy of classes—may owe more to the deep influences of expanding numbers than to Lenin or to Nicholas; and the disruptive powers of excessive national fecundity may have played a greater part in bursting the bonds of convention than either the power of ideas or the errors of autocracy.

Organization. The delicate organization by which these peoples lived depended partly on factors internal to the system.

The interference of frontiers and of tariffs was reduced to a minimum, and not far short of three hundred millions of people lived within the three empires of Russia, Germany, and Austria-Hungary. The various currencies, which were all maintained on a stable basis in relation to gold and to one another, facilitated the easy flow of capital and of trade to an extent the full value of which we only realize now, when we are deprived of its advantages. Over this great area there was an almost absolute security of property and of person.

These factors of order, security, and uniformity, which Europe had never before enjoyed over so wide and populous a territory or for so long a period, prepared the way for the organization of that vast mechanism of transport, coal distribution, and foreign trade which made possible an industrial order of life in the dense urban centers of new population. This is too well known to require detailed substantiation with figures. But it may be illustrated by the figures for coal, which has been the key to the industrial growth of Central Europe hardly less than of England; the output of German coal grew from 30,000,000 tons in 1871 to 70,000,000 tons in 1890, 110,000,000 tons in 1900, and 190,000,000 tons in 1913.

Round Germany as a central support the rest of the European economic system grouped itself, and on the prosperity and enterprise of Germany the prosperity of the rest of the Continent mainly depended. The increasing pace of Germany gave her neighbors an outlet for their products, in exchange for which the enterprise of the German merchant supplied them with their chief requirements at a low price.

The statistics of the economic interdependence of Germany and her neighbors are overwhelming. Germany was the best customer of Russia, Norway, Holland, Belgium, Switzerland, Italy, and Austria-Hungary; she was the second best customer of Great Britain, Sweden, and Denmark; and the third best customer of France. She was the largest source of supply to Russia, Norway, Sweden, Denmark, Holland, Switzerland, Italy, Austria-Hungary, Rumania, and Bulgaria; and the second largest source of supply to Great Britain, Belgium, and France.

In our own [i.e. British] case we sent more exports to Germany than to any other country in the world except India, and we bought more from her than from any other country in the world except the United States.

There was no European country except those west of Germany which did not do more than a quarter of their total trade with her; and in the case of Russia, Austria-Hungary, and Holland the proportion was far greater.

Germany not only furnished these countries with trade, but, in the case of some of them, supplied a great part of the capital needed for their own development. Of Germany's prewar foreign investments, amounting in all to about $6,250,000,000, not far short of $2,500,000,000 was invested in Russia, Austria-Hungary, Bulgaria, Rumania, and Turkey. And by the system of "peaceful penetration" she gave these countries not only capital, but, what they needed hardly less, organization. The whole of Europe east of the Rhine thus fell into the German industrial orbit, and its economic life was adjusted accordingly.

But these internal factors would not have been sufficient to enable the population to support itself without the cooperation of external factors also and of certain general dispositions common to the whole of Europe. Many of the circumstances already treated were true of Europe as a whole, and were not peculiar to the Central Empires. But all of what follows was common to the whole European system.

The Psychology of Society. Europe was so organized socially and economically as to secure the maximum accumulation of capital. While there was some continuous improvement in the daily conditions of life of the mass of the population, Society was so framed as to throw a great part of the increased income into the control of the class least likely to consume it. The new rich of the nineteenth century were not brought up to large expenditures, and preferred the power which investment gave them to the pleasures of immediate consumption. In fact, it was precisely the *in-*

equality of the distribution of wealth which made possible those vast accumulations of fixed wealth and of capital improvements which distinguished that age from all others. Herein lay, in fact, the main justification of the Capitalist System. If the rich had spent their new wealth on their own enjoyments, the world would long ago have found such a regime intolerable. But like bees they saved and accumulated, not less to the advantage of the whole community because they themselves held narrower ends in prospect.

The immense accumulations of fixed capital which, to the great benefit of mankind, were built up during the half century before the war, could never have come about in a society where wealth was divided equitably. The railways of the world, which that age built as a monument to posterity, were, not less than the Pyramids of Egypt, the work of labor which was not free to consume in immediate enjoyment the full equivalent of its efforts.

Thus this remarkable system depended for its growth on a double bluff or deception. On the one hand the laboring classes accepted from ignorance or powerlessness, or were compelled, persuaded, or cajoled by custom, convention, authority, and the well-established order of society into accepting, a situation in which they could call their own very little of the cake that they and nature and the capitalists were cooperating to produce. And on the other hand the capitalist classes were allowed to call the best part of the cake theirs and were theoretically free to consume it, on the tacit underlying condition that they consumed very little of it in practice. The duty of "saving" became nine-tenths of virtue and the growth of the cake the object of true religion. There grew round the non-consumption of the cake all those instincts of puritanism which in other ages has withdrawn itself from the world and has neglected the arts of production as well as those of enjoyment. And so the cake increased; but to what end was not clearly contemplated. Individuals would be exhorted not so much to abstain as to defer, and to cultivate the pleasures of security and anticipation. Saving was for old age or for your children; but this was only in theory—the virtue of the cake was that it was never to be consumed, neither by you nor by your children after you.

In writing thus I do not necessarily disparage the practices of that generation. In the unconscious recesses of its being society knew what it was about. The cake was really very small in proportion to the appetites of consumption, and no one, if it were shared all round, would be much the better off by the cutting of it. Society was working not for the small pleasures of today but for the future security and improvement of the race—in fact for "progress." If only the cake were not cut but was allowed to grow in the geometrical proportion predicted by Malthus of population, but not less true of compound interest, perhaps a day might come when there would at last be enough to go round, and when posterity could enter into the enjoyment of *our* labors. In that day overwork, overcrowding, and underfeeding would have come to an end, and men, secure of the comforts and necessities of the body, could proceed to the nobler exercises of their faculties. One geometrical ratio might cancel another, and the nineteenth century was able to forget the fertility of the species in a contemplation of the dizzy virtues of compound interest.

There were two pitfalls in this prospect: lest, population still outstripping accumulation, our self-denials promote not happiness but numbers; and lest the cake be after all consumed, prematurely, in war, the consumer of all such hopes.

But these thoughts lead too far from my present purpose. I seek only to point out that the principle of accumulation based on inequality was a vital part of the prewar order of society and of progress as we then understood it, and to emphasize that this principle depended on unstable psychological conditions, which it may be impossible to recreate. It was not natural for a population, of whom so few enjoyed the comforts of life, to accumulate so hugely. The war has disclosed the possibility of consumption to all and the vanity of abstinence to many. Thus the bluff is discovered; the laboring classes may be no longer willing to forego so largely, and the capitalist classes no longer confident of the future, may seek to enjoy more fully their liberties of consumption so long as they last, and thus precipitate the hour of their confiscation.

The Relation of the Old World to the New. The accumulative habits of Europe before the war were the necessary condition of the greatest of the external factors which maintained the European equipoise.

Of the surplus capital goods accumulated by Europe a substantial part was exported abroad, where its investment made possible the development of the new resources of food, materials, and transport, and at the same time enabled the Old World to stake out a claim in the natural wealth and virgin potentialities of the New. This last factor came to be of the vastest importance. The Old World employed with an immense prudence the annual tribute it was thus entitled to draw. The benefit of cheap and abundant supplies, resulting from the new developments which its surplus capital had made possible, was, it is true, enjoyed and not postponed. But the greater part of the money interest accruing on these foreign investments was reinvested and allowed to accumulate, as a reserve (it was then hoped) against the less happy day when the industrial labor of Europe could no longer purchase on such easy terms the produce of other continents, and when the due balance would be threatened between its historical civilizations and the multiplying races of other climates and environments. Thus the whole of the European races tended to benefit alike from the development of new resources whether they pursued their culture at home or adventured it abroad.

Even before the war, however, the equilibrium thus established between old civilizations and new resources was being threatened. The prosperity of Europe was based on the facts that, owing to the large exportable surplus of foodstuffs in America, she was able to purchase food at a cheap rate measured in terms of the labor required to produce her own exports, and that, as a result of her previous investments of capital, she was entitled to a substantial amount annually without any payment in return at all. The second of these factors then seemed out of danger, but, as a result of the growth of population overseas, chiefly in the United States, the first was not so secure.

When first the virgin soils of America came into bearing, the proportions of the population of those continents themselves, and consequently of their own local requirements, to those of Europe were very small. As lately as 1890 Europe had a population three times that of North and South America added together. But by 1914 the domestic requirements of the United States for wheat were approaching their production, and the date was evidently near when there would be an exportable surplus only in years of exceptionally favorable harvest. Indeed, the present domestic requirements of the United States are estimated at more than 90 per cent of the average yield of the five years 1909-1913. At that time, however, the tendency toward stringency was showing itself, not so much in a lack of abundance as in a steady increase of real cost. That is to say, taking the world as a whole, there was no deficiency of wheat, but in order to call forth an adequate supply it was necessary to offer a higher real price. The most favorable factor in the situation was to be found in the extent to which Central and Western Europe was being fed from the exportable surplus of Russia and Rumania.

In short, Europe's claim on the resources of the New World was becoming precarious; the law of diminishing returns was at last reasserting itself, and was making it necessary year by year for Europe to offer a greater quantity of other commodities to obtain the same amount of bread; and Europe, therefore, could by no means afford the disorganization of any of her principal sources of supply.

Much else might be said in an attempt to portray the economic peculiarities of the Europe of 1914. I have selected for emphasis the three or four greatest factors of instability—the instability of an excessive population dependent for its livelihood on a complicated and artificial organization, the psychological instability of the laboring and capitalist classes, and the instability of Europe's claim, coupled with the completeness of her dependence, on the food supplies of the New World.

The war had so shaken this system as to endanger the life of Europe altogether. A great part of the Continent was sick and dying; its population was greatly in excess of the numbers for which a livelihood was available; its organization was destroyed, its transport system ruptured, and its food supplies terribly impaired.

It was the task of the Peace Conference to honor engagements and to satisfy justice; but not less to reestablish life and to heal wounds. These tasks were dictated as much by prudence as by the magnanimity which the wisdom of antiquity approved in victors. . . .

EUROPE BETWEEN WARS

By André Siegfried

From chap. 2 of *Europe's Crisis,* by A. Siegfried. Published by John Wiley & Sons, New York; reproduced by permission of Jonathan Cape, Ltd., London. The author is a leading French geographer and economist.

THE irresistible domination that Europe exerted over the rest of the world until the beginning of the twentieth century is now challenged. . . .

. . . The breaking up of the European monopoly was caused by forces which were already at work in the last quarter of the nineteenth century.

In order to realize this fully, we must study the economic history of England, since, so far as industry is concerned, she has always been in the vanguard of Europe. As early as the 'eighties we begin to perceive certain signs of weakness in her supremacy, which hitherto had been triumphant and uncontested. Overseas markets began to shut out her imports when they created industries of their own, so that her export trade no longer made such astonishing progress as before. In this matter England was typical of the rest of the Continent, except that since she had advanced further along the road to industrialization, she was more exposed and vulnerable.

It is hardly accurate to say that the war [of 1914-1918] created a competition which was specifically new, but

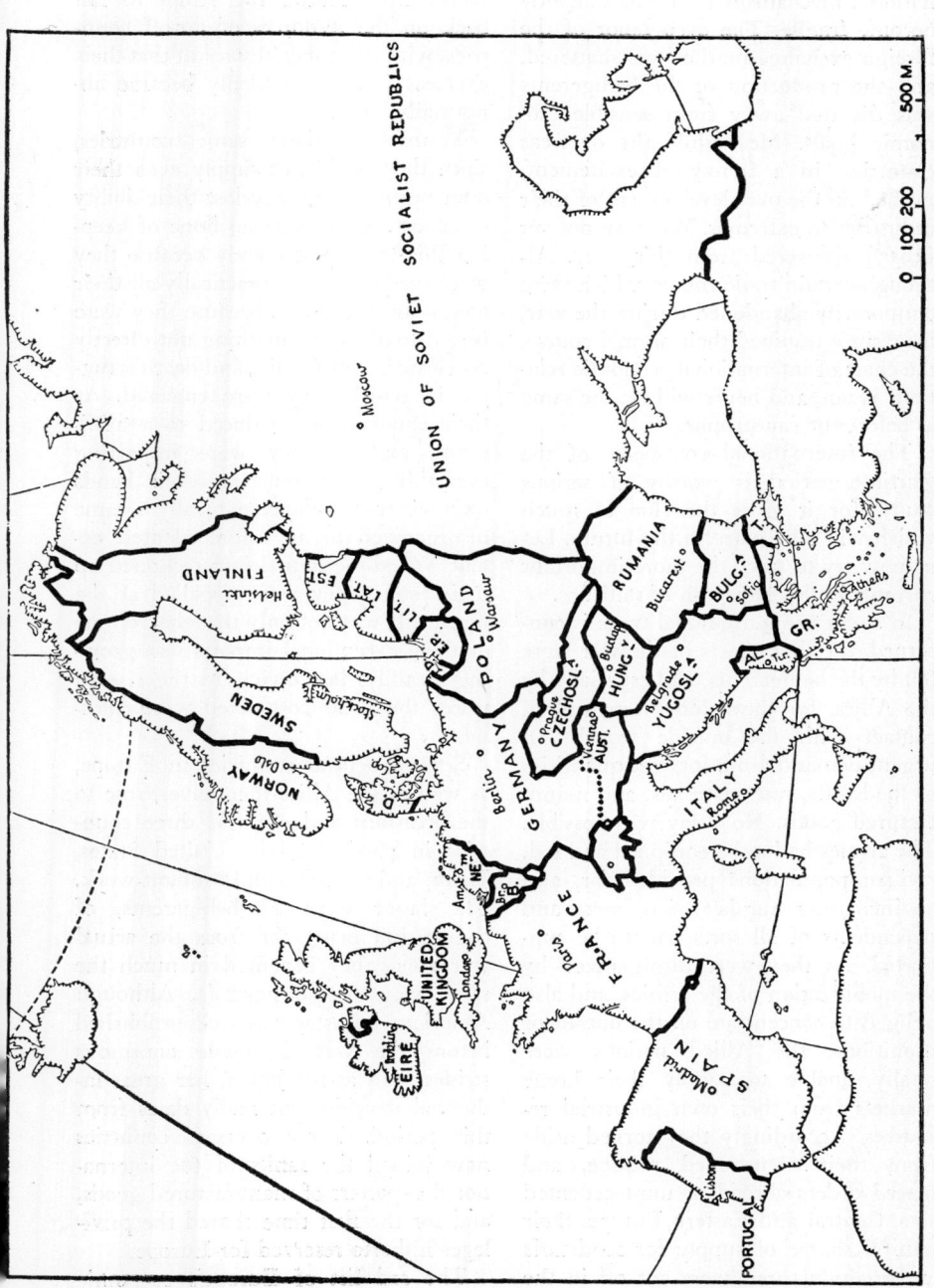

Fig. 10. Europe between Wars. This map shows the political boundaries of Europe as these were defined by the peace settlement of 1919.

From M. Rajchman, *Europe, An Atlas of Human Geography*. Copyright 1944 by William Morrow & Co., New York; reproduced by permission.

undoubtedly it did upset a delicate international mechanism which had already become fragile. The even tenor of the foreign exchange market was shattered, and the production of the belligerents was diverted away from sensible economic goals. Meanwhile the overseas countries, in a frenzy of excitement, pushed on the overdevelopment of their industries to extremes. We have not yet [1935] recovered from this orgy. Although certain trade routes, which were temporarily abandoned during the war, have since resumed their normal course, the chart of international economic relations is not, and never will be, the same as before the catastrophe.

The international commerce of the wartime period is worthy of serious study, for it gives the clue to much which will take place in the future. Let us now try to trace the more important currents in this labyrinth of statistics.

In so far as international trade is concerned, the first effects of the war were felt by the belligerents, and especially by the Allies, for they alone were still in contact with the outside world. An urgent demand arose for vast quantities of foodstuffs, raw materials, and manufactured goods. No delay was possible. The armies had to be equipped and fed, civilian populations provided for, and an increasing number of refugees and dependents of all sorts had to be supported. As they were disorganized by the mobilization of the armies, and also obliged to concentrate on the output of munitions, the Allied nations were totally unable to supply their home markets from their own industrial resources. Accordingly they turned aside from their accustomed routine, and placed orders abroad of unprecedented size. Central and Eastern Europe, their natural source of supply for foodstuffs and manufactures, were cut off in the twinkling of an eye when commerce with the enemy became a criminal offence. This caused the Allies to fall back on the resources of far-off countries, with the unhealthy result that their overseas imports suddenly became abnormally large.

Meanwhile, these same countries, since they could not supply even their own needs, necessarily lost their ability to export. There was no hope of keeping this trade, not merely because they were swallowing up practically all their own output, but also because they were forced to abandon anything not directly concerned with the life-and-death struggle in which they were engaged. As their exports were reduced to a minimum, and as they were importing everything they could lay their hands on, their trade balance naturally became disorganized to an unprecedented extent. When the statisticians reckoned up their totals, they were appalled at the figures. It was not only that the volume of these exceptional imports was growing steadily, but owing to the rise in prices the debts contracted were colossal. . . .

Several neutral countries in Europe, as well as the Allies themselves, rose to the occasion; and overseas three countries in particular—the United States, Japan, and Canada—did brilliant work. The latter were all belligerents, of course, but being far from the actual war zone, they benefited in much the same way as the neutrals. Although American industry was well established before the war, it made enormous strides; and as for Japan, her great industrial development really dates from this period. These overseas countries now joined the ranks of the international exporters of manufactured goods, and for the first time shared the privileges hitherto reserved for Europe.

The sad list of Europe's economic losses during these black years does not end here, however, for we still have to consider the indirect effect of the war on the overseas countries in so far as they were markets for manufactured goods. When these far-off nations were suddenly enriched by an exceptional demand for their products at unheard-of prices, their purchasing power shot up with the force of a geyser. Easy come, easy go—people made money so quickly that they never thought of saving it. Their one idea was to spend it, no matter how. The usual exporting nations had practically dropped out of the running, for although Europe was still able to export a little, the dangers of ocean transport and high freight rates proved a hindrance. The immediate result was that European goods failed to arrive just at a time when the new countries were feeling rich. Two adaptations quickly occurred. First, the non-European industries stepped into the breach, and secondly, local industries increased their output, while in some cases entirely new industries sprang up.

This trend did more than anything else to industrialize the world outside the boundaries of Europe, and in opposition to her. The urge to construct factories was irresistible. The effects of the conditions which prevailed everywhere in those extraordinary years have not been counteracted either by the return to peace, or by the lesson of the two economic depressions which have since taken place.

Protection is hardly needed, and yet governments have been granting it with great gusto, imposing all manner of restrictions, especially on luxuries. These severe import regulations, sometimes amounting to embargoes, have provided a shelter behind which national industries have been created, or have been able to grow at their ease.

New industries have been springing up like mushrooms after the rain, but as we have learned by experience, once they have been created, enterprises usually manage to survive, especially when they can count on government support. While assistance of this type is likely to be given to the manufacturer to protect his investment, it is practically certain to be granted to the workman to consolidate the trade on which his living depends. Quite apart from the United States and Japan, this applies to Australia, Brazil, Canada, and a dozen other overseas countries where new industries were established during the war.

The most developed of these young countries took the place of Europe, and began to fill the wants of the others. In the past the Old Continent was in the center of the picture, but new commercial relations were now beginning to be established without reference to her. For example, the United States got into direct contact with South America, and also with the Far East via Panama, while Japan began to trade direct with South America, Australasia, and India. Certain of these trade routes were already in existence, but others were entirely new. Europe's role in this international commerce declined, and the result was a dislocation which will never be readjusted. Conditions during the war undoubtedly were exceptional, but their repercussions have come to stay.... No doubt we shall regain some of the markets which the fatal years of the war lost for us, but others will elude our grasp. Not without a struggle will the other continents give up the advantages which they obtained owing to what were exceptional circumstances. The interests which have gained by the change are only too anxious to consolidate it, and no matter what economic arguments are brought forward, politics are always dragged in to their assistance. We have only to look around us to see that this is being done every day. Therefore, the industrialization of the world, even when condemned as uneconomic, is destined to endure. When Europe tries to recover her lost markets she is confronted with the exasperated nationalism of thirty overseas countries, who are in revolt against the old conception of international division of labor and complementary trade.

Regarded from every angle, the ultimate effect of this widespread crisis has been to undermine Europe's former role of leadership. . . . The Old Continent is no longer strong enough to impress her own traditions as in the past and make the world react to a single impulse.

In place of this single driving force, the world is being divided up into various spheres of influence. The European sector is still intact, and still extensive, but on leaving these shores the traveler soon encounters that of the United States. Meanwhile several zones are taking shape in Asia, where they seem to have broken as completely away from America as they have from Europe. Considered on a plane far above the realm of politics in the accepted sense of the term, one easily perceives the three or four different paths along which the world is traveling, in marked contrast to the extraordinary unity of the earlier inspiration, when the power of the Old Continent was without effective counterpart. Instinctively we recall the last chapters of ancient history and the breaking up of the *Pax Romana.*

WHAT IS EUROPE'S FUTURE?

The effects of the Second World War on Europe's future role in world affairs is today a subject of heated debate. The following two selections are believed to be representative of current thought on the question.

THE OLD EUROPE IS GONE

By Jan C. Smuts

From an address by Field Marshal Jan Christian Smuts, Prime Minister of South Africa, delivered before the British Empire Parliamentary Association in London November 25, 1943. Excerpts quoted in *New York Times,* December 12, 1943, VI, 9.

We have moved into a strange world, a world such as has not been seen for hundreds of years, perhaps not for 1,000 years. Europe is completely changing. The old Europe has gone. The map is being rolled up and a new map is unrolling before us. We shall have to do a great deal of fundamental thinking and scrapping of old points of view before we find our way through that new continent which now opens up before us.

Just look, for a moment, at what is happening and what will be the state of affairs at the end of war in Europe. Three of the five Great Powers will have disappeared. That will be a unique development. France has gone, and if ever she returns it will be a hard and a long upward pull for her to emerge again. A nation that has once been overtaken by a catastrophe such as she has suffered, reaching to the foundations of her nationhood, will not easily resume her old place again. . . . We are dealing with one of the greatest and most far-reaching catastrophes in history, the like of which I have never read. . . .

Italy has completely disappeared and may never be a Great Power again. Germany, at the end of the war, will have disappeared perhaps never to emerge again in the old form. The Germans are a great people with great qualities, and

Germany is inherently a great country, but after the smash that will follow this war Germany will be written off the slate in Europe for long, long years, and after that a new world may have arisen.

We are, therefore, left with Great Britain and with Russia. Russia is the new colossus in Europe, the new colossus that bestrides this continent. When we consider all that has happened in Russia within the last twenty-five years and we see Russia's inexplicable rise, we can only call it one of the great phenomena in history. It is the sort of thing to which there is no parallel in history, but it has come about.

What the after-effects of that will be, nobody can say. We can but recognize that this is a new fact to reckon with, and we must reckon with it coldly and objectively. With the others down and out and Russia the mistress of the Continent, her power will not only be great on that account but it will be still greater because the Japanese Empire will also have gone the way of all flesh. Therefore any check or balance that might have arisen in the East will have disappeared You will have Russia in a position which no country has ever occupied in the history of Europe.

Then you will have Great Britain, with a glory and an honor and a prestige such as perhaps no nation has ever enjoyed in history, recognized as possessing a greatness of soul that has entered into the very substance of world history. But from a material economic point of view she will be a poor country. She has put in her all. The British Empire and the British Commonwealth remain as one of the greatest things of the world and of history, and nothing can touch that fact. But you must remember that the Empire and the Commonwealth are mostly extra-European. Those are the overflows of this great British system to other continents. . . .

EUROPE WILL RECOVER

By Friedrich Baerwald

From "The Future of Europe," by F. Baerwald, in *Thought*, September 1944. Copyright 1944 by Fordham University; reproduced by permission.

There is a widespread school of thought that has "written off" Europe. They count the dead, the diseased, the underfed, the dispersed and they cannot see how any group of people having suffered so terribly can ever recover again; they view the Second World War as final evidence that Europe cannot solve its national and political problems or forget its ancient hatreds. The cultural heritage of the Old World is considered by them at best as a museum piece incapable of further growth. This picture of decay is then contrasted with the spectacle of the vitality of the dynamic and young people of the United States and of the Soviet Union, later to be joined in their advance into a new world by the awakening people of China and India. That the British Empire will continue in one form or another is mostly conceded, but its share in world leadership is expected to decline sharply.

Inasmuch as problems of changes in international political and cultural leadership and in the relative strength of nations and continents play an important part in our considerations, it is advisable to state first the factors that bring about the rise of Great Powers and centers of culture. Mere numbers of people, the mere existence of natural resources, the endowment of a people with a genius for business and technology do not in themselves guarantee effective participation in world leadership. Power and cultural influence of a nation or of a continent are never, as it were, gifts of nature. They are the results of decisions and the ability and willingness of people to see them through and to exert themselves continuously to maintain their lofty position once it is reached. All this is so important that often in history internal strength has made up for the deficiency of nations in manpower and wealth, and has given them superiority over more richly endowed but inefficient states....

We have stressed already that mere numbers are not decisive. However, the trend of quantitative change of a population is important. We have become used to base a generally optimistic outlook on an expectation of the growth in population. Conversely, actual or potential decline of population very often creates an atmosphere of political and cultural defeatism. Thus great concern has been expressed about the outlook for the European population, especially as compared to the probable development of the people of the Soviet Union. It is necessary to see these discernible trends in their proper proportion. This will dispel easy optimism as well as unjustifiable despair.

The rate of growth of the population has declined sharply in Europe in recent decades. This trend was stronger in the West and North than in the South and East of the Continent. By the end of this century, this will have resulted in a marked numerical ascendancy especially of the Slavic nations. Between 1900 and 1910, the rate of population growth in Europe was 9.4 per cent. It dropped to 1.8 per cent between 1910 and 1920 and between 1930 and 1939, it was only 6.1 per cent. Yet in absolute numbers, the European population was just below 400 million in 1939. That is to say, even then, the population of Europe was more than twice as large as the population of the North American continent where, in 1939, 184 million inhabitants were living. However, the North American continent has an area of 8,664,860 square miles whereas Europe has only 2,092,664 square miles. Or in round figures before the Second World War, Europe housed double the population of the North American continent on one quarter of the territory of that continent. In the future the relative proportion of the population of Europe and the North American continent will not change radically. According to the most recent estimates taking already into account the impact of the Second World War, the population of Europe will become stationary sometime between 1960 and 1970 at a level of about 417 million people. From then on, it is expected to decline unless the already mentioned change in public opinion and the proposed scheme for the support of large families reverse the trend. The population of the United States will also become almost stationary at approximately the same time. Around 1970, it will be just slightly above 150 million. Shortly after that date, it also is expected to decrease slowly. To round out this picture of relative strength, we now turn our attention to the population of the U.S.S.R. There, the population in 1940 was estimated at 174 million. It is expected to increase to about 251 million in 1970. This means that at that time, the U.S.S.R. will be far more populous than the North American continent, but Europe proper, which geographically speaking is only a promontory of the huge land mass occupied by Russia, will be far more populous than the Soviet Union.

This survey of the population trends in Europe indicates that even on purely quantitative grounds, it will retain a position of great preeminence in the world. But will this not be offset by a decline in the quality of its human material suffering as it will at the end of the war from complete general exhaustion developing into unwillingness and inability to continue its former great designs and objectives? . . .

The ability of physical and mental recuperation of people has often surprised the cautious experts. Widespread malnutrition during the First World War has not interfered with a rapid improvement above and beyond the prewar level of health standards in most European countries. Since the progress in medical science and in health services continues at a rapid pace, there is no reason to assume this to be different after this war. There has also been no decline in technical skills. On the contrary, the productivity of farming and industry in Europe has increased in the interwar period. Industrialization has spread to formerly undeveloped areas. . . .

But . . . how can Europe recover from the large-scale destruction of its cities, industries and transportation systems? Surely a real restoration is inconceivable as far as historical monuments are concerned. . . . It is different with the reconstruction of dwellings and industries. What can be expected there is largely an improvement. Technology and city planning have not stood still in these years of crisis. The tremendous scope of the required program will create the economies of large-scale operations and facilitate coordination of all the new developments. It will also for years solve the problem of unemployment in Europe.

Now all these reconstruction programs cannot be solved on a local or even a national level. For instance, before the rebuilding of textile plants and workers' settlements in Poland can be planned rationally, it will be necessary to determine just what the place of that Polish industry will be in relation to the European textile industry as a whole. What will be its line of specialization? What should be its size? To what extent would it merely duplicate, let us say, the Dutch textile industry and thereby lead to a renewal of unwholesome trade policies? It is not at all necessary for the governments to solve all these problems for the industries. But the European industries must do it themselves and they can succeed only within a continental European framework, taking also into account the channels of exports to other areas. Whenever this spontaneous cooperation of industries does not develop, governments must take the initiative to secure economic integration.

It is important to realize that a very considerable degree of economic unification has actually taken place in Europe in recent years. The fact that this particular type of unification must be changed because it served merely the interests of the Nazi state and its collaborators does not militate against this idea as such. . . .

One might ask whether this picture of a reinvigorated Europe creating an integrated economic system is not altogether chimerical. The accumulation of hatred engendered by years of Nazi occupation and the intensification of nationalistic feeling created by it seems to justify these doubts. But it would be an error to take the present psychological condition of some groups in Europe as an indication of the long-run development of European sentiment. The underlying European realities will reassert themselves. . . .

The prospects . . . are that out of this war there will emerge a Europe at first weakened physically and economically but also endowed with a new vision of its own position and possibilities. Regardless of what people in other global spheres may think, the Europeans will not consider themselves as mere pawns in the hands of World Powers. . . .

Chapter 6

Great Britain

GREAT BRITAIN, more than any other European power, forms a connecting link between the United States and the European realm. Hence the fortunes of the British nation are of vital concern to the United States. Americans may "twist the Lion's tail" and otherwise irritate their British cousins. But in moments of grave peril ancient grudges are pushed into the background, and the Anglo-Saxon peoples stand shoulder to shoulder against the common enemy.

Twice, in 1917 and again in 1940, we have mobilized our great strength in support of Britain. In doing so, many Americans were doubtless moved by sentiment. But deeper than sentiment was widespread realization, usually unexpressed, that defeat of Britain and break-up of the British Empire would seriously weaken American defenses, if not imperil the very existence of the United States.

One hears it often said that the British navy has been America's first line of defense in the Atlantic. There is a large measure of truth in this proposition. But it is easily subject to misinterpretation. England has not maintained a navy for the purpose of defending the United States. The Royal Navy exists for the defense of the British Isles and the oceanic supply lines of the British Empire. In performing those functions, however, British sea power has incidentally, and in varying degrees from time to time, strengthened the defenses of the United States. Without the British navy we would have needed a stronger navy of our own.

This was the case even back in the nineteenth century when Americans still regarded England with distrust, and still contemplated the possibility of a third war with that country. Even in those days, British sea power was in many respects an asset to the United States. This was so because British statecraft, for purely British reasons, generally stood in the way of other European powers extending their sway into the Western Hemisphere. Thus, while we still viewed England as a source of potential danger, we simultaneously and incidentally derived benefit from Britain's long indisputable command of the seas.

American reliance upon British sea power took on a more formal character after the First World War. During the period between wars we entrusted our defense in the Atlantic almost exclusively to Great Britain. The Royal Navy's command of European waters permitted the concentration of American naval strength in the Pacific, to the mutual advantage of both nations.

It is easy today to forget the unique position once held by Great Britain. During the nineteenth century, Britain was not merely one of the Great Powers. Victorian England was the first and only World Power.

For various reasons, discussed in the following pages, England experienced the industrial revolution earlier than other countries. The application of mechanical power to manufacturing, and the resulting growth of commerce and accumulation of capital, began earlier and proceeded more rapidly in England than upon the Continent or in North America. British imports of food and raw materials, and exports of coal and manufactures, came in the nineteenth century to comprise a large proportion of the world's commerce. London became the business and financial center of an economic community which spread over the globe. This economic commonwealth embraced not only the British Empire but also many independent countries upon several continents.

The British navy, exercising virtually world-wide command of the seas, gave to the members of this family of nations a fair assurance of uninterrupted trade and continued peace. Industrial leadership and a far-flung commerce, backed up by financial and naval primacy, enabled British statesmen to wield an influence which approached, even if it never attained, the dimensions of global sovereignty and a world government.

Toward the end of the century, however, there were accumulating signs that these halcyon days were drawing to a close. Developments of various kinds in many parts of the world were beginning to eat away the foundations of the *Pax Britannica*, or British Peace, as the Victorian era was sometimes aptly called. One of the most disquieting signs of the times was the rapid growth of German power, following the Franco-Prussian war of 1870 and the consequent unification of the Germanic peoples.

Alarmed by the increasingly aggressive trend of German naval and foreign policies, as well as by other unsettling developments in Europe and the Far East, British statesmen began to look abroad for new friends and allies. One result was marked improvement in Anglo-American relations, dating from about the time of our war of 1898 with Spain. As time passed, Britain came increasingly to value the friendship of the United States, and Americans came also to recognize more clearly our own stake in the survival of a strong, friendly Britain.

Unfortunately, both Englishmen and Americans were slow to grasp, or at least to acknowledge, the full extent and implications of the changes then taking place in the strategical position and over-all situation of Great Britain. Americans in particular tended to overestimate the military strength and resources of Britain. Because British sea power had formerly reigned supreme in every ocean and in most of the adjoining narrow seas, Americans in the twentieth century continued in the main to assume that Britain unaided could still take care of herself against any probable enemies.

Even the First World War failed to drive home fully the lesson of Britain's increasing vulnerability to attack from the Continent. The fall of France, accompanied by the British retreat from Dunkirk, and followed by the German assault on Britain itself, came as a terrible shock to most Americans who suddenly awoke to the frightening possibility of Britain going down in defeat and the eastern Atlantic passing under the hostile sway of Hitler's Third Reich.

That experience, together with what has happened since, has demonstrated how closely related are the fortunes of the Atlantic peoples. New developments in amphibious warfare, the ever-lengthening range of piloted planes, the introduction of pilotless aerial weapons, and other military developments, as well as profound changes in economic and political relations, all seem likely to increase the mutual dependence of the two peoples in the future.

If this is so, it is plain that we must have the clearest possible picture of Great Britain's changing world position. Whence came the strength that supported the *Pax Britannica* of the last century? Why is Britain unable to play the same historic role in our time? What are the elements of strength and of weakness in Britain's present military, political, and economic position? What future trends may be anticipated in the light of the Second World War? These are questions which deeply concern Americans, and it is with these and similar questions in view that the following readings have been selected.

GREAT BRITAIN'S GEOGRAPHICAL POSITION

By Halford J. Mackinder

From chap. 1 of *Britain and the British Seas*, by Sir Halford J. Mackinder. Oxford University Press, Oxford, 1906, 2nd ed. 1930; reproduced by permission. The author is a famous British geographer, formerly director of the School of Economics in the University of London, and Member of Parliament.

Before the great geographical discoveries of the fifteenth and sixteenth centuries, the known lands lay almost wholly in the Northern Hemisphere and spread in a single continent from the shores of Spain to those of Cathay. Britain was then at the end of the world—almost out of the world. At one point her white cliffs might be seen from the mainland, and from this she stretched, northward and westward, away from the life of Europe. . . . During two thousand years Britain was at the margin, not in the center, of the theater of politics. . . .

The historical meaning of the Columbian discoveries can best be realized by turning a terrestrial globe so that Britain may be at the point nearest to the eye (see Fig. 8, p. 125 above). Europe, Asia, Africa, and the two Americas are thus included within the visible hemisphere; but the chief feature even of the land-half of the globe is a great arm of mediterranean ocean, Atlantic and Arctic, winding northward through the midst of the lands to encircle the pole, and to end beyond on the shores of Alaska and Siberia. There, across the narrow and shallow Bering Strait, the mountains of America are visible from the Asiatic coast and the ocean-end is almost land-girt. The southern entry, from the water hemisphere, is an ocean-bay between Cape Horn and the Cape of Good Hope, which narrows somewhat toward the Equator, and is there half-closed by the western wing of Africa. A wide passage is left, some fifteen hundred miles in breadth, which leads into the triangular basin of the North Atlantic, essentially only the vastest of lakes. Two of the sides are the coasts of South and North America, where they recede into the West Indian Gulf; the third is the edge of Europe and Africa northward and southward of the Strait of Gibraltar. No flat chart can give a correct impression of the form of the North Atlantic. Only a globe can suggest its vast bulging center, and the relative insignificance of its Arctic, Mediterranean, and Caribbean recesses. A broad channel, with parallel shores trending northeastward, connects the North Atlantic with the Polar Sea. Iceland stands in the midst of this entry; Greenland defines it on the one hand, and Britain and Scandinavia on the other. Practically, however, this, like Davis Strait, is a mere gulf of the North Atlantic, extending only to the edge of the ice-pack. For most purposes, therefore, the North Atlantic is a rounded basin, with eastward, northward, and westward gulfs, and a southern exit. But the five historic parts of the world are accessible from its waters, and for the generations that followed Columbus history centered increasingly round its shores. Thus Britain gradually became the central, rather than the terminal, land of the world. . . .

. . . For many centuries the English

were a race of shepherds rather than mariners, and the most significant feature of British geography was not the limitless ocean, but the approach of the southeastern corner of the islands to within sight of the Continent. Kent was the window by which England looked into the great world, and the foreground of that world, visible from Dover Castle, had no ordinary character. Immediately to the east of Calais is the end of the linguistic frontier which, crossing Europe from south to north, divides the two great races, Romance and Teutonic, whose interaction has made European history. From Calais eastward, in succession, were nations of Germanic seamen—Flemings, Hollanders, Frieslanders, Hansards, and Vikings. Westward was the Frenchman, and behind him the Spaniard and the Italian. To the Teutons—"Easterlings" and "Norsemen"—England owes her civil institutions and her language; to the peoples of the west and south, her Christianity and her scholarship. Two distinct streams of ethical and artistic influence converged upon the island from the Rhine delta and from the estuary of the Seine; . . .

Behind Europe, and seen through Europe as through a colored glass, lay the imagined wealth of the Indies; and it is not without significance that the lie of the physical features—gulfs, rivers, and peninsulas—drew the great roads from the Indies northwestward through Persia, Mesopotamia, and Egypt—by the Danube, the Adriatic, and the Rhone—to Flanders and Paris, and so to Kent and to London.

Seen thus in relation to earlier and to later history, Britain is possessed of two geographical qualities, complementary rather than antagonistic: insularity and universality. Before Columbus, the insularity was more evident than the universality. Within closed coasts, impregnable when valiantly held, but in sight of the world and open to stimulus —Teutonic, Romantic, and Oriental— her people were able to advance with Europe, and yet, protected from military necessities, to avoid tyranny and to retain the legacy of freedom bequeathed in the German forests. Ordered liberty, fitted to the complex conditions of modern civilization, needed centuries of slow experimental growth, and was naturally cradled in a land insulated yet not isolated.

After Columbus, value began to attach to the ocean-highway, which is in its nature universal. Even the great continents are only vast islands and discontinuous; but every part of the ocean is accessible from every other part. . . . The unity of the ocean is the simple physical fact underlying the dominant value of sea-power in the modern globe-wide world. Britain—*of* Europe, yet not *in* Europe—was free to devote resources, drawn ultimately from the Continent, to the expansion of civilization beyond the ocean. The sea preserved liberty, and allowed of a fertility of private initiative which was incompatible with supreme military organization. The same sea, by reducing the reserve of men and material needed for the protection of the island home, has permitted the devotion of British initiative and energy to trade and rule abroad. Great consequences lie in the simple statements that Britain is an island group, set in the ocean, but off the shores of the great Continent; that the opposing shores are indented; and that the domains of two historic races come down to the sea precisely at the narrowest strait between the mainland and the island. . . .

POLITICAL SIGNIFICANCE OF BRITAIN'S GEOGRAPHICAL POSITION

By C. B. Fawcett

From chap. 8 of *A Political Geography of the British Empire*, by C. B. Fawcett. Ginn & Co., London & Boston, 1933; reproduced by permission of the University of London Press. The author is Professor of Economics and Geography in the University of London.

PHYSICALLY the British Isles are a part of the European subcontinent. They lie on the continental shelf of northwest Europe, and are marked off from the rest of Europe only by the shallow seas which have been formed by the flooding of a part of the Great Lowland since the last Ice Age. They lie just off the northwestern edge of the Continent, with their fertile lowlands near to it and their more barren highlands along the oceanic margins of the islands....

At the Strait of Dover, off the southeastern corner of England, our island is separated from the Continent by a distance of only twenty-one miles. For three hundred miles westward along the English Channel this distance gradually increases until from Cornwall to Brittany it is over a hundred miles. Northward from Dover the sea separating us from the Continent widens steadily to a hundred miles between East Anglia and north Holland, and beyond that very sharply to more than four hundred miles between Scotland and Jutland. But farther north the westward projection of Norway combines with the easterly trend of northern Scotland to reduce the northern opening of the North Sea to a width of barely two hundred miles between Shetland and west Norway.

Just to the south of the Narrow Seas the western end of the Mid-World Mountain Belt comes to the Atlantic coast in northern Spain, and approaches it in the Alps and the western outliers of highland in central France. To the northwest these Narrow Seas penetrate the breaks between the highlands of Norway, Scotland, and northwest Ireland, which belong to one and the same geological structural series. To the north of the Mid-World Mountains, from the Alps and Carpathians to the Caucasus and the Hindu Kush, lies the Great Lowland of Eurasia, which extends for some four thousand miles eastward from the shores of the Narrow Seas to the foot of the East Siberian and Altai Highlands. This is the greatest continuous expanse of lowland on the globe. To the south and east it is bordered by great mountains and wide, often desert, plateaus and to the north by the icebound margins of the North Polar Sea; only to the west does it come into direct contact with seas open to navigation. Here is the "Ocean Gate" of Europe, between Brittany and Norway. And here the British Isles lie between it and the open ocean, stretching across it for seven hundred miles like a vast breakwater; so that all the ocean traffic of the populous west of the Great Lowland must pass by the shores of Great Britain; and the Strait of Dover is the busiest channel of all the high seas (see Fig. 9, p. 130, above).

... The chief land routes of the Great Lowland meet the ocean routes between Norway and Brittany; and here, chiefly round the southern half of the North Sea, is the chief node of world routes. Here also is the center of the Land Hemisphere of the world, which contains about nine-tenths of the total area of habitable land, so that this nodal region is also in a high degree a central region of the inhabited world. Thus the position of Great Britain here is one of great strategical value in culture, in commerce, and in war; and, while her position as the chief naval power in the Narrow Seas is essential to her own life and security so long as war on the seas is probable, it is nonetheless capable of being regarded as a menace to the European powers. It could not be maintained against a really united Europe, whose land base is so much greater than that formed by the British Isles. . . .

A little more than a century after the voyages of Columbus the first English colonies were founded in North America; and from that time the relations of the British Isles with the New World have been continuously expanding and becoming closer until they are now in some respects more important than her relations with Europe. In the seventeenth century England, and after 1707 Great Britain, steadily became the leader among the colonizing powers, a position which was greatly facilitated by the relative freedom from the continental entanglements and dangers of her rivals which she owed to her insular position and the loss of the last of her medieval possessions on the mainland in the sixteenth century. By the end of the eighteenth century the rivalry between the colonizing powers had ended in the establishment of the decisive naval supremacy of Britain, a supremacy which was unchallenged from 1805 to 1898. During these same centuries the Industrial Revolution transformed a large part of both the internal and external economic and geographical conditions of Britain, the country in which it originated and in which its effects have been most fully felt. The population of Great Britain has increased more than fourfold within the island, while it has also sent out emigrants whose total numbers are greater than those of the population of the homeland at the beginning of this period of expansion; and the transoceanic intercourse and trade has steadily grown, both absolutely and relatively to the total external exchanges, until now it far exceeds that maintained across the Narrow Seas. In the sixteenth century Britain began the modern age as an outlying fragment of Europe. By the eighteenth century she had become the chief outpost of Europe toward the New World beyond the oceans. The growth of her connections with that New World has placed her between it and Europe; and the pull on her of all the links which now attach her to the younger lands is so great that it is arguable that in this twentieth century she is more closely bound to her daughter lands beyond the oceans than to the old Europe of which she was once a part. . . .

The nineteenth century was the century of Great Britain. In no previous century of the modern world was the economic and political leadership of one state so decisive. And there is no present probability that any one country will ever be able to repeat that unquestioned leadership. Note that from 1815 to 1898 the supremacy of the British Navy was never challenged. In 1815 Great Britain was supreme on the high seas of the world and was also the only one of the Great Powers whose home territory had not suffered invasion during the Napoleonic Wars. Europe was exhausted, and the United States still in its infancy. Great Britain alone at that time possessed readily accessible deposits of good coal. Here the Industrial Age began; and it concentrated in this country its first great accumulations of population, of wealth, and of economic and political power, to such an extent that during the first half of the Industrial Age, Great Britain had no serious rival.

At the beginning of the nineteenth century the British Empire outside the home countries consisted almost wholly of a few footholds on the edges of vast empty territories. Canada was British, but was still very weak and threatened by the annexationist policy of some parties in her growing though very youthful neighbor—a policy decisively defeated in 1812. In Australia and South Africa the Empire had only a foothold, and little more than that in India; while New Zealand was still unexplored and unsettled.

The feebleness, slowness, and uncertainty of long oversea communications at that time, made the communications between all these territories and the homeland small and slow; while the general belief, based mainly on the experience with the Thirteen Colonies and on that of Spain and Portugal in Latin America, was that all these colonies would naturally and inevitably separate from the homeland when they grew up. Hence these oversea lands counted for little in the life of Great Britain, certainly far less than did the more accessible and populous countries of Europe.

Also, on the smaller scale of human political and economic organization before the Age of Steamships and Railways, Great Britain was a relatively large country. The huge area of such an empire as that of Russia was so fully counterbalanced by the difficulties and slowness of transport over its vast distances that it counted for less than did France or Great Britain. The infant United States suffered from the same handicap. Until the coming of railways the handicap of mere distance prevented the effective consolidation of any lands of sub-continental magnitude. It may be argued that the breakup of the First British Empire in the latter part of the eighteenth century was due largely to the fact that the Atlantic was then at least six weeks wide, and that therefore no close or frequent intercourse between the peoples or the governments was possible. Such distances made continuous effective cooperation between peoples of distant lands quite impossible; and the strongest states of the period, the Great Powers of Europe, were all based on territories of moderate extent, from the hundred thousand square miles of Prussia or Britain to nearly double that area for Austria and France. Further, it is noteworthy that no state whose territory extended to much more than three hundred miles away from its metropolitan district escaped some movements of secession in such distant areas during the century which preceded the first railway.

The invention and development of the steamship gave a more reliable and rapid means of ocean transport; and it enabled Great Britain to build up her overseas connections and strengthen her influence on all the shores of the oceans. There is some truth in the assertions that the British Empire of today is a product of the steamship; and that it is British because Great Britain was the maritime state which took the lead in the development and exploitation of the steamship. In the same way the railway made it possible to link together effectively the widely separated areas of one continuous land mass in the temperate zones; and the United States is as much a product of the railway as the British Empire is of the steamship.

These mechanical inventions, supplemented by the telegraph and later improvements in communications, changed the whole scale of economic and political geography. They provided some of the material pre-requisites for growth and organization of far vaster powers than the Great Powers of eighteenth century Europe. But only three important states in the world were in a position to make any full use of them during the nineteenth century. The British peoples, primarily by means of the steamship, but in the larger dominions and dependencies also by the railway, built up a vast empire along the seaways; while the United States and Russia each built up a land empire of sub-continental magnitude by means of the railway. . . .

BRITAIN'S INDUSTRIAL LEADERSHIP, 1775-1870

By E. C. Eckel

From chap. 1 of *Coal, Iron and War*, by E. C. Eckel. Copyright 1920 by Henry Holt & Co., N.Y.; reproduced by permission. This author was for many years a geologist in the service of the U.S. government. He served as an engineering officer in the A.E.F. during the First World War.

As late as the middle of the eighteenth century, England's industrial future was by no means certain or assured. The manufacture of woolen goods, taken up much later than in France and Germany, had at length been brought to a point of importance, and the time had definitely gone by when all of England's exports consisted of raw materials, such as tin, lead and wool. But the iron industry had not secured a firm foothold, and . . . it had in common with some other industries, reached a point of extreme depression. . . .

. . . There was apparently nothing on the industrial horizon to offer hope for the British iron industry in particular, and yet it was on the verge of such an expansion as the world had never seen before in connection with any industry in any land. Furthermore, this great expansion was to come not only in this one great basal industry, but it was to spread out, enlarging and remodeling the entire industrial structure of the country, and to ultimately bring about great social and political changes.

. . . In England, and for that matter elsewhere, just before the beginning of the period of rapid expansion in manufactures . . . most industries were still of the household or neighborhood type, carried on by individuals, by families, or by very small groups of employed workers. The power available for manufactures was merely manual, except that in favored localities a small water-power development was in use. The steam engine—of modern type—did not exist. . . . Transportation of commodities was not a matter of prime importance, for when production was on such a very small scale, the commodity could in general be made close to its market. . . . There were of course no railroads, there were no canals, and the common roads were very bad indeed. Coal was used chiefly as a domestic heat producer, and since there were no adequate means for unwatering the coal mines, both its consumption and its production were limited.

Under these conditions the result was a small-scale and widely scattered production of most manufactured commodities. There was no way under which large accumulations of capital could be profitably applied to industry under such conditions; and even if the way had been open, there were few large individual or corporate accumulations of capital to be so used. . . . There was no intimation that within a half-century this type of British industry was to be swept away as completely as had been the ancient civilizations of the East. . . .

The awakening in England. . . . Between 1760 and 1810 the organization of British industry was changed throughout, and the bulk of the changes were at least commenced during the first three decades of that period. During that brief space of time came a series of remarkable improvements in spinning and weaving machinery, which would make it both possible and profitable for the textile industries to group workmen in factories or other large operating units if the necessary power could be secured. And, as if in prompt response to this demand, came the modern steam engine to furnish the power. The steam engine furnished power not only to the manufacturer, but it enabled economic pumping, deepening and hoisting at the coal and iron-ore mines, so that the fuel and ore required by the new industrialism could be provided cheaply and in ample quantities. And, in turn, the engine required better steel and better shopwork than had been needed previously, both of which requirements were met by inventions and improvements. Finally, the grouping of the industries in large units having now become feasible and economically necessary, the transportation of both the raw materials and the product of these large units became a matter of serious importance. So we have the beginning of highway and canal development, and a very little later the commencement of steam navigation and of railroads.

. . . The new organization of transport and industry which was brought about by all these changes had two very distinct though related effects, not only upon the coal and iron trades, but upon most other manufacturing industries. From this time on there were much larger and wider markets for manufactured products and for raw materials, so that tonnages or quantities produced could be greatly increased: and it would also be physically possible and economically necessary to produce these increased tonnages in larger and more closely grouped plants. The day of the small forge and furnace and mill had passed away; the day of the small individual proprietor, too, was passing. From that day on to the present the trend of development in these two regards has never changed; and the huge industrial plants and organizations of today are but logical and necessary results of the changes which took place in British industry over a century ago. . . .

The growth of markets, 1700 to 1775. During this preparatory period the English iron output as earlier stated showed little or no growth. . . . The annual rate of growth from 1700 to 1775 was, so far as can be determined, less than 1 per cent. This rate was far lower than anything which followed for the next hundred years, and it was not until 1890 that English iron growth again fell as low. We have no good population figures prior to 1800, but it seems certain that during this first period the amount of iron produced in England actually showed a decreasing number of pounds per year per capita. At the close of the period the population of Great Britain was probably in the neighborhood of eight million. The annual output of pig iron therefor amounted to perhaps three to five pounds for each person. . . . In the years immediately preceding the [First] World War, the outputs of America, Germany and Great Britain ranged from five hundred to one thousand pounds per capita each year. . . .

The Industrial Revolution in England, 1775-1815. The forty years here grouped can be considered as covering the period of wonderfully rapid development in all industrial lines which is commonly called the Industrial Revolution. . . .

Of the forty years included in this period, Great Britain was at war for thirty. The almost continuous struggle affected industrial development, but it did not cause it. On the contrary, it may be said that *in spite* of these wars industries were able to develop in Great Britain, thanks to certain special features which in her case limited the evil effects of the conflicts. With the exception of one very brief period in 1781, the British Navy held the seas. Behind that shelter crops could be gathered in peace, industries could develop unchecked, and goods could be shipped to the markets of all the world. English contributions in men were not large, and losses were light. At the close of four decades of war Great Britain emerged with a largely increased population, with highly developed industries, and an enormously expanded foreign trade. Most of the American colonies had been lost, but the American trade had been held and even increased.

During those forty years the rate of increase of British iron output averaged about 8 per cent annually. The output had risen, at the close of the period, to over eighty pounds per year per capita. In other lines of manufacture the increase had been almost as great, and much more striking in some ways, so that in considering this period attention is often concentrated disproportionately on the textile industries, for example. The advances in these latter, however, were effects and not causes of the industrial revolution. That had originated in the forcing effects of ready access to wider markets, and had developed thanks to the coal and iron resources of Great Britain. Comparisons with the condition in other countries at the same period brings out this latter point very clearly, and when we come to consider the growth at various periods of the United States, of Germany and of France we will see the same sequence of phenomena repeated in each case.

. . . With increased access to Asiatic and the growing American markets, there would have been steady increase in commercial and manufacturing growth in any case, but this growth would have been at a rate limited by primitive methods of production and transport. What gave this period its entirely new type of activities was the improvement of the steam engine under Watts and Boulton, which offered an efficient source of power. It could be seen immediately that this new power could be developed in large units, so that a great increase and concentration in manufactures were possible. It would be seen almost as quickly that the new power was not fixed in position, like a water wheel or windmill, so that soon it was applied to revolutionizing the methods of transport.

The second point relates to the material conditions under which the new power could best be developed—and this could be seen immediately to require access to coal and iron. At the time Great Britain was the most fortunately located of all the nations with respect to these two necessary materials, for the coal fields of the United States were still unknown and those of Germany were far inland. Steam shipping, then as always, fell to the nation which could supply cheap bunker coal; and Great Britain assumed a lead both in manufactures and in commerce which was retained for over a century.

Undisputed world leadership, 1815-1870. During the fifty-five years which followed Waterloo there was great and relatively steady industrial development throughout the world, in which Great Britain took the leading part. There was, at the close of the Napoleonic Wars, a decade of serious depression. . . . But around 1825 there were compensations for the losses of the wars, and world progress was resumed. The gold supply began to be heavily increased from Russian and Siberian discoveries, the Spanish colonies finally freed took up a new growth, and the United States and Canada spread out far to the westward of their older settled limits. New markets again brought new manufacturing activity.

For the period which followed, Great Britain was the undisputed industrial leader of the world, and her iron and other great industries found at least their share of the market. Cheap bunker coal meant cheap freights, and imported food supplies permitted Great Britain to be turned essentially into one vast workshop. So long as her coal supply was the cheapest and most accessible in the

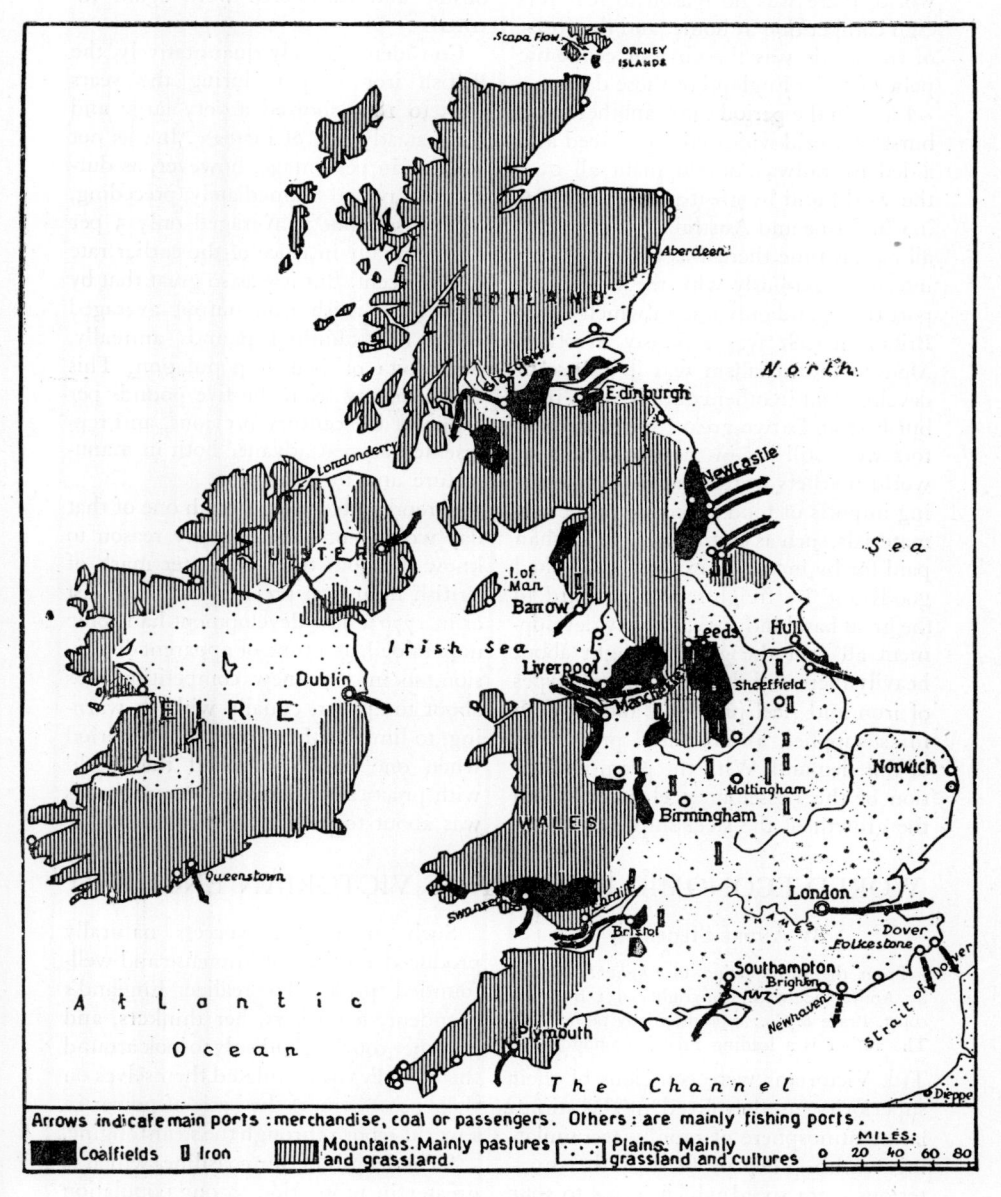

FIG. 11. Physical Foundations of British Economic Development. Note the proximity of coal, iron, and easy access to the sea.

From M. Rajchman, *Europe, An Atlas of Human Geography*. Copyright 1944 by William Morrow & Co., New York; reproduced by permission.

world, there was no reason to fear foreign competition at home, and the freest of free trade was the obvious economic policy for the England of those days. . . .

Later in the period came another great burst of world-wide activity, forced and aided by railway development all over the world and by great gold discoveries in California and Australia. Throughout all of this time there was no war which interfered seriously with the British export trade, and only one in which Great Britain herself was seriously involved. Modern industrialism was in course of development in other countries, it is true, but England's two great future competitors were still far in the rear, so far as world markets were concerned. Increasing imports of food supplies and of raw materials, such as cotton, were more than paid for by increased exports of finished goods and by freights. With regard to the great basal industry, railway development all over the globe brought about heavily increased demand for new types of iron and steel products, and English mills supplied a very large proportion of this demand. With the prompt adoption of the Bessemer steel process, and the growth of the steel ship, British industry and commerce were again favored.

Considered merely quantitatively, the British iron output during the years 1815 to 1870 showed a very large and quite steady rate of increase. It was not so large in percentage, however, as during the period immediately preceding, for we see that it averaged only 5 per cent annually in place of the earlier rate of 8 per cent. But it was so great that by 1870 the British iron output averaged about five hundred pounds annually, per capita of British population. This was a far cry from the five pounds per capita of the century previous, and represented a great advance both in manufacture and in utilization.

It represented also, though one of that day would not have had any reason to know it, about the high-water mark of British industrial preeminence. For just as in 1770 a new development had come unheralded, at a time of apparent depression, so in 1870 new competition was about to appear, equally without warning, to limit further growth. The period when one nation supplied the world with practically all manufactured goods was about to pass.

WORLD ECONOMIC PRIMACY OF VICTORIAN ENGLAND

By André Siegfried

From the Introduction to *England's Crisis*, by André Siegfried. Copyright 1931 by Harcourt, Brace & Co.; reproduced by permission. The author is a leading French economist.

THE Victorians were conscious of their superiority, as they lived in the stimulating atmosphere of rapidly accumulating wealth. They profited by that mysterious extra speed which seems to spur on those who start first, for they were the first fully to exploit the Industrial Revolution which transformed the world, and gave to Europe uncontested economic control. . . .

Such magnificent success naturally produced a feeling of immense and well-founded pride. To realize England's grandeur, her rulers, her thinkers, and even her tourists, had only to look around them. They congratulated themselves on their possession of the basis of power in a world reborn through the steam engine.

"The length of our coastline, which is greater in proportion to our population and territory than in the case of any other nation, assures our strength and maritime superiority. Iron and coal—the nerves of industry—give our manufacturers great advantages over our rivals, and our capital exceeds what they can dispose of. In invention, in energy, in ability, we yield to no one. Our national character, the free institutions under which we live, our liberty of thought and action, our untrammelled press which spreads abroad our discoveries and progress—all these things place us in the forefront of the nations which develop mutually by the free exchange of their products. Is this a country which should fear competition?" In his great speech in the House of Commons in 1846, on the Abolition of the Corn Laws, Sir Robert Peel made the above simple statement of incontestable facts. The preeminence of coal and iron carried everything before it. . . .

Twenty years later, . . . the situation was even more favorable. . . . In 1866 Stanley Jevons . . . wrote as follows: "Unfettered commerce, founded on the basis of our coal resources, has made the several quarters of the globe our willing tributaries. The plains of North America and Russia are our cornfields; Chicago and Odessa our granaries; Canada and the Baltic our forests; Australasia contains our sheep farms, and in South America are our herds of oxen. Peru sends her silver, and the gold of California and Australia flows to London; the Chinese grow tea for us, and coffee, sugar and spice arrive from the East Indian plantations. Spain and France are our vineyards, and the Mediterranean our fruit garden; our cotton grounds, which formerly occupied the Southern United States, are now everywhere in the many regions of the earth. . . ."

At about the same time Sir Charles Dilke, who on leaving the university made a voyage around the world, completed his surveys on a triumphant political note: "In 1866 and 1867 I followed England around the world; everywhere I was in English-speaking or in English-governed lands. . . . The idea which in all my travels has been at once my fellow and my guide is a conception, however imperfect, of the grandeur of our race. . . ."

The initiators of [England's nineteenth century] economic regime . . . clearly realized the sacrifices that would accompany the wholehearted adoption of free trade. The eventual decline of agriculture had to be faced, for a policy of low prices necessitates unrestricted imports, which are apt to be contrary to the best interests of the farming community. The nation, therefore, had to learn to live on imported food, and the factories to use foreign raw materials in steadily growing quantities. These purchases abroad were to be paid for by exports. Since both soil and climate are mediocre in Great Britain, industrialism had to be pushed relentlessly to its utmost limits. There could be no possible hope of economic independence, for not merely had Britain to accept a division of labor which led to specialization, but also the risks which accompany international interdependence. Still, the advantages could be amazing. . . .

International division of labor had to be accepted without question, making England, and to a lesser extent Western Europe, the highly specialized workshop of the world. . . . The colonies were to produce the raw materials which the mother country reserved the right to transform into manufactured goods, and it was assumed that the non-European countries would maintain toward Europe the deferential attitude of a colony toward the motherland. Otherwise there would have been no sense in the concentration on a few square miles in the British Isles of an overdeveloped industry, and the accumulation there of a dense population which in the last resource must depend for its existence less on the products of the soil than on the margin of profit realized by the exporting industries. There was [however] no guarantee that the new countries would not one day wish to manufacture their own raw materials, nor that England's costs of production would always be lower than that of her competitors. . . .

[The predominance of nineteenth century Britain rested also upon] absolute free trade, not only internationally, but within the country itself. Tariff freedom should be accompanied by liberty in labor and wages, which should react spontaneously to any change in prices. It was not without reason that Cobden and his epoch viewed with suspicion the social aspects of the labor problem. The Liberal school considered labor as merchandise, and refused to speak of it except in economic terms. About 1840, when they extolled the free entry of foreign wheat, they argued that if bread were cheaper, wages would be lowered, and thus without affecting the standard of living of the workmen, manufacturing costs could be considerably relieved. If wages had been blocked by social legislation, the reaction on which they counted would not have taken place, and the system would not have worked.

Finally it was essential that coal should enjoy the monopoly bestowed upon it by the steam engine, and that England should maintain her extraordinary lead in this field. In 1860-1870, out of the world's coal production of 130 million tons, England accounted for 80 millions. But would Prussia always turn out only 12 million tons, and the United States only 14 millions?

These hypotheses were readily admitted by contemporary thinkers, but today we realize the imprudence of accepting as normal a mere stage in the economic evolution of the world, and of constructing on this foundation an edifice which it is now difficult to modify. . . .

LONDON, ECONOMIC CAPITAL OF THE WORLD

By Stephen King-Hall

From chap. 1 of *Our Own Times*, by Stephen King-Hall. Nicholson & Watson, London, 1935; reproduced by permission. This author is a prominent British writer on international affairs, associated with the Royal Institute of International Affairs.

The artisans who made Great Britain the workshop of the world were fed and clothed by imported food and wool and cotton from overseas lands. These countries were developed by British credit founded upon the enormous savings derived from the profits of British industry. The development of the overseas lands set in motion prolonged and extensive movements of human migration across the oceans and laid the foundations of new national states. In order to assist international trade the British perfected and operated a technique of world money called the Gold Standard. This device subtly linked together the national economic systems of the principal trading states and was by common consent controlled from London, the capital market place of the world. The British built up and operated a merchant shipping service which carried nearly half of the seaborne trade of the world. Through the words and deeds of its British high-priests the nineteenth century industrial revolution offered men a new world in exchange for the old, and though the acceptance of the offer necessarily involved tremendous readjustments in national social systems and the creation of a new international economic society, men followed the lead of the British and signed the bond, little realizing the consequences of failure to carry out the terms of the cooperative contract. Between 1914 and 1918 they were to discover the nature of the penalties.

One of the most far-reaching consequences of the British policy was that the inhabitants of nineteenth century Britain were prepared to accept the implications of being the world's greatest creditor nation, even though this involved them in an almost complete dependence upon sea-borne food, and hence heavy expenditure upon a navy maintained to ensure the due arrival in British ports of these essential overseas supplies. . . .

BRITISH SEA POWER IN THE VICTORIAN ERA

By Harold and Margaret Sprout

From "Command of the Atlantic Ocean," by Harold and Margaret Sprout, in *Encyclopaedia Britannica*, 1943 edition. Copyright 1943 by Encyclopaedia Britannica, Inc.; reproduced by permission.

The voyages of exploration, dating from the later fifteenth century, shifted the maritime center of gravity from the Mediterranean Sea to the Atlantic Ocean. . . .

Transformation of the Atlantic from a deserted waste into a vast arena of commercial and military activity, profoundly altered power relationships in the Old World. Lands fronting only on the Mediterranean lost in relation to those facing the Atlantic. In a long succession of wars . . . Britain successfully contested the sea power of Spain, Holland and France. As a result of this epic struggle, Great Britain became the dominant Atlantic power. By 1815, after the victorious close of the Napoleonic Wars, British sea power had come literally to envelop the vast land mass of Eurasia-Africa from the North Cape to the coast of China.

This far-flung *Pax Britannica*, as it was sometimes called, rested upon a remarkable combination of political, military, and technological factors. . . . England experienced the industrial revolution earlier than its continental rivals. British imports of foodstuffs and raw materials and exports of manufactures flowed in ever increasing volume along the ship lanes to and from the British Isles. The profits from this traffic were divided between further industrial development and support of the Royal Navy which guarded the life lines of Britain's global empire.

Geography facilitated this task of the Royal Navy. The British Isles interposed a great barrier between northern Europe and the Atlantic Ocean. To reach the ocean all sea-borne commerce to or from that region had to pass through the English Channel or round the stormy northern tip of Scotland. The Rock of Gibraltar, taken by British arms in 1704, guarded the narrow strait which afforded the only marine exit from the Mediterranean down to the opening of the Suez Canal. In Gibraltar, moreover, Britain possessed a formidable military stronghold separating the Atlantic and Mediterranean coasts both of France and of Spain. The island of Malta, which passed into British hands during the Napoleonic Wars, somewhat similarly divided the eastern and western basins of the Mediterranean. Portugal was the only European country which suffered no strategical handicap that rendered it inherently vulnerable to the pressure of British sea power; but Portugal possessed neither the manpower nor the material resources necessary to remain a serious contender for the Atlantic trident after the onset of the Industrial Revolution.

Geography thus compelled most of the transatlantic, and much of the coastal, traffic of Europe to pass through narrow seas under the guns of the Royal Navy. British squadrons, patrolling the Channel and the North Sea within easy reach of their protected anchorages, afforded a constant reminder that British sea power had repeatedly in the past, and presumably could again, cut off northern Europe from sea-borne supplies. British squadrons in the Mediterranean afforded an equally impressive reminder of Britain's presumptive ability to halt the flow of traffic to and from the ports of southern Europe. British France, the country generally regarded during the nineteenth century as Britain's most dangerous maritime rival.

Primitive overland communications prevailing in Europe well down through the nineteenth century enhanced the strategical advantage which Britain derived from geographical position and a

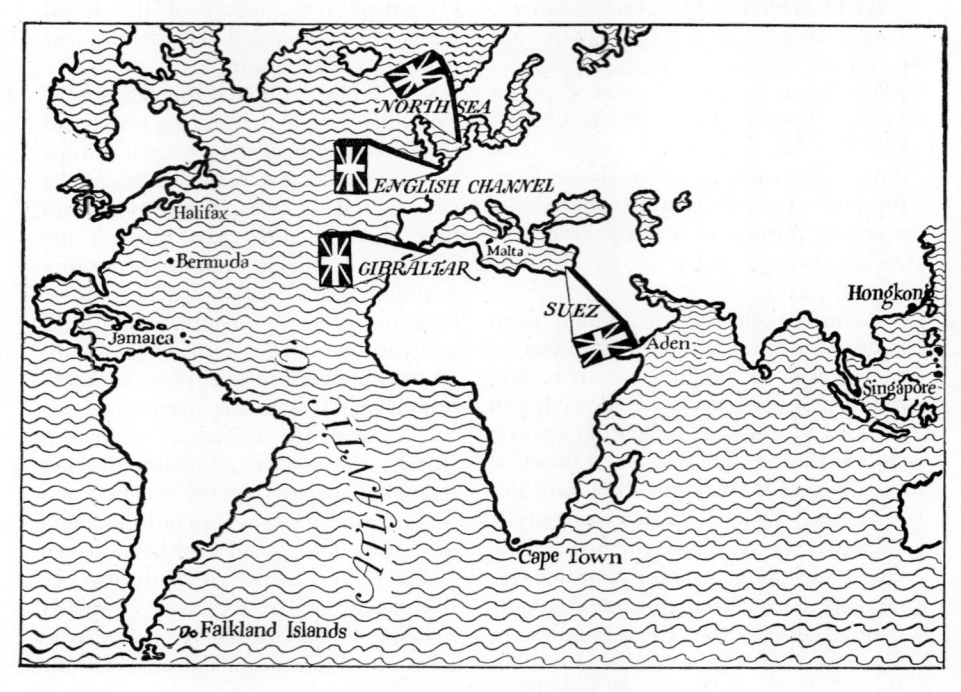

FIG. 12. Geography and British Sea Power.
From H. & M. Sprout, *Toward a New Order of Sea Power*. Copyright 1940 by Princeton University Press.

fleets could usually engage their continental foes without uncovering either the British Isles or a safe line of retreat to their own defended bases. British forces in the Channel and North Sea were favorably situated to interrupt communications between any hostile coalition of northern and western continental powers. By blockading the Strait of Gibraltar, Britain could divide the naval strength of Spain, and especially of strong navy. There were no motor vehicles, almost no all-weather highways, and only the rude beginnings of a railway system upon the European mainland. Large-scale movements of people or freight were next to impossible except by sea—and Great Britain commanded the sea right up to the coast of Europe. There was no escape from the paralyzing effects of sea blockade, and no way of countering the superior mobility which gave British sea power such a leverage on the Continent.

Defensively, Britain's position was likewise secure. The fleets which stood ready to block the ocean portals of Europe, simultaneously barred hostile approach to the British Isles. The automotive torpedo did not appear until 1860, and did not pass into general use for several decades thereafter. There were no submarines to steal through the blockade and raid British merchant shipping on the high sea. There were no bombing planes to rain destruction upon the ships, docks, and factories of Great Britain.

British sea power dominated not only the ocean portals of Europe, but all navigable passages leading from the Atlantic to the Indian and Pacific Oceans as well. Acquisition of the Cape of Good Hope (1805) and of the Falkland Islands (1832) clinched the Royal Navy's hold on the only two sea routes to India and the Far East down to the opening of the Suez Canal. Occupation of a strategical site in the Gulf of Aden at the foot of the Red Sea (1839), together with naval stations at Gibraltar and Malta, assured Britain a secure hold on that marine short-cut which connected the Mediterranean Sea with the Indian Ocean in 1869.

British sea power likewise dominated the western Atlantic down to the end of the nineteenth century. During the American Revolution, it is true, the French fleet of Admiral François J. P. de Grasse had wrested control of North American waters long enough to compel the surrender of Cornwallis at Yorktown in 1781. The resulting establishment of the United States raised a potential threat to Britain's permanent dominance in that region by laying the foundations for an independent, well-located, and ultimately formidable power center in North America. But it was more than a century before the new republic developed into a serious contender for command of the American sea. Meanwhile, from its bases in Nova Scotia, Bermuda and the West Indies, the Royal Navy continued to exert strong influence on sea communications throughout the western Atlantic. Squadrons operating from these bases blockaded United States ports in the War of 1812; and repeatedly thereafter the pressure of British sea power made itself felt at critical stages in Anglo-American diplomacy.

This was especially the case during the long struggle for control of the Central American isthmus and of the Atlantic approaches thereto. Britain already possessed Jamaica, Trinidad and other strategical positions in this region. In addition, British leaders coveted the Spanish Island of Cuba which screened the gulf coast of the United States in much the same manner as the British Isles covered the coastline of northern Europe. Another British objective was to control the various routes for a ship canal to the Pacific. Success in those aims would have strengthened British influence throughout the Western Hemisphere, and in particular would have given Britain a leverage on the United States comparable to that which it already held over Europe.

American statesmen were awake to this danger. In framing the Monroe Doctrine (1823), in which the United States warned the monarchies of continental Europe to keep their hands off the newly liberated Spanish colonies in the Western Hemisphere, Secretary of State John Quincy Adams rejected overtures for a joint Anglo-American declaration, lest such a move estop the United States later from turning the Monroe Doctrine against Great Britain itself. That contingency actually arose in the 1840's when Britain and the United

States began a seesaw struggle for key positions in the Caribbean and in Central America, on the outcome of which depended the future command of the western Atlantic.

An uneasy truce was reached in the Clayton-Bulwer Treaty of 1850. British pressure in this region was further eased from time to time by the diversionary effects of the Crimean War and subsequent European developments involving British interests. The phenomenal rise of United States industrial and military potential during and after the Civil War (1861-1865), culminating in rapid naval expansion toward the close of the century, confronted Britain with the choice either of steadily strengthening its naval establishments in the American seas, or of gradually losing command of those waters and therewith any possibility of controlling the future isthmian canal.

European complications again resolved this dilemma in favor of the United States. At the close of the Napoleonic Wars, the Royal Navy was safely superior to all continental rivals. The long struggle had produced no radical changes in naval design. Technical stability meant slow obsolescence, a decided advantage to the leading naval power. By mid-century, however, a technical revolution was in full swing. The transition from sails to steam, from solid shot to explosive shells, from smoothbores to rifles, from wooden walls to armor—all these and other technical advances speeded obsolescence, and gave Britain's continental rivals a chance to compete on more nearly even terms. These technical developments also produced unsettling effects on political relations and behavior, which in turn stimulated naval expansion. The resulting sense of insecurity was further aggravated by the growth of German power potential after the Franco-Prussian War (1870), and by the world-wide struggle for colonies, raw materials, protected markets and other imperialistic phenomena, which accompanied the later stages of the industrial revolution. . . .

BRITISH SEA POWER IN THE WRITINGS OF CAPTAIN ALFRED THAYER MAHAN

By Harold and Margaret Sprout

From chap. 1 of *Toward a New Order of Sea Power*, by Harold and Margaret Sprout. Rev. ed. Copyright 1943 by Princeton University Press, Princeton.

The growth and achievements of British power, especially British naval power, made a deep impression upon the thinking of Captain Alfred Thayer Mahan, USN, an American naval officer who became in the 1890's the world's foremost writer on sea power and the influence of sea power upon history.

According to Mahan, history taught that nations may rise or decline but never stand still. Expansion—political, economic, cultural—was the essence of national greatness. To support a program of expansion, a government must have access to accumulated wealth. A large and flourishing foreign commerce was the surest means of accumulating wealth. But a vigorous and growing foreign commerce was not to be had merely for the asking. To compete successfully in the world-wide struggle for markets, a country must maintain a large merchant marine. In addition, such a marine would itself contribute materially to a nation's wealth, by sharing in a carrying trade that would otherwise go to the ships of competing nations.

These valuable assets all required protection. To provide its merchantmen with secure havens on their outward as well as on their homeward voyages, a country must have oversea colonies. To guard these vessels upon the high seas, a strong navy was indispensable. Such a navy was likewise essential to defend the sea approaches to the mother country and to its oversea colonies. And the colonies, in turn, provided sites for bases and stations to support the navy overseas.

While a strong navy was necessary to guarantee security to a country's shipping, a prosperous merchant marine was, at the same time, the backbone of its naval power. Such a marine fostered seafaring and maritime industries. Merchant shipping, a seafaring class, and strong maritime industries provided a "shield of defensive power behind which" a people could gain time in an emergency to "develop its reserve of strength." And in countries with a representative form of government, such maritime interests could be depended upon, in turn, to exert the political pressure and influence necessary to keep the navy at a high standard of strength and excellence.

Mahan's interpretation of history was largely and more or less admittedly rationalized and generalized from the simultaneous rise of the British Navy and the British Empire. The principal sea routes of the world had become the internal communications of that Empire. The security of those communications which radiated in every direction from the British Isles, crossing and crisscrossing all the oceans and larger seas, depended ultimately upon armed force. And that force was supplied in the main by the British Navy which, as previously noted, had by the nineteenth century come to exercise a virtually world-wide command of the seas.

England's naval dominance Mahan attributed largely, though not quite exclusively, to certain strategic dispositions and tactical formations which, after generations of trial and error, had come to govern British naval operations in war. England's remarkable security, he pointed out, had not been achieved by dispersing the British Navy along the coasts of the British Isles or by distributing its ships among the oversea colonies. The British Admiralty in time of war had not guarded the Empire's global sea communications by scattering its men-of-war around the world by ones and twos. Such operations were sometimes useful; but they were distinctly secondary to the primary objective which was to search out the enemy's forces, and to destroy or drive them from the seas, as a necessary preliminary to the wholesale destruction of enemy commerce, and to the protection of England's own merchant shipping upon the high seas.

From his interpretation of British naval history, Mahan deduced a fundamental principle: the doctrine of concentration of power; in its applied form, the doctrine of battle-fleet supremacy. This doctrine he endorsed and supported with reasoning which ran somewhat as follows: Local floating defenses might supplement land forces in repelling an invader; but these could neither prevent nor break up sea blockades. Solitary roving cruisers might raid the enemy's coast and commerce, and conceivably do a great deal of damage. But commerce raiding could never in itself yield decisive results. And it could not even seriously harass the enemy unless one's cruisers could restock and refit at ports conveniently near to the heavily traveled lanes of enemy commerce.

History, as Mahan read it, taught the inescapable lesson that this kind of hit-and-run guerrilla warfare, while often a useful supplement to, was not an effective substitute for, command of the sea by a massed fleet of line-of-battle ships capable of destroying the enemy's armed forces or of driving them to cover; of blockading their seaports and thereby disrupting their oversea communications at the source; and of supporting one's own cruisers patrolling the sea routes and escorting one's own transports and cargo shipping through zones of special danger.

It is important to remember, however, though all too frequently forgotten or ignored, that British sea power rested upon a number of things besides a big navy and a particular strategic doctrine. England owed its global command of the seas also and quite as much to a remarkable and unique concurrence of conditions—geographical, technological, economic, and political—which began to take shape in the seventeenth century and lasted down to about the close of the nineteenth century. Without this favorable setting a vastly greater expenditure of military effort would have been required to achieve the same preponderance of power, if indeed it would have been achieved at all.

The first requisite of military power is a secure primary base. Countries vary widely in the natural strength of their frontiers, and hence in the proportion of their national effort that must be devoted to purely defensive purposes. England was most favorably situated in this respect. England alone among the European powers enjoyed the decisive advantage of insularity. The British Isles provided a national seat of military power of great natural strength, one that could be made secure without the continuous and heavy outlays that were necessary for the defense of European land frontiers.

There was never any doubt in the mind of Mahan that England's insularity had played a vital role in the spectacular rise of British sea power. He repeatedly stressed this point in his historical accounts of England's successive and successful struggles with the sea power of Spain, Holland, and France. In one of his most emphatic utterances. Mahan declared: "History has conclusively demonstrated the inability of a state with even a single continental frontier to compete in naval development with one that is insular, although of smaller population and resources."

British fleets also enjoyed secure havens overseas. Through a remarkable combination of muddling and foresight, England gradually acquired during the eighteenth and nineteenth centuries a world-wide network of advanced naval bases. Almost without exception these outlying stations resembled the British Isles in their natural defensive strength under conditions then prevailing. One of the earliest to pass into British hands was the Rock of Gibraltar, wrested from Spain in 1704. Connected with the mainland by only a narrow isthmus, this massive natural fortress had all the advantages of complete insularity. Malta, occupied during the Napoleonic Wars, was an island in the central narrows of the Mediterranean. The port of Alexandria, eventually to become a main citadel of British power in the eastern Mediterranean, lay on the Nile delta flanked by formidable deserts.

The Cape of Good Hope, which passed into British hands in 1805, had no overland communication whatever with the European world. Aden, occupied in 1839, was set upon a desert coast at the foot of the Red Sea, with land access only across the forbidding waterless waste of southern Arabia. Ceylon, on which another British depot developed, was an island off the tip of India. The British position in India itself was protected by the lofty Himalayan mountain mass which stood athwart the land approaches from Central Asia. A long chain of British island possessions extended southeastward from Singapore to Australia and New Zealand. And British shipping had, in the island of Hong Kong, a secure haven off the great port of Canton in the China Sea.

In American waters the situation was much the same. Bermuda, several West Indian stations, and the Falkland Islands provided England easily defended bases at safe distances from the mainland. Halifax in Nova Scotia was England's only continental American base easily accessible from the hinterland. Thus, from Canada to Cape Horn, and from the British Isles to the China coast, British warships and merchantmen were always within reach of a haven of refuge and supply. These protected ports, of which there were many more besides those specifically mentioned, were with very few exceptions invulnerable to attack from the rear; and as long as British fleets held sway upon the oceans, they were reasonably secure against attack by sea.

This global network of British naval stations possessed not only great defensive strength but incomparable offensive value as well. Admiral Lord Fisher once declared that England held the "five keys" which "lock up the world" —Dover, Gibraltar, Alexandria, the Cape of Good Hope, and Singapore. This figure of speech aptly summed up both the nature and the geographical extent of the influence wielded by the British Navy at the apex of its power.

The British Isles were the master key to this whole structure of power. England and Scotland lay between northern Europe and the Atlantic Ocean. This forced the deep-sea commerce of all northern Europe, from the farthest reaches of the Baltic, to pass through the narrow Strait of Dover under the guns of the British Navy. The only alternative was to make the long and difficult detour around to the north of Scotland with no assurance even then of escaping British cruisers patrolling those northern waters. British squadrons from a central position within easy reach of their home dockyards could blockade the Atlantic and Channel ports of France, close the Dover Strait, patrol the North Sea, and even make sweeps into the Baltic. By concentrating superior force in these narrow seas, England could prevent the junction of hostile forces from northern and from western Europe, and pretty thoroughly disrupt the flow of sea-borne commerce to and from the Continent all the way from St. Petersburg to Brest. And the same British forces which denied continental access to the Atlantic, simultaneously provided a strong shield against counterattack either on the British Isles or on British cargo shipping in the Atlantic.

The Rock of Gibraltar dominated even more completely the narrow strait which provided the only marine exit from the Mediterranean prior to the construction of the Suez Canal. All sea-borne commerce to and from eastern Spain, southern France, the whole of Italy, the Balkan peninsula, the Levant, and the Black Sea hinterland had to pass through this bottleneck. The Rock also constituted a formidable military barrier between the Atlantic and Mediterranean coasts of France and of Spain. The British fortress of Malta constituted a similar barrier dominating the flow of commerce between the eastern and western basins of the Mediterranean.

The opening of the Suez Canal in 1869 placed a heavier burden on British sea power but in no sense weakened England's grip on the ports of southern Europe. The British Admiralty already possessed a naval station at Aden near the Red Sea exit into the Indian Ocean. Alexandria was later developed into a strong base near the northern terminus of the Canal. These positions, together with Malta and Gibraltar, commanded every narrow strait along this short-cut to India and the Far East, which, though legally an international thoroughfare, was actually in a military sense a British waterway.

Thus through its hold on four narrow seas—the Suez Canal, the Mediterranean, the English Channel, and the North Sea—Great Britain could virtually dictate the terms of Europe's access to the "outer world." Under conditions prevailing until near the end of the nineteenth century, control of these four narrow seas had political and military effects felt around the globe. As long as no important center of naval power existed outside Europe, England's grip on the ocean portals of that continent constituted in effect a global command of the seas.

Mahan eventually grasped the unique character of this *Pax Britannica*, but only after it had begun seriously to crumble under the impact of changing conditions. In 1910 he pointed out, with reference to German naval expansion and its menace to Great Britain, that England defended its scattered dominions and colonies "not indeed by local superiorities in their several waters, an object at once unattainable and needless, but by concentrated superiority of naval force in Europe, which as yet remains the base, at once of defense and of attack, as far as other quarters of the world are concerned." The following year he observed that "so long as the British fleet can maintain and assert superiority in the North Sea and around the British Isles, the entire imperial system stands secure."

This incomparable position vis-à-vis Europe was, as we have already emphasized, the key to England's global sea power. Because of its hold on the ocean portals of Europe, the British Admiralty rarely had to station especially strong squadrons in the more distant seas. But the bases were there when needed. British detachments operating from Halifax, Bermuda, and the West Indies maintained a tight blockade of United States ports in the War of 1812. From the Falkland Islands and from the Cape of Good Hope, British naval power dominated the older sea routes to India and the Far East. From other positions already described, British sea power held every passage leading into the Indian Ocean, and penetrated into the farthest reaches of the Pacific.

There were some exceptions and qualifications of course. Britain's command of the seas approached, but never quite attained, the point of incontestability. No sea blockade was ever completely effective. The British Navy passed through periods of decay and mismanagement. There was always a possibility, usually a fairly remote one, that the continental powers would successfully combine against England. A momentary loss of command in the Atlantic contributed materially to the winning of American independence. Certain marine areas were never brought permanently under British naval domination. And other qualifying details might be added. But such details, even in the aggregate, detract but little from a totality of power and a leverage on world politics without precedent in naval annals; a position which, for geographical reasons, no other power could hope to approach; and a position which even Great Britain itself could not sustain after the rise of modern fleets in the Western Hemisphere and the Far East, and after the rise of submarine and air power in the opening decades of the twentieth century.

BRITAIN'S CHANGING WORLD POSITION, 1890-1914

By Harold and Margaret Sprout

From chap. 2 of *Toward a New Order of Sea Power*, by Harold and Margaret Sprout. Rev. ed. Copyright 1943 by Princeton University Press.

Mahan's master work on sea power, and the subsequent books and essays that streamed from his hurrying pen, had world-wide repercussions on naval development and world politics. Mahan's interpretation of history excited expansionist forces already stirring in Europe, in America, and in the Far East. His strategic ideas, derived largely from British naval history, were accepted as precepts of universal application and utility, without qualification as to time or place. And the impact of these ideas was widely felt in accelerated naval development which, inside of two decades, was to alter profoundly the balance of naval power, with political repercussions in every quarter of the globe.

This changing order of sea power was but one of many shifts in international power relations which accompanied the spread of the industrial revolution. For several generations British coal and manufactures had dominated the world economy. But industrialization had gradually taken root elsewhere, often with the aid of British capital. In the closing years of the nineteenth century these new industries in Europe, America, and elsewhere were rapidly becoming serious rivals of the older mines and factories of the British Isles.

The growth of mutually competitive industrial economies on the European Continent, in the United States, and in other lands, inaugurated a new era of imperialism which in certain respects closely resembled the mercantilistic imperialism of the eighteenth century. This new imperialism received in the 1890's a tremendous stimulus from the vision of power, glory, profits, and moral destiny, set forth with crusading zeal in Mahan's prolific writings. These as well as the trend of political and economic events, stimulated the growth of navies which supported and at the same time fostered the new imperialism. The rising wave of imperialism further accelerated the pace of naval expansion the world over. And this in turn undermined the historic world-wide naval dominance of Great Britain.

That dominance rested not only upon British ships and sailors, but also upon the incomparable strategical position of the British Isles. Battle-fleet supremacy in the North Sea, in the English Channel, in the Mediterranean, and in the adjacent reaches of the eastern Atlantic, gave England naval dominance over the powers of continental Europe. As long as those continental European powers were the only rivals possessing strong navies, this local primacy gave Britain a virtually world-wide command of the seas.

The rise of Japanese naval power undermined England's strategic dominance, and hence political influence, in the Far East. Through one of the ironies of history, Englishmen themselves contributed to their own eclipse in the Pacific. British shipyards in the 1880's and 1890's built one warship after another for Japan. And British naval officers were loaned to the Mikado's government to teach the elements of naval science and administration.

It could be argued, of course, that someone else would have built the ships and provided the advice and technical assistance if England had refused. It could also be argued that Great Britain needed a counterpoise to Russian imperialism which was at that time encroaching on British preserves in Asia.

But all that does not alter the fact that a modern Japanese fleet in Asiatic waters fundamentally changed the strategic situation to the ultimate serious disadvantage of Great Britain; that British squadrons guarding the English Channel, the North Sea, and the Mediterranean no longer *ipso facto* dominated the sea communications of the Far East.

Meanwhile, parallel developments were taking place in the Western Hemisphere. Prior to the Civil War, the United States had both a navy and a naval policy. But neither our navy nor our naval policy affected the main currents of world politics in any large or continuing manner. Even within the Western Hemisphere, England rather than the United States was the dominant naval power most of the time. The Civil War brought about a mushroom naval development in the United States. But that was followed by rapid deterioration and a prolonged eclipse. American naval reconstruction commenced in the 1880's, and by 1890 was acquiring some momentum. Mahan's writings, in conjunction with other influences, accelerated the pace and changed the direction of American naval development. By 1898 the United States Navy had evolved from a handful of commerce-raiding cruisers and coast-defense monitors into a rapidly growing fleet of first-class seagoing battleships. Control of Europe's narrow seas no longer assured to Great Britain the command of the American seas.

Only by progressively strengthening its oversea squadrons could the British Admiralty have preserved even a semblance of its former primacy in American and Far Eastern waters. Whatever the desires and inclinations of British naval authorities, developments nearer home soon rendered such a course practically impossible. . . .

ANGLO-AMERICAN REORIENTATION

By Harold and Margaret Sprout

From "Command of the Atlantic Ocean," by Harold and Margaret Sprout, in *Encyclopaedia Britannica*, 1943 edition. Copyright 1943 by Encyclopaedia Britannica, Inc.; reproduced by permission.

In the late 1870's, France, Russia, Italy, and then Germany all began modernizing and expanding their navies. For a time the British government tended to regard France and Russia as the most dangerous rivals. With that combination in view, the British Admiralty in 1889 publicly announced a "two-power standard" as the irreducible minimum to ensure Britain's control of European waters and of the long sea routes to India and the Far East. Gradually, however, British anxiety was transferred to Germany. The British watched German industrial and military growth with misgivings, heightened after 1890 by the aggressive overtones of German foreign policy. When Germany in 1900 launched a naval building program designed to break Britain's exclusive grip on the European seas, the effect was to bring about a fundamental reorientation of British policy.

To meet the rising German threat required the utmost concentration of British naval strength in European waters. Simultaneously to contest in the American seas the rapidly growing naval power of the United States was out of the question. Britain had no choice but to recognize American primacy in the western Atlantic; and British statecraft proceeded with considerable finesse to derive from this necessity as much benefit as possible. A continuing and generally successful effort was made to settle outstanding disputes with the United States and to cultivate American goodwill in order that that country might safely be stricken from Britain's list of potential enemies. In the Hay-Pauncefote Treaty of 1901, British statesmen even relinquished their long-cherished ambition to share in the control of the future isthmian canal. And by 1904 the British Admiralty had begun reducing its squadrons in American waters.

The first fruits of this reorientation were soon apparent. When European sympathies ranged almost solidly against Britain during the Boer War (1899-1902), American statesmen countered with quiet but unwavering diplomatic support. Thereafter, as crisis followed crisis in Europe, and as the German Empire made increasingly menacing gestures towards the Western Hemisphere the weight of the United States was ranged consistently on the side of Great Britain in a manner that strongly suggested the possibility of an Anglo-American naval coalition if such were necessary to hold the Atlantic against the steadily encroaching menace from the European Continent. . . .

THE ANGLO-JAPANESE ALLIANCE

BY HAROLD AND MARGARET SPROUT

From chap. 2 of *Toward a New Order of Sea Power*, by Harold and Margaret Sprout. Rev. ed. Copyright 1943 by Princeton University Press.

GREAT BRITAIN's growing commitments in Europe and shrinking power overseas profoundly affected international politics in the Far East. Security for British interests in Asia was sought through a multilateral equipoise stable enough to support the *status quo* in that remote sector. Englishmen encouraged our annexation of the Philippine Islands in 1898, regarding the United States as a friendly steadying influence in the Far East. When they failed to secure a formal alliance with the United States, they entered into a military partnership with Japan, directed first against Russia, later against Germany. And in various other ways they labored to fashion a political substitute for their former naval dominance in the Far East.

BRITISH SEA POWER IN THE 20TH CENTURY

BY HAROLD AND MARGARET SPROUT

From "Command of the Atlantic Ocean," by Harold and Margaret Sprout, in *Encyclopaedia Britannica*, 1943 edition; reproduced by permission.

THE German menace had the further effect of suppressing at least temporarily the ancient rivalry between Great Britain and France. The Anglo-French Entente of 1904 left Britain free to develop a fleet base at Alexandria near the Mediterranean terminus of the Suez Canal; and recognized a French protectorate over Morocco except for a coastal strip facing Gibraltar. This understanding was accompanied by marked improvement in Anglo-French naval relations, permitting withdrawal of British fleet units from the Mediterranean. The entente thus brought about a further strengthening of the northern sea frontier; but, like the Anglo-Japanese Alliance and the parallel if less formal understanding with the United States, this step, too, represented a dissipation of that exclusive command of the Atlantic which had once been the cornerstone of British naval policy.

While bargaining for allies and simplifying their strategic commitments, British statesmen steadily enlarged and strengthened the Royal Navy. Despite Germany's utmost efforts, the Royal Navy held its lead. In first-class capital ships, then regarded as the true index of naval power, the British fleet outranked Germany's in 1914 by a ratio of three to two. And the Anglo-French coalition, to which was added the naval resources of Russia, Japan, later Italy, and eventually the United States, held an overwhelming preponderance of naval force measured in tons and guns.

Following the outbreak of war in 1914, the Allies, under the leadership of Great Britain, skillfully translated this mathematical primacy into an effective command of the Atlantic and adjoining narrow seas. Within a few days their naval forces drove the German merchant flag from the high seas. Within a few weeks the German oversea cruiser squadrons were run down and destroyed or driven to cover. The main British fleet screened the transport of the British army to France, while the German fleet lay at anchor or cruised near its home bases in the North Sea, unwilling to risk a decisive battle and powerless to break up the blockade which the Allies drew tighter during the winter of 1914-1915.

In February 1915, the German command countered the Allied blockade with a submarine offensive against merchant shipping in a "war zone" surrounding the British Isles. Shortage of submarines, threats of American intervention, and other factors presently led to partial relaxation of this initial assault on Allied communications, but not until it had revealed the frightful commerce-destroying ability of the submarine, previously regarded with scepticism as a more or less useful auxiliary of the fighting fleets.

The temporary slackening of the submarine offensive was followed by increased activity on the part of the German High Sea Fleet. Late in May 1916 the German and British fleets met in the Battle of Jutland. In this, the only major fleet action of the whole war, the fate of the Allies hung momentarily in the balance. A decisive defeat, shattering British sea power and transferring command of the Atlantic to Germany, would have constituted irretrievable disaster. No such catastrophe occurred. The German fleet, with skillful handling and exceptional luck, managed to inflict serious injury and then escape, though not without substantial casualties, from the annihilation that would certainly have been the outcome of a finish fight with Britain's Grand Fleet.

The Battle of Jutland apparently convinced the German command of its inability in this way to smash the Anglo-French command of the Atlantic and thereby to raise the blockade. Only the submarine remained. U-boat construction was stepped up. The scope and area of submarine operations were gradually enlarged. Finally in February 1917 the German command ordered a general submarine offensive against all merchant shipping, neutral as well as belligerent, in a desperate gambling attempt to starve Britain into surrender before an effective anti-submarine defense could be developed, and before the eventually certain intervention of the United States could turn the tide for the Allies.

This plan almost succeeded. When the United States entered the war in April 1917, the U-boats were sinking merchant ships at an appalling rate. Existing defensive measures—chiefly arming merchantmen and patrolling the ship lanes—were proving totally inadequate. The logical recourse was to convoy cargo ships in groups under armed escort, a device already tried and proved in the case of troopships. Now with American bases and naval reinforcements, a general convoy system became feasible and was successfully put into operation. In the intensified war against the U-boats, raids were carried out against the German submarine bases, mine fields were laid across the two Atlantic exits from the North Sea, and acoustical devices were developed for detecting the presence of submerged U-boats. With the aid of these and other defensive measures, foodstuffs, raw materials, and munitions continued to flow along the Atlantic sea lanes to the British Isles, across the Channel to France, and through the Mediterranean to Italy and the Near East. An American army, eventually 2,000,000 strong, was ferried safely across the Atlantic to the battlefields of Europe; and simultaneously the Allies drew steadily tighter the blockade of the Central Powers, which, starving their peoples and their war industries, prepared the way for their political and military collapse in 1918.

The victory of 1918 completely altered the balance of naval forces in the Atlantic. The destruction of German sea power removed the threat which had chained the Royal Navy to European waters; which had suppressed the ancient antagonism of France and Britain; which had driven Great Britain and America into something approaching an alliance; which had compelled the Royal Navy to relinquish without a struggle its primacy in the American seas. Temporarily at least, British sea power held exclusive and undisputed sway over the eastern Atlantic and adjoining narrow seas. And following the victory over Germany there were accumulating indications that British statesmen and their naval advisers looked forward to early restoration of their former global command of the seas.

This trend had disturbing repercussions on Anglo-American relations. The war had caused an upsurge of navalism within the United States. Congress in 1916 had voted a construction program designed to give the United States a "navy second to none." Late in 1918 the administration had thrown its weight behind a supplementary building program which, if and when carried out, would have given the United States incomparably the strongest navy in the world. These mutually conflicting aims caused the close wartime association of Britain and America to cool rapidly after the Armistice. Anglo-American relations began to show an alarming tendency to revert to their nineteenth century pattern of mutual distrust and animosity.

One especially aggravating factor from the American point of view was the continued existence of the Anglo-Japanese Alliance. The reason for that pact had disappeared with the defeat of Germany, but neither party seemed willing to terminate it while the United States went on expanding its navy. American statesmen, in turn, were just as unwilling to modify their naval plans as long as the Anglo-Japanese Alliance remained in force, since its mere existence was felt to involve at least a theoretical possibility of simultaneous attack in two oceans.

The Washington Conference for the limitation of armaments (1921-1922) broke this deadlock. The Anglo-Japanese Alliance was abrogated; naval building programs were drastically curtailed; a large number of older capital ships were scrapped; and the British, American and Japanese battleship fleets were stabilized in the ratio of 5-5-3. The United States, in effect, recognized Britain's paramount strategic interest throughout the eastern Atlantic and European narrow seas. Britain, in turn, tacitly disavowed any intention of contesting United States control of the American seas.

The consequent improvement of Anglo-American relations opened the way for a mutually advantageous redisposition of naval forces. The United States gradually shifted almost all its major fleet units to the Pacific. Britain postponed indefinitely the planned reestablishment of a battleship fleet in that ocean and concentrated British naval strength in European waters. Whether or not these dispositions reflected some definite understanding between the two governments, it is certain that the United States fleet came widely to be regarded as a symbol of Anglo-American solidarity in the Pacific, and British sea power in European waters as America's first line of defense in the Atlantic.

The Washington Conference achieved no such happy solution of European naval problems. Irreconcilable differences between France and Britain on the one hand, and France and Italy on the other, appeared early in the negotiations. These differences grew out of the general failure to establish a stable power equilibrium in Europe after the war. At the outset it was largely an Anglo-French controversy. The British did not wholly share French fears of future aggression from a resurgent vengeful Germany. They believed rigorous repression of that country would seriously retard economic recovery. The prospect of French military hegemony over the continent aroused deep-seated opposition. The British ideal was still avoidance of military guarantees, a balance of power on the Continent, and a two-power naval standard for European waters.

No continental power was able, or even seriously disposed at that time, to contest Britain's two-power standard in the capital-ship category. But capital ships were no longer the only index of naval power. The late war had hastened the development of two new weapons which were to play an increasing role in the control of the seas, especially narrow seas such as the Mediterranean, the Channel, and the North Sea.

One of these new weapons, the submarine, had forced Britain to the brink of disaster, despite the Royal Navy's command of the ocean's surface. The other new weapon, the airplane, promised to develop into an even greater threat not only to shipping but also to the ports and industrial installations of the British Isles. The terms of peace prohibited Germany from possessing these newer weapons. But France suffered no such restriction and was geographically situated to use both submarines and planes against Britain with maximum effect. These weapons were consequently valuable diplomatic levers to be relinquished only in return for British guarantees to France. Moreover, if France were left to depend solely on its own defensive resources, a larger force of cruisers and destroyers would be required to ensure safe passage across the Mediterranean for French colonial troops from Africa.

Another source of French intransigence was Italy's emergence as a serious contender for control of the Mediterranean. The Italian Navy was decidedly inferior to that of France, but the Italian government insisted on the right to match France in every category of naval craft. Since Italy was exclusively a Mediterranean country, whereas France fronted on the Atlantic as well, to accept naval parity with Italy was equivalent, in French eyes, to surrendering control of the Mediterranean, and with it the assured flow of supply and reinforcements from Africa.

The French finally yielded with respect to capital ships and aircraft carriers, and in these two categories accepted parity with Italy and tonnage quotas low enough to preserve Britain's two-power standard for European waters. But every proposal to limit submarines and aircraft broke against the unsatisfied French demand for guarantees. Neither France nor Great Britain could agree on cruiser quotas acceptable to each other or to the other naval powers. The most that could be achieved was a qualitative restriction limiting individual cruisers to 10,000 tons displacement and 8-inch guns. Thus the way was left open for renewal of competitive warship construction.

The Fascist revolution of 1922 provided just the stimulus needed to produce this result. To the Fascists the Mediterranean was Italy's *mare nostrum*. Mussolini boasted his determination to carve from its borderlands a modern counterpart of the classical Roman empire. Since control of the Mediterranean was an essential feature of his imperial pipe dream, Mussolini had no interest in naval limitation save as a means of cheaply improving Italy's naval position at the expense of France and Great Britain.

In 1927 the United States sponsored a second naval conference, called to deal specifically with the cruiser problem. Neither France nor Italy took any part in this conference, which was thus foredoomed to failure. Its sessions, held at Geneva, quickly deteriorated into an Anglo-American wrangle in which technical arguments and considerations were allowed to revive the ancient feud over freedom of the seas, and to recast the two great Atlantic powers in their abandoned roles of naval rivals and potential enemies.

A change of government in both countries inspired a fresh start. A third conference was held at London in 1930. Here some of the damage to Anglo-American relations was repaired, and a provisional solution of the cruiser controversy was achieved. But the continued intransigence of France and Italy still prevented any stable adjustment of naval relations among the Atlantic and Mediterranean powers.

Likewise inimical to this end was the naval resurgence of Germany. Under the Treaty of Versailles Germany was forbidden to acquire any modern armored ship displacing over 10,000 tons. To circumvent this restriction, German naval architects created the so-called pocket-battleships, *Deutschland, Admiral Scheer,* and *Admiral Graf Spee.* These ships, designed as commerce raiders, technically conformed to the Versailles limitation, but their 11-inch guns definitely outclassed the 8-inch weapons allowed on cruisers built by signatories of the Washington Naval Treaty. These ships upset existing arrangements for the protection of commerce, compelled every Atlantic power to reconsider its naval program, and in conjunction with other developments started a fresh cycle of competitive building.

One of these contributing causes was the Nazi revolution of 1933, followed by Hitler's denunciation of the Versailles Treaty. Naval rearmament accelerated rapidly under the Nazis. Profiting from past experience, they concentrated mainly on commerce-raiding weapons. Their battle-cruisers, *Scharnhorst* and *Gneisenau* (laid down in 1934), and even their great battleships, *Bismarck* and *Tirpitz* (1937), were conceived less as components of a massed fleet than as super-raiders for attacking convoys on the high sea. The same objective was implicit in Germany's resumption of submarine building on a large scale. Yet in the face of these preparations manifestly directed primarily against Great Britain, Hitler won London's consent in 1935 to further German naval expansion up to 35 per cent of British strength, with the possibility of eventual parity in submarines!

The Ethiopian crisis later in 1935 focused attention on the deterioration which was taking place in the strategical position of France and Britain in the Mediterranean. Both London and Paris showed the greatest reluctance to take any steps which might force hostilities with Italy and doubts were expressed in many quarters regarding the Royal Navy's continued ability to hold the Mediterranean against the air and sea power of Italy.

Formation of the Rome-Berlin Axis in 1936 formally linked the growing danger in northern and in southern waters, and inclined the naval balance still more strongly against the Atlantic powers. But this event, followed by rapid deterioration of world conditions, provided the necessary stimulus for strenuous if tardy counter measures which were well under way when war intervened in September 1939.

The first phase of the ensuing battle for the Atlantic lasted until the fall of France in June 1940. During this period the Anglo-French coalition drove German merchant shipping from the Atlantic, and maintained a fairly effective long-range blockade on the general model of the previous war. The German-controlled zone in the North Sea was somewhat broader than in 1914-1918, mainly because of the maritime role now played by shore-based aviation. It was consequently more difficult to intercept German blockade-runners entering or leaving the North Sea. The blockade in the Mediterranean also fell somewhat short, thanks to Italy's "non-belligerent" help in forwarding sea-borne supplies to Germany. But these handicaps were offset by the close cooperation of the United States and other oversea countries in the use of various devices—pre-emptive buying, "navicerts," etc.—designed to cut at the source all traffic with the Axis.

On the defensive side, the initial non-belligerency of Italy postponed a show-down in the Mediterranean with resulting advantage to the Allies. Also the exclusion of Axis men-of-war from a Western Hemisphere "safety zone," guarded by a "neutrality patrol" under United States leadership, afforded considerable protection to Allied shipping entering and leaving North and South American ports. On the other hand, the modern submarine proved to be a far more difficult weapon to combat than the primitive U-boats of 1918, and the Allies were dangerously short of anti-submarine equipment during the early months of the struggle. Early raids by the pocket-battleships, and threatened raids by the more formidable German battle-cruisers, compelled the Allies to deplete their main fleets in order to provide battleship escort for their troop and cargo convoys. And the lengthening range of German air power, especially after the occupation of Norway, gradually curtailed British use of the North Sea.

The battle for the Atlantic took a radically different turn following conquest of the Low Countries, the fall of France, and Italy's entry into the war. Britain lost French naval support at the very moment when its own sea power was seriously crippled by losses incurred in the retreat from Narvik and evacuation from Dunkirk. The sea and air power of Italy, reinforced by German units, imperiled and eventually barred the direct route to Suez, forcing British shipping to use the long alternative route around the Cape of Good Hope. This cut the total cargo-carrying capacity of the British merchant marine almost in half at the very moment when German acquisition of naval and air bases on the Channel and on the west coast of France foreshadowed more destructive attacks on shipping in northern waters.

At this critical juncture, the United States, though still technically a non-belligerent, assumed a more positive role in the battle for the Atlantic. Fifty American destroyers were turned over to Great Britain to make good previous naval losses. In return, the United States received long-term leases for ship and plane bases in Newfoundland, Bermuda and numerous points in the Caribbean. Congress voted a 70 per cent increase in the navy, and early in 1941 a separate Atlantic Fleet was established. American units were sent to relieve the British garrison in Iceland, which had become a vital convoy depot and focus of anti-submarine activity. Greenland was occupied to provide additional facilities for the Anglo-American sea and air patrol rapidly spreading over the North Atlantic. Transatlantic air-ferry service was developed for the delivery of planes and for the rapid transportation of important freight and personnel.

Early in 1942, after the United States had become a full belligerent, the Axis opened a large-scale submarine offensive against coastal shipping in American waters. German U-boats also operated in considerable force along the South Atlantic ship lanes to India and the Middle East. The Allied campaign (1942-1943) to reopen the Mediterranean depended almost entirely upon seaborne supply shipped through submarine-infested waters. Allied convoys approaching the British Isles, and those bound for the Russian ports of Murmansk and Archangel, had to battle their way against savage air and undersea attacks. It was publicly estimated at the close of 1942 that Allied shipping losses, chiefly from planes and U-boats, still exceeded those suffered during the worst period of 1917. And a considerable weight of Allied naval power had to be kept constantly available in northern waters in case Germany's formidable surface raiders, especially the superbattleship *Tirpitz*, should break into the Atlantic shipping lanes as the *Bismarck* did briefly in 1941.

On the other side of the ledger was the ever tightening Allied blockade of Axis Europe, and perceptible, if slow, progress in combating the Axis war on shipping. With more and better equipment, the convoy system was strengthened and extended. Unprecedented ship building, especially in American yards, caught up with and then began to forge ahead of losses, though the latter still remained dangerously high. Bombing raids on Axis ports and industrial centers progressively impaired Germany's capacity to build and service submarines and aircraft. Transoceanic cargo planes provided for the United Nations an increasingly important alternative means of transport beyond the reach of enemy raiders. Brazil's entry into the war strengthened the Allied position in the South Atlantic. The occupation of virtually all west African ports, including the French naval bases at Casablanca and Dakar, denied to Axis raiders their last possible havens in southern waters. All these and other developments foreshadowed ultimate failure of the Axis sea strategy which aimed at halting the flow of American armies and matériel across the Atlantic to the battlefields of Europe and Africa; at starving Great Britain into submission; at preventing sea-borne supplies from reaching Soviet Russia; and at breaking the United Nations' blockade of Axis Europe.

Victory in the Atlantic represented the collective effort of the United Nations, but chiefly of Britain, Canada, and the United States. The strength of this coalition was derived in no small degree from the successful reintegration of the fundamental components of sea power. These components are: (1) a secure primary base, (2) relatively superior resources, and (3) favorable strategical position. Britain formerly possessed all three vis-à-vis both Europe and America. The rise of United States power potential, coinciding with changing conditions in Europe, had compelled Great Britain to recognize American primacy in the western Atlantic. The tremendous industrial growth of Germany, coinciding with the development of submarines and later aircraft, undermined the security of England's island base off the coast of Europe, endangered the far-flung network of sea communications which supplied British industry, and thereby weakened the whole structure of British sea power. The United States lacked England's favorable strategical positions for offensive action vis-à-vis continental Europe. But the United States enjoyed a secure base thousands of miles from Europe and Asia. The United States also possessed resources and industrial potential surpassing those of any other country. Britain could no longer command the Atlantic singlehanded against a determined war on commerce backed up by the industrial resources of continental Europe. The United States could not play Great Britain's historic role singlehanded, without huge continuing outlays for armaments on a scale sufficient to compensate for the lack of key strategical positions bearing on the nerve centers of the Old World. Together Britain and America possessed in large degree the fundamental requisites for continued command of the Atlantic and adjoining narrow seas. Still it was by no means conclusive that even an Anglo-American coalition could hold these waters indefinitely unless some means were devised to control the European development of submarines, aircraft and other new weapons. Thus the problem of command of the Atlantic was destined at the close of World War II to merge into the larger problem of future power relationships within Europe and between Europe and the other continents facing the Atlantic. In this region, Britain and the United States in concert presented the strongest single power combination. Depending on the terms of peace following World War II, and on the future trend of Anglo-American relations, the English-speaking countries facing the Atlantic might come to represent a coalition of sea power as formidable, as stable, and as useful in the future as British sea power was in the period following the Napoleonic Wars.

THE CHALLENGE OF LAND POWER

By Robert Strausz-Hupé

From chap. 18 of *Geopolitics, The Struggle for Space and Power*, by Robert Strausz-Hupé. Copyright 1942 by Robert Strausz-Hupé. G. P. Putnam's Sons, New York; reproduced by permission. The author is professor of political science at the University of Pennsylvania.

Long and spectacular as had been the reign of sea power, by the close of the nineteenth century, political and scientific developments had begun to undermine the foundations on which the single mastery of the seas had rested. A great mobility of organized military force has been, throughout history, the attribute of all the states which established themselves as world powers. Roman techniques of road and ship construction, the superior marching powers of the Roman legion, and maneuverability of Roman fighting vessels assured Rome military superiority over all the nations of the ancient world. Likewise a highly developed system of postal and military communications, no less than highly original cavalry tactics, assured the Mongol hordes of Genghis Khan and Tamerlane military superiority over their slower-moving foes.

In the Franco-Prussian War of 1870, the Prussian forces were carried to the

French frontiers by rail, thus gaining an all-important head start over the French armies. The French military leaders insisted upon moving their troops by road and on foot, and at once lost the initiative to their Prussian foes, who had enlisted the cooperation of the steam engine.

British world rule by the single mastery of the seas was established in the age of sail. Up to the development, in the 1830's, of the railway, the sailing ship was the fastest means of locomotion. Notwithstanding a few celebrated records of mail service by coach and rider, established on such important routes as the London-Dover and Paris-Calais roads, nothing on land could rival the speed and carrying capacity of the sailing ship. Moreover, the sailing ship was a highly self-sufficient unit and could stay at sea for considerable periods of time. The coming of steam did not bring about an immediate revolution either in the strategic concepts of British sea power or in the sea-power–land-power relationships. For Great Britain had acquired in the age of sail a large number of suitable naval bases, most of which lent themselves to the establishment of convenient coaling stations. The British Admiralty was quick to urge the acquisition of additional points suitable for the servicing of steam vessels. This required on the part of Britain's naval strategy no profound changes in strategic dispositions, for the dominant trend in Britain's policy had always been a continued struggle for naval bases. This is what Oswald Spengler meant when he said that the **Royal Navy was not built for the British Empire but on the contrary the Empire was created for the fleet.**

At the end of the nineteenth century it was railroad strategy, superior in mobility to naval strategy, which challenged British world supremacy established through sea power. . . .

The first step was the integration by Russia of a large part of the Asiatic land mass through railway communications. The construction of strategic railroads linked European Russia with Tashkent and Merv, Kushka and Ashkabad, and thus with the Afghan and Persian borderlands. Likewise, the completion of the Trans-Siberian Railroad established Russia's effective control over the vast reaches of Siberia and brought Russian land power to the coasts of the Sea of Japan and the China Sea and thus to the Pacific Ocean. Russian land power, disposing of strategic railroads, exerted an increasing pressure upon Britain's strategic frontiers in the Near and Middle East. It was this pressure which the traditional arrangement of British sea power was not able to meet.

Admittedly, Britain could still control the Indian Ocean without detaching so much as one battleship or heavy cruiser from her fleet in European waters. Even after its victory at Tsushima the Japanese fleet was not considered a potential rival in Asiatic waters, and for all practical purposes the Indian Ocean remained what it had been for a hundred years, a British "closed sea." Nonetheless, the increasing pressure of rail-borne Russian land power upon the buffer states of Afghanistan and Persia, which guarded the approaches to India, appeared to be leading to an inevitable collision between the world's greatest sea power and the world's largest land power.

The agreement of 1907 between Russia and Great Britain over their respective stakes in Asia averted this collision. But, while Russian pressure had abated, another railway line menacingly approached the Indian Ocean and threatened to "out-flank" British sea power. The Anatolian Railroad—so enthusiastically advocated by Dr. Rohrbach—and its projected extension to Bagdad bade fair to carry German land power to the Persian Gulf. Similarly Turkish railway lines, built with the assistance of German capital and engineers, were linking Turkish Anatolia with the Levant and Arabia, and thus carried the threat of the land power of Germany, Turkey's ally, to the immediate vicinity of Suez. It was indeed this double threat to Egypt and to India which Great Britain in 1914 was forced to meet in Palestine and Mesopotamia with a large-scale and costly deployment of land power.

Railroads rendered the proximity of Russia and later of Turkey, supported by Germany, an effective threat to the British Empire which neither British sea power nor Britain's traditional diplomacy was able to avert. It was this threat which forced Great Britain to enter the ranks of land powers while still remaining a sea power, thus robbing her of the economic advantage which insularity once had vouchsafed her.

By the end of the First World War, a British mass army stood in France, and powerful British forces were concentrated in Palestine and Syria. Britain had attained formidable power on land —only to let it lapse as soon as victory had been won. In spite of the object lesson of the geographic strategy of the First World War, Britain pared down its land forces to approximately their prewar strength. To have retained in peacetime the status of a great land power would have meant revolutionary changes in Britain's social and economic organization, and these changes British statesmen were not ready to propose.

Thus the fall of France [in 1940] caught Britain a third-rate land power. Sea power, effectively seconded by air power, saved the British Isles but was no longer in a position to safeguard the Empire. The advantage of interior lines now favored German land power in its operations against Britain's attempts to establish footholds on the Continent and against Britain's own positions in Egypt. By contrast, Britain's land armies had to be supplied by extended exterior lines. Similarly, it was the weakness of British land power in Asia in December 1941 which opened the way to Japan's easy initial successes.

Britain's position on the eve of the Second World War was decidedly less favorable than it had been in the First. She was relatively poorer in resources, and the dual strain upon her strength of maintaining her fleet and matching the multiplying threats of enemy land power was by far greater. It is mainly this fact which explains the long list of British failures from Dunkirk to Mandalay. The ineptness of the brass hats and politicians probably hastened Britain's retreat from ramparts once believed impregnable. But neither dexterous strategy nor brilliant diplomacy could have substantially modified developments which had been predetermined by geography. That Britain—her strategic weaknesses notwithstanding—withstood the onslaught of her enemies after the fall of France is one development which undoubtedly had not entered into the calculations of the Geopolitikers. For the entrance of Russia and the United States into the war added their vast land power, effective and potential, to Britain's force, and thus brought into being the greatest alliance of land and sea power of all time.

When Mahan wrote, railroads were only just beginning to lay the foundations of the superiority of land power. By the time of the First World War, the change of Britain's strategic position had become fully apparent. The vast deployment of British troops on

French battlefields obscured it temporarily. But Britain's forces on the Continent, notwithstanding their unprecedented size, were essentially marginal, and they carried over the tradition of the armies which Marlborough and, a hundred years later, Wellington had led to the European mainland. Britain had, in the days of Marlborough and Wellington, been able to spare her manpower for decisive intervention on the side of her European allies, the grand finale, precisely because her navy ruled the waves and guaranteed the safety of Britain's possessions overseas. But in the First World War these possessions were for the first time threatened by circuitous landward thrusts—thrusts pressed home by German-Turkish land power operating along rail lines flung to the gates of Egypt and to the shores of the Persian Gulf.

Seen in true historical perspective, the development of the submarine and of air power merely reinforced the effects of the technological revolution which had begun with the introduction of the steam engine. The new weapons of the twentieth century now imperiled the home base itself of Britain's sea power. But the world political potential of sea power had been in full retreat before the rapidly increasing potential of land power long before the first submarine had plunged below the surface and the first plane had taken to the air. The railroad had set in motion the cartographic revolution which placed the richest possessions of the British Empire within the effective range of hostile land power. It is this fundamental weakness of Britain, the result of globally distributed commitments and profound changes in geographic strategy, which the German geopolitical thinkers clearly apprehended long before it had become apparent to most other observers. Their reasoning, it now may seem, proceeded from the obvious and led to a fairly simple conclusion. Yet all great strategic concepts are essentially simple. . . .

BRITAIN'S CHANGING ECONOMIC POSITION

By the Editors

In the economic sphere, Britain's relative position has suffered a comparable decline. As late as 1850, England produced over one-half of the world's iron and steel. Before the close of the nineteenth century both Germany and the United States had forged ahead of England. In the 1930's the Soviet Union also passed Great Britain, which now stood fourth in this important category of industrial power.

All this does not mean that British production of steel was declining. On the contrary, it has been increasing more or less steadily over the past century. What has declined has been Britain's share, or percentage, of the world total. Or to put it another way, British production has increased less rapidly than that of the newer industrial countries.

What has been true of steel has been true also of other industrial components of British power. The picture is much the same with respect to coal, merchant shipping tonnage, exports and imports of commodities, and other indices of economic life and power.

The gradual deterioration of Britain's economic position has received much attention, and the following selections by André Siegfried and E. H. Carr can be taken as typical samples of a growing literature analyzing the economic as well as political and military aspects of England's changing power position.

EARLY IMPACT UPON BRITISH OPINION

By André Siegfried

From the Introduction to *England's Crisis,* by André Siegfried. Copyright 1931 by Harcourt, Brace & Co.; reproduced by permission.

If we begin our study of England at the economic high-water mark of 1860-1870, we can soon trace the first symptoms of decline, for the sources of the present crisis are to be found as far back as 1880. It was then that the first serious rivals began to appear, for hitherto British industry had stood alone. The report, published in 1886, by the Royal Commission appointed to inquire into the Depression of Trade and Industry, leaves no doubt on this score. Conditions were already disquieting, and England should have made an effort to recover or at least to adapt herself to the changes that were then taking place. Instead we find her calmly resting on her laurels. She enjoyed a complete monopoly not only in distant countries, but even in Europe, where industrialism was still backward, and, without realizing it, she was accustomed to all that this monopoly entailed. She honestly believed that she was competing internationally under normal conditions, without guile and according to the rules of free trade. In reality, however, her commercial victories were less important than she thought, because she had not encountered a dangerous rival until she met the Germany of Wilhelm II. . . .

If at this point in her destiny England had been forced by some accident to reform, who knows what might have happened? Suppose that instead of a few colonial expeditions she had been engaged in a really serious war, or suppose that the long-drawn-out Victorian era had come prematurely to an end! The Old Queen was the symbol of the eternal, changeless stability of things, of the abundance in which the English had lived for generations, and the easy profits they still earned with no serious effort to reorganize. The whole structure of the kingdom seemed justified. It was an acquired situation, consolidated by Providence, and destined to endure forever.

Meanwhile, contemporary thinkers, with characteristic British honesty, observed and commented on the first disquieting symptoms of decline. The report of the Commission of Enquiry into the Economic Depression (1886) is a monument of lucid objectivity, and a dozen similar reports have followed it. "What courage!" we exclaim. "What realists! How calmly they look straight into the bottom of the abyss!" For over forty years the Blue Books have been perpetually repeating the same grave warnings. "We are no longer alone. More active rivals with better equipment are springing up and leaving us behind. . . ." So ran the Enquiry in 1886 and in 1930 in his report on British Commerce in South America Lord d'Abernon uses the same terms, makes the same reproaches, and reveals the same defects in the Britain of today.

. . . Intellectually the Englishman reads and appreciates these warnings, but by instinct he refuses to believe them. His unshaken confidence in his country, his pride, and an extraordinary faculty of not seeing what he prefers to ignore, all rebel against the lesson. He juggles with it, and finally drops it altogether. A sanctimonious and inherent optimism whispers that he will pull through somehow, not because he has seen how his methods can be reformed, or his equipment renewed, but simply because he is an Englishman. "We will muddle through," he says. . .

A BRITISH ANALYSIS

By E. H. Carr

From chap. 7 of *Conditions of the Peace*, by E. H. Carr. Copyright 1942 by the Macmillan Co., New York; reproduced by permission. The author is professor of international politics in the University College of Wales; he was for many years a member of the British diplomatic service and an officer of the British Foreign Office.

It is extremely important that there should be, at the end of this war, a clear understanding of the changed position of Great Britain since the palmy days of the nineteenth century. Lack of this understanding was responsible for many of the disastrous incidents of the period 1919-1939. The confusions of British foreign policy in this period were rather the result than the cause of the decline in British power and prestige in international affairs, and they occurred because the change in the situation was not realized and faced either by British statesmen or by the British public. The uniqueness of the British position in modern history is due to one central fact. Thanks in part to the skill and inventiveness of her people, in part to the comparatively high degree of political development already attained by her before 1800, but most of all to the fortunate disposition of her natural resources, Great Britain had a long start over the rest of the world in that vast process of industrial development which made the nineteenth century one of the most remarkable periods of recorded history. Throughout the middle years of the century, Great Britain was the principal supplier to the world of nearly all staple industrial products, drawing in return from the rest of the world supplies of foodstuffs, raw materials, and a few specialized luxuries. She was thus able to lead the way in a remarkable rise in the standard of living, and to acquire an overwhelming preponderance in that form of military power which best suited her needs—the first, and down to the end of the century the only, large-scale mechanized navy. The solid basis of the two-power naval standard and of all that it implied was the fact that, as lately as the 1870's, British exports exceeded those of the two next greatest powers combined. This disparity could not possibly endure. Great Britain possessed no monopoly of natural resources or capacities. Where she had led, other favorably situated countries, having larger territories and larger populations, could follow. By 1913 Great Britain, Germany, and the United States ranked approximately equal as exporting countries. The total production of Germany was as great—that of the United States more than twice as great—as that of Britain.

These changes were quickly reflected in the international situation. The Boer War gave Britain an unwonted and transient sense of failure, and showed the rest of the world that she was less invincible and less invulnerable than had been supposed. The configuration of European politics was quickly reshaped. The German threat to British supremacy took more obvious and more aggressive forms. The German naval program, by compelling Great Britain to accelerate construction and to concentrate her fleet in the North Sea, was a grave embarrassment to Britain as a world power. Great Britain replied by taking France into her defensive system, thereby revealing her weakness and insensibly modifying the whole basis of her policy. Meanwhile the picturesque career of Theodore Roosevelt hastened the process of drawing the United States closer to Europe. A basis of common tradition with Great Britain, as well as the fact that Germany was the spearhead of an attack on those free and liberal nineteenth century ways of life which belonged as much to the American as to the British tradition, made it certain that in the new three-cornered distribution of world power, the United States would ultimately throw her weight on the British, not on the German, side.

Though Britain's unique supremacy in industrial power had disappeared before 1914, many of its adjuncts—especially her undisputed preeminence in finance and shipping—still remained almost intact. The war undermined these, and thus further weakened her position as a world power. She was no longer the greatest producing or the greatest exporting country in the world. She was still, in virtue of her vast nineteenth century investments, the largest creditor country. But she sold large blocks of her investments to the United States in order to finance the war; and the income from the remainder, instead of being reinvested abroad as in prosperous nineteenth century days, was increasingly required in the period between the two wars to pay for the excess of imports over exports. In shipping she still led the way. But the overwhelming predominance which had once given her, with a few minor countries, a virtual monopoly of the carrying trade of the world belonged to a distant past. This decline in economic power was reflected in a falling-off of military strength. After 1918 a revival of the two-power naval standard was not to be thought of; and the comparatively small margin of British naval superiority over the Japanese Navy gave Japan an effective preponderance of power over Great Britain in the Far East. In the air, Great Britain did not attempt seriously to compete with other European powers.

These conditions explain the most distressing and unsatisfactory feature of British foreign policy between the two wars—its failure to establish any proper coordination between ends and means. Public opinion expected, and ministers too often encouraged it to expect, a policy which, if it were to be effective, implied both capacity and readiness to take immediate military action in almost any part of the world to enforce it. At no time after 1919 did Great Britain possess that comfortable and easy margin of military superiority which alone makes such a policy possible. The root of this discrepancy between policy and resources lay in the traditional character of the British outlook and in the obstinate refusal of the British people—admirable in many respects, yet dangerous—to recognize that Great Britain no longer occupied the same position of effortless supremacy which she had enjoyed almost throughout the nineteenth century. One thing which made it easy to entertain this comforting illusion was that the decline had been relative, not absolute. The standard of living was still rising. The general structure of British economic life was unaltered. In spite of unemployment—and the unemployed, having little political influence, were too often treated as a minor incident—Great Britain seemed to be still moving upward in the scale of prosperity. While Germany, having lost the war, knew that her international position had been compromised and took heroic steps to retrieve it, Great Britain relapsed easily into the comfortable belief that, having won the war, she was stronger and more impregnable than ever, and that no special exertions were called for on her part. It was readily assumed that the international status of Great Britain was unchanged, or had even been enhanced by the victory of 1918; and any qualms were silenced by vague perorations about the League of Nations or Anglo-American cooperation.

The illusion received added encouragement from a corresponding failure on the other side of the Atlantic to realize the fundamental transformation which had come over the international scene. At the end of the war it was assumed in many quarters as a matter of course that the hegemony of the world had passed from London to Washington. Max Weber, writing in Germany in November 1918, believed that the world supremacy of America was "as inevitable as that of Rome in the ancient world after the Punic War." But the transfer was not so quickly or easily effected. The United States was as reluctant to assume, as Great Britain was to abandon, the prerogatives of military and economic predominance. Hence there was, throughout the twenty years between the two wars, a constant failure on both sides to make the necessary adjustments to the changed situation. The Washington Conference [for the limitation of naval armaments, 1921-22] proceeded on the tacit assumption that Great Britain and the United States were henceforth equal partners in world supremacy. But no political partnership between states is ever equal except in name (which helps to explain why the pretence of equality is always so rigidly kept up); and no provision was made, at Washington or elsewhere, for that effective leadership without which effective action is impossible. Hence Great Britain embarked on policies, at Geneva and elsewhere, which could not have been consistently maintained—and ought not to have been initiated—unless American power had been at the disposal of Great Britain; and the people of the United States, far from casting themselves for the role of world leadership, confined their policy for the most part to the defense of American interests, narrowly interpreted. The period between the two wars was an interregnum in international leadership, due to the inability of Great Britain to perform her old function and the unwillingness of the United States to assume it.

Failure to recognize this fact led to misunderstandings, of which the most curious and most revealing arose over the affairs of the Far East. After 1931 Great Britain was patently unable by herself to curb the power of Japan. The United States, lacking the psychology of leadership and taking refuge in the irrelevant point that British financial interests in the Far East were larger than American, were unprepared for any concrete action. In 1932 American diplomacy by half-promises of sympathy and support busily encouraged Great Britain to act, and discredited the British Government for its failure to do so. But in 1937, when British diplomacy more cleverly declared itself ready to participate in any action initiated by the United States, the latter developed the same inertia as Great Britain had displayed five years earlier. From 1936 onwards American opinion severely condemned Great Britain for her failure to intervene effectively in the affairs of Europe. But this condemnation did not imply on the part of the United States any corresponding readiness to act themselves. After the present war broke out, many people in Great Britain found it difficult to understand the passionate desire of Americans to encourage and assist the British war effort, combined with an equally passionate determination not to involve their own country in the war. The psychological basis of the American attitude to international affairs for the past twenty years has been the conviction that Great Britain has a prescriptive and immemorial right and duty to take the lead where a strong lead is required, and that it is the business of good Americans to encourage and support Great Britain in so far as they approve what she is doing. Throughout the whole period, both Great Britain and the United States constantly attempted to pursue political and economic policies based on their respective nineteenth century traditions and incommensurate with their present power, and confusion and misunderstanding were the inevitable result. The conception of a responsibility for leadership resting on the United States has hardly yet begun to take root.

Nothing can be more important, in framing Great Britain's post-war international policy, than to form as clear a view as possible of the changes in her status which the war will have brought about. One of the primary needs for readjustment will be psychological. At the close of the war, however favorable its issue, Great Britain will have little temptation to repeat the error of supposing that victory has enhanced her military or economic power. Behind the short-lived exultation of victory her self-confidence will have received a salutary shock. In 1918 it could reasonably be felt that British sea power had been the predominant factor in the defeat of the enemy. French military power had no doubt also been invaluable; but this could equally be counted on in any further struggle against Germany. The assistance of the United States in money, in material, and in manpower had substantially eased the later stages of the war and perhaps hastened the victory. But there was no sufficient ground to suppose that victory could not ultimately have been achieved without it. The lighthearted boasting of irresponsible Americans that they had won the war provoked amusement rather than indignation. Now all this is changed. The assumption that French military and naval forces constituted a reliable and permanent adjunct of the British defenses—a convenient assumption under which Great Britain concealed from herself the relative decline in her own power—has been shattered. It is clear, and has been frankly admitted, that Great Britain could not defeat Germany in the present war singlehanded without American aid in the things which she most needs. The realization of this fact will have psychological consequences whose character and extent can as yet hardly be estimated. In any event, one result of the change can hardly fail to be a temporary, if not a permanent, weakening of Great Britain and of Western Europe as a whole in relation to the United States and to the non-European world as a whole. Much will depend on the success of British policy at home in recovering a sense of moral purpose, in reorganizing the life of the community and in increasing the national capacity for production. Much also will depend on the success of British foreign policy . . . in bringing about a tolerable economic reconstruction of Europe. But it is difficult to imagine any contingency—other than a complete German victory over the United States as well as over Great Britain—in which Europe or any European country would be likely to remain the undisputed center of the world. The world of the twentieth century may eventually find its center of gravity across the Atlantic, or it may continue to have many centers. But it will not, like the nineteenth century world, have a single center in Europe—or, more specifically, in London. The revolutionary change in Great Britain's status may be expressed by saying that, instead of being the one great world power, she will become one of two or three, or perhaps more, world powers.

This change will have economic symptoms and implications. The most important of these is that the world will no longer have a single economic and financial center. It is still not clearly enough recognized that the nineteenth century system of relatively free trade and a single international currency standard depended on the fact that a large proportion of the international trade of the world was negotiated and financed in London. Modern talk of "managed" trade and "managed" currencies sometimes carries with it the implication that nineteenth century trade and nineteenth century currency required no management, and that management is not only unnecessary but intrinsically undesirable. This is an illusion. The international trade of the nineteenth century was "managed" by the merchants of Great Britain, who offered the readiest and most convenient market for a large proportion of the merchandise of the world. The international currency was "managed" by the City of London, which discounted bills, made loans and advances, adjusted exchange values and arranged the necessary minimum transfers of gold. London ceased to play this role in 1914, has never regained it, and cannot now regain it. Failure to find some other orderly method of conducting and financing international trade, or even to perceive that some other method was required, has been responsible for the economic and financial anarchy of the ensuing period. After twenty-five years it is time to understand that international trade and finance must be organized on a new basis and that nineteenth century precedents are valueless and misleading. Counsel has too long been darkened by idle dreams of a return to free trade or a restoration of the gold standard.

Another aspect of the change which will present peculiar difficulties to Great Britain—and not only to her—is the impending radical modification of Great Britain's status as a creditor nation. In the days of her nineteenth century prosperity, Great Britain helped to create markets for herself in almost every part of the world by loans designed to promote the development of the borrowing countries. Moreover, she did not normally, before 1914, retain the interest paid on these loans; she reinvested it in the same or other overseas countries, thereby rendering the whole process cumulative. This revenue did not, therefore, really enter into the balance of payments, and British imports were fully paid for by British exports and by receipts from British shipping and other services. As we have already seen, the situation was modified by the war of 1914-1918 in two important ways. In the first place, Great Britain was compelled by the necessity of financing purchases from abroad, especially from the United States, to sell a substantial part of her overseas investments; and after 1918 the interest derived by Great Britain from such investments never attained anything like its pre-1914 dimensions. Secondly, the interest received by Great Britain from her remaining overseas investments became for the first time after 1918 an indispensable item in her balance of payments. There was now a considerable gap between British imports on the one side and British exports and shipping and other services on the other. Interest on overseas investments was no longer reinvested abroad, except in small and diminishing amounts, but was used to bridge this gap.

The modification of Great Britain's economic status in the world after the present war will therefore be profound. She will have parted, directly or indirectly, with a large proportion of her most lucrative overseas investments, so that instead of an income from this source of £200,000,000 a year—the estimated figure for 1938—she may be able to count on not more than, say, £50,000,000 a year. Moreover, this revenue may be offset by obligations contracted during the war, so that Great Britain might conceivably end the war on balance as a debtor, not a creditor, nation. Even if this extreme contingency is not realized, there is no doubt that Great Britain after the war, in order to make her balance of payments meet, will have either to import considerably less than she did before the war or to export considerably more. Some fall in imports might not prove incompatible with the maintenance of the 1938 standard of living. But it should be borne in mind that any such reduction in foreign trade would react detrimentally on our shipping and on the revenue derived from it, and thereby aggravate the problems of making both ends meet; and it is difficult to believe that, if the reduction were at all considerable, the general level of prosperity would not suffer. Great Britain will therefore be faced, if her standard of living is to be maintained, with the difficult task of increasing her exports at a time when a large number of other countries both in Europe and elsewhere are better equipped than ever to produce many of those goods which they formerly imported from Great Britain. There are only two ways of escape from this dilemma. Britain can only regain her prosperity if she develops new lines of production, and thus puts herself once more in the forefront of the producing world; and she can only regain her prosperity if the standard of living, and consequently consumption, all over the world, undergoes a substantial increase and thus provides once more that expanding market which was the basis of nineteenth century well-being. This means in practice two things. Great Britain will have to produce more than before in order to maintain—and a fortiori to increase—her present standards of living; and she will have to regard rising standards of living in other countries as a matter of direct interest to herself.

This change in Britain's position will also have its repercussions in every country whose trade with Great Britain has been an important factor in its economic life—that is to say, throughout a large part of the world. Of late years it has sometimes appeared to be taken as a matter of course in commercial negotiations between Great Britain and other countries that the trade balance should be "passive" for Great Britain and "active" for the other country, this condition being the natural reflection of Great Britain's position as the major creditor nation and purveyor of shipping and financial services. In the decade before the war, some countries had begun to realize that the only way to maintain a market for their own produce in Great Britain was themselves to buy more British goods. But the economic and psychological strain of readjustment to a new situation in which other countries will be unable to sell to British importers substantially more than they buy from British exporters is bound to be considerable. It will be greatest of all in the United States, which will, according to all reasonable expectation, replace Great Britain as the principal creditor country and the most important financial center in the world. It is difficult to see how disaster can be avoided unless the people of the United States adjust themselves fairly rapidly to the view that this position can only be maintained, as Britain maintained it in the nineteenth century, by offering a large and expanding market to the products of the rest of the world. But it should be recognized that such an adjustment will involve a profound modification of tradition, an abandonment of deep-seated prejudices and, above all, an unusual readiness to override sectional interests, in a country where a high degree of natural economic self-sufficiency has hitherto made foreign trade seem relatively unimportant.

Of all countries affected by the changed status of Great Britain, the United States will be affected most. The problems of adjustment confronting Great Britain are matched by problems of adjustment equally difficult and delicate confronting the United States. Both sets of problems are interconnected, being often merely opposite facets of the same situation. There is a dangerous tendency in some quarters to assume that the close cooperation and consciousness of common interests and policy established between the two countries during the war will remain unimpaired in the post-war period; in other quarters an equally dangerous tendency to assume a return to conditions approximately the same as those prevailing before the war. Neither of these prognostications is likely to be fulfilled. The end of the war will bring to light again many of the rivalries and jealousies temporarily suppressed by the sense of common danger and common effort. But the whole picture will have been transformed, both by the tremendous experience through which both countries will have passed and by the changed character, psychological and economic, of the relations between them; and while some old problems will have disappeared, new ones will be found to have arisen. The problems of readjustment to a new status which will confront both countries after the war will present themselves mainly in the concrete form of problems of Anglo-American relations. If the position of Great Britain as a world power has since 1919 been dependent in large part on the character of her relations with the United States, this will be still more conspicuously true after the present war. . . .

The discussion of Anglo-American relations, while it remains a capital problem of British post-war policy, cannot be carried at the present stage to any conclusion; for too much depends on factors which are largely beyond British control. But the more the underlying conditions and psychological difficulties of readjustment are understood on both sides of the Atlantic, the less likelihood there will be of a recrudescence of dangerous jealousies and frictions. The same is true in the main of British relations with the other countries of the English-speaking world; for most of the same forces have been at work, though in a modified degree. The second world war in a quarter of a century has for the second time rallied the British Dominions spontaneously to the support of the mother country, and provided powerful evidence that they, too, cannot afford to disinterest themselves in the destinies of Europe. On the other hand, strategic interests will tend in the future to strengthen the ties of three at least of the Dominions—Canada, Australia, and New Zealand—with the United States. Financial interests may point in the same direction. Little has been said in public about wartime financial arrangements between Great Britain and the Dominions. Canada may well emerge from the war as a creditor of Great Britain, though she will doubtless remain a debtor of the United States; and it is not impossible that a common interest in gold may forge new links between the United States and South Africa. It is perhaps unlikely that Great Britain will be in a position to resume lending to the Dominions on anything like the old scale. But she will be able, if she pursues a wise policy, to offer the same extensive market as of old to Dominions produce —a market which neither the United States nor any other country can readily provide—though it will have to be recognized in the Dominions that the days of an overwhelmingly "active" trade balance with the mother country are past.

Post-war relations between Great Britain and the Dominions present a less difficult problem than relations between Great Britain and the United States, both because the required readjustment will be less radical and because mutual understanding is closer and more deeply rooted in tradition. But the two problems will be similar in kind, arising as they do from shifts in the balance of military and economic power and complicated as they are by many cross-currents of sentiment and tradition. Moreover, they will react on each other; for they are in a sense merely two aspects of the same problem—the organization of the English-speaking world. But it is important to remember that the solution of this problem must be sought in the first instance in the realm not of constitution-making, but of military, economic, and psychological readjustment.

Beyond the confines of the English-speaking world the course of British policy can be more confidently charted. In the Far East, it is true, Great Britain's role must on the whole remain a subsidiary one. She cannot act effectively there unless the full weight of the United States is thrown into the scale, and she may fairly expect to leave the main initiative to Washington. But elsewhere it would be fatal for her, both politically and economically, to have the air merely of waiting to see what the United States will propose. In large parts of Europe and Africa and in the Middle East, Great Britain—if she sets a wise course and recovers that sense of a mission which alone can preserve her from decay—will continue to exercise a role of leadership and preeminence. How much she can achieve will no doubt be influenced, here too, by the amount of moral and material support which she receives from the rest of the English-speaking world. But a clear and decided British policy will make the active cooperation of the United States and the Dominions more, not less, certain. The tradition of waiting for a British lead is still firmly ingrained in American minds; and almost everywhere a strong British lead will be welcomed, not resented, by the other English-speaking countries. This is particularly true of Europe—a continent against which Americans retain all their prejudices and where they are particularly reluctant to assume responsibilities except of a humanitarian order. Europe is still the danger zone. The future power and prestige of Great Britain are most intimately involved in her handling of the European problem.

THE BRITISH EMPIRE: STRUCTURE AND ORGANIZATION

By C. B. Fawcett

From chaps. 1-2 of A Political Geography of the British Empire, by C. B. Fawcett. Ginn & Co., London and Boston, 1933; reproduced by permission of the University of London Press.

THE British Empire of today occupies more than a quarter of the land area of the globe and counts nearly a quarter of mankind in its population. . . . Its lands extend by the shores of all the oceans, into every type of major geographical region, and on to every continent; while its peoples include members of every considerable racial and religious division of mankind, at all existing levels of culture and social development. Hence it is preeminently a world state, perhaps the only state which is fully entitled to that description; for its politico-geographical relations and problems extend into every considerable region of the world, and bring it into contact in some degree with every other independent state on the earth. No other power has so many, so varied, and so widely dis-

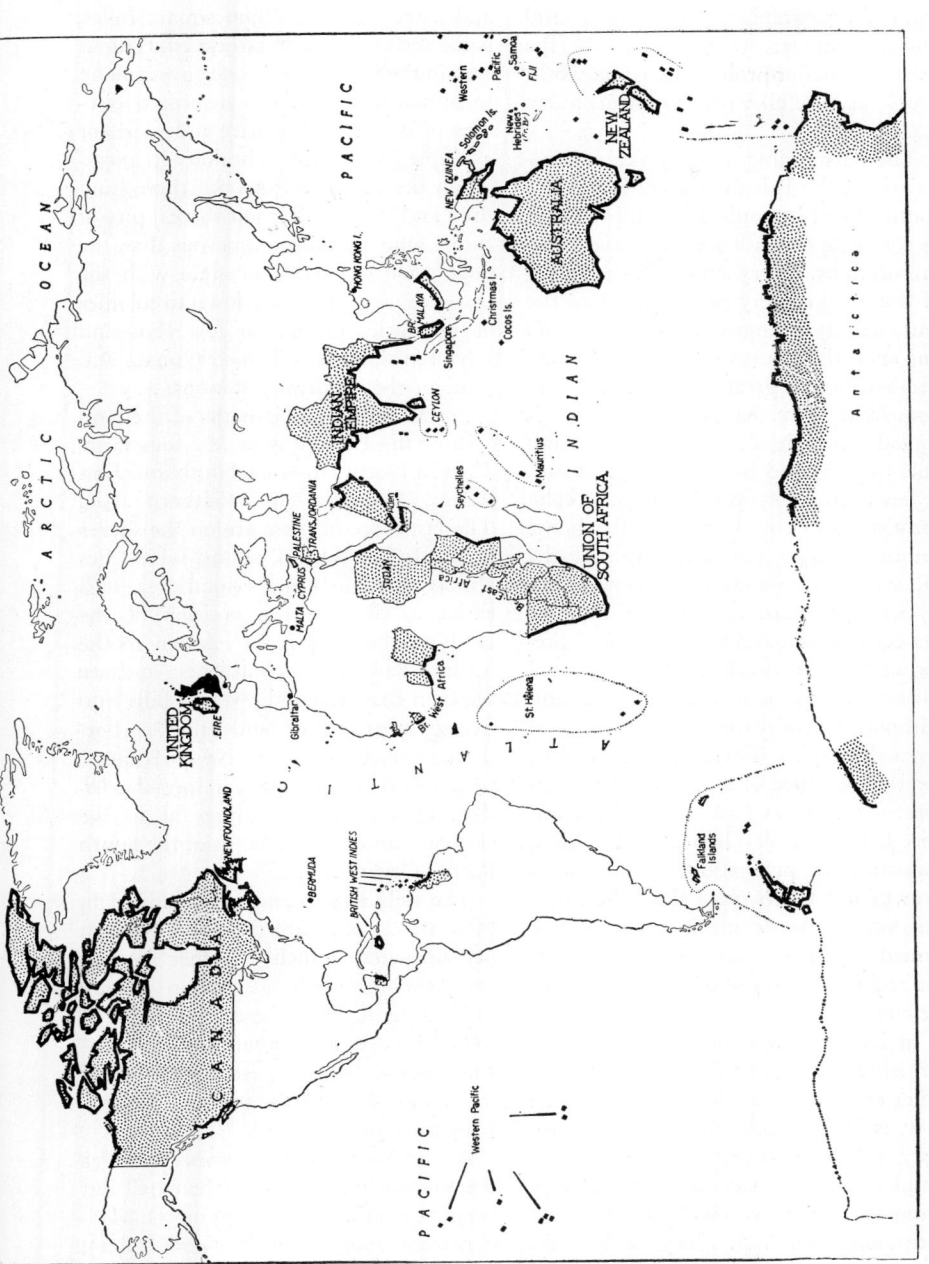

Fig. 13. Geographical Structure of the British Empire. Note the grouping of British lands around the Indian and North Atlantic oceans.

From E. A. Mowrer and M. Rajchman, *Global War, An Atlas of World Strategy*. Copyright 1942 by William Morrow & Co., New York; reproduced by permission.

tributed geographical, economic, and political contacts with the rest of the world. Its major problems are also world problems, and all world problems affect it. . . .

The outstanding geographical characteristic of the British Empire is the discontinuity of its lands. From this follows its complete dependence on oversea communications. Every other Great Power of today, like every great empire of the past, has its strength concentrated into one area; though it may also control dependencies at a great distance from that homeland. But the British Empire is spread through all the latitudes from pole to pole, and besides all the oceans. It has been built up by discovery, colonization, and conquest from the home countries along the seaways; and the links between its component parts are all across the seas. The physical unity of the oceans was, and is, an essential prerequisite for its origin and its continued existence. The seas are all one: and without that unity there could have been no such empire. There is no precedent for the existence of so scattered an empire; it could not have come into existence before the development of efficient transoceanic navigation; its greatest growth has taken place since the introduction of the steamship; and its continued existence is completely dependent on its freedom to use the seaways under all circumstances.

In its political organization also the British Empire is as different from any other empire the world has ever known as it is in its geographical distribution. Its governments range from typical examples of modern democratic and representative systems to absolute, if benevolent, autocracies. . . . Its governmental units vary almost as much in extent and population as in their political forms. In area they range downward from the Dominion of Canada, which, with three and three-quarter million square miles, is the second or third largest continuous area in the world under one government, to miniature dominions or crown colonies of only a few square miles, as for example Jersey and Gibraltar. In population the range is from the three hundred and sixty millions of the Empire of India, who are more numerous than the population of any other state with the one exception of China, down to colonies or territories of only a few thousand inhabitants, such as British Guiana and some of the small way stations. . . .

. . . More than nine-tenths of the land area of the Empire is in . . . four large areas in North America, South and East Africa, Australia, and southern Asia. The last three of these are on the shores of the Indian Ocean, round which lies almost two-thirds of the total area. It is easier to describe the position of the lands of the Empire in relation to the oceans than to the continents; and we see then that nearly the whole falls into two great groups of lands, the one bordering the shores of the North Atlantic Ocean and the other encircling the Indian Ocean and extending far to the eastward among the islands of the South Pacific Ocean. . . .

The only large areas not included in these two groups are the West African dependencies, which together occupy approximately half a million square miles of land. These lie on the shores of the South Atlantic Ocean, in which the Empire also holds the island stations of the Falkland Islands and St. Helena, with their dependencies.

Away from these three ocean areas the Empire includes only the small but very important way stations on the Mediterranean route (Gibraltar and Malta), with Cyprus and the mandated area of Palestine and Transjordan, and Hong Kong in the Far East.

Thus we may say that the lands of the

British Empire are included in two great groups, respectively about the North Atlantic and the Indian Oceans, and along the seaways which connect these by way of the "open-sea route" through the South Atlantic Ocean, and the "inland-sea route," through the Mediterranean Sea and Suez Canal and the Red Sea, respectively. . . .

While the distribution of the lands of the Empire is perhaps most easily described in relation to the oceans . . . it is also possible and useful to describe their position in relation to the chief land mass on the earth—the Old World. . . .

[Defining the Old World as that part of Eurasia-Africa that was accessible to the civilized peoples of Europe and Asia before the great explorations of the fifteenth and sixteenth centuries], it is at once evident that the British Empire is essentially marginal and outlying in respect to the great Continent [of Eurasia]. And in their location round the Old World its lands fall into two well-marked concentric series, an Inner and an Outer.

The lands of the Inner Series are on, or just off the margin of, the Old World Continent. They include British Isles and the Indian Empire, together with a number of smaller territories on the inland-sea route between Great Britain and India, and other territories in Malaya, Borneo, and Hong Kong on the extension of that route to the Far East. . . .

The sub-continent of India is part of the Old World Continent; but it is so far cut off from the interior of the Continent by great mountain and desert barriers that it is mainly peninsular in its location, and by far the greater part of its intercourse with other lands is overseas. India has, under normal conditions, much less direct intercourse with the Continent than have the British Isles themselves; though here, to the north-west of India, is the chief military land frontier of the Empire.

Only at Gibraltar does the British Empire extend onto the mainland of Europe, its smallest foothold on any of the continents, but in southern Asia it includes about one and three-quarter million square miles on the mainland without reckoning mandate territories.

These lands of the Inner Series include the two most populous lands of the Empire, India and Great Britain; and while their area is somewhat less than one-sixth of the whole, their population is not less than four-fifths of the total. They form a broken fringe round the western and southern shores of Eurasia, from Norway to China. The seaway along which they are strung is one of the principal ways of communication within the Empire. It is also the coasting route of the Continent; and as such it is an important route to many other powers as well as to the British Empire, which here as elsewhere is therefore very intimately associated with the non-British world.

The lands of the Outer Series include all the rest of the Empire, more than five-sixths of its area, and are all situated in the New World. They form an irregular series round the Old World at distances of from two to five thousand miles from it. The continuity of this series of lands is interrupted by wide stretches of ocean and large areas of non-British territory; while it is also entirely broken by the North Polar Ice Barrier. Hence it is a very fragmentary ring. Most of its more important segments are in more frequent and more direct communication with the British Isles than they are with one another. . . .

Such a summary statement of the location of the British Empire in relation to the Old World brings out very vividly the fact that it is mainly in the New World. Its homelands in the British Isles are themselves capable of being regarded either as an outpost of the Old World of Europe toward the New World beyond the oceans, or alternatively as an outpost of that New World toward Europe. And it seems clear that the growth of the younger Dominions, and their resultant increasing weight in the councils of the Empire, is steadily tending to make the Commonwealth as a whole more and more a part of the New World.

BASES OF BRITISH FOREIGN POLICY

By Eyre Crowe

From Eyre Crowe's "Memorandum on the Present State of British Relations with France and Germany," British Foreign Office, January 1, 1907; published in vol. 3 of *British Documents on the Origins of the War*, edited by G. P. Gooch. H. M. Stationery Office, London, 1928. The author of the paper from which this selection is taken was an officer of the British Foreign Office.

The general character of England's foreign policy is determined by the immutable conditions of her geographical situation on the ocean flank of Europe as an island state with vast oversea colonies and dependencies, whose existence and survival as an independent community are inseparably bound up with the possession of preponderant sea power. The tremendous influence of such preponderance has been described in the classical pages of Captain Mahan. No one now disputes it. Sea power is more potent than land power, because it is as pervading as the element in which it moves and has its being. Its formidable character makes itself felt the more directly that a maritime state is, in the literal sense of the word, the neighbor of every country accessible by sea. It would, therefore, be but natural that the power of a state supreme at sea should inspire universal jealousy and fear, and be ever exposed to the danger of being overthrown by a general combination of the world. Against such a combination no single nation could in the long run stand, least of all a small island kingdom not possessed of the military strength of a people trained to arms, and dependent for its food supply on oversea commerce. The danger can in practice only be averted—and history shows that it has been so averted—on condition that the national policy of the insular and naval state is so directed as to harmonize with the general desires and ideals common to all mankind, and more particularly that it is closely identified with the primary and vital interests of a majority, or as many as possible, of the other nations. Now, the first interest of all countries is the preservation of national independence. It follows that England, more than any other non-insular power, has a direct and positive interest in the maintenance of the independence of nations, and therefore must be the natural enemy of any country threatening the independence of others, and the natural protector of the weaker communities.

Second only to the ideal of independence, nations have always cherished the right of free intercourse and trade in the world's markets, and in proportion as England champions the principle of the largest measure of general freedom of commerce, she undoubtedly strengthens her hold on the interest and friendship of other nations, at least to the extent of making them feel less apprehensive of naval supremacy in the hands of a free-trade England than they would in the face of a predominant protectionist power. This is an aspect of the free-trade question which is apt to be overlooked. It has been well said that every country, if it had the option, would, of course, prefer itself to hold the power of supremacy at sea, but that, this choice being excluded, it would rather see England hold that power than any other state.

History shows that the danger threatening the independence of this or that nation has generally arisen, at least in part, out of the momentary predominance of a neighboring state at once militarily powerful, economically efficient, and ambitious to extend its frontiers or spread its influence, the danger being directly proportionate to the degree of its power and efficiency, and to the spontaneity or "inevitableness" of its ambitions. The only check on the abuse of political predominance derived from such a position has always consisted in the opposition of an equally formidable rival, or a combination of several countries forming leagues of defense. The equilibrium established by such a grouping of forces is technically known as the balance of power, and it has become almost an historical truism to identify England's secular policy with the maintenance of this balance by throwing her weight now in this scale and now in that, but ever on the side opposed to the political dictatorship of the strongest single state or group at a given time. . . .

BRITISH FOREIGN POLICY BETWEEN WARS

By Austen Chamberlain

From "The Permanent Bases of British Foreign Policy," by Austen Chamberlain. *Foreign Affairs*, July 1931. Copyright 1931 by Council on Foreign Relations, New York; reproduced by permission. Sir Austen Chamberlain, who died in 1937, was a prominent British statesman and diplomat.

THREE geographical facts have been decisive for the course of British history and explain, just as they dictate, the main principles of British policy and the preoccupations of British statesmen. First, Great Britain is an island, but, secondly, this island is separated only by a narrow streak of water from the Continent of Europe. Thirdly, this island has become the center of a wide-flung empire whose arterial roads are on the oceans and through the narrow seas.

Great Britain is an island state. She has no land frontiers. Her pretensions to become a continental power, to expand as her rivals were expanding, by continental conquest or inheritance, were finally settled by the Hundred Years War. Since then she has looked to the sea as at once her defense and her opportunity. Her land forces have been kept at a minimum. They have never been sufficient to wage a continental war except in alliance with some great military power; but, thrown into the scales on one side or the other in a struggle between the continental giants, their weight and the bulldog tenacity of the race when once engaged in a fight have more than once been decisive of the issue. At sea, on the other hand, she has—until these latter days when she has admitted American parity—jealously guarded her naval superiority, for to deny the passage of the narrow seas to her enemy was her only defense, to keep them and the oceans open to her own ships was a necessity of her daily existence and a condition of her imperial power.

But though Great Britain is an island, detached from the Continent and prone to regard herself as unaffected by those cares which occupy the first place in the minds of the inhabitants of continental countries, the waters which divide her from western Europe are so narrow that she can never for long remain indifferent to what happens on the opposite shores of the Channel or the North Sea. Steam brought the coasts nearer and rendered the movement of ships independent of the winds which played so large a part in the days of Nelson and Cornwallis. The development of aeronautics has further impaired our insular security and has given fresh force to the secular principle of British policy that the independence of the Low Countries is a British interest, that their frontiers are in fact our frontiers, their independence the condition of our independence, their safety inseparable from our own. It was to secure the independence of the Low Countries that we fought Spain in the sixteenth century, that we fought Napoleon in the nineteenth and that we fought Germany in the twentieth. Here, at any rate, we find a permanent basis of British policy. . . .

There have been times in her history when England has sought to free herself from all interest in or dependence on the affairs of the Continent, but they have never lasted long nor has the result of such isolation, whether "glorious" or not, been encouraging. Nature has placed our island too close to the shores of Europe for us to remain unaffected by the storms which burst there, whilst the development of communications and the course of scientific invention have increased our vulnerability. There are many who would be glad to see England as free from European entanglements as the United States, though, as the [First World War] shows, even America may be involved by a general European conflagration. But for us the peril is closer, the danger more imminent, and we best insure against it not by abstention until war has actually broken out but by throwing our weight beforehand into the scale of peace. . . .

. . . Outside Europe the maintenance of her imperial communications and the interests of the Dominions, colonies and dependencies become dominant. But for India and the Dominions of Australia and New Zealand, there would have been no British occupation of Egypt, no reconquest of the Sudan for civilization, and the great work accomplished by Lord Cromer and his assistants would have remained unattempted. The fact that Egypt commands in the Suez Canal the main artery of communication between England on the one hand and India and Australasia on the other is what took us to Egypt and keeps us there. We cannot afford to see Egypt and the Canal dominated by another country any more than the United States could tolerate the domination of the Panama Canal by a foreign power. We cannot, therefore, allow abuses or disorders to arise in Egypt which would justify or excuse foreign intervention; but, subject to this overriding necessity, it is the policy of Great Britain to leave the management of Egyptian affairs as far as possible to the Egyptians themselves, and to confine our interference to the defense of our vital interests and the discharge of our obligations to other nations to whom we have formally declared that we should regard any interference by them in the internal affairs of Egypt as "an unfriendly act" and "any aggression against its territory as an act to be repelled with all the means at our command. . . ."

Passing to the Near and Middle East, we find that here also the permanent basis of British policy is fixed by the existence of the Indian Empire. No British Government desires to extend its liabilities in the Red Sea, the Persian Gulf or on the shores of the Indian Ocean, and, indeed, in Iraq we reduced them as rapidly as the circumstances of the case and our mandatory obligations to the League of Nations would admit; but the safety of our communications is vital to us. With no aggressive intentions ourselves, we shall be content if no other power cherishes aggressive designs. Our interest lies only in the maintenance of peace and of the *status quo*. Stable governments, able to defend their independence and to preserve their territory from attack best serve British interests alike in Iraq, Persia and Afghanistan....

Passing now to the Far East . . . it is too soon to forecast what the turn of events may bring forth; but if I were to hazard a prediction, it would be that the course of British policy will be largely determined by that of the United States and by the extent of the understanding which it may be found possible to establish between our two nations in a sphere where their interests are identical....

The interests of Great Britain in China are entirely commercial. There, more than anywhere else, our policy is the policy of "a nation of shopkeepers." At no time have we cherished any territorial ambitions, . . . here, as elsewhere, British interests would best be served by the establishment of a strong national government able both to preserve internal order and to protect Chinese territory from external aggression....

I have left to the last the consideration of British relations with America....

It is an axiom of British policy that we should always seek to preserve the most friendly relations with America. Sentiment and interest combine to impose this attitude upon us. War between us is, we hope, unthinkable. . . . I can say with confidence, after a cabinet experience of more than a quarter of a century, that such a possibility has never entered into Great Britain's consideration of her requirements for defense and has never influenced the strength of the forces maintained by her, whether on land or sea. The 3,000-mile frontier which marks the boundary between the United States and Canada remains unfortified—at once the symbol and the pledge of enduring peace between the British Empire and the United States.

But merely to preserve peace would be a wholly inadequate and negative expression of British policy. We desire much more than the maintenance of peace. We wish by all means in our power to remove all causes of friction, to wipe out the memory of old quarrels and to place and keep our relations on a footing of cordial friendship and good understanding....

It can safely be said that no government will ever command or retain the support of the British people which is thought for a moment needlessly to jeopardize the good relations of the two peoples. It is our earnest prayer that, in whatever differences the future bring forth, we may meet with a like spirit across the Atlantic Ocean.

THE PLACE OF MILITARY INSTITUTIONS IN ENGLISH SOCIETY

By D. W. Brogan

From chap. 7 of *The English People*, by D. W. Brogan. Copyright 1943 by D. W. Brogan. Alfred A. Knopf, New York; reproduced by permission. The author is professor of political science in Cambridge University.

"The Meteor Flag of England shall yet terrific burn." Thomas Campbell had no ironic intention when he wrote the line. But the Englishman may be forgiven if he stresses the "yet" in a "jam tomorrow" spirit, for not only has hope been long deferred in most British wars; it has become a national habit to assume that it will be so and, in a sense, should be so. No people is less surprised by reverses or less easily cast down by them. When a war has been a series of brilliant successes, the public has forgotten it. Thus the great Duke of Marlborough has never had the popular fame of the Duke of Wellington, who is pictured as performing the simple role of putting a number of English infantry regiments on a hill and letting the French exhaust themselves trying to persuade them that all was lost. But in the army and outside it, much less successful generals have been much more popular. The army, that is, has never been taken with sufficient seriousness. Its moral rather than its intellectual qualities have been stressed, and victories won with the odds on the side of the victors, the object of good generalship, are less popular than victories won against the odds. Getting there "fustest with the mostest" may be a motto worthy of American or other foreign generals, but in the confused image of war that does duty for history in the English mind, it is not how the deeds that won the Empire were done.

Of course, this attitude reflects the unconscious arrogance of a country that could afford a good deal of military inefficiency because it was an island—and a safely guarded island. . . . Because she was an island, England escaped that militarization that overtook Europe in the late sixteenth and early seventeenth centuries. She escaped the identification of the gentry with an officer class and, no doubt, paid a price for that escape in an insufficiently professional attitude in those members of the ruling class who did become, for longer or for shorter periods, officers in the little army that adequately served the purposes of the great sea power.

The contrast between England and the continental nations became more striking with the transformation wrought by the French Revolution. On one side of the Channel, the nation in arms; on the other, a rather random handful of the gentry controlling a small army of poor men, enlisted for simple material motives, living apart from the nation in the new barracks, serving for twenty-one years, often thousands of miles away from home. Such an army was not part of the nation as the French Army was, still less the armature of the whole state as the Prussian Army was. The rising middle class might not have a single soldier in its acquaintanceship; the rank and file were too poor, the officers too exclusive, to have anything in common with the merchants of Manchester or Birmingham. . . .

Wars took place, but off stage. There were victories and defeats, Tel-el-Kebir and Maiwand, from which bronzed commissionaires and slightly crippled doctors like John Watson returned to the full civilian life of Victorian London. There were reforms in the army; the old long-service army gave place to a more modern professional army, imitating in an English half-hearted way the Prussian helmet and the Prussian staff. But the army was still a minor and slightly un-English institution. At the time when its literary apotheosis was complete, came the humiliations of the South African War. And when the next test came, the old professional army, almost bled to death in the first months of the war, was merged, swamped in the first great national army, millions strong, that was needed to destroy German power. For the first time the average Englishman of all classes knew the army at first hand . . . as an institution whose strength and weakness was a matter of life and death for the individual and the nation. Into the army were sucked some of the most critical minds in England, to whom almost everything in the army was equally new and equally odd. As the bloody battles succeeded one another, with no visible result, the stereotype of battles in which the incompetence of the leaders was too much for the courage of the led, was stamped on the public mind. . . .

When peace came, the first desire of the millions of citizen soldiers was to get back to civil life as fast as they could. Attempts to build up a soldiers' vote, or a soldiers' bloc, failed. The English veteran of three or four years' service ... had no desire to be reminded of his past ordeal. The British Legion, as a lobby or as an institution, quickly sank into comparative obscurity. Once a year, on Armistice Day, its members paraded in shabby civilian clothes, with their medals on their chests, unimpressive figures trudging through the November mists to the local war memorial. How unlike the organized glorifications of their achievements that marked such German veterans' organizations as the Stahlhelm! How unlike the saturnalia of an American Legion convention turning Cleveland into Paris for a week! Never was English life so civilian in tone as when most vigorous male adults had been soldiers.

It was the epoch when the Oxford Union voted not to "fight for its King and Country," a resolution immediately and widely misunderstood, but which did represent a natural reaction against "mere" patriotism, and a very English but dangerous belief that what was out of date in Oxford must be out of date everywhere. But for once Oxford abandoned a lost cause long before it was lost and the English intellectual assumed too easily that all colonels were Blimps or even that Blimp was always wrong.

The return to the old professional army system broke the brief contact between the soldier and the public. Less than ever was soldiering a career that could appeal to the intelligent young man who had no emotional bias towards it—and to admit such an emotional bias was to write yourself down a gangster, a sadist, or a fool. The old view of the honor of the profession of arms seemed dead.

It was inevitable, then, that only the most conservative minds were attracted to the army. Prospects in it were not bright. Had the last war not been fought to end war? Endless peacetime preparation for a most unlikely eventuality, a spell of service in the tropics, made only mildly interesting by a feeble Burmese rebellion, retiral on not very handsome pensions in early middle age—these were the prospects offered to the would-be officer. There might, indeed, have been no officers at all, but for the survival in many otherwise cultivated breasts of the old bias in favor of the soldier's career being possibly the most brilliant of all. And in addition to those who took Dr. Johnson's view of the matter, there were enough families where the army was a tradition, as the pulpit had been among the New England Brahmins, or where the social prestige of the officer counted to tip the scale against the English equivalents of selling bonds or insurance or entering a good law firm.

It would have been idle to expect of officers so recruited a ready welcome for all modern ideas. If they had been open to all the winds of current doctrine, they would have been at least as tempted to leave the army altogether as to try to modernize it or themselves. When the intellectuals did turn to military matters, it was to quote Clemenceau to the effect that war was too serious a matter to leave to soldiers—and then to leave it to soldiers.

Interest in military matters was confined to the reduction of military science to staying on the defensive and on winning wars without very much blood and tears. But, until the Spanish Civil War, there was no real interest on the Left at all. War was a sin to most of the leaders of the Labor Party who had been pacifists in the last war. The Spanish War did open the eyes of many of the Left to the sad truth enunciated by Mr.

Dooley. You can refuse to love a man or to lend him money, but if he wants a fight you have got to oblige him. Yet, contemplating the Spanish War, not enough attention was paid to the fact that the Fascists won it and never, except for a brief moment, looked like losing it. And if that victory was due to German and Italian aid, that showed how formidable international Fascism was. Yet the Labor Party took no critical interest in British armament policy and, on the very eve of the war, when Hitler and English public opinion had at last forced some semblance of realism on the Chamberlain Government, the party that had been most vociferously in favor of standing up to Hitler voted against conscription. It was against their principles; so were war, disease, poverty, rain on May Day, and many other disagreeable aspects of this vale of tears. . . .

The record of the Conservative (or National) Government is, of course, worse. They were the Government; they were paid to see that no harm befell the Commonwealth, and the Conservatives were the traditionally patriotic, not to say jingo, party. Yet in 1939 England was less well prepared on land than she had been in 1914.

There is a special as well as a general reason why Britain was less well prepared for war in 1939 than in 1914. In the critical period before the war of 1914 England had a Liberal Government. And the old Liberal Party was far better equipped to prepare for war than either a Conservative or Labor Government could be. The Liberals were by tradition anti-militarist, sceptical of the beneficent effects of war and of the worth of military glory. For two generations, at least, the assets of military glory had been taken over by the Tories. The last attempt by a Liberal to cash in on the political profits of a belligerent foreign policy had been made by Palmerston. And Palmerston's success had been purely personal; by a noisy "Liberal" foreign policy, by ostentatious attention to armaments, he had been able to follow out a profoundly conservative policy at home. The Liberals learned their lesson. They benefited by public reaction against expensive and unsuccessful imperialism in Afghanistan and South Africa. They made a mess of it when they attempted, in a half-hearted way in the Sudan, to rescue General Gordon, with due attention to Liberal principles in finance and Liberal principles in matters like the slave trade. They were the party of "peace, retrenchment, and reform."

But although they were the party of peace, they realized that it took only one to make a quarrel; no number of pious resolutions could guarantee peace. So there was nothing illiberal in making preparations for war while hoping and expecting to avoid war. But they were also the party of retrenchment. And waste was rampant in the military establishments—waste of a kind which the Liberals were well equipped to spot. For the "pride, pomp and circumstance of glorious war" made little appeal and the fine feathers and social graces of the army were among the most obvious forms of conspicuous waste. Then the beneficiaries of this waste were nearly all stout Tories to whom the army was something not to be administered in any narrow functional sense, but something as wrapped up in sacred ritual as cricket or the hunting field. So it was easy for a Liberal government to lay radical and sacrilegious hands on these parts of the military establishment most treasured by the Tories and least relevant to military efficiency. And such economies could be accompanied by reform since reform, again, took the form of stressing the professional as against the ornamental and conservative side of the army. So the great reforming ministers were radicals like Cardwell and Campbell-Bannerman and Haldane. They undertook to provide and did provide a cheaper, more efficient, less conservative army. In doing this they made many deeper but few new enemies and they alienated no friends. To carry out valuable reforms entirely at the expense of the vested interests of the rival party is a dream of every politician. Of course, it required more than a steady indifference to the lamentations of the foe. There must be a positive content to the reform as well. But two great Liberal war ministers, Cardwell and Haldane, were first-class administrators who thought the problems of military administration worthy of the full exercise of their energies. And the Liberal prime ministers who chose and supported them thought the War Office a worthwhile job.

The navy was less of a mere vested interest, its reform more divorced from party and social politics, but the Liberal government in 1914 had shown full appreciation of the importance of naval efficiency, not only by its readiness to spend money, but by the appointment to the Admiralty of one of the two rising hopes of the party, Mr. Churchill.

Alas, the parties which alternated in power after 1922 were not run by realist Liberals, but by two different kinds of sentimentalists. The Conservative war ministers never got down to thinking out the problem of what preparation for war meant, in either the diplomatic or the military field. The old ways were good enough for them. A Conservative government tackling the cavalry stranglehold on the army should be like a Conservative government making the public schools really public, and anti-Conservative government.

But there were other than narrow party reasons why England was ill prepared for war in 1939, reasons, indeed, that make it almost creditable that she was so ill prepared. For the change in the character of modern war made it impossible for a democracy to prepare adequately in a time of formal peace. In 1914 the Queen of Battles was the machine-gun and, to a lesser extent, the quick-firing field-gun, both defensive weapons. So the initial weakness of the Allies could be prevented from being fatal to them. The tactics imposed on both sides by the nature of the weapons available helped, in the long run, the side that had unmobilized resources. But in this war the decisive weapons, the tank and the airplane, helped the offensive. The victorious onslaught of the superior army paid its old dividends in accumulating strength on one side and debility on the other. It is obvious now (though it was not obvious in 1940) that the hopes of a second Battle of the Marne entertained by many people up till the fall of Paris were illusions, based on inadequate knowledge of the nature of modern war. The success with which the Germans drove to the Volga and the Caucasus shows what little chance the French had of resisting the power of the German armed might. Our admiration for what the Russians have done is proof enough of how we have accepted the fact of the overmastering power of a well-equipped modern army on the offensive against an inferior foe. . . .

But the preparation of this German might had involved so profound a distortion of "normal" German life that only a country in which the difference between war and peace was purely formal could have endured the strain. Freedom of all kinds had to be suppressed to make the arming of Germany practicable. All doubts as to the necessity of the war plan had to be suppressed; all means of judging had to be removed; enemies had to be provided, Jews, then Czechs, then Poles, then English. The immense diversion of economic resources had to be kept from producing its natural result, an increased demand for consumer's goods. Germany conquered unemployment by abolishing the normal reasons for employment. . . .

Only an authoritarian government can refuse to let the workers spend their wages, can depress the standard of living, can give cannon instead of butter. A free government can only do this in presence of imminent and immediate danger. That there was such danger was obvious to those who can face unpleasant truths, but they are always a minority. . . . Only when the danger was so obvious that all but the most pertinacious optimists or partisans were silent could a free government at last begin to do, with general assent, what the authoritarian governments do by mere decree and by the manufacture of public opinion. And by that time it was too late. The totalitarian power had gained a great start; it is that start in the race which is belatedly perceived and which at last breaks down the natural reluctance of the citizen of the free state to sacrifice some of his freedom. And it is doubtful if anything but actual war, or even actual imminent danger, a Dunkirk or a Pearl Harbor, really shakes the mass of men out of their complacency.

The Conservative Government in England was faced with the dilemma of admitting openly that German rearmament was a grave and increasing danger to England and demanding full powers to deal with it and, at the same time, preserving normal diplomatic relations, playing the comedy of being just big boys together. A very strong, farsighted, daring ruler or rulers might have taken the risk. But the English people had not elected MacDonalds or Baldwins for their energy or daring. They were no Dantons awaiting the chance to show boldness; no Pitts confident that they could save the country and that no one else could. So we had chaotic policies like the Anglo-German Naval Treaty that had any value only if German good faith could be counted on and an attempt, at the same time in a sheepish and inadequate way, to make the R.A.F. the equal of the Luftwaffe. The public could see the inconsistency and was deaf to the timid suggestions that the situation, though well in hand, was serious all the same.

It is true that the English Government before 1939 made all the extra mistakes possible, down to the nonsensical promise of "peace in our time," accompanied by more armaments, but although no government could have done much worse, no democratic government of the usual type, in which the customer —that is, the voter—is always right, could have done much better.

Leaders whose more or less avowed principle is that they know no more than the average man or that, if they do, they must not act on this knowledge are not confined to England. So Mr. Churchill was kept out of office, and in the United States the vigilance of the President in naval and diplomatic matters was taken as a hobby of an otherwise sagacious executive, when it was not taken as the hallucination of a man who had not the profound knowledge of the outside world that inspired Senator Borah. As far as their political systems are truly representative, England did not deserve to have Mr. Churchill in reserve, any more than the United States deserved to have Mr. Roosevelt in office. . . . France, which had neither a Churchill nor a Roosevelt, had to fall back on superannuated soldiers and political admirals, neither of them worthy rulers of the country of the Revolution or of 1914. . . .

The English Army in 1939 was too small, too ill provided with modern weapons, too much impressed with the lessons and the personalities of the last war to play anything like the role it had played in 1914. The war was even less like what had been foreseen than it had been in 1914; the bad diplomatic preparation made the British share of the military effort more inadequate to the needs of the alliance. Instead of a retreat from Mons, the Marne, the Aisne, Ypres, there was disaster and the abandonment of the Continent.

Menaced with invasion, forced to fight with inadequate forces far from its bases and to fight alone, it was no wonder that the British military record was poor. Military thought had not been encouraged during the long armistice years, and an army needs constant stimulus to thought. Nor was this initial defect easily remedied. Germany had gained a good deal of technical knowledge, cheaply, in the Spanish War; every victorious campaign taught her more. But the English Army was always laboring behindhand with no time to seek perfect or even adequate solutions. Where the barest minimum of equipment was scarce, fine improvements in design were easily neglected. Where the nearest approach to modern equipment that was available had to be sent on a voyage of 14,000 miles, a voyage taking months to make, it was natural not to wait on perfection.

And for modern war of armored divisions striking like thunderbolts over great stretches of country, no country could be a poorer training ground than the crowded island. The nearest approach to an open maneuver area such as the Germans have and the Russians have and the Americans have is Salisbury Plain, which a good-going Panzer division could cross in an hour. There is no English equivalent of Pomeranian heaths or Louisiana swamps, where mimic war can be practiced with some reasonably close approximation to the real thing.

So, for two years, the British Army had to fight battles at the end of one of the longest communication lines in history, or to train in a crowded island where real battle conditions were almost impossible. The army so constituted had to find its officers from a mass of not highly military young men whose very virtues were not always assets. Quite often the new junior officers were much cleverer than their professional chiefs; even more often they thought they were; it took time and the stern test of war to find leaders. . . .

The British Army is a very English institution, even to letting the chief credit for its not infrequent victories go to the Scotch and the Irish and the Australians and other peoples with more taste for martial glory than the nation of shopkeepers, the most soldierly of unmilitary peoples.

The English are a nation of players of team games and makers of engines and runners of races. So the success of the R.A.F. has nothing surprising in it. The countrymen of Watt and Parsons and Rolls were not at a loss, mechanically, nor were the countrymen of the great sailors or the great aviators of the last war unworthy of their predecessors. It is unnecessary to insist that the R.A.F. was a good thing; even those who have not watched their arabesques in the air over London in September 1940 realize that in the fate of the handful of fighter pilots who then defeated the invading aerial army lay the immediate destiny of the world. It was a Thermopylæ that succeeded. And the new Spartans were largely the products of the new secondary schools that had conformed, from necessity, largely to Athenian standards.

There is one permanent exception to English irony, resignation, indifference, or whatever you like to call it. Ships and the sea, above all the Royal Navy, are exempted from this complacency. In the last war, as in this, it was naval disasters or failures that astounded and angered the man in the street—and almost everybody lives in this street. It is not merely that Britain is an island, that the sea is all around and near at hand, that no one lives more than thirty or forty miles from tidal water or that there are few fields that have never seen a sea-gull. It may be because these are basic facts that the devotion to the Royal Navy is so deep and wide, but that devotion is now a thing in itself.

The military tradition is one of victory, but of victory by muddling through, of success won mainly by toughness, of not knowing when you are beaten and of applying horse sense. English war on land is (in the national tradition) an extension of sport, last-minute victories won by gentlemen over players. Some of the most popular English soldiers have been not notably successful, but unsuccessful admirals do not become heroes, if only because the Englishman never remembers that there have been any. His picture of naval war in the past is a picture of endless victories, won often against formal odds, but won by skill, by energy, by initiative. The typical English land victory, as seen through the eyes of the man in the street, is won by standing an attack until the attackers get tired of it. Such was the great symbolical victory of the last war, First Ypres. Such was Waterloo. Such was not Trafalgar or the Nile or the Baltic. It is not Wellington waiting till the French had got tired of attacking—and until Blücher turned up—but Nelson who is the national hero. Nelson finding excuses for not receiving orders that might have kept him from attacking, Nelson breaking through French and Spanish fleets like a modern Panzer division, as Rodney and Hawke had done before him, Nelson winning with sailors and ships at the highest degree of technical efficiency. The British Army traditionally has got along by taking it, the Navy by dishing it out.

It is because the Englishman has thought himself immune from invasion at home that he has been able to afford the luxury of his imperial commitments over all the seven seas. It was because the Royal Navy saved England from the militarization imposed on all other European countries that capital and energy, human and material, could be sent off to points as remote as Hong Kong or Aden. It was this political freedom of action that gave what truth there was to the old claim that English naval supremacy maintained order on the oceans, put down piracy in the China Sea or slave-trading in the Persian Gulf. But such police work did not call for the great battle-fleets that cruised in the Mediterranean or the North Sea. Much smaller fleets would have kept Malayan seas safe for commerce, or protected missionaries in the Solomons. But it was because the home of the merchants—and the missionaries—was saved from exterior political pressure by the great fleets at home that much smaller investments of the power paid such handsome dividends to British and all other business civilizations in the last century. A serious threat to naval supremacy at home weakened English power to the ends of the earth; the rise of a first-class naval power in the Pacific presented a problem that could only be solved if there was no threat to British security in Europe. A Berlin-Tokyo Axis was in the nature of things; a power seeking to establish a new empire in Asia was, in fact, dependent on the appearance of another would-be world empire-builder in Europe. This is the basic explanation of the fall of Singapore and of Burma.

But, of course, there are other reasons, too. Nearly every technical improvement in shipping methods, or in the character of modern war, has told against English sea power, has made its traditional task more difficult. The change-over from coal to oil has made the fleet dependent on a foreign source of power; the coming of the submarine and the airplane has made the command of the surface of the sea less decisive. The decline in international trade, a decline that has affected England more than any other country, the growth of subsidized mercantile marines, has reduced the English share of world shipping, the great pool on which the navy draws for men, for ships, for technical resources of all kinds. At the same time defeat on land made the long coastline from Narvik to Biarritz one great base from which the Germans, with perfected weapons [could] carry on a more deadly war than they did even at the height of their naval power in the last war. . . .

In their attitude to other navies and other maritime peoples, the English are, if not arrogant, at least paternal. Only fleets that have fought great actions against the Royal Navy really count. Great admirals like Santa Cruz and Duquesne or Farragut are forgotten because they did not win or lose a battle against a British fleet. De Ruyter, Van Tromp, Tourville, Hipper, Suffren, these are great names: as Villeneuve, Grasse, De Winter, Von Spee are honored names. They all played in the World Series that is always won, in the last game, by the same team. . . .

GREAT BRITAIN'S WORLD POSITION TODAY

By the Editors of "Planning"

From *Planning*, No. 201, February 9, 1943. Broadsheet issued by Political and Economic Planning, London.

The world conflict for whose settlement [British statesmen] must prepare is . . . the culminating episode of a major revolution which is transforming the whole shape of civilization. Both in our national society and in international society a new pattern is emerging. In these circumstances the basic presuppositions on which our foreign relations in the nineteenth century were based, and which permitted of a remarkable stability and continuity of policy, can no longer be accepted as valid. The very fundamentals of our policy have to be rethought, and new presuppositions hammered out which will permit of similar continuity of policy in the coming years. This means thinking in terms, not merely of this year and next, but of decades and even half-centuries, not merely of diplomatic relations between sovereign governments, but of the whole range of relations between the peoples of the world—political, economic, social and cultural. . . .

It is now widely recognized that the two world wars of the twentieth century and the intervening period of armistice must be regarded as episodes in a major revolution which is reshaping the whole pattern of civilized society. No one can hope to sketch out even the bare outlines of a foreign policy for Britain in the coming years who has not first grasped the nature of this revolution, for it determines the conditions within which policy must be formulated, perhaps for the next half-century. In this revolution three main elements stand out as having a particular bearing on foreign policy:

The first and most obvious is the high degree of integration and interdependence in human affairs which technical advance has brought about. . . .

The second relevant factor in this revolution is the change which it has brought about in the role played by the state within the community. . . . Gradually at first, rapidly as a result of the war, the state has been reaching out its powers of direction and control into every sphere of the community's activity. . . . In all countries the process is, in its general direction, irreversible, because it is the inevitable consequence of modern technical conditions. . . .

The third relevant factor in this revolution is the profound change which has been effected in the constituents of national power. The technical conditions which made possible the coexistence of a patchwork of scores of completely independent, and theoretically equal, sovereign national states or "powers" of varying size and strength have passed once and for all. . . . Whether we like it or not, the world politics of the postwar years will, in fact, be shaped primarily in terms of the relations between three or four great world powers; and this is the fact which must determine the outlines of the new international system which we aim to create.

To qualify for the onerous role of world power a nation must possess a formidable combination of resources. It must possess an extensive and highly developed industrial potential; the ability to control or ensure the supply of vast quantities of raw materials, often from sources scattered throughout the world; a high order of technical and administrative skill; and, last but not least, the ability in its leaders to command the continued and active support of the increasingly powerful and politically conscious masses.

But it must also possess something further. The type of association between a powerful nation and a group of smaller peoples which modern conditions require will only be durable if that nation possesses in exceptional degree a capacity for leadership—a leadership which is willingly accepted because it is recognized, not as the selfish attempt of the stronger to impose his will by force on the weaker, but as the most farsighted and disinterested expression of the common interests and purposes of all.

It is this moral element in power which, if there is any validity in the idea of the twentieth century as the century of the common man, must and will become increasingly fundamental to the whole concept of power and its exercise in the modern world. It is precisely in this respect that Hitlerism, with its self-centered lust for "racial" domination and its belief in the omnipotence of force, has most obviously and disastrously failed, thereby forfeiting Germany's claim to be a world power. It is precisely in this respect that the British people can hope to find a lasting source of strength, thanks to the value which their long experience in democratic evolution, both at home and within the Commonwealth, has taught them to set on this element in power.

But we must first analyze in greater detail both the weakness and the strength of Britain's world position in the light of these new conditions.

Of our weaknesses, the first and most obvious is that our material power has declined and is declining relatively to that of the other world powers. The material preeminence which was ours in the nineteenth century has passed once for all. Our now almost stationary and aging population of less than fifty millions is less than half that of the United States and barely a quarter that of the U.S.S.R. The days of a "two-power standard," based on a navy which was undisputed mistress of the seas, are gone for good. Unlike the U.S.A. and U.S.S.R. we only contain within our own island territory a small proportion of the vital raw materials upon which industrial power is built. The rest, together with the greater part of our foodstuffs, we must draw from the four corners of the world over long and vulnerable lines of communication from sources often not in our own control.

Even more important is the passing of our preeminence as the workshop of the world, the mainspring of the world's commerce and capital investment, and the master-mechanic of the world's financial machinery. The centers of gravity of the world's heavy industry have shifted eastward and westward. In steel production, which is the hard core of industrial power in the modern world, the United States could show an output in peacetime of 51 million metric tons (1937) and the U.S.S.R. 19 millions (1939), as against Britain's 13 millions (1937).

Our other basic weakness lies in a less material sphere. Living on the moral capital of our past greatness, we have still failed to adapt ourselves sufficiently to the realities of our new situation. We have been too slow in shaking off the outworn attitudes of mind and social and economic forms which once stood us in good stead, but now clog our thinking and frustrate our national will and energy. Though second to none in inventiveness, we have been shy in the application of new methods and techniques, whether in the sphere of warfare, industry, or social organization.

Lastly, we have been content to present to the world an incomplete and distorted picture of ourselves, or rather to leave its presentation in the hands of a type of Englishman who has become increasingly unrepresentative of the life in Britain. And, what is even more important, we have so far failed to generate, either in our domestic or foreign affairs a sense of mission, of standing for a set of values and a way of life. Of all the powers which in recent years have made a bid for world status, each one, Germany, the U.S.S.R., America, Japan, even Italy, has in its different way generated a sense of mission, has offered the world an ideal. We alone, though we had at least as much to offer as any other, were content to offer nothing but merely negative appeasement and the stale appeal of past ideals.

These weaknesses are fundamental, and it is essential that in the framing of our foreign policy they should be squarely faced. But it is equally essential that they should not be exaggerated and made into excuses for inaction and timidity. Even in the material sphere what will count above all will be not the absolute amount of our resources, but our will to use them. If we listen to the pessimists who trounce every bold proposal with the cry that we cannot afford it, or that the British public will not stomach it, then, whatever the extent of our ultimate resources, we shall condemn ourselves to the status of a second-rate power. If on the other hand we have the will, the administrative capacity and the leadership to mobilize our resources as fully for peace as for war, accepting sacrifices in peacetime of the same order as those we have accepted in war, then, as our wartime achievements have shown, we need have little fear of the limits imposed by our physical resources. And as to our more intangible weaknesses, these, though highly damaging, are even more remediable by our own efforts. Not the least of the tasks awaiting the framers of our foreign policy will be the exercise of such imaginative leadership as will ensure that those efforts are forthcoming.

Moreover, against these weaknesses we must put into the balance the durable elements of our strength. First, there is our geographical position between Europe and America, a position reinforced by our historical role as the bridge between the old world and the new. There is our position as the nucleus of a world-wide commonwealth of free peoples—an association whose cohesion the war has once again strikingly demonstrated, and for which the more rationally planned world of the future will open up new possibilities of intimate collaboration, imparting new strength to all its member nations.

In the sphere of industry there is the high degree of technical skill and the high quality of British workmanship—to which our achievements in the air and in many other phases of the war bear witness, and which has been yet further enhanced by the extensive development in training and technical skill resulting from the war. This will qualify us to play a leading part in a world economy directed toward rising living standards.

In the cultural and intellectual field, quite apart from our inherent potentialities, we shall have a special position for two reasons: first, because the people of war-ravaged Europe will look to us, as the temporary repository of European culture, for help and guidance in picking up again the scattered threads of the European tradition, and in rebuilding the institutions—churches, universities, trade unions and many others —in which it is largely embodied. Secondly, in a world where English will become more and more the language of international intercourse, we shall share with the other English-speaking peoples the benefits of that development.

But it is in the social and political field that our greatest potential strength lies. Here geography and history have endowed us with an exceptional wealth of experience, expressing itself in our capacity for tolerance and compromise and for combining change with continuity; in the strong sense of national unity which we combine with a development of the free institutions and associations that give vigor and variety to a modern community; in our social and political inventiveness and adaptability. . . .

The same factors of history and geography have given us, through our world-wide associations, great experience in the handling of world affairs and of relations with foreign peoples, from the most advanced to the most backward; and they have had another and even more important consequence. The British people have begun to learn, as other nations of world importance have often failed to learn, the necessity of harmonizing their own national aims and aspirations with the basic aims and values of civilization. That most deep-rooted and powerful of social instincts, the instinct of patriotism, which in Nazi Germany or Fascist Italy has been mobilized for ends fundamentally in conflict with the basic values of civilization, can in Britain be summoned up for ends which are of world-wide appeal.

Such are the potentialities in the British people which the framers of our foreign policy must turn to account. By no means all of them are fully realized in our society as it is now organized. Many of them have long been frustrated by economic and social inequality, by the persistence of obsolete ideas and methods, by the obstruction of vested interests, by timid and unimaginative leadership. Given the necessary adaptation of our society and a courageous leadership, both in home and foreign affairs, which will release these latent potentialities, they will be enough not merely to outweigh our material weaknesses, but to carry us on to what may be one of the great periods of our history. . . .

Chapter 7

France

IN 1919 President Wilson brought back from the Paris Peace Conference a treaty pledging U.S. military aid to France in case of another German invasion. The Senate never acted on the treaty, so it did not go into effect. But its terms expressed none the less faithfully the great importance which many Americans then attached to safeguarding France in the future.

As the First World War faded into the past, Americans tended to forget their debt to France. There was a general disposition to discount French fears of German revenge. As a nation we showed very little grasp of the French view that only superior armed force could keep Germany within bounds. Americans generally were impatient with French insistence that military guarantees from the Great Powers, including the United States, must precede any substantial weakening of the army and other defenses of France.

Americans too often failed during this inter-war period, to realize how much they relied upon France as well as Great Britain to guard the Atlantic rimland of Europe. The defeat of France in 1940 came as a terrifying shock to the American people who had taken at face value comforting assurances that the French army was fully adequate for the defense of Western Europe.

The German break-through to the Atlantic compelled us for the first time really to take stock of what we had at stake in Western Europe. For the first time in this century, we faced a potentially hostile Great Power on the opposite shore of the Atlantic. The fall of France gave the Axis submarine bases and flying fields flanking the Atlantic approaches to the British Isles, temporary control of the Mediterranean, and, above all, a springboard for attacks on southern England. German occupation of France transformed the French colonies in Africa and in the Western Hemisphere into sources of potential danger to the United States. Hitler secured a direct overland link with Falangist Spain, and thereby closer contacts with Fascist groups within some of the American republics. French imperial defenses in the Far East all but collapsed, opening Indo-China to Japan for subsequent use as a jumping-off point for the assault on Malaya, Singapore, and the East Indies.

Only time can reveal the full impact of the Second World War upon Franco-American relations. The French Empire as well as metropolitan France include numerous military positions of growing strategic importance in relation to the future defense of the United States. At the same time, there is no prospect that either France or the French colonies will become derelicts upon the ocean of world politics. Though physically weakened, France may yet emerge from the present war spiritually invigorated and internally more united. Time alone will show whether France can fully regain its pre-war standing among the powers. But General DeGaulle's renewal of the historic French tie with Russia not only foreshadows a vigilant watch on the Rhine but also makes France a pivotal state in the future relations of the United States and Great Britain with the Soviet Union.

All this does not mean that the new France will, or can, play in the new Europe the same role that the old France played in the old Europe. We shall be in danger of making grave mistakes if we assume that the clock can be pushed back to 1939, 1933, or 1919. In the case of France, as in the case of Great Britain, we are confronted with a new situation. But this emerging situation is the outgrowth of what has gone before, and to understand the France of today and tomorrow, we must know something of the France of yesterday and the day before.

France was once the most populous and the most powerful state in Europe. By 1914, however, Russia, Germany, and Great Britain had outstripped France in population. Germany had displaced France as the foremost land power in Europe. Only in alliance with Russia and Great Britain was France able to stem the German assault on Paris. In 1917 it required the intervention of the United States to break the long stalemate on the Western Front and accomplish the defeat of Germany.

The victory of 1918 temporarily restored the historic primacy of France in Europe. Germany was crushed and compelled to surrender most of its arms. The Austro-Hungarian Empire had collapsed and dissolved into its constituent ethnic elements. Italy tottered on the verge of revolution. Russia had plunged into the revolutionary abyss, and was racked by bitter civil war. England showed no disposition to assume political leadership over the Continent.

France, though internally shaken by four years of battles on its own soil, and terribly weakened by frightful casualties, was nevertheless the strongest power upon the Continent in 1919, and thereafter became the keystone of a structure of alliances and other arrangements designed to enforce peace in Europe for a long time to come.

Twenty-one years later, in 1940, the France which had emerged triumphant from the First World War crashed down in defeat under the shattering impact of yet another German invasion.

This disaster cannot be explained simply by comparing military equipment, numbers of soldiers and workers, stocks of raw materials, capacity of mines and factories, and other tangibles. The intangibles also must be taken into account. One must attempt to answer such questions as: Why did France in the inter-war period fail to make more effective use of the many strategic assets which she possessed? Why were French statesmen in the 1930's unable to maintain the alliances and other security arrangements so painstakingly erected in the 1920's? Why was the French nation unable to enter into an effective alliance with Soviet Russia, and thereby ensure the encirclement of Germany? Why did most French military experts fail to estimate realistically either the potentialities of new weapons and tactics or the military strength of their friends and probable enemies? Why did other peoples, including ourselves, fail to estimate more accurately the relative strength of France in that tragic period? In the light of all that has happened, what factors are shaping the role which France can play in the future? And how will the emerging situation and policies of the new France affect the security of the United States?

THE FACE OF MODERN FRANCE

By Pierre Maillaud

From chap. I of *France*, by Pierre Maillaud. The World Today Series. Copyright 1943 by Oxford University Press, London and New York; reproduced by permission. The author is a well-known French journalist.

The French Republic in 1939 was a state of some forty-two million inhabitants, including three million foreigners.

... Frenchmen, before their country was struck down, were still living at ease and with some elbow room in a wide and fertile country.... This land was still capable of development in every direction. Never had the French been compelled to look with anxiety across the sea for their food supplies. Never had they, like Antonio, waited till their ship came home to fulfill their obligations. They could dig their good earth and make it pay.

Geography has made France a natural economic unit, because of a diversity after the last war when he remarked that "any French child can draw from memory a fairly accurate map of his own country." In fact, only the northern frontier (less than 400 miles out of

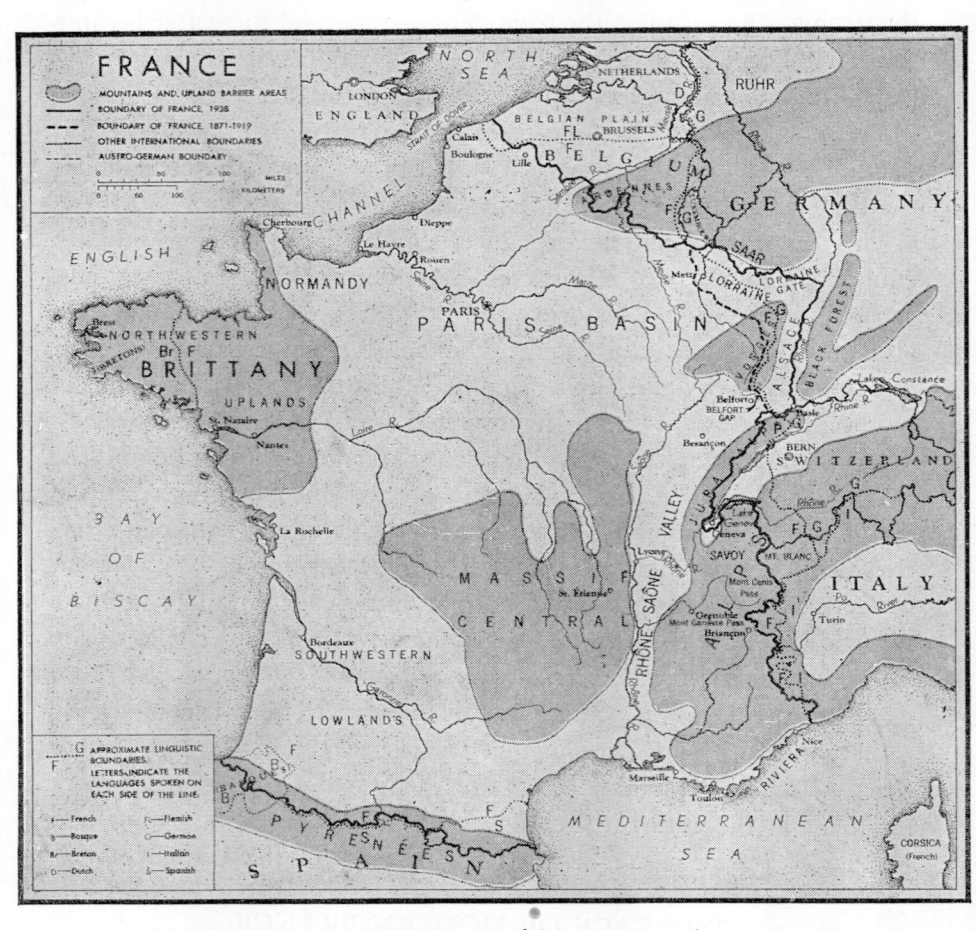

FIG. 14. France: Geographic Regions and Linguistic and Strategic Frontiers.
Prepared for the War Department by the Office of Strategic Services; reproduced from *Geographical Foundations of National Power*. Army Service Forces Manual M-103-1. Government Printing Office, 1944.

unparalleled in Europe. Indeed, the combination of unity and diversity is perhaps the most distinctive feature of metropolitan France. The geographical unity was somewhat naïvely acknowledged by a German professor shortly nearly 3,500) might cause the child to hesitate over the drawing-paper: it is the only one not clearly defined by sea, mountain, or river. France's diversity is even more conspicuous. To this quality the Frenchman is very much alive, as well as to the singularity of this phenomenon in Europe, and the most uncouth French peasant will draw the foreigner's attention to its practical value.

This diversity expresses itself in every form: variety of produce, climate, scenery, people, habits, and traditions.

The temperature sometimes falls to 40 degrees of frost east of Besançon, in the most continental part of France, when it may well reach 58 degrees Fahrenheit in the most sheltered part of the Riviera, and the winter sports fans may open the skiing season in Mégève when the last bathers begin to shiver on the beach of St. Tropez.

The farmer of Flanders and Artois can grow sugar beetroot, whilst oranges are picked in Nice and tobacco leaves dried in Languedoc. Soon after millions of bushels of wheat have been harvested in the central plains of France, the orchards of Guyenne yield thousands of tons of peaches and plums. And when the last apples and pears of Normandy are gathered and crushed for cider, cartload after cartload of grapes redden or gild first the sunny roads of the Bordelais and then the lanes of Anjou and the hilly paths of Burgundy. Breton fishermen sail their frail fleets toward Newfoundland for cod-fishing while the richest cattle herds in Western Europe are being driven down from mountain to plain. Wood-cutters begin their hard tasks in the melancholy forests of Sologne when the shepherds of Savoy at the crack of dawn marshal their sheep away to some new pasture to graze 10,000 feet above sea-level.

Variety in habits, costume, and mood, is no less marked: as the first white-aproned waiter lifts the shutters of his small provincial café with his double-pronged pole, a peasant in a little church of Finistère, 300 miles away, is kneeling down to pray, his round black hat held against his stomach, an ivory cross dangling over his short velvet jacket, his baggy brown breeches spreading over the straw seat of his chair. At the same hour one of the belated revellers in Paris waves his top hat and white scarf to hail a racing taxi, whilst a cowboy of the Camargue carefully polishes his brand new maroquine riding-boots and star-shaped spurs to make his debut on the Arles arena early in the afternoon.

These and other images of France are within the compass of every schoolboy's memory or imagination. But this double notion of unity and diversity does not suffice to define the main characteristics of the French land. In order to complete the picture, another and very specifically French notion must be added: the notion of balance between these various elements. Two thousand years ago, Caesar compared France to a human body in which no organ is missing, of which no organ is superfluous. The balance between plain and mountain, between continental and maritime regions, between pastures and agricultural zones, between water and earth is so striking that it appears from a glance at a map. The accidents of terrain are nowhere so abrupt as to make any part of France uninhabitable. The system of waterways is by far the most complete and orderly in Europe. It never falls short of the need nor does it anywhere exceed it.

Rivers have played a great part in the life and development of France. Within her frontiers, they serve as a guide to the traveler. They show him where to look for mountains, where they widen and spread into the plains, inviting industry, luxury, and art, and where to find the main ports, like gates opening on the sea. Thanks to this unique system of waterways, nowhere turbulent and uncontrollable, and which has been improved by a number of canals, very few parts of France are deserted. It brings everywhere a sense of life active yet gentle, of strength within order and measure.

This is, no doubt, the reason why the most essentially French part of France's civilization was born on her rivers. Her most prosperous towns are built on them. Her finest cathedrals rise from their banks. The turrets of her most graceful castles are reflected in their waters. Her great economic regions are easily definable through them.

These great French waterways, from the Somme to the Garonne and the Rhone, had already sketched out the first map of France long before any policy of natural frontiers had been dreamt of. Perhaps it was no mere coincidence that the first French political thinker, Louis XI, in his castle of Plessis-les-Tours, on the banks of the Loire, foresaw the French "realm to be," one hundred years before Henri IV set out to achieve its unification. It was also from the banks of the Loire that a clearly marked French culture began to spread, as the heir and successor to the great Italian Age, less rich in art but greater in thought, since it broke away from the scholastic rule and ushered in modern ethics.

France has over two thousand miles of seacoast and approximately the same length of land frontiers. She lies between the Continent and the sea, firmly bound to the one and yet wide open to the other. Her unequalled network of rivers provides the links between land and sea. It is almost as though it symbolized the French compromise between the continental and the maritime extremes and perhaps the great dilemma in many French minds between a continental and an imperial policy.

The same quality of balance also appears in the distribution of the French population over the territory. Partly because of its harmonious geography and partly because of its system of waterways, the population of France is more evenly spread over the land than that of the other great European nations. Its density is naturally greater in the northern parts of the country, which contain most of the great industrial centers, with the exception of Le Creusot, Lyons, and St. Etienne. Besides, the expansion of trade during the nineteenth century increased the maritime population. But the process of concentration of population which has been a notable feature in world evolution during the last hundred years has been slower and more limited in France than elsewhere. In 1939, more than 55 per cent of the population lived in hamlets or towns of less than 4,000 inhabitants. Problems of supply or accommodation which assail a country with a highly centralized and concentrated population, did not arise. Regional migration and especially national migration was never a necessity.

The French, therefore, in spite of their colonial conquests and of the progress of communications, were inclined to a sedentary life, not only nationally but also regionally. Traveling was a pleasure and a luxury rather than a need. Work, entertainment, or repose were never out of reach.

Paris had become an increasingly powerful magnet. But, although a hundred and fifty years of administrative and cultural centralization had reduced the political importance of provincial capitals, many towns in addition to Paris had remained, in various degrees, effective centers of gravitation. . . .

. . . In 1939, despite economic, social, and political crises, the country's great natural assets still made individual life in France happier than it had become in most parts of Europe. These assets, which were to prove heavy liabilities in terms of international power, still remained valuable in terms of "life within the nation," even in the midst of profound and far-reaching changes.

But this "French way of living," which the Germans envied as a boon undeserved by its possessors, was not merely the product of a fortunate land. It had been dearly bought. The riches and harmony of nature were a geographical fact; but its exploitation had been a human accomplishment repeatedly threatened from within and without. . . .

When the French defenses broke down under the German onslaught and the German mechanized hordes were let loose over this fertile and flourishing land, it was not the first time that a civilization which has been and remains essential to the progress of Europe had been threatened with extinction.

Indeed this civilization had sprung from its physical and cultural struggle with Germany. Its birth, its crystallization, its radiation throughout Europe and the world, are inseparable from the national resistance of France to German nomadic instincts and tribal migrations. Its role as a guardian of Western culture has only been fulfilled through the centuries in so far as France was also able to perform the function of keeper of her own realm. . . .

STRATEGICAL POSITION OF FRANCE

By David Thomson

From *French Foreign Policy*, by David Thomson. Oxford Pamphlets on World Affairs, no. 67; Oxford University Press, London, 1944; reproduced by permission.

THE constant reason for France's importance in Europe is her geographical position. Since the kingdom of France first took recognizable shape some six hundred years ago, it has mattered in Europe because it links the Atlantic seaboard and the English Channel with the western basin of the Mediterranean. Behind the strong natural defenses of these coastlines and the Pyrenees and the Alps, a single national community under a single royal government was able to grow up, holding at bay Saracens and Spaniards on the south, Teutons on the east, and English on the north. A single bloc of this size, shape, and position naturally played a decisive part in the balance of power in Europe. Its rich diversity of soil and climate produced men and materials which a strong monarchy could harness to national purposes; and France became the first great nation-state on the continent.

DEFENSE FRONTIERS

By Samuel Van Valkenburg

From chap. 3 of *Elements of Political Geography*, by S. Van Valkenburg. Copyright 1939 by Prentice-Hall, Inc., New York; reproduced by permission. The author is professor of geography at Clark University.

Size. France, with an area of 207,000 square miles, is the largest country in Europe, excluding Soviet Russia and since 1938 also Germany. On the other hand, it is less than four-fifths the size of the State of Texas. . . .

Location. France is located between the latitudes 44° and 55°N on the west side of the greatest land mass of the world, namely Eurasia. Disregarding the climatic implications of this position, which will later be shown as favoring national development, it may be said that France possesses one of the most valuable locations in the world. Location does not concern latitude alone; the vicinal factor must be considered as well. On the east, France borders Central Europe, one of the world's most productive areas; while on the west it faces the commercially important Atlantic and the Americas. . . . This location has many commercial and cultural advantages, and, although the danger of war, as a result of immediate contacts with powerful dynamic neighbors, may be listed as a disadvantage, one thing is certain—this location gives France a central position. Half of the length of the French boundary is seacoast. Because France borders upon the Mediterranean and North Seas, as well as upon the Atlantic, the nation's commercial and political interests extend over those waters. This would make the sea location perfect, were it not for the fact that the connections between these bodies of water are dominated by a foreign, though friendly, nation.

Shape. The shape of France is remarkably compact. . . . A circle with a 300-mile radius described from the geographic center of the country encloses nearly all of France. The sectors without the circle, when totaled, amount to but a small portion of the country's area. It is interesting to note the center of the circle, the theoretical heart of France. It is located south of the Loire River, not far from the historic town of Bourges. Paris, the capital, has an eccentric location, and, since it is nearer to the northern boundary, it is more vulnerable in time of war. This disadvantage came strongly to the fore during the World War, when in the fall of 1914 and again in the spring of 1918, the German armies came almost within sight of the capital, while throughout the last part of the war the city was under enemy gunfire.

Relief. . . . Relief together with climate has been an important factor in the development of France into one of the great world powers today.

One singular feature of the topography of France deserves special mention because of its strategic value. This feature is the series of escarpments around the Paris Basin. The geologically young Paris Basin is located inside a frame of uplands and mountains which offer real obstacles to an enemy approaching Paris in time of war. Only small, disconnected army divisions can operate in these mountain sections. The Ardennes in the north are the first unit in this frame, with the winding narrow valley of the Meuse as the only break. Beyond the Moselle are the hills of the Hunsrück and the Palatinate, farther south the Vosges, the Jura, and finally the Central Plateau. The western part of this mountain frame, the Armorican uplands, does not enter in this military evaluation except in case of a sea attack. Between these topographic obstacles are the gateways into France; the Flanders opening between Ardennes and the coast; the gate of Lorraine between Hunsrück and Vosges; the gate of Burgundy between Vosges and Jura; and finally the Rhone-Saône depression between Alps-Jura on the east and the Central Plateau on the west. But nature has gone even further in its protection of France, for these gateways are controlled through a concentric alignment of the escarpments, whose outer steep slopes, several hundred feet high, face the enemy. These slopes are due to outcropping hard layers of rock which dip toward the interior of the basin, at the geographical and geological center of which lies Paris. They were used by France as a basis for the defense system during the [First] World War, and such names as Côte de Meuse (near Verdun), the Argonne Forest, and Chemin des Dames (near Reims) frequently appeared in the newspapers, for they were centers of fighting.

The weak part of the natural system of defense is in the north where the escarpment is much lower, permitting the enemy to enter the country and advance up to the inner escarpments immediately around Paris. This was the case in August 1914, when the right wing of the German army moved rapidly through Belgium and northern France, threatening to take Paris and encircle the French Army. Fortunately for the Allied cause the battle of the Marne brought relief.

Land boundaries. The land boundaries of France are for the most part based on physical features. . . .

The Pyrenees have often been cited as an excellent example of a mountain boundary. On wall maps and in atlases they appear as a great barrier separating France from Spain. Undoubtedly, they have served well as a frontier zone, but in reality they are not a complete barrier. . . .

The eastern French boundary from the Mediterranean to the Lake of Geneva follows essentially the crest of the main Alpine range, except in the Swiss portion, where it follows a secondary range west of the Swiss portion of the Rhone. Taken as a whole the barrier here, too, is not complete, for six highways connect the two sides of the range and could easily be used in case of war. Consequently, the French have built heavy fortifications at the weak spots, principally around Briançon, the French military center in the Alps. . . .

The Jura boundary between France and Switzerland has no physiographic basis other than that it follows generally the trend of the mountains. Many passes which make transit easy render this a mediocre boundary from the standpoint of military defense, and France regards with concern the possibility of a German march through Switzerland in case of war. Beyond the Burgundy Gate the boundary extends across the rolling topography to the Rhine, which, since 1918, has been the boundary between France and Germany. Under present conditions of military technique, rivers no longer constitute a barrier in case of war. Nevertheless, rivers as boundaries have the advantage of being rather definite even when, as in this case, they divide a valley so that the two parts which have natural and economic interests in common find themselves separated by a political break. The Vosges are the natural protection of France, and while the French lines of defense are immediately along the river front, these mountains serve as a buttress which, incidentally, separates Alsace from the rest of France.

The boundary line between the Rhine and the Ardennes runs over the Lorraine Plateau, which is another gateway into France. This boundary has no definite physiographic basis. Its origin has to be explained historically as an agreement between the two countries concerned. It is heavily fortified, and the above-mentioned escarpments are reinforced. The south foot of the thickly forested Ardennes provides a rather good boundary between the Moselle and the northern lowlands, with the spur of Givet on the Meuse protecting the only good approach. The [First] World War showed that the Ardennes are not well suited to major operations of modern warfare.

Of all the French boundaries, that passing through the northern lowlands is the least satisfactory. It is not only superimposed on the lowland topography but it separates people of the same language, tradition and economy. Although it has existed in its present form for centuries, it has not matured but shows all the signs of interference with natural conditions. Strategically, it is the weakest spot in the French defense, as was illustrated by the [First] World War when only the heroic defense of the Allied armies kept the enemy in check and away from the Channel ports.

RESOURCES, INDUSTRIES, AND COMMUNICATIONS

By Samuel Van Valkenburg and
Ellsworth Huntington

From chap. 29 of *Europe*, by S. Van Valkenburg and E. Huntington. Copyright 1935 by John Wiley & Sons, New York; reproduced by permission.

France is an unusually stable, well-balanced, and mature country. . . . The balanced quality of the country, resulting in part at least from favorable conditions of climate, relief, soils, power, and mineral resources, is evident in the fact that among the large European countries France is the one which could best maintain its present economic status if all foreign trade were suddenly abolished. Only in the field of textiles would this cause really serious limitations, for France raises no cotton. . . .

Geographical Assets. Located on both the Atlantic and the Mediterranean, and touching the North Sea, France has a wider range of maritime opportunities than any other European country not even excepting Spain. The western Mediterranean admits the country to northern Africa where the colonies of Algiers, Tunis, and Morocco are almost an integral part of France. They serve as a stepping-stone to the great French colonial empire in the Sudan and equatorial Africa. The Atlantic gave France a share in the exploitation of the world in the sixteenth and seventeenth centuries. Most of the fruits of this are lost, as in the case of Canada, but commercial as well as cultural contacts still remain.

A second geographical factor which favors France is its climate, which is an almost perfect blending of three different types, the Western European, the Mediterranean, and the Central European. Cyclonic control is dominant, but is less vigorous than in countries farther north. Hence the French climate is on the whole less stimulating than the less agreeable climates of its northern neighbors.

The relief of the surface is another asset, for only locally is France seriously rugged. The wide rolling plains, the uplands and plateaus, and the mountain ranges induce diversity of production to the great profit of the country as a whole. Moreover, in spite of high mountains, the relief permits easy connections between the different French regions and permits France to have an admirable system of roads, canals, and railroads.

France is also rather well provided with mineral resources. The coal production, it is true, does not equal the consumption, but the waterpower, especially of the Pyrenees and Alps, partially offsets this deficit. Potash, rock salt, and bauxite are valuable French mining products, but the chief factor in France's mineral output is the abundance of iron ore, for which France is the second world producer.

Finally, the last but not the least French asset is the population itself. This mixture of ancient Celts and later Germanic invaders shows strong ethnic unity, and for centuries has withstood the shocks of national existence.

THE LAND AND ITS USES

By R. H. Whitbeck and
V. C. Finch

From chap. 24 of *Economic Geography*, by R. H. Whitbeck and V. C. Finch. Revised edition copyright 1941 by R. H. Whitbeck and V. C. Finch. McGraw-Hill Book Co., New York; reproduced by permission. The late Dr. Whitbeck was professor of geography in the University of Wisconsin, where Dr. Finch holds a similar position.

The area of France is about one and three-fourths times that of the British Isles, but its population is slightly less.

Physiographic and climatic features divide the country into several contrasting regions. These may be arranged in groups which include: (1) The well-watered and generally fertile northern and western lowlands, containing the basins of the Garonne, Loire, Seine, and several smaller rivers. The northern part of this region is often called the "Paris Basin." (2) The hill lands of Brittany and of central France with their hard rocks and poor granitic soils. (3) The rugged lands of the Alps and the Pyrenees. (4) The Rhone Valley and the southern coastlands with the dry summers of the Mediterranean climate. Over one-half of France is lowland of more than average fertility; 50 per cent of the total area is under cultivation in field crops, vineyards, orchards, and gardens; and 20 per cent is devoted to pasturage. France has more farmland of excellent quality than any other European country except Russia. Nearly 40 per cent of the population is engaged in farming, as against 7 per cent in the United Kingdom. Moreover, the greater part of the farms are tilled by their owners, a highly desirable condition but not one that prevails generally throughout Europe. The farms, which average 20 to 40 acres in size, are industriously but not scientifically cultivated. . . . The land of France is naturally more productive than that of Germany, but the farming is so much less scientifically done that crop yields have generally been lower.

FOOD SUPPLY AND DEFENSE

By Samuel Van Valkenburg

From chap. 4 of Elements of Political Geography, *by S. Van Valkenburg. Copyright 1939 by Prentice-Hall, Inc., New York; reproduced by permission.*

Seen from the air most of France shows an intricate system of farm plots, which appear to fit together like parts of a jigsaw puzzle. One is tempted to dwell upon the beauty of the French farmlands and the great care taken by the peasants to make the land productive, but in a political-geographical study it is only necessary to emphasize the fact that agriculture is still one of the major occupations of the people of France. . . . There is a steady decline in agricultural intensity from north to south, and second, the harvest in the north is far more secure than in the south. . . . When during the [First] World War the Germans entered northern France, they occupied a large percentage of the most important agricultural land of the country, which resulted in a serious food shortage for the duration of the war. In other words, the best agricultural sections of France are also the most vulnerable sections.

France is often cited as an example of a country which because of favorable physical conditions and an industrious population is able to feed itself. This is, however, not the case. . . . The cereal consumption is much larger than the production. . . . Using a five-year average (1930-1934), the following are percentages of self-sufficiency for various grains: wheat, 89 per cent; rye, 95 per cent; barley, 79 per cent; oats, 99 per cent, and corn, 37 per cent. Similar deficits exist for fruits, sugar, rice, vegetables, and wine. . . .

The deficit of the homeland is partly canceled by a surplus of those products in the colonies. In fact, only coffee (Brazil), fruits (Spain), and oilseeds (Argentina) are left as important deficits. At this point it is necessary to distinguish between colonies near at hand (North Africa) which supply the homeland with cereals, wine, and vegetables, and those more distant (French Indo-China and French West Africa) which supply rice and oilseeds. The need for this distinction is the fact that long distances increase the vulnerability of the food supply in case of war. . . . Nevertheless, in contrast to many countries in Europe, France, with a change and a slight decrease in her food consumption, would be able to feed herself even if cut off entirely from the outside. It is, therefore, not the food supply which really worries the French economists when they check the resources of their nation.

MINERAL RESOURCES

By R. H. WHITBECK AND V. C. FINCH

From chap. 24 of *Economic Geography*, by R. H. Whitbeck and V. C. Finch. Revised edition copyright 1941 by R. H. Whitbeck and V. C. Finch. McGraw-Hill, Inc., New York; reproduced by permission.

IN one resource France has led all Europe—the iron-ore reserves of Lorraine, which nearly equal in quantity those of all the rest of Europe and have given to France a practically unlimited supply of that metal. The ore bodies are of sedimentary origin; they are partly on the French side and partly on the German side of the boundary as it existed from 1871 to 1919. One of the reasons for Germany's tremendous industrial growth was the possession of the iron-ore deposits taken from France in 1871 and developed by efficient German methods. These "minette" ores are not high in metallic iron (average, 30 to 40 per cent), and they contain so much phosphorous that some of them could not be economically used for making steel until the discovery of the Thomas process (about 1880). The quantity of ore, however, is enormous; and with the return of Alsace-Lorraine to France, Germany lost over two-thirds of her iron ore, and France came into possession of these reserves and of the furnaces and steel mills that the Germans had built. Control of this resource . . . again returned to German hands [after the fall of France in 1940, and remained so until the autumn of 1944]. Besides these major ore bodies in Lorraine, France has iron ores elsewhere, including those of Normandy and Brittany in the north, those of the eastern Pyrenees in the south, and those in her colonial possessions in northern Africa. However, upward of 90 per cent of the ore mined in France comes from the minette ores of Lorraine. Germany has also the necessary coal for smelting the iron ore, which France does not have. With her coal and iron so largely in the northern and eastern part of the country the French steel industries naturally center in that part of the country (see Fig. 21, p. 323).

France is poor in coal. The chief coal field is in the extreme north, extending across the boundary into Belgium, and minor coal fields are located in various other parts of the country. As a whole, the coal of France is of only moderate quality and is expensive to mine and hence is more costly to the users than is British, German, or American coal. After the First World War, France imported, mainly from Britain, nearly half as much coal as her mines produced and also some of the coke with which to smelt her iron ores. Undoubtedly the different character of the manufacturing industries that have developed in France as compared with those in the United States, Great Britain, and Germany is partly due to her inadequate coal resources.

France is poor in nearly all metals excepting iron and aluminum. Copper, lead, zinc, gold, silver, tin, and nickel are either wholly lacking or very scarce. France has one of the two largest known reserves of bauxite, the principal ore of aluminum, in Europe or in the world, the other being in Hungary. . . . France is also one of the two leading producers of antimony, used in various alloys, including type metal. China clays of the finest quality exist and are used in making the beautiful French pottery at Limoges and elsewhere.

The enforced expansion of manufacturing into other parts of France during the four years of the First World War, when the Germans held the principal French coal field, led to a rapid development of hydroelectric power. France has great potential waterpower in the Pyrenees, the Alps, the Vosges, and the Auvergne regions. The amount of such power in use more than doubled between 1913 and 1921, and France now has more than a third as much waterpower in use as the United States has and more than any other European country except Italy. This is one method by which France can make up for her shortage of coal.

MANUFACTURING INDUSTRIES AND DEFENSE

By Derwent Whittlesey and J. K. Wright

From chap. 2 of *Geographical Foundations of National Power*. Army Service Forces Manual M-103-1, Government Printing Office, Washington, 1944. Dr. Whittlesey is professor of geography at Harvard University; Dr. Wright is director of the American Geographical Society.

France ranks as one of the leading manufacturing states of Europe. Nevertheless, it lags far behind Germany and Great Britain in aggregate output of manufactured goods. The character of its manufactured products, mainly articles requiring skill and taste, differentiates it still more sharply from countries which have developed an industrial life symmetrically pyramided on a base of coal and iron.

There are four principal manufacturing areas: (1) in the northeast in the vicinity of the coal fields near the Belgium border and beyond it in Belgium, (2) in the iron-mining region of Lorraine, (3) in Paris and its suburbs, and (4) in and near Lyons.

France's iron and steel industry is handicapped by the geographical distribution of the iron and coal and the lack of alloy minerals. The leading pig-iron center is the iron field of Lorraine, which operates largely on German coal. The leading steel and chemical-producing section is the northeastern region, where most of the country's coal is mined (see Fig. 21, p. 323, below). The earliest steel center grew up on a coal field at St. Etienne, not far from Lyons. It specialized in equipment for war but remains small because of the restricted local supply of coal and iron. Electrical machinery and cutlery are the chief steel products of Lyons and its satellite towns. In the Parisian suburbs is concentrated the manufacturing of many metal products, particularly automobiles, aircraft, and munitions. Shipbuilding is centered chiefly in Brittany, on the lower Loire, and in Normandy.

The main centers of textile manufacture are along the northeastern frontier. Lille, the largest of the mill towns, is the fourth largest city in France. In French Flanders on the border of Belgium, local flax has attracted an important linen industry, and an equally significant woolen textile industry has grown up here. Cotton has been added to the raw materials consumed in this region, and cotton manufacturing is important in Alsace also. Lyons was the first place in the Western World to develop silk manufacturing; the mulberry leaves for the cocoons were grown in the mild Rhone valley. The Lyons silk mills have retained preeminence and have added rayon to their products.

Chemical products, including explosives, are produced both in the Alps, where there is abundant waterpower, and in the northeast on the coal fields. Lyons also is a major center of chemical manufacturing.

In 1936 the French government embarked upon a program of relocating certain strategic manufactures. It was planned to move certain industries, particularly aircraft, to the southwestern part of the country. A law was then passed permitting nationalization of factories that make equipment for war or, alternatively, state control of their output. Because of the expense involved in moving and because of political pressure exerted against change, little had been done before the outbreak of the war. It was decided to apply the law only to the final stages of manufacturing, in any event. Under this plan, about a dozen industries were expropriated, including the Renault automotive works and the munitions plants of Schneider and Brandt. The government bought into the aircraft industry by purchasing two-thirds of the productive capacity of the country.

Degree of Self-Sufficiency. It will be evident from the preceding discussion that the self-sufficiency of France is only partial, even taking into account the supplementary resources of the Empire. It might be possible for France to feed its population without outside supplies during a long war, although there is some question as to the adequacy of the grain supply in poor years. The production of war materials and munitions could probably be increased by a more intensive use of the labor and natural resources than was in effect in 1938. On the other hand, the industries in time of war are basically dependent on an uninterrupted supply of strategic minerals from overseas.

INTERNAL COMMUNICATIONS

By Derwent Whittlesey
and J. K. Wright

From chap. 2 of *Geographical Foundations of National Power*. Army Service Forces Manual M-103-1, Government Printing Office, Washington, 1944.

All the main streams of France are navigable at least for small boats, although the Rhone is too swift for full utility, and the Loire is handicapped by sandbars and shifting channels. There are also more than 8,000 miles of canals. So low are the passes between them that the principal river systems are merged into one by means of barge canals. Altogether the waterways carry approximately one-ninth of the total French internal traffic.

Roads and railroads parallel the streams and canals and take shortcuts between them, making an intricate network of routes. About a ninth of the total traffic of France is carried by the highways, of which there are nearly 400,000 miles. Fifty thousand miles of these are maintained by the state, in part for purposes of military mobilization. Paris is the hub of the road system, including the principal "national routes." The main spokes in the wheel pattern of motor roads have existed for centuries. . . .

The railroads include 44,000 miles of trunk lines and 11,000 miles of local lines. They carry seven-ninths of the total traffic. Railroads follow the natural routes marked out by streams and roads, though they generally stick closer to the valleys than do the roads, particularly the straight roads first laid out for the Roman legions. All French railroads are of standard gauge except for minor lines in the mountains. Some of them in the Alps and Pyrenees are electrified, but otherwise coal is the fuel used. Military strategy has modified the location of some routes in the vicinity of the eastern frontier. Extensions of the main railroad lines reach into all the countries of central Europe and, with a change of gauge, into Spain. Most of the railroads in the colonies are isolated lines, not linked into networks, and are generally of a narrow gauge, a meter in width.

It has often been remarked that it takes less time and energy to travel from one part of France to another by way of Paris than to go direct, even when points of departure and destination are close together. The wheel-shaped pattern of both roads and railroads, adjusted largely to the distribution of hills and valleys, focuses economic life upon Paris to a superlative degree.

However advantageous that may be for business, it puts the country at a disadvantage in case of war. Invaders are led directly to the political heart of the country, and defenders are handicapped by the lack of a sufficient number of lateral routes, or belt lines, in deploying their forces along a broad base behind the fighting frontier.

In 1938 the air routes over France were both internal and international. From Paris as a center, local routes radiated, following the major pattern of the rails and roads. Transcontinental routes linked England with Italy by way of France, and connected France with all the European countries to the eastward.

POPULATION AND MANPOWER

By Derwent Whittlesey
and J. K. Wright

From chap. 2 of *Geographical Foundations of National Power*. Army Service Forces Manual M-103-1, Government Printing Office, Washington, 1944.

The French Empire boasts a total population of over a hundred million persons. For metropolitan France the figure is about 42 million people, including 2½ million foreigners. The population of the colonies is estimated at 65 million. The population of France itself is roughly equal to that of Italy or the United Kingdom. Germany has left all these powers far behind.

Until 1850 France had been the most populous state in Europe with the exception of Russia. In the following decade, Germany usurped the lead. Before long, two other states had surpassed France in population: Austria-Hungary in 1880, and the United Kingdom in 1890.

France reached its highest point of natural population increase more than a hundred years ago. From that peak, the average annual increase diminished slowly until the middle of the century after which it dropped sharply. Influenza epidemics combined with a declining birth rate to produce actual deficits in 1890, 1891, 1895, and 1900, and deficits again occurred in 1907 and 1909 which were in no way attributable to epidemics or other external causes.

The First World War cost France nearly 2 million people. Even with the acquisition of Alsace and Lorraine, the population of France in 1921 fell short of . . . 1911 by nearly 400,000. The usual post-war increase in the birth rate enabled France to replace its losses in part, but even this could not compensate for the gaps left in the ranks of the young men of France or for their children who were never born. In fact, France's only salvation during the 'twenties was organized, large-scale immigration. The percentage of foreigners, mostly Italians and Poles, was particularly high in mining and manufacturing, in the North, in Lorraine, and in the Paris area,

Since 1935 the mortality rate in France has exceeded the birth rate. In that year the surplus of deaths over births was 18,000, and every year since has witnessed a decrease in population. Austria is the only other European country with an annual deficit. The situation in France is made worse by an unfavorable age-group distribution. Of all the Great Powers, France has the highest proportion of middle-aged and old people. Its working and fighting population is therefore relatively small compared to the total figure. In the long run, the decline in population alone may result in the reduction of France to the rank of a second-rate power.

POPULATION AFTER THE FIRST WORLD WAR

By Pierre Maillaud

From chap. 5 of *France*, by Pierre Maillaud. The World Today Series. Copyright 1943 by Oxford University Press, London and New York; reproduced by permission.

According to the official records of the American War Department, the French casualties during the First World War stood at: officially killed, 1,357,000; wounded, 4,266,000; missing, 537,000 (of whom over 200,000 were in fact dead). The total figure amounts to 73 per cent of the number of men mobilized in four years and three months of war, i.e., 8,410,000. (In Great Britain the proportion was 35.8 per cent.) Out of this total, nearly one million men were maimed, and several hundred thousands partly disabled. It is therefore not surprising that in 1939, in spite of the recovery of Alsace-Lorraine, the French-born population of France should not have exceeded the 1913 figure. Yet the census is misleading, for it supplies a total figure of population which is partly irrelevant in terms of manpower. In 1939, the male population capable of active service was very noticeably below the 1913 figure; the classes of conscripts called to the colors were only beginning to equal those of 1913, and the reserves, in terms of able-bodied men, could only have reached the 1913 figure toward 1950. Finally, part of the able-bodied population had been directly under the physical and moral strain of the previous war. It is quite clear that in 1939, the cumulative effect of all these factors was still telling heavily on the French nation.

TREND OF POPULATION GROWTH

By F. W. Notestein et al.

From chap. 2 of *The Future Population of Europe and the Soviet Union*, by F. W. Notestein et al. League of Nations, Geneva, 1944. The authors are respectively director and research associates of the Office of Population Research at Princeton University.

In the early eighteenth century France was probably the most populous country in Europe. She was passed by Russia in the eighteenth century, by Germany about 1870, by the British Isles about 1900, and by Italy about 1930. . . . Of the major powers France alone failed to share in the very rapid growth of the last century. Her rate of growth was the lowest in Europe, aside from Ireland, and in recent decades even that was maintained only through immigration. Since 1935 actual decline has begun. Almost all other countries were growing and, barring war, would have continued to grow for a few years. Rapid increase in the past has left them with an abnormally large proportion of the total population in the young adult ages producing all the births and few of the deaths. France, on the other hand, cannot grow from this source. Her population has aged into the position that

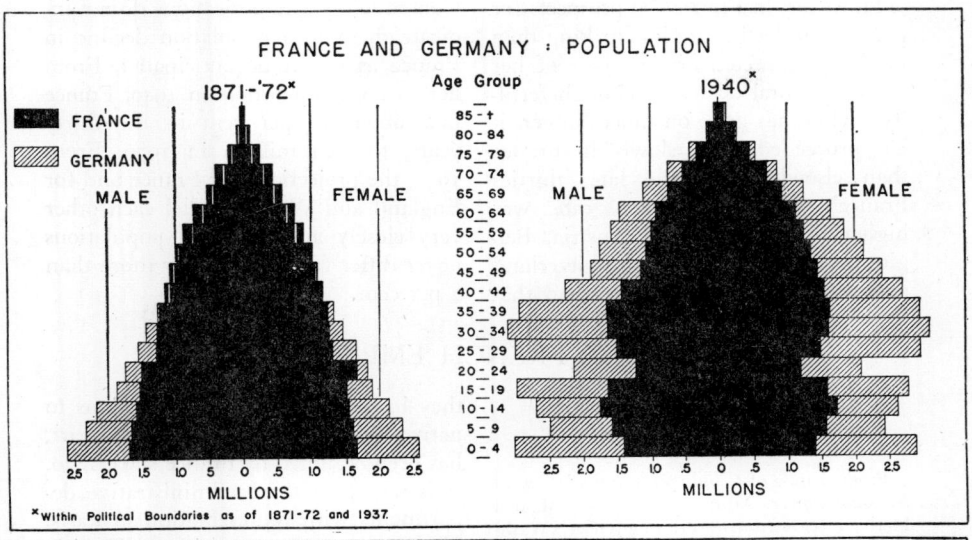

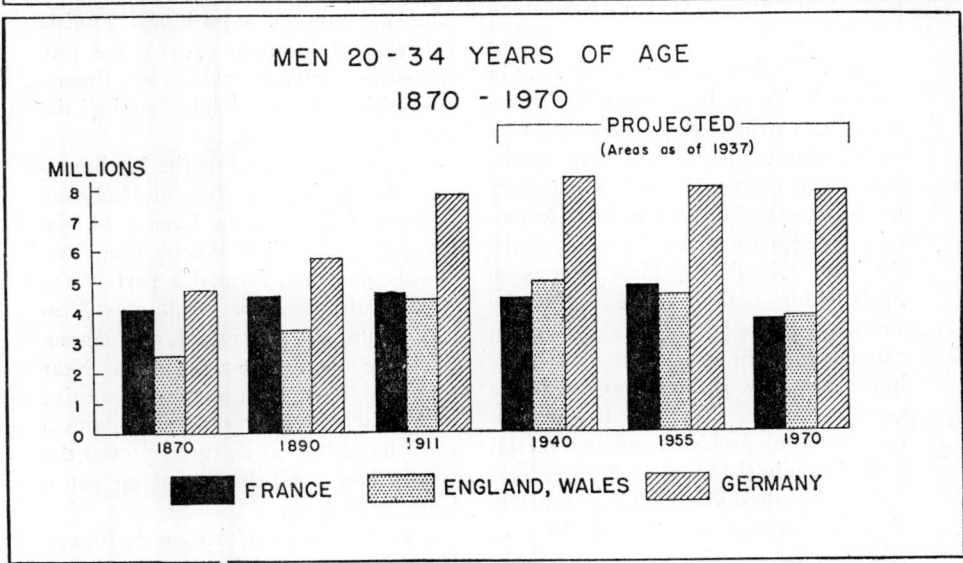

FIG. 15. Population Trends in France and in Germany.

Prepared for the Department of State by the Office of Population Research at Princeton University; reproduced by permission.

other countries will approach in the future.

However, in France the prospects for population decline are less striking than might be expected on the basis of her prewar natural decrease. Though fertility decline has gone on much longer, it has proceeded more slowly in France than elsewhere. In the late 'thirties France's net reproduction rate was higher than the rates of Austria, Belgium, Czechoslovakia, and Switzerland and was substantially higher than that of Germany before the introduction of National Socialist pro-natalist policies. Consequently, the projections do not indicate so rapid a population decline in France as might be anticipated. From her 41.2 million people in 1940, France falls about 10 per cent in the thirty years, to 36.9 million in 1970. From 1945, the projections for France and for England and Wales parallel each other very closely and the total populations never differ from each other more than 2 per cent.

THE FRENCH EMPIRE

By Derwent Whittlesey
and J. K. Wright

From chap. 2 of *Geographical Foundations of National Power*. Army Service Forces Manual M-103-1, Government Printing Office, Washington, 1944.

Trans-Mediterranean France. ... On the south side of the western Mediterranean lies a strip of rugged country, like an island of populated land between the sea and the desert. Through it and along its desert margin, rise the Atlas Mountains. Except for a small area near the Strait of Gibraltar, which belongs to Spain, this region is controlled by France, and the French view it as an extension of France. It is but thirty hours away by sea and has much the same climate as the Midi. Its environment poses no problems new to a person brought up in the south of France.

It is by all odds the most valuable French territory outside of Europe. About 1,200,000 French people have made their permanent home here and have overlaid the native life with French civilization. They cultivate some of the land to produce crops for export to France; they control most of the mining and modern transportation systems; and they have built European extensions to native cities. Algeria, the central part, has been occupied by France since 1830. It is set up as three administrative departments with representation in Paris. The more recent acquisitions, Tunisia (1881) and Morocco (1911), are protectorates, actually ruled by French authorities who ostensibly "advise" the native governments. ...

At the eastern end of the Mediterranean, France has held Syria and Lebanon under mandates of the League of Nations since the First World War. Previously they had formed a part of the Turkish Empire. The inhabitants, Moslem Arabs and Christians, are among the more advanced peoples of the Near East and have been somewhat restive under French rule. France maintains a small naval base at Beirut to protect the terminal of a pipeline bringing petroleum from Iraq.

French West Africa and French Equatorial Africa. The vast, unpeopled space of the French Sahara separates North Africa from the remainder of French territory on that continent far more effectively than the Mediterranean Sea separates North Africa from metropolitan France. The political boundaries of Algeria extend far into the desert. Beyond them, the southern Sahara and the French colonies (which become progressively less dry as one goes southward) are assembled into two administrative units, French West Africa and French Equatorial Africa. Together, these form a continuous tract in the interior, connected with the coast by a number of projecting arms of French

Indian Ocean Possessions. While the position of France in the Indian Ocean is inescapably secondary to that of Great Britain, France has an interest in maintaining steppingstones on the routes from the home base to the Far East and especially to Indo-China, a potentially lucrative colony of the empire on this route. The potential value of Madagascar, somewhat larger than

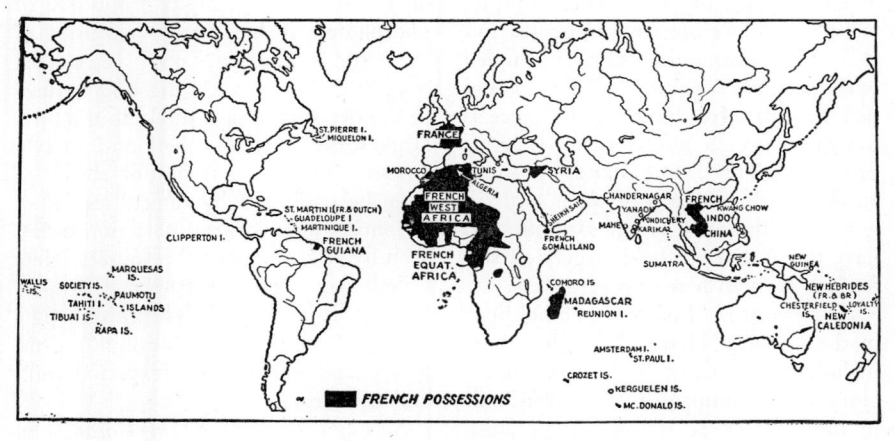

FIG. 16. The French Empire.

From W. O. Blanchard and S. S. Visher, *Economic Geography of Europe.* Copyright 1931 by McGraw-Hill Book Co., New York; reproduced by permission.

territory that are separated from one another by British and Portuguese colonies and the republic of Liberia. . . .

Dakar, on Cape Verde at the westernmost extremity of the African continent, is the capital of French West Africa and the most important French city south of the North African coast. Its easy contact by railroad and river with the interior, especially with the Sudan, is one reason for its importance. The harbor has been made adequate to accommodate all the merchant ships that wish to use it and has also been developed as a naval base. It has become one of the vital points under French control and has been called the **African Gibraltar**. . . .

France, is mainly economic. . . . At the north end of the island, the excellent harbor of Diego Suarez has been developed as a naval base, the only important non-British base in the Indian Ocean.

On the route from France to the Far East via the Suez Canal lies the small colony of French Somaliland. Its port, Jibuti, is the principal outlet of Ethiopia, with whose capital it is connected by a railroad. . . .

On the coasts of India, France still retains a few small relics of the great empire of the eighteenth century . . . with a total population of less than 300,000 persons and an aggregate area of only 196 square miles.

Colonies in the Far East and the Pacific. French Indo-China (286,000 square miles) is almost exactly the size of Texas and has a population of nearly 24 million. Its coastal lowlands are the centers of old civilizations. . . . France holds scattered islands in the Southwestern Pacific, also, of which New Caledonia (7,200 square miles) is the largest and most productive.

These parts of the French Empire yield valuable crops and minerals, but their high economic value is coupled with political weakness. They cannot defend themselves alone, and France is too far away to afford them effective protection. The Pacific islands are interspersed with holdings of other nations, especially those of Great Britain, and have therefore been held largely on sufferance of British sea power. . . .

Possessions in America. The holdings in the Western Hemisphere, like those in India, are relics of eighteenth century glory. They comprise two small islands in the Gulf of St. Lawrence . . . important as fishing centers, the islands of Martinique and Guadeloupe in the West Indies, and French Guiana, a largely undeveloped territory, long used as a penal settlement, on the north coast of South America. . . .

Manpower and Natural Resources of the Empire. In 1939 it was estimated that the total mobilizable manpower of France consisted of approximately 7,300,000 men of whom 1,575,000 were non-French natives of the empire. . . . The oversea empire, especially the African territories, is thus considered a valuable asset by a France faced with a shortage of manpower. Nor is it merely a matter of numbers. Traditionally superb fighting men, the Moroccans, Algerians, Senegalese, and certain of the others, with sound training, provide the equal of first-class European units in modern warfare.

As a source of economic strength, the oversea empire is of considerable value to France but not nearly to the extent that its vast area might lead one to expect. So far as is known, no petroleum of important consequence is available, but large coal deposits are known in Indo-China and Madagascar. French North Africa, however, has a wide variety of mineral resources. It is one of the world's greatest producers of phosphates; it has large quantities of iron and manganese ores, substantial quantities of lead and zinc, and a number of deposits of ores rarely found on a large scale, such as cobalt and molybdenum. The mineral output seems to have been limited by difficulties either of marketing or of transportation rather than by lack of potential resources. New Caledonia, in the far Pacific, is important for its nickel and chromium. The colonies have not been thoroughly prospected and may yield unexpected mineral treasures. . . .

Strategic Position of the Colonies in Relation to Other Powers. . . . Fully as important [as the elements of economic and military strength or weakness which the colonies contributed directly to France] is the position in which they stand . . . in relation to the other powers, especially the British Empire and the United States. . . .

France and its North African territories lie athwart Britain's life line through the Mediterranean to India, the Far East, and Australia. The naval and air bases at Dakar and at Diego Suarez, in Madagascar, are close to Britain's alternate route to the East around Africa. Dakar is also within easy range of the sea lanes from Brazil and the Argentine to Great Britain and the United States, and from the Indian Ocean to the United States. The French colonies in the West Indies lie near the sea routes from Great Britain and the

United States to the Panama Canal, and from the United States to eastern South America. Indo-China is on the route from China and Britain's colony of Hong Kong to the Indian Ocean; and New Caledonia is on the main routes from the United States and the Panama Canal to Australia and New Zealand. Imperial France thus holds highly critical positions near lines of communication vital to both the British Empire and the United States. . . .

In the Far East, French Indo-China held a position in relation to Singapore, Britain's gateway to the China Seas, somewhat comparable to that held by French North Africa in relation to Gibraltar, Britain's gateway to the Mediterranean. French Indo-China was practically handed over outright to the Japanese by the Vichy government, and it was used as a base for the Japanese conquest of Singapore and Burma in 1942.

By refusing to follow the lead of Vichy, the Free French in New Caledonia were able to place that island at the disposal of the United States, both for protection of the route to Australia and for use as a base for the counter-offensive launched against Japan in the Solomon Islands in 1942. Remote French Equatorial Africa, the center of Free French activities, also emerged for a time as an area of notable strategic importance. During the period when the central Mediterranean was practically closed to Allied shipping, air and land routes across Equatorial Africa, supplementing the long and hazardous sea journey around the Cape, formed a link by which British and American men and materials of war could be brought to the eastern Mediterranean.

THE FRENCH QUEST FOR SECURITY

By Pierre Maillaud

From chap. 2 of *France*, by Pierre Maillaud. The World Today Series. Copyright 1943 by Oxford University Press, London and New York; reproduced by permission.

For sixteen centuries France's history is identified with her struggle for self-preservation. For sixteen centuries French culture has developed and flourished in proportion to the degree of success attending that struggle. For sixteen centuries self-preservation has dictated to French statesmanship a policy which has endured and never changed even through dynastic and social upheavals. . . .

This policy has been alternately defensive and preventive. From the partition of Charlemagne's Empire in 843 to the time of Richelieu, its aim was to reclaim the lands lost by the dismemberment of that Empire. For eight hundred years France fought to protect against the foreign foe a realm patiently reconstructed, and she nearly collapsed forever in the sixteenth century when Charles V of Hapsburg gathered under his scepter every one of the lands which surrounded her. . . .

Richelieu's greatness lies in the fact that he evolved something more than a mere defensive policy: a preventive one. Its fundamental aim was to keep the peoples of Germany divided. This much-disputed principle is nothing more than a French version of the English system which is based on a "balance of power." It was as imperative for France to keep in a state of division the vast reservoir of men beyond the Rhine, whence so many invasions had started, as for England to prevent the establishment of a crushing combination of powers on the Continent. . . .

By the Treaty of Westphalia in 1648, which was the posthumous outcome of

Richelieu's diplomacy, German unity was postponed for over two centuries. Although this diplomacy has remained to this day a veritable charter for French statesmen, it was misunderstood during the eighteenth century, when French policy for the first time lost sight of the true German menace and was thus partly responsible for the growth of the Prussian State as heir to the scheme of German unification. . . .

[Not until after the defeat of Bonaparte in 1815 did France return to its historic policy, and even then French statesmen could not undo all the damage, since Prussia had greatly increased her territories on the left bank of the Rhine.]

If Prussia did not achieve more, France owed it to a diplomat of the traditional school . . . , Talleyrand, who, at the Congress of Vienna in 1815, displayed remarkable skill in exploiting differences between the Allies. His greatest merit lay perhaps in that he clearly discerned the true interests of France in the long run. . . . that Prussian expansion and not England was the real threat to the existence of France. Acting on his assessment of the situation, he succeeded in limiting the effects of a Napoleonic policy which had brought France to a state of military collapse and utter physical exhaustion.

[The policy of Louis-Napoleon III was a caricature of the first Napoleon's.] . . . The crowning result of Napoleon III's policy was the war of 1870-1871, in which Bismarck gave himself the supreme luxury of saddling France with the apparent responsibility of the conflict, when in fact this great German statesman had trapped Napoleon into joining issue with Prussia under the worst conditions. Napoleon's preparations had been on a par with his diplomacy. The worst effect of the French defeat was not the annexation of Alsace-Lorraine [to Prussia]; it was the unification of Germany under Prussian rule.

[After that event] . . . the French Republic found an international situation which for several reasons was more unfavorable to France than almost any in the nation's previous history. Before the colossal power of Germany, the country was weakened in every respect. For the first time since the beginning of the Thirty Years War, her manpower and physical resources of all kinds were inferior to those of Germany, whose population and industrial might were rapidly increasing. The Second Empire had estranged every possible friend and ally, and the First Empire's legacy of French unpopularity survived in Europe. Faced with such odds, the Third Republic achieved together two tremendous tasks which neither the decaying monarchy of the eighteenth century nor the genius of Napoleon had succeeded in carrying out: it rebuilt France's position in Europe and gave her a vast colonial empire.

Whilst in the eighteenth century France's colonial expansion had antagonized England, not only did the Republic conquer huge territories without damaging its relations with her (a hope also fondly entertained by Germany), but it succeeded in cementing a friendship with Great Britain which saved Europe in 1914. It restored French military power as a barrier to German expansionism.

The weight of France in the seventeenth century was not to be regained. The inescapable fact was that, in 1914, Germany had 70 million inhabitants and France 39 million. The counterpoise to Germany could not be found only in military might. It had to be found in diplomacy. A foreign policy which succeeded in that endeavor while at the same time allowing France to conquer the second largest colonial empire in the world can hardly be considered a failure. It was in fact a great historical achievement.

With resources relatively more restricted than at any previous time in her national life, France, under the Third Republic, from 1875 to 1919, accomplished one of the chief objects of her traditional policy, dictated by her situation on a continent where she lies more exposed than any other nation: the unity and power of the realm. . . .

THE QUEST FOR SECURITY BETWEEN WARS, 1919-1939

By Arnold Wolfers

From chap. 1 of *Britain and France between Two Wars*, by Arnold Wolfers. Copyright 1940 by Harcourt, Brace & Co., New York; reproduced by permission. The author is professor of international relations in Yale University and a member of the research staff of the Yale Institute of International Studies which sponsored the publication of his book.

Ever since the [First] World War *"sécurité"* has been the keynote of French foreign policy. . . . This term, taken by itself, does not throw much light on the particular character of French policy. After all, almost every government in the world professes to be seeking peace, safety, and security. The specific meaning of the term becomes more apparent when the French speak of their desire for *"garanties de sécurité contre une agression de l'Allemagne."* France was obsessed by the fear of a new war with Germany. [At the Peace Conference of 1919] she was almost exclusively occupied with efforts to obtain protection from the menace of future German aggression. But the settlements reached at the Peace Conference did not allay her fears; she continued ever after to seek new guaranties. This psychological background has to be remembered in order to understand a policy of security such as France came to pursue. It was a policy directed not merely toward the defense and enforcement of the Treaty of Versailles (which was regarded as the minimum requirement for French security), but also toward the erection of still more safeguards against Germany.

At first sight it seems astonishing to find France already hypnotized by the "German menace," at a time when Germany was prostrate, exhausted, and internally disrupted. Many British observers considered this French preoccupation as evidencing an almost hysterical nervousness, "a sort of pathological obsession," if not, in fact, a cloak for imperialist designs for conquest and revenge. But the French were not concerned about the near future; they were convinced that the advantages France had gained, great although they might be at the time, were only temporary and precarious. . . . Because the dangers that threatened the *status quo* were still remote, there was all the more reason to fear lest countries which were less vitally concerned and more prone to optimism, like Britain, fail to take the threats with proper seriousness and refuse to prepare in time the means with which to meet them.

Overshadowing all other considerations was the knowledge that Germany was potentially far stronger than France. A country of 40 million inhabitants was facing one of 70 million. Add to this the French belief that the Germans were a particularly aggressive and military nation, which had been the cause of all previous encounters and which would seek revenge if given an opportunity, and the conclusions are obvious. On the basis of these assumptions, France could feel secure only if two conditions were fulfilled. She and the countries on whose assistance she could rely would have to be made capable of holding Germany permanently in a state of "artificial inferiority." In addition, France would have to possess sufficient military superiority of her own to ward off German invasion until her allies could come to her support. This was a program calling for a reversal of the natural order of power on the Rhine. It was a difficult and, in any event, a precarious undertaking.

It is only fair to add that the French insisted that they were seeking not superiority or hegemony, but merely trying to equalize Germany's natural advantages. But this is only a matter of terminology. What France wanted to equal was not Germany's actual power, but her potential strength. . . .

A policy such as France set out to pursue was in danger of becoming involved in a vicious circle. If Germany was regarded as so dangerous and potentially so powerful that the free development of her forces would have to be permanently crippled and parts of her territory taken away or put under military control, it was inevitable that her resentment would be aroused and her "aggressiveness" heightened. The British, as we shall see, never ceased to emphasize this fact. Was not the danger intensified by the very means which were designed to remove it? But the French believed that they had no alternative, since they could see no other way of eliminating the German menace. This accounts for the demands which they presented at Versailles and afterwards, the object of which was to defeat in advance even the most violent future German revolt.

The French Government did not propose the extreme program that some Frenchmen advocated. This would have consisted in breaking up Germany into small states and putting an end to the existence of an overpowering neighbor. Instead, France demanded that her strategic frontier be on the Rhine. "*Quand on est maître du Rhin, on est maître de tout le pays* [meaning the Rhineland]. *Quand on n'est pas sur le Rhin, on a tout perdu*," declared Foch in May 1919. This was an age-old French credo. "*Sécurité totale*" for France—and, if the French were right, for the Anglo-Saxon democracies—required that the German territory on the left bank of the Rhine, as well as the Rhine bridges, be placed permanently under French or Allied military control. The Anglo-Saxon countries refused to accept this thesis. Instead, the treaty provided for the permanent demilitarization of the Rhineland and for its temporary military occupation by Allied troops. To this, however, were added pacts of guarantee in which the United States and Great Britain promised to assist France in the case of unprovoked German aggression. These pacts and the provisions concerning the Rhineland were together considered by France's allies to be a satisfactory substitute for the establishment of the Rhine as a military frontier. The intention was to remove the danger of a sudden invasion of French soil by the demilitarization provisions and thus to give the Anglo-Saxon allies or guarantors time to come to France's assistance if Germany should nevertheless try to attack her. The French, not without bitterness and disappointment, bowed to this compromise, rather than lose the friendship and future support of their great allies. What made them feel that they had "lost the peace" was the failure of these treaties to become effective, thereby destroying what France had even then regarded as only a second-best solution to her problem. Not only was the strategic superiority of France now brought far below her expectations, but the most effective promises of assistance for which France could hope had vanished. At the same time Germany's dissatisfaction was by no means removed.

At Versailles, France wavered between two methods by which Germany might be kept in check. Either she could try to rely largely on making herself superior in power and thus become less dependent on outside help, or she could put her faith primarily in the military assistance which she could obtain from others. At no stage of the negotiations, however, was the French Government ready to drop the demand for what she came to call *"la solidarité des alliés."* Even the strategic frontier on the Rhine was, Marshal Foch argued, to be a part of *"l'organisation défensive de la Coalition."* A coalition comprising all of the Great Powers with the exception of the two Central European Empires had been necessary to defeat Germany. The *"caractère interallié de sa victoire,"* as Tardieu put it, was not forgotten by France. It convinced the French that Germany could be held in check only with the help of allies. . . . In some form or other the grand coalition of the [First] World War would have to be carried over into peacetime.

This accounts for the intense dismay of the French when, even before the adjournment of the Versailles Conference, they found themselves deserted by almost all of their great allies. Some of them were never to be recovered. Russia was struggling in the throes of the Bolshevist Revolution, and was for a long time considered as an enemy rather than as a friend. More than once during the post-war years she was on the verge of alignment with Germany. Next, the United States turned her back on Europe and refused even to ratify the Versailles Treaty. Not only did the pact of guarantee which Wilson had negotiated with Clemenceau fail to materialize, but the pledges of assistance contained in the League Covenant did not become binding on the United States. Two other Great Powers on the side of the victors, Japan and Italy, left the conference so dissatisfied that they could not be relied upon to defend the new order. As a result, Britain was the only Great Power from which any semblance of "Allied solidarity" could be expected.

Relations with Britain therefore became one of France's major preoccupations. But even there she had to cope not merely with resistance in minor matters, but with a complete lack of agreement on what was for France the crux of the whole matter, namely, the necessity of enforcing the treaties upon Germany and of supplementing the guarantees of security which they contained.

While it may not be hard to understand why French demands for security against a German attack from across the Rhine should have been so extensive, there is another and more perplexing aspect of her policy. . . . France, despite her fear, did not limit herself to preparations for the protection of her own soil, but left no doubt that she was determined to enforce the Peace Treaties in their entirety and to defend the whole new continental *status quo*. She wished to be regarded not merely as *"la garde du Rhin"*; her army was also to be *"la garantie de la stabilité politique de l'Europe,"* the defender not only of her own frontiers, *"mais . . . de toutes les frontières, . . . de tous les peuples."* It would seem that this was greatly multiplying the dangers by which she was threatened. Was she not entangling herself unnecessarily in Germany's quarrels in remote regions and drawing the wrath of the revisionist powers upon herself? If by nature she was as much weaker than Germany as she claimed, could she afford to take on responsibilities of a continental scale?

There seems at first sight to be such incongruity in this attitude that some people have doubted the sincerity of French fears and have believed that her clamor for more security was but a façade hiding a desire to enjoy supremacy or hegemony on the Continent. More flattering to France, and more in line with many declarations by her statesmen, would be the supposition that, apart from considerations of her own security, she was genuinely and generously concerned in the fate of the new Slavic states in Central Europe which she, as a defender of the small powers, sought to protect from German aggression.

While we cannot hope to penetrate into the real and decisive motives behind French policy—and they probably varied from period to period and from statesman to statesman—it seems most likely that France was again involved in the same vicious circle. She had two obvious reasons for pledging assistance to countries like Poland or Czechoslovakia. She feared, for one thing, that Germany, if she were able to expand in the East, would become so powerful that she could turn around and attack France successfully. Also she wished to assure herself of the assistance of those countries, whose military strength was by no means negligible as long as Germany was held to the provisions of the Versailles Treaty in regard to armaments. They were substitutes for France's prewar ally, Czarist Russia.

But, while France was acquiring the support from them which she had not been able to obtain from the Great Powers, she was at the same time incurring grave new risks. The defenses in the East might prove to be not only inadequate but a source of German exasperation and a major cause of conflict. French entanglement, in that case, might be the surest means of bringing about the new war on the Rhine against which she was seeking to protect herself. Not until the French policy had met with serious setbacks did some Frenchmen, after 1936, come to express the opinion that the far-flung commitments were a mistake and that France should seek security by entrenching herself behind the Maginot Line.

By making the sanctity of treaties and the strict enforcement of the *status quo* the fundamental principle of her foreign policy, France became involved in the same contradictions which had afflicted her commitments in the East. She believed it necessary for her security not to allow any provisions of the Peace Treaties to be violated with impunity or changed in favor of Germany. . . . But in order to prevent any precedent from serving as a wedge by which Germany might start a general assault on the order of Versailles, France made herself the target for all revisionist attacks. If she was to adhere to her purpose consistently, she had to oppose changes of the post-war settlements, even though they might conceivably have satisfied the Germans and thus have removed the dangers which she was trying to avert.

The specific connotation of the term "*sécurité*" as it was used by the French to explain their objective now becomes clearer. It referred to a state of things in which not only was the danger of a German invasion of French soil to be eliminated—security in the narrow sense of the word—but in which the entire new *status quo* as established in the Peace Treaties would be firmly protected by the superiority of the powers which were ready to defend it. "Security" came to play such an important role in post-war diplomacy that it is worth keeping this original French meaning in mind. Committees on "security" were established; pacts of "security" were negotiated; the relation of disarmament to "security" was debated at length. Later, interest came to center on "collective security." But even then something of the original French connotation was attached to the term. It was still an attempt to lay the specter of a German revisionist "explosion" against the established order by assigning superior force to the defenders of the "law."

WHY FRANCE FELL: A FRENCH INTERPRETATION

By Pierre Cot

From chap. 2 of *The Triumph of Treason*, by Pierre Cot. Copyright 1944 by Ziff-Davis Publishing Co., Chicago; reproduced by permission. The author is a well-known French statesman. He was Minister of Aviation in one of the prewar French Cabinets.

The essential cause of the defeat [in 1940] was the isolation of France, resulting from the failure of collective security. . . .

The second cause was the weakness of the French Army. . . .

The third cause was the moral disunity of the French nation and, more specifically, the moral collapse of the ruling classes. . . .

The Isolation of France: the Collapse of the Franco-Soviet Pact. France was conquered because in September 1940 she did not have indispensable allies. . . .

France's military weakness, compared to Germany's strength, made a war without allies unthinkable. The number of Frenchmen who could be mobilized was half that of the Germans; the number of qualified workers, the quantity of tools, the availability of natural resources and industrial equipment—in short, all that makes a country able to produce—were in the ratio of approximately one to three. With the same effort and using the same methods, France could not have opposed Germany on the battlefield with more than one French soldier as against two Germans, and one French cannon as against three German. Consequently, the cornerstone of French security was collective security. This categorical imperative, resulting from necessity, was understood perfectly by Herriot, Briand, Paul-Boncour, and Blum, by Reynaud and Mandel, and, to a lesser degree, by Poincaré, the jurist, and Tardieu the nationalist. With collective security France could have barred the way to aggressors. . . . On the other hand, all that weakened the bonds of collective security, nullified the League of Nations Pact, and contributed to the success of aggressor states, brought about the isolation of France and prepared the conditions of her defeat.

We know what France's choice, or rather her choices, were. After 1919 France worked with all her might for the organization of collective security; she wearied the League of Nations' Assemblies and Committees with her insistence on the problem of security. Later, however, France let the Fascist powers destroy, stone by stone, what she had constructed so painstakingly. Sanctions were not properly imposed against Italian or Japanese aggressors, the Spanish Republic was abandoned, Czechoslovakia was betrayed. France neglected her duties, her partners, and her agreements in such a way that by 1939 she had lost the majority of her friends. . . . She entered the war with only Poland and England on her side. The Polish Army resisted magnificently, but its fight, without Soviet backing, was clearly hopeless. England sent France more soldiers, airplanes, and arms than the French General Staff had asked for or anticipated; but Chamberlain's England was incapable of playing its traditional policeman's role on a continent where Hitler had been given every means of arming himself and defying the police.

What France lacked in 1939 was the support of Russia. Because this aid was the *sine qua non* of collective security, it was the *sine qua non* of French resistance. French diplomacy should have done everything to ensure this aid. . . . It is an historical fact, shown by the Napoleonic campaigns and especially by the wars of 1870 and 1914, that without a Russian alliance, France has always been defeated in Europe, but when allied with Russia, she has always been victorious.

Russian aid was essential to France in 1914. What was true in 1914 was still more true in 1939, because the German and Russian armies had become relatively stronger, and the French Army relatively weaker. . . .

When the obvious interest of France, confronted by a growing Nazi threat, would have been to strengthen a rapprochement with Russia, French policy did nothing but undermine the Franco-Soviet Pact [of 1935] and violate its spirit. . . . In short, by her attitude during the Spanish war, by her treatment of Czechoslovakia, and by the signing of the Bonnet-von Ribbentrop Pact, France slowly detached herself from Russia.

At the end of 1938 the Franco-Soviet Pact was no longer a living treaty, but a dead text. . . . Bonnet's policy had made it clear to the Soviet government that Russia could not count on France. . . . In addition, during the winter of 1938-1939, Germany hastened to complete the construction of the Siegfried Line. These fortifications, incomplete at the time of Munich, became impassable for the French Army in the course of the winter. By the beginning of 1939 Russia knew that the French Army could not aid her effectively.

. . . The Soviet government actually had no alternative but to try one supreme effort with France and England, and to inform the French government discreetly that if this effort failed, Russia, following Bonnet's example, would be obliged to "revise her alliances" and to modify the general course of her policy. [The result was the well-known Soviet pact concluded with Hitler in August 1939.]

. . . French security was never greater than when it was founded on the strength of the Red Army and the bastion of Czechoslovakia; and French security was never so precarious as when France lost both Czechoslovakia and the confidence of the Soviets. Before September 1938, France was in little danger of attack and in no danger of defeat; after August 23, 1939, France was sure to be attacked and in grave danger of defeat.

The Military Weakness of France: the Mistakes of the General Staff. The second cause of France's defeat was the weakness of her Army. Opposed by the German forces, the French Army revealed itself to be inferior, in quality more than in quantity. . . .

Foreign public opinion has a tendency to think that the morale of the French Army was lower than that of the German. The fact is that the latter was composed of fanatics who were well-trained and who were proud to die for their Führer, while the French soldiers were somewhat disillusioned—they had not been told what they were fighting for, and they lacked confidence in their officers, many of whom hated democracy and preferred "Hitler to Léon Blum." The evidence offered at the Riom trial showed that the moral inferiority of the French Army proceeded from a lack of technical education and training, not from lack of individual courage. Soldiers and officers were surprised by a type of war—the Blitzkrieg, whose rudiments their leaders had not taught them. And all evidence disclosed that the morale of the soldiers and of the troop officers was higher than that of the General Staff in charge of directing the war. . . .

A more important element of weakness was the insufficiency of matériel at the soldiers' disposal. The Riom trial made curious revelations on this point and proved that France had more matériel than had been supposed, although it was less modern than the German matériel. About 40 per cent of the tanks and 60 per cent of the airplanes were *never used in the war*.

. . . In a war of machines, military and industrial strength are linked closely. . . . In the days of infantry and cavalry battles, the advantage was with agricultural and pastoral peoples rather than with nations of merchants and artisans, because the best cavalrymen and foot-soldiers were recruited from among farmers and horse-drivers. In the days of tank battles and aerial combat, the advantage is with industrial nations, for the modern soldier is a mechanic and a technician, supported by other mechanics and technicians. Germany therefore had a great advantage over France.

The inferiority of French matériel was caused, in part, by prewar differences in French and German production of war equipment.

First, the productive capacities of French factories in the years preceding the war were about a third of the capacity of German factories. France produced approximately one-third of the amount of steel and aluminum that Germany did. Even if France had concentrated the same proportion of her productive capacity on armament manufacture as had Germany, she would still have produced only one cannon, one tank, and one airplane to Germany's three. Second, according to a study published by the Foreign Policy Association, Germany spent four times as much as France on national defense between 1934 and 1938. This means that Germany concentrated a greater proportion of her productive capacity on war preparations than did France, and that the cost of national defense was twice as much for each of the 80 million Germans as for each of the 40 million Frenchmen. The French had "butter" and the Germans "cannon." Third, in planning her national defense and her armament programs, Germany was giving more importance than France to aviation and tanks. France concentrated on other armaments; the French fleet was almost twice as strong as the German, and France, until 1938, had more soldiers and officers under arms than Germany. The result was that, spending four times less for her entire national defense, and maintaining a stronger navy and a larger army than Germany, France built not three or four but five or six times fewer airplanes and tanks than did Germany. . . .

But the most important factor of French military weakness was the mediocrity of the High Command and of the General Staff. . . .

Broadly summarized, the war doctrine of the French General Staff was that of defense and a war of position, as opposed to the doctrine of offense and a war of movement, the basis for the German Blitzkrieg. . . . Just a few months before the war, General Chauvineau presented this doctrine with great talent in a book, *Is Invasion Still Possible?* He answered his own question in the negative; he foresaw stabilization of fronts and the war of attrition. "The tank has failed as a means of breaking through," wrote this French doctrinal prophet. None other than

Marshal Henri Philippe Pétain, the highest military authority in all France, wrote the preface and recommended that all officers read Chauvineau's book.

Chauvineau claimed that the General Staff's doctrine was motivated by prudence and realism; actually it was characterized by archaism and lack of daring. Said to be founded on the lessons of 1914-1918, it interpreted them wrongly and merely expounded the ideas which Pétain had developed before 1914 as a colonel, and professor at the École Supérieure de Guerre. Good in its youth, the doctrine had grown old. It failed to allow for the revolution in warfare produced by the discoveries of science and by the progress of industry in general and the internal combustion motor in particular. It failed to allow for the transformation wrought by tanks and airplanes. It was a conservative doctrine, contradicting the revolutionary conceptions being developed in Germany and Russia and the modern ideas of warfare a few French officers tried vainly to force into the minds of their leaders.

Among these nonconformist officers the most brilliant was General de Gaulle. In 1935 . . . he published his daring book on the use of tanks, the formation of armored divisions, and the creation of a modern army. While Germany attentively studied his ideas, the French General Staff distrusted the young officer who had ventured to have ideas of his own and who was capable of substituting thought for obedience.

The German General Staff, eager for new ideas, encouraged its officers to do historical research and to write intellectual studies and even polemics, while the French General Staff forbade criticism and discouraged thought. The abundance and richness of German military literature between 1920 and 1940 is remarkable compared with the poverty and weakness of French military literature in the same period. The French Army did not think. Its leaders shrugged their shoulders when you spoke to them of German conceptions or Russian methods, when you cited the articles of General Erfuhrt and the books of Major Guderian, or when you mentioned the experience of the Red Army and the lessons of the Spanish War. They were not interested. . . . Thus the French Army went to war in 1939 fortified with a doctrine, theories, and "Regulations" perfectly suited to the conditions of war in 1918.

It is all the more necessary to study the causes of the General Staff's stubbornness and intellectual poverty when one remembers that France almost lost the war in 1914 because of the bad military doctrine of its General Staff, which, as has been said, is always late by one idea and one war. . . . From 1918 to 1939 the German generals, chastened by the defeat of 1918, sought in the analysis of the causes of their defeat the avoidance of future errors—while the French generals had become unbearably conceited as a result of the victory of 1918, which they claimed to have won by superiority of methods. Moreover, the average age of the German generals in June 1940 was ten years below that of the French generals, and experience has taught us that men of fifty can adapt themselves more rapidly to unforeseen situations than men of sixty. . . .

The French war plans—which were supposed to envisage all possibilities—obviously did not provide for the breaking force and rapidity of penetration of the German motorized columns. No preparation had been made for the destruction of the bridges over the Seine or the Loire, just as no provision had been made for the defense or abandonment of Paris. Such operations hardly can be improvised; thus, when the French armies were obliged to fall back south of Paris, the artillery was rendered useless because it had no maps of the country where the battle was developing. . . .

Deprived of Russian aid, badly prepared for modern warfare, and badly directed on the battlefield, the French Army was bound to be conquered on the European continent. The mistakes that the military leaders had piled up in ten years could not be repaired in a few months. With a different Chief of Staff and a different leader of the government, the defeat might have been limited to the military domain and would not have become a national disaster. Beaten on the Meuse, the Seine, and the Loire, the French Army still could have fallen back, inflicting severe losses on the enemy; at the worst, it would have been possible, with the aid of the English fleet, to organize a second Dunkirk and to send to North Africa the tanks and the planes that General Weygand had hesitated to use against the German Army.

To accomplish this, Weygand and Pétain would have had to be animated by the will to resist and conquer; they would have had to wish ardently for the collapse of Hitlerism and Fascism, for the victory of the democracies. Had they any such wish?

The Moral Disunity of the French People: Fifth Column Activity. One must examine here not the morale of the Army, but the morale of the nation as a whole. . . .

Modern warfare, with its multiple aspects and scientific techniques, has revived the importance of the moral factor as an instrument of victory or defeat. . . .

If the political parties are not united in a single effort, if the social classes are opposed to one another, if the privileged class uses the war to reinforce or maintain its privileges, if the sacrifices are shared unequally and the rewards distributed unjustly, if goods are not conscripted as well as men, one can hardly expect national morale to remain at a high level. Then the morale of the army will quickly reflect the morale of the nation. . . .

The morale of France at war was weak in that the French nation was not united behind the government. The Fifth Column provoked a disunity which the common people resisted as best they could and which the government did not fight strenuously enough. . . .

In September 1939 the French people entered the war without enthusiasm but with discipline. The mobilization was completed without incident. The men said: "We must finish with *that* once and for all." *That*, to them, meant Hitler's policy of aggression and force. They were not going to fight for Poland or against the German people, but against methods and doctrines which constantly imperiled the peace of the world. The common people, with greater intelligence than their rulers, grasped the meaning of the war. They should be praised all the more for it because they were deeply attached to peace and had suffered greatly from the previous war.

. . . France had mobilized and lost more men in the course of World War I than any other belligerent nation. . . . Consequently, the number of young men brought up in the horror of war by a disabled father or a widowed mother was greater in France than in Germany. Again, as a result of the defeat of the peace treaty, of the policy of reparations, and of the Hitlerian doctrine, a great number of young Germans had been brought up in the cult of revenge, while young Frenchmen of the working classes, temperamentally inclined toward conciliation, repeated that the worst international agreement was better than the best of wars.

For a multitude of reasons, then, it was at the same time easy and necessary for the government to explain constantly to the French people why France was fighting at the side of England. . . . It was particularly dangerous not to emphasize the ideological aspect of the war, because it was France and England who, to maintain international order, had declared war on Germany. . . . Not to emphasize this aspect was to play into the hands of German propaganda . . . that Germany had been the object of an unjust aggression and that France was fighting England's battle; its most dangerous slogan was: "The English supply the machines, the French supply the men." To counteract this campaign French propaganda should have said: "We are fighting for democracy and international order"; instead, it limited itself to saying: "We are fighting today for fear of being attacked tomorrow."

The French people were offered nothing but the mediocre arguments of preventive war; their cause was cheapened, not ennobled. Moreover, the French were now told about Poland the opposite of what, a year earlier, they had heard about Czechoslovakia; and, as in England, it was the same government that upheld these contradictory theses. The French government failed to oppose Hitler's holy war with a holy war of liberty. Its leaders seemed ashamed to speak of democracy, thus depriving themselves of their best trump for national and international order.

Deprived by her inadequate propaganda of the necessary spur, France, after the first weeks of the war, sank into indifference. Her war did not interest her; during the winter of 1939-1940 France was bored. This indifference proved fertile soil for the Fifth Column.

The activity of the Fifth Column will not be considered by historians as a special phenomenon of French public life, but as an integral part of Fascism. The Fifth Column has appeared wherever Fascism has tried to gain a foothold. . . . By the Fifth Column I do not mean only spies and licensed traitors. The Fifth Column includes all who, by accepting Fascist doctrines or methods, become the conscious or unconscious accomplices of a foreign power. . . . Through hate of the Popular Front, good Frenchmen, or men who considered themselves such, served Hitler gratuitously by doing work to which they would never have consented, had they been offered payment. Why? Because they detested the Republic and democracy more than they loved France. They accepted the idea of the defeat as a necessary evil which permitted them to rid France of the democratic system and to keep in power, in the neighboring countries, the Fascist dictators whom they considered solely capable of maintaining order in Europe. They afterwards became unconscious collaborators of these dictators. . . .

France received no exceptional treatment from Hitler and Fascism. A general plan coordinated the activity of the Fifth Columns all over the world. All were recruited from the same circles and had the same social and political composition. The object was the same everywhere; to divide and unnerve public opinion, weaken the resistance of the regime, and prepare a governmental group ready to execute a Fascist *coup d'etat* at a moment of trouble or confusion. The methods were the same everywhere: cultivation of the seeds of disunity which normally exist among free men and in free countries, exaggeration and inflammation of all racial and religious conflicts, all class rivalries, all political antagonisms, gradual conversion of opposition and dissent into hate, creation of an atmosphere of civil war. . . .

The Fifth Column was able to carry on its work because of the feebleness of governmental action against it. The government, of course, took measures against spies and traitors; but these terms were applied only to agents sent directly from Germany, and these agents were the least numerous and dangerous. No measures were taken against native Fascists and friends of the Nazi regime. The government, counting on their "patriotism," left them a clear field. . . . Just as the Fascist dictators had profited by the weakness and complacency of the French, English and American democracies to obtain strategic positions for the execution of their plans before the war, so the French Fascists gained positions during the war to carry out their *coup d'etat* at the moment of defeat. A great network of intrigue enveloped France, its meshes growing ever tighter and stronger.

The government reserved all its harshness for the Communists. After the signing of the Russo-German Pact and the invasion of Poland, it was considered more reprehensible to be the friend of Stalin, with whom France was not at war, than the friend of Hitler, whose armies were preparing to invade France. It was more suspect to be a partisan of Franco-Russian rapprochement than to be a partisan of a Franco-Hitlerian entente. . . .

Meanwhile, the government's economic and social policy became more and more reactionary. Greater sacrifices were asked of workers than of employers. The right to strike, along with all social legislation, was suspended, but the right to huge profits continued in full force. Right or wrong, the government's policy seemed to be directed against the Popular Front in general and Communism in particular rather than against Fascism in general and Hitlerism in particular. Anti-Communist feeling reached its climax with the Russo-Finnish War; a veritable wave of madness swept over Parliament, where Pierre-Etienne Flandin demanded that France declare war on Russia. As France obviously could not fight Russia and Germany at the same time, this policy would have resulted in peace negotiations with Germany. Daladier, then President of the Council, and General Gamelin, then Chief of Staff, resisted this dangerous move as best they could. But, generally speaking, the Fascists had their own way in the country at large and in the Army. The anti-Communist agitation was a smoke screen behind which was being prepared the great political conspiracy that was to paralyze France and facilitate Hitler's work. By its repressive policy toward the workers and its indulgent treatment of the Fascists, the government prevented the soldiers' war from becoming a people's war—a tranformation which alone could have produced the great burst of enthusiasm and energy necessary for the conquest of France's internal and external foes.

In spite of the action of the Fifth Column and the inaction of the government, however, the morale of the common people remained intact until June 1940. It is a point on which I must insist, because one obtains exactly the opposite impression from most of the books on the fall of France hitherto published in the United States.

. . . The authors of these books described what they saw; they believed in the decay of France because they saw around them the decay of the French bourgeoisie. None of them had any contact with the workers and peasants who form the immense majority of the French people. . . .

. . . To describe their state of mind, I cannot do better than report what was told me by Alexis Leger, former general secretary of the Ministry of Foreign Affairs. . . . When the members of the government, abandoning Paris on Weygand's advice, were moving to Tours before going to Bordeaux, Paul Reynaud's automobile was stopped by hordes of refugees on the roads. The people who stopped him were peasants driving their carts, workers tightly packed into trucks, and pedestrians and bicyclists; they were coming from the north; and had been bombed and machine-gunned by German airplanes. Reynaud was recognized and cries went up. Having been told by his associates that the people wanted peace at any price, Reynaud grew pale when he heard the crowds muttering, until he realized that they were shouting: "Hold fast, Reynaud! *Vive la France! On les aura!*" The French people's last word to Reynaud was to "hold fast," but the advice of Pétain and Weygand was to ask for an armistice. The Fifth Column had not poisoned the common people; it had converted the military leaders. . . .

At the end of June 1940, France certainly had enough troops and war matériel to resist in North Africa; the fleet was intact, and, combined with the British fleet, would have had absolute control of the Mediterranean. The Air Force possessed 2,100 first-line airplanes which could have been sent to North Africa without difficulty. France had an army of 400,000 men in Syria and North Africa (Morocco, Algeria, Tunisia), larger, better equipped, and more easily supplied than the Italian Army in Libya. The African Army could have been reinforced by troops and matériel from France, the safe evacuation of which was ensured from both Atlantic and Mediterranean ports by the British and French fleets. A report sent by General Noguès, commander-in-chief of the North African Army, informed the government that Germany could not invade North Africa so long as the British and French fleets were in control of the Mediterranean. Albert Lebrun, President of the Republic, decided to leave for North Africa with some of the ministers and parliamentarians who were then at Bordeaux, but Laval threatened to establish a dissident government if Lebrun proceeded with his plans. . . .

It is hardly necessary to stress the consequences of the decision taken by Pétain, Weygand, Laval, and their accomplices. Had the Pétain government decided to go to North Africa, the whole course of the war might have been different. . . .

How explain the role played by Pétain and Weygand in that decisive phase of the defeat of France? Why did they act as if they had been agents of the Fifth Column, favoring Hitler's cause both in the decisions they took and in the advice they gave? Why did they follow a line contrary to the French interest?

Concerning these men, the hypotheses of treason cannot be accepted without proof. History will search for this proof. Until further information is available the best explanation for their attitude is their admiration for Fascism and the hate for democracy which had dominated them for many years.

These sentiments led them to overestimate Hitler's force and to underestimate the British capacity for resistance. . . . Their admiration for Fascism and for National Socialism made them believe that it was possible to reach an understanding with Hitler; they thought that Hitler as conqueror would be satisfied with tearing up the

Versailles Treaty and retaking the provinces of Alsace and Lorraine. Pétain spoke of a "negotiated peace between soldiers"; he believed that a France, purged of democracy, should be associated with the direction of the European New Order. Acceptance of military defeat gave them an opportunity to overthrow the Republic and to establish a military dictatorship leading the French nation back to the discipline of the *ancien régime*. They hoped for a monarchic restoration, which they would serve as guides and advisers. They needed military dictatorship to blur the mistakes committed by them and their colleagues of the General Staff. Here facts speak for themselves. As soon as they had seized power amid the confusion of the collapse, Pétain and Weygand, with the help of Laval and Darlan, hastened to suppress all political liberties . . . and set up a Fascist regime.

Theories Advanced to Explain the Defeat. How did France, before and during the war, come to commit so many blunders in her foreign, domestic, and military policies?

Three general explanations have been advanced: the aging of the French nation, the Popular Front, and the rallying of the French bourgeoisie to Fascism.

(1) *The Aging of the French Nation.* . . . The old age of France manifested itself only in the fields of military science and industrial organization. France's contributions to civilization in the advancement of sciences and liberal arts between 1920 and 1940 were not inferior to those of Germany and Italy. . . . Finally, the [subsequent] resistance of the French masses to Fascism and Hitlerism, their participation in the underground struggle and in sabotage, reveals an energy and courage, which cannot be reconciled with the general theory of the nation's old age.

(2) *The Policy of the Popular Front.* According to Vichy, the Popular Front put France in a state of least resistance. . . . No one, unless he is trying to mask the errors of the appeasement policy, the mistakes of the General Staff, and the activity of the Fifth Column, can charge the Popular Front with the exclusive, or even the principal, responsibility for the defeat.

(3) *Conversion of the French Bourgeoisie to Fascism.* I consider the rallying of the French bourgeoisie to Fascism the most acceptable explanation. It alone permits us to understand all the aspects and causes of the French defeat and reveals an element of truth in the theory of France's old age. The French people although no older than the other European peoples, was led by the oldest and weakest of its social classes. This class was too blinded by its own interests to be capable of working for the nation as a whole, and too much fettered by its prejudices to master the problems of modern life. This theory illuminates, furthermore, the mistakes of French foreign policy, which stemmed from the bourgeois horror of an alliance with Russia and its desire to see the authoritarian systems maintained in Germany, Italy, and Spain. It also explains the intellectual inferiority of a General Staff that was the military expression of the bourgeoisie. . . . The last explanation also throws light on the activity of the Fifth Column, four-fifths of whose members were recruited from the bourgeoisie.

This conversion to Fascism was not sudden and complete, but gradual and partial. . . . The Fascist and pro-Fascist organizations in France before the war . . . had an almost exclusively bourgeois membership. The most active anti-Fascist organizations, on the other hand, recruited their members chiefly from the common people. . . . The

French bourgeoisie, gradually abandoning its eighteenth century heritage of rationalist and liberal thought, as expressed in a democratic society, regressed toward a hierarchic social order and an authoritarian form of government, such as the *ancien régime* had been. . . .

As the bourgeoisie was predominant in French politics, this progressive conversion had important consequences. The Third Republic was largely a democracy in name only. Within governmental and administrative institutions the power of the bourgeoisie had grown stronger and stronger at the expense of the common people. The will of the majority was no longer sovereign. Most of the members of the government, most of the civil servants, and all the Army leaders belonged to the bourgeoisie. Unconsciously at times, they behaved less as representatives of the French nation than as representatives of the bourgeois circles to which they were attached by family, education, and way of life; because of them, the governmental and administrative machinery was controlled not by the majority of the people, but by a wealthy minority. France was under the yoke of a bourgeois dictatorship. The bourgeoisie, when it succumbed to the Fascist powers, handed over to them a state well under its control.

Weakness of French Democracy. French democracy . . . had its strong and its weak points. Its particular character was shaped by economic and social circumstances and, in its most individual aspects, by historical circumstances.

The strength of French democracy came from its revolutionary tradition. Unlike the more peaceful and steady development of the Anglo-Saxon democracies, the French was created by revolutions—the Revolutions of 1789-1793, of 1830, 1848, and 1871. . . .

This democratic tradition has taken two principal forms. The first is the attachment of the *petite bourgeoisie* to the republican form of government. The common people love the Republic. For one hundred and fifty years . . . the common people of city and country have devoted themselves to creating the Republic, defending it when it was in danger, recreating it when it has been destroyed. For it they have fought on the barricades. To save it they have opposed all of the forces of reaction—Church, Army, Aristocracy, and Industry. The second expression of the French democratic tradition has been the political orientation of the labor organizations. . . . They concerned themselves with the form of government, the economic system, and with international relations, and always had a political and social program. . . . They [were] in the front line of the anti-Fascist struggle between 1934 and 1940. They have been the leaders of the underground battle against Hitler and the Vichy government. The attachment of the common people to the Republic and the political power of the labor organizations were the armor of democracy, and this armor would have been sufficiently strong if the military defeat, caused and utilized by the enemies of democracy, had not overturned the political situation to the benefit of Fascism, and permitted Pétain, with Hitler's support, to crush the Third Republic.

The weakness of French democracy has two causes. The first factor is . . . the persistence, on the part of the haute bourgeoisie, of an anti-democratic tradition. . . . According to the historians, there have been, for the past hundred and fifty years, two Frances: one, a liberal and democratic France, the France of the Revolution and of the Declaration of the Rights of Man, and the other, a reactionary, militaristic, and nationalistic France, the France of the Restoration and of the Empire, of the MacMahon regime and of the Dreyfus affair. The two Frances have been constantly at war; the adversaries of democracy have never disarmed and have never accepted the political new deal of the French Revolution. For a century and a half, all Frenchmen—consciously or unconsciously, depending on the degree of their political education—have been divided into two spiritual families, partisans or enemies of the Revolution. The political history of contemporary France is the history of the struggle between these two families.

... The French conservatives ... have been not only guardians of established order and opponents of social progress, but also enemies of the republican system.... They have supported, in varying circumstances, the King, the Emperor, Marshal MacMahon, General Boulanger, and Pétain. Tomorrow they will support anyone who seems capable of delivering them from the democratic menace. They feel that democracy, with its principle of majority rule, represents a threat to their privileges....

This small but permanent nucleus of anti-democrats was the rallying point for French Fascism....

The second circumstance favorable to the development of French Fascism has been the progressive degeneration of the democratic institutions. Few realize how undemocratic these had become.

From its beginning the Third Republic was not very democratic. Its system was fixed by the constitutional laws of 1875. ... They had been drafted and passed by a National Assembly composed largely of royalists and conservatives. The National Assembly accepted the republican principle because its members, split into rival groups, could not agree on a monarchic formula. Some favored an absolute monarchy and others a constitutional monarchy.... Still more important for the understanding of its constitutional weakness is the fact that the republican regime, from 1920 to 1940, suffered a progressive degradation, resulting not from actual modifications of the constitutional laws, but from their application and interpretation by Parliament....

This transformation has rarely been described. Since the French Republic was a parliamentary democracy, Parliament had legislative power as well as the control of the executive power, the cabinet being politically responsible to it. The French Parliament, like the British, was divided into two houses, the Chamber of Deputies and the Senate. Only the Chamber was elected by direct universal suffrage. The Senate, similar to the English House of Lords, represented the most conservative elements of the nation—chiefly the middle class and the "rural bourgeoisie." In senatorial elections the rural bourgeoisie had an advantage; those Frenchmen who lived in the country and small towns elected proportionately three times as many Senators as those who lived in the big cities. ... The result was that only the Chamber of Deputies was representative of the whole nation (including its radical elements), while the Senate was the political expression of the conservative bourgeoisie.

This created no serious difficulties before the war of 1914. During the 1875-1914 period the political powers of the Senate were less extensive than those of the Chamber of Deputies; it was generally understood that the Senate could not overthrow the cabinet, and that after using its "right of remonstrance," it had to bow before the will of the Chamber in financial matters, since the Chamber had the right to apply the "doctrine of the last word." After the First World War, however, these wise constitutional guarantees were abandoned. The Senate now considered its powers equal to those of the Chamber, caused its will to prevail in financial matters, and claimed the right to overthrow the cabinet.

In practice, the extension of the Senate's political power resulted in legislative paralysis and ministerial instability, in short, governmental impotence. Differently constituted and representing the will of often irreconcilable social groups, the Chamber and Senate were bound to have divergent political orientations. As the cabinet, to exist, needed the confidence of both houses, it was always obliged to seek a compromise between the will of the people and that of the conservative bourgeoisie. When the cabinet's attitude pleased the Chamber, it displeased the Senate, and vice versa. A survey of the many ministerial crises between 1920 and 1940, one of the weaknesses of the Third Republic, reveals that 80 per cent of them were caused, directly or indirectly, by the disagreement between Chamber and Senate on financial matters. Every cabinet that showed progressive tendencies was pitilessly overthrown by the Senate. . . .

From 1920 to 1940, in three general elections out of four, the French people chose progressive governments; and every time the wealthy minority, whether by the manipulation of its economic power or through the Senate, compelled these governments to follow a conservative policy or overthrew them. . . . Big business rather than the common man dominated the Third Republic.

An important consequence of this "dictatorship of the bourgeoisie" was the increasing impatience of the masses and of organized labor with the Third Republic. The French workers felt that the will of the people was no longer sovereign, that it could never prevail, especially in social questions, against the will of the minority. . . . Anglo-Saxons have wondered what it was that encouraged the growth of revolutionary parties in France; it was largely the impotence of the democratic mechanism. Revolution appeared as the alternative to reformism.

It was not because it was too democratic, but because it was not democratic enough, that the Third Republic weakened and was conquered. Politics cannot be explained by hypotheses, much less by regrets. But if the French governmental institutions had been truly democratic, the Popular Front cabinets would not have been overthrown; had the Senate not held a reactionary mortgage on Parliament, the French government would have supported the Spanish Republic and would have continued to work for a Franco-Soviet rapprochement—for such was the feeling of the majority. The war and the defeat would have been avoided. . . .

The adhesion of the reactionary bourgeoisie to Fascism was thus the decisive element in the French defeat; it was the cause of causes, the common denominator for the factors of the defeat. . . .

The defeat of France appears to me as a tragedy in three acts: it was prepared by France's isolation, chiefly caused by the rupture of the Franco-Soviet Pact; it was consummated by the military weakness of France, chiefly caused by the General Staff's professional and intellectual inferiority; it ended with the fall of the Third Republic and the policy of collaboration, chiefly caused by Fifth Column activity. Each of these determinants played its special role. Yet the three acts form a coherent whole: at every juncture, the treason of the French *haute bourgeoisie* appears. . . .

WHY FRANCE FELL: A BRITISH INTERPRETATION

By D. W. Brogan

From D. W. Brogan's Introduction to The Twilight of France, *by A. Werth. Copyright 1942 by Harper & Brothers, New York; reproduced by permission. Dr. Brogan is professor of political science at Cambridge University, and is a life-long student of French politics.*

The political life of a nation does not often illustrate its virtues and achievements at their best. . . . In the France of the last twenty years the difference between the achievements of the French nation and the French state was even more striking than usual. It was not merely that France was as fertile as ever in talent and in genius, that her primacy in the arts was undisputed, her leadership in the sciences contested by few. Her moral life, too, seemed to be renewing itself; there were everywhere signs of a second spring.

Not quite everywhere; the state, the political organization, seemed unchanged or changed only for the worse. The French state was still capable of great material achievements: the restoration of the devastated regions, the development of the Empire. These were among the greatest successful efforts in construction of our times. But the political direction of these plans grew feebler and the political machine functioned more and more slowly, was less and less capable of mechanical efficiency. Where it acted effectively, it was in an extremely wasteful fashion, and often, in the most important spheres, it did not act at all. . . .

Such a decline had happened before and had gone to extreme lengths before it was noticed. Louis XVI was still issuing edicts *"de par le roi,"* still dismissing the Parliament of Paris in the manner of Louis XIV, at a time when his authority was already a sham. And so Prime Ministers sat in the place of Ferry and Clemenceau and Poincaré, Ministers of the Interior in the place of Rouher and Constans, Foreign Ministers in the place of Vergennes and Delcassé, when the effective powers of these offices had evaporated. With a fine dramatic sense, Dumas opens *Twenty Years After* in the Palais Royal, with Mazarin as the shade of Richelieu. But the change from Richelieu to Mazarin was as nothing to the change whose consequences are illustrated here. The authority of the executive had been destroyed. . . .

Political authority had passed (for what it was worth) to Parliament, to the thousand deputies and senators. . . .

Most of the senators and deputies were neither fools nor knaves. But they were members of a morally dangerous trade. The French have a proverb that "a door must be open or shut." The French parliamentary system existed to confute this belief. Had France been a physical as well as psychological island, her happy state might have made her the envy of the world. She had her problems, her stresses and strains, but her natural wealth, the industry and tenacity of her inhabitants, the stabilizing effect of widely distributed property, the comparative absence of that wrecker of modern states, prolonged and general unemployment, made it possible to avoid answering some of the most difficult questions put to the rulers of the great industrial states. French politics could, therefore, be about "principles," not about the application of those principles. They could be, and were, passionate, stirring, entertaining, but they did not reflect the urgency of modern economic problems. Elections could still be fought on fine old irrelevant slogans, and whole communes of Kulaks vote the Communist ticket without provoking more than an indulgent smile.

For there was a sense in which politics in France had become very pure, had acquired some, though not all, of the character of art for art's sake that was shown by American politics in the boom days of Coolidge. It was often as difficult to explain, on rational grounds of choice, the political color of similar French regions as it was to explain why the slum dwellers of Philadelphia voted the Republican and their brethren in New York the Democratic ticket. Elections, the right to vote, the legal equality of Frenchmen, these were an important part of French social life. There was not much reason to complain of indifference or of failure to vote. But what was being voted for or against was harder to define. Men still voted for and against the Revolution, the Church, the Commune, but what they voted for or against in the current situation was harder to discover.... All that one could safely say of the results of a general election was that it changed to some degree the political personnel, and gave an indication of the names which the President of the Republic would have to consider *for the first few months* of the Parliament in looking for ministers. But there was nothing that Rousseau would have called a general will revealed by the consultation of the electors—as the language of politics unconsciously revealed.

There used to recur in French political jargon, above all on the Left, a technical term whose popularity was depressingly significant. How often has a measure been opposed in the name of "universal suffrage"; how often has a politician (whose own weight was light) proudly spoken as the "delegate of universal suffrage"; how often has what is, after all, a term describing a piece of electoral machinery, been hypostatized into an independent power whose presumed will was to be blindly obeyed! Such verbal idolatry was not insignificant. The older French republican tradition spoke of "the sovereign people" as the Constitution of the United States speaks of "We, the People of the United States 'who' *do* ordain and establish" the form of government which is to give effect to their continuing sovereign will. To a philosopher, the fiction of the People having a continuing will may be distasteful, but it is as a working political idea more real and more dignified than "universal suffrage." You can make a song about it. The soldiers of the Revolution could sing *"le peuple souverain s'avance"* as they dethroned kings and liberated peoples. Try to sing *"le suffrage universel s'avance"* as a battlecry!

The verdict of universal suffrage was a verdict in favor of a number of candidates professing certain doctrines and making certain promises over a number of candidates professing not very different doctrines and making very similar promises. It had no more positive content, as was speedily found by such victors as put on airs as mandatories of the popular will. French elections never produced landslides of the American or British types. A defective electoral system gave exaggerated parliamentary majorities which never represented overwhelming majorities in votes cast. And in a country where women played so decisive a role in family and economic life, women did not vote. The sole animating force of the French political system was a Parliament so chosen. Once the elections were over, it remained for the successful candidates to give the machine of government, it would be too much to say its impetus, but those little jerks forward and backward that gave the electors an impression of something happening. French politics took a fairly uniform development, at any rate, from 1924 on, when the "Left" recovered its normal electoral predominance. Electors returned a coalition majority which began by promising and even trying to put into effect some of the promises made during the campaign. Within a period that was never more than two years long, the balance of power in the Chamber had shifted toward the Right and the electors learned with more or less resignation that, for various "technical" (i.e. financial) reasons, the goods promised could not be delivered. If the technical problems were really serious, Parliament abandoned any pretense of dealing with them, and gave "full powers" to a Prime Minister to do by decree what the deputies could not bring themselves to do by law. The responsibility was thus put on the shoulders of Poincaré or Doumergue or Laval or Daladier. When the crisis was over, politics were resumed, credit taken and responsibility disowned.

In normal times, the damage done by such a system could be exaggerated by the captious critic. The elector was less deceived than it was customary to pretend. He wanted his deputy or senator to do his best, but he did not expect much, and in rural France did not want much, in the way of change. The elected did not really deceive the electors. No doubt there were hundreds of thousands of sincere *militants* on the Left who suffered from these repeated deceptions, as they saw their leaders make necessary, if ignominious, compromises. No doubt there were hundreds of thousands of sincere pessimists on the Right who believed that, to use the old Bonapartist phrase, it was necessary first to "strangle the slut" before France could be restored to political health. But the average Frenchman had the resigned pessimism of the peasant. Good harvests mean bad prices; no autumn ever fully justifies the hopes of spring.

The temptation this attitude put in the way of the politician was very great. He knew that profound changes were not wanted and that even substantial changes were very difficult. He knew that all sections of the French political world would combine against a man, a section, or a group, that seemed to have a chance to use the machinery of the state vigorously. All parties, therefore, agreed that, since they could not have their own way, no one should. What was left was too often what Burke called "a confused and scuffling bustle of local agency." Each deputy and senator did his best for his constituents, in the hope that the aggregate of these competing bests would add up to the good of the French state. But that is the kind of political arithmetic of which states die. . . . Schemes of reform or of change boldly proposed [were] not so much rejected as smothered. The fate of Tardieu was the fate of Blum; the fate of Briand was the fate of Paul-Boncour and would probably have been the fate of Barthou had he lived. The policies of these men differed; what they had in common was a desire to give effect to a policy—and the chambers were not ready to support the effort necessary to make any real, coherent, decisive policy work.

It was this situation that made possible the career of what in seventeenth century England was called the "undertaker," the manipulator of parliament whose pretensions to policy or principle were hardly taken seriously even by his own electoral committee, but who was a master of what Italians call *combinazioni*. . . . There is, for example, Chautemps, highly cultivated, with hereditary claims to Radical loyalty, master of passing the responsibility for decision on to others. But the perfect specimen of the type is, of course, Laval. Here he is, with his teeth not much dirtier than his "white" cravat or his hands. Like so many agents of the Right, he got his start by the profession of the most violent, intolerant left-wing sentiments. But once elected to the Chamber, he made friends, friends on all sides—and it must be remembered that he *kept* friends on all sides. Even when he was the incarnation (for the purposes of public meetings) of all that the Left detested, he did not break off his useful connections with his old friends on the Left—either in Aubervilliers or Auvergne. He was a lawyer, and it was impossible for him to make fine distinctions between his clients in Parliament and in the courts. But Laval, if the most finished specimen of the political adventurer, was only the most successful representative of a class. And that he had friends on all sides was not surprising, for the Chamber was a club; it was suspicious of members who were not on easy terms of familiarity with the other members. Barrès might object to being *tutoyé* by strangers who were merely colleagues, but Barrès was not a typical deputy. No, outside the Communist Party (if that exception is valid) it was true in 1939 as it was when Robert de Jouvenel laid down the law before the war of 1914; "There is more in common between two deputies, one of whom is a revolutionary, than between two revolutionaries, one of whom is a deputy."

For all its faults and falseness, the French political system might have continued to permit good, the development of the humane, critical, rich French civilization, and not have done irremediable harm, if France had been, let us say, an island more isolated than New Zealand is from the stormy outside world. But France was a neighbor of Germany. By a combination of heroism, skill and luck, France had been the victor in 1918. But, intrinsically, for the purposes of modern war, France was hopelessly inferior to her formidable neighbor. Once Austria was added to the Reich, there were twice as many Germans as there were Frenchmen. Nor was this all; because her population of military age in 1914 was disproportionately lower than that of Germany (as a pioneer in birth-control, the population of France was older), the fact that her military losses were disproportionately *higher* made the position of France vis-à-vis Germany still worse. And because in modern war, industrial potential is even more important than manpower, France was still weaker. Then, although this grim truth was hidden from all but the few real experts like General de Gaulle, who understood modern war, the weaker, less completely prepared nations would not, this time, be given a chance to pull themselves together. In 1914, the machine-gun, the quick-firing field-gun, were the weapons that made the defensive possible and made vain the German dream of "a battle without a morrow." In 1940, the dive-bomber and the tank had given reality to the dreams of Schlieffen.

. . . There were, possibly, two policies to be adopted toward Germany. While there was yet time, the Weimar Republic might have been buttressed and threatened; helped on promises of effective good behavior. Or, when that policy had been tried and failed, or simply not tried, the realities of the Hitlerian Revolution might have been faced. The enemies of Hitler in Germany told the German people that he was asking them to commit suicide, that Germany's neck was in a rope, and that, if the hands which held it in Paris, Warsaw, Prague, were frightened by Nazi threats, they would pull the rope. Hitler called that bluff; it was his greatest internal victory.

All the former victors were to blame, but the French failure was inherent in the French political system. To choose one or other line of action was to commit the French state to one resolute policy, carried out without flinching, without compromise. At home and abroad the Third Republic had lost all power to carry out any coherent, long-term policy. No doubt . . . Barthou saw what needed to be done. But had he not been physically assassinated at Marseilles he would have been politically assassinated in Parliament. The fact that the French talked of Hitler, even after 1934, as "Chancellor Hitler" was a disquieting symptom. So he was just a politician like Brüning or Blum? Alas! he was not.

The failure of the French to understand, in time, what was the full import of the Nazi revolution was due to virtues as well as to vices. Accustomed in their own country to vehement words covering moderate and reasonable projects, the genuine German extravagance, an extravagance of content as well as of form, was discounted by the man in the shop and on the farm who, for too long, took the bellowings of the Führer as bluff and bluster. How could a primary schoolteacher, convinced that the only real obstacle to the spread of enlightenment, of rational pacifism, of the religion of humanity was the Church, understand the demonic power of the Nazi religion? His education narrowed him by its very generality. Men could not because they should not believe such things, and if, by an incredible hypothesis, they *did* believe them, their belief need have no result in action. It was both natural and disastrous that the schoolteachers, all over rural France the molders of the political mind of the country, should have been uncritical and optimistic pacifists. From this well-meaning, but as far as the outside world was concerned, ill-equipped body, came some of the most effective pacifist propaganda of 1938. . . . Not until it was too late did the profession that regarded itself as, in a special sense, the guardians of the Republic realize that it had helped to destroy its own work.

But it was not only the primary schoolteachers who were at fault. The master whom the Left intelligentsia among the university and secondary schoolteachers most delighted to honor, "Alain," was a dangerous dissolvent of the sense of realism. For the France, tolerant, sceptical, anarchical which Alain wished to preserve or create, was a Utopia in the modern world of heavy industry and nationalist passion. And it was another university teacher, Déat . . . [who] moved from the candid if impracticable selfishness of "Why die for Danzig?" to preaching to the Frenchmen of 1941 the duty of dying to make Moscow German.

There was even some justice in the criticism passed on a leading *universitaire* who, in his role as a statesman, never fell into the more absurd or base aberrations of Alain or Déat. It was of M. Herriot, confronted with Germanic hysteria, that Bainville wrote, "A Cartesian Frenchman like M. Herriot will rub his eyes when he has read these documents. He will ask himself if he is dreaming. It is another world of ideas, another universe. Without a preliminary study, you might believe it was an affair of a bet, of a paradox or of an aberration." The gullible English spectator of the madness of the Third Reich thought that all this extravagance covered a fundamental soundness of practice and aims, that the frenzies of a Nuremberg Party Day were merely a Teutonic version of an Aldershot tattoo plus a Scout jamboree. The gullible Frenchman thought they were mere declamation. He thought the ideals proclaimed were detestable, but he thought they had no chance of being put into practice. It was a more respectable error, but its consequences were the same—and in France they were not mitigated by the existence of the Channel.

But this was not all. Those sections

of French opinion which had boasted of their realism, which had prided themselves on their knowledge of the modern world, a world in which the optimistic generalities of 1789 had no place, were incapable of putting their realism to any good use. As German power grew, as the primary need of the French state was a most vigorous, uncontested, and rapid assertion of its dwindling military superiority, the Right in France found other fish to fry. It feared, or professed to fear, that Russia was as great a danger as Germany; in some cases it was found convenient to pretend that Russia was a greater danger. And, suffering from an illusion common to the Right in all countries (and not confined to the Right), the revolutionary character of Nazism was ignored. In Germany Hitler was a "restorer of order." ... The popular basis of Nazism, those elements in it which gave it its explosive power, were underestimated by the Right to whom they were in fact too much like the emotional forces behind the *Front Populaire* to be palatable. The idea of a European order in which Germany would preserve the existing class structure was an illusion which clouded some professedly clear minds. And more were blinded by the fantastic vision of an Italian counterpoise to Germany, by ideas of a Latin union based on classical virtues of order and clarity. It was a literary illusion. No amount of mythical nonsense about the German language and the German race would have mattered much, if there had not been so many Germans, if there had not been German heavy industry to arm them and the Prussian military tradition to make the Wehrmacht something that rhetoric could not alone have made, and once made could not alone destroy. ...

In the crisis of June 1940 what was lacking to set against a natural resentment and despair was *political* authority. The defeatism of the generals was natural enough. They had done all they knew how to do—and it had not been enough. They were chess players who knew that they had lost. But the art of war is more than a military art, and statesmen of authority might have countered the professional despair of the soldiers. They might have estimated, more justly, the power and will of Britain to resist. They might have estimated, more justly, the possibilities of imperial resistance. Above all, they might have denounced as suicidal illusion that pathetic belief in an honorable peace "between soldiers," that professional self-deception of Marshal Pétain, that ignorant refusal to see the Nazi revolution as it really was. But it was just this independent political authority that was lacking. M. Paul Reynaud had shown foresight and energy, but his own political position was weak. A man of the Right, he had been disowned by his own supporters without being accepted by the Left. The President of the Republic was filling, worthily, an office which had long since lost all authority and had only formal prestige. Parliament was a body which had failed to carry out the policy of the *Front Populaire* without finding any substitute, which had not even openly ratified the declaration of war, and which was soon to perform its final abdication, to crown its series of resignations of responsibility by giving dictatorial powers to Marshal Pétain.

There was no center of authority left. A generation of open fear of great personalities, a generation of temporary alliances to weaken any over-mighty minister, had reduced the personal authority of the parliamentarians to nothing. Against the palace revolution of the Bordeaux cabinet crisis, only a political counterrevolution could have been effective. And where were the leaders of such a counterrevolution to be found? Only Georges Mandel was of the stuff of which Gambettas are made —and Mandel, even less than Reynaud, had a political position worthy of his talents and courage. He had been the right-hand of Clemenceau—and the Left had spent twenty years explaining away its sin in producing the dictator who, in 1917 and 1918, had saved France. No precaution had been omitted which would help to make it certain that no new Clemenceau could appear. Nor did one.

. . . Both the Chamber and the Senate were too well provided with men who, because they were orators, thought themselves statesmen, and who thought that a successful speech was a solution in itself, a complete action. There are, of course, speeches that are complete acts, speeches that secure for a moment the emotional and moral adherence of the audience, that prevent a collapse or generate a new and necessary burst of energy. . . . But the great and effective orators of today are popular orators, the movers of great masses, the dominators of great crowds or the men who, at the microphone, can hold the attention and control the judgment of many millions. Such were not the masters of the French tribune. No more than so many eminent lawyers did the virtuosi of the Chamber have an equivalent power of effective speech outside the arena whose rules and temper they knew so well. This had not always been so. Gambetta, Déroulède, Clemenceau, above all, Jaurès, could dominate both the Senate and the people. But in the period between the two wars, the leaders of French politics were less and less concerned with the outside world, less and less able to repeat their parliamentary successes outside. Their rhetoric was often generous, even moving, as it was when M. Herriot appealed to the great and true commonplaces of the republican tradition, but it was not a call to action, at best it was an appeal for resistance.

This decline in the power of the political leaders to move the man in the street was crucial in a country where government by speech was so important. As long as power went to the masters of parliamentary tactics (of which a great part was the skillful use of parliamentary oratory) this did not much matter. But in a crisis where it was no longer enough to modify or to express the opinion of the Palais Bourbon, when the Chamber had no opinion or dared not express what opinion it had, the lack of tribunes of the people was felt. France was provided with masters of formal rhetoric, fit for the 14th of July; she was even better provided with masters of debate fit for the daily rhetorical games of Parliament. She was not provided, as both Britain and America were provided in their great crises, with masters of public and general speech. . . . Political questions were, indeed, discussed at a higher level than they usually were at Westminster or at Washington. But it was not unimportant that the most brilliant debater and reasoner of the Left, M. Blum, was not merely lacking in popular appeal but normally and wisely did not pretend to have it. And as far as the Right had a master of doctrine and an inspirer of action, it was Charles Maurras, almost stone deaf, a man of the study and of the docile, listening group. . . .

It was not that there were not men of courage and ability, of understanding and energy, but how was the people to distinguish between the forcible and the forcible-feeble, between the men whose energies were aroused by dangers and the men who were numbed by it? The creation of such personal, non-parliamentary reputations was made as difficult as possible. So when the great crisis came, the bewildered, desperate, betrayed French people turned to the one emblem of independent authority that remained, to a Marshal of France. There were so few Marshals; there were so many ex-Prime Ministers, leaders of the Chamber and the House, masters of the arts that control debating bodies, parliaments and party congresses, *voces et praeterea nihil*. It was, in fact, the politicians, MM. Lebrun, Herriot, Reynaud, who were in favor of carrying on the war from Africa; as happened in Germany in 1918, it was the nerves and resolution of the great military chiefs which snapped first. Ludendorff preceded Pétain, both in despairing of the military situation, in throwing up the sponge and in placing the blame on civilian shoulders. But that the French people took the word of the Marshal, that the Third Republic collapsed with as little resistance as the Second Empire, is a lesson that Frenchmen and friends of popular government everywhere must ponder. In 1871, Daumier drew his Bonapartist peasant looking at the ruins of his house and reflecting on the overwhelming support he and his class had given to Napoleon III less than a year before: "We didn't vote for that." So said the Frenchman of 1940; so would have said the Englishman or the American had he had to face such disasters under such leadership. . . .

TOWARD THE NEW FRANCE

By C. A. Micaud and Robert Strausz-Hupé

From "The New France," by C. A. Micaud and Robert Strausz-Hupé, in *The Yale Review*, Autumn 1944. Copyright 1944 by Yale University Press; reproduced by permission.

FRANCE—in full partnership with Britain—is the one nucleus around which the new Europe can be built. Paradoxically, defeat in war and treason at Vichy will have rid France of the deadweight of the past; she will be free to resume her European mission. France is on her way to a political, social, and economic renaissance.

How new will the new France be? We cannot answer this question unless we understand past and present political alignments, the real issues dividing the forces of collaboration and resistance.

In spite of the spectacular victory of the Popular Front, the France of 1936 was very much like the France of 1900. Three main groups, almost three classes, continued their struggle for power.

The first group, the so-called Right, or "Old France," had never reconciled itself to the ideals of the French Revolution. It looked discontentedly to a past it longed to recreate. The Rightists believed in tradition, authority, hierarchy; the revolutionary ideas of progress, liberty and equality were to them senseless and dangerous slogans incompatible with a pessimistic philosophy of life that denied the democratic premises of man's goodness and perfectibility. The masses, unable to choose their leaders, should be ruled from above, by an élite whose claims to leadership were based on birth and wealth. . . .

The second group, "Republican France," was born of the French Revolution and remained true to its philosophical and ethical foundations. Liberty was its motto; individualism its religion. The Radical-Socialists, who together with some smaller parties, represented it in Parliament, traditionally fought against the past, the reactionary pretensions of Old France, but they fought also against the future, the collectivism inherent in modern industrial economy, whether capitalistic or social-istic. Their suspicion of authority was matched by their dislike of a radical shake-up of economic and social institutions. Republican France was made up of independent farmers and *petits bourgeois*, shopkeepers, *fonctionnaires*, artisans—mostly people in towns and villages. It, too, belonged to a pre-industrial age and represented the little man's aspirations to rural democracy. Republican France saw no good in abandoning the peaceful idyl of today for the disquieting future of giant industries and collective bargaining. It was radical in politics but conservative when it came to economic and financial matters. Since the Radical-Socialists held the balance of power, they could wage effectively their dual struggle against reaction and progress while keeping the republic alive and relatively prosperous.

The third group, "Socialist France," was born of the Industrial Revolution; its aim was economic and social equality. Not only factory workers but intellectuals and discontented *petits bourgeois* and peasants swelled the socialist parties until they came to number well over one-third of the electorate; at the last general elections, in 1936 one Frenchman out of five cast his ballot for the United Socialist Party ticket, and one out of seven voted Communist. The Socialists had come to accept governmental responsibility and were reconciled to a slow and gradual elimination of capitalism. The Communists led the more radical elements of the working classes into uncompromising opposition to bourgeois society. Only in 1935 did they join the grand coalition of Republican France and Socialist France against the growing threat of the pro-Fascist leagues.

The coexistence of these three groups —products of three ages in the life of the country—explains not only the past difficulties and weaknesses of France, but the fundamental issues in the struggle between the partisans of collaboration with Germany and those of resistance.

France's economic and social problem transcends in importance the more spectacular political struggle. Two groups with a pre-industrial outlook have dominated the political scene and imposed their policies on a third, at the expense not only of the working classes but of the industrial development of the country. Up-to-date labor legislation was enacted only in 1936. Yet the Popular Front, which had sponsored it, died an inglorious death at the hand of the *petits bourgeois*; the pendulum had once more swung from Left to Right as economics clashed with politics. For Republican France, although the enemy of Old France on ideological grounds, held the same orthodox views in economics that in practice amounted to a policy of agricultural preference and relative scarcity.

Before the First World War it could be argued plausibly that lack of coal and iron deposits compelled France to maintain a predominantly agricultural economy. The situation changed radically after 1918: not only did France recover her iron mines of Lorraine and modernize her industrial equipment, but her enormous potential of hydroelectric power and high-grade bauxite deposits invited a large industrial development. Such a policy would have necessitated profound structural changes—a shift of population from country to city, adequate social legislation, state credits and public works, and finally reform of agricultural methods along the lines of specialization and mechanization. This was too bold a program for the *petits bourgeois*, as well as the upper classes. Instead, France clung to a policy of deflation and protection of agricultural interests: high tariffs maintained prices of foodstuffs well above world market prices. Agricultural protection conserved the socially and economically least desirable forms of agriculture. Poor lands were kept under cultivation; on small marginal holdings the introduction of modern farming methods could not be afforded. The standard of living of the French peasant was below that of Dutch and Danish farmers with their intensive, specialized forms of production. Agricultural protection exposed French trade to retaliatory tariffs abroad and was paid for, as it is paid for everywhere, by the domestic consumer. Hence industry lacked sufficient foreign and domestic markets, and it was the working classes which footed the bill of a policy of scarcity.

Agrarian interests cloaked their demands for protection in military arguments: in war, France was to be self-sufficient in foodstuffs; France was to replenish her declining manpower from a sturdy peasantry. Agricultural production was thus assumed to be more important for maintaining French power than a large industrial potential. Yet homegrown food did not stop Germany's mechanized armies; moreover population statistics showed that some of the richest farming districts in Normandy, the Channel coast, and Touraine had had, for many years, only a slightly higher birth rate and a higher mortality rate than the cities.

In fact, the Right was determined to maintain a rural, that is conservative, majority of hard working, law-abiding citizens, and Vichy's policy of the "return to the land" had no other foundation. To avoid the contagion of dangerous socialist ideas they were quite willing to trade the prospects of industrial expansion for the political "safety" of millions of small farmers, not too prosperous and not too poor. Surprisingly enough, this policy was encouraged by Republican France, which did not realize that democracy can flourish only in a land of prosperous farmers and contented workers. It was also encouraged by many industrialists who preferred "order" and security to expanding production and larger profits.

The democratic method of government could survive in a country divided on fundamental issues only as long as both extremes hoped to ensure the final triumph of their ideals and interests through parliamentary procedures. Before the First World War, the Republic had secure foundations: the upper classes were largely reconciled to a regime that had proved tamer than anticipated, and the Socialists, trusting in the slow but steady evolution to the Left, believed that power would be theirs in the not too distant future.

This was no longer the case in the last decade of the Third Republic. The successes of Communism and Fascism in Europe enabled French extremist factions to make spectacular gains at the expense of the democratic Center. . . . Pierre-Etienne Flandin, then still a leader of the moderate Rightists, declared at the end of 1937 that "the democratic regime is surviving much more because of the rivalry of the two opposing totalitarian tendencies than by virtue of its own force."

Shortly afterwards, this same Flandin became parliamentary champion of appeasement. For domestic and foreign policy could no longer be separated. The Rightists, formerly the jealous defenders of France's national interests, were now defending the dictators against economic sanctions and a "preventive war." They fought against military agreement with Soviet Russia, economic and military sanctions against Italy, intervention in Spain against the rebels, mobilization at the time of the Rhineland coup, and a policy of firmness in the days of the Austrian *Anschluss* and the Munich Conference. All these measures were advocated by most Leftists—whom the former militarists of the Right now labelled jingoist and pro-Russian.

After the First World War the nationalists of the Right had opposed the Left's conciliatory policy towards Germany: the questions of reparations, disarmament, and revision of the peace treaties were taboo. Yet, by 1936, many of these same die-hards had become converted to Hitler's crusade against Bolshevism. They urged capitulation to German demands and opposed the policy of firmness advocated by the majority of the Left. Class interests and ideological bias had proved stronger than patriotism. Not Hitler but Stalin was public enemy No. 1. Some even said, "Rather Hitler than Blum." . . .

Appeasement led to collaboration, just as an anti-democratic bias and the pathological fear of a social upheaval led to the active acceptance of the Vichy regime. . . .

French Fascism is not the product of monopoly capitalism much less of deficit finance, but of the unhappy wedding of a surviving feudal philosophy with the great bourgeois fear of social upheaval.

Vichy's policy of a "return to the land" was officially presented as a measure for restoring family life and increasing the physical and moral health of the population. Actually it was a logical fulfillment of the desire to recreate the patterns of the past. It is characteristic of this policy that mechanized agriculture is frowned upon as sternly as large-scale manufacturing. Vichy's concept of a France made up of a majority of small landowners and artisans fitted perfectly with Nazi plans for a New Order in which France was to be one of the granaries of industrial Germany, forever a vassal state. Vichy acceded easily to the transfer of titles to industrial property into German hands and organized dutifully the shipment of skilled and semi-skilled workers to the Reich. In compensation for this policy of agricultural preference, industrialists (who are mostly representatives of the cartels) were placed at the head of a regimented economic system under the purely nominal control of the state. They were thus in a position to secure to themselves handsome profits. The working classes have been consistently discriminated against in spite of early promises and of the grant of utterly inadequate old-age pensions. Not only have independent labor unions been suppressed and the right to strike abolished, but the standard of living has steadily declined. Room has been made for the unemployed at the expense of women, foreigners or what Vichy laws designate as such, and, of course, those supplied with a one-way ticket to Germany. It is not surprising that Vichy incurred the hatred of the working men, who . . . in thousands joined the underground organizations. . . .

By contrast, the resistance movements are looking toward a future prosperity and true democracy—economic as well as political. Definite trends, if not specific policies, are taking shape both in official declarations and the Underground press, pointing to radical changes in the economic, social, and political structure of the republic. . . .

Concerning France's economic and social problem, nationalists of the de Gaulle type are coming to agree with Socialists that industry must be expanded vigorously if France is to be both strong and prosperous. War has taught France one bitter lesson. The lonely champion of mechanized warfare was right in preferring an army of mechanics to one of shopkeepers and peasants. Industrial potential is more important in modern warfare than self-sufficiency in foodstuffs. Moreover, the answer to the social question lies not in a return to a pre-industrial age, but in a bold adaptation to new conditions and new possibilities. France can be a leading industrial country with generous labor legislation and a contented working class. Her policy of self-sufficiency must be abandoned for one of international cooperation and union. Agriculture need not suffer from this new orientation: modernization of agricultural methods, specialization in crops according to climate and soil, elimination of marginal lands, and production of high grade foodstuffs, a better marketing system, and an extensive use of machinery through the development of cooperatives will raise total output, yet give greater comfort and buying power to a smaller rural population. Such a program, which is now beginning to take shape, would, of course involve government control of credit and industries, a planned economy not necessarily exclusive of capitalistic methods. The only alternative to this "mixed" economy, making for enlarged production and better distribution, would be the disastrous continuation of class warfare and perhaps a successful attempt by the embittered workers to impose a dictatorship of the proletariat. If this fundamental issue is clearly presented to the electorate, it is thought that Republican France, remembering the consequences of its narrow economic conservatism, will reconcile itself to the necessity of profound structural changes. . . .

If an adequate answer is given to the economic and social questions, the political problem will solve itself with relative ease. Even the issue of authority, of "efficiency without dictatorship," will not be insurmountable. The constitutional reforms to be adopted—no agreement obtains yet on that score except that they are needed—will provide the framework of the new society. But they cannot guarantee its stability. It must rest upon a new equilibrium between bourgeoisie and proletariat, and between the *idées-forces* of authority, liberty, and equality. Only then will constitutional procedures be respected and the Fourth Republic rest on solid foundations.

FRANCE IN THE NEW EUROPE

By André Géraud

From *Free World*, May 1944. Copyright 1944 by Free World Inc.; reproduced by permission. The author, better known by his penname Pertinax, is a leading French journalist.

THAT France must play a great part in the moral and material reconstruction of the European Continent no student of international affairs, no statesman acquainted with the task ahead, will even think of denying. Personally I do not believe that the schemes of European unity can lead to anything more than was achieved in Geneva. I am not prepared to regard the European Continent as an organic whole whose scattered limbs wise statesmanship could bring together. It is enough to remark that the promoters of a European federation invariably founder on the hard fact that the British Empire and Russia must be left outside. There is more in common between the members of the Atlantic community—America, England, France, the Low Countries, and the Scandinavian kingdoms—than between them and, let us say, Germany and Russia. But all idea of a federated Continent aside, France is probably the power best fitted to weld together the national policies of the greatest number of European states; and even now French culture is a common denominator for which there is no substitute. France, therefore, cannot but be rated an indispensable "associate" of the major powers of today. ...

But, after her terrible trial, will France have enough strength left in her to impress others? No, curtly said General Smuts some months ago. Of course I don't agree. The irrepressible hope of a Frenchman is that a rebirth of his nation will take place and that, in the twentieth century, his nation will manage to retain something of its former great leadership. At the same time I don't want to indulge in a perfunctory show of optimism. We have to admit that the rebirth of France cannot be taken for granted, that France will not survive as a potent maker of history unless recast in a new moral, political and social mold. In foretelling the future of France we must guard against paying undue heed to the magnitude of the military disaster which befell her in 1940. But for their sea frontiers, England and America would not have fared better; and the crisis which at the outset put the Third Republic on its mettle— the reintegration of labor in the national community on more generous terms than before—was by no means specific to French history. Furthermore, in a world devoted to mass production our national qualities are set at a disadvantage. To recoup ourselves we shall have to overcome greater difficulties than those with which other nations have to contend.

What we shall be able to achieve no prophet can appraise. At any rate a preliminary condition must be fulfilled. As I see it, little headway will be made unless a movement of reform, a new inspiration, sweeps French society off its old bourgeois foundations. A new France must come into its own—as far removed from the France of 1789 as the latter was from the royal or from the medieval France which preceded it. Will that regenerated France be brought into being under the impact of the Resistance Movements? ... An encouraging fact is to be detected in those Resistance Movements. They cut across all social strata. Conservatives, Liberals, Socialists, Communists are being carried along in the same surging wave of patriotism. When weighed against the aim in view, the liberation of the country, none of the participants feels that his earthly possessions count for much. To anyone who remembers the French society of 1939, which the fear of a social upheaval blinded to the Hitler menace, this is a tremendous change. If the French community as a whole follows suit, then a great revival can be expected and at last we shall see light after darkness. ...

... National unity is to be sought for in new ideas, in a new personnel— and not in a resurrection of the dead.

FOREIGN POLICY OF THE NEW FRANCE

From "Free World"

From an interview with George Bidault, French Foreign Minister, in *Free World*, February 1945. Copyright 1945 by Free World Inc.; reproduced by permission.

We must think courageously and honestly about the security of our country, of Europe and of the world, if justice is to be revived.

On this subject, less than on any other, should realism be set against ideals. To be realist is to admit that the duty of maintaining security must be in the hands of those who have the means to assure it. They, in combining army, fleet and powerful aviation forces, foresee the functioning of the mechanism of these forces against the danger of war. To be realist is also to foresee a method by which the legal dispositions which will govern this security mechanism shall not create the risk of interfering with its functioning.

The whole world, all nations of goodwill, must be associated in maintaining the peace. But if a definite threat develops and measures must be taken to overcome it, how shall the necessary decisions be made? Evidently by a vote of all the associated nations. But is it desirable, is it logical, that in this vote nations the farthest removed from the danger under consideration, and those, on the other hand, whose military and economic contribution is the least, should have exactly the same voice in the Council as those nations directly exposed, and those whose resources make them preeminently responsible for security? I do not think so. That's what I want to say in expressing a warning against the arithmetic of weakness and the geometry of distances in relation to danger.

... What we are trying for is a universal system. In order to obtain it we must not fall into the trap of certain terminologies. We do not want blocs. No principle of separation must govern the organization of Europe, and there is here not only a question of words but also a question of spirit. The bloc suggests the idea of an original organization which is sufficient to itself but which is susceptible of bringing about a policy of separateness.

Now, it is obvious that just as the Soviet Union cannot remain indifferent regarding the region bordering on her territory, we likewise must regard as of primary importance to us those regions which lie next to us. This doesn't mean that we should have nothing to say on matters far removed from us, but that we ought also and especially to think about those that are close to us. It comes down to saying that a spirit of solidarity must prevail, able to take into account, if it is to be effective, the fact of geography.

It is we who are on the Rhine, where we have the right to do certain things that are important to us and to the world. No separate action certainly, but let us not forget that this is a matter of taking a measure for public safety in which there is risk of losing sight of the fact that we cannot roll on wheels toward the west. For us the Rhine is always there. Always a source of worry. It is essential that this eternal worry be ended forever. The question of the left bank of the Rhine is raised. The territories which compose it—and one must add to them the Ruhr—will no longer be governed militarily, economically, administratively, by Berlin.

What regime shall prevail in these regions? It is because of the necessity of reaching an accord on this point with the Allies and because of the uncertainty regarding the disposition of the Rhineland populations that it is impossible for me to give precise details. From today, in any case, France, the first in danger and periodically invaded, lays claim with determination to a share of authority proportionate to the risk she runs. We will protect ourselves with our own means in agreement with our Allies. They cannot ignore the fact that in no case will anything be done by us except in strict conformity to that public law to which France will always remain faithful, according to the commandment of her Christian and humanist tradition which has inspired her whole history.

We do not wish for a peace of vengeance. We wish for a peace of justice. Justice means the protection of the innocent and the punishment of the guilty. When the same guilty one hurls himself at regular intervals on the same victim he is a repeater and justice demands that all measures be taken in order that the victim may in future be forearmed and that the aggressor once and for all shall be restrained.

It goes without saying that we do not for a moment propose to take decisions separately from the others in this secular quarrel which has already caused the flow of so much blood and tears.

We want a world organization effectively capable of maintaining peace. In order to arrive at it, France, on the morrow of disaster and of her resurrection, lays claim, according to what is the hope of many peoples and her own imperative destiny, to her full place in the midst of the nations charged with guiding the new world. We have the habit of expressing ourselves in universal terms. Rendered attentive by such a succession of trials to our own interest, so often neglected, we abdicate nothing of that mission with which we feel ourselves charged from the earliest times to the furthest future. The absence of France from the world counsels would not only be intolerable to Frenchmen, we believe profoundly that her voice is necessary to the peace and that it is to the interest of all that she shall make herself heard. Moreover we know that this voice is awaited and that it will be heard.

Chapter 8

Mediterranean and Middle East

THE region bounded by the highlands of middle Europe and the deserts of Africa and Arabia, and reaching from the Atlantic to the Indian Ocean, is the historic home of western civilization. It was the seat of most of the great empires of ancient times. In modern times this region has become increasingly an arena of struggle among greater empires located wholly or mainly outside the Mediterranean basin. In the twentieth century Italy has been the only strictly Mediterranean country to be counted among the Great Powers. Italy's claim to Great Power standing has always been dubious, and will become even more so as the result of the war. For reasons that will emerge in the course of this chapter, there is little prospect of any Mediterranean or Middle Eastern country becoming a major power in the world of tomorrow.

This does not mean that the region's international importance is negligible. The Middle East is believed to contain the world's largest remaining oil reserves, a factor in itself sufficient to make the region a focus of international politics. The Mediterranean and the Middle East together constitute a transit zone of the greatest strategical importance. What happens within this region has a direct bearing on the security of several Great Powers.

"In politics," writes one authority on the Mediterranean, "its significance has been that of a passage, or a megaphone, or a knuckleduster. It has always been a route to somewhere, or the string which when pulled, reveals that its other end is in India, Vladivostok, the Middle Danube, or Mosul. You cannot write on it without also writing on imperial policy, Moslem policy, European policy. You cannot write on it without considering the policy of five or six Great Powers, and as many satellites, all of whom, when the storm threatens, react differently." (*The Mediterranean in Politics,* by Elizabeth Monroe. 1938, Oxford University Press, London.)

The Mediterranean and Middle East, in short, has been and seems likely to be in the future an arena of Great Power politics. Conflicting Great Power interests have caused strife and conflict there in the past.

In no region will there be a sterner test of the ability of the principal United Nations to work together for peace as well as for war.

American interests in the Mediterranean and Middle East have been predominantly humanitarian and commercial in the past. American money and effort have supported missions and educational institutions in the Near East. The United States government has interceded verbally on numerous occasions on behalf of oppressed minorities in that area. American archeologists have played an active role in uncovering and preserving the relics of classical civilization. American business has participated in numerous enterprises, and today has a large stake in the development of Middle Eastern oil. The American Navy in its earliest years took the lead in suppressing the pirates of the North African Barbary coast. And throughout our history Americans have carried on a flourishing commerce with the Mediterranean borderlands.

American political interests in this region have been more restricted and are, in the main, of comparatively recent origin. As far back as the 1820's, it is true, American statesmen spoke out for the Greeks struggling for independence from the Ottoman Empire. Again in the 1900's, to cite another instance, President Theodore Roosevelt strongly backed up France and Great Britain in their opposition to German attempts to gain a foothold in North Africa. But a few years later at the close of the First World War, the United States refused absolutely to assume any political responsibility for the Armenians or other minority fragments of the shattered Ottoman Empire.

Recent events have involved the United States more deeply in the Mediterranean and Middle East. In 1935 it was President Franklin Roosevelt, more than any other single statesman, who led in the abortive attempt to organize international resistance to Mussolini's conquest of Ethiopia. Again in 1939-1940, American pressure was applied in an equally unsuccessful effort to keep Mussolini from joining Hitler in the assault on France and Great Britain. Our policy of material aid to Britain and (after June 1941) to the Soviet Union led to the opening of an American air transport service across Africa to Egypt and the Middle East. In fulfillment of the same policy, we have built port installations and assembly plants on the shores of the Red Sea. American troops have fought in North Africa and in southern Europe, and American service forces have operated a large-scale transportation service from the Persian Gulf across Iran to the southern border of the Soviet Union.

The future of American political and military commitments in the Mediterranean and Middle East has not yet been revealed. It is quite possible that we may not be able to withdraw completely from this region for a considerable time. Something will depend upon the importance attached to our stake in Middle Eastern oil and other resources. More will depend, perhaps, upon the future course of Anglo-Soviet relations in the Middle East. In the long run, American political or strategic interests in the area seem likely to be more general than specific, more indirect than direct, and much less vital on the whole than the Mediterranean and Near Eastern interests of several European powers. But Americans cannot be wholly indifferent to a region which figures so vitally in the security of France and Great Britain. Nor can we safely ignore possible future difficulties that may arise among the European powers in a region of great and increasing importance to the Soviet Union.

THE MEDITERRANEAN AND MIDDLE EAST

By the Editors

Broadly speaking, four groups of territories comprise the region of the Mediterranean and Middle East. These are: (1) the peninsulas or promontories of southern Europe; (2) the fertile margin of northern Africa; (3) the fertile east shore of the Mediterranean; and (4) the semi-arid to arid peninsula of southeastern Asia.

Most of Saudi Arabia, Iraq, and Iran, it should be noted, are geographically part of the drainage basin of the Indian Ocean. In certain respects, they belong in a political and strategical sense with the Afro-Asian Realm of which the Indian Ocean basin is so important a part. At the same time, however, these lands of southeastern Asia constitute a transit zone or strategic "bridge" *from* Europe *to* the Indian Ocean, and hence are an extension of the political and strategic zone of the eastern Mediterranean.

The northern boundary of the Mediterranean region is formed by a broken system of highlands and mountain ranges which extend eastward across Europe from the Pyrenees to the Caucasus. Three great promontories reach southward from this highland demarcation zone. These are: (1) the Iberian peninsula occupied by Spain and Portugal; (2) the Italian peninsula; and (3) the Balkan peninsula occupied by Albania, Jugoslavia, Bulgaria, and Greece.

All of these countries have a hilly to mountainous terrain. With the exception of Italy, none of them has ever possessed an adequate modern transportation system. All of them are more or less cut off by mountains and meager communications from middle Europe.

Facing Europe across the Mediterra-

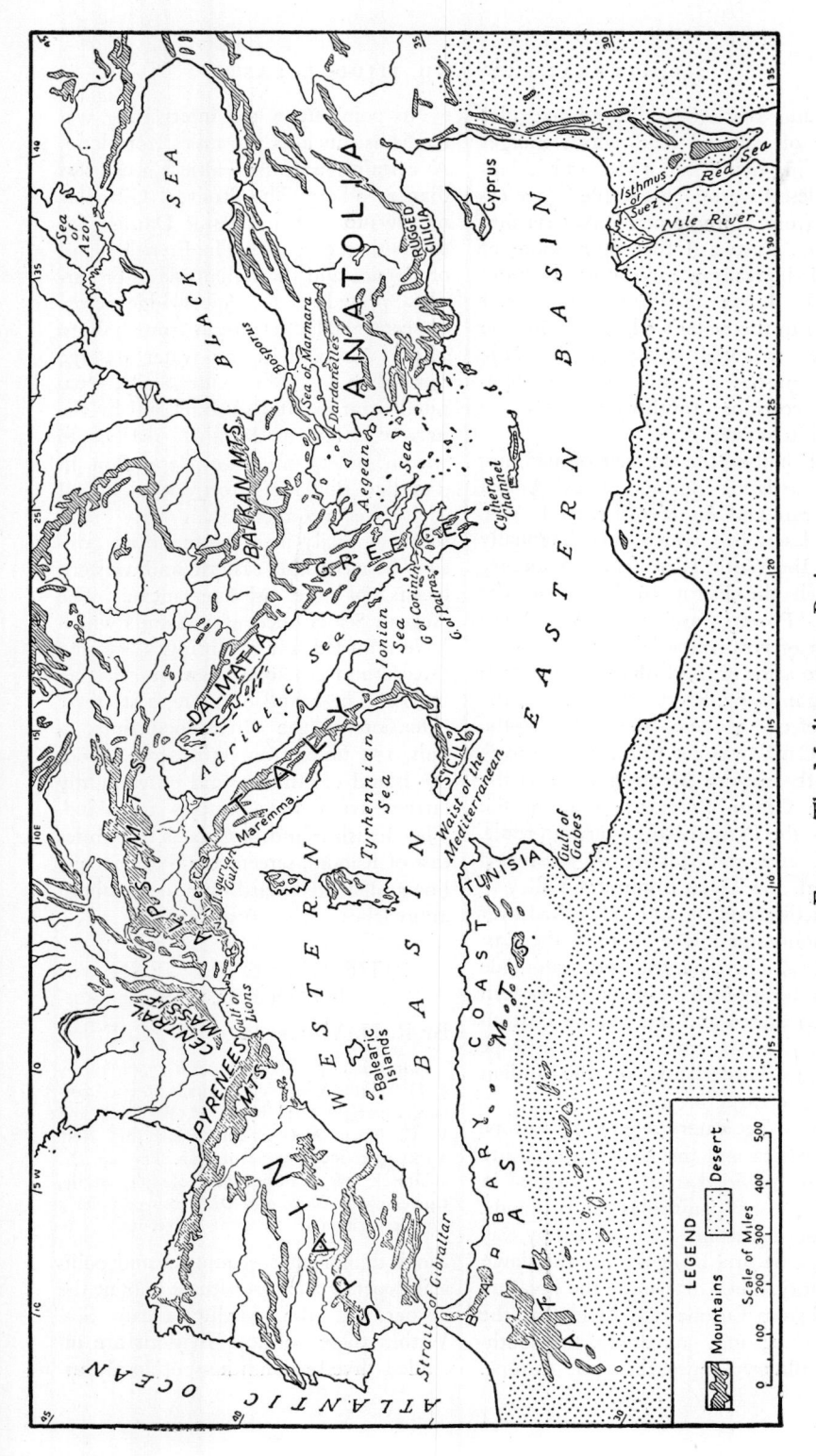

FIG. 17. The Mediterranean Basin.

From D. Whittlesey, *The Earth and the State*. Copyright 1939 by Henry Holt & Co., New York; reproduced by permission.

nean and Black Seas lies an irregular fringe of watered land which merges at varying depth into a vast and forbidding desert waste. This fertile fringe extends from Morocco across Algeria into Tunisia. Eastward the south shore of the Mediterranean rapidly grows more arid. In Libya and Egypt the desert thrusts to the water's edge, save for the narrow irrigated valley of the Nile which pushes a fertile, densely populated corridor southward into the waterless waste.

East of the Nile the belt of arid and semi-arid lands continues across Arabia into Iran and on across central Asia. This desert belt which cuts diagonally across the World Island is the boundary between the European Realm of the Great Powers and the Afro-Asian Realm of rival imperialisms.

Two arms of the Indian Ocean reach deeply into the desert barrier. From the head of one of these—the Red Sea—the Suez Canal was cut to form a shipway from the eastern Mediterranean to the Indian Ocean. From the head of the other—the Persian Gulf—caravan trails, roads, and railroads reach westward through the Tigris-Euphrates Valley to the Mediterranean, and northward over the mountains to the shore of the Caspian Sea. These natural and man-made communications have made the eastern Mediterranean and the Middle East an historic transit zone between Europe and the borderlands of the Indian Ocean.

Across the waters separating Europe from Africa and the Near East, nature has also provided strategic "bridges" in the form of peninsulas and islands. Conquering armies have crossed by way of these natural bridges since the dawn of history. They determine the invasion routes from Europe into Africa and the Near East; and, conversely, the southern military approaches to Europe.

No point upon the intervening waters is as much as 200 miles from land. At certain places the width is much less than at others. The Strait of Gibraltar narrows to eight miles; the Dardanelles to less than one mile. The French island of Corsica and the Italian island of Sardinia provide a strategic bridge across the central Mediterranean from Italy to North Africa, with no water passage more than 110 miles wide. Sicily, separated from the Italian mainland by the narrow Strait of Messina, reaches to within ninety miles of Cape Bon in Tunisia. England's fortress island of Malta lies no more than sixty miles south of Sicily in a commanding position between the eastern and western basins of the Mediterranean. The Aegean Sea is filled with islands which have afforded military bridges between Greece and Anatolia from time immemorial. The island of Crete, a strategic extension of the Greek peninsula, is only 175 miles from Africa, 100 from the island of Rhodes, and only slightly farther from the Turkish mainland. The British island of Cyprus, 250 miles east of Rhodes, screens the Syrian coastline and stands guard over the northern approaches to the Suez Canal.

THE MEDITERRANEAN BORDERLANDS

By R. H. Whitbeck and V. C. Finch

From chap. 27 of *Economic Geography*, by R. H. Whitbeck and V. C. Finch. Revised edition, copyright 1941 by R. H. Whitbeck and V. C. Finch. McGraw-Hill Book Co., New York; reproduced by permission. The late Dr. Whitbeck was professor of geography at the University of Wisconsin. Dr. Finch occupies a similar position in the same university.

More than a dozen countries and political dependencies are situated about the borders of the Mediterranean Sea. Within these political divisions are included diverse conditions of local surface features and climate, many peoples and many languages. Yet . . . they have a sufficient number of conditions in common to permit their being grouped together into one of the primary geographic regions of the world. The most fundamental of the unifying conditions is (1) similarity of climate. Others of consequence are (2) lack of extensive plains lands, (3) common frontage upon an inland sea, (4) a degree of similarity in location with respect to the principal land masses of the world, and (5) a general meagerness of those natural resources which are fundamental to large industrial and commercial development.

Climatic Conditions and Associated Features. A combination of climatic elements so distinctive as to have acquired the name "Mediterranean" characterizes all but the Libyan and Egyptian parts of the borderlands of the Mediterranean Sea. The outstanding features of this climate are (1) subtropical temperatures with smaller annual range than the average for the latitude; (2) low annual rainfall, with a winter maximum and dry summers; (3) a high percentage of sunshine. So characteristic is this type of climate that it is known by the name "Mediterranean" wherever it may be found, as in California, Chile, or Australia. The present region may, in fact, be further defined by it. On this basis the Mediterranean lands include southern Europe, Turkey, Syria, Palestine, and the coastal slopes of Tunisia, Algeria, and Morocco. Egypt and Libya are not included, since they get very little rainfall and may better be discussed later in connection with the deserts of northern Africa.

This type of climate, although it is favorable to certain crops and industries, imposes strict limits upon the development of others. The perennial crops must be those which are able to withstand summer heat and drought, such as the olive and the grapevine, or those which thrive under irrigation, such as citrus fruits. Fall-sown cereals which, in the mild winter temperatures, can make use of the winter rains furnish the staple foods. Because of the summer drought, good pastures are difficult to maintain, and their scantiness is evidenced by many sheep and goats but a relatively smaller number of cattle. The mild and sunny winters of the Mediterranean shores have made the region a winter resort for people of the more gloomy north European countries. Even northern Italy has 25 per cent of possible sunshine in its most rainy month.

Surface Configuration. The geologic history of the Mediterranean region has left its mark upon the coastal outline of the land and upon the configuration of its surface. A series of subsidences along the southern margin of the older land masses of Central Europe are responsible for the creation of the basin of the Mediterranean Sea. With these same processes were associated some of the mountain-building forces that have resulted in the hemming in of the region as a whole by mountains from whose northern axis project southward a series of peninsulas: Iberia, Italy, and the Balkan Peninsula. Fringing this irregular margin are the unsubmerged portions of other mountains which appear as islands, large and small.

Not only do mountains such as the Pyrenees, Alps, Balkans, and Atlas provide margins for the region, but other and lesser mountains characterize its surface. A degree of unity in the Mediterranean surface features may be indicated by calling attention to some of the repeating features. These include (1) limited coastal plains, as in southern Portugal, eastern Tunisia, and western Turkey; (2) alluvial basins and deltas, as in southern Spain and France and the Po Valley of Italy; (3) broad, dry plateaus broken by ranges of mountains as in central Spain, the plateau of the Shotts in Algeria, and the Anatolian Plateau of Turkey; (4) the many included and rimming mountain ranges themselves.

The separation of the borderlands of the Mediterranean into many distinct physical units has had a profound influence upon the history of mankind. The total area of all the Mediterranean lands is not half so great as the area of the United States, yet they include, wholly or in part, eight independent states and several dependencies, at least eight distinct languages, and a large number of dialects. The latter, as in all old countries, are to be attributed in part to historic conquests and migrations and to the long separation of small groups of people by barriers that prevented easy intercommunication.

Frontage upon the Mediterranean. There can be little doubt that, in the early stages of human development upon the shores of the Mediterranean, the sea was a barrier to human intercourse. Yet at a very early date the Phoenicians, who inhabited a part of the narrow plain at the eastern end of the Mediterranean, had pushed out from their shores to near-by islands and coasts. With this beginning they progressed from one island and peninsula to another until they penetrated to every corner of the sea and beyond its western portal. After them came the Greeks, the Romans, the Venetians, and the Genoese. The Mediterranean ceased to be a barrier and became a unifying influence, and powerful conquerors arose who welded these borderlands into great empires. Yet none has been powerful enough permanently to overcome the tendency to political disunion imposed by the expanses of sea and by the mountainous and disjointed surface features.

The Location of the Mediterranean among the Land Masses. European civilization owes much of its character to the peoples who inhabited the shores of the Mediterranean, and modern commerce has sprung from beginnings in the same region. During the Middle Ages the Mediterranean was the great commercial thoroughfare of the world. The merchants of Venice and Genoa controlled a large part of the world's trade that flowed between northwestern Europe and the East. But historical events and important discoveries shifted the world's trade to the Atlantic Ocean, and the Mediterranean became for several centuries only a byway in the commerce of the world. Its importance was later increased by the reopening of connection with the East through the Suez Canal, yet its ancient position of predominance has not been regained. The closure of this route during the struggle to wrest its control from Great Britain is evidence of the fact that world trade may continue to flow without using the Mediterranean although not so abundantly or conveniently.

Character of Natural Resources. T e early traders and merchants of the Mediterranean borders found in the natural resources of the region a wealth of materials for their purposes. For the craftsmen of the Middle Ages local raw materials were, in the main, sufficient. In this respect also the world has changed. Iron and steel have replaced wood and copper and bronze, and the energy of coal has replaced hand power. In the race for modern industrial and commercial supremacy the Mediterranean borderlands have been left behind, for nature did not abundantly endow them with the materials upon which modern commerce and industry depend.

Importance of Agriculture. Agriculture has developed in the Mediterranean lands under many discouragements. The hot, dry summers restrict the range of possible crops and of livestock industries. The rough surface and many steep slopes put large areas beyond the possibility of cultivation. In Italy less than one-half, in Spain only one-third, and in Greece one-twelfth of the land is under tillage. These proportions average higher than the 20 per cent attained in the United States; and the percentage for Italy ranks among the highest in the world. That this is true attests dense and industrious populations dependent mainly upon the land for a living. About 45 per cent of the persons in all occupations in Italy and 50 per cent of those in Portugal are engaged in agriculture. In Greece 60 per cent and in Algeria 70 per cent are farmers. These figures may be contrasted with those of industrial countries—such as the United States, 22 per cent; Germany, 29 per cent; or the United Kingdom, 6 per cent—to get the full measure of the importance of agriculture to the people of the Mediterranean region....

Forest Resources. In ancient times the more rainy parts of the Mediterranean border, such as the eastern shores of the Adriatic Sea, appear to have had considerable forest wealth of oak, chestnut, beech, pine, and other valuable timber trees, mainly hardwood. The drier portions probably never had more than the present shrub forests, or *maqui,* the European equivalent of the chaparral of California. Fire, destructive lumbering for more than 2,000 years, indiscriminate wood cutting, and the unrestricted browsing of sheep and goats have left for present generations but a small part of the forest resource. In most of the countries the supply of timber barely serves to meet the local needs, limited as the requirements are through poverty and lack of commercial and industrial development....

Sources of Fuel and Power. A survey of the fuel and power resources of the Mediterranean countries provides at once an explanation of the predominance of agricultural pursuits and a basis for estimating some aspects of future developments in these lands. Of coal there is, in the entire Mediterranean region, extremely little. Of all the countries, Spain is best provided; yet its maximum output of coal and lignite is barely enough for a limited domestic requirement, and some is imported. Small amounts are mined in Italy, northern Africa, and other parts of the region, but they generally are not sufficient for local needs. Turkey produces less than Spain; but its requirements are less, and a small surplus has been available for export. Growing industries probably will require the total output shortly and perhaps need imported coal in addition. Italy, the most industrialized of the Mediterranean countries, has produced as much as 1 million tons of lignite in a year from its own mines, but generally its output is much less. Of good coal it has almost none. Imports of coal, principally from Germany and Britain, average about 12 million tons per year. Thus Italian industry is placed in a vulnerable position, and Italian politics are tied to the facts of resource distribution. In time of war between Britain and Germany the only route open for the export of German coal to Italy, so long as Britain commands the sea, is the expensive rail route across the mountains. The Mediterranean countries share with those of northern Europe a lack of domestic petroleum....

The waterpower resources of the Mediterranean region are considerable, much greater than the coal resources. The low average rainfall and its great variability is not well suited to power production, yet the high altitudes and many steep slopes and mountain valleys provide the necessary fall and also provide favorable conditions for storage reservoirs. In general, the shorter streams and the lower and more erratic rainfall of North Africa and of the eastern end of the Mediterranean region are not favorable for power development. Spain and Italy have the most waterpower in use and the greatest prospects for the future. The principal waterpowers of Spain, both developed and prospective, lie in the more rainy northern part of the country, especially on the southern slopes of the Pyrenees Mountains. However, the estimated resources, although greater than those of Sweden, for example, are much less than those of Norway, and only one-fourth the available resource is actually developed. For similar cause the principal waterpowers of Italy are in the north. The provinces at the foot of the Alps are particularly favored in this respect because of (1) the high altitudes and steep slopes of the mountains and their valleys, (2) the heavy rainfall fairly well distributed throughout the year, (3) natural regulation of stream flow due to (a) the summer melting of Alpine glaciers and (b) the presence of the large glacial lakes, such as Como and Garda, in the Alpine valleys. Italy's great need for power has led to the rapid development of her waterpower resource in recent years. Storage reservoirs have been provided, and the 6 million horsepower now developed actually exceeds the total potential horsepower of the country as estimated on the basis of ordinary minimum stream flow. Italy has therefore more waterpower in use than any other country in the world except the United States and Canada, and its power resources are more completely utilized than those of any other country except France and Germany.

Sources of Mineral Wealth. Metals and minerals of moderate value and variety are found in the Mediterranean region, and a few of the deposits have had an important place in the history of the world's industrial development. The Rio Tinto copper mines in southwestern Spain, for example, have been worked since the days of the Phoenicians and still are among the larger producers in Europe, although they yield a comparatively small part of the world's output. The quarries of Carrara, Italy, and the Parian quarries of Greece yielded marbles for ancient works of art and are still producing for domestic use and for export. The mineral products of the Mediterranean region have, in general, been far excelled in value by the products of other regions of greater extent or of richer ores. In the supply of only a few of these substances do the Mediterranean countries rank high in world output. Examples are pyrite, of which Spain, Italy, Portugal, and the island of Cyprus mine one-third of the world supply; and sulphur, of which Italy and Spain are the only important producers outside the United States and Japan. They are minerals that are abundant and cheap elsewhere but that are produced in the Mediterranean countries also because of cheap labor. Large resources of phosphate rock are located in Tunisia and Morocco, and the produce of these mines is second only to that of the United States; they constitute more than one-fourth of the world's present supply.

Iron ores are found at several places in the Mediterranean countries; but since there is little coal with which to smelt them locally, large quantities are exported. The largest supplies are found in Spain, particularly the Viscaya district of the north. Nearly two-thirds of the quantity mined is sent in normal times to England, Germany, and the Netherlands, mainly through the northern ports of Bilboa and Santander. These ores are almost as conveniently located with respect to the northern European smelting centers as are the Lake Superior ores with respect to the Lake Erie smelters and Pittsburgh. Other important iron-ore reserves are located in Algeria, Morocco, and Tunisia. The combined output of these African sources totals only about 5 million tons per year, equal to only a small part of the average annual production of the United States but very important to Europe. Italy, unfortunately for that country, has no adequate domestic supply of ore. There are several small reserves of low-grade ores, but only by the greatest of national efforts, projected but not yet realized, can she produce as much as half her requirements at home.

THE MEDITERRANEAN IN GREAT-POWER POLITICS

By the Editors

The Mediterranean basin was once the primary seat of political power in the Eurasian Realm. As Mackinder has so vividly described (see pp. 87ff., above), first Egypt, then Crete, then the Greek peninsula, then the westward-reaching Persian Empire, then the Macedonian Empire, then Carthage in North Africa, and finally Rome were in turn the dominant power centers of the middle sea. Later, the Moslem Empire from its center in the Near East threatened to embrace all Europe in its two arms thrust up the Danube Valley and around through Spain. Still later, for reasons to be taken up in due course, the center of political struggle shifted outside the Mediterranean basin altogether.

Mediterranean military history is, in the main, a record of recurring struggle between land and sea power. Military power wielded from ships cannot operate without shore bases. The classic strategy of the inland rival, as of the weaker sea power, has been to capture these vital bases from the rear. Such seems to have been the larger strategic purpose of the famous flanking marches around the eastern or western ends of the Mediterranean, undertaken by the armies of the Persian ruler Xerxes, by Alexander the Great of Macedonia, and by Hannibal of Carthage. Such, at a later date, was substantially the strategy of the Moslem pincers on medieval Europe.

In our time, after several centuries of maritime dominance, the historic challenge to sea power in the Mediterranean has been reenacted once again. The current phase dates back into the nineteenth century. The principal contestants have been Great Britain, France, Italy, Germany, and Russia. Of these, only two—France and Italy—front directly on the Mediterranean. Only one —Italy—has no frontage on the oceans. For Russia and for Great Britain, the Mediterranean has been important chiefly as a highway. Germany, the fifth contender, has no frontage on the Mediterranean, and no vital interest in transit through the middle sea. Hitler's Third Reich, as the Empire of Wilhelm II, coveted the Mediterranean borderlands partly for exploitation, but more especially for strategic positions from which to pull down the other Great Powers and to launch imperialistic campaigns in Africa and in Asia.

The political and strategical importance of this transit land has fluctuated greatly through the centuries. Before

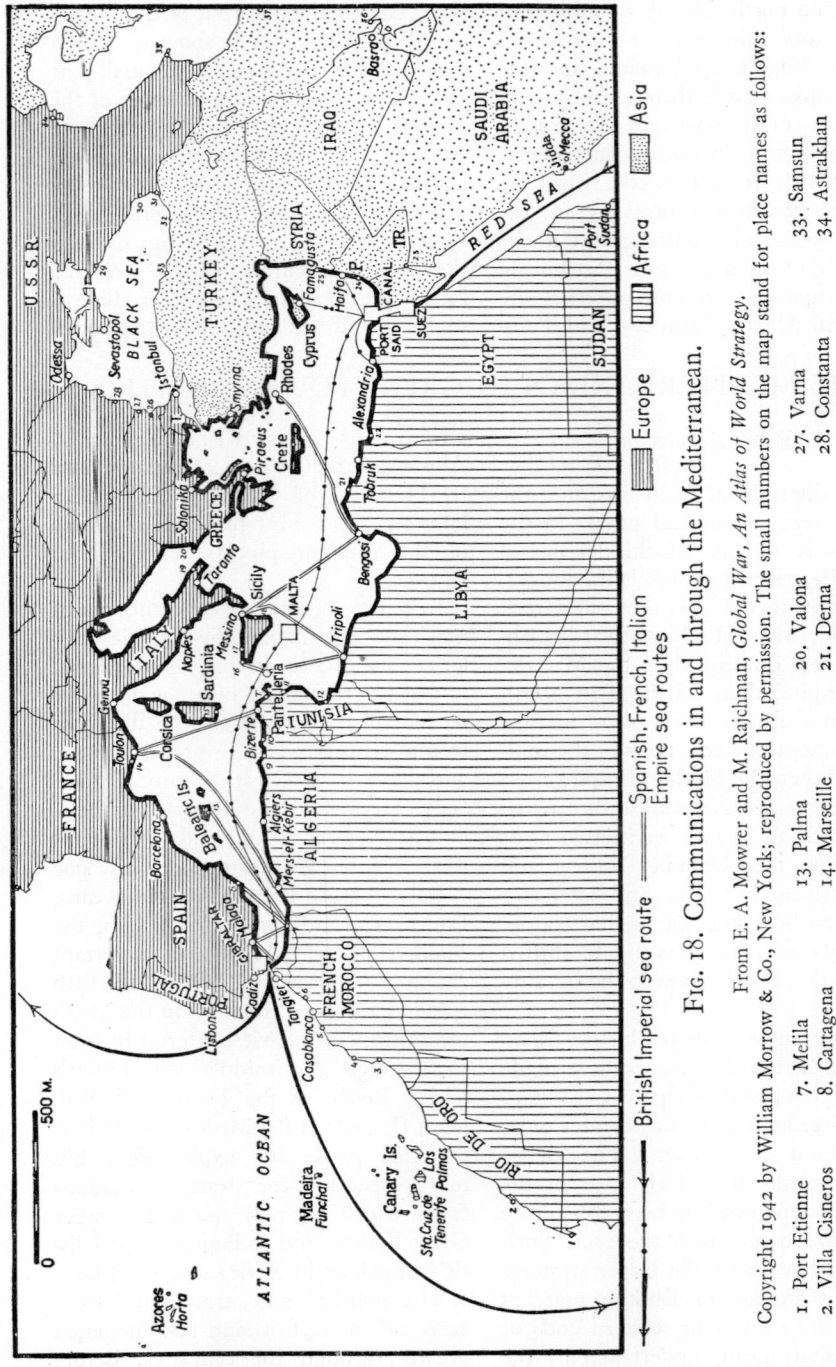

FIG. 18. Communications in and through the Mediterranean.

From E. A. Mowrer and M. Rajchman, *Global War, An Atlas of World Strategy*, New York; reproduced by permission. The small numbers on the map stand for place names as follows:

Copyright 1942 by William Morrow & Co.,

1. Port Etienne
2. Villa Cisneros
3. Agadir
4. Mogador
5. Mazagan
6. Rabat
7. Melila
8. Cartagena
9. Philippeville
10. Bone
11. Susa
12. Gabès
13. Palma
14. Marseille
15. Cagliari
16. Trapani
17. Palermo
18. Catania
19. Brindisi
20. Valona
21. Derna
22. Sollum
23. Aqaba
24. Jaffa
25. Beirut
26. Burgas
27. Varna
28. Constanta
29. Novorossiisk
30. Poti
31. Batum
32. Trabzon
33. Samsun
34. Astrakhan
35. Baku
36. Bandar Shahpur
37. Tehran
T. Tunis

the Christian era, waterways were almost the only communication routes between the peoples living around the shores of the Mediterranean. Medieval Europe's only commercial route to the Far East ran through the Mediterranean and thence by caravan across the Near and Middle East. The discoveries of the fifteenth and sixteenth centuries opened up the all-sea routes via the Cape of Good Hope and Cape Horn. The Mediterranean became a backwash and a dead-end road, and remained so until after the middle of the nineteenth century.

The Suez Canal, completed in 1869, opened up a shipway through the desert barrier from the Mediterranean to the Red Sea. This navigable short-cut to the Indian Ocean profoundly altered the strategic geography not only of the Mediterranean basin itself but also of every maritime country in the world.

Before the present war the Mediterranean artery to the Orient was one of the world's busiest thoroughfares. Ships carrying rubber and tin from southeastern Asia and the East Indies, wool from Australia, gold from the Transvaal, oil from the Persian Gulf, cotton from India, and countless other products of Asia, Africa, and Oceania, all converged on Suez. Eastbound ships from England, western Europe, and the Americas, converged similarly on Gibraltar, bringing coal, manufactures, and other products of the West. Through the Mediterranean steamed an endless procession of ships, both east and west, carrying a huge and infinitely varied cargo, of which a great deal originated or terminated somewhere in the British Empire.

Defense of this imperial artery was naturally a major aim of British strategy. To achieve this the British Navy was long maintained at a strength greater than any two European navies combined. To support the ships, the British Admiralty developed fortified havens and maintenance stations at the Rock of Gibraltar, on the islands of Malta and Cyprus, at Alexandria in Egypt, and in the Gulf of Aden at the foot of the Red Sea.

Measures taken for the security of England's Mediterranean "lifeline" impinged at many points upon the interests or ambitions of other European powers. If the British Navy was to be strong enough to ensure delivery of supplies through this sea in wartime, it could by the same token deny to England's enemies the use of the Mediterranean. Conversely, in the highly charged international atmosphere of the past seventy-five years, every move on the part of those powers to improve their relative military position in this region was bound to call forth counter-measures on the part of Great Britain.

For a long time England maintained a tight grip on the Mediterranean despite all competition. But eventually the introduction of new weapons, accompanied by other changes in the European political and military situation, undermined British primacy in these waters. The development of torpedo warfare, especially in connection with the submarine, increased the wartime hazard to shipping in narrow seas. The rise of air power doubled and redoubled that hazard within the range of shore-based planes; and, as previously noted, no point in the Mediterranean is beyond that range today.

For Great Britain the Mediterranean has been and is an imperial highway, a shortcut to the Indian Ocean. But the use of that highway in wartime has come to involve more than naval control of Mediterranean waters. Command of the air is also necessary; and that requires a much more extensive territorial base than England has ever possessed in this area in the past. Indeed, it may be that this sea will henceforth be a wartime highway only for that state or coalition which holds at least one of the Mediterranean coastlines throughout most of its length.

For Russia as for Great Britain the Mediterranean has been a highway. But there the parallel ends. Southwestern Russia has direct access to blue water only through the Black Sea and the Mediterranean. Control of the Bosporus and the Dardanelles has been one of the historic objectives of Russian statecraft. This would not give Russia any doorways opening on the oceans. But it would help to ensure against the blockades which in both World Wars have isolated Russia from her West European and oversea allies.

The blockade of Russia in the present war has also focused attention on the Middle East. Iran, Iraq, and Arabia contain the world's largest known petroleum reserves. Iran has also become a corridor land of great strategic importance to the Soviet Union.

Southern France fronts directly on the Mediterranean, and through that sea run the principal lines of communication with the French Empire in Africa, the Near East, the Indian Ocean, and southeastern Asia.

This empire, especially the provinces and dependencies in Africa, has played an important role in French military strategy. Never since the political unification of Germany in 1870 has European France alone contained the manpower necessary to assure the security of its eastern frontier without aid from overseas. For this reason, France has come to rely heavily upon both white and colored troops from North and West Africa. France, like England, has a Mediterranean lifeline, one running north and south from Marseilles to Tunis, Algiers, Casablanca, Dakar.

France also has strategic interests in the eastern Mediterranean and in the sea route to the Indian Ocean and Far East. Under the terms of the peace settlement following the First World War, Syria has been governed under a mandate to France. And the main line of communication with Madagascar, Indo-China and other French dependencies in the Indian Ocean and Pacific parallels the British line via Suez.

Italy's situation is unique. Italy alone among the Great Powers has no ocean frontier. That country's only access to the oceans is through the Mediterranean. The Italian mainland is a long narrow peninsula. Few points on that peninsula are more than seventy-five miles from the sea, none more than 150.

For these reasons and others to be discussed later, Italy is inherently a weak country, exposed to attack by sea and by air, and extremely vulnerable to blockade. Hence the diplomatic axiom that Italy can never, without courting disaster, break with that power or coalition which holds the sea gates of the Mediterranean. Hence also the Fascist ambition to rule not only the waters of that sea but also the passage ways from the Mediterranean into the Atlantic and Indian Oceans. "Mare nostrum"—our sea—was the slogan of Fascist Italy, a slogan which voiced an aspiration, never realized, to wrest from Great Britain the keys to Gibraltar and Suez.

Germany is not a Mediterranean country, but German empire-builders have long cherished large ambitions within and beyond the Mediterranean region. Wilhelm II intrigued and maneuvered, but without success, to obtain a foothold in Morocco from which to exert a leverage on French North Africa and British Gibraltar. He also sponsored a project for a German-owned railroad from Berlin-to-Bagdad, and thence to the Persian Gulf. War interrupted this project in 1914. But had it been completed, Germany would have secured an option on the oil fields of Iraq and Persia, and a naval port on the Indian Ocean from which to threaten the British Empire from the rear.

Hitler followed in the Kaiser's footsteps. Though the Third Reich never published an official blueprint, Nazi spokesmen have repeatedly discussed German aims in and around the Mediterranean. From their utterances, one can piece together a program of aggression designed to carry the swastika to the Persian Gulf and to the Cape of Good Hope.

The keys to success in this region, according to Nazi doctrine, were the western Mediterranean and the Near and Middle East. Once in possession of these two critical zones, British sea power could be driven from the middle sea, and brought under punishing attack in both the South Atlantic and Indian Oceans. The French Empire in Africa and the Moslem communities of the Middle East would fall like ripe plums into the Nazi basket, and become springboards for further swift and irresistible advances through southern Asia and across the South Atlantic.

An Axis break-through to the Middle East and Indian Ocean would have constituted an all but irreparable military disaster for the United Nations. Such a break-through would have opened to the Axis the oil reserves of the Persian Gulf region, while denying those resources to the Allies. It would have presaged large-scale submarine warfare against Allied shipping in the Indian Ocean. The southern supply line to Russia, and (after 1941) the only supply route to India and China, would have been blocked. The United Nations would have been split asunder, while the two halves of the Axis would have been joined by a sea and air link across the Indian Ocean and southern Asia for the exchange of weapons and raw materials.

Scarcely less damaging would have been a major Axis break-through into West Africa. With the Mediterranean temporarily closed by Axis air and undersea power, and with Japanese conquests blocking the transpacific route to the Far East, the South Atlantic supply line via the Cape of Good Hope and the trans-African airline became the slender threads joining the production centers of Britain and North America with the hard-pressed defenders of Egypt, the Middle East, India, and free China. Fall of Gibraltar and conquest of West Africa would have put German bombers and submarines astride these vital supply links, while giving the enemy new doorways into South America.

Thus, in the Second World War, as in previous conflicts, the Great Powers have played for high stakes in the Mediterranean and the Middle East.

ITALIAN WEAKNESS AND FASCIST AMBITION

By the Editors

The late Frank Simonds, journalist and student of world affairs, described in the following words Italy's situation after the First World War:

"After 1919, as before, Italy was a second-class state with the aspirations and appetites of a Great Power. Great Britain and France had expanded their colonial empires. Even Belgium had acquired provinces on the borders of her Congo Empire, but abroad Italy remained where she had stood in 1914, her overseas empire limited to the Tripolitan and Erythean façades to barren hinterlands. And these desert possessions, representing vast costs in blood and treasure, were set in immediate and vivid contrast to a French Empire, which on the Mediterranean included Tunis, Algeria, and Morocco, and extended inland to the Niger and the Congo.

"Beyond the Isonzo [the river which flows into the head of the Adriatic Sea], the Hapsburg Monarchy had disintegrated, but in its place had risen a large and virile Jugoslavia. In Anatolia the dream of an Italian sphere of influence had fallen swiftly before the power of Kemal Pasha, although in adjoining Syria, French power was seated alike at Beirut and at Damascus. In Central Europe the development of the Little Entente quickly closed the door to Italian influence. Even on her own frontiers Italy was presently confronted by a military alliance between France and Jugoslavia, while in all international meetings, the association of Poland and the Little Entente [of Czechoslovakia, Rumania, and Yugoslavia] with France, reduced Italian influence to zero." (*Can Europe Keep the Peace?* by F. H. Simonds. Copyright 1931 by F. H. Simonds; Harper & Bros., New York.)

Thus, Italy, though numbered among the victors of the First World War, emerged from that struggle in moral revolt against the terms of the peace. Coupled with outraged national feelings and chaotic internal conditions went a growing sense of frustration which presently found expression in Mussolini's march on Rome and the overturn of constitutional parliamentary government.

The aims of the Fascist regime which seized power in 1922 have been described many times. To quote again from Frank Simonds writing in 1931:

"Not liberty, not unity, not security ... is at stake in the Italian case, only power. The right to a place in the sun, the old and once familiar demand of Pan-Germanism, inspires Italian policy. ... The purpose of the men and the party today dominant in the peninsula is to exploit every political development on the Continent to the greater glory of Italy, and to the expansion of Italian prestige and power."

The bombastic utterances with which Mussolini proclaimed Italy's right to a place in the sun left no doubt as to the aims and methods of Fascist statecraft.

In 1925 Mussolini still spoke with some caution and restraint: "Every nation with a vital capacity for progress is compelled by its own qualities to develop its own productive forces and its thought, to increase its pacific and economic penetration in the world, and to expand beyond its own confines its power and its intellectual and moral prestige."

By 1927, he spoke in a more confident tone: "The precise, fundamental and paramount duty of Fascist Italy is that of putting in a state of preparedness all her armed forces on land, sea, and in the air. We must be in a position at a given moment to mobilize five million men, and we must be in a position to arm them. Our navy must be reinforced, and our air force ... must be so numerous and so powerful that the roar of its engines will drown any other noise in the peninsula, and the span of its wings hide the sun from our country. We shall be in a position then —tomorrow—when, between 1935 and 1940, we shall find ourselves at a point which I would call a crucial point in European history—we shall be in a position to make our voice felt, and at last to see our rights recognized."

Two years later, in 1929, Mussolini was still more sure of his position. "Today we can say, without exaggeration and with a quiet conviction, that Italy is heard and respected, and we can add that, with the continuance of the Fascist regime, the Italy of tomorrow will be still more respected and, if necessary, feared."

In 1936, after his conquest of Ethiopia in defiance of the greater powers and the League of Nations: "I hold out a great olive branch to the world. This olive branch springs from an immense force of eight million bayonets, well sharpened and thrust from intrepid young hearts." (Quoted in *The Mediterranean in Politics*, by Elizabeth Monroe. Oxford University Press, London, 1938.)

The territorial limits of Fascist ambition grew with success. By 1942, on the eve of the great debacle, Virginio Gayda, editor of the Fascist newspaper *Giornale d'Italia*, drew the future boundaries of the new Roman Empire along lines that out-Caesar-ed the Caesars. After asserting that for Italy, "freedom of the Mediterranean" included, first of all, the "return of Corsica, Dalmatia, Malta, and other islands" in the Mediterranean Sea, Gayda continued as follows:

"Freedom in the Mediterranean means the demolition of the gates that close the international sea passage toward the oceans: Gibraltar and Suez. In addition to the above, all of the colonial spaces with the restoration of the whole east African Empire. . . . It also means the development and unification of North African possessions which must be returned and which France and England have seized. In addition to these all the other territories which mark the historical aspirations and are in the hearts of all Italians. It finally means the addition of territories which from east Africa extend out toward the Atlantic. Here appears also the solution of the vital Italian problem of the free access to the seas. Out of Libya is the deep region of Lake Chad which belonged to Turkey as an integral part of the Libyan territory and therefore by right should go to Italy but which is now unjustly occupied by France. From this region there extends toward the southwest extensive territory which reaches the sea directly, Nigeria, a British colony. This complex of territory which lies between Libya, the Mediterranean, and the Atlantic Ocean must naturally enter the sphere of economic and political influence of the Italian colonial system."

Italy's resources for any such undertaking were pitifully inadequate. The sources of Italian weakness have already been indicated in a general way in the preceding sections. They can be summarized briefly.

One of Italy's most serious handicaps is the country's geographical position inside the Mediterranean, the gates of which are held by other and greater powers. Fascist writers never tired of asking the question: "Is the Mediterranean Sea a maritime highway like other great bodies of water, or is it our prison?"

One dispassionate student of Mediterranean politics writes as follows of Italy's vulnerable strategical position: ". . . this weakness has hampered Italy again and again. It has forced her to sit on the fence; to tell Germany and Austria in 1896 that, while recognizing her obligations to the Triple Alliance, she could never participate in a war in which England was fighting on the other side; to wait and see, and come into every firm of allies as the junior partner; to make amends for every fling with a conciliatory gesture. During her expansionist period, it explains why her relations with her neighbors swing like a pendulum from breach to treaty and back again. Yet the vulnerability of

Italy is often forgotten. Dictators are the champion exponents of the doctrine of Coué. They proclaim that they are getting stronger and stronger. They say it so loud and clear that, besides raising the morale of their own people, they hypnotize others." (*The Mediterranean in Politics*, by Elizabeth Monroe. 1938. Oxford University Press, London.)

Within the Mediterranean itself, Italy occupies a central position of considerable strength. The Italian peninsula and the island of Sicily, as previously noted, divide the sea into two basins connected by a passageway less than 100 miles wide. This central position "was not the least important factor in the building of the Roman Empire and in the early blossoming of the Italian cities in the Middle Ages. To their undoing, the Fascists in recent years came to believe that they could emulate ancient Rome by capitalizing on this central position and making Italy once again predominant in the Mediterranean." (*Geographical Foundations of National Power*. Army Service Forces Manual M-103-1, 1944.)

What the Fascists failed to recognize, or at least to admit, was the altered value of Italy's geographical position in the modern industrial age. Italy is especially poor in the raw materials of heavy industry, and hence of modern military power. As already noted, the country has little iron, less coal, and virtually no petroleum. Italian production of mineral fuels before the war was about 0.2 of 1 per cent of that of the United States.

The country's over-all raw-material situation is not much better. "The only nonferrous metals which Italy has in any quantity are mercury, lead, zinc, bauxite, and magnesium. Italy produces more sulphur and borax than it requires for domestic demand. She has only insignificant amounts, or none at all, of copper, chromium, tungsten, tin, nickel, molybdenum, phosphates, mica, and platinum, while sources of antimony, graphite, and asbestos fall far short of meeting basic requirements.

"In view of the shortage of solid and liquid fuels, the production of hydroelectric power is of the utmost importance to Italy. Italy has made tremendous strides since the last war in harnessing the streams, and the electricity thereby produced is Italy's most valuable raw material." (*Geographical Foundations of National Power*. Army Service Forces Manual M-103-1.)

Apart from hydroelectric power labor has been the only abundant factor in Italy's industrial economy. The Italian population is about 45 millions. Before the war the birth rate was relatively high, and sufficiently higher than the death rate to produce an annual increase of nearly one per cent. The birth rate was falling as in other European countries. But Italy was still in an earlier stage of demographic development than was France, England, or even Germany, and the outlook was for a maximum population of about 50 millions.

These, then, were the conditions and materials with which Mussolini and his Fascist colleagues had to work. It is scarcely necessary to dwell on the disparity between Italian resources and Fascist ambition. The Fascists' problem was one of making bricks without straw, or, to use another figure of speech, of lifting Italy by her boot straps. Specifically, their problem was to overcome by human effort and organization the handicaps imposed upon Italy by geography and poverty of natural resources.

For a time, it seemed as if the Fascists were in process of achieving their aims. Italy emerged slowly from the economic and social chaos which gripped the country following the First World War. Foreign tourists remarked upon the improved appearance of Italian cities and the absence of beggars. Trains ran on time. Beautiful new Italian liners plied the sea lanes. The rapidly growing navy, army, and air force gave the impression of high quality, efficiency, and smartness. By 1937 Mussolini had made a superficially impressive start on his new Roman empire, with a colonial domain ten times as large as Italy, Sardinia, and Sicily combined, and a subject population of over 14,000,000 people.

Down to that point Mussolini had bluffed his way without fighting any major power. But his task grew rapidly more difficult after the conquest of Ethiopia. The Fascist blueprint called for acquisition of French territories in North Africa. Italian domination of the Balkan countries, and expulsion of British sea power from Gibraltar, Malta, and Suez. These larger aims lay beyond Mussolini's severely limited resources. To achieve them he would have to have a helping hand.

The only available partner was Nazi Germany. This was a risky association for Italy. German ambition covered many of the same objectives, and German military potential was so vastly greater as to put Italy at the mercy of the Third Reich. Mussolini, however, took the risk, formed with Hitler the infamous Rome-Berlin Axis, and was reduced by inexorable stages to the status of a helpless vassal or satellite of the Nazi dictator.

The rest is well-known. The colonies were lost one by one. Italy was invaded and became a bitterly contested battlefield. The country was laid waste, inescapably by the advancing Allies, wantonly by the retreating Germans. The Fascist cement dissolved, the constitutional monarch reassumed his authority, the provisional government surrendered, and "free" Italy reentered the struggle on the side of the Allies.

CAN ITALY RECOVER THE STATUS OF A GREAT POWER?

By the Editors

Italy has paid a heavy price for its adventures under Fascism and its association with Nazi Germany. A visitor to Italy in the summer of 1944 brought back this description of conditions in the wake of the advancing Allied armies:

"The Italy of today is a land in which the people's stomachs are empty and in which the masses lack both shelter and food. The war-born destruction which has brought about this situation is beyond imagination. In Naples, Umbria, and Calabria, and in the Abruzzi Mountains there is hardly a bridge, large or small, which has not been blown up. . . . While it is true that the work of reconstruction is proceeding rapidly, with many bridges rebuilt from one week to the other, for the time being only those bridges are being reconstructed which pass the test of military necessity.

"The destruction of the buildings is hardly less devastating than that of the bridges. In Naples all buildings around the port are more or less leveled. In Terni, the Pittsburgh of Central Italy, 90 per cent of the buildings are destroyed. Although Rome, Assisi, and Siena have escaped destruction . . . there has been enough of it in the vicinity of Rome. In Florence all bridges have been destroyed except the Ponte Vecchio. . . .

"The Italy of today faces ruin everywhere. Places like Capua, Terracina, Velletri, and Cinzano are nothing but ruins, worse than Pompeii. . . . Even in Sicily, which was liberated many months earlier than southern and central Italy, the picture is hardly different, and it will take many years to rebuild the island.

"The destruction of power plants and of the transportation system offers particularly difficult problems. Practically every power plant was destroyed by the retreating German armies in an extremely effective way. But the power plants are all the more important because Italy is a country without coal.

"The breakdown of the transportation system has led to a complete interruption of communications, except by radio, and to grave disturbance of the markets. . . ." ("The Italy of Today," by Luigi Antonini, in *International Post-War Problems, The Quarterly Review of the American Labor Conference on International Affairs*, January 1945. The author visited Italy as the representative of the American Federation of Labor.)

Wrecked ports, demolished bridges, ruined buildings, and smashed machinery can be repaired or replaced in time, given the necessary materials and labor. Italy has the labor. Whether the bankrupt Italian state can as easily lay hands on the materials for reconstruction is more doubtful. How long it will take to put the political and social machinery of Italy into running order again, no one can say.

But certain facts cannot be disputed. Italy cannot escape the limitations of its geographical position or its poverty in essential raw materials. Indeed, the whole trend of technology is such as to accentuate those limitations. If Italy before the war was the weakest of the Great Powers, it is difficult to see how Italy after the war can hope to regain Great Power status at all.

The United Nations have yet to announce the role which Italy is to play in the post-war society of nations. But it may be doubted whether Italy after defeat and devastation can retrieve any semblance of the prestige and influence which Mussolini snatched from the ruins after the First World War.

SPAIN TODAY AND TOMORROW

By the Editors

"If Spain," write the editors of *Fortune* magazine, "were a tiny country lost in the vast expanse of South America or the Asiatic mainland, its internal struggles would arouse in the outside world nothing more than intellectual curiosity. But Spain is an explosive entity within the unstable European continent. Should Spain become a modern, powerful country it could control the gateway to the western Mediterranean, the shipping lanes between France and her empire in North Africa. As the country that discovered the Western Hemisphere and colonized a large part of it, it could influence South American countries. Furthermore, the special position of the Catholic Church in Spain is a matter of prime interest to the entire Catholic world and consequently to all Western civilization. And finally, the possibility of another civil war in Spain hangs over all efforts to evolve social and economic order in liberated European countries." ("Spain: Unfinished Business," in *Fortune* magazine, March 1945.)

Another observer, Thomas J. Hamilton, writing in *Foreign Affairs* (April 1944), puts the same problem in different words. "Spanish imperialism is . . . a force capable of creating a great deal of trouble in the world." This imperialism, like the Fascism which has given it recent verbal expression, is "an outburst against nearly three centuries of humiliation." According to Spanish fascists, "wherever either Spain or Portugal had once ruled, or even been first in the line of discoverers, Spain was entitled to rule again. In view of the fact that

Spain's possessions at one time and another had embraced half the world, this was a far-reaching program." It was never possible of fulfillment, of course, save on the assumption of a German victory, and probably not even then. As long as Spain is ruled by a reactionary and strongly nationalist government, Spanish "dreams of empire" will remain a force to be reckoned with wherever the Spanish language is spoken. And the greater the power and prestige of such a reactionary Spain, the more disturbing may be the force of frustrated Spanish imperialism in the world of tomorrow.

For this reason alone, it would be necessary to estimate the potentialities of modern Spain.

A bare inventory of national resources would put Spain ahead of Italy in several of the basic elements of political and military power. Spain has greater mineral wealth than Italy, more arable land, a more varied and on the whole not less favorable climate. Spain has the immense strategical advantage of direct frontage on the Atlantic, and a position dominating the British Rock of Gibraltar. The wide use of the Spanish language throughout most of Latin America, and to a lesser extent in the Philippines and in northwest Africa, gives Spain a cultural lever which Italy could never hope to match.

Yet Spain falls far behind Italy in the efficient use of its national resources. The Spanish population is smaller— about 25 million as compared with Italy's 45 million. The pre-war standard of living in Spain was lower. The Spanish death rate was higher, the amount and quality of food per capita was lower, the transportation system was far less adequate, the country was less industrialized, its military power low, its political prestige almost zero.

Today Spain is still suffering the after-effects of a bloody civil war which was the proving ground for Axis weapons and tactics later used against the greater powers of Europe. What is the outlook for the Spain of tomorrow? What role may it play in the new world order?

These questions the editors of *Fortune* magazine attempted recently to answer in an article entitled "Spain: Unfinished Business" (March issue 1945). The following selection is reproduced by permission from that article; copyright 1945 by Time Inc.:

SPAIN: UNFINISHED BUSINESS

By the Editors of "Fortune"

The Falange has totally controlled Spain for six years and is today the reason Franco stays in power. There is no freedom of press, religious worship, or public assembly. Four different kinds of secret police and armed guards spy on the populace. Travel in Spain is possible only after the police have given permission. Travel abroad is impossible for any but a favored few. Employment in civil service and in private offices, factories, and on the land depends upon the good will of the Falange, which supervises or manages all production and distribution. Four hundred thousand of Spain's skilled and unskilled workers, engineers, and managers fled from Spain at the end of the civil war to escape the Falange. Since 1939 a million and a half men and women have been in and out of Falange concentration camps and prisons. Falange vengeance hinders reconstruction and prevents reconciliation. Since the liberation of France many previously released political prisoners have been rearrested and summary executions, without charge or trial, have increased. The Falange rules by martial law.

Nevertheless, people in the street, in

city cafes and country taverns, and in their homes, speak their minds freely without fear, without looking over their shoulders. Even a totalitarian government cannot impose silence by terror when it exercises power without any significant popular support. . . . Hence it is easy to poll opinion in Spain and to discover that the political, religious, and economic divergences of the country have remained substantially as they were before the civil war.

The Falange was founded by José Antonio Primo de Rivera, son of the dictator who ruled Spain from 1923 to 1930. . . . José Antonio . . . believed in the inevitability of totalitarianism in the modern world. "Unless *we* establish the totalitarian state," he proclaimed to his followers, "the Communists will."

But no totalitarian state can come into being without some popular support, and until the civil war the Falange labored against a great handicap. Fascism cannot grow unless it feeds on the fear of a growing Communist movement. But Spain had no Communist movement. . . .

The common people of Spain, of course, would have none of the Falange. Spain's revolutionary movement is traditionally anarchistic—opposed to statism and dictatorships of the left as well as the right. Whatever may be said against the Spanish Anarchists, no one can see the people of Spain in action and remain unmoved by their exalted devotion to individual liberty. . . . The Falange became a political force during the civil war, when the ne'er-do-wells and dubious intellectuals in the middle class and the nobility and the *pistoleros* of the underworld saw a chance to advance themselves under the aegis of the Germans and Italians aiding Franco. The Falange did not get into the political big time until Franco wanted to advance himself over the army officers who had appointed him Generalissimo and Chief of State. To gain ascendancy he needed political support, and the Falange—modeled after the Fascist and Nazi parties—suited the times and his purpose. During the course of the civil war he diverted more and more jobs and power to members of the Falange. By the time the war ended the Falange was the government. . . .

After the Falange acquired absolute control of Spain's governmental apparatus, it set out to control the entire Spanish economy by creating a so-called "national syndicate" for each industry and each branch of agriculture. All employers, workers, and distributors of an industry must belong to these syndicates. In addition to this regimentation, the Falange formed regional syndicates, composed of representatives of the national syndicates within a province, as, for example, Valencia. The civil governor of the province, appointed by Franco, is the chief of the regional syndicate. The heads of the regional syndicates and of the national syndicates make up the Falange's National Council—about ninety members. These are the men who administer and control Spain. The new Cortes [i.e. parliament] that Franco created is a rubber stamp.

All this sounds like Mussolini's corporations and the fascist corporative state. But the Falange's syndicates were originally patterned after the anarchosyndicalist unions and conceived as a bait to catch the million and a quarter Spanish workers who are Anarchists. . . . The similarity between anarchosyndicalist unions and the Falange syndicates is of course factitious. The anarchist unions had elaborate safeguards against the concentration of power in a few hands. . . . But in the Falange syndicates all decisions are made at the top. Theoretically at least, not a single legitimate business transaction can take place in Spain today without the approval of the Franco-appointed chief of the appropriate national syndicate or syndicates.

The *promises* with which the Falange endeavored to beguile the Spanish people were the same mess of pottage proffered by Mussolini and Hitler to the Italians and Germans. The Falange boasted that the power and glory of Spain under Charles V would be re-achieved if not surpassed. This would be accomplished by breaking up the large estates, the latifundia; by industrializing Spain; by making Spain self-sufficient; by devoting all Spanish resources, human and material, to the creation of the greatest military might Spain had ever possessed. All this was set forth with the obscurantist bravura for which Fascism is notable, in a program of twenty-six points. When boiled down, the twenty-six points amounted to a ten-year plan for the industrialization of Spain; a labor charter granting workers vacations with pay and health insurance and subsidies to large families; and *Hispanidad*, i.e. exporting Falangism to Spanish-speaking people throughout the world and winning them to the cause of an awakened and expanding Spain. . . .

The most important and also the most indisputable fact about the Falange economy is that the ten-year plan is still only a blueprint. Its realization depended upon the creation of new sources of coal and hydroelectric power, and none have been developed. The electrification of the railroads was one of the key items in the plan, since it would eliminate the necessity of importing about 700,000 tons of British coal annually. Of 4,000 kilometers scheduled for electrification, fourteen have been electrified, and these fourteen are on the line connecting Madrid and the Escorial, the museum of past monarchical glories. The railroads have been nationalized, however, as the plan provided.

Coal production has been stepped up no more than 20 per cent above the 1935 figures. Shipbuilding, which the plan said would be 125,000 tons a year, amounted to 75,000 tons in 1943. The new factories envisaged in the plan to make synthetic rubber and fibers, nitrate for fertilizer and explosives, and gasoline and oil from lignite, do not exist. Nor have the plan's agricultural aspects been realized. The proposal to break up the latifundia by buying land has resulted in the settlement of only 600 families. The high prices demanded by the landowners and Falangist "administrative expenses" consumed $11 million—or more than $18,000 per family.

Total expenditures on the ten-year plan have never been announced. It is known, however, that about $230 million was allocated for each of the following: hydroelectric development, electrification of the railroads, shipbuilding, settlement, and public works. Very little was spent for these purposes. Most of it was spent on the army. The internal public debt increased from $2.1 billion in 1940 to about $3 billion by 1944.

The result is that the abysmally low living standard of the Spanish peasant and worker has fallen further. Wages have been frozen at the 1936 level and rigorously kept there despite the fact that the combined index of prices in Spain has risen from 100 in 1935 to 450 in 1944. . . .

The official explanation of why food must be rationed in Spain is that a shortage of fertilizers has reduced the crop yields. Despite the annual importation of 500,000 tons of Argentinian wheat, Spain today consumes from 15 to 25 per cent less wheat than it did before the civil war. The harvests of other cereals are similarly below the pre-civil-war averages, according to official statistics. Meat and milk are not rationed because in Spain they are luxury foods beyond the reach of three-fourths of the population.

It would naturally be supposed that the shortage of fertilizer would also affect the yields of those luxury crops of interest to the export trade, such as oranges, almonds, and grapes (for wine). But the yields of these crops have been normal and better than normal, and Spain, short of staples, is glutted with wine, brandy, oranges, and almonds, because export markets have been disrupted by the war. The people of Spain thought the lack of staples was the result of enormous exports to Germany. But the shortages continued after the liberation of France. Another and better explanation is the business activity of the Falange.

The farmers and landowners of Spain have been at war with the agricultural syndicates ever since they were created by the Falange. The farmers and landowners try to withhold from the syndicates as much of their produce as they can because the syndicates pay only the ceiling prices. The syndicates try to extract as much as they can in order to sell on the black market, where they compete with the farmers and landowners. The result is two black markets: one illegally run by private enterprise, the *mercado negro,* where the trader is subject to heavy fines and imprisonment when caught; and the "official" illegal black market operated without risk by the syndicates and nicknamed *"estraperlo,"* a word coined by the operator of a gambling house. It describes any violation of its own laws by the government.

Prices on the black market are commensurate with the risks. Hence three prices operate in the Falange economy; the ceiling price on rationed goods, the *estraperlo* price, and the black-market price. For example: the ceiling price for a liter of olive oil is 4.6 pesetas (nominally 41 cents). The *estraperlo* price is 10 pesetas; and the black-market price is 14 pesetas in season and 19 out. . . . There are four prices for bread because another competitor has to be reckoned with—the army. It gets enough bread to allow it to sell a surplus in the black market.

. . . The amount of a rationed article distributed depends on the civil governor of the province. The Falange custom is to allocate to the ration market only what cannot be absorbed by the black markets or be exported. . . .

The conflict between private business and Franco's state is bitter beyond description and even finds its way into the trade press and economic journals, though censorship keeps it out of the daily press. . . .

What does not get into the press comes out without reserve in speech. The antechambers of the ministers of state overflow with businessmen, industrialists, and landowners protesting against arbitrary acts and regulations and corruption of Falange officials. . . .

In any other totalitarian state such talk would be impossible. In Spain it is a daily occurrence. "Who is the greatest general in Spain today?" is one of the current jokes. The answer is not General Franco. It is "General Protest."

The top army officers have become as antagonistic to the Falange as the businessmen. The junta of lieutenant generals who made Franco Chief of State correctly fear that the Falange's expanding power jeopardizes their own. After the fall of Mussolini the generals wrote to Franco demanding the restoration of the monarchy. Franco's reply to this maneuver for power was to incorporate the best elements of the Falange militia into the army with a rank just below that of the lieutenant generals. He has resisted all demands that he restore the monarchy because if he yields, his own power will vanish.

And finally, the Church has begun to oppose the Falange.

Accustomed for centuries to a position of power in Spain sometimes equaling that of the state, the Church is often isolated from the people. Before the civil war only from 10 to 15 per cent of the Spanish population (26,000,000) were active Catholics. Most of the others were indifferent, anticlerical, or atheist. The Church's support of Franco during the civil war alienated a great many of those who had remained faithful. What the Church could call her own she retained by her command of the schools, by establishing Catholic trade unions in certain parts of the country, and by creating agrarian credit banks in old Castile. The Falange has dissolved the Catholic trade unions along with those of the Socialists and Anarchists. It has, through its youth movements, loosened the Church's hold upon the young. Most serious of all, Franco won, after a protracted battle with the Vatican, the right to designate the bishops. These actions outweigh the things Franco has done for the Church: restoration of property and schools to the religious orders and of the state grant to the Church ($5,800,000 a year). . . .

The root cause of Spain's troubles is the same under Franco as it was before he overthrew the Republic and as it will be when Franco is eliminated. In a word, it is the fact that Spain has never had an industrial revolution. When the Church lands and the common lands were seized in the nineteenth century, they were not made available to the peasants; they were offered at public sale; only the well-to-do could buy them. A third of the Spanish latifundia, the large landed estates, are owned by the nobles and grandees, two-thirds by urban *nouveaux riches,* none of whom work the land. The peasants, when there is work for them, do not earn enough to buy the products of what little industry Spain has, situated chiefly in the north, in Catalonia and the Basque provinces.

The Catalans and Basques have always resented the political hegemony of Castile—that mountain-encircled plateau of central Spain where the monarchy, the landowners, the Church hierarchy, and the perennial juntas of army generals have cohered and quarreled and maintained a highly centralized government. . . . The Republic of 1931-1936 granted a bit of home rule to Catalonia and in the course of the civil war to the Basques and the Galicians. But the attempt was as halfhearted as the Republic's efforts to buy up the latifundia and sell the land to the peasants on terms within the reach of those destitute and desperate men.

The typical Castilian—that is, the typical exponent of all-powerful centralized government dedicated to perpetuating the status quo—is today terrified of the Spanish people. . . .

It is also said that the Spanish people are lazy and uncooperative. Americans managing business enterprises in Spain have not found them so. . . .

As one descends the social scale in Spain one meets astonishing cases of cooperation. . . . In fact, the principle of local self-administration has pervaded much of the history of Spain. It is the reason why Spain has survived catastrophic government for three or four centuries. It is the true wealth of Spain. Even the Falange has not succeeded in destroying it. . . .

The nub of the Spanish dilemma is how an agrarian revolution can occur in the south and west without engulfing all Spain. Spanish politicians—in Spain and in exile—are no more agreed on how this can be accomplished than they have ever been. . . .

Whether Franco departs peacefully or violently, the perennial problem of Spain will still have to be settled. Until the land has been given the peasants in the South, and industry in the North gets an opportunity to develop, Spain will continue to be the most explosive element in western Europe.

THE NEAR AND MIDDLE EAST

By J. S. Badeau

From *East and West of Suez*, by J. S. Badeau. Headline Series No. 39. Copyright 1943 by Foreign Policy Association, New York; reproduced by permission. The author is Dean of the Arts and Sciences at the American University of Cairo, Egypt.

There exists around the eastern end of the Mediterranean a group of lands to which both geography and history have given an inevitable unity. Since "Near East" is the most common and inclusive term, we will adopt it for that area "east and west of Suez" that has become of such strategic importance to the Western world. [It should be noted that this author uses the term "Near East" to include part of what is more commonly called the "Middle East."]

Bridge to Asia. . . . Europe and Asia . . . face each other across the land mass that lies between the Mediterranean Sea and the Indian Ocean. "Bridge to Asia" would be the accurate name for this connecting tract. . . .

This bridging function determines the geographical limits of the area. At its center lie those lands that must be traversed in passing by direct route from Europe to Asia. The northern border is a natural frontier formed by the Black and Caspian Seas with their connecting mountain wall, and [east of the Caspian Sea] the desolate wastes of the Kara Kum desert which turn the traveler away from Central Asia. Far to the south and west are the sands of the Libyan Desert, crowding Egypt away from Africa. Between northern mountains and southern desert lies a vast, land-locked isthmus, projecting from the Indian Ocean to the very doorstep of the Mediterranean world. . . .

Within the borders of the bridge to Asia lie the political divisions of Turkey, Egypt, the Lebanon and Syrian Republics, Palestine, Trans-Jordan, the Arabian states (Saudi Arabia, Yemen, Oman, and the Trucial Sheikhdoms of the Persian Gulf), Iraq, and Iran. The combined area of these countries is about two and one half million square miles—roughly the size of the United States with Washington, Oregon, California, and Idaho left out. . . .

The Desert and the Sown. . . . The most striking feature of Near Eastern geography is its sharp contrast between arid wilderness and tilled field, the "desert and the sown," as the Arab calls them. In few places is there a continuous landscape of green; vegetation is usually confined to more or less sharply defined areas around which barren steppes or rocky hills close in. . . .

In many lands of the Near East, there is far more desert than sown. Egypt is 97 per cent arid land, Trans-Jordan 80 per cent, Syria 50 per cent; while the Arabian peninsula exceeds even these high figures. Among the mountain ranges of Iraq and Iran, where melting snows and spring rain give a more adequate water supply, the fields huddle together in the valleys or on the lower slopes of the hills, standing out in welcome relief against the tawny limestone cliffs that rise about them. Only on

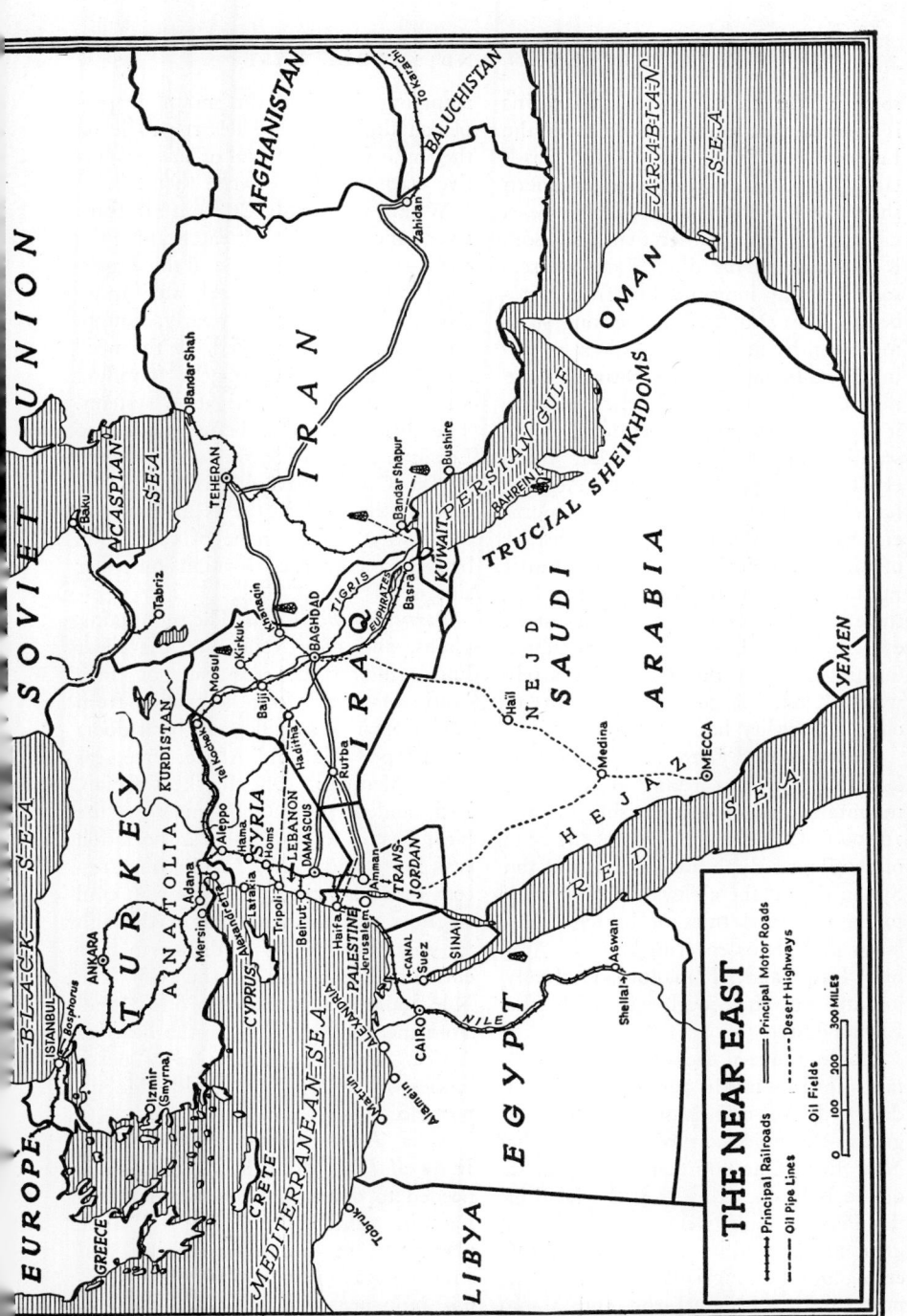

FIG. 19. Communications Through the Near East.
From J. S. Badeau, *East and West of Suez*. Headline Series, No. 39.
Copyright 1943 by Foreign Policy Association, New York; reproduced by permission.

some of the coastal slopes and plains is there a year-round green; as in the Lebanons of Syria, the Aegean headlands of Turkey, and the southern shores of the Black and Caspian Seas.

Lack of water, rather than poor soil, is the cause of infertility. Rains are seasonal, coming intermittently from October to May and leaving the long summer months unrelieved of their parching heat. In most of the Near East the rainfall is less than ten inches, making it impossible to grow anything but the scantiest crops without irrigation. Western Turkey, especially along the Aegean, has abundant rain, while on the southern shore of the Caspian is a district of almost tropical fertility, the annual rainfall approximating sixty inches. But these are the exceptions; to Western eyes the Near East does not suggest a farming country but rather a sparsely watered land, largely desert, with an oasis of fertility here and there.

Mountain and Plain. . . . Across Turkey and Iran runs a tangled system of mountains and plateaus, rising to over 16,000 feet. Ending abruptly at the edge of the Tigris-Euphrates Valley and the Syrian desert, these elevations give way to an extended tract of barren tablelands and plains covering most of Arabia, Iraq, and Trans-Jordan, finally joining on the southwest with the Libyan desert.

Holding apart the chain of mountains in the north and the chain of deserts in the south is a narrow strip of green—the most coveted region in the Near East. One end rests on the delta of the Nile, the other is at the head of the Persian Gulf; between stretches a great arc of fertility which follows the curve of the Tigris-Euphrates valley north and west, then turns south along the Syrian and Palestinian coast until it reaches Egypt. . . . The whole history of the Near East could be written as the recurring clash between mountain people on the north and desert people on the south for the control of this productive tract that lies between them.

Within the Fertile Crescent are three river valleys. The two greatest are at the ends—the Nile in Egypt and the Tigris-Euphrates in Iraq. In each an impressive civilization arose very early, brought on, it has been suggested, by the need for community effort in the founding and maintaining of irrigation systems. The third valley lies between the two Lebanon ranges of Syria, and is watered by the Orontes river. It is one of the most fertile spots in the Near East and has always been a bone of contention between the great civilizations on either side of it.

Portico to the World. The mountains, plains, and river valleys of the Near East stand at the crossroads of three continents; they form a portico from which open front, side, and back doors to Europe, Asia, and Africa. Five seas —the Mediterranean, Black, Caspian, Red, and Persian Gulf—meet in the Near East to furnish easy transportation east, north and south. The Fertile Crescent opens a well-watered caravan trail to India and the East. Passes through the mountain chains of the north give entree to Russia and Central Asia. The Nile Valley offers the only direct road from the Mediterranean to the heart of Africa. Such a concentration of possibilities will always have world-wide importance.

Near Eastern Peoples and Their Ways of Life. More than geography is needed to define the role of the Near East in world affairs. To the static placement of mountain chains and strategic seas must be added the dynamic influence of human life—the outlook, attitudes and resources of the people who live in the geographic setting. . . .

... Few lands have seen such a confusion of tongues and diversity of races as the Near East. There has always been pressure from the peoples on either side to take advantage of its routes and control its resources....

Today four major groups stand out clearly. The heart of the Near East is possessed by the Semitic Arabs, who hold most of Iraq, Arabia, Syria, Palestine, Trans-Jordan and the nomad lands of Egypt. Each of these countries has its own variant of the parent stock, and each speaks some version of the original Arabic. To their north lie Iran and Turkey, containing what is left of the Persian and Ottoman Empires and their founders. Each of these speaks its own language and continues in the consciousness of its own racial and cultural heritage. On the south is Egypt, whose upper classes are a mixture of Turkish and Arab blood, but whose peasants differ little from their ancestors of Pharaonic times. The Coptic language, a survivor from pre-Islamic days, is kept alive in church liturgies, but the speech of the people is a dialect of Arabic.

Within these major groupings are many local variations and unabsorbed minorities.... No exact figures for racial distribution are available, but even the passing tourist cannot escape the impression of the mixture of races and confusion of tongues that still characterize the land of the Tower of Babel.

Near Eastern life is further divided by social and economic strata. Three main divisions occur: the nomad, the peasant, and the townsman. The nomad is the herdsman whose only home is the tent. He may be Turkoman, Lur, Kurd, or Arab, but whatever his race or tongue, he is characterized by a proud impatience with restraint and a loyalty to his immediate leaders that make him politically unstable. His cultural level is low, for he is usually illiterate and unacquainted with the arts and crafts of settled life. Arabia is par excellence the home of the nomad, but in all other parts of the Near East he is to be found, forming a floating group but lightly attached to national life.

The peasant is little higher in the social scale than the nomad, but his attachment to the soil and his unending struggle to wring a living from unpropitious nature have produced in him a shrewd and obstinate mind. He is so steeped in tradition, and his margin of profit is so small, that he is loath to experiment with new implements and improved methods. Only when some strong arm, like that of Kemal Atatürk, founder of modern Turkey, gets behind him can he be forced into progress. Yet the peasant is a hard worker, resourceful in using his primitive tools and capable of great development under the programs of education and social reform that many countries of the Near East are undertaking. It is the peasant who forms the base of Near Eastern life, for from 60 to 80 per cent of the population outside of Arabia belong to this class.

The townsman is quite a different character. He is the product of the cities that sprang up along the trade routes—Alexandria, Damascus, Bagdad, Teheran. Rubbing shoulders with the trade and traders of the world has given him a cosmopolitan outlook, a respect for culture, a smattering of several languages, and an awareness of outside political affairs. Out of his ranks in the past came many of the scholars and government officials; today he is producing a new middle class whose ambitions are the mainspring of nationalism and whose youth fill the new schools. Heir to a long tradition of culture and newly awakened to the possibilities of modern political life, he is the creative center of the renaissance of the Near East.

Despite the divisive elements of race, language, nationality, and social status, certain common heritages and popular attitudes are found in the Near East that bind its people together. Iranian, Turk, and Arab, peasant and city trader, look out on the world through much the same glasses. There is a certain unity to the human life of the Near East.

The basis of this unity lies partly in the great past to which the present generation is heir. For this past, the man of the Near East does not return to the days of antiquity when Egypt, Assyria, and Persia were world powers. His roots are in a more immediate era, when for nearly seven hundred years (from the eighth to the fifteenth centuries A.D.) the lands of the eastern Mediterranean dominated the civilized world. Part of this leadership was *political*. At its height in the eighth century, the Moslem Empire exceeded that of imperial Rome; it ruled from the Pyrenees in Spain to the Oxus in central Asia, giving new substance to Alexander the Great's dream of East and West united into a single state. As this vast empire fell apart, it was succeeded by lesser states that continued to give some political unity to large portions of the Near East. . . . Finally the rise of the Ottoman Turks in the fourteenth century, and the continuation of their empire until the eve of the First World War gave renewed impetus to the political importance of the Near East. Thus there is in the mind of Near Easterners a memory of past political significance, when their states and peoples held weight in the counsels of the West, and were not considered merely as areas for possible control or imperial colonization.

No less is the heritage of the past one of *cultural leadership*. The conquests of Islam drew into fertile cooperation many types of ancient culture—Persian, Byzantine, Egyptian, Syrian—out of which came the many-faceted brilliance of medieval Moslem civilization. . . . Although after the twelfth century the Near East gradually lost this cultural leadership, the memory of its glory still remains, giving the man of the Near East a sense of inherent cultural worth and dignity that reacts strongly against easily-assumed western superiority.

One of the most enduring bonds of the past is language. Arabic, the tongue of the conquering Moslem tribes of Arabia, has become the common language of the Near East for all except Iranians, Turks, and a few minorities like the Kurds and Assyrians. . . .

Binding the heritage of government, culture, literature, and language together is the pervasive influence of *religion*. Ninety-two per cent of the people of the Near East are Moslems. Although this dominant faith is divided into a number of sects, it produces a typical mind in its adherents. Under Islam, religion is a much more pervasive influence than it is in the West, for it not only creates personal beliefs about God, but gives form and substance to communal life. . . .

These common roots in the past give the peoples of the Near East a common viewpoint on the modern world. They come to our era conscious (either vaguely or distinctly) of centuries of past leadership; yet they now discover that this leadership has vanished and the culture on which it rested is no longer significant in the eyes of the dominant West. To maintain their dignity, they must not only show that equally with the European they can master the new ways, but also affirm dogmatically the value of their own traditional culture, often reading into it thoughts and discoveries that never existed in historical reality. . . .

Patterns of Today. . . . Foremost among these patterns is that of *nationalism*. The westerner first notices it as vociferous resentment and turbulent agitation against the political control of foreign powers. Yet if he observes carefully, he soon discovers that it goes on to include the restriction of foreign commercial enterprise (as the cancellation of the original oil concessions by Iran), the founding of modern, state-controlled education (as in Egypt), programs of forced social change (as the abolition of the veil by decree in Turkey), and a general reluctance to accept criticism from the foreigner (as in all parts of the world). Outside the Arabian peninsula, all countries of the Near East have exhibited some of these tendencies during the past century, but more especially, since the last war. Turkey has gone the farthest in recreating her national life, Egypt and Iran come next, while Syria and Palestine for various reasons lag behind.

In reality, nationalism is more than the revival of patriotic feeling; it is the discovery of a new concept of corporate life. Original Islam knew nothing of nationality as such; indeed it deliberately set itself to abolish racial and national divisions by substituting for them a fraternity of faith led by a theocratic ruler. The great political systems of the Near East were expressions of this religious state, and owed their power to the dominance of an individual leader (like Ibn-Saud of today) rather than to any upthrust of popular, patriotic feeling. Under nationalism, the state is replacing religion as the ultimate social organism. Turkey has rejected Islam as a basis for the state, while Iran has seriously curtailed its scope. Even in Iraq and Egypt where a Moslem revival is part of the national plan, the actual principle upon which the new social programs are based is the welfare of the nation rather than the demands of traditional religion.

The rise of nationalism has killed all hope of reviving the pan-Islamic political schemes of the past century. . . . Yet in dissolving the last traces of medieval political unity, nationalism has not completely destroyed the kindred feelings among the peoples of the Near East; they all unite in demanding political independence and cultural respect from the West.

Accompanying nationalism is a second pattern found in many parts of the Near East today—that of the *discovery of the common man*. For centuries the toilers of the fields and the artisans of the towns were only the milch cows of the government, producing the wealth by which it lived. Now they are discovering that the nation is not simply "they," the men at the top—pashas, sultans, scholars, high commissioners; but "we," the great mass of country and village folk. Especially is this true of the newly-formed middle class whose political ambitions have been the mainspring of the struggle for independence. Out of their ranks came most of the leaders of nationalism. From this same class come the increasing numbers of students who are flocking to government schools, seeing in education their surest hope for political and economic security.

This discovery is far from complete. Only Turkey, Egypt, Iraq, and Syria have any form of popularly elected governments, and in most of these countries the peasant is just beginning to take an interest in political life. Yet even this beginning is a portentous sign in an area where from antiquity the common man was never more than a hewer of wood and a drawer of water.

The third common pattern in the modern outlook of the Near East is the most basic; it is a *change in atmosphere*. Heretofore each rising generation has looked to the past for its guidance, satisfied with its achievements and seeking only to follow in its ways. Now youth feels the pressure of the present and the future, and is eager to fit itself for participation in the modern world.

One evidence of this is interest in education. Every new state in the Near East has made one of its chief tasks the founding of a modern school system. Egypt, for example, spends 11 per cent of its national budget on education—as compared with 7 per cent in Great Britain and 8½ per cent in France. Turkey has 8,169 public schools with a total enrollment of 943,000 pupils; Iran has 4,939 schools with 273,000 pupils; Iraq has 737 schools with 102,000 pupils. These schools give training in the modern scientific studies of the West, producing pupils whose mental world is far removed from the traditional concepts of the past Near East.

Another evidence of changing atmosphere is the interest in programs of social betterment. The very fact that ordered social change is considered possible is highly significant in a land where poverty and disease have always been accepted as the will of Allah. Egypt and Iraq have Ministries of Social Welfare, charged with the direction of social experiment and legislation; Iraq, Turkey and Iran have Ministries of Public Health to enforce sanitary regulations. Even Arabia is not behind in this respect, for in 1926 Ibn-Saud created a sanitary service for Mecca and the Hejaz, and added further measures in 1931....

TURKEY

At its apex in the sixteenth century under Suleiman II [the Ottoman Empire] had penetrated three continents, embraced more than 1,700,000 square miles of territory, and ruled over a polyglot population of 40,000,000 subjects. Yet scarcely had this supremacy been achieved when its foundations began to crumble, first through rebellion and misgovernment from within, and later the ambitions of European powers from without. In 1829 Greece won her war of freedom. Serbia became practically independent in 1829 and was followed by the other Balkan States, who administered their final *coup de grâce* to the Turk in the First Balkan War (1911-1912). At the same time Turkey's possessions in Africa were slipping away; Mohammed Ali won practical independence for Egypt in 1841, France seized Algeria in 1830 and Tunisia in 1881, and Italy received most of Libya as the spoils of the Turkish-Italian war of 1911. Such a weakening of Ottoman power would undoubtedly have brought about the collapse of Turkey had not the Great Powers intervened from time to time, each fearing to see the corpse of the Sick Man fall into the other's hands.

The defeat of the Central Powers in 1918 was the final blow. In the Treaty of Sèvres (August 10, 1920) the sultan was forced to renounce his sovereignty over Mesopotamia, Trans-Jordan, Palestine, Syria, and Arabia, and formally recognize the previous loss of Egypt, Cyprus, and North Africa. Armenia was to become an independent state and Kurdistan an autonomous territory; Greece and Italy were awarded certain islands in the Aegean and coastal regions of Turkey proper; and the military and economic administration of Turkey itself was placed under an Allied regulation that really robbed the nation of all vital independence. Thus the victors proposed to divide the greatest territorial spoils in modern history.

Yet the division was not even momentarily satisfactory and was never fully carried out. . . . The Turkish National Assembly refused to ratify it, taking advantage of inter-Allied rivalries to stave off its execution. After the fierce, but successful, war with Greece, in which the new Turkey of Mustafa Kemal [Kemal Atatürk] was born, a second settlement of the Near East was made at Lausanne, when a treaty was finally signed on July 24, 1923, by which Turkey was freed from most of the proposed restrictions on her economic, military, and judicial life, and received back parts of her European possessions together with all of Asia Minor. . . .

The rebirth of Turkey under the National Assembly and its first leader, Mustafa Kemal (later known as "Atatürk" or "Father of the Turks") is one of the most amazing stories of our times. Not only has the nation won a national sovereignty that makes it truly a modern state, but the whole of its economic and cultural life has been permeated by new and progressive programs that are giving the West a revised estimate of that once scornful term, "Turk." The basic change is political. For the despotic sultanate and inadequate parliament of Ottoman days, the Constitution of 1924 substituted the framework of a radically republican state.

All power is vested in the National Assembly, which is elected every four years by popular vote and chooses the President from among its own members. Under this system, Mustafa Kemal emerged as virtual dictator, not by defying the constitutional limits to his power, but by creating a one-party system (Republican People's Party) that gave the National Assembly unity with its leader. In 1930 an attempt was made with the consent of Mustafa Kemal to introduce a second party (Free Republican), but this experiment was not successful. Yet to infer that the democratic ideal of the Constitution is only the façade for permanent dictatorship is unjustified. The problem of bringing to political responsibility an illiterate generation nurtured in the heritage of Ottoman despotism could only be accomplished by determined and dictatorial leadership for several decades. The fact that Turkish progress did not collapse with the death of Mustafa Kemal in 1938 but has continued through the trying years of war under Ismet Inönü is evidence that it is rooted in something more than the will of one man.

Turkey's first concern was to regain full national sovereignty among the European powers. In the Treaty of Sèvres the high-water mark of foreign interference in Turkey's internal affairs was reached, but the provisions of the treaty were never fully applied, and many of them were removed by the subsequent Lausanne Conference. Turkey's program now became one of friendship with Soviet Russia, whose support she used in making headway against the pressure of the Great Powers. The dispute with Great Britain over the demarcation of the Iraqi-Turkish frontier was settled in 1926, treaties of friendship with Italy, France, and Greece followed, and admission into the League of Nations came in 1932. In 1936, taking advantage of the growing tensions in Europe, Turkey pressed for, and obtained, a revision of the Straits settlement of 1923, by which the Dardanelles had been demilitarized and largely taken from Turkish control. The return of this strategic area to Turkish administration and military protection marked the restoration of full national sovereignty. Turkey had at last become master in her own house.

While the nation was struggling to

regain its place in the world, it was also reshaping its own internal life. The problem was twofold: economic and cultural.

Old Turkey, like most oriental countries, had exported raw materials and imported manufactured goods. She now undertook to supply her own consumer needs by a program of careful economic planning. Part of the program was agricultural, aimed at diversifying crops and utilizing unproductive, or half-productive soil. Between 1925 and 1939 the wheat acreage increased 57 per cent, the total yield 125 per cent; maize acreage 120 per cent, the total yield 180 per cent; rye acreage 120 per cent, the total yield 180 per cent. At the same time industrial enterprises were started, textile and sugar mills taking the lead since their products were the chief articles of import in spite of the fact that their raw materials were readily available in Turkey. The road system was improved, railways extended, and in 1939 the first blast furnace opened its doors. To finance such undertakings a series of national banks was founded, to relieve Turkish enterprise of its complete dependence upon foreign-controlled capital. Following Russia's example, an agricultural Four Year Plan and an industrial Five Year Plan were introduced, although like most such schemes their full program was not realized.

The cultural task was that of translating the common people from the religion-dominated world of the historic Orient to the modern era of western science. This has involved drastic social legislation; the abolition of the fez and the veil, the forbidding of polygamy, the disestablishment of Islam as the religion of the state, and the substitution of the western Sunday for the Moslem Friday day of rest. Perhaps the most far-reaching change came in the abandonment of the Arabic for the Latin alphabet and the program of adult literacy that followed, for no less than 2,000,000 adults learned to read through this change. Traditional titles of rank and nobility such as Pasha, Effendi, and Hajji were forbidden, and all Turks became plain Bey (man) and Beyin (woman). A system of state schools was created, which in 1939 enrolled nearly a million pupils out of some seven million under twenty years of age. . . .

EGYPT

On the eve of the First World War, Egypt's political situation was peculiar. Nominally she was still a part of the Ottoman Empire, ruled by a khedive who recognized the suzerainty of the Turkish sultan. Yet since 1882 British troops had occupied the country, and British advisers controlled its finances and exerted pressure on its politics. . . .

Turkey's entrance in the [First] World War on the side of Germany made Egypt of paramount importance to the Allies as the protector of the Suez Canal and the naval base of the eastern Mediterranean. Because of his pro-Turkish sympathies, the ruling khedive (Abbas Hilmi) was deposed by the British, who in December 1914 proclaimed Egypt a British protectorate governed by a sultan, to which position a relative of Abbas was elevated. At the close of the war there was strong Egyptian agitation for independence, led by Saad Zaghlul. A delegation sought to represent Egypt at the Peace Conference, but this was denied to them, and their leaders, including Saad Zaghlul, were exiled. Nationalist agitation continued, however, and in 1922 Great Britain formally gave Egypt its independence, raising its sultan, Fuad, to the position of king.

In granting independence Great Britain "absolutely reserved" her rights in the Sudan and the defense of the Suez Canal, the latter necessitating the presence of British garrisons in Cairo and other cities. These reservations were the target of renewed nationalist agitation, still led by Saad Zaghlul and supported chiefly by the popular political party of the Wafd or "Delegation." Opposing the program of the Wafd were not only British imperial interests, but the king of Egypt, who did not want to see a strong parliamentary regime emerge. Zaghlul's death in 1927 robbed the nationalists of their most able leader, and for a period the power of the palace was dominant, supporting an almost dictatorial prime minister. However, the break-up of European unity with the "Ethiopian incident" of 1935 made both England and the nationalists realize that in the event of war they would need each other's support. On August 26, 1936, an Anglo-Egyptian Treaty of Alliance was signed which really marked the beginning of Egypt's full independence. The present leader of the Wafd party is Nahas Pasha, who negotiated the treaty, while the king is Farouk I, son of the first king Fuad I, and tenth ruler of the dynasty of Mohammed Ali.

The form of government in Egypt was set by the original Constitution of 1923, later suspended by the King and temporarily replaced by a new constitution in 1930. Under it the nation is governed by a hereditary king, his ministers, and an elected parliament of two houses.

Egypt's chief problem is that of simple bread and butter. Its population is the densest in the world (1,045 per habitable square mile) and is increasing at a rate that promises to double the present figure within a century. . . .

The independence Egypt seeks is not merely from foreign political control; she equally desires to become free from poverty, ignorance, and disease.

SYRIA

Unlike Turkey and Egypt, Syria had no independent political life before the First World War. For her the struggle was one of liberation from Ottoman rule, long resented by the Arabs. As early as 1875 there were revolutionary secret societies preaching Arab independence, and by the time Turkey joined the Central Powers in 1914, Arab Nationalism was a full-fledged movement. Its cause was strengthened by similar aspirations in the Hejaz, where Sherif Hussein, the guardian of Mecca, had long fretted under Turkish rule. The outbreak of war confronted these nationalists with a dilemma of strategy: Should they uphold the hands of their Moslem brothers, the Turks, winning post-war independence in gratitude for help given? Or must Turkey be left to her own decay in the hope that a free Arab state might emerge from her defeat? At the moment of indecision, exiled Arab leaders in Cairo were approached by the British authorities (*not* Lawrence, but Ronald Storrs, Reginald Wingate, and others), seeking to persuade them that the future of Arab independence lay in revolt against the Turks and an alliance with England.

In an exchange of notes between the high commissioner of Egypt (Sir Henry McMahon) and the sherif of Mecca (Hussein), the matter was concluded. England asked that the Arabs rise against the Turks and thus break the power of Germany in the East. On her part, she promised to "recognize and uphold the independence of all Arabs" in what is now the Hejaz, Trans-Jordan, Syria, and Iraq, excepting only two non-Arab districts in the extreme north (Mersin and Alexandretta) and that part of Syria which lies "west of Damascus, Homs, Hama and Aleppo." Whether Palestine was part of the excluded district has been a debated point, although those who read the Arabic text of the agreement readily understand how the Arabs have claimed that it was not. On the strength of these promises, the Arab "Revolt in the Desert" took place (1916), contributing immeasurably to the final Allied victory in the East.

But when it came to the Peace Conference, there was a different story to tell. In addition to the conversations with the Arabs, Great Britain had entered into some nineteen other commitments, many of them secret, involving the post-war status of the Near East. Chief among them was the Sykes-Picot Agreement, in which the promises made the Arabs were ostensibly squared with France's demands for the recognition of her *"droit historique"* (historic right) in Syria. By this agreement, the Arabs' best lands were to be cut into mandates and spheres of influence, France receiving as her share a large slice of Anatolian Turkey as well as all Syria north of Palestine—including even the Mosul district in Mesopotamia. . . .

The Peace Conference thus had to deal with a clash of conflicting interests; the Arabs wanted the unity and independence they felt they had been promised; the French wanted to safeguard their influence in Syria and checkmate the rise of a preponderant British influence that might undermine it; the British wanted to keep the support of France in the post-war world, yet fulfill (at least in part) their promises to Sherif Hussein, at the same time creating a pro-English Arab East. . . .

What emerged from the protracted skirmishing of the Powers . . . was the division of Greater Syria into three mandated areas: Palestine (England), Iraq (England), Syria and Lebanon (France).

France's plan in Syria was "divide and rule." To the historic separation of Syria and the Lebanon . . . were added three other divisions, thus splitting a population of some 3,200,000 people into five political units—the State of Syria, the State of Greater Lebanon, the State of Jebel Druze, the Government of Latakia, and the Sanjak of Alexandretta (part of Syria, but under separate administration). This was done under the plea that it but recognized existing religious and racial divisions; actually it struck at the unity of the Arab National movement by fostering local loyalties.

The years that followed were not unnaturally marked by continued friction between the people of Syria and the French administration, there being no less than eighteen uprisings between 1919 (when French troops first took possession) and 1941. At first French control was essentially a military occupation, but after the great Druze rebellion of 1925-1927, the policy began to change. Lebanon was declared a republic in 1926, and Syria in 1930. In 1936 treaties of alliance were signed which promised independence within three years with the abolition of the mandate and support to Syria and Lebanon in applying for membership in the League of Nations. Under these treaties France still retained considerable power, being permitted to keep designated garrisons in Jebel Druze and Latakia, and unlimited troops in Lebanon. The outbreak of the Second World War frustrated Syrian hopes under this treaty, but when the Free French and the British occupied the country in 1941, they proclaimed the complete and immediate independence of both Syria and the Lebanon. The Sanjak of Alexandretta, essentially Turkish in speech and sympathy, was returned to Turkey by France in 1939.

The record of economic progress in Syria is less impressive than that in

Turkey or Egypt. France's first need was for military facilities, so her engineers produced a system of excellent roads and continued the development of the railway. By tying the Syrian lira to the franc, trade with France was given a preferential position, yet as late as 1938 the value of English imports exceeded French by nearly 25 per cent. French cultural influences were furthered by French schools and the official use of the French language; yet no extensive system of public education has been founded, there being in 1939 twice as many private as public schools. A few small-scale industries have been started, but most of these are the result of the initiative and capital of Syrian-American immigrants who have returned to their home land.

PALESTINE

... Palestine is the scene of a head-on clash between two nationalisms, born at about the same time and focused on the same area. Arab Nationalism came into being during the last quarter of the nineteenth century, accompanied by a renaissance of literature and thought that marked it as something more than the political tool of dissatisfied leaders. During the same period Jewish Nationalism was being born in the program of political Zionism, having as its immediate object the relief of oppressed Jews and the creation of a state where they might live in peace and freedom. For both movements, Palestine had a peculiar attraction. For the Hebrew it was the home of his religion, the only land in which he had ever enjoyed a national existence. For the Arab it was the third sacred site of his faith (Abraham, Moses, David and Jesus are all *Moslem* prophets), and a land in which he had dwelt for over thirteen hundred years....

Both these nationalisms received their accolade from the Allies during the First World War. The McMahon-Hussein Agreements promised British support for Arab independence in an area understood by the Arab leaders to include Palestine. Although England has always denied that understanding, the fact is that nowhere in the correspondence was Palestine excluded *by name*; only by inference can the exclusion be maintained—and this seems to the Arabs distinctly artificial and forced. On the other hand, the Balfour Declaration of November 2, 1917 announced to the world that "His Majesty's Government views with favor the establishment in Palestine of a national home for the Jewish people," providing that "nothing shall be done which may prejudice the civil and religious rights of existing non-Jewish communities in Palestine." Both Arab and Jew thus entertained a justifiable claim to the country based on solemn promises, and, in the Arab case, on national military participation in the war as an ally.

But the position of Palestine was not only the result of tensions between Zionism and Arab Nationalism. England had her interests to serve as well. The creation of a large French mandate in Syria and the growing nationalist sentiment in Egypt imperilled British influence near the most vital link in the lifeline to India—the Suez Canal. Whatever form the future of Palestine was to take, England wanted to have it under some measure of British control....

The mandate that was assigned to Great Britain in 1922 has not proved the easy solution to any of these hopes....

At the close of the World War there were about 55,000 Jews in Palestine, forming 8 per cent of the population. Some of these descended from ancient Hebrews; others were colonists planted in the early decades of the original Zionist movement. With the inauguration of the British mandate committed to furthering a national home for the Jewish people, planned immigration became part of the Government program. Between 1922 and 1941, the Jewish population of Palestine increased by approximately 380,000, four-fifths of this being due to immigration. This made the Jews 31 per cent of the total population. During the same period, the Arab (Moslem) population increased by some 356,000, due chiefly to a high birth rate. . . .

The Zionist influx resulted in a remarkable stimulation of life and business. Citrus culture, already practiced for generations by the Arabs, was developed into a principal industry (7,595,645 boxes of fruit were exported in 1939). The chemicals of the Dead Sea were exploited, and the manufacture of soap, chemicals, medicines, perfumes, cement, and numerous other products, was undertaken. In every field the determination and ingenuity of the Jewish colonist was shown.

Yet Arab resentment continued, even increased. It was not basically anti-Semitism, for on the whole the historic record of the Moslem Near East in its treatment of Jewish minorities is better than the record of Christian Central Europe. The root of the trouble was in the announced *political* objective of Zionism to create in Palestine, not a national *home,* but a national *state*—which could only be a Jewish state, which therefore could not be an Arab state. What the Arab objected to was the intrusion (to him) of a foreign people, apparently bent on gaining political control of his country with the help of money and protection supplied by the West. . . .

In 1936 a Royal Commission of Inquiry was sent out by the British government to make a thorough investigation.

. . . The upshot of the investigation was a proposal that Palestine should be divided politically between the Jews and Arabs, with Britain retaining a permanent mandate over the Holy Places. This partition scheme pleased no one. . . .

Renewed Arab disorders broke out, settling down to a banditti warfare that only stopped when the outbreak of the Second World War flooded Palestine with British troops.

Trans-Jordan, the land lying across the Jordan from Palestine, was included in the Palestine mandate assigned to Great Britain, but with the proviso that it be excluded from the proposed national home for the Jews. It is headed by Emir Abdullah, a son of Sherif Hussein, whose independent government was recognized by England in 1929. The High Commissioner for Palestine is also High Commissioner for Trans-Jordan. . . .

IRAQ

. . . When England bought off France's claims to Iraq by giving her a share in the Mosul oil, and thus received the entire mandate for herself (San Remo, 1920) the country needed above all else a strong and capable leader who could bridge the gap between local aspirations and mandatory interests. The rebellion that broke out when the mandate award was made served notice on Britain that she could not dictate the status of Iraq; some recognition of local political aspirations was necessary. It was therefore proposed that an independent Iraq government should be set up, with whom the mandatory power could enter into negotiation and treaty.

By a British-supervised popular vote, Emir Feisal was chosen to head this government. On August 23, 1921, he was proclaimed king, becoming the first independent sovereign the nation had had since A.D. 1258. Under Feisal's rule, Iraq made remarkable progress in political development. In 1924 parliamentary government was instituted, and in 1930 a treaty was negotiated that promised the termination of the mandate. Under its provisions Great Britain was to aid Iraq in entering the League of Nations, at which time the mandate should cease, being replaced by a Treaty of Alliance between the two sovereign states. This occurred two years later (1932), and thus the first of the mandates awarded by the San Remo conference came to its end.

King Feisal died in the fall of 1933. ... Robbed of this commanding leader, Iraq has had a hard time in maintaining her political stability.... The outbreak of the Second World War plunged Iraq into the turmoil of international tensions; for as one of the principal petroleum-producing countries in the Near East and guardian of the overland route to the Persian Gulf and India, its control was vital to the Allies and coveted by the Axis. By a *coup d'état*, which took place five days after the fall of Athens (April 1941) a former prime minister and pro-Axis nationalist, Rashid Ali Gailani, seized the government, forcing the Regent to flee the country. British troops were landed, and with the help of the Trans-Jordan Desert Corps the faction of Rashid Ali was defeated and a pro-British government came into office. In January 1943 Iraq declared war on the Axis.

Despite the disappointing conclusion to the political development made under Feisal, Iraq has done much to advance her national life. Extensive irrigation projects, culminating in the Habbaniyah Outlet, have restored part of the ancient fertility that made Iraq a granary of the Near East. Better varieties of wheat have been introduced, and cotton cultivation has been started. In 1940 the last portion of the "Berlin to Bagdad" railroad was completed, by which Basra, at the head of the Persian Gulf, is linked directly with the rail systems of Europe. Nearly 4,000 miles of road make auto transportation possible, strengthening the hold of the central government and spreading travel and commerce through the villages and towns. Much energy has been put into the development of a modern school system, patterned largely on Egyptian lines, which provides technical as well as scholastic training. Shut off for centuries from the life of the West by the barren expanse of the Syrian desert, Iraq is beginning to stir with the same life and aspirations that have made Turkey and Egypt modern states.

SAUDI ARABIA

The history of the Arabian peninsula has always been the history of personalities. The Arab nomads, mercurial in temperament and fiercely tribal in political loyalty, have only coalesced into a nation under the driving force of a great leader. In our day that leader is Abd el Aziz ibn-Saud, king of Saudi Arabia. ...

Under Ibn-Saud the regions of the Nejd were consolidated into a single Kingdom of Saudi Arabia, whose borders stretch from Iraq to the Red Sea, from the Syrian desert to Yemen. ...

Ibn-Saud is more than a political leader seeking power; he is a reformer striving to bring Arabia into the current of the modern world. The introduction of the motorcar, telephone, and radio have strengthened the hold of the central government while sternly applied laws against intertribal warfare have at last convinced the fighting Bedouin that peace is to be the normal state of Arabia.

In addition to the dominant state of

Ibn-Saud, the Arabian peninsula contains the region of Yemen on its southwest coast, an independent state ruled by Imam Yahya and containing some 2,500,000 inhabitants. Along the Persian Gulf stretch a series of minor states, each independent but allied by treaty with Great Britain. They are Oman and Muscat, the Trucial Sheikhdoms, Bahrein and Kuwait.

IRAN

[In 1925] Reza Shah Pahlevi announced ... that his nation would no longer be known by its foreign Greek name of "Persia," but would take for its own the ancient title of "Iran." Behind this announcement lay more than a salute to past glory; it was a declaration of national selfhood, proclaiming that something of the independence of past days had been recaptured.

Persia was the first oriental nation to wring a modern constitution from its hereditary ruler. Until 1906 the sl ıh had been absolute, his power limited only by the authority of the religious leaders of Shiite Islam—the Mujtahid en. In that year he came face to face with demands for national reform, and was forced to establish a National Assembly, followed by the proclamation of a constitution. That the National Assembly meant business was shown two years later, when it deposed the shah and set his son on the throne.

Yet the new nationalists had scarcely started to wrestle with the financial and administrative chaos of the country when they were blocked by a combination too strong to be resisted. Throughout the nineteenth century, Russia had frankly pursued the aim of incorporating Persia into her empire; she now joined hands with the shah and a section of the hereditary nobility to make any program of reform impossible. At the same time, Great Britain was interested in the country, in whose independence she saw a barrier to Russian expansion toward India. Yet her desire was not for a too-strong nation which might resist her influence, but one just free enough to challenge the ambitions of others. On the eve of the First World War it seemed as though these rival influences were about to make an end of the Persian national state, for the Russian annexation of the northern provinces was imminent and Great Britain would undoubtedly have claimed the oversight of the remaining southern part.

It was the Russian revolution that saved the day. Under its policy of repudiating the imperialism of the czars, the Soviet Government called an abrupt halt to its interference in Persian affairs, and even enabled the nation to make a new beginning by renouncing Persia's debt to Russia, abolishing the Capitulations, and turning over to the Persian Government all Russian state and church property in the country. A new national government was formed under the impetus of this friendship, but in 1919 Great Britain succeeded in having a pro-British ministry come to power, under which a treaty of support was concluded with England. By the terms of this treaty Britain would have a predominant place in Persian affairs. Her advisers would assist in government, her capital and engineers build railroads, her officers train the army, her financial experts reorganize the customs. It seemed as though the nation had escaped from one foreign imperialism only to run straight into the arms of another.

At this juncture appeared the man of the hour, Reza Khan, commander of the army. Like Mustafa Kemal, he found in threatened domination of his country the tocsin to awaken national revival. By a *coup d'état* he seized the government in 1921, driving out the pro-British cabinet, denouncing the treaty, and installing himself as prime minister. His aim was to found a controlled republic modelled after Turkey. But finding the opposition of the Mujtahideen too powerful, he became hereditary shah in 1925, using his autocratic power to drive the country into progress.

Iran's reconstruction has in general followed Turkey's program, although at a much slower pace. Islam has not been discarded as the religion of the state, but its place is restricted and its leaders shorn of much of their traditional power. Cultural changes like the abolition of the veil and the wearing of European hats have been legally enforced, yet the oriental character of marriage and divorce is left untouched. Great attention has been paid to the founding of a modern, state-controlled system of education. Between 1921 and 1937 the total number of schools increased from 612 to 4,939 and the pupils enrolled from 55,000 to 273,000.

Economically, Iran has sought increasing freedom within her own boundaries. The note-issuing privileges previously granted the Bank of Persia (a British institution) were withdrawn, and the telephone and telegraph systems, owned by British companies, were taken over by the Iranian government. Perhaps the greatest triumph of all came in the successful insistence that the terms of the oil concessions be reviewed. After reference to the League of Nations, Iran carried her point, and in 1935 a new agreement with the Anglo-Iranian Oil Company was signed. By its terms the area of exploitation is limited, increased royalties are paid the government, and more Iranians are trained and employed by the company.

These promising signs of national rebirth were checked abruptly by the outbreak of the Second World War. As a possible back door to the Near East, Iran became the target for intense Axis propaganda and infiltration and when the Shah refused to run the interlopers out at the dictation of the Allies, Russian and British troops occupied the country (August 25, 1941). The shah forthwith abdicated in favor of his son, Mohammed Reza, under whom a pro-Allied regime has been established and a treaty of alliance with England and Russia concluded. . . .

NEAR EAST IN WORLD POLITICS

Bottleneck of Communications

. . . Between the Caspian and the Nile there come to a focus all the principal, direct routes by which the life of the Occident reaches the life of the Orient. . . . When history first lifts the curtain on ancient civilization, the Egyptians were getting myrrh and indigo dye for mummy wrappings from India via the Red Sea, and the Babylonians were dealing in teak wood, copper, and pearls that reached them from south Asia by way of the Persian Gulf.

. . . Medieval housewives depended on spices to preserve their food, and these spices came from the Orient across the historic routes of the Near East. But the rise of the Ottoman Turks in the fifteenth century stopped the flow of goods from the East; tariffs became exorbitantly high and unchecked brigandage made the roads unsafe. Spices became difficult to get and expensive to buy; there was consternation in the kitchens of Europe no less than in the directors' meetings of Venice, whose trade was slowly being ruined. Expeditions were hurriedly sent out to find "the lands where spices are procured," and explorers were commissioned to discover some new road to the Orient. It was Vasco da Gama who opened the way. By sailing to India around Africa

(1497-98) he opened up a new route to "Calicut and Cathay" that completely avoided the "terrible Turk" and his extortions. For three hundred years most of the eastern trade went this long way round, leaving the Near East to stagnate in the back-waters of the Mediterranean. . . .

The Suez Canal [was] opened in 1869 [and] cut the land link between Asia and Africa, shortened the route to India by four thousand miles, and rerouted the entire commerce of the world. . . . Once again the Near East possesses the major communication tie between East and West.

Despite its international significance, the Suez Canal is basically a commercial enterprise. Ferdinand de Lesseps, its designer and builder, received from the khedive of Egypt a concession to form the "Universal Company of the Suez Maritime Canal." To provide funds for construction, this company offered its shares on the bourses of Europe. In the first issue 51 per cent of the stock was bought by French interests, 44 per cent was acquired by the khedive of Egypt, and the rest was scattered among other continental investors. . . . In 1875 the khedive, embarrassed by his mounting debts, was glad to sell his canal shares to Great Britain, who thus became a major partner with France in the Suez enterprise.

Ever since the acquisition of the canal shares, British influence has been dominant in the Suez zone. As chief commercial user of the canal (50 per cent of the 1938 transit tonnage was British) and largest imperial power in the East, England has maintained a steady interest in safeguarding this area of the Near East from the ambitions of other nations. By occupying Egypt in 1882 she established control of one flank of the canal, and through the Palestine mandate of 1922 she protected the other flank. When Egypt sought complete independence from British control in 1922, one of the questions "absolutely reserved" for the discretion of the British government was the defense of the Canal Zone—a proviso that also appeared in the Anglo-Egyptian Treaty of Alliance signed in 1936. . . .

The original concession under which the canal company was formed expires in 1968, when the Suez Canal will revert to the Egyptian government. In 1909 the company sought an extension for another forty years (until 2008) but such a storm of protest arose from the awakening nationalists of Egypt that the proposal was dropped. After 1968 Egypt expects to control and use the canal as her own property, reaping the profits she lost when the prodigal khedive sold his shares to England. Yet she can scarcely hope to assume complete responsibility for such a major link in international communications without the support of the Great Powers, who will always be on guard lest some single nation seize the canal and close it to the free traffic of the world.

The opening of the Suez Canal restored the historic sea-route to the Orient; another ancient path awaited revival—the old caravan trail across Asia Minor to the head of the Persian Gulf. This became the concern of Germany, who saw in its development both a check to the dominant influence of Britain, and an instrument for accomplishing the *Drang nach Osten* (drive to the East) that played so large a part in her foreign policy. Under this plan England's sea route to India would be counterbalanced by a German overland route, leading from Central Europe to the Indian Ocean.

The scheme took the form of a railway line, some 1,500 miles long, to connect the Bosporus with the Persian Gulf. The German Anatolian Railway

Company received its first concession from the Turkish Government, in 1888 and began the construction of portions of this line. . . .

At the outbreak of the war [in 1914], about 1,200 miles of railroad had been built. The difficult sector through the Taurus Mountains to Aleppo was constructed by the Germans during the war, and the British built the stretch from Basra to Bagdad to facilitate troop movements during the Mesopotamian campaign. Not until 1936 was the final link begun, when the Iraq government undertook to connect Baiji in Iraq with Tel Kochek in Syria. On July 20, 1940, the first through train reached Ankara from Bagdad; British engineers had completed what the Germans had begun.

Despite its grand conception, the Berlin-to-Bagdad railway has not become the major link with the East the Germans had hoped. With the breakup of the old Turkish Empire after the war, the rail route became the property of three separate national territories (Turkey, Syria, Iraq) and so lacks the unified control that might make it a rival of the Suez Canal. Moreover, other means of land transport have diminished its significance and opened competing routes. Its chief function has been to stimulate trade and tie the isolated hinterlands of the Near East to the Mediterranean world.

Other rail lines have been built in the Near East, following for the most part old trade routes. Leaving the Berlin-to-Bagdad trunk line at Aleppo (Syria) is a connection for Cairo that runs via Damascus, Haifa, and the Sinai seacoast. From Cairo the first link of Cecil Rhodes' "Cairo-to-Cape Town" line runs southward through the rich Nile Valley for 554 miles, ending at Shellal near Aswan, where a steamer makes connections with the Sudan Railway.

Iran has built a railroad from the Persian Gulf to the Caspian Sea, and is building a branch between Teheran and Tabriz that will connect with the Russian system, opening the back door to the heart of Eurasia.

Such a network of rail connection is rapidly making the Near East as central in oriental-occidental land travel as the Suez Canal did in sea travel. It is possible today to go from Murmansk on the Arctic Ocean to Basra at the head of the Persian Gulf by rail; tomorrow we may step on the train in Paris and, with only one auto-portage, alight in Calcutta.

While rail and sea routes are still the main arteries of international communications, the real revolution in Near Eastern travel has been worked by the automobile. Nature has provided miles of touring space on the hard gravel plains of the desert, and even difficult mountain passes can be negotiated with a minimum of road, a maximum of faith in the protection of Allah—and a high-slung car.

The chief auto route cuts straight across the Syrian desert from Damascus to Bagdad. These arid plains were sometimes crossed in the old days by fast-riding mail couriers mounted on fleet racing camels, but the heavy caravans generally went further to the north, keeping nearer to the green belt of the Fertile Crescent. Now freight trucks ply regularly between the Mediterranean and the Persian Gulf, stopping only for a brief pause at Rutba Wells, in the middle of the desert. Air-conditioned buses carry a large passenger traffic, and convoys of small cars care for the less luxurious traveler and the mail. Opened in 1923, this route has become the principal land link between Syria and the Persian Gulf, operating so successfully that long-standing plans for a Bagdad-to-Haifa railroad have been dropped in favor of a paved desert highway.

A road of nearly equal importance runs from the railhead at Khanaqin (Iraq) to Teheran, where it connects with the Iranian Railway. There is a similar auto connection between Teheran and Zahidan, the terminus of the Karachi branch of the Indian Railway. Even the Arabian desert is being crossed by motor car, Iranian and Iraqi pilgrim bands now driving direct from Bagdad to Mecca across north Arabia.

Such routes do not have the political overtones that accompany railway lines and canals. They can be built without a heavy outlay of capital—thus avoiding foreign investment and control, they can be shifted to alternate areas without much loss [but] they are scarcely adequate to carry the bulk of heavy commerce. Yet this road system has been by far the most penetrating communication influence in the local life of the Near East. It brings the European world and its goods to the back door of every village and makes possible the control of centralized government. Furthermore, auto transport forms the "missing link" between uncompleted rail lines, making it possible, for instance, for America to send supplies to Russia via Iran even though the Iranian rail system is far from complete.

Of much greater potential *political* significance is the development of air travel. The coming of the airplane has not only brought the East to within a few days of the West, but it has robbed of their historic—and therefore political—significance natural barriers like mountains, deserts, and seas. The first regular air mail service in the Near East was organized by Britain's Royal Air Force in 1921, and ran between Cairo and Bagdad. In 1929 this was taken over by the great British air company, Imperial Airways, and made a part of its network of imperial communications. Political rivalry developed at once, and other European powers hastened to stake their claims in the new development of the Near East. Iran (possibly under German pressure) objected to any flying over south Persian territory, and forced the British to use the much less attractive Arabian side of the Persian Gulf. In 1927 the German Junkers air company gained a concession from Iran and opened four airlines radiating from Teheran. The Dutch K.L.M. service was extended to the Netherlands East Indies, making Bagdad its Near Eastern base. The French Air Orient (later "Air France") pushed its lines toward the French colonies in the Far East, flying via Beirut, Damascus, Bagdad, and Basra. By 1932 the aircraft of four great European nations met at the Bagdad Airport, which had become the halfway house of all the air routes to the East.

The enormous development of air transportation by the war will place the Near East directly in the center of the struggle for post-war communications. Already it is planned to make Alexandria the base for four air trunk lines —one running south through the heart of Africa, one east to India and Australia, one north to Russia and Central Asia, and one to western Europe. These are European plans—but American airlines are already claiming their share. At present our men and equipment are reaching the Near East via Brazil, Nigeria, and Khartoum, and undoubtedly Pan American Airways hopes to develop this as a major route at the close of the war.

The opening of oil fields in Iran and Iraq demanded yet another type of communication—the pipeline. The Persian and Mesopotamian oil centers are near the Persian Gulf, to which pipe lines were early built; but the most pressing demand for Near Eastern oil came from the Mediterranean, where it could be used to refuel naval fleets. In 1935 the world's longest welded pipeline (1,150 miles) was opened from Kirkuk beyond the Tigris to the seacoast at Haifa. Great Britain hoped to keep this line entirely within territory over which she had military control, but under French protest a branch was built from Haditha (Iraq) to Tripoli in French Syria. Thus both England and France assured themselves of direct—almost monopolistic—access to the fuel supplies of the Near East. After the fall of France in 1940, the British temporarily closed the Tripoli branch of the pipeline, fearing that the oil might fall into the hands of the Axis via Vichy France.

Germany's defeat in the last war was due in part to her failure to capture the Near East and cut Britain's imperial communications. This lesson was not forgotten, and when the Axis powers engineered a new war for world conquest, the occupation of the Near East was a basic item of strategy. . . .

While the Axis was busy trying to throttle the Near East from the west, the Allies were opening a new and vital artery of war supplies in the East. From the head of the Persian Gulf to Russia runs the Near East equivalent of the Burma Road—a combined rail-truck route over which war supplies can be delivered behind the lines of the Caucasus front, direct to the heart of unoccupied Russia. It was the strategic importance of this back door to Russia that made the Allies so concerned about the anti-British regime of Reza Shah Pahlevi, finally leading to the Anglo-Russian occupation of Iran in 1941.

Near Eastern Resources. A second factor entangling the Near East in the life of the world is its possession of needed natural resources. . . .

These resources are *marginal* in their significance. Small in themselves, their possession may lend a Great Power just the necessary edge of superiority in a world fiercely competing for the supply and control of raw materials.

One of the chief raw materials of western industry is cotton. . . .

[As a result of the American Civil War] India was developed as an important source of cheap cotton, but Egypt quickly became the principal producer of long-staple fiber, its cotton being the finest in the world. Between the Civil War and the present decade, Egypt's cotton production increased by slightly over 600 per cent, the total crop in 1938 being 1,900,000 bales. This makes Egypt sixth in the world production of raw cotton, although she is first in the amount of cotton grown per inhabitant. . . .

Like cotton, the oil of the Near East is only a small part of the [current] world supply, yet it is large enough to cause constant involvement in the West's struggles for raw materials. Sixty per cent of the world's petroleum comes from the United States; of the remaining 40 per cent slightly more than one-seventh comes from the oil fields of the Near East. But these figures do not tell the full story. In spite of its huge production, the United States has only a modest fraction of the world's available oil resources, and what it does have is being drained away at a rapid rate. What of the future, when yields are low and supplementary supplies must be sought abroad? Here the true oil-significance of the Near East appears, for this area has nearly as much petroleum as the United States. . . .

In addition to the great oil fields of Iraq and Iran, petroleum is produced in the Red Sea regions of Egypt, and on the island of Bahrein in the Persian Gulf [and in still other localities]. The

Egyptian holdings have been worked by British companies since 1907, but since the First World War some American production has started. Bahrein, where a concession was granted to American interests in 1930, has rapidly become an important oil and refining center, being the twelfth largest oil-producing country in the world.

While cotton and oil are the chief economic resources of the Near East, there are other products that have significance in world economy. One-sixth of the total chrome ore is produced in Turkey, one-twelfth of the olive oil comes from Syria and Palestine, one-fourteenth of the barley is grown in Turkey and Iraq. Tobacco, wheat, wool, and sesame seed are produced in smaller amounts and find their way to the markets of the world....

Fulcrum of the Moslem World. Geography and resources alone would give the Near East world significance. But these lands of the eastern Mediterranean are not only the focus of oriental-occidental communications; they are also the focus of the consciousness and outlook of two hundred and fifty million Moslem people.

Scattered across Asia and Africa, these followers of Mohammed form one of the most significant blocs in the East today. No other group is so far-flung, or penetrates so many vital areas. China has at least ten million Moslems, seventeen million more live in Soviet Russia, every fourth Indian is a Moslem. The Dutch East Indies are 98 per cent Moslem, while even our own Philippine Islands have an important minority of half a million Moslems we know as Moros. From the steppes of Central Asia to the jungles of central Africa, the *overwhelming majority of native peoples* are Moslem. Two hundred and fifty million strong, the Moslem world is something to reckon with!

Although the Moslem peoples include practically all the races and nationalities of the East, they form one of the most self-conscious blocs in the world today. Islam has always been more than a religious belief; it is a legal code, a social order and a cultural pattern as well. Wherever it has gone it has stamped a common design on the daily life of its followers and given them a consciousness of an international brotherhood that is more basic than loyalty to nation or race. Original Islam knew nothing of nationality; religious brotherhood was its organizing concept. Believers were Moslems first, and Indians, Persians, and Arabs only by accident.

Nationalism is making inroads on this unity, but has not yet worked its complete destruction. With the defeat of Turkey and the abolition of the caliphate, the dream of Pan-Islamism died, carrying with it the last vestiges of the political unity of the Moslem world. Yet a certain atmosphere of world fellowship remains. The national awakening of traditional Moslem countries, like Iraq and Egypt, tends to emphasize the Islamic heritage and make of it a political instrument against Western control. In non-Moslem countries, the aggressive nationalism of the majority frequently drives the Moslem minority further from national unity and closer to the bonds of world Islam. The self-consciousness of the Moslem bloc helps to make a united, nationalistic India impossible at the present time. Fearful of Hindu domination, the powerful Moslem League is more loyal to religious allegiance than to the national movement.

Yet the center of gravity of the Moslem bloc still lies in the Near East. Here are forty-eight million Moslems standing at the geographical center of the world of Islam. Here are the sacred shrines of religion to which all Moslems turn in daily prayer, and tens of thousands visit at the time of the yearly Pilgrimage. Here is the living home of the Arabic language and culture that sets the atmosphere of the world Moslem mind. Here are the independent Moslem powers—Iran, Iraq, Turkey, Egypt, Saudi Arabia—in whom the scattered Moslem minorities of Africa and Asia find the promise of their political selfhood. Above all, here is the great, creative, intellectual center of Islam, furnishing the materials of thought to the Moslem world. Egypt alone prints nearly three hundred Arabic periodicals and newspapers, about one-half of which go out to the far places of the Moslem faith. Standard theological works, dictionaries, volumes of polemics, histories, literary reviews, political studies, and a host of minor tracts, are prepared in Cairo and Damascus to form the standard reading of the leaders of traditional Islam across the world. Moreover, Cairo is the home of the Azhar—the Oxford of Islam and the world's oldest university. Founded nearly a thousand years ago, this institution has for centuries trained the professional Moslem leaders in law and religion. Its present enrollment of thirteen thousand students is drawn from every land in the eastern hemisphere where Islam is known. In 1938 a delegation of some twenty Chinese Moslems arrived in Cairo, having come overland from North China to train in the Azhar. After remaining there for from seven to fourteen years, they will return to their Chinese Moslem communities their minds and outlooks saturated with the Near East.

The attitude of the Moslem peoples of the Near East is thus significant far beyond the geographical borders of the Levant. Influences are here injected into the bloodstream of the Moslem bloc that makes themselves felt wherever the Call to Prayer marks the presence of the Faithful. The Near East is still the area in which the religious and cultural consciousness of world Islam comes to a focus.

The West has not been blind to the influence of the Near East in the Moslem world. During the last war, Germany inveigled the sultan of Turkey (who was also the caliph of Islam) into proclaiming a jihad, or Holy War, hoping thus to marshal the Mohammedan millions against the Allies. The plan eventually failed, partly because it lacked the support of the religious leaders of Mecca, partly because autocratic and reactionary Turkey was not the kind of political leader desired by awakening Moslem communities, partly because Moslems saw the humor in one Christian nation calling for an Islamic jihad against another Christian nation. In India and Egypt there was some pro-Turkish agitation, but nowhere did the caliph's call lead to the active uprisings Germany had hoped.

With the close of the war, the victorious Allies saw to it that no coalition of Moslem peoples emerged as the predominant influence in the Near East. By dividing the lands of the Arab movement between England and France, any hope of reviving a pan-Islamic consciousness was checkmated, and the heart of the Moslem world was reserved for divisive nationalistic and European influences. . . .

That is why the Near East has been the scene of one of the most intense propaganda campaigns of the present war. The Axis knows that the attitude of Near Eastern people, no less than the possession of Near Eastern resources, is of world importance.

Long before Graziani started his desert campaign, Italy and Germany were attacking the Allied position in the Near East with a barrage of cleverly insinuated accusations and suggestion. Schools, consulates, archeological expeditions, military missions—all were in reality part of the propaganda army. Through local newspapers that readily accepted foreign subsidies, nationalistic criticism of English and French colonial policy was kept hot, and clever radio programs carried Goebbels' views of history to the furthest dweller of the desert. . . .

With the outbreak of war [in 1939], propaganda efforts redoubled. The Axis plan followed that of the British during the last war. Its basis was agitation against the ruling power (then Turkey, now England); its instrument was the political ambitions of a disgruntled Arab leader (then Sherif Hussein of Mecca, now the grand mufti of Jerusalem); its fuel was the nationalistic temper of awakening Near Eastern life (then the Arab movement, now the nationalisms of the several countries). These elements were utilized to the full by the power of the radio, now one of the most pervasive influences in the Near East. When it is remembered that Egypt has 70,000 receiving sets, Syria 18,000, Turkey 29,000 and that even the sheikh's tent on the desert may resound with the voices of the world, it is seen that radio has become a powerful instrument of warfare in seeking to capture the heart of the Moslem world. From the powerful short-wave stations at Bari and Berlin, daily newscasts in flawless Arabic were beamed to every part of the Near East. Pro-Axis Arab leaders, forced to flee from Iraq and Syria, formed an "Arab Government in Exile" and used the "Free Arabia" radio station at Athens to exhort the Arab world to "continue to fight against England and you will soon be free from the Anglo-Jewish yoke." Even the tribesman of the Nejd heard the voice of Berlin on the coffee-house radio, and since that voice spoke through a renegade Iraqi with a flair for beautiful and passionate Arabic, he could not but be impressed.

In all this the prize the Axis was angling for was not simply the support of the peoples of the Near East. With dissatisfaction in India (where there are 80,000,000 Moslems), the Japanese invasion of the Dutch East Indies (98 per cent Moslem) divided loyalties in South Africa (where there are considerable Moslem minorities), and Allied occupation of North Africa (solidly Moslem) any trouble stirred up in the Near East might have repercussions across the whole of Asia and Africa.

. . . Vital communications, needed raw materials, influence on a world bloc, have so bound the lands of the Near East to the advancing life of the great civilizations, East and West, that some measure of entanglement in their affairs is inescapable. The question is not "to be interfered with or not to be interfered with"—history and geography have already answered that irrevocably; it is "to be interfered with—by whom and in what spirit?" . . .

Chapter 9

Germany

For the second time within a generation American soldiers have fought Germans upon European soil. For the second time within a generation we laid aside the pursuits of peace and joined with other liberty-loving peoples to put down a German menace.

American fear of German aggression reaches back into the last century. The German Empire's aggressive attitude and ill-concealed latent hostility toward the United States during our war with Spain in 1898 was deeply resented in this country. Recurrent meddling in Latin American countries convinced many people of Germany's intention to violate our cherished Monroe Doctrine at the earliest opportunity. For these and other reasons, Germany became the No. 1 probable enemy in the eyes of President Theodore Roosevelt and his military and diplomatic advisers. Under his leadership American support was extended in various ways to the emerging anti-German coalition in Europe during the early years of this century. Henry Adams, great-grandson of our second President, summed up the growing anxiety in American official circles when he wrote in 1906, that "we have got to fortify the Atlantic System . . . for if Germany breaks down England . . . she becomes the center of a military world, and we are lost."

Probably the vast majority of Americans before the First World War never formulated their ideas about Germany in precisely those terms. But they resented German arrogance and the Kaiser's "saber-rattling" speeches. Almost everywhere one turned within the United States, he encountered smoldering anti-German feeling which was fanned into flame in 1914 by Germany's seemingly unprovoked march through Belgium on the road to Paris.

But moral indignation did not immediately impel Americans to action. Central Europe seemed a faraway place to most people in the United States. The war was brought home to us by the sinking of the *Lusitania* and other German aggressions against neutrals upon the high seas. But even our entry into the struggle in 1917, and the departure of millions of hastily trained American troops to turn the tide of battle on the Western Front, did not dispel permanently the illusion of remoteness and detachment with which Americans had traditionally viewed happenings in Germany and in other European countries. To Americans generally, the war of 1917 was more a crusade to save democracy for the other fellow than a desperate struggle for our own liberties and independence.

Passions ran high while the war lasted, but cooled down quickly after the Armistice. Americans increasingly turned their backs on the Old World in their eagerness for a "return to normalcy" at home. The Senate rejected the League of Nations, and never seriously considered the treaty of guarantee which President Wilson had signed pledging aid to France in case of another German invasion.

Post-mortems on the war raised doubts in American minds, particularly in youthful American minds, whether Germany had really been the chief aggressor after all. The Versailles Treaty was criticized as too severe. It was called a vindictive, Punic Peace. French fears of German military revival and renewed aggression were commonly dismissed in America as unrealistic, if not pathological. Earlier American fears of German ambition and resentment of German bluster were largely forgotten in the palmy days of the Coolidge bull market.

This reaction from the First World War, accentuated by our geographical remoteness from the Old World, prepared Americans badly for the rise of Hitler, for the Nazi Revolution, and for the crescendo of brutality and aggression that followed. For several years there was absolutely no consensus of American opinion as to what the rebirth of German power and the expansionist program of the Third Reich portended for the United States. Millions of Americans clung to the hope that "we could do business with Hitler," and drowned their misgivings in comforting self-assurances that we would be safe in any case behind our wide oceanic moat.

Events themselves abruptly ended this faith in American invulnerability. The fall of France, the aerial assault on England, the drive on Suez, the invasion of Russia, the growth of Nazi fifth-columns in Latin America and even inside the United States, the conclusion of the anti-American Berlin-Tokyo alliance, and other events shattered the refuge of neutrality and passive defense into which so many Americans had retreated during the 1930's. Confronted with rapidly growing perils on both our eastern and our western horizons, American diplomatic influence, material resources, and manpower were progressively thrown into the struggle overseas, until the Japanese attack on Pearl Harbor swept away the pretense of neutrality altogether.

In the light of these events, it is scarcely necessary to labor the point of our obvious and vital concern with the terms of peace with Germany and with that country's prospects for recovery and capacity for future mischief. The Germans have tried twice to break through into our oceanic realm and into the vast Heartland of Eurasia. Many observers are convinced that they will try still a third time if given the slightest opportunity to do so. Others believe that Germany—the most populous, most centrally located, and most highly skilled and industrialized European country west of the Soviet Union—must play a constructive role if Europe is to be rescued from its misery and chaos.

What is the course of wisdom at this fateful crossroads of history? Later on (Chapter 17) we shall present some specific proposals for dealing with Germany in the future. We need first, however, to turn the spotlight on this extraordinary nation which has contributed so much both to the art and culture and to the misery of mankind. We need to learn all we can of this people, their discipline and organization, their genius for science and technology, their national aims and patterns of behavior, their past successes and failures, their resources and equipment, their presumptive capacity for further mischief or, conversely, the possibility of their playing a constructive and law-abiding role in a new world order.

THE GERMAN REICH

By Derwent Whittlesey
and J. K. Wright

From chap. 3 of *Geographical Foundations of National Power*. Army Service Forces Manual M-103-1, Government Printing Office, 1944. Dr. Whittlesey is professor of geography at Harvard University. Dr. Wright is director of the American Geographical Society.

In ancient and medieval times Germanic peoples overran large parts of Europe. Having invaded the ancient Roman Empire, they settled down in various parts of the conquered lands and were eventually absorbed by the native populace. Later conquests led in the ninth century to the creation of the Holy Roman Empire of the German Nation [the First Reich]. This loose congeries of petty German states finally expired in the time of Napoleon (1806) because of internal weaknesses. Voltaire said it was "neither holy, nor Roman, nor an Empire," and despite its name it was certainly not a national state in the modern sense.

Except for Italy, Germany was the last of the Great Powers to achieve national unity. During the centuries from the close of the Middle Ages down to 1870, while Great Britain, France, and Russia were strong and united, Germany remained subdivided among petty states, and its people as a whole felt little national consciousness. In political loyalty they were Prussians or Bavarians or Saxons, and Germans only in speech and culture.

Unification was a slow process, accomplished under the leadership of Prussia, which from about 1740 on gradually extended its own territories to include the whole of northern Germany. In 1871 Bismarck's statesmanship brought South Germany also into a new state, over which the King of Prussia was crowned as Emperor Wilhelm I. Thus was created the second German Empire, a firmly knit national federation under Prussian domination. After the defeat of its armies on the Western Front and the abdication of the Kaiser [Emperor] in 1918, the second Empire was succeeded by a republic, which lasted until 1933, but under both the republic and the Nazi regime which replaced it in that year, the process of national integration continued apace. The Nazis called the reorganized Germany which they set up the Third Reich (i.e. the Third Empire). . . .

GERMANY'S CENTRAL POSITION

By the Editors

GERMANY occupies the heart of Europe. The shortest routes between eastern and western Europe lie in most instances across lands inhabited by people of Germanic speech and culture. Germany in 1939 had a common land frontier with eleven countries, five more than any other wholly European state (see Fig. 10, p. 141, above).

A country so situated is the natural economic focus for a large surrounding region. This point was well stated by the late Frank H. Simonds. Discussing the conflicting pulls of France and Germany on the countries of eastern and southeastern Europe during the 1920's he observed that "politically, the interests of all the peoples of the Little Entente are with Paris, but economically all are unmistakably, and even almost irresistibly, drawn into the orbits of Berlin and Vienna. It is the German and Austrian markets in which Yugoslavia and Rumania would naturally sell their agricultural products, and from them that they would draw their industrial supplies and factory-made goods. In this region France sells little and buys less. She can lend her allies money, but she cannot absorb their products. And loans are a transitory episode; markets, a continuing necessity" (*Can Europe Keep the Peace?* Copyright 1931 by F. H. Simonds. Harper & Brothers, New York; reproduced by permission).

Others have expressed the same thought in different ways. J. F. Bogardus, for example, observes that Germany's central position "is a decided advantage from an economic viewpoint. Such bordering nations as France, Switzerland, Belgium, Denmark, and the Netherlands are among the most densely populated and most productive in Europe. Consequently they constitute a tremendous market for German goods. . . . The neighboring states also produce surpluses which are in great demand within Germany itself. Thus there has arisen the basis for a sufficiently great trade to make Germany the most important commercial nation on the continent.

"Its commercial advantages have been increased because of its location between eastern and western Europe. Germany has consequently been a transit zone through which the streams of commerce have had to flow in passing between those two areas. This trade has increased its contacts with the east and west, and has made Germany an important transshipment center." (*Europe, a Geographical Survey*. Copyright 1934 by Harper & Brothers, New York; reproduced by permission.)

German statecraft has systematically exploited for political and military purposes the economic needs of the border countries. Geography plus industrialization has made Germany the natural market for food and raw materials, supplier of manufactures, coal, and fertilizers, entrepôt and broker for a large surrounding region. If Germany should recover its prewar industrial and commercial dominance in central and western Europe, it may be difficult in the future as in the past to prevent that economic primacy from giving Germany a corresponding political leadership in Europe.

The strategical qualities of Germany's central position have been most striking in time of war. It is axiomatic that such a position has military advantages. Interior lines are generally shorter in length. Given an efficient transportation system shorter hauls mean less elapsed time between the fighting fronts and the arsenals, supply depots, troop centers, and other points in the rear.

As a rule men and matériel can be concentrated for offensive purposes at any selected point on the outer rim of the central position more rapidly than opposing forces can be shifted outside the rim to parry them. Conversely, possession of interior lines generally facilitates the transfer of forces from one front to another to meet attacks on the outer ramparts. Each military unit, in short, represents more effective power when operating along interior lines from a central position.

The central position, however, has certain drawbacks. It is more susceptible to blockade, especially when, as in the case of Germany, the country has no unimpeded outlets to the oceans. Unless the centrally located belligerent can keep open a supply corridor to the outside world or is self-sufficient in foodstuffs and raw materials, it will inexorably feel and may finally succumb to blockade.

The central position can also be attacked simultaneously on two or more fronts. The necessity of fighting on several fronts, while subjected to a strangling blockade, brought about the defeat of Germany in the First World War. The recurrence of these conditions, together with a new strategic factor, broke the back of German resistance in the Second World War.

The new factor is air power. Development of the heavy bomber largely cancelled out, in this later struggle, the advantages which Germany previously derived from its central position. Mines, factories, supply dumps, railroads, canals, and other vital installations deep inside German frontiers and far beyond range of attack in previous wars, were subjected to shattering aerial bombardment from bases along the rim of Fortress Germania as the Nazis called their beleaguered country in the later stages of the war.

Since air power is still in process of rapid development, it is too early to venture positive judgments. Evidence to date, however, suggests strongly that heavy and sustained aerial attacks—certainly possible with piloted planes, perhaps possible in the future with robot weapons as well—can shake morale, disrupt production, slow or paralyze troop movement, and otherwise prevent the centrally located belligerent from exploiting fully the advantage of interior lines.

GERMANY'S PREWAR FRONTIERS

By Derwent Whittlesey and J. K. Wright

From chap. 3 of *Geographical Foundations of National Power*. Army Service Forces Manual M-103-1, Government Printing Office, 1944.

[In reading the following selection, it should be kept constantly in mind that the frontiers described are those existing before the Second World War.]

Sea Frontiers. Germany has a somewhat restricted coastline. Its seacoasts make a little less than a third of the total length of the boundary of Germany proper. . . . The salt-water boundaries are divided between the Baltic and North Seas. Nearly four-fifths faces the Baltic, an enclosed sea with only one outlet navigable by ocean vessels—the narrow strait between Denmark and Sweden. German Baltic ports would therefore be penned in if an enemy were to seize the strait. To avoid this military danger, Germany has built the deep-water Kiel Canal on German territory across the base of the Danish peninsula.

The one-fifth of the German coastline which faces the North Sea is by all odds Germany's most valuable contact with the world ocean. . . . The coastline is low, and Germany's largest ports have grown up on the estuaries of the two main rivers, Elbe and Weser, which reach the North Sea in German territory. Other ports on the German section of the Rhine make contact with the sea through the Netherlands.

Land Frontiers. Germany has land boundaries on all four sides, and the length of them is a potential source of military weakness.

In the north, the boundary with Denmark crosses the plains near the base of the Danish peninsula. In 1864 it was pushed northward to give Prussia control of the best route for a canal connecting the Baltic with the North Sea; later, after the First World War, it was moved a little to the south. The Kiel Canal is the critical feature of this zone. . . .

There are three main avenues of advance from Germany into France, these being, in order from south to north, the Belfort Gap, the Lorraine Gate, and the Belgian Plain. . . . [The invasion routes between Germany and France have been previously described. See p. 218 above, and Fig. 14, p. 214, above.]

Viewed in the large, Germany is protected from invasion from the south . . . by what may be regarded as a single major barrier, the Alps and their lower eastern continuation, the Carpathians, with a secondary line of barriers to the north on the Czechoslovakian frontier. The only large breach in the major defensive wall is the gap in which Vienna stands. The political boundary, however, follows the Alps-Carpathian barrier only for a short distance in the eastern Alps. At the western end of the southern frontier region neutral Switzerland intervenes between South Germany and the Alps. North of the middle part of the major barrier, on both sides of the Vienna Gap, Czechoslovakia forms a broad, blunt projection extending into Germany to within 110 miles of Berlin. Farther east, Poland separates the Carpathians from eastern Germany. . . .

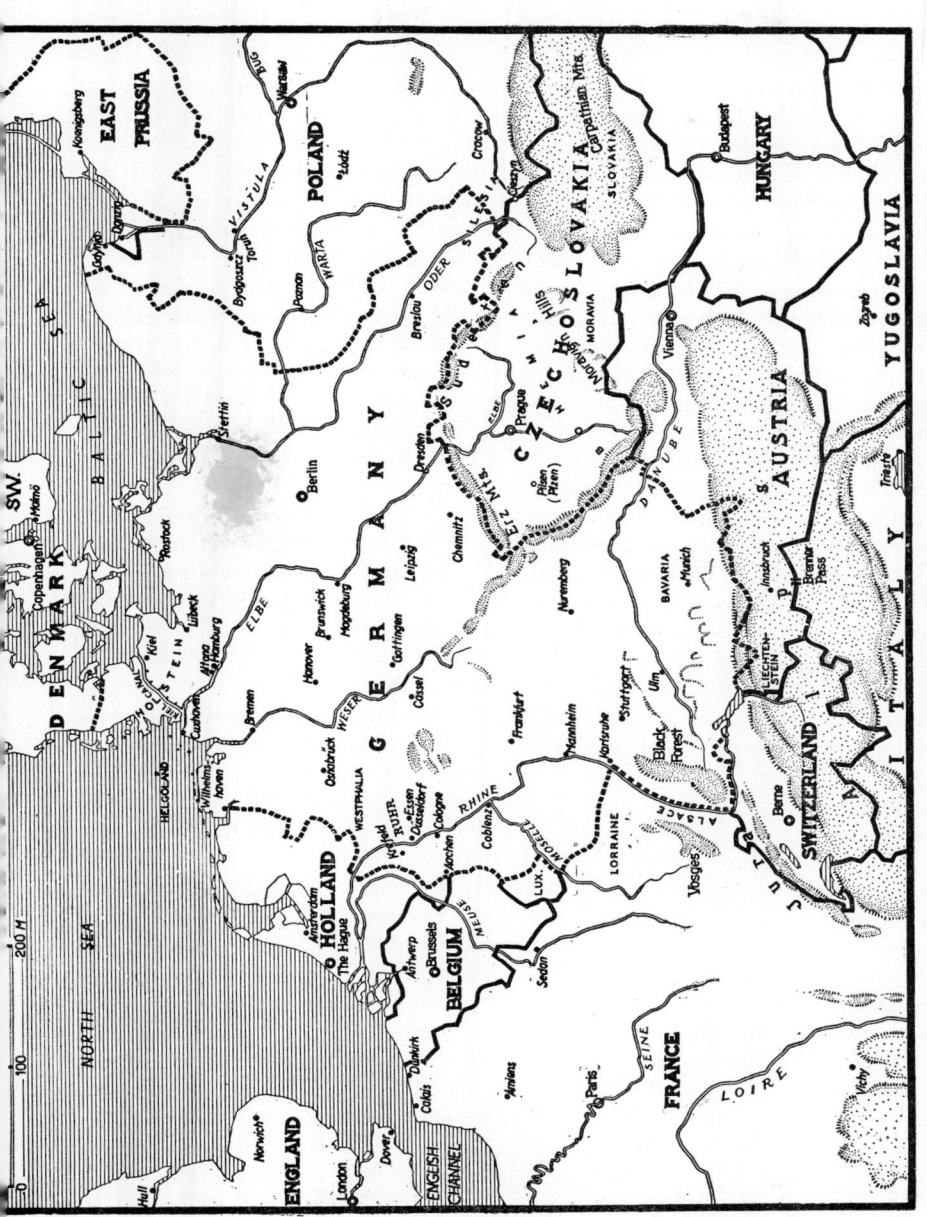

FIG. 20. Germany's Pre-War Frontiers.

From E. A. Mowrer and M. Rajchman, *Global War, An Atlas of World Strategy*. Copyright 1942 by William Morrow & Co., New York; reproduced by permission.

Bohemia and Moravia form the geographical as well as the political and economic 'head" of Czechoslovakia, around which two arms of the German state, Austria and Silesia, seem to clutch at the "neck" of that unfortunate country. Three ranges of low mountains (the Bohemian Forest on the southwest, the Ore [Erz] mountains on the north, and the Sudetens on the northeast), which constitute the secondary line of barriers to which we have referred, provide the "head" with a protective "skull," although a somewhat soft one because conversion of many slopes from forest to farmland has deprived these ranges of much of their barrier character. The "neck" itself is unprotected by nature. From the Danube near Vienna a lowland passageway extends completely across it and on through a narrower gap, known as the Moravian Gate, between the Sudeten Mountains and the Carpathians. This passageway is the main link between eastern Germany and Austria. With the Danube Valley above Vienna it also provides a natural highway connecting southern Germany ... with Poland (and Russia beyond). Furthermore, armies approaching Germany from the Middle Danube Basin, having forced the breach in the main mountain barrier at Vienna, would have two alternative natural avenues of advance: either eastward up the Danube into southern Germany or northeastward through the "neck" of Czechoslovakia into upper Silesia and eastern Germany. No wonder the Vienna Gap and Moravian Gate rank with the Lorraine Gate and the Belgian Plain among the most highly critical spots in the strategic geography of Europe. In the Moravian Gate, Napoleon fought and won a great victory over the Russians at Austerlitz in 1805.

Germany's eastern frontier (prewar) lies wide open to invasion. From Upper Silesia to the Baltic Sea the political boundary between Germany and Poland wends an apparently irresponsible course across the North European Plain....

Critical Areas from the Political Point of View. The frequent changes in the land boundaries of the German state illustrate most of the issues that arise from the necessity of superimposing a political line on a zone of transition between different nationalities or between economic regions. No other country in Europe has so many unstable frontier areas. Movements of autonomy or independence arise on both sides of the political border, sometimes in favor of Germany, sometimes in favor of Germany's neighbors.

The location of Germany's most valuable coal fields close to the frontier is a danger, just as is the case for France with its coal and iron ore. Germany's risk [has been] mitigated [most of the time] by a powerful military establishment which antedates the Industrial Revolution. At the same time the marginal location of the coal attracts to it a large part of the iron of western and central continental Europe and thus drains Germany's neighbors for Germany's benefit.

On the west, along the Rhine, Alsace, and Lorraine ... a problem arises based on linguistic grounds, on historical claims, and on natural resources, particularly iron ore. The Netherlands and Belgium control the mouths of the Rhine, natural outlet of Germany's largest industrial region. Across Belgium's coastal plain and through its Sambre Valley lie the two easiest routes to France. From the Belgian and adjacent French coast is the most direct approach to England.

On the south, the Alpine zone is a transit land between northern and Mediterranean Europe, regions with sharply contrasting climates and reciprocal economy. The area of German speech has long since overflowed into all reaches of this zone. Here Austria grew to power as the center of a great empire of non-Germanic peoples and nations, comprising at its height a large part of southeastern Europe. As rulers of this empire, the Austrians developed a proud national spirit of their own, a spirit that resented the rise of Prussia and contested attempts at mastery over southern Germany proper until the question was settled by the swift defeat of Austria by Prussia in 1866. As the center of the empire, Vienna became a great metropolis, partly because it was the political capital and partly because of its advantageous position at the crossing of routes of trade. The World War of 1914-1918 caused the breakup of the Austro-Hungarian Empire, and thus paved the way for Austria's subordination to Berlin when the Nazis marched into Vienna in 1938. The line of national cleavage, however, still remains across the territory of the German state.

Bohemia and Moravia in Czechoslovakia are not only a distinct physical and economic unit, but also a homeland of Slavic culture, language, and history. The Bohemian upland basin is almost surrounded by mountains, and from the standpoint of Germany is a readily fortified wedge thrust halfway across the block of German speech. Germany considers domination of Bohemia-Moravia, with the Moravian Gate, vital to her control of Middle Europe. A further complication here is that the entire mountain rim, or "skull," of Czechoslovakia is inhabited on both sides of the political boundary by a German-speaking population (the Sudeten Germans) and that two wedges of German settlement have been thrust into the "neck" of Czechoslovakia from neighboring Austria and Silesia. It must be remembered, however, that prior to 1938, the Sudeten Germans had never lived under the German flag.

On the east ... the German boundary ... has fluctuated more frequently and over a wider zone than elsewhere. At its southern end, from 1748 until 1919 the whole Upper Silesian coal field and associated industrial towns were comprised within Prussia. The linguistic frontier between Polish and German speech runs through this industrial region, and after the First World War the political boundary was established approximately along the linguistic line, dividing the region between the two nations, somewhat as if an international boundary were laid through the suburbs of Pittsburgh. The Polish part contained the only important coal deposits and the only industrial area of any magnitude in the revived Poland; without them Poland can be only an agricultural nation.

Hardly less vital to Poland's economic prosperity and power is the access to the sea that came with the restoration in 1919 of the Polish Corridor between East Prussia and the rest of Germany, a narrow strip of land that had belonged to Poland until 1772. East Prussia, except for a broad southern strip where the Poles predominate, has been solidly German for centuries, and is connected with the rest of Germany by a bridge of German settlement across the Corridor. Between Upper Silesia and the Corridor lies Posen, a fertile farmland predominantly of Polish speech and nationality. Here the Polish-language border approaches within 150 miles of Berlin. Posen was a part of Prussia from 1793 to 1919.

Stretching eastward from Upper Silesia along the most fertile part of the plain at the foot of the Carpathians is the productive farming country of Galicia. Although inhabited almost entirely by Poles, it was part of the Austrian monarchy for nearly two centuries. With German annexation of Austria, Germany inherited Austrian claims to Galicia.

Throughout this whole eastern frontier region Germans and Austrians settled in many of the Polish cities during the period when the region was partitioned between Germany and Austria. The desire to take advantage of their presence, resentment over the isolation of East Prussia, and a studiously cultivated contempt of the Poles and the large Jewish population in Poland as "inferior races," all inspired the Nazis in their attempt . . . to wipe out Polish national existence.

GERMAN RESOURCES AND INDUSTRIES

By R. H. Whitbeck and V. C. Finch

From chapter 25 of *Economic Geography*, by R. H. Whitbeck and V. C. Finch. Revised edition, copyright 1941 by R. H. Whitbeck and V. C. Finch. McGraw-Hill Book Company, New York; reproduced by permission. The late Dr. Whitbeck was professor of geography at the University of Wisconsin. Dr. Finch holds a similar position at the same university.

The increase in manufacturing, commerce, and national prestige achieved by the German Empire in its forty-seven years of existence was phenomenal. The causes and conditions that promoted this achievement lay partly in the people and partly in the situation and resources of their country. . . .

The German lands, i.e. those in which people of German language predominate, . . . are physically divisible into two strongly contrasting parts. These are (1) the North German Plain and (2) the southern highlands, basins, and valleys.

The northern plain of Germany is part of the great North European Plain. It is a region of low relief covered by glacial deposits and morainic ridges. In the west especially, near the Netherlands border, it includes sandy heath lands and coastal marshes and peat bogs. In the central and eastern parts, extending into East Prussia and Poland, are other morainic ridges also interspersed with numerous glacial lakes and swamps. It is a surface comparable with that of central Minnesota, parts of Wisconsin, or southern Michigan. . . . In general, the North German Plain is one of undulating surface and soils of moderate to low fertility interspersed with areas of poor drainage. It is narrow in the west but broadens eastward toward Russia.

The southern region of highlands, basins, and valleys is one of extreme variety. It includes such ancient hills as those bordering the Rhine Gorge, the Black Forest, the Harz Mountains, and the mountainous rim of Bohemia. These are mainly dissected plateaus and short or broken ranges, some of them the eroded remnants of highlands once greater in both height and area. Included among them are basins and valleys. Some are of low elevation, such as the plains bordering the lower and upper Rhine. Others are higher and are traversed by bold ridges. Such are the basins of Thuringia, Bavaria and Bohemia, the uplands of Saxony, and the Alpine foreland. In general, the elevations increase southward in this region, ending in the high Alps of Austria. The basins include many districts of fertile soil and great agricultural productivity, but even the hill regions are cultivated on their gentler slopes, and the less tillable areas are devoted to forests. Within these highlands are most of the famous scenic places of Germany which, under normal conditions, are themselves a great resource, attracting thousands of foreign visitors and yielding a large revenue to the country.

The climate of western Germany has a strong marine influence; the winters are relatively mild; and the coast is free from ice. Eastward the average annual precipitation decreases from more than 30 to less than 25 inches, but it is everywhere sufficient for agriculture. The winters of eastern Germany are severe, and the use of the Baltic seaports is hampered by ice. The summer temperatures are warm but not warm enough to mature maize. Altogether it may be said that the climate of eastern Germany and Poland is somewhat like that of the northern Great Lakes district of the United States.

Until about 1890 Germany was more an agricultural than an industrial nation, but after that time industrialization progressed rapidly. At present less than a third of the population lives in rural districts and in villages of less than 2,000 inhabitants; more than two-thirds live in larger towns and cities. There are about 60 cities of more than 100,000 population each in Germany proper, and at least a dozen more in Austria, Bohemia, and the German section of Poland. In spite of a high degree of urbanization, Germany is more nearly self-sufficing in farm produce than Britain. This cannot be attributed to the natural fertility of the German soil and its climatic versatility but rather to the scientific methods of agriculture and the comparatively low standard of living that the German people as a whole have been willing to accept as a means of economic defense.

It has been stated already that much of the land is of poor agricultural quality. Some very sandy lands and marshes in the northern plain and some steep and thin-soiled slopes in the south are farmed with difficulty or are incapable of tillage. Yet a surprising proportion of the total area in Germany proper is productive. About 40 per cent is in tilled crops and orchards; 17 per cent is in meadows and pastures; and more than a quarter of the total area is in carefully tended forests. There is no uniformity in the system or size of land holdings for there are many large landed estates, especially in the eastern districts, and also a large number of small and medium-sized holdings (under 25 acres). As a rule the smaller farms are owned by the farmers who work them, but only a part of them live on their land. As is true in France and many other sections of Europe, it is common for the farmers to live in rural villages, from which they go out to till their near-by fields. The owners of the landed estates, especially in eastern Prussia, constitute a form of aristocracy who have long been a power in German political and military affairs, but their land also is worked by village peasants. The same is true in Poland.

Hay and root crops for the feeding of livestock occupy more land than any other single use, for Germany has a large and varied animal industry to be supported. Of the cereal crops, rye and oats are much more extensively grown than wheat and barley. Among other crops potatoes and sugar beets hold the leading places. . . .

Germany reduced forestry to a science. More than one-fourth of the land in Germany proper and nearly half that of Austria is too hilly or mountainous or has soil too poor to be profitably used for agriculture. Such lands are set apart and studied to ascertain what use can best be made of them; if they can support forests of one kind or another, they are devoted to that use. Trained foresters manage these forests and determine what species of trees are best suited to the conditions, how thick the stand of timber should be, and what trees are ready for cutting. As fast as the mature trees are removed, young trees are allowed to grow up in their places, or others are set out from nurseries. So carefully are the forest resources husbanded that Germany is able to produce a large part, but not all, of her requirements of firewood, lumber, timber, paper pulp, and other wood products. Moreover, the forests protect the steeper slopes from soil wash and regulate the runoff. Largely under the influence of German methods, many other countries, including the United States, are introducing scientific forestry.

Germany has very large coal resources. Its most productive field and the one containing the best coking coal is in the Ruhr Valley of Westphalia in western Prussia, and 80 per cent of the good bituminous coal of the country is mined there and in the near-by Saar Basin. Germany's greatest manufacturing region is situated on both sides of the Rhine in and adjacent to these coal fields. The next most important field is in Upper Silesia in the extreme southeast of Germany. Since 1918 and until recently the Silesian deposits have been so partitioned that part of them were in Germany, part in Czechoslovakia, and the larger part in Poland. They were the basis of the Polish industrial development near Cracow. Most of this coal is of lower grade than that of Westphalia. Other and smaller deposits of bituminous coal are located in the central provinces, especially in Saxony. Germany's total coal production of more than 300 million tons a year is somewhat larger than that of Great Britain and nearly equal to the bituminous coal output of the United States in recent years. However, more than half the tonnage of coal mined in Germany has been lignite, which has little more than two-thirds the heating value of good bituminous coal and is quite unsuited to some industrial uses. The principal lignite fields are in the central region. The possession of great coal deposits by Germany was one of the most fundamental factors in the expansion of its manufacturing and commerce, but coal probably did not play so large a part in German industrial and commercial development as in that of Great Britain.

Germany has only a small domestic petroleum supply. The reported output of 3 or 4 million barrels per year in recent years is much more than formerly, probably as a measure of preparation for war, yet it equals little more than 10 per cent of the recent imports of foreign petroleum into Germany. Even with the additional supply available through the occupation of Poland, domestic production can provide only a small part of the German petroleum requirement, especially in time of war.

The waterpowers available in Germany and its recent territorial additions are a valuable part of the total energy resources of the country. A moderate and well-distributed rainfall and numerous hill and mountain districts with glacial features and forested slopes give rise to extensive waterpowers and numerous power sites. These have been developed with characteristic German thoroughness, supported by the need to utilize all their natural resources. Moreover, most of the power sites are located within easy hydroelectric-transmission distance from urban and industrial markets for light and power. The quantity of power now developed in Germany, Austria, and Czechoslovakia is more than one-fourth that in use in the United States and about three-fourths that in France. In Germany proper the power possibilities are most highly developed, and the amount

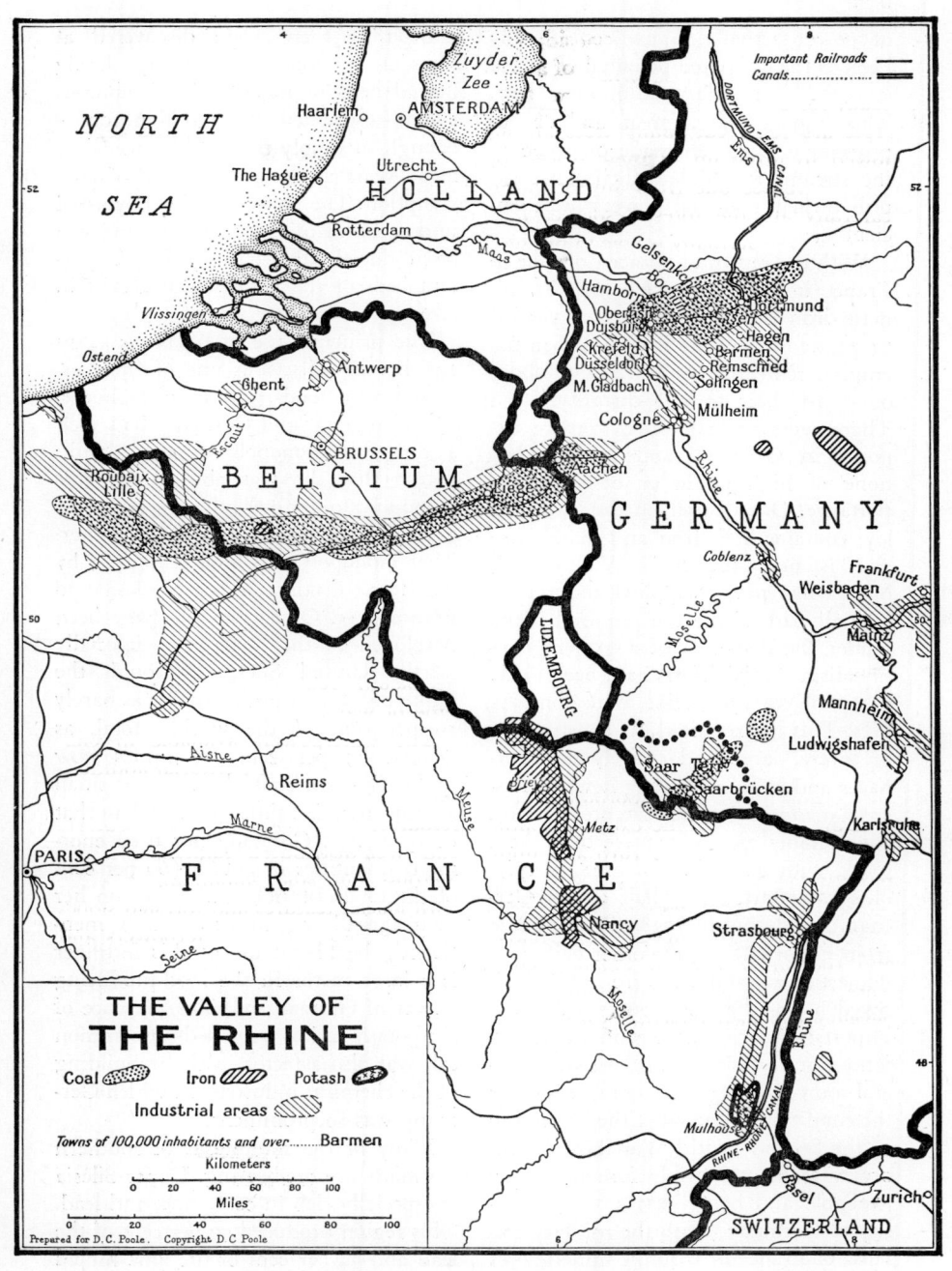

FIG. 21. The Rhine Valley: Raw Materials and Industrial Areas.
Copyright 1936 by DeWitt C. Poole; reproduced by permission.

of power actually in use considerably exceeds the estimated potential of all the streams at ordinary minimum flow. This implies that a great deal of improvement has been made on some of the streams to regulate their flow and utilize their potential powers most efficiently.

With the return of Alsace-Lorraine to France in 1918, Germany lost the minette iron deposits which had yielded 75 per cent of all the iron mined in the empire, reducing her reserves to about one-third their former quantity. . . . There were several other iron-ore deposits in Germany and Austria, but none of high grade or of large importance. One district, in the Sieg Valley, contains both iron and manganese and is near the Ruhr Valley coal, but it has never supplied more than a small part of the ore required there. Under the demands of a growing nationalism special efforts have been made in recent years to utilize more domestic ores. This has required the construction of several large and entirely new furnaces and steel mills using new processes of manufacture, but the products are considerably more expensive than those made with good foreign ores. In spite of great effort, about half of the German iron output in 1938 still was made from imported ores, the other half from domestic ores and scrap iron reworked. Sweden was the chief source of the ore imports; France was second in importance but declining; and there were several sources of minor importance. Under the conditions imposed at the beginning of the Second World War the Swedish ore was about the only foreign supply available and hence was a vital necessity to Germany. With the military collapse of France in 1940 the minette ores again became freely available for German use, and Belgian and French coal and steel-making facilities as well.

In 1843 there were discovered at Stassfurt in central Germany deeply buried beds of potash salt of fabulous extent—estimated at 20 billion tons—enough to supply the world's needs for 2,000 years at the present rate of consumption. The potash is mined by usual underground mining methods and can be produced rather cheaply. Less important beds of the same salt also exist in Alsace.

The principal use of potash is as an enricher of soils; it is one of three essential plant foods (potash, phosphorus, and nitrogen), and Germany had such a complete monopoly of the world's potash that she was able to use this monopoly to compel other countries to grant certain trade concessions to her. That monopoly was broken in 1918 by the loss of the Alsace deposits to France. . . . Other deposits have been developed in the meantime, especially in the United States. Although the United States output in 1938 was barely 10 per cent of the world's total, as against 75 per cent for mines now under German control, even that small amount was five times greater than that of 1932. . . . Germany has used enormous quantities of potash (60 per cent of the total output) in building up her own agriculture, and, as already mentioned, the liberal use of this fertilizer is a large factor in the food-producing power of German soil. The presence of the potash and of large beds of common salt was also a factor in the upbuilding of the chemical industries in which Germany was so prominent.

Many of the mountains of southern Germany are ore-bearing. Upper Silesia is especially rich in coal, zinc, and lead. This region produced 57 per cent of the lead and 72 per cent of the zinc mined in Germany before 1914, but since then the industry has been largely in Polish hands. Only in 1939 was it returned to

German control as a result of the conquest of Poland. Moderate quantities of graphite, pyrite, copper, and silver are mined—not enough, however, for the country's needs. As a by-product of iron-ore smelting by the Thomas process, large quantities of phosphate (for fertilizer) are produced.

The rise of manufacturing in Germany during the generation preceding the First World War was very rapid, and in 1914 that country ranked at least third and possibly second among the manufacturing nations of the world. For such an industrial expansion many conditions in Germany were highly favorable:

1. The geographical location of the empire gave it easy access to the markets of practically every European country.

2. It had ample supplies of coal, well distributed in various parts of the country.

3. It had iron, zinc, copper, lead, potash, salt, pottery clays, and a number of lesser minerals.

4. It produced a considerable variety of other raw materials including wood, sugar beets, hides, coal-tar products, and other chemical materials.

5. The government actively interested itself in everything that aided the upbuilding of industry—enacted a protective tariff, assisted the merchant marine, developed waterways, gave favorable rates on the state-owned railroads, actively promoted technical education, and encouraged scientific research.

Germany had for many years a place of world leadership in the varied field of chemical industries. This was based upon two main factors: 1. Its mineral wealth, especially coal, salt, and potash. 2. The scientific interests and training of its people, especially in the field of chemistry.

. . . The scientific leanings of the Germans were reflected in the remarkable development of their chemical industries. In the manufacture of aniline dyes, for example, Germany formerly had almost a monopoly—manufacturing about three times the quantity made by all the rest of the world. These dyes are made from coal tar obtained as a by-product of coke manufacture, and at the outbreak of the war of 1914-1918 Germany was in almost complete control of the secret formulas. But during the war other countries developed their dye industries. In scores of other phases of the chemical industries, including tanning, brewing, distilling, and the manufacture of drugs, medicines, explosives, glass, fertilizers, soaps, plastics, rayon, and other artificial fibers Germany was a leader. In these industries conditions have changed greatly in a quarter of a century. In recent years the German chemical industries have faced strong competition from Britain, Russia, France, and other European countries, also from Japan, and especially the United States which now has the largest and most varied chemical industries in the world.

With her basic resource of coal Germany [before the war] produced more raw iron than any other country except the United States—more than Russia and, in recent years, as much as France and Britain together. This serves as raw material for a variety of metal industries. The industries include shipbuilding; arms manufacture; and the making of electrical and other machinery, vehicles, implements, and precision instruments for many uses. In part these manufactures require other metals, such as copper, zinc, and lead, of which the domestic supply has been insufficient. The recovery of the lead and zinc mines of Upper Silesia from Poland will increase the supply of those metals, but imports will still be necessary.

The industrial region of Westphalia includes the principal center for the manufacture of iron and steelwares of all kinds, although many of the lighter wares are produced in other parts of the country also. The great arms and heavy steel industries of Essen have long been famous. . . .

It has already been pointed out that textiles and steel products are the leading articles of manufacture in practically all industrial nations. This is because they serve fundamental and widespread human wants. Germany, like the other manufacturing nations of Europe, produces only a minor part of the raw materials for its textile mills. Cotton is imported, about half of it from the United States, and enters through the port of Bremen. Silk comes from the Orient, wool from Argentina and Australia, flax from Russia, and coarse fibers from many lands. The importance of textile manufactures is seen in the fact that cotton, silk, rayon, and woolen fabrics and the manufacture of clothing from them normally employ more workers than any other German industry, even including the metalworking industries or the preparation of food products. . . .

Germany has a highly developed and integrated system of communications. It includes nearly 34,000 miles of railway, largely owned and operated by the government, more than 200,000 miles of highways, some of which are paved through-roads of the most modern type, and nearly 5,000 miles of inland waterways. The latter are comprised of about 1,000 miles of canals and nearly 4,000 miles of improved river routes. They are much more used than are the waterways in most other countries.

The average density of the railway pattern is high. Each mile of track must serve only 5.3 square miles of area. This is more than twice the average density in the whole United States and nearly as high as that in the Great Lakes-New England industrial regions. Much of the transport system has been designed with an eye to its military as well as its commercial utility. The rail network is well distributed over the country, but its focus is Berlin. From this center the lines of transportation radiate to all sections of the country, as do those of France from Paris.

Because the German waterways are so much more used than those of other countries, they may be described here in greater detail. First, it may be noted that the arrangement of the rivers is most fortunate. Flowing from the highlands of the south, the five great rivers trend not north but generally northwest, following the slope of the plain. Thus the Rhine, Weser, and Elbe all empty into the North Sea, and only the Oder and the Vistula flow into the ice-hampered Baltic. The ample precipitation of the whole of central Europe gives these major streams considerable volume, making them commercially usable. Cutting the central part of the German plain transversely to the trend of the major streams are several large stream channels now occupied only by small tributary streams. These are the graded courses, or spillways, of the large streams that carried the great volume of drainage from the continental glaciers westward along the ice fronts during the period of glaciation. Being already graded they are easily canalized and thus serve to link together the main rivers. By this means traffic originating far inland on the Vistula can be carried westward to the Elbe or the Weser and thus to the North Sea ports.

The Rhine is the most important commercial river of Europe. It rises in Switzerland and enters the sea through the Netherlands and has been under the control of an international commission. The Rhine is not quite so long (800 miles) as the Ohio River but carries vastly more commerce than the whole Mississippi system. It has been dredged and straightened and otherwise improved, and the many cities on its banks have built docks equipped with modern devices for loading and unloading cargoes. It is not a deep river, ranging between 6½ feet in the upper stretches to 10 feet in the lower. ... The Rhine has some 20 important cities on the river or directly tributary to it. Great coal and iron mines are near by, and a large tonnage of heavy low-grade freight is available.

The Elbe and the Oder are the other German rivers of most usefulness. Near the mouth of the Elbe is the great port of Hamburg, whose peacetime river traffic, like that of Rotterdam at the mouth of the Rhine, was greater than its rail traffic. The river rises in Bohemia and is navigable throughout its entire course across Germany; by means of this river Bohemia is made tributary to the North Sea rather than to the Mediterranean. The Oder is less used than the Elbe, and the Vistula, mainly in Poland, still less; yet all are used more than similar rivers in the United States.

Canals connect the German rivers not only with one another but with rivers in the Netherlands, Belgium, France, and other countries. By means of canals now under construction [in 1940] the Rhine is to be connected with the Danube and the Vistula with the Dnieper in Russia. There will then be two water routes from western Germany to the Black Sea. Certain ones of these canals are used a great deal, especially for the shipping of coal, iron ore, and building materials. ...

The Kiel Canal connects the North and Baltic Seas across the narrow neck of land south of Denmark. The original canal, completed in 1895, had a depth of 29½ feet and proved to be too shallow. Just before the First World War the depth was increased to 36 feet, and the canal was otherwise enlarged to accommodate the largest battleships and liners. ...

POPULATION AND POWER IN GERMANY

By the Editors

At the close of the Napoleonic Wars (1815), about 25 million people lived upon the lands later incorporated into the German Empire. At that date and until after mid-century, the population of France exceeded that of the disunited German states. But the Germanic peoples were increasing rapidly, more rapidly than France or any other nation in central and western Europe. The German Empire at its birth in 1871 contained 41 million people, a total considerably greater than that of France. By 1910 the population of Germany had increased to 64 millions, and four years later, at the outbreak of the First World War, it was estimated to be nearly 69 millions. This total made Germany the most populous European state except Russia.

The political importance of this fact was enhanced by the concurrent growth of German industry and by the systematic integration of men and machines into a highly organized military establishment. As a result of these and other related developments, the military power of Germany rose rapidly during the period 1871-1914, more rapidly than that of any other European state. Germany in 1914 was easily the strongest military power in Europe.

In some degree at least, the growth of German manpower was attributable not only to natural increase but also to declining emigration brought about deliberately by governmental policy.

In 1913, Dr. Karl Helfferich, director of the Deutsche Bank, observed that "emigration, which in the 'eighties of the last century still reached enormous proportions, has dropped almost to insignificance. This development cannot be measured in its full extent till we compare the number of emigrants with the excess of births. In the decade 1881-1890 there were 1,342,000 German emigrants, as against a total birth-excess of 5,500,000; in the following decade there were still 528,000 emigrants to 7,300,000 net births; but in the decade 1901-1910, when the birth-excess rose to 8,670,000, the number of emigrants sank to 220,000. In the year 1912 the number of emigrants was only 18,500. If, while considering emigration from Germany, we also take into account immigration into Germany, a still brighter color is given to the picture. Whereas Germany always had formerly a more or less considerable excess of emigration over immigration, there has been an excess of immigration since the middle of the 'nineties. After having been an emigrant land, Germany is becoming an immigrant land.

"All this proves," Helfferich concluded, "that economic opportunities have grown more rapidly in Germany during recent decades than the population. The demand for labor, the opportunity for remunerative employment has expanded even faster than the population has grown" (*Germany's Economic Progress, 1888-1913*. 1913. Georg Stilke, Berlin. The Germanistic Society of America).

According to one view, this shrinkage of emigration from Germany, accompanied by rising demand for labor inside Germany, was the result of policies deliberately introduced for the specific purpose of increasing German military power.

"From 1878," writes Sir Halford Mackinder, "Germany began to build up her manpower by stimulating employment at home. One of her methods was the scientific tariff, a sieve through which imports were 'screened,' so that they should contain a minimum of labor and especially skilled labor. But every other means was resorted to for the purpose of raising a Going Concern which should yield a great production at home. The railways were bought by the state, and preferential rates granted. The banks were brought under the control of the state by a system of interlocked shareholding, and credit was organized for industry. Cartels and combines reduced the cost of production and distribution. The result was that about the year 1900 German emigration, which had been steadily falling, ceased altogether, except in so far as balanced by immigration. . . .

"The rapid German growth," Mackinder concludes, "was a triumph of organization. . . . The fundamental scientific ideas were, most of them, imported, and the vaunted German technical education was merely a form of organization. The whole system was based on a clear understanding of the reality of the Going Concern—organized manpower" (*Democratic Ideals and Reality*. Copyright 1919 and 1942 by Henry Holt & Co., New York; reproduced by permission).

SCIENCE, TECHNOLOGY, AND ECONOMICS

By Derwent Whittlesey

From chap. 2 of *German Strategy of World Conquest*, by Derwent Whittlesey et al. Copyright 1942 by National Planning Association. Farrar & Rinehart, New York; reproduced by permission. Dr. Whittlesey is professor of geography at Harvard University.

No part of Europe escaped the impact of science during the nineteenth century, least of all Germany. . . . The rapidly changing political structure of the German world at that period made it easy for states in flux to try out new intellectual formulas of government, and to apply them to novel utilization of natural resources. This in turn affected the thinking of German theorists in economics. Within the new German boundaries were rich mineral treasures, including coal and iron. On the base provided by such natural resources, with the help of a fast-growing understanding of natural science, the modern economic world has been erected.

The full flowering of the scientific method in Central Europe came after Germany's political consolidation in 1870. Its growth had accompanied the expansion of Prussia during the preceding half century. Coal is the physical base of the industrial pyramid. Prussia found itself in control of two of the major continental deposits of coal west of Russia. It also controlled large reserves of potash and salt. These three minerals are the base on which the chemical industry rests.

Exploitation of these tremendous physical resources unleashed a threefold revolution in German society. Increased production created a demand for labor. Industrial cities and a money economy grew up in the midst of the old subsistence agriculture and handicrafts. Mass production also created a surplus of manufactured goods and a shortage of raw materials that forced the country into trade with the outside world. The inevitable result was commercial expansion. A merchant marine began to grow, to be followed by a navy. There was a demand for colonies as potential markets and as sources of raw materials. It was no accident, therefore, that Prussia took the lead among German states in fostering scientific discovery and in making practical applications of the findings. Its transformation from a poor to a rich state follows the pattern of a growing industrial society. Foreign and colonial commerce grew, feeding upon the new manufactures. Scientific agriculture so increased the production of foodstuffs on German farms that this manufactural society came close to being able to provide its own subsistence. This was a new thing among the industrial nations which lacked farmland outside their manufacturing regions. . . .

Germany was set apart from the rest of the western world by its unique economic practices and theories, which accompanied the rise of scientific technology. War was the favored means of Prussian territorial expansion, but victories were consolidated by economic devices. The earliest of these was the customs union. . . . Prussia abolished internal tariffs as part of its post-Napoleonic rejuvenation. Every subsequent annexation of territory was followed by the abolition of customs duties unless this step had already been undertaken. Independent German states, particularly if they lay between parts of the scattered Prussian territory, were encouraged to obtain the advantages of trading in a large area by entering the Prussian customs union. Such a move proved doubly advantageous to Prussia because for many a German state it was the first step toward incorporation with Prussia. Even the large states of South

Germany entered the customs union some years before they became members of the Empire. In 1841, Friedrich List (1789-1846), the most influential economist in Germany, urged the extension of the customs union to all of Germanic Central Europe.

His proposed economic "Pan-Germany" did not work out, but within the customs union his theories were put into successful operation. The union adopted a policy of stiff protective tariffs against the non-German world. This policy was suggested by the position of the country, embedded in the heart of Europe and surrounded by potential enemies. It had access to the world ocean only by way of the North Sea, a water semi-enclosed by other nations. A state so located, it was argued, must prepare to withstand the closing of its frontiers by war. This attitude set Germany apart from the rest of the western world, which at just this time became committed to specialization and interchange. This was particularly true of Great Britain, which carried the doctrine to its logical conclusion—international free trade.

The chief support of protection naturally came from the rising industrial areas, and for a time German landholders opposed it. The creation of the Empire as a result of the Franco-Prussian War released for joint economic advancement the energy which had previously been dissipated among the several German states. The central government took a large slice of the wealth made available. The army received a generous part, and because the army was the pride of the landholders they permitted an increase in tariffs for the benefit of the manufacturing sections. Since then, tariffs have been increased at intervals of about twenty years. Rising tariffs have led naturally to the [German] ideal of autarky. . . .

With protection as a fixed policy after the Franco-Prussian War, German factory production shot up at a rate faster than that of any other country, including the United States. Adhering to the Prussian tradition, the imperial government held the throttle of the economic machine. By this means the state has been able to allocate the nation's wealth among the three elements that make the economic machine run—labor, capital, and technology. But first it drew off what it required for the army, which is traditionally looked upon as a guarantee of the state's existence. It is by far the largest unproductive load borne by the German economic structure, costing in peacetime more than that of any other nation. German financiers and entrepreneurs have received a small fraction of the total wealth as compared to those in other leading manufacturing countries. This practice bears out the teachings of List, who argued that private self-interest might not coincide with the higher good of the state, and that wealth does not lie in exchange values but in the full development of the three productive powers: agriculture, manufacturing, and commerce. He also insisted that agriculture is naturally subordinate to the other two. He assumed a reciprocal relation between a subordinate agriculture and a dominant industry. In this concept is also the germ of the modern proposals to reduce non-German Europe to an agricultural (and ipso facto subordinate) basis.

Chemistry, physics, biology, and economics were the four supports upon which Germany's material advancement rested. They came into play a century or more ago, and have functioned at an accelerating rate. A familiar example from the early period was the development of the sugar beet, begun when continental Europe was cut off from cane sugar by Britain's blockade of

Napoleon's Empire. A century later Germany freed itself from dependence on external sources of nitrates—valuable as fertilizers and for munitions of war —with the invention of the Haber process of fixation from the air. This was only two years before the outbreak of the war of 1914-1918, and is believed by many to have made that war possible.

Psychology and geography developed later, and were not formulated to serve the evolving German state until the end of the nineteenth century. . . . In a pedantic people like the Germans, the initial contribution of psychology to practical statecraft lay chiefly in awakening in the German mass mind a strong sense of the unique mission of Germany as a world leader. . . . Later on psychology was deliberately invoked to sway the mob. Conviction of German racial superiority was then symbolized by the *Blut* in the slogan *Blut und Boden*.

The *Boden* symbolized the German emphasis on geography. As a modern science, geography like psychology was developed earlier in Germany than in the rest of the world. Although it was not formulated as a tool of state until the present century, aspects of it had been exploited for specific practical ends decades earlier. . . .

From its beginning the German imperial government supported expeditions [for geographical exploration]. These . . . covered nearly all the little-known lands of the earth. It is only recently that the non-German world has realized that, outside its colonies, the most intensive German studies were made in areas which Germany might make use of as sources of raw materials, as markets for manufactured goods, and as potential lands for military conquest. . . .

Generations of German schoolchildren have been taught to *read* maps, not merely to look at them. . . . Familiarity with maps has trained the German public mind to think in terms of space on the earth's surface. . . .

In Prussia it was early realized that the higher officers, entrusted with the larger strategy . . . must have additional knowledge of the earth and be able to range more widely and thrust more deeply into scientific geography. The creation of the general staff put these larger matters of geography into the hands of a continuing body of staff officers charged with organizing and directing the nation's armed forces. . . .

From a beginning confined to tactics and strategy, the work of the general staff has expanded to incorporate in its war plans all the resources of the state. In doing so, it has proceeded along the same path taken by the rapidly growing science of geography. From responsibility for little more than the deployment of troops on varied terrain and plans of strategy for defense and for conquest in Central Europe, the general staff has become a clearinghouse for all the available information about the natural resources of every part of the world in which Germany has taken an interest. To this end, officers have been detailed to study geography in the universities, and geographers have been brought into the system of military education. Officers thus trained have been detailed as observers in foreign countries. There they have cast a practiced eye over the economic and political geography of the state as well as its military geography in the traditional, narrower meaning.

This is not to say that the study of geography in the larger sense was left solely to the general staff. On the contrary, the consolidation of the three hundred German states of the late eighteenth century into the world power of the nineteenth was paralleled by the establishment of modern geography in German universities. The two phenomena were, moreover, closely related. Professors in the new or rejuvenated universities were generally paid by the state, and several of the most accomplished geographers occupied administrative posts in the government. With the rise and spread of the factory system, and the consequent flowering of world trade, economic geography took its place alongside the older branches, physiography and climatology. The central position of Germany in Europe ensured an interest also in the political values and handicaps of such a location, and toward the end of the century produced the first comprehensive formulation of political geography. Such a work could hardly have been written outside Germany, one of the lands occupying a central position among the occidental nations and the only country recently expanded from a small core to one of the largest states in Europe. . . .

TECHNOLOGY AND STEEL

By E. C. Eckel

From chap. 3 of *Coal, Iron and War*, by E. C. Eckel. Copyright 1920 by Henry Holt & Co., New York; reproduced by permission. The author was for many years a geologist in the service of the U.S. Government.

In 1830 the states which later made up the German Empire . . . [were] producing about 120,000 tons of pig-iron, as against perhaps 190,000 tons in the States; but on the other hand the German output of coal was then about five times as great as the American, being 1,500 thousand tons against 300 thousand. We can assume, then, that though in iron production the United States was already well in the lead, the German states were probably much further ahead in general manufactures. Both countries, of course, were still unimportant by comparison with Great Britain, which at that date was producing some 700,000 tons of pig-iron and probably well over twenty million tons of coal annually. . . .

The first sharp increase in rate of growth, so far as the coal and iron industries [of the German states] were concerned, took place after the revolutionary movement of 1848 in Europe had subsided. . . . Soon after Europe came back to stable even if autocratic government, internal improvements were commenced. Among these was the early Prussian system of state railways, and by 1860 there were close to seven thousand miles of railroad in Germany, as contrasted with 340 miles open in 1840. This growth directly and indirectly aided the iron and coal industries, and the output of iron showed its first great jump about 1853. . . .

In 1850 Germany was making about 400 thousand tons of pig-iron; by 1870 this had more than tripled. The rate of growth was not as rapid as that of the American industry, but the fluctuations from year to year were less. There was promise of a sound and steady development in this as in other industries, in the German states as constituted and organized in 1869. But this status was not to endure, for in that year the German states were on the threshold of a decade of very remarkable military and political change—a period whose ideas at first remarkably favorable to intensive industrial growth, were later to have fatal developments.

. . . In 1870 Germany had a population of around 39 millions, an increase of some 45 per cent over that of 1830. But her iron output was now 1,400 thousand tons, an increase of over 1,000 per cent, while her coal production had risen to 34 million tons, an increase of almost 2,200 per cent. England was still far in the lead in both respects, but since 1830 both the United States and Germany had gained at a far more rapid rate, and were gradually closing up the gap. Turning to a closer competitor, Germany had during those four decades of peaceful growth passed France as a producer both of coal and of iron, though as regards iron the lead was very trifling. But ... both Germany and France had reached close to the maximum of possible development with the ores and processes then available. The process that would make a cheap competitive steel possible was still in the future; the ores that could be utilized by such a process were still, so far as Germany was concerned, across a frontier. The next stage in advance is marked by the acquisition of the ores and the development of the process. . . .

The Franco-Prussian war made very remarkable additions to the material bases upon which any future industrial development must rest, and also brought about changes in political conditions which would ultimately be of service in future industrial growth. . . .

The results of this war had very great ultimate effects on Germany, on France, on England, and on the rest of the world. These effects were not only political and military, but industrial. . . .

But ... when we go back to the books and papers of that period, in an attempt to discover just how the matter impressed the people of 1871, we find little trace of any recognition that anything serious had happened to the world. In France, 1870 was looked upon as a purely military and political humiliation, which the nation would hope to avenge some day by equally purely military means. In England, there was at first frank pleasure over the final elimination of Louis Napoleon, and perhaps a little quiet relief that the historic enemy across the Channel would be likely to give little occasion for alarm for some time . . . [and] not a trace, so far as can be found in the literature or speeches of the day, to suggest that anyone recognized the fact that a new and far more dangerous opponent had come to power. In Germany itself the war seems to have been regarded, even by the statesman who conducted it, as a military and political success, which aided German unity, gave a good frontier—and nothing more. Throughout the world there was not one trace of the idea, now generally accepted, that very obviously a new and dangerous military and industrial power had appeared, with aims different from those of other powers, and with different ideas as to the possible means for carrying those aims into effect. . . .

This . . . is very surprising, for . . . the outstanding result of the Franco-Prussian war was industrial. [Victorious Prussia redrew the Franco-German frontier] so as to give Germany half of the most valuable iron-ore deposit in Europe, and one of the largest in the world. . . .

That it included so much seems to have been due to the direct efforts of German geologists; that it did not take in all of the field was due, partly to scientific stupidity and partly to an excusable lack of prevision. From the memoirs and letters that have been published, we see that neither Bismarck nor the army leaders cared much about the matter, but did want an extension [of the frontier] to cover Belfort. But France was obdurate about Belfort, and as a choice between two evils, preferred to give up more of Lorraine; while an eminent German geologist laid stress upon the importance of taking in the iron-ore territory. The idea was sound but the execution was shockingly bad. . . . As we know, the Lorraine ores are of sedimentary origin, forming true flat-lying beds, and can be followed underground for great distances, like coal seams. But in 1870 the weight of scientific authority held . . . that they originated by replacement from the surface, and that therefore the ore would disappear a short distance below the outcrop. . . .

Under the influence of this idea, the boundary was finally drawn a relatively short distance back of the outcrop; and most of the known and visible ores passed into German control. Years later, the use of brains and drilling machinery demonstrated that the ores did persist in depth, and that the region that had been left in French hands was underlain by much more ore than had been turned over to Germany. . . . [Even that portion of the ore field transferred to Germany had decidedly limited value under metallurgical conditions existing in 1870.]

The Lorraine ores are typically high in phosphorus, and the pig-iron made from them is of course very high indeed in that element. That meant that in 1870 they were not ores that could be used in the steel industry, for the Bessemer process, as at first introduced, did not eliminate phosphorus at all. A pig-iron suitable for the original Bessemer process had to be practically free from phosphorus. This limitation left the Lorraine ores, as were our own Alabama ores at the same date, entirely worthless from the steel-maker's standpoint, but free for use where a very fluid cast iron was desired. They were strictly foundry irons, not steel-making irons. And the industrial world was then, under the stimulus of the large tonnages of cheap steel which the Bessemer process could yield, turning from the use of iron to the use of steel. Lorraine in 1870 seemed to have a good but very limited future.

But . . . Lorraine was not the only region which had an over-supply of phosphoric iron ores. England was similarly placed with regard to her cheapest ores, Alabama was in the same straits, and the vast Newfoundland deposits later developed would show the same difficulty. So there was a direct incentive to the study of possible processes for making good and cheap steel from a high-phosphorus pig-iron. In 1870, however, there was no such process in actual use, or even well advanced experimentally.

The solution was to come from England, but not until 1879. In that year Thomas and Gilchrist, two remarkable cousins, gave to the industrial world a very convincing demonstration of a new steel-making process. . . . This was the basic Bessemer or Thomas-Gilchrist process, whose essential feature was the use of a basic (lime or magnesia), lining to the Bessemer converter, this lining making almost complete removal of any phosphorus contained in the pig-iron. Seemingly a very simple matter, the new process was in reality a very brilliant technical achievement, which resulted in widespread industrial changes. Primarily, it made it possible to utilize the cheaply operated Bessemer converter for making steel from a phosphoric pig-iron; but secondarily it put an actual premium on the use of such irons, for it was soon found that the phosphorus eliminated from the iron combined with the lime to form a phosphoric slag, valuable as a fertilizer. By crediting the sales value of this by-product against the cost of steel-making, the new basic Bessemer process showed cheaper steel than did the old or acid Bessemer method. Iron ores high in phosphorus now had a new place in the industrial world, and the Lorraine iron region would come into its own. . . .

In following out the later developments which gave the Lorraine ores their high recent value, we have overrun somewhat the story of industrial growth after the [Franco-Prussian] war.

Industrially considered, the actual spoils of the war were great enough even at their then value. The conquerors received the five milliards of gold, which incidentally was currently credited with being in large part the inciting cause of the great German industrial activity of the years which immediately followed, though this is a question. But in real assets they received an industrious population of one and a half millions, a large wheat area, a thriving cotton industry, and a well developed iron region. As regards this latter more particularly, we may say that it included not only the greater part of the outcrop of the Lorraine iron ore field, but a group of iron-making plants. The eight or more plants which now found themselves on the German side of the frontier had an output, just before the war, of some half million tons of pig-iron annually. Further, Germany also received that portion of the Saar coalfield which had been left French in 1815— a portion which represented perhaps a fourth of the entire field.

The direct and immediate gains through this affair were therefore considerable, and showed promptly in the swelling of the production returns of Germany with a corresponding falling off in French output in the years following the war. The iron output in Germany proper, excluding Luxemburg, was, for example in the year before the war, 1,290 thousand tons; in the year after the close of war 1,810 thousand tons; the gain represented almost exactly the product of the French furnaces acquired.

During the decade which succeeded the war, the Lorraine ores were still limited in use, owing to the conditions previously discussed, and the iron output of Germany rose only some 50 per cent in the ten years. But with the invention of the basic Bessemer process in England and its prompt adoption in Germany, the rate of growth quickens immediately. In the decade 1880-1890 the German pig-iron production increased almost 100 per cent; and in the two succeeding decades the same rate of progress was maintained. By 1910, therefore, Germany was producing close to fifteen million tons of pig-iron annually, as compared with the 1,400 thousand tons of 1870 and the 120 thousand of 1830. Though the United States was still far in the lead as an iron producer, Great Britain had been passed by Germany around 1900, and industrial progress in other directions had been equally surprising.

"A PLACE IN THE SUN"

By Eyre Crowe

From "Memorandum on the Present State of British Relations with France and Germany, January 1, 1907," by Eyre Crowe. This famous document has been published under various imprints. The following excerpt is quoted from *British Documents on the Origins of the War, 1898-1914,* edited by G. P. Gooch and H. Temperley. 1928. H. M. Stationery Office, London. The author of the Crowe Memorandum was a high official in the British Foreign Office.

For purposes of foreign policy the modern German Empire may be regarded as the heir, or descendant of Prussia. Of the history of Prussia, perhaps the most remarkable feature, next to the succession of talented sovereigns and to the energy and love of honest work characteristic of their subjects, is the process by which on the narrow foundation of the modest Margraviate of Brandenburg there was erected, in the space of a comparatively short period, the solid fabric of a European Great Power. That process was one of systematic territorial aggrandizement achieved mainly at the point of the sword, the most important and decisive conquests being deliberately embarked upon by ambitious rulers or statesmen for the avowed object of securing for Prussia the size, the cohesion, the square miles and the population necessary to elevate her to the rank and influence of a first class state. . . .

With the events of 1871 the spirit of Prussia passed into the new Germany. In no other country is there a conviction so deeply rooted in the very body and soul of all classes of the population that the preservation of national rights and the realization of national ideals rest absolutely on the readiness of every citizen in the last resort to stake himself and his state on their assertion and vindication. With "blood and iron" Prussia had forged her position in the councils of the Great Powers of Europe. In due course it came to pass that, with the impetus given to every branch of national activity by the newly-won unity, and more especially by the growing development of oversea trade flowing in ever-increasing volume through the new imperial ports of the formerly "independent" but politically insignificant Hanse Towns, the young empire found opened to its energy a whole world outside Europe, of which it had previously hardly had the opportunity to become more than dimly conscious. Sailing across the ocean in German ships, German merchants began for the first time to divine the true position of countries such as England, the United States, France, and even the Netherlands, whose political influence extends to distant seas and continents. The colonies and foreign possessions of England more especially were seen to give to that country a recognized and enviable status in a world where the name of Germany, if mentioned at all, excited no particular interest. The effect of this discovery upon the German mind was curious and instructive. Here was a vast province of human activity to which the mere title and rank of a European Great Power were not in themselves a sufficient passport. Here in a field of portentous magnitude, dwarfing altogether the proportions of European countries, others, who had been perhaps rather looked down upon as comparatively smaller folk, were at home and commanded, whilst Germany was at best received but as an honored guest. Here was distinct inequality, with a heavy bias in favor of the maritime and colonizing powers.

Such a state of things was not welcome to German patriotic pride. Germany had won her place as one of the leading, if not, in fact, the foremost power on the European continent. But over and beyond the European Great Powers there seemed to stand the "World Powers." It was at once clear that Germany must become a "World Power." The evolution of this idea and its translation into practical politics followed with singular consistency the line of thought that had inspired the Prussian kings in their efforts to make Prussia great. "If Prussia," said Frederick the Great, "is to count for something in the councils of Europe, she must be made a Great Power." And the echo: "If Germany wants to have a voice in the affairs of the larger oceanic world she must be made a World Power." "I want more territory," said Prussia. "Germany must have colonies," says the new world-policy. And colonies were accordingly established, in such spots as were found to be still unappropriated, or out of which others could be pushed by the vigorous assertion of a

German demand for a "place in the sun." ... When the final reckoning was made up the actual German gains seemed, even in German eyes, somewhat meager ... assets of somewhat doubtful value.

Meanwhile the dream of a colonial empire had taken deep hold on the German imagination. Emperor, statesmen, journalists, geographers, economists, commercial and shipping houses, and the whole mass of educated and uneducated public opinion continue with one voice to declare: We *must* have real colonies, where German emigrants can settle and spread the national ideals of the Fatherland, and we *must* have a fleet and coaling stations to keep together the colonies which we are bound to acquire. To the question: "Why *must?*" the ready answer is: "A healthy and powerful State like Germany, with its 60,000,000 inhabitants, must expand, it cannot stand still, it must have territories to which its overflowing population can emigrate without giving up its nationality." When it is objected that the world is now actually parcelled out among independent states, and that territory for colonization cannot be had except by taking it from the rightful possessor, the reply again is: "We cannot enter into such considerations. Necessity knows no law. The world belongs to the strong. A vigorous nation cannot allow its growth to be hampered by blind adherence to the status quo. We have no designs on other people's possessions, but where states are too feeble to put their territory to the best possible use, it is the manifest destiny of those who can and will do so to take their places."

No one who has a knowledge of German political thought, and who enjoys the confidence of German friends speaking their minds openly and freely, can deny that these are the ideas which are proclaimed on the housetops, and that inability to sympathize with them is regarded in Germany as the mark of the prejudiced foreigner who cannot enter into the real feelings of Germans. Nor is it amiss to refer in this connection to the series of imperial apothegms, which have from time to time served to crystallize the prevailing German sentiments. ... "Our future lies on the water." "The trident must be in our hand." "Germany must reenter into her heritage of maritime dominion once unchallenged in the hands of the old Hansa." "No question of world politics must be settled without the consent of the German Emperor." "The Emperor of the Atlantic greets the Emperor of the Pacific," etc.

The significance of these individual utterances may easily be exaggerated. Taken together, their cumulative effect is to confirm the impression that Germany distinctly aims at playing on the world's political stage a much larger and much more dominant part than she finds allotted to herself under the present distribution of material power. ...

FOREIGN POLICY 1871-1914
By Derwent Whittlesey

From chap. 3 of *German Strategy of World Conquest*, by Derwent Whittlesey *et al*. Copyright 1942 by National Planning Association. Farrar and Rinehart, New York; reproduced by permission.

[The German Emperor] exercised nearly absolute power. His position was akin to the absolute monarchies found earlier in every European country. It was a modification of the absolutism of Prussia, a state which had evolved in a rural society of great landowners and servile peasants. The core of Prussia ... remained unchanged throughout the political upheavals following the French Revolution, and even through the still more profound industrial revolution which altered the rest of Germany during the succeeding century. In this region the German imperial house had its traditional seat. Old Brandenburg-Prussia, the stronghold of the ruling class ... exerted far more political power than its wealth or population deserved.

In all of older Prussia only Berlin had become a considerable manufacturing city. Industry had been induced there not because of local advantages, but because the nation's railway net focused for strategic reasons upon the capital of the Prussian state and the German nation. The emperor, resident in Berlin, could not overlook the urban, commercial, and manufactural districts which surrounded his palace. Still less could he disregard the rising wealth and population of other parts of Germany, mainly in the west, led by the Prussian Rhineland.

An ambitious emperor, taking advantage of unwavering support by the "solid" agrarian east, had the power of directing the increasing force of the industrial west to a degree unmatched in competing states. Elsewhere the rise of manufacturing and trade had been paralleled by the growth of liberal democracy, acting as a check on absolute political authority.

The split in the nation between agrarian east and urban west permitted (or perhaps compelled) the adoption of policies at variance with each other. Continued expansion landward (*Drang nach Osten*) had to be matched by overseas expansion into colonies and economic penetration into lands already allotted to other nations. The first required a powerful army, the second a large navy.

The army, true to Prussian tradition, was in full vigor, organized and directed by its general staff. This body had strategic and tactical plans for the defense of the German borders, and for offensives in every neighboring country. A clue to its activity after 1890 is found in the reversal within ten years of the policy of reducing frontier fortresses. It not only strengthened those existing but also built new ones.

The army was a going concern, but the navy had to be created. A beginning had been made before 1890, and construction was pushed thereafter. The step was a challenge to the supremacy of Great Britain on the seas. . . .

Within Germany, propaganda was launched to win support for ambitious imperial projects. On numerous earlier occasions the fire of patriotic loyalty to individual German states had been stirred up. Sometimes it had ignited spontaneously, as in the reaction to Napoleon's military conquest. Sometimes it had been cunningly fanned, as in the publication of the altered French dispatches which brought South German states to the side of Prussia [in 1870]. Now it was prepared ahead, as organized, long-term propaganda, for the whole of Germany and for all people of German origin, wherever they might reside.

It has been charged that the general staff of the army and the Emperor William II himself sponsored or perhaps devised some of the plans for German aggrandizement published during the two decades before the World War of 1914-1918. There is no documentary proof of this. Nevertheless, the autocratic German government might easily have put a stop to the flood of publications and public utterances attacking friendly nations so violently as to embarrass responsible authorities. But it did not. Instead, the government became more and more inclined toward "saber rattling," until its culmination during the flush of military success in the early years [of the First World War]. . . .

GERMANY BEFORE 1914: AN ENGLISHMAN'S IMPRESSIONS

By Harold Butler

From chap. 4 of *The Lost Peace*, by Harold Butler. Copyright 1941 by Harcourt, Brace & Co., New York; reproduced by permission. The author is a British statesman with a long and distinguished diplomatic career.

My first acquaintance with Germany was in 1906. . . . German life was pleasant enough in those days. The country was comfortable and well to do. Though the Kaiser was always clamoring for a place in the sun, Germany was a sunny land. Expanding industry was reducing emigration. The standard of living was steadily rising. There was no Versailles-Diktat, no craving for revenge, no economic collapse, which its leaders could use to goad the people into war. They had only to go on working to become the greatest and richest nation on the Continent, if they had not already achieved that ambition. But that was not enough. The whole German soul was shot through with a megalomaniac lust for power, dressed up in all the romantic trappings which appeal to it so irresistibly. The Nibelung saga was not just a gorgeous fantasy of poetry and music. It was the call of the blood. In it the heroic and tragic destiny of the Teutonic race found its highest expression. When he listened to Siegfried's horn or to the rushing music of the Valkyries' ride or to the devouring crackle of the fire music, the stolid German's visionary soul was filled with rhapsody. He dreamt dazzling dreams of mighty struggles and world-shaking cataclysms, in which he was cast for the role of the sublime warrior. He liked to think of his natural kindliness being transmuted into the ruthless stuff of which Attilas are made. His incurable romanticism was untamed by the hard common sense of the English or by the cold logic of the French. He was at the mercy of a leader who flashed the mirage of victory and conquest before his eyes. *Weltmacht oder Niedergang*, world power or extinction, became the slogan of a German crusade against humanity. . . .

One did not have to live long in the old Germany to become aware of a fanatical devotion to this national myth of war and power underlying the placid, plodding exterior of Hans and Gretel. However good-natured and harmless they might seem as individuals, as particles of the national mass they were ready to be transformed into pitiless disciples of blood and iron when the word was given from on high. For the vast majority was devoid of any critical faculty. They had never been spiritually free. Their whole training from infancy had been in obedience to authority. . . . The German people had never controlled its own destiny. Unlike the English and the French, it had never taken its fate into its own hands and made the popular will the source of authority. It had never beheaded or exiled a king. It had never acquired the instincts of democracy by daring all in the cause of political and personal liberty. It had never produced a Hampden or a Cromwell, a Robespierre or a Lenin. In consequence it knew nothing of liberty. Its attitude to the state was the attitude of the Middle Ages, when kings ruled by divine right. The German had never attained the status of free citizenship, which gives every individual some responsibility for shaping the policy of the nation. That was determined by a "higher authority," whose behests he executed almost automatically. The Englishman, the Frenchman, or the American thinks that he is as good a man as his rulers and that he has a right to be heard as to how he should be ruled. Not so the German. He does not trust his own judgment. He leaves the affairs of state to be settled by an élite, to whom he regards himself as inferior and whose decisions he does not really feel entitled to question. Having no belief in his own rights, he has little conception of the rights of others. Distrusting his own political capacity, he wants to be led. Being unaccustomed to exercise his political intelligence, he is ready to give blind obedience to leadership, as long as it purports to be leading him to national greatness.

In those bygone days nothing was so surprising to the stranger as the meek acceptance of authority by the great mass of Germans. One heard of Liberals and Socialists who were opposed to the imperialist policies of the Kaiser, but when one met them, their timidity was devastating. At the time when the outcry against Chinese labor on the Rand was still echoing through Britain, I remember discussing the massacre of the Herreros in Southwest Africa with a German Liberal. He expressed disapproval in principle of such colonial methods, but he thought any public protest would be not only futile but wrong, as the authorities must know their own business best. The most spirited opposition came from *Simplicissimus,* the famous Munich weekly, whose brilliant cartoons and biting satire fought a vain but valiant battle against Prussianism and reaction. Other papers such as the Socialist *Vorwärts* indulged in milder but regular criticism of the government, none of which would be tolerated for a moment by the Nazis. In words the Opposition was often effective, but when it came to deeds, it was deplorably feeble. At international congresses the Socialists talked boldly of declaring a general strike to stop war, but when it came to the point they voted the military budget in 1914 unanimously and enthusiastically. At heart they were as German as the rest. . . .

But however anxious the left-wing parties might have been to preserve peace, they waged a hopeless fight against the weight of authority among people who were predisposed to accept any official utterance at its face value. That meant not merely that what the government said was fairly certain to be swallowed unhesitatingly, but that what professors and school teachers said was almost equally certain of credence. A professor was after all a higher official. He belonged to the third grade of the complicated hierarchy of officialdom. He was inferior to the nobility, to the higher officers of the army and navy, and to the heads of civil service, but superior to anyone else. He ranked above an industrialist or a banker, unless the latter had managed to infiltrate into the aristocracy, and his pronouncements based on his lofty position in the state and the reputation for immense erudition which German professors had acquired were accordingly treated as oracles. . . .

Even in those days when the press was largely free and there was no hindrance to German intercourse with the outside world, when foreigners could enter and travel about the country without a passport, the German remained incredibly ignorant of international realities. He was told that the British and the French were too soft to fight, and he believed it. He was told that these same decadent peoples in alliance with the Russians, who were too corrupt and ignorant to fight, were preparing a monstrous plot to encircle and crush Germany by force, and he believed it. He was told that after a sharp, jolly war he would have the world at his feet, and he believed it. The great mass of the German people did not want war, but they were the slaves of the national myth, so when the order came they obeyed it with tremendous enthusiasm. They were gullible, and they had been gulled into a great military adventure prepared for many years in advance before the eyes of the world. They fought bravely and according to their lights cleanly. They were still a Christian people, who in their private lives observed a fairly high standard of decency, piety, and honesty. But because they had never been spiritually free, they made no attempt to impose any standards of international conduct upon their rulers. Though they had long since been released from the external shackles of subjection to land-owner or employer, they had never experienced that liberation from within which, as Heine saw, was still needed to complete their emancipation. The result was a terrible Nemesis, another luckless and bloodstained page in the tragic history of Germany....

WAR AND DEFEAT, 1914-1918

By the Editors

WHETHER the unification of the Germanic peoples in 1871 was the match which lighted the powder train leading to the First World War is open to debate. But there can be no doubt that the ensuing rapid use of German power, accompanied by an expansionist propaganda, an intransigent diplomacy and an increasingly aggressive foreign policy, contributed to the growing atmosphere of insecurity in Europe, which exploded into war following assassination of the Austrian crown prince in 1914.

The ensuing war revealed the truly formidable military stature of the Second Reich. Germany towered above her chief ally, the Austro-Hungarian Empire, and her satellites, Turkey and Bulgaria. It was German industry, discipline and organization that sustained the cause of the Central Powers for over four years. On land at least, the German Empire proved more than a match in the end for all her European enemies combined.

The Kaiser's armies overran Belgium and northeastern France, and drove almost to Paris and to the English Channel in the first rush. The fronts were stabilized by a combination of Allied heroism and luck, and the war settled down to a gigantic siege, in which the Allied armies ringed the Central Powers while Allied sea power tightened the screws of another great continental blockade.

Unable to break the deadlock on the Western Front, German inventive genius developed in the submarine a commerce-destroying weapon which came perilously near to breaking the back of Britain's war effort. Then in 1917 Russia collapsed, and in the spring of 1918 German might was once more concentrated for a grand assault in the West. Once again the German armies almost reached Paris and the Channel. But time was now running out. German victories had gradually rallied the oceanic world, including the United States, to the support of the hard-pressed Western Allies. In the autumn of 1918 the forces of this global coalition, spearheaded by a huge and rapidly growing American army in France, rolled back the Germans in crushing defeats while the German home front crumbled under the cumulative effects of war fatigue and the strangling Allied blockade. One by one the Central Powers gave up the struggle until Germany stood alone.

Faced with irretrievable disaster, the German High Command ordered the civil government to start peace negotiations. Then to escape responsibility for defeat the Military repudiated the negotiations. But to no avail. Mutiny broke out within the armed forces followed by revolt on the home front. The Kaiser abdicated and fled to Holland, and on November 11, 1918, the Germans laid down their arms in surrender.

The peace terms of 1919 indicated the completeness of Germany's defeat. The German Republic, which rose from the ashes of defeat, was compelled to assume responsibility for the war and for all damage caused to the Allies. Germany was saddled with a heavy reparations bill. The defeated Reich was compelled to surrender its telegraphic submarine cables, most of its merchant marine, the coal mines of the Saar valley, and many other valuable economic assets.

The territorial clauses were no less severe. Germany lost her oversea colonies. Alsace and Lorraine were returned to France. Poland was given a corridor through East Prussia to the Baltic. Through these and other boundary changes, Germany lost control of about 25,000 square miles of territory inhabited by some six million people.

The military clauses were drawn with the deliberate purpose of keeping Germany weak. The Reich was ordered to disband its general staff and to abolish conscription. Its army was limited to 100,000, to be raised by voluntary long-term enlistment so as to prevent the accumulation of trained reserves. Germany was denied tanks, heavy artillery, military planes, or other weapons necessary to spearhead offensive operations. The German navy was similarly reduced and limited. No fortifications were to be built on either side of the Rhine, and Allied armies were to occupy the area west of that river for fifteen years. Comparable, if less rigorous, restrictions were placed on the construction of military works along Germany's other frontiers. The Reich was forbidden to unite with Austria, the Germanic remnant of the defunct Austro-Hungarian Empire. And still other provisions were imposed with the view to preventing the revival of German military power. If the peace terms of 1919 had been rigorously enforced, there could have been no revival of German military power.

But the terms were not strictly enforced, especially those relating to the surrender of German weapons. This indulgence resulted largely from the fear of Communist revolution in Germany and of Russian Bolshevist expansion into Central Europe. Later the German Republic secured successive modifications of the reparations terms. The Allied occupation was terminated sooner than planned. In still other ways the terms of peace were subsequently lightened. But in 1919 most of these changes lay in the future. Germany was beaten and crushed. German military power was shattered. And few, if any, of the framers of the peace envisaged the re-emergence of the German menace within a generation.

GERMAN STATECRAFT UNDER THE REPUBLIC

By the Editors

The German nation accepted the peace settlement under duress. But they showed themselves incapable of accepting, or even grasping, the magnitude and consequences of their defeat. Largely stripped of arms, there could be no early renewal of hostilities to overturn what they all but unanimously regarded as a vindictive, unjust peace. But Germany, though disarmed, still possessed political and psychological weapons.

One of these was the "menace of Bolshevism." In 1922 the Germans thoroughly frightened the peoples of the West by concluding with the Soviet Union a commercial treaty that seemed to foreshadow the delivery of Central Europe to Bolshevism. Actually, the conservative forces who had reasserted control in Germany by that time, had no such intention. But they were willing to play with fire in order to create panic and confusion within the ranks of their former enemies.

Another weapon in the German arsenal was passive resistance. All sorts of delays occurred in carrying out the terms of peace. The mark steadily depreciated in value, retarding economic recovery in Central Europe. Reparations payments dropped farther and farther in arrears.

These tactics brought on crisis after crisis. Cracks opened up in the relations of the Allies until no semblance of a united front was left. To collect reparations, the French in 1923 marched troops into the Ruhr industrial region against the protest not only of the Germans but of their own British allies. This step knocked the remaining props from beneath the tottering German economy. Inflation soared unchecked, until British and American finance stepped in to salvage the wreck in return for German acquiescence in somewhat modified conditions of peace.

This settlement, known as the Dawes Plan, was a turning point in German policy. The strategy of sabotage and passive resistance was abandoned in return for financial assistance and French withdrawal from the Ruhr. The German Republic, under the leadership of its foreign minister, Gustav Stresemann, seemed reconciled to the new *status quo* and willing to win its way back to freedom and good standing by good behavior and hard work.

This avowed change of heart was expressed in the famous Locarno Treaties of 1925, in which Germany joined her former enemies in recognizing the permanency of the new frontiers. The following year Germany accepted the obligations of the League of Nations and was admitted to membership with a permanent seat beside the other Great Powers on the Council. At that juncture the outlook for peace seemed never brighter.

The leader of this seeming reorientation of German policy was Foreign Minister Stresemann. Until his death in 1929, he was the outspoken mouthpiece of the policy of reconciliation. The following selection from one of his public addresses is typical of the era of good feeling in which the German Republic momentarily accepted, at least outwardly, the new international order.

THE POLICY OF RECONCILIATION

By Gustav Stresemann

From "The Way of the New Germany," an address by Gustav Stresemann, June 29, 1927, at Oslo University, Norway. Reprinted in *Germany: A Self-Portrait*, edited by H. R. Crippen. Copyright 1944, by Oxford University Press, New York; reproduced by permission.

IN the course of the past few years I have had, at times, to fight a hard battle on behalf of German foreign policy. For that reason I am perhaps the man best fitted to answer the question that is so frequently put regarding the mental attitude of present-day Germany.

In their estimation of this mental attitude, people abroad are variously inclined to be appreciative, skeptical, critical, or hostile. Let me endeavor, so far as is possible in view of the inadequate historical perspective afforded by the short space of time that has elapsed since the war, to reply to those who ask what are the leading spiritual and political tendencies in . . . the new Germany.

A description of the old prewar Germany is an essential preliminary to any such attempt. Old Germany . . . was a land of progress in the field of social politics; it was much less narrow, less under the influence of the Manchester school [of *laissez-faire,* free-trade economics] than other states. . . . It was the land of barracks, of universal compulsory military service, of sympathy with things military; but it was also the land of technical achievements, of applied chemistry, of modern research. In that land old things and new struggled to take form. He who would write its history must see to it that he look deep down and not be content to rest on the surface. . . .

The Great War caused this older Germany to collapse. The collapse extended to its constitution, its social institutions, its economic structure. Its thoughts and feelings have been transformed; and no man can say that this process has reached its completion. . . .

He who analyzes the experiences and sentiments of the early post-war period will hardly be accused of lack of objectivity when he says that it is easier for the victor than for the vanquished to express thoughts of peace. For the victor peace obviously means the consecration of the position of power in which his victory placed him, whereas to the vanquished it means acceptance of what position may remain to him. To lag behind on the path you have trod side by side with another, and let him take precedence without thought of envy in your heart, is a hard thing to do; hard for an individual, hard for a people. Still harder by far is it for the human soul to have believed, after half a century of development, that the summit had been reached, and then to be cast from the summit. The psychology of a people that has gone through that experience is not so easy to grasp, nor to transform, as many people seem to believe.

That was precisely the problem with which the New Germany was faced. The entrance of Germany into the League of Nations was not rendered easy to Germany. The courtesy that is so fitting a trait in a victor, was long in manifesting itself. The obligations which the people had to undertake were superhuman, and never could the nation have borne them, had it not had as the heritage of centuries the consciousness of duty to the state. To this day the historian often sees in the outcome of the war for Germany merely a tale of lost territories, abandonment of practical colonial activity, loss of national and private capital. He frequently overlooks the heaviest loss Germany had to endure. I take that heaviest loss to have lain in the fact that the intellectual and professional middle class that bore in itself the traditions of the state, had to pay in the war for its loyal devotion to the state at war, with a complete sacrifice of its fortune and became proletarian. How far state policy was justified in demanding from an entire generation so great a sacrifice, owing to the depreciation beyond recovery of the currency issued by the state, and the fact that the capital was not refunded, is a point round which the clash of expert opinions, and perhaps even that of practical legislators, endures to this day undecided. But everything that happened in Germany in the period since the war, must be considered in the light of these feelings of an uprooted class of society. That class also included, as a consequence of the provisions of the Treaty of Versailles, the officers of the old army, and further that portion of the growing generation whose lot in the old Germany had been cast mainly in the sphere of military or civil state service. This was a case of an economic uprooting. But to those who found themselves, mentally and politically speaking, suddenly bereft of a stable basis for their thought and feeling, must be added all those in whose heart and mind the idea of the monarchy had implanted itself firmly by virtue of its existence for the past five hundred years. They had, during the war, endured the ebbs and tides of varying fortune, but none of them had ever expected such a crash. They would not break with old established things, for they were incapable of realizing what had gone before. To these considerations has to be added, as has so often been the case in history, the excess of zeal of the partisans of the new order, who set out that new order in too crass a contrast, instead of trying in some measure to graft it on to the old.

Humbled and downtrodden, beggars that had once been leaders, the men of this class, with a bitterness easy to understand in view of their pessimism, threw themselves in trenchant criticism of unjust attacks from abroad, and of contempt of tradition at home. The downfall of this class of heretofore leaders—and by that phrase I do not mean the nobility or the landed gentry, but the middle class that saw its hard-won possessions, worked for in a lifetime, dwindle steadily, and had to start their life anew with nothing—led to the social order of the old Germany being shaken to its very foundations. There came a further political tremor: the Ruhr struggle [resulting from French occupation of the Ruhr industrial region in 1923 to enforce German compliance with the terms of the peace]. Once more the feeling of being subjected to violence fanned resentment into flames of desperate resistance. But with a difference this time: a distinction began to be drawn between those who seemed still to wish to pursue the fight against Germany, and those who deemed such a continuation not justifiable. From the United States of America voices came wafted over the ocean which indicated that America wished for a peaceful and united Europe as a groundwork for common effort and common work. The London Conference on the Dawes Plan took place. In lieu of economists and bankers, statesmen took the boards. . . .

For the first time, the German people, wounded and sore, saw its representatives no longer the object of ordinances issued by others, but negotiating with them, and from Monsieur Herriot it received the assurance of the evacuation of the Ruhr. Out of this keen fight between the pessimists who could not believe in a change in the world's spirit, and those who consciously marched on in an opposite direction, the latter emerged the victors. With them stood arrayed not only those few who had trod that path with them from the beginning but also the working classes who, though not less nationally minded than any other portion of the people, had picked up the threads of old associations and hoped, in their comrades of political and trade-union fields, to find fellow workers in the cause of international cooperation.

As Herriot's successor, Monsieur Briand took up the reins of French foreign policy and honored the promise to evacuate the Ruhr. Then, following on the German initiative of February 9, 1925, the policy of Locarno was inaugurated. It would be inaccurate to say that from the outset this policy met with joyful and hearty support. Distrust abroad hindered a prompt response to the German *démarche*. Misrepresentation at home was a further obstacle; a misrepresentation that saw merely weak resignation in what was in reality the beginning of an active line of policy. From the other side new questions were thrown into the debate in order to test the genuineness of Germany's desire for peace. Entrance into the League of Nations was put forward as a condition for ratification of the Locarno treaties.

What a curious change became manifest here! In 1919, Germany herself had wished to join the League, and had been foiled in this desire by shortsighted and undiscerning people. Now her adhesion was asked for. The League of Nations, established as a league of victors, now sighed for reconciliation and cooperation with the strongest opponent in the Great War. Here, too, there were strong obstacles to be overcome. For, in the German view, the right of self-determination of populations had not always been observed by the League of Nations in its decisions as to the fate of former German territories. After many vacillations between confidence and distrust, agreement was reached on the treaties. Then came mistakes in tactics, a certain false sensitiveness, that again, in March 1926, made Germany's entrance into the League impossible. As against that, there was recorded the famous decision of the former Allies that, even in the absence of Germany's formal entrance, they would proceed as if Germany were a member of the League.

In September Germany entered the League, and on that occasion Monsieur Briand delivered a speech that resounded to the furthest corners of the earth, in which he mentioned that the time had come when guns and machine guns should be dispensed with, and uttered words that should be engraved over our country: that the two great nations, Germans and Frenchmen, had won so many laurels in battle against each other, that the future should only see them in friendly competition for the great aims and ideals of mankind.

. . . The period that ensued had heights to show, and deep valleys; budding confidence was often followed by snows of distrust. Even now [1927] it shows rather a crisis of confidence in the whole evolution of peace than unanimous assent on the part of the peoples of the earth. . . .

Because the evolution was no straight one, because disappointments followed closely upon high-pitched hopes, the mental evolution of Germany could not follow a straight line either. A people of strong individualists, such as the Germans, does not easily allow its feelings and sentiments to be reduced to a common denominator. Yet it is possible to assert today [1927]—and the last debates in the Reichstag have demonstrated this—that the overwhelming majority of the German people is united in determination for peace and understanding.

AN ENGLISHMAN'S IMPRESSIONS OF GERMANY BETWEEN WARS

By Harold Butler

From chap. 4 of The Lost Peace, *by Harold Butler. Copyright 1941 by Harcourt, Brace & Co., New York; reproduced by permission. The author is a leading British statesman and diplomat.*

When I returned to Berlin early in 1921, it was a shabby, miserable, half-starved city shorn of all its imperial pomp and splendor. There were no more swanking monocled officers in gorgeous many-colored uniforms; their place had been taken by the neat sober gray of the Reichswehr officers, who went about quietly and modestly as befitted the servants of a republic. Altogether soldiers were few and far between. Germany had become outwardly demilitarized. It was now a civilian nation, and one could not help noticing how badly dressed it looked. Of course textile materials were scarce and the country had been ruined by the war, but even with the return of apparent prosperity five years later, the Germans did not learn how to wear their clothes. For some occult reason their tailors, who knew how to cut a smart uniform as well as any in the world, never discovered the art of turning out a well-fitting lounge suit. Whether this was the fault of the cutter, or whether the German body like the German soul could only adapt itself to the stiff garments of regimentation, I was never able to decide. But the Nazis followed the national instinct when they put everybody back into uniform, not merely by embodying millions into the army, the Storm Troopers, the Labor Corps, the Hitler Youth, the German Girls' Corps, and so on, but by inventing uniforms, badges and insignia of all kinds for diplomats, officials, and even journalists. By pandering to the innate German love of parade and decoration they struck a shrewd blow at the drabness and dullness of the civilian republic, which had always been one of its chief weaknesses. The German always felt slightly ashamed of himself in mufti, a little bit lost and forlorn, as if to find himself just a solitary individual, his own master instead of a unit in a disciplined throng, gave him a chilly sense of isolation and bewilderment. Put him into uniform, however, and his chest swelled, his self-esteem was restored, he was part of an organized mass, only called upon to obey orders instead of having to make his own decisions. . . . This collectivist psychology is one of the most deeply rooted German traits. The Republic was totally unable to satisfy it, but Hitler understood it. His vast parades with waving flags and blaring music restored to the average German, and particularly to the women, something which they loved and of which they felt themselves unjustly deprived. Nor was it merely the pomp and the showmanship which they wanted, but the comfortable sense of being one of a crowd again instead of lone individuals. The herd spirit is stronger among the Germans than among any other western people. The great majority have never valued personal liberty, perhaps because, as the Nazi leaders assert, they have never felt the want of it.

Still, in 1921 Germany was a republic, and there were other signs besides its civilian exterior to suggest that the "revolution" had really changed things. The old rigid class distinctions had gone. The social superiority of the aristocracy, the army and the officials was no longer aggressively proclaimed. There was less ceremonious bowing and heel-clicking. The relations between people of all ranks were less constrained. But with the loosening of the old social order had gone a general relaxation of morals, both public and private. The terrible strain of the war years, the bitter disillusionment of defeat, the impoverishment of all classes and the chaos of the demobilization period had all contributed to this decline. The atmosphere was full of violence and murder. The Free Corps of disbanded soldiers were always looking for trouble. One *putsch* followed another. First the Spartakists, then Kapp, then the Saxon Communists, then Hitler, were bloodily suppressed. Kurt Eisner, Karl Liebknecht, Rosa

Luxemburg, Mathias Erzberger, Walter Rathenau, and many lesser men were successfully assassinated by the disciples of reaction. The rule of law was spasmodic and precarious. Shady finance, dishonest trade and wild speculation were rampant in the commercial community. In the great cities the ordinary social restraints were openly defied. In large sections of the upper and middle classes religion and respectability were thrown to the winds. Berlin night life reached a pitch of licentiousness never equalled in modern Europe. Vice of every kind was flaunted in the Kurfürstendamm with an ostentation at which Paris would have blushed. The first five postwar years culminating in the total collapse of the currency witnessed a demoralization from which the nation never really recovered.

But when one looked for signs that the revolution had converted Germany to democracy, one began to doubt whether it had ever taken place at all. Though the outward appearance had changed, the internal balance of forces, the real springs of power, remained the same. Behind the façade of a humdrum, mostly middle class parliament, the army and the civil service were still supreme, and at heart they were the same army and the same civil service. It was characteristic of the German "revolution" that it had failed to alter the structure of the state, without which it could not be a real revolution at all. In November 1918 there had been some real fervor for political emancipation. The working class had turned against the old order, but it did not find the vigorous leadership without which no great revolution has ever been accomplished. Its own leaders, drawn from the old majority socialists, who had supported the Kaiser and the war from the beginning until very near the end, possessed neither the will nor the ability to remold the political and social traditions of the country. To establish any kind of democracy the first task was to destroy the power of the army and to subordinate it to the people. This task was never attempted. The first act of the new popular government was to entrust the withdrawal of the troops from the front and their demobilization to von Hindenburg and the old General Staff. When in January 1919 the Spartakists made an ill-planned attempt to establish the authority of the people, Noske, the Socialist Minister of War, entrusted the preservation of order not to a militia drawn from old soldiers sympathetic to the republic, which might readily have been formed on the model of the Austrian *Volkswehr,* but to troops organized by a typical collection of generals and "vons" of the old Prussian school—von Luttwitz, von Hoffmann, von Roeder and the rest. These were the men who in fact crushed the "revolution" within two months of its birth. They did it with the approval and support of the majority Socialists, who in their brief hour of authority threw overboard most of the principles which they had protested since the days of Karl Marx. Not being strong men themselves, they were always conscious and apprehensive of the reactionary forces arrayed against them. As one close observer remarked, "even after the revolution it could not be said that there was a bare majority of the German people for democracy and parliamentary government." The fact was that there was only an abdication of power by the old regime when defeat stared it in the face, never that uprising of a great democratic majority of the nation in which most people in the Allied countries fondly believed.

Having quickly learnt to lean upon the old army diehards, the republican government made little effort to suppress the Free Corps composed of mercenaries and adventurers and commanded by notoriously reactionary officers, who breathed uncompromising hatred of the republic and all its works. From their ranks came the murderers of the few genuine revolutionaries such as Eisner, Liebknecht, and Luxemburg, and of mild but able reformers such as Erzberger and Rathenau, who they feared might consolidate the democratic system. Though they suffered a temporary setback with the failure of the Kapp *putsch,* the Free Corps with the Reichswehr secretly arming and encouraging them, became a real power in the state against which the civil authorities were helpless. Even if the government had had the means to repress them, it may be doubted whether they would have used them. Successive republican governments did nothing to prevent the gradual recovery of its old domination by the army, its progressive defiance of the military clauses of the treaty, or its scarcely concealed expansion by the arming and training of "Security Police" and civil militia. During all the years from 1919 to 1933 the army was slowly laying fresh foundations of military power, which might some day bring revenge within their grasp, while Parliament and people stood passively by. They probably did not know what was going on underneath, but if they had, would the majority have offered more opposition than they did to the reintroduction of conscription in 1935? There is indeed little doubt that the army was almost as responsible for the second counter-revolution under Hitler as it was for the first counter-revolution under Noske fourteen years earlier. At no time had its authority been seriously shaken or even seriously challenged. By throwing the responsibility of making peace upon the "democrats," it had brought off a brilliant double coup. Not only did it evade its responsibility for the defeat, but it rendered "democracy" hateful in the eyes of the people by saddling it with the odium of the humiliating peace, to which the blunders and follies of the old regime had condemned Germany. But then the army knew, as Hitler knew, that few things are easier than to mislead the German people.

If the political power of the army was never destroyed, that of the civil service remained equally intact. When I first went back to Berlin after the war, I made some inquiries about civil servants whom I had known as members of the German delegation in Paris in 1910. If I had imagined that they had been thrown out as scions of the old anti-democratic bureaucracy, I was quickly undeceived. There they were still in their old places, as authoritative and as authoritarian as ever. As I was brought into close contact with various departments, I soon realized that little had really changed. The permanent heads were as powerful as ever, and most of them hardly troubled to conceal the fact that they were still as anti-democratic as ever. . . . No government, certainly not a reforming government, least of all a "revolutionary" government, can hope to succeed unless it can count upon the loyalty of its officials, but there was little of that quality to be found in the heavy well-appointed offices of the Berlin bureaucracy when it came to executing democratic reforms. A few new men with a more or less democratic outlook were brought in, but they were not allowed much rope by the permanent officials. . . . The civil service, like the army, was never democratized and never stripped of its power. The absence of any real revolution in Germany was proved by nothing so clearly as by the fact that the higher civil service survived the upheavals both of 1918 and of 1933 almost unscathed. Men trained in the Prussian bureaucracy who had been loyal to the Kaiser could not bring loyalty to the republic. Still less could men who had been loyal to the republic have brought loyalty to Hitler, and yet the Nazis, with all their heresy-hunting and all their thirst for well-paid jobs, could find few higher civil servants unworthy of the confidence of the Fuehrer. . . .

And so the new Germany began almost where the old Germany left off. *Deutschland ueber alles* remained the national anthem of the republic as it was of the Empire and was to be of the Third Reich. Its ideas were unchanged, its law courts were unchanged, its machinery of government was unchanged. The failure of its spiritual revolution was manifest long before the Treaty of Versailles was signed, and became more manifest every year as the forces of reaction gradually recovered their grip.

But surely, it may be said, democracy would not have perished if the Treaty had not imposed an impossible reparations burden, if Germany had been admitted to the League, if Poincaré had not occupied the Ruhr, if inflation had not spread ruin and despair throughout the country. These are the familiar German pleas by which the Nazis justified their revolution of nihilism and by which the democrats excused their failure to prevent it. No doubt the economic chapters of the Treaty were folly, no doubt the occupation of the Ruhr was a political and economic blunder, but whether they were responsible for the breakdown of German democracy is quite another question. That they gave the counter-revolutionaries a splendid opportunity of discrediting the republican government which had signed the peace is certain. With Germany a member of the League at its birth the democratic forces in the nation might have been strengthened and their hesitant leaders encouraged. If the reparations burden had been lighter, the charge of ruining the nation could not have been so readily laid at their door or at the door of the Allies. If their troops had never occupied the Ruhr, the French could not have been saddled with the blame for inflation. But Germany was in any case economically exhausted by the war. She must in any case have passed through a period of dire distress. Inflation on a large scale had already begun before a single French soldier entered the Ruhr [in 1923]. . . . Without the complete dislocation of German industry caused by the occupation, the collapse of the currency might not have attained the astronomic proportions which it finally achieved, but under the most favorable circumstances Germany could not have escaped the ruin which the huge drain on her resources ending in defeat entailed. But is it to be supposed that the army and the reactionaries would have tamely admitted that this ruin was caused by their blunder in plunging into war and by their military failures? Deprived of the reparations slogan, would they not have claimed that ruin was due to the loss of the iron-ore of Alsace-Lorraine and of the coal of Silesia? Their outcry against the territorial clauses of the Treaty would have been just as loud as the uproar over paying a fraction of the indemnity which was wrung from France in 1940. In the face of such an outcry it is unlikely that the republicans would have stood much more firmly than they actually did. If the fear of the Allies had been less, they might even have been driven from power earlier rather than later. When the Rhineland was evacuated, Wilhelm Foerster prophesied with perfect accuracy that it would be the signal for a military and nationalist reaction, which might have taken place even sooner, if the Rhineland had never been occupied. Though all such speculation on what might have been is necessarily vain, there is certainly no reason to think that the failure of German democracy was primarily due to the Treaty. To suppose that a peace without reparation or indemnity would have scotched the militarist and reactionary elements in Germany rests on a reading of its history and psychology which is difficult to sustain. It is at least as arguable that in no circumstances were the democratic aspirations of the nation sufficiently virile to revolutionize the whole German outlook and tradition, without which they could not prevail.

A different conclusion might suggest itself if democracy had made vigorous efforts to assert itself during the five years which followed the evacuation of the Ruhr. During that time Germany staged a recovery which astonished and deceived the majority of Germans and the majority of the outside world as well. Production rose rapidly, unemployment declined sharply, to such an extent, indeed, that by 1928 the number of people receiving relief in Germany was only 600,000, half the number in Great Britain, with a population 30 per cent smaller. In those days the country seemed to be recovering its old prosperity. Beer flowed freely once more, food was good and plentiful. Municipalities went in for ambitious schemes of development financed by money borrowed in London and New York. Not content with model housing estates and sanatoria, they launched out into luxury expenditure on mammoth halls, athletic grounds, swimming pools, and planetaria. . . . The German love of the grandiose and the spectacular was able to find expression once more at great cost to the foreigner. It has been calculated that out of one pocket Germany paid £400 millions in reparations under the Dawes plan during these five golden years, while into the other she took £750 millions derived from the trusting bankers of Lombard Street and Wall Street. So on balance the country was doing well, and seemed to be rapidly making good the losses of war and inflation. The Republic could no longer be charged with having cursed the people with perpetual poverty, nor, as the French and British troops began to leave the Rhineland long before their time, could the Allies be charged with undying vindictiveness. There seemed a fair prospect for democratic government in Germany and for continuous peace in Europe.

These appearances were, however, deceptive. It is true that the wave of crime and disorder had subsided. The Nazi Party, with about 100,000 members, was still a negligible factor in politics. I used to see its flaming red posters on the hoardings at election times and was told it was run by an obscure lunatic called Adolf Hitler. Stresemann had a long and copious lunch with Briand in the grubby little inn at Thoiry. Germany made full use of her membership in the League to push her claims in every direction, but not to show any active sympathy with its aims and principles. When she was admitted, a deputy of the Reichstag said "the League will find us uncomfortable people," and it did. At times I was disposed to think that Germany did not receive a fair deal at Geneva. Her officials in the Secretariat were not given much scope, and her representatives in the Assembly were always regarded with some suspicion. But when one looks at their previous records and their subsequent performances, one realizes that the German officials of the League were with hardly any exceptions alien to the whole conception of international cooperation. They were interested in Germany, but not in the League. Many of them had been officials saturated with the ideas of the old order and became enthusiastic Nazis when Hitler climbed to power. The remainder, who were dubious about him at first, hastened to make their peace when they saw that he was leading Germany back towards domination in Europe....

The same tendencies were creeping out in German politics. The Republic, despite the prevailing prosperity and its increasing prestige abroad, was losing rather than gaining ground in the hearts of the people. Its very existence was already becoming precarious. As early as 1925 the writing on the wall had become plainly legible. When President Ebert died, the contest for the Presidency of the Republic lay between von Hindenburg, the figurehead of the old regime, and Marx, the candidate of the Catholic party. The old Marshal won by a handsome majority, while Thaelmann, the only "revolutionary" candidate, polled only two million of the thirty million votes cast. From that time onward the ascendancy of the army was unquestioned and unquestionable. The President appointed one of his old staff officers, General Groener, as Minister of the Reichswehr, and allowed no civil interference in military affairs. The secret funds of the army, which were shielded from any republican prying, were swollen by all sorts of dubious methods and devoted to building up the power of the war-machine and its masters....

Nor were other signs lacking that the second phase of the counter-revolution, which culminated in the election of Von Hindenburg, was but the forerunner of a third phase, which would see the overthrow of the whole republican edifice by violence. Uniforms were once more becoming prominent in the streets, not the battle-gray of the Reichswehr, which still kept discreetly in the background, but the varied uniforms of the private political armies. There was the Stahlhelm (Steel helmets), mostly ex-service men organized by ex-officers and subsidized by big business, who constituted an anti-democratic reserve running into hundreds of thousands. There was the Reichsbanner (flag of the Reich), recruited for the defense of the Republic and wearing its black, red, and gold colors. If this corps had been formed in the early days, it might possibly have enabled the government to disband the Free Corps and really to assert its authority in the country, but when it was organized in 1924, it came five years too late. There was the Red Front of the Communist Party, and there were Hitler's Storm Troopers. The stage was in fact set for civil war. Political manifestations came to assume the form not so much of public meetings and Reichstag debates as of Sunday parades and nightly brawls between the rival gangs. No serious attempt was made by the government to dissolve these illegal organizations or to ban the wearing of private uniforms. Any such measure could only have been carried through with the consent of the army, which would doubtless have undertaken to break up the Red Front and the Reichsbanner with alacrity, but which would certainly not have raised a rifle to suppress the Stahlhelm or the Storm Troops.

Thus the Republic was slipping toward extinction even in the halcyon days of fictitious prosperity....

But its fate was sealed by the onset of the great slump of 1929. With the collapse of the inflated values of Wall Street the flow of American credit across the Atlantic dried up and with it the balloon of German prosperity came sagging to the ground....

Though during the good times the Nazi ranks had not attracted many recruits, with the pricking of the economic bubble a startling change came over their fortunes. As the unemployment figures mounted, so did those of the Nazi Party. Its double appeal to nationalism and to socialism, its double promise to smash the Versailles Treaty and to cure unemployment began to sweep the country, and particularly its youth. Stark poverty was now gripping Germany once more. The comfortable mirage of the past five years had suddenly vanished into thin air. To a people of little political intelligence all the old parties seemed to have failed, and in despair millions of them turned to Hitler. The world was astounded and perturbed when at the election of 1930 the Nazi vote bounded at one jump from 810,000 to 6,401,000. The end of the Republic was in sight.

When the crash came, it came easily and without resistance. To the end all the party leaders clung to the vain hope of a compromise with Hitler, which would permit the parliamentary game to go decently on. Even the trade-union chiefs deluded themselves into the same sense of false security. A few days after Hitler became Chancellor, one of them assured me that nothing would really be altered, but that they would come to some arrangement. He was soon in prison, poor fellow, and went on to a concentration camp. The leaders could not bring themselves to risk all the wealth and power of the great trade-union movement by calling a general strike. Had there been one such man at the top, millions might have followed him. It would probably have been a forlorn hope, but at least the minority who believed in freedom would have made an honorable fight for it. As it was, they were wiped off the map. One May morning Dr. Ley quietly took over the buildings and the accumulated savings of the strongest working-class organization in the world, without lifting a finger. . . .

Hitler had not been many months in power before he severed all ties with Geneva. That was the logical and necessary consequence not only of all his agitation, but of all his purposes. He did not leave the League because he objected to this or that clause in the Disarmament Convention, but because it was his intention to rearm to the limit. He cut loose simultaneously from the I.L.O., not because Germany had not equal rights there (which she had always had), but because it was a necessary step to rearmament. To achieve that object he required not a 48-hour week, still less a 40-hour week, but a 60- or 70-hour week or even longer. . . . From the day of his assumption of office, Hitler's objective was the constitution of overwhelming military power, which would enable him not merely to regain Germany's lost provinces, but to extend her rule over Europe and then beyond the seas by the sword.

But Hitler's weapon was not the sword alone. The path to military victory was to be prepared by the poisoned pen and the corrupting word of propaganda. Long before Germany possessed an army and an air force, he had won a resounding victory by persuading the wealthy in many countries that he alone stood between Europe and Bolshevism. He did it in Germany, he did it in France, he even did it to some extent in Britain. On the day when he sent his troops into the Rhineland, I happened to meet a prominent British banker, who stoutly maintained that London ought to lend Germany all the money it needed, "because Hitler was the great barrier against Communism." He had innocently accepted the Nazi propaganda at its face value, oblivious of the fact that at no time since January 1919 had Germany stood in the faintest danger of a Communist revolution. Successive general elections, the overwhelming power of the Reichswehr, the police and the private armies of the Right, the passive conservatism of the people, all rendered such an explanation of the Nazi revolution a fantastic absurdity to anyone who knew the country. But the majority of foreigners, including a considerable number of influential Englishmen, did not know it. They were obsessed by the red bogy. They cheered Hitler's diatribes against Stalin and his henchmen, and naively looked on him as the savior of Western civilization.

And yet there was much in her recent history to suggest that Germany's eyes always instinctively turned to the East. The *Drang nach Osten*, the eastward urge, still haunted the minds of her leaders. The General Staff had always seen in Russia the final reinsurance against a British blockade. As early as 1922 Rathenau had torpedoed the Rapallo Conference by announcing his treaty with Lenin and Chicherin to the dismay of Mr. Lloyd George and Monsieur Barthou. In 1926 Stresemann had prefaced his entry into the League of Nations by a new treaty with Russia declining to accept any military obligation of the League of which the Soviet government might disapprove. Hitler reversed this policy in appearance, but his aim remained the same, if his method was different. He toyed with a nationalist revolt in the Ukraine. In the light of what we now know of German fifth-column activities there is no reason why the evidence of a German attempt to suborn Marshal Tukhachevski and to undermine the Red Army furnished by the Moscow trial of 1937 should not be genuine. Whether by force or by agreement the German plan to acquire control of the vast resources of Russia was never dropped. Hitler himself made no secret of it. In 1936 he said to the Labor Front: "If we had at our disposal the incalculable wealth and stores of raw material of the Ural Mountains and the unending fertile plains of the Ukraine to be exploited under National Socialist leadership, then we would produce and our German people would swim in plenty." It was only a question of the timing and the method by which this dream was to be realized. A year before the event, Rauschning, who was familiar with the inner forces molding German policy, forecast the Nazi-Soviet pact. "There are many well-known political elements," he wrote, "who desire a solution of this sort. . . . If Germany and Russia were to join together, the western powers and the small states would be compelled to capitulate without a struggle. There is a good deal of evidence that this policy might prove attractive for reasons of internal politics. In any case dynamism sees in the *volte-face* of an alliance with Soviet Russia a last chance which might be of incalculable revolutionary effect. That trump card was played unblushingly by Hitler in August 1939. It served his purpose by sealing the fate of Poland and avoiding a war on two fronts for a time. But as he has now confessed, it was a temporary arrangement rendered cynically expedient by the needs of the moment, which he meant to throw overboard at the earliest convenient occasion, that is to say, when he had extracted the maximum profit from perfidy. In the last resort the mastery of Russian foodstuffs and raw materials was indispensable to his survival in a struggle against the British Empire and the United States, and his dream of European hegemony was in jeopardy as long as Russia remained a Great Power.

There is no need to recapitulate the stages of Hitler's progress. By now they are sufficiently well known and understood even by those who would not see. The kernel of his whole effort has been to uproot every democratic seedling in German life. He has done it with characteristic thoroughness and ruthlessness, and it would be foolish to suppose that he has not largely succeeded. Every official, every university teacher, every schoolmaster, with a tinge of liberal sentiment was summarily ejected, unless he could give plain proof of his conversion to the Nazi creed. No newspaper, no book, no film, no play was tolerated which did not harmonize with the Nazi view of life. Every instrument of education and propaganda was turned to its inculcation. Fairy stories and school books were rewritten, science was falsified, economics and history travestied, in order to ensure that no word of any other doctrine should penetrate into the minds of the young. Lest a new intelligentsia should arise which might be the source of heresy, brawn was deliberately cultivated instead of brain. After six months' physical toil in a labor camp followed by two years' gruelling in the ranks of the army, the critical faculties of the most promising scholar might be safely regarded as atrophied. In the old imperial days military service was adapted to the needs of the budding student. He was a one-year volunteer, who did not serve his time as an ordinary private in the ranks, and whose duties were often related to his intellectual interests. The opposite was rather the case with the Nazis. The whole object of their system of education was to eradicate individualism and independent thinking. The future leaders picked for special training were chosen for their physique, character, and devotion to the ideals of Hitlerism rather than for their mental capacity. The clever boy was generally discouraged and reduced to mediocrity. The result of the system is a generation of narrow-minded fanatics imbued with a blind worship of the Fuehrer and a total inability to think for themselves. To suppose that among them are to be found thousands of good democrats thirsting to throw off the Nazi yoke and to cooperate in building a new world with their youthful contemporaries in other countries is just pure illusion. One of the most baffling of future problems will be the youth of Germany, whose mental horizon is bounded by Hitlerdom and whose stunted intelligence is probably incapable of conceiving any other view of life. To convert them into rational beings, to say nothing of decent members of civilized society, will be a task of herculean difficulty.

The Nazis boast that the Germans have never belonged to the West and its civilization. They claim that through the centuries they have fought a long fight against the culture of Greece and Rome and against the teachings of Christ. Their true ancestry always derived from the old pagan gods and from the barbarians of the primeval forests, who threw back Varus and his legions. The claim is not wholly false. Though they produced Luther, Jakob Boehme, Kant, Goethe, and Beethoven, the Germans have never wholly assimilated the spirit of the Occident. As a nation they have never spoken its language fluently or shared its ideals fully. At heart they have always retained something of the outlook of primitive man, something of the tribal conception of society. They have continued to confound violence with virility, to venerate as leaders generals rather than statesmen, to honor the virtues of the warrior and to despise those of the saint. To them the action of the individual has always been subjected to the law of the tribe. His right to lead his own life has been subordinated to his duty to the state. For ninety years and more every liberal tendency has been systematically crushed out, and increasing homage paid to the traditions of savagery and brutality inherited from primitive Germanity. The Nazi revolution was the climax of this process. It carried the doctrines of Pan-Germanism and racialism, which had long been gathering force, to their violent and logical conclusion. It put the clock back by several centuries. How can it be put forward again? It cannot be done in minutes or in months. To reverse the whole trend of German development over a century will be a matter of years, if not of generations. It can only be done by the Germans themselves. Like every other people they can only gain their freedom by their own exertions; it cannot be imposed upon them from without. To achieve reality it must come from within. Until this spiritual revolution has occurred, Germany will remain a danger, actual or potential, to the rest of the world. We who know what freedom is can encourage its growth by precept and example, but we must leave Germany to fight out her own salvation, whatever its price in blood and tears. Until she has found it, it is idle to suppose that Germany will take her place as a willing partner in a new world order based upon the principles of liberty and democracy. To cure her economic evils will not be enough, for German nationalism becomes more overweening in good times than in bad. . . .

ORIGINS OF THE THIRD REICH

By F. L. Schuman

From chap. 10 of *International Politics*, by F. L. Schuman. 2nd edition. Copyright 1937 by McGraw-Hill Book Co., New York; reproduced by permission. Dr. Schuman is professor of political science at Williams College, and author of books and articles on Nazi Germany.

Republican Germany's foreign policy encountered a succession of defeats at the hands of France and attained none of its major objectives. This circumstance helped to discredit democracy. The psychic insecurities bred of national defeat and impotence were aggravated by social insecurities engendered by currency inflation and general impoverishment. Even in its early days, the Weimar Republic was bitterly assailed by monarchists, ultra-patriots, and adventurous leaders of disgruntled ex-soldiers. Liberals and Social-Democrats, in the name of freedom, tolerated reactionary enemies of the Republic on the Right and Communist enemies of the Republic on the Left and were denounced by each for tolerating the other. Junkers and industrialists, unconverted to Liberalism and still in possession of much of their old power and prestige, dreamed of glory and profit and schemed with reactionary conspirators against the new regime. The dark years after Versailles created a following for anti-republican plotters. The Kapp *putsch* of March 1920 was frustrated only by a general strike. In November 1923, during the French occupation of the Ruhr, an obscure ex-corporal of Austrian birth, preaching anti-Semitism and the glory of the Treaty of Brest-Litovsk and leading a "National Socialist German Workers' Party" attempted a *putsch* in Munich. It was suppressed. He was tried and lightly sentenced. He resumed political activity in 1925, but converted few to his cause so long as the new prosperity of the middle 'twenties caused the lower middle classes, the proletariat, and the peasantry to turn deaf ears to agitators and fanatics. His name was Adolf Hitler.

When the Great Depression descended upon the Reich, it created potentially revolutionary conditions once more. Jobless workers flocked to the Communist Party. The impoverished peasantry and Kleinbürgertum, terrified at the economic collapse and fearful of Communism, flocked to Hitler's Nazis who promised to save them from Bolshevism and the Jews. Industrialists and Junkers perceived an opportunity to use Hitler to destroy the trade unions and the liberal and radical parties. The forces of democracy were paralyzed. The Communists were incapable of undertaking proletarian revolution. The Nazi messiah appealed to the masses by combining the vocabulary of socialism with the language of impassioned chauvinism and racial hatred. He and his aides cried from the housetops that the German armies were undefeated in 1918, but had been "stabbed in the back" by the Marxists and Jews; that democracy and Communism were destroying German *Kultur;* that the "Weimar Jew Republic" was shameful and corrupt; that the glories of the Hohenstauffen and Hohenzollern Empires must be recaptured in a glorious "Third Reich," strong, authoritarian, and ready to restore to Germany her rightful place in the sun.

With banners, drums, and trumpets the brown-shirted Nazi Storm Troopers, subsidized by businessmen and aristocrats, carried the *Hakenkreuz* flag of anti-semitism throughout the land and shouted their battlecries: "Freedom and bread!" "Out with the Jews!" "Break the bonds of interest slavery!" and "Germany awake!" In the Reichstag election of September 14, 1930, they won 6,400,000 votes. In the presidential election of April 10, 1932, in which the "wooden Titan," Von Hindenburg, was re-elected by a slim margin, 13,400,000 votes were cast for Hitler. In the Reichstag election of July 31, 1932, 13,745,000 Nazi votes were cast—37 per cent of the total. Hitler seemed about to be swept into power by a great mass movement which would give him a majority of the electorate. But business conditions improved slightly in the autumn of 1932 and in the Reichstag balloting of November 6, 1932 (the last free election in Germany), the Nazis polled only 11,737,000 votes—less than one-third of the total. By the end of the year their movement was bankrupt and disintegrating.

The Reich was delivered to Fascism not by an electoral victory but by a conspiracy, entered into against the last republican Chancellor, Kurt von Schleicher, whose old friend, Franz von Papen, resolved to use Hitler to put himself back in power. Papen, arch muddler of the German reaction, had been head of the "Baron's Cabinet" which Hindenburg had appointed after ousting Chancellor Heinrich Bruening in May 1932. In January 1933 Papen spun his plot. His tools, so he thought, were Hitler, the mob hypnotist; Hugenberg, the ultra-nationalist publisher; Fritz Thyssen, the steel magnate; the *Reichsverband der Industrie;* and the *Junker Landbund.* Hindenburg, who had been reelected to the Presidency nine months previously by the support of Bruening and of all the liberals and Socialists in order that he might save the Reich from Hitler was persuaded to "save agriculture" (i.e. the Junkers) from "agrarian Bolshevism" (i.e. an exposure of the use to which they had put state subsidies) by dismissing Schleicher on January 30, 1933, and appointing Hitler Chancellor, Papen Vice-Chancellor, Hugenberg Minister of

Economics, and other reactionaries to the remaining posts.

The story of how Hitler astutely tricked his non-Nazi colleagues, wiped out all other parties, suppressed the social radicals in his own ranks, and established the Nazi dictatorship cannot be reviewed here. Suffice it to note that the multitudes were exalted by the mass pageantry of great festivals, by the masterly propaganda of Goebbels and by the demagoguery of Der Führer. They were prevailed upon to give the regime almost unanimous support in a series of referenda. Dissidence was suppressed by the ruthlessness of Goering and the espionage of Himmler. Heavy industry and the Junkers had paid the piper and were, to a considerable degree, able to call the tune. On "Bloody Saturday," June 30, 1934, critics within the ranks were silenced and old scores were settled. Among those shot for treason were Gregor Strasser, Ernst Roehm, Karl Ernst, and other Nazi radicals who resented Hitler's dependence on the propertied classes or who aspired to replace the Junker-controlled Reichswehr with the Storm Troopers as Germany's new army; the aides of the incautious von Papen, who barely escaped death and was bundled off to Vienna as German ambassador; Kurt von Schleicher and his wife; Erich Klausener, General von Bredow and scores of others.

With Hindenburg's death on August 2, 1934, and Hitler's assumption of the powers of the Presidency, Der Führer's control of the German state became absolute. Hjalmar Schacht remained his liaison with big business. Defense Minister Blomberg and the General Staff remained his liaison with the Junkers. With the trade unions abolished and strikes forbidden, with the press, radio, cinema, theater, and school system shackled, and with all social organizations "coordinated" under Nazi control, the dictatorship was as unlimited as human ingenuity and lust for power could make it. Popular unrest was deflected into Jew-baiting and into hatred of foreign enemies. Germany thus became a new citadel of Fascist totalitarianism, dedicated to militarism, revenge and imperial expansion.

METHODS OF NAZI STATECRAFT

By E. M. Earle

From "The Nazi Concept of War," by E. M. Earle, in *Makers of Modern Strategy*, edited by E. M. Earle. Copyright 1943 by Princeton University Press. Dr. Earle is professor in the Institute for Advanced Study.

To the Nazis the armed forces of the Reich were only the cutting edge of the war machine. In their totalitarian strategy, military operations and war were ... but a regrettable and unavoidable last resort, after all other methods of conquest had been exhausted. Hitler's greatest period of success, therefore, was his long series of bloodless victories up to and including Munich. Thereafter the battle rested largely with the soldiers, and there is not much evidence available to show that Hitler's military strategy will compare favorably with his triumphs in the realm of psychological and political warfare.

An indispensable first step in the war of nerves was the welding of the German people into a unity which was terrifying to the outside world. This was accomplished partly by the ruthless suppression of all internal dissent from the Nazi program—particularly by the destruction or the "coordination" of the Jews, the churches, the universities, the trade unions, the socialists, the communists, and all others who were suspected of internationalism or pacifism.

It was done partly by skillful propaganda of press and radio, reinforced by party discipline and appeals to national pride. Militarism, Pan-Germanism, anti-semitism, racial superiority, worship of the state, and other features of Hitler's program were deeply rooted in German history and were exploited by the Nazis to their own ends. "Any resurrection of the German people," wrote Hitler, "can take place only by way of regaining external power. But the prerequisites for this are not arms, as our bourgeois 'statesmen' always babble, but the forces of will power. . . . The best arms are dead and useless material as long as the spirit is missing which is ready, willing, and determined to use them." Therefore, "the question of regaining Germany's power is not, perhaps, How can we manufacture arms, but, How can we produce that spirit which enables the people to bear arms."

It is not necessary to describe in detail the manner in which Hitler created the will to fight by bringing about the psychological and emotional mobilization of the German nation. He took over from Hindenburg and other army leaders the stab-in-the-back legend, designed to show that the German army had not been defeated in 1918 but had been betrayed on the home front, and gave the legend a popularity and degree of credence it could not otherwise have attained. He led the German people to believe that in November 1918 they had voluntarily laid down their arms on promises from Woodrow Wilson of a just and generous peace and that Wilson had defaulted on his promises in the "greatest betrayal in all history." By these and other devices he bred in the hearts of all classes a consuming sense of injustice over the *Diktat* of Versailles, and among large numbers of Germans he aroused a spirit of vengeance. He revived the pre-1914 theory that a peaceful Germany was being encircled by jealous and hostile states. Among German youth he developed a cult of Spartanism, a fanatical German nationalism, and an unquestioned loyalty to the Führer which boded no good for the peace of the world. By maintaining the largest private army in modern history, the S.A., and a corps of janissaries, the S.S., Hitler even before he came to power as Chancellor spread the spirit of militarism throughout the land. . . . The function of the state, said Hitler, is to unite all Germans, and "to lead them, gradually and safely, to a dominating position" in the world.

The story of German economic mobilization, *Wehrwirtschaft* and *Kriegswirtschaft*, has been told often. . . . It must be noted, however, that from the General Staff the Nazis took over the idea that the "total" war of 1914-1918 was not total enough; that adequate measures—such as the development of synthetic raw materials and the building up of stockpiles of critical minerals—must be taken against blockade; that the home front must be solidified economically, as well as psychologically, in support of the war effort which was to come. The Four Year Plans, under the general administration of Goering with the assistance of Major Generals Fritz Loeb, Georg Thomas, and Hermann von Hanneken, among others, brought about the complete militarization of German economy. As a result, the German army entered the war in 1939 better equipped, and with larger reserves of matériel, than any other modern army. The Nazi concept of total war was inherent in their theories of the totalitarian state.

Force alone, however, was never considered by Hitler to be an effective weapon. Force and the threat of force must be supplemented by words, slogans, ideas, which are among the most powerful of all weapons, as was demonstrated by the French Revolution, by Woodrow Wilson, and by the Bolsheviks. Therefore the National Socialist movement was offered the Germans and the world as a basis for a New Order, which would replace the old "chaos" and "inefficiency." Because it had about it a character of inevitability—because, in the words of an American, it was the "wave of the future"—it was on the offensive, the rest of the world on the defensive. Only the ideological offensive—a fanatical belief in one's own view of life—can give victory, said Hitler. Thus the Nazi revolution was to serve not merely as an instrumentality for unifying the German people but a means, as well, of disunifying those countries which stood in the way of German expansion.... The revolutionary struggle in Germany was to be transformed by Hitler into a European and worldwide civil war.

Hitler was a master at throwing apples of discord among other nations. He knew of the critical differences of opinion in France, Great Britain, and America, and exploited them to the full. He always succeeded in discussing the issues of European politics not in terms in which he really viewed them—as questions of power—but in terms which would cause the maximum division in public opinion abroad. "Mental confusion, contradiction of feeling, indecisiveness, panic: these are our weapons," he told Rauschning. Thus the alliance with Japan was first presented to a credulous world as the Anti-Comintern Pact and hence as an attack on Bolshevism. The fear of Bolshevism, Hitler correctly suspected, was so strong among the conservatives of Britain, France and the United States that they altogether overlooked the portent to their own security in the Pacific of the camouflaged alliance. To the conservatives, also, Hitler was one who had "solved the labor problem," not one who conscripted the labor force for the manufacture of armaments. Liberals in Britain and America were befuddled by attacks on Versailles, by appeals to the sacred right of Germans in Czechoslovakia and elsewhere to be "reunited" with the motherland, and by the claims of Germany to "fair play." Anti-semitism was bait for so many different classes in so many different places as to be a catch-all for the unwary everywhere. Those who advocated resistance to Hitler were represented to peaceful peoples as "war mongers."

In this manner, so much confusion was spread abroad that the statesmen of Europe seemed unable to see their interest and act on it. Of this, of course, Spain was the classic example. Ciano might realize in regard to Spain that "there no longer are frontiers, only strategic positions," but non-fascists could be persuaded by fascist propaganda that the struggle for control of Spain involved only Bolshevism and Catholicism. In short, the Nazis undermined morale and the will to resist everywhere, except at home, by fostering pacifism, defeatism, and "corroding uneasiness, doubt, and fear." By these methods Hitler softened up his victims, lulled them into a false sense of security, and ultimately rendered them incapable of successful armed resistance. Thus Czechoslovakia, at the beginning of 1938, was a relatively prosperous state, secure behind a bulwark of powerful fortifications ... a magnificent army ... powerful allies in both east and west; nine months later she found herself unable to stave off disintegration, in which her friends lent her enemies a helping hand. If he had accomplished nothing but the conquest of Czechoslovakia without firing a shot, Hitler would have to be recorded on the pages of history as a master of political warfare. Although Goebbels and Goering played their parts, and although the Wehrmacht always stood in the foreground, it was Hitler who set the pace, called the tune, and reaped rewards.

Nazi strategy, indeed, drew no clearly defined line between war and peace and considered war, not peace, the normal state of society. Since war to the Nazis no longer consisted solely, or even primarily, of military operations, the policy of the state in time of so-called peace was only a "broadened strategy" involving economic, psychological, and other non-military weapons. Political warfare was constantly carried on, writes a former member of Hitler's entourage, "not only to render the tactical situation favorable to a succession of bloodless victories, but also to determine the particular issues which the general political situation may make ripe for settlement in accordance with the aims of National Socialism. These political activities find their explanation in the novel character of the important moves to come—pressure combined with sudden threats, now at one point and now at another, in an unending activity that tires out opponents, enabling particular questions to be isolated, divisions to be created in the opposing camp, and problems to be simplified until they become capable of solution without complications [i.e. without war]." The military preparations of Nazi Germany were only one aspect of its revolutionary activities, which were designed to make armed aggression superfluous, or, if necessary, certain of success. "The aim is not simply the expansion of frontiers and the acquisition of new territory, but at the same time the extension of the totalitarian revolutionary movement into other countries. All this is virtually the transfer [to the international sphere] of the modern technique of the *coup d'etat*," with the Nazi military establishment having the same function as armed revolutionaries in a domestic insurrection. By these means Hitler found it possible to bring about far-reaching political changes without bloodshed, with his enormous armaments intended to be a threat of war, rather than an instrument of actual combat.

Sir Eric Phipps, the British ambassador in Berlin, warned his government in November 1933 that the conditions in Germany under Hitler "are not those of a normal civilized country, and the German government is not a normal civilized government and cannot be dealt with as if it were." But Sir Eric did not find a sympathetic ear in Whitehall, where the belief prevailed that Nazism was "a healthy national revival" rather than armed Jacobinism.

Hitler's strategy, both in peace and war, was a strategy of terror. In order to come to . . . stay in power he tortured and imprisoned and murdered his opponents; in order to have his way in Europe he projected the same methods beyond the boundaries of the Reich. The Luftwaffe, especially, was intended to be a means of terrorization and perhaps more than any other single weapon at Hitler's command was responsible for the Munich capitulation of Britain and France. . . .

HITLER'S GRAND STRATEGY

By THE EDITORS

THE grand design of world conquest, which put down roots during the years of the Republic, and burst into full bloom after the Nazi revolution, embraced two ultimate objectives. One was to break the grip of the maritime powers—Great Britain and the United States

—on the sea communications of Europe and on the oceanic realm bordering the Atlantic, Pacific, and Indian Oceans. The second was to gain control over the manpower and physical resources of the continental realm of Eurasia. The second objective was the more immediate, indeed the necessary preliminary to the first.

The step-by-step process by which Hitler set out to make himself master, first of Europe, and then of Eurasia, has been recounted by Harold Sprout in *Geographical Foundations of National Power* (Army Service Forces Manual M-103-3, Government Printing Office, Washington, 1944), from which the following paragraphs are adapted.

The subjugation of Europe commenced with the plebiscite, held in 1935, to decide the fate of the Saar District. This coal-mining valley, wedged in between Lorraine and the Rhineland, had been detached from Germany by the Versailles Treaty. The mines had been turned over to France, and the land and people organized as an autonomous district under supervision of the League of Nations. After fifteen years the population of the Saar was to be allowed to vote on reunion with Germany. Whipped up by Nazi propaganda and terrorism, the predominantly German population voted almost unanimously to rejoin the Reich. This outcome increased German manpower by nearly a million, and gave Hitler the valuable coal mines and the closely built-up manufacturing centers of the Saar Valley.

But the Saar lay in a vulnerable spot, close to the French border and within the demilitarized zone. This undefended western frontier put Nazi statecraft in a straitjacket. Without the heavy industry of the Rhine and tributary valleys, Germany could not fight a major war. Without fortification and other military installations in the Rhineland, the Reich could not defend this vital region against invading French armies. The inexorable logic of military geography compelled Hitler to look to the remilitarization of the Rhineland before he could take any step involving serious risk of armed conflict with France.

Remilitarization of the Rhineland. The opportunity for such a move at a minimum risk came early in 1936. It was created by the confusion into which Europe had been thrown by Mussolini's conquest of Ethiopia. In March of that year Hitler sent troops into the demilitarized zone and began work on a system of fortifications. A diplomatic crisis resulted but no effective counteraction. The democratic powers hesitated, then acquiesced. In doing so they relinquished, without firing a gun, a military advantage upon which hinged in no small degree their future ability to restrain Germany without fighting a major war.

Remilitarization of the Rhineland meant that French armies could no longer march virtually unopposed into western Germany. They could no longer cut off the German armies from their industrial base in the Ruhr. They could no longer advance swiftly across southern Germany to join forces with their Czech allies. Germany could henceforth fight a stubborn defensive campaign in the west if necessary to hold off the French army while cutting down the allies of France in the east.

Formation of the Berlin-Rome Axis. The next step in the progressive immobilization of France—and of England as well—was the formation of the Berlin-Rome Axis. It created a diversionary menace in the Mediterranean, a region of vital concern both to France and to Great Britain. Axis pressure in that region might, almost certainly would, prove a deterrent to French and British counter-action against Germany elsewhere in Europe.

Axis Intervention in the Spanish Civil War. The dangerous potentialities of this Fascist combine were immediately apparent when Hitler and Mussolini began sending "volunteers" to help Franco install a Fascist regime in Spain where civil strife had broken out in the summer of 1936. This intervention provided a means of testing Axis military equipment, tactics, and training. It also confronted France with the specter of a land war on two fronts, and Great Britain with the menace of devastating air and land attack on Gibraltar from Spanish territory on either side of the strait.

Occupation of Austria. The deterrent effect of the foregoing aggressions began to be apparent early in 1938 when Hitler made his first major move in Central Europe, the occupation of Austria. Such action had been prohibited by the Versailles Treaty for precisely the reasons that the Nazi dictator now desired to do it. German troops marched into Vienna unopposed, and Austria was absorbed into the expanding Reich. A diplomatic crisis was precipitated but that was all. Once again the democratic powers hesitated, and then faced an accomplished fact which only a war could undo. Their inaction gave Hitler 7,000,000 more people, valuable mineral resources, and the developed manufacturing area in and around Vienna. Even more important from a military standpoint, occupation of Austria opened for Hitler a doorway into Czechoslovakia, key to the whole security system of eastern Europe.

Czechoslovakia reaches westward into southern Germany. This huge salient comprises the ancient province of Bohemia. It has been likened to a vast saucer surrounded by ranges of wooded hills and mountains. On the north, west, and southwest, Bohemia presents a strong military front. The western boundary of Czechoslovakia is one of Europe's stronger natural frontiers. The only relatively easy invasion route into Czechoslovakia is by way of the south. Through this gap in the highlands invasion by motorized forces was feasible. With Germany in possession of Austria, Hitler had marshalled the forces inherent in geography to bring heavy pressure to bear on Czechoslovakia, backed by armed forces if necessary.

Dismemberment of Czechoslovakia. Pressure on the Czechoslovak Republic began immediately. It took the form of stirring up unrest among the German-speaking inhabitants of the Sudetenland, and of supporting their inspired demands for autonomy and union with the Reich. The Sudeten people had never lived under the German flag. Their trumped-up clamor was a clever pretext to disguise the underlying strategic aim. Hitler's real objective was the acquisition of Czechoslovakia's northern frontier, a region in which the Czechs had made the most of strong natural defenses to guard the republic's mountain-rimmed western boundary. Once that line of fortresses was gone, Czechoslovakia's resistance would be futile.

Despite previous concessions to appease the dictators, and despite the resulting loss of strategical advantages, the situation of the anti-Fascist coalition was not yet hopeless. Though German forces stood poised at the southern border, the Czechoslovak army was well trained, well equipped, mobilized, and ready to fight. In spite of East European rivalries, almost every country on Germany's eastern and southern frontiers would have rallied to the defense of Czechoslovakia, for that state occupied the geographical position which blocked

German aggression both east and southeast. Once more, however, the democratic powers gave in without a struggle. At Munich in late September 1938 British and French statesmen made another pact with Hitler, and the Nazis made another bloodless conquest.

The dismemberment of Czechoslovakia began immediately. By successive steps that country was broken up and absorbed into the Reich. The long western salient was thus eliminated. In its place Hitler acquired in the province of Slovakia his own deep salient reaching eastward almost to the boundary of the Soviet Union. With it went coal and iron mines, factories, munitions centers, in fact the most highly industrialized region of East Central Europe.

German occupation of Czechoslovakia radically altered the military map of Eastern Europe. It placed Nazi troops all along the northern border of Hungary and southern boundary of Poland. The Polish state, sprawled over the east European plain, had notoriously weak frontiers. In the summer of 1939, after Hitler's occupation of Czechoslovakia, Poland faced Germany along a vast and indefensible arc reaching from East Prussia to the apex of the long Slovakian salient. The destruction of Czechoslovakia thus prepared the way for German assault on Poland, next on the Nazi agenda of aggression, and shattered beyond repair the geographical framework of the East European front which France had forged at such great pains and expense after the First World War.

Nazi-Soviet Non-Aggression Pact. Destruction of Czech military power and loss of the Bohemian salient threw Poland and the West European powers back upon the Soviet Union. Russia alone could give effective aid when Hitler struck at Poland. But neither that state nor the Atlantic powers were able to come to terms with Stalin during the fateful summer of 1939. In August, while they procrastinated, Hitler stole another march with his surprise announcement that he and Stalin had concluded a non-aggression pact. Polish independence was doomed. For Hitler that pact was another bloodless triumph, assuring Soviet inaction while Germany overran Poland and then turned west to strike down the military power of France, before the final reckoning with the Soviet Union.

Conquest of Poland. The Nazi-Soviet non-aggression pact galvanized the democratic powers into action. Britain and France, awake at last to the rapidly growing menace in Central and Eastern Europe, encouraged Poland to make a stand, and met the German assault on that country with declarations of war on the Reich. Unhappily, there was little that the Anglo-French combine could do at the moment. Hitler now reaped the fruits of his earlier aggressions. Germany's strongly fortified West Wall blocked Allied occupation of the Industrial Ruhr. The Czechoslovak army had ceased to exist. The Soviet Union was at least temporarily immobilized.

The lightning conquest of Poland, carried out in September 1939, together with Hitler's pact with the U.S.S.R., momentarily gave Germany a secure eastern frontier. He could now turn westward against the Low Countries and France. But first he took the precaution of safeguarding Germany's exposed northern flank and the supply line which brought high-grade iron ore from Sweden to feed the war industries of the Reich.

Occupation of Denmark and Norway. The occupation of Denmark and the swift conquest of Norway, carried out in the early spring of 1940, further strengthened the military position of Germany. It gave Hitler enough leverage on Sweden to ensure continued delivery of Swedish iron ore via Norwegian coastal waters. Occupation of Norway also gave Germany additional gateways to the Atlantic. These were immediately useful for stepping up blockade running and the campaign against British shipping in the Atlantic. Later, Hitler was to use Norwegian ports and flying fields with still more deadly effect in making savage attacks on British and American convoys bound for the Arctic ports of the Soviet Union.

Conquest of the Low Countries and France. By May 1940 the stage was set for Hitler's grand assault on Western Europe. Much of what had gone before was preparatory for this great offensive. Hitler had broken up the French block in Eastern Europe. He had taken the necessary steps to protect his southern and northern flanks. His truce with Stalin temporarily assured an inactive Russia. The German armies could now be massed in the west to deliver a smashing blow at France and the Low Countries. Within five days the Netherlands was driven from the struggle, and Belgian resistance collapsed in nineteen days. Meanwhile, the drive appeared to be following the 1914 invasion route into northern France, but this was only a diversion to conceal a smashing surprise attack in great force through Luxemburg and the broken Ardennes district. It struck with shattering impact at the northern hinge of the Maginot Line near Sedan. Breaking through the French defenses, the German vanguard raced across northern France to Abbeville on the Channel coast.

The Allied armies were split apart, their communications disrupted. Most of the forces to the north of the German salient escaped to England through the port of Dunkirk. Those to the south were swiftly encircled, cut off, and captured, as Paris fell and France went down to defeat and total disaster. A bare six weeks of Blitzkrieg sufficed to destroy French resistance.

Hitler had wrecked the European state system. Each step in the amazing sequence of aggressions, beginning with the remilitarization of the Rhineland back in 1936, was the logical consequence of steps previously taken. Each opened a path for the next in the sequence. The geographical logic of this process was inexorable. Down to the summer of 1940 it unfolded without a blunder in conception and with scarcely a hitch in execution.

Hitler's Assault on the British Isles. Conquest of France placed the Wehrmacht in position to attack and invade the British Isles. German arms commanded the European coastline from Spain to the North Cape. German submarines now possessed bases fronting directly upon the Atlantic, so situated as to dominate the main sea approaches to Great Britain. The Luftwaffe's planes stood poised for attack along a thousand-mile arc reaching from southern Norway to the Brittany peninsula. Only the English Channel, scarcely more than twenty miles wide at Dover, separated Britain from the invasion army massing in northern France.

To meet the threat, England had only the exhausted remnants of the army evacuated from Dunkirk, an army which had left all its tanks and heavy equipment in France. The British Navy had suffered heavy losses in carrying out the evacuation and in the simultaneous withdrawal of the last British troops from northern Norway. The Royal Air Force had likewise suffered, and possessed all too few planes for the supreme test that now lay ahead.

Twentieth century developments in military technology heightened England's peril at this critical juncture. Sea power alone could no longer defend the British Isles as in the past. Without mastery of the air, British battleships and other surface craft could not even operate in the narrow waters separating England from the mainland. With submarines and bombing planes, an enemy in possession of the nearby Continent could do serious, possibly fatal, injury to England before ever landing a soldier upon British soil.

The defense of Great Britain in 1940 thus turned on air power as well as naval power. If the numerically stronger Luftwaffe could knock out the Royal Air Force, England's plight would become desperate. Without aerial cover the British Navy would be sunk or driven from the Channel and North Sea. German armies under their own aerial umbrella could stream across these narrow waters, force a landing upon the British coast, and strike inland to encircle and cut off the defending armies, just as they had done repeatedly in the Battle of France.

But the Luftwaffe had first to win mastery of the air. As long as the R.A.F. ruled the sky over England and the surrounding coastal waters, no army could force a landing upon the shores of Great Britain.

From early August to the end of October 1940 the Luftwaffe battered at the aerial defenses of England—and failed.

The air blitz caused enormous damage. Ports were smashed; factories were burned; production disrupted; communications repeatedly paralyzed. The rain of bombs continued throughout the winter and spring. But time was running short. Hitler's timetable called for a smashing surprise blow at the Soviet Union as soon as the ground was dry in Eastern Europe. Accordingly the Luftwaffe was shifted to the east in May in preparation for the coming offensive.

But England still stood, damaged but defiant and undefeated. Hitler had suffered his first major defeat, a defeat so serious as to affect the outcome of every ensuing campaign.

Consequences of Hitler's Failure to Conquer Britain. Conquest and occupation of the British Isles would have clinched Hitler's hold on western Europe. No reinvasion of Europe was conceivable without an operating base adequate for this purpose. The fall of England would have ended also the blockade of Axis Europe. Even if the British government had moved to Canada and tried to continue the struggle from North America, the key geographical position covering the sea approaches to northern Europe would have been lost. With Germany in possession of the British Isles, nothing could have kept German shipping off the high seas.

Conquest of Britain would have had shattering repercussions in the Mediterranean theater. With a secure Atlantic frontier, Hitler could have shifted large forces to the Mediterranean and Middle East. The thin line of British defenses in that region could in all probability have been overwhelmed, opening a road to the oil-fields of Iraq and Iran, and to the borderlands of the Indian Ocean. Lastly Britain's collapse would have placed in German hands the industrial and labor resources of the British Isles. That increment might conceivably have been sufficient to carry the Wehrmacht to victory over the Soviet Union.

In any case, German occupation of the British Isles would have isolated the U.S.S.R. It would have placed German air and sea power in position to cut the north Atlantic supply line to Murmansk and Archangel. An accompanying collapse in the Middle East would have blocked the alternative route via the Persian Gulf. Whether the Soviet Union alone could have withstood the German onslaught no one can say. But no one can deny that the flow of food, raw materials, and equipment made possible by Allied control of the Atlantic and Indian Oceans was a vital factor in hastening the German debacle in Russia.

Hitler's failure to conquer Britain produced other results just as decisive. England undefeated presented a terrific threat to Germany's rear. The British Isles constitute a formidable military base essentially as near to the heart of Axis Europe as is Long Island to that of North America. London was the capital of a world empire with immense if scattered military resources. British sea and air power blocked Nazi expansion overseas.

From England was to come much of the inspiration which kept alive the spark of revolt in occupied Europe. From England was to come the great bombing offensive, compared with which the Luftwaffe's efforts pale into insignificance. From England sped the nerve impulses which drew ever tighter the sea and air blockade of Axis Europe. Into England were to pour the reinforcements which one day would batter down the western bastions of Hitler's European Fortress.

These were the stakes for which Hitler played in the Battle of Britain. These are some of the reasons why the Luftwaffe's defeat in the skies over England will go down to posterity as a major German defeat which affected the later course of the Second World War.

Nazi Strategy in the Mediterranean and Near East.

Hitler followed in the Kaiser's footsteps in this region. By helping to put Franco in power in Spain, he won a potential foothold menacing Gibraltar. His partnership with Mussolini promised access to strategical points commanding the central narrows of the Mediterranean. The Balkans, Egypt, Turkey, and the farther Middle Eastern countries were all subjected to propaganda and other pressures designed to promote German influence throughout this region. The fall of France and Mussolini's entry into the war opened North Africa to the Nazis and cleared the way for direct assault on the British-held corridors to the Persian Gulf and Indian Ocean.

The Axis played for high stakes in the Mediterranean. The Allies could suffer temporary loss of the use of their Mediterranean lifeline, and still carry on—albeit with difficulty—by air transport across central Africa and the long sea route around the Cape of Good Hope. But an Axis break-through to the Indian Ocean would have split the anti-Axis coalition asunder. It would have opened to Germany, and denied to the Allies, the oilfields of the Middle East and the raw materials of the Indian Ocean borderlands. The southern supply route to Russia would have been sealed. India would have fallen. China would have been totally isolated. Japan would have gained access to the desperately needed products of Europe's industries and to wanted raw materials. The strategical unity of the United Nations would have been shattered; the two isolated halves of the Axis would have been joined together.

Despite the high stakes involved, the Axis effort in the Eastern Mediterranean never attained the proportions of other major campaigns. It never approached the dimensions of the attack on France or the action on the Russian front. The difficulty of supplying large forces in the desert unquestionably limited the scale of operations. The Allied forces further had the very real advantage of abundant fuel brought by pipeline to the east shore of the Mediterranean. But in most other respects, the Axis had the stronger position. When all is said and done, the fact remains that Hitler sent inadequate forces and matériel for the job—and failed. The result was another Axis defeat, as costly perhaps as Hitler's failure to conquer Britain.

Nazi Designs on the Heartland. Hitler's attack on the Soviet Union translated into action the supreme declared aim of Nazi strategy in Eurasia. There, as in various other sectors, Hitler followed hard in the Kaiser's footsteps. Germans have long coveted the manpower and resources of Russia. They have conversely feared the growth of a great industrial-military power to the east. The war of 1914-1918 confirmed their worst forebodings and whetted their rising ambitions in that direction.

The Russian Revolution of 1917 momentarily gave them a chance. German armies overran the Russian borderlands. A puppet state was set up in the Ukraine, a fertile well-watered agrarian province larger than the state of Montana. In 1918 German forces occupied the Donets industrial region, and penetrated deep into the Caucasus. The short-lived and now all-but-forgotten Treaty of Brest-Litovsk, forced upon the new Soviet regime in March 1918, disclosed the sweeping aims of German policy. Germany was to have a stranglegrip on all the strategic gateways into European Russia from the Baltic to the Black Seas, and was to manage the future development of the agricultural and mineral resources of southern Russia.

The German defeat in the west brought this grandiose project crashing down in ruins. But the dream did not fade. The idea of "living space" in the east figured constantly in the thinking of those German intellectuals who, under the leadership of one General Karl Haushofer, helped to plant the seeds and to cultivate the ground from which sprang the Nazi dictatorship.

In developing their plans for empire in the east, these Germans derived no little guidance and inspiration from numerous foreign geographers and historians. They studied with particular zeal the writings of Sir Halford Mackinder, dean of British geographers, who had warned his countrymen in 1919 that they had won a war but might still lose the peace. If the scientific talents, discipline, and organization which had made Germany the strongest power in Europe were to be joined with the vast resources of Russia, German statecraft might yet forge a military power with which to conquer and rule the world.

Mackinder's warning, set forth in his book, *Democratic Ideals and Reality*, passed virtually unnoticed within the victorious countries, but not in Germany. In that country, Mackinder's thesis was avidly studied and discussed, and became one of the guiding lights of the Institut für Geopolitik which undertook in the 1920's to lay the intellectual foundations for a new program of expansion.

General Haushofer, leading publicist of *Geopolitik* as the German doctrines of "space and power" came to be known, ignored no part of the globe. But he devoted most attention to the Heartland, the name which Mackinder had given to the vast interior of Eurasia. There, according to the exponents of *Geopolitik*, lay the "living space" for the Greater Germany to come.

Haushofer doubted Germany's ability to wrest the Heartland from the Soviet Union by force. But he had great confidence in German ability to achieve the same end by subtler means. He looked forward to a partnership in which Germany, the senior partner, would increasingly direct the economic growth and political destiny of Soviet Russia.

Haushofer is said to have wielded considerable influence over Hitler's thinking. Many of his ideas were early woven into the creed of the Nazi Party. But Hitler's own utterances took on a violence largely absent from the less passionate writings of the geopolitical theorists.

Mein Kampf, written in 1924, is full of incendiary utterances on the subject of Russia. Hitler referred repeatedly to the Russians as an inferior race. He castigated the Soviet regime for its Communism and for its alleged subservience to the Jews.

Germany, Hitler declared, would be either a "world power" or nothing at all. To become a world power Germany must have more space, a larger and more populous industrial and military base. This was not to be found in the "south and west of Europe" but in the "lands of the east."

"The political testament of the German nation," he declared, must always be "never to tolerate the establishment of two continental powers in Europe," and always "to see an attack on Germany in any such attempt to organize a military power on the frontiers of Germany, be it only in the form of the creation of a State capable of becoming a military power, and, in that case, regard it not only a right, but a duty, to prevent the establishment of such a state by all means including the application of armed force, or, in the event that such a one be already founded, to repress it."

Again, "if the Urals with their incalculable wealth of raw materials, the rich forests of Siberia, and the unending cornfields of the Ukraine lay within Germany, under National Socialist leadership the country would swim in plenty."

From such utterances as these, it was generally believed in Europe and in America that Nazi aggressions in Central Europe were preparing the way for an early attack on the Soviet Union.

Hitler's non-aggression pact with Russia on the eve of war in 1939 seemed for a brief time to constitute an about-face. A stunned world interpreted the pact as an alliance among the dictators to divide eastern Europe. Haushofer is said to have hailed the pact as a victory for his own program of bloodless penetration of the Heartland. But that fateful pact was neither of these things. The Nazis had discovered, if the rest of the world had not, that the time had passed when any outsider could dictate the destiny of the Soviet Union, yet they had to defeat the Red Army and have access to the resources of the Heartland as well as a secure eastern frontier before they dared embark upon larger ventures overseas. Thus Hitler had either to destroy the Red Army or abandon his whole strategy of world conquest. But he apparently dared not attack Russia with the combined military strength of France and Great Britain poised ready to strike at his rear. The pact with the Soviet Union gave Germany time to conquer Western Europe before undertaking the greater task in the east.

Hitler's Assault on the Soviet Union. The timing of Hitler's assault on Russia is one of the war's unsolved riddles. In June 1941 he had still to secure his rear and southern flank from dangerous counterattacks. He had still to possess an assured oil supply for a long-drawn-out campaign across the vast Russian plain. He had still to gain the strategical positions from which to block the flow of military equipment and other supplies from Britain and America to the Soviet Union.

Three times, in 1941, in 1942, and again in 1943, Hitler hurled the Wehrmacht against the Red Army—and failed. With that failure vanished the dream of a German empire reaching from the shores of the Atlantic to the heart of Asia. And beyond this colossal disappointment loomed the impossibility of realizing German ambitions in the more distant realm beyond the oceans.

GERMANY IN DEFEAT: THE OUTLOOK FOR RECOVERY

By the Editors

Hitler's Germany reached its high-water mark in the autumn of 1942. At that time Rommel's famed Afrika Korps stood deep inside Egypt awaiting reinforcements to crack the last line guarding the Suez Canal and the road to the Indian Ocean. Far to the north, Leningrad was cut off and subjected to incessant bombardment. German armies crowded the approaches to Moscow from the west. The Ukraine, the Donets Basin, and most of the Caucasus—the richest food and mineral-producing area of the Soviet Union—were in German hands. Hitler was confidently predicting the early fall of Stalingrad, key to future Soviet resistance and gateway to the Middle East.

In terms of increased military potential, the Nazi achievement was no less impressive. Axis Europe—Germany, the satellite states, and the occupied countries, not to mention the tribute-paying neutrals—covered two million square miles, two-thirds the area of the United States. The population under German domination or influence exceeded 300 millions at that time. The Wehrmacht numbered several million veteran troops, finely equipped, fanatically loyal to the Führer, and supported by the labor of possibly 50-60 million workers.

In the Ukraine Hitler possessed Europe's richest granary. He had a firm grip on the iron ores of Lorraine and Krivoi Rog, and seemingly indisputable access to the high-grade ores of Sweden in addition. He had the coal of the Donets Basin and the Ruhr, the manganese of Nikopol, the Maikop and Grozny oilfields, the bauxite of France, Hungary, and Yugoslavia, and other strategic minerals to make Axis Europe all but self-sufficient for a war of indefinite duration. In addition, German armies had captured more or less intact the industrial machinery of Western and Southern Europe, and with a little time the efficient Germans could restore the wrecked mines and ruined factories of occupied Russia.

The tables have been turned. Never in modern times has a great nation suffered so crushing a defeat. Not even in the Russian Revolution a generation ago did physical devastation, social disintegration, and human depravity engulf a people so completely as Germany in the Second World War.

Can Germany recover from this catastrophe, regain the status of a Great Power, and play a role for good or for evil in the future society of nations? No one can answer this question with any certainty today. The final terms of peace have yet to be formulated. Time alone can show whether the victors have the will to enforce those terms during the critical years to come. Nor is it possible as yet to appraise the recuperative powers of the German people themselves. About all that can be done at this time is to review certain basic realities and trends, and to suggest certain provisional conclusions deduced from these facts viewed in the light of the emerging world situation.

Population Trend. Before the war the population of Germany was larger than that of any other European nation except Soviet Russia. But Germany like France and England was entering a period of incipient population decline.

The population policies of the Nazi regime succeeded in checking this trend somewhat, but only partially and probably only temporarily. Even had there been no war the outlook for long-continued population growth was not favorable. Total defeat, accompanied by widespread physical devastation and social chaos, may well hasten the decline of population.

In any case, German population growth will be slower during the next generation than that of the Soviet Union. In terms of manpower Germany will probably never again stand in a position relative to Russia as favorable as in 1941.

At the same time the Germanic peoples will probably continue after the war to be the largest national group in Central and Western Europe.

Material Resources. Germany in 1933 was either largely or entirely dependent upon foreign sources for all the most essential raw materials except coal, nitrates, and potash. German efforts to exploit domestic low-grade ores were only partially successful. Development of synthetic substitutes relieved some of the most critical shortages, such as rubber and petroleum, but at high labor cost.

Except for the items noted above, German rearmament was carried out mainly with imported mineral supplies. A series of bloodless conquests, followed by the lightning campaigns of 1939-1940 and the costly but deep invasion of Russia, gave the Nazis temporary control of Europe's main production centers and mineral reserves. For a time, as previously noted, Greater Germany came close to achieving the self-sufficiency necessary to withstand blockade and a long war of attrition.

The fall of Hitler's satellites and liberation of Nazi-occupied countries has thrown Germany back upon her own limited resources. If Silesia is transferred to Poland, and Lorraine, Alsace, the Saar, and part of the Rhineland to France, if the Germans are denied control of the Ruhr, and if territorial adjustments are made in favor of Belgium, Holland, and perhaps other states as well, post-war Germany will have a mineral base little if any stronger than Italy's.

Industrial Plant and Communications. Germany will start on the road to recovery with badly damaged mines, factories, and communications. How much, if any, aid the Germans will receive toward reconstruction will depend upon the terms of peace and the post-war policies of the principal United Nations.

There has been a strong movement to prohibit German industrial recovery, in whole or in part, as insurance against future aggression. Others contend that any such course would prevent not only German but also European recovery. According to this view, Germany is inescapably the industrial heart of Europe.

Under the most favorable circumstances Germany will be confronted with a gigantic task of reconstruction. At the same time, it must be admitted, much of Europe will face the same kind of problem. Given permission to rebuild, Germany's situation in relation to other European countries may not be relatively so unfavorable. And it should also be recognized that the recuperative powers of modern industry are much greater than is sometimes assumed.

The German State. Whether and in what form German political unity will survive defeat will depend both upon the terms of peace and upon the qualities of the German people themselves.

There seems to be no doubt that Germany will be occupied for a considerable period, perhaps for several years. Various proposals have been put forward for permanently breaking up the Reich into three or four separate states. It is impossible, however, to forecast the eventual solution of this crucial problem.

The German People. The impact of defeat and the residual effects of Nazism upon the German people constitute additional imponderables in the future of Germany. Germans have long been distinguished for their scientific and technical aptitudes, their genius for organization, and their capacity for disciplined achievement. Will these qualities survive the crash?

What is the outlook for moral regeneration in Germany? What behavior can be expected, for example, from the millions of German youth who have grown up under Nazism? The answer lies hidden in the future. But the weight of experience and informed opinion is darkly pessimistic. If events justify this pessimism, it may be decades before vigilance can be safely relaxed, before Germany can be readmitted as an equal partner in the society of nations.

Political Relations. The danger of a recalcitrant Germany recovering power and capacity for mischief will depend in large degree upon the trend of relations among the principal United Nations. As long as the Soviet Union, Great Britain, France, and the United States continue to act in concert, Germany can be kept within bounds, no matter what the possibilities of German moral regeneration. Only a schism between the Soviet Union and the Atlantic powers will give vengeful and recalcitrant Germans an opportunity to stage a comeback.

Strategical Position. Germany in defeat is still a nation of 70-odd million people occupying the geographical heart of Europe. In the future as in the past, Germany almost inevitably becomes the storm center in the tragic event of mutual distrust and antagonism between the Soviet Union and the Atlantic peoples.

Anglo-French appeasement of Hitler during the later 1930's, interpreted in Moscow as a strategy for deflecting Nazi aggression toward Russia, produced the opposite result of driving Stalin into a temporary truce with the Third Reich. Stalin's own appeasement of Hitler, in the Nazi-Soviet non-aggression pact of 1939, in turn loosed the Wehrmacht on Western Europe.

German leaders can be expected to make the most of their strategical position. They will understand only too well that their one chance of military and political recovery will lie in stirring up trouble between their eastern and their western neighbors. Eternal vigilance and skillful statesmanship will be needed to maintain the vital solidarity of the principal United Nations in the face of German intrigue and propaganda.

In conclusion, it may be said with some assurance that there is small prospect of Germany quickly regaining a commanding position in Europe. Taking a longer view the outlook is less clear. Some fear German ability to circumvent any terms of peace. Equally careful observers doubt Germany's capacity ever again to become a great military power. In any case, as has been frequently emphasized in these readings, the center of power in the Old World, which in the nineteenth century shifted from Western to Central Europe, seems now to be shifting again to the east toward the Soviet Union.

Chapter 10

Eastern and Southeastern Europe

EAST and southeast of the lands of Germanic speech, a physically and culturally fragmented region extends eastward to the Soviet Union and southward to the Adriatic and Aegean Seas. The Germans call this region the *Trümmerzone,* or zone of debris. It has been more realistically called the "crush zone" of Eastern Europe.

Because of its location, this region is an historic battleground and buffer zone between Russia and the Moslem Near East on the one hand, and Central and Western Europe on the other. Across this wide belt of territory have flowed the tides of migration and conquest since before the dawn of recorded history.

In few regions has terrain fixed more rigidly the lines of human movement. Only in the north does nature interpose comparatively few obstacles. There the great European Plain stretches eastward from Germany across Poland into Russia. This plain terminates abruptly on the south in the hilly-to-mountainous ridges which define the northern border of Czechoslovakia. Czechoslovakia itself is a long narrow country lying athwart the watershed of Eastern Europe. Its most prominent strategic feature is the mountain-rimmed western salient of Bohemia which thrusts its spear-shaped head deeply into southern Germany. South of the east-west watershed lies a plain, almost completely surrounded by mountains. Through this plain flows the great Danube River from southern Germany to the Black Sea. Still farther south the mountainous ramparts of Yugoslavia, Albania, Bulgaria, and Greece drop abruptly to the shores of the Adriatic, Mediterranean, and Aegean Seas.

The valley of the Danube is the main east-west highway through southeastern Europe. Through the Danubian cities of Vienna and Budapest pass all the north-south main roads and railroads from Poland and Germany into the Balkans, and one of the principal routes into northern Italy. Nazi possession of Vienna was necessary to crack the defenses of Czechoslovakia, the strategic key to all of Eastern Europe. Occupation of Austria and Czechoslovakia opened the way for Nazi

FIG. 22. Europe's Cross-Roads.
From E. A. Mowrer and M. Rajchman, *Global War, An Atlas of World Strategy.*
Copyright 1942 by William Morrow & Co., New York; reproduced by permission.

FIG. 23. Nationalities of Eastern and Southeastern Europe.

From M. Rajchman, *Europe, An Atlas of Human Geography.* Copyright 1944 by William Morrow & Co., New York; reproduced by permission. Symbols on the map indicate the following:

B. Bulgarians
G. Germans
Gr. Greeks
H. Hungarians
I. Italians
K. Karelians
L. Lithuanians
P. Poles
R. Rumanians
Ru. Ruthenians
S. Serbs
Sw. Swedes
T. Turks
U. Ukrainians
WH. White Russians

armies to pour into the Balkans in the spring of 1941. Soviet drives up the Danube, and the capture of Budapest and Vienna, in turn, cut Axis Europe in two and smashed-in the doors of southern Germany. Vienna and Budapest were the twin capitals of the former Austro-Hungarian Empire, and they will doubtless play a strategic role in the future development and external relations of the Danubian basin.

East-central and southeastern Europe presents a confusing patchwork of nationalities. Traveling from the Baltic to the Aegean Seas, one encounters many languages and dialects. In some localities linguistic boundaries are blurred and overlapping. In others, marching and countermarching armies, and the ebb and flow of migration in the past, have left ethnic and linguistic islands, often cut off by rugged terrain from populations of different speech and culture (see Fig. 23, p. 375).

The pattern of economic life shows wide variations. Though the region has considerable coal, iron, oil, light metals, and other mineral resources, the chief occupation is still agriculture, carried on in many localities under oppressive conditions with the most primitive tools. There are industrial areas, notably in western Poland, Czechoslovakia, and around Vienna. Many new industries have been started in recent years. But these have not yet altered substantially the over-all picture of rural populations toiling for a living from the land.

As in most rural societies, birth- and death-rates are high. The differential yields a slow increase, with every improvement in sanitation, medical service, nutrition, or other betterment of living conditions promptly translated into more rapid growth of population.

Before the First World War the "crush zone" of Eastern Europe was an arena of struggle among the Russian, German, Austro-Hungarian, and Ottoman Empires. The area of Polish speech was divided among Germany, Austria, and Russia. The Hapsburg Empire occupied most of the Danube basin, giving to that area an integrated transportation system, free-trade, and a fairly well balanced economy. But most of the nationalities which composed that empire resented a rule which was always arbitrary, often oppressive, and occasionally brutal.

The war of 1914-1918 gave these nationalities the opportunity to revolt. Defeat and revolution brought down the empires of Romanoffs, Hapsburgs, and Hohenzollerns. In President Wilson the oppressed nationalities of Eastern Europe found a champion for their demands for self-determination and independence. The political fragmentation of this region also served the ends of France and Great Britain. A tier of independent states reaching from the Baltic to the Mediterranean would provide a buffer zone between Germany and Russia.

Such a buffer zone was desired for two purposes. One was to keep Germany in chains, in particular to prevent a resurgent Germany from gaining control over the manpower and resources of the Ukraine and other parts of the great Eurasian Heartland. The other purpose was to throw a blockade—a *cordon sanitaire*—around Bolshevist Russia whose program of revolutionary Communism thoroughly alarmed the statesmen of Western Europe.

The peace settlement of 1919 broke up the region into nine independent states—Poland, Czechoslovakia, Austria, Hungary, Rumania, Yugoslavia, Albania, Bulgaria, and Greece. If the Baltic states are included, the number is thirteen. In the course of time the key states of the region—Poland, Czechoslovakia, Rumania, and Yugoslavia entered into mutual-assistance pacts which were further buttressed by alliances with France.

All these arrangements, however, proved unavailing in the end. France could provide loans, but Germany could offer a market for the foodstuffs and raw materials of eastern and southeastern Europe. Under Nazi leadership, Germany's natural economic advantages were skillfully exploited to gain political ends. German demands, backed up by threats and display of force, won the key positions—Austria and Czechoslovakia—in the fateful year of 1938. This opened the way for the assault on Poland and for the conquest of the Balkans in the early years of the Second World War.

Much water has flowed over the dam since the Wehrmacht roared through the Balkans in the spring of 1941. Under Nazi occupation all the countries of eastern and southeastern Europe were mercilessly pillaged and despoiled. Some factories were moved from Germany into these countries in an attempt to put them beyond reach of Allied air power. But the Nazis looked upon these satellite and occupied countries chiefly as producers of food and raw materials in their long-term plans for a "new order" in Europe.

The devastation and shattering defeat of Germany, accompanied by the spectacular rise of Soviet power and prestige, have profoundly altered the balance of political forces in eastern and southeastern Europe. It is now clear that this region has ceased to be a crush zone merely between Russia and Germany. Eastern Europe and the Balkans *plus Germany* are in the way of becoming a connecting zone between the Western Powers and the Soviet Union. The respective policies of these remaining Great Powers and their mutual relations vis-à-vis this larger pressure zone have yet to be fully revealed. But inter-Allied discussion regarding the boundaries and government of Poland and other countries in the area indicate the nature and complexity of the problems which in the days to come will severely test the solidarity of the principal United Nations.

"THE MOST DIFFICULT PART OF THE WORLD"

By Richard Hartshorne

From "The United States and the 'Shatter Zone' of Europe," by Richard Hartshorne, in *Compass of the World,* edited by H. W. Weigert and V. Stefansson. Copyright 1944 by the Macmillan Co., New York; reproduced by permission. Dr. Hartshorne is professor of geography at the University of Wisconsin.

Of all the areas of the world, none presents such a multiplicity of territorial problems as the belt of Eastern Europe lying east of a line from the Baltic to the Adriatic, including in 1938 some thirteen countries situated between Scandinavia, Germany, and Italy on the one hand, and the Soviet Union and Turkey on the other. Although we have heard much of this area as the "shatter zone" of Europe, in the words of German propaganda of the interwar period, most Americans other than the several million who emigrated, or whose parents emigrated, from those countries have little familiarity with it. Normally it seems too remote to require our direct attention. But for the second time in a generation we are engaged in a war that originated in that belt. Why should the United States in these two wars be concerned with an area that was of so little importance to us through over a century of our national life, an area in which we have had relatively minor economic relations, whether of trade or of competition, an area that has never produced a political or military power that could seriously endanger us?

Since it is natural for people to think of the history of any foreign area primarily in terms of our interest in it, we tend to think of the history of this belt of Eastern Europe as though the year 1914, or 1917, were its baseline. Common thought among Americans therefore tends to assume that the situation in Eastern Europe prior to the First World War was more or less satisfactory so far as this country was concerned, but that after we were drawn into that war along with Western European countries our representatives joined theirs in committing the blunder of dividing large unit areas into a great number of individual independent states, in mistaken obedience to the principle of nationality. This division ignored the necessities of modern economic geography; the structure was therefore unsound, and in less than a score of years collapsed—one is almost led to suppose—from its internal difficulties. Hence, it is thought by many, a more secure system for this part of the world must not be based upon the bankrupt principle of nationality.

That this line of thought is false to very recent, as well as more remote, history should not require demonstration. In one respect, however, it contains a germ of truth; namely, this is an area where international events of major importance are determined from without rather than from within. It is hardly possible to conceive of any political development intrinsic to this belt producing results within it that could ever endanger the United States. What does concern this country is the fact that while political instability is characteristic of this zone, as it has been for centuries, it offers a tempting opportunity to any large state in the neighborhood to expand its territory and thereby augment its military power.

The expansion of any land power in Europe was never of major concern directly to the United States, as long as that power was limited to the land areas of Europe. In 1815, therefore, it was of no direct concern to the United States that the Congress of Vienna divided all Eastern Europe among four land powers—Russia, Turkey, Austria, and Prussia. Likewise the rising movement of nationalism that immediately began to undermine this imperial structure and continued to attack it for over a century concerned us only in terms of political ideals. For none of the naval powers of Atlantic Europe could effectively exploit this unstable situation to secure mastery of the Continent, and then consider transatlantic attack on the United States. Domination of the Continent was never possible for Britain. The one great attempt of France, under Napoleon, had failed before many Americans could realize that it might well have proved serious for us. Spain had ceased to be a major naval power and had long since been eliminated from territorial control in Central or Eastern Europe. Obviously none of the smaller western countries, such as Holland or Sweden, could play a major role in Eastern Europe.

The formation of the German Empire in 1870-1871 made it finally impossible for any Atlantic power to exploit the insecurity of Eastern Europe for its own enlargement. At the same time, however, this created the more real danger that the new Germany, a land power which began also to develop naval power, might be able to utilize the opportunity to secure domination in Central and Eastern Europe. But any German ambitions for such a course of conquest in the east were checked by the "balance of powers"— more particularly by the opposition of those Great Powers that bordered directly on Germany. In allying herself, in this situation, with the Hapsburg empire of Austria-Hungary, Germany became a supporter of the imperial *status quo* in the very area where national disintegration might have provided her with easy opportunity for expansion. It was true that the alliance might be converted into a tool for conquest, but it could be only a cumbersome and unreliable tool, both because of the independence of Austria from Berlin and because of the large degree of independence of Hungary from Austria.

In the First World War this situation was changed in ways that presumably no one had anticipated: while Germany by the end of 1916 had been able to conquer large areas of the opposing states on both the east and the west, her allies, Turkey and notably Austria-Hungary, had been so weakened by internal disintegration under war pressure as to open up a real possibility for expansion of a German power far into the southeast—and simultaneously there developed the unexpected chance to destroy British sea power by strangulation of its base through submarine warfare.

The failure of the submarine campaign saved the old order in Western Europe; but that of Eastern Europe could not be saved, even had the enemies of Germany and Austria-Hungary wished to save it, for it was already destroyed from within. Since Germany itself escaped disintegration, the new geographic situation in Europe established by the peace treaties was one which made a German conquest of Europe relatively easy—once Germany had time to recover from the immediate effects of the war and to escape from the military limitations imposed by her opponents.

From the Baltic to the Aegean, the new system in Eastern Europe included no obstacle to German advance comparable with the Hapsburg empire of Austria-Hungary. This could have been accomplished only by a close combination of the several units into which it had split. Because these included the former dominators with those who had been dominated, any such combination was politically difficult if not impossible. Further, the freed peoples had mutual enmities that were almost as great. All these animosities were increased by the numerous minority problems inevitable in a region where it is impossible to draw boundaries mutually satisfactory even to reasonable people.

Theoretically there was one basis on which security might have been established in this region of small states— namely, the maintenance by the three Great Powers bordering it of a large buffer zone against one another, like the maintenance by the powers of Western Europe, each for its own purposes, of the independence of the Netherlands, Belgium, and Switzerland. But none of these neighboring Great Powers—Russia, Germany, or Italy—had had a major hand in setting up the new system, and each had reasons of its own for favoring change, with hope that such change might be to its advantage, rather than to the others'; and finally, in each of them there came to absolute power a government committed to attack on the *status quo*.

In contrast with the neighboring Great Powers opposed to the *status quo*, the powers interested in maintaining it —France, Britain, and, so far as we recognized our interest, the United States—were geographically and psychologically so remote that they gradually lost interest. The continuous difficulties, inevitable in any new structure of young states, made the people of the Western Powers more and more ready to wash their hands of Eastern Europe as time enabled them to forget its dangers to them—even though those were actually increasing.

That the new politico-geographic system of Eastern Europe would inevitably face great difficulties was certainly not unknown to the statesmen who took part in its establishment. Just because it was almost completely new, they recognized that for a long time it would suffer the insecurity of immaturity. But they were dealing with a part of the world that had never known political security, that had never developed mature, well established states loyally accepted by the peoples included in them.

Unlike Western Europe, Eastern Europe had not experienced a long continuous evolution of states each based on the national loyalties of its people, but rather had endured a meaningless series of conquests with more or less peaceful interludes marked by opposition of the many national groups to whatever imperial power had conquered their territories. If any developmental trend could be read in its history, it was that of the rising authority of national units in opposition to imperial rulers, which had increased progressively for over a century. Most of these national groups, however, had attained to actual governmental control but very recently —some as early as 1830, but over most areas only as a result of the series of Balkan Wars that began in 1912 and terminated, apparently, in 1918. (From the point of view of Eastern Europe the war of 1914-1918 can be considered as simply a widely extended "Third Balkan War.")

Consequently all these new states were cursed with the ills of youth, as well as handicapped by lack of strength.

Because the cultural geography of Eastern Europe—as revealed in maps of languages, or religions, or economic standards, or of such social factors as literacy—is so much more confused than that of Western Europe, it was impossible to represent the different national units by simple national states of internal integrity. Save for the remnant of defeated Austria, all were plagued by linguistic minorities, accentuated in many cases by religious and other social cleavages inherited from previous political divisions, and aggravated particularly by the socio-economic problem of landownership in a region emerging belatedly from feudalism.

In nearly all the new states German minorities provided an ever-ready tool for German expansion propaganda. Had the number of German minorities been reduced by applying the principle of nationality where it favored Germany, the result would have given Germany— as it later did give her—a stranglehold over the westernmost states bordering Germany, and thereby indirectly over the others.

Finally, both the location of all these states in relation to the western half of Europe and the agricultural character of their economy provided a basis under which Germany was naturally the single largest factor in their foreign trade. Once the German government established rigid control of all German foreign trade, it was relatively easy for it to extend economic domination over the individual small states trading with it.

In brief, the ultimate change in the politico-geographical situation caused by the conflict of 1914-1918 was that Germany, by extending the struggle to the utmost, caused the destruction of its ally Austria-Hungary, so that the peoples of southeastern Europe, after a short period of life under small national states, were exposed to piecemeal conquest by a reorganized Germany.

It is extremely unfortunate that the period of grace granted the new states of the shatter zone was too short to permit of much change in inherited feelings or to develop new habits and associations. For a nation is an entity that must be developed through common political life. Even where the territory of the state is homogeneous in culture, this requires time. For the new states of Eastern Europe, each with its various minority problems, several generations of time were needed.

Indeed the period has been too short even for experimental purposes: to demonstrate whether or not the system set up could be made lasting. For it is essential to remember that great as have been the problems within each of these new states and the animosities between them, their current destruction has not been caused by these forces but plainly and simply by conquest from an outside state that would not have hesitated in its conquest had all those difficulties been absent. In other words, the present war, in demonstrating that Germany could conquer Yugoslavia—or for that matter Denmark—tells us nothing that was not obvious before.

On the other hand the experience of the new states during the 'twenties and 'thirties does emphasize certain conclusions which though not unknown in 1919 were not sufficiently recognized by those in authority. Of these, perhaps the most important is that the identification of the national political unit with an independent economic unit cannot work effectively in a region where national areas are so small. In other words, the necessary economic basis for anything approaching well-being of the peoples of Eastern Europe cannot be attained in a system of small states each operating its economy independently and, most often, in opposition to the others. But as long as security is based on the complete sovereignty of each political unit, such economic independence is essential for national security. Consequently, it was obvious, long before the war broke out, that in this part of Europe two things were incompatible—economic well-being and national security based on national sovereignty. The war has merely demonstrated a more obvious point; namely, that national sovereignty for these small states provided no national security.

. . . What can be done with this most difficult part of the world? The consideration of that problem must recognize the reality of three major factors, the combination of which presents such apparently insurmountable difficulties that anyone attempting to solve the problem is tempted to ignore one or more of them. But we should consider sceptically, if not immediately dismiss, any plan for settlement that does not give due consideration to each of these factors.

The first is so widely recognized today that there is little likelihood that anyone will ignore it, as many no doubt did in 1918. Whatever criteria are used for determining nationality, the national map of Eastern Europe does not permit of division into clear-cut national states comparable with the system of national states in Western Europe. If anyone charges the statesmen of 1919 with failure in this part of Europe, he must realize that the error was not in having failed to establish *just* boundaries, for that is impossible in this region, but rather in failing to recognize this fact and therefore to attempt an entirely different basis of state construction.

Those who are most impressed by the first postulate might wish to ignore the second; namely, that, however impossible it is to draw clear-cut boundaries between the national units of Eastern Europe, each of a large number of national units is a definite reality possessing a strong geographic core area, and no politico-geographic system can be expected to succeed that does not give expression to each of these national areas, that does not permit each national group the exercise of those functions of government in which cultural differences are vitally important. Space does not permit further demonstration of this proposition than the bare statement that every government in this area that has ignored it has been able to rule its domain only by the elimination of all the freedoms we regard as essential to decent human life. And where these freedoms are denied, we can expect no political security.

The third postulate is that the area of German nationality—at least as large as the Germany of 1920—by reason of its location, resources, economy, and population, possesses permanently the power to destroy whatever political structure is set up in Eastern Europe, unless the structure is effectively designed to prevent that outcome.

The politico-geographic structure established at the end of the last war was in no way equipped to prevent its own destruction. The one major alliance within the area, the Little Entente, was directed not at Germany but only at another small state, Hungary, which is now also a victim. The support of the system depended almost exclusively on the Western Powers, whether in terms of direct alliance, as with France and— too late—with Great Britain, or in terms of the League of Nations, which was helpless when abandoned by the powers that had established it (the United States, Great Britain, and France), or in terms of the disarmament of Germany, to maintain which the Western Powers were not willing to fight.

To be sure, the fact that in this case the Western Powers failed to maintain the necessary support does not prove that, after learning the disastrous effects of that failure, they would act the same way again. But the peoples of Eastern Europe will indeed be blind if they again place their security in the hands of many small national states supported only by remote powers.

Chapter 11

The Soviet Union

THE rise of Soviet power is one of the most important developments of our time. No less important is the role which the Soviet Union is playing today and seems fated to play in the years to come. Moscow is the capital of a world power just as surely as is London or Washington. Satisfactory political relations with Moscow will be as vital to winning the peace as it has been in winning the war.

Recognition of this fact represents a full swing of the pendulum from the situation that existed after the First World War. For in those years the peoples of Western Europe and America viewed the newly installed Soviet regime as a quasi-outlaw in the society of nations, the prime source of world-wide revolutionary Communism, and a menace to be quarantined and resisted with every available weapon.

The international standing of the Soviet Union commenced to improve during the early 1930's. Fear of Russian Communism subsided gradually as the Soviet government, under the leadership of Stalin, showed a growing desire to reach an accommodation with the capitalist nations. One after another, most of the great and lesser powers entered into more normal relations with Moscow.

The United States recognized the Soviet regime in 1933. The U.S.S.R. became a member of the League of Nations the following year. At Geneva the Soviet representative actively sponsored movements for disarmament and for strengthening the peace machinery. Meanwhile Moscow was entering into non-aggression pacts with most of the countries bordering its far-flung frontiers. Almost alone the Soviet Union aided the republican government of Spain in its bloody and futile civil war against the Axis-supported Franco rebellion.

During the later 1930's, however, Soviet relations with the Atlantic democracies deteriorated. The purge, by means of which Stalin rooted out disloyal elements in the Communist Party, in the Red Army, and in the Soviet industrial and governmental bureaucracies, deeply shocked democratic peoples. Worse, it shook their gradually emerging faith in the strength and stability of Stalin's regime.

In turn, the Anglo-French appeasement of Hitler revived Russian distrust of the Western Powers. The ill-fated Munich agreement of 1938, which gave Hitler a free hand in Czechoslovakia and thus shattered the eastern bulwarks of defense against Nazi aggression, assumed in Russian eyes the image of a dark plot to remove the obstacles to an early German assault on the Soviet Union. This image was sharpened during the following months by the hesitation and delays which attended every French and British step in last-minute attempts to include Russia in a defensive coalition against the unappeasable Nazis.

Stalin's pact with Hitler in the summer of 1939 dealt the final blow to Soviet relations with the democratic front. This pact, followed by Soviet occupation of eastern Poland, the Baltic countries, and Bessarabia, was widely viewed as a cynical Nazi-Communist conspiracy to divide up eastern Europe. The Soviet campaign against Finland, undertaken in the winter of 1939-1940 to rectify the frontier just north of Leningrad, was likewise interpreted as evidence of an aggressive trend in Soviet policy. It was not until after the German invasion of Russia in June 1941 that the Atlantic peoples began to appreciate the essentially defensive character of these Soviet moves and their crucial importance in the life-and-death struggle with the Third Reich.

Since the dark days of 1939-1940 the pendulum has swung back again. The Soviet Union became one of the principal United Nations. The Moscow conference, followed by the Roosevelt-Stalin-Churchill meeting at Teheran in 1943, the Dumbarton Oaks Conference, the Yalta meeting, the San Francisco Conference, and many other events all reflect and underline the change that has taken place in the international position of the Soviet Union. We have beheld the Prime Minister of Great Britain and the President of the United States traveling thousands of miles to confer with the head of the Soviet state—upon Russian soil. We have witnessed the phenomenal growth of Soviet influence throughout eastern and southeastern Europe as the Red Army overran the Axis satellite states and liberated the conquered peoples. We have seen Great Britain enter into a long-term alliance with the Soviet Union. We have watched the French nation, under General DeGaulle's leadership, swing back into its historic alignment with Russia. We have witnessed the steady rise of Soviet prestige and influence throughout the Near and Middle East; and one may look forward to comparable developments in the Far East and perhaps in other regions as well. Moscow, in short, has become a factor, active or latent, in almost every international situation.

This fact alters the international position and foreign relations of all nations. The impact of Soviet prestige and influence is felt especially by Great Britain and the United States, whose interests reach out into every ocean and continent, and which, together with the Soviet Union, will be the custodians of greatest power in the days ahead.

It is frequently said that almost any terms of peace, almost any plan of post-war reconstruction, almost any kind of international security organization will succeed, provided the Soviet Union, Great Britain, and the United States continue to work harmoniously together. It is argued, conversely, that no peace can endure and no world organization can function if these World Powers drift into a state of active or even incipient hostility towards each other.

Such statements oversimplify an extremely complex problem. They overlook, for example, the vital role which other nations must play if peace and justice are again to prevail in our time. But it would be difficult to exaggerate the supreme importance of Big Three solidarity. Such emphasis sharply and very properly calls attention to the immense weight of these super-powers, and their consequent responsibility not only to support a world security charter but also to adjust and accommodate their own far-flung interests without recourse to violence.

Only a rupture of the Big Three coalition would give the defeated enemy nations the opportunity for again disturbing the peace. But such a rupture might well provide exactly the conditions that would enable them to escape the terms of the forthcoming settlement. As Walter Lippmann has said: "the whole world would know at once that the preliminaries of the Third World War had occurred," if either the Soviet Union or the oceanic powers entered into alliance with Germany or Japan. Such an event "would be the certain sign that the structure of the peace had been fatally broken."

It may not be easy to avoid or to allay the mutual distrust which could lead to such a fatal breach of the grand coalition. Both the Atlantic and the Soviet peoples have inherited a legacy of prejudice and misunderstanding dating from the First World War and the Russian Revolution. The democratic countries have not yet forgotten the earlier menace of revolutionary Communism directed from Moscow. The Russian people, in turn, have not forgotten how their allies in the First World War gave armed support to counter-revolutionaries fighting to overthrow the Soviet regime, and thereby prolonged the agonies of civil strife and devastation.

In these and in other respects a wide chasm has separated the Soviet Union and the Atlantic powers. The problem is to overcome these old prejudices and suspicions so that the Soviet Union and the western democracies can live side by side in peace, and work side by side for peace. It will require patience, tolerance, and understanding to bring this about. It cannot be achieved by expecting one side to make all the concessions. But it would be unrealistic to assume, in the light of present evidence, that the Russians are any less anxious than we to promote a stable world order, or that they will be any less willing than we to make reasonable concessions and adjustments in order to achieve it.

On this point we have the emphatic testimony of Mr. Churchill in his parliamentary report on the Crimean conference. "I decline absolutely," he declared, "to embark here upon a discussion about Russian good faith. It is quite evident that these matters touch the whole future of the world. Terrible, indeed, would be the fortunes of mankind if some awful schism arose between the western democracies and the Russian people, if all future world organizations were rent asunder and a new cataclysm of inconceivable violence destroyed what is left of the treaties and liberties of mankind."

But Mr. Churchill did not anticipate any such "schism." On the contrary, he said: "The impression that I brought back from the Crimea and from all my other contacts is that Marshal Stalin and the other Soviet leaders wish to live in honorable friendship with the western democracies. I also feel that no government stands more to its obligations than the Russian Soviet government."

Any suggestion of irreconcilable conflict of interest between the Soviet Union and the United States must be subjected to most careful scrutiny. Down to the First World War the record of Russo-American relations was one of uninterrupted friendship, despite fundamental differences in the Russian and American ways of life. At several critical moments in American history, Russian support was a decided asset to the United States.

Following the Russian Revolution, it is true, American troops, along with British and other Allied contingents, were landed at Archangel and Vladivostok to support counter-revolutionary movements against the newly installed Soviet regime. But in one respect at least, even this seemingly hostile enterprise worked ultimately to Russian advantage. For the presence of American troops in the Russian Far East helped measurably to block Japan's ambition to annex that whole region while Russia was paralyzed by revolution and civil war.

In the present war we took a stand alongside the Soviet Union soon after the Wehrmacht struck in June 1941. Supplies and equipment from the United States have been a material factor in hastening the victories of the Red Army. In the final phase of the European struggle, as the Red armies drove ever deeper into central Europe, there were some symptoms of doubt and misgiving as to what this might portend for us in the future. Such sentiments were forcefully dealt with by the *New York Times* (January 28, 1945) in the following words:

"It is as though some observers desired Russia to be strong to ensure an Allied victory but not quite as strong as she actually is. Curiously enough, some of these same observers not many months ago were fearful lest the Russian armies halt on some prearranged line and there make a truce which would release Nazi soldiers for the Western Front. But obviously we cannot have it both ways. Russia fighting on the line of the Volga could contribute little to the common victory. Russia crossing the Oder is serving purposes of her own, but she is serving the common cause too. Regardless of suspicions, jealousies and possibly conflicting aims, our armies fight for Russia on the Western Front and hers fight for us on the Eastern Front. The historic choice was between a strong Russia and a strong Nazi Germany. It has been made, and well made."

Many facts support the wisdom of that "historic choice." The aims of the Soviet Union, like those of Great Britain and the United States, are essentially defensive so far as we can ascertain today. The Russians have no "master-race" delusions, no insane ambition to rule the world. There is good reason to believe that they desire security and a long period of peace in which to rebuild their shattered cities and devastated countryside, and to develop their vast pioneer realm in inner Asia. The Soviet Union possesses in Siberia a huge frontier somewhat comparable to our own Middle and Far West seventy-five years ago. With this beckoning frontier within their own borders, it is hard to imagine the Russian people setting out, like the Germans, to conquer "living space" or a "place in the sun."

If the Soviet government seems determined to tolerate no potentially unfriendly regimes in bordering countries, it is equally true that this Soviet quest for security conflicts with American vital interests at few if any points upon the globe. Some mutual adjustment and compromise may be necessary in certain areas. But given the seeming disposition on both sides to live-and-let-live, it is difficult to believe that these two great continental nations will direct their enormous resources and energies to preparations for their mutual destruction. On the contrary, as Mr. Churchill and many other qualified observers have stated, there is growing evidence of Russian as well as British and American desire to compromise conflicting aims, to make reasonable concessions, and to take other steps that may be necessary to ensure winning the peace.

If we really mean to do our utmost to bring American relations with the Soviet Union into a friendly and stable equilibrium, we shall need, first of all, to enlarge our meager knowledge and understanding of the aims, the strength, and the potentialities of this greatest power in the Old World. Knowledge and understanding will not alone suffice. In addition, it will require imagination, courage, and a high order of statesmanship to direct our course wisely in the light of all the knowledge obtainable. But without the knowledge, and a balanced estimate of Soviet power and policies based upon that knowledge, we shall have neither chart nor compass with which to guide our ship of state.

The inadequacy of earlier information and judgments was reflected in American surprise and bewilderment at the Wehrmacht's failure to "go through Russia like a knife through butter." When the Nazi armies ground to a standstill before Leningrad, Moscow, and Stalingrad, the question upon American lips was: How did the Russians do it? How could the Soviet Union stand before blows more shattering than those which felled the Czar's regime in the last war?

The answers to these questions are not to be found in the bare facts of natural resources and population statistics. Soviet boundaries in 1941 were certainly no stronger than those of the Russian Empire in 1914. Soviet Russia has the same relief and ground-cover, the same soils and climates, much the same fuel and mineral resources. Population has increased substantially, but the Russia of 1914, like the Soviet Union today, was by far the most populous European country. To explain Russian failure in the First World War, and Soviet success in the Second, one must analyze not merely the physical bases of Soviet strength, but also the structure and functioning of the Soviet state, its policies, and the morale and other qualities of its peoples.

It is difficult for many reasons to reach a balanced judgment as regards either the past accomplishments or the future trend of Soviet power and policy. Estimates of Russian strength have varied widely, more widely perhaps than those with respect to any other power. Often the conclusions reached by different persons, even those with comparable opportunities for observation and study, have been utterly contradictory. About no other Great Power has there been so much difference of opinion and judgment.

Controversy and disagreement as to the present and probable future strength and policies of the Soviet Union arise from several sources. Many pre-1941 estimates reflected conclusions based upon Russian performance in the First World War and in the initial phase of the Russo-Finnish War of 1939-1940. American judgment was also colored in many instances by prejudices inherited from the period of revolutionary Communism and social chaos which followed the break-up of Czarist Russia. At no time since the birth of the present Soviet regime, it must be admitted, has it been easy to obtain sufficient trustworthy information upon which to found estimates of Soviet power and policy. At times very little reliable information could be obtained at all. The Soviet government controlled the flow of intelligence across its frontiers. The outside world knew only what passed a vigilant censorship and what foreign observers were permitted to see.

Today, in spite of greatly improved relations and better opportunities for observation, Soviet Russia still remains a good deal of an enigma. Great effort has been made, in selecting readings for this chapter, to give a fair and balanced picture of Russian development, present strength, and future potentialities. But the impressions derived from these, or indeed from any selection of materials on Russia, should be regarded as tentative and necessarily provisional, subject to possible revision in the light of fuller and more accurate knowledge.

LAND OF THE SOVIETS

By Sir Bernard Pares

From chap. 1 of Russia, by Sir Bernard Pares. New American edition. Copyright 1943 by Penguin Books, Inc., New York. The author is England's foremost student of Russian civilization. He has made many trips to Russia extending over half a century. He has traveled widely in that vast country and lived there for extended periods. Until 1939 he was Director of Slavonic Studies at the University of London.

Russia is a country covering about one-sixth of the land surface of the world. ... Its history has been one of continuous colonization—for the most part less by governments than by peoples, prompted by a desire to escape the close attention of governments. ...

In European Russia, as it is now, the mountains are all on the circumference—in the east the Urals, which are not very high; in the southeast, the far higher Caucasus; the natural boundary on the southwest, which even after the latest annexations still lies outside the Russian state, is the Carpathians, from which in early history much of the Russian or eastern branch of the great Slavonic family migrated on its march of eastward colonization. The bulk of present European Russia is a vast plain resting on a granite foundation, with a wide central plateau, which forms the main basis of Russian history; this plateau is only slightly elevated, but with the clear crisp air it makes one feel quite high up: I have had that feeling when standing all night in the Kremlin.

The most definite thing in Russian geography is the rivers. ... They originate in great reservoirs of marsh: there is a greater proportion of marsh in Russia than anywhere else in Europe. It was not difficult, even in early Russian history, to connect them by "portages," so that light boats could be carried from one water system to another. The rivers flow quietly onward through a crumbly soil, which assists their power of fertilization. In a present-day Russian railway guide, something like a third will be taken up by the water routes. Moscow owed her importance largely to the fact that she controlled the headwaters of the various systems, which were at first her refuge from invasion and later the roads of her imperial advance. The rivers of Siberia, which are even greater than those of European Russia, nearly all flow northwards into the Arctic Ocean—which very much tends to limit their usefulness, but here, too, the process of colonial advance, easy enough in almost unpopulated country, was an advance from one river system to another. It was just in the most confused and disorderly period of Russian history that this advance eastwards took the biggest dimensions.

The Russian rivers were the main roads of Russian history. Between them lay vast hinterlands of forest or marsh, or both together, in which the harassed population might find a refuge. One river after another would light up into a history of its own: the Dnieper system with its capital at Kiev, the Volga system with Moscow, the Volkhov-Neva road, first with Novgorod the Great, now almost a village, but once the greatest merchant city in Russia, and later, near the end of its course to the sea, with St. Petersburg [Leningrad] planned by Peter the Great as his window opening on Europe. The main rivers—Dnieper, Don, Volga—through most of their way flow from north to south, and by a curious "tilt of the earth"—as it has been described by Russian scholars—the western bank, the line of defense against the invading nomads, is generally considerably higher than the eastern—almost like a series of steep

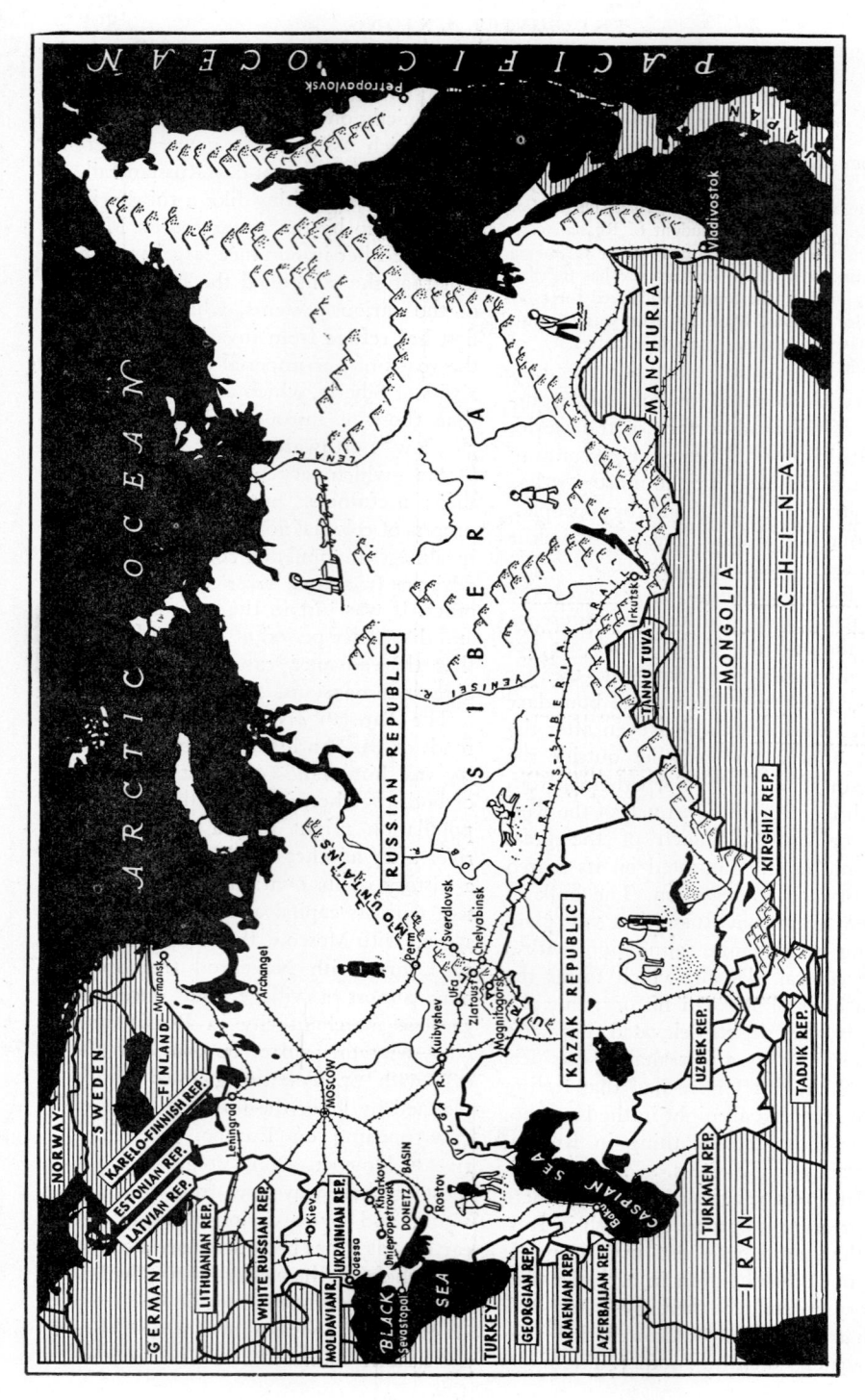

FIG. 24. The U.S.S.R.

From V. M. Dean, *Russia at War*. Headline Series No. 34. Copyright 1942 by Foreign Policy Association, New York; reproduced by permission.

ramparts against Asiatic invasion. The lordly rivers of Siberia flow northwards through vast park-like tracts of virgin forest, almost uncharted and unexplored. At Krasnoyarsk a piece of this virgin forest was left untouched as the park of the new town.

As the rivers were the only lines of light on the map, they were practically the only centers of traffic; so much so, that the early Scandinavian Vikings, advancing along the great water road of their time, described Russia as Garderyk, or the Kingdom of Towns. An ancient monkist chronicler, in his just claim that early Russian history belongs to Europe, tells how the waterway of Volkhov-Dnieper is only the eastern link to a vast belt of water communication completed by the Baltic, the North Sea, the Atlantic, the Mediterranean, and the Black Sea. And the Vikings, who were the first founders of the Russian state and not long afterwards accepted Christianity, did indeed traverse this round route, and the easiest part of their navigation was through that eastern link formed by the rivers of Russia, which were also the eastern belt of Europe and Christendom, and were defended by them against the nomads who unceasingly poured in from Asia.

The northern mass of European Russia was, and largely still is, thick forest. It was through unending forest that Napoleon marched to Moscow in 1812. Silver birches, pines and firs; firs, pines and silver birches. It is far easier to lose one's way in a square half-mile of these forests than in a square mile of our [English] smaller ones. . . . Here Russian peasantry, seeking shelter in the woods from the invading nomads, blended with the primitive Finns, who racially belong to Asia, and formed the Great Russian family, perhaps now the largest national block in the world. Even well into the nineteenth century the majority of Russians lived in forest.

Agriculture was hard in these surroundings and in this climate—far harder than on the wonderful southern soil from which they had been driven. The great water-roads had fostered that vast and broad sociability which is today the charm of Russia for every western visitor, and it was this that has given the guarantee of state unity. It was not natural that the dominion over any of these great water-roads should have been for long divided. But here in the remote backwoods, near the headwaters of smaller, tributary rivers—each of which in that time of divisions might form a separate little principality united to others only by a loose family tie—it was fear and caution that prevailed. The lonely worker in the forest, as he blazed the roots of trees to obtain a short-lived stimulus from the poor clay soil before moving on further, did not know what danger of man or beast might spring out on him from behind any tree. It was the forest that made that constant wariness which is the chief characteristic of the Great Russian peasant, as also it made that world of fancies and musings in which he is absorbed, especially in the long winter nights. It was first the forest that made the Russian peasant, or the Russian peasant soldier, the champion evader in the world.

He has a native instinct for the slightest gradation of cover. So one thought as one saw him crawling forward on his belly into No Man's Land when on the attack [in the First World War]. A soldier, guiding me at night through the same "interesting" region—that was their word—kept turning from right to left and back without any apparent reason. "Why do you do that?" I asked. "I feel it in my legs," he said simply, and I think I know what he meant.

South of this great mass of forest which covers most of the north of European Russia and most of Siberia, lies another great belt of almost treeless plain. It is the famous "black soil" formed by the attrition of glacial action, which provides the greatest granary in Europe, the long-sought goal of German ambitions. It is called Ukraine, or Borderland, and its people speak a strong variant of Russian. They have not the Finnish admixture of the north; and, indeed, the early Russian state, of which Kiev was the capital, was based on this part, though it covered a lot of the north, and its reigning family later migrated thither, ultimately to center itself at Moscow. In this great plain, reeds grew high enough to give cover to man and horse, but it is a land of vast horizons, and it was over this most fertile country that the nomads, in their time of predominance, advanced on Europe. History long eschewed the forest world, but was early at work on the black soil, and it was therefore a land of constant struggle and combat and deeds of daring, such as filled up the lives of the free Cossacks who escaped hither from the serfdom which grew up in the north. Here the fighting man had his value—and this life of adventure has contributed greatly to Russian poetry and to that spirit of daring in thought and action which is another of the great charms of Russia. The Ukrainians have never had a real state of their own. A legend says that when the Creator distributed his gifts to others, he left them out, but in the end he comforted them with the gift of song; and, indeed, the folk song of Ukraine, deeper than the German and more melodious than the Great Russian, is probably the most beautiful in the world.

Yet forest and plain, traversed alike by the great rivers, were designed by nature to be one great state. There are no natural boundaries to divide them; and economically they are vital to each other and interdependent. Moscow, at the headwaters, stands almost at the junction of the two. And over them alike, in the absence of mountains, flows evenly with only gradual variation, the same stern climate, becoming more and more continental as it approaches the great block of Asia, with sharper extremes of heat and cold. The deserts of Central Asia send their harsh and blasting winds into European Russia, and it is only in the northwest, which originally was not inside the Russian frontiers but later housed the artificial capital of Peter the Great, that there penetrate feeble offshoots of the beneficent and moderating seawinds of Europe. The good that they do here, by the way, is little enough, and the damp and dreary climate of Leningrad is far more trying to the health than the strong and stimulating air of Siberia.

The Russian climate is a stern one, with long months of winter and, in the north, of darkness, when no agricultural work can be done. Yet the frosty sky is bright and blue and the hard, powdered snows make a merry road to anywhere. Then comes the sudden spring, when all movement seems forbidden, while the great snows and the great river ice melt; and then wild flowers break out everywhere, so that to the Russian peasant it can seem no mere fiction that death is followed by resurrection; and Easter, like so many saint's days that mark in his calendar the changes of the seasons, seems indeed also a great feast of nature. It is not long before the summer becomes hard and brazen and dry, and gradually breaks in heavy thunderstorms. The early autumn is wonderfully even and beautiful, and everyone and everything again recover their balance. Then another period of cold rain and broken roads till King Frost resumes his cheery rule.

The Russians do not disregard their climate as we do; they defend themselves against it. The houses, even of the peasants, are terribly overheated. Even the trains have double doors, so that the passengers, after fastening themselves well up, can pass by gradations into the cold outer air; and foreigners will probably find that they have to show something like the same respect for the climate as the Russians.

The potential wealth of Russia was always prodigious: there can hardly be any country which could be richer or anywhere the natural resources have been more neglected or wasted. In the earliest times Constantinople was so dependent on Russian supplies that it made the most precise trade treaties by which the Russian traders obtained unusual privileges and facilities: they carried thither in small ships down the Dnieper waterway the forest wealth: furs, honey, wax—and slaves. In the Middle Ages Novgorod the Great possessed vast reserves of forest wealth, coveted by the German cities of the Hansa League. Peter the Great, in his masterful way, did all he could to develop this wealth; but after him Russia had to wait for further development till the economic revolution initiated by the emancipation of the serfs in 1861, which was led into profitable channels by three notable Finance Ministers—Vyshnegradsky, Witte and Kokovtsev—who brought the country to its highest level of prosperity in the period before the Great War [of 1914-1918].

Russians were always talking of their "inexhaustible treasure house" and dreaming hazy dreams about the future, but ordinarily the country was content to jog along on a level which quite often sank below that of starvation. Famine would come almost periodically for three years at a time. The country was divided into the producing provinces in the south and east and the consuming provinces in the north. Even more than half-way southward from Petersburg [Leningrad] to Moscow there will hardly be a week of summer without one night of frost. The black soil of the south is twice the size of France, and as good as the best land in France or Belgium, but it has to supply the poor clay soil of the north. It takes no more than a breakdown of transport to produce a famine. Western Siberia is one of the greatest areas for farm products in the world, and cold storage made them invaluable to Western Europe, yet an idiotic internal customs duty was laid on them to hamper their competition with the producers of European Russia. It was only the railway-building of Witte that made these supplies readily available.

Yet agriculture is far and away the most important industry of Russia. From unknown antiquity up to 1906 northern Russia was farmed on the primitive principle of communal land tenure, which till the eighteenth century prevailed all over Europe, but was abandoned then because it was a hopeless obstacle to initiative and improvement. In Russia it was preserved even after the emancipation of the peasants in 1861 because it offered a lazy and inadequate substitute for poor-law relief. The land belonged to the village community as a whole, and each member was therefore supposed to be assured of "a bit of bread"; but for the sake of fairness—a very strong instinct in the Russian peasantry—it was divided up into innumerable cumbrous strips, constantly diminished in width by the rise of population; I have frequently met peasants who had one hundred and fifty scattered over many square miles, and probably the man had only one horse—some had none. I have stretched my legs across a strip so narrow that an ordinary plough had no room to turn round on it. Then, as the state balance chiefly depended on the export of grain, huge amounts were sent abroad which were sorely needed at home; a correspondent of *The Times* [of London] once wrote that our food supply was largely dependent on the mortality of Russian children!

Yet, however ill-managed in the past, the output of Russian agriculture was very impressive. Before the south was developed, the flax of the north had a special importance for British traders, particularly of the "Russia Company" endowed with great privileges by John the Terrible, and supplied rigging for the English navy. The Russian rye crop is of special interest to Germany. The black soil yields great quantities of wheat. But there are lots of other crops in that part. I remember looking out of a train at dawn and seeing a vast unbroken stretch—there are no hedges in Russia—of sunflowers, grown for their seeds and oil, making their morning bow to the sun. Another district, in the north, is devoted mainly to medicinal herbs. There are extensive cotton fields in Russian Central Asia, which began to be properly developed during the American Civil War, and now, thanks to long-pursued work of irrigation, are of growing value. Russia gets tasteful wines from Crimea and the Caucasus and has also a variety of agreeable mineral waters. She has her own tobacco from Crimea, Caucasus and Turkestan, where she also grows some rice. . . .

After agriculture comes the vast mileage of virgin forest, whose great belt extends all through northern Russia and northern Siberia. There was reckless wastage. On either side of the great Trans-Siberian Railway, the finest achievement of Witte, the forests were blazed by the contemptuous use of wood fuel, in a country overrunning with petroleum. The forests only began to be really profitable in the period of the Duma, the first Russian Parliament (1906-1917), and the railways only began to give a profit in the same period.

Fisheries are among the great treasures of Russia—on the northern and Siberian coasts and on the magnificent rivers—rich in a great variety of fish, many of which are unknown to us. They give the impression of astonishing profusion. At Omsk, on the Irtysh, sitting waiting for a boat beside the town pier, I saw two fishermen, in biblically primitive costume, holding the two ends of a net, walk several times into the river and literally scoop the fish out, as if there were hardly room for them there. When I expressed my surprise to a Siberian business friend, he was only surprised at my surprise. When the coarse salmon go down the broad Amur, one of the biggest rivers in Siberia, they say it almost looks as if you could walk across on their backs. . . .

I am looking at a large economic wall map of the whole state: how tiny little Europe looks in comparison! Almost every kind of metal or mineral leaves its mark on it. Goldfields are sprinkled about over nearly the whole of the vast eastern half of Siberia—on the Lena, in the Altai Mountains, and down the coast as far as Vladivostok. . . . Russia already apparently takes second place in the world in gold output, and she has other great reserves charted but as yet unworked. The Urals give gold, platinum, a number of curious minor precious stones. It was the discovery of coal and iron in close neighborhood in the Don Basin that attracted the lately liberated serfs and built up a new industrial Russia in the south. There are also big coalfields in the Urals, Central Asia, the Altais, on the Lena, and on the coasts of the Pacific and Arctic Oceans, and iron is only less generously distributed. Two big coalfields were discovered in the eight months that I spent in Siberia in 1919. There are also reserves of copper, lead, zinc, nickel and aluminium. Of manganese, mostly in the Caucasus but also in parts of the Urals, Russia has vastly the greater part of the whole world supply.

Everyone knows of Russia's stores of petrol. On the Volga one was always passing the tankers bringing it up from Baku, the main center of supply; but a so-called "second Baku" is being developed in the Urals, and there are even workings close to the Arctic coast on the Pechora. But enough has been said to show that Russia was already more than ripe for state planning.

Russia has nearly everything that could make her self-supporting; and yet she lived on foreign loans, sought her technical experts from abroad, and had to send thither for spare parts when, as so often, her machinery broke down. It is not surprising that Lenin should have declared her to be a colonial dominion.

SOVIET POLITICAL GEOGRAPHY

By G. B. Cressey

From chap. 15 of *Asia's Lands and Peoples*, by G. B. Cressey. Copyright 1944 by McGraw-Hill Book Co., New York; reproduced by permission. The author, a leading authority on the geography of Russia and Asia, is professor of geography at Stanford University.

WITHIN the Soviet Union is room for all of the United States, Alaska, Canada, and Mexico. From Leningrad to Vladivostok is as far as from San Francisco to London—nine and a half days by the Trans-Siberian Express. There are continental extremes in temperature, rainfall, natural vegetation, usability, and accessibility.

Too much of the land is too cold, or too dry, or too wet, or too infertile, or too mountainous, or too inaccessible, or too something else. Good agricultural land covers no more than a million square miles, largely within a narrow triangle or wedge bounded in the west by Leningrad and the Black Sea and tapering eastward toward Lake Baikal. Elsewhere there may be the attraction of minerals or timber or local oases, but climatic barriers have restricted normal settlement over vast areas.

Although landlocked continentality is obvious, the Soviet Union at the same time has the longest coastline of any country, and the most useless. Frozen seas bar access for most of the year. Even the rivers flow in the wrong direction. The Volga ends in the isolated Caspian, and the Ob, Yenisei, and Lena point to the Arctic Ocean. Even the Amur bends north before joining the Pacific. The Don and the Dnieper enter the Black Sea but it, too, is enclosed. Nowhere does the country border an open ice-free ocean except at Murmansk in the extreme northwest. . . .

The Czarist regime made feeble efforts to navigate the Arctic, but the Soviets are actively developing the Northern Sea Route. Scores of steamers call at Siberian ports during the brief summer period of open water, and a few dozen make the complete transit from Murmansk to Vladivostok, aided by ice-breakers and scouting planes. If Arctic navigation proves dependable in linking the Atlantic and Pacific coasts of the Union, it may compare in significance with the Panama Canal for the United States.

Like the United States, the U.S.S.R. faces two ways and has interests in both Europe and Asia. America's neighbors are across the seas, while those of the Soviet Union, on all frontiers except the west, lie across deserts and mountains. The country is influenced by its position in an isolated part of Asia and the climatically least desirable portion of Europe, remote from the Atlantic. This position would be a disadvantage were not the Union's economy largely self-sufficient because of the abundant resources within the country.

Custom has divided Russia into European and Asiatic sections, but this tradition has little geographic validity. Various maps disagree as to the continental limits and do not even consistently follow the crest of the Urals. These mountains are no more of a continental barrier than the Appalachians. No political boundary has followed the Urals for centuries; neither do they mark any conspicuous change in climate, crops, nationalities, or economic activities. ... The Soviet Union is a single geographic realm; in culture she is knit to Europe, but by nature she stands between two worlds, the Orient and the Occident.

The factors that give the Soviet Union its geographic coherence are its great expanse of level land; its isolation by oceans, deserts, and mountains; the pioneering achievements in agriculture, and industry which are transforming the landscape; and its unique political structure. These all make it a phenomenon as well as a place. This unity is offset by the diversity of nationalities, by the wide contrasts in climate and usability, and by the difficulty of communications. ...

It is well to remember that the geography of much of the U.S.S.R. is more easily comparable with that of Canada than with the United States. Climatic conditions place severe limitations on agricultural possibilities in each continent. Almost all of the Soviet Union lies north of the United States, for the Black and Caspian Seas are in the latitude of the Great Lakes. Fortunately no Rocky Mountains keep out moderating Atlantic influences. Where the Union extends farthest south in Middle Asia, conditions resemble Nebraska and Utah. The exceptions are the cotton and fig country of the southern oases, the citrus and tea east of the Black Sea, and the rice of the Pacific Maritime Province. ...

Through the course of Russian history settlement has pushed into Asia as an advancing wedge. To the north of the occupied land lies the great coniferous forest with acid podsol soils; to the south is the steppe, fertile but precariously dry. Each eastward advance of the wedge of settlement brings a corresponding expansion to the north and to the south. Population pressure and pioneering lure combine to press cultivation eastward, and at the same time north and south. The northward course of agriculture has already moved the frontier into lands of precariously short growing season, while southward expansion is at the expense of drought. Both movements involve the hazard of famine. The southward thrust is more attractive since there are no forests to be cleared and the soils are exceptionally fertile; in good years, rainfall is adequate but, too often, a limited amount or poor distribution results in widespread starvation.

Siberia has been Russia's pioneer east, just as Anglo-Saxon settlement pressed westward into the New World. The dates are comparable since Tomsk was founded in 1604 and Jamestown in 1607. Siberia was occupied rapidly but thinly, with Yakutsk on the Lena dating from 1632, whereas Hartford was not founded until 1638. On the other hand, the Trans-Siberian Railway was not completed until thirty years after the Union Pacific. . . .

The Union of Soviet Socialist Republics is one of the richest countries in the world. Her coal reserves exceed a trillion and a half tons, second only to the United States. Petroleum reserves are more difficult to estimate, but Soviet geologists credit their country with more oil than any other. Hydroelectric possibilities are great. Iron ore deposits are huge, and within the country are manganese, copper, lead, zinc, gold, platinum, aluminum, and even nickel. Commercial timber covers a million square miles, and there is four times as much rich chernozem soil as in the United States. Here is one land where a self-sufficient national economy is almost feasible. . . .

It is probable that no nation has ever transformed its economic life so rapidly as has the U.S.S.R. since 1928. The goal is nothing short of overtaking and surpassing all other nations. As a result, millions of people have been moved from farms into factories. Illiterate peasants whose mechanical experience was limited to a plow and a hoe now operate complex machinery. Thousands of miles of new railways have been laid down, thousands of new locomotives built, factory cities of 200,000 people replace tiny villages, and large areas of virgin steppe have been plowed for the first time in history. . . .

. . . No one can travel across the country without being impressed by the material results of the Five Year Plans. The capacity of the government to achieve is obvious. The pioneering spirit that typifies all parts of the Union is unique. Nowhere else in temperate lands is there so much good undeveloped farm land. Nowhere else is the rural or urban landscape in such transformation.

All this must be viewed in relative terms and properly adjusted for the social factor. In comparison with Czarist times, the changes are stupendous. Yet in comparison with Western Europe, the country still has a long way to go. Prior to the Second World War, the Union boasted that within Europe it had become the second producer of steel, occupied third place in coal, and led in oil. This did not mean that there were as many automobiles on the streets, or that the trains were adequate or clean, or that people were dressed as in Berlin or London.

To the outside world, the Soviet Union has variously appeared as a "big bad wolf" about to devour the rest of civilization, a Utopia that may solve all our ills, or an incomprehensible riddle. In reality it is none of these, and yet in some measure all. Climate, soil, and topography impose permanent restrictions in some respects, but in other ways it is evident that the land of the Soviets has become one of the major world powers.

The term Russia should be used only historically or in a very loose sense. Russian people live in most of the country, but alongside them are Ukrainians, Georgians, and other national groups, each in its separate republic. Where racial minorities were suppressed under the Czar, each culture is now encouraged.

The Union of Soviet Socialist Republics is a federation of republics, some of which also include autonomous republics. The fundamental basis of political regionalization is twofold: economic and racial. On these bases, sometimes conflicting, the local *okrugs* (districts), *oblasts* (regions), *rayons* (subdistricts), and autonomous areas are grouped into larger *krais* (territories) and republics, and they in turn into Union republics. One of the latter is very large and complex, others small and with few subdivisions. Boundaries are fluid so that changes in economic developments may be quickly reflected in the political structure. . . .

The first of these republics, the Russian S.F.S.R., is by far the largest and most powerful. . . . It occupies three-quarters of the area and dominates the political life of the U.S.S.R. This is the only part of the Union to which the term Russia might properly be applied.

SPACE AND TERRAIN IN THE DEFENSE OF THE SOVIET UNION

By Derwent Whittlesey and J. K. Wright

From chap. 6 of *Geographical Foundations of National Power*. Army Service Forces Manual M-103-2. Government Printing Office, Washington, 1944. Dr. Whittlesey is professor of geography at Harvard University. Dr. Wright is director of the American Geographical Society.

No other country, when considered as a whole, is so nearly invulnerable as the Soviet Union. . . .

Sea Frontiers. The Union's available seacoast consists principally of four short openings, each of them barred off from the ocean by foreign territory.

The longest strip of such coast is the northern shore of the Black Sea, but to reach the open ocean it is necessary to pass through Turkish territory in straits (the Bosporus and the Dardanelles) only a mile wide, to run the gauntlet of the Aegean Islands, and then to go either through the narrows of the central Mediterranean and the Strait of Gibraltar or through the Suez Canal, the Red Sea. . . .

The Union's point of contact with the Baltic is through the Gulf of Finland. . . . The natural outlet of the Baltic Sea is a strait three miles wide between Sweden and Denmark, with an alternative outlet by the Kiel Canal through German territory.

In the extreme northwest a short strip of the Union's Arctic coast is ice-free throughout the year. There the port of Murmansk has been built and connected by rail with the heart of the country. Ships using this route must ordinarily pass close to the Norwegian coast to avoid the ice.

The fourth outlet is in the Far East, where the port of Vladivostok at the end of the Trans-Siberian Railroad is kept open in winter by ice-breakers. It lies on the Sea of Japan, all the entrances to which are controlled by the Japanese islands. [For development of additional Pacific ports, see the section on "The Soviet Far East" below.]

From the White Sea eastward the [Arctic Ocean] coast is practically ice-bound nine to ten months in the year; ephemeral "leads" (channels) of open water are navigable during the warmest months. . . . The Soviet government has established a coasting route kept open by ice-breakers during the two months of least cold weather. . . . The government also proposes to establish air communication across the polar regions to North America. The projected flights would be lateral extensions of an air route skirting the northern coast that has occasionally been flown and is tied to the southerly east-west route by north-south lines.

In order to keep ships afloat and planes aloft, the government maintains an elaborate meteorological and oceanographic service throughout its northern territories. This is in reality a powerful military weapon, since no other country possesses the information concerning the sea or the weather necessary for waging war in this large and remote sector of the earth.

Land Frontiers. Long sections of the land frontier are barriers of the first order.... The deserts and high mountains of interior Asia form a wide protective belt on the southern boundaries all the way from the Caspian Sea to Manchuria. In the Far East, however, the boundary with Japanese-dominated Manchuria is a treaty line marked by the Amur and certain of its tributaries for about 1,500 miles. These river valleys form the most densely settled parts of this district. A further weakness here lies in the proximity to the border of the Trans-Siberian Railroad which follows a roundabout route wholly within the territory of the Soviet Union....

Between the Caspian and Black Seas the international boundary separates the U.S.S.R. from Turkey in the west and from Iran in the east. The line has been drawn in such a way as to give the Soviet Union control of the mountains bordering the Caucasian trough on the south. Part of the way it follows the Aras River, cutting Armenia in two. Batum, the best natural harbor at the eastern end of the Black Sea, is just inside Soviet territory. The Caucasian range, 200 miles farther north, is lofty, with peaks reaching above 18,000 feet; a few passes cross it, the lowest being at about 8,000 feet; the coastal lowland strip between the Caucasus and the Caspian Sea is narrow and that along the Black Sea, much narrower....

The Soviet Union's western boundary during the last 200 years has fluctuated across a frontier zone extending from the Arctic Ocean south to the Carpathians, and from the approximate position of the 1939 boundary on the east to the Baltic Sea and the heart of Poland on the west....

The only mountain barrier is the Carpathian range on the southwest, where Russian armies have more than once been halted in their advance toward the plains of Hungary. There are, however, other barriers. Except for a narrow passageway along the north shore of the Gulf of Finland, the whole of Finland might be so considered. Much of that country is low, rugged, forested, ice-scoured, and strewn with innumerable lakes and marshes.... Military operations are difficult there at all times of the year, though less so in winter when the waters are frozen.

Between the Gulf of Finland and the Carpathians, the extensive Pripet Marshes in White Russia ... are the most formidable barrier anywhere on the Union's western frontier. The terrain between the Pripet Marshes and the Gulf, however, is not without its obstacles in the form of lakes, smaller marsh lands, and forests. Farther south the rivers flowing into the Black Sea have long been considered important lines of military defense, especially in the case of the Dnieper, which covers a wide strip of low ground when in flood, and the Dniester, a tortuous stream in a narrow gorge....

Two principal natural avenues for military movements lead across the Soviet Union's western frontier zone, one along the northern side of the Pripet Marshes on the direct line from Berlin to Moscow; the other over a broad, well-drained, and largely treeless upland between the marshes and the Carpathians. The first of these was the route taken by Napoleon in his disastrous campaign of 1812. The second was followed by the German armies in 1941 and 1942 in their eastward advance across the Ukraine and far beyond to Stalingrad on the Volga. . . .

SPACE AND TERRAIN

By the Editors

The German invasion of the Soviet Union in June 1941 was launched from a front over 500 miles long. Because of the wedge-like shape of western Russia, this front increased in length as the Germans advanced eastward. Within a few weeks the armies were deployed along a front reaching from the Arctic Ocean to the Black Sea, a development ultimately to Russian advantage because of the larger reserves of the Red Army.

The battlefield was also one of great strategic depth. When the invaders stood before the Soviet capital, they had conquered an area comparable to all the United States east of the Mississippi River.

Except along the southern margin of the Crimea, this battlefield is a more or less continuous plain. It is an extension of the plain reaching eastward across northern Germany and Poland. In the south it is largely treeless, agriculturally and to some extent physically the counterpart of the North American prairie. Farther north the Russian plain is more rolling and progressively more wooded. The country between Warsaw and Moscow bears considerable resemblance to parts of Ohio and Indiana. Still farther north lies a heavily forested belt, broken by thousands of lakes and clearings, not unlike northern Michigan and Wisconsin fifty to seventy-five years ago.

As noted in the preceding selection, large rivers flow across the west-Russian plain—northwest to the Baltic, southeast to the Black and Caspian Seas. These rivers—especially the Dnieper—have more than ordinary military value in a country possessing comparatively few natural obstacles to military movements. Owing to the geological structure, the west banks of these rivers are generally higher than the east banks. Hence they afford more protection, and constitute less of a military obstacle, to an army facing east than to one facing west, a factor in Germany's favor at every stage of the struggle inside the Soviet borders.

Almost nowhere in western Russia is there sufficient slope to give rapid surface drainage. There are many swamps and marshes, some of them covering hundreds of square miles. The most famous, the Pripet Marshes east of Brest-Litovsk, have already been mentioned in the preceding selection.

The Pripet Marshes and the wooded and swampy plains farther north and east provide abundant ground cover. The Red Army and the Soviet guerilla bands made skillful use of this terrain, carrying out incessant forays from woods and marshes on the flanks and rear of the invading German armies.

Poor drainage lengthens the period of mud in fall and spring. Mud is king for weeks at a stretch. During such periods railways provide almost the only means of moving large bodies of troops and matériel. In dry weather, however, much of western Russia, especially the treeless Ukraine, constitutes an ideal battlefield for deploying huge armies in a war of rapid movement. The terrain is such that an army dislodged from one defensive position may have to retreat a hundred miles or more before reaching another. But in this country of wide spaces there is room to retreat and to absorb the shock of such tremendous blows as the Wehrmacht dealt in the summers of 1941 and 1942.

But space, so vital for a defense in depth, also imposes limitations upon the defenders. Vast distances separate the Soviet Union's various frontiers from each other. In the main these isolated frontiers are also remote from the newer industrial centers. Long overland hauls reduce the mobility of Soviet defenses. This partially offsets the advantage of interior lines, and ties down manpower in transportation, frontier garrisons, etc.

The country's huge size and vast internal distances, as well as the strategic vulnerability of its older industrial regions in the west, are responsible for a Soviet policy of duplicating essential industries in different parts of the country. Industrial decentralization and duplication strengthen Soviet border defenses and relieve the strain on internal communications. But such a policy is costly to the extent that the newer industries are less economical than the older ones, as they indubitably are in certain instances. Where such is the case, additional labor is expended, reducing still further the effective differential in manpower between Russia and less populous nations.

THE PEOPLES OF THE SOVIET UNION

By G. B. Cressey

From chap. 15 of *Asia's Lands and Peoples*, by G. B. Cressey. Copyright 1944 by McGraw-Hill Book Co., New York; reproduced by permission.

ALTHOUGH the Russians are clearly of European origin, two centuries of Mongol domination and the later Siberian expansion brought in an Asiatic element. The plains of Russia were a melting pot akin to those of North America. The genealogical register of the sixteenth century shows that 17 per cent of the noble families were of Tatar and oriental origin while 25 per cent were of German and west European extraction. To speak of the Russians as Asiatics with a European veneer is surely incorrect. . . . Their alphabet is from the Greeks, but in their midcontinental environment they have acquired a mixed culture. The Russians are at the same time the most eastern of European peoples and the most western of Asiatic.

No less than 169 ethnic groups are recognized within the Union, although only 50 number more than 20,000 representatives. Slavs account for three quarters of the population, while most of the remainder are Mongoloid, Persian, or Turkic divisions. . . .

Slavs occupy the bulk of Eastern Europe and have spread across Siberia along railways and rivers. Turkic peoples are concentrated in Middle Asia with extensions into the Tatar Republic and Bashkiria in the Volga Valley, and in Yakutia. Mongol peoples live around Lake Baikal, and along the lower Volga. In the extreme north and northwest are relic races such as the Finns and Nentsi, while the northeast has Paleo-Asiatics and Tungus.

Only three census enumerations have ever been made. In 1897, the total was found to be 129,200,200, while in 1926 it was 146,989,460. These figures are not comparable as to area, for after the Revolution the country lost 27,000,000 people in Finland, Poland, and the other frontiers, and there was great loss of life during the First World War and the ensuing years. The 1939 total was 170,467,186. . . .

As a result of the Five Year Plans, cities have grown enormously. In fact, it is hard to find a center that did not double in the period between the First and Second World Wars. Moscow and

Leningrad are the two giant cities, but no others exceed a million. Between the latter figure and half a million came Kiev, Kharkov, Baku, Gorki, Odessa, Tashkent, Tbilisi, Rostov-on-Don, and Dniepropetrovsk. In 1939 the Union had 82 cities in excess of 100,000 population as against 31 in 1926 and 14 in 1897.

This is a nation of young people, most of them born since the Revolution and therefore with no memories of Czarism. In 1939, 63 per cent were under 30 years of age. . . .

[Soviet population is largely concentrated in a vast triangle. The base of this triangle lies along the western frontier. Its apex reaches deep into Siberia. This triangle encloses the largest area of fertile land with sufficient rainfall to support agriculture.] The center of population lies west of the Volga, but with the development of Siberia, it should gradually approach the Urals.

THE RUSSIAN REVOLUTION

By W. H. Chamberlin

From chap. 1 of *Soviet Russia,* by W. H. Chamberlin. Copyright 1931 by Little, Brown & Co., Boston; reproduced by permission. Mr. Chamberlin, formerly a newspaper correspondent in Moscow, is the author of several books on Russia.

On the eve of the [First] World War, which was destined to be the decisive factor in bringing about the long-threatened Russian Revolution, a keen observer could scarcely fail to have been impressed by the striking contrasts and contradictions in the political, economic, and social structure of the Russian Empire. The original Muscovite state had swelled to gigantic proportions over a long period of conquest and colonization; it occupied almost a sixth of the surface of the globe, with a population estimated at 180,000,000. But it was so backward in technical development and methods of administration that it repeatedly suffered defeat in wars with countries much smaller in area and population.

Two hundred thousand landlords, owning something over a quarter of the arable land in European Russia, were an object of sullen envy and hatred on the part of the vast majority of the sixteen million peasant households, which lived in a state of dire poverty. Against the rapid pace of industrial development in Russia, the growth of production, and the enrichment of individual manufacturers had to be set the profound dissatisfaction of the two and a half million Russian industrial workers, all the more potentially dangerous as a class because they were denied any means of legal expression. The Czarist policy of oppression and discrimination against the non-Russian nationalities which constituted more than half the population of the Empire fed the flames of centrifugal nationalism and made it certain that Poles and Letts, Finns and Ukrainians, Jews and Caucasians, would play an active part in any movement tending toward the disintegration of the Empire.

. . . The contrasts in pre-revolutionary Russia were extraordinarily sharp. The Russian intelligentsia was second to none in the world in range and breadth of intellectual interests, in warmth and subtlety of artistic appreciation. There was no field of art or science in which Russia could not point to great names; one thinks instinctively of Tolstoy, Dostoevsky, Turgeniev, Moussorgsky, Tschaikovsky, Repin, Bechterev, Metchnikov, and Pavlov. But these brilliant achievements of the educated minority were the full property of only a very small percentage of the Russian population; with an illiteracy figure of over 60 per cent Russia could not possess a broad popular culture like that of England, France, or Germany.

As the wiser conservatives among the Czar's counselors had foreseen, the Czarist system, which had been severely shaken by the minor shock of the Japanese War, succumbed completely to the infinitely greater strain of the [First] World War.... The tremendous problems involved in the conduct of the war proved quite beyond the capacity of the corrupt and incompetent civilian and military bureaucracy. The casualty lists mounted higher and higher, and the Russian armies went from defeat to defeat, partly as a result of bad leadership and general inferiority of preparation as compared with the German troops against which they were pitted, partly as a result of the inadequate supply of shells and other munitions.

The internal situation of the country deteriorated rapidly; the harvest fields were denuded of working hands as a result of the constant mobilizations; the transportation system broke down under the strain of military requirements; the bread lines in the cities grew longer and longer....

An unplanned and unorganized popular tumult in the streets of Petrograd [formerly St. Petersburg, later Leningrad], growing out of the shortage of bread and a labor dispute at the big Putilov factory, was all that was necessary to bring down the rotting structure of the monarchy in March 1917. A few regiments of disciplined soldiers could have dispersed the rioters, who lacked both arms and organized leadership; but the turning point of the whole movement came on March 12, when regiment after regiment refused to obey orders to fire and went over to the insurgents....

The history of the period from the fall of the autocracy in March to the triumph of Bolshevism in November is a record of the vain efforts of the Liberals and moderate Socialists ... to check and deflect by eloquence and parliamentary maneuvering a tremendous fourfold revolutionary process which had set in motion tens of millions of people.

The first of the four aspects of this process was the disintegration of the Russian army, the greatest mutiny in history....

The second element in the revolutionary process was the seizure of land by the peasants, who quickly realized the absence of any governmental restraint and began to drive the landlords from their estates. Sometimes the peasant land-seizures were peaceful; sometimes they were accompanied by violence and murder; but in any event the actual transfer of land to the peasantry, to a large extent, preceded the Bolshevik Revolution and the promulgation of the decree nationalizing the land.

Side by side with the mutiny of the army and the agrarian upheaval in the countryside went the workers' revolt in the cities. Starting with demands for the eight-hour working day and for wage increases, the labor movement became increasingly radical as the Bolsheviks captured the leadership in the factories and most of the trade-unions from the Mensheviks, and by October and November the workers were filling the ranks of the Red Guard, or insurgent armed force, and demanding complete control over production, in some cases driving owners and foremen out of the factories.

Finally, as the fourth element in the process of old Russia's disintegration, must be noted the demands for separation, or at least for very broad autonomy, which emanated from all but the most backward of the non-Russian nationalities. . . .

All these manifestations had their root in Russian history; they were far too sweeping and elemental to be ascribed to the handiwork of any group of agitators or conspirators, however active and energetic. But the Bolshevik Party unquestionably furnished an indispensable leaven of unifying leadership for all these elements of popular revolt. Under the leadership of Lenin, who returned from his exile in Switzerland across Germany in a sealed train about a month after the March Revolution, the Bolsheviks proclaimed a thoroughgoing revolutionary program. They demanded immediate peace negotiations, transfer of political power to the Soviets, confiscation of all the lands of the estate owners for the benefit of the peasants, and fullest freedom for the non-Russian nationalities. The upward curve of revolution was temporarily halted in July, . . . but the ground lost in July was made up ten times over again in September, when the commander-in-chief of the army, General Kornilov, apparently instigated by some of the conservative Duma leaders, who saw in a military dictatorship the only alternative to anarchy, and laboring under the mistaken impression that Premier Kerensky sympathized with his project, attempted to proclaim himself the supreme authority in the land. This unsuccessful attempted coup was followed by a great swing to the left throughout the country; the Soviets, which had hitherto been under the control of the Mensheviks and Social Revolutionists, began to pass over to the Bolsheviks in the biggest industrial centers.

On October 23 the Central Committee of the Bolshevik Party, under ceaseless prodding from Lenin . . . resolved on an armed uprising; and on November 6 and 7 the Bolsheviks, supported by armed workers, sailors, and sympathetic units of the garrison, seized Petrograd and presented a *fait accompli* to the Second Congress of Soviets, which was meeting just at that time, with a majority of Bolshevik delegates. The coup in Petrograd was gradually extended over the country, with some resistance in Moscow and other provincial centers, but in general with relatively little bloodshed. The new government, which called itself a Council of People's Commissars, hastened to consolidate its position by issuing three decrees, ratifying the triumph of the revolutionary movement: a decree proposing immediate peace to all the warring countries; a second declaring landlord property in land abolished forever and pronouncing the land the property of the state, to be used by the peasants on a basis of personal labor; and a third establishing the control of workers' committees over industrial plants.

Limitations of space make it impracticable to go beyond a very brief review and characterization of the main elements in the struggle which the Soviet government was obliged to maintain against foreign and domestic enemies before its position was firmly stabilized. From the beginning it was an Ishmael among the governments of the world; Lenin and other Bolshevik leaders were firmly convinced that the Russian Bolshevik revolution was only the beginning of a world socialist revolution, which, according to their theory, had to develop out of the economic ruin and physical suffering caused by the war. Russia's withdrawal from the war and the conclusion of a separate peace with the Central Powers at Brest-Litovsk were bitterly resented in the Allied countries; and another cause of friction was provided by the Soviet decrees repudiating Russia's prewar and war debts and nationalizing foreign industrial enterprises. At first the absorption of the Allied powers in the World War prevented them from undertaking any hostilities against the new Soviet state; but in the spring and summer of 1918 there were interventionist descents of Allied troops upon the Russian ports of Archangel, Vladivostok, and Baku; and throughout the civil war the Allied governments, especially England and France, supported the Whites (as the anti-Bolshevik forces came to be known) with munitions and technical aid, simultaneously enforcing a strict blockade against Soviet Russia.

The issue of this civil war, which occasionally seemed likely to assume an international character, wavered greatly from time to time. In the summer of 1918 the territory under Soviet control shrank to a few starving provinces around Petrograd and Moscow; and only the most desperate display of revolutionary energy staved off what seemed to be an inevitable collapse. The breakdown of the Central Powers, which coincided with the development into an effective fighting force of the Red Army created by the Soviet government, brought a dramatic reversal of the situation; Ukraine, which had been under German occupation, was rapidly overrun by the Bolshevik forces; in the spring and summer of 1919 there were Soviet republics in Bavaria and Hungary, and the existence of the new non-Bolshevik states in Eastern Europe was, to say the least, precarious.

In the autumn of 1919 the fortunes of the Russian civil war again took an unfavorable turn for the Soviet forces; the White army of General Denikin reached a point less than two hundred miles distant from Moscow, and another White general, Yudenitch, was barely beaten off from the very gates of Petrograd. The White armies were decisively defeated in the autumn and winter of 1919; and in the summer of 1920 the Red Army, after routing the Poles, who invaded Ukraine, penetrated almost to Warsaw; and the specter of the spread of Bolshevism over Eastern Europe again loomed up. The defeat of the Red Army before Warsaw, which was soon offset by the smashing of the last of the White armies, that of General Wrangel, determined, at least for the time being, the fate and limitations of the Bolshevik Revolution: it triumphed in Russia, but stopped at Russia's frontiers.

The civil war in Russia was fought along class rather than territorial lines, the Bolsheviks finding their chief support in the industrial workers, while the motive power in the White movement was furnished by the former propertied and official classes, which had suffered most in the revolutionary upheaval. The peasantry, which constituted the majority of the population, wavered uncertainly in its attitude, now raising insurrections against the ruthless grain requisitions which the Bolsheviks employed to feed the starving cities, now turning sharply against the Whites when they saw that the victory of the latter threatened the return of the hated landlords. If one may judge from the intensity and scope of the insurrections, the peasants regarded the Bolsheviks as the lesser of the two evils, perhaps because they felt that some day the requisitions would cease, whereas the return of the landlords would mean the permanent loss of the land which they had seized in the first period of the revolution.

The struggle was fought on both sides with a fierceness commensurate with the great social issues at stake, and with the grim traditions of Russian history. . . . The most eminent victims of the Red Terror, which struck pitilessly at all the classes most closely bound up with the old regime, aristocrats and officers, landlords and big merchants, priests and higher ecclesiastics, were the members of the imperial family. Every revolution of the scope of the Bolshevik upheaval demands the head of the former ruling monarch; and the execution of the Czar would most probably have occurred even if events had taken a more quiet course. . . .

Whenever the Whites temporarily occupied a stretch of territory they wreaked on all persons suspected of Bolshevik sympathies the cruel vengeance that invariably marks the return of an ousted privileged class. Anti-Semitism was a psychological trump card of nearly all the White leaders; and the progress of the army of General Deniken and of the Ukrainian nationalist leader Petlura (subsequently assassinated by a Jew in Paris) through Ukraine was marked by terrific pogroms in which tens of thousands of people lost their lives.

Not the least of the factors in the final victory of the Bolsheviks (or, as they began to call themselves in 1918, the Communists) was their party organization, in which every member was at the disposition of the Central Committee. If a section of the front wavered, a picked group of Communists, prepared neither to ask nor to expect quarter, was rushed to strengthen it. If a city or a district had to be evacuated, a little band of Communists was always left behind for the dangerous work of carrying on underground propaganda and stirring up revolt in the White rear. . . .

Moreover, with all due allowance for the presence in the anti-Bolshevik camp of people of varying political and social views, the predominant ideology in the most important White governments, those of Admiral Kolchak in Siberia and that of General Denikin in South Russia, may fairly be described as restorationist. The chief posts in these governments were held by military and civilian officials of the old regime, who saw in the whole Revolution of 1917 nothing but a detestable and monstrous outburst of mob violence and anarchy, which had to be broken up as thoroughly and completely as possible. Consequently, while some lip service was paid to democratic ideals in official pronouncements, the actual administrative practice of the White regimes usually strengthened the Communist propaganda to the effect that the civil war was a struggle of the poor against the rich, of workers and peasants against capitalist and landowners. . . .

Despite their victories on the military fronts, the Communists found themselves in a very difficult position in the winter of 1920-1921. The World War had placed a severe strain upon industry and transport; and the disastrous consequences of the civil war, with its accompaniment of blockade, flight and sabotage of many members of the administrative and technical personnel of the factories, physical destruction as a result of military operations, and severance of the industrial centers of northern and central Russia from the sources of food and raw material in the south and east, can scarcely be overstated. Industrial production had sunk to 15 or 20 per cent of the prewar level; large numbers of workers had fled from the cities to the country as a result of the lack of food; the productivity of agriculture had fallen catastrophically, and in more than one province the peasants were in armed revolt against the requisitions, which still did not yield enough to feed the hungry cities.

It was against this background of economic collapse that Lenin formulated the emergency program that acquired the name of New Economic Policy, generally shortened in Russia to Nep. The basic feature of the Nep, which was promulgated at the Tenth Communist Party Congress in March 1921, and gradually went into effect during succeeding months, was the substitution of taxation for the former system of requisitioning all the peasant's surplus grain. Permission to sell his surplus in the market revived the peasant's interest in sowing and harvesting larger crops; and the rise of agriculture in turn constituted the necessary prerequisite for the revival of the depopulated cities and the stagnant industries. Under the New Economic Policy the state management and operation of the country's industries and transport remained; but the previous system, under which the industries turned over their products to the state and received, or were supposed to receive, their supplies of food for the workers and raw materials for the plants through a highly bureaucratized and inefficient distributive apparatus, was reorganized in a manner calculated to give the individual industrial units more initiative and more responsibility. Money and banking and other elements of capitalist technique, which had been discarded or had largely lost significance during the so-called war communism of the preceding period, again found a place under the Nep.

A fearful drought, coming immediately on the heels of the ruin and devastation wrought by seven years of war, inflicted on Russia the worst famine of its history in the autumn and winter of 1921-1922. The famine was most extended in the Volga, but also affected southern Ukraine and the Crimea. There is no accurate record of the number of people who perished in this great natural catastrophe, but it probably ranged from one to two millions. Help rendered by the American Relief Administration and other foreign organizations averted an even greater loss of life.

However, despite the shadow which the famine cast over the first year of its working, the New Economic Policy marked a turning point in the history of the Russian Revolution. Its adoption, which coincided with the stoppage of attacks from without and the gradual restoration of peace and order within the country, marks the dividing line between the destruction of the old and the building up of the new Russian social order. . . .

MACHINERY BEFORE BUTTER

By Maurice Edelman

From chap. 3 of *How Russia Prepared*, by M. Edelman. Penguin Books, Ltd., London; reproduced by permission. The author is a British businessman who had exceptional opportunities for observing Soviet industrial development before the war.

The death of Lenin on January 21, 1924, was followed by a conflict . . . among the executors of his political testament. Trotsky, Kamenev and Stalin had each made notable contributions to the revolution, and each had the authority of service in its cause. For the policies which they advocated, they each claimed that they were continuing the tradition of Lenin, who had established three cardinal principles—to keep the Soviet Union out of war, to build up its military strength, and to prepare a socialist economy based on the dictatorship of the proletariat. Trotsky, in association with Kamenev and Zinoviev, formed a bloc in 1926 in opposition to Stalin and the Central Committee who in 1925 at the fourteenth Party Conference had successfully proposed further concessions to the "middle" peasants as an extension of the New Economic Policy. Trotsky's Communism had an equalitarian basis, and he was intolerant of any concessions, even strategic, to the capitalist system. At Brest-Litovsk, in 1918, when parleying with the Germans for peace, his uncompromising and inflexible resistance to their proposals, summarized in the formula "neither peace nor war," lost for Russia the Baltic States which a subtler negotiator would have retained.

From his experience of life in the U.S.A., where he had spent his early years, he regarded the plans for the industrial development of backward Russia as idealistic, and for immediate purposes illusory. In the U.S.A. he had seen how enormous capital investments in heavy industry, despite the traditional technical skill of the American working class, had only become economically productive after many years. How then, he asked, could the Soviet Union hope to become industrialized without making (for untold generations) sacrifices which might mortally weaken the state before their benefits could be gathered.

On the other hand, he saw the western democracies, highly industrialized with a vigorous working class, ready for revolution. This, Trotsky said, is the way to socialism for the Soviet Union. The duty of the Communist International must be to stimulate revolutionary activity throughout the world. Whatever its result, it will necessarily weaken capitalist governments, and so prevent them from waging war against the Soviet Union. Under an international banner, inscribed "Workers of all lands, unite," the Soviet Union will lead a Permanent Revolution, bringing proletarian power to industrialized countries like Germany and Britain, who will then be able to send their manufactured goods to the Soviet Union and receive in exchange raw materials. During the Permanent Revolution, according to Trotsky, the Soviet Union would only export raw materials in exchange for consumers' goods. In this way the standard of life would be raised, an equalitarian communism could be introduced, Nep abolished and the principles of the revolution secured.

This was an attractive policy, particularly for those who had no stomach for the long years of sacrifice which the alternative policy of industrialization promised. In the summer of 1927, Trotsky organized a demonstration in the Red Square in support of his policy and addressed a huge public meeting, the last which he addressed in Russia. By the decision of the Central Committee he, Kamenev and Zinoviev were expelled from the Party in November of that year. Only a negligible number of Communists followed Trotsky in his secession. It was a triumph as much for the discipline of the Communist Party which Stalin, the secretary, directed as for the policy itself. . . .

The conference which expelled the opposition decided also to end the New Economic Policy and reorganize the economy of the Soviet Union on socialist principles, by the industrialization of the whole country on an intensive scale and by the amalgamation of individual peasant farms into state farms (Sovkhozi) and collective farms (Kolkhozi).

The Soviet Union was in a strong position on October 1, 1928, to begin its First Five Year Plan. Both agriculture and industry had almost reached prewar level; the capitalist states had also shown a more conciliatory attitude. Stalin believed that by utilizing the vast productive resources of the Soviet Union he could make it economically autarkic and independent, in peace or war, of its capitalist neighbors on whose moods and prejudices it still depended. The conception of the plan was Lenin's; Stalin carried it out; its instrument was the Russian people. In exchange for a socialist future, Stalin could only offer them a present life of toil in which their familiar necessities—butter, eggs, and even wheat—were exported to raise currency for the purchase of machinery. As earnest of the new life, the social reforms of the Communist Party were extended and emphasized—the seven-hour working day, holidays with pay, free medical care and crèches for children. The realization of social progress gave the workers faith in economic progress.

The Five Year Plans for the socialization of industry and agriculture were complementary. Without mechanization it was impossible to create the large agricultural units on which the success of collectivization depended. Without collectivization it was impossible to produce the grain and livestock surplus necessary to feed the growing industrial populations. Agricultural industry, particularly the production of tractors, was and is directly related to the defense industry of the U.S.S.R., since, by an historical and technical coincidence, the tractor plant is readily converted into a tank plant.

Stalin gave this dialectical answer to Trotsky: Sacrifice, he said, would ensure the construction of heavy industry; heavy industry would create simultaneously a tractor and a defense industry; the tractor industry would increase agricultural output; agricultural output would raise the standard of living; war industry would defend it, and the rise in the standard of living would close the era of sacrifice and prepare the way for socialism.

The workers of the U.S.S.R. accepted this thesis with enthusiasm. The motto, "The Five Year Plan in Four," was translated into action through the belief that a socialist synthesis would come from their sacrifice and toil. "Sobbotniki," men and women shock-brigade workers, voluntarily worked on their rest day in order to accelerate the fulfilment of the plan. Like an army going into battle, the Soviet working class under the direction of its general staff, the Communist Party and its G.O.C., Stalin, fought the resistance of human and material inertia. Rich peasants opposed the plan by killing livestock and refusing to sow. The bright tractors proudly dispatched from Kharkov, were ignored and left to rust in fields where the peasants continued to scratch the soil with their wooden ploughs. Stalin in his report to the Central Committee in 1933 on the results of the First Five Year Plan described sabotage in these words, "They [the saboteurs] set fire to warehouses and break machines. They organize sabotage in the collective farms and state farms, and some of them go so far as to inject the germs of bubonic plague and anthrax into the cattle and help to spread meningitis among the horses." . . .

Despite these difficulties, the masses of the peasants were solidly behind Stalin who released them from the Kulaks.

In the speech quoted above, Stalin said, "Three or four years ago, the poor stratum of our peasantry represented not less than 60 per cent of the peasant population. Who are the poor peasants? They are those who usually lacked either seeds, or horses, or implements, or all of these, for the purpose of carrying on their husbandry. The poor peasants are those who lived in a state of semi-starvation and as a rule were in bondage to the Kulaks and the landlords. Not so long ago, about one and half million, and sometimes two million, poor peasants used to go seeking work every year in the south—in the north Caucasus and the Ukraine, to hire themselves to the Kulaks, and still earlier—to the Kulaks and the landlords. Still larger numbers used to come every year to the factory gates and fill the ranks of the unemployed. And it was not only the poor peasants who found themselves in this unenviable position. A good half of the middle peasants found themselves in the same state of poverty and privation as the poor peasants. The peasants have managed to forget about all this now.

"What has the Five Year Plan in Four Years given to the poor peasant and to the lower stratum of the middle peasants? It has undermined the Kulaks as a class, and has liberated the poor peasant and a good half of the middle peasants from bondage to the Kulaks. It has brought them into the collective farms and put them in a firm position."

As for the workers, Stalin could say, "One of the principal gains of the Five Year Plan in Four Years is that we have abolished unemployment and have relieved the workers of the U.S.S.R. from its horrors." . . .

The Five Year Plans were more than economic plans; they were the General Plan of the Soviet Union for the war regarded as inevitable from the day when the Soviets first seized power. Lenin recognized that it would not be enough to industrialize Russia; the industries would have to be removed from the western parts of Russia, from the Leningrad, Ivanovo and Moscow districts and the Ukraine, where they had been established for the sake of commercial relationship with the western states, which now were the enemies of the Soviet Union. Before the revolution, according to the official figures of the State Planning Commission, the whole of Russia's industry was concentrated in 5.8 per cent of her territory. To reconstruct industry within this limited scope which might fall to one rush of the enemy, was not in accordance with Lenin's wide vision of the Soviet Union as a teeming and prosperous series of states, stretching from the Baltic Sea to the Pacific, in which an interrelation of merchandized agriculture and industry would gradually obliterate the differences between town and country. . . . The First and Second Five Year Plans laid the foundations of the Urals war industry; the Third Five Year Plan which the German invasion interrupted, witnesses the Urals fulfilling not only an economic plan, but also its function in the grand strategy of the Soviet Union.

PREPARATION FOR TOTAL WAR

By Nikolaus Basseches

From chap. 7 of *The Unknown Army*, by N. Basseches. Copyright 1943 by Viking Press, New York; reproduced by permission. The author was an Austrian newspaper man stationed in the Soviet Union for twenty years.

If the war of 1914 provided a foretaste of total war, the Russian civil war was a total war in the fullest sense of the word. . . .

Everything to the last nail, to the last box of toothpowder, was put at the service of the war. The revolution had, on its own account, ruined industry in general. Now, in order to keep war production barely functioning, the last remnant of civilian industry had to be suspended. . . .

When Russia's ruined industry had barely been put back on its feet—about 1928—the Soviet Union embarked upon the task of building up, as fast as possible, a modern industry adequate to the needs of an army of millions in a protracted war. The leaders in the Kremlin had always believed that war might break out at any moment. . . . That explains the whole character of the first Five Year Plan—a plan for heavy industry. It also explains a series of extraordinary phenomena which accompanied it. Russia was to be given, with the greatest possible speed, a gigantic raw-materials base for this heavy industry. And the means of production for developing this base were to be imported from abroad.

This method of procedure demanded terrible sacrifices of the Russian people. It imposed superhuman efforts on the national economy as a whole. . . . The population was deprived of everything; every resource was mobilized, the people were put on hunger rations—all in order to provide an immediate metallurgical base for Russian industry. Haste was made without regard to human sacrifice. . . .

This whole industrial expansion was undertaken without regard to economic gain. There could be no thought of profit when anything and everything was exported that could be exported, at any price, in order to procure the foreign currency necessary for the purchase of machinery. Even more characteristic was the fact that these machines, imported at such expense, were not treated with corresponding care. No crews of schooled technicians and qualified workers were brought in to work them, even at first. The shining new modern machines, of the latest models, were set going—and workmen were brought from the villages to run them. Usually, the first lot of these machines was quickly ruined by these unskilled workers. Whereupon a second lot was imported, then a third, until finally the plant functioned. This almost had the appearance of industrial vandalism; but actually it was all part of the race against time. Only in this way, only by ruining gigantic accumulations of machines for educational purposes was it possible to train a large industrial army in so short a time.

The building up of this industry also demanded terrible human sacrifice. In order to gain illusory hours, human lives were taken; people immolated themselves to relieve a bottleneck or to prevent a hiatus in the work. It was not at all a peaceful economic development, but a campaign, a war with dead, wounded and prisoners, with mobilization and major battles.

How did the populace survive all this? What made them hold through to the end? After the civil war there had been a military but not a moral demobilization. The war had clothed the villages of Russia in army drab. During the revolution the army storehouses had scattered their provisions over the land. In those days the soldiers' coat and the soldiers' cap served as a protection and sometimes as camouflage. People who at that time were still in mufti hid themselves in the uniform, and remained in it long after the necessity had passed. Officials in essentially peaceful functions went about in high boots as late as 1940, wearing military uniforms without any particular insignia. Clothes inevitably influence a man's mentality. But besides the clothing, military customs lingered on. Every industrial leader had been a military commander in the civil war. His orders had been issued in writing, in military style. He had maintained discipline among his subordinates; handed down daily written reprimands, and imposed penalties.

The military forms and the military terminology persisted in peace. The industries continued to issue their "orders" in military style, "orders" in which appointments, demotions, and the detailing of personnel were announced, reprimands administered and praises bestowed. There was talk of "campaigns" in industry, of "storm attacks" and "storm troops," of "breakthroughs" and "battles," of "captains" of economics and of industry.

The Soviet government never allowed people to slip back into the restfulness of peace. Again and again, at the slightest provocation, official propaganda and the press sounded the alarm. World events were interpreted so as to give the impression that war against the Soviets was imminent, that time and again only a miracle—and the genius of Soviet diplomacy—had prevented the war, and prolonged Russia's breathing space.

All pacifistic propaganda was choked off at an early stage in the Soviet Union, and every horrifying description of war was avoided. It is not surprising that in this state of mind the great mass of the Russian people took it for granted that their economic expansion was carried out in the manner of a war.

The geographical distribution of the new industries was governed by military necessity.

The Soviets had declared in their economic program that the new industries would be distributed over the surface of the country, not with regard to commercial profit, but in accordance with a prearranged plan to secure maximum practicability—that is, from the point of view of a national, and not a private enterprise, economy. But already during the first Five Year Plan military rather than economic considerations prevailed. In 1918 a large part of South Russia, including the whole Donets Basin, was occupied, first by the Central Powers and later by the counter-revolutionary forces. The Whites managed to advance northward as far as Orel. When they were superseded by the Soviets, the development of the Donets Basin was, of course, continued; but the center of gravity of Soviet reconstruction was shifted to the Urals and Siberia. . . . As there was not enough coal in the Urals area, the Kuznetsk coal basin in southern Siberia was extensively exploited at the same time. One of the first railroads built by the Soviets was the coal transportation line from the Kuznetsk Basin to the Urals. Thus the whole Ural mountain area became a gigantic arsenal, while the metal resources of the Donets Basin (except for some war factories of rather local importance) were reserved almost exclusively for civilian requirements. All through the Urals there arose, in place of small factories, enormous modern plants employing tens of thousands of workers—from the rifle works of Perm to the electro-steel mills of Zlataust. The Kuznetsk Basin served both peace and war. It became the industrial base of Siberia and, at the same time, supplied Russia's battlefront in Asia with the heavy industries of war.

The same principle which had governed the choice of sites for the heavy industries was now applied to the armament plants, namely that all these works should be situated as far as possible from Russia's frontiers. Besides these remote centers, an important war industry also grew up in Leningrad. Other Leningrad industries, already in existence, like the Putilov works, were modernized and enlarged. But in so far as they did not manufacture armaments for the navy, they chiefly produced special parts for armaments, such as optical and precision instruments, electrical motors and specialized machinery. The first airplane factories in Russia were in Moscow. The major automobile industry is located in Gorki (formerly Nizhny Novgorod) which was expanded into a Russian Detroit. All along the Volga, and even more through the forests that cover the great territories between the Volga and the Urals, there are large factories for war industries. The main centers of Russian industry are beyond the reach of any enemy.

At the end of the second Five Year Plan the Russian armament industry had reached a point where it could provide for a large army in a long war. While important industrial products for peacetime use were still lacking, the army had the most modern means of warfare, and even though the ruined machines had cost the state billions of roubles, Russia now had a large army of qualified industrial workers. . . .

In 1935 military industry was reorganized. The law of 1936 regarding the officers' corps provided for a special corps of military technicians and military engineers. And this corps comprised not only the military technicians of the army and the army administration, but the personnel of the armament industry as well. . . .

At the beginning of the nineteenth century a Russian engineer wore the uniform of a military officer. Military discipline and customs prevailed in the factories. Only in 1864 had the corps of the mining officers and that of transport engineers become civil services. Now once again the military uniforms returned, military discipline was reintroduced, and the Russian armament industry became an integral part of the armed forces. Here, too, the past had been a harbinger of the present.

Naturally, the question of food was not treated as a solely military problem. But the timing of the solution of the various stages of the problem, as they developed, showed that the future war was being borne in mind. The way in which the Soviet state was constituted made the collectivization of agriculture necessary. In the long run the opposing elements of a controlled industry and a privately run agriculture were bound to bring about the collapse of the regime. But actually there was no immediate need for haste. Forced collectivization brought about a frightful conflict. If the Soviets had first completed their industrial structure, they could have dominated the villages by supplying them with industrial articles. In that case the collectivization would have proceeded painlessly and with relative ease. But the precipitate dual process of collectivization and industrialization was undertaken in the expectation of war.

The split in the Russian village had started long ago; but it engendered a fierce struggle after the revolution, following the break-up of the large estates. Economically the two factions were poles apart. The ground-tenants, the new class of big-scale peasants, quite naturally wanted to burst the constricting fetters of the Bolshevik economic system. They were a danger to the regime in time of war. They were a disintegrating force in the village, which was the great human reservoir for the army. Collectivization, cruel as it was in its execution, became one of the means of hastening the synthesis of all Russian forces, of mobilizing all the human reserves and identifying agriculture with the methods of the total war. In the civil war a separate army had been needed—the *prodarmia* (food army)—to force the peasants to give up the food essential for carrying on the war.

In the First World War and in the civil war, the Ukraine, at that time Russia's granary, was occupied by the enemy. But in western Siberia, with Semipalatinsk as its center, there was a much larger and more suitable region for planting great areas with grain. The only trouble was that the inadequate transportation facilities made this section practically useless. The great Trans-Siberian Railway merely skirted the territory without opening it up. Therefore the building of the Turkestan-Siberia Railway (Turk-Sib) was made a part of the first Five Year Plan, so that Russian Central Asia should have a direct connection with Siberia. In this way not only western Siberia was opened up, but also Kazakhstan, formerly known as the Kirghizian steppe. The transplanting of emigrants to the Kazakh Soviet Socialist Republic and the permanent settling of nomads turned this territory into a rich source of foodstuffs. Russia's grain supply thus became independent of the Ukraine.

Incidentally the Turk-Sib Railway was also the solution of a strategic problem. This railway made it possible for troops and reserves from Russian Central Asia to be carried to the Far Eastern front much more quickly than from European Russia. Of course, it also strengthened the defenses on the borders of Afghanistan and Iran.

But although the Russians built, during the course of the various Five Year Plans, over 30,000 kilometers of new railroads, tens of thousands of kilometers of motor highways, as well as the Baltic-White Sea canal and part of the Volga-Don canal, they did not succeed in solving Russia's vast transportation problem. For the completion of their railroad system they had to wait until their heavy industries were sufficiently productive. And even then, and at the greatest speed, it will be a matter of decades. It is not only a question of extending and adding to the great transcontinental lines by which the troops could be transported to the borders. It is equally, if not more, important to have a close network of railroads which could rapidly take reserve troops to their assembly points and thence to the various army units. With the help of the radio and the expanded telegraph network, orders now quickly reach the smallest and remotest villages. It is no longer, as formerly, a matter of weeks before a messenger on foot or horseback notifies the elder of the village of the call to arms. But even so the Russian recruit still requires many days before he is definitely inducted. Thousands and tens of thousands have had to go many miles on foot in order to reach their assembly points. From there it has required days and sometimes weeks before they have arrived at their training centers.

Since war threatened time and again on the Far Eastern borders during the last two decades, since the Far Eastern problems seemed more urgent than the European one, the Soviets proceeded to double-track the Trans-Siberian Railway. These thousands of kilometers of additional tracks placed the Russians in an entirely different situation from that of the Russo-Japanese War of 1904. Yet their failure to solve the Russian transportation problem in its entirety left an important advantage to Russia's enemies, for the better and more closely knit network of transport lines of Western Europe gave the Germans numerical superiority in men and materials during the first months of the war.

Russia's industrialization completely changed the armament situation of the Russian army. At the turn of the century Russia produced less than 2 million tons of pig iron a year. After her industrialization she produced 22 million tons. Before 1914 Russia stood fifth among the world's producers of pig iron; now she stood second. . . .

The preparation of human reserves was begun long before the production of matériel. Modern warfare demands all available human reserves and economical use of them. Their proper distribution between armed forces and industry is, in the last analysis, the decisive factor in victory. Russia always believed that her human material was inexhaustible. She was always wasteful in its exploitation. The Bolsheviks, like their predecessors, carried out the collectivization of agriculture and the expansion of industry regardless of the human sacrifice they entailed. But the execution of the first Five Year Plan showed that, in spite of the high absolute number of its inhabitants, Russia was relatively poor in human material, that is, poor in relation to the area which had to be administered and economically organized. It was a land poor in population, which in case of a total war would need a large internal industrial army solely for the mastery over space. There was a scarcity of people everywhere in Russia both during and after the first Five Year Plan.

The question of military reserves was comparatively easy to solve. Already during the civil war the Soviets had begun to prepare the untrained reserves for war. They created the organization known as *Vseobutsh* (universal military training) whose function was to prepare all untrained reservists in civilian life for future military service. When the new defense laws of 1923-1924 went into effect, the preparation for military service (aside from this voluntary paramilitary organization) became obligatory. The young Russian was obliged to undergo military preparation two years before he entered active service. Military posts were established in every large factory, in every college, in the large government services with numerous personnel, and others were provided for the millions working in scattered localities. In these posts, young people at the age of eighteen were drilled several times a week. Practical instruction was given, along with first lessons in theory. But the military rounding-up of the population did not stop there. At an early stage two large associations were founded. One was the Society of the Friends of the Air Force, the other the Society of the Friends of Chemistry. Later on they were combined and fused with the Society for Promoting the Defense of the Soviet Union. Another large society, the Osoaviochim, sprang up. This enormous quasi-volunteer organization absorbed all the draft-exempt elements of the population (including women). It is devoted to the auxiliary preparation of the reserves. Naturally it has enormous means at its disposal. It even has its own industrial plants. An entire army of former professional officers and well-educated military instructors, who had found no place in the active army were assigned to this organization as professional instructors, organizers, and managers. These military instructors, who are at the disposal of the army, wear the same uniforms as the officers, except that their rank is indicated by stars instead of squares, bars, and rhomboids.

The society was divided into numerous specialized groups. They had their rifle ranges and exercise grounds throughout the country. They encouraged shooting as a sport by every means at their command. There was not a village in the Soviet Union without its rifle range; every citizen could take examinations in shooting; if he passed, he received a medal. . . . The Osoaviochim went about its promotion of shooting with thoroughly "American" promotion technique. Famous actresses mounted the shooting stands, took part in the exercises, won the medals and wore them with pride on every festive occasion. Millions of young men and women followed their lead. The regiments of the Osoaviochim took part in the general army maneuvers. In every thickly populated district the Osoaviochim erected military museums. Societies and seminars for all branches of military science had already been available all over Russia for a decade. Some people studied chemical warfare, others trained for service with the motorized troops, still others devoted themselves to the scientific aspects of artillery. There were even courses for military bookkeepers and for women who were to be employed in the commissariat department.

The Osoaviochim aviation auxiliary is a story in itself. In every village high towers were erected for the purpose of teaching the public the fundamentals of parachuting. Lectures were organized everywhere. Elementary pilot courses could be had in the smallest communities. Glider flying was promoted all over the country, and all the equipment for it was provided free of charge. There were courses for draftsmen, mechanics, and code operators. The Osoaviochim had at its disposal large flying fields, some of them the largest in the Soviet Union, such as the famous Tushino airdrome near Moscow. The society also had a large fleet of modern planes.

Osoaviochim, too, employed all the methods of modern publicity and propaganda in order to make the people air-conscious. Every year great aviation festivals were organized and drew millions of spectators. The employment of parachutists for military purposes was actually an invention of the Osoaviochim. In order to encourage parachute jumping, groups of professional parachutists were set up. The Russians soon discovered that sex appeal could be used as an incentive, so the Osoaviochim organized a whole staff of famous parachute-jumperettes, distinguishable by their elegant uniforms. Their records were widely publicized, their portraits were printed in the daily press. During the Kiev maneuvers of 1934, for the first time in military history an entire infantry brigade with artillery and light tanks was dropped from the air, before the very eyes of the astonished foreign military attaches. From that time on, parachutes were a prominent item in the great aviation festivals of Tushino. Hundreds of people jumped; machine guns and live cows were landed from the air. The program always ended with the jumping of an enormous military band whose members played a march as they fell. All young people in Russia wore parachute medals which bore the number of their jumps. The activities of the Osoaviochim eventually reached every member of the population who could in any way be utilized in the event of war.

There were other organizations which served the purposes of preparedness for war. The Red Cross, for instance, adopted the methods of Osoaviochim. They set up health centers in all parts of the country. People who were not members of the Osoaviochim, especially women, trained themselves in the various branches of the medical service for the eventuality of war. The Red Cross provided a program of training and appropriate examinations. Besides the men wearing the medals of Voroshilov marksmen or parachutists, there were great numbers of women sporting medals bearing the words "I am prepared for medical defense."

Still another factor in securing the full utilization of the general public in the event of war was sports. Sports in Russia from the very beginning of the Soviet regime had been subordinated to the military authority. At the head of Russian sports there was always a general of the reserve. It was relatively easy to rally the entire population for sports, because the sports clubs were attached to the great collectives. The playing fields and equipment were paid for partly out of the budgets of local authorities and factories, partly by the unions, and partly by the sports authorities themselves. Therefore Russia acquired a remarkably large number of stadiums in an extremely short time. All along the Moskva in Moscow, or the Dnieper in Kiev, one could see large numbers of well-constructed water-sports installations. These were the water-sports headquarters of the unions, of various large government departments, and individual plants. Some were under joint control, such as the sports club "Dynamo" which belonged to the political police and the electric-motor factory Dynamo. Every kind of sport was cultivated—football and tennis, shooting and riding. Skiing was particularly encouraged. But these were all intended to serve military ends, as was revealed by the fact that the sports authority, too, had set up a many-graded system of examinations for proficiency. Its very name revealed the purpose, and the sports medal had this inscription: "I am prepared for work and defense (G. T.O.)." At the great sports demonstration in Moscow tens of thousands of men and women gave a display of bayonet fighting.

So we see that in the course of the last ten years everything possible had been done in the Soviet Union to prepare the population, including the women, for service in war. Since everything in the Union is subject to centralized planning, it was natural to proceed more and more to a planned regimentation of the people. After 1932 freedom of movement for all practical purposes was abolished. In reality the people were tied to their places of residence and their jobs. This simplified military control considerably. It is important to remember that from its very beginning the Soviet regime tried to draw women into gainful employment. It was one of the first principles of the new regime that a woman not only should be paid the same as a man but that women were capable of filling all the jobs which hitherto had been reserved for men. This had made it possible, even in times of peace, to employ large contingents of women, not only in the usual light industries but in heavy industry as well—and in the army. Under Russian law women were obliged to serve in case of war, though not as combatants. They were, moreover, permitted to volunteer for armed service. Therefore the Red Army and the war industries always had had large contingents of women; that was not a new phenomenon in Russian life. And since Russian empresses had worn military uniforms it is easy to understand that Russian women should be somewhat accustomed to the idea. Many women had entered the army as telephone operators even in Kerensky's times, before the Bolshevik revolution. At that time, too, several female "death battalions" (shock battalions) were organized, which as a matter of fact were not very successful. The civil war brought tens of thousands of women into the Red Army, not only as relief workers, propagandists, and commissars, but also as machine-gunners, and even as cavalrymen. Later, at the big parades on the Moscow Red Square, a company of women was to be seen attached to every military academy and to most of the military schools that marched past. They wore blouses and uniform coats of the same style as the men. The half-length skirt was of the same material as officers' trousers. They wore high boots and on their heads they had blue berets with star cockades worn on the left.

We know that the Russian military

academies had a number of different faculties. The "command faculties"—in other words, for service in the front lines—did not include women. On the other hand, many women studied at the Frunze Military Academy, which prepared students for higher staff service. . . . The more highly placed interpreters with the troops in Asia are often women and reach the rank of colonel. Women study in the engineer and construction faculties in the various technical military academies. And in the Aviation Academy (the only one) women are permitted in the command faculty.

Even in peacetime many of the military as well as civilian pilots were women, and they held fairly high military ranks. In the intelligence service, in the commissariat departments, and in the medical corps there were, of course, large numbers of women.

The Soviets had managed, even in times of peace, to bring about a great reshuffling of classes. Since a large number of posts that did not require the direct handling of weapons . . . were filled by women, large numbers of men were freed for direct combatant service. Here the Russians developed considerable organizing talent. For some years past women in officers' uniforms have been a part of Moscow's social picture. The thorough military education of the population, together with the well-regulated service which brought this entire population into close contact with the army, and the extension of military service to all the peoples of the Soviet Union greatly increased the Soviets' reserves of military manpower as compared with the period before the revolution. Normally it is reckoned that 10 per cent of the population can be mobilized in case of war; and 12 per cent is considered to be the highest possible limit. According to this the Soviets, on the basis of their population, should have been able to mobilize from eighteen to twenty million people. But owing to the fact that women were, to a great extent, taken into the armed services, that in most cases they were able to replace men without previous preparation, and finally because the Soviets were in an exceptionally advantageous demographic situation from a military point of view (namely, of having a great many persons of suitable military age and relatively few old people)—owing to all these things, the number of mobilizable people in the Soviet Union was very considerably expanded. The entire army, with all its staffs and administrations, together with the available trained women, must be estimated at not less than thirty million people. The Soviets have succeeded in accomplishing the most thorough and widespread military training of a population that history has ever known.

THE SOVIET MIDDLE EAST

By A. J. Steiger

From "The Soviet Middle East," by A. J. Steiger, in *Survey Graphic*, February 1944. Copyright 1944 by Survey Associates, Inc.; reproduced by permission. Mr. Steiger brings to the analysis of Soviet industrial development a background of training in social psychology, industrial employment, journalism, and extended residence and travel in the regions of which he writes.

Half way round the 40th parallel from our own Middle West, Russia has opened up her Middle East on the other side of the globe. . . .

Russia's Middle East is as vast as the whole United States. Its wide open spaces—west to east—may be said to reach from the Volga to central western China and the Yenisei. . . .

The southernmost reaches of this territory lie as close to the 40th parallel as Chicago, or New York or San Francisco; its northernmost as far up the map as Hudson Bay. It has soil as frozen as any in Alaska but also deserts hot as any in Arizona; windswept plains like those where our buffalo once grazed; mountains and sunny uplands like California's.

Within less than three years, twelve to fifteen million hardworking people have moved in. They have joined earlier settlers there as well as its native inhabitants, along this eastward-moving industrial frontier. . . .

Defense against invasion, both from west and east, was a keynote in the master plan for Soviet industrialization. Drawn up with the aid of the 200-year-old Russian Academy of Sciences, the program provided for shifting the industrial base east of the Volga. When the Wehrmacht invaded in 1941, the Russians were prepared not only to yield territory in the west but to evacuate the industrial vitals of the Ukraine. The Kazakh branch of the Academy of Sciences, with headquarters in Alma-Ata—which is actually nearer to Chungking than to Moscow—reported a dozen expeditions in the field, plotting new mineral deposits. Some of the foremost scientists of the Academy in Moscow reassessed resources in the Urals and beyond.

The Nazi invasion had been under way less than six weeks when Hermann Habicht, an American businessman turned correspondent, left Moscow in August on the Trans-Siberian express and reported trainload after trainload of plant, equipment, and people moving eastward. Journeying on to Vladivostok on the Pacific, he encountered women and children now being evacuated westward from the areas east of Lake Baikal in anticipation of a simultaneous invasion by the Japanese.

Two months later, when Robert Magidoff, NBC correspondent, joined the diplomats shuttled from invested Moscow to the wartime capital at Kuibyshev on the Volga, he found traffic so congested, not only with westbound troop trains but with evacuated plants and their crews moving east, that the 36-hour trip took six days.

Russia's Middle East had thus become the safety zone between threatened frontiers on two continents. . . .

The abundant wealth of [this] Russian area was revealed by discoveries of copper, gold, silver, lead, and zinc ores in the eighteenth century. This led to the rise of a flourishing artisan smelting industry, the products of which are symbolized today in museum exhibits of brass cannon and Russian samovars. Some Ural iron works are as old as the Bear Mountain furnaces near West Point, which were the source of muskets for the Continentals in the American Revolution. The Russian "blue iron" produced on charcoal fires ranked with Sweden's as the finest in the world. Its permanent bluish shine was the joy of engine-wipers on the seven seas.

Middle Eastern coal deposits now estimated in trillions of tons, awaited the rise of blast furnaces. Before 1917 the Trans-Siberian Railway had absorbed what little was mined in the Kuznetsk Basin. Siberian manganese deposits and fireclay, nickel ores in the southern Urals, oil at Emba and in Uzbekistan, copper at Balkhash, potash salts in Kazakhstan, iron at Magnitogorsk, nonferrous metals at Norilsk within the Arctic circle—all these lay buried, waiting for prospector, miner and engineer. . . .

The development of an industrial bastion here has been a signal feature in all of the Soviet Five Year Plans. New railways were driven to vital industrial deposits and urban centers sprang up along them as they had along the older Trans-Siberian and Central Asian Railways. By 1940 there were a score of cities in the Soviet Middle East with populations that ranged above 100,000. Alma-Ata, Krasnoyarsk, Magnitogorsk, and Stalinsk were twice that in size, and three cities—Sverdlovsk, Novosibirsk, and Tashkent—each ranged around 500,000. (That is comparable to Buffalo or Cincinnati.) For the most part, as modern industrial centers, these communities have had their rise in the last fifteen years.

... In your mind's eye, lay a transparent map of Russia's Middle East at the right of an ordinary map (same scale) of our own Middle West. Then turn it back, like the next page of a book. You will be surprised at what you see. For, if you tilt it a bit, you will find that these key cities, now in reverse from east to west, fall directly over what from the standpoint of social economy might well be called their American counterparts.

Thus, Sverdlovsk, with its heavy industries, would overlay the steel city of Pittsburgh. Novosibirsk, in the heart of rich Siberian wheatlands, would be near the western border of Kansas. Tashkent, in the heart of Central Asia's cottonlands, would overlap the Gulf of Mexico, just south of our own cotton belt. Krasnoyarsk, with its pulp mills and mining machinery, would be near Salt Lake City.

The coal, oil, and iron of the Urals would rest on our Appalachians, and herds of Kazakhstan livestock would graze over our own southwestern grasslands. Passing east through the industrial center of it all would be like traveling from Pittsburgh west through St. Louis and beyond.

These names will recur in what follows, and perhaps I can give you a sense of what they mean to me. For in the early '30's my research work in industrial accidents at the Sverdlovsk Psycho-Technical Institute gave occasion for visits to most of the major projects under way in the region.

Sverdlovsk itself, with its half million people by 1940, was then just emerging as a center of heavy industry. Side by side with vast construction projects, like a machine-building works designed to produce heavy mill equipment, were landmarks of the old provincial town of Ekaterinburg (population 70,000 in 1920). I have in mind, for example, a diamond mill, driven by a water wheel, and making ornaments of jasper, topaz, and aquamarine.

Impounded by the mill dam near the center of the old town was an extensive lagoon, a common feature of the Ural landscape. Here, sturdily built log cabins stood their ground against modern apartment dwellings. But all around were evidences of feverish building activity—a medical center in an extensive quadrangle of many buildings; a rambling engineering training college with freshly-boarded walls smelling still of the sawmill; an airdrome newly laid out in the wild grassland of the town's environs.

The new city of Sverdlovsk was just emerging above the tree tops of the surrounding forests. But when I visited an electrolytic copper refinery twenty miles out of town, I found it had been designed by an American engineer, Archer E. Wheeler, in a skyscraper overlooking Battery Park. The Urals are a long way from Canada, but it was here that I came to know Walter Arnold Rukeyser, another American engineer who was advising the Russians on new asbestos mining and processing plants after the latest Quebec models....

A signpost along the railway near Chelyabinsk marks the boundary line between Europe and Asia. Through the car window, you could see an enormous tractor plant designed in Detroit. Going by rail also, through the open prairies of the southern Urals in the spring of 1933, I could see far off to the east the smoke of campfires made by nomad herdsmen of Kazakhstan. Swinging in a wide curve around a small mountain, we suddenly came on to a valley full of smoking industry. This was the Magnitogorsk steel mill being built beside this mountain full of iron ore, and aid in its design had come from Arthur G. McKee and Co. of Cleveland. It was here that I met John Scott, who has told the full story of this mill in his book *Behind the Urals*.

Far out in Siberia another new steel mill was coming into operation in the Kuznetsk Basin at Stalinsk (population, 3,000 in 1917; 220,000 in 1939). Nearby is Novosibirsk, sometimes called the "Chicago of Siberia.". . .

In 1936, I found Novosibirsk developing a skyline of impressive buildings. Huge new structures lined the river Ob, crossed by two railway bridges. The open country is never far removed from the new cities of Russia's Middle East and on the outskirts here you could see old-fashioned Siberian cabins. Yet here, as at Magnitogorsk, electric lighting had been carried to the remotest hut. . . . The streets were lined with newly planted shade trees and were being paved, but sidewalks were still scarce and you had to watch your step or lose your rubbers in mud much as Chicagoans in 1850 might have waded through.

From Novosibirsk, trains run south along China's western frontier over the Turkestan-Siberian Railway into Central Asia. . . . An important stop on this line is Semipalatinsk, or literally "the Seven Tents," a city with a modern meat-packing plant noted, like Kansas City, for its cattle runs, the livestock coming in from the Kazakhstan grasslands and from western China.

Two days' travel along the Turk-Sib brought me to Alma-Ata. Founded by Cossack frontiersmen, this city of 250,000 nestles like Denver in towering rocky mountains. Along its steep streets run gutters of mountain water that irrigate rows of tall shade trees. With abundant sunshine and pure mountain air, the place has become a Hollywood of Soviet filmdom. . . .

From Alma-Ata, the Central Asian Railway runs westward through fertile uplands and semi-desert plains to Tashkent and on to the Caspian seaport of Krasnovodsk. Tashkent I have never visited myself. Half a million strong, it has become one of the fastest growing industrial centers of the East. It is the capital of Uzbekistan where, as in our southern states, cotton is king. Huge textile mills have been erected there.

Prior to the Nazi occupation, half the total Soviet output of coal, as well as iron and steel, came from the Ukraine. While machines can be moved, iron and coal mines like power dams are rooted in the earth, and, as we have seen, the Soviets had to resort largely to new mines and mills to the east. As American and other foreign engineers had for the most part long since gone, they had to rely largely on their own engineering talent. . . .

To meet wartime needs, the new mideastern mills have been greatly expanded. Last November, *Pravda* reported that output in the Urals had been "trebled" in 1942 and was well on its way to being "doubled" again in 1943. Another announcement told that in 1942 alone six new iron and steel plants and seven new iron and manganese mines were opened east of the Urals. What this meant was that iron miners from Krivoi Rog had been brought to the Bakal mines, where output [was] reported to have been augmented eight times over. Manganese mined in the Urals [was] sufficient to replace the loss of the Nikopol deposits. During 1942, the Ural output of aluminum exceeded that of the entire country before the war. The output of special steels has been increased eight times over at Magnitogorsk, which began to produce armorplate after the war began. The Urals have become the chief center for essential ferro-alloys.

Expansion of Middle Eastern blast furnaces, however, has as yet [winter 1943-1944] recaptured only about one-fifth of the potential lost when the Nazis occupied the Ukraine, for that had produced more than 60 per cent of Soviet pig iron. Provisional estimates, however, do not include the 1,700-cubic-yard-capacity Furnace No. 6 blown in at Magnitogorsk in January 1944, nor the iron and steel works being built in Kazakhstan and Uzbekistan or those operating beyond Lake Baikal farther east.

Any estimates of steel capacity, moreover, will have to take into account the smelting of scrap metal retrieved from wrecked tanks and guns, of which there is a bumper crop as the Red Army advances. The "largest electric steel smelting plant in the U.S.S.R." was set going during 1942 in the Chelyabinsk region. During the first six months of 1943, three more electric steel smelters were opened there, and plans for the second half-year called for the construction of four new blast furnaces, two coke-oven batteries, nine open-hearth furnaces, four electric furnaces, two tube-rolling mills, and an automobile factory, the first in the region. Open-hearth capacity has been greatly expanded also at Omsk, Zlatoust, and elsewhere.

Strong emphasis is now placed on restoring the iron and steel industry of the reoccupied areas in the Donbas and the Ukraine. Immense demand for blast-furnace and rolling-mill equipment is reported there. At Stalingrad, one blast furnace is already in operation. . . .

The reports are that power-plant capacity in the Urals was upped 250 per cent during 1942 alone. Moreover, new stations like the Irtish project in Siberia will soon make themselves felt as well as the huge Farkhad hydroelectric station on the Syr-Darya river in Uzbekistan.

Meantime, come plans to turn ancient dam sites to account. Long ago, mills were built beside impounded lagoons along the numerous small rivers of the Urals, much as early American industry first sprang up along the streams of New England and Virginia. Many of these water wheels are now in disrepair, but one Soviet commission estimated that by erecting small electric stations at the existing dams in the Nizhni Tagil region, up to four million kilowatts of cheap electric power could be produced. "Down by the old mill stream" may thus come to have a new meaning in Western Asia as in our eastern states.

. . . The communications system has likewise been expanded in the Soviet Middle East. In May 1943, the Commissar for Communications declared that during the previous eighteen months more copper wire had been strung than in the preceding five years. Here, American lend-lease shipments have been a genuine factor—as in the case of rails, block signals, jeeps, and trucks.

Alongside reports about such general expansion one can also read of industrial equipment unutilized for want of power or effective personnel. Recent travelers over the Trans-Siberian tell of seeing many engines and freight cars hauled on to sidings in disrepair. Although the Kuzbas coal mines have expanded output to double the prewar level, it was estimated in June 1943 that the existing mines were being operated at less than half capacity. About 40 per cent of the working force at Magnitogorsk are new people, predominantly women and youth who entered industry after the war began. . . .

Americans who have been in Russia have diverse opinions regarding the efficiency of Russian industry. After visiting a war plant on the Volga, Wendell Willkie declared: "If I had not known I was in Russia, I should have thought I was in Detroit or Hartford. I have been greatly struck by the high degree of skill and organization and I speak as an American used to high standards of efficiency.". . .

[As the author says, there is considerable disagreement among American observers as to Russian efficiency. This question will be taken up again in a later section on "The Soviet Peoples at Work and at War."]

THE SOVIET FAR EAST

By Harriet Moore

From "Where East Meets West Again," by H. L. Moore, in *Survey Graphic*, February 1944. Copyright 1944 by Survey Associates, Inc.; reproduced by permission. The writer is research director of the American-Russian Institute.

The Soviet Far East—that huge area beyond Lake Baikal—is a rugged, cold, sparsely populated but potentially rich area which the Soviets have been developing at "double-quick" since Japan's invasion of Manchuria in 1931. Today, thousands of miles of Soviet-Japanese border are patrolled by sentries and bristle with armaments. And behind this frontier is the new Soviet East. . . .

The old paths of settlement to the East were trod successively by traders, Cossacks, convicts, and peasants squeezed off the crowded lands of European Russia. . . . As in Alaska and the Canadian Northwest, it was fur and then gold that lured the traders. . . . As time passed, some farming was developed; coal was found and mined; lead, zinc, and other metals were exploited by foreign companies along the Pacific Coast; and the Japanese developed the fisheries and lumber, discovered the oil and coal on Sakhalin. Thus it was when in 1925 the last Japanese soldier left Soviet soil and the new government took over in full charge. There were few more than 3,000,000 people living in the area. It had a tiny industry and was not nearly self-sufficient in food. Its main products were still gold, furs, and timber. It was the Soviet intention, judging from the first published plans, to let the area develop slowly; provide the non-Russian populations with alphabets; improve education, health and agriculture; develop existing industries. The rapid exploitation—even exploration—of its resources was to wait on the completion of the steel and heavy industry centers in the Urals and in western Siberia at Kuznetsk.

But September 18, 1931, changed the schedule. Japan had once before seized the Russian East and had not revised her ambitions. To turn Russia's Far East into a bastion was the immediate Soviet reaction to Japan's new continental invasion. But this required everything from people and transportation facilities to agriculture, industry, and armies. Though for the past decade most of the activity in the Soviet Far East has been in the category of military secrets, the changes have been so great that an idea of what is going on can be pieced together from newspaper reports and accounts of travelers.

The men to build the new frontier were not too easily found, for the Soviets with their gigantic program of construction from Leningrad to Vladivostok and from the Arctic to the deserts of Central Asia had no surfeit of people. Moreover, it was not a land of milk and honey, of pleasant climate and easy living to which people were being asked to move. The Far East has one of the least hospitable climates of the entire Soviet Union: bitterly cold in winter, rainy and foggy in the summer.

Much of its land is plagued with problems of "perpetual frost." The earth remains frozen the year round and the surface alone thaws so that, lacking drainage through the deeper soil, it becomes a great swamp in summer. Difficult for building, perpetually frozen soil is also bad for farming; and it is a mecca for mosquitoes and other waterbred insects that torture mankind. So much of the area is mountainous and forested that habitation, by and large, is confined to the great river valleys, though the Buryats range with their cattle over the arid highlands east of Baikal.

The Soviets had never thought to populate this area heavily for, as in the Arctic, they aimed to develop resources and necessary transportation with a minimum of manpower. Yet for a fortress area—and that is the concept of the Far East—there must be a garrison. It has been to the Red Army and to the youth that the patriotic appeal has been made, accompanied as always in the U.S.S.R., with material reward as well. Before the war, men doing their service in the Red Army in the Far East were urged to settle there following the completion of their training. They were given special credit facilities and subsidies to move their families and establish themselves as farmers or workers in this area. Today, the farms along the Amur and Ussuri are collectives of Red Army men who were trained in the special Red Banner Far Eastern Armies. . . .

To the youth fell the opportunity to do the most dramatic job of all—the building and populating of the new key industrial center of the Far East—Komsomolsk, named after the Soviet youth organization. This city is situated at the point where the Amur ceases to be navigable for ocean-going vessels of any size. It is two hundred miles north of Khabarovsk and was literally hewn out of the dense forest and swampland by the Komsomols—members of the Union of Communist Youth. The challenge to build it was taken up by the Komsomol in 1932, and by 1939 the city had 70,000 inhabitants. Pavlenko's novel, *Red Planes Fly East,* tells the dramatic story of setbacks and sacrifices, of death and disaster, which made up the early years of Komsomolsk but which were in the end crowned with success.

Today it can be assumed that Komsomolsk has 300,000 inhabitants; it is a big ship-building center, has a steel mill, is a rail and river transportation junction and, lying well behind the Soviet frontier, it is a pivotal point in the Soviets' military might in the East.

This is but one of the stories of industrial development. Other Far Eastern cities have grown immensely in the last ten years and other new industries have been established where there were none before. The bulk of the people moving into the area have been industrial workers prevailed upon to move east in a spirit of patriotism or adventure, or in response to the higher wage paid and other financial inducements offered. The result was that from 1926 to 1939 the urban population in eastern

Siberia and the Far East trebled, while the rural population only increased by 17.5 per cent. This meant 800,000 more farmers in the area but 2,090,000 more industrial workers.

In the last few years before the Nazi invasion of the U.S.S.R., steps were being taken to redress the balance. Previously the more or less haphazard movement of farmers to the East often met a corresponding flow westward of settlers who had not been able to make a go of farming under the difficult pioneering conditions. To avoid this wasteful shifting of families, improved procedures were being devised....

To resettle farmers in the East meant complex problems of moving entire collectives with their livestock, supplying them with cleared land, or sending the men ahead to clear the land and build homes, financing them until the first harvest was in, providing agricultural machinery such as they were accustomed to in the farms which they were leaving. Methods of handling these problems were being worked out successfully so that 10,000 households moved East in 1939 and in 1940 the figure was expected to rise to 35,000 families or 140,000 persons. Without an even larger flow of farmers to the East, the Soviet Far Eastern bastion would be in danger of defeat by siege. It could not feed itself if it were cut off for long from the West It was to meet this threat that the third Five Year Plan originally called for a 30 per cent increase in cultivated acreage in the Far East. And to achieve this the farmers had to be lured eastward....

The lifeline of the Soviet East remains the Trans-Siberian Railway, skirting dangerously near the Japanese-held frontier of Manchuria. The railroad is today double-tracked and equipped, it is rumored, with two sets of bridges, tunnels, stations, and so on, in case of military emergency. Though much has been written of the Baikal-Amur-Magistral line, better known as BAM, no one really knows how near completion it may be. Designed to run north of Lake Baikal, through the Lena gold fields and on eastward to Komsomolsk and the Pacific, it will be safe from surprise assaults from the south. But it passes through extremely difficult mountainous terrain and whether in wartime the Soviets have been able to spare the men and materials to complete the project remains a military secret.... To supplement the Trans-Siberian Railway, there are but three types of transport....

1. One is by air, from the east or west, from Alaska or Siberia. Both these lines have been tried out; ... for years the Soviets have been using aviation to reach remote points in the east and north, carrying in mail, men, and medicines, carrying out the valuable furs and gold to speed them to market. The airline map of the Soviet Far East shows many miles of regular transport routes along the coasts, parallel to the rivers, and cross-country from river to river.

2. The second line of supply is by sea from America....

3. The third line—the Northern Sea Route—is far more spectacular in its nature than in its carrying capacity. It has brought ships from the outside world at least once a year. But still relatively few ships make their way along the entire northern coast in the short three-month navigation season. Many more ply between Vladivostok and the mouth of the Lena than pass eastward from Archangel around the hump of the Taimyr Peninsula. But it is the latter run that would be needed to replace the Trans-Siberian Railway.

Statistics for recent years are, of course, unavailable, but it is perfectly obvious that there is no substitute for the Trans-Siberian to supply the Soviet

East in time of emergency except BAM, and that is probably not yet complete.

That is why the Soviets have forced economic development in the Far East way out of proportion to the population and the discovered resources. In the old days, only the obvious and accessible were produced—gold from the Lena and Aldan; furs from Yakut and the north generally; oil and coal from Sakhalin; fish from the Pacific; lumber. But today virtually everything is produced in some measure east of Baikal.

Coal and iron ore, tin, molybdenum, tungsten, and salt are mined; heavy industry has been built up in Ulan Ude, Petrovsk, Komsomolsk, Khabarovsk, and Vladivostok. Airplanes are assembled, ships are launched, oil is refined, textiles are woven, sugar beets processed. Again, lacking statistics, it is only possible to guess and that guess would be that, for peacetime purposes, the Soviet Far East can supply itself almost completely with consumer goods, including food and light industrial products. It can repair and build its own cargo ships. It can assemble its cars, trucks, and planes and manufacture some of its railway rolling stock. But the Trans-Siberian must still haul in the heavy industrial equipment for new enterprises and for war. . . .

As a military base . . . the Soviet Far East remains an outpost that must be fed and supplied from outside in any long conflict. Its thin line of settlement along the very frontier is vulnerable to sudden attack and its lifeline in danger of being cut. It is no wonder that the Special Red Banner Far Eastern Armies hold such a unique place in the Soviet defense establishment. . . .

THE SOVIET PEOPLES AT WORK AND AT WAR

FOREIGN observers have come away from the Soviet Union with diverse impressions of Russian spirit and efficiency. There is no longer disposition to belittle the giant strides taken since the overthrow of the Czarist regime. There is also agreement, by American observers, that the Soviet Union still lags behind the United States in technology, industrial organization, assembly-line "know-how," and other important respects. Beyond that there is much difference of opinion, so much that it would be utterly useless to search for any single representative sample. The following selections are believed to be fairly typical samples of American eye-witness impressions of the Soviet peoples at work and at war.

The first one deals with the evacuation of Soviet industries from western Russia to the Urals in the fall of 1941. When it was reported in American newspapers that the Russians were evacuating scores and hundreds of factories—machinery and workers together—from the path of the advancing Wehrmacht, there was much scepticism in the United States. Businessmen, engineers, editors, and others asserted flatly that such a migration was impossible. The following eye-witness account by a trustworthy American reporter is a revelation of the spirit and organization which executed one of the most extraordinary migrations in history.

MIGRATION TO THE URALS

BY LARRY LESUEUR

From *Twelve Months that Changed the World*, by Larry Lesueur. Copyright 1943 by Larry Lesueur, published by Alfred A. Knopf, Inc., New York; reproduced by permission.

As we neared the Urals, the countryside began to resemble the rolling hillsides of New England. The tracks of the Trans-Siberian ran through gashes in the old worn-down mountain range dividing Europe from Asia. Ancient and eroded by the centuries, the Urals seemed to be only a series of foothills compared to our own Rocky Mountains....

That night, to our surprise, we began to speed past modern floodlit towns. At four o'clock in the morning I looked out the frosted windows on a large collection of new yellow wooden factory buildings and dormitories crouching on the wooded hillsides of the Urals. Although dawn would not come for another four hours, the snowy streets of this new city were crowded with pedestrians. I knew it must be one of the newly founded cities of the Urals, working right around the clock on war production.

We passed another and another of these mushroom towns, and although I possessed an excellent *National Geographic* map of Soviet Russia, they were uncharted. I knew we were among the shadow cities of the Urals, hastily thrown up to house the factories and workers which were leapfrogging across the plains of Russia. I saw carpenters clinging to the snowy roofs slapping up the newly finished pine boards. Work was going on throughout the night under the golden gleam of powerful arc lights. New railroad spurs were laid through the center of the towns, and the refugee factory workers and dismantled machinery were arriving from the conquered west. I saw whole families of workers down to the small children hauling the heavy machinery off the flatcars onto trucks and sleds. We could actually see the new cities coming to life before our eyes....

As our train slid down the grades of the Urals into Asia we saw a vast flat snow-covered plain unrolling in front of us. Siberia did not look much different from European Russia. Then we chugged into the great railroad yards of Sverdlovsk, the former city of Ekaterinburg, where Czar Nicholas and his family met their death. It was a busy boom town. The freight yards were an impressive sight. I saw that many of the countless refugee factories had reached their destination. The workers who had camped for weeks on sidings all the way across Russia jammed the station. Many were busy unloading the snow-covered machinery. The yards were piled high with odd bits of machinery like a gigantic jig-saw puzzle. Crowds of men and women refugees wearing black, shapeless overcoats whose drabness matched the grimness of the Russian landscape stood in line before make-shift canteens waiting to get their first good meal since they left their homes, thousands of miles to the west....

The railroad yards of Sverdlovsk, chief city of the Urals, were a steaming arena of vast movements, far removed from the threat of German bombing. Troop trains were being assembled for the west, supply trains were arriving from the eastern interior of Siberia, and new loads of evacuated machinery and workers were arriving constantly. The yards were jammed with massive diesel locomotives stamped with the name of Stalin or Djerzhinsky....

Our train pulled out for Chelyabinsk, the next big factory city of Asia. As we moved slowly through the night, we saw the mining cities of the Urals on every side turning out the ore for tanks and guns so that Russia might live. There could be no slackening now that the Germans had begun their great plan of surrounding Moscow; the snow-filled darkness was lurid with the sparks of blast furnaces....

We had hopes of getting a plane to fly us across the Urals again to Kuibyshev on the Volga. Flying conditions were bad, however. . . .

A yard engine poked us across the tracks past scores of big idle locomotives and hundreds of empty box cars, many of them bearing the marks of Kiev, Odessa, Minsk, and Kharkov. There were hundreds of cars stamped with the Latin lettering of the Baltic States—Estonia, Latvia, Lithuania. The factory people of these newly incorporated Soviet Republics had also been moved to Asia. We could see there could be no shortage of rolling stock in the Soviet Union, if all these engines and cars lay idle even while Russia battled the greatest army in Europe in front of Moscow. These were the trains the Germans hoped to capture by their lightning invasion, but it was obvious that the Russians had been quick enough to save them.

Our car clanked up against the waiting troop train and then we jumped out to see who our new companions were. It was a Cossack cavalry regiment. . . .

Attached to the troop train, we rushed at unprecedented speed back across the Urals, again passing the ubiquitous trainloads of evacuated machinery waiting to go east on the single-track line. I spotted several more unmapped towns, snuggled in the heavily wooded hills. Floodlit at night for maximum output, they gleamed against the fresh falling snow like spotlighted dance floors. . . .

We were on the last lap of our long ride toward Kuibyshev, and the weather on the European side of the Urals was cold and clear. I had expected it to be warmer here than in Siberia, but the temperature remained at ten below zero and the sky a pale cheerless blue. . . .

We passed over a long steel bridge thrown across a deep ravine. A few hundred yards from the steel bridge lay a brand-new wooden bridge, half concealed in the wood. It was an alternate bridge in case the steel span was bombed. In no other warring country had I seen such foresight. I knew there must be some highly developed organization behind this preparedness, some unseen factor that made this limited network of single-track railroads function as competently as it did. I remembered that I had not seen a wreck or any evidence of a derailment. There must be some hidden strength which few of us in America and England were aware of, else we never could have predicted Soviet Russia's speedy collapse.

Great crowds of refugees were sleeping in the railroad station at Ufa, and the tracks were banked for miles with snow-covered machinery from the western factories. Here the railroad branched off to Magnitogorsk, the Siberian city of steel and iron, to Bokhara on the Persian frontier, to golden Samarkand and the Tomb of Tamerlane, and to Tashkent on the Afghanistan border. Those were the forbidden frontier areas, which no foreigner had visited in years. Behind us stretched the vastness of Russia, curving around half the world, with its cities ancient as time. In front of us was European Russia and Moscow, where the most gigantic armies in history were locked in a battle that would decide the fate of Europe. . . .

SOVIET INDUSTRY AT WORK

By Wendell Willkie

From chap. 4 of *One World,* by Wendell Willkie. Copyright 1943 by Simon & Schuster, New York; reproduced by permission. Mr. Willkie, it will be recalled, visited the Soviet Union during the dark days of autumn 1942 when the Germans were fighting in the streets of Stalingrad.

I SPENT one day looking at a Soviet aviation plant. I saw other factories in Russia, candy factories, munition factories, foundries, canneries, and power plants. But this aviation plant, now located outside of Moscow, remains most vivid in my memory.

It was a big place. My guess would be that some 30,000 workers were running three shifts and that they were making a very presentable number of airplanes every day. The plane produced was the now-famous Stormovik, a single-engined, heavily armored fighting model which has been developed by the Russians as one of the really novel weapons of the war. . . .

Parts of the manufacturing process were crudely organized. The wings of the Stormovik are made of plywood, compressed under steam pressure, and then covered with canvas. The woodworking shops seemed to me to rely too much on hand labor and their product showed it. Also, some of the electrical and plating shops were on the primitive side.

With these exceptions, the plant would compare favorably in output and efficiency with any I have ever seen. I walked through shop after shop of lathes and punching presses. I saw machine tools assembled from all over the world, their trade-names showing they came from Chemnitz, from Skoda, from Sheffield, from Cincinnati, from Sverdlovsk, from Antwerp. They were being efficiently used.

More than 35 per cent of the labor in the plant was done by women. Among the workers we saw boys not more than ten years old, all dressed in blue blouses and looking like apprentice students, even though the officials of the factory pulled no punches in admitting that the children work, in many of the shops, the full sixty-six-hour week worked by the adults. Many of the boys were doing skilled jobs on lathes, and seemed to be doing them extremely well.

On the whole, the plant seemed to us Americans to be overstaffed. There were more workers than would be found in a comparable American factory. But hanging over every third or fourth machine was a special sign, indicating that its worker was a "Stakhanovite," pledged to overfulfill his or her norm of production. The Stakhanovites, strange as it may seem to us, are actually pieceworkers, paid at a progressively increasing rate on a speed-up system which is like an accelerated Bedeaux system. The Russian industrial system is a strange paradox to an American. The method of employing and paying labor would satisfy our most unsocial industrialist. And the way capital is treated would, I believe, completely satisfy a Norman Thomas. The walls of the factory carried fresh and obviously honored lists of those workers and those shops which were leading in what was apparently a ceaseless competition for more and better output. A fair conclusion would be that this extra incentive, which was apparent in the conversation of any worker we stopped to talk to at random, made up for a large part, but not all, of the handicap of relative lack of skill. The productivity of each individual worker was lower than in the United States. Russian officials admitted this to me freely. Until they can change this by education and training, they explained, they must offset it by putting great emphasis on patriotic drives for output and by recruiting all the labor power, even that of children and old women, that they can find. . . .

Russia's farms, just as much as its factories, have been mobilized for total war, and their capacity to support a fighting nation has been one of Hitler's most profound miscalculations and one of the world's surprises.

Day after day we flew over these

farms, all the way from the front itself, at Rzhev, to the farthest limits of cultivation in Central Asia and Siberia. For Russia's farming lands stretch nearly six thousand miles behind the front. Only from the air, I suspect, can one get any sense of the immensity of this farming land, or of its infinite variety. . . .

We left the Volga bend to drive inland to a collective farm which had formerly been a hunting estate of a member of the lesser nobility. It had some 8,000 acres, with fifty-five families living on it, a ratio of about 140 acres per family, which is about the size of the average farm in Rush County, Indiana.

The soil was good—a dark, rich loam—but the rainfall was slight, only some thirteen inches per year. In Indiana we have about forty. Crops were cultivated without benefit of fertilizer, and cultivation was almost exclusively mechanical. Largely wheat and rye and other small grains were grown. The season's average yield per acre of wheat was fifteen and one-half bushels; of rye a little less, which I thought pretty good under the circumstances. . . .

Each of the fifty-five families on the farm was allowed to own one cow; the scraggly herd, consisting of every known mixture as to breed, grazed together on a common near a cluster of small houses in which the families lived. But the collectivist farm itself owned 800 head of cattle, 250 of them cows, of excellent stock and all well cared for. The cattle barns were of brick and large; the floors were concrete and the stanchions modern. The calves were almost tenderly watched over, in clean neat stalls, and women who were in charge of the barns explained to me their methods of improving the stock by care and breeding. The methods were scientific and modern.

I saw only one able-bodied man on the farm; he was the manager. Most of the workers were women or children, with a few old men. For the farms of Russia have been the enormous reservoir from which the Red Army has been recruited, and the wives and children of Red Army soldiers are today feeding the country. . . .

I learned later that this farm was somewhat above the average in physical equipment. But it was run much like 250,000 other collective farms in the Soviet Union. And I began to realize how the collective farms constituted the very backbone of Russia's tough resistance. . . .

SECRET OF SOVIET STRENGTH

By C. L. Sulzberger

From the New York Times, *June 8, 1945; reproduced by permission. The author has been one of the* Times' *Moscow correspondents during the war period.*

THE war has left the Russians impoverished and decimated, but instinctively able to surmount wounds as they have so often in the past. They are united under a firm, tough leadership and are beholden to nobody.

They are masters of their own lands and confident in their own political philosophy, even though it has not yet matured into that communism it sets out to be and still aims to achieve. Toward that ideal they still are working.

Many foreigners stress certain minor tendencies in the Soviet Union's wartime economy as evidencing a trend toward free enterprise and capitalism. Close scrutiny, however, contradicts such an impression. Moscow has made no basic concessions to private enterprise; the Government retains all ownership of land, resources and means of production.

The Russian people, with probably

more innate self-confidence than at any time in their past, look for glory, prosperity and a role in history from power without precedent. The Kremlin, during recent years, has been skillfully linking their present spiritual life with the traditions and culture of the Russian past. Tolstoy still is the most popular author of the Russians.

The not particularly audacious experiments of the Moscow Art Theatre and the classic ballets of Tchaikovsky seem to satisfy the curious conservatism of the present Russian mood, despite the people's amazing instinctive quest for knowledge and intellectual experience. Even among relatively new artistic figures those linked most closely to the past, such as Maxim Gorky and Alexander Bulgakoff, have the greatest hold.

Although the technical competence of the Russians has developed truly amazingly with the wholesale introduction of mechanization, they remain essentially unsophisticated and their unspoiled, if hard life, rendered not nearly so nervous by artificial stimulus as that in many Western lands, leaves them with a strong emotional vigor to face the future.

Despite the intellectual atrophy brought about by the purge period, which removed the cream of that great intelligentsia that mushroomed into Soviet life after the revolution, there is unquestionably rooted in the mass Russian psyche a freshness, a curiosity and an energy that belie the popular instinct toward traditionalism.

These statements all appear paradoxical, but to the Western mind the Russian soul is a paradox and only occasionally and in flashes completely understandable. This is one reason, and an important one, for the continual disagreement among observers on all subjects Russian, for tendencies toward exaggeration such as prewar minimization of the strength in Russia of the Soviet system and possibly toward maximization of the same.

It permits the Government, a vast majority of whose officials appear to have a positive physical fear of taking any decision whatsoever, to be at crucial times the most efficient Government in the world. It allows an Army whose organization and method often seem to violate all orthodoxy in warfare, both classical and most modern, to loom unrivaled.

THE SOVIET UNION TOMORROW

By the Editors

Soviet military achievements in the Second World War have invalidated most earlier estimates of the strength and potentialities of the Soviet Union. That this vast country is today one of the world's strongest powers, few will any longer deny. That the Soviet Union is emerging from the war the dominant power in Eurasia is the opinion of an increasing number of competent observers and analysts. That Soviet strength will grow rapidly in the years to come seems almost beyond debate.

The Soviet Union has suffered frightful physical devastation and terrible human losses. But Soviet recuperative powers are great. For in that country one witnesses the phenomenon of a very large, youthful, resilient, and rapidly growing population, in possession of vast material resources and a dynamic state organization, and swiftly acquiring the tools and skills of modern industrial society.

Population. The population of the Soviet Union, after the annexations of 1939-1940, probably exceeded 190 millions. The U.S.S.R. thus outnumbered the United States by about 55 millions, Greater Germany by about 110 millions, and Great Britain by about 145 millions.

There can be no reliable estimate of Soviet population today. How many millions have perished on the battlefields, in German-occupied areas, and on the Russian home front, no one knows, probably not even the Soviet authorities themselves. Current estimates of total losses vary widely, ranging from 10 to 20 millions.

On the eve of the Second World War, the disparity of military manpower between the Soviet Union and the western nations was greater than the disparity of total numbers. In 1940 the male population of the Soviet Union within the age group 15-34 years exceeded 30 millions. This figure nearly equalled the comparable manpower of Germany, France, England, and Italy combined. It was about 9 millions larger than that of the United States. The Soviet Union thus had not only a much larger but also a considerably more youthful population than did the nations of central and western Europe and the United States.

Numbers and age distribution, however, do not tell the whole story. These factors must be evaluated in the light of comparative levels of health, literacy, skills, morale, and other qualities. The man-hours of work required on the average to produce a given result varies widely from one country to another. People's capacity to bear up and carry on under hardship and suffering is just as variable. Such intangibles as morale cannot be measured with a slide-rule.

Despite great strides during recent years, the Soviet economy functions less efficiently than our own. The Soviet peoples, though endowed with amazing stamina and high morale, represent considerably less per capita achievement on the whole than do the populations of the more highly industrialized countries in general, and the United States in particular.

During the coming generation, the numerical disparity between Soviet and western peoples seems virtually certain to increase markedly. The total population of the Soviet Union is expected to reach a figure somewhere between 225 and 250 millions by 1970. The higher figure is what might have been realized with negligible war losses. The lower figure is more nearly what may be expected in the light of the very heavy losses sustained. Thus, at a minimum, the increase in Soviet population may exceed the total population of Great Britain or France in 1940.

In contrast to Russian prospects the population of the United States by 1970 seems unlikely to exceed a total of about 165 millions, a net gain of some 30 millions at most. And the population of central and northwestern Europe will almost certainly decline substantially during this same period.

In terms of military manpower the contrasts seem likely to be even greater. Allowing for maximum war losses, Russian males within the 15-34 year age group will probably equal the comparable manpower of all the countries of central and northwestern Europe combined by 1970. In the same period the military manpower of the United States will expand slowly, possibly reaching a total of about 25 millions as compared with a possible Russian total of some 43 millions.

According to the Office of Population Research at Princeton University (*The Future Population of Europe and the Soviet Union,* League of Nations, Geneva, 1944; reproduced by permission), the relationship between the "changing balance of military manpower in Europe" and the over-all balance of political and military power is exceedingly complex, "too complex to permit the generalization that this shift in manpower balance to the east necessarily means an equivalent shift of military potential. The latter is a composite of manpower, natural resources, technology, economic organization, national psychology, and political alliances. . . .

"Manpower, to be effective, must be implemented with effective economic and military weapons and organized in the context of political unity. However, it seems reasonable to suppose that the past history of diffusing industrial civilization will continue. From its nucleus in England, the Low Countries, northern France, and western Germany this technological civilization has spread in widening concentric circles to include Scandinavia, Germany, Bohemia-Moravia, Austria, northern Italy, and northern Spain. In embryonic stage, it has become established in the capitals and larger cities of Eastern Europe. In Russia, through vigorous governmental action, the transition from a feudal to an industrial society has been made in little more than a generation. With

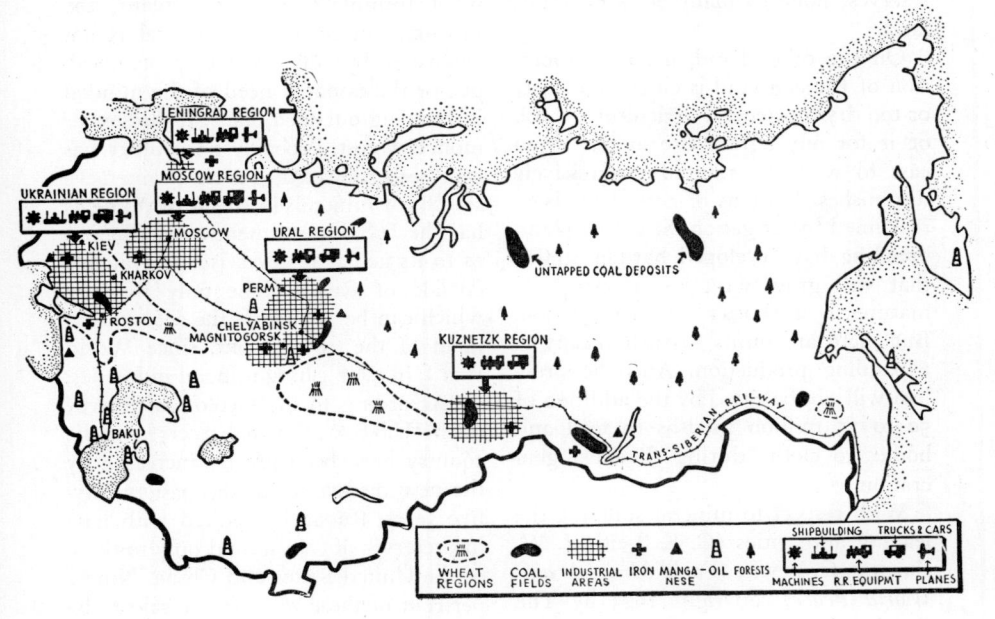

FIG. 25. Soviet Resources.
From V. M. Dean, *Russia at War*. Headline Series No. 34. Copyright 1942 by Foreign Policy Association, New York; reproduced by permission.

political security there is an almost irreversible trend toward an increasingly effective industrialized economy. At the same time that the manpower of Eastern Europe and the U.S.S.R. is becoming much larger relative to that of Western Europe, this formerly backward area is also finding the tools to make its manpower effective."

Natural resources. With respect to food and raw materials, Soviet Russia's position is one of great potential strength. No other single political area except the United States can become in case of necessity so nearly self-sufficient in the material elements of national power.

With respect to soil and climate, the source of food, and of vegetable and animal raw materials, the Russian picture presents both lights and shadows. No other country has such large forest reserves; none so many acres of arable land.

On the other hand, a large proportion of Russian land is either too frosty or too dry for general agriculture, much of it for any agriculture at all. From east to west the rainfall progressively diminishes. Millions of acres have been reclaimed by irrigation. Scientific plant-breeding has developed hardier strains that will grow with less moisture or mature in a shorter frost-free season. But there are limits to such means of expanding production. And the problem will not be eased by the addition of 50 to 75 million mouths to feed and bodies to clothe during the next generation.

With respect to mineral supplies, the leading authorities (C. K. Leith, J. W. Furness, C. Lewis, *World Minerals and World Peace,* copyright 1943 by The Brookings Institution, Washington; reproduced by permission) write as follows:

"From what is authentically known, the resources of the U.S.S.R. in coal, iron ore, petroleum, manganese, chromium, potash, phosphates and zinc are sufficient to meet growing domestic needs for many years to come. Important copper deposits have been developed east of the Urals, but Russia still imports substantial amounts. For such minerals as nickel, tungsten, vanadium, titanium, antimony, tin, mercury, sulphur, certain grades of mica, and lead, there is at present either a total lack or a deficiency. Further geological surveying and prospecting undoubtedly will add to the country's resources many of these minerals, and may eventuate in complete self-sufficiency in some cases. . . ."

"Any discussion of Russia's mineral expansion," continue these authorities, "must take into consideration certain fundamental facts: When the government formulates industrial plans, the procurement of a basic mineral is not evaluated by any monetary standard, but by the essential need of the mineral in carrying out such plans, regardless of monetary cost. Probably no country has ever been subjected to such an intensive search for minerals in so short a time as has the U.S.S.R. Authentic information as to its actual reserves is not available outside of Russia. The only measure which can be applied is the accomplishment of the government, since World War I, in establishing mineral industries.

"According to the Geological Survey of the U.S.S.R., the coal reserves of the country have been greatly increased by the new discoveries of the past twenty-five years. Russia is credited with having reserves of coal second only to those of the United States and China. Ninety per cent of these reserves are said to be in Siberia. Prior to the present war, annual production of coal reached 146,800,000 metric tons.

"The petroleum reserves have been greatly augmented and many promising areas are as yet undeveloped. No longer does Russia depend entirely upon the production of the Baku district for its requirements. It is claimed by the Geological Survey that in the Urals and the area west to the Volga River, reserves have been indicated of a greater magnitude than those of the Baku district. There seems little doubt that new fields will be developed southeast of the Caspian Sea.

"Under the regime of the Czars, the only large iron ore production was from the Krivoi Rog district in the Ukraine. This district has continued to be the main source of iron ore as well as pig iron. Large deposits of iron ore, much of it low-grade and requiring concentration, have been discovered in the Magnitogorsk, Sverdlovsk, and Nizhui-Tagil districts, and these have been developed in part. The reserves of iron ore in the Ural Mountains alone are estimated to be well in excess of a billion metric tons of all grades.

"A steel industry has been based on the Magnitogorsk deposits and the coal of the Kuznetsk Basin a thousand miles to the east, with plants in both places and a shuttle exchange of iron ore and coal between these points. While costs are higher than in the Krivoi Rog district, the new industry is less vulnerable to attack.

"Among the nonferrous metals, copper, lead, and zinc production has been greatly increased. It is claimed that large, undeveloped deposits of these metals have been discovered in the ranges of mountains forming the southeastern boundary of Siberia, but the best information is that these are still insufficient for Russia's needs.

"It is believed, in spite of extravagant claims to the contrary, that the manganese reserves of Russia have not been augmented. The deposits of the Caucasus are known to be among the largest of high-grade now known. Those of the Ukraine, while of lower grade, contain a large tonnage.

"New placer deposits of platinum, deposits of off-grade chromite, and adequate deposits of potash and magnesite have been developed during the past 20 years. Also, silver, and to a lesser degree, nickel and tungsten, are produced. Next to Canada and South Africa, Russia has become the largest producer of high-grade asbestos.

"Bauxite deposits have been developed, but in the main they are not high grade. Their extent is unknown.

"Perhaps the most outstanding achievement in Russia's mineral program has been the discovery and development of new alluvial gold in Siberian rivers draining into the Arctic Ocean. However, the location and extent of these deposits are not fully known outside Russia. Reported production would bring Russia up to second or third place among gold-producing countries, but there is some scepticism outside Russia about the validity of the published figures."

The over-all picture which one derives from the above and from other sources is one of great potential strength in terms of the basic essentials of industrialization and of military power. But it should be emphasized that the intensive development of these resources was just beginning in the decade before the war. Some of Russia's best ores are still entirely or largely untouched. England, Germany, the United States, and other industrialized countries, in contrast, have used up some of their best and most accessible ores. American resources in particular are undergoing abnormally rapid depletion under the insatiable demands for matériel in the present war.

What all this portends for the future is not altogether clear. But it is entirely possible that the Soviet Union will eventually become the world's foremost producer of industrial minerals, with all that implies as to military power and political influence.

Industrial potential. From what has already been said, it is apparent that the Soviet Union is still a pioneer country in the early stages of industrialization. This point can be demonstrated in various ways.

Use of energy resources furnishes one crude index of a country's relative industrial development. It has been estimated that the 135 million people of the United States utilize annually the mechanical equivalent—coal, oil, electric power, etc.—of the labor of some 16 billion human beings. In contrast to this astronomical figure, it has been roughly estimated that the nearly 200 million people of the Soviet Union use annually no more than the mechanical equivalent of 6 billion laborers. The contrast is increased, moreover, by the larger area of the Soviet Union (2½ times the United States), and the consequent consumption of a larger proportion of the country's energy output for transport and communications.

Not only the size but also the geographical structure and climate of Soviet Russia all have a bearing on the development and exploitation of Russian resources. Distances are vast. Energy resources and other mineral deposits are not uniformly well distributed for economical exploitation. The Urals industrial region, for example, depends heavily upon coal hauled 500 to 1,000 miles by rail, a costly business any way one looks at it. Frost is a grim enemy in much of Soviet Russia for several months each year, requiring large outlays of energy resources for heating human habitations.

These and other obstacles that might be mentioned are not fatal handicaps. But they do curtail the efficiency of the Russian economy. The long overland hauls, for example, to bring iron and coal together for smelting require more man-hours of work to produce a ton of steel than are required under more favorable geographical conditions in the United States, in the Rhineland, or even in Great Britain. Longer hauls and other geographical handicaps partially offset Russia's advantage in manpower and may be expected to do so for an indefinite time to come.

Another factor bearing on Russia's future power position is the physical destruction wrought by the German armies and occupation forces. The full extent of this devastation is not yet known. But there can be no doubt that the destruction of Russian cities, factories, mines, railroads, and other capital equipment presents a huge problem of reconstruction, and places a heavy mortgage on the future.

As indicated by the conflicting impressions of the American observers quoted in earlier pages of this book, the efficiency of Soviet industry is in dispute. The prevailing view seems to be that Russia has taken giant strides forward during recent years, but that the Soviet Union still has a long road to travel to master fully the techniques of modern industrialism.

State structure and organization. The Soviet Union is a one-party, totalitarian state, with a socialized economy. All transportation, mining, and manufacturing are state-owned and state-operated. Agricultural production is carried on mainly by state farms or peasant cooperatives under strict state control. Economic planning and direction is a state monopoly down to the smallest details. The government allows no public debate on national issues and policies. There is no private enterprise, no economic competition, in the American sense. A huge bureaucracy, responsible to highly centralized state authority, runs the vast and far-flung political and economic machinery of the Soviet Union, administering an area roughly 2½ times the size of the United States.

At the planning level the Soviet system seems to work smoothly and with considerable flexibility. Moscow can make and scrap policies without consulting press or parliament. Stalin can alter the structure of the government or change the direction of Soviet policy merely by signing a decree. Russian authorities carry out the government's orders with a ruthlessness which often appalls foreign observers.

Whether a more democratic system could have reorganized and relocated Soviet industry and speeded up production in time to meet the Nazi menace, no one can say. But it may be doubted whether a less authoritarian regime could have survived the shock of the German invasion and the subsequent temporary loss of the country's richest agricultural and industrial area.

Despite unlimited power at the center, perhaps because of it, the Soviet system has shown a certain rigidity in operation. A dictatorship can arbitrarily fix hours of work, direct the flow of labor and raw materials, reward achievement, and punish failure. But the Russian dictatorship has yet to approach the over-all ability of the American system to organize and carry out the complicated processes of modern economic production and distribution.

Our achievement is not merely a product of individual skills and mechanical proficiency in the use of tools. Nor is it the result merely of our long head start. Equally important are the underlying human relationships, the organization which makes the machinery run. It is a deeply rooted American faith that the competition of private enterprisers, together with a maximum of individual liberty, is the secret of American economic achievement.

The Russians, with their highly centralized political and economic system, may eventually arrive at the same goal. It would be utterly reckless to assume that they will not acquire in time the industrial and technological "know-how" which has given our more liberal economy such flexibility, productivity, and strength. But, as previously noted, it is the general verdict of competent American observers that the Soviets are still a long way from that goal today.

The *strategical position* of the Soviet Union also has a very great bearing on the role which Moscow can play in the post-war world. Strategical position, as repeatedly emphasized in this book, is the political and military meaning which technology and the international distribution of power give to a country's geographical position at any particular time. A country's defensive strength or weakness, and its opportunities for bringing influence to bear beyond its own frontiers, change—sometimes slightly, sometimes profoundly—with new developments in weapons and transport, and with the rise and decline of other nations.

Germany's shattering military defeat has immensely strengthened the geographically weak western frontier of the Soviet Union. No remaining centers of power, or combination thereof, in central or southeastern Europe could present by themselves a serious military danger to this Soviet frontier. On present evidence it is difficult to imagine any real threat to Soviet security developing in this region, except as the result of some coalition between the East European border states and a resurgent Germany backed up by the Great Powers of Western Europe and the United States.

The expulsion of Japan from the Asiatic mainland will measurably strengthen the Soviet border facing Manchuria and Mongolia. Demilitarization of Japan itself will comparably improve the defensive position of the Soviet maritime frontier in the Far East. The ways in which, and the exact degree to which, the post-war settlements in the Pacific and in Asia may benefit the Soviet Union will depend in part, of course, on the role which Soviet forces play in the final defeat of Japan.

In the short view at least, the unprecedented physical devastation, famine, and chaos throughout most of Europe and the Far East—part of the heavy price of victory over the Axis—seem to render even more remote any possibility of hostile movements against the territory of the Soviet Union.

Much the same factors—geography, technology, devastation, and social chaos—seem likely to determine Moscow's ability in the future to influence the course of world affairs beyond the frontiers of the Soviet Union. That Russian influence will largely predominate throughout a zone bordering Soviet frontiers on the west seems altogether probable. It is more difficult to forecast Soviet influence in other parts of Europe, in the Near and Middle East, in India, in China, or beyond the seas. Soviet influence, like that of other nations, will depend upon economic and ideological as well as purely military factors. In general, the more distant the area, the more heavily will Soviet statecraft have to rely upon essentially nonmilitary instruments of policy.

From a military point of view, the Soviet Union is preeminently a land power. It occupies the heart of the greatest land-mass upon the globe. It is one of the most populous and by far the largest politically unified block of real estate in the world. Like the United States, the Soviet Union stands in a central position in relation to Europe and the Far East. But unlike the United States, its linkage with these critical areas is by land rather than by sea.

By virtue of its large and rapidly growing population, its vast and largely untouched resources, its economic, political, and military development, and last but not least the shattering of all dangerously strong neighbors, the Soviet Union is in process of becoming the foremost, probably the dominant, land power throughout most of the immense area reaching from the Pacific Ocean to the Elbe, and from the Arctic Ocean to the great desert-mountain barrier of the Middle East and inner Asia.

Greater obstacles, however, stand in the way of the Soviet Union becoming a sea power of comparable magnitude. It has no portals on the Indian Ocean. Its Pacific frontier is screened by offshore islands. The Arctic ports of Siberia are open only a few months in the year. To reach the oceans from Russian Black Sea ports, ships must pass through long reaches of narrow seas culminating in either the Suez Canal or the Strait of Gibraltar. In the northwest, Russian sea traffic can reach the Atlantic only through the landlocked Baltic or around the North Cape.

It is perfectly possible that some of these conditions may change in due course to the advantage of the Soviet Union. Destruction of Japanese power will markedly enlarge Russian strategic opportunities in the Pacific. The elimination of Germany has already improved Moscow's strategical position vis-à-vis the Atlantic. It would not be surprising if Soviet access to the Mediterranean is placed on a more secure footing in the near future. And it is by no means impossible that the U.S.S.R. may eventually gain direct outlets on the North Sea and on the Indian Ocean.

All these gains together, however, would not overcome a more serious limitation on the extension of Soviet power into the oceanic realm. This limitation arises from the discontinuity of the Union's maritime frontiers. All sea routes between those frontiers involve long and roundabout voyages. To move by water between any two of them, it is necessary at some point to pass through narrow straits or around a continental promontory. All of these strategic bottlenecks are controlled by either Great Britain or the United States, or both together. In the main these bottlenecks lie far beyond the present reach of Soviet land power or land-based air power. The nature of this geographical handicap was dramatically illustrated over fifty years ago in the disastrous attempt to move the Russian Baltic fleet to the Pacific in the Russo-Japanese war of 1904-1905. Russia's opportunities on the oceans are many times more limited than were those of the United States before the building of the Panama Canal.

Soviet maritime frontiers are relatively strong in terms of defense. There can be no doubt of Russian ability to provide sea and air forces fully adequate for the protection of these shores, disconnected though they are. But the Soviet Union would enter any competition for oceanic sea power under handicaps so severe as to cause the great maritime nations little concern, at least under prevailing conditions as to weapons and communications.

SOVIET AIMS AND POLICIES PAST, PRESENT, AND FUTURE

By Sumner Welles

From chap. 8 of *The Time for Decision*, by Sumner Welles. Copyright 1944 by Sumner Welles; Harper & Bros., New York; reproduced by permission. Mr. Welles was Assistant Secretary of State 1933-1937, and Under Secretary 1937-1943.

In the first post-war years the two greatest powers, both from a material as well as from a military standpoint, will be the United States and the Union of Soviet Socialist Republics. . . .

The maintenance of world peace and the progress of humanity is going to depend upon the desire and the capacity of the peoples of the two countries to work together. It will depend upon their ability to replace their relationship of the past quarter of a century, which has not only been negative but marked by fanatical suspicion and deep-rooted hostility on both sides, with one that is positive and constructive.

During the period between the two wars the people of the United States lacked even the desire for a common understanding with the Russian people. Popular opinion in this country was molded by an almost unanimous detestation for Communism in all its aspects—particularly for its doctrine of world revolution—and by the violent and justifiable revulsion against the bloody excesses of the Soviet government, especially during the first years after the Bolshevik revolution of 1917. . . .

For their part, the Soviet leaders and the Russian people as a whole have seen the United States and the other so-called capitalist countries erect against them a wall of political antagonism. Quite naturally, they have been prone to interpret this in the light of the open efforts of the Allied governments, upon the conclusion of the First World War, to assist reactionary elements within Russia to overthrow the revolutionary government and to substitute for it a conservative regime subservient to the desires of the western world. They have also seen the western powers agree to the transfer to other peoples of territory which had for many years formed an integral part of Greater Russia. They had some reason to believe not long ago that the western nations, in the hope of keeping the robber powers out of their own preserves, were ready and willing to sanction the notorious plan of the German General Staff to divide additional spoils torn from Russia between Germany and Japan. And at one time they were led to the conclusion that the policy of this country was dominated by those financial interests which demanded the full payment with compound interest of the debts incurred by the imperial governments of Russia.... In the years when Hitler was poising himself for his final thrust against the rest of civilized mankind, statesmen as well as important newspapers in all the western countries loudly proclaimed that were Hitler to overwhelm Communist Russia the rest of the world would be the gainer thereby.

In brief, the record is far from one-sided. Recent events, political trends, the very conditions in which the world has lived during this past generation have all tended to create in each country a mass of deep-rooted resentments and prejudices which only statesmanship of the highest order and joint determination can hope to eradicate.

Far too many influential figures in this country have been glibly announcing that the fact that our two nations are joined today in the war against Hitlerism is sufficient to ensure complete understanding and enduring friendship in the years to come. No talk could be more intrinsically harmful. Such assertions tend to blind public opinion to the thorny truth that there is as yet no common understanding; that there are major problems to be solved before any such understanding can be achieved; and that our foreign policy today has no more difficult task before it. Unless both governments and both peoples make a sincere and determined attempt to find a new foundation for the relationship between the two nations, the very cornerstone of any future international organization will be lacking.

Such an effort on our part will be made much easier if we keep in mind certain salient factors in the history of the Russian people, as well as the policies of their governments both before and after the revolution of 1917. For one thing must be remembered . . . that, during the last fifteen years of the Soviet regime, the policy of Russia toward the other nations of Europe and the world objectives sought by her strikingly parallel the policies followed and the objectives sought by Russian governments during the preceding two centuries. The basic truth of this assertion is not changed by the fact that the Soviet government, primarily as a weapon for defense, has sought at times to utilize the Communist International to further a world revolution. That hope, incidentally, was obviously becoming more and more a fantastic and forlorn delusion in the years prior to this war.

Too many of us are apt to forget that, until the year 1861, the overwhelming majority of the Russian people were serfs. . . . The tidal waves which recurrently swept Europe as a result of the French Revolution in 1789 and which culminated in the revolutionary year of 1848 were barely felt within imperial Russia. The servitude of the masses and their total illiteracy made it possible for successive Czars to close Russia's doors hermetically to any foreign revolutionary doctrines. . . .

It was only after Alexander II emancipated the serfs in 1861 that a tremendous social force began to ferment in Russia. From time to time appearing upon the surface during the closing years of the nineteenth century, it had its being largely underground. It culminated finally in the Bolshevik Revolution of 1917. . . .

Each attempt during the nineteenth century to accomplish a gradual transformation from absolutism to constitutional monarchy was subsequently reversed by ukase. Even the half-hearted effort in the reign of the last Czar, Nicholas II, to lay rudimentary foundations for constitutional government by the creation of the Russian Duma was frustrated by the elements of black reaction surrounding that weak and unhappy monarch.

What must not be forgotten, therefore, is that before 1917 the Russian people as a whole never had the slightest voice in the policy of their government. Only in the past twenty-five years has the determining force within Russia come from the masses as well as from an autocratic few at the top. It is easy to assert that the Russian, as an individual, is still merely a cog in the wheel turned by a highly centralized dictatorship. From the standpoint of our western tradition, that is superficially true. From the standpoint of the Russian people, it is a hopelessly inadequate appraisal. The Russian people today are satisfied that their government is devoted to the popular interest. While the methods by which popular reactions are made apparent within the Soviet Union are totally different from those within the western democracies, and particularly within the United States, the Soviet government today is guided by the popular will, and ultimately depends upon that will for its existence. Certainly in the immediate future the foreign policy of the Soviet government will continue to represent what the people want. . . .

Various aspects of Russian foreign policy during the past two and a half centuries are strangely significant in the light of the present. It was Peter the Great who wrought the first great change in Russian history. By wresting the Baltic provinces from Sweden, he obtained for Russia the "windows to the west"—the vital outlet to the Baltic Sea without which she could scarcely have become a European power. Catherine the Great and Potemkin gained from Turkey mastery of the Black Sea, and by doing so began that long duel with Great Britain for control of the Dardanelles which in Russian hands would have made Russia a Mediterranean power. It was Catherine who was primarily responsible for one of the greatest international crimes of history, by conniving with, and even inducing, Prussia and Austria to participate in three successive encroachments upon the territory of Poland. Finally, through the third partition in 1795, Poland ceased to exist. . . . Paul I, in conjunction with Napoleon, planned for the overland invasion of India, and thus engendered that continuing series of nightmares which disturbed the sleep of all British Prime Ministers and Viceroys of India throughout the nineteenth century.

Every successive Czar during two centuries, from 1689 to 1869, fostered the gradual, steady expansion of the Russian people through the Siberian wastes to the Pacific Ocean. This finally resulted in the firm establishment of Russia as a Pacific power with full domination as far south as the banks of the Amur River.

While successive imperial governments, during the earlier part of the nineteenth century, had intervened repeatedly on behalf of the Slavonic Christians, who were still suffering under Turkish rule over the Balkan provinces, it was under Alexander II and Alexander III that Russia's Pan-Slavic doctrines were first proclaimed as cardinal principles of Russian foreign policy.

The significance of these aspects of Russia's traditional foreign policy and of their hold upon the imagination of the Russian people themselves should not be minimized, for much of European history has turned upon these policies of the past. In my opinion such policies will soon again play an important part.

By the time the Russian people finally rose to overthrow the hopelessly incompetent government of the last Czar in 1917, Russia had not only assimilated her territorial acquisitions, but she had even been assured by the Allied governments that at the close of the war she would at last be given control over the Dardanelles.

After the Bolshevik government had been forced to conclude the Treaty of Brest-Litovsk with an apparently victorious Germany in March 1918, she was stripped of all the territories in Central and Eastern Europe which she had obtained since the time of Peter the Great. Immediately thereafter Finland, by force of arms, won its independence of Russian control, an independence sanctioned by the Soviet government itself. The Baltic provinces of Latvia and Estonia likewise achieved their freedom. The remaining province of Lithuania was granted its independence by the Treaty of Versailles. So Russia's entrance to the Baltic, obtained for her by Peter the Great, was closed.

By the Treaty of Riga, which the Soviet government was forced to conclude with the reconstituted Poland in 1921 after the Polish armies, assisted by the French, had defeated the Russian troops at the gates of Warsaw, she was deprived of vast additional territories. They had at one time been under Polish sovereignty, it is true, but in a great portion of them the Polish population did not exceed 10 per cent of the total. Much of the Ukraine was thereby wrested from her. By the Treaty of Versailles the province of Bessarabia had already been incorporated within the new Rumania.

Russia thus entered the post-war period, under her new revolutionary government, stripped of far-reaching territories in Eastern Europe. She regarded these not only as vital to her security but as indispensable to her position as a European power. At the same time her Siberian provinces were being invaded by Japan and other Allied powers bent upon fostering that counter-revolution which it was thought might result in the establishment of a more responsive and amenable government in Moscow.

Granted the history of the Russian people, and the fact that the masses themselves now believed that they were at last on the path to the enjoyment of popular rights, it is hardly surprising that they should have been fertile ground for propaganda against the "predatory capitalist nations" of the West.

There was, of course, one way in which the breach between the Soviet Union and the western powers might have been avoided. It was the way Woodrow Wilson advocated. But it called for sufficient vision and constructive statesmanship on the part of the powers represented in the Council of the League of Nations to realize that a League without the Soviet Union could not long function successfully in Europe.

Post-war Europe was a desperately shaken community. That same strange contagion of panic which swept Europe at the close of the eighteenth century again gripped the continent in the early twenties of this century. Governments and the wealthier classes saw the specter of Bolshevism in every sign of unrest, political or social. Not only the British and French governments, but [the U.S.] government as well, were firm in the illusion that through a rigidly enforced quarantine the miasma emanating from Moscow could be prevented from spreading its ills abroad. Both the British and French governments, therefore, steadfastly refused to consider the possibility that the League of Nations should be called upon to deal with the Soviet government except at very long range indeed. It must be admitted, however, that Lenin's anathema of the League as a tool of the capitalistic powers was not conducive to a change of sentiment on the part of the Council of the League.

When Soviet delegates were permitted to come to Rapallo in 1922 [in connection with a conference of European states called to discuss economic reconstruction and relations with Russia], they were isolated as if they were lepers. Their conclusion there with Germany of the Treaty of Rapallo made it evident to some of the more clearsighted leaders in the western powers that the German General Staff was far from moribund, and that Germany had been enabled to gain a great advantage, tragically and shortsightedly rejected by Great Britain and by France. German foreign policy throughout the Stresemann period used this understanding with Russia as its chief card in all dealings with the Western European powers. Russian policy was thereby turned back from the democratic West, and encouraged to brood for more than a decade upon the destructive dogmas of world revolution rather than upon the constructive possibilities of world cooperation inherent in the League.

But in any event Russia was at that time principally concerned with her internal problems. Bolshevism had been founded upon the doctrines of Karl Marx, which were first made known in Russia in 1872, and which were applicable, in the concept of their author, to economies that were primarily industrial. The new government had to adjust the Marxist theories to a national economy where the industrial population was only an infinitesimal percentage of the agricultural population. The impossibility of applying the pure Marxist philosophy, under such conditions, and the violent rivalries, both individual and doctrinary, which were constantly coming to the fore, demanded the first attention of the revolutionary leaders. As the one practical solution of these initial problems, Lenin assumed dictatorial authority in 1921. Upon his death in 1924, the supreme control passed into the hands of Stalin, Kamenev, and Zinoviev.

Any hopes that Lenin or the more doctrinaire of his associates may have had that Communism in its revolutionary aspect would spread throughout the world were shown to be illusory. In none of the western powers of Europe, much less in the United States, did the doctrines of world Communism meet with any popular support. Even among the sorely beset and suffering peoples of Central and Southeastern Europe the flare-up of Communism lasted but a brief moment.

Russia itself gradually swung back from the early and fantastic extremes of the Trotskyist school of violence. . . . In the realm of economics, the stubborn refusal of the Russian peasant to produce more than he required for his own consumption unless he were permitted some reasonable profit, after a series of famines and highly disruptive disorders, forced a return to a more rational basis for collective farming.

The 1920's were necessarily dedicated to the readjustment made necessary by the growing breach between the Soviet leaders, such as Zinoviev, who were determined to concentrate upon the plans for world revolution, formulated by the Comintern, and the leaders who followed Stalin in desiring to set the course back toward the establishment of a workable form of state socialism. The long-protracted and bitter controversy ended only in 1928 with the final victory of Stalin, and the expulsion of Trotsky from Russian soil.

The year 1929 marked the turning point in modern Russian history. In that year the [first] Five Year Plan was announced to the Russian people. It had as its chief objective a self-sufficient Russia—self-sufficient not only in an industrial sense, but likewise in a military sense. For Stalin already saw clearly that unless the Russian people themselves could rapidly produce the necessary means of self-defense, through their internal economy as well as through their armies, the country would be unable to survive the dangers ahead.

Under the conditions which then existed, the rapid industrialization of Russia could be achieved only by means of foreign credits. In view of the Soviet government's repudiation of the national debts incurred by preceding governments, and in view of the suspicion with which the West still regarded any contact with Russia, credits, except on the shortest terms and at an inordinate rate of interest, were almost unprocurable. The situation, however, had to be met, and it was met in large part by the exportation of raw materials, desperately needed at home, in payment for what was required from abroad.

To satisfy the more extreme of the doctrinaires, further efforts were made, even during this critical period, to put an end to religious education as well as instruction in independent schools which refused to make Communism the basis for their teaching. But, as in the earlier years of the revolutionary period, both efforts proved futile and were slowly abandoned. . . .

Each year that passed marked an advance from the earlier stages of impractical and unproductive Communism toward state socialism. By 1935 the basis for a practical, rather than an ideological, state education had been reestablished; the staggering percentage of national illiteracy was being sharply reduced; family ties were once more respected; and various categories of personal property were sanctioned. By 1936 a new constitution had been proclaimed and approved. This established the right to hold property (exceedingly limited in practice, as to both quantities and categories) and, nominally at least, the rights of universal and equal suffrage, freedom of worship, freedom of the press, and freedom of speech and assembly. While it is true that the exercise of these rights was initially greatly restricted, it is noteworthy that their enjoyment has expanded each year since the Constitution was proclaimed. . . .

The election of President Roosevelt in 1932 brought with it the end of a sterile chapter in American foreign policy. The refusal of this government during the preceding twelve years to maintain any official relations with the government of Russia raised some grave questions as to the realism of the policies of the American statesmen who had been shaping the foreign policy of this nation. . . .

There was every reason in 1933 to seek an end to the deadlock between the two countries. President Roosevelt, prior to his inauguration, had determined, as a basic part of his foreign policy, to rectify this condition. It was, of course, necessary for him to be guided during the negotiations by the clear requirements of legitimate United States interests. But he had also to take into consideration the almost insuperable wall of public prejudice which had been built up against everything relating to Soviet activities. The moment the possibility of establishing any relationship with the Soviet Union was even mentioned, a loud clamor arose. It was claimed that such a course would open the door to a flood of Communist agents.

Tentative soundings taken during the summer of 1933 gave assurance that a reasonable foundation existed for the resumption of official relations between the two countries, and in the late autumn of that year the Soviet Foreign Commissar, Maxim Litvinov, came to the United States. In the ensuing conversations, the President and the Foreign Commissar reached satisfactory agreements on the question with which popular opinion was then chiefly concerned: the guarantee that subversive activities within this country would not be undertaken by agents, indirect or direct, of the Soviet government. However, they came to no satisfactory understanding on the question of the debts incurred either by the imperial Russian governments or by the short-lived Kerensky government. This matter was consequently postponed for settlement at a future time.

Official relations were immediately established by the reciprocal appointment of ambassadors. If the two governments had shown more concern in following up this beginning, they might well have reached a satisfactory working understanding far more speedily than they did. Unfortunately, the supervision of Soviet-American relations in both Washington and Moscow was largely entrusted by [the U.S.] government to men who proved incapable and unsympathetic to the task of bettering the ties between the two countries. Nor, it must be frankly stated, were more friendly relations encouraged by the continued subversive activities of Communist International agents in other parts of the Western Hemisphere, notably in Mexico, Uruguay, and Brazil.

The fact is that official relations between the two countries were purely nominal and almost entirely static until Joseph E. Davies was sent as Ambassador to Moscow by President Roosevelt in the first days of 1937. I doubt whether people in this country as yet realize sufficiently the concrete value of the work accomplished by Ambassador Davies during his relatively brief mission to the Soviet Union. Entirely devoid of any ideological sympathy for Communism, and by no means captivated by certain policies of the Soviet government, Ambassador Davies brought to his task an open mind, a completely objective point of view, and a wealth of political and practical experience. Above all else, he was governed by a deep-seated conviction that, in view of the increasingly dark international horizon, a way must be found to remove every unnecessary obstacle to the establishment of a closer understanding between the two peoples. He has himself written about his mission. But his achievements can properly be evaluated today only in the light of the war years. Had the foundations not been laid, the efforts of both governments to find a common meeting ground in 1941 would have been far more difficult.

It was during the years before Munich that Maxim Litvinov at last had an opportunity to demonstrate the quality of his outstanding talents. For it was then, with her internal conditions well in hand, that Russia at last sought to play a more cooperative part in European affairs. And Great Britain and France now finally, although hesitatingly, accepted her cooperation. In 1934 she became a member of the League of Nations and immediately, through the energy and inspiration of Litvinov himself, became a prime factor in League affairs.

These were years of constantly mounting difficulties for the Soviet Union. The dangers in the world situation were always obvious to the realistic vision of Stalin and Litvinov. In the Far East,

Japan, by her invasion of Manchuria, threatened the vital interests of Russia in her Siberian reaches. With the consolidation of Japanese control in North China and in Inner Mongolia, the Soviet government was forced to relinquish its interest in the Chinese Eastern Railway. Although Russia assumed protection of Outer Mongolia and Chinese Turkestan, she was pushed back by Japanese encroachments to the line of the Amur River. Even this tactical withdrawal did not prevent constant border clashes with the Japanese militarists, any one of which might unexpectedly have proved the forerunner of a major conflagration.

In Europe, first the growth of Fascism in Italy and then the far graver peril of Hitlerism in Germany only too obviously threatened the existence of the Soviet state. It did not need the conclusion of the Anti-Comintern Pact between Germany and Japan to tell the Soviet leaders that the German General Staff was planning the dismemberment of Russia through simultaneous attacks by Germany on one side and by Japan on the other. The German army's perpetual ambition to rob Russia of the Ukraine, even though a part of Ukraine territory had now become a portion of the new Poland, was once more uppermost.

To guard against these dangers, the Soviet government attempted both to reinforce the power of the League of Nations and to achieve a measure of security through the negotiation of special agreements with France and other powers directly allied to France. The Protocol of Mutual Assistance, signed by France and Russia in 1934, was supplemented by a further pact in May, 1935, together with a Soviet-Czechoslovak Pact of Mutual Assistance signed on May 16 of the same year.

The ability of the Soviet government to complete its task of internal reconstruction, in order to be ready to defend Russia against what seemed an inevitable war in the east as well as in the west, depended upon its ability to gain time and to make the western democracies realize that they themselves were endangered.

Litvinov became the foremost prophet of the basic principles underlying the Covenant of the League of Nations. No responsible European statesman in the decade of the 'thirties saw more clearly or spoke more truly. Unfortunately, he proved to be a prophet crying in the wilderness. His insistence that peace is indivisible fell on deaf ears. His demand that the western powers join with the Soviet Union in recognizing the dangers inherent in the rearmament of Germany was disregarded. In the light of present events, no statesman of those years, with the exception of Winston Churchill, has been proved more consistently right....

In those prewar years, great financial and commercial interests of the western democracies, including many in the United States, were firm in the belief that war between the Soviet Union and Hitlerite Germany could only be favorable to their own interests. They maintained that Russia would necessarily be defeated, and with this defeat Communism would be destroyed; also that Germany would be so weakened as a result of the conflict that for many years thereafter she would be incapable of any real threat to the rest of the world.

This stupendous lack of realism on the part of the so-called realists did incalculable damage in its effect upon the sentiments of the Russian people and the policies of the Soviet government. By the end of 1938 the Soviet government had reached the conclusion that it could not expect any sincere assistance from the western powers, and that such armed assistance as they could give, even were it definitely forthcoming, could be of only minor avail.

Internally, Stalin had already cleaned house. The notorious and much-dramatized purges had eliminated from positions of authority within the Soviet Union, and particularly within the Soviet Army, those individuals who had been suborned by the German General Staff.

From the standpoint of foreign policy, a radical readjustment was determined upon. The views of the Soviet government in 1938 are concisely set forth in a report sent to Washington by Ambassador Davies at that time.

"Litvinov's position and the attitude of this country definitely is that a Fascist peace is being imposed on Europe; that ultimately Europe will be completely Fascist with the exception of England and the Soviet Union; and that finally Italy will desert Germany as she did during the great war [of 1914-1918]; that Soviet Russia must count on no outside aid and in fact must be and is completely self-contained and independent; that France cannot be depended upon; that there is no hope for the maintenance of law and order based on public morality between nations until the reactionary elements in England in power are overthrown; that they see no immediate prospect of this."

The agreements of Munich confirmed the conviction of the Soviet government that the western powers strove to keep Germany from the west only by turning her to the east. . . .

In March of 1939, in an address delivered to the Party Congress of the Soviet Union, Stalin seized the opportunity to warn the western powers finally that continued appeasement of Hitler and of the Fascist government of Italy would end in ruin. He added a characteristic blunt declaration that Russia would under no conditions pull the chestnuts out of the fire for the western powers. That was the last warning given. Early in May, Molotov replaced Litvinov as Foreign Commissar and the first steps were taken toward finding the basis for an uneasy truce between Hitlerism and the Soviet Union.

The replacement of Maxim Litvinov under these conditions had been inevitable. In the councils of Europe, Litvinov had gained an outstanding position. He had won for himself recognition of his real, if frequently brutal, sincerity. He had seen clearly and he had spoken the truth. But the policy for which he stood was the policy that "peace is indivisible" —which he had in his hoarse and gutteral voice preached so often to deaf ears at Geneva. He was identified, consequently, with a policy of international cooperation for which the League of Nations stood, but which, through no fault of his, it had failed to carry out. . . .

In the summer of 1939, the Soviet government not only believed her potential allies to be weak and ineffective, but also feared that, should war break out, they would seek to throw the major burden upon the Russian people.

The history of the negotiations undertaken in the early spring of 1939 between the British and French governments and the Soviet Union for the purpose of agreeing upon joint action in the event of German aggression anywhere in Europe makes painful reading. The negotiations lasted four months. Ostensibly they collapsed because the western democracies were unwilling to let Russia impair the integrity of the smaller countries of Eastern Europe. Actually they broke down because the Soviet government had already determined that two could play at the same game. It suspected that the western powers were doing everything they could to turn Hitler to the east and therefore decided to checkmate them by turning him to the west. The protracted ostracism of Russia, her abstention from the League until five short years before, the hostility with which the Soviet government had long been treated in the West, had all combined to create so much suspicion and distrust on both sides that any real agreement was impossible. No greater error in policy was ever committed either by the Soviet Union or by the western democracies.

Throughout the discussions with the British and French representatives the Soviet government was secretly bargaining with Germany. The end came while the representatives of Great Britain and of France were still in Moscow. On August 23 agreement between Germany and the Soviet Union was proclaimed to the world. Nine days later Hitler launched his attack on Poland.

This agreement was profoundly alarming to everyone in this country who believed that it might well result in the defeat of Great Britain and France. But from a practical standpoint it is important to observe how it enabled the Soviet government to achieve advantages which proved to be of inestimable value to her two years later when the anticipated German aggression finally took place, and to note how Soviet diplomacy consistently hoodwinked Hitler and his egregious Foreign Minister von Ribbentrop. The secret agreements concluded with Germany in August and during the second visit of Ribbentrop to Moscow in September, while giving Hitler temporary security on his eastern frontier, gave Russia some vital advantages. She occupied the Baltic States. She occupied eastern Poland. She occupied Bessarabia. And with the reluctant acquiescence of Germany, Soviet troops on November 30 invaded Finland. Through the terms of the armistice concluded with that republic in March 1940 the Soviet government obtained military control of strategic territory which later enabled it to prevent Germany from occupying Leningrad.

Employing precisely the same methods, Stalin in April, 1941, further checkmated Germany by concluding a neutrality pact with Japan's Foreign Minister Matsuoka. This immediately blasted the hopes of the German General Staff for an attack by Japan upon the Soviet Union when Hitler should determine that the time for it had come.... While the Japanese signature to the Neutrality Pact was obviously not worth the paper it was written on, it was evidence that Japan was not prepared to follow her German partner blindly....

It is no longer a secret that even the highest military authorities in this country and in Britain did not believe in the summer of 1941 that Russia could possibly resist the German onslaught for any appreciable length of time. They had been persuaded that alleged inferiority in Russian military equipment and what they believed was a lack of effective discipline within the Russian Army would necessarily bring about, sooner rather than later, an inevitable Russian collapse. They had refused to listen to the repeated reports on the strength of Soviet morale and on the might of Soviet mechanized equipment and aviation sent to them by General Philip Faymonville, long stationed as a military attaché in Moscow. Of all our observers at that time, General Faymonville was by far the best qualified to speak, for he possessed a sympathetic understanding of the Russian people which did not distinguish many of his colleagues, who were hypnotized by a belief in Nazi invincibility. Fortunately, General Faymonville's predictions, and not those of the majority of the high military authorities of the western powers, were justified. . . .

When the United States was brought into the war six months after the attack by Germany upon the Soviet Union, this government immediately made every effort to establish closer relationships between Moscow and Washington in the political, as well as in the military, sphere.

After an initial delay, due largely to Russia's unfamiliarity with the operating methods of the American government, an increasingly workable arrangement was found to supply the equipment and raw materials so urgently needed by the Soviet authorities. It was long, however, before anything approaching satisfactory arrangements for the interchange of military information took place. In the political field, not until very recently—in fact, not until the conferences at Moscow and Teheran in October and November, 1943—has there been any satisfactory opportunity for a joint clarification of the war aims and peace aims of our two countries.

At the moment when I write these lines [1944], there have suddenly developed glaring evidences of a tragic lack of accord between the Soviet Union and the British Empire and the United States concerning the solution of various fundamental political problems—fundamental in that they directly affect not only Russia's vital interests, but likewise the ability of the United Nations to construct a durable and workable international organization when the war is won.

As I have emphasized before, there are no traditional or material grounds for antagonism between the Russian people and the people of the United States. And, although only a tentative beginning has been made, the United States is the one major power, from Russia's point of view, with whom an enduring friendship should be most easily possible. As yet, however, little real progress has been made in this direction. The time for it, of course, was while our partnership in the war was young, and before any of the major powers had assumed open and intransigent positions on important political questions. Recollections of western policy during the past twenty years and the necessary but ingrained caution of the Soviet civil and military authorities about permitting alien governments to obtain accurate or detailed information on Russia's internal and military affairs have created among the Russian people a deep suspicion of all western powers, including the United States.

This prejudicial state of affairs has been overcome partly by the highly important military assistance given the Soviet government by the United States, and partly by President Roosevelt's never faltering insistence that in the interest of both countries and of the world at large a personal relationship be instituted between Marshal Stalin and himself.

His insistence was rewarded at the Moscow Conference, and at the conference a month later at Teheran, when the President and Marshal Stalin finally met face to face. The four-power declaration was the first marker on the road toward the establishment of a workable international organization in the post-war period, for it pledged the four major powers to continued cooperation not only until the war was won but afterward. The announcements made as a result of the Cairo Conference, which obviously could not have been released without the prior agreement of the Soviet government, proclaimed the post-war objectives of the United Nations in the Far East. The

Declarations of Teheran gave a heartening indication that the Soviet government intends to fortify the independence of Iran in the years to come and is apparently wholehearted in its desire to collaborate with the two major western powers in post-war reconstruction. Unfortunately, these declarations were followed a few weeks later by danger signals indicating that the Soviet government was bitterly opposed to any intervention by the western powers in Russia's relationships with the nations of Eastern Europe.

Had the government of the United States determined in the early days of 1943 that time would not permit any delay in establishing, at least in rudimentary form, an executive council of the United Nations, in all probability most of the problems which now loom so large could have been avoided. An executive council composed of representatives of the four major powers and representatives of the smaller powers could have paved the way for a more comprehensive organization in the future and in the meantime could have threshed out and settled political questions as they arose, at least in principle. It was hardly wise to postpone the effort to solve so extremely delicate a question as the Polish frontiers, for example, until the armies of triumphant Russia had actually occupied the territories involved or to put off creating an international agency, which would have simplified the solution of such questions, until the various governments concerned had taken stands that made any joint solution highly doubtful.

In recent years the Soviet government has discarded many of the more radical forms of political organization which time and experience have proved to be inefficient. This has been particularly noticeable in the army, which has recently adopted the methods of organization and discipline that centuries of experience have shown to be conducive to efficient military procedure. Even the traditional titles have been resumed. With the successful progress of the Soviet campaign against Germany, the Russian army has assumed an increasingly important place in the Russian state. Stalin's assumption of the title of marshal a few months ago has made this clear, if any confirmation were required. Consequently, any conjecture as to the future international policies of the Soviet Union must take into account the opinions and ambitions of Russia's military leaders.

What does Russia want? On the answer to that question depends the ability of the United Nations to set up an international organization that will be able to keep peace in the world and successfully undertake the task of reconstruction. And in the success or failure of that adventure will be found the answer to the question which underlies all others: Is a third World War ahead of us? . . .

So far as one can judge, the Soviet government is reverting to the concept of Russia's world interests that was held by her governments prior to 1918 and 1919. In exploring the future it is well to keep in mind the historical Russian objectives.

It seems to me that in the Pacific the Soviet government, at the conclusion of the war, will seek first, either by actually joining in the war against Japan or by facilitating her defeat by the other three major powers, to reduce her to a position where she can no longer threaten Russian supremacy. The United States, Great Britain, and China have declared that Japan is to be forced lock, stock, and barrel out of the Asiatic mainland. In such event, it would be logical for the Soviet Union to demand that Russia be restored to the position she occupied in northeastern Asia prior to 1906, which included sovereignty over the whole of Sakhalin, that her present position in Sinkiang and Outer Mongolia be confirmed, and that her financial and commercial interests in Inner Mongolia be fully protected. It also seems not only logical but eminently desirable that the Soviet government be assured of her rightful place in any international trusteeship which may be established on behalf of the Korean people. Finally, Russia's legitimate interests in the fisheries of the northwestern Pacific must be fully protected.

I also hope that under a future world organization the Soviet Union will be willing to share with the United States, the Dominion of Canada, and China the responsibility for safeguarding peace in the regions of the northern Pacific.

In the Near East, the Declaration of Teheran concerning Iran seems convincing proof that the Soviet Union desires only equal protection with other powers of her legitimate trade in the regions north of the Persian Gulf. It is more difficult to forecast Russian policy in Eastern Europe and the Balkans. At the end of 1916 both the British and French governments officially informed the imperial Russian government that the question of the Straits and of Constantinople would be settled in the manner Russia had so long desired. That assurance was given because of the participation of Turkey in the First World War against the Allied powers, and was later nullified as a result of the Russian Revolution of 1917. At the same time the imperial Russian government demanded a part of East Prussia and a western frontier on the Carpathians, which would have brought Galicia and a large part of the Bukovina under Russian sovereignty. The changes which she then apparently desired in the Balkans would have assured her of a political "sphere of influence" without, however, any direct acquisition of territory within that area.

From present indications, the ambitions of the Soviet government today are by no means dissimilar. It refuses to discuss the matter of the incorporation within the Soviet Union of the three Baltic republics, which had been an integral part of Russian territory until the termination of the First World War. In so far as Poland is concerned, the Soviet government has made it clear both publicly and privately that, while it desires to see Poland reconstituted as a strong, independent state, it will insist that the Polish eastern frontier run more or less along the lines set down by the so-called Curzon Line of 1919.

In this the Soviet government is adopting an attitude similar to that assumed by the short-lived Kerensky government of 1917, which likewise proclaimed the independence of Poland and announced that "the creation of an independent Polish state, comprising all lands inhabited by a majority of Poles, [was] a reliable guarantee of peace in a future renovated Europe." The Curzon Line, drawn at the Versailles Peace Conference, was from the outset protested by the new Polish state on the ground that the frontiers of Poland as they existed prior to the first partition of Poland in 1772 should be reestablished. When the Allied governments in 1920 refused to alter their decision that the new republic of Poland should incorporate only territories which were indisputably Polish in their population, Marshal Pilsudski attempted to satisfy Polish aspirations by armed force. After initial successes and, subsequently, more serious reverses, the Polish armies with French assistance finally forced Russian capitulation in the autumn of 1920, and in March of 1921 the Peace of Riga was concluded between the Polish and Soviet governments. As a result of that treaty, the Polish frontiers were so drawn as to incorporate Russian, White Russian, and Ukrainian populations amounting to many times the strictly Polish population of those areas.

There is nothing sacrosanct about the Polish eastern frontier as established by the Peace of Riga. The Curzon Line would establish a boundary far more in accordance with the principle of self-determination, and consequently far more likely to assure stability in that grievously afflicted portion of Eastern Europe.

Every impartial observer must have great admiration for the magnificent faith and patriotism of the Polish people. These qualities have survived a century of national extinction and all the efforts of the most brutal and reactionary forces of Europe to suffocate them. But the Polish people can hardly maintain that the nations of the world must today consider as sacred the Polish frontiers of 1772, which had themselves been established by shifting tides of conquest. Even in the modified form laid down by the Treaty of Riga, supposing it were conceivable that the Soviet government would agree, these frontiers would today bring under Polish sovereignty peoples violently hostile to such an arrangement.

The maintenance of Poland's western frontiers, as they existed in 1939, would offer even less assurance to the peace of Europe. The arrangement which gave Poland her only access to the sea through a corridor separating one portion of Germany from the rest, promised trouble from the moment it was made.

A surgical operation will be required to lay down frontiers that will ensure the existence in the future of that "strong" Poland which both the Soviet government and this government desire to see. That operation will involve the elimination of the Polish Corridor, the humane and orderly transfer, under international regulation, of German populations from East Prussia and their replacement with Polish nationals, and an adjustment of Poland's eastern frontier with Russia in such manner as to incorporate within eastern Poland only areas in which Polish majorities predominate. The true friends of Poland can only favor a solution which by fixing permanent frontiers will at last give a homogeneous Polish people the opportunity to turn their thoughts to the peaceful development of their resources.

The Soviet government has made repeated announcements, recently confirmed by President Beneš of Czechoslovakia, that Russia desires the independence of Finland, Austria, Hungary, Rumania, and the remaining Balkan States. In so far as her frontiers with Finland are involved, Russia will undoubtedly demand as a minimum a confirmation of the frontiers established by the Armistice of 1940 as a measure of security upon which she must insist. The lamentable unwillingness of the Finnish government to make peace with the Soviet government when it could in April 1944, may result in far more onerous terms later on. In the south the Soviet government will recover, and should recover, the province of Bessarabia wrested from her in 1919.

The Slavophile policies pursued by the imperial governments of Russia in the first decade of the twentieth century have by no means been abandoned. At the end of the present war Russia will undoubtedly seek to have the Balkan states set up governments whose policies are in harmony with hers.

As for the Dardanelles, for so many generations a dominating factor in Russian foreign policy, the development of aviation has considerably reduced their strategic significance from the point of view of Russian security. I can see no reason why a continuation of the Montreux Agreement, which governed the status of the Straits prior to 1939, should not prove satisfactory. Only if there is no world organization in which the Soviet Union takes part, and Turkish policy appears to menace Russia's vital interests, need the historic question of the Straits once more provoke trouble.

The Soviet government is as legitimately entitled to promote a regional system of Eastern Europe, composed of cooperative and well-disposed independent governments among the countries adjacent to Russia, as the United States has been justified in promoting an inter-American system of the twenty-one sovereign American republics of the Western Hemisphere. I can only assume, until evidence to the contrary is presented, that the recent constitutional modification of the Soviet Union, as a result of which a federal system of sixteen nominally autonomous Soviet republics has been established, is the first step in this direction, motivated by the Soviet government's belief that regional arrangements can thus more readily be perfected.

If the Soviet Union attempts to use such a regional system for the purpose of imposing a series of protectorates, as a preliminary to their subsequent incorporation within the Soviet Union itself, the other nations of the world can only regard it as an unmistakable sign that Russia is embarking upon a policy of expansion, whether by military force or by the domination of the internal affairs of independent states. If, on the other hand, such a system is based upon the same general foundations as the inter-American system, in which the sovereign independence of each state is assured, it should readily become one of the cornerstones of a stable world organization. . . .

Russia can become the greatest menace that the world has yet seen. It is potentially the greatest power of the world. It can equally well become the greatest force for peace and for orderly development in the world. It is, I think, no exaggeration to say that Russia's future course depends very largely on whether the United States can persuade the Russian people and their government that their permanent and truest interest lies in cooperating with us in the creation and maintenance of a democratic and effective world organization.

Part III

The Afro-Asian Realm of Rival Imperialisms

Chapter 12

The Afro-Asian Realm

SOUTH and southeast of the vast desert-mountain belt which cuts diagonally across the World Island, there stands a group of disconnected lands which together constitute what we have called the Afro-Asian Realm of Rival Imperialisms. These lands reach from the South Atlantic coast of Africa across the Indian Ocean to the Pacific. They include all of Africa south of the Sahara, the borderlands of the Indian Ocean, China, and the larger islands of the Western Pacific.

These Afro-Asian lands support about two-thirds of the world's population, or approximately twice as many people as Europe, the Soviet Union, and the Americas combined. Except for a few localities, chiefly within the British Commonwealth, the vast majority of the people live in grinding poverty. Their birth-rates, with a few exceptions, are among the highest in the world. But high birth-rates are largely offset by high death-rates, resulting from disease, famine, and other consequences of sub-marginal living standards.

Broadly speaking, the Afro-Asian Realm has been mainly an arena of struggle, the "happy hunting ground" of rival empire-builders, chiefly Europeans. The island kingdom of Japan, located on the far outer periphery of the realm, is thus far the only state throughout the entire area to develop military power and political prestige and influence comparable to the Great Powers of Europe and North America.

Many factors have contributed to the political, economic, and social backwardness of the Afro-Asian peoples. Their lands lie mainly within a tropical zone ravaged by malaria, dysentery, and many other incapacitating diseases. With few exceptions they live in climates less stimulating and less conducive to health and material progress than are those of Europe. Relative to the population there is far less arable land, and most of that which is arable is less fertile than the better lands of Europe and the Americas. There is nowhere in the Afro-Asian Realm a food-growing area comparable to the black-earth belt of Russia, to the North American prairie, or the Argentine pampas. Other natural resources are not lacking, but they are, in the main, neither so abundant nor so well distributed nor so accessible as in Europe and North America. There are large reserves of petroleum in the Middle East, in the East Indies, and perhaps in a few other places. There is some coal in Africa and in India and a great deal in China. But large areas are deficient in usable energy sources; and in very few places can good coal, iron ore, and limestone—the basic raw materials of heavy industry—be brought together cheaply and in quantity. On present evidence the industrial potentialities of the Afro-Asian Realm seem to be very much lower than those of either Europe, northern Eurasia, or the Western Hemisphere.

Historically most of the Afro-Asian Realm has had closest political and commercial ties with the oceanic countries of Europe and America. For centuries the desert barrier largely cut off eastern Europe and northern Asia from central and southern Africa, India, China, and the East Indies. The long sea voyages around the Cape of Good Hope or Cape Horn were usually far cheaper in effort than the caravan hauls across the deserts of Africa, the Near and Middle East, or Inner Asia.

Construction of the Suez Canal opened up a direct water route across the desert barrier. But this short-cut was from the outset, and has remained to this day, in possession of the oceanic powers, chiefly Great Britain. The historic dominance of those powers over all easy routes around or across the barrier deserts is reflected in the location and structure of the colonial empires of Great Britain, France, Belgium, Portugal, and the Netherlands.

The Western European maritime states, however, have not enjoyed undisturbed primacy over the Afro-Asian Realm. From the east shore of the Mediterranean to the mountain bastions of northern India, the desert belt has been for over a century an unstable pressure zone between the maritime empires of Great Britain and the continental empire of Russia. From the Near East to northwest Africa, German land power has tried repeatedly to outflank and thereby collapse the enveloping sea power of Great Britain. The pivotal points in these historic struggles include many names famous in the annals of world politics—Morocco, Egypt, Berlin-to-Bagdad, Iran, Afghanistan, Khyber Pass, and many others.

The rise of Japanese power threatened the tenure of all European empires in the Afro-Asian Realm. Previously the Afro-Asian lands had been arenas of struggle chiefly among the Europeans themselves. The emergence of Japan as a strong military state with large imperial ambitions not only threatened Russian and western colonial and commercial interests directly. It also provided a ferment which has rendered increasingly difficult all relations between the white and colored races throughout the vast colonial domains in Africa, southern Asia, and the southwestern Pacific.

Cautiously at first, but with increasing boldness, Japan's empire-builders set out to make their will supreme over a large and expanding domain. Their ambition grew with success until eventually they came to covet a huge sprawling empire reaching from mid-Pacific to inner Asia and to the farther shores of the Indian Ocean. The Japanese have been stopped and their ill-gotten empire taken from them, but only after a desperate struggle which has shaken all human relations in the Afro-Asian Realm.

Early Axis victories, especially Japan's Blitzkrieg in Southeast Asia and the Indies, dealt shattering blows to the white man's prestige. In China the long up-hill struggle has intensified awakening Chinese nationalism. This in turn is stiffening Chinese resistance to all external dictation from whatever source. While the modernization of that country may proceed more slowly than we have been led to expect, the ferment is working. That the clock can be put back, and China returned to a state of semi-vassalage to the West—its status for a hundred years—seems doubtful to say the least. That China may eventually emerge as the dominant national state in the Far East is certainly a possibility with which to reckon.

A similar nationalistic awakening is taking place in India. The peculiar social structure of that country and the diverse religious faiths of its peoples may retard economic progress and delay political unification. But few observers anticipate indefinite continuance of British rule, at least in its present form. With respect to India, as in the case of China, the great question is not whether modernization, industrialization, and political integration will take place. The more important question is whether these developments involving nearly one-half the human race will be orderly in the main, or whether they will explode in destructive and revolutionary violence that will shake the foundations of society and the relations of nations all over the world.

Africa, too, has felt the impact of the war, though less violently than the Far East. The Dark Continent has not been a major war theater, except along its Mediterranean margin. But Allied military airlines have spanned that continent, and Allied troops have been stationed at many points. Sorely needed raw materials have poured from Africa's forests, mines, and plantations. Scarcely a corner of the continent has escaped the impact of the struggle or the stimulus of war-induced prosperity.

German conquest of Belgium and France, Italy's entry into the struggle and subsequent inglorious collapse, Nazi pressure on Spain and Portugal, and many related events have all had repercussions in the colonial domains of Africa. While the colored peoples of that continent do not yet present the spectacle of an awakening and inflammatory nationalism, they have nevertheless been catapulted into the white man's battles, with what ultimate consequences remain to be seen.

The American people have much at stake in all these happenings within the Afro-Asian Realm. At some points our stake is immediate and obvious. At others the connection may be less apparent, but none the less real.

With the phenomenal rise of air power we have become acutely aware of the huge West African bulge which reaches to within 1,600 miles of the shoulder of Brazil. After the fall of France, Dakar suddenly jumped into the news and remained there until Allied victories in the Mediterranean theater removed the enemy's dark shadow from the southern continent. That particular threat is long since past, but we can never safely forget it, or remain indifferent to what happens upon the long coastline of West Africa.

Americans have less immediate concern with the future of India and with other lands bordering the north rim of the Indian Ocean. But we do have considerable stake in the oil reserves of Saudi Arabia. We have a much greater stake in promoting peace and harmony in the zone of historic Anglo-Russian rivalry in the Middle East and inner Asia. Continued turmoil and violence in India would almost certainly affect adversely the smooth course of Anglo-American relations.

Turning to China, the United States is the traditional champion of that beleaguered country. In the past we have repeatedly opposed attempts by various combinations of European and Japanese imperialists to carve up China into spheres of special interest. We have steadfastly insisted that a strong, united, and democratic China is the best bulwark of peace and security in the Far East. As a result of the present war we have become more deeply involved than ever in the fortunes of China, and all signs suggest that we shall remain so for an indefinite time to come.

Our commitments in the Philippine Islands are both specific and heavy. We have granted political independence to the Filipinos. But the Philippine archipelago is one of the key positions in the Pacific Ocean. What happens to the Philippines has a direct bearing not only on other American interests in the Far East, but also on the strategic security of the United States itself. This is so because of the shape of the Pacific Ocean, the pattern of island chains reaching out to mid-ocean from the mainland of Asia, and the greatly increased range of fighting ships and naval air power.

The war has further opened our eyes to America's stake in Southeast Asia and the East Indies. It may be that we shall never be so dependent again upon Far Eastern rubber, tin, quinine, and other products as we were before the war. But we cannot afford to forget our discovery that Australia and New Zealand are outer bastions of our continental homeland, and that their first line of defense lies along the island chains connecting them with the Asiatic mainland.

We have an additional, if less direct, interest in the rehabilitation of Southeast Asia and the Indies. American imports from those territories in the past have been a very considerable factor in sustaining the economy, and hence the potential military strength, of Great Britain. If we regard Britain as a vital bulwark of American security in the Atlantic, and such is the purport of American policy during the past half-century, we cannot but be concerned with helping to restore and maintain the sources of British strength; and of these, Britain's Pacific and Indian Ocean domains are among the most important.

Americans habitually speak their minds with brutal frankness when discussing the East Indies, Southeast Asia, India, and other colonial domains in the Afro-Asian Realm. We are severely critical of the European rulers of African and Asiatic peoples. Such criticism often reflects a perfectly laudable humanitarianism. But too often we speak with little knowledge of peoples and conditions, and there is frequently imperfect understanding of our own national interests in the Afro-Asian Realm.

The remainder of this chapter is devoted to Africa, India, and to larger aspects of the Far East in general. Separate chapters will be devoted to a more detailed discussion of China and Japan.

AFRICA

By the Editors

AFRICA is the largest land-mass in the Afro-Asian Realm. It can be likened to a gigantic promontory jutting southward from Eurasia. This huge promontory is nearly three times the size of Europe. From the eastern tip of former Italian Somaliland across the western bulge to French Dakar, the distance is roughly the same as that between New York and Moscow. North and south, Africa extends from the latitude of Norfolk, Virginia, to that of Buenos Aires, about 5,000 miles, or twice the airline distance from New York to San Francisco.

The political map of Africa is a mosaic of European sovereignties. This continent is the home of no major power. Its strongest political unit is the Union of South Africa, located at the southern end of the great promontory. The Union, a member of the British Commonwealth of Nations, has a white population of only two millions, and a total population of only ten millions. Besides the Union there are only three nominally independent states. Of these, one is Egypt, a densely populated nation occupying the narrow Nile valley, long under British protection, and strategically as well as historically a part of the Near East. Another nominally independent state is Ethiopia, an extremely mountainous country south of the Red Sea, inhabited by several million primitive people chiefly of Hamitic race, recently liberated from Italian rule, with a future as yet undetermined. Liberia, the third nominally independent state, is a tiny Negro republic in West Africa, founded over a century ago by freed slaves from the United States. The rest of Africa is divided among the empires of the European powers—France, Britain, Belgium, Portugal, and Spain.

WHY AFRICA HAS BEEN THE DARK CONTINENT

By S. W. Boggs

From "Africa: Maps and Man," by S. W. Boggs, in The Department of State Bulletin, *September 18, 1943. Dr. Boggs is the chief geographer of the Department of State.*

NOTHING in the annals of geographic discovery seems stranger than the belatedness of African exploration. Although ancient civilizations flourished in Mediterranean Africa, it was only within the lifetime of men still among us that the elementary geography of the interior of the continent became known. The great rivers and lakes of North and South America were better known within two centuries of Columbus' voyages than were the Nile, the Niger, the Congo, and the Zambezi and the great African lakes a hundred years ago. By 1850 even the exploration of the Arctic and Antarctic left problems perhaps no more baffling than those of central Africa. This apparent anomaly in geographic exploration is not an historical accident, however, but due in large part to the character of Africa's coasts and ocean currents, its topog-

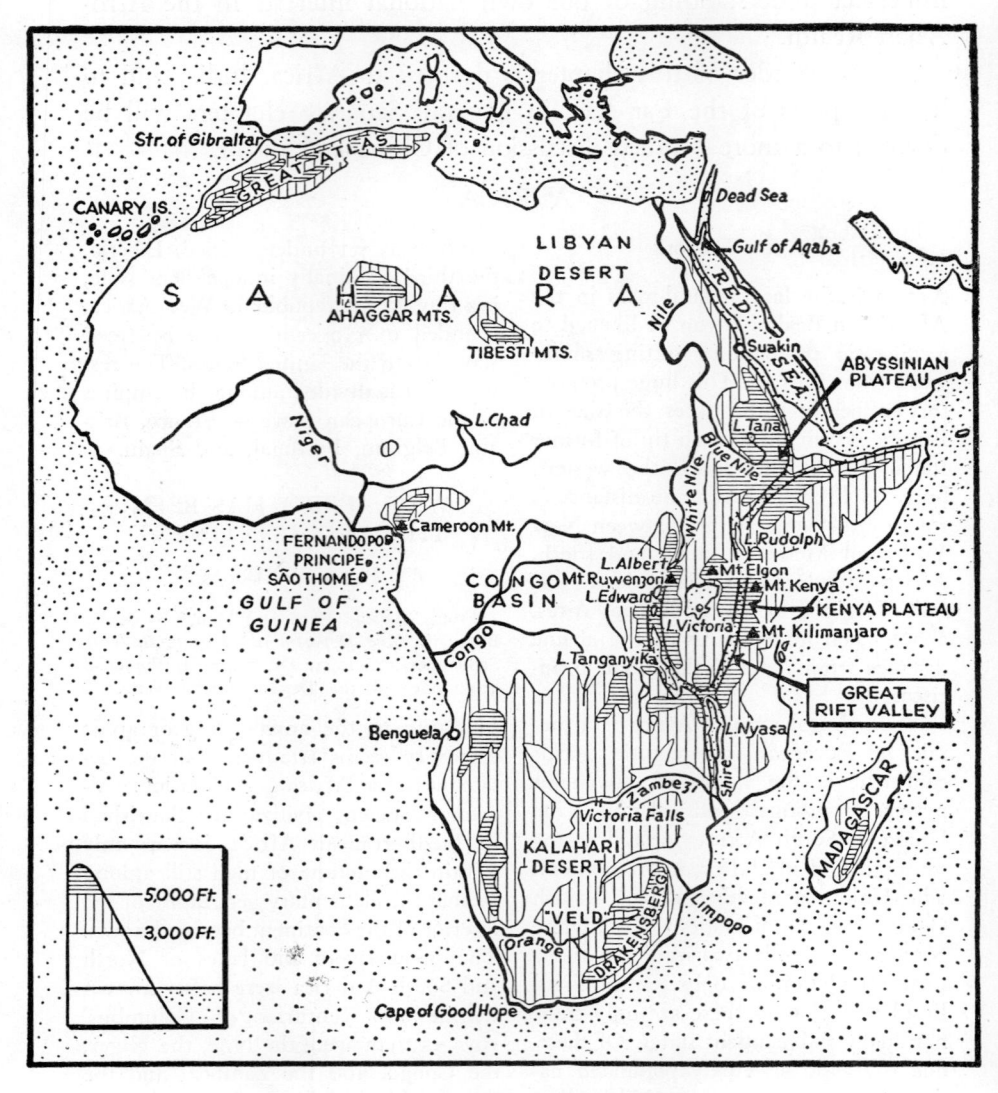

FIG. 26. Africa: Geographic Regions.
From W. G. and M. S. Woolbert, *Look at Africa*.
Headline Series No. 43. Copyright 1943 by Foreign Policy Association,
New York; reproduced by permission.

raphy, climate, and vegetation—factors that affect Africa's future as certainly as they have influenced its past. . . .

What have the physical features of Africa to do with this remarkable delay in the exploration of almost the entire continent south of the part that belongs more to Europe than to Africa?

First, the Sahara is an obstacle even greater than its vast size suggests. . . .

Second, the nature of the coasts is a serious handicap. With an area three times that of Europe, the coastline of Africa is only about four-fifths as long— in spite of Europe's broad attachment to Asia. The remarkably smooth, curved coastline is nearly harborless. . . .

Third, the currents and winds in general favored clockwise navigation of sailing ships, down the east coast and up the west. Arab penetration from the east was thus assisted by nature. The going south from Europe was much more difficult and hazardous.

Fourth, the continent is largely a plateau and is like an inverted saucer, with very narrow coastal plains. The great rivers are not navigable from the sea and their interior courses are broken by falls and cataracts, notably the Congo. There are no navigable rivers comparable with the Amazon, the Mississippi, the St. Lawrence, the Rhine, the Danube, the Yangtze.

Fifth, climate and vegetation, which is immediately dependent upon it, added greatly to the obstacles of exploration. Only a portion of the southern tip of Africa enjoys a Mediterranean type of climate similar to a narrow coastal strip of Morocco, Algeria, and Tunisia. Africa is the most tropical of the continents. Luxuriant vegetation flourishes in steaming, torrid heat and high humidity. The tropical rain forest, tropical grassland or savanna, and the hot desert, all have great heat in common.

Furthermore, it should be remembered that continental unity has little reality save as a continuous obstacle to navigation by sea. It may be easier to circumnavigate the earth in a sailing vessel than to make a long overland journey on foot or even up unknown rivers. . . .

AFRICA'S ROLE IN WORLD POLITICS

By Nicholas J. Spykman

From chap. 4 of America's Strategy in World Politics, by N. J. Spykman. Copyright 1942 by Harcourt, Brace & Co., New York; reproduced by permission. The late Dr. Spykman was Sterling professor of international relations at Yale University and formerly director of the Yale Institute of International Studies, which sponsored publication of the book quoted.

Geography has not dealt kindly with the Dark Continent. It consists mainly of a great table land. The rivers which flow from the plateau country drop to the narrow coastal plains by a series of falls and rapids and are not navigable inland for any distance from the coast. This feature, together with unfavorable winds, lack of harbors, and inhospitable and fever-infested shores, is responsible for the fact that although the continent has been circumnavigated for more than three hundred years, it was explored and opened up only in the second half of the nineteenth century. Most of the areas except Egypt are thinly populated and lack an adequate labor supply, which explains in part why the Asiatic equatorial zone, and not Africa, although it is nearer to Europe, provides the great tropical staples for the European economy.

The African continent lacks the raw materials, the manpower, the culture, and the technology necessary for the development of indigenous states with military power. As a colonial world, it has been asked to contribute raw materials and soldiers to the strength of European states, but since Ancient Egypt, Carthage, and the Arab kingdoms no political units have developed strong enough to threaten continental Europe. Africa is important in the struggle for power partly because of its production of gold and certain important raw materials, but primarily because of its strategic location in regard to the great sea routes. The North African coast plays an important role in the power struggles of the European Mediterranean. South Africa and Cape Town flank the turning point on the route to India. They were of enormous importance in the days before the opening of the Suez Canal and are again benefiting from the closing of the Mediterranean passage. [In the Second World War] They have once more become a significant pivot in the imperial lane to Asia and the Far East. Most important, however, is the coastal zone from the Strait of Gibraltar to Liberia with the chain of offshore islands from Madeira to the Cape Verde group. This section not only flanks the European routes to the Cape but also to South America, and contains between Dakar and the Gold Coast the territory nearest to the Western Hemisphere.

THE INDIAN OCEAN IN WORLD POLITICS

BY E. A. MOWRER AND
MARTHE RAJCHMAN

From *Global War, An Atlas of World Strategy*, by E. A. Mowrer and M. Rajchman. Copyright 1942 by William Morrow & Co., New York; reproduced by permission. E. A. Mowrer is an American journalist; Marthe Rajchman is a well-known cartographer.

THE Indian Ocean is hardly an ocean at all; just a tremendous bay opening off the Antarctic, which is itself hardly an ocean but just a name given to the southern sections of the other oceans contiguous to the Antarctic Continent. Considering the Indian Ocean as merely the piece of water between the Cape of Good Hope and Cape Leeuwen in Australia and north of a line connecting them, it is still a tidy piece. From Cape Town to Freemantle, Australia, is 4,711 sea miles. From the line connecting the two to the top of the tremendous bay, say to Karachi in India, is over 4,000 sea miles.

This "ocean" is bounded on the west by Africa and the thousand-mile-long coast of Arabia called the Hadhramaut, on the east by Burma and Thailand and the Malay Peninsula, the Dutch East Indies and Australia. At the top (the north) it forks into two—the Arabian Sea and the Bay of Bengal, with, between them, the steaming peninsula of India.

In the northwest corner are two water pockets with holes in them, the Gulf of Aden and the Gulf of Oman; the one hole leads to the Red Sea and through the Suez Canal to Europe, the other to the Persian Gulf, which gives on Iraq and the roads to the Black Sea, the Dardanelles and Soviet Russia. From either the Gulf of Aden or the Gulf of Oman northwest to the North Sea is the shortest and most practical line along which to cut the land-mass of Europe-Asia-Africa neatly in two and dominate it strategically.

In the northeast corner, at the top of the Bay of Bengal, start the overland roads to China, bad roads but the only ones there are. Between the Malay mainland and the Indies and Australia to the east, are three main passages (among many minor ones) leading to the China Sea; the Strait of Malacca; the Timor Sea-Arafura Sea-Torres Strait into the Coral Sea that is part of the Pacific;

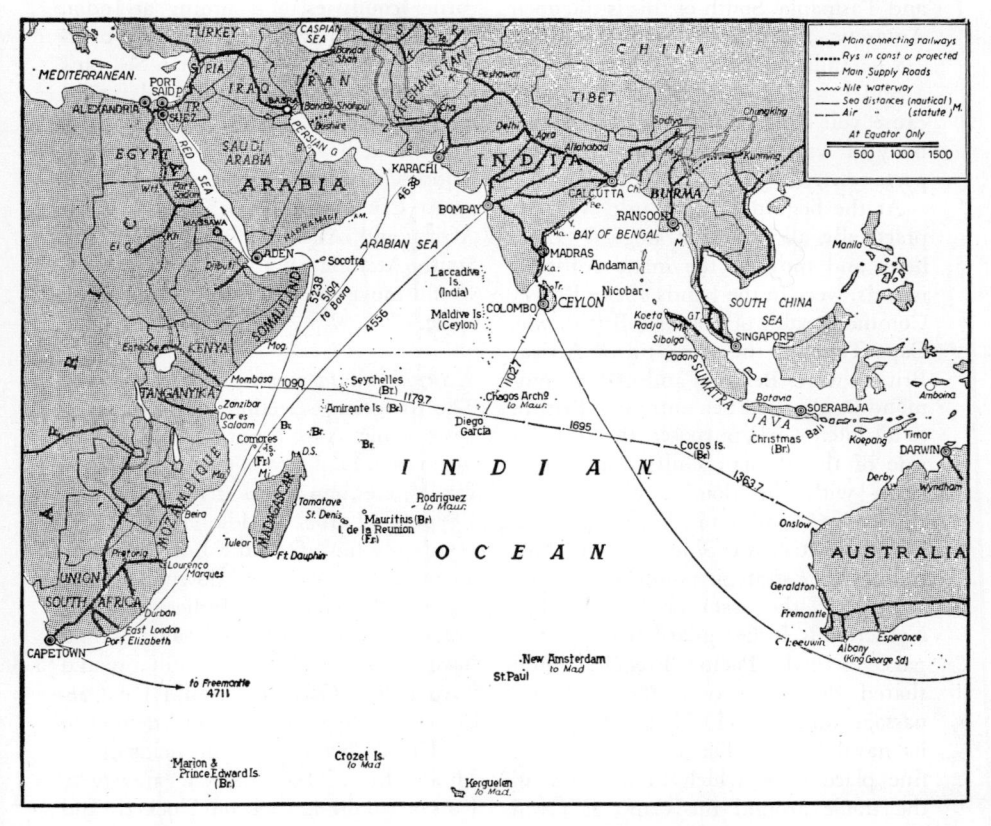

FIG. 27. The Indian Ocean and Its Borderlands.
From E. A. Mowrer and M. Rajchman, *Global War, An Atlas of World Strategy.*
Copyright 1942 by William Morrow & Co., New York; reproduced by permission.
Symbols on the map indicate the following:

B. Bahrein Is.	Kh. Khartoum	Te. Termez
Be. Berhampur	L. Lashio	TR. Transjordania
Ch. Chittagong	M. Moulmein	Tr. Trincomalee
Cha. Chaman	Ma. Masulipatam	WH. Wadi Halfa
DS. Diego Suarez	Me. Medan	Y. Yanaon
ElO. El Obeid	Mj. Majunga	Z. Zahidan
G. Gwadar	Mo. Mozambique	
GT. Georgetown	Mog. Mogadiscio	Br. British
K. Kushka	My. Myitkyina	Fr. French
Ka. Karikal (Fr)	P. Palestine	

and the Bass Strait between Australia and Tasmania. South of this is the open Antarctic. . . .

The Indian Ocean . . . is essentially a center from which to go places. Because you can go so many places, this body of water is of great strategic importance. . . .

At the beginning of World War II, practically all of the strategical points here, and most of the many scattered islands, were in the hands of the British Commonwealth of Nations. British was Cape Town at the south tip of Africa; British were Berbera and Aden commanding the Red Sea entrance; British, to all intents and purposes, the Arabian side of the Persian Gulf; British was India with the dominating bases at Bombay, Colombo and Trincomalee in Ceylon; British was Singapore and Australia. Other strategic points were either Dutch (to the east) or French. The Netherlands Indies guarded the minor passages to the Pacific. French Djibuti shared dominion over the Red Sea passage and French Madagascar with its naval base at Diego Suarez was a fine place from which to threaten all the traffic around the Cape of Good Hope. Yet so long as a non-British "intruder" into the Indian Ocean grabbed bases on only one side, sea traffic could proceed, though adventurously. If, however, it seized bases on both sides, or worse, successfully snatched Ceylon, then the Indian Ocean would be transformed from a vast network of British sea lanes into a theater of air and naval warfare—and not much else. A superior enemy fleet operating from Indian Ocean bases would split the British Commonwealth wide open.

Short of this, the British positions in the Indian Ocean would have to be "flanked" by land operations, presumably in the northwest and northeast corner countries, and aiming at India. These corners would have to be overcome. Germans in the Arabian Sea plus Japanese in the Bay of Bengal would have denatured the ocean, almost regardless of how many island bases the British Commonwealth was able to hold on to. Communications between South Africa and Australia, or between the South Atlantic and the South Pacific, would move into the Antarctic or cease to be.

Supplementary note by the Editors. The foregoing selection was written in 1942 while Axis armies were still on the march. Had they continued their advances, German forces driving through Egypt and the Middle East would eventually have forged a link with Japanese forces coming down through Southeast Asia and the Indies. Had this occurred, the United Nations would have been split asunder. India would have fallen. Germany would have acquired for her own use, and denied to the United Nations, the oil fields of the Middle East. The southern gateway to Russia would have been blocked, and China would have been completely isolated.

These disasters came close to happening. The German drive was halted just short of Suez and the Near East. The Japanese actually breached the east wall of the Indian Ocean. Eventually, the Japanese and the Germans were both driven back. The great French island of Madagascar was wrested from the servile hand of Vichy. The oil of the Middle East continued to flow to the Allied fronts in the Mediterranean and in Asia. And the global strategic unity of the United Nations was saved.

INDIA

By the Editors

Northeast of the great southern promontory of Africa, half-way across the Indian Ocean, another broad promontory juts southward from the desert-mountain barrier. This is India which, though smaller than Africa south of the Sahara, is nevertheless of sub-continental dimensions.

India is approximately one-half the size of the United States, and supports a population nearly three times as large. It is roughly equal in area and in population to Europe west of the Soviet Union, and like Europe is a peninsula attached along a broad base to the compact central land-mass of Asia.

The salient physical features of India stand in marked contrast to those of Europe, however. The latter lies north of the 35th parallel; almost all of India lies south of that latitude. In the words of C. B. Fawcett (chap. 17 of *A Political Geography of the British Empire,* Copyright 1933 by Ginn & Co., Boston; reproduced by permission): "Europe has cool or cold winters; and only in the warmer parts of its Mediterranean lands are the winter temperatures as high as those of the northern parts of the Indian lowlands. India is a hot land; and owing to the mountains which shelter it on the north the winters of its northern plains are much warmer than those of places in the same latitudes in North America. On the plains of India frost is rare, and snow is almost unknown. Indian civilization has not been influenced by either the difficulties or the stimulus of a cold or cool winter.

"Europe is a peninsula of peninsulas," Fawcett continues, "in close touch with the seas which penetrate far into it and have led many of its peoples out on to the seaways. India is a very compact sub-continental land mass, with few gulfs or islands or minor peninsulas to bring it into intimate contact with the ocean to which it has given its name. . . . Throughout the great part of India's long history the sea has counted for little in the life of its peoples."

India, moreover, has never achieved an international position commensurate with its population and resources. Though their land contains coal, iron, and many other raw materials, the vast majority of the Indian people have yet to emerge from an extremely primitive way of life.

India, however, has been an imperial prize of immense value. It is also a strategic focus of the other British domains bordering the Indian Ocean all the way from South Africa to Australia. Today it is one of the storm centers of our troubled world. It very nearly became a major battleground in the war against the Axis. Its development and external relations will have a bearing on the future of every part of the Afro-Asian Realm.

INDIA TODAY

By John Fischer

From "India's Insoluble Hunger," by John Fischer, in *Harper's,* April 1945. Copyright 1945 by Harper & Brothers; reproduced by permission. Mr. Fischer is one of the editors of *Harper's.* He served a year in India recently with the Foreign Economic Administration.

Late on the night of August 22, 1943, I stepped off a train at Howrah Station in Calcutta. The city was blacked out, because at that time Japanese planes still were shuttling across the Bay of Bengal on occasional bombing raids. In the dim glow from the locomotive firebox, the station floor seemed to be paved with some kind of irregular black-and-white flagging. Then, as my eyes got accustomed to the steamy, stinking half-light, I saw that the floor was covered with huddled bodies, some wrapped in strips of dirty white cotton, most of them naked. They were crowded hip to hip, and as I picked my way toward the street I couldn't help stepping on many of them. Only a few groaned or whimpered. Even the babies —and there were hundreds of them— lay limp and quiet, apparently too weak to cry. And it was plain that some of those people on the station floor were dead, and had been dead for a long time.

That week the newly formed Municipal Corpse Disposal Squad removed 112 bodies from the streets. More—to this day nobody knows how many— were taken away by charitable organizations and private citizens. Still others lay for days on the sidewalks and in gutters; no one can tell the caste or religion of a naked cadaver, and naturally few Hindus, or Moslems either, cared to risk spiritual defilement by touching the body of a possible infidel or outcaste. The *Statesman,* one of India's leading newspapers and normally an apologist for the government, observed that "those who carry away the dead found in the streets do noble work," and complained of the "red tape" which "necessitated their rotting publicly for hours or days."

That week, and for many weeks to follow, starving families continued to pour into Howrah Station and the great Maidan Park in the center of Calcutta and into every alley and doorway and air-raid shelter where there was room to lie down. The stronger ones fought for garbage around the curbing trash bins; the weak begged silently by slapping their bellies every time an Englishman or American walked past. There was some talk of rationing and of prosecuting grain speculators; the Great Eastern Hotel, where I lived, voluntarily cut its menu from eleven to nine courses; and a few of the more extreme newspapers even suggested that the Calcutta racing season be suspended, so that the overstrained railway system might haul in rice instead of horses and fodder. Such irresponsible suggestions were, of course, given no consideration.

Still the hungry came, because they heard rumors that the government might some day set up gruel kitchens in Calcutta, and because the famine was still worse in the country districts. An official of the Friends' Ambulance Unit reported from Contai that "a fight between vultures and dogs over a corpse is no rare sight . . . there are not enough able-bodied men to burn the dead, which often are just pushed into the nearest canal." Many desperate families offered their female children for sale. One rupee, eight annas, or about forty-five cents, seemed to be the standard asking price for a girl six to ten years old, if she was still in good enough condition to stand alone.

Through all these months the white Brahmin cattle wandered by the hundreds through the streets of Calcutta, as they always have, stepping placidly over the bodies of the dead and near-dead, scratching their plump haunches on taxi fenders, sunning themselves on the steps of the great Clive Street banks. No one ever ate a cow; no one ever dreamed of it. I never heard of a Bengali Hindu who would not perish with all his family rather than taste meat. Nor was there any violence. No grocery stall, no rice warehouse, none of the wealthy clubs or restaurants ever was threatened by a hungry mob. The Bengalis just died with that bottomless docility which, to most Americans, is the most shocking thing about India.

How many died? No one, of course,

really knows. By October, when Lord Wavell took over the government and finally set the army to distributing food on a systematic basis, the *Statesman* was estimating the deaths throughout Bengal at some ten thousand a week. The official figures were much lower; many calculations by private relief organizations were higher. None pretended to be entirely accurate or complete. After comparing many different estimates, my own guess—and I believe it to be conservative—is that the 1943 famine, plus the epidemics of malaria, smallpox, dysentery, and dengue fever which followed in its train, probably wiped out about three million people.

If there were no reliable statistics on the famine, there were at least plenty of explanations. The Indian Nationalists blamed the British—with some justice, since the Central Government in India is one of the feeblest and most ineffective ever endured by a major nation. Even the English editor of the *Statesman* described the famine as "the worst and most reprehensible administrative breakdown in India since the political disorders of 1930-31," and added: "Under the present system of government, responsibility for breakdown inescapably rests upon Authority in Britain, and its immediate representatives here. Every British citizen is necessarily shamed and sullied. . . ."

Privately many of the British blamed the corruption and bickering of the native provincial politicians—again with some accuracy, since most of the honest, patriotic, and able native leaders were in political prisons, not provincial ministries. Everybody blamed the floods which disrupted the main rail lines into Bengal, the hurricane which had devastated farms along the east coast, and the Japanese who had cut off rice imports from Burma.

In each of these explanations there was unquestionably much truth. Yet beneath them all lay another fact more ominous, more difficult to cure. It is simply this: there are too many Indians.

There are some 400 million of them —as many people as there are in all of Europe, aside from Russia. They are crowded into a land which cannot at the moment support half that number on what most Americans would regard as the barest level of decency. For every square mile of farm land, there are 423 Indians; and eight out of ten depend for their living on farming. (Perhaps 2 per cent of the Indian people work in modern industries; while 3 or 4 per cent more sweat out some kind of living in cottage industries and handicraft trades.) Moreover, the Indian peasant is one of the worst farmers in the world. His methods are incredibly primitive; his soil has been drained of its fertility for centuries; his yields are far below the world average. His farm is rarely larger than five or ten acres; his plow is a crooked stick dragged by a water buffalo; his home is a one-room mud hut, which is quite likely to wash away every rainy season. Normally he is up to his ears in debt, on which he may pay up to 100 per cent interest, and he could not afford better equipment if he wanted it. He seldom does; the old ways seem best, just because they are old and probably sacred.

The result of all this is that more than half of all the people in India are always underfed. Probably 80 million of them never once get a full belly from birth until the day they die. (Once I threw a banana peel out the window of a train to a monkey sitting on a station platform. The monkey never got it; a pack of naked brown children beat him to it, and nearly clawed each other to pieces before the biggest one gulped it down. Not a banana—just the skin; and that was not a famine area.) If you feed a rat on the diet of a Bengali peasant, the rat will die. So, of course, will the Indian, although not quite so soon; his life expectancy is about thirty-two years.

Yet every year there are 5 million more mouths which have to be fed, somehow, from India's weary, eroded land. Since World War II began, the *increase* in India's population has nearly equaled the *total* population of England. Within the past twenty years, it has amounted to more than the entire population of Germany. And if present trends continue until 1960, India's growth will reach the neighborhood of 12 million every year.

Under these circumstances, famines like that of 1943 are inevitable—and they are likely to increase both in frequency and severity. As long as the population continues to crowd so heavily on the thin margin of subsistence, any failure of the monsoon, any prolonged breakdown of transport is almost certain to sweep whole provinces over the edge of starvation.

One Indian businessman, who is neither cynical nor especially cold-blooded, summed it up in these terms: "From a strictly economic point of view, the 1943 famine was a failure. At most, it killed only three or four million people, which means that it still lagged far behind the birth rate. And that means a few handfuls less rice for everybody next year."

This relentless fertility, with all the economic consequences it entails, is the basic problem of India. The political problem, which is absorbing nearly all the attention of educated Indians and their British rulers alike, is—I am convinced—almost trivial in comparison. Like most Americans, I have a strong instinctive sympathy for Indian independence, simply because I believe that every people has a right to govern (or misgovern) itself any way it sees fit. Yet, for reasons outlined later in this article, I cannot share the hopes of my Indian friends who see independence as the sole, sure-fire remedy for all their ills. Independence *alone* won't really solve anything; perhaps its greatest blessing may be to relieve the Indian leaders from their preoccupation with British-hating, and let them buckle down to the long, hard job of getting India's deteriorating economy back under control. To the Indian peasant, plagued with malaria, dysentery, and too many children, wondering every hour where his next mouthful of rice is coming from, it can't make much difference what flag flies over the Secretariat in Delhi—not so long as India's population goes on climbing at the rate of a steady 1.2 per cent every year.

Is there any answer?

Not from the British. I have questioned scores of English officials, from the Viceroy's staff down to local tax collectors, without finding one who thought he could see a way out. Typically, they shrug their shoulders and say something like this:

"After all, that's not my pigeon. I've got troubles enough in my own department—and in five or six years I'll be going home on a pension. Besides, we British don't dare interfere with the native customs and religions which lie at the root of the population problem. And there would be no use interfering anyway, because nobody can do anything with these Indians. The Congress wallahs can do the worrying when they finally throw us out, as I suppose they will one of these days."

In short, a kind of tacit confession of Imperial bankruptcy. The surest indication that British rule in India is not likely to survive much longer, it seems to me, lies in this failure to face up to the essential tasks of government. A much more brutal, more tyrannical regime might last indefinitely, if it had some bold plan for grappling with the country's fundamental troubles. The British in India are neither brutal nor very tyrannical; indeed, they often go to absurd lengths in a hopeless effort to placate their native critics. They are merely ineffectual; they lack confidence in themselves; they hold out no real hope that they can improve the lot of the average Indian; and such governments seldom hang on long.

It is true, of course, that in the past the British Raj has made strenuous efforts (in certain limited fields) to fight off the constant threat of starvation. It has carried through the greatest system of irrigation projects in the world. It has built a rail network capable of shuttling food supplies from surplus to shortage areas, thus eliminating the minor, local famines. In addition, it has started a rudimentary public health program, which already has had a notable effect on the death rate. The net result has been merely a spurt in the rate of population growth—especially in the period since 1921, during which it has been the most rapid in the country's history. Consequently, the British economic program has not meant a better life for the average Indian; it has just meant more Indians.

It also is true that the government of India has set up an impressive array of post-war planning committees and agencies; but so far they have produced no program of the heroic scope which the situation requires. Nor are they likely to. The purpose of these committees, I suspect, is primarily political. They are meant to serve as an answer to the far-reaching post-war proposals being pushed forward by the Indian National Congress.

For the Indian Nationalists have an answer, or think they have. Their solution for India's economic nightmare is industrialization, plus a tremendous increase in agricultural production. It has been most widely publicized in the form of the Bombay Plan, a scheme of economic development drawn up by a group of the ablest and most powerful native industrialists.

The objective of the plan is to treble the national income within a period of fifteen years after the war. To reach this goal, farm output would be doubled, and industrial production would be stepped up five-fold. Allowing for a constant population growth during this period of 5 million a year, the plan calculates that the per capita income would be doubled.

Although the plan itself does not go so far, most of its proponents argue along these lines: We realize, of course, that even these substantial gains in production can provide only a temporary relief for India's grinding poverty, if the population keeps on rising at its present rate. Eventually, however, our population ought to stop growing of its own accord. That happens in every nation, as it becomes industrialized and raises its standard of living. It is happening right now in Great Britain, and it is beginning to happen in America—although both of these countries grew even more rapidly during the last century than India is growing today. And there can be little question of India's ability to industrialize herself in short order, once we throw off the dead hand of British Imperialism. Look at Russia—with its Five Year Plans it built an even greater industrial plant in less time.

These are brave, hopeful words—the most hopeful being uttered in India today. And they are based on more than hope. Unquestionably India has many of the raw materials for building a modern industrial state. Her deposits of high-grade iron ore, still only partially explored, may prove to be among the most valuable in the world. Bauxite, sulphur, manganese, mica, and many another industrial mineral are plentiful. Her rivers, pouring off the Himalayas and the Deccan Plateau, offer a tremendous waterpower potential, so far only about 4 per cent developed. (But there also are serious gaps in the raw materials arsenal, as we shall see.)

Moreover, at least a few Indians have demonstrated a genuine capacity for industrial operations. The Tata steel mills, for example, are the largest in the British Empire, and some of their most modern departments operate more efficiently than any in the United States. Good machine tools are being made in India already; and the country has produced more than a handful of competent engineers, chemists, and mechanics.

Perhaps more important still, the nation's industrial leaders are almost fanatically determined to reach their goal. Mr. G. D. Birla, for example, insists that he will some day establish a full-fledged automobile factory in India, even though the scarcity of roads and purchasers may force it to operate at a loss for years on end. He is not really interested in profits; he already is making plenty in a dozen other industries. To Birla, an auto factory is a symbol of national pride—no modern state is complete without one. And he has his counterparts in many other fields, all bent on building some kind of factory virtually without regard to cost. The bitterest accusation that they hurl against the British is the charge that England has deliberately discouraged the growth of industry in India, to prevent competition with her own plants.

All this adds up to a strong probability that India will accomplish a considerable degree of industrialization during the next generation, although not necessarily on the scale set forth in the Bombay Plan. At the same time, food production no doubt can be stepped up substantially; as much as 75 million acres of additional land might be brought under cultivation, and the use of fertilizers and better farming methods theoretically might double the yield from the present farms.

Nevertheless, I do not think the Bombay Plan is likely to achieve its basic purpose: to create a higher standard of living by shoving production well ahead of the rise in population *and keeping it ahead*.

In the first place, there are strong reasons to believe that the Bombay Planners set their sights too high, that a five-fold increase in industrial production cannot possibly be carried through within fifteen years. And secondly, even if the plan could be fulfilled down to the last ton of steel, there is little prospect that it actually would result in checking the cancerlike growth of India's population.

Indian Nationalists are fond of pointing to the Russian example, and in many respects the Bombay Plan is modeled frankly after the Soviet Five Year Plans. Like them, it calls for a massive investment of labor and material in heavy industrial plant—steel mills, machine tool factories, chemical and power projects—within a very brief period. The Indians, however, are apt to gloss over the methods Russia had to use. The Soviets carried through their Five Year Plans by cutting sharply the consumption of the people and throwing the resources thus saved into a rapid building up of capital equipment. That entailed a ruthless and efficient dictatorship, willing to plunge ahead regardless of the cost in suffering and human life.

Now a Free India government is

likely to find that it cannot follow the Russian example, for four reasons:

1. Although India's natural resources are impressive, they do *not* include some of the key raw materials on which Russia (and every other modern industrial state) has built its economy. The most serious lacks are petroleum and coking coal. The coal shortage, in fact, has proved the most serious bottleneck in the Indian war effort. Production of coal still falls short of 25 million tons a year—as compared with America's 620 million—and almost all of it is awkwardly located in the northeast corner of the peninsula, so that its distribution involves long and costly train hauls.

2. In Russia, even after the devastation of World War I and the Revolution, the people as a whole had a standard of living considerably above the subsistence level. There was some fat on the economy, which could be shaved off and diverted to the building of industrial plant. In India there is no such margin. Present living standards cannot be hammered much lower—for whatever worthy purpose—without causing wholesale starvation.

3. There is little prospect that a Free India would have a government strong enough to impose great sacrifices on its people, even if they had anything much to sacrifice. (Many British officials predict that India could never form any stable government at all; and the current deadlock between the Congress Party and the Moslem League makes it difficult to answer these predictions.) At best, any independent Indian government is likely to be an uneasy coalition, constantly preoccupied with balancing and compromising the conflicting demands of scores of different racial, religious, and political groups. Such a government could not afford to act ruthlessly; if it did, it would be tossed out of office overnight. On the other hand, if any one group—such as the Congress Party—should be able to dominate the government and should attempt to impose a drastic economic program on the other factions, the result quite possibly would be civil war.

4. Finally, the Russians started their great experiment with an energetic people, braced by a rigorous climate and fairly bulging with a vitality which even such Americans as Wendell Willkie and Eric Johnston have found a little overwhelming. In contrast, the great mass of the Indian people have been enervated for generations by hunger, tropical diseases (at least 25 per cent have malaria), and a climate which will almost wilt a bulldozer. No one who has not lived in India can quite imagine the effect of that climate—a smothering, bone-melting heat, in which every movement requires a separate effort of the will. It is no reflection on the Indians to suggest that such a climate is a major obstacle to any plan for a rapid and vigorous reconstruction. It sweats the energy out of the Englishman in India, just as it does the native. It would do the same to you.

Let's assume, however, that all these difficulties by some miracle might be overcome. Suppose that the Bombay Plan could be carried out on schedule, and that all its most optimistic goals could be achieved. Would the resulting rise in living standards actually slam an automatic brake on the rate of population growth, as its supporters believe?

The answer almost certainly is no. By the end of its fifteen years, the Bombay Plan is intended to lift the income of the average Indian to 135 rupees, or $45 *a year*. It is true that this would be about double the present per capita income; but even so, it would not amount to one-tenth of the earnings of the average American. It is hard to believe that an income of $45 a year would be large enough to set in motion those sweeping changes in living standards, habits, and education which have been responsible for a declining birth rate in the Western world

Moreover, it is doubtful whether a rise in income—no matter how large—would have the same effect on India's population trends that it has had in Europe and the United States. The simple rule of thumb, "Higher income = lower birth-rate," may not apply in India, simply because her culture, religions, and habit patterns are too different.

First of all, the great emphasis which both Mohammedanism and Hinduism place on the family and on sexual relationships would probably rule out any widespread practice of birth control. The creation of a son is the first duty of every Hindu; the sexual act itself is a religious rite. With many Indians, sex seems to have become almost an obsession. (Witness the countless—and admirably explicit—volumes on the arts of love which crowd every bookstore; the aphrodisiac advertisements in every newspaper; the native state where the chief industry is the manufacture of phallic symbols from pink marble.)

Doctors, missionaries, public health workers, sociologists—Indian, British, and American—all told me the same story: any attempt to change the Indian's breeding habits can show results only after generations of persistent and tactful education. For these cultural patterns are more rigidly fixed, more resistant to change than those of any other major people. Indeed, the dominant characteristic of India is an inert, rocklike conservatism which the western mind finds almost impossible to grasp.

Consequently, it seems likely that a doubling of the per capita income under the Bombay Plan might well lead to a *rising* birth-rate, rather than the expected decline. At the same time the death-rate presumably would slump, since the plan calls for a great expansion in sanitation and public health facilities. If this should prove true, the Bombay Plan then would arrive at precisely the same kind of result as the British-sponsored irrigation schemes—a still faster population growth, a still sharper pressure on the means of subsistence, continuing poverty for the average Indian.

This gloomy conclusion is borne out by the studies of two of India's most competent and searching economists, P. A. Wadia and K. T. Merchant. In *Our Economic Problem*, one of the most painstaking analyses published in India in recent years, they conclude that "it is obvious that so long as we have a high birth rate, it is difficult to think of any immediate change for the better in our material condition. We shall continue to grow at the rate of about 10 to 13 per thousand every year, unless our numbers are seriously affected . . . by natural calamities. . . . The problem in the coming two or three decades will be that of the impact of a progressively increasing population on our ill-balanced and deteriorating economic and social structure."

Does this mean that there is *no* solution for India's economic problem?

So far as I can see, it probably does—at least for the predictable future. I arrived at this hopeless sort of answer reluctantly, over a period of many months, and the process was one of the most painful experiences I have ever undergone.

When I went to India, I believed in a kind of inarticulate, unconscious fashion that there *must* be some kind of solution for every problem. Perhaps it might be only a theoretical solution, not immediately practical; but with enough effort and good will it ought to be possible at least to figure out some line of attack on any set of difficulties. I think nearly all Americans feel the same way—we've never yet been up against anything we couldn't lick, somehow.

It was a considerable shock, therefore, to run into a situation to which I could not find even a theoretical answer. Nor anyone who believed, with real confidence, that *he* had the answer. (Even the most enthusiastic of the Bombay Plan's proponents have a few private doubts.) And it was especially numbing to realize that this apparently insoluble problem may mean suffering and death on a staggering scale, for many generations to come.

There is always a hope, of course, that some new kind of solution may yet turn up. For example, Jawaharlal Nehru, leader of the left wing of the Indian National Congress, has sketched the outlines of a program which would take into account many of the difficulties the Bombay Plan avoids, and would attack them in a much more drastic fashion. He demands a revolution; and "revolution" is precisely what he means. The Nehru program proposes nationalization of heavy industry, collective farms to replace the present tiny peasant holdings, and—by implication—a frontal assault on the whole archaic social structure of India, with its incrustations of caste, superstition, and blind conservatism. Because Nehru has spent much of his mature life in prison, he has never had a chance to translate these proposals into a detailed, specific plan of action. In any case, there is no prospect that his program will get a trial within the foreseeable future, because the big industrialists who finance and dominate the Congress Party are implacably opposed. And during his present term of political imprisonment Nehru apparently has lost much of his mass following.

Maybe Nehru is on the right track. Certainly some such bold and imaginative surgery would seem to be indicated. It is questionable, however, whether any revolution, however drastic, would be enough. How can India lift herself by her bootstraps, when there isn't enough strap to get hold of—when there is so little margin beyond bare subsistence to use for the task of reconstruction?

The essential thing, which Nehru's program (like all the others) seems to lack, is the injection *from outside India* of a tremendous stream of equipment and capital and technical skill. Incalculable amounts of money and energy would have to be poured out, first of all, on a campaign of education and public health in the thousands of Indian villages. Such a campaign in the very long run might bring the birthrate under control, clean up the malaria and cholera and typhoid, and prepare the Indian people physically and mentally to remake their own destiny. On top of that, more billions would be needed to get a modern industry under way on a scale capable of filling the needs of 400 million people.

The mere statement of these needs indicates how little chance there is of meeting them. No nation or group of nations would be willing to make such an investment, because much of it—certainly that part spent on education and health—could never be repaid. Furthermore, India would not be willing to accept really large-scale investment from abroad, because both business and political leaders are profoundly suspicious of foreign economic penetration. (They are especially wary of American "dollar imperialism." I know dozens of intelligent Indian businessmen who honestly believe that lend-lease is simply a subterfuge under which the United States is scheming to grab control, somehow, of the Indian economy.) Even the

Bombay Plan would permit foreign financing only to the extent of a little more than $2 billion over a fifteen-year period, and then only "if it is not accompanied by political influence or interference of foreign vested interests."

The best hope for a boost from overseas lies in the debt which Great Britain owes to India. It is perhaps not generally realized that during the course of the war India has substantially achieved her financial independence from the British—and more. Britain has purchased huge tonnages of raw materials from India; since she could not pay in cash, she has jotted down a credit to India on her books, with a promise to pay at some unspecified date after the war. Long ago India piled up enough of these blocked sterling credits to wipe out all the debt she previously had owed England. The credits are still piling up, so rapidly that Britain probably will be in debt to India to the tune of $3 or $4 billion by the war's end.

If India could take payment for this debt in machinery and other capital equipment for her industrialization program, it might serve as a real help towards a new start. It seems more likely, however, that England will want to pay off as much as possible with consumers' goods which would compete with, rather than aid, India's fledgling industries. Some Indian Nationalists even believe—or profess to believe—that the British will cheat them out of this money somehow, by outright repudiation of the debt or perhaps by some juggling of the sterling-rupee exchange rate. So it appears probable that India will have to tackle her reconstruction largely on her own steam—and it also seems evident that there just isn't enough steam there.

This dismal account may at least cast some light on the peculiar behavior of a good many Americans who have been handling war jobs in India. When they arrive, they generally are more than eager to engage in the time-honored American pastime of British-baiting. Within a few weeks, as they get their first good look at the lackadaisical performance of the British bureaucracy, they pull out all the stops and voice their criticisms in a full-throated bellow. About six months later, however, something apparently happens to the vocal cords. The jibes tend to fade away to a whisper, and sometimes they stop altogether.

The explanation, of course, is simple enough. Sooner or later, nearly every American begins to wonder what *he* would do if he had to run India—and lapses into a thoughtful and chastened silence. (After all, can we afford to brag about our record in Puerto Rico, which presents much the same problems on an infinitely smaller and more manageable scale?)

One morning, during the worst of the hot weather, an American general sat down at my breakfast table looking uncommonly haggard and worn. He said he hadn't slept well. "As a matter of fact," he added, "I've been having a perfectly horrible nightmare. I dreamed that all the Englishmen quietly slipped out of this country during the night, and left us Americans holding the bag. Can you imagine anything worse?"

INDIA'S PHYSICAL FOUNDATIONS

By G. B. Cressey

From chap. 29 of *Asia's Lands and Peoples*, by G. B. Cressey. Copyright 1944 by McGraw-Hill Book Co., New York; reproduced by permission. The author, a leading authority on Asia, is professor of geography at Stanford University.

EXTRAORDINARY physical contrasts characterize India. It contains one of the wettest spots on earth as well as one of the driest; the highest and largest of all mountain ranges border vast river lowlands; dense rain forests contrast with lifeless desert; in some areas the problem of agriculture is too much water while elsewhere there is too little. All of these are India. Unlike Japan, with its pattern of microscopic detail, the topographic features of India group themselves into simple major units. Local contrasts exist but are subordinate.

India has charm and glamor, but it also has poverty and problems. The cultural landscape everywhere reflects the intensity of man's quest for livelihood in a land of uncertain rainfall. Wherever the environment permits, crops are grown to the limit. Here is monsoon Asia at its climax, with a seasonal rhythm of rainfall which affects all of man's activities Although the average rainfall is generally high, its effectiveness is restricted by high temperatures and high evaporation. Surprisingly large parts of the subcontinent are semiarid and even desert.

One of the great problems of India is that it appears to have too many people; it scarcely seems possible that so many can live on so little and have much opportunity for the obviously needed increase in standards of living. The population increased between 1931 and 1941 by 50 million, to reach a total of 388 million in all India. How long can this continue?

India, like China, is not merely a place on the map; here is a rich culture, the product of centuries of contemplative living. Whatever the political future of this land, it has a notable contribution to the trade and civilization of the rest of the world.

Within India are 1,808,679 square miles of mountains, hills, and plains. From the borders of Iran eastward to the frontier of China is about 2,300 miles, while from the southern tip of the peninsula to northern Kashmir is 2,000 miles. The Tropic of Cancer cuts midway between north and south, but all of India south of the mountain wall is essentially tropical. . . .

Geology and Land Forms. Within the Indian realm are three entirely different areas, unlike in geological history, surface configuration, and utilization. These are the mountain wall of the Himalaya and other encircling ranges; the plains of Hindustan drained by the Indus, Ganges, and Brahmaputra; and the dissected plateau in the peninsula to the south. . . .

Climate. . . . India has three seasons. The arrival of the monsoon in June inaugurates the wet season. This is really India's spring, for nature then comes to life. Despite the high sun, the ocean air and clouds keep the day temperature in the nineties. The heat increases from south to north as the winds lose their effect. Humidity is high, but breezes make it bearable. In Bombay, June to September temperatures average 82° F. for day and night, while in Calcutta the figure is 84° F. Conditions are even more unpleasant just after the rains, for the humidity is high and, although the thermometer is lower, sensible temperatures increase. During the rainy period, it is difficult to dry one's clothing except over a fire. Furniture put together with glue is apt to come apart. Books and shoes mildew overnight.

Following the cessation of the rains, temperatures decrease; the cool season extends from late November, or December in the south, through February. Light frosts occur in the Ganges Valley, and the clear skies make the climate attractive to the European although poorly clad Indians may complain bitterly of the cold.

The hot season begins in March.

Temperatures rise to 100° F. or more in the daytime, but the nights are cooler. The sun is nearly vertical in April and May and the air relatively still. All work is suspended at midday, for heat and glare are intense as the molten sun shines from a cloudless sky. Dust storms and tornadoes are locally destructive....

Mineral Resources. The mineral wealth of India is strikingly concentrated in the uplands 200 miles west of Calcutta. Coal, iron ore, limestone, manganese, copper and mica are in fair proximity, out of which has grown a large iron and steel industry. Elsewhere mineral deposits are widely scattered. Taken as a whole, the [Indian] Empire is not an important mineral producer. Extensive geological studies under British direction make it unlikely that significant reserves remain undiscovered. In terms of both area and population, the known reserves are exceptionally low. Only a tenth of 1 per cent of the people are engaged in mining....

Coal reserves are variously estimated from 54 to 79 billion tons. Most of this is good bituminous coal.... One seam in the Bokaro field is 126 feet thick. Only limited amounts are suitable for metallurgical coke. Largely undeveloped Tertiary lignite reserves are present in Assam and the Punjab. Production in 1938 reached 28,000,000 long tons, including a small export to Japan. The supply is adequate for the local needs of transportation, textile factories, and smelting. Household consumption in all India totals only two million tons annually. After the United Kingdom, India is the largest coal producer in the British Empire.

Petroleum is entirely lacking in Hindustan and the plateau, but there is a small output in the Punjab and in Assam. The small oil production in the Punjab and Baluchistan represents the eastern margin of the Mesopotamian and Iran district.

The wide distribution of the native iron industry suggests a similarly extensive occurrence of iron ore. Such is the case, although most deposits are not of modern economic significance.... One of the largest iron ore bodies of the world is in the Salem district southwest of Madras. The ore is a rich magnetite but is not suited for modern blast-furnace treatment, and there is no near-by coal....

Hematite ore of exceptionally high quality is present in the northeastern plateau, chiefly in the Singhbhum district in Bihar and Orissa. The chief outcrop is a range 30 miles long in the native state of Bonai where it is mined cheaply by open-cut methods. The ore is associated with banded jasper, and the average iron content exceeds 60 per cent. Both quality and tonnage are said to equal those of Lake Superior, with conservative estimates of a billion tons of "actual" ore and another billion of "potential" ore. Indian statistics give the reserves of the district as 3,600,000,000 tons, and for the entire country at several billion more. This iron belt is by far the largest and best reserve in all Asia, with the possible exception of those in the Soviet Union.

Iron ore is widely distributed in Mysore, with hematite schist and limonite mined in the Bababudan hills. Other high-grade ores are present in Portuguese Goa, within four miles of a harbor. Gwalior has several ore deposits but they are remote from coal. Lateritic ores with 30 per cent iron are widespread in the peninsula. The 1937 production of iron ore was 2,870,832 tons.

Three-quarters of the world's manganese is mined in the Soviet Union and India. Production of this ferroalloy fluctuates with the world output of steel, in which it is used to remove oxygen and sulphur, or in some cases as a toughening alloy. India's yield in 1937 was 1,051,594 long tons, somewhat below the average, and about a third that of the U.S.S.R. ...

Two characteristic Indian minerals are mica and graphite. Over three-quarters of the world's sheet mica comes from India. . . . India is deficient in nonferrous minerals, with no zinc, little lead, and no tin.

The unproductive state of the mineral industry in the Indian Empire is indicated by the following figures of production, the rough annual average for the decade of 1930 in millions of United States dollars: coal 23, gold 11, lead 5, manganese 5, silver 4, tin 3, salt 3, and tungsten, iron ore, and mica 1 each. Note that these represent the yield for 1,800,000 square miles and over 350 million people.

INDIA'S PEOPLE AND THEIR WAYS OF LIFE

By G. B. Cressey

From chap. 30 of *Asia's Lands and Peoples,* by G. B. Cressey. Copyright 1944 by McGraw-Hill Book Co., New York; reproduced by permission.

In all of Asia there is nowhere else the cultural heterogeneity found in India. The political unity imposed by Great Britain tends to obscure the internal diversity in race, language, religion, and material civilization. India is a land of widest contrasts; congestion and poverty are countered by wealth and spiritual insight. The system of caste has compartmentalized social and economic activities among Hindus, although Mohammedans and the other sects tend to be democratic.

Few generalizations apply everywhere. The Sikhs of the Punjab with their splendid physique and casteless society have little in common with the impoverished outcastes of Madras. Primitive hill tribes in Assam and educated Mohammedans, city students and illiterate peasants or ryots, wealthy Parsees in Bombay; all these make national coherence difficult.

More than elsewhere in monsoon Asia outside of Japan, India has accepted the material culture and veneer of European civilization. But despite the long exposure there has been little modification of the nonmaterial aspects of social organization and ideas. In the industrial cities there is a slight modification of minor aspects of caste, but the basic provisions against intermarriage and social intercourse in general remain.

The political structure of India is as complex as the social. Two-thirds of the country is included in the twelve provinces of British India. Since 1935 Burma has been set apart as a separate country. Ceylon has always been a crown colony. Several small Portuguese and French possessions remain along the coast as souvenirs of earlier conquests. The rest of India is divided into some 560 Indian states, some of them very large, others but a few square miles in size. Each state is more or less sovereign in internal affairs but has been bound by a variety of treaties to the old British East India Company, or to the British government, or to the King of England ruling as Emperor of India. They are thus under varying degrees of British supervision. . . .

Since many of these states enjoy different degrees of autonomy, the constitutional problem of an All-India Federation is exceedingly complicated. Some of the native rulers cling to ancient customs and refuse to cooperate in any scheme for unification. Added to this is the more serious problem of bringing together the Hindus and the Mohammedans. In most independent districts there is a British Resident, as representative of the Viceroy, whose unofficial authority usually increases as the area of states diminishes. A few of the larger states have their own railway systems with a distinctive gauge, independent postal administration, coinage, army, and customs regulations.

The political pattern of present-day India represents a crystallization of the chaos that England found, and produced, when the East India Company carried on its operations in the seventeenth and eighteenth centuries. . . .

The British came originally for trade rather than conquest. As warehouses were established along the coast, the East India Company entered into political relations with whoever ruled the region. In most areas these were the local governors, and in some cases even rebel chieftains. When civil difficulties arose, the British found it necessary to employ police to guard their possessions, and from this they expanded to militia and to the aid of their political favorites. Successive events, in part accidental, in part manipulated, gave the East India Company and its militarily supported native rulers increased political control. In places, this expansion was piecemeal, the frontier advancing as it was expedient to quell disturbances in bordering territory; elsewhere whole provinces were transferred to British administration, either under their official Mogul governor or under rebellious leaders. . . .

The nearly 400 million people of India have nine great religions, and over 200 languages of which 20 are spoken by at least a million people each. Even the name India was not applied to all of the country until modern times. There has never been a common tongue throughout the realm until the introduction of English, which is spoken by less than three million. Hindustani is widely used in the Ganges Plain, Bengali in Bengal, Telegu and Tamil in Madras, and Punjabi in the Indus lowland. This language distribution has little relation to provincial boundaries or to religion.

There are more than 2,000 castes in Hindu society, with the Brahmans at the top and the "untouchables" or depressed classes, which are outside the caste system, at the base. These latter number over fifty million people. . . . The class stratification of Hindu society is a serious barrier to modernization.

The restrictions of language and religion divide people into isolated cultural communities which make government and business difficult. In social, linguistic, and political structure, the peninsula of India is more complex than anything the peninsula of Europe has ever known. Without external guidance, national coherence is very difficult.

Toward the end of the sixteenth century, the total population of India was approximately 100 millions; by the first census of 1872 the number rose to 206 millions. The population of India, including both British India and the Indian States, at the 1941 census was 388,800,000, an increase of 13 per cent in a decade. . . . Half these people live in Hindustan, which occupies but one-fifth the area. In the lower Ganges Valley, population densities exceed 1,000 per square mile, while parts of the desert and delta jungles are essentially empty. Only a tenth of the total live in cities of 5,000 or over, for India is the most rural of all the large countries of the world. Literacy in 1939 was 12 per cent, with the largest numbers in Bengal and Madras. With a birth rate of 34 and a death rate of 24, the average expectation of life is but 27 years, as compared with 58 in Great Britain. . . .

Indian agricultural economy is based on rice, except in the northwest or specialized areas such as those devoted to cotton or jute. Since flooded fields require level land, hills are often sparsely populated....

Two factors guide population distributions in India: level alluvium and adequate water. Densities are high in the Ganges lowland and along both coasts. The Indus lowland has good soil but is too dry for agriculture, except where irrigated. The blankest areas on the population map are the arid lands of Rajputana and Baluchistan in the northwest, and the mountains of Kashmir. India's problem, like China's, is agricultural overpopulation....

Agriculture. The world of the average Indian farmer ends at his horizon. His interest is centered in the village where he lives except for an occasional journey of a few miles to a bazaar or fair....

The agricultural landscape differs with the season and from north to south, but everywhere below the Himalaya it has a characteristic Indian touch. The foliage is tropical and luxuriant, cultivated fields are tiny and of irregular shape as the result of generations of repeated subdivision, and livestock is abundant. The poverty of the people and houses of mud and straw reflect the marginal livelihood of the overcrowded land.

India is a land of villages, over two-thirds of a million in number. Most of them are located away from paved roads or railways and are but little affected by the tides of nationalism that sweep the cities. Each settlement is nearly self-sufficient with its own artisans, carpenters, and blacksmiths who furnish all needed tools. A shop or two supply the few material wants, and a temple or mosque cares for the religious needs. Traditional practices still suffice, and the high percentage of illiteracy makes changes difficult. Outside markets for farm produce are limited, so that increased labor brings few rewards. Recurrent years of poor crops pile up indebtedness to the local moneylender.

Despite extensive government efforts for agricultural improvement, the sheer magnitude of the reform problem means that for most farmers cultivation is still rudimentary. Plows are simple iron-tipped sticks which stir but do not overturn the soil. In most areas they are light enough to be carried to the fields on the farmer's back, but in the black soils of the Deccan the plows are heavier and require up to six yoke of oxen. Crops are reaped with a sickle, threshed by the feet of cattle, and winnowed in the wind. The mattock is used in place of a spade.

Some progress has been made in consolidating scattered holdings, but many farmers with no more than three or four acres in all till one or two dozen farm plots....

The Indian income needs desperately to be raised, but there is little hope of this through mining, lumbering, fishing, animal husbandry, or industry. Agriculture remains the dominant occupation, yet the cultivated area can scarcely be enlarged further without prohibitive expense. The crop area rose 14 per cent during the first quarter of the century, but population increased nearly as much. Only one-seventh of the land is double-cropped, but only modest increases are feasible here. Probably the most hopeful prospect is through better seed selection and increased returns per acre. Present acre yields are much below world averages.

Fertilizing would materially increase the harvest, but farmers are too poor to purchase commercial preparations. Unfortunately for the future, India does not appear to have phosphates or other raw materials for the manufacture of mineral fertilizers. The large number of farm animals suggests the availability of manure, but in the absence of other fuel for domestic needs, cattle and buffalo dung is made into cakes and burned. Compost piles are used somewhat, and there is a limited plowing under of legumes for green fertilizer. Rotation and fallowing are common practices, and the interplanting of legumes and grains also helps to maintain fertility.

Without irrigation India would be a different country. Seasonal rainfall, often irregular, leaves much of the land a semi-desert for half the year. In the northwest there is never enough precipitation. Irrigation is an old practice, greatly expanded under the British. Water is supplied by wells, reservoirs, and canals, and the irrigated area amounts to over 20 per cent of the total under cultivation. . . .

India is credited with nearly half the world's cattle. Humped cows or oxen and water buffalo are found everywhere, with camels in the dry northwest and elephants in the wetter east. Hindus hold the cow in religious esteem and, since the taking of life is forbidden, the animals are never killed no matter how feeble or diseased. Working bullocks must be fed, but cows are usually left to pick up what they can find. Millions of useless cattle compete for food urgently needed for work animals. . . .

Industry. Five primary activities contribute to the wealth of a nation: agriculture, animal husbandry, forestry, mining, and fishing. Only the first is of major significance in India. Secondary production involves the manufacture of these primary materials, but modern Indian industry is restricted to the products of agriculture and the few mines. The arrival of a significant industrial era for India has long been forecast, but its appearance seems to be gradual and its future problematical. . . .

In 1936 there were only 10,000 modern factories in all India, with a daily average of 1,652,147 workers. These are strikingly localized, largely in or near Calcutta, which is far in the lead, Bombay, Ahmedabad, Cawnpore, Jamshedpur, Madras, and Sholapur. No other city had more than 20,000 factory workers in 1936. The highly uneven distribution of modern industry and its concentration on cotton and jute are noteworthy features of India today. Conspicuous developments occurred during both the First and Second World Wars. . . .

Coal production is localized in the Chota Nagpur Plateau of Bengal and Bihar. . . . The output is barely sufficient for Indian needs so that the west coast imports South African coal. Despite cheap labor and shallow workings, the coal industry is not prosperous. . . .

Hydroelectricity is a new development. The largest installation is in the Western Ghats near Bombay where pipes descend 1,725 feet and develop a pressure of 750 pounds per square inch against the turbines. Railways near Bombay are mostly electrified. Electric power is also developed on the Jhelum in Kashmir, the Cauvery in Madras, and elsewhere. All these sources may be enlarged to a limited extent, but their distribution is highly regional. On account of seasonal rainfall, expensive reservoirs are needed. Most of the country has no prospective source of industrial power.

Pig iron is produced at Burnpur near Asansol, at Kulti in Bengal, and at Badravati in Mysore; and both pig and steel at the new center of Jamshedpur. The location of raw materials is the dominating factor, and few other Indian centers seem feasible.

The greatest steel plant is that of the

Tata Iron and Steel Company, Ltd., at Jamshedpur, 155 miles west of Calcutta. Production started in 1911 and the plant respresents an investment of $100,000,000. All of this is Indian capital, and the industry is the pride of the Nationalists. Jamshedpur holds thirtieth place among world steel centers. Rich 60 per cent hematite ore comes 45 miles from Gurumaishini in the Singhbhum district; coal is brought 115 miles from Jherria; and dolomite flux is transported 40 miles. Manganese is near by. Assembly costs are less than half those in the United States or England, and the Tata plant is the cheapest producer of pig iron in the world. Steel costs are high since there is little scrap for melting. . . .

The five blast furnaces produced nearly two million tons of pig iron in 1940, and the steel output from seven open-hearth furnaces was about one million tons. This is three-fourths of India's production of pig, and nearly all its steel. This is said to be the largest iron and steel works in the British Empire.

Although the capacity of the Tata works has been enlarged several times and there is a protective tariff, production still fails to meet the needs or to keep out steel imports. There is normally an annual importation of 300,000 to 400,000 tons of steel from England, and an export of iron ore and pig iron to Japan. Some Jamshedpur steel is profitably shipped to California.

The Kulti plant of the Bengal Iron Company has five furnaces with a capacity of 300,000 tons; no steel is produced. There are also two blast furnaces at Burnpure and one in Mysore.

Aluminum was not produced until 1939 when a plant was opened in Bengal with a capacity of 3,000 tons annually. Copper ores from the Singhbhum district are smelted at Mandhandar in Bihar. There is little refining of other metals. Suitable raw materials for cement are widespread, but transportation costs for coal are high since none of the plants is near the mines. Bombay and Calcutta are the chief markets, yet there are no cement works within 300 miles of either city. The total production could meet nearly all needs, but rail costs to the seaboard counterbalance ocean freight so that imported cement is used along the coast. Railway industries are one of the largest of all employers.

Chemicals are an essential part of modern industry and are so interdependent that the absence of one link may handicap many others. Most of the raw materials are available in India, but they are seldom near to both power and markets. Adequate supplies of sulphuric acid are produced from imported materials, but in the case of most other chemicals the output is on an experimental basis. The necessary skilled workers are few in number.

Textiles are India's characteristic industries, chiefly cotton mills around Bombay and jute mills near Calcutta. . . .

Jute production goes back a century. It is the cheapest of all fibers, and India dominates the world market. The material is used for gunnysacks, burlap, coarse carpets, and cordage. . . .

The bulk of India's present industry is made up of consumers' goods rather than machines or tools or producers' goods. It may be a long while before India becomes a great primary manufacturing region.

Communications. Since the Europeans approached India from the sea, coastwise shipping was developed before internal communications. Unfortunately the country has few harbors. Coral reefs, delta shoals, and monsoon winds make it necessary at many ports for vessels to discharge cargo into lighters several miles offshore. Several of the few good harbors along the coast of the peninsula are cut off from their hinterland by the Ghats.

Internal communications have been equally unsatisfactory. Rivers are alternately in flood or reduced to a mere trickle and are unfit for dependable transportation. The plains of Hindustan are entirely without road-making materials, and local travel is difficult during the muddy season. Neighboring villages are even now cut off from each other during the rains, so that trade is limited.

Railway construction began in 1853. Unfortunately, several rail gauges have been used so that passengers must sometimes change cars, and freight must break bulk en route. . . . In 1937 the broad-gauge systems totaled 21,197 miles, the meter-gauge 17,773 miles, and the narrow-gauge 4,158 miles, a total of 43,128 miles. India thus ranks third in mileage, preceded by the United States with 238,539 miles (1937) and the Soviet Union with 52,425 miles (1936). . . .

There is still no line connecting Burma with India, although surveys have been made both along the coast as well as via the Hukong Valley in the north. Ceylon is but 22 miles by boat from India, and there are intervening islands and sand bars known as Adam's Bridge which might make railway construction feasible. Proposals to link up the Indian system with Europe involve the politically undesirable route through Afghanistan to Soviet Middle Asia, or a line by way of the deserts of Iran to Bagdad. The present rail net provides adequate coverage for most of the country. . . .

India has four major automobile highways, following a framework that dates back into the remote past. The most famous is the Grand Trunk road, from the Khyber Pass via Delhi to Calcutta. The others connect Calcutta with Madras, Madras with Bombay, and Bombay with Delhi. It has proved very difficult to provide a satisfactory system of improved automobile roads; in many areas they cost almost as much as railways. Only 200 miles of the Grand Trunk highway are paved with asphalt; elsewhere water-bound macadam is the rule. Numerous rivers are unbridged, and sections of many important roads are liable to be inundated.

The total length of all highways in 1938 was 319,131 miles, of which 66,000 miles were water-bound macadam and 122,000 miles good-weather roads. The best subsidiary roads are in south India. In 1941, there were 123,400 motor vehicles of which 77,000 were passenger cars.

The lack of good roads has always been one of India's handicaps, whether in trade, social coherence, or political unity. Nor has there been well-developed water transportation by river, canal, or coastwise vessels to take its place. Cultural stagnation was ineviable. . . . Regional isolation has been the rule. Each invading monarchy has found India relatively easy to subdue but difficult to organize.

THE FAR EAST

By the Editors

The principal components of the region covered by the term "Far East" include China, the easternmost reaches of Siberia, Korea, Southeast Asia, Japan, and Oceania. Except for part of the Soviet Far East (already described in the preceding chapter on the U.S.S.R.), these territories, like the rest of the Afro-Asian Realm, lie south or southeast of the barrier deserts and mountains which set off this whole realm from Europe and northwestern Asia.

HISTORIC ISOLATION OF THE FAR EAST

By G. F. Hudson and Marthe Rajchman

From chap. 1 of *An Atlas of Far Eastern Politics*, by G. F. Hudson and M. Rajchman. Revised edition. Copyright 1942 by the Secretariat, Institute of Pacific Relations, New York. Published by the John Day Co., New York; reproduced by permission. G. F. Hudson is a leading British authority on the Far East. Marthe Rajchman is a well-known cartographer.

There have been in history three ways of approach to the region of the world known as the Far East: the first, by sea from the Indian Ocean; the second, overland from the countries of the Middle East; and the third, across the Pacific from North or South America....

The approaches by sea and land from the Middle East . . . have been in use from remote antiquity, and an account of them must reveal the natural boundaries of the Far Eastern region. . . .

Leaving out of account the Arctic littoral, Asia has three coastlines: to the west the Mediterranean and Black Sea, to the south the Indian Ocean, and to the east the Pacific. Before the making of the canal, the isthmus of Suez barred any access for shipping from the Mediterranean to the Indian Ocean, and even now it remains a very definite dividing line. From the Indian Ocean to the Pacific there is a continuous natural seaway, but the Malay Peninsula, reaching south to within two degrees of the Equator, makes a very sharp corner at the southeastern extremity of Asia, and Singapore is no less of a boundary than Suez. The three Asiatic coastlines are thus clearly separated, and their hinterlands may be identified with the three regions of the East; by this criterion the Near East includes Turkey and Syria (with Egypt), the Middle East, Arabia, Iraq, Iran and India, and the Far East, Indo-China and China.

These divisions by relation to coastline would not, however, have so much significance if they did not correspond to two well-marked insulating barriers inland. The Ararat highlands and the Hamad (Syrian desert) intervene between the Mediterranean and Persian Gulf lands. . . . Similarly, a vast mountain system comprising the Pamirs-Tibet and Yunnan-Burma highlands shuts off China from India and Iran, the mountains being reinforced to the north of Tibet by the deserts of Sinkiang. These two great ramparts of natural obstruction may be regarded as fixing the confines of the Near, Middle and Far Eastern regions.

The Pamirs-Burma mountain system affords by far the more impervious barrier of the two, and accounts for the high degree of isolation which was the condition of Far Eastern history until quite recently. Though the isolation of the Far East has often been exaggerated, it remains true that China has been in the past more secluded from cultural contact and interaction with an outer world than any section of the region extending from Spain to Bengal. . . .

By longitude Tibet and Sinkiang, lying north of the Ganges plain, should be comprised within the Middle East, but the course of history which has made them to this day—at least nominally—parts of China, corresponds to a strong geographical predisposition; they are more accessible from the east than from the south or west, though just lately, since the construction of the Turksib Railway, the gravitational pull of the Soviet Union has been very

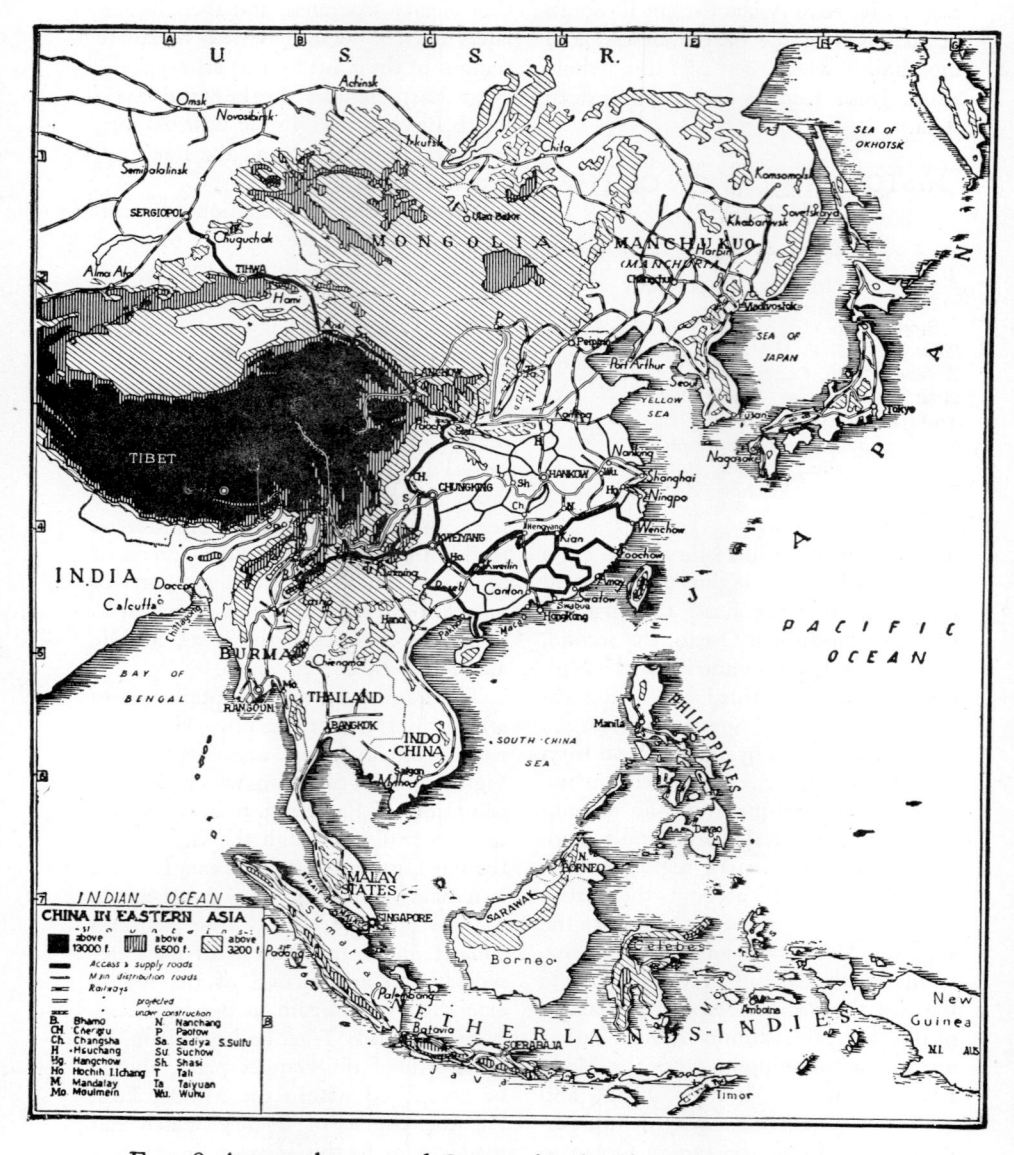

FIG. 28. Approaches to and Geographical Isolation of the Far East.
From M. Rajchman, *A New Atlas of China*. Published by the John Day Co. for *Asia* Magazine. Copyright 1941 by the John Day Co.

strong in Sinkiang. . . . The formal frontier of China follows the line of the most tremendous mountain rampart in the world. The T'ien-shan, the Pamirs, the Karakorum and the Himalayas are all mountain ranges on a grand scale, and the last-named is backed by the vast plateau of Tibet. . . .

It is possible to avoid the high mountains by going to the north of the T'ien-shan and then southeast to China via Hami. There is a clear way from west to east across Asia through the gap between the T'ien-shan and the mountains of the Altai system. This way went the caravan route from the Sea of Azov to Peiping described by Pegolotti in the fourteenth century, and this way runs the road from the Turksib Railway to Lanchow by which Russian munitions are supplied to China in the present war. But for access to China from India or Persia such a route has always meant a long detour added onto a distance already excessive for commerce before the age of mechanical transport. . . . The same applies in an even greater degree to the open country to the north of the Altai; here there could be no question of a route from Indian or Mediterranean countries to the Far East, and the opening of trans-Asian communications in such high latitudes depended on the development of Russia and her expansion eastward through Siberia—it dates, therefore, only from the seventeenth century.

Turning from the north to the south of the great central mountain block of Asia, we find obstruction of a somewhat different kind, but no less formidable. From the southeastern corner of the Tibetan plateau mountain ranges splay out toward the south, reaching the sea in Tenasserim, where the Malay Peninsula juts out from the land-mass of Indo-China. These mountains diminish rapidly in height from north to south.

. . . But an exceptionally high annual rainfall . . . clothes the hill tracts facing the Bay of Bengal with dense tropical vegetation, which makes them hardly less difficult to traverse than the loftier heights of the Pamirs or Himalayas. . . . An environment of mountain forests has kept a wide region in the interior of Indo-China in various stages of primitive culture more or less impervious to influences from areas of higher civilization to west, east and south. . . .

With such obstacles to overland communication between the Middle and Far East, it might seem, nevertheless, that the continuous seaway from the Indian Ocean into the Pacific would afford a sufficiently close contact. Yet the Malay Peninsula has been up to modern times a strong factor of separation, for not only did it mean a long, roundabout voyage from the Bay of Bengal to the South China Sea, but it diverted maritime traffic into waters where piracy used to flourish with peculiar vigor. . . .

In view of the length and dangers of the voyage through the Straits of Malacca and round Malaya, trade tended to make use of a portage across the isthmus of Kra, renouncing the advantages of continuous voyage, but reducing the risks from piracy. . . .

With or without the Kra short-cut, however, the "southeast passage" failed throughout ancient and medieval times to attain primacy as a means of access to the Far East, and the overland routes through Sinkiang, in spite of their difficulties, retained most of the traffic there was. . . .

From India and from the Bay of Bengal there were two direct overland routes to China: one across the Himalayas and Tibet via Lhasa, and the other by Burma and Yunnan. So great were the disadvantages, however, of both these ways that the main lines of communication between India and China, during the period when Buddhism was propagated from India all over the Far East, were through Sinkiang. . . .

After the arrival of European shipping in the Indian Ocean with the voyage of Vasco da Gama in 1498, the sea route round Malaya was opened up more than ever before, and became by far the most important approach to the Far East. The traditional overland routes fell into decline. . . . On the other hand, the last four centuries have seen the development by western powers of two new lines of approach: the trans-Siberian and trans-Pacific.

The Russians, pressing eastward to the north of the Altai, reached Lake Baikal early in the seventeenth century and opened trade with China across Mongolia along the route Irkutsk-Kiakhta-Urga-Peiping. But when in the last decade of the nineteenth century the building of a transcontinental railway was undertaken by Russia, it was decided to carry it, not across the Gobi to Peiping and Tientsin, but to the most southerly Russian port on the Pacific. The political situation in 1896 having enabled the Russians to get permission from China to build the line through Manchuria, it became possible to approach China overland from Russia without having to cross either high mountains or deserts. The Trans-Siberian was eventually linked with the Chinese railway system by the connection Harbin-Mukden-Peiping, entering China not from the northwest or north, but from the *northeast*. The Russians have had plans ever since the 'nineties for a short-cut line from the Trans-Siberian to China proper via Urga or Hami, but no such railway has yet been built, though there is now a line as far as Urga (Ulan Bator, the capital of Outer Mongolia).

The approach to Asia across the Pacific dates only . . . from Magellan's voyage in 1519. Up to about 1850 ships came from the direction of Cape Horn or the Magellan Straits, having sailed round South America from Europe or New England; or they came from the Pacific ports of Latin America, Mexico being the most northerly region of European settlement on the Pacific coast. Then, with the rapid growth of San Francisco as a port of the U.S.A. from 1848 onward, shipping began to sail thence almost due west—actually with a slant southward through six degrees of latitude—to Shanghai, which had been first opened to foreign trade in 1842. Japan, which had hitherto held place as the far end of the Far East, the Cipangu which Marco Polo heard of but never reached, lay in the path of the new oceanic trade route, and it was the Americans coming across the Pacific, not the Europeans approaching from the south, who in 1853 compelled the self-secluded Japanese to enter into relations with the outer world.

POLITICAL GEOGRAPHY OF THE FAR EAST

By Nicholas J. Spykman

From chap. 5 of *America's Strategy in World Politics*, by N. J. Spykman. Copyright 1942 by Harcourt, Brace & Co., New York; reproduced by permission. The late Dr. Spykman was Sterling professor of international relations at Yale University and formerly director of the Yale Institute of International Studies, which sponsored the publication of the book quoted.

[NATIONAL OCCUPANCY AND CONTROL OF THE PARTS OF THE FAR EAST ARE DESCRIBED IN THIS SELECTION AS OF THE START OF THE SECOND WORLD WAR.]

THE transpacific zone, like the transatlantic zone and the Western Hemisphere itself, consists of a northern and a southern continent with a mediterranean region in between. The southern continent is the national domain same as the United States or Canada. The land mass is divided by the Tropic of Capricorn with the smaller section in the tropics and the larger half in the

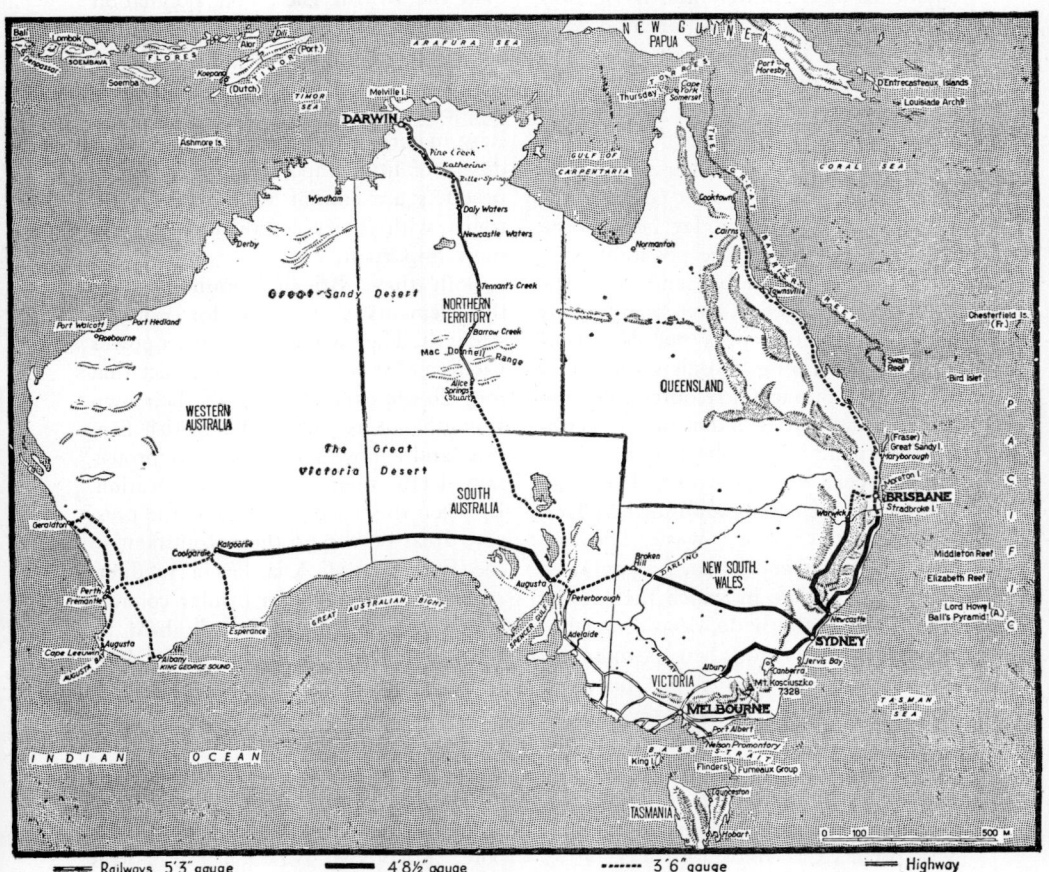

FIG. 29. Australia.

From E. A. Mowrer and M. Rajchman, *Global War, An Atlas of World Strategy.* Copyright 1942 by William Morrow & Co., New York; reproduced by permission.

of the Commonwealth of Australia. The east coast of this great island faces the Pacific, the west coast the Indian Ocean, and the north coast the Asiatic "Mediterranean." Australia is three million square miles in size, approximately the south temperate zone. The greater part of the continent, especially the west, consists of a desert plateau, and economic life is concentrated along the eastern and southern rim where an adequate, though irregular, rainfall permits agriculture, and a mild climate makes the land suitable for white colonization. Communication between the different coastal regions is maintained by means of circumferential navigation instead of overland transportation partly because of lower cost, but principally because the great desert belt that occupies most of the center of the continent acts as a barrier.

In Australia, as in other new countries, men have dreamt dreams of growth and expansion far beyond the limits of the geographic possibilities in terms of climate, arable land, and natural resources. They have seen visions of a great future, of a populous continent maintaining a high standard of living on rich natural resources. But the truth of the matter is that in this southern continent across the Pacific nature has not been very generous. There are productive areas only around the edges, and the center is empty waste. The land mass has been compared, not unfairly, with a soup plate in which the soup is found not in the wide, deep center but on the narrow rim. There is room for additional population along the coast, and the northern tropical region is a desirable zone of emigration for the crowded Asiatics of the northern continent, but the dominion is firmly committed to an immigration policy that will preserve a white Australia.

Australia has considerable mineral resources: gold, copper, silver, lead, fairly good coal, and some iron. She has developed behind a protective tariff a small steel and machine industry and some light manufacturing, but she remains primarily a country with an extractive economy whose main emphasis is on agriculture and whose largest exports are wool, mutton, wheat, and other grains. Approximately twelve hundred miles east of Australia lies a second British dominion, New Zealand, consisting of two large islands and a number of smaller ones. She covers a total area of approximately a hundred thousand square miles, slightly larger than the British Isles. Her population is less than a million and a half, but it has managed to create a high standard of living from a predominantly extractive economy of an agrarian nature. Raw materials are insignificant and industry of little importance. Her export products are similar to those of Australia with dairy products relatively more important.

Both these British dominions lack the elements that make for military strength. They would represent a power vacuum if it were not for the fact that they do not exist in terms of their own strength but as part of the British Empire and enjoy a considerable protection from their geographic location. Between this weak world and the pressure areas on the northern continent in the Far East of Asia lies a mediterranean buffer zone, an insular colonial world at present still largely held by western sea power and the naval base of Singapore.

The Asiatic "Mediterranean" lies between Asia and Australia and between the Pacific and the Indian Oceans. This middle sea has a roughly triangular shape with corners at Formosa, Singapore, and Cape York on the Torres Strait near the northern tip of Australia. The rim includes the Philippines, Halmahera, New Guinea, the north coast of Australia, the Dutch East Indies, British Malaya, Siam, French Indo-China, and the southern coast of China up to Amoy. . . .

The continental littoral stretches from Amoy to Singapore, the base which controls the Strait of Malacca and the exit to the Indian Ocean. The southwestern rim, 3,000 miles long, from the tip of Sumatra to Port Darwin consists of the

Greater and Lesser Sunda Islands belonging to the Netherlands, except the eastern half of Timor, which is Portuguese. There are a small number of passages between the islands of this chain, but they can be easily closed by mines and submarines. Port Darwin controls the exits from the Banda Sea to the Indian Ocean and the Torres Strait. British, Dutch, and Australian naval cooperation can, therefore, close all the passages from the Pacific to the Indian Ocean and force a detour around the Australian Continent. This fact is responsible for the special importance of Singapore and the geopolitical similarity of its location with that of Panama. The eastern rim which extends from Amoy to New Guinea includes Formosa, the Philippines, and Halmahera. . . . In the center of this large middle sea lie the great islands of Celebes and Borneo and innumerable smaller ones. The Asiatic "Mediterranean" zone is an insular world par excellence.

This region is a tropical area, rich in minerals and endowed in certain sections with an extremely fertile soil. The Archipelago contains important oil fields, coal, and iron, and a large potential waterpower, precious minerals, and the largest tin deposits in the world. Good soil, plenty of rainfall, and an ample labor supply eminently suited for plantation work have combined to make this region the most important exporter of the products of tropical agriculture, far surpassing in output the African or the American tropics. It supplies its own neighboring continents as well as America and Europe with coffee, tea, copra, palm oil, quinine, rubber and various other products.

The total population along the littoral and island rims of this mediterranean basin is approximately 125 million people, not counting the people of southern China. From this Chinese coast there comes an outward thrust of economic expansion in the form of emigration of labor, traders, and capital. In many regions, a Chinese middle class layer has worked itself in between the native barter economy and the western capitalist system with its large-scale production and long-term credit. This Chinese economic penetration has so far not been accompanied by any political control partly because of the nature of present-day Chinese society, partly because of the non-existence of Chinese naval power. The area is, therefore, dominated not by the littoral state with the largest population and the greatest economic potential but by distant naval powers. . . .

The northern continent of the transpacific zone consists of the mainland of Asia and a chain of offshore islands. The Pacific drainage area of the continent north of the Asiatic Mediterranean is the land mass east of the Tibetan highland and the Mongolian plateau. It consists of China, Mongolia, Manchuria, Korea, and a section of northeastern Siberia. The economic life of China lies primarily in the river basins of three great streams, the Hwang-Ho, the Yangtze Kiang, and the Si-Kiang. The latter reaches the sea near Canton and Hong Kong and is, therefore, part of the drainage area of the Asiatic Mediterranean. The lower valleys of the two northern rivers join to form the great plain of North China which reaches the coast on both sides of the Shantung peninsula. This concentration of population and economic life in three parallel river zones with difficult mountain territory between is responsible for the recurring tendency toward regionalism in Chinese history and forms an obstacle to effective political integration.

The power resources for an industrial

civilization in China are fair but by no means abundant. There are so far no indications of rich oil fields and the waterpower potential, viewed in the light of the very large population, is not overwhelming. There are, however, considerable coal deposits in different parts of the country. Iron is available but not in great amounts, and the country contains other mineral ores that must await development of transportation facilities before large-scale exploitation can begin. The raw material basis is, therefore, not as favorable as that of the industrial sections of Europe and the United States, but a judicious application of western technology to the resources available, combined with a population of three hundred million and a country of enormous size, could create a considerable war potential.

East of the Khingan Mountains between Mongolia and Korea and detached from China proper lies Manchuria and the river basin of the Amur. Southern Manchuria drains into the Gulf of Chih-Li west of the Liao-tung peninsula, and the Amur River reaches the coast at Vladivostok on the Japanese Sea. Manchuria and Eastern Siberia are rich in lumber and mineral resources and represent, compared to China proper, almost undeveloped virgin land. They have been exploited only during the last fifty years and still offer enormous possibilities for growth notwithstanding the limitations of a very severe winter climate. It was through the valleys of the Amur and the Ussuri that Russian eastern expansion reached the Pacific, and it is through the same depression that the great Siberian plain, west of Lake Baikal, finds an eastern outlet to the sea. North of Vladivostok lies the barren Asiatic littoral of the largest political unit in the world . . . the Union of Soviet Socialist Republics.

The mainland of Asia is separated from the Pacific by a number of marginal seas closed in by peninsulas and island chains: the East China Sea and the Yellow Sea bordered by Formosa, the Ryukyu groups, the southern island of Japan and Korea; the Japanese Sea, fringed by Honshu, Hokkaido, and the main islands of Japan; and the Sea of Okhotsk, bounded by the Kurile group and Kamchatka. On Kyushu, Shikoku, Honshu, Hokkaido and Karafuto rests the military strength and sea power of the Land of the Mikado. These islands alone are inadequate as a food and raw material basis for a highly industrialized nation with a dense population. Because of the mountainous and volcanic nature of the country, the percentage of arable land is very small. Improved agricultural technique has increased the yield of the rice fields, but Japan is a net importer of food. The deficiencies are made up by imports from Korea and Manchuria on the mainland and from French Indo-China and Siam in the Asiatic Mediterranean.

In regard to the power basis of industry, her position is equally unfavorable. Waterpower is plentiful, but coal is inadequate and oil production covers only 30 per cent of consumption. The whole metal industry is dependent on imports which include iron ore, pig iron, and scrap iron; the alloy metals, manganese and tungsten; and a large part of the requirements of bauxite, copper, lead, nickel, tin, and zinc. Even the textile industry must use imported wool, cotton, and wood pulp for rayon. Compared to China, the Japanese power potential is small indeed, but available resources have been developed to a much greater extent so that actual war industry is far more productive on the island empire than on the mainland. In the transpacific zone as elsewhere it is the northern continent that contains the great power potentials. . . .

Chapter 13

Japan

THE Japanese were the first oriental nation to adopt the discipline, tools, and weapons of western industrial society. Japan was consequently the first oriental nation to play an active role in world politics. The rise of Japanese power, accompanied by an increasingly aggressive trend in Japanese statecraft, has profoundly altered the pattern of human relations within the Afro-Asian Realm and between the peoples of that realm and the colonial powers of the Occident.

Japanese economic competition early aroused anxiety among the western peoples. Japan's success in escaping from a semi-colonial dependence upon the western powers has directly or indirectly stimulated a spirit of revolt and nationalism within other Asiatic countries, notably in China and India. The Japanese victories of 1941-1942 dealt shattering blows to occidental prestige throughout the Orient, posing difficult and dangerous problems for the future relations of the western powers with the colonial peoples of the Afro-Asian Realm.

Japan's adventures in empire-building go back many years. Long before the present war Japan's ruling classes dreamed of a vast continental-oceanic empire in the Far East. Some Nipponese extremists talked recklessly of extending their sway over all Asia, and even into Europe, Africa, and the Americas. Japanese army and navy officers wrote serious books describing how they would conquer those distant lands. But Japan's more realistic empire-builders devoted their energies mainly to Eastern and Southeastern Asia and the Pacific Ocean.

The Japanese never officially blueprinted the boundaries of their projected realm. Japanese ambition grew with success. But it is now reasonably clear that the "Greater East Asia Co-Prosperity Sphere," the grandiose and misleading name given to their expanding empire, was eventually to reach deep into Asia and far out into the Pacific Ocean.

Throughout an immense domain, bounded roughly by India, Lake Baikal, Alaska, Hawaii, New Zealand, Australia, and the East Indies, the Japanese were to have a monopoly of arms, and a near-monopoly of heavy industry. The subjugated peoples were to be "hewers of wood and drawers of water," producing food and raw materials for their Japanese lords and masters.

The steps taken to carry out this grandiose project fall into a logical strategic sequence or pattern. Each move represented an attempt to circumvent some geographical handicap, to overcome some strategical weakness, or to exploit some natural advantage. Each territorial accession prepared the way for the next, and down to the middle of 1942 the pattern unfolded in a manner and with a success which seemed momentarily to invalidate all previous assumptions regarding the inherent weakness of the mushrooming island empire. But the Japanese like the Nazis fatally miscalculated the forces that could be arrayed against them, and in the end their victories turned to ashes as they strove desperately to hold their crumbling ramparts against the inexorable advance of vastly superior forces.

The American people have played a major role in the rise and fall of the Japanese Empire. To the growth of no power have we contributed more than to Japan. With no other have our vital interests more frequently or more violently clashed. The leaders of no other nation have depended upon us more heavily or hated us more bitterly. From no power have we suffered more humiliating defeats. Against no other, in turn, have we dealt more shattering blows.

Not so long ago, while mobilizing world opinion against Japanese aggressions in Asia, we were simultaneously supplying, for a price, a sizable proportion of the scrap metal, gasoline, machine tools, aircraft engines, and other materials which made that aggression possible. More recently, while Japanese diplomats played for time in Washington, the Japanese High Command was secretly preparing the initial blows against Hawaii and the Philippines.

Such has been the checkered and paradoxical record of American relations with Japan through the years.

Prior to the winter of 1941-1942, Americans generally failed to take too seriously the looming shadow in the Pacific. We had long regarded the Japanese as clever imitators of western ways and as dangerous economic competitors. But we had not as a rule thought of Japan as a military power in the same class with the United States or the greater states of Europe.

From many sources we were assured that Japan had "feet of clay." Geographers and geologists had described the paucity of nature's gifts to the island kingdom. Economists had stressed the weak spots in Japan's industrial potential. Military strategists had emphasized the country's extreme vulnerability to blockade. Statesmen had counted heavily upon the presumed reluctance of Japan's rulers to risk pitting their inferior strength against the immensely greater resources of the United States. The course of the undeclared war on China, begun in 1937, Japan's seeming inability to crush Chiang Kai-shek's poorly trained, miserably armed, under-fed troops, confirmed and strengthened the widespread American belief in the inherent weakness of the island empire.

It took bombs falling upon Pearl Harbor to awaken the American people to the perils of their previous complacence. The attack on Hawaii and the swift advances against the Philippines, Malaya, Burma, and East Indies, brought dawning realization of the stature as well as the intentions of our Pacific enemy. The speed and skill of the amphibious Blitzkrieg revealed not only the weakness of Allied forces available in the Pacific and Far East, but also the degree to which we had underrated Japanese power and ignored the real sources of Japanese strength.

We were psychologically as well as materially unprepared for the drives which carried Japanese arms in less than six months to the borders of India and Australia. Once more, as in the cases of France, Germany, the Soviet Union, and other countries, we had to learn the hard way how vital it is to know the true measure both of one's friends and of one's possible enemies.

Prewar estimates of Japanese strength erred in several important respects. From a survey of Japan's inadequate soil resources, limited coal, iron, and oil reserves, shortages of other raw materials, narrow margin of food supply, etc., it was too easy to reach the conclusion that Japan could never fight a long war of attrition against the greater powers. What was too often neglected was the character of the Japanese way of life, Japanese ability to do without, the stamina, discipline, morale, and fanaticism of the Japanese people.

We knew, for example, that Japanese cities were made largely of wood and paper. We knew, too, in a vague general way that the

Japanese people had few automobiles, refrigerators, radios, and the thousand-and-one metal gadgets so abundant in the United States. From these facts, it was usually inferred that large-scale incendiary bombing would start unextinguishable conflagrations, and that the lower Japanese standard of living somehow indicated a correspondingly lower military potential. What was too often overlooked was that the scarcity of metal in Japanese civil life was the result not merely of smaller output but also of deliberate denial of metal products to all but the capital-goods industries and military-equipment factories. Japan's steel production was never more than a minute fraction of our own. But the steel that Japan did make went almost exclusively into war and preparation for war.

Still more disastrous was our ignorance of the qualities of the Japanese people. We knew next to nothing of the discipline, the living habits, the ideals and the moral drives which governed Japanese behavior. In consequence we were largely unprepared for the fanatical qualities of the Japanese soldier in battle. We lacked standards for estimating the ability of the Japanese home front to carry on in the face of hunger, privation, and mounting disaster.

It would be difficult to exaggerate the importance of such intangibles in the rise and achievements of modern Japan. These factors are basic to any realistic estimate of the future behavior of the Japanese. At the same time, Japanese behavior patterns differ so from our own, that Americans experience the greatest difficulty in really understanding this oriental people. Hence, in the readings that follow, relatively less space is devoted to the more obvious tangible elements of Japanese strength and weakness, and more to the intangible factors which have enabled the Japanese to go so far with so little, but which in the end have contributed measurably to their undoing.

HISTORICAL FOUNDATIONS OF MODERN JAPAN

By Sir George Sansom

From *Japan,* by Sir George Sansom. Oxford Pamphlets on World Affairs, no. 70. Oxford University Press, New York and London; reproduced by permission. The author is a distinguished British scholar, an authority on Japanese history and civilization, and a high ranking member of the British diplomatic service.

We are now finding the measure of the Japanese in war, but there is still much to learn about them as a nation. Even after defeat, they will have to be taken seriously into account. They number some 75 million and the presence in the Pacific area of 75 million discontented and ambitious people, even stripped of power to do positive damage, will bode ill for permanent peace in that region unless some means can be found of adjusting and reconciling them to a new international order. It therefore behooves us to study the Japanese so that we may know what kind of people we shall have to deal with, what their past has been and how, in the light of their past, they are likely to behave in future.

Early Japanese history can be very briefly summarized. Japan was living in her late Stone Age until the beginning of the Christian era, and some parts of the country remained in that condition for several centuries more. It was to China that the Japanese people owed their emergence from primitive conditions, since it was from the Chinese that they learned directly, or by way of Korea, first the use of bronze and iron, then the art of writing, and later, about A.D. 550, the elements of Chinese social and political philosophy and the doctrines of Buddhism. It is of course no shame to the Japanese that they should have taken over the elements of a civilization so manifestly superior to their own. China was a vast and ancient continental state, enjoying an advanced culture that already reached back to high antiquity when Japanese tribal leaders first began to covet Chinese goods and copy Chinese methods. Indeed, what is remarkable and creditable is that the Japanese set about learning from their Chinese tutors not under compulsion but willingly and energetically. The Chinese pattern of life was not imposed upon them by invasion, as the Roman or Norman patterns were imposed upon the British Isles. It was the Japanese themselves who recognized the benefits of the Chinese way of life, and set about adopting it with diligence. Here, in the earliest phases of their history, we can discern already at work a characteristic national trait—a desire to better themselves, a tireless ambition, a determination to profit by the knowledge and experience of others.

Many observers of modern Japan, thinking chiefly in terms of mechanical inventions borrowed from the West by the Japanese, have said that they are mere imitators, that they have no power to originate and invent. But, whatever else may be said about Japanese originality, Japanese civilization was, and perhaps remains, unique. This distinctive quality of Japanese civilization is apparent in its earliest history; for as the Japanese took over and assimilated Chinese institutions, they managed to imprint upon them a most decided Japanese character, to give them an unmistakable Japanese flavor. By the end of the ninth century, though the forms borrowed from China remained, their content was changed almost beyond recognition. The administrative system, in the beginning almost slavishly imitated from Chinese models, developed into something which, though retaining its original structure, was in practice refashioned to suit Japanese ways of thinking and behaving. The great corpus of Chinese philosophy, respectfully followed as to its texts, was so transmuted, by changes of emphasis or by reinterpretation, that it conformed to traditional Japanese sentiments; and even the powerful doctrines of Buddhism were in some respects so modified as not to conflict with secular Japanese beliefs and customs.

The same tendency can be observed throughout the history of the Japanese people. Their tenacious culture seeks always to transform invading influences, to assimilate them without doing violence to itself. Even when they exposed themselves to the very dominating forces of western civilization in the nineteenth century, they were at pains to conserve habits which to an outside observer seem incompatible with modern life. Therefore, in the study of Japanese behavior, we must expect to find underlying the most familiar appearances a reality peculiarly and intensely native to the Japanese soil, and not easy to comprehend in terms of our own occidental experience. . . .

There was little real intercourse between Japan and the Asiatic mainland throughout the Middle Ages. There was some going and coming of Buddhist monks, of scholars and artists and of traders, for the Japanese generally contrived to keep abreast of cultural developments in China. Their political relations were, however, of a tenuous kind, partly because the attention of the Chinese was traditionally centered upon their land frontiers and rarely directed overseas, but chiefly because the Japanese were absorbed in their own domestic affairs. In the years from about A.D. 1100, when provincial warlords rose to power and the authority of the Emperor began to collapse, to about 1600, they were fighting among themselves an almost unbroken series of feudal wars, in which various factions strove for dominance in ever-changing combinations. It was in these years that there was built up the fighting habit, the military caste, and the so-called warriors' code known to us as Bushido. Only once during these centuries were the Japanese disturbed by threats from the world outside. This was at the time of the Mongol invasions when (in 1274 and again in 1281) Khubla Khan sent armies to conquer Japan, but failed in his enterprise largely because of inadequate sea power. The Japanese, having been saved from the Mongols by a storm which scattered the invasion fleet, resumed their quarrels at home; and it was not until the early seventeenth century that stable and effective centralized government was reestablished in Japan, under military dictators (Shoguns) of the feudal family named Tokugawa, whom the fortunes of civil war had brought to a position of dominance throughout the country.

Meanwhile certain events happening in other parts of the world had, unknown to the Japanese, played an important part in determining their future. The great age of maritime discovery by western peoples had now begun, and European vessels were gradually opening a way into the Pacific. . . . The Japanese had not deliberately cut themselves off from the rest of the world. Indeed their ships had not ceased to trade with China, and in the years from 1400 to 1600 in particular, Japanese vessels sailed far and wide in the Western Pacific. Japan seemed to be emerging from her shell, but this was a matter of individual enterprise rather than of national policy. As a nation she was still looking inwards rather than outwards when in 1542 . . . two Portuguese travelers landed under stress of weather on a small island in southwest Japan. Their arrival caused the greatest excitement, and the firearms which they carried much impressed the Japanese. Indeed it may be said that this incident marked the beginning of a new epoch in Japanese history, since now for the first time the great voyages of the seafaring nations of Europe had brought Japan into contact with western peoples, who were thenceforward to influence the life of all countries in the Pacific Ocean. Within a few years Portuguese vessels had entered Japanese harbors, Portuguese traders and Jesuit missionaries had visited Japanese cities. These and later Spanish, Dutch, and English travelers were made welcome because they brought new knowledge.

The Japanese showed an interest in the Christian religion, which some of them at first supposed to be a new form of Buddhism, and they were enthusiastic about firearms and sailing ships because they soon saw that these were important instruments of power. For a time the rulers of Japan were on cordial terms with both missionaries and traders, but suspicions of the motives of these strangers began to grow in their minds until suddenly, without warning, an edict was issued in 1587 banishing all missionaries from Japan. The edict was not enforced, because the feudal rulers were in doubt as to whether they could admit the merchants while keeping out the priests. They wanted the knowledge which Europeans could supply, but wanted to preserve their native institutions unchanged, and uncontaminated by western influences. They played for a time with plans of compromise, hoping to find ways of keeping out dangerous ideas while letting in useful goods. So in 1597 they proscribed Christianity and persecuted Christians while allowing the continuance of foreign trade. But gradually they came to the conclusion that any form of direct intercourse with foreigners was dangerous.

They had gained considerable knowledge of the political rivalries and armed conflicts that were common among European powers, and they were well aware of the ambitions of the Portuguese and the Spaniards, followed by the English and the Dutch, to establish themselves in Eastern Asia. By the year 1600 there were few places in the Far East that Japanese travelers had not visited and a decade later many Japanese adventurers were trading or fighting, as merchants or pirates or mercenaries, in the Philippines, Indo-China, Malaya, and Siam. In a sea fight with Japanese corsairs off Singapore in 1604 a British East Indiaman suffered heavy losses. Such incidents were not uncommon, and the Japanese soon came to be feared in those southern seas as desperate and ruthless fighters.

It is one of the curious accidents of history that the Japanese, thus prepared for a career of conquest in the Pacific, should have suddenly withdrawn and left the field to Europeans. They seem to have concluded that they could not withstand the material power of the western nations, who had at their command superior resources. . . .

The foreigners were all expelled. Severe edicts were issued, forbidding all Japanese to leave their country, under pain of death. These laws were enforced with increasing rigor. Native Christians were massacred, foreign missionaries were executed, the building of ocean-going ships was prohibited, and foreign vessels venturing into Japanese ports were destroyed. By 1640 Japan had entered upon a period of almost complete seclusion, which lasted for some two hundred years.

This decision of the Japanese people to cut themselves off from the world at large, although the steps by which it was reached are fairly clear, is none the less mysterious. Only a few years before, not only had Japanese ships been ranging far and wide in the south seas, but the military leaders of the country, having overcome their opponents at home, had begun to look abroad for further conquests. In 1598 they sent a great expedition to Korea, with the object of invading and subduing China. This venture failed, and their armies returned home somewhat ingloriously. No further attempt was made. It is strange that so combative a people should have so suddenly renounced their ambitions, and so easily settled down to centuries of peace and isolation. It seems as if they have always been torn between a desire to expand and a fear lest the outside world should contaminate their cherished institutions.

Their decision to withdraw from the world gave to the Japanese an experience which few other peoples can have known. For more than two hundred years they lived in isolation, at peace, under an administration which was highly organized and efficiently conducted. They were governed by a military oligarchy composed of members of an hereditary caste who, though they no longer exercised the profession of arms, did not abandon their military outlook upon life. They stood for discipline, for the division of society into rigid classes, each with clearly defined functions. First came the soldier, then the farmer, then the craftsman, and last the merchant. The arts of peace were by no means neglected. Painters, poets, and philosophers had their place in this regulated world. Learning and aesthetic pursuits were regarded as next in dignity to martial exercises. It was a mature and static feudalism in which the virtues of obedience and loyalty were prized beyond all others. Within its limitations it was a very advanced society, based upon law and privilege, harsh in principle but in practice not without urbanity and elegance. Probably no contemporary European community was more civilized and polished.

Yet something was wrong with this society. It was a well contrived, well balanced arrangement of people and property, but it was not a living, growing organism. It must either change or collapse, and those who presided over it did not desire change. The precautions of the feudal rulers did not, however, in the long run prevent change. By the beginning of the nineteenth century the feudal structure was showing signs of weakness. There was discontent among the military class, the provincial clans began to chafe under the rule of their feudal overlords, while economic distress was stirring feelings of revolt among peasants and soldiers alike. So when in 1853 the American, Commodore Perry, came with his warships and under veiled threat requested Japan to open her doors, the long period of isolation came to a sudden end. There was internal turmoil and strife. There was a flare-up of anti-foreign sentiment combined with a strong movement to overthrow the feudal usurpers and restore to the Imperial House the power which it had not exercised for many centuries past. The watchword for the moment was "Restore the Emperor and Expel the Barbarians." But the forces in favor of opening the country were too strong and in the end the Emperor was restored while the barbarians were admitted. By 1868 Japan had fully emerged from seclusion. . . .

When Japan was faced at this time with problems which were no longer confined to those of internal administration, when she had to prepare herself for entry into an unfamiliar world, a thoughtful Japanese surveying his country's prospects may well have felt grave misgivings. He would know, from reports that had reached Japan through channels deliberately left open during the years of seclusion, that the western nations had for long past been engaged in warfare one with another, that they were strongly armed, and that the trading nations among them were bringing strong pressure to bear upon distant regions of the globe. Through a trickle of foreign books and from the reports of a few Dutch merchants who were, by exception, allowed to reside in close confinement in a small trading station at Nagasaki, he would have heard of the French Revolution, of the Napoleonic Wars, of the Crimean War, of the Indian Mutiny, and of wars against China in 1841 and 1857; and he would have concluded that the most important task of Japan was to conserve and develop her moral and material strength for her future protection.

This was the line which the rulers of Japan then followed. We know now that they were not thinking only in terms of defense, but that visions of domination in Asia were already in their mind's eye. But for the moment they were concerned to build up their country's strength. There were dangers ahead, for the Japanese people, released from the worst rigors of feudal discipline, were beginning to think for themselves and were inclined to demand new privileges, to break down the old feudal structure and to erect in its place a new form of government in which they would play a major part. The rulers of Japan did not approve of these aspirations. . . . They were for the most part members of the military caste, who had by no means abandoned ideas of feudal privilege. They held that the feudal order was a source of strength and unity, and that the Japanese tradition of obedience and loyalty was a most valuable asset. They were, of course, by their own training and temperament, opposed to popular rights. They felt, moreover, and not without reason, that if Japan were to embark now upon new political experiments, if she were to listen to the democratic doctrines that were now pervading western nations, she would be bound to go through a period of confusion which would delay, and perhaps even prevent her growth as a strong power.

Both their tradition and their judgment disposed them . . . to strive to incorporate foreign elements in the national life without changing its essence. This had been the way in which Japan had reacted to Chinese influences in the past, and this was the way in which she faced the problem of building upon a medieval foundation the apparatus of a modern westernized state.

The task of the leaders was not an easy one. Until the middle of the nineteenth century Japan had been an agrarian state, composed of a large number of feudal regimes, all owing allegiance to a supreme feudal ruler but at the same time preserving local independence in varying degree. If a strong national government was to be established and if ambitious economic and military plans were to be carried out, it was necessary not only to replace regional authority by central authority, but also to promote a national allegiance to take the place of those local or personal allegiances upon which the feudal system depended. The forms of centralized government were easy enough to devise. Its nucleus already existed, and there were plenty of useful models in western countries. But some means had to be found of focusing the loyalty of the Japanese people upon a supreme object. The obvious solution of this problem was to restore the prestige of the Emperor, who had for centuries past been kept in seclusion while one dynasty after another of feudal dictators exercised power in his name.

This plan lessened the risk of a return to feudal rivalry, while it enabled the effective leaders of Japan, no longer as feudal usurpers but as appointed statesmen and officials, to exercise power in the imperial name, once they could establish in the popular mind the idea of the supremacy of imperial rule. It was true that for long past the Emperor had been an aloof and shadowy figure venerated but playing no active part in the national life; but this very remoteness made it easy for the leaders to strengthen and inculcate a popular conception of the sovereign as an almost divine being, descendant of a long line of ancestors reaching back to the gods who, so the native myth pretended, were the founders of Japan.

A very deliberate process of indoctrination was carried out, by which this legendary belief was turned into a political axiom. It has been described by good authorities on modern Japanese history as the invention of a new religion. The earliest animistic creed of the Japanese, which was a worship of the powers of nature, was, in combination with their ancient custom of ancestor worship, ingeniously developed into a kind of state religion. In this cult (known as Shinto, the way of the Gods, in contrast to Butsudo, the way of the Buddha) the Emperor figures as both monarch and priest, ruling over the people as their supreme parent, and worshipping the divine ancestors on their behalf.

Obviously such doctrines could not have been imposed upon a people not prepared to accept them. Though they exaggerate in form, they represent in substance a body of traditional sentiment. It can be argued that the term "Emperor-worship" gives a wrong impression of the attitude of the Japanese people toward their sovereign, since divinity means less to them than to a people brought up in a monotheistic faith. It is true, however, that a great number of them do regard the Emperor with something like religious awe, and that most of the remainder, whether by force of habit or out of purely cynical acceptance of a politically useful convention, tend to subscribe to the doctrine that he is of divine origin and has divine authority. It is difficult to say how deeply rooted are these beliefs. In their extreme form they would probably not survive a great national disaster, in so far as they are a result of artificial propaganda rather than a genuine product of history. It is, however, not unlikely that even after defeat and internal confusion, the mass of the Japanese people will continue to regard the Imperial House with trust if not with veneration, as a stabilizing force in the national life.

These are only speculations; but it is certain that in the history of Japan's development as a modern state the principle of so-called divine rule has played an important part in concentrating upon national purposes the powerful spirit of loyalty which has been the distinguishing feature of the social system of the Japanese since early times. It is a significant thing that their native vocabulary contains many words which express the idea of duty or obligation, but none which corresponds closely to our western notion of individual rights. Much that seems strange in Japanese behavior can be understood if we remember that, throughout Japanese history, the moral law has been concerned not with the duty of the individual to himself, but with his duty to his family, to his teacher, to his employer, to his superior in the social hierarchy, to his community and to the state. Nobody who knows the Japanese well will contend that they are a cowed and docile people. Throughout their history they have shown themselves on occasion intractable and turbulent, ready to sacrifice their lives for religious or political beliefs. The humble peasant, goaded by oppression, has revolted against his feudal masters just as the arrogant Samurai, the member of the hereditary military caste, has fought against his feudal enemies. But all of them have for generation after generation been conditioned to obedience. In this respect social pressure has been intense and unremitting—so intense indeed that, when it is removed, the reaction is violent, leading to excesses which revolt and astonish those who have seen the Japanese only under discipline.

It was upon such foundations that modern Japan was built. . . .

JAPAN'S ISLAND HOME

By Philip Dunaway

From chap. 8 of *Geographical Foundations of National Power*. Army Service Forces Manual M-103-2. Government Printing Office, Washington, 1944. The author of this chapter has been an officer of the Foreign Economic Administration.

The homeland of Japan proper consists of four large volcanic islands—Honshu, Hokkaido, Shikoku and Kyushu—and several hundred smaller islands in the same arc-shaped chain.

The ends of the arc are each less than 200 miles from the continent, but the center is more than 600 miles away. The nearest neighbors of Japan proper are on the west: the U.S.S.R. (Vladivostok—Tsuruga, 490 miles; Vladivostok—Hakodate, 437 miles); Korea (Fusan—Moji, 123 miles); and China (Shanghai—Nagasaki, 463 miles). To the north, the island of Sakhalin and the Kuriles approach the islands of Japan proper. To the south the Ryukyu Archipelago and the Bonin-Volcano Island series form connecting links with Formosa and the Micronesian Island group respectively. To the east the nearest notable island is Midway (2,250 miles from Yokohama).

The position of the Japanese islands off the continent of Asia has often been compared to that of the British Isles (see Fig. 28, p. 488, above). In each case, the combination of proximity to and comparative isolation from the continent has permitted a semi-detached historical development. In each case there is inevitably an emphasis upon sea power. In each case industrialization occurred earlier than in the neighboring continental countries, and the search for markets for industrial goods has been accompanied by the acquisition of an oversea empire.

The differences, however, are fundamental. The British Isles [see chapter 6 above] lie nearly at the center of the hemisphere containing the land masses of the world. Japan lies on the outer margin of this hemisphere. . . . It possesses centrality only with respect to the North Pacific sea routes, a trade channel of considerable importance but fairly minor in comparison with the North Atlantic or Mediterranean trunk lines. Moreover, the neighboring continent is less rich in natural resources and productive population than the European continent. Because Japan lies on the eastern rather than the western margin of the continent, its climate differs markedly from that of Great Britain and is, on the whole, less healthful.

The area of Japan proper, 148,000 square miles, is seven-tenths that of France and almost exactly that of Montana. Honshu, the largest island, has an area a little less than the combined areas of New York and Pennsylvania but with more than double their population. Hokkaido, lying in about the same latitude as Maine, has approximately the same area and four times the population. Shikoku, in the general latitude of South Carolina, has less than one-fourth the area but almost double the population. Kyushu, between the same parallels as Georgia, has one-fourth the area and almost five times the population.

The irregularly shaped islands at no place are more than 260 miles in width. Most inland points are considerably less than 100 miles from the sea. If the interior were extensively developed and heavily settled, the protection afforded by the mountainous relief would compensate in part for the lack of protection in depth. There is, however, little to defend in the interior since the areas important to the Japanese economy and culture lie on the coasts.

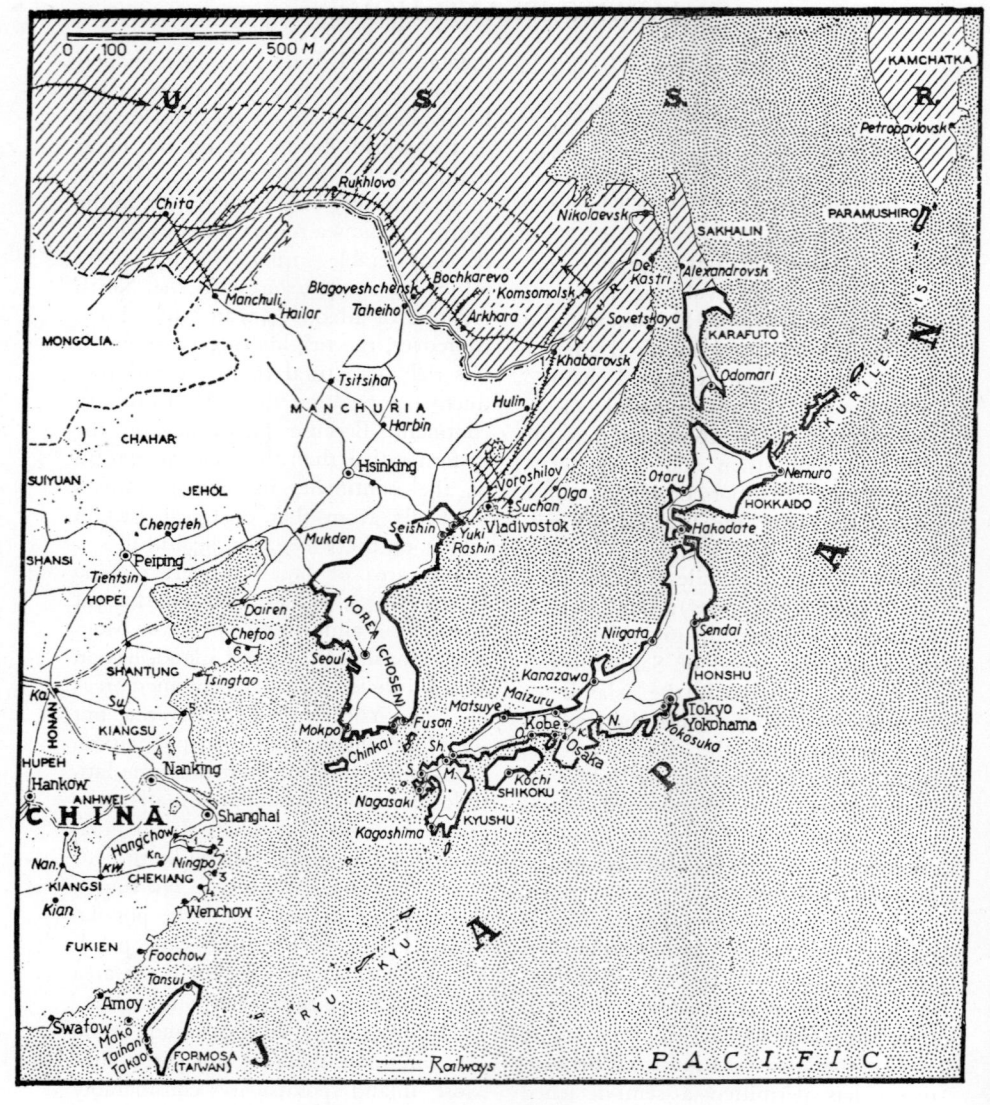

Fig. 30. Japan and Eastern Asia.
From E. A. Mowrer and M. Rajchman, *Global War, An Atlas of World Strategy*.
Copyright 1942 by William Morrow & Co., New York; reproduced by permission.
Symbols on the map indicate the following:

K	Kyoto	M	Moji	S	Sasebo	1	Shaohing	4	Haimen
Ka	Kaifeng	N	Nagoya	Sh	Shimonoseki	2	Chinhai	5	Haichow
Kn	Kinhwa	Nan	Nanchang	Su	Suchow	3	Shipu	6	Weihaiwei
Kw	Kweiki	O	Okayama						

NATURE'S GIFTS TO THE JAPANESE

By G. B. Cressey

From chap. 10 of *Asia's Lands and Peoples*, by G. B. Cressey. Copyright 1944 by McGraw-Hill Book Co., New York; reproduced by permission. The writer, professor of geography at Stanford University, is a recognized authority on the Far East.

The Japanese Empire is both insular and mountainous. Land and water are everywhere near each other, and the few plains are so small that one is almost always within sight of mountains. The encircling seas have such a large role that the geography of Japan is nearly as much hydrography as topography. . . .

The Pacific Ocean is encircled by a series of rugged Tertiary mountains from Cape Horn through Alaska to Australia. Along the coast of Asia these form a festoon of mountainous island arcs, each with its ends curving inward towards the continent. Japan proper occupies one of these arcs, while the island possessions of the Chishima (Kuriles) and the Ryukyu are similar arcs to the north and south. From north to south these arcs enclose the Sea of Okhotsk, Sea of Japan, and East China Sea.

If we could take away the encircling ocean, the Japanese archipelago would stand out as a great mountain range, with peaks rising five and six miles above their base. And if we could change geological history to moving picture speed, we might observe the frequency with which volcanoes and block faulting and crustal folding have disturbed the configuration of Japan. Scattered sedimentary rocks reveal that the islands have been submerged at various times since the Pre-Cambrian, while widespread lava flows, ash deposits, and intrusions betray repeated igneous activity. In tectonics and topography, Japan is so young that there has not been time to round off the edges. Slopes are unusually steep and summits jagged. . . .

Land that is even approximately level is limited to discontinuous fragments of uplifted sea floor, interior basins filled with debris, alluvial flood plains and deltas, and the dissected terraces of earlier streams or marine plains. Valley floors have a noticeable slope, and down them during the rainy season flow turbulent yet overloaded mountain streams, whose braided courses are strewn with sand and cobbles. On either side dikes guard the adjoining fields, for so much deposition has occurred that the bed of the stream may be level with or above the surrounding countryside.

Not all of the nearly level land is usable. Coastal swamps and stony river beds almost defy reclamation. The largest areas of unused level land are the old flood plains and coastal plains which now stand as terraces a few tens or even hundreds of feet above present stream levels. These former surfaces, graded to sea level when the land was lower but now uplifted and dissected, are known as diluvial terraces, in contrast to the present-day undissected surfaces called alluvial. In some plains they cover a quarter to a half the lowland area. Since diluvial terraces are built of sand and gravel and have a low water table, they are of limited use for Japan's great crop, rice. Irrigation is difficult.

These isolated and discontinuous plains, peripheral and interior, form the principal home for the 70 million Japanese who live within Japan proper. The total level area does not exceed 20,000 square miles, no larger than half the state of Ohio. The four main islands contain about three dozen lowland areas large enough to identify, ranging from the Kwanto Plain near

Tokyo, with an area of about 2,500 square miles, of which more than half is diluvial, to strips a few hundred yards in width and a few miles in length. . . .

Japanese rivers are short, with the longest but 229 miles. Few of them are suitable for navigation, owing to their swiftness as well as to the variation in seasonal flow. There are many possibilities for hydroelectric power development, but sites for adequate reservoir storage are seldom available. . . .

Fringing the sea are two types of coastline, one with cliffs and offshore islands, the other low and often swampy and usually near the mouth of a short torrential stream. The coast is highly irregular and has numerous large embayments on the Pacific side. The ratio of 1 mile of coastline to 8.5 square miles of area, in contrast to 1 to 13 for Great Britain, reflects the [extent to which the Japanese live near the sea]. . . .

With only one-seventh of the land approximately level, and much of the rest too steep to be terraced or otherwise utilized except for forests, the Japanese face inescapable problems. Viewed from the sea, Japan rises hill upon hill; seen from the land the panorama is water, water everywhere. The two dominant aspects of her physical setting are thus the restricted extent of level land and insularity. Over large areas the Japanese are plainsmen enveloped in mountains; elsewhere they became fishermen.

Climate. Japan's climate cannot be judged by latitude and solar insolation alone. It is warmer than comparable parts of China to the west, yet cooler than Mediterranean lands on the same parallel. Since the islands lie off the east coast of a great land mass, powerful continental influences are modified by marine conditions.

No simple summary can give an adequate picture of Japanese climate. The main islands have a latitudinal extent of a thousand miles, and the irregularities of topography introduce sharp vertical contrasts. If placed along the Atlantic seaboard, Japan proper would reach from Maine to Georgia, while the Empire would extend from Labrador to Brazil. Although summer conditions in Japan closely correspond to those in the northeastern United States, Japanese winters are colder. At both seasons Japan has higher humidity. The most populous part of Japan lies in the latitude of the Carolinas, 400 miles south of the American center of population.

During the summer, a flow of hot moist air moves over Japan from the Pacific. In winter months conditions are reversed with strong winds, cold and dry, from Siberia. Thus tropical Pacific air masses dominate one season, while polar continental air masses rule the other; of these the latter are the more dynamic. . . .

All parts of the four main islands have adequate precipitation, but the pattern is very patchy, owing to relief. Several stations in the south along the Pacific receive over 125 inches and there is a similar precipitation maximum along the central part of the Japan Sea side. Rainfall in interior basins only drops below 40 inches in a few localities. Except along the west coast, the precipitation maximum occurs at most stations of Old Japan during the summer. . . . Winter winds are dry as they blow out from the interior of Asia, but in crossing the Japan Sea they acquire some moisture and yield heavy snowfall on the western slopes of Honshu and Hokkaido. Snow remains on the ground along the west coast as far south as central Honshu; on the Pacific side, in contrast, only the northern end of the island has a snow cover.

August is the hottest month except in Formosa where July temperatures reach the maximum. Tropical clothing is worn everywhere during the summer even in Hokkaido, and the high humidity and sultry air are enervating. South of Tokyo, books, shoes, and clothing are quickly covered with mildew in summer. Mosquito nets are required almost the year around in southern Japan. The July temperature difference from southern Kyushu to central Hokkaido is but 9° F., whereas in January the range is 29° F. . . .

The frost-free period, essentially equivalent to the growing season, ranges from 120 days in the interior of Hokkaido and 160 days in the mountainous Honshu to 240 days along the southeastern coast. Thus two crops of rice may be grown in parts of Kyushu, Shikoku, and the southern peninsulas of Honshu. . . .

Forests and Soils. Half of Japan is still covered with forests, though little of it is virgin growth. . . . Charcoal is an important forest product and the chief household fuel. Its value is almost equal to all timber. Many villages have their communal areas where it is produced for domestic needs, and it is a common sight to see lines of people coming out of the woods laden with bundles of charcoal. The annual value of charcoal is three-fourths the value of sawn timber. Whereas the latter is largely from conifers, hardwoods are preferred for the former.

Despite improvements in all aspects of forestry, the supply is inadequate, so that both timber and wood pulp are imported. Oregon, Washington, and British Columbia are a large source of supply, and Manchuria is increasingly important. Hokkaido and Korea have the largest domestic reserves. . . .

Mineral Resources. The story of Japan's mineral wealth is easily told. There is a wide variety of natural resources within Old Japan, but practically none of them is adequate for current industrial needs. Only coal, copper, gold, silver, and sulphur are present in large quantities, and of these only sulphur and gold are available for export. In normal years the Japanese Empire as a whole produces but two-thirds of her copper, one-third of her zinc, one-third of her salt, one-fourth of her tin, one-twelfth of her lead, one-sixth of her iron, and one-tenth of her consumption of petroleum. Nickel, aluminum, and magnesium are entirely lacking. Even the domestic production of coal is but nine-tenths of the consumption, largely because of the necessity of importing special coking coals.

. . . Despite her material handicaps at home, Japan has achieved a great industrial development on the basis of imported raw materials, such as oil and scrap steel from the United States, and iron ore from the South Seas.

. . . Japan is comfortably supplied with coal and hydroelectricity but has very little oil and no natural gas. Coal is widely distributed and predominantly bituminous of only fair quality. Almost none is suitable for high-grade metallurgical coke.

The official reserves as estimated in 1932 are as follows:

Proved reserves...... 5,960,000,000 tons
Probable reserves.... 4,045,000,000 "
Possible reserves...... 6,685,000,000 "

Total reserves........ 16,690,000,000 "

. . . In 1941 production probably amounted to 55,500,000 metric tons within the Empire, which includes imports amounting to 5,000,000 metric tons from Korea, 2,500,000 each from Formosa and Sakhalin, and 4,000,000 metric tons from outside the Empire, largely China and Indo-China. . . .

Since domestic coal is generally unfit for metallurgical coke, it is necessary to import suitable coal from Penhsihu in Manchuria, Kaiping in north China, and Hongay in Indo-China.

Japan's per capita reserves, even including all possible deposits, amount to but 238 tons per capita as compared with 4,070 for the United Kingdom and 27,500 for the United States. Although production may be expected to continue for many years and should prove adequate for domestic needs in time of peace, there is no likelihood that Japan can increase her production of this basic source of power so as to compete in heavy industries with the leading countries of the world. Any great industrialization must rest on imported coal.

The second great source of modern power is petroleum. Japan's two dozen producing districts extend from Karafuto in the north to Formosa in the south, with the principal area in the Niigata and Akita prefectures on the Japan Sea side of Honshu. There are about 4,000 wells, yielding an average production of less than two barrels per day. The 1941 production in Japan proper of 2,659,000 barrels is approximately equal to the daily yield in the United States, and represents but 0.1 per cent of the world production. An additional 1,000,000 barrels is secured from Formosa and concessions in Soviet Sakhalin. Despite strenuous governmental efforts over the past decade, there is little geological prospect that the output can be materially increased. . . . By 1939 imports had increased to over eight times domestic production.

In addition to large imports from the United States and the Netherlands Indies prior to the Second World War, fuel oil for the navy was distilled from oil shale in Manchuria. In 1939 the consumption of oil products in Japan amounted to 25,400,000 barrels. No commercial supplies of natural gas are reported.

The rugged topography and heavy precipitation of the central mountainous area lend themselves to the development of waterpower. In 1936 the total consumption of hydroelectric power amounted to nearly 20 billion kilowatt-hours as compared with nearly 5 billion kilowatt-hours of electricity produced by coal. Despite the 50 per cent growth of hydroelectric power in the previous five years, it was not possible to meet the demands, so that the use of thermal-electric power increased by 250 per cent. Japan still has undeveloped waterpower sites, but they are mostly small in size and lack adequate reservoir storage to equalize the highly seasonal flow. Out of an ultimate theoretical production of 10 million kw., half is already in use. . . .

Japan's resources of iron ore are especially insufficient. Reserves for the entire Empire are estimated at 90,000,000 metric tons, of which 10,000,000 are in Korea. This compares with some 5,000,000,000 tons in the United States. Less than a dozen deposits are in commercial production in Japan proper. Domestic output of iron ore in Japan proper for 1941 amounted to 935,000 metric tons largely in Hokkaido, which was but 13 per cent of the requirements. The fivefold increase in the preceding decade reflects strenuous mining efforts rather than large reserves. The deficiency was met by importations from Korea, Tayeh in the central Yangtze Valley amounting to nearly 500,000 metric tons in 1940, Johore and elsewhere in Malaya to the extent of 1,874,000 metric tons in 1940, and the Philippine Islands which supplied 1,236,000 metric tons in the same year. British India has supplied as much as 1,000,000 tons annually plus 300,000 tons of pig iron. Australia has shipped several hundred thousand tons a year.

Although Japan imported 35 per cent of her pig iron, the use of large quantities of imported scrap enabled her to carry on a slight export of steel, chiefly to her colonies and to Manchuria.

Copper was the second most important mineral product in Japan until 1935, and the country ranks seventh in world production. At one time Japan had a large surplus for export, but prior to the Second World War she found it necessary to import substantial quantities of copper, largely from the United States. . . .

Zinc is much more plentiful than lead, amounting to about 60,000 and 15,000 tons, respectively. There is also some production of tin and chromium. There are no domestic ores of aluminum in Japan proper. . . . Less than half Japan's manganese is obtained at home. Korea contributes nearly 80,000 tons of graphite.

The most noteworthy nonmetallic resource of the islands is sulphur, one of the basic tonnage materials needed for industry. High-grade deposits are widely distributed, usually in association with volcanic rocks. . . . Availability of sulphur furnishes a basis for the growth of such industries as paper, celluloid, and rayon. About a third of the production is available for export. . . .

Salt is obtained from sea water, but the high humidity does not favor solar evaporation. Production around the Inland Sea is barely sufficient for salt in foodstuffs, and most of the industrial needs, which are twice those of foodstuff salt, are secured from East Africa and the North China coast.

Despite strenuous efforts for many years to increase the home supply of minerals, the percentage of import remains high. Thus in 1931 production of natural resources within the Empire amounted to 283,000,000 yen, with supplementary imports of 220,000,000 yen, a total sufficiency of 60 per cent. In 1936 the internal supply . . . accounted for 61 per cent of the total. . . .

It may be of interest to compare the production of certain basic resources in the Japanese Empire with those in the United States. America's output of copper is 7 times that of Japan; coal 10 times; iron 40 times; and oil 432 times. . . .

The geology of Japan and her possessions is now well enough known to make it abundantly clear that there is no likelihood of great industrial developments in terms of her own mineral resources. There is not even enough for domestic needs, let alone world trade. Fortunately, Japan does have coal, although it lacks coking qualities. Economic or political conditions may make it feasible to import ores from the mainland, but it does not seem likely that Japan can permanently enjoy a dominant position in the mineral industry of eastern Asia. Her industrial future would appear to rely upon such resources as cheap labor, limited agricultural products, and skill.

JAPAN'S HUMAN RESOURCES

By the Editors

The population of Japan changed but little in size during the two centuries in which that country lived a hermit existence. At the time of Commodore Perry's visit in 1853, the total number living in the Japanese islands probably did not exceed 30 millions. Thereafter the total increased steadily. By 1910 it was about 50 millions. The first systematic census, taken in 1920, showed a population of nearly 56 millions. By 1940 this had grown to 73 millions.

The growth of numbers has been accompanied by a shift in the distribution between city and country. In 1920 approximately 38 million Japanese lived in communities of less than 10,000. Twenty years later the number was less than 37 millions. In the same period the city-dwellers increased from 18 millions to over 36 millions. In terms of percentage, the rural population declined from 68 to 51 per cent of the total, while the urban population increased from 32 to 49 per cent. During this period the combined population of the six largest cities grew from 5.5 millions to 14.4 millions.

MEANING OF RECENT POPULATION TRENDS

By G. T. Trewartha

From chap. 5 of *Japan, A Physical and Regional Geography*, by G. T. Trewartha. Copyright 1945 by the University of Wisconsin Press, Madison; reproduced by permission. The author is professor of geography at the University of Wisconsin.

With a time lag of about half a century, Japan is duplicating the population history of Western Europe and the United States. The only reason that its large numerical increases are so conspicuous is that they come at a time when population growth in many western countries has begun to level off. The intercensal increase in population was 6.7 per cent in 1920-1925, 7.9 per cent in 1925-1930, 7.5 per cent in 1930-1935, and 5.6 per cent in 1935-1940. The quinquennium 1930-1935 saw a maximum absolute increase of 4.8 millions, which declined to 3.9 millions in the next five-year intercensal period.

The large annual increment to Japan's already very large and dense population, together with such impedimenta to trade as high tariffs, empire preference, quotas, and exchange restrictions, which became increasingly prevalent during the past decade, made it more and more difficult for resource-poor Japan to exchange her manufactures for raw materials on world markets. In the face of this situation the military and nationalist elements in Japan found it easy to convince themselves that economic and strategic security required control of southeastern Asia, which could be developed both as a market for manufactures and as a source of raw materials and food. This was the theme of the propaganda disseminated to prepare the country for the present war.

The crude birth-rate for Japan for about forty years prior to 1935 was between 30 and 36 per 1,000 population. This is about double the crude birth-rate of Northern and Western Europe and of the United States during the past decade. Since 1930 when the rate reached its all-time high of 36.2, it has declined steadily; in 1935 it was 31.6, and in 1938, 27.0. More refined measurements clearly establish the fact that fertility in Japan began a definite downward trend as early as about 1920. The number of births per 1,000 women in the reproductive period of life decreased from 169.4 in 1920 to 142.6 in 1935. Penrose attributes this partly to the increasingly widespread practice of birth control by the rapidly expanding urban population, which recognized the handicap of large families in city living.

But despite this decline in reproduction rates for nearly all ages of mothers, there has been no commensurate reduction in the annual increment of population; on the contrary, it actually increased somewhat between 1920 and 1935. The reason is that mortality rates have declined more rapidly than the birth-rate. Thus the crude death-rate in Japan declined from 26.8 in 1918 to 25.4 in 1920 to 16.7 in 1935. Infant mortality especially showed a sharp decline; from 166 deaths under age one per 1,000 live births in 1920 to 106 in 1937. Nevertheless the mortality figures of Japan are still 4 to 6 per 1,000 higher than in Northern and Western Europe.

It is, then, Japan's oriental birth-rate and occidental death-rate that produced, until about 1935 or a little later, an annual increase in population of almost a million despite a falling reproduction rate. If the war in China, and thereafter World War II, had not interrupted normal living in Japan, mortality rates would probably have continued to decline, but it is dubious whether they could have kept pace with the decline in reproduction rates. Ultimately the net rate of population increase would have begun to fall. Until 1935 the annual rate of population increase actually mounted; in the period 1930-1935 it rose to 1.5 per cent. During the next five years, however, it declined to 1.1 per cent. Thus the problem created by a rapid increase in population would slowly have disappeared. Nevertheless the age distribution of the Japanese population, characterized by a large proportion of young people, indicates that rapid growth is possible for some time to come. In this respect Japan resembles Eastern Europe and Soviet Russia more than Western and Northern Europe, where the percentages of mature and older people are greater. In 1935 almost 40 per cent of Nippon's population was under fifteen years of age, as compared with 22 per cent in the British Isles, 24 per cent in Western and Central Europe, and about 25 per cent in the United States. Only 7.8 per cent of Japan's population is between the ages of fifty and fifty-nine, as compared with nearly 10 per cent in the United States and over 11 per cent in France. With such an age distribution Japan may not feel the full effects of declining fertility for several decades. Before the outbreak of the Sino-Japanese War in 1937 it was estimated that the population of Nippon would reach 80 million by 1950 and 105 million by 1970. Dr. Ueda, however, concluded that it could never reach 100 million. Under present conditions all such prophecies are of course meaningless, for no one knows what the conditions will be in Japan after this war.

Since the outbreak of the Sino-Japanese War in 1937 population growth has been abnormal. Statistics on births, deaths, and marriages have not been published since 1939, but the figures for 1938 reveal that certain trends had begun to accelerate. In that year as compared with 1937 there was an increase in total deaths and a sharp decline in births, and hence a sharp decline in the excess of births over deaths. In 1938 the crude birth-rate (26.7 per 1,000) was the lowest it had been in many decades, and the population increase (9.3 per 1,000) was about 33 per cent less than in the previous year. In the fourth quarter of 1938 there were 20 per cent fewer births than in the same period of 1937. Even if the rate declined no further, the total births in 1939 would have fallen to about 1,750,000, the lowest figure since 1920. As reckoned from October to October the net population growth of 970,000 in the 1937-1938 period would have declined to 653,000 in 1938-1939 and to 239,000 in 1939-1940. It may have become nearly static by 1940. All this of course reflects the military mobilization for the Sino-Japanese War and the emigration of civilian war workers to the industrial centers of Manchuria, Korea, and China, which is attended by increasing separation of the sexes. The rise in mortality in 1938 seems to indicate a decline in Japan's national health as a result of the war in China and the exertion being made for the more serious conflict to follow. Since 1940 the situation has been aggravated by the much greater manpower mobilization, the higher mortality due to military casualties, and the weakened resistance to disease induced by the decreased food supply, the crowded conditions in industrial cities, and the shortage of domestic fuel.

Strangely enough, the decline in the birth-rate and more recently in the rate of population growth have alarmed official circles. . . .

JAPAN'S ECONOMIC POTENTIAL

By Philip Dunaway

Adapted from chap. 8 of *Geographical Foundations of National Power*. Army Service Forces Manual M-103-2. Government Printing Office, Washington, 1944.

In the economy of Japan as it was organized before the war, the home country had an abundance of only four important elements: fish, raw silk, electric power, and human labor.

The resources of Japan proper would probably have been adequate to provide a subsistence diet for the population, but in practice the resources of the dependencies were made use of to supplement the domestic supply, especially of rice, sugar, fruits, and soya beans. Rice was imported from Formosa and Korea, sugar and fruits from Formosa, and soya beans principally from Manchuria. There were small imports of wheat, meat, fish, and dairy products from foreign countries, and there were exportable surpluses of fish and tea.

Although Japanese agriculture supplies four-fifths of the national requirement of rice and one-third of the soya beans, the naturally poor soil of Japan has been depleted by intensive cropping and requires fertilizer on an ever-increasing scale. To provide this, aside from fish residue, beancake, and ammonium, Japan must import potash, nitrates, and phosphates. Because agriculture has been organized on the basis of surplus farm labor, production necessarily suffers when war calls vast numbers of men to the colors.

The metal and machinery industries can probably be operated so long as Japan obtains iron ore and pig iron from Manchuria and coking coal from North China, and supplements the stockpile of imported steel scrap with domestic scrap and scrap from the battlefields. General manufacturing in Japan proper is wholly dependent on imports for its supply of raw cotton, rubber, and most light metals. So long as Japan dominated the Netherlands East Indies and Malaya and could supply shipping, there was ample rubber and petroleum, adequate quantities of bauxite, and a small amount of nickel for war industries. Once these sources were lost, Japan had to rely on stockpiles and the output of synthetic industry at home and in Manchuria and Korea. Coal liquefaction plants were in operation by 1938, but there is no record of synthetic rubber development. . . .

INDUSTRIAL EXPANSION FOR WAR

By A. J. Grajdanzev

From "Japan's Economy Since Pearl Harbor," by A. J. Grajdanzev, in *Far Eastern Survey*, June 14, 1943. Published by the American Council, Institute of Pacific Relations, New York; reproduced by permission.

The present war in the Pacific would have been impossible without a major development of industry in Japan and fundamental changes in its structure. In 1929 Japan was a great textile power; her industry was predominantly so-called light industry, specializing particularly in the production of textiles. In the same year, her production of coal was less than 7 per cent and of steel and machinery less than 5 per cent of United States' production. . . .

The ten years between the occupation of Manchuria and the Pacific war were used by Japan in securing her rear by wars in China; in the advance to the south, obtaining the sources of raw materials; in expanding production facilities in Japan proper. . . .

The textile industry, which held first place in 1929, dropped to second place in 1938; no doubt by 1941 it had dropped to fourth place, after metals, machinery and tools, and chemicals. Metals and machinery production, responsible for 17.7 per cent of the total gross value of production in 1929, rose to 43.2 per cent in 1938 and continued to rise thereafter.

But these figures do not tell the whole story. Civilian needs in metals, tools, and machines have been almost completely neglected and production today is limited to war demands. Civilians cannot buy even nails. In this way, the munitions industry between July 1937 and December 1941 was expanded "seven- or eight-fold" and the productive capacity of aircraft industry increased "more than ten times." These results convinced the Japanese militarists that after the occupation of Southeast Asia they could do even better.

Shoji Watanabe, Director of Mitsui Seimei (Mitsui Life Insurance Co.), declared: "The future demands that Japan should increase in strength more than eight times that of her present status. Japan must be prepared for at least twenty more years of war. There is no need to fear that, for the success of the Imperial forces has assured that she will not suffer from the lack of necessary raw materials. . . ."

The Japanese economy today is one of extreme scarcity; there are shortages everywhere. Under these conditions it is important to know which industries are getting first claim, i.e., what is the system of priorities, and also within each industry who is getting the raw materials? The question was answered by Lt. Gen. Suzuki (President of the Cabinet of the Planning Board). In May 1942 he listed the following order of priorities to meet competing demands: "(1) Adequate supply of war materials. (2) Security of supplying power and of the production required for replenishment of war materials. (3) Supply of materials absolutely necessary for the expansion of productivity, which is essential for the successful prosecution of protracted warfare. (4) Stabilization of livelihood."

In other words, first come all the supplies for the actual prosecution of the war; second, for tomorrow's war; third, for the long-term war; and fourth, what is left, for civilian consumption. . . .

JAPAN'S ECONOMIC DILEMMA

By the Editors of "Fortune"

From "Little Industry, Big War," in *Fortune* magazine, April 1944. Copyright 1944 by Time Inc.; reproduced by permission. This entire issue was devoted to various aspects of Japan's power and policies in the present war.

WHEN Japan went to war with China [in 1937] her industry was defective in two respects. It was light. Far too many Japanese mills and factories produced textiles and consumer goods, too few produced steel, machinery, and chemicals. And Japan was poor in raw materials. Of coal, iron, and oil, the trinity of indispensables, she had sufficient supplies only of coal.

Japan built steel mills, chemical works, automotive plants, and other heavy industry with astonishing speed. After fighting five years . . . she had acquired all the raw materials she needed. Indeed, totting up what she found in the Philippines, Malaya, Thailand, Borneo, Sumatra, Java, and Burma, she made a fabulous haul. But then Japan's good fortune came to an end. To use these imperial riches to enlarge her new, compact industry Japan needed time. She also needed peace. With these in her favor, she might well have become one of the strongest industrial powers of all time. But having taken up the sword to gain an empire, she could not lay down the sword while she developed the empire. Back of Japan's inability to exploit her new wealth, lies the half-completed story of the greatest miscarriage of modern imperialism.

Japanese industry is very new. When it was launched in the last quarter of the last century, England's black country had been black for nearly a hundred years. Even the Ruhr and the Monongahela were already lined with furnaces and factories. And Japan began in the 'eighties and 'nineties not with steel but with raw silk, which paid for spindles and looms. The factories that today supply the army and navy of the Emperor have been built within the last twenty-five years, well within the active lifetime of the middle-aged men who run Japan.

This industry is also compact. Along the southern coast of Honshu, the main island of Japan, are six great industrial cities all within an airline distance no greater than that from New York to Washington. In 1936 these six cities accounted for more than a third of the value of all factory production of Japan. Five of them are clustered in two great metropolitan seaport zones.

Midway along the coast is the Kwanto—the metropolitan area that includes Tokyo and its adjacent seaport, Yokohama. Here is the capital of empire, the headquarters of Japanese industry, commerce, and finance, and the seat of the great industrial families (with one exception). Here also is one of the great centers of Japanese heavy industry.

Two hundred and fifty miles to the west is the Kinki. This is a triangle with sides fifteen to thirty miles long and, as its points, the cities of Osaka, Kyoto, and Kobe. With a population of 5 million in 1935 (compared to 11 million in the Kwanto) the Kinki was the peacetime home of light industry, the arts and crafts. It has now become Japan's leading center of war production. Osaka, largest city of the three, is the seat of the Sumitomo—the metals and machinery family of Japan.

About 100 miles from Osaka on the road to Tokyo is Nagoya. Though it now has a population of well over a million, Nagoya is the newest of the industrial cities of Japan. Before the war it made porcelain and wove some of the fine fabrics to which Japan, having already captured the market for coarser counts, was turning.

Far to the west on the island of Kyushu is Nagasaki, long a port of call for the China trade. And 100 miles northeast of Nagasaki are the strategic coal and steel towns of Fukuoka and Yawata. In Manchuria are coke ovens and blast furnaces (about one-fifth of Japan's pig iron now comes from Manchuria) and even automobile factories. These outlands are important. But the heart of Japan's industrial empire could be viewed from a DC-3 in an hour and a half.

That is how it was and that is how it probably remains. . . .

That Japan has moved some highly strategic industry and workers out of the large cities may be assumed. New war industries have probably been located with an eye to decentralization. That most prewar industry remains where it can employ the people of the six big cities is certain.

The compact geography of Japan's industry is less remarkable than its compact ownership. . . . The corporation, the holding company, and the trust are all in the business lexicon of Japan. But the word Zaibatsu (wealthy family) is more important than any of these. The most distinctive feature of Japanese business is this handful of great families that monopolize it. . . .

When Japan went to war with China in 1937 some fifteen interests controlled more than two-thirds of the country's trade and industry. The four great family houses, Mitsui, Mitsubishi, Sumitomo, and Yasuda, controlled close to one-third. Mitsui, biggest of them all, did well over a tenth of the business of the island empire. . . .

Until the 'thirties the great monopolists also monopolized the affairs of state. They invested in the two indistinguishably respectable parties in the Diet; watched the police keep the Japanese proletariat from showing any obvious discontent; remained unworried by Japan's miniscule labor movement; and expanded their enterprises and their profits prodigiously. The depression, which came to Japan in the late 'twenties, wiped out or crippled thousands of small businesses—many of them in debt to the big families. Mitsui, Mitsubishi, et al came through unscathed and superficially more powerful than ever.

Actually they were weaker. Public opinion or whatever in Japan passes for it turned against the big families. Most of all it turned against Mitsui. . . .

In 1931, while Mitsui was in trouble in Tokyo, the officers of the Kwantung Army led their men into Manchuria. Development of the territory was to be a military project; the young officers announced to all Japan that the Zaibatsu would participate in production and profits in Manchuria only as the well-regulated guests of the army. The army wanted the money of the big families. The big families were reluctant to invest and develop on the army's terms so the army tried to find businessmen of its own.

For a while the job of developing Manchuria was given to the South Manchuria Railway, which, in turn, was under close army control. Then in 1937 management of all coal and metals mining and heavy manufacture was turned over to the army-sponsored Manchuria Industrial Development Co. headed by Yoshisuke Aikawa. . . .

The big houses heartily disliked this new army-sponsored competition. The army bitterly resented the reluctance of the large houses to invest in its new enterprise.

When war with China broke out, the rivalry between the old business interests and the army took a new turn. At stake now was the control over the machinery of war mobilization. The fight over this was deep and bitter—and it was by no means settled when Kwantung-trained General Tojo became Premier in 1941. The shifts and countershifts, the improvisation and compromise that have since occurred in Japanese war organization make Washington, by contrast, seem a model of well-organized stability. . . .

Like all countries heading for industrialization, Japan began with textiles. She built, by mechanical standards, the most efficient textile mills in the world. The workers were disciplined. Their real income, though good by oriental standards, was unbelievably low by standards of the West. Cloth could be sold at bargain prices. In 1933 Japan passed Britain as a world exporter of textiles and from then on led the field.

To textiles, in the years following the First World War, Japan added a wide assortment of other light consumer goods. Throughout the world the imprint "Made in Japan" became synonymous with cheap, and sometimes incredibly cheap, sneakers, flashlights, bicycles, ash trays, golf balls, and patriotic emblems for loyal citizens of the importing country.

But textiles were the heart of Japanese industry until the decade before she went to war. In 1930 one out of every four of her industrial workers made textiles; one in three made textiles or clothing. The textile industry was typical also of the way Japan did business with the world. Raw cotton was imported from the U.S., India, Brazil, Egypt, and China. Even rayon pulp was purchased from the U.S., Canada, and Scandinavia, while the home forests were saved. The cloth was sold in India, China, Indonesia, Africa, and South America. Japan processed the raw materials of foreigners for foreigners.

To prepare for war, Japan needed first to build a heavy industry. This she did. Aided by a fortunately timed currency depreciation and, perhaps, a resiliency the western countries lacked, Japan recovered early from the depression. Production rose while U.S. and even German industry remained in the doldrums. And production rose most in the heavy industries, in steel, shipbuilding, and machinery. Some increase in heavy industry is normal in a young country. More of the increase in Japan was deliberately ordered by the Japanese government.

In the late summer of 1937 textile manufacture and other light industry were classed as "non-essential" and virtually forbidden to borrow money for expansion. . . . Steel and other heavy producers, on the other hand, were exempted from direct taxation and liberally supplied with loans. The Japanese Industrial Bank, Japan's equivalent of the Defense Plant Corporation, was greatly expanded after the outbreak of the China war. Its job was to see that heavy industry had lots of money.

In July 1938, the famous Link system was introduced. Japanese business houses were allowed to import raw cotton (and subsequently wool and synthetic fiber) only if an equivalent quantity of finished cloth was exported. By this device all raw cotton imports—normally Japan's biggest purchases from abroad—were re-exported; none was wasted on the people of Japan. Whatever value the little girls in the textile mills of Nagoya added to the Mississippi cotton they spun could all be spent abroad for oil, machine tools, and scrap. So even the textile mills became the full-time servant of heavy industry.

Finally, in 1941, with freezing of her assets and then the war, many of the textile mills were closed down. So were other civilian industries. In Japan's war economy, manpower and materials are strictly reserved for war. A category of essential civilian goods scarcely exists. The civilian does without.

Steel mills and shipyards are not enough: there must be factories to manufacture *every* kind of equipment that modern war requires, for in wartime the gaps cannot be filled by imports. In the 'thirties Japan needed to make certain that heavy industry was complete.

The consensus is that in most respects she succeeded. In all western countries an automobile industry fathered the manufacture of tanks and aircraft, as well as other combat vehicles and trucks. In 1929 the Japanese automobile industry produced just 437 cars. But Japan did create an automobile industry. Most of it was built after 1936 (when 9,600 cars were manufactured) and most of the expansion of the aircraft industry is believed to have occurred after 1938.

Japan began making machine tools in 1932. The output to this day is small —General Motors would have needed the entire production for two or three years to tool its war plants. But Japan imported large numbers of tools before the war and she seized a few in Manila and Singapore. Tools are durable. With what she has and can make, Japan can get along. . . .

[In] January [1944] the Japanese Diet was asked for 100 million yen to be paid in rewards to inventors who contributed to what Representative Hajime Hoshi declared had become a "war of inventions." This might once have been considered a feeble effort to compensate for lack of innovating power in Japanese industry. But the myth that the Japanese are only imitators has now been exploded—exploded by aircraft, ordnance, and ship design that show authentic originality. Japanese industry does not have the leadership of a self-assured scientific tradition as do U.S., British, or German manufacturers. But this weakness, we do well to remember, is less a fault of temperament or intellect than of youth. . . .

Estimates of Japanese national income, the best clue to over-all industrial size, are available and few exercises are so unrewarding as their study. For six years yen and dollars have been exchanged mostly in black markets; under any circumstances, it is hard to compare the amount of war material a dollar and a yen will pay for in the two countries. Nevertheless economists have tried; they place the *real* income of Japan between one-seventh and one-eighth of that of the U.S. These estimates mean that Japan, as an industrial power, has not made the major league.

The key statistic of war economy is production of steel. A working estimate of Japan's steel production is 12 million ingot tons, one million plus or two million minus. Beside the 88 million total of the U.S. this looks small. However, men who have related steel to war output think it remarkably large. Britain began the war with a capacity of only 15,500,000 tons; Russia for two years has fought the biggest war of all time with available capacity of not over 12 million tons.

With 12 million tons of steel Japan cannot build as the U.S. builds. She cannot launch 19 million tons of merchant shipping in a year or build and equip an entire munitions industry in twenty-four months. But . . . Japan could not do these things anyway. For what Japan can do, she has [had] no shortage of steel. . . .

For two years (1942 and 1943) Japan's enemies have had another war to fight. Why, Americans have asked, [didn't] Japan seize the opportunity to expand and entrench . . . ?

The answer to this question begins with the geography of the new Japanese Empire and the line between inner empire and outer empire. The inner empire includes what the Diet [in] October [1943] heard described as the "firm-as-a-rock safety zone" in which would be built a "firm-as-a-rock food structure."

The inner empire is the islands of Japan proper, Korea, and Manchuria. At the extreme edge are North China and the strategic and long-held Chinese island of Formosa. The outer reaches of empire include South China, the Philippines, Indo-China, the Netherlands Indies, Thailand, Malaya, and most remote of all, Burma.

The inner empire, like other things Japanese, is compact. The lines of communication are short—from Japan proper to Korea only five hours; five hours by rail from the Korean border to Mukden. With the exception of the route to Formosa, these lines of communication are protected from sea attack by the mainland of Japan itself.

To the outer empire, distances are great. From Yokohama to Batavia is farther than from New York to Liverpool. The U.S. supply line to Naples is shorter by 400 miles than that of the Japanese to Rangoon. And although the outer empire has everything Japan needs, the inner empire has not.

For meager rations there is enough food in the inner empire; in this respect the island economy of Japan differs emphatically from the island economy of Britain. Before the war Japan proper supplied from 80 to 85 per cent of the rice requirements. The remainder came from Korea and Formosa, principally Korea. The inner empire also provides slender supplies of fish, grain, and soybean curd.

The men who run Japan intend to continue to feed their people from the inner zone. . . . But food sufficiency in the inner empire has its price; the price is what agricultural economists call a labor-intensive agriculture. On the rice lands of the Sacramento Valley in California the seed is spread on the flooded fields by plane. On Japan's compact farms—they average less than three acres—each rice plant is transplanted from the seedbed where it was sprouted to the paddy field where it grows. From this lavish use of man- and woman-power come the high yields that make Japan self-sufficient or nearly so. If Japan should practice Californian or Arkansan methods—saving labor by profligate use of land—she would have to import or starve.

Though Japan's army of four million men is not large in relation to her total population, the manpower shortage is serious. Males from twelve to sixty are subject to labor conscription. So are unmarried women from twelve to forty. The Japanese have hesitated some over drafting married women but no similar delicacy is evident in selecting the jobs to which women are assigned. . . .

The root cause of this shortage in a country of 73 million people is the need to keep a minimum of 40 per cent of the people on the farms of the inner empire. The effort to supply food at home and the need to bring materials from the outer margin are Japan's problem of empire. They will remain so while Japan is at war and ships are scarce. . . .

Had her enemies left her completely undisturbed during the last two years, Japan could have entrenched herself as many feared. She could have turned little industry at home into big industry. Her people could have been drawn into that industry. Raw materials and food could have been brought from the empire; cloth and bicycles and rubber sneakers could have been supplied in return. Ships, naval bases, and above all an air fleet and supporting aircraft industry could have been created to make the supply lines secure.

Japan's historic misfortune is that when she most needed peace she had war. . . .

The men who run Japan know the extent of their misfortune. The opportunity to develop an empire and build an industry as strong as that of the U.S. or Britain has been lost. . . .

There may be some who have another hope. The men who within a decade or two converted a light consumer-goods industry into a balanced producer of modern armament had competence and energy. After the war if they still have that industry and access to raw materials they could work wonders. In ten years of a favorable peace Japan *could* turn little industry into big industry.

When peace comes Japan's steel mills, shipyards, automobile factories, chemical plants, and machine shops—or some of them—will still be there. They will pose a decisively important problem for the peacemakers....

THE JAPANESE STATE IN ACTION

By T. A. Bisson

From "Japan as a Political Organism," by T. A. Bisson, in *Pacific Affairs,* December 1944. Copyright 1944 by The Institute of Pacific Relations, New York; reproduced by permission. The author is a member of the research staff of the Institute of Pacific Relations.

Japan presents no such clear-cut picture either in the content or operation of its political order [as did Hitler's Third Reich].... Responsibility for policy and action in Japan is not centered at any one point, but diffused over a number of groups.... Failure to give due recognition to this fact encourages a futile search for the particular "devil" in Japan's political organization....

The Japanese political system ... is an amalgam of feudal, theocratic, and democratic elements. While each element possesses an institutional structure and mode of operation of its own, the whole system or the net political outcome at any given time is constituted by the interaction of all three. Perhaps the most basic—and most disastrous—error of appraisal in the past has been the failure to recognize that the feudal and theocratic elements, rather than the democratic, have represented the determining motivation and source of authority for the total system....

An effectively representative government could not possibly emerge within the Japanese constitutional framework. The feudal architects who fashioned the system in the 'eighties had no such end in view, and the strength with which they endowed the non-democratic elements proved itself in the test. Institutionally, both in the Diet and in certain electoral procedures, the democratic element has remained part of even the presently existing system. Its relatively easy subordination, however, together with the effects on the minds of the party leaders who lent themselves to the betrayal, raises obvious questions as to the usefulness of the existing democratic forms and of the men who have worked through these forms in posts of authority during recent years. Their allegiance was to the dictatorial regime of which they formed a part, not to the Japanese people. The democratic element in the system was thus a façade, behind which lay the real structure. This façade, nevertheless, with its House of Representatives, its general elections, its parties and party leaders, and its cabinet, modeled deliberately by its architects on European constitutional forms, made it fatally easy to overlook what was going on inside the house.

... The controlling force in modern Japanese politics has never expressed itself exclusively through a single group. No one political vehicle through which power is solely conducted exists in Japan or can exist there under the present system. It is easy to see that no Hitler can emerge out of the conditions of group responsibility which actually prevail. It is more difficult to recognize that no one group or agency, such as the militarists or the IRAA (Imperial Rule Assistance Association), can form the sole channel of political authority and preferment.... Not the dominance of one group interest but the accommodation of several, all within a single dictatorial coalition, is the typical expression of the Japanese system. . . .

Each group is intent on increasing its power within the coalition, on maximizing its economic advantages, on limiting the cost which it must bear of any common effort. These are conflicts incident to any coalition of diverse groups. Under conditions of extreme stress, the strife might become so intense as to disrupt the coalition and destroy its political effectiveness. Thus far in Japan's modern history, even in cases of such extreme friction as to lead to assassination and armed uprising, there has been no break in political continuity. After each crisis the ruling coalition has immediately reformed on a new basis and continued to operate in the old way. Factors conducing to this result, i.e. the pressures which hold the coalition together, may be grouped under three heads: first, the need to maintain the coalition's dictatorial power; second, the common acceptance of the task of Empire aggrandizement; and, third, the key role of the Emperor in "holding the ring."

Up to the present, disagreements leading to crisis in Japan have as a rule been intra-coalition disagreements. The single exception that comes to mind is that of the "rice riots" of 1918. In this case the dictatorial position of the coalition was temporarily shaken by a threat coming from a force wholly outside it—that is, the Japanese people. Here, of course, is one of the main centripetal influences acting upon the coalition. The four groups are unitedly determined that their ruling position at home should not be overthrown by popular forces striving to attain genuine democratic rights. Their system is intrinsically authoritarian and undemocratic. All decisions that matter are made by a relatively small group operating behind the scenes and not amenable to popular control. Even an overwhelming popular mandate can be disregarded and swept into the ashcan by the groups in control, as has happened more than once. Intra-coalition struggles must obviously be subordinated to the overriding necessity of maintaining the dictatorial system as a whole.

For all groups, in the second place, the cornerstone of policy and action is the "divine mission" of the Empire. Expansion of the "master race," based squarely on theocratic principle, is a concept more universal and more firmly grounded even than in Germany. At this point, which should be the clearest of all, misuse of the terms "moderate" and "extremist," abetted by wishful thinking and in some cases perhaps by willful deception, has confused outside world opinion and worked to Japan's advantage. Applied to foreign policy, these terms are descriptive of differences in *method* not in *objective*. The distinction is fundamental. If it is not made, the foreign observer is continually nourishing the delusion that he has allies inside the gates of the Japanese state regime. He has none. A Japanese "moderate" is not a pacifist, nor a good internationalist, nor is he opposed to Japanese aggrandizement. He is rather more cautious than the "extremist" and may differ over the incidentals of timing and tactic, yet he is thoroughly willing to move his pins forward on the map when additional territory has been occupied. In the past his most useful role has been in the Foreign Office when the army was running amok, since he could then act as polite screen, apologist, and general scapegoat. It may yet be shown that he can perform an even more effective job when it comes to obtaining the best possible peace after a disastrous war.

Thus it must be stressed that, in the overall operation and activity of the coalition, foreign policy is not a *divisive* but a *unifying* force. Even more it is a useful tool, skillfully and ruthlessly wielded, to channel popular discontents outward against the foreign enemy of the moment (actual or invented) instead of inward against the regime. Too much experience has been had in the wielding of this weapon for the wielders thereof to turn it recklessly in upon themselves. It is of course possible that in the unprecedented conditions of total defeat in war the coalition may disintegrate into irreconcilably antagonistic elements. But it is also possible, and much more to be feared, that all four groups will be unitedly seeking to find the best way out of the disaster threatening to engulf them. On such an occasion it will be vital that loose handling of terms does not again lead to a transvaluation of judgments, to the confusion of Anglo-American and the benefit of Japanese diplomacy. Past experience seems to indicate that there is no weapon labeled "disunity over foreign policy" that can be turned inward against Japan. The same experience shows that foreign hands that try to grasp such a weapon will themselves be cut, since it will prove to be wielded by the Japanese. A "moderate," to the extent that he is taken as our ally, is Japan's diplomatic ace-in-the-hole. As manipulated by Japan's ruling coalition, relations with foreign powers are made to contribute to national unity and strength; they are not a weakness to be exploited. When the most colossal error in foreign policy ever committed by Japan's ruling forces has become an historical fact, and is leading to an overwhelming defeat in war, it would be the height of folly to strike hands with the double face of our enemy as soon as the last shot is fired. A second, and even a third, look must be taken at all the "liberal friends" who offer themselves from within the existing Japanese regime. Lurking behind them in the shadows will be their real allies, waiting for the time when they too can again come forward to join forces with the "moderates" on the old dictatorial and expansionist program.

The Emperor bears a significant relation to both these centripetal pressures acting upon the ruling coalition. He is the stanchest bulwark of the coalition's dictatorship. His most important "gift" to the people was the 1889 Constitution, beside whose full-blooded authoritarianism all other organic acts pale into insignificance. In his name, under the peace preservation laws and other associated statutes and ordinances, the countless acts of daily tyranny visited upon liberal or radical opponents of the regime are sanctioned. As to the Emperor's influence with respect to aggression and territorial aggrandizement, no elaboration need be made. He supplies the tribal ideology which knits the coalition together, with its unrivalled motivation of the "sacred mission" of a "master race." The aggressive instincts of Japan's dominant groups are buttressed by a divine imperative: to extend the "benevolent sway" of the Emperor over previously unfavored regions. Under these conditions, with an imperial influence tending invariably in a given direction, the effort sometimes made to pass off the Emperor as a puppet without political responsibility of any kind or as an institution which can be directed toward good ends hardly merits serious consideration. . . .

The Emperor plays yet another special political role of vital importance in ensuring the continued unity of the coalition. He acts as the fulcrum of the whole system. The permanent dictatorship functions under the shadow of his authority. To him the ruling groups are always under the necessity of presenting an appearance of unity, even if the reality is lacking. The significance of this factor cannot be overestimated, and constitutes further evidence that the Emperor exerts an influence that extends far beyond that which could be attributed to a despised tool and puppet. It means that the coalition's representatives in the seats of power must continually bear in mind their ultimate responsibility to the Emperor. The visits which the chief ministers of state are obliged to pay to the Ise shrine are a constant reminder of this responsibility. They are well aware that if their conflicts should pass beyond the bounds of propriety, if they should finally develop into irreconcilable fissures in the state structure, the ark of the covenant would be broken. The steady pressure which this awareness exerts on Japan's ruling coalition is one of the major incentives to adjustment and compromise, to restraint on irrevocable acts that would break political continuity and wash away the foundations of unity. Without the ever-present safeguard of the Emperor's presence, the unbridled will of one or more of the ruling groups might long since have broken through the bands that harness them to an ineluctable cooperation. . . .

In its flexibility and tensile strength Japan's political system is akin to a living organism. Its intrinsic authoritarianism is the product of continually repeated adjustments made by businessmen and the militarists, bureaucrats and the party leaders. In this group dictatorship, no one man can set himself up as the undisputed and all-powerful dictator. The leader at any given moment registers the net group adjustment and functions as the temporary representative of the existing balance of power within the coalition. His position is as impermanent as the shifting basis of the successive intra-coalition adjustments, in response to the declining strength of one group or the growing power of another. The Emperor, not the Premier, is the center of the system. As a real functionary, and as an ideological symbol of overpowering importance, the Emperor occupies the key position in the regime. He is the crucial element in the whole apparatus of rule through which the coalition maintains the unity and permanence of its group dictatorship. Beside him even a Tojo fades into relative insignificance and can be hustled off the political stage without ceremony. The system makes a new adjustment, places another temporary leader in power, and continues to operate in its accustomed manner.

WHO RULES JAPAN?

By the Editors of "Fortune"

From "Who Runs the Emperor?" in *Fortune* magazine, April 1944. Copyright 1944 by Time Inc.; reproduced by permission.

A MAN called Hirohito happens to be the Emperor of Japan, but the Emperor is neither a man nor a ruler. Nor is he simply a god living in Tokyo. He is a spiritual institution in which center the energy, the loyalty, and even the morality of the Japanese; he is the divine source of temporal power and the fountain of honors; for the Japanese he is the reason for existing and also the reason for dying. . . . The Japanese people are expected to serve him and to "set his mind at rest." He is the physical incarnation of the state. He is Japan. . . .

His value to Japan is his value as a myth, and the myth has been artfully assembled and cleverly merchandised. He is the offspring by direct descent of the Emperor Jimmu, founder in 660 B.C. of Japan, and great-great-grandson of the sun goddess Amaterasu. He is the inheritor of the divine command of Hakko Ichiu—to bring the eight corners of the world under one Japanese roof. He is the center of the religion that deifies him. He is the custodian of three sacred treasures, articles bequeathed by ancient gods, that prove his divinity: the sacred mirror and the sacred jewels, which were used to lure the sun goddess out of a cave and restore light to the world, and the sacred sword, which was found by the sun goddess's brother in the tail of a dragon. The jewels are kept in the Imperial Palace, the sword in the Atsuta Shrine, and the mirror, an eight-sided bronze, at the ancestral shrine at the great religious center of Ise. Here the Emperor personally reports great events to his sacred forebears; here cabinet ministers, ambassadors, and generals bow in reverence before assuming office.

The religion is called Shinto, the way of the gods. It is the agency by which the Emperor is made identical with the country in the minds of the people. It relies not on theology or dogma, but on simple acts of loyalty, repeated time and again in the schools, in the barracks, and in the homes, and reinforced by the pageantry and pomp of official ceremony. . . .

But there are more homely means of emphasizing emperor-worship. Japanese are taught to consider the name of the Emperor too awful to utter and certainly too sacred to print. The Japanese know the names *Aramikami, Akitsukami, Kamigoichinin,* and *Otenshisama* —Incarnate God, Manifest Deity, Upper Exalted Foremost Being, and, most common, Honorable Son of Heaven. The Japanese know that after the Emperor's death they can call him by the title of his reign—Showa, radiant peace. Few of them, however, know the name Hirohito, although they do know the story of the Yokohama father who inadvertently gave the not-to-be-named name to his son and atoned by killing the boy and himself as soon as he learned of his sacrilege. The Japanese are instructed also in the protocol of avoiding less obvious acts of lese majesty. No one can look down on the Emperor, and therefore no one can put up high buildings in the vicinity of the palace. Shades must be drawn in all upper windows whenever the Emperor goes out into the streets, and the police must go ahead to make certain of obedience. When he passes all heads must be bowed in abject humility; few eyes dare to look directly at his august presence. No one may ride a white horse, because the Emperor rides one. No one may picture the sacred sixteen-petaled chrysanthemum. And great emphasis is given to proper courtesy and respect to the Emperor's picture and the imperial rescripts. There are minute regulations as to how these shall be stored, carried, and bowed to, and heroic tales are circulated of teachers and students who burned to death trying to save the picture and the rescript on education. . . . The Japanese seldom see their Emperor, but they are in daily touch with the paraphernalia of reverence. Continual emphasis on imperial protocol has made him the center of the subservience that has always been exacted from the Japanese people.

Who the Emperor is is unimportant. . . . What the Emperor does is not particularly important either. . . . It is always the name and not the man that carries weight. The name approves plans, and makes decisions theoretically immutable. The name under an imperial rescript—whether the Emperor writes it or not—gives to a declaration of war or to a statement on the duties of soldiers the awesome attribute of divine law. The Rescript of December

8, 1941, which declares that "the entire nation with a united will shall mobilize their total strength so that nothing will miscarry," has the force of a categorical imperative. So has the famous Meiji Rescript to Soldiers and Sailors, the Bible of the Army and Navy, read with ceremonious awe in all garrisons and ships. One of its lines reads, "Bear in mind that duty is weightier than a mountain, while death is lighter than a feather." The imperial name turns this figure of speech into a strict moral compulsion. Any Japanese who disobeys it by surrender automatically becomes a traitor to his Emperor and thus to his country and to his religion and to his family, and expects to be punished accordingly. . . .

The Emperor is . . . insulated not only by ritual and ceremony but by various groups of personal advisers, through whom imperial matters proceed with proper Japanese dignity. He is watched, protected, and guided by patriarchal palace advisers appointed by the government. Most important of these are the Lord Keeper of the Privy Seal and the Minister of the Imperial Household, who manage the great wealth of the imperial house. No visitors can see the Emperor without their permission—an important function in a country in which ideas gain respectability only by being rehearsed in front of the Emperor. Scarcely beneath them in the hierarchy is the Grand Chamberlain, the great stage manager of imperial ceremonies and pageants and Shinto pilgrimages and war-front visits. These men are the heirs of the old Japanese court officialdom; they give to the government a traditional and ceremonial tone. The household ministers by no means control the use of the imperial name, and therefore are limited in power. But their access to the imperial ear enables them to channel certain ideas to the throne and certain ideas away from it. They have been important enough to be assassinated.

Further imperial insulation is provided by the Privy Council, an organization formed in 1888 to discuss the constitution. This body officially advises the Emperor, but it does not often offer independent advice. Its twenty-six members are chosen by the Premier, although formally appointed for life by the Emperor. Venerable and ancient men, they do not as a group live long enough to interfere seriously with major political changes. Furthermore they are joined ex officio by all the cabinet members. Essentially the council preserves the Emperor from too mundane connections with government activity and helps shield his name from unsuccessful policy. It is an organization in which imperial divinity and governmental practicality can meet with proper dignity.

None of the old Genro, the oligarchy that in the early days wielded power, still lives, but the device of a stopgap between cabinet turnovers proved highly useful. Some years before his death in 1940, Prince Kimmochi Saionji, last of the old Genro, took to consulting the former Premiers and, among others, the President of the Privy Council. This group is being elevated as a new Genro into an extra-constitutional sacrosanct organization, which apparently shares with the Privy Council the responsibility for major policies that go wrong. They are supposed to advise the Emperor whenever a new Premier is about to be appointed . . . but they have nothing to do with day-to-day affairs. It may be that they will be judges to decide what shall be done and who shall bear the onus for defeat in war. Their tendencies are conservative, their precise functions are undefined, but they are publicly referred to only in most respectful and flowery terms.

Politics in Japan are in certain respects the same as politics the world over. There are political deals of a sort that would not seem out of place in the West; there is a bureaucracy, efficient in operation and distinguished in tradition, not unlike the German civil service. There is a mass party that has points of resemblance to Fascist parties in Europe. Particularly, the aims of government in Japan are comparable to the aims of government in Nazi Germany; in both lands service to the state is supposed to be the purpose of life and the individual is held to be of only ephemeral importance; in both, a small group of men wields a totalitarian power that permeates the entire political, economic, cultural, and religious life.... This article, however, is concerned with a description of what is particularly Japanese in the political structure rather than with resemblances to the structure of other countries.

These Japanese features center around the imperial institution. The Emperor is the source of all power; he is as sovereign in his country as the people are sovereign in ours. But there is a curious anomaly in his position. In the U.S., political policies inevitably go before the people, who have final decision as to what party shall govern and what policies shall rule. Even between elections their opinion is potent. In Japan the Emperor can settle nothing. He has all the trappings of a myth, but he has also all a myth's weakness. He has no say.

Who has the say? Certainly not the Japanese people. No other country in the world ... listens less to its people. Modern Japanese rulers have followed the tradition of exhorting the people instead of consulting them. The people vote, but nothing comes of their voting. Even when political parties existed in some strength, they were largely the playthings of powerful business interests.... The people may have wished to register their opinions and to resist increasing totalitarianism but no effective channels existed.

In the early days of modern Japan the clansmen who deposed the shogun and restored the Emperor had the say; but the feudal clans could not survive as power centers in a modern world. When their power lapsed, two conflicting yet mutually dependent groups of businessmen and militarists took their place. The power of these groups fluctuates continually, and the composition of the Japanese government, particularly of the Japanese cabinet, is an almost exact measure of the relative power of the two groups.

But who actually decides how much power each group shall have? The Emperor does not and the people do not. The decision is made by the opposing groups themselves. There are only a few industrialists; there are only a few top-ranking generals and admirals. They form their separate policies in their own political councils, but they settle the question of who shall run the country and who shall have the balance of power by talking to each other and by talking to the imperial satellites.

This conversation is the fulcrum of Japanese politics; its essence is compromise and its manifestation is coalition between rival groups motivated by similar nationalistic aims. It is quite true that the extremists in the army group have resorted occasionally to assassination, and that businessmen who pursue strong anti-military policies have at times been in no position to sleep tranquilly in bed. It is also true that each group is quick to capitalize on the other's political mistakes. Murder and castigation, however, are not characteristic of most Japanese political strategy. A Japanese businessman will seek power to run Japan his way, not the army way, but he knows that he cannot run the Japanese army; therefore he must cooperate with the militarists. Likewise, an army officer knows that he cannot run Japanese factories; he too must cooperate.

Mutual recognition of shifts of power is the real basis of political maneuvering. To put it positively, the balance of power between big business and the military depends at any given time on their relative value to the nationalist, expansionist aims of the country. To put it negatively, the balance of power tips in favor of the group that could cause the most difficulty by declining to cooperate. Big business can embarrass an army government by saying in effect: all right, you run the factories. And the army, with of course the support of the navy, can embarrass a business government by saying: all right, build your economic empire without the aid of military force. . . .

In this game the military have an edge. They have the right to appoint the Minister of War and the Minister of the Navy. If the military dislike the composition of a government, they can prevent its formation by refusing to appoint their own ministers. Thus they exercise effective veto power, which is reinforced by their right of direct access to the Emperor, and by their complete freedom from any sort of civilian control.

On the basis of conversation of this sort, the Japanese overlords determine the degree to which each of the conflicting power groups can use the name of the Emperor. Much of the conversation is carried on in the cabinet, the chief organ of Japanese government, where the various ministers, acting not as individuals, but as representatives of groups, try to harmonize divergent viewpoints into national policy. If the political balance fails, the cabinet falls —cabinets have fallen frequently—and the informal discussion starts all over again.

The Emperor is run by men, but the men are not primarily important as individuals. In this, Japanese politics have been compared to a flight of Tokyo pigeons. As the flock zooms to one side, one pigeon seems to appear as a leader; but by the time the flock has circled to the other side, a different pigeon seems to be out in front. It is quite difficult to tell one pigeon from the next. But there are two groups of them.

The industrialists are able to keep their identity largely because they built modern industrial Japan. The Meiji Restoration was financed by merchants, particularly by the house of Mitsui, and Japan's economy was westernized by big business. Industrialization was rapid; a shower of government subsidies fell upon the relatively few moneyed families. Japan had always planned her affairs from above, and in the race for industrialization there was neither time nor inclination for a period of *laissez faire*. The country jumped from feudalism to monopoly capitalism, and as a consequence, economic power never was widely diffused. Two hundred families are said to have run France; sixty families are said to control much of American enterprise; but six families actually do manage the bulk of Japanese industry.

The zenith of big-business control of the country was in 1930. Japan's rich families—known as the Zaibatsu—had taken over and developed two political parties, the Seiyukai and the Minseito, which, although conservative, were relatively popular organizations. For nearly ten years the industrialists had controlled the cabinet and ruled in the Emperor's name, and the militarists had even taken to wearing civilian clothes on the streets. Foreign trade was booming; the capitalists were rich. The influence of Elder Statesman Prince Saionji was directed toward westernization of the country and toward the forms of parliamentary government. The Zaibatsu were powerful. A Minister of Education had once said, "Suppose that you dreamed Japan had adopted a republican system of government, a Mitsui or a Mitsubishi would immediately become the presidential candidate." (This dream was a political mistake. The intimation that Japan could be a republic was denounced as sacrilege, and the cabinet forced to resign.)

But at the moment when the industrialists appeared strongest, their power began to crumble. The London Naval Treaty of 1930 had just been concluded and the militarists, enraged by big-business encroachments upon their private preserves, used their right of access to the Emperor to demand that the treaty be discarded. Premier Hamaguchi and his cabinet demanded en bloc that it be approved. Discussion followed, but the big-business representatives—believers in stable international relations—stood firm, and the treaty went through. But the militarists had not stopped fighting, and they had only begun plotting. Nationalistic fervor increased. The Premier was assassinated. A constitutional authority who had been called in to formalize the right of the cabinet to supersede the will of the armed forces was denounced later on when military power was stronger, because he had referred in his books to the Emperor as only the highest organ of the state. His books were suppressed; his friends took no steps to defend him; he was forced to resign his position in the honorific House of Peers; he was even shot at by an assassin. In 1931 the militarists moved into Manchuria; in 1936 they got rid of the naval treaty. Thereafter the political power of the military grew apace—war abroad and assassination at home strengthened it greatly—and by 1941 the militarists were ready to take control. . . .

During the period of increasing militarism big business and the army and navy were bound to differ. The industrialists wanted to control their own monopolies. The militarists wanted to control the entire economy, though not necessarily to direct it. The industrialists wanted steady profits; the militarists wanted quick seizures of territory. The industrialists looked with favor on gradual changes; the militarists, more impatient, believed in direct action.

But the difference was not wide. The two groups disagreed on matters of method and of timing. They did not disagree on matters so important as Japanese expansion. Expansion meant wealth for the one group, and for the other glory. When Admiral Sekine, in discussing the development of East Asia, wrote, "If the great Central China, rich in agricultural and mineral products, and inhabited by 200 million obedient masses, is industrialized, the mere imagination of it would give a sudden solvent effect on all residues we have in our stomachs," he was expressing an appetite for huge enterprise common both to the military and to big business. Controversy hinged basically on the question of whether, regardless of profits, the whole economic structure should be taken apart and put directly to war uses, or whether profits should be protected during the period of military action. Yet the military by no means wanted to strip big business of all power; they looked to the monopolists to keep Japan rich just as much as the monopolists looked to them to keep Japan safe.

Today the military get along with big business partly because big business, like other Japanese power groups, is not entirely homogeneous in interest. Some of the capitalists cooperate intimately with the army; others keep a distance. Smaller businessmen are even more reserved, for their existence is threatened by the increasing centralization of economic effort. Furthermore, business attitudes toward the military government vary somewhat according to the excess-profit tax rate, and according to the degree of military dictation of the economy. The shipbuilders for a time were enthusiastic over their increasing fleets. They lost enthusiasm when the military began dictating ship movements and sending whole fleets into hazardous waters without indemnities. . . .

The military who now run the Emperor give all the appearance of a solid front, but among them are personalities and groups as varied in opinion as individual businessmen. There is widespread diffusion of authority. There are not only separate army and navy commands, but a separate self-perpetuating army triumvirate and navy partnership. The army has a Chief of Staff, a Minister of War, and an Inspector General of Military Education. The navy has a Chief of Staff and a Minister of the Navy. Men who hold these positions do not have superiors and subordinates; they have colleagues, with whom they share responsibility for whatever goes wrong. There is further diffusion of responsibility between the advisory Supreme War Council—the front organization that meets to discuss vital moves—and Imperial Headquarters, the working group that maps strategy and plans tactics. In the field, separation of authority goes even further. Prince Ito wrote that: "The exercise of the right of warfare in the field . . . as the exigency of circumstances may require, may be entrusted to the commanding officer of the place, who is allowed to take actual steps his discretion dictates, and then to report to the government." This clause has been used to perpetuate army power and also to justify army decisions on war and peace. A commanding officer was used to touch off the attack on Manchuria in 1931; another was used in 1937 to commit the country to the war with China. In 1940 the North China Army engineered incidents against foreigners, which embarrassed the government in Tokyo; and the Central China Army, not the Foreign Office, installed Wang Ching-wei as puppet in Occupied China.

The result has been the development of distinct subgroups within the army political machine. . . . Despite intrigue, perhaps because of it, army prestige is high. The militarists are the heirs of Prince Yamagata, the clansman who built Japan's modern army and created her empire. In Japan the sword is the symbol of authority and the source of conventional morality. To be a soldier or sailor has always been a distinction, and Yamagata's success against China, Korea, and Russia only gave added importance to a group preeminent in Japanese life. For many years the Japanese Army has appealed strongly to the ambitions of bright young men, who see in a military career the chance for high social prestige and for personal advancement.

The real progenitor of the present power of the military is the early power of the Kwantung Army in Manchuria. The war in Manchuria in 1931 was one of the first victories of the militarists over big business, which wanted expansion at a slower and safer pace. The militarists did not yet have the political potency to do all they wanted in Japan proper; therefore they turned Manchuria into a training place for men and for organization methods. They were determined that Manchuria should be their private schoolroom, and they worked out effective and total controls of everything from major economic and political matters to the daily comings and goings of the inhabitants. A spy system was set up inside the army and the government. A single political party—the Kyowakai, or Concordia Society—was established and all government officials were forced to belong. A police-control system was later created inside the Kyowakai by forming within neighborhood groups the five-man system of joint responsibility. Army control of the economy was established, and after the China war began a law was enacted to expedite the Five Year Plan requiring government permission before initiating any kind of industry, floating debentures, merging, or even increasing capitalization. Japanese industrialists were put to school in this tightly controlled power center, and under the restrictions businessmen who were ready to follow the army lead were permitted to profit. The profits were high, and the businessmen, whatever their private worries over forthright state economic control, were publicly enthusiastic. "Manchukuo," Toyotaro Yuki announced in 1933, "owes a great deal to the military."

Actually the military owed a great deal to Manchuria. There they trained their political front men: Tojo, for instance, operated for a time as head of the army gendarmerie. There they developed a backlog of power that considerably strengthened their position in politics at home. Within ten years the direct-action theories of the military in Manchuria spread everywhere through the Army. Officers of less extreme opinion were retired and discharged. One of them was assassinated during the murder spree of 1936, when the Lord Keeper of the Privy Seal and the Finance Minister were also slain. (The Premier escaped because his brother-in-law was mistaken for him.)

By the time of the assassination, the army was ready to move with more directness. Five men in the Supreme War Council resigned, and the army political machine, in a show of strength, installed as Premier one Koki Hirota, whose education had been guided by the rabid nationalistic gangster, Toyama, sponsor of the Black Dragon Society. This cabinet handed over 46 per cent of the entire budget to the military and, at army urging, signed the Anti-Comintern Pact with Germany. When this and other army policies drew criticism, the army wasted no political time. War Minister Terauchi promptly resigned and the cabinet fell. When the relatively moderate General Ugaki was suggested as the new Premier early in 1937, the army refused to appoint a War Minister. The cabinets that followed fitted closer to military ideas; thenceforth no members were allowed to retain political party affiliations. The military had finally tipped the balance of power. By October 18, 1941, when Tojo became Premier, they had almost complete control of the government....

How is Japan run [in 1944]? In part it is run like a conquered country—for Japan is being treated in the 'forties along the same lines Manchuria was treated in the 'thirties. The military have done over much of the economic structure. They have had the government buy into the holdings of Zaibatsu companies. Ever since 1937 they have been forcing monopolies to specialize. They have established nine regional blocs for administering political and economic policies and for regulating the transfer of labor. These blocs are important politically because they have the power to enforce the cooperation of industrialists, landowners, and the people generally in the new economic structure. . . .

The older government institutions are under complete military control. The Premier is responsible not to the Diet but to the Emperor, and the Premier can use the Emperor to dissolve the Diet. In ordinary times members are allowed to initiate laws, but they seldom do. Today the hand-picked Diet acts as a rubber stamp, though there are signs that the members do not wish to be pushed permanently aside.

Local government falls under military control since the heads of the nine regional blocs are chosen by the Premier and appointed by the Emperor. The Home Minister chooses the governors of the forty-six prefectures (which correspond to our counties); the governors in turn appoint the mayors of the townships. These officials run the local councils, which, though elected by the people, are uniformly docile. This system is important in laying the will of the government upon the people. Its symbol is the police station, where information is card-indexed for every person in the area: birth, sickness, marriage, jobs, travels, parents, grandparents, children. . . .

The military run the Emperor, but they have no more been able to do without industrial power than the big businessmen were able to do without army power when the Emperor was under their control. Japanese government still rests on a coalition of rival groups, each of which must rely on the other; and even the rival groups themselves are coalitions of subgroups of opposing aims and interests. Everything depends on merging differences of opinion. But the degree of cohesion in the coalitions varies with the intensity of the crisis, and only success and mutual profit keep the groups together. Crisis and failure do not, as in certain other countries, bring them closer. . . . Thought of the impending defeat even now multiplies differences of opinion and makes political argument more bitter. The warlords run the government, but their government can be no stronger than their own now-retreating war machine. . . .

THE JAPANESE WAY

By Helen Mears

From "The Japanese Riddle," by Helen Mears, in *The Atlantic Monthly*, September 1943. Copyright 1943 by Atlantic Monthly Co.; reproduced by permission. The author of this article speaks from close personal observation during extended residence in Japan.

THE Japanese are slaves to their own special habits, which differ widely from ours. So do their attitudes toward facts, toward authority in human relations, toward money and possessions. Even our ideas of politeness are so different that although the Japanese at home have a reputation for being the politest people in the world, from an American point of view their politeness often seems simple rudeness.

This is the kind of thing that may happen to you when you are living in Japan:

You are having lunch with a Japanese friend in a "modern style" restaurant, where the menu is printed in a kind of Japanese-English. You order from the menu. The waitress suggests that something else is very nice, but you prefer your own choice and stick to it. An hour or more elapses. When the waitress finally returns, she brings you not what you ordered but what she suggested. Your Japanese friend accepts for you with courteous phrases, dismisses the waitress with bows and smiles, and gives you no explanation.

According to Japanese custom, it is rude ever to refuse a request directly. The waitress, in suggesting some other dish, was explaining that they did not have what was ordered. Since the foreigner, not understanding, persisted, she merely waited, knowing that in time hunger would persuade him to take what was given. The Japanese companion understood this but found it difficult to explain the matter to a foreigner. A Japanese, of course, would accept the waitress's suggestion at once.

Or you are walking in the country with a Japanese interpreter, looking for a specific village for a specific purpose. You come to a crossroad and, not knowing which direction to take, you gesture toward one and ask, "Is this the right road?" The interpreter at once bows and smiles and sets off down this road. An hour later you discover that you have been going in the wrong direction —and it is clear that the interpreter knew all the time it was wrong!

It is impolite in Japan ever to suggest that someone is wrong. Since the foreigner had seemed to choose one of two crossroads . . . the interpreter had no choice but to take that road. It was unthinkable that the interpreter should tell a foreigner he was mistaken.

Or you may be staying at a Japanese Inn. For breakfast you have a treat—an egg. It is, however, served raw with some bitter seaweed. You would prefer it cooked and suggest that it be scrambled. You tell your Japanese companion, who has traveled in America and has had scrambled eggs. She explains to the maid. The maid bows and smiles and assents—and departs, leaving you with your egg raw.

The maid had never before encountered such an oddity as a scrambled egg and simply could not understand that anyone would want an egg prepared that way. It would have been rude of her to admit she did not understand, or to refuse to scramble the egg. So she merely agreed politely and forgot all about it.

Or you are at the Mitsui Bank, getting some money on your letter of credit. During the negotiations the letter is mislaid. You see a corps of clerks madly searching for it—in desk drawers, under desks, in wastepaper baskets—while you get more and more jittery. At last the head clerk summons you to a window. You expect him to reassure you and possibly to suggest that if it does not turn up, the bank will guarantee the loss. Instead, he leans toward you confidentially and in excellent English inquires, "Do you care for music?"

The Japanese solve unpleasantness by pretending the unpleasantness does not exist. It is rude ever to intrude your own feeling on anyone else. The Mitsui clerk was in a panic about the lost letter of credit, so it was necessary for him to behave as though the whole affair were of no importance.

Or you are sitting in at a weekly session of a "Men's English-Study Club" in Tokyo. You mention the "Manchurian Incident" unfavorably and everyone deplores it, explaining that the Japanese people are against the "incident" and favor "universal peace." You think this fine, until later on another foreigner present expresses sympathy with the Japanese military point of view, and at once the group agrees with him as warmly as it previously agreed with you.

When they came out for universal peace the members of the "Men's English-Study Club" were obeying the rule of politeness which dictates that you must give the answer that will be pleasing to the questioner. A Japanese answers a question—even a question involving a statement of fact—by saying not what is so, but what he thinks the questioner would like to hear. When the second foreigner voiced a different point of view from the first, the club politely agreed with him also.

In all these incidents the difficulty was caused by the clash of Japanese custom with American. A Japanese would have understood at once what was meant in each case and there would have been no difficulty. Such incidents, however, once we have calmed down enough to study them, tell us much about Japanese behavior. All exhibit the effort of the Japanese, inside the frame of their own customs, to avoid unpleasantness in human relations. They do this by evading reality. They avoid argument by assenting; they do not assert their opinion against another's; they ignore unpleasant facts; they deal not with an objective situation but with an imaginary situation—a situation that exists in their own minds because it has been put there by education based on a centuries-long conditioning process.

This evasion of reality, this ability to live in a make-believe world, is an inescapable behavior pattern of the Japanese. It can be found at the bottom of their social relations, their economic life, and their political life. Today it even operates to confound international relations.

The Japanese solve their problems of human relations by pretending that, as individuals, they have no feelings, desires, emotions, or ideas. There is no room in Japan for individual spontaneity or temperament: they have therefore trained themselves to behave as if such things do not exist. Seventy-two million Japanese live in a space about the size of California. As a result the average Japanese is accustomed to cramped quarters and to a complete lack of privacy. The average Japanese family of five lives in a single room that would be close quarters for one adult American. In the cities the small houses are packed closely together; and in summer each family lives in view of its neighbors, since the paper walls are seldom closed. A Japanese almost never does anything alone: he travels with a group, takes his recreation at some neighborhood festival, and even bathes with his neighbors at the public bath.

To make human relations endurable under these conditions of crowding and lack of privacy the Japanese have developed a civilization that represses the individual in both body and mind. The Japanese begins his life tightly strapped in a kind of harness dangling from the back of his mother, and he spends the rest of it in as little space as possible. He learns to sit cross-legged or to squat or kneel, absolutely motionless, for hours at a stretch, and to sleep in any position.

He also learns to live according to rule. He does not behave the way he chooses, but in the way society has decided will prevent friction. How he says good morning to his wife, what he has for lunch, how he sits on the mats, how his wife opens and closes a door, how she prepares breakfast, even how he commits suicide, are not acts of personal preference; they are reflexes, habits learned as a child—easily learned since they have been national practice for centuries.

In the ordinary round of daily life you will never hear a Japanese admit that he is hungry or tired or uncomfortable. He will never express personal pleasure or irritation. He accepts whatever comes, bows, smiles, utters the correct courtesy phrases with the imperturbability of an automaton.

The Japanese is repressed socially. He

is taught that he is not an individual but a member of a family—a private family and a national family. There is no informal social life, no free meeting between young men and young women. Marriages are arranged by families, and the wife literally belongs to her husband. A Japanese woman has no legal existence except as a daughter, wife, or mother. As a small child at home a Japanese girl is taught "etiquette"—the rules of correct behavior that will govern her relations with her husband as well as with her neighbors and those in authority. She is taught frugality, loyalty, and obedience.

In pre-modern Japan education of women was forbidden on the theory that a woman who was encouraged to think was likely to "question the authority of her elders." Although today Japanese girls are required to go to school, the basis of the education they receive in the compulsory primary grades is still character-building, the family system, and the national mythology. Little girls learn that it is their lot in life to be obedient daughters, good wives, and wise mothers. They are taught that they belong to their fathers because they belong to the Divine Emperor who is descended from the sun goddess and therefore is the father of the Japanese people.

The Japanese is repressed intellectually. Thinking is discouraged; there is a government bureau whose function is thought-control. There is no tradition in Japan of discussion of ideas or exchange of opinion. Average Japanese tell each other not what they think or what is so, but what they think will give pleasure or prevent friction. Even the university students, who represent the vanguard of westernization, have great difficulty in getting over this inhibition. The emphasis in education is practical, and vocational schools are numerous. The masses of the people do not have to bother to discuss national or international politics. Their leaders tell them what they ought to know.

The Japanese solves his economic problems by pretending he doesn't have any. The average Japanese has a minimum of money and possessions. He has no furniture in his minute house. He sits on the mats and leaves his street shoes outside to save wear and tear. His diet is extremely restricted. For heat and cooking he uses a small charcoal brazier. Even running cold water is a luxury. He owns nothing but a few clothes, bedding, and a few utensils for cooking and laundry. The Japanese evades his material poverty by pretending both that he does not care for wealth and that he has it.

The Japanese is taught to believe that one should not be interested in material rewards or possessions—that money is vulgar. The Mitsui clerk who tried to hide his distress at a mislaid letter of credit by discussing "culture" was illustrating how ingrained in national custom the ancient Japanese rules still are. Even in a bank one must not admit any crass concern about money. The pre-modern Japanese society put "tradesmen and moneylenders" at the bottom of the social scale, and in Japan today the average Japanese is uncomfortable when he is dealing with money. He wants it, of course, but at the same time he has been trained to feel he ought not to want it, that it is un-Japanese to want it; so he pretends not to be interested.

Social and business life in Japan are full of small devices for seeming to ignore money. When you buy food from a roadside vendor he will usually decline payment. The polite thing is to thank him for his generosity and leave the money hidden under the bowl. Life is also full of small devices for doing without money. At a wedding, for instance, it is the custom for the bride and groom to go through the form of exchanging gifts. But instead of exchanging real gifts, each makes out a list of presents and they merely exchange the lists.

The Japanese need less money than any other people of comparable importance in world affairs because they are largely living in a world that is still almost half agricultural and three-fourths primitive in its lack of modern tools and conveniences. They use seaweed for food, soap, fertilizer—and get foreign exchange from it as well, since it is an important export product for biological laboratories. The farmer uses his rice straw for a half-dozen different purposes—thatch for his roof, sandals, rope, raincoats, mats, barrels. The small tradesman does not use expensive paper and cord to wrap up his wares when a cornucopia of bamboo leaf will do, and the housewife cooperates by always carrying a colored handkerchief in which to tie her bundles. The Japanese waste nothing. To save materials, they have made a cult of smallness and produce everything under the sun on a miniature scale, from art objects and houses and toys to airplanes and submarines.

The Japanese pretends that he has wealth—that is, variety and freedom of choice—by playing an elaborate game of make-believe. For instance, the Japanese diet is extremely limited and monotonous. But the Japanese, in their formal dinners, give themselves an illusion of variety by elaborate service, and decoration, and poetic names. They insist that "food is art"—that what you eat is of less importance than the way it is served, the way it looks, and the poetic or moral ideas each dish can symbolize. A Japanese can celebrate every family and national holiday throughout his life by eating a flavorless candy made from soybeans. By calling the candy by a special name for each occasion, and serving it with some different garnish of flower petals or bamboo or maple leaves, he can pretend that he has something special and different each time.

This ingrained frugality, this ability to "do without" and remain contented, this capacity to be satisfied with imaginary satisfactions in place of real satisfactions—these are all recognizable behavior patterns of the Japanese. They have been of the utmost importance in building up the military machine of "Japan the Great Power."

The Japanese get along politically by pretending that their Emperor is a god and that he is ruling the country. In practice the rulers are the representatives of big business and the military, but the decisions they reach, if the decisions affect the life of the nation as a whole, are given out as "imperial rescripts"—laws pronounced by the Emperor—and as such these have the force of divine decree for the people.

The people worship the Emperor as high priest of the national religion, Shinto, and as a symbol for their divine islands. To have such a symbol as titular center of the political state gives the Japanese incredible unity. The people are emotionally devoted to their islands. Their love of country, however, is normally not so much patriotism as nature worship, a literal worship of the land itself. In times of crisis, propaganda can turn this love of country into fanatic nationalism.

The Japanese solve their international problems by pretending that they are as powerful as they care to be. They claim that their Empire is over 2,600 years old, but this is a mythological empire, founded by a god in the Age of Gods. The real Empire is actually about fifty years old, for the Japanese controlled no territories outside their own small islands until the end of the nineteenth century.

The Japanese have no "glorious imperial past" to refer to. Mussolini could exhort his tired people to new efforts by recalling the splendors of ancient Rome, but the Japanese have no such history behind them. Japanese pre-modern empire-building was limited to the confines of their own small islands; and their national heroes are all of a strange, improbable sort, whose exploits usually include some touch of the supernatural. To bolster national morale, therefore, the Japanese must refer to his glorious *mythological* past.

The Japanese are told that the blood of heroes courses through their veins— not mere human heroes, but gods who conquered their enemies by waving magic swords, under the protection of the sun goddess. The Sacred Sword of the sun goddess is enshrined in Japan today, and the peasant soldiers are told that this sword will make them invincible against actual enemies, as in the mythological age it made the descendants of gods invincible against their mythological foes.

The Japanese character and civilization have always been a riddle. There seems to be no connection at all between what the individual Japanese is like in his own country and what the nation is like in its international relations, particularly in recent years. At home the individual seems unambitious, unenergetic, easily led, a slave to custom; yet in their national activities the Japanese have appeared to be ruthlessly aggressive, efficient, remarkably adaptable. Actually this state of affairs is not so contradictory as it seems.

The more unenergetic as individuals the people of a country are, the easier it is to regiment them. Japan's pre-modern civilization was a controlled society with only a subsistence standard of living. In the modern period it developed into the first totalitarian state. An aggressive leadership was able to apply machine technology and western organization to build up a modern export industry and a modern military machine by using the regimented society and low standard of living as the foundation to support it.

The pre-modern Japanese developed a special civilization that was based on an economy of scarcity. This civilization adapted itself to the special conditions of their small, steamy, mountainous, poverty-stricken islands. They accepted the conditions of crowded poverty and set about making such conditions livable by evolving various devices designed to restrict individual initiative, on the one hand, and on the other, to create an illusion of harmony, an illusion of space, an illusion of extravagance.

This civilization carried over into the modern age. And because the individuals were content with non-material rewards and satisfactions, the new wealth that came to Japan in the modern age could be absorbed by export industry and the military machine.

What does all this tell us about the Japanese as soldiers, military strategists, and empire-builders? It suggests, at least, that Japan the World Menace is to a large extent an illusion. The Japanese is no aggressive superman who will put the world in his kimono sleeve. For the purpose of all-out war his civilization and character gave him certain initial advantages, but the same factors may prove to be a source of weakness. . . .

The strength and weakness of the Japanese as empire-builders comes from the same source—the concentration of their culture and character. This concentration makes them fanatic, unified, strong in war as long as they have the offensive and can call the turns. It makes them unadaptable, unequal to rapid shifts in plan, unstable emotionally when frustrated. It makes them little to be feared as empire-builders, for they are still much too insular and unschooled in the psychology of other peoples to organize into a paying proposition territories they take in war—even if they could hold them. There is also their lack of basic wealth and capital to finance their empire-building, but that is another story.

The Japanese military, however, will not be stopped from action by facts. They will not recognize the impossible. They will hide from an uncomfortable reality by pretending that it is not there. The gamble of their attacks against Singapore and Pearl Harbor is a fine example of the lack of realism in their military activities. Their successes on those occasions were due less to Japanese prowess than to the failure of the United Nations to be on the job. This situation has already been . . . remedied. The next time the Japanese military dive for a wall, pretending it is not there, they may hit a real wall and smash themselves against it.

STRATEGY AND FRUITS OF JAPANESE IMPERIALISM

By the Editors

The Japanese embarked upon their quest for empire with few natural assets and many liabilities. The limitations imposed by scarcity of arable land and paucity of mineral resources have been reviewed in earlier sections of this chapter. Yet despite those handicaps, the Japanese succeeded in building one of the greatest empires in modern times.

Many factors contributed to this achievement, including a few geographical assets, a great deal of hard work, smart strategy, considerable treachery, and phenomenal luck up to a certain point. By drawing heavily upon the freely proffered aid of Europe and America, and by cultivating a spartan way of life, the "Children of the Rising Sun" succeeded in accumulating the arms necessary to take the first steps in empire-building during the later years of the nineteenth century. By diverting their meager resources increasingly into military channels, and by exploiting recurrent strife among the western powers, they were able to achieve important successes at a cost well within their limited resources. Cheap victories gave them either new sources of raw materials or greater leverage on other states, or both together in some instances. By this means they progressively enlarged the industrial base of their military power and proportionately freed their country from economic bondage to the West.

Geographical remoteness from the main seats of political power contributed not a little to Japan's rise. The military development of China and of the Russian Far East is of recent date, and still lags far behind that of Europe and North America. The principal European powers and the United States all have colonial possessions or other interests in the Pacific or Far East. But their principal industrial centers are located far away upon the opposite face of the globe. Japan, like the United States, derived great advantage during the early stages of its development from the vast distances separating it from strong powers which might have desired to curtail or at least control its growth.

Nature also gave Japan a commanding position off the coast of Asia. Japan's home islands, like those of Great Britain, are separated from yet close to the continental mainland. In an earlier chapter we have described the political and military value of Britain's strategical position, under conditions prevailing until recent years. For much the same reasons, Japan's strategical position also was strong, though not as strong as that of Great Britain.

The difference arose partly from the political situation in Eastern Asia, partly from the island structure of the Western Pacific. The retarded political and economic development of the Far East gave Japan fewer military leverages and commercial opportunities than were open to Britain. The island structure of the Western Pacific made Japan more vulnerable to attack, on the one hand, but also opened up unique opportunities for expansion, on the other.

Japan is the focus of several festoons or chains of islands. These have been likened both to stepping stones and to the rungs of a ladder. Starting from Tokyo, it is possible to advance either across the North Pacific to Alaska or through the South Pacific to the East Indies, Australia, New Zealand, and on clear to the Marquesas, without ever making a water jump of more than 500 miles, and usually very much less. These island chains thus provide natural pathways for amphibious armies either toward or away from Japan.

To enhance the security of their island home, and to preempt the military routes for later expansion, Japanese statesmen set out methodically during the last quarter of the nineteenth century to acquire the island chains which fix the routes of attack and retreat across the vast reaches of the Pacific.

Their first step was acquisition of the Kurile chain which encloses the Okhotsk Sea and, together with the Aleutian chain, closely parallels the great circle route from North America. In 1875, the Kurile islands, previously claimed by Russia, were transferred to Japan in return for recognition of Russian claims to the larger island of Sakhalin which all but blocks the northern exits from the Japan Sea.

In 1876, the Japanese reached out to the south to occupy the Bonin islands. This chain of islets forms one of the northerly links in a long festoon connecting central Japan with the East Indies via the Marianas, Palau, and Moluccas. Fifteen years later, in 1891, the Japanese moved on to the next "rung" of that ladder, occupying the tiny Volcano group, of which the most important today is Iwo.

Meanwhile, in 1879, the Japanese had seized the Ryukyu chain which encloses the East China Sea. Those islands extend southwestward from Kyushu almost to the great island of Formosa. In taking the Ryukyus the Japanese ignored the Chinese Empire's nebulous historic claim to them, and the Chinese by that time were too weak and internally divided to make any effective protest.

The next prize was Formosa. That large island was indisputably part of the Chinese Empire. But the Japanese greatly desired it, largely because of its immense strategic value, located between Luzon and the China coast, and between the East and South China Seas. With its seizure after military victory over China in 1895, Japan held interlocking chains of islands that screened the coast of Asia from the Russian peninsula of Kamchatka in the north to the coast of southern China in the south.

During the same war, Japanese forces also occupied the Liaotung peninsula of southern Manchuria. China was compelled to cede that territory also to Japan. But the European powers decreed otherwise. Japan was not strong enough yet to defy them, and was obliged to relinquish its foothold in Manchuria.

Japan's next bid for territory was equally unsuccessful. Tokyo objected to United States annexation of Hawaii in the vain hope, apparently, that Japan itself might acquire that commanding position. The Japanese also tried, with no better success, to gain some kind of foothold in the Philippines at the time the United States took over those islands from Spain.

Their next attempt in Manchuria, however, succeeded. Russo-Japanese rivalry in that region led to war in 1904-1905. The Russians, fighting at the end of a 5,000-mile, single-track railroad, were worsted. By that victory Japan secured: (1) the foothold in south Manchuria denied to her ten years before; (2) the southern half of Sakhalin which she had renounced back in 1875; and (3) a protectorate over the nominally independent state of Korea occupying the long peninsula which the Japanese likened to a "dagger pointed at the heart of Japan."

The First World War gave Japan the opportunity to extend a long arm out towards the Hawaiian islands. Taking advantage of their alliance with Great Britain, the Japanese immediately entered that conflict in 1914, and dispatched armed forces to occupy Germany's Pacific possessions as far south as the equator. These included the Marianas (except Guam), the Caroline, and the Marshall islands. The Marianas form part of the north-south festoon previously described. Connecting with this festoon just north of the equator, the Caroline islands extend eastward some 1,500 miles to a point connecting with another north-south festoon, of which the Marshall group forms the most northerly link. These acquisitions gave Japan strategic positions closely paralleling the American military route from Hawaii to the Philippines via Midway, Wake, and Guam.

Japan's island screen afforded little or no protection, however, against long-range blockade. To this form of pressure the island kingdom was peculiarly sensitive. Japan depended heavily upon imports of raw materials and industrial equipment. These were brought from points as far away as the Americas and Europe. Two main arteries connected Japan with these oversea sources of supply. One ran parallel to the Asiatic coastline, through the South China Sea, and thence into the Indian Ocean and beyond. The other crossed the Pacific to the Western Hemisphere. Both of them reached far beyond the range of Japanese naval power.

The British Empire held the commanding positions along the southwestern rim of the Pacific. American sea power held sway over the eastern reaches of that ocean. Between them Great Britain and the United States controlled all the passageways between the Pacific and the Indian, Arctic, and Atlantic Oceans, as well as the sea approaches to the Americas, to the East Indies, and to Southeast Asia. The Japanese navy might dominate a considerable area in the Western Pacific. But as long as the United States and the British Empire held the more remote borderlands and the exits from that ocean, Japan was and would remain a prisoner within a circumscribed region bounded roughly by the International Date Line and the Equator.

Partly to escape the leverages which geography thus gave to Britain and the United States, Japanese leaders vigorously pushed their quest for empire in Eastern Asia. This program, as we have seen, long antedated the First World War, but that struggle gave it impetus and direction. The war created a partial political vacuum in the Far East. European forces were largely withdrawn; the danger of European interference with Japanese plans largely removed for the time being. The United States was left virtually sole guardian of western interests in Eastern Asia. But even the United States was forced momentarily into a relatively passive role as the American people became deeply involved in the European struggle.

Japan made the most of this opportunity. In 1914 the Japanese seized the German concession in the Chinese province of Shantung on the long peninsula facing Korea. In 1915 China was presented with a series of "demands" designed to bring that country completely under Japanese domination. In 1918, following the Russian Revolution, Japanese troops swarmed into eastern Siberia with the manifest purpose of permanently occupying the whole region. Though local resistance and western pressures eventually compelled the Japanese to suspend both of these aggressive enterprises, there was no longer any mistaking the trend and purport of Japanese ambition in the Far East.

This trend became still more pronounced in the growing struggle for control of Manchuria. The area bearing that name comprises the three northern provinces of Greater China. These lie northwest of the Korean peninsula in a pocket formed by that Japanese dependency, eastern Siberia, Mongolia, and North China proper. Japanese strategists and empire-builders have long regarded Manchuria as the key position in their struggle for eastern Asia.

They have coveted Manchuria for three principal reasons. First, that region contains valuable raw materials— iron and coal in particular—which supplement the weak industrial base of Japan proper. Second, Japanese strategists have desired Manchuria to prevent it from ever becoming a springboard for an attack on Korea, or even on Japan itself. Third, they have viewed this region as a strategic lever with which to pry open the doorways into eastern Siberia, into Central Asia, and into North China.

Any map of this region shows the extraordinary strategic importance of Manchuria's position. With the Japanese in Manchuria, Vladivostok stands at the apex of a long narrow salient exposed to attack on three sides. Northern Manchuria in turn thrusts a broad and deep salient into Soviet Asia. From southern Manchuria opens an historic gateway into Mongolia, through which an army could strike deep in the rear of Soviet defenses in the Far East.

Finally, Manchuria provides the easiest route into North China, a region of immense value to the Japanese Empire. Within the five Chinese provinces of Shantung, Shansi, Hopei, Suiyuan, and Chahar, are located the richest known coal fields in the Far East. Shansi alone has thirty times as much coal as all the Japanese islands. In addition there are substantial deposits of other minerals, especially iron ore. The ores of Chahar alone are said to exceed the total iron reserves of Korea and Japan combined.

Without the fuels and metals of this region, China would have little chance of ever becoming a major military power. With the resources of North China and Manchuria combined, the Japanese could build upon the Asiatic mainland a supplementary industrial base to bolster the shaky foundations of their greater empire.

In 1931, when the peoples of Europe and the United States were mired in the great depression, the Japanese army took over Manchuria. Shortly thereafter, they extended their hold to the neighboring province of Jehol. These territories they grouped together to form the puppet state of Manchukuo. From that strategic fulcrum they commenced prying their way into North China, and in July 1937 they struck the opening blow of the greater war in Eastern Asia.

Without entering at this point into the reasons for Japan's failure to finish promptly this "China incident" (as Nipponese spokesmen long persisted in calling their undeclared war on China), it may be noted that by the summer of 1941 Japanese strategy in Eastern Asia was rapidly approaching bankruptcy. Direct attack had won victories and carried Japanese armies deep into China, but had failed to force a decision. Years of attrition warfare had caused untold misery to China's suffering millions, but had failed to break the resistance of the Chinese national government. The blockade, principal instrument of the attrition strategy, showed an incurable tendency to develop leaks through which continuously trickled sorely needed supplies from the United States and other countries. Traffic on the Burma Road was increasing, and Japan was powerless to stop it without precipitating armed conflict with Great Britain and the United States.

Fresh clouds, moreover, were darkening Japan's eastern and southern horizons. China's struggle was gradually becoming the common cause of other nations. The flow of supplies along the Burma Road symbolized the growing alarm with which the English-speaking peoples watched the struggle in China. An emerging will to resist the spreading menace was reflected in active if belated preparations for the concerted defense of British, Dutch, and American territories in the Far East. The Dutch were defiantly resisting Japanese demands on the oil and other resources of the East Indies. The British Empire and the United States were cutting down exports of critical war-making materials to Japan. These trade restrictions were developing into a virtual counter-blockade which undermined the shaky structure of Japanese military power and threatened disaster to Japan's deadlocked armies in Asia.

To conquer China, Japan had to stop the leaks in the blockade and, above all, close the Burma Road. To break the counter-blockade rising up against Japan itself, Tokyo's military masters saw no alternative but to seize the sources of raw materials in the Philippines, in Southeastern Asia, and in the East Indies. To do any of these things, they had first to smash the British-Dutch-American coalition taking form in the Pacific.

This was a large order. American military potential alone was at least ten times that of Japan. But late 1941 was a time uniquely favorable for Japan's desperate enterprise. The Wehrmacht had overrun Western Europe. The British were fighting for their very existence. German armies stood at the gates of Leningrad and Moscow. The United States had withdrawn large elements of the American navy to help Britain fight the Battle of the Atlantic. The United States was beginning to mobilize its enormous resources, but months if not years would elapse before the new American army would be ready for fighting overseas. If the risks confronting Japan were great, so also was the opportunity. The rest is history.

The initial successes of the Japanese Blitzkrieg are history also, too recent and too well known to need retelling here. Not so widely appreciated perhaps were the effects of early Japanese victories in augmenting the military potential and in buttressing the defenses of the Japanese Empire.

By mid-1942 Japan held in uneasy subjection an imperial domain reaching deep into Asia and far out into the Pacific Ocean. This empire was roughly triangular in shape. Its northwestern border extended across Asia from the India-Burma border to the captured American island of Kiska. The eastern side of this vast triangle stretched from Kiska to the Gilbert atolls in mid-Pacific. The southern side was a long curving line which passed through the upper Solomons and New Guinea, bent south of Java and Sumatra, and then turned northwest across the Bay of Bengal to the India-Burma frontier.

This triangle enclosed a land and water area several times as large as the continental United States. Its land surface alone exceeded three million square miles, one and one-half times the size of Axis Europe at the pinnacle of Nazi success. Its population, 400-500 millions, embraced fully 20 per cent of the human race. Its natural resources provided the foundation for a truly formidable military power.

Before the war the area conquered by Japan produced 95 per cent of the world's natural rubber, 90 per cent of the quinine, 80 per cent of the copra, 70 per cent of the tin, and smaller proportions of a great many other essential raw materials. In North China, the Japanese had possession of one of the world's great unexploited coalfields, by far the greatest in the Afro-Asian Realm. In Southeast Asia and the East Indies, they had oil reserves sufficient for generations to come. They had control of large if not over-abundant supplies of iron-ore, plenty of manganese, chromium, and other ferro-alloys. There was bauxite in ample quantity, raw materials for expanding chemical industries, indeed almost everything needed for the invincible military state envisaged in Tokyo. But the Japanese had yet to consolidate their gains.

Compare the situation of the Japanese Empire with that of Axis Europe in that same year of 1942. The Emperor's armies, like Hitler's, had conquered a rich and populous domain. But both were surrounded by undefeated enemies bent on regaining what they had lost and on destroying the military power of the aggressor.

Japan was more isolated than Germany from its most dangerous foes. In this respect Japan's position was defensively stronger. But the distance which partially protected Japan for the time being also rendered Nipponese forces incapable of striking body blows at the main citadels of Allied strength. At no point in their advance did the Japanese gain a secure foothold within 4,000 miles of the main production centers of the United States.

Japan, furthermore, held more scattered territories than those comprising Axis Europe. These territories were knit together by long and exposed sea lines. Japan's scattered empire contrasted with Hitler's compact continental bloc. Nazi communications were being attacked by bombers ranging deep inside "Fortress Europe." But German communications were no more vulnerable than the long sea lines reaching out from Japan to Southeast Asia, to the East Indies, and to the scattered islands of the South Seas.

Japan, moreover, was more dependent than Germany upon outlying areas. Japan proper has nothing equivalent to the coal and iron producing district along the lower Rhine. Japan's vital resources were more scattered. Thrown back upon the resources of its home islands, Japan's material strength would drop rapidly to the level of Italy. Thus for Japan everything depended upon keeping open the shipping lanes which knit together the home islands with the Asiatic mainland and with the East Indies.

Japan's situation also differed from Germany's in the nature of the booty conquered. Hitler won not only forests, crop lands, mines, and oil wells, but also blast furnaces, steel mills, tractor plants, aircraft factories, and all the other paraphernalia of modern industrialism. With these went a large reservoir of human skills. Germany had only to repair what the armies had damaged and put the conquered peoples back to work in order to increase rapidly the industrial output of the expanding Reich. The colonial lands of Southeastern Asia, on the contrary, were chiefly producers of food and raw materials. These products had, in the main, to be hauled back to Japan for processing. But Japan lacked the ships to transport all this tonnage and simultaneously to carry on large-scale military operations along the rim of its sprawling empire. Japan also needed more smelters and factories in order to utilize fully the glut of raw materials which began piling up in the conquered territories. The island empire, in short, faced a gigantic problem of capital development to realize the potentialities of its windfall conquests of 1941-1942. Japan's empire-builders desperately needed a breathing space in which to enlarge their industrial plant and digest the fruits of successful aggression.

Conquest of Australia, New Zealand, Hawaii, and Alaska would have given them the needed respite. Occupation of those key positions would have deprived the Allies of the advanced bases from which to launch early counteroffensives. Had Japan won the Battles of the Coral Sea and Midway, or even the long-drawn-out struggle for Guadalcanal, she would have gained time—certainly months, perhaps years—in which to exploit the newly conquered riches of her inflated empire and build a nearly invincible military power in the Far East.

But Japan did not win those crucial battles of 1942. The labor and raw materials that might otherwise have gone into building new plants and enlarging old ones, had largely to be used to replace the ships, planes, and other matériel lost in the Coral Sea, at Midway, in the western Aleutians, in New Guinea, in the Solomons, and along the extended sea routes relentlessly patrolled by increasing numbers of American submarines.

By the end of 1942 Japan's overall position was seriously deteriorating. Rice rotted in the warehouses of Burma while Japan's weary war workers eked out a bare subsistence. Japan possessed limitless oil in the East Indies, but not enough tankers to haul it to the fighting fronts. The shortage of ships grew more and more acute, though Japan possessed in Manchuria, North China, and elsewhere all the coal and iron needed to build a cargo marine of any size. The plain truth was that Japan had more raw materials than she could use with her existing industrial plant. And increasing pressure on the military fronts prevented any large-scale diversion of effort from munitions production to industrial expansion.

This military pressure reflected the rapid growth of Allied strength in the Pacific. This was partly a result of the astonishing pace of American industrial mobilization. But it was the result also of global improvement in the strategic situation of the United Nations. The German defeat at Stalingrad, the Soviet counteroffensives, Rommel's expulsion from Egypt, the Anglo-American invasion of North Africa, the reopening of the Mediterranean, the increasing fury of the air war over Germany, and other developments all reflected the changing tide of war; all affected the disposition of Allied forces and the military balance in the Pacific.

Equally ominous for Japan were accumulating signs of Allied technical superiority. The Japanese won their amphibious Blitzkrieg against outnumbered defenders fighting largely with obsolete or obsolescent weapons. In the summer of 1942 the Japanese met the "first team" and were routed. Allied sea, air, and land equipment was proving technically superior in almost every category. By the end of 1942, Japan's early advantage in numbers of men and quantity of equipment was also disappearing. Early 1943 brought accumulating evidence that Japan, like Germany, was digging in for a bitter defensive struggle on the outer rim of its widely extended empire.

There were also indications that Tokyo's master strategists were beginning to study seriously the possibility of losing their outlying conquests. Capital development in the Philippines, East Indies, and Southeast Asia was being held to a bare minimum. The conquered areas were being looted of everything movable. The Japanese were striving desperately to build up large stockpiles of tin, rubber, bauxite, manganese, and other essential raw materials produced in the outer regions.

Confronted with disaster in their Outer Fortress, Nipponese spokesmen dwelt more and more upon the defensive strength of their Inner Fortress. This so-called Inner Fortress consisted of Japan proper, Korea, Manchuria, North China, Formosa, and minor intervening islands. Within that area were located most of the industrial centers. Within it, too, were the principal beds of high-grade coal, and sufficient iron ore to feed Japan's blast furnaces for many years. The Inner Fortress could also produce the food and textile-fibers necessary to keep soldiers and workers alive and clothed on a bare subsistence basis. Local production, with the aid of built-up stockpiles, could be made to provide enough ferro-alloys, chemicals, copper, and certain other essentials to get along for a while.

But the Inner Fortress lacked, partially or totally such essentials as petroleum, rubber, tin, and light metals. It was thus wanting in some of the most vital elements of modern military power. Cut off from the outer empire, Japan could carry on only to the limit of its precious stockpiles. How long would depend largely upon the scale and pace of the war and consequent rate of military consumption.

1943, 1944, 1945 were years of disaster for Japan. By mid-1945 the Japanese fleet was reduced to the strength of a mere task force. Burma and the Philippines were lost. Supplies were again moving overland into China. The Marianas and Iwo were in American hands. Okinawa had fallen. The home islands were almost completely cut off from Southeast Asia and the East Indies. The shorter sea links with Manchuria, North China, and the Yangtze Valley were largely blocked. Hopelessly outclassed in the air, the Japanese were powerless to stop the ever larger flights of super-bombers which poured incendiaries and explosives upon the homeland's inflammable factory cities.

But the Japanese people still showed no signs of early collapse. The discipline and other qualities which had enabled them to do so much with so little, might become in the end a contributing cause to a defeat even more overwhelming than that suffered by Hitler's Third Reich.

Chapter 14

China: Past, Present, and Future

CHINA occupies a unique position in the thoughts and feelings of Americans. As a nation we really know very little about this ancient country. Only a few of us have ever visited it. We are only just beginning to study Chinese civilization seriously in our colleges and universities. Yet countless Americans feel a warm sympathy for the Chinese, wholly unlike their feeling toward any other country in the world.

Missionary influence undoubtedly has been a large factor in the growth of this sentiment. But American interest in China is also of commercial origin. During most of the nineteenth century, China was a place where one went in the famous clipper ships to buy exotic goods highly prized in Europe and America. Toward the end of the century the emphasis gradually shifted from imports to exports. China came to be regarded more as a place to sell than to buy. The crowded millions of eastern Asia were looked upon as a vast potential market for the manufactures pouring in a rising flood from the smoking factories of the West. In the crude idiom of that day, the Occident yearned for the Chinese to add the proverbial inch to their shirts and thereby solve the problem of distributing for profit the mass-produced goods of western industrialism.

The European approach to the China market was generally imperialistic. Each of the competing powers tried to monopolize as much of the trade as possible for its own citizens. The means ranged from schemes for outright seizure of Chinese territory to regimes of special privilege in "spheres of influence" nominally under Chinese rule. At the close of the nineteenth century, the European powers and Japan were pressing on the moribund Chinese Empire from all sides. There was great danger that China would suffer the fate of Poland in the preceding century—be partitioned among the competing powers and cease to exist as an independent state.

For various reasons, it was contrary to American traditions, and repugnant to American feelings and policy, to join in the scramble to stake out exclusive trading preserves in eastern Asia. Instead, the United States, with some support from Great Britain, undertook to establish a counter-trend summed up in the familiar phrases: "open door" and "integrity of China."

This American policy grew out of our commercial treaties with China. These treaties granted Americans the right to carry on commerce with China on equal terms with all other foreigners. This was the principle of the open door. This treaty right applied, of course, only within the recognized geographical boundaries of the Chinese state. If those boundaries were pushed inward by pressure from outside —if, in other words, the territory of the Chinese state diminished—the geographical area to which our open door right applied would shrink proportionately. If China were completely partitioned and ceased to exist as a recognized independent state, our commercial rights derived from treaties with China would disappear along with it.

The United States gradually devised both a short-term and a long-term policy to deal with this problem. The short-term policy was to secure from the other Great Powers some kind of general agreement to respect the territory and political existence of China. This policy was summed up in the phrase "territorial and administrative integrity of China." The longer-term policy was to help strengthen the Chinese state to the point where the Chinese themselves could resist the encroachments of European and Japanese imperialists.

Neither policy was followed with complete consistency or with unqualified success. The Manchu dynasty collapsed in 1911. The republican regime which followed was never more than a shadow government. For many years the country was ruled by provincial chieftains who waged intermittent gangster warfare upon each other. Even today, despite the achievements of the national regime of Chiang Kai-shek, China still lacks a government which can command the allegiance of all classes and sections. Yet despite internal disunity and lack of modern weapons and equipment, the Chinese have fought bravely and stubbornly against the Japanese invaders.

China's heroic defense and critically important strategical position have won for the Chinese a provisional status and a voice in international affairs out of all proportion to the realities of their power today. China is treated as one of the principal United Nations. In December

1943 at the Cairo Conference on the aims and strategy of the war against Japan, General Chiang Kai-shek sat with President Roosevelt and Prime Minister Churchill as spokesman for one of the "three great allies" in the Far Eastern struggle. At no stage in the creation of a world security organization has anyone seriously proposed denying China a permanent seat, along with the other Great Powers, in the Executive Council of the organization.

Yet, by any objective test, China is not a Great Power today. The country has almost no modern industrial plant. What little existed before the war has been, or will be, mostly destroyed as the result of the war. The country has only the rudiments of a modern transportation system. The Chinese people have yet to achieve political unity. They still live under the shadow of civil war and continuing revolution.

But what of the future? Will China become in actuality the Great Power envisaged by most Americans? China is a big country. The Chinese outnumber every other nationality in the world. Their birthrate is among the highest. Only a shockingly high death-rate prevents rapid growth of population. Does the country also have the necessary stores of mechanical energy and the requisite raw materials to support large-scale industrialization? Can the Chinese adapt their ancient culture to the necessities of modern industrialism?

These are not easy questions. Life-long residents and trained observers do not wholly agree as to the potentialities of China. On the whole, the disagreement seems to be not so much whether China can become a Great Power, but rather as to when it may become one. This latter question is critically important. For upon the question: when will China become a Great Power? hangs the future of international relations in eastern Asia.

As a nation we have got to answer this question. For our own safety and for the safety of our posterity, the answer had better be right. For upon this answer will depend some fateful decisions.

If the outlook in China is for indefinite civil war, anarchy, and famine, China may continue to be the virtual political vacuum that it was during the early years of the century. If this is what is in prospect, heroic measures will be required to prevent eastern Asia from becoming an arena of dangerous struggle among the British Empire, the Soviet Union, and the United States. Disagreement over a prostrate

China is one of many things that could disrupt the Big Three coalition without which there can scarcely be an enduring peace.

If, on the other hand, the outlook in China is for fairly rapid modernization and industrialization, accompanied by internal consolidation of power, China can become the strong independent state which Americans have long held to be an essential element of stability, order, and peace in the Far East.

The following readings are addressed to these crucial questions. They do not speak the final word on China. But they do reflect personal observation as well as long and profound study of political trends in the Far East.

THE FACE OF CHINA

By G. B. Cressey

From chap. 3 of *Asia's Lands and Peoples*, by G. B. Cressey. Copyright 1944 by McGraw-Hill Book Co., New York; reproduced by permission. The author is professor of geography at Stanford University, and a recognized authority on the geography of China.

CHINA is more than a place on the map. Here is a unique phenomenon. Other lands are older and others more beautiful, but nowhere else have so many people lived so close to nature and with such cultural continuity as in China. The landscape everywhere reflects the intensity of man's occupance. The culture of the ages has permeated all levels of society so that even the ricksha coolie quotes Confucius. No land on earth is so mature. . . .

The roots of the Chinese go deep into the earth. The carefully tilled gardens, the hand-plucked harvest, and the earthen homes all tell the story of man's intimate association with nature. On every hand a substantial peasantry labors industriously to wrest a meager livelihood from the tiny fields. Innumerable groups of farm buildings, half hidden in clumps of bamboo or willow, suggest the intensity of man's quest for food, and the ever-present grave mounds serve as reminders of the heritage of this venerable land.

The most significant element in the Chinese landscape is thus not the soil or vegetation or the climate, but the people. Everywhere there are human beings. In this old, old land, one can scarcely find a spot unmodified by man and his activities. Whereas life has been profoundly influenced by the environment, it is equally true that man has reshaped and modified nature and given it a human stamp. The Chinese landscape is a biophysical unity, knit together as intimately as a tree and the soil from which it grows. So deeply is man rooted in the earth that there is but one all-inclusive unity—not man and nature as separate phenomena but a single organic whole. The cheerful peasants at work in the fields are as much a part of nature as the very hills themselves. So, too, the carefully tended rice fields are an inescapable element in the human panorama.

No mere photographic portrayal of China can reveal all the varied ties that bind man and the soil together. Crisscross through the visible scene run innumerable threads of relationship. The landscape is a mosaic of many diverse elements, some dependent upon the vagaries of a none-too-certain rainfall, some conditioned by the limitations of the soil, still others molded by the force of tradition. All of these are linked together into a synthetic, animated picture. . . .

China is not only rich in her culture, she is diverse in her physical environment. Few countries have greater contrasts. Rainfall varies from an inch a year in the desert to nearly a hundred inches along the coastal mountains. Extensive forests stand in contrast to denuded hillsides. Rice is eaten three times a day in the south, but is a once-a-year luxury elsewhere. Shanghai may be a cosmopolitan city of the world, but one has to go only a few hundred yards beyond its borders to find a primitive countryside.

Whereas the United States and the Soviet Union extend from east to west, China trends north and south. From the far south of Hainan to the northernmost bend of the Amur River is 2,500 miles. These extremes reach from well inside the tropics to within 13° from the Arctic Circle. Thus agricultural possibilities and means of livelihood vary notably. If superimposed on North America, China would spread from Puerto Rico to Hudson Bay, with the Yangtze Valley in the latitude of New Orleans.

Few large countries have such a large percentage of hilly or otherwise uncultivable land. Only through prodigious effort and painstaking care have the Chinese been able to support so large a population. This topographic diversity has divided China into many regions, each with its personality and often with rivalries with other regions. The Chinese of the various provinces differ in physical appearance, in language, and in psychology. . . .

Despite these contrasts, China has a distinct homogeneity. Dialects may differ but the written language is the same. The degree of modernization may vary but everywhere is a coherent ideology, in large measure the heritage of Confucius and the sages. It is this way of life, of getting along with each other and with nature, that makes the Chinese so genuine. . . .

The earliest written records date from 1200 B.C., and earlier dates are known to be fictitious. The first nationwide dynasty is the Han, 206 B.C. to A.D. 220. Later came the Tang, 618 to 907, the Sung, 960 to 1280, the Ming or Mongol, 1368 to 1644, and the Ching or Manchu, 1644 to 1911. Most of these major dynasties have been times of stability and progress; between them have been intervals of chaos and confusion. It is unfortunate that we of the Occident should be learning of China during one of these transition intervals, unrepresentative of the country at its best.

The present political era dates from the Revolution of 1911 which overthrew the Manchus, and the subsequent establishment of the Nationalist government under Chiang Kai-shek in 1928. With the establishment of that government, the capital was removed from Peking to Nanking. Later on, during the Japanese invasion, it was temporarily located at Chungking. Although the rest of the world failed to appreciate the situation at the time, it is now clear that the Second World War began with the Mukden Incident of September 18, 1931, when Manchuria was overrun by the Japanese. The second phase of the Sino-Japanese War dates from July 7, 1937.

China's history is a by-product of her geography. Southeastern Asia is almost an oasis, largely self-sufficient and isolated from the rest of mankind. Until the era of modern travel, the most perfect barriers surrounded China on all sides. Towering plateaus, arid deserts, tropical forests, and the widest of the oceans all helped to preserve the unity of China. Nowhere near by was there an equal neighbor, except in India which was months away....

The most dangerous of these frontiers was in the north, for the Mongols gave the Chinese more trouble than all other "barbarians" put together. Hence the Great Wall was built, linked together out of earlier parts by the Emperor Chin Shih about 220 B.C. Unfortunately this rampart failed to achieve the desired result. In times of greater rainfall, the Chinese farmers were not willing to stay on their side of the fence and pushed cultivation into the grasslands to the north, while, during decades of drought, the wandering Mongol shepherds sought pasturage in the more humid lands within the Wall.

Only a few travelers reached China from Europe, notably Marco Polo and the Jesuit missionaries. Only occasional Chinese pilgrims went westward, but even in 128 B.C. the explorer Chang Chien crossed the Pamirs and reached Bukhara. The first Chinese to visit India was Fa Hsien in A.D. 413; like other pilgrims in quest of Buddhism he traveled via Sinkiang. Most of this contact with the West was overland, but a few Arab vessels came to Canton and Hangchow, even as early as A.D. 300. (See Fig. 28, p. 488, above.)

In so far as China had a front door, it was the Jade Gate at the Tibetan end of the Great Wall, named from the caravans that brought jade, properly nephrite, from the Kuen Lun Mountains. Out through it passed other caravans carrying silk and porcelains, some of which were carried as far as Roman Britain. China thus faced toward Inner Asia, and Japan was only of incidental concern. With the arrival of Europeans and the development of Canton, Shanghai, and Tientsin a century ago, these seaports became the new front doors of China. Instead of being a barrier, the ocean is now a highway. The Jade Gate faded into a poetic memory. Through the new coastal cities has flowed a tide of ideas which have altered the superficial life of many Chinese. Large countries do not easily change their cultural momentum or orientation, hence the reconstruction of a nation as big and numerous and ancient as China has created major problems....

China has had few years of normal opportunity since the Revolution of 1911, but the resiliency of trade and the cultural progress in times of peace have been amazing. Japan doubtless invaded China when she did because of the realization that another decade of internal development might make conquest impossible. From the beginning of the Manchurian conquest in 1931, it was clear that China was not yet strong enough to defeat Japan; what did not become evident until later was the fact that Japan could not conquer and develop China. Until outside aid arrived, the situation is aptly described by the Chinese proverb of a man riding a tiger; the tiger could not get at the man but the rider was afraid to get off. China's assets proved to be an unsuspected patriotism and defense in depth. With plenty of room into which to retire, China could afford to sell space in order to buy time.

China's international boundaries have never remained fixed for more than a few centuries at a time. Some Chinese dynasties on occasion have included areas west of the Pamirs, on the south slopes of the Himalaya, in northern Indo-China, along the left bank of the Amur River, as well as Korea, Formosa, and the Liuchiu Islands.

Under the last or Ching Dynasty, China was divided into 18 provinces

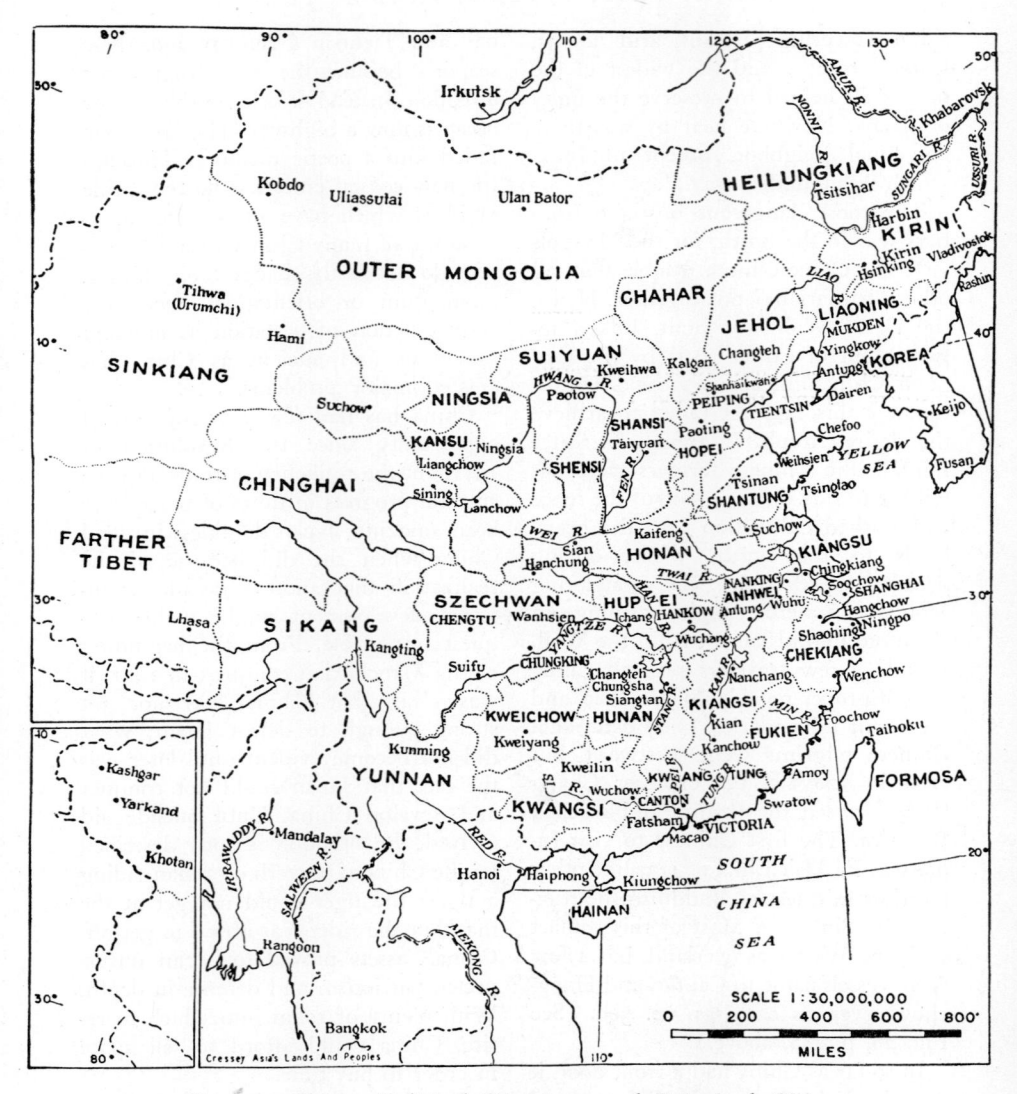

FIG. 31. China: Political Divisions and Principal Cities.

China is composed of 28 provinces and 2 outer territories. Three of her major cities are in the north: Peiping, Tientsin, and Mukden; five are in the Yangtze Valley: Shanghai, Nanking, Hankow, Chungking, and Chengtu; while two others are in the south: Canton, and Victoria on the island of Hongkong.

From G. B. Cressey, *Asia's Lands and Peoples*. Copyright 1944 by McGraw-Hill Book Co., New York; reproduced by permission.

and four dependencies. Several of the provinces were united at times, but it is customary for the Chinese to refer to the traditional part of their country south of the Great Wall as "the Eighteen Provinces." . . .

The nineteenth province was created in 1878 when Sinkiang was raised from territorial status.

Manchuria was divided into three provinces in 1903 and was rearranged by the Japanese into 19 administrative districts during the period of "Manchoukuo."

Mongolia has two parts: Inner Mongolia next to the Great Wall and thus closer to Peking, and Outer Mongolia. In 1912 the former was divided into four provinces.

Outer Mongolia has been independent since 1921, and is made up of two states under the protection of the Soviet Union, not recognized by China or by other foreign powers. One is the Mongolian People's Republic, with its capital at Ulan Bator, formerly Urga, and the other is the Tuvinian People's Republic, whose capital is Kizil Khoto. . . .

Tibet is also made up of two sections: Nearer Tibet and Farther Tibet. The latter is a semi-independent territory with its capital at Lhasa. . . . The former is divided into two provinces, thus bringing the total to 28.

Greater China . . . has an area of 4,380,535 square miles, of which 3,386,966 lies within the provinces. . . .

CHINA'S POLITICAL AND MILITARY POSITION

By David Nelson Rowe

From chaps. 1-9 of *China Among the Powers*, by D. N. Rowe. Copyright 1945 by Harcourt, Brace & Co., New York; reproduced by permission. The author is associate professor of international relations at Yale University, and a member of the Yale Institute of International Studies which sponsored the work resulting in his book.

China's long years of war against Japan have brought about a revolutionary change in her international position. When the war began in 1937, China could hardly be classed as a leading power. She had been under continuous Japanese military or political pressure during the six years since the invasion of Manchuria in 1931. As a result, she had lost much of her richest territory and in 1937 it seemed doubtful that she could hold out long against Japan. Yet today China stands with Britain, the Soviet Union and the United States as one of the Great Powers, and few would question her right to such a position in world affairs. . . .

China's place in maintaining the peace will depend to a great extent upon the amount and the nature of her military power at the close of the war and on the possibilities for its development thereafter. Since war is the final testing ground for demonstrating national strength or weakness, a study of China's war against Japan should tell us much about her military position at present and as it is likely to be at war's end. In addition, a thorough investigation of her basic resources and of the means for their utilization will allow us to estimate her future military possibilities. . . .

CHINA AS A MILITARY POWER TODAY

Except for her present war against Japan, China has lost every war she has waged against foreign powers during the past century. As a result she has from time to time lost much of her border territory, chiefly to Britain,

France, Russia, and Japan. By the end of the nineteenth century China had become so weak militarily that she was a negligible factor as a contestant for power even within her own borders. As a result, she became a battleground for the rivalries of the powers. The Russo-Japanese war ending in 1905 was a contest between those two nations over the Chinese territory of Manchuria, and was largely fought on Chinese soil. Again in the First World War, Japan fought Germany on the Chinese soil of Shantung Province, with the aim of establishing her own control over that region.

Finally, since 1931, the cycle has swung back again, and Japan, partly as a means of attacking the interests of the other powers in China, engaged in war against China itself. This was a logical result of the decreased military strength of the other nations in the Far East after the First World War, and particularly after the Washington Conference of 1922. It was also caused by Japan's fears of the possible results of China's new nationalism after 1927, that is, the development of political integration and military strength in China. Any developments along these lines had to be prevented before they had progressed sufficiently to become a real problem.

In this connection it should be remembered that although the Japanese policy of expansion in Asia has always been strongly supported by the Japanese people, the attack in Manchuria in 1931 was made on the direct initiative of the Japanese army. It was doubtless aimed to strike a disintegrating blow at the growth of Chinese political organization before it could bear fruit in an increase of military strength which might obstruct further Japanese expansion.

In fact, however, after the Revolution in 1911 Manchuria had never been a source of real support for any of the legal or *de facto* central regimes in China. Its economic development had been dominated by Japan. Its complete amputation from the body of China after 1931 therefore did not materially decrease the prospects for the immediate growth of Chinese military strength. In fact, the decision of the Chinese Nationalists after 1927 to locate their regime in the Central China city of Nanking, instead of at Peking under the shadow of the Great Wall, was of great importance. It moved the political center of China away from the zone of Japanese military and economic domination in Shantung and Manchuria, and based it solidly on the revenues and financial resources of the lower Yangtze River Valley. As a result, the long expected Japanese move to take North China, which came in 1937, found the Nationalist government with the beginning, though a minor one, of a modern army. This army was totally dependent on foreign imports for all heavy artillery, automotive equipment, airplane engines, etc., and its supplies of those items were very small.

In building China's military strength, Generalissimo Chiang seems to have thought primarily in terms of land power. At any rate it is doubtful whether any appreciable naval strength could have been developed in the short time and with the limited resources at his disposal. Under the circumstances, the dominant Japanese sea power soon cut off the chief sources of Chinese replenishment in matériel, and, although the advance of the Japanese forces in China was sometimes delayed, it continued steadily for over two years.

After 1939 the war between China and Japan developed into a condition of stalemate. From that time, as is well known, Japan held not only all of Manchuria, but also large portions of the vital plains of North China and the Yangtze Valley. She also seized most of China's railroads and occupied or blockaded the entire Chinese coast. Why was she unable to advance far enough, to secure the capitulation of the Chinese government? On the other hand, given China's power to resist, why was she in turn powerless to drive Japan from her territory? Only by answering these questions may we arrive at a real understanding of the extent and nature of Chinese military power today.

The answer to the first question is that the Japanese never clearly understood the real nature of their military task in China. They continued to think in terms of the old China, which during the middle of the nineteenth century had repeatedly been defeated in war by opponents who took advantage of her peculiar weakness. This weakness lay in the fact that she was in the process of political disintegration, and that the alien ruling dynasty thus found it impossible to use effectively even those archaic elements of armed force which it controlled. This made it possible for the westerners to employ against China the methods of what may be termed "colonial warfare." This consisted in the use of small concentrations of military force of a vastly superior technological type, against overwhelming numbers of opposing forces handicapped by inferiority of weapons and above all by low political morale. Under these circumstances, while battles were sometimes difficult to win, campaigns were relatively easy, due to progressive deterioration of the already poor morale of the opposing forces.

It should have been apparent to the Japanese from their experiences with the Chinese in the fighting around Shanghai in 1932 that the obvious technical superiority of their forces would not in itself suffice to win military success. Yet in 1937 at Shanghai and elsewhere they repeated exactly their mistake of five years earlier. Relying on their technical superiority, they failed to concentrate sufficient quantities of troops and matériel to give them a quick decision. Their final success in forcing the Chinese troops to withdraw from their positions around Shanghai came only after several months and by means of a major flanking operation. . . .

The mistake of the Japanese at Shanghai was a fundamental and persistent one; from its effects they have never recovered. This error was to be seen in all their operations at the outset of the China war, which they attempted to label a mere "incident." . . .

The error of coming with "too little" had its clear results in North China and at Shanghai in the failure to secure a quick decision. But its results were disastrous when, after securing control of the seaports and proceeding inland, the Japanese began to engage in land warfare in China's interior. Here they were still further handicapped by their failure to anticipate the extent of the task of liquidating their enemy, whose movements could take advantage of the size of the country. The Japanese showed no realization of their need to marshal sufficient forces to make their power felt in a large geographical area. . . .

Without this initial and cumulatively fatal error on the part of the Japanese, the Chinese would soon have found themselves without means of continuing military resistance. Their weakness in modern armaments has already been mentioned. The numerous troops in the various armies were equipped with rifles and machine guns of a variety of types and patterns, including half a dozen different makes, using non-interchangeable ammunition. The same variety was to be found in the artillery, which was for the most part of foreign manufacture and of very limited quantity. Up to 1937, most of the few arsenals in China had been operated by the various provincial governors for their personal armies, and were far from modern or efficient. Most military equipment had to be imported, at considerable cost. In 1930 the expenditures on arms imports represented a considerable portion of the estimated $100,000,000 U.S. spent each year on munitions of war.

This sum is not large by present-day standards, but in relation to the Chinese economy it was then and still is an important amount. Yet it was insufficient to secure any really large quantities of modern arms. The small Chinese air force, for instance, barely lasted out the first six months of the war, though a few planes remained thereafter and were for a time supplemented by Russian planes and pilots.

China's defenselessness was clearly recognized by Generalissimo Chiang. In a series of speeches delivered to his Officers' Training Corps in July 1934 he accurately assessed the extent and nature of China's military weakness. . . . He predicted that China would be unable to "put up a successful resistance to Japan," and stated that war with Japan at that time would "amount to suicide."

Perhaps lest his listeners should consider these words an excuse for a mere temporary policy of appeasing Japan, the Generalissimo went on to warn that to make material preparations for war with Japan, even a period of thirty years would be insufficient! The Japanese, he stated, would probably not allow China this much time in which to prepare, nor could the existent Chinese economy or technology support adequate military preparations.

This being the case, how could China possibly defend herself against continued Japanese aggression? In effect, the reply of Chiang Kai-shek to his subordinates was that China's resistance must be compounded of three elements. The most important element was political mobilization. Here the Nationalist leader put his finger on the old weakness which had caused China's defeat so many times in the past. . . .

The primary backwardness of China was political, and unity could do something to offset the enemy's obvious technological superiority. This would make it possible to use "manpower to fight the material equipment of the enemy!"

But that this alone could not succeed was clear. The second element in China's defense was to be the use of her large continental area into which to draw the enemy, in order to cause his technical superiority to be diluted by spatial dispersion. The Generalissimo's estimate that the Japanese could occupy the eighteen provinces south of the Wall in eighteen months was later to be proved unduly pessimistic. But his general conception was sound, and here he introduced the third element in China's defense, namely, the certainty that if a quick Japanese victory could be avoided, there would be "changes in the international situation." He saw correctly that stalemate, produced by united Chinese resistance . . . could not by any means or for any reason be considered a victory for China, and that for China to win the decision must be supplied from other centers of power. His estimate of the world situation was correct. Japan's adherence, in November 1936, to the Berlin-Tokyo Anti-Comintern Pact made the Soviet Union a potential ally of great strength for China. It made logical the speedy creation thereafter of the United Front between the Chinese Nationalists and Communists.

Chiang himself had always considered that, to the Japanese, Russia was the supreme enemy. The Soviet belief that Japan was an enemy of Russia was indicated by Stalin's aid to Chiang Kai-shek after 1937. For several years the Soviet Union was the only power to give actual military support to China in substantial quantities. The formal expansion of the Anti-Comintern Pact into a Rome-Berlin-Tokyo Axis, directed against the United States and Britain as well as Russia, meant the complete development of those "changes in the international situation" upon which Chiang Kai-shek relied and which, with Pearl Harbor, brought Britain and the United States into his war with Japan.

At this point it must be clearly stated that the success of the entire Chinese program of resistance to Japan depended vitally in the first instance on the Japanese error of underestimating the enemy's power to resist. Given the failure of the Japanese to win a decision quickly and to annihilate the forces of Chinese resistance, it then became possible to develop further the Chinese strategy. The Chinese plan for prolonged resistance was announced by the Generalissimo on October 31, 1938. It divided the war into three stages. These were, first, a retreat to optimum defense positions in Central and Western China, second a defense at these positions combined with the carrying on of guerrilla warfare behind the Japanese lines, and, third, the final counteroffensive. The counteroffensive was to be based on the exhaustion of the enemy achieved in the two prior stages, and on a continued growth in Chinese strength coupled with foreign help. . . .

The continuing military failure of the Japanese was practically ensured by the geography of China's west. Not only did this region comprise a vast area, but the nature of the terrain was such that the Japanese found it impossible to continue their advance at even its previous slow rate. Not far above Hankow the Yangtze River changes from a broad open stream deep enough for ocean freighters to a swift narrow channel with frequent rapids. It is navigable only by native junks pulled by trackers or by specially built steamers with powerful engines.

Such vessels the Japanese could have supplied, but to risk them in the narrow gorges . . . would have been an invitation to Chinese mountain artillerymen. The river served the Japanese only as far as the beginning of the gorges at Ichang, where they were already 1,000 miles from the sea at Shanghai. They never advanced westward any distance beyond Ichang. At this point they based the bombers which later flew over the mountains to Chungking.

Transportation westward by land was even more difficult. The Japanese advances had brought them by 1939 to the edge of the great semicircle of mountains which enclose the Chinese coastal plains and river valleys. Here the terrain, in effect, robbed them of mechanical transport and thus deprived them of a large measure of their technological superiority over the Chinese. The best example of this is to be seen in the various Japanese campaigns in the northern province of Shansi. An American newspaper correspondent describes the situation there as follows:

"It is practically impossible at any time to transport guns of any caliber up and down the high cliffs and deep gorges. When it rains it is even impossible to get supplies to the men engaged in the mountains.

"There are no roads which can be used for communication lines, making it necessary to use experienced mountain climbers, not only to do the fighting, but also to supply food and ammunition to the troops."

Deprived thus of their technological advantages, the Japanese were at the disadvantage of confronting the vastly superior numbers of their enemy, who were fighting on familiar ground and on the defensive. This latter fact is of primary importance. For, while it is a mistake to speak of the Chinese people as pacifist and peace-loving, the Chinese themselves admit that their forces make a better showing in defense than in offense. All efforts of foreign military instructors to change this characteristic have failed. Actually, as Owen Lattimore correctly states, "western military science, in fact, affects only the tactics, never the strategy of Chinese warfare." This is particularly true in the matter of defensive versus offensive warfare. To the Chinese way of thinking, a successful repulse of the enemy constitutes a victory over him. . . .

For this kind of warfare the armaments used by the Chinese troops, consisting of rifles, machine guns, and mortars, together with hand grenades, can all be manufactured in the arsenals of Free China. But China is still unable to manufacture any heavy weapons of war in her own factories, nor will she be able to do so at the war's end.

When the war is over, the Chinese army may well possess a small nucleus of an air force, the personnel having been trained in the United States and flying American planes. All replacements of personnel and matériel must come from abroad, as must all gasoline with which to fly the planes. And all the heavy artillery and its ammunition, with which to blast the Japanese from their defense positions 1,000 miles inside China, must also be supplied to China from abroad, as it was before the war. . . .

MANPOWER

Among the factors determining the military power of a state, none is more basic than its population. . . . The use of machines in warfare has not eliminated the need of mass armies. And the requirements of supply for mechanized warfare have greatly increased the needs of manpower on the home front and the lines of communication. It is as unnecessary to determine the relative importance of these two wartime uses of manpower as it is essential to state their absolute interdependence in the waging of war.

It is impossible to secure reliable statistics regarding the population of China. . . . The average of twenty-five representative estimates . . . made between 1900 and 1943 is approximately 411,333,400. For China today this is in all likelihood too low a figure. The latest Chinese official estimate is 459,339,764. . . . China's population is thus the largest of any state located in a single territorial area. . . .

The population of China is highly concentrated in the regions of good agricultural land. These, however, are scattered widely from North to Central China and from east to west. The western province of Szechwan, for example, has an estimated population of 52,703,210 and the two other southwestern provinces of Yunnan and Kweichow together add an estimated total of 21,960,951. This amounts to a figure of 74,664,161 for these three interior provinces, which together provided a strong basis for China's resistance to Japan. . . . Of China's twenty-eight provinces these three together have a population exceeding that of any European country except Germany and U.S.S.R. . . .

China's population problems are those of surplus, not of shortage. For the predictable future she will have no worries regarding adequate supplies of manpower. Her problem will be to prevent her population from increasing more rapidly than she can increase the facilities for their support and for their efficient employment both in peace and in war. The rate of increase of the Chinese population is quite high. It is probable that in spite of all the wars, famines, and natural disasters of the last thirty years, China's total population has increased. If the coming of political stability in the future means a reduction of these natural checks on population increase, it is probable that within one or two generations the population would increase from 75 to 100 per cent.

Such an increase would be a disaster to China, resulting in strong adverse effects on her military power position. This is true because the result of such an expansion in population would be to lessen the possible use of the national wealth for military purposes, by forcing its absorption in the ordinary task of supporting the population. For this, the improvement or expansion of Chinese agriculture can only partly suffice. It is merely necessary to state that almost all arable land in China has already been taken up.

The huge Chinese population is about 75 per cent agricultural. Compared with western countries, a large proportion of the people is in the young and middle-aged groups. This reflects the prevailing high birth-rate and short life span. A smaller proportion than in western countries is above the age of fifty. This . . . increases the proportion of the population which is capable of bearing arms and of producing for war. . . .

Because of the lack of exact data, it is difficult to secure an accurate estimate of the total number of men in China of military age. If we take the relatively safe figure of 450,000,000 for the total population, the number of males would be approximately 225,000,000. Of these perhaps one-third would be of military age. Even if only one-third of them are fit to serve or can be spared from civilian life, China still has a military manpower pool of over 20,000,000 men. This is approximately double the size of the armed forces of the United States [in 1945].

At present this is a much greater number than she can effectively arm or employ. Figures for the total number of front-line and reserve troops mobilized for the war against Japan vary from 4,000,000 to 15,000,000. Actual combat troops provided with the simplest of arms probably do not number more than 3,000,000 men. But this number reflects not available manpower, but technological backwardness.

Not only is the span of life short in China, but the general health of the people is poor. Endemic malaria, dysentery, hookworm, and tuberculosis are important not only as they affect the death-rate. Their chief effect on the people comes from the fact that they do not usually kill quickly, but slowly devitalize their victims, who may suffer from several of them more or less constantly. The result is a general decrease in working efficiency, which in turn prevents the individual from taking measures to improve his health. The only escape from this vicious circle lies in improving the ratio between the amount of wealth produced and the number of people to share it. Merely to improve health conditions increases the problem by increasing the population.

The government attack on the problem of public health through the

National Health Administration was planned as a part of the national reconstruction movement. After the beginning of the war, public health work was extended into the interior of China where in most localities modern medicine was previously almost nonexistent. Health work in those regions was carried on against great odds. The lack of trained personnel, drugs, and equipment alone would constitute serious obstacles. But to them were added the prevalence of obstinate public superstitions in some localities and the climatic and geographic difficulties. . . . The health problem still remains critical.

Its bearing on the military potential of China is clear. Not only do disease-ridden populations make poor material for armies, but the whole fabric of any national military effort would be vitiated by a lack of health among the population. In time of war, deficiencies in the organization of health measures show up clearly.

The critical shortage of doctors and nurses in China is a result of educational backwardness. The Chinese army can secure only about one-thirtieth of the number of medical personnel judged necessary for an efficient army medical service. . . .

Added to the lack of trained personnel is a lack of organization and of adequate transportation facilities. All these things combine to produce a type of treatment of the wounded and sick in Chinese armies that can justly be termed barbarous, and which is partly caused by a lack of common sympathy of the commanding officers for their men. Corrupt practices among officers also play a part in preventing food supplies from reaching the troops. Inadequate and improper food is the general rule in the Chinese army. Thus the army is for the most part powerless even to maintain, let alone improve, the unsatisfactory level of health prevailing among the masses of its recruits. This is certainly of no less importance in a non-mechanized army built on the unlimited use of manpower than in a modern mechanized force.

China's military manpower is unsatisfactory not only from the point of view of health. There is also the problem of illiteracy. In 1938 the Chinese Ministry of Education estimated that there were 360,000,000 illiterate persons in China. This is nearly 80 per cent of the total population, and is probably a conservative estimate.

Of the officially estimated total of 360,000,000 illiterate persons in 1938, 165,000,000 were in the age bracket of 15 to 45 years, which includes practically all men of military age. This group of illiterates alone makes up about one-third of the total population of China.

Between 1938 and 1940 the Ministry of Education claimed to have educated about 25,000,000 persons in the 15-45 year age group, who were therefore no longer to be classed as illiterate. This gives a clue to the official definition of literacy, for these persons would be able to receive only the barest elements of training in reading in the short time available and with the lack of facilities for training. . . .

All this indicates that the problem of illiteracy is a serious one in China and cannot be solved quickly. It is a great handicap in the military field, particularly since in China the armies are conscripted from the lowest social and economic levels. Such better educated groups as college students or the sons of rich gentry are practically immune to the demands of the military.

It is in the more advanced fields of the technology of war that illiteracy will provide a particularly serious bar to the modernization of China's mass armies. This drawback can be overcome, but it will take considerable time and the expenditure of large sums to wipe out illiteracy in China.

At the same time, the problem of raising the level of technical knowledge and skill among the population is also a formidable one. At present, the vast majority of the population is backward in this respect, as would be expected in a society at least 75 per cent of whose members are engaged in entirely non-mechanized farming. It will be easier to secure from this reservoir of manpower sufficient workers for large-scale industry than to secure large numbers of men for the armed forces who are capable of maintaining and operating complex war machines. In the case of industry for mass production, many mechanical procedures can be broken down and simplified for continuous repetition by unskilled workers. But no such system can be adopted for the operation of war machines. For the most part their manipulation demands far more complicated skills. In addition, mechanized troops must combine discipline with individual initiative under combat conditions. These characteristics are rarely to be found in individuals whose environment is characterized by an almost entire lack of mechanical sophistication. Such individuals rarely have the opportunity to acquire skill in the manipulation of machinery. Also, and still more important, they are seldom conditioned during childhood to form such habits of correlated group responsibility and individual initiative as are connected with the mass operation of mechanical devices.

For example, the poor performances sometimes turned in by Chinese pursuit aviation squadrons early in the war were not exclusively caused by poor flying ability. Though pilots often failed to adhere to disciplined mechanical procedures, in the air they equaled the best Japanese fliers. Their fatal defect was the tendency to break formation in combat, often causing them to be shot down one by one. They needed flying skill less than they needed discipline in fighting the enemy.

However, the maintenance of machines presents even greater problems in China than training workers to operate them. In this connection it must be emphasized that such traditions of manual precision as are in the Chinese heritage are not typically connected with impersonal discipline, but with the individualism of the artist and craftsman. The artist and craftsman must be a master of manual workmanship, but the products which he turns out are not characterized by uniformity. They are, in fact, differentiated and individualized. In contrast, modern mass-produced machines, whatever their esthetic shortcomings, demand impersonal and disciplined adherence to prescribed procedures, for both manufacture and maintenance. Otherwise the organized and complex system of operations into which they fit, both in peace and in war, falls to pieces.

Leaving aside the question of value-judgments, one cannot expect to discover habits of devotion to legalistic rules and regulations widespread among members of the Chinese society. Their social values, it must be remembered, are the product of historical causations quite different from those of Europe and America. To say this is but to indicate one of the problems of utilizing the masses of the Chinese population for building state power on the western model. It may be argued that such an end is undesirable, but it is nonetheless recognized by China's leaders as necessary for the continued existence of Chinese independence. Indoctrination in mechanical precision and discipline is but one aspect of a general process of changing the place of the individual in Chinese society. The pattern shifts, but in as vast an organism as China such great changes take generations to accomplish.

A further question relating to military manpower is that of popular attitudes to war.... Here again the answer is found in the general social environment. It must be remembered that in China political feudalism gradually went out of existence and finally disappeared about two thousand years ago. With it went the organized fostering of the martial spirit by the feudal politico-military elite. There is some reason to believe that the old Chinese aristocratic fighting class was already non-existent at the time of the unification of China out of a collection of feudal states in the second century B.C. With the formation of the Chinese Empire and the abolition of feudal titles, the association between military skills and political and social advancement was very much lessened. The conduct of government was taken from the hands of military experts by the organized Confucian intellectual aristocracy. This new hierarchical elite has held the real power in Chinese society almost continuously since that time.

Here is to be found a chief cause of the progressive deterioration of the social and political position of military men during the last two thousand years of Chinese history. The Chinese have indulged in imperialistic expansion on several occasions during this long time, but the preponderance of foreign wars were defensive in nature. No great military tradition can be expected to maintain itself among people who adopt the defensive approach as a solution of their foreign military problems.

It should be noted that this attitude toward the outer barbarians was already beginning to develop before China's unification in the second century B.C. The Great Wall was its symbol. This great rampart had been largely built by the feudal principalities on the northern border as a series of defense works and was later joined into one system under the Empire. It was always more of a symbol than an effective barrier. For social pressures and forces on both sides of the Wall have always been more important than the man-made structure which was supposed to keep them from conflict.

Taking all these things into consideration, it is not surprising that in China armies came to be considered "a necessary or even unnecessary evil." Under these handicaps there was little motive for the best qualified men to enter upon military careers. It was the exception for such persons, or even for the ordinary peasant, artisan, or trader, to enter the armed forces out of any basic sympathy with the military profession. In times of peace the militia could be driven into the ranks only by hunger. In times of war they were forced in by a conscription system which exempted the wealthy gentry who could pay the necessary bribes to the recruiting officers.

This feature of the system is still in operation in China today. And since the officers come largely from the more privileged classes, there is a conspicuous lack of mutual sympathy between them and the men in the ranks. This is accentuated by the necessarily heavy sacrifices of untrained men when the Chinese army meets the technologically superior enemy. Such sacrifice and such differentiation are made natural in turn by the cheapness of human life in overpopulated China, with its high birthrate and heavy mortality.

Thus the very attitudes of the Chinese toward war are partly determined by demographic factors. This is only to indicate the difficulty of changing them. Popular attitudes toward war will not change until the individual can be convinced that his part in it will carry less than its present risk and yield more than its present profit both to himself as an individual and to his society as a whole. To increase the national per capita income would help produce this conviction. It would give the individual soldier better material support in time of war and a greater reason for wanting to win wars. But China's rapidly growing population is likely to increase more quickly than its means of producing wealth. Even if it were attempted to produce a change in attitudes purely by education and indoctrination, the costs of this could only be met from an increased national income.

The great need is for limitation on the growth of Chinese population. Otherwise the improvement of the health and technical efficiency of the population will be prevented since, under these circumstances, modernization cannot provide the necessary margin of economic income. It is, however, difficult to foresee any radical decrease in the Chinese birth-rate during the next generation or two. As the death-rate is likely to be lowered by the furtherance of internal peace and the institution of preventive medicine, it is not probable that China will soon emerge from her present overpopulation and accompanying economic poverty. This will definitely detract from her military power potential.

USE OF THE LAND IN CHINA

Agriculture has a two-fold significance in relation to China's military potential. There is first the factor of agricultural production, which in quantity relative to demand is an important element in the war potential, and includes such items as food, clothing, and materials produced for industry or for export.

In addition, however, there is what may be termed the agrarian order, which is of particular importance in China. If agriculture itself may be considered as a system of production, the agrarian order may be considered as a way of life for the 75 or 80 per cent of the Chinese people who get their living from cultivating the soil. The study of the Chinese agrarian order involves the analysis of the fundamentals of the Chinese society. Because military power stands upon and is limited by the social organization and social trends in the state, the agrarian order is now, and will be for some time, inescapably involved in any study of the constituents of state military power for China. . . .

Chinese agriculture as a producing system suffers all the handicaps of a primitive technology. Although crop yields per acre are high, they are achieved only by the most intensive hand labor. In such districts as the Yangtze Delta this is so much the case that farming on the crowded land resembles gardening more than anything else.

In light of the extreme crowding on the good agricultural land it is not surprising to find that in normal prewar years China did not produce enough food for her people. . . .

Rice is China's most important crop, occupying 21 per cent of the total crop-producing area. But it is not an important crop in the region north of the Yangtze Valley, where it occupies only 2 per cent of the producing area. In North China the dominant crop is wheat, consumed for the most part in the shape of bread. In this crop also there is an insufficient production for the demands of China as a whole. . . .

Rice, wheat products, and sugar represent the chief food imports of prewar and present-day China. The monetary cost of these imports alone is not serious, though it may come to $50,000,000 U.S. in a year, and after the war China will need all her available foreign exchange for purchases of material for reconstruction. What is serious is the complex of conditions which makes necessary the importation of quantities of basic foods, and the implications of these conditions for China's national power in the future.

The increase in the population is the most important among the major factors making necessary the importation of food into a once self-sufficient China. At the same time the prevalence of civil disorder and misgovernment during the last thirty years has been a major drawback to agricultural production. . . . As a result of impossible conditions thousands of peasants have left good lands empty and migrated to poorer regions or taken up careers as bandits. . . .

The small beginnings of industrialization in China before 1937 actually heightened the problem. Food imports became increasingly necessary as people came into the industrial cities of the coastal region. The surrounding countryside could not expand production sufficiently to feed the additional population, and undeveloped transport made it difficult to draw on the more remote hinterland. Therefore food was imported from abroad for the coastal regions where industry began.

In the production of food, quantity is not the sole criterion of success. There is also the question of quality. The deficiency diseases which are caused by lack of protective vitamins interfere quite as much with the wartime efficiency of populations as the lack of energy which comes from a shortage of calories. Calorie shortages were found by Buck in farm diets in almost one-half the localities studied in his important survey. Extreme conditions resulting from famine were not included in this analysis, and it is probable that the survey gives a correct picture of the usual conditions in agricultural China, including 75 or 80 per cent of the population. In quality the food of agricultural China is even less satisfactory than in quantity. There is a general deficiency of vitamins and fats, and the protein intake, though for the most part sufficient, is not of high quality. The diet is in general 97 per cent vegetarian, and is about 92 per cent composed of cereals. The reason for this is that the population density forces concentration on cereals. A greater caloric value per acre can be produced from cereals than from other farm crops.

Overcrowding on the land thus prevents an adequate production of meat in China. Instead of feeding grain to animals it is directly consumed by the farmer himself. The resulting economy of calories deprives the farmer of the better quality protein derived from meat and milk. . . . It should be remembered that after the rather lengthy nursing period, Chinese children get practically no milk. It is difficult to see how an extensive dairying industry can develop in the present Chinese farm economy, with its poverty of land and resources per capita of the population.

This is not to underestimate the possibilities for technical improvement of such animal husbandry as exists. Measures can and will be taken to reduce the epidemics which in the two provinces of Szechwan and Sikang alone are estimated to kill 300,000 head of cattle each year. . . .

In 1933 the estimated loss of livestock (including poultry) in all China . . . came to about 20 per cent of the estimated value of all livestock in China for the year. If these losses could be eliminated, the meat supply of China would be materially increased. But it is doubtful whether it could be increased rapidly enough to surpass the probable population increases after the war and thus better the per capita consumption of animal food products. . . .

Animal husbandry is important not only in the production of food, but of raw materials for the making of clothing. The most important wool-producing regions of China are in the north and west. Unfortunately the Chinese wool is not satisfactory for making cloth. In normal times most of it is exported, chiefly to the United States where it is used for rug-making. The limited manufacture of woolen fabric for clothing in mills in the Chinese coastal cities was based upon imports of woolen yarn, largely from the United States. Some efforts have been made to improve the wool-bearing qualities of Chinese sheep, but this work was not far advanced before the war and has not progressed materially since.

Also connected with animal husbandry is the production of hides and leather. Most hides produced in China are exported in normal years, as there has been only a very small domestic tanning business. It is probable that 85 to 90 per cent of the Chinese people do not wear shoes made of leather, so that the exporting of most of the hides is not as serious as it might seem. It is probable that after the war modern tanning industries will be established, and will guarantee an adequate domestic supply of leather for all military uses. At present the troops for the most part still wear the straw shoes or sandals to which they are accustomed in ordinary life, and are quite capable of going barefoot if necessary.

The all-important agricultural product for clothing in China is cotton. The crop averages about 500,000 tons each year and constitutes between 5 and 10 per cent of world production. It provides only about three-quarters of China's own requirements, the remainder being imported cotton of higher grades. To make up for such imports, considerable Chinese raw cotton [was] exported [before the war], chiefly to Japan. It is quite possible that in the future, Chinese cotton may be improved in quality and quantity, to replace cotton now imported from other regions.

Cotton clothing is ideal for the warm summers which are typical of China. But for winter use its poor insulating qualities make it inferior for protection against cold. Nevertheless it is almost universally used. Its poor insulating qualities are partly compensated for by its cheapness. Thus garments are frequently quilted, the padding being made of wadded cotton batting. This accounts for the bulkiness of much of the winter clothing in Central and North China, which constitutes an impediment to mobility. In addition its wearing qualities are not high and the cotton padding is an ideal habitat for body parasites.

Clothing for the Chinese armed forces at present differs little in type from that of the civilian population. A general use of wool for winter clothing of the troops would provide superior wearing qualities. It would also contribute to the efficiency of the troops and to their health. The use of wool for clothing, however, would necessitate considerable imports from abroad. This would constitute a drain on needed foreign exchange, at least until the domestic wool crop could be much improved in quality. To do so would take considerable time and money, and would depend to a considerable extent on effective Chinese civil control in the border regions of Sinkiang, northwestern China, and Mongolia where most of the wool is now produced.

Clothing manufacture creates the chief demand for agricultural materials outside of foodstuffs. But it is closely rivaled by industry and the export market. Such items as soy beans and soy bean products, wood oil, and silk have in the past been exported in considerable quantities, and have thus helped to pay for imports of industrial products. Of these the most important have been soy beans, bean oil, and bean cakes. It is probable that, with the development of the plastics industry, this crop may become even more important than in the past. . . .

The history of the Chinese silk and tea trade may well serve to illustrate the problems incidental to increasing China's exports of agricultural products. These two commodities were among the earliest exports to western countries, and were greatly in demand. But the raising and processing of tea in China is still carried out by the same primitive hand methods as were used a century ago. This leads to great diversity in type and quality, so that China produces a great variety of teas. One result is to prevent the effective use of mass advertising, which would be necessary in order to foster the sale of Chinese tea abroad. Thus far, the conservatism and superstition of the producers have made it impossible to introduce modern methods of manufacturing to any great extent. . . .

For silk the history is similar to that of tea. Chinese silk was formerly dominant in the world market. But it could not compete with the Japanese product in either price or standards of uniformity, once the Japanese instituted modern production methods and rigid standards and specifications. These were of great importance, for the American market demanded a uniform product of raw silk, capable of machine fabrication.

It would be difficult to calculate the monetary losses China has suffered from failure to apply modern standards in the production and sale of agricultural raw materials. These losses are not limited to the export field. One result of unstandardized or adulterated raw materials is the invasion of the Chinese domestic market by foreign products, which may cost more per unit but be less expensive in the long run than unsatisfactory Chinese materials. . . .

It is not enough to lay the responsibility for change in this field on the government, and to expect results from its fiat. A government with power to regulate would itself be first-hand evidence of the basic change in the social psychology of China necessary to allow such regulations to become effective. Previous attempts of the government to institute such simple changes as standardization of weights and measures have thus far met with failure. As a result of such attempts the government has simply added new varieties of weights and measures to the old ones, never displacing them, and has thus only increased the confusion. Attempts to establish government inspection of raw products have proved quite expensive, and have frequently led to corrupt practices by the inspecting officials.

The importance of these factors to China's military strength comes from the fact that for a long time to come China's economy must remain predominantly agricultural. Agriculture can contribute to China's national strength not only by producing quantities of good-quality food and clothing, but by helping to pay for imports of machinery and industrial goods. To do this, China must modernize the production and sale of her agricultural raw materials and must compete in the world markets. Such modernization is not impossible, but it faces many serious obstacles and cannot be quickly accomplished.

Finally, China's agricultural economy is militarily important because its conditions determine the way of life of 80 per cent of her people. The agrarian situation in general is characterized by the increasing concentration of land ownership. This in itself may or may not be considered an evil, but it unquestionably is an evil when combined with exorbitant rents, usurious rates of interest, and heavy taxes and other levies. . . .

Concentration of land-holdings is more severe in some localities than in others, but it predominates in all regions. It is greater in South China than in the north. In the delta regions of the Yangtze and Pearl rivers, 70 per cent of all inhabitants of agricultural villages are tenants. In northern Kiangsu Province, landlords owning up to 3,000 acres live in mud castles, having their own armed forces with which they control both the local magistrates and the peasantry. In the same region there are large tracts of land belonging to temples. One of these amounts to about 30,000 acres. Such temples also have their own private armed forces. They can easily dominate the local government and prevent the central government from carrying out its policies in the area. . . .

On the whole it can be stated that in China the landlords, forming about 5 per cent of the population, possess about 50 per cent of the cultivated land. On the other hand the poor peasants, who make up about 70 per cent of the population, possess only about 20 per cent of the land.

. . . Rents are usually paid in kind, which gives the landlords complete protection from rising prices on their own purchases, while preventing the farmer from taking advantage of the increased price of his produce. When prices fall the farmer pays the same amount to the landlord, who cannot suffer loss in a situation of falling prices. Land rent in the Szechwan area often represents considerably more than half the total crop yield. As Dr. Sun Fo has stated, in China "the lion's share of the land's yield goes into the pockets of the landlords." In a good year in Szechwan this means that some 2,750,000 tons of rice are paid to landlords as rent.

The situation in Szechwan is not untypical. In southern Anhwei Province before the war the payment of half the crop to the landlord was not unusual. But heavy rents were far from being the only burdens on the farmers. Because of the relatively narrow margin of income over subsistence, the farmers were virtually without working capital with which to tide themselves over bad seasons or the unproductive winters. This meant that in case of need they had no recourse but to borrow. For such loans the landlords and merchants were the chief sources, together supplying directly about 50 per cent of all loans to farmers. This does not count the loans which they made through pawnshops and stores. On all such loans, interest rates were high. More than one-third were made at 20-30 per cent per annum, and nearly one-third more were made at 30-40 per cent per annum. . . . Thus the monopolistic character of Chinese landlordism is reinforced by its control over rural finance, through which the pressure on the peasantry became intensified to an often unbearable degree.

But to complete the picture, the relations between the landlord's economic power and his political privileges must be indicated. As has already been stated, the landlords were frequently able to control the officials of the local government in their neighborhood. Their political power often did not stop there, but extended to the actual holding of political office itself. Thus local government was closely controlled by the gentry, whose economic position was in this way rounded off by control over the collection of taxes and the local expenditure of government funds. . . .

The policy of the dominant politico-economic class was actually one which in many cases led to the destruction of the working peasantry and the land on which they lived. In the province of Kwangtung, for instance, much valuable rice land simply went out of production because of heavy migrations of the population to the South Seas. This was caused by intolerable rents and taxes and failure of the ruling gentry to maintain the public works by which agriculture in the region survived.

The civil wars of the last thirty or more years not only permitted such occurrences by loosening the ties of governmental regulation. They also added directly to the burdens of the peasantry in the shape of military requisitions and levies. Such requisitions have become more prevalent now than at any previous time in Chinese history. They have been expanded in scope to include not only food, clothing, housing, and transport, but a hundred other items. . . .

Thus the situation of many Chinese peasants is close to slavery. In some cases, particularly with the women of the poor peasantry, the condition resembles slavery itself. . . .

. . . What could be more natural in such a situation than for the peasants finally to revolt? In so doing they are united against the gentry and magistrates, whose economic position is reinforced by political power.

Previously, when this happened over wide areas, the revolts, whether finally successful or not, actually lessened the social pressures which gave rise to them, for they caused the death of large numbers of people and redistributed property among the survivors. . . .

With this traditional background in mind, it is not surprising to find a Chinese social scientist in 1930 speaking of the Chinese farmers' leagues as the probable "vanguards of an agrarian revolution in the near future." In the same vein, Professor C. Dragoni, a League of Nations agricultural expert in China during 1932-1933, warned that unless steps were taken to prevent the growth of discontent among the peasantry, they might "take action which would gravely endanger social and political stability."

Of course these warnings came long after the issues involved had been well defined in the politics of Nationalist China. By this time Generalissimo Chiang Kai-shek's ten-year war against the Chinese Communists which ended in 1936 was past the half-way mark. It should be noted that the Communists had entrenched themselves in the agricultural region of the south-central Yangtze Valley, chiefly in the province of Kiangsi. This was a natural result of the forcible liquidation of their relatively insignificant proletarian forces in the cities, who had been vulnerable partly because of their concentration in large centers. It was natural also in view of the central importance of the agrarian question in China's society.

Thus it was that for the Communists the land-tenure question became "an essential part of their whole revolutionary system." They proceeded at first to liquidate the class of landlords, gentry, and local officials. After thus breaking the system of political and economic controls, they distributed land to the peasants, dividing it, but not nationalizing it. They then organized local government by soviets, in which the agricultural laborers were given strongest representation. The land program was nothing less than a well-organized and somewhat dressed-up following out of the old patterns of Chinese agrarian revolt. It was based not on doctrinaire socialist desires to abolish the right of private property, but on adherence to that right as first established in China over two thousand years before. . . .

The need for agrarian reform is constantly referred to in the speeches of Chiang Kai-shek. In one of his earlier messages to the Kuomintang [Nationalist party], he declared the equalization of land ownership to be the policy of the party. . . .

The Nationalist government has yet to outline any program which will do this. No proposals carrying real threats to the privileged position of the landlord class are likely to come from the Nationalist party government as long as it continues to be dominated by members of that class. And neither the Nationalists nor the Communists have any remedy for the basic fact that China's population will probably increase more rapidly as measures are taken to increase total production and to improve the distribution of agricultural income. It has been well and truly said that this is "the tragic dilemma in which those who would improve village life in China will certainly find themselves." . . .

CHINA'S INDUSTRIAL RAW MATERIALS

It is universally recognized that the military power of a state in the present age depends heavily on its capacity to fabricate quickly large quantities of the materials of war. In the existing condition of technology, war materials and the apparatus for making them are predominantly made of various minerals. However, vast quantities of other materials are required. It is necessary to base war industries upon those raw materials available within a state or in areas under its military dominance and control. . . .

In making war on China, Japan was attacking a nation whose resources were for the most part unused. As China has found out since, unrealized potentialities do not win wars. In addition, the creation of wealth out of material potentialities depends strongly on political and sociological factors.

For China the development of national power through industry lies in the future. The most important questions which must be answered in this connection are as follows:

1. Where are the available sources of mechanical power in China, such as coal, oil, and waterpower, and how extensive are they?

2. What material resources does China possess or have secure access to, out of which she can fabricate products contributing to state power?

3. To what extent can China's human resources for labor, management, and planning contribute both to industrialization and to the operation of industry?

4. What are the possible sources of capital for the building of modern industry in China? What does the answer indicate in terms of foreign participa-

tion or of control by private or governmental agencies?

In order to answer fully these questions it would be necessary to secure a great deal of detailed information which is not available even in Chinese official circles. . . .

On the other hand, enough information is already available to make possible a general evaluation of China's probable industrial potentialities within the next twenty-five or fifty years. For this purpose it is not necessary to fill in all the precise details of quantities, qualities, and locations of raw material resources. Investigation by the National Geological Survey of China has already proceeded far enough so that the general picture of China's resources is now "reasonably clear," for the chief items and in all but the more remote regions.

In spite of this, current writers both Chinese and foreign are often prone to overestimate the extent of China's industrial raw materials. The terms "unlimited," "inexhaustible," "enormously rich," or even "abundant," cannot be indiscriminately applied to China's mineral resources. Nor is it correct to say that "five years of war have changed the vast interior of China from a medieval into a modern economic state," particularly in respect to industrial production. In fact, the total value of all civilian industrial production in China in 1940 was only about 4 per cent of the first American lend-lease appropriation. . . .

At the very foundation of modern industry are the available sources of mechanical power. China does not utilize mechanical power and equipment as is done by the United States. As a result, the per capita output of Chinese labor is only one-fortieth that of American labor. The three chief sources of power for modern industry are coal, petroleum, and waterpower. The entire continent of Asia produces from coal only 11.3 per cent of all power produced from this source in the world, 8.8 per cent of all power produced from petroleum, and 9 per cent of all power produced from water.

China's coal reserves are her greatest potential source of power, and her greatest single mineral asset. Her total deposits are estimated at about 236,000,000,000 tons. This is less than one-tenth the proved and probable reserves of the United States, and somewhat more than one-third of those of Canada. Thus China's per capita reserves of coal are only 3 or 4 per cent of those of the United States. It is significant that, as time goes on and China's coal resources are more carefully explored, the various estimates of reserves tend to become more uniform. The gross over- and under-estimates are now things of the past.

Nearly 85 per cent of China's coal is located in the two adjoining provinces of Shansi and Shensi in North China. This great concentration is particularly suitable for industrial utilization. . . . The province of Szechwan ranks next to Shansi and Shensi in coal deposits, with about 4 per cent of the national holdings. The other 11 per cent of China's coal is scattered among the remaining twenty-five provinces, providing only meager sources of local coal for most of China's most heavily populated centers. Adequate facilities for the economical transport of coal are an absolute requirement for any widespread industrialization in China. . . .

It is also important to note that China's coal is about 80 per cent bituminous. The quantity suitable for making coke is substantial, but its location is for the most part remote from the sources of iron ore.

Before the war the total annual production of coal in China was only about

150 lbs. per person. This compares with a figure of nearly 10,000 lbs. consumed per capita in the United States, and about 1,100 lbs. in Japan. Only 55 per cent of the prewar Chinese consumption was for industrial uses, the balance being used for domestic heating. This contrasts with an 83 per cent industrial use and a 17 per cent domestic use in the world as a whole.

[During] the war, the Japanese secured control of about 90 per cent of the prewar sources of coal in China. Consequently, the Chinese government undertook the development under its auspices of new mines in West China. . . .

These new developments, according to the Chinese Ministry of Information, resulted in an increase of coal production in Free China from 3,600,000 tons in 1937 to 5,700,000 tons in 1940. . . .

The wartime development of coal mining in Free China will be of permanent value for the prosperity of China's western regions. But the chief increases in coal production must come in Shansi and Shensi where 85 per cent of China's deposits are concentrated. Very little of the area of these provinces is under the control of the Chinese national government at Chungking. Even [with] the Japanese gone there will remain the problem of the Communists who now occupy much of the region. Without a previous settlement of the Nationalist-Communist issue, no attempts to modernize the transport facilities of the area can succeed. On the other hand, this mountainous territory can never be brought under the control of the central government without the development of modern communication and transport facilities. This is a typical case of the political-geographic dilemma which makes difficult the creation of a modern state in China, in the same way as it makes almost impossible a Japanese conquest of the whole of the country. . . .

Manchuria's coal deposits have been developed by Japanese capital to accompany the development of transport and metallurgical industries. Japanese surveys of coal deposits in Manchuria led them to assert that previous estimates were much too low and should be multiplied by five. . . . The importance of these deposits lies not in their size, nor in their quality, for Manchuria as a whole lacks good metallurgical coal. It lies in their accessibility to modern transport by rail and water, which makes the coal deposits available for incorporation into an integrated economy. In the future the Manchurian coal can be shipped by water and become the source of power for industry as far south as the Yangtze Delta region. It will doubtless be supplanted for metallurgical purposes by the coal of Hopeh Province, which is superior for the production of coke.

All things considered, the available coal supply of China is adequate for its needs for a very long time to come. But it must be remembered that new railroads are required to tap the Shansi-Shensi deposits, and that the necessary coal for the production of power after the war will probably come from expansion of mining in Manchuria, Hopeh, and the Yangtze Valley, in addition to increased use of local deposits elsewhere.

Quite in contrast to the plentiful supply of coal is the distinct lack of petroleum in China. Before the war, oil produced about 76 per cent of all power in America, but in Asia it produced only about 9 per cent of all power. . . . Only 640,000 barrels were produced in Chinese territory. This was extracted from shale by the Japanese in Manchuria. In 1940 it was reported that production from this source had been increased to 3,000,000 barrels a year. This production was heavily susidized by the Japanese Navy, and was definitely uneconomical. . . .

Natural petroleum has been known to exist in China for many centuries, but has never been produced in large quantities. About thirty years ago, extensive investigations in North and Northwest China and Szechwan were made by American geologists. It was concluded that oil deposits in commercial quantities did not exist there. Furthermore, the general view was that the geological structure of China, except for the two regions of northern Shensi and Szechwan, is definitely unfavorable to the existence of large oil deposits, and that the total oil reserves of China were probably less than 1 per cent of those of the United States.

. . . Wells in Kansu were producing about 60,000 gallons of crude oil a month in 1941. It was converted into gasoline locally, and used for the most part in the northwest, where it helped to fuel traffic on the road to Russia. But the prospect for any large production there after the war is slight. Even at present the efforts to expand production in Kansu are meeting with great difficulties because of the generally undeveloped character of the region, the resulting shortages of foodstuffs and manpower, and the great difficulties of communication. After the fall of Burma, new machinery for drilling and for refineries could not be brought in from the United States.

To make up for the lack of oil after the Japanese blockade shut off imports, the government fostered the distilling of alcohol from vegetable matter. Wartime shortages of foodstuffs, however, placed a limit on this expedient. Certain vegetable oils such as tung oil, camphor oil, and peanut oil also were used as fuel for modified diesel engines.

The oil of Sinkiang, in China's far west, has been locally exploited for some time. . . . Nevertheless, it is unlikely that this oil could be of much use in Central or South China, on account of the vast distances which intervene and the lack of modern transport facilities.

The oil of Szechwan, if recent reports are to be believed, may be of primary importance to post-war China. According to the Ministry of Information, the National Geological Survey of China estimates the Szechwan deposits at about 400,000,000 barrels. A recent news dispatch from Chungking states that professors from Szechwan University estimate deposits in the Kiangyü district of Szechwan alone sufficient to supply China's requirements "for several centuries."

Unless the size of these deposits has been grossly overestimated, which only time can tell, this will prove of great importance. For the Kiangyü district is only about 225 miles from the Yangtze River, close enough to make quite feasible the construction of a pipeline connecting with tankers on China's main river artery. . . .

In case the size of the Szechwan oil deposits does not come up to present expectations, it is probable that, as with coal, Manchuria and North China will again prove the first source of supply. . . . In 1940 the Japanese, who had previously relied on shale oil and coal liquefaction in Manchuria, brought in a well flowing with natural petroleum. The field, located near railway transport in the northeastern province of Jehol, was considered potentially important. . . .

Although the oil from these sources may be unable to compete in price with imports from abroad immediately after the war, it is essential that oil resources inside China be utilized. . . . In time of war dependence on foreign supplies would be disastrous. . . .

The third major source of mechanical

power in the world is waterpower. Asia produces less than 10 per cent of the world's waterpower. The amount China produces is very small. The Chinese National Resources Commission estimates that in all China the streams can produce about 22,000,000 horsepower available 95 per cent of the time and about 41,000,000 horsepower available 50 per cent of the time. If it were technically and economically feasible to develop all this available potential, the result would be waterpower considerably greater than that of the United States at the beginning of 1941. At best, however, this would require the work of half a century. It is likely that the heavy construction costs and the general lack of capacity for use of the power will limit utilization to between one-tenth and one-twentieth of available resources during the next twenty-five years.

Regarding the over-all development of power resources in China after the war, it will be essential to plan the location of power production and industries near each other. This will not be unduly difficult for the consumer industries which fabricate raw materials of relative lightness and compactness. But for heavy industry the problem is not so easily solved.

The steel industry is a case in point. China's iron ore resources are not great. The most generous estimate gives a total of 1,694,000,000 tons for all China. . . . The diffusion of iron ores over the entire area of China, added to a general low iron content, makes it economically unjustifiable to plan for any large-scale steel industry, based on Chinese ores, in the post-war generation.

. . . Profitable operations in a given locality cannot be undertaken without a concentration in one place of iron ores to the amount of at least 10,000,000 tons. This provides the material necessary to produce enough pig iron to pay costs of plant, transportation facilities, operations, etc., and return a profit. In all China there are less than a dozen localities in which a concentration of 10,000,000 tons or more of iron ore exists. Only two of these localities contain as much ore as the American steel industry uses in one year of peacetime production. These two localities are in the northern frontier province of Chahar and in southern and eastern Manchuria. The Chahar deposits are estimated at more than 90,000,000 tons of high-grade ore. Those of Manchuria are far larger and may contain over 1,000,000,000 tons, but they are mostly of low iron content.

To exploit the Chahar deposits would require no great development of transport facilities. . . .

[These] deposits could be made the basis for a small annual steel production over the next twenty-five years. For this period they could at best provide a maximum of 2,000,000 tons of steel per year, one-fourteenth that of Greater Germany in 1940, one-third that of Japan for the same year, and less than 4 per cent of the average United States production for 1935-1941 inclusive. . . .

Although the Japanese probably produced as much as 1,700,000 tons of pig iron and 700,000 tons of steel in South Manchuria in 1942, it is most doubtful whether these products could compete in price with the output of plants in the United States, England, Germany, or India. . . . Japanese production was heavily subsidized, primarily for military reasons. . . . Any attempt to build up a . . . domestic steel industry, even if based on better grade ores than those used by the Japanese in Manchuria, would have to be heavily subsidized by the Chinese government through direct grants of capital and heavy tariff protection.

As a matter of fact, the trend in

China is clearly toward domination and control of heavy industry by the national government.... Such a policy would assure the greatest possible development of a domestic steel industry for China, to be justified on grounds of military necessity. There is no denying its bearing on the problem of China's military strength....

An average production of 2,000,000 tons of steel each year for the next twenty-five years cannot give China sufficient industrial strength for major military power. It would not even be enough to give China a thoroughly modern economic structure. This is not to say that, particularly if supplemented by normal peacetime steel imports, such a steel production could not greatly influence the Chinese economy. Under favorable conditions of finance, labor and management, and granted the major ingredient of political stability, China during the twenty-five years following the war could see a great and profitable development of light industry for the production of consumers' goods. It was in this field that most of her industrial development took place in the years before 1937. That it was only just a beginning can be seen from the fact that in 1936 there were only 625 factories in all China making machinery. The value of the average annual production of each plant was less than $10,000 U.S.

Since these plants were for the most part located near the seacoast, most of them were destroyed or captured by the Japanese. Those which were moved to Free China in 1937-1938 have been supplemented by new machine shops established since then. The total number is small, however, and the plants are probably smaller on the average than those existing before 1937. After the war, as before 1937, equipment for the machine production of consumers' goods must for the most part be imported from abroad. This is necessitated by the almost total absence of a machine tool industry in China....

... Among the products in which [China] has a leading position in world trade are two minerals, tungsten and antimony. She produced just before the war approximately 40 per cent of the world's tungsten.... Of antimony China normally provides nearly two-thirds of the total world production. ... At the highest price ever quoted (1916), and at the maximum rate of production (1937), China's yearly export of tungsten would bring about $600,000 U.S. in the American market. ... The Chinese production [of antimony] in 1937 was worth about $4,500,-000 U.S. in the American market....

China may have a reserve of 22,-000,000 tons of [manganese] ore of 45 per cent metallic content. Her estimated production of 120,000 tons of ore in 1937 is more than is required for the present small steel industry. Vanadium, nickel, and chromium, also of great importance for hardening steel, are all either lacking in China or present only in very small quantities, so far as is known at present. The province of Sikang, on the eastern border of Tibet, is said to have a deposit of 340,000 tons of nickel ore. In copper, China is probably not rich. Her reserves are not large and are scattered over a large area. They have been mined for centuries by primitive methods and have produced an aggregate amount of metal which is large. Many previously worked deposits are now exhausted.

In lead and zinc China is probably not well supplied. Chinese writers disagree radically in their estimates, but in all probability there are only limited quantities available. Resources in tin are better. The production in 1938 from Southwest China deposits was about 12,500 tons of metallic tin. Production is backed up by a reserve of about 1,417,000 tons for all of China, which will allow large exports for a long time after the war.

Regarding China's holdings of aluminum and magnesium, the light metals so important in war, there can be even less certainty than with some of those resources already scanned. Dr. G. B. Cressey characterizes China's reserves of bauxite as "modest." However, a Chinese writer in 1935 indicated a total deposit of 188,000,000 tons of bauxite in the two provinces of Shantung in northern China and Liaoning in southern Manchuria. This would amount to more than a hundred times the average annual world production of bauxite ores for the ten years 1928-1937, and would make China exceptionally rich in this ore. More recent estimates would even raise the figure to 271,000,000 tons for Shantung and to 461,000,000 tons for Manchuria and the northwestern province of Kansu!

Even if these figures were found to be only 50 per cent correct, it would be natural to develop an extensive light metals industry in China, utilizing the large coal resources of northern China as a source of power for smelting the ores. . . .

Minerals are not the only materials in which China will find herself lacking. . . . Such a common material as lumber is basic for all kinds of heavy construction work such as mines, railroads, factories, etc. For a variety of reasons, much of China has been denuded of its forests. The problem of afforestation is one of the most critical in a long list of conservation projects facing post-war China. Its bearing on the general economy does not derive solely from the present lack of forestry products in China, but also from the need of afforestation as an aid to erosion control and flood prevention. . . .

PROBLEMS OF INDUSTRIAL DEVELOPMENT IN CHINA

China's post-war industrialization depends quite as strongly on an adequate supply of personnel and capital as on her raw-material resources. . . .

Before the war only a small proportion of China's large population was employed in industry. Factory workers were estimated at one million and a quarter in 1930. Seven years later the figure was set at two million, with another million employed in modern mines and communications. This figure represents less an increase in the number of factory workers than an improved estimate of their numbers. With the disruption of industry which has resulted from the war, the number of workers in industry has doubtless decreased. . . .

Just as it is dangerous to assume that mass manpower will always be suitable for modern armies, in the same way, mass populations do not always comprise immediate reservoirs of industrial labor. As a matter of fact, the rapid increase of China's population . . . will be a handicap to industry, and will inhibit the rapid development of an efficient labor corps.

To demonstrate the truth of this it is only necessary to remind ourselves that the law of supply and demand operates in the field of labor. As a result, so long as there is an oversupply of labor, this labor will tend to remain cheap. . . .

Disregarding . . . the humanitarian factors involved, low wages in industry help to prevent the growth of a body of skilled, efficient labor. They foster . . . low standards of life and work among industrial laborers, and thus diminish seriously any chances for education and training. In addition they keep down the standards of health and sanitation, and thus prevent high efficiency. . . .

The cheapness of Chinese labor and its accompanying low standards of efficiency tend to cause wasteful use of labor resources. Large numbers of laborers have to be secured to perform work which could be done more efficiently, and with less material waste, by fewer but better trained workers or with the use of machines. If the need for such numbers of workmen be reduced by modern machinery, the old Chinese rule that no one is to be deprived of his "bowl of rice" makes it difficult to dismiss them. As a result, they would all have the privilege of starving together. . . .

The psychology of the Chinese industrial laborer is not in harmony with modern machine industry as it is known in the West. . . . The handicraft worker proceeds on his own terms and at his own pace. The products of his skill and precision, as has already been stated, embody the advantages and disadvantages of artistic individualism, with all that it connotes in low volume of production and variability of result. . . .

The current political revolution in China has not yet brought with it the necessary accompanying revolution in the sphere of social psychology. Beginnings there naturally are, but only beginnings. To give an example of the problems involved, the primitive collectivism of the Chinese family system often results in the distribution of a worker's wages among a number of more or less distant relatives. There is therefore in many cases little incentive for the worker to improve his training and efficiency as a means of bettering his own financial lot. And there is less incentive for the employer to raise the wage scale, since increased wages will not produce a corresponding degree of improvement in the living standards and efficiency of his employees. . . .

The first and fundamental personnel problem for industry in China is that of building a body of skilled mechanics. Chiang Kai-shek has recognized the need for this type of program. His ten-year plan calls for turning out 2,460,000 graduates of various grades of technical and vocational schools. Unless some such program is adopted, no large program for the utilization of unskilled workers in industry can succeed. The task is likely to prove slow and costly. . . .

As a matter of fact, social and ethical indoctrination must be combined with technical training, if the suggested program is to succeed. Graduate mechanics must not, as in the past, be allowed to feel that their newly acquired skill has so improved their social position as to make it below their dignity to be called on to soil their hands with manual labor! It may seem incongruous to speak of intellectual arrogance on the part of auto mechanics, but in China this is all a part of the mentality associated with the orthodox Confucian emphasis on social status. Indoctrination must substitute for this a psychology of cooperation and self-sacrifice, which can best be inculcated not in a vacuum, but in connection with practical training.

. . . The need for [trained] personnel is apparent to the most casual observer in China, and is proved by the figures. In 1936, the year before the war, there were in the six Chinese provinces of Kiangsu, Chekiang, Anhwei, Kiangsi, Hupeh, and Hunan only 1,867 auto mechanics who could qualify as "skilled hands." This is roughly one auto mechanic for every 200 square miles of territory. . . .

Too much must not be expected, however, from technical training alone. Until China is liberated from the shackles of age-old conservatism in the field of social organization and brought forward toward modern political statehood, efforts at organized technical advance will suffer the handicaps already mentioned. The desirable changes in the popular psychology which have come from the war cannot well be furthered by overdoses of ideological nationalism, backed up by distorted interpretations of what purports to be Chinese history.

As has already been stated, the Chinese government will have an important place in supplying personnel for industry in the future. One vital question to be decided is that of the official attitude toward organized labor.

Labor unions and collective bargaining in China do not, as is sometimes claimed, owe their existence to recent Communist influence.... Attempts in 1923 to gain the legalization of labor unions by the republican government at Peking did not succeed, but in the following year the right to establish labor unions and the right to strike were granted by the revolutionary Nationalist government at Canton. This was at least partly the result of the weakness of the Nationalist party and of its desire to strengthen the laboring element as an instrument for its revolution.

Under these circumstances, labor unions in China underwent a phenomenal development up to 1927. Following the rupture in that year between the right and left wings of the Kuomintang, and the domination of the party by the rightists headed by Chiang Kai-shek, the official attitude toward unions underwent swift and violent change. The Nationalist government undertook the strict regulation of labor unions, in order to prevent their use as centers of Communist opposition. It also used its powers of regulation to suppress the activities of unions and thus to prevent them from promoting the interests of labor. The suppression of the right to strike, for instance, robbed the unions of any real power to advance the interests of their members....

The government policy regarding labor has naturally been confirmed and strengthened by the necessities of total mobilization during the war....

Government control over industry in post-war China will extend far beyond the sphere of labor. It will involve basic questions of capitalization, control, and actual operation of industry.... China's poverty of natural resources would make it extremely difficult for her to embark on a completely independent course of national development.

China cannot ... do as the Russians did, that is, secure the capital for rapidly modernizing her economy through a reduction in the national standard of living.... The necessary margins simply do not exist. A still further lowering of the standard of living in China would merely increase the ever-present possibilities for mass starvation. For quick modernization China must depend on capital support from abroad. Possibilities in this respect are at least partly dependent on the policy of the government in respect to promotion, control, operation, and ownership of industry.

... Before the war, modern industrial capital in China did not amount to more than $1,300,000,000 U.S., of which only one-quarter was owned by Chinese nationals. Almost all enterprises were on a small scale of capital and operations. This was caused not only by scarcity of capital, but in addition by reluctance on the part of the Chinese public to invest in joint-stock companies with the operation of which they were unfamiliar.

The basic factor, however, in the scarcity of capital funds has been the simple lack of available and utilized economic wealth in China. The economic life of the country has been too close to the subsistence level to allow the accumulation of surpluses to be used later for purposes of production....

It was inevitable that the impact of the West on China would have destructive effects on the old Chinese society and economy. The destruction would have been less severe if the causes of social disintegration had been limited to those of foreign origin. As it was, the slight measure of western economic advance in China was built on a system of special privileges for foreigners. This was induced by the political weakness of China, and this political weakness was accentuated by the tendency of the capital accumulated from agriculture to seek the security of the foreign concessions.

In the concessions, such capital was immune from control by the Chinese and secure from the instability resulting from revolution, but the country paid heavily for this protection. For China, as a part of her subjection to foreign control, was prohibited from the use of tariffs to protect her industry. It was partly as a result of this that such manufacture of iron and steel as was begun during the First World War quickly died out when the price of steel went down after 1918....

The fact that this era of special privilege in China has been ended by [Anglo-American] agreement can be explained largely in terms of the new political forces present in China. China's new nationalism has made it possible for her to carry on a primitive war of resistance against Japan, so that Japan was forced to expand the area of conflict in order to have any chance of winning. As a result, the other powers of the Southwest Pacific were forced into the war. These powers [were then] obliged by the necessities of political warfare against Japan to recede from their former position of privilege in China....

In this connection a definite possibility exists that the Chinese government will attempt to control completely the course of national economic development.... There are certain consistent lines of development visible during the past twenty years.

In 1922, Dr. Sun Yat-sen, the recognized founder of the Nationalist party, conceived a plan for state-controlled modernization of China by the use of foreign capital.... In 1932, after Japan's attack on Manchuria, the National Defense Planning Committee was established. Its function was to investigate the natural resources of China and to originate policies for national defense. Later reorganized as the National Resources Commission and placed in the Ministry of Economic Affairs, its functions were officially described as follows:

To develop, operate, and control basic industries ... important mining enterprises ... electrical power enterprises ... and to administer other enterprises as designated by the government.

In August 1936, this organization announced a three-year plan for the general development of industries producing motors, electrical equipment, tools, and machinery. In addition, plants were to be built to produce increased quantities of metals, coal, gasoline, chemicals, etc....

The war interrupted this program and forced the transfer of activities to West China. By 1941 the Commission had developed seventy-one industrial and mining projects there....

This type of government activity in business had been forecast by Chiang Kai-shek when, in July 1937, he stated that China must develop "state capital" for the conduct of "independent enterprises and those which private capital cannot handle, and for large-scale projects related to our national economic program." At the same time he emphasized the need to protect private business, in the interest of securing maximum production.

By 1942, enterprises under the control of the National Resources Commission had increased to ninety-eight. At that time a much greater development of state enterprises was foreshadowed for the post-war period by Dr. Wong Wen-hao, Minister of Economic Affairs since 1938, and chairman of the National Resources Commission. . . . [He listed the following] among goals to be achieved within ten years:

1. A total output of 14,000,000 tons of steel, with a tenth-year output of 5,000,000 tons.
2. A total output of 500,000,000 tons of coal, with a tenth-year output of 100,000,000 tons.
3. A total output of 3,360,000 tons of steel rails.
4. The construction of 2,400 locomotives.
5. The construction of 3,000,000 tons of steamships.

The Commission was at the same time considering still another plan to cover a five-year period. To carry it out would require an estimated 30,000 engineers and 800,000 skilled workers. In 1942 the Commission could discover only one-third of that number of engineers and one-fifth of that number of skilled workmen. This plan was aimed at raising the living standard of the people and strengthening China's national defenses. It was admitted that this official plan could not be carried out without foreign technical and financial assistance.

No clear line of policy exists as to the future division of effort between government owned and controlled enterprises and those owned by private concerns. Chiang Kai-shek's doctrine of 1937 that both state-owned and privately owned business were to exist in China was reiterated by Dr. Wong Wen-hao in 1941. The government was "to lead in the founding of heavy industries and the creation and development of main industrial areas." But "every possible encouragement" should be given private business, including cooperation from government enterprises. An increasing function of the Ministry of Economic Affairs was to be the "promotion" of private concerns. The extension of government financial aid to private business was to play its part in this.

The statement of the Chinese Ministry of Information in 1943 regarding the sphere for development of state-owned enterprises . . . [limits government ownership] to the following types of enterprises:

1. Those "relating to national defense."
2. Those to be operated on a large scale and which "private interests are not in a position to undertake."
3. Those which "require wholesale planning and control."
4. Necessary, but unprofitable or poorly paying enterprises.
5. Industries supplying power or fuel.
6. "Those enterprises specially designated by the Government."

This definition of the scope of state control over the future economy of China is sufficiently broad to allow complete domination of all business by the government after the war. . . .

The entire development of industry is to be protected and promoted by tariffs, and by government control over imports, exports, and foreign exchange. Tariff protection may be more necessary for light industries which are privately owned than for government-financed heavy industries. In any case tariffs for China could serve to lessen her present condition of economic dependence on the more advanced nations with which she will be dealing after the war. Such dependence will be considerable even with strong government controls and protection. Without them China would probably remain in the position of economic colonialism which she has come to occupy during the past century. . . .

The advisability of this type of trade and financial policy for post-war China is even more open to question than its feasibility. For purposes of political and economic stability, post-war China must raise the living standard of her own people. During the next generation at least, this will be incompatible with a policy of pushing large exports of consumers' goods. . . .

All in all it seems quite possible that in China after the war, foreign capital will be fitted into an over-all national economy in which only secondary attention will be given to the general well-being of the people. Primary attention may be given to building of state power for military purposes. In spite of the need for military strength in post-war China, too much concentration on this would sacrifice long-term strength to short-term requirements. . . .

Finally, no matter how much we assist in building up Chinese industry in the generation after the war, we cannot by any means make her capable of a self-sustained defense of her territory in case she is strongly attacked. Even less would she be able to take over large responsibilities for the maintenance of peace in Asia. . . .

TRANSPORT AND COMMUNICATIONS IN CHINA

The primitive condition of China's transport system has affected every aspect of her life, in both war and peace. Lack of transport facilities in the vast hinterland has effectively blocked the Japanese invasion and made resistance possible, but it has also reduced that resistance to a strategy of the defensive. China's primitive agrarian economy cannot support offensive warfare to a great extent because of its lack of modern means of transport.

Even that measure of defensive warfare which China has managed to carry on has been severely handicapped by the poor transport facilities of her base in the western part of the country. Many times the necessary reinforcements have arrived at the front too late or not at all. . . .

Supplies to accompany troops on the march must for the most part be moved by coolie transport. The entire tempo of movement is slowed to the pace of men carrying heavy burdens. Shortages in food supply are an inevitable result which in turn help cause malnutrition among the troops.

It is because of the almost total lack of modern transport that in the Chinese army a soldier who receives a serious wound is nearly as good as dead. . . . Only those whose wounds are so light as to enable them to walk to treatment stand a good chance of recovery. No conceivable surplus of manpower can make up for the waste of time, labor, and material invested in the training of troops who are sacrificed to transport inadequacies of this kind.

If transportation has become a critical problem in time of war, it is largely because of its inadequacy as a part of the normal peacetime economy of China. The effects of this on agriculture and industry have already been mentioned. The demand for transport development after the war will come from all fields of the economy. Industry and trade cannot be developed without transportation to assemble raw materials and carry away finished products. . . .

From the increase of transport facilities and the accompanying regional specialization, there will inevitably result a change in the very structure of Chinese society itself. Local independence will diminish, and for it will be substituted increased unity and interdependence. The effects of interdependence in the economic field will be surpassed in importance only by its results in the field of politics. No modern state can be formed in China until social and political localism has been broken down by the realities of economic interdependence. This can come only with the modernization of transport, which will supply the physical media through which political unity can be promoted and expressed.

Thus, for military, economic, and political reasons, the present condition and future development of transport in China are of basic importance. Any attempt to evaluate the present or future status of China as a power must include careful study of this factor.

It would be inaccurate to characterize transport in China as completely primitive. Elements of modernity have been introduced, in the shape of airways, railroads, steamship lines, and automotive traffic. But, as is the case with modern industry, these modern elements form a small minority of the total. The overwhelming bulk of transport is still carried on by those same primitive means which have been in use for centuries. Wind or currents of water are used for moving boats; animals are used in some regions to carry or haul loads, but the chief motive power for transport comes from man himself. Most goods are carried from place to place on the backs of coolie porters, or are pulled or pushed along by them in boats, rickshas, carts, or wheelbarrows.

These methods of transport persist not because they are less costly than more modern methods, but simply because adequate modern facilities do not exist. Coolie carriers and wheelbarrows, for example, are much more expensive for transport of goods than are railroads. In 1934 the cost of moving a ton of freight one kilometer by wheelbarrow was six times greater than the cost of moving the most bulky and least perishable goods by rail. . . .

In West China, similar cost advantages are discoverable for motor transport, over caravans or human carriers. . . .

However, costs are not the only factors limiting the usefulness of coolie transport. Certain goods, such as heavy and unwieldy pieces of lumber, cannot be cut up to form small loads, and are transported through rough country by porters only with the greatest difficulty. . . .

Even in regions where motor roads exist, great quantities of freight are still transported by human and animal carriers. For example, the exchange of goods between China and Soviet Russia over the western route between Alma-Ata and Lanchow depends heavily on camel caravans and coolie porters. In 1941 these methods of transport moved more than 500,000 tons of goods a total distance of 19,000 miles between the two countries. The gasoline for motor trucks on the eastern section of the highway was brought in from western Sinkiang by camel caravans. . . .

Twenty years ago there were only about 1,000 miles of surfaced motor roads in all China, with an additional 10,000 miles of graded dirt roads. By July 1937 these totals had increased to approximately 15,500 and 52,500, respectively. A considerable amount of construction has taken place during the past seven years of war, but China's highway system is still totally inadequate for the full utilization of her natural resources. . . .

The great advantage of road construction in China is its cheapness. The chief requirement for building unsurfaced dirt roads is a plentiful supply of labor. This is easily requisitioned from the Chinese countryside. . . .

In road-building as elsewhere, the "cheap" Chinese labor is not always inexpensive. But however expensive, hand labor is likely to remain the chief means of road building and maintenance in China for some time after the war. The mechanization of road-building would require heavy imports of machinery, such as bulldozers, rollers, etc., and the fuel for powering their motors. This would cause a further drain on China's resources of foreign exchange. These funds should be conserved for absolutely necessary imports, such as heavy industrial machinery, for which human labor cannot be substituted. . . .

Smoother surfaces provide higher speeds at lower rates of fuel consumption. Speeds of travel are particularly low on the new roads in China's west, where poor surfaces combine with extreme grades. An average speed of more than twenty miles an hour while driving over the Burma Road was considered impracticable. On the road from western Szechwan into Sikang, opened to traffic in January 1941, speeds are still lower. Trucks travel this road at an average of 67.5 miles per day. Passenger cars can average about 100 miles in a day's driving. This is a far faster rate of travel than was possible in that region before the construction of the road. Speeds as low as this detract from the economies of motor transport by increasing ton-mile costs of vehicle maintenance, and also indicate road conditions which must shorten greatly the life of automotive equipment.

It is probably a fact, however, that conditions of the road surface have been blamed too much for the rapid deterioration of cars and trucks in China. Actually, the lack of training and discipline among the drivers is largely responsible. On the Burma Road, trucks in charge of Chinese drivers had the shockingly brief life of only six months. The chief cause of this was the inexcusable abuse of their equipment by truck drivers. This represented only one feature of the general mismanagement of the Burma Road on the part of the Chinese authorities.

. . . Chinese drivers are prone to treat their vehicles as though they were farm animals. They will overload them critically, and often fail to provide them with an adequate "diet" of water or lubricating oil. Unfortunately, the truck cannot, like a mule, refuse to move if dangerously overloaded. Nor can it forage for its own food and drink if neglected by the driver. The mechanical appliance rewards only those who are capable of following exact procedures in a disciplined way. . . .

It is a serious question whether after the war the type of car or truck normally put out by American manufacturers will prove desirable for use in China. . . . In chassis and body construction they are far too light for the very rough roads of China's interior. In addition, their gasoline engines are expensive to operate. Diesel motors would give much greater economy. This is particularly important because China must buy practically all her petroleum products abroad. . . .

A trend toward diesel-engined transport on China's roads had begun well before the war. . . .

When it becomes possible to supply a uniform quality of soy bean or other vegetable oils from China's great production, there is no doubt that China will see an even greater demand for diesel-engined trucks and buses than before the war. It has been estimated that vegetable oils are in normal times 86 per cent cheaper per gallon than imported gasoline. . . .

No matter what the development of roads and of automotive transport, China cannot hope to avoid the need to develop railways and water transport. It is quite unlikely that trucks will supplant rail and water in the shipment of heavy and bulky goods over any distance. This is particularly true of such goods as iron ore and coal.

Water transport has always been of great importance in China. There are an estimated 40,000 miles of canal systems, located particularly in the Yangtze River valley, which provide channels for shallow-draft boats. The Yangtze itself is the country's chief avenue of inland transport. It is navigable most of the year by 10,000-ton ocean freighters as far upstream as Hankow. Its channel is thirty feet deep as far as Ichang, about 1,000 miles by river from the sea at Shanghai. The Upper Yangtze and its tributaries are navigable by shallow-draft steamers or by small Chinese craft. The latter are propelled by wind or current, or pulled upstream by trackers on the river bank. . . .

The sea is important for transport between northeastern and southeastern China. . . .

The lack of railroads in Western China has thrown fresh emphasis on water transport. The largest part of all freight in Free China is carried by small boats and steamers over an extensive network of rivers. . . .

The small steamers and launches plying the rivers of Free China amount only to a total capacity of some 25,000 tons. . . . Junks and other craft amount to a tonnage of well over half a million. A few of these are of improved construction, and still fewer of them have been supplied with charcoal-burning auxiliary engines. The chief handicaps of these primitive craft are their slowness and the irregularity and uncertainty of operations, which result from their dependence on wind, current, and human muscle for propulsion.

There is no doubt that China's postwar development would be facilitated by a great expansion of modern shipping facilities. It is equally certain that, at first, most of the equipment and the trained personnel to direct its operation must come from abroad. . . .

The great need of China in this and other respects is the rapid development of her internal economy. The development of internal and coastwise shipping will lay a solid foundation of experience for possible later development of oceanic shipping. The creation of an adequate merchant marine for coastal and inland waters is a task to occupy all the resources available for this purpose for the next twenty or twenty-five years. . . .

Shanghai is the only Chinese port with a ready-made avenue of transport to the remote interior, provided for it by the Yangtze River. All other ports should be developed only in coordination with the expansion of China's railway system. . . .

The need for a great increase in railways in China is apparent. The three provinces of Manchuria are the only ones in which a nearly adequate railway system exists. This system has been built for the most part by the Japanese, with other construction by the Russians and Chinese. . . .

China's needs for railroads can be easily seen from a few illustrative facts. In the entire province of Szechwan, with its 45,000,000 or more inhabitants, there are only about ten miles of railroads, comprising a narrow-gauge line for hauling coal produced by a mine northwest of Chungking. The area of Szechwan is about 142,500 square miles. The rivers of this vast province provide better transport facilities than are usual elsewhere, but speed, certainty, and economy of transport can only be secured for much of this rich agricultural region by the construction of rail lines to supplement waterways.

Eight other provinces are, like Szechwan, almost totally lacking in railroads. Together these nine provinces comprise more than one-third of the total area of China. If to them are added Outer Mongolia and Tibet, which also lack railways, it appears that well over one-half the area of China is totally lacking in railroads. The importance of this lies in the fact that, with one exception, the nine provinces which have no rail lines are in the far western and northern regions of China. . . .

As has been pointed out already in respect to mineral deposits, most of the economic potential of China lies in regions most easily accessible from the seacoast. This is fortunate in view of China's shortages of such minerals as iron. The presence of iron in such areas as the Philippines and Malaya, where there are no coal deposits, would make it logical to import iron ore by water to Manchuria, North China, or the Yangtze Valley. In turn, this gives first priority to the development of transport facilities in regions nearer the seacoast, and makes the total absence of railways in the far west less of a handicap to the development of China after the war. . . .

Naturally, if all other relevant geographical factors could be disregarded, the greatest possible safety from attack would be secured by locating strategic industries at the geographic center of China. Here they would have maximum remoteness from possible foreign attack. But even for countries the size of China, such a protective feature will probably be nullified within a generation by the development of air power.

The conditions which inhibited the building of railroads in prewar China were similar to those which have been already pointed out as restricting the development of industry. The complex of causes included political and social disorganization, lack of capital, and a state of partial foreign economic control. . . .

The civil wars attendant on the establishment of Nationalist supremacy between 1923 and 1936 virtually wrecked the railway plant of China. . . . The war with Japan . . . caused the destruction of much of the existing facilities. Retreating Chinese armies tore up rails and ties, transporting them westward for use in extending the railways in Free China. In the first six months of the war, some 47,000 tons of material had thus been salvaged. . . .

Of far greater importance than the question of just how many miles of new lines should be built within a given period, after the war, is that of their precise location. . . .

The known and possible presence of minerals and other resources in the border regions must be balanced against their remoteness from population centers. A further item is the cost of constructing long rail lines through much empty country to reach resources more easily available elsewhere. From the strategic viewpoint, until China's military strength is greatly increased, lines into border areas must logically be regarded as possible avenues of hostile invasion of China. They cannot be thought of solely as possible "backdoor" lines of supply in case of war. Necessary trade with these regions, and between them and foreign countries, can easily be handled by increased truck and airplane traffic. Air transport can supply the needs of politics and government. In the case of Outer Mongolia, the construction of railroads by the Chinese would raise serious political questions. . . .

Decisions on questions of total requirements, costs, and locations of railway lines will not suffice. Of necessity there would also be extensive changes in the administration of railways. The first of these should consist in the amalgamation of existing lines into several main systems....

This reform, however, must be accompanied by the development of a higher level of administrative efficiency than has heretofore been prevalent. Difficult as it may prove to be, railway administration must be detached from internal politics. Railway expansion will require the training of numerous administrative personnel in addition to mechanical and technical staffs. Since the railways are operated by the national government, their administrative staffs should be placed under civil service regulations as to qualifications, salary and tenure. This will be most difficult of accomplishment....

... Equality of opportunity for the shipment of goods and freedom of shippers from corrupt exactions by officials are necessary if trade is to be fostered and placed on the most economic basis. In addition, the government must supply adequate policing to safeguard rail shipments from plundering and brigandage....

There should be no feeling of apprehension on the part of China's planners that the necessity for railways will be eliminated by the development of transport by air....

China does constitute a natural area for the development of air transport. Within its boundaries, extreme weather conditions are the exception, rather than the rule. The large size of the country and the distances it provides combine with the total absence of modern transport to create a particularly strong demand for air transportation. The great advantage of the airplane is that it requires only a short time to construct the needed facilities for its operation at far distant points on the surface of the earth. Whereas a railway to western Sinkiang would require years to build, the necessary landing fields for aircraft took but a short time to construct and were already in use before the war.

Thus, for express passengers, mail, and some freight, the airplane should be employed in all the farther regions of China where more modern means of transport are lacking. The development of these regions may be accelerated in this way and their political relation to the rest of China strengthened.... At the same time, this method of military domination and political control does not in itself open China to attacks in reverse....

The increasing demand for air transport in China can be seen from prewar developments. The China National Aviation Company, commonly referred to as CNAC, began operations in 1929. In that year its planes flew approximately 58,350 miles, carrying only 220 passengers and 8,650 pounds of mail. In 1936 the mileage flown had increased to approximately 1,550,000 or nearly 27 times the 1929 total. The number of passengers carried had increased by more than 70 times, and the weight of mail by nearly 30 times....

The history of CNAC in both peace and war demonstrates the future possibilities for air transport in China....

The radio will be increasingly employed by the government for purposes of political indoctrination. The establishment of a national network of stations centering in the capital city is probable after the war.

Yet until education eliminates the extreme differences in language between regions in China, it will be difficult to secure all the advantages of a national network. To do so, the government must reaffirm its policy of compulsory education of primary-school students in the Mandarin dialect, which has been chosen as the national language. . . .

Hence it is that the telephone and radio-telephone constitute imperfect instruments for the general transmission of intelligence in China. In addition to the dialects, there is the problem of the sound-structure of the Chinese language, with its large number of homophones or syllables of an identical sound. The absence of any alphabet or system of phonetic writing in China makes it impossible to spell out words over the telephone, so as to distinguish as in English among "rays," "raze," and "raise." . . .

The use of the telegraph in China has been faced with some similar difficulties. Lack of an alphabetical script forces the use of a code to indicate the different characters. Coding and decoding are thus necessary even for ordinary messages. This clumsy system can be eliminated. The future introduction of an alphabetized script in place of the Chinese characters is quite possible. . . .

Facsimile transmission can be used by radio as well as by telegraph. Radio photo-telegram service between the United States and China has been in existence since December 1942. . . .

CHINA'S POLITICAL AND SOCIAL ORGANIZATION

How will the probable development of China's government and society influence the growth of her national strength in the generation after the war? . . .

The traditional pattern of the Chinese "national" government was laid down some two thousand years ago. . . .

The character of the Chinese imperial regime resulted from the size of the geographic area over which its influence extended and within which it served chiefly as the symbol of a prevalent cultural homogeneity. Over the vast area in which Chinese culture existed, the constant and continued use of direct governing authority by the central imperial regime was technically unfeasible, in view of the difficulty of communications. This did not result in the total destruction of the principle of political centrality. It did make necessary an effective and far-reaching compromise of that principle in favor of the principle of local and small-group control. . . .

In essence the maintenance of a central regime, so strongly compromised by surrender to political and social localism as was that of traditional China, was possible only because of the nature of that self-perpetuating and bureaucratic elite into whose hands was given the power to represent the Imperial House in the localities. This elite was predominantly composed of persons adept in the formal manipulation of verbal symbols. It was notably deficient in the possession of other technical skills, unless we except the ability to acquire material wealth in the conduct of official duties. . . .

National unity existed largely in the abstract. The preservation of local order was naturally a concern of the magistrates delegated by the central regime to operate in local areas. . . . Chief military reliance for the suppression of any large-scale civil disorder was placed on local levies of militia, whose military inexpertness was countered by their numbers. . . .

A further and more pressing concern of the local delegates of the central regime was the collection of taxes. The taxes were necessary to maintain the bureaucracy. They also supported the Imperial House on such a level as effectively to complicate and enrich the panoply of its symbolism and thus help induce popular respect for the imperial regime.

The Imperial House ostensibly held absolute powers, but it was committed by the facts of geography to a policy of tolerating local self-government. By far the greater number and weight of normal human concerns were immune from regulation by the central government and from any other kind of formal governmental control.

As a substitute for formal governmental control, the Chinese possessed numerous devices for ensuring orderly relationships in society and for fostering the interests of organized groups. Most of these devices were organized functionally or *ad hoc,* and by organizational, regional, or purely personal groupings of individuals. . . . Typical of these organizations were the mercantile guilds of the commercial cities, the insurance societies connected with localities or provinces, and the omnipresent secret societies of towns or rural areas.

Such groups often had great power over individuals, for whom their word was law. The supreme organization, however, was and still is the family, obligation to which has always transcended in strength that to any other social group in China. In rural China the family gave rise to the village, the government of which was in the hands of family patriarchs. These elders ruled by virtue of the family system and had power of life and death over village residents. They exercised control under the limiting restraints of custom and public opinion, and their acts were sanctioned by the authority of filial respect. Of their authority there was no doubt. Their powers were ill-defined, but were nonetheless real.

Seen in this way, government and social control in traditional China cannot be characterized as negative or passive. Actually, it was shot through with the tightest compulsions and controls, albeit these were private and local in origin and did not emanate from a central source of political authority. The Chinese dislike for public and legal means of preserving private interests is not based on abstract anti-constitutionalism. It is derived largely from the failure of centrally controlled courts and officials to function honestly and effectively in an empire of vast size and primitive communications. . . .

[There are] three great traditional vices, from the western point of view, of Chinese politics and government. The first of these is Face, which means laying primary emphasis on personal prestige factors and on formal manifestations instead of positive realities. This principle permeates Chinese social and political relations. The second is Favor, or the notion that politics and government are based on humanistic pragmatism and not on abstract principle. They are, therefore, at best to be conducted on a basis of *quid pro quo,* and at worst on a basis of complete corruption. The third is Approximation, the practice of which both Face and Favor make inevitable, and which militates against the exact enforcement of rules or precise obedience to orders. . . .

These vices are not exclusively Chinese. They can be found to a greater or less degree in all governments. But they have become uniquely entrenched in Chinese politics and in the psychology of the Chinese. . . .

After nearly thirty-five years of the revolution, the present government of China has yet to secure complete authority as the successor to political power for all China. The years following the abdication of the Manchu Dynasty saw attempts to reconstitute imperial rule. The generally artificial and uninspired efforts at that time to establish a constitutional republic met with the opposition of influential and militarily powerful figures. . . .

Since neither a monarchy nor a republic could be constituted as a means of governing, China rapidly broke up into a collection of warring satrapies, headed by a diverse congeries of local chieftains, usually known as Tuchün or warlords. . . .

All of these local warlords were potential aspirants to the political succession. They achieved various degrees of success in moving toward this ambitious goal, but their methods were essentially similar. By violence or threat of violence, they secured control over sources of revenue in their localities, using them to enrich themselves and to purchase western armaments. . . .

During the first fifteen years of this chaotic process of political selection, there was in existence a nominally national government of China at Peking. . . .

The chief rival of the Peking regime, in its claim to the revolutionary succession, was to be found at Canton. Here were the followers of Dr. Sun Yat-sen, whose early anti-monarchic and revolutionary career guaranteed him a following in the struggle to create effective national governing power in China. . . .

As a matter of fact, the success which the Kuomintang has enjoyed since 1923 in establishing a claim to the character of a national government, is much more to be attributed to Chiang Kai-shek than to Dr. Sun. Chiang Kai-shek's technical training was in the military field. Unlike that of Dr. Sun, which was in medicine, his particular skill proved directly applicable to the solution of China's political problems. Polished by four years in Japanese army schools, his military ability served as a superbly useful accompaniment to his natural skill as a political manipulator. . . .

To recognize the contribution of Chiang Kai-shek is not to attribute to the government dominated by him the character of a generally accepted successor to the old regime. Support for the Nationalist government is strictly limited by locality and by social and economic groups, and is weakened by factionalism of all types. In specific areas not under Japanese control, the localism of the warlord period still survives. These facts have been recognized by Chiang Kai-shek himself. . . .

In regions more remote from the capital at Chungking, the presence of fully autonomous local regimes must be noted. Best known of these is of course the Communist regime of Northern and Western China, centered in northern Shensi. This regime exercises all the functions of government for an estimated population of 50-60,000,000. . . .

Political regimes of the southwestern provinces have in varying degrees lost their autonomy since the temporary wartime shift of the seat of the central government to Chungking. . . .

The Chinese government is aware of the lack of political unity. . . . This is to be seen in its efforts to regulate or prohibit the growth of organizations which might prove focal points for the development of informal social control in the old Chinese manner. The official opposition to independent labor unions and cooperatives has already been noted. The Ministry of Social Welfare, a party organ, attempts also to control and supervise all other organizations having a regularly constituted membership. The Ministry tries to regulate rigidly the constitutional organization of social groups in an effort to make political orthodoxy in the Kuomintang pattern a requirement for membership.

In addition, the Nationalist party has

promoted its own official organizations, some of them for the masses and others for elite bodies. Of the former, the New Life Movement is the outstanding example. In its inception, at least, it owed much of its inspiration to German and Italian fascist models. . . .

An official Party organization of a somewhat different type is the *San Min Chu I* Youth Corps (Three People's Principles Youth Corps). Membership of the Corps comprises about 500,000 of the youth of both sexes between the ages of 16 and 25. As officially stated, the purpose of the Corps is "to assist in national mobilization and to lay the foundation of a powerful nucleus to carry out future reconstruction." . . .

Contrary to what one might expect from the discipline in its organizations, factionalism is one of the major characteristics of the Nationalist party itself. Chiang Kai-shek has succeeded in elevating to high positions as policymakers a considerable number of his fellow-provincials from Chekiang. These individuals all speak the same language, in more ways than one, and are bound together not so much by their politics as by their origin in the same locality. Common local origin is traditionally one of the strongest bonds of identity in China, and its power in Chinese politics today should not be forgotten. Factional groupings appear, however, even among these fellow-provincials, some of whom are the most energetic in their efforts to extend party dominance.

The Kuomintang hierarchy is at best a collection of cliques among which Chiang Kai-shek acts as a moderator and preserves his own interests by the immemorial practice of playing one group off against another. This does not imply for him a merely negative role. On the contrary it describes a normal Chinese system of political operations, natural in the almost total absence of fixed political formalism in the Chinese scene. Intolerable as such a situation might appear to the western political mind, one must expect this characteristic of traditional Chinese politics to persist in the future. In spite of present and future appearances of institutional forms and constitutional framework, no great shift away from it is likely during the next generation. . . .

Full acceptance everywhere in China of the authority of one central government as a successor to the dynasty which abdicated in 1912 will be fostered by the victory over Japan. The central importance of Chiang Kai-shek to that victory will enhance his prestige both nationally and internationally, and thus aid the process of political consolidation. National unity, however, will be of real importance to China only to the extent that it is accompanied by basic changes in the functioning of government. . . .

Nothing is a more serious bar to political and economic modernization in China than its present critical lack of personnel trained in scientific techniques. Without such personnel no modern government is possible. . . .

For the next generation, however, no material shift away from oligarchic government is to be expected in China. . . . Soon after the war, China will doubtless receive a constitution by gift of the ruling oligarchy. By its terms, the election of officials, definite allocations of governmental powers, and reservation of individual rights may well be secured. But the road to democratic constitutionalism is a long one, and there is no indication that the Chinese will attempt to cover it in a few quick steps. . . . The present official Draft Constitution would concentrate executive power in the hands of one man and would make him virtually impregnable to direct control by representatives of the people. . . .

The Draft Constitution comprises for

the most part a modified sketch of institutions now operating in Nationalist China. It consolidates and stabilizes the present condition of oligarchic centralism visible in the present Kuomintang-dominated government. By its very slight broadening of the base of popular consent for such an oligarchy, it indicates the extreme gradualism of the large majority of leaders of China's governing party. That party comprises a carefully recruited political elite.... It is strongly entrenched at present, and will be still more strongly in control when the proposed Constitution comes up for adoption. It is therefore clear that no radical venture into popular democracy is to be contemplated for China in the near future....

The improbability of the development in China within the next generation of anything like what Americans think of as working democracy should not be allowed to obscure the chief issues, which concern the content of socio-economic policy. For these are the issues which will determine how soon and to what extent China can strengthen herself in order to participate in the maintenance of peace and security in the post-war world....

CHINA IN THE WORLD OF TOMORROW

Such are the massive problems to the solution of which China's energies must be devoted for the next half century. Seen together, they make it most unlikely that, for at least twenty-five years after the present war, China will be able to develop such technical capacity as to allow her to rely primarily on her own strength to guarantee her security. Even less will she be in a position to participate positively in any system to provide security for other areas or countries of the Far East. This means, among other things, that for the policing of Japan after the war, it will be impossible to place primary reliance on China.

It would be a gross error to conclude from these facts that China will not attempt to develop her military power immediately after the war. Some such development is inevitable, if only for purposes of internal political consolidation. If it were limited to purposes of internal policing, a moderate effort would suffice.

If, on the other hand, the postwar position of China were one of obvious insecurity, there is no doubt that her leaders would channel every constructive effort... into the building of all the military strength that China's potential would permit. Her very weakness today and her relative poverty of resources would, under these conditions, demand concentration on armaments to the exclusion of production of civilian goods. This would serve to support the consolidation of total political controls which it would make necessary, if not completely effective. At the same time it would postpone indefinitely any major attempt to solve China's basic social and economic problems, and would thus in reality inhibit the development of a fundamentally strong and unified Chinese state.

Such a strong Chinese state must in the final analysis rest upon the consent of the masses of the population. If there is to be permanent mass dissatisfaction, the result, in view of the latent power of Chinese individualism, can only be eventual political subversion. The internal weakness of China resulting from this would in turn tend to attract foreign intervention or aggression as it has during the past century, and instead of making China a center of international order, would preserve her as an area of international power rivalries.

Conversely, the only way in which to guarantee China a long-term role in the preservation of international peace and order is to induce really basic socio-economic reform designed to advance the welfare of her population. This long-range task is beset with many internal difficulties and obstacles in China. The great efforts necessary for their solution will occupy all available energies for the next twenty-five to fifty years.

This task will not even be attempted, however, unless a general settlement for Asia and the Pacific can be evolved after the war which will provide all peaceful states, including China, with security against attack. Unless such a settlement results from the present war, the Chinese will feel it necessary to build their military power as rapidly as possible to its potential maximum, giving only incidental attention to the inevitably evil results of this policy on their internal politics and social problems.

This situation can only result in the creation in China of another Japan out to seize from others those necessary components of military self-sufficiency which she lacks within her own borders and justifying such action on the grounds of necessity for defense against possible military aggression. As in the case of modern Japan, such a course of conquest might well serve to conceal for a time the real weaknesses of her social order and to prevent their solution by internal measures. That such a course of conquest would carry serious threats to general peace and security cannot be doubted. That it might be undertaken even against serious odds seems likely. . . .

[For Dr. Rowe's further conclusions regarding peace and international security in the Far East, see chap. 17, page 730, below.]

CHINESE POLITICS AND THE WAR WITH JAPAN

By Owen Lattimore

From chap. 3 of *Solution in Asia*, by Owen Lattimore. Copyright 1945 by Owen Lattimore. Little, Brown & Co., Boston; reproduced by permission. The author, formerly political adviser to General Chiang Kai-shek, is director of the Page School of International Relations at The Johns Hopkins University.

One of Chiang Kai-shek's most solid claims to a place in history is that he personally was responsible for the decision to risk China's very existence as a nation in a final stand against Japan. . . .

There can be no doubt that when the foreigners, both businessmen and diplomats, came to terms with the government controlled by Chiang Kai-shek, they thought they had found the man they wanted to rule China in their interest. Nor can there be any doubt that Chiang saw what the game was and knew that the dice were loaded, but still thought that he could play the game and win—and he did win. . . .

Through civil war against the Communists [1928-1936] Chiang was able to regulate the interests of the varied groups within the Kuomintang coalition. In effect, he could say to any of these groups when he was called on to adjust their differences, "You must accept my solution, otherwise the Communist situation will get out of hand, and that will be worse for you than what I now propose." In the same way, the civil war could be used to improve his bargaining position in negotiations with foreign powers. In effect, he could say to them, "You must concede me the minimum that I ask in negotiating credits, tariff revisions, the gradual adjustment of the old unequal treaties in China's favor, because otherwise people will begin to go over to the Communists, whose demands are much more extreme than mine." Even in evading and fencing with the Japanese the same kind of argument could be used. . . .

Finally, the war against the Communists was used to build up a national army in the face of the conventional thinking of the imperial powers who favored a Chinese army of a colonial type—one that would enable Chiang to crush peasant rebellions and keep provincial warlords in line, but not one that would enable him to face an invading army on equal terms. It was easy and profitable to unload obsolete tanks, second-line planes, and all kinds of surplus equipment on China. It was not to the interests of the Japanese militarists, however, even to allow all the provincial militarists to be subordinated to the national government. It was their set policy to oppose unity in China, and they therefore sold arms both to Chiang Kai-shek's government and to warlords who opposed Chiang Kai-shek.

In spite of all difficulties, however, Chiang succeeded in building up an army not only good enough to give him superiority in civil war, but good enough to face an invasion. . . .

. . . There were several phases of this war and its accompanying political developments. . . . The first phase was one of extremism. Although many besides the Communists had their doubts in 1928 whether the time had really come for a right-wing compromise within the Kuomintang, and a compromise between the Chinese Revolution and the foreign interests whose controls it was attempting to throw off, only the hardest-minded men were willing to carry their opposition to the length of civil war.

From the beginning the extremists were dominated by the Communists. The great majority of the professional officers went with the Kuomintang and Chiang Kai-shek. As was to be expected, the troops who stood by them were the most professional troops, those who had been longest under discipline and had the best equipment. Most of the warlord troops, whose morale was of a half-feudal kind, colored by personal allegiance to the warlord who paid them, were also against the Communists. This left the Communists with a military nucleus of men who were either armed industrial workers or peasants who had a high revolutionary morale but comparatively little training as professional soldiers.

One wing of the Communists believed in revolutionary ardor and the offensive at all costs. The leaders who tried to make this the "party line" threw away their best troops in trying to take cities and important strategic centers. The leadership then passed to Mao Tze-tung and Chu Teh, the men who have since become the legendary figures of Chinese Communism. These men foresaw a long struggle against superior forces with better equipment. They needed time to train their men in the kind of war they foresaw, and they believed it imperative to get behind them a solid civilian support. Under Chinese conditions this meant that they had to retire to an area of undeveloped communications and few large cities and base themselves on the support of poor peasants. . . .

The Communists could not survive unless they got food, shelter, guides to show them the terrain, and information about the movements of the enemy. They could not win over the peasants by giving lectures on Marxism. They had to do things which would utterly and irrevocably commit them to the peasant cause. . . .

There was only one thing to do: take land from the landlords, give it to the peasants, and then join with the peasants in defending the land against both the landlords and the Kuomintang's armies.... Often the landlords resisted expropriation. They were killed —there being no time to persuade them —in a Red Terror. Later, as the fight for survival became desperate and bitter, the Red Terror turned not only against those who resisted, but against anyone whose loyalty was in doubt. Both sides, in fact, fought a merciless, Old Testament, Hebrew-and-Philistine war...."

... For every landlord or "bourgeois" killed, scores of peasants were slaughtered, tortured, or burned in their villages.... In China, as in Pilsudski's Poland, in the Baltic States, and in Mannerheim's Finland, the White Terror was worse than the Red because in a peasant country revolution attempts to break the grip of a minority, while counterrevolution attempts to break the will of a majority.

Among the Communists in this period the processes of coalition were unimportant. The vast majority were peasants. There were intellectuals and urban proletarian workers among the leaders, but these were people who had been torn from their origins and local contacts. There was no question of compromise between the Communists and foreign interests, if only for the reason that the Communists were geographically not in contact with foreign interests. Even more important is the fact that the Chinese Communists were so isolated, south of the Yangtze and far inland from the coast, that they could not receive arms or any other help from Russia, while the intensity of the fight for survival made it impossible for them to slacken or strengthen their civil-war efforts in accordance with "directives" from either the Third International or the Soviet government. They were on their own.

A second phase of the civil war can be dated approximately from the Japanese invasion of Manchuria in 1931. The shock of this invasion was important in two ways. First it tended to support the opinion of those, including many who had not gone along with the Communists, who had all along contended that China in 1926-1927 had not loosened the foreign grip enough to make herself safe. Second, it followed a peaceful agreement by which the Northeastern Provinces (Manchuria) had submitted to the National government without civil war—an omen that it was not yet safe for China to consolidate in peace without being prepared to defend her consolidations against foreign attack.

Five months later, in February 1932, the Chinese Communists "declared war" against the Japanese—a declaration which has to be cited in quotation marks, because there was no way in which the Communists could get at the Japanese to fight them. At the same time the Communists issued an appeal for a United Front. In 1933 this appeal was followed up by an offer to cooperate with any Kuomintang army against the Japanese; but the government ignored the appeal and kept up the civil war relentlessly, forcing the Communists to begin, in 1934, their famous Long March from south of the Yangtze westward to the edges of Tibet and then northward and northeastward to the Yellow River province of Shensi, in the northern part of which they consolidated themselves in 1935 and 1936. Mao Tze-tung confessed to Edgar Snow that this move was partly made necessary by losses suffered in a mistaken attempt to fight the Kuomintang armies in positional warfare; but he claimed also to have made the move partly in order to get into a better position to deal with the situation arising out of Japanese aggression.

There were two main characteristics of this second phase. On the one hand the Communists, though still not in a position to convert themselves into a coalition party, began to acquire a significant number of sympathizers within the much greater territory controlled by the Kuomintang, because of their demand for an end to civil war and a united stand against the Japanese. On the other hand, events outside of the Kuomintang-Communist civil war were forcing a final crisis between China and Japan.

1. The Germans and Italians in Europe, and the Japanese in Asia, were working a seesaw—but against whom? The most influential American and European experts held that it was against Russia, or could be turned against Russia. Actually, the indications are that the Rome-Berlin-Tokyo Axis had decided, long before the appeasement powers were aware of it, to leave Russia alone for the time being and attack the appeasement powers first. In view of our policy in Spain, our attitude toward Hitler at the time of Munich and after Munich, and our Asiatic policy of protest without resistance, America must be included with the appeasement powers. . . .

2. In China all through the year 1936 the Japanese hoped that Chiang Kai-shek could be bluffed into letting them occupy a big and strategically vital territory between the Great Wall and the Yellow River. The coalition headed by Chiang was known to be badly split. Wang Ching-wei, who later went over to the Japanese, held at that time the position equivalent to Premier in the Chinese government, and was known to be defeatist. Many of China's industrialists and bankers were known to be for peace at any price, because their main wealth was in factories, machines, and warehouses in the port cities, defenseless against the Japanese navy.

3. If the Chinese were to resist, there was the further question of timing the call to the nation to resist. Chiang had faced the ultimate necessity for resistance as early as 1931-1932, and had worked steadily to prepare for the war, knowing that he would at first get only wobbly "moral support" from America and Britain, but believing that in the end Japanese encroachment on American and British interests would force more positive aid. . . .

In holding to this line he was supported, or at least not restrained, by American and British policy. In view of the fact that our present policy openly encourages a negotiated settlement between Kuomintang and Communists, and deplores the possibility of civil war, it is important to recall that in all the published American official documents covering policy in the years between the invasion of Manchuria in 1931 and the invasion of the main body of China in 1937, there is not a hint that we ever urged a negotiated national unity in China. In my opinion this forces us to draw a very sobering inference: the unity of China was not a prime requisite because in Washington and London, too, we were at this time either fumbling instinctively or working calculatedly toward a "settlement" which would allow Japan actual gains at the expense of China, while impairing as little as possible the legal purity and financial value of our own rights and privileges.

During this period the Communists pressed and propagandized for a negotiated end to the civil war and a full stand against Japan at the earliest possible moment rather than the last possible moment. . . . They ceased to be merely a party which *opposed* the policy of the government and became a party with a policy *alternative* to that of the government. Furthermore, although they remained a one-doctrine party and could not yet broaden out into a coalition, they became potentially the focus of a new coalition because a number of movements outside of Communist territory, and not in the least Communist in character, began to urge the National government to accede to the policy advocated by the Communists.

At Christmas time in 1936 the electric question of sooner or later was decided. With this decision the civil-war phase of China's internal politics passed into a new phase of war for national survival. Some of the troops lined up against the Communists in Northwest China had become impatient of civil war and eager to fight Japan instead, and had even begun to fraternize with the Communists. At a time when probably not one of the generals under him would have had the courage to do so, Chiang Kai-shek went personally to the center of disaffection to restore discipline, and was kidnaped by the mutineers. There were three immediate reactions to the kidnaping. There were popular demonstrations all over the country . . . hailing Chiang Kai-shek as the national leader and representative of the whole people, and demanding that he be released immediately. The Communists themselves joined in this demand for unconditional release, sending a representative to the center of the mutiny to take part in negotiations. On the other hand, some of the more rigidly military minds in the National government wanted to send a punitive expedition against the mutineers, regardless of whether this might cost the Generalissimo his life.

. . . The Generalissimo himself took a line of the severest dignity and courage, refusing to discuss any conditions whatever and insisting on the duty of the mutineers to submit to their commander in chief. He won. It was the greatest victory of his life, and it united China. Although no bargain had been struck, the way was now open for a negotiated United Front between the Kuomintang and its only armed opponents, the Communists, and consequently for a united stand against the Japanese.

. . . It was plain to the Japanese that they had to strike before the new unity could solidify. They struck at the Marco Polo Bridge, six months later, on July 7, 1937. They failed to engineer a limited war, and found themselves swept into the unlimited war which [lasted until 1945]. . . .

From the outbreak of war in 1937 to the fall of Canton and Hankow, in October 1938, China showed a political cohesion that astonished foreign observers. By taking Shanghai, the Japanese themselves prevented any important appeasement by wealthy Chinese. . . . At the same time all Chinese were inspired by the stubborn defense of Shanghai, which proved once for all that the Japanese were no supermen, even when relative superiority of naval guns, planes, tanks, and artillery ought to have made them supermen. The Chinese were also buoyed up by the conviction that by forcing the Japanese out of a "limited war" in North China into a general war all over China, and by completely upsetting the Japanese timetable, they had by their own will and courage imposed a long war on the Japanese instead of a Blitzkrieg. Since this was a defeat of Japan's master strategy, it held out hopes for eventual Chinese victory. In this period there was remarkably good coordination between the Communist troops and the national armies, considering that the United Front had been formed only at the last minute and considering the distrust and enmity accumulated during ten years of civil war. There was also a heartening fervor in the spread of guerrilla war behind the Japanese lines.

There was a change, radical in nature though gradual in development, after the fall of Hankow and Canton, which divided China into a Northwestern area and a Southwestern area, not too efficiently joined together (because of transport difficulties) by the province of Szechwan, in which stands Chungking, the wartime capital.

In this situation China began to fight a stalemate war, in the strategy of which there was an important assumption: that Japanese failure to win a decision would generate pressures forcing Japan to encroach on the interests of other nations and forcing these nations to line up definitely with China. . . .

The assumption was correct, as Pearl Harbor proved; but there was one doubtful factor, the factor of time. If Japan had moved against the western powers earlier, the approaches to China might still have been kept open, and relief from the West might have come in such a form and at such a time that the National government would have emerged with a clear ascendancy over the Communists. The fact that the Japanese delayed the attack on Pearl Harbor until the very end of 1941 gave time for a full development of the differences between government policy and Communist policy. In addition, the differences between the two policies were emphasized by the isolation of China when the Philippines, Hong Kong, Singapore, and Burma fell so rapidly, cutting China off from supplies in quantity, while simultaneously Russia was extended to the utmost in checking the huge weight of the German assault.

During this period the Kuomintang underwent a transformation. . . . Of the coalition composing the Kuomintang, the bankers and industrialists, by being driven into the far interior, had lost most of the tangible property and the structure of trading connections on which their power and political influence were based. Consequently, there began a subtle change in the relations between them and the Kuomintang party functionaries and government administrators. Once their opinions and wishes had had great influence on party decisions and government policies. Now, it was they who had to defer to bureaucrats and functionaries. The pitifully small percentage of machinery which had been salvaged from the industrial cities could not be set up again without consulting officials who knew the government's war plans. Even more important, the government, because of the terrible dislocation of the whole country's financial structure, became rapidly more important as the major source of both investment capital and working capital, provided through grants and subsidies. Government functionaries, in a word, became members of boards of directors, while former managing directors and members of boards became subsidiary business bureaucrats.

Increase of bureaucratic authority in an agrarian society is incapable of mobilizing a war economy efficiently. . . . In China a high proportion of the personnel of bureaucracy sympathize not with the need for efficiency but with those who demand special favors—which, in an agrarian society, means the influential landlords. . . .

Just before the war, the largest and most calculable single source of government revenue had been the customs duties collected on import and export trade. With the loss of the seaports, this revenue was abruptly cut down. Farm production now became the most important national source of revenue, in addition to being by far the most important economic activity in Free China. . . .

In every rural district the landlords, and the merchants and bailiffs whose interests are allied with theirs, are literate; the majority of the peasants are not. A large proportion of county magistrates and lesser officials, therefore, come from landlord families, and an overwhelming proportion have interests or connections allied to those of the landlords. Consequently, it is simply impossible to collect the land tax without the good will of the landlords, and usually this good will boils down to a simple proposition: the landlord must be called in to help; he must be allowed to pass on his share of the tax to the peasants, in the form of increased rent, and if the government wishes to increase its revenues, the landlord must be allowed to increase his also.

The outcome is as simple as the explanation. The influence of landlords over party functionaries and government officials has grown greater at the same time that the influence of party functionaries and government officials over bankers and industrialists and businessmen has grown greater. Thus the Kuomintang, with few overt changes to mark the transition, has in fact largely ceased to function as a coalition party, and has become more and more a landlord party. Business interests have not been eliminated and they have not ceased to make money, but they have become subordinate where they were once dominant. Since they alone cannot offset the landlord interest, they need a widening of the coalition in order to regain their ascendancy, and they are therefore less implacably hostile to the groups led by the Communists than are the landlords.

While the Kuomintang was moving from a coalition of interests toward a monopoly of one interest, the Communists were moving in the opposite direction. From being a one-doctrine party, they were tending to become a coalition party. This trend was produced by imperative pressures. During the ten years of civil war the Communists, cut off from cities and urban workers, had become a peasant party. They had been able to survive only by winning to their support the largest possible number of peasants, no matter how bloody and merciless the war in which this policy involved them with the landlords. In a war against the Japanese, however, this policy would have meant annihilation, not survival. Japanese political warfare relied strongly on persuading the landlords that Japan would defend them against Bolshevism. It would have been fatal to drive a whole class of Chinese, and many of those dependent on them, into alliance with the Japanese.

The Communists therefore changed their policy. They ceased to expropriate land, unless the landlord went over to the Japanese. They left the landlord on his land, and they defended the land for him against the Japanese; but in return they drastically limited the amount of rent which he was allowed to collect from his tenants. The reduction of rent, in turn, was large enough to retain the allegiance of the peasants. A parallel policy was adopted in production and trade. With the big cities all in the hands of the Japanese, the Communists had nothing to fear from Chinese big business. With nothing to rely on but rural resources, they did need to fear economic paralysis. They therefore thought it to their interest to encourage and protect both private enterprise and cooperative enterprise, and to allow room for private profit as the quickest and surest stimulus for production and distribution.

Finally, having created nothing less than a new coalition of group interests, they took the logical step of allowing political expression for all groups within the coalition. Probably the most significant report brought back by the American newspapermen who visited the Communist area in the summer of 1944 was the confirmation of what was previously known only through Communist propaganda: actual operation of the Communist one-in-three system limiting Communist membership in committees and local governing bodies and the higher councils of the whole area to one-third of the total membership. This is the most positive step yet taken in China by any party away from dictatorship and toward democracy. It confirms the graduation of the Communists from being a perpetual minority opposition party to the status of a party which has good claims to a position within a coalition government.

These comparisons of change and trend are important because of a factor whose importance is not discussed often enough in America. Up to 1944 the Japanese had occupied only about a third of China's territory; but that third was the home of about half of China's population—and the half which before 1937 contained by far the largest proportions of prosperous, educated, and politically sophisticated people. It is this part of China, including the Northeastern Provinces (Manchuria), which has actually experienced what Japanese rule means. It is in this part of China also that the chief contact between the people and their distant government in Chungking has been through propaganda. A major emphasis in that propaganda has been on the future democracy for which China is fighting.

[After] the Japanese are driven out, the political program of the forces which drive them out or follow them up will be of critical importance. If the actual policy put into practice is not one of free political organization and representation, or at the very least a coalition policy representing all major groups, there will be terrible disillusionment and political unrest. In view of all this it is realistic to allow for the fact that the Kuomintang has been weakened by the trend toward landlord domination during the war years, because the landlord interest will instinctively move toward control of the peasants, not toward allowing them political representation, when Occupied China is liberated from the Japanese. Conversely, the coalition trend of the Communists has put them in a strong position to make a bid for wider allegiances when, on the heels of the Japanese, their columns march parallel with those of the National government into recovered territory.

THE OUTLOOK FOR CHINESE DEVELOPMENT

By G. B. Cressey

From chap. 9 of *Asia's Lands and Peoples,* by G. B. Cressey. Copyright 1944 by McGraw-Hill Book Co., New York; reproduced by permission.

The three great geographic assets of China are coal, manpower, and location. Minerals are present in only modest amounts and the soil is good but so inadequate in terms of population that there is little room for industrial crops or export surplus. Extensive forests may be grown on hillsides. The country almost lacks petroleum, and where waterpower is available it is also seasonal. Despite such shortages, China can look forward to a far greater industrial future. Certainly no other country in eastern Asia is so well endowed as a nation; per capita possibilities are more modest.

The mineral resources of China are varied, and their exploitation is a matter of metallurgy, economics, and political policy. Location and world prices are quite as important as geological origin. It is possible that China has enough of most metals to supply all the industries that can be built for several decades. Coal without iron ore is better than iron without coal, for coal is the key to chemical industries, to cement, and to power. China's coal supply is very great and well distributed, though not all is of metallurgical quality.

China's millions provide the world's largest source of labor. At present they are inefficient, but there is no reason why two generations of training may not make labor as skilled as in Europe. A limited diet and a somewhat enervating climate are handicaps, but the sheer bulk of China's manpower is impressive. The new China has an enormous amount of work to be done in building roads, controlling rivers, improving agriculture, developing forests, operating factories, and improving housing. The people to do the job are available.

Location is a geographic resource, for the possession of material assets is of little value in Antarctica or central Africa. Most of China's economic potential lies in areas accessible to the seacoast, which in turn is at the meeting point on the main sea routes from Europe and from North America. In the territory between India, Australia, and Soviet Siberia, China has no possible rival except Japan, which is dynamic but poor.

Starting with the early 1930's, China was experiencing spectacular developments in road building, city rehabilitation, and education, all of which were arrested by the Japanese invasion. Postwar China faces exceedingly urgent economic needs that touch all of her life. To list some of them alphabetically, they include agriculture, consumer goods, export products, housing and sanitation, hydroelectric power, industry both heavy and light, land reclamation and resettlement, military defense, mining, reforestation, river conservancy, roads and railways, shipping and port facilities, and urban reconstruction.

Some plan is essential. When the Soviet Union started its five-year programs it ruthlessly postponed the manufacture of consumer goods and started at the bottom with mining, transportation, heavy industry, and defense. Some such emphasis is needed in China, but other needs will not wait. Nor is it possible to duplicate the Soviet program here, even with comparable political and social ideology, for China lacks the mineral wealth of the U.S.S.R. and does not possess even the initial tools.

China's first need is inventory. Few major developments are justified until the possibilities are all clear. This was illustrated in the Soviet Union by the creation of steel mills in the Kuznetsk coal basin prior to the discovery of Karaganda coal much closer to the iron ore. China should not plan for heavy industry until the location of all available resources is known. Does China have unused land with soil and climate suitable for crops? Is the flow of certain rivers dependable enough to justify large hydroelectric installations? Can the metal of various ores be extracted economically? What population trends may be counted on? What areas if any will be strategically safe from invasion during the next war?

Within the first decade of peace, China must catch up with a century of progress in the west. For this she needs vast amounts of capital. As of 1937 and excluding the Manchurian provinces, the total modern industrial capital of China amounted to 3,807 million Chinese dollars, of which 74 per cent represented foreign investments. Japanese investments in Manchuria reached five billion yen by 1941. This averaged less than $2 per capita accumulated by Chinese themselves. In contrast to this, the figure in the United States in 1930 was $430 U.S. or $1,433 in Chinese currency. Or if machinery per inhabitant is considered, prewar northwestern Europe has an index figure of 100, the United States 405, China less than 1. . . .

China emerges from the Second World War as one of the Big Four of the United Nations, weakest in actual achievement but with a very great potential in area and position. Before the end of the twentieth century she will probably have caught up with the West and regained her historic leadership in the East, provided that civil war does not retard her progress.

In this era of material civilization and power politics, China is well endowed with the essentials of political geography. These include large size, compact shape, advantageous location, natural boundaries, access to the ocean, reasonably satisfactory land forms, diversified if none too abundant minerals, and an agriculturally productive climate. . . .

If China had not been huge, she might not have survived the Japanese invasion. One of a nation's greatest military assets is defense in depth. Without the ability to trade space for time, China could scarcely have held out. Even omitting the sparsely populated areas of Mongolia, Sinkiang, and Tibet, two million square miles remain. Large size is not synonymous with self-sufficiency, but within the diverse environments of Greater China there is a wide variety of resources. A large size at the same time brings problems in communications and the welding together of diverse peoples.

China's location is not of first rank for world commerce, but she is well situated with respect to a large trade area within which as a whole are exceedingly great resources and attractive markets. Her location is both continental and maritime. Two great ocean highways meet along the China coast; one from Europe via Singapore, the other from North America. Overland communications with the Soviet Union and India are inadequate but can be improved.

Many international disputes arise from unsatisfactory boundaries. China's frontier with India along the Himalaya is easily defined and defended. Next to Soviet Siberia the broad Gobi Desert interposes a different environment but there is no sharply defined boundary. A strong China pushes her control to the north of the desert, a strong U.S.S.R. pushes her influence to the southern margin in the form of the Mongolian People's Republic. The only part of China across which a foreign power might legitimately wish a transit route is in the far northeast where Manchuria projects into Soviet territory and blocks the normal avenue from Lake Baikal to Vladivostok.

China has a coastline 4,000 miles in length, without measuring irregularities. In comparison, the land frontier is 9,500 miles. The delta sections are deficient in good harbors, but on the whole there are adequate port possibilities and good access to the hinterland. The coastal Chinese have a long record of maritime interests, with native junks reaching Ceylon early in the Christian era. Nevertheless, China as a whole has been continental minded, and one of her current problems is to reorient her economic and social interests.

Whereas China has a long coastline, she does not enjoy unrestricted access to the sea. Korea and the Maritime Provinces of the Soviet Union block access to the Sea of Japan, hence the importance of the new Korean gateway at Rashin. To the east of Shanghai are the Liuchiu or Ryukyu Islands, once a Chinese dependency but taken over by the Japanese late in the nineteenth century. Formosa screens the Fukien coast, while the Philippines lie to the southeast. It is but natural that as large a power as China with historic claims to Formosa and the Liuchius should demand their retrocession.

The strategic advantages and disadvantages of topography were repeatedly illustrated during the war with Japan. Invasion was blocked by mountains, but internal strength is also handicapped. Towering mountains to the west and a broad desert to the north provide buffer zones. Except for the Central Mountain Belt, eastern China has no mountains higher or more rugged than the Appalachians, nor hills more difficult of access and utilization than the Appalachian Plateaus.

The mineral picture has already been considered in detail. With superabundant coal and passable iron ore, China is moderately well equipped for industrialization. Southeast Asia as a whole, including the adjoining islands, is exceptionally rich. A strong China will presumably wish assured access to the South Seas, from where she will have to draw numerous mineral and agricultural products.

Too little attention is given to the importance of climate. . . . Agriculture is intimately related to temperature and rainfall, but human health and energy are also tied up with climatic stimulus. World maps of climatic energy give intermediate rank to China. . . .

Leadership in any part of the world depends partly upon factors such as these. China has a large and secure home base, and a commanding position in her larger region. Japan's location is as good but she lacks the security, the resources, the number of people, and the psychology of leadership.

. . . Although it is impossible to foresee distant centuries, it does not appear likely that China will become a threat to the rest of the world. The Chinese have a peaceful and democratic tradition and, whereas they will be supreme in their own realm, their country lacks the geographic factors that might make for world dominance. Under able leadership, China will find that she has the geographic resources with which to meet her geographic needs, provided her population remains within bounds.

Part IV

The American Realm between
Europe and Asia

Chapter 15

The American Realm

THE American Realm constitutes the third great political division of our world. Various names have set off this region from the European and Afro-Asian realms. To successive generations of immigrants, the Americas have been the "New World," lands of opportunity for the oppressed and down-trodden of the "Old World." In the days when Europe was the political center of the globe, it was natural to call the Americas the Western Hemisphere, i.e. the hemisphere west of Europe. In the original words of the Monroe Doctrine, the American continents are designated simply as "this hemisphere."

What precisely does "this hemisphere" include today? Maps labelled "Western Hemisphere" usually show that half of the globe which reaches westward from the 20th meridian west longitude to the 160th east longitude. But that demarcation is not official; nor is it the only one. According to the Geographer of the State Department, "there is no dispute regarding the continents and related islands which are embraced within the Western Hemisphere." These are "North America (including Central America and the West Indies and Greenland) and South America, together with all islands appertaining to the two continents." Uncertainty exists only with respect to the oceanic areas to be included. As will be shown later in this chapter, the commonly accepted boundaries no longer express satisfactorily the political and military realities of our age. Hence, the advantage of some term less geographical than "hemisphere" to denote the political realm of the Americas.

It is sometimes argued that there is no American Realm in any but a purely geographical sense. According to this view, Canada and the South American countries have closer ties outside than inside the Americas. The idea of an inter-American community, it is said, is purely a creature of United States policy with very little vitality even within the United States. These are extreme views, not shared by some of the most competent students of inter-American relations. That the American Realm is different in almost every respect from the European and Afro-Asian Realms is readily conceded. But the war has demonstrated, if there was doubt before, that the peoples of North and South America do constitute a "commonwealth of nations" despite linguistic, economic, political, and other differences in background and outlook.

The American Realm is a community of independent states with only vestigial remnants of the European empires which once covered the two continents and their insular outposts. Partly because of the great strength of the United States, partly because of the American policy first enunciated in the Monroe Doctrine, the Western Hemisphere has been relatively free of the Great Power rivalries and struggles which have kept the Old World in a turmoil. Though semi-colonial economic conditions still prevail in certain parts of the American region, no non-American state wields significant military power or political influence in the Western Hemisphere today. Increasingly the American nations are coming to act in concert, especially on matters affecting their political and strategic security.

The lands of the American Realm comprise but a small fraction of any hemisphere drawn upon the globe. Altogether they add up to scarcely one-twelfth of the earth's surface. The conventional Western Hemisphere—between 20° W and 160° E—is about five-sixths water. This fact clearly suggests the insular character of the American Realm.

Other facts also contribute to its insular quality. Though Alaska and Siberia nearly join in the Far North, all the more important approaches to the Americas, commercial as well as military, lie across wide bodies of water. This is almost as true of heavily used air routes as of sea routes. The European and Afro-Asian Realms face each other across barrier deserts and mountains. But the Americas stand apart, separated by oceans from the nations of the Old World.

Insularity, however, does not mean isolation. The oceans are the world's most efficient highways, vastly easier to traverse than the deserts and mountains of Africa and Asia. Maps in common use, moreover, give a distorted view of these oceans. Two maps in particular have fostered erroneous thinking about the relations of the New World to the Old. These are the rectangular Mercator map of the world and the map of the Eurasian and American hemispheres joined at the equator. The Mercator projection progressively exaggerates areas and distances in the higher latitudes. Consequently it pictures the North Atlantic and North Pacific Oceans relatively wider than they really are. On the joined-hemispheres map, these water areas are split apart and made to look wider still. Areas south of the equator are similarly distorted, of course, but with less serious effects on political thinking since most of the sea and air links connecting the Americas with the Old World reach into the middle or higher northern latitudes.

Not only is the American Realm insular as regards Europe, Africa, and Asia; it is insular also in terms of its respective parts. North and South America, though formerly joined by a narrow isthmus, have always stood to each other in the relation of islands. Though there may some day be an all-America highway, the connecting links today are by water or by air over water. The sea, moreover, is the only means of moving heavy freight between most of the South American countries. Only in the United States and Canada is there a highly developed grid of railroads and highways reaching from coast to coast.

The total land area of the American Realm is less than half the size of the Great Continent of Eurasia-Africa. It is only three-quarters as large as Eurasia alone. The population of the Old World is nine times that of the New, and, except in Western Europe and a few other localities, is increasing more rapidly. The Old World probably has greater untapped resources, and should these ever come under efficient unified control the balance of power might tip decisively against the Americas.

Mackinder classified the Americas as mere insular satellites of the Great Continent of Eurasia-Africa (see p. 96, above). Events have shown conclusively that our realm is very much more than that. But the American peoples should never belittle their handicaps and limitations, or ignore the essential features of their political situation.

The United States occupies some of the best lands in the Americas— best in climate, resources, terrain, and world location. Partly, perhaps largely, as a result of these advantages, the United States is today the strongest political unit in the American Realm. This fact carries inescapable corollaries of leadership and responsibility.

The people of the United States have traditionally regarded the independence and defense of the other American nations as of vital concern to their own security. But in times past they were reluctant to put the military defense of this hemisphere upon a collaborative basis. The Monroe Doctrine stated the presumptive hostility of the United States to any European (or Asiatic) power threatening the territories or institutions of other American states. But it was long contrary to United

States policy to guarantee such protection or to enter into agreements for the joint defense of the Americas.

The Latin American republics have been comparably reluctant to tie their destinies exclusively to the United States. Propinquity, as well as an enormous power differential, has created special relationships between the United States, on the one hand, and Mexico, the Central American countries, and the Caribbean lands, on the other. But the more remote republics of South America, Argentina in particular, long maintained closer relationships with Europe than with the U.S.

Common danger drew most of the American nations closer together during the Second World War. That conflict likewise disrupted many of the economic bonds between Europe and Latin America. In certain instances, notably Brazil, the United States government has actively assisted in economic and military development. U.S. statecraft today places great emphasis upon better understanding and closer ties between all American countries and the United States.

Obstacles stand in the way of achieving rapidly a great deal in this direction. The culture patterns of Latin America are fundamentally different from that of the United States. In some instances Latin American economies are more competitive than complementary to our own. Some of the countries of South America are farther from the United States than are the countries of Western Europe. Above all, the power differential itself creates barriers to intimate political relations.

The readings for this chapter have been selected with a view to showing the geographical structure of the American Realm, its connections with the European and Afro-Asian Realms, the uneven distribution of resources and other advantages within the Americas, and other factors bearing upon international relationships within the New World and between the New World and the Old.

THE AMERICAN HEMISPHERE

BY S. W. BOGGS

From "This Hemisphere," by S. W. Boggs, in *U.S. Department of State Bulletin*, May 6, 1945. The writer is chief geographer of the Department of State. The maps in this article have been furnished through the courtesy of Dr. Boggs.

ALL hemispheres are round—on the earth itself and therefore on the globe. A hemisphere is usually mapped within a circle which faintly suggests the roundness of the whole world. A hemisphere is mapped in perspective (on the "orthographic projection") or more usually it is flattened after the manner of other maps—to represent areas truly or to confer upon the map some other desirable property. However, a hemisphere may be mapped within a rectangle or within many other geometric limits.

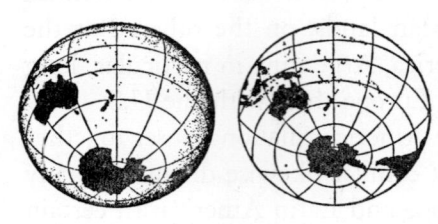

FIG. 32. THE WATER HEMISPHERE

The hemisphere with the maximum water area and minimum land (88.8 per cent water, 6.2 per cent land, 5.0 per cent Antarctic icecap). About 6 per cent of the world's population lives here on 12 per cent of the world's land area (excluding Antarctica). On the left it is shown on the orthographic projection (that is, in perspective, with parallel rays of vision, like the sun's rays lighting the earth), the earth's surface receding near the edge; it is shaded here as if lighted directly in front. On the right it is "flattened" on the azimuthal equal-area projection. No part of the United States lies within the "water hemisphere."

Americans frequently speak of "this hemisphere," meaning *the* hemisphere in which the United States finds itself. They will better grasp the "global" relationships of the United States if they get a true mental picture of some of the many hemispheres in which the United States is located.

Hemispheres are infinite in number. Rest a transparent glass or plastic geographical globe on its south pole, half fill it with water exactly to the line of the equator, and seal it shut. Roll it into any position whatever; the bottom hemisphere will be filled with water and the top with air. The water level will always be a plane passing through the center of the globe. The visible water-line will invariably be a "great circle"—a circle greater than any that can be described on the globe with a radius either less or more than the interval between one of the poles and the equator. Any two points on the earth's surface lie on one of these great circles—which constitutes the shortest route between them. Therefore, with surface features and weather permitting, great-circle routes between ports are naturally preferred by both steamships and airplanes.

The Northern Hemisphere. Any hemisphere may be identified and distinguished from all other hemispheres by its center point. Conversely, any point on the earth's surface is the center of a hemisphere which somewhat differs from all other hemispheres.

The United States is in the Northern Hemisphere, nearly half way between the Equator and the North Pole, the

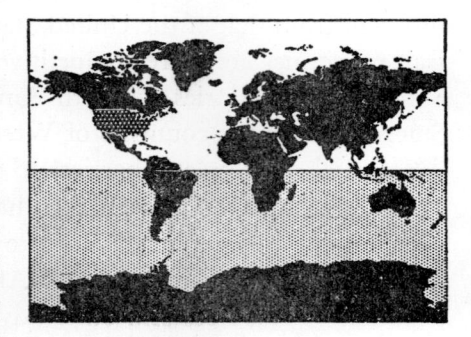

FIG. 33. THE NORTHERN HEMISPHERE

The center is the North Pole, and the limiting great circle is the Equator. The unshaded portion of the world map on the Miller projection corresponds to the hemisphere map below.

45th parallel of latitude coinciding with the northern boundary of New York State and with the Montana-Wyoming boundary.

The northern and southern hemispheres are the only hemispheres whose common boundary has any geographic significance. The seasons on opposite sides of the Equator are antipodal, since it is summer in one when it is winter in the other.

Approximately 37,570,000 square miles (74 per cent of the world's 50,973,000 square miles of land area, exclusive of the icecaps in Greenland and Antarctica), with a population of approximately 1,968,577,000 (constituting 91 per cent of the world's population of approximately 2,166,879,000), are to be found in the northern hemisphere. This hemisphere includes all of North America, Europe and continental Asia, part of South America (17 per cent of its area and 15 per cent of its population), and part of Africa (67 per cent of its area and 68 per cent of its population).

The So-Called "Western Hemisphere." The concept of the "Western Hemisphere" or New World, comprising the American continents and islands, is very important, both historically and politically. But this so-called "Western Hemisphere" is inadvisedly called "western" and does not deserve the appellation "hemisphere."

Because the Americas are west of Europe, Europeans and their descendants on this side of the Atlantic frequently call them "the Western Hemisphere." The American continents are, however, east of Asia and of the whole of the so-called "Eastern Hemisphere" quite as much as they are west of it. . . . If the Chinese or Japanese had crossed the broad Pacific and had discovered the Americas they might have called these continents the "Eastern Hemisphere."

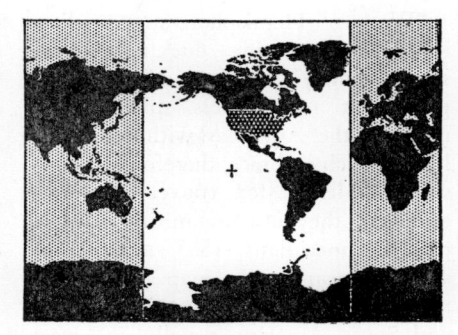

Fig. 34. The Map-Maker's Conventional "Western Hemisphere"

The meridians 20° W and 160° E of Greenwich constitute the conventional limit of this hemisphere. The center is a point in the Pacific Ocean, on the Equator, in 110° west longitude, about 1,250 statute miles from the nearest point on the American continents, near Acapulco, Mexico, and more than 2,000 miles from the Panama Canal. The unshaded portion of the world map comprises this conventional "western hemisphere," and the shaded portion is the "eastern hemisphere." The letters around the circular hemisphere map signify: N, North Pole; I, Iceland; A, Azores; C, Canary Islands; S, South Pole; NZ, New Zealand; and G, Guadalcanal Island in the Solomon group.

The Americas comprise only about 30 per cent of the world's land area and contain about 13 per cent of its population. As may be seen in Figure 35, the American continents and islands, including Greenland, lie wholly within one half of a certain hemisphere, and in that quarter-sphere there is twice as much water as land. The Americas therefore scarcely deserve to be called a "hemisphere."

"Western" Hemisphere suggests limiting lines running due north and south, namely meridians. Now it happens that map-makers make many maps of the Americas within circular limits which embrace, therefore, a hemisphere. Merely for convenience and economy, they utilize limiting lines, a pair of meridians 180° apart, that would appear on the map anyway. So they take a meridian between Africa and South America, usually 20° west of Greenwich (if that is used as the prime meridian for the map), and then necessarily employ its anti-meridian, 160° east longitude.

The center of this conventional hemisphere is in the Pacific Ocean, on the Equator, in 110° W longitude. It is about 1,250 statute miles from the nearest point on the American mainland, west of Acapulco, Mexico, and 1,850 miles from the nearest point in the United States, near Brownsville, Texas. Clearly this center point is without geographic significance.

The limiting meridians of this so-called "Western Hemisphere" have no political, historic, geographic, or economic significance. If we were to follow the ancient custom of "beating the bounds" . . . we would traverse open ocean most of the time. Going north on the 20th meridian we would cross part of Antarctica, Iceland, and a mere northeastern tip of Greenland; going south on the 160th meridian we would cross the eastern tip of Siberia including the Kamchatka peninsula, the island of Guadalcanal in the Solomons, and part of Antarctica. Within this hemisphere are found the Cape Verde Islands, the Azores, the western third of Iceland with its capital city, almost all of Greenland, eastern Siberia, thousands of Pacific islands, all of New Zealand, and a large part of the Antarctic continent—in addition to North and South America. The Atlantic and Pacific islands and the eastern portion of Asia within this hemisphere comprise only 1.1 per cent of the world's land area, with 0.5 per cent of its population.

This hemisphere, mapped by itself, induces complacency in Americans. It embraces almost the maximum area of ocean in any hemisphere which contains all of North and South America. Like an ostrich with its head in the sand, we avoid seeing the other half of the world, much of it surprisingly near.

People in the United States sometimes identify this so-called "Western Hemisphere" with the Monroe Doctrine. The term "Western Hemisphere," however, was not employed in the message of President Monroe to the Congress in 1823. The terms "the American continents" and "this hemisphere" were used, evidently synonymously; Russia was in mind at that time and certainly no part of Siberia was thought of as part of "this hemisphere." Neither were New Zealand, part of the Solomon Islands, Samoa, the Fijis, and other Pacific islands, nor was any part of Antarctica (of which they knew almost nothing) contemplated when men spoke of "the American continents" and "this hemisphere" in 1823. . . .

A More Significant Hemisphere for Americans. A hemisphere centered in the north Atlantic Ocean, at 28° N and 31° W, is much more significant for all people in North and South America than is the map-maker's "Western Hemisphere" centered in the Pacific on the Equator. This hemisphere, illustrated in Figure 35, includes all of the Americas except the westernmost Aleutian Islands, and all of Europe and Africa and more than 40 per cent of Asia. Altogether it comprises 76 per cent of the world's land area, with fully 50 per cent of its population.

THE AMERICAN REALM

other. It has been found to have its center in western France, near Nantes, in about 47°13' north latitude, 1°32' west longitude. On its 44,904,000 square miles of land (88 per cent of the world's land area) live about 2,035,000,-000 people (94 per cent of the world's population). In addition to all of Europe and Africa and North America, the land hemisphere includes nearly 88 per cent of Asia's territory and nearly 92 per cent of its population (the Philippines, Netherlands Indies, British Malaya, and parts of French Indo-China and Thailand being excluded); the land hemisphere also embraces about 79 per cent of the area of South America with 73 per cent of its population.

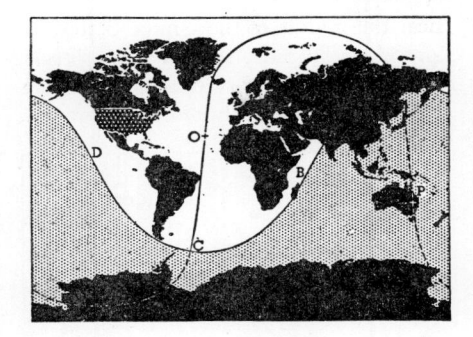

FIG. 35. HEMISPHERE CENTERED AT 28° N 31° W

The straight line AOC through the center divides it into quarter-spheres. The western quarter-sphere contains all of North and South America, including Greenland, and a portion of Siberia. The eastern quarter-sphere comprises all of Europe and Africa (except a small part of Madagascar) and about 42 per cent of the area of Asia. The limit of the hemisphere, ABCDA on both maps, is a complete great circle (like the Equator or any meridian circle) while the line AOC which divides it into halves is half of such a great circle, the other half being APC as shown in a dotted line on the world map.

This might be called a "western-civilization hemisphere," since it embraces Europe and the Americas (but with all of Africa and much of Asia besides). Only Australia and New Zealand are outside its bounds. Both history and geography make this hemisphere important to peoples on both sides of the Atlantic.

The Land Hemisphere. Geographers have made careful determinations to ascertain which hemisphere contains a larger percentage of land area than any

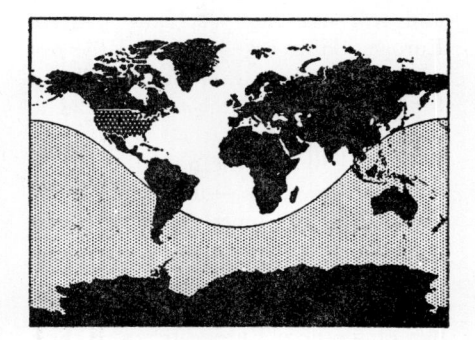

FIG. 36. THE LAND HEMISPHERE

The hemisphere with the maximum land area (45.6 per cent land, 53.7 per cent water, 0.7 per cent Greenland icecap). About 94 per cent of the world's population lives here on 88 per cent of the world's land area. On the world map, the shaded area is the water hemisphere (see Fig. 32).

This hemisphere includes all of the United States and all of its non-contiguous territories except those in the Pacific. The United States is located near the edge of the hemisphere. Considering the vast area and the enormous population, the resources and the industrial development, the land hemisphere may be regarded as the most important hemisphere. The advantages of central location, particularly in a military sense, have not been overlooked by Germany. Commercially the situation is different, in part because ocean transport costs roughly only a tenth as much a ton-mile as railroad transport.

From the center of the land hemisphere, in Western Europe, one can account for the origin of major regional terms which Americans have inherited and still use. To people in Western Europe, China and Japan and the rest of eastern Asia is the "Far East." But for Americans it is the nearest land to the west, and is reached by starting north and west to the north Pacific, or by air over Alaska—it is our "Near West." For the Chinese it is neither east nor west. The Chinese name for China is "Middle Country" or "Middle Flowery People's Country"—just as the peoples of southern Europe regarded their sea as the middle of the land area, the Mediterranean. Objective geographic terms, such as "the Americas" or "the American continents," and "eastern Asia" or "the Western Pacific," are accurate and of universal applicability, since they are acceptable to the people who live in the regions concerned.

Hemisphere Centered Within the United States. In all four hemispheres just described (Figures 33 to 36) the United States is found somewhere near the edge, or at least the center of the United States lies about half way between the center and the edge of the hemisphere. A hemisphere centered near the middle of the United States, in 40° north latitude, 100° west longitude (near Beaver City, Nebraska, and Norton, Kansas), is illustrated in Figure 37.

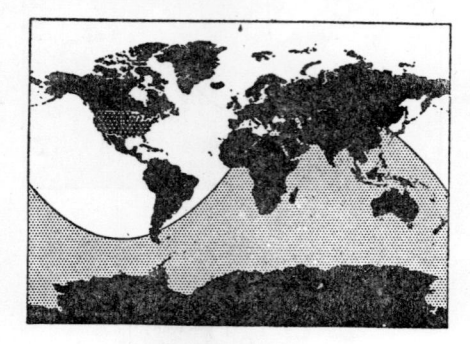

FIG. 37. HEMISPHERE CENTERED NEAR THE CENTER OF THE UNITED STATES

A hemisphere centered at 40° N 100° W is shown here. Although it does not include the southern tip of South America, it does include all of Europe, part of Africa, and, in Asia, part of Turkey, most of Russian Asia, most of Manchuria and Japan.

This hemisphere fails to embrace the southern end of South America, but it includes all of Europe except the island of Crete, about 30 per cent of the area of Africa, and more than 10 per cent of the area of Asia; it includes all of the Arctic Ocean, a very large portion of the Atlantic Ocean, and an even greater area in the Pacific. Asia and Africa are nearer to the United States than most Americans realize. Dakar, Moscow, and northern Manchuria are nearer to the center of the United States than is Buenos Aires. The actual "global" relations of the United States, which are remarkably different from the conceptions many people cherish, based on Mercator maps, have suddenly acquired heightened importance in these days of airplanes and radio.

Hemispheres à la Carte for Americans. If Americans were curious to ascertain how much of the world can be included in some hemisphere that includes all of the United States (the 48 States and the District of Columbia) they would be greatly surprised. They can order almost any hemisphere they like *à la carte* in more than one sense. A series of hemispheres, with the United States at the very edge of each, reveals relations of this country to the rest of the world that few people appreciate. Three such hemispheres are illustrated below, in Figures 38, 39, and 40.

(a) Northern boundary of the United States at hemisphere's edge. If the northern edge of a hemisphere is placed on the northwestern corner and the northeastern tip of the United States there will be included, in addition to all of the United States and a narrow strip of Canada, all of Mexico, Central America, the Caribbean, South America, Antarctica, New Zealand, a portion of Australia, and the tip of South Africa, still larger areas of the Atlantic and Pacific Oceans, and a portion of the Indian Ocean near the Antarctic continent.

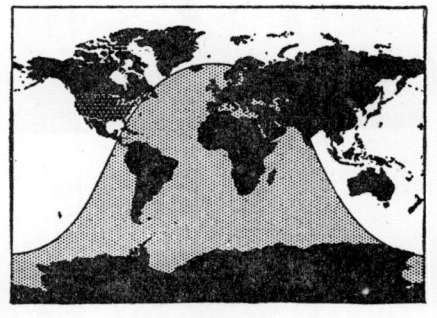

Fig. 39. Hemisphere with the Eastern Coast of the United States at Its Edge

The center of this hemisphere is in the North Pacific, near 24° north latitude and 177° east longitude.

(b) Atlantic coast of the United States at hemisphere's edge. If the northeastern and southeastern extremities of the United States are placed at the edge of a hemisphere, almost all of Canada, Labrador, and Greenland, all of Mexico and part of Central America, a very great part of Asia and the northern tip of Europe, all of Australia and

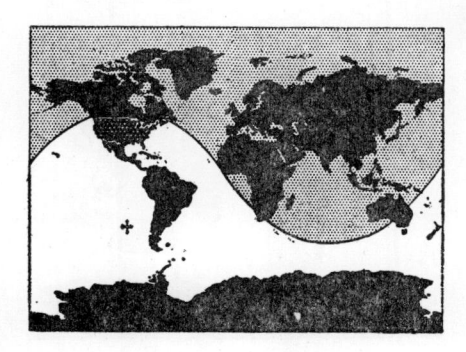

Fig. 38. Hemisphere with the Northern Limits of the United States at Its Edge

The center of this hemisphere is in the South Pacific, near 38° south latitude and 98° west longitude.

New Zealand, all of the Arctic, most of the Pacific, and the eastern edge of the Indian Ocean will be included.

(c) *Southern boundary of the United States at hemisphere's edge.* A hemisphere which has Brownsville, Texas, and San Diego, California, on its southern edge will include not only all of Canada, Alaska, and Greenland but also all of Europe, Africa, and Asia, except a small portion of the Netherlands Indies and large parts of the Atlantic, Pacific, and Indian Oceans.

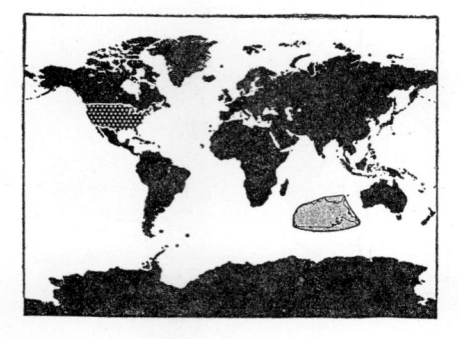

(d) *Sum of all hemispheres containing all of the United States.* Similarly, a hemisphere whose edge touches Key West, Florida, and Brownsville, Texas, embraces all of Europe and Asia and most of Africa, and the northern fringe of Australia. A series of hemispheres touching pairs of points of the Pacific coast of the United States will necessarily duplicate areas already included in hemispheres described above, because together they include all the land on earth except Kerguelen Island in the Indian Ocean (one of the world's most desolate spots), both polar regions, and all of the oceans with the exception of the area in the Indian Ocean which is not much larger than the United States. The limits of this excluded area comprise a series of great circles tangent to a mirror image of the United States in the South Indian Ocean.

The global relations of the United States are disclosed in a rather remarkable way by a series of hemispheres such as those shown above. When a person speaks of "this hemisphere" as the one in which the United States of America is located, one may well inquire, "Which hemisphere?"

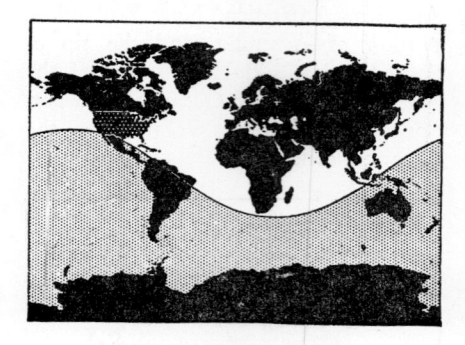

Fig. 40. Hemisphere with the Southern Limits of the United States at Its Edge

The center of this hemisphere is west of Moscow near 55° north latitude and 35° east longitude.

Fig. 41. The Sum of All Hemispheres Containing All of the United States

The sum of the hemispheres shown in Figs. 38, 39, and 40, and of others that might be added in which points on the Pacific coast of the United States are on the edge of one or another hemisphere, is indicated by the unshaded area on this map. The shaded area in the Indian Ocean (about 4,180,000 square miles) is the only portion of the earth's surface which can not be included in some hemisphere that covers all of the United States. Kerguelen Island is the only land in that area, and it has no recorded population.

POLITICAL GEOGRAPHY OF THE AMERICAS

By Nicholas J. Spykman

From chap. 2 of *America's Strategy in World Politics*, by N. J. Spykman. Copyright 1942 by Harcourt, Brace & Co., New York. The late Dr. Spykman was Sterling professor of international relations at Yale University and a member of the research staff of the Yale Institute of International Studies, which sponsored the work resulting in his book.

Since the piercing of the Old and the New Worlds by the canals of Suez and Panama, the great land masses on the earth's surface consist of five continental islands. The three which lie in the Southern Hemisphere, Australia, South America, and Africa, are true islands which permit of circumnavigation. The two biggest, which lie in the Northern Hemisphere, North America and Eurasia, although true islands in a geographic sense, function in terms of navigation as peninsulas because of the ice cap in the North Polar Sea. Of these two northern continents, Eurasia is by far the larger. Its area is more than two and one-half times that of North America and it contains ten times the population. Because the political power of the world is for the most part concentrated in the temperate zones, location with reference to the Equator will not only determine climate but also proximity to centers of power. Ocean currents, altitudes, and other modifying influences may alter the normal climatic conditions, but, in general, history is made in the temperate latitudes, and, because very little of the land mass of the Southern Hemisphere lies in this zone, history is made in the temperate latitudes of the Northern Hemisphere.

The fact that the greater land masses lie in the north and that the largest land areas that do exist in the Southern Hemisphere lie in the tropics has certain obvious implications. From an economic, political, and military point of view the northern half of the world will always be more important than the southern half, and relations between various continents of the northern half will have more influence on the history of the world than relations across the Equator on the same continent. The location of a state north or south of the Equator will, therefore, play a large part in determining the political significance of that state, the nature of its international relations, and the problems of its foreign policy.

The Western Hemisphere is an island realm surrounded by the Atlantic, the Pacific, and the Arctic Oceans. It lies between the European and Asiatic ocean fronts of the Eurasian Continent and covers a huge area of about 15 million square miles. This great land mass consists of the two continents of North and South America separated by an American "Mediterranean." The continent of North America has the form of an inverted triangle. Its coastlines flare out toward Alaska and Greenland with the result that the most northern outposts are nearest to Asia and Europe. The South American continent is also shaped like an inverted triangle but placed far to the east of the northern land mass with the bulge of Brazil near the shoulder of Africa. In between these two continental masses lies the American "Mediterranean," providing a transit zone between North and South America and between the Atlantic and the Pacific.

The United States occupies a unique position in the world. Her territory lies in the northern half of the globe, in the area of the great land masses, and is of continental dimensions with all that this implies in terms of economic strength. Fronting on two oceans, the United States has direct access to the most important trading arteries of the world. Her domain is situated between two clusters of dense population in Western Europe and Eastern Asia and, therefore, between the most important economic, political, and military zones.

The continental domain of the United States is an area of about three million square miles between Canada and Mexico, rich in natural resources, with a national economy of great productivity and a population of one hundred thirty-five million. The location and direction of the Rocky Mountains makes the country primarily an area of Atlantic drainage, and variety in topography and climate gives to each section of the country a distinct economic character. The Northeast contains the centers of population and of industrial and commercial activity. The Middle West is essentially agricultural, while the West largely accounts for the stock-raising and non-ferrous metal production of the country.

The section of the hemisphere nearest to Asia is the territory of Alaska. This peninsula, surrounded by the Arctic, the Bering Sea, and the Pacific, has an area of more than half a million square miles, greater than the surface of the Scandinavian countries and Finland. There is probably a hundred thousand square miles of grazing land, and the country is rich in waterpower and a great variety of minerals. It is a land of great potential possibilities, but its population of sixty thousand is bound to grow only very slowly. Climate, topography, and distance from areas of dense population and commercial activity will inevitably retard its development until resources nearer the industrial centers of the United States are exhausted.

The part of the Western Hemisphere nearest to Europe is the huge ice-covered island of Greenland which approaches Iceland and Spitsbergen. Except for a small area of about one hundred thousand square miles, an ice sheet covers the whole island. The North Atlantic Drift gives the southwest coast a warm climate and a heavy rainfall which permit the growth of a luxuriant vegetation during the summer months. The island produces two important raw materials in great abundance. Cryolite, which accounts for four-fifths of the exports, is mined at Ivigtut, and graphite is found on the west and southwest coasts. The island, except for climatological limitations, would be the natural vestibule for air approaches to this continent.

Between these two continental outposts and the United States lies the Dominion of Canada. It covers an area larger than the forty-eight states but has a population of only about twelve million, a fact largely explained by climate and topography which restrict the economic use of a large part of the area and leave much of it an arctic waste. The great geographic regions of the country are practically prolongations of those in the United States giving rise to similar economic specialization. The eastern section extends from the Atlantic to a little beyond Lake Superior, about halfway across the continent. The central region—the prairie country—rolls for nearly eight hundred miles to the foothills of the Rocky Mountains. The western zone, mostly occupied by British Columbia, commences high up in the rugged mountain chains of the Rockies and the Selkirks, which parallel the seacoast, and reaches westward toward the Pacific. The West represents forestry, grazing and mining; the great prairie provinces, agriculture and particularly wheat growing; and the East, mining, industry, and commerce. An iron and steel industry has been started with mills in Ontario, operating on ore and coal both imported from the United States, and in Nova Scotia, operating with ore from Newfoundland. Of the principal energy resources only waterpower is in abundance in the industrial region.

The Canadian economy shows a great similarity to that of the United States. It is characterized by a high productivity per capita and a resulting high standard of living. Although much of the area will forever remain sparsely populated because of climatological and other geographic reasons, the development of natural resources has only begun, and Canada has a future of expansion ahead of her.

By far the greater part of the life of Canada clusters in a narrow belt from one to two hundred miles in width along the Canadian-American border, and of that more than 90 per cent of all that is vital and active is concentrated in the eastern half of the country in the provinces of Ontario, Quebec, New Brunswick, Prince Edward Island, and Nova Scotia. Here is found the great bulk of Canada's population, her principal industrial, banking, and commercial centers, and her largest cities and chief ocean ports.

Tucked away under the protecting overhang of Labrador, across the Gulf of Saint Lawrence, lies Newfoundland, bare, rocky, exposed to the icy blast of winter, and half-hidden in fog in summer. It is a land of hardship and poverty on which lumbering, mining, and fishing provide a bare subsistence for a population of three hundred thousand. Unimportant economically, bankrupt financially, it is of consequence only because of its strategic location at the entrance gate of Canada.

The frontier between the United States and Canada was established long before the acquisition of Alaska, and between the Alaskan and American borders lies the corridor of British Columbia which provides access to the Pacific for western Canada through the Fraser and Skeena river valleys. This Canadian territory between the Straits of Juan de Fuca and Dixon Entrance prevents direct overland access from the United States to her northern territory. The situation seems at first sight to resemble the Polish Corridor without the ethnic question. A more careful analysis, however, shows a basic difference. The Polish Corridor is a lowland containing old and well-established roads and railroads which maintain communication between East and West Prussia. British Columbia is highly mountainous and provides no easy route for north-south communication. Conquest or purchase cannot change these facts of topography. The state of Washington and Alaska have always communicated by sea and will undoubtedly continue to do so, at least in peacetime.

While Canada is in many ways a northern extension of the type of society found in the United States, the lands below the Rio Grande represent a different world, the world of Latin America. It is perhaps unfortunate that the English and Latin speaking parts of the continent should both be called America, thereby unconsciously evoking an expectation of similarity which does not exist. Only if it is realized that the countries to the south are different from the United States in essential geographic features, in racial and ethnic composition, in economic life, and in social customs, ideology, and cultural tradition can we evaluate the significance of this area for our national life and estimate correctly the likelihood of an effective cooperation in a common policy of hemisphere defense.

The Latin American world faces the United States across the Mexican land frontier and from beyond the American "Mediterranean" of which our country is itself the most important littoral state. The drainage area of the remaining coastal states and the islands along the eastern rim include a territory of almost two million square miles which contains approximately fifty million people. It consists of a large part of Mexico, of Central America, Colombia, Venezuela, and of the chain of islands stretching in a great arc from the east of Venezuela to the western end of Cuba which is one hundred fifty miles from Yucatan and seventy-five miles from Key West. East of Florida and the Greater Antilles lies a second island chain, the Bahamas, which, like a line of closely spaced sentinels, stand guard before the entrance to the Mexican Gulf. Like its European counterpart, the American "Mediterranean" is divided into a western "Mediterranean"—the Gulf of Mexico—and an eastern "Mediterranean"—the Caribbean Sea. The distance from New Orleans to Trinidad is roughly comparable to that between Batum and Gibraltar, and the areas of the tributary coastal regions of the two seas are approximately equal.

The mountain ranges of Mexico and Central America provide an easier slope and broader coastal plains on the east than on the west and so facilitate an eastern orientation and flow of trade. Yucatan and the plains of Guatemala, Honduras, and Nicaragua face the Gulf and the Caribbean, and only in Panama does the greater part of the lowland region face the Pacific. Salvador is the only exclusively Pacific state in the region, and for her a connection with the railroads of Guatemala provides an Atlantic outlet. In Colombia the Andes range presses close to the Pacific and approaches the Caribbean at right angles in three parallel spurs, permitting an outflow to the eastern sea through the valleys of the Atrate and the Magdalena and their tributaries. Topography makes Venezuela, except for the depression of Lake Maracaibo, a land of Atlantic rather than Caribbean drainage, but climate and distribution of natural resources have made her economically a Caribbean state. The Orinoco Valley is as yet of little significance, and the highlands of the Guianas are practically unexplored. Economic life is concentrated on the northern coast where the mountain range offers relief from the tropical heat and short railways connect with good harbors.

Mexico, although large in area compared to the Great Powers of Europe, is a small country compared to the United States, and, as in the case of Canada, her relative power position is not likely to change much. Shape, location, topography, aridity, and soil conditions preclude the development of great economic and military strength. Where the country is broad, from the United States border to the Tropic of Cancer, it is, except on the Gulf coast, a continuation of the desert and semi-desert region of southern California and Arizona and predestined, apart from mineral development, to a pastoral economy. There are several other regions with great variations in altitude, temperature, and rainfall, and, therefore, diverse economic possibilities, but topography has placed barriers against effective economic and political integration which railroads have only partially overcome. Even after the natural resources are much further developed than at present, the center of economic and military strength will remain on the high central plateau in the south. This region, which contains the capital and 40 per cent of the population, obtains access to the outside world through Tampico and Vera Cruz and the American-controlled Gulf of Mexico.

Mexico and the other states on the mainland have a large percentage of Indian population and are in general under-populated, while the island rim, with a very large percentage of Negro population, is, particularly in some of the Lesser Antilles, an area of high population density. At first sight the descendants of the plantation slaves seem to live in a tropical paradise. The broken line of green volcanic islands stretches in infinite variety of shape and contour through the blue sea. Palm-fringed beaches border gentle slopes rich in cultivation, and steep symmetrical cones reach for white clouds. Charming country roads, fringed with the color of many-hued flowers, ramble from village to village, past sugar plantations, banana groves, and citrus trees. But poverty lies next to the flowering swamp, and sickness scourges the mountain slopes. Yellow fever is under control, but hookworm and malaria aid the tropical sun in sapping the energy of a vitamin-starved population.

The countries of this "Mediterranean" world are similar in geological origin, geographic features, and in indigenous plant life and crops. They lie in the northern tropics and the eastern trade winds and at various altitudes show parallel climatic zones. The area is important not only as an exporter of tropical products but also because of great mineral wealth.

Its economic importance lies in the fact that it provides the United States with a tropical raw-material zone, practically in her backyard, which, except for an inadequate and badly distributed labor supply, might produce many of the articles now imported from the Asiatic and African tropics. Its chief agricultural products, except sugar, do not compete with the agrarian products of the Middle West, and its minerals provide essential raw materials for our industrial East.

The strategic significance of the American "Mediterranean" derives not only from the fact that it lies between North and South America, but also from the fact that it lies between the Atlantic and Pacific, a significance enhanced but not created by the construction of the Panama Canal, as the relations between Panama and the Philippines in Spanish times testify. This passageway, completed in 1914, gives the United States the full benefit of her geographic location on two oceans. The canal, although outside the borders, is, none the less, an important link in our coastal navigation and has shortened the sailing distance between Atlantic and Pacific ports by eight thousand miles. Even more important is the fact that it shortened the route from the Pacific states to Europe and from the Atlantic states to Asia, where their respective products are in demand.

The two states along the north coast of South America, Colombia and Venezuela, have been included as part of the American "Mediterranean" zone. From a strict geographic point of view, they are, of course, part of the southern continent, but from a geo-political point of view they belong to the intermediate world between the northern and southern continents. Geographic factors are responsible for the fact that these two countries maintain more intimate contact with the opposite coast of the middle sea, with North America, than with the rest of South America. A similar situation is observable in regard to the other Mediterranean seas. North Africa has been more intimately related with Europe than with the equatorial belt beyond the Sahara, and Northern Australia is closer to Singapore than to Melbourne which lies on the other side of the broad Australian desert.

The barrier between North and South America is not the Caribbean Sea but the nature of the territory along the Equator. The mountain ranges which bend eastward from the Andes, separate the Amazon basin from the valleys of the Magdalena and the Orinoco and form the southern boundaries of the Guianas. Beyond this lies the enormous impenetrable jungle and tropical forest of the Amazon Valley. The river and its tributaries offer an excellent system of communications from west to east but they do not provide transportation for movements north and south. Not only are North and South America two separate continents instead of a single continent as is sometimes erroneously suggested, but the South American continent itself does not function as a single continental mass in terms of overland communication.

South America beyond the Equator can be reached only by sea. This applies not only to the United States but also to the republics of Colombia and Venezuela, which lack adequate land communication with their southern neighbors. The main area of the southern continent will continue to function in American foreign policy not in terms of a continental neighbor but in terms of overseas territory. It is true that the original approach of the Spaniards was overland by a road which started in Cartagena and followed the Andean plateau and that a Pan-American highway is planned to follow the same general route, but under modern conditions this overland approach cannot possibly compete with maritime routes either in commercial or strategic significance.

The other geographic features which determine the relations between North and South America are the position of the great mountain chains and the eastward projection of the southern half of the continent. The meridian of New York is also the meridian of Valparaiso and cuts the southern continent far west of its center. The southern land mass not only has a main axis, the Andes, which runs north and south, but also a secondary axis formed by the Brazilian ranges. The direction of this massif is southwest and northeast which makes the continent broad in the north, that is, in the tropics, and narrow in the south, in the temperate zone. Moreover, its mass juts out far into the Atlantic toward West Africa, with the result that all points below Pernambuco are slightly nearer to Lisbon than to New York.

The Rocky Mountains, the Sierras, and the Andes make the whole hemisphere primarily an area of Atlantic drainage, with the main centers of economic, military, and political strength on the east coast. This means that the most important relations between North America and South America lie within the confines of the same ocean, the Atlantic. The building of the Panama Canal did not affect them. It has given added significance to the littoral of the American "Mediterranean" including Colombia and Venezuela, and it has brought the west coast of South America closer to the United States than to any other power, but it shortened neither the route from New York to Buenos Aires, nor the distance from either place to Europe.

Since the construction of the Panama Canal, the economic centers of the United States have been brought in close contact with the west coast of South America, for a long time one of the most isolated regions in the world. Not until the nineteenth century and the development of the guano and nitrate deposits was there anything approaching regular contact with Europe by way of the Strait of Magellan. The canal brought a competitive advantage to the United States which is expressed in trade figures, but the fact remains that the economic and political possibilities of the region are severely restricted by geographic factors.

The west coast is the land of the Andes, except for Tibet, the highest mountain region in the world. It varies in width from one hundred to four hundred miles and is made up of parallel ranges with peaks up to twenty-five thousand feet and with few passes below fifteen thousand feet except in the south. Rising sharply from the coast, the massive, crenelated mountain wall reaches its crest in most places well within a hundred miles of the sea. The coastal valleys are extremely narrow except in a small area in Ecuador, northern Peru, and Chile, where the Central Valley is both the heart of the country and the center of its agriculture. The few rivers that do exist cannot serve navigation purposes and, with few exceptions in the extreme south, are inadequate even for the development of waterpower.

The nature of the mountain territory is responsible for a very low percentage of arable land in proportion to the total surface and creates such obstacles to the construction of effective means of communication that high freight rates must remain a retarding influence on all economic development, be it in agriculture, mining, or industry. This difficulty is further increased by the fact that on almost the whole length of the coast there are no good harbors. It is true that aviation has been of great assistance to the region, but there are definite limits to its usefulness. Exploration has been facilitated, new regions made accessible, communication speeded up between cities, and capitals brought within a few days' travel from the United States, but aviation has so far not been able to solve the basic transportation problem which is moving bulk freight at low cost.

In this enormous mountain belt of about 5,000 miles in length, there is little land suited for settlement. Agriculture is restricted to the coastal valleys and to the depressions and plateaus between the ranges, and climate reduces even this relatively small area. The prevailing westerly winds bring heavy rainfall to southern Chile, and Ecuador lies in the tropical rain belt, but many parts of Peru, Chile, and Bolivia are barren or even desert. The coastal valleys of northern Chile and southern Peru are, therefore, entirely dependent on irrigation for the cultivation of their crops of sugar and cotton, and the development of irrigation is possible only within restricted limits. Even in the temperate climate of the Central Chilean Valley, between the coast range and the high cordillera the normal rain supply must be supplemented by irrigation since the rain falls mostly in the winter.

Except for central and southern Chile, all of South America's west coast lies in the tropics. Only high up in the mountains is the climate suited for permanent settlement by white men, and then only as employers of native labor. On the plateaus of Ecuador, Peru, and Bolivia the Indian alone is sufficiently adjusted to the rarefied atmosphere to be able to do manual labor. The only region which contains the elements necessary for an agrarian economy based on white labor is Chile, and no other section holds promise of great agricultural development. Large parts of Chile have a temperate, mediterranean climate, and there is an area of land suitable for crops or pasturage of about twelve million acres, of which approximately two million are at present under cultivation. With further development of irrigation, she should be able to sustain a population at least as large as that of Italy.

Except in southern Chile, the west coast is poor in forest and pasture land and will never equal the Argentine in animal husbandry. Sheep giving a fair weight of fleece are pastured in the highlands of Peru and Chile, and there has been a considerable development in sheep raising in southern Chile. In the high valleys of Peru and Bolivia are bred the llama, the beast of burden of high altitudes, and the related alpaca and the vicuña, the former famous for its long heavy wool and the latter for its silken coat. Chile has cattle ranches, but there is nothing here which compares with the huge grassland zone that is the basis of Argentine beef export.

If much of the topsoil of the west coast is unproductive, the subsoil partly compensates by extraordinary richness. Only Ecuador is unimportant as a mineral producer. For the other republics, minerals represent the most important export and the greatest source of foreign exchange. Copper, with gold and silver as by-products, vanadium, tin, tungsten, lead, borax, bismuth, and nitrates flow from here to the industrial centers of the world. The great handicaps under which the mining industry operates are high transportation cost and lack of fuel. Peru produces oil in the north near the Ecuadorian boundary and also coal, of poor coking quality. Peru and Chile have created a light industry of consumers' goods with government aid and tariff protection, but everything conspires to postpone until an indefinite future the type of industrialization that is necessary for great military strength.

Distance and isolation, topography and climate all have contributed to discourage immigration from Europe, with the result that the growth of population has been much smaller than on the east coast. Ecuador has a population of two and a half millions, and Bolivia, with a half a million square miles of territory, has only about three million. She lost her access to the coast in the War of the Pacific (1879-1884), and although most of her products still move across the Andes to the western ocean, Bolivia is none the less orienting herself more and more in the direction of the Atlantic. Peru and Chile have respectively six and four million people, most of whom remain employed in agriculture, notwithstanding the national importance of mining and the growth of small industry.

The building of the canal could not, of course, alter the location of the Atlantic drainage area which is the largest part of the South American continent. Below Venezuela along the east coast lie the Guianas, vestiges of colonial days, possessions of the European powers, Great Britain, the Netherlands, and France. The Guiana colonies have been a disappointment to their owners. The coastal plains are unsuited for white settlement, and manual labor depends on imported Asiatics or on a Negro population ravaged by tropical disease. The colonies export chiefly sugar, cacao, and coffee, and contain valuable tropical forest resources in the interior, but these must await exploitation until transportation cost to the coast can be considerably lowered. From the Dutch and the British colonies come some gold and a small quantity of diamonds, and the important mineral bauxite, the aluminum ore, which goes mostly to the United States.

Beyond these European colonies lies the state of Brazil with forty-four million people and the largest area of any country in the Western Hemisphere, most of it unexplored wilderness. It consists of the Amazon basin in the north, the drainage area of the Paraná in the southern interior, and the highlands of the east. The Amazon drainage area is the greatest tropical forest zone in the world. It has a rainfall of seventy to one hundred inches, and a dense luxuriant vegetation which constantly threatens to engulf the plantations. Like all tropical forests the region has a limited economic value. Clearing is very expensive, soils are subject to excessive leaching and soon become deficient in plant food, and the area lacks an adequate labor supply with which to undertake large-scale plantation agriculture.

The future of Brazil lies neither in the Amazon basin nor in the interior provinces of Goyaz and Matto Grosso but on the eastern highland, near the Tropic of Capricorn, far beyond the bulge of Pernambuco and 5,500 miles from New York. The real heart of the country is the central section with the coffee state of São Paulo and the mineral state of Minas Geraes. Elevations up to four thousand feet reduce the heat and permit an economy based on white labor, and valleys and contours are sufficiently gentle to permit cultivation without wasteful soil wash. These two states, together with the small coastal states of Rio de Janeiro and Espirito Santo, represent 12 per cent of the area of Brazil, but contain 40 per cent of the population and the center of her economic life and include the two great cities of Rio de Janeiro and São Paulo.

Enormous size and distribution over wide latitudes give Brazil different regional economies and a great variety of products. The north is tropical and exports sugar, cacao, and forest products; the south lies in the temperate zone and raises sheep, cattle, hogs, and wheat; while the central section of the highlands produces cotton and coffee. The potential resources are only partially developed and there is still room for considerable growth, even if the geographic limitations of the interior provinces are taken into consideration. Less than 5 per cent of the total area is at present under cultivation, and improved transportation should open great areas to westward expansion.

The agricultural resources of Brazil alone are greater than those of the whole of the west coast, but it is quite probable that the eastern highlands are less generously endowed with minerals than the Andes. However, there has never been a systematic geological survey of the country, and both Brazil and the outside world may yet be pleasantly surprised by the discovery of new resources. In the state of Minas Geraes lies the greatest body of high-grade iron ore in the world, estimated at twelve billion tons. Brazilian coal is scarce and not of good coking quality, but a new process has been designed for its use in the manufacture of pig iron and with the technical help of the United States steel industry and the financial help of the United States government, the country has begun the construction of a steel and iron industry designed for an output of half a million tons of pig iron a year. This will supplement the manufacture of consumers' goods flourishing behind tariff protection and form another step in the program for industrialization designed to reduce the dependence of its extractive economy on foreign markets.

Brazil is practically devoid of good roads outside the immediate vicinity of the large cities, and aside from a few short lines in the northeast the railroads are all concentrated in the states of São Paulo and Minas Geraes. There is one cross-country line which connects São Paulo with Corumba on the Paraguay River and with the southeastern section of Bolivia, and a short line around the rapids of the Madeira River which provides an outlet to the Amazon basin for the northeastern section of Bolivia. The other international line is the road from São Paulo through the southern states, connecting with the Uruguayan railroad net and Montevideo.

Through the port of Santos and the harbor of Rio de Janeiro move the cotton and coffee crop which represent more than 50 per cent of the export of the country. Rio, a white city against blue hills, meeting the ocean across silver half-moon beaches, is the economic and political heart of an empire and the center of its social and cultural life. Through a federal government, its authority extends to the swamps and hills of the Matto Grosso and the Upper Amazon tributaries near the Colombian borders, but the authority is a symbol rather than a fact. It will take a long time, even with the aid of modern techniques of transportation and communication, before the three million square miles of territory of the "Colossus of the South" become fully integrated into an effective economic and political unit.

To the west and southwest of the Brazilian highlands lies the large drainage area of the La Plata River system. It is smaller than the Amazon basin but larger than the Mississippi Valley and contains a population of twenty million. At the river mouth in the position of New Orleans lies Buenos Aires. This drainage basin extends from the tropics in the north to the temperate zone at the mouth of the river and includes the eastern part of Bolivia, a large part of Paraguay, and the Matto Grosso section of Brazil.

Paraguay is the northernmost state lying entirely in the La Plata basin. She has a population of one million, largely Guarani Indians, a low economic and cultural level, and a tradition of dictatorship. West of the Paraguay River lies the Gran Chaco which extends into Argentina and Bolivia. Paraguay is a source of quebracho, the valuable tanning product, and her open savannas are well suited for cattle breeding. But large parts of the country are useless to man. They are inadequately drained and turn into swampland during the summer floods, while absence of springs and shortage of water make them uninhabitable in winter. Only after the most prodigious expenditure of capital for drainage and water supply could this area be made into an agricultural region, a development not likely to come as long as there is plenty of better land available elsewhere in the drainage basin.

The smallest political unit in the La Plata region is the state of Uruguay with a population of two million and seventy-two thousand square miles of land. Her economy is predominantly pastoral, and she exports cattle and sheep. Agriculture is developing only very slowly. There is an adequate railway net feeding Montevideo, the capital and principal port, and a standard of living of the population which is one of the highest in South America.

The rest of the La Plata drainage basin is occupied by the second largest state of the southern continent, Argentina. She is favored by topography and climate and is potentially one of the greatest food-producing regions of the world. Her present population of thirteen million is only a small fraction of what her territory could sustain, the rate of population increase is high, and if immigration is ever resumed, she will again become one of the fastest-growing countries in the world.

The northern tropical region of Argentina has products similar to those of Paraguay. To the south lies a region of 165,000 square miles suitable for the cultivation of cotton, as large an area as Georgia, Alabama, and North Carolina. The soil is rich, land cheap, labor costs low, and the yield twice that of the cotton lands of the United States. Further south lies the cattle and wheat region of the Pampas and beyond, the sheep country of Patagonia. The Pampas are an ideal grazing area with native grasses of great nutritive value and excellent land for alfalfa. Much of the grazing land is also suitable for crops and would bring a higher return per acre if it were under cultivation. At the present the most important products are wheat, alfalfa, and flax. The total area under plow is probably not more than thirty-five million acres or about 25 per cent of the land suitable for tillage, and possibilities of increased production lie not only in unused land, but also in an increase of the yield which is at present far below that of the United States and Western Europe.

Argentina, with the richest agricultural resources of the continent, is least well provided with mineral resources. Her territory contains no iron, no coal, but considerable oil in the northwest and in Patagonia, and a fair supply of waterpower although not in the regions where it would be most useful. Unimportant quantities of gold, silver, copper, lead, tungsten, and zinc have been mined, and no large-scale mineral development is in sight. There is a probability that the eastern slopes of the Andes range contain as yet unexplored deposits, but the transportation problem is bound to retard development here as it does in the West.

Like all South American republics, Argentina is trying to achieve a certain diversification in her economic structure and to build with the protection of a high tariff at least a light industry to supplement her agrarian extractive economy. The country is, however, poorly endowed for industrialization, and her main function in world economy will have to remain that of an exporter of agricultural products, presumably to Europe and in direct competition with many of the products of the United States.

The low level of industrialization does not prevent the Argentine from cherishing imperial ambitions. The population of the Argentine is predominantly white, more white than that of the United States, and based largely on Spanish and Italian immigration. It lives in a temperate climate, and like the population of Chile displays energy, drive, and initiative. The immigrant origin of many of the people does not prevent a fervent patriotism, and the fact that the population is less than one-third as large as that of Brazil does not induce any false modesty toward the northern neighbor. In the city of the "Good Airs" lives a race of strong men. In their cosmopolitan city where the Latin exuberance of public buildings meets the functional starkness of warehouse and factory, they dream gracious dreams of an economic empire. In certain circles the whole of the La Plata drainage basin including the tributary zones in Uruguay, Brazil, Paraguay, and Bolivia is an area to which "manifest destiny" calls. The Argentinians are determined that their state shall be the most important political unit on the southern continent and fully the equal of the United States in the Western Hemisphere.

History has treated us kindly; geography has endowed us greatly; the opportunities have been well used; and the result is that our country is today the most important political unit in the New World. Geographic and strategic factors, raw materials and population density, economic structure and technological advancement all contribute to give the United States a position of hegemony over a large part of the Western Hemisphere.

The United States is blessed by the happy circumstance that she is a strong power between two weak powers. She need fear no direct assault on her land boundaries, and her security problem is not one of frontier defense. The military equipment of Canada is modest, and her naval power slight. In the technical aspects of the military arm and in strategic position, there is no comparison between the two countries. The advantage is overwhelmingly with the United States. Geology, topography, and climate give the latter the entire continent to draw upon while the same factors sharply restrict what Canada can use of her own domain. The United States excels in manpower and resources, has more military aircraft, a greater army and navy, and can seriously cripple both the internal and external communications of her neighbors. In strategic location, as in all other factors of war, the U.S. dominates Canada.

The defense problem on the southern border resembles in some respects that of the north. The same disparities that give the United States predominance over Canada also favor her against Mexico. The total Mexican population is only about one-eighth that of the United States, and natural resources and industrial capacity are even more meager. There is no navy, an army of approximately fifty thousand men, and a small air force, but neither is well equipped, and the country has had no experience with modern warfare.

It is, therefore, perfectly obvious that the land neighbors of the United States cannot menace her boundaries. Regional location gives our country a position of unrivaled territorial security. Canada and Mexico are not in a position to threaten us now and are prevented by geography and lack of resources from ever becoming strong military powers. They affect the defense problem of the United States, not as primary sources of danger, but only as possible advance bases for enemies from across the oceans.

The American "Mediterranean" is today a zone in which the United States holds a position of unquestioned naval and air supremacy. This body of water is now to all intents and purposes a closed sea to which the United States holds the keys, a strategic situation approached only by Great Britain in the Indian Ocean and by Japan in the marginal seas off the coast of northeastern Asia. No serious threat against the position of the United States can arise in the region itself. The islands are of limited size, and the topography of Central America, like that of the Balkan peninsula in the European Mediterranean, favors small political units. Even the countries of large size like Mexico, Colombia, and Venezuela are precluded by topography, climate, and absence of strategic raw materials from becoming great naval powers. The supremacy of the United States in this area can, therefore, be challenged only by forces from outside the zone, either in South America or in Europe or Asia.

The international trade of the region is at the mercy of the United States, and the littoral states can be blockaded and cut from their access to the world market with the greatest of ease. For Mexico, Colombia, and Venezuela this means a position of absolute dependence on the United States, of freedom in name only, and, therefore, a situation which the proud citizens of those republics must resent as deeply as the Italians have resented their position on a closed European Mediterranean. Only a very skillful diplomacy and a very thick velvet glove will be able to make the reality of the power relationship tolerable to our good neighbors.

There is no likelihood that the west coast of South America will ever become the seat of great naval strength, although the Chilean navy was strong enough at the time of the Pacific War [1879-1884] to discourage the United States from backing up with force her demands for a revision of the peace terms. The political units are small in population, backward industrially, and lack the facilities for building modern armaments. Since the building of the Panama Canal, the comparative naval strength in the region is expressed less in terms of the small local navies than in terms of distance from the bases of the major naval powers. This means a position of relative advantage for the United States. Operating from the Canal Zone she can exert naval pressure far down the coast beyond the southern border of Peru, and only the economic and political center of Chile enjoys the protection which distance and a small air force provide against effective blockade.

In the Atlantic drainage area of South America, beyond the buffer zone of the American "Mediterranean" and accessible only by sea, lie the two most powerful states of the southern continent. Geographic analysis, however, dispels the illusion of an economic war potential. Brazil is larger than the United States, but much of her territory consists of a tropical forest zone, and the much narrower zone in which her economic life is centered lacks the energy resources and the economic productivity necessary to sustain military power. Argentina, with greater possibilities as an agrarian state because of her location in the temperate zone, is very much smaller than the United States and lacks the basic raw materials for heavy industry without which war strength is unreal. Even combined, these two states could offer no serious threat, and alliance is highly improbable in the light of the inherent conflict that flows from their geographic location.

Relative strength gives the United States an enormous advantage, but relative distance gives these southern states considerable protection. It is true that our navy, operating from bases in the American "Mediterranean," could blockade the exit of the Amazon basin and the ports of northern Brazil, but the real political and economic center of that country lies beyond the bulge and outside the radius of simple naval operations. Buenos Aires and the La Plata region are even farther away from Washington, approximately 7,000 miles, or twice as far as Europe. If the United States were willing to go to war and exert herself fully, she could of course defeat both Brazil and the Argentine with comparative ease if the South American opponents found no allies among the naval powers of Europe. But the fact remains that the temperate zone of the southern continent lies too far away from the center of our power to be easily intimidated by measures short of war. The result is that the nations of the extreme south enjoy a sense of relative independence from the United States which the smaller political units of the American "Mediterranean" can never possess. The A.B.C. states [Argentina, Brazil, Chile] represent a region in the hemisphere where our hegemony, if challenged, can be asserted only at the cost of war.

The United States is today the strongest power in the New World. How has her power been used? Compared with the general practice in Europe and Asia, it has been exercised with a good deal of moderation and restraint. Uncle Sam has respected frontiers for almost half a century. He has been a fairly lenient creditor for the last two decades and has permitted his southern friends a good deal of liberty in their treatment of his property. In his Good Neighbor Policy he has promulgated a self-denying ordinance seldom recorded in the annals of diplomacy. The non-intervention doctrine is a declaration that the supremacy of power which hegemony provides is not to be used as an instrument of national policy. It is an invitation to the states of Latin America to cease worrying about our strength and start rejoicing in our good intentions.

. . . Our Latin American friends have heard our protestations of good intentions and are watching with keen interest to see whether the reform will stick.

To our neighbors below the Rio Grande we remain the "Colossus of the North" which in a world of power politics can mean only one thing, danger. Good will is fine, but balanced power is a greater security. This means that those countries outside the zone of our immediate predominance, the larger states of South America, must try to counterbalance our strength through common action and through the use of weights from outside the hemisphere. They rejoice in the competition for their favors between Uncle Sam and the European states and try to play one off against the other. Europe seems far away, much farther than Washington. It is to them neither a danger nor an abomination but a weight with which to balance the "Colossus of the North."

NORTH AND SOUTH AMERICA: CONSEQUENCES OF LATITUDE AND ALTITUDE

By Samuel Flagg Bemis

From chap. 1 of *The Latin American Policy of the United States*, by S. F. Bemis. Copyright 1943 by Harcourt, Brace & Co., New York; reproduced by permission. The author is Sterling professor of diplomatic history at Yale University. His book was published under the auspices of the Yale Institute of International Studies.

Before we consider the geographical relationship of North America and South America to each other it is well to recall their relationship to Asia, Europe, and Africa. In the northernmost latitudes the New World is really very close to the Old World. Siberia lies nearly in sight of Alaska across Bering Strait. The Aleutians almost chain together Asia and North America, and it was along these islands that our first inhabitants reached this continent. The first visitors from Europe to North America also came by way of short water passages between islands in northern latitudes: from Norway to the Orkneys, to Iceland, to Greenland, to the continent. Nor is South America so far from Europe and Africa as most North Americans conceived it to be before the age of aerial navigation. From the westernmost point of Africa to the eastern bulge of Brazil is but eighteen hundred miles, and here the Portuguese voyagers to India accidentally touched America on their way around Africa in 1500; Cabral would have discovered the New World then if Columbus had not found it in 1492. Nevertheless, separation of the two hemispheres in the habitable latitudes was so pronounced as to keep them unknown to each other until nearly a thousand years ago, and without historical significance to each other or influence on each other until nearly five hundred years ago.

In terms of longitude the axis of the New World runs along the line Montreal-New York-Guantánamo-Panama-Lima-Santiago. From this axis,

South America, hinging on the Andes, extends its vast lowlands far to the eastward; North America swings oppositely far westward. Thanks to the Panama Canal, the entire west coast of South America and the northern shore of that continent are much closer to both coasts of the United States than to any other land-mass. On the other hand, the southeastern shore of South America, from Cape San Roque to the Plata River region, is as close (or almost as close) to Europe as to the United States, and, of course, much nearer to Africa than to either. The longitudinal relationship of the New World to the Old also emphasizes the extreme separation of South America from Asia. They scarcely appear together on the same hemisphere.

North America and South America seem at first to have a certain symmetry and even similarity. Both are widest in the north. Both taper off to the south. Both have new high cordilleras thrown up on their western edges. Both have geologically old blocks of land rising in the east. Both have great interior valleys with continental drainage. Even in shape they are not altogether dissimilar, particularly when seen on a globe rather than on a Mercator projection.

Such a superficial similarity is deceptive A vast and fundamental difference exists between the two continents; that is their respective latitudes. The widest part of North America lies in the arctic and subarctic, the narrowest part in the tropics and subtropics. The widest part of South America is in the tropics—almost on the Equator, in fact; the narrowing part falls in the subtropics; only tapering Argentina and Chile are left in the temperate zone, and, of those parts, the southern extremities are bleak and barren.

This fundamental difference is all the more striking when we compare the interiors of the northern and southern continents as dwelling places for civilized man. In South America the heart of the continent is the Amazon Valley, least favored for human abode of all great expanses of non-arid and non-arctic land. In North America the heart of the continent is the upper Mississippi Valley and the Great Lakes region, choicest area on the globe for the habitation and sustenance of civilization: fertile, rich in varied natural resources including food, fuel, minerals and waterpower, combined with easy resources of transportation; and—most important—endowed with a climatological optimum for man, so necessary for the best of human health, physical and mental energy, and social progress. One of the great natural handicaps of what we call Latin America is that it has no share at all of the climatological optimum. Only in a belt of land across Chile and Argentina, of which the northern boundary is the latitude of Buenos Aires, do we find a second-best zone of climatic energy. . . .

If the continents of the New World, even in their temperate latitudes, are so different, each is also divided within itself by geographical obstructions, differences more pronounced in South America than in North America. In North America the mountain ranges and lowland regions have had comparatively little influence in separating nation from nation; in South America they have had a profound and enduring effect, both during the colonial regime, and in the national period of the last hundred years. This is . . . principally because of the different latitudes of the two continents. When the land lies altogether in a temperate zone, the geographical division of mountains and lowlands is not such a permanent barrier to the uniform settlement of a new continent by civilized people living through freezing winters in heated houses. Therefore geographical barriers have not served much as national frontiers in North America, although rivers and lakes, as well as lines of longitude and latitude, have made convenient boundaries when political forces have divided homogeneous areas.

In South America, on the other hand, the falling of the land into highlands and lowlands is not only more pronounced in its sudden variations of altitude and of rainfall, but the location of by far the greater part of the continent causes these changes in altitude to become also differences between temperate plateaus and hot tropical jungles—note in this respect the striking difference between the valleys of the Amazon and the Mississippi—a regional separation that has had a deep sociological effect since mankind first peopled the continent. The more abrupt character of the mountain ascents also delayed development of modern transportation and, in at least the case of Chile and Argentina, served, even in the temperate zone, as a natural and impressive geographical frontier. . . .

More rain falls on South America than on North America, but it falls mostly on the right places in North America and mostly on the wrong places in South America. In North America the eastern seaboard west to the 100th meridian, north to include the St. Lawrence-Great Lakes basin, and south to the Gulf of Mexico, as well as the West Indies and Central America (exclusive of the highlands of Mexico), has an adequate supply of rain for staple crops, and there is enough in the western plains of the United States and southern Canada for dry wheat-farming and grazing. Deficiencies are mostly in the mountain states where rain is least useful.

Most rain falls on South America in the more uninhabitable regions of the tropical Amazon basin, and the least rain falls in the Andean highlands and on the Pacific coast, otherwise most habitable to man. Of the choice temperate regions only the Plata basin and central Chile get enough to support a thriving civilization; even there agriculture could well do with more rain, particularly in Chile. In much of South America rain is highly seasonal: long rainy seasons alternate with long dry seasons, which is not so sustaining for staple crops as a more even distribution throughout the year. Generally good rainfall in North America combines with a large area of other desirable climatic conditions. In South America most abundant rainfall comes within a climatic zone of low human energy. The result of this on crop yields, nutrition, health, and human vigor is profound. It exercises an ineluctable enervating effect on the peoples and governments of the tropical lowlands, and on their economy, sociology, culture, and politics, both national and international. They cannot get away from it.

LATIN AMERICA: PATTERN OF DEVELOPMENT

By P. E. James

From chap. 1 of *Latin America,* by P. E. James. Copyright 1942 by The Odyssey Press, Inc., New York; reproduced by permission. The author is professor of geography at the University of Michigan.

LATIN AMERICA is not a new land. This is a fact which many North Americans find difficulty in understanding. Some of the lands which lie to the south of the United States had been exploited and abandoned by the Indians before the arrival of Columbus. In the centuries which followed Columbus the so-called "New World" was ransacked by Spaniards, Portuguese, English, French, Dutch, and other peoples of European origin. There are many parts of Latin America for which up-to-date information is lacking, for which there are not even reliable maps; but there are few parts which have not been explored and exploited first by one group and then by another. Actually Latin America is not a virgin land, awaiting the arrival of the pioneer—it is an old land, tramped over, many of its sources of accumulated treasure exploited and abandoned, many of its landscapes profoundly altered by the hand of man. Yet it is a land in which large areas remain comparatively empty of human inhabitants.

Now, more than 400 years after the nations of Western Europe began to plunder the New World, three chief groups have emerged in political control of the larger part of the hemisphere: the Anglo-Americans, the Spanish-Americans, and the Portuguese-Americans. In the twenty-one independent states included in the Pan American Union there are approximately 258 million people. Of these about 132 millions are in the United States. Latin America has about 78 million people in states which are descended from Spain, about 45 million people in Portuguese Brazil, and about 3 millions in the Negro republic of Haiti, which was once a colony of France. In addition there are some 5 million people in small units still under the sovereignty of European nations or recently acquired by the United States. . . .

The 8 million square miles of land in the part of the Western Hemisphere which lies south of continental United States represents about 19 per cent of the total area of the world's inhabited continents; but the 130 million people make up only about 6 per cent of the world's population. The largest political unit in Latin America both in area and in population is Brazil; yet Brazil's 45 million people—approximately equal to the number of people in Italy—occupy a territory which is as large as all of Europe without the Scandinavian Peninsula, and larger than that of continental United States. Only two countries in mainland Latin America make effective use of all parts of their national territories—these are little Salvador and Uruguay. . . .

The normal pattern of Occidental settlement in a pioneer land is one of scattered clusters, commonly strung together along a line of travel. . . . In the course of time the original areas of settlement of Europe and of eastern North America were enlarged until they grew together, little by little filling in the scantily occupied territory which once separated them; but in Latin America the clusters still remain generally distinct from one another in an elementary pattern which has never been filled in. . . .

In the midst of each of the population clusters, even the smallest, there is an urban core or nucleus, and because the areas of concentrated settlement still remain distinct from one another, there is little overlap between the territory served by one city and that served by a neighboring one. . . .

Today the urban nucleus of a Latin American area of settlement exerts such a strong attraction that the tendency is for people to move in toward that center rather than to expand the frontier into a new pioneer zone. There are many expanding frontiers in Latin America, but most of them are hollow ones, that is, they represent waves of exploitation moving across a country, followed by abandonment and population decline. Such is the sugar frontier of Cuba, or the coffee frontier of São Paulo. These frontiers produce no net gain in the density of settlement. There are, however, in four parts of mainland Latin America—that is, excluding the West Indies—zones of concentrated settlement which are expanding, and their expansion is not accompanied by a decrease of the density of population in the original nuclei. These four places are: the Highlands of Costa Rica, the highlands of Antioquia in Colombia, the Central Valley of Chile, and the three southern states of Brazil. . . .

The clustered pattern of population bears a simple relationship to the political units. . . . Only one central cluster of people marks the core of such political units as Chile, Uruguay, Paraguay, and El Salvador. In most of the countries the population clusters form the cores of the major subdivisions—states, departments, or provinces. It is less common to find two clusters in one state, or one cluster divided between two states. . . .

One result of this simple relation of the population pattern to the political areas is that the political boundaries generally pass through the scantily occupied territory between the clusters. . . . A second result of the clustered pattern of population is the necessity for recognizing two kinds of political area. There is the *total national territory* over which a politically organized group claims jurisdiction—the whole area within the national boundaries. But only that part of the total territory which actually contributes to the economic support of the citizens of the country can be called the *effective national territory* (sometimes called the *ekumene*).

Finally, a third result of the clustered pattern of population is the nature of the transportation problems which Latin Americans have to face. Throughout most of South and Middle America the overland routes of travel lead from the interior to the nearest or most accessible ports; the land routes which connect one region of concentrated settlement with another, even within the same country, are developed only poorly. . . .

. . . The chief highways of approach to Latin America and the chief lines of connection between the isolated centers of population are the oceans. Even if airplanes are now changing the nature of the transportation problem for passengers and mail, the movement of commodities is still largely dependent on ships.

Whether the approach to Latin America from other parts of the world is by ship or by air the relative remoteness of the continent must be observed. South America is literally one of the ends of the habitable earth. . . . [It] is equally remote from the centers of commercial activity in the modern world which are located on either side of the North Atlantic in eastern North America and Western Europe. . . .

The population clusters appear on the map to be all alike; but actually they are composed of an extraordinary variety of racial and cultural elements, combined in many different proportions. . . . Race mixture has gone on with little restriction or taboo, and today more than half of the one hundred and thirty million Latin Americans are of mixed ancestry. Furthermore, the ingredients are highly diverse. There are, to be sure, the three main elements—Indian, Negro, and white or European (including people born in America of European ancestry); but each of these elements includes a wide variety of kinds of people. . . .

Racial diversity, however, is not the only source of disharmony within Latin-American society. There are social and economic cleavages which divide communities into sharply contrasted classes.

Some of these class distinctions are inherent in the society of traditional Latin America; but in the modern period the arrival of the urban industrial way of living has developed a new kind of difference separating the people of the larger cities from the people of the rural districts.

In traditional Latin America the economic and social life is dominated by the large estate. For want of a better term we shall describe this kind of society as *feudal,* although this implies none of the specific characteristics of the European feudal political system. Prestige and security in a feudal society are gained first through the ownership of a large tract of land. A very minor proportion of the total population forms the landed aristocracy, and is enabled to live in comfort and security and with a relatively high standard because of the large area from which income is derived and because of the relatively low cost of labor. When land is no longer available, prestige, if not security, can be gained by finding a position in the government service or by winning a commission in the army, or by entering the priesthood. But these various forms of life are open only to the fortunate minority: the vast majority of the members of a feudal society are landless workers—peons, sharecroppers, tenants, or others. Usually they are permitted to make use of small areas for the production of their own food, and for the materials necessary for clothing and shelter; they repay the owner by providing him with wage laborers, or by paying him rent for the use of land for commercial crops. This is the Latin America of the semi-independent large landowner, who wishes above all to be left alone by all government authority; it is also the Latin America of political insecurity, in which first one group and then another plots to overthrow those who are in power, rarely because of genuine differences of ideology, usually because of the desire for the rich rewards of office-holding. This is the Latin America which verges on internal chaos to such an extent that it can be held together only by the successful operation of military dictatorship. This is the Latin America in which the army is the most powerful force in political life. . . .

. . . In Latin America, the impact of the industrial society with the traditional feudal society is now going on. Where the industrial way of living has become established, a new and still more profound line of cleavage has been formed across all the previous diversities of Latin American society. . . .

. . . The use of controlled inanimate power changes the emphasis from production by cheap labor to production by machines or, in terms of economics, capital investment assumes a position of preponderant importance, and the owners of capital rather than the owners of land assume places of the highest prestige and political power. Production is enormously increased, not only total production, but also per capita production. This leads to specialization and exchange, and hence to interdependence over wide areas. . . .

. . . Life becomes more speculative, less certain, but with rewards for the successful which are in a material way far beyond anything the world has offered before. . . . The vague concepts of feudal society, such as *por la mañana, por la tarde,* must be given up for more precise concepts, such as 9:45 a.m. or 3:10 p.m. Behavior of all sorts becomes more standardized. The picturesqueness of provincial costumes disappears under a uniform cover of blue denim overalls; . . . local differences in manners and customs are modified by the impact of the new patterns of life. In the big cosmopolitan centers of Latin America life follows the same routine as in North American or European cities... in short, the whole aspect of life is changed from its variegated feudal base to a uniformity repeated in all the occidental urban centers....

A COMMONWEALTH OF NATIONS?

By Frank Tannenbaum

From "An American Commonwealth of Nations," by Frank Tannenbaum, in *Foreign Affairs*, July 1944. Copyright 1944 by Council on Foreign Relations, New York; reproduced by permission. The author is professor of Latin American History at Columbia University.

The future historian will note, when he deals with America's participation in the Second World War, that for most purposes it was in effect a hemispheric undertaking. True, the brunt of the effort has of necessity fallen upon the United States, but given the distribution of effective power and interests in the Western World this is neither surprising nor unexpected. What may seem to call for special comment is that of the 20 republics south of the Rio Grande, only one—Argentina—should seemingly have remained indifferent to the issues involved or even in some measure friendly to our enemies. But even in this case, the Argentine Government belatedly broke off relations with the Axis Powers and their satellites; and there is evidence that the majority of the people have from the beginning been on the side of the Allies in this war.

This very remarkable moral, political, and, in a sense, military alignment of the Western World on the same side in a great war has illumined an accepted assumption—the unity of this hemisphere. The idea is old, as old at least as Bolívar; but it was the visible threat of a German victory in Europe that at last gave it unmistakable expression. In spite of Latin American fear of the United States, so well and so long fostered by agents of Hitler and before him by others (including Latin Americans like Vasconcelos, Ugarte, Fombona and Pereyra), it became evident that the link that tied North and South America together was more than physical—it was political and spiritual as well. There had been, before the storm clouds gathered, in an age that now seems far off and a little unreal, much discursive and eloquent writing and preaching upon the sharp differences between the peoples and cultures of the United States and Latin America. One was Anglo-Saxon, the other Latin; one was Protestant, the other Catholic; one was material, the other spiritual; the culture of the United States was, as the tale was told, crass, coarse, and corrupted by an unholy zeal for money making. We had not only a "dollar diplomacy," but also a dollar-seeking way of life. Every item in the life of the United States that could be made to brand our culture as barbarous, uncouth and grasping was emphasized and exaggerated.... The "ideological warfare" was in full swing before its name had been invented.

And yet, when the crisis came, the discord so busily sown in previous decades was largely washed away and an essential identity in attitude and community of interest quickly prevailed. This "revelation," for so it might be described, reflected the fact that the people of this hemisphere, when looking out upon the world, had a common view of the universe. For it is true that the familiar list of differences between the United States and Latin American peoples is only partially descriptive and denies the imprint of their experience in this hemisphere. The conquest and settlement of the Americas has molded all of the peoples on this side of the Atlantic into a recognizable folk in a way not shown by the ordinary catalogue of their varying characteristics. This uniqueness of outlook and attitude, of feeling and philosophy, is a by-product of the sharing by Americans everywhere of certain profound experiences in their common history in this hemisphere which have left their residue in attitude, notion, belief, practice, values, habit, language and mannerism. More than four centuries of a common heritage have implanted in all of us a "something" that is American rather than European. It is discernible in our prose and poetry, politics and polity, in our popular heroes and folk tales, in the stories told to children, and in the moral issues that burden the grown-ups.

That something is a by-product of the essentially universal American experience with the Indian, the Negro, the open spaces and wide horizon, the unfilled areas, the peculiar use of the horse (the cowboy, the gaucho, the llanero, the vaquero are brothers under the skin), the peculiar American experience with ranching: of driving cattle a thousand miles as is still done in Brazil, for instance. It is the persistent tradition of a culture uprooted in the Old World and replanted and developed in the New, the common experience of the mixture of races and peoples in their varying degrees, of the constant flow of immigrants and their amazingly rapid metamorphosis into something essentially different from what they were, in the evidence of social and physical mobility, in the pride and self-assurance born from a world easily molded and changed.

It stems from the common belief in progress, from the common notion that government is a human and malleable instrument subject to pressure and open to change by political "revolt" at the ballot box or by a "revolution," from the fact that all of the nations in the hemisphere achieved their independence by revolution, and that their greatest heroes are all successful "rebels" against Old World "tyranny." It derives from the fact that the belief in democracy is ingrained even in areas where the "caudillo" and the "political boss" is a persistent and sometimes sinister figure, and from the fact that all political upheavals have—with very few exceptions indeed—been at least in the name of democracy.

Those influences under varying forms and in different degrees have given Americans a common psychological and spiritual heritage deeper than the traditional, obvious differences that separate them. This identity of experience extends even to the feeling of isolation, of being set apart from the rest of the world, of being separated and protected by both the Pacific and the Atlantic Oceans. When they speak from the depths, Americans talk about the same things and say essentially the same things about them. Even a cursory knowledge of the truly national literature of this hemisphere will make this clear.

It was consistent with the basic experience of the folk in the Western World that when face to face with the greatest moral and political conflagration of modern times they should react to it in very much the same way—as in fact they have done. Psychologically and morally the American people everywhere responded to the alternative offered by Hitler by almost spontaneous opposition. This was what their common experience dictated.

The identity of North and South was

enhanced by the common peril. Danger made clear the helplessness of the Latin American countries, individually and even collectively, in the face of a ruthless military power bent upon conquest. It also made evident the dependence of the United States upon both moral and material support from those countries for the defense of its own or any other part of the hemisphere against aggression from abroad. The military need to keep the Panama Canal and the passage around Magellan Strait open to United States shipping and closed to that of our enemies made the cooperation of the countries in Latin America essential to us. By the same token, the survival of the Latin American countries as individual nations depended upon the military strength of the United States. It was unmistakably clear that the countries of this hemisphere are in the same boat militarily and politically, and no words can hide the fact. This military and diplomatic unity was born of necessity and made easier and more logical by the common historical experience of North and South.

It would, however, be unrealistic and misleading to gloss over the persistent stress and strain that prevail between the United States and the countries of Latin America. The talk in the nations to the south about the differences, the emphasis upon the cultural and spiritual divergence, the warnings of danger, have a basis in the bigness, power, organized energy, wealth and military strength of the United States. We are the great nation in this hemisphere. Our mere size and power are like a permanent shadow, protective or threatening as you will, but inescapable and unavoidable. Our protestations of affection and concern are, in spite of our best diplomatic efforts, the protestations of the big brother; our very manner if not mannerism reflects that. This is the fact and no one can conceal it—not even by studiously avoiding mention of it. So, too, the protestations of the Latin Americans that they love us, admire us, respect us—or the opposite—are in effect the behavior of a little brother, and nothing can hide the fact, neither humility, nor bravado, nor even studious indifference. Anyone who has attended any Pan American conference will readily identify the attitudes, speeches, disclaimers and protestations, the deference and implicit jealousy or fear that reflect the simple fact of our bigness. The overflow of American energy in the past and its possible overflow in the future are a constant theme song, accompanying every political argument, every projection into the future.

Diplomatically this gulf between the one Great Power and a number of small ones has been bridged by the doctrine of equal sovereignty, a doctrine that makes Haiti and Santo Domingo—to use just two instances—equal entities with the United States in a diplomatic argument, if in nothing else. This doctrine has its numerous corollaries, the most important of which is the principle of non-intervention in the internal and external affairs of any one of the 20 Latin American republics. Equal sovereignty as a theory and non-intervention as a policy are really deliberate attempts to redress the balance in this hemisphere between one very powerful and a number of weak nations. And, as a matter of fact, they do redress the balance in a certain way and within certain limits; they tend to defend the dignity and justify the confidence of the weaker political units in their dealings with the United States. They also tend to give Pan Americanism a kind of moral basis which it lacked until these policies were fully acquiesced in by the United States. The effect is to provide a basis of security, especially as we have actually implemented these measures in various ways, such as converting the Monroe Doctrine from a unilateral to a multilateral instrument. It cannot be denied that these changes in attitude and practice have been effective in deflecting the preoccupation of the Latin Americans with the "bigness" of the United States, for the time being. But perhaps their most important immediate consequence has been their influence upon the United States, where they have led to the writing and acceptance of a "self-denying ordinance." They have led us to behave as if the theory of sovereign equality were true and not merely an operational formula.

These doctrines and the conventions based upon them, useful as they may be as operational tools in a very complex and ill-balanced international structure, are nevertheless pure fictions. The theory of the equality of sovereignty, the non-intervention policy, the Monroe Doctrine and its various corollaries, the policy of recognition, whatever it may be at the moment, and even the Good Neighbor Policy, are in effect intervention. In the nature of the case, given the difference of power and the inner lack of political balance in most of the countries in Latin America, whatever we do or fail to do has the force of intervention. Our policy, whatever it is, our attitude, whatever it is, has a significant influence, in many instances a decisive one, upon both the internal and the external policy of most, perhaps all, the countries in Latin America. Our power is such that we are a party to every transaction, even against our will. We are a weight in every balance. We are an influence in every political judgment, every decision. When we refuse to intervene, we merely intervene on the other side. When we do not support our friends, we in effect support our enemies; when we will not intervene on the side we believe in, we intervene on the side we do not believe in. We cannot escape the consequence of our power; we may refuse to exercise our responsibility, but in doing that we merely exercise it on the wrong side.

In a political world so unstable as Latin America, where government in most cases rests upon a slender and tentative alignment of political groups and personalities and where the individual factor plays so large and significant a role, any move that appears to favor those in power strengthens them in their hold upon public office and tends to perpetuate it, and every move that looks like indifference on our part carries an implication of censure, weakening those who hold political power, strengthening the opposition and hastening the day of revolution. The one thing we cannot achieve in Latin America is neutrality; our very declaration of a policy of "hands off" has the effect of lending support to one or another group contending for place and position. The Good Neighbor Policy, effective as it has been, and so valuable in promoting a moral alignment against aggression at the time when the alignment had to be made, was in effect intervention on the side of the governments in power. Any favor extended, any courtesy shown, increased the prestige and hold of the personalities in office and tended to perpetuate them in that place.

To say this is not to suggest that any other policy would have been more desirable or that any other policy would have made us less interventionist. It is merely to point out for the sake of "realism" and practical politics that the doctrine of non-intervention has a much more limited meaning than it implies. Both the internal and the external policies of the countries of Latin America are sharply responsive to our mere presence; anything we do or say—even if we say or do nothing at all—has the effect of intervention. It is no accident that in many Latin American countries the American ambassador is the most important political personage in the country, even if he does his best to be the least important one.

It need only be added that our failure to admit or our refusal to exercise the inevitable influence that stems from our position may become a contributing cause of political chaos and disillusionment. Our moral responsibility equals our power, and the awareness of that reality is, or ought to be, the first thought in shaping our Latin American policies.

Though much has been written on the subject, we perhaps do not yet realize how greatly the Latin American countries have contributed to the fulfillment of our wartime objectives in this hemisphere. As a background for examining some of the concrete evidence of this cooperation we might first remind ourselves what our policy was in the days when our danger of becoming involved in the war was growing. Summarized, our objectives then were: (1) To organize and arm the hemisphere for defense. (2) To destroy any attempt to use any part of it for direct or indirect military operations such as espionage, the construction of submarine bases, propaganda, sabotage, or for the supply of valuable raw materials to the enemy. (3) To obtain bases for our military and naval forces. (4) To acquire as rapidly as possible the available raw materials for our own needs. (5) To achieve hemispheric unity both for political and military ends. (6) To obtain military aid from Latin America by the organization, arming and training of local troops for use in actual combat if and when need and opportunity offered. (7) To maintain the peace in the area as an essential means of achieving some or all of these objectives.

First and perhaps most important, we should note what may be called the spiritual preparation of the Latin American countries. Long before we were involved in the war they evidenced a growing sympathy for the cause of the Allies, an increasing shift toward cooperation with the United States, and at the same time a growing fear and repudiation of the doctrines and aspirations of Germany. Fully a year before December 7, 1941, there were many signs that the various nations in the Western Hemisphere were forging a common policy. Even an incomplete citation of the available material provides impressive testimony . . . that a ground swell in favor of cooperation with the United States had been developing in Latin America before Pearl Harbor. The fatal events of that day produced a unity of action and policy in this hemisphere barely equalled and certainly not exceeded by the British Commonwealth of Nations. Even more significant, perhaps, is the fact that without the formal political unity of the British Commonwealth, and without the common background of language and culture, the nations in the Western World in a moment of crisis behaved in fact as if they belonged together, as indeed they did, in the face of a common danger.

. . . The American nations accepted and reacted to the attack against the United States as an attack against themselves, and . . . with amazing speed and thoroughness they united against the aggressors. By the end of January 1942—that is to say, within six weeks of Pearl Harbor—all of the nations except Chile and Argentina had either declared war or broken relations with the Axis, and [subsequently] both of these followed suit. There [remained] not a single nation in the hemisphere which [did] not cut its official contacts with the Axis Powers.

This moral cooperation was accompanied by a military effort which must be judged by its potential importance. Save for naval battles, the actual conflict did not extend to this hemisphere; the war did not reach either the Pacific or the Atlantic coasts of any of the Latin American nations. But it is clear from the evidence at hand that both preceding Pearl Harbor and immediately following it the American nations were preparing for such a possibility, and it may be assumed that they would have accepted the physical challenge of the Axis Powers as in fact they accepted the moral challenge. . . .

Our own aid to the military rearming of Latin America [was] extensive. . . . Lend-lease agreements [were] entered into with every country in Latin America except Argentina and Panama (the last-named received aid under different provisions). Of the amount assigned [down to July 1944], one-half [went] to Brazil, and three-fourths [went] to Brazil, Chile, Mexico and Peru. . . . Every country except Argentina received a certain amount of modern military equipment. But the amounts expended under lend-lease are after all only a part of the total sum of money either loaned, invested, or given to the different countries for a great variety of purposes, all of them designed to increase hemispheric solidarity, to develop and make available the raw materials needed for the war effort, and to increase the effectiveness of the Latin American nations in the general enterprise of winning both the war and the peace. . . .

The economic and military contributions by the United States have increased the prestige of the governments in power. There is, however, no reason to assume that they have materially affected political habits in Latin America, or even the basic instability there. Nothing that happen[ed] during the war will lessen the personal emphasis upon honor and prestige, the extreme individualism that borders on the anarchic, and the importance of the *personaje*. Nor will it have seriously broken down the isolation of the various classes from each other; the role of the Indian, the *roto*, the peon, will remain substantially unchanged. So too will that of the *gamonal*, the *hacendado*, the *amo*, and the *señor*; and the prestige of the military will, if anything, have increased. We have in effect armed the continent as it has never been armed before. In the sphere of domestic affairs, ambitious generals will have better means at their disposal for playing the game of "revolution," and the governments will have more effective tools at their disposal for the suppression of "popular" uprisings. . . . We may have made the "normal" dictatorships more permanent, and therefore less palatable, and in consequence more tyrannical and efficient. . . .

Perhaps more serious than the predictable stirrings of domestic political ambitions as a result of the military equipment we have placed in the hands of local army chieftains is the very real danger, if not the likelihood, that these new tools may be used in older quarrels between Latin American nations. It must always be remembered that international quarrels in Latin America have all too frequently served internal political ends. What assurance is there that the arming of Peru and Ecuador will not lead to a renewal of the old animosity settled under duress after Pearl Harbor? What certainty is there that the arming of Bolivia and Chile will not lead to an attempt to satisfy an old ambition and to rectify an essentially unstable boundary situation? What, further, is the assurance that the arming of Brazil may not lead to that country's military embroilment with Argentina? To raise these questions is not to predict that any such consequences are inevitable; but it is important to repeat here that unless the United States shows a sense of responsibility proportionate to its power in this hemisphere, the arming of the Latin American countries may, and in all probability will, have consequences other than those it had in view when it placed arms at the disposal of the governments of Latin America.

It must be remembered that there is no reason to assume that political attitudes, and the persistent feeling that a government in power is a usurper, have been in any important way modified. Political practices will remain as they were before the war; so will the essential instability of the political structure; so will the artificial character of political parties. Revolution will still be the one sure means of changing government; suppression of opposition by more or less drastic means will still continue a favorite political technique. The source of the difficulty lies beyond immediate cure, and certainly beyond cure from the outside. The political form is a function of the structure of society in all its ramifications, and the things that can be added by an outside paternalism will not have any serious effect upon the system as it exists.

If there is a "solution" for the political instability, it must come from a better balancing of the inner forces, a greater evening-up of incomes within the different countries, a more general identification of the governments with the people, a larger participation in effective politics by the mass of the community, and a greater responsibility of political parties both in and out of government. But such a consummation, if it comes at all, will take a long time, a very long time. What we have done is to strengthen the governments in power. These governments came to power in most places—we need not specify—by arbitrary means, by revolutions, by pronouncements, by the suppression of the legislature, by "unanimous elections," by plebiscites (voluntary and popular, if we are to believe the governments), by every means except that of the accurate counting of votes freely given. The question of democracy is really irrelevant to the point. If the governments in power had not thus come to office, others in their place would have achieved public control by the same sort of "democratic" means. Democracy in our sense is not at issue. Nor is there any question as to the inevitability of our behavior during a war of the proportions of the present conflict. The simple point is that we have become identified with strengthening, favoring and maintaining the present governments. We are being held responsible for saddling the present "tyrannies" upon the people. The words "present tyrannies" are used advisedly, for in their place other tyrannies would have been equally "good" or equally "bad," and they would have come to office by the "natural" process of substitution. But we have impeded this natural process of Latin American "democracy," have dammed the process, and when the dam breaks, as it will, as indeed . . . it is already breaking, we shall be blamed for the revolutions as we are now blamed for the tyrannies. The democratic groups accuse us of maintaining the dictatorships in office. They would equally blame us if we interfered against them.

The difficulties and perplexities are numerous. One of them that most Americans, official and unofficial alike, will not recognize is that our influence, our democratic influence, is essentially revolutionary in Latin America. If we really mean what we say, if the preaching of the Four Freedoms is to be taken literally, then we are vehicles of social revolutions in most, perhaps all, of the Latin American countries. Revolution, bloody conflict, and prolonged social chaos: there is at present no other road to achieve the Four Freedoms. If we do not mean what we say, then we are going to be accused—are already being accused—of hypocrisy, of supporting the "evil powers," of conniving at the suppression of democracy, of saddling arbitrary and anti-democratic government upon the peoples. For it is true that the Four Freedoms, if they are ever to be achieved, involve a basic change in the land structure of Latin America, everywhere except in Mexico and Costa Rica; and this means prolonged social strife and at least temporary agricultural depression, and involves the transfer of political power and prestige from the present small and divided upper class to the large mass of the people. There is no assurance that anything that can be done will, within any reasonable time, have that effect; it might even prove to have the opposite effect. But the doing of it, whatever that implies, is a task beyond the means, purpose or ken of what we can either propose or execute.

This conclusion might lead profitably to a detailed analysis of the economic consequence to Latin America of the war and of the financial and material contributions received from us. All that can be said on that score here is that the immediate inflation has increased discontent and raised a very real threat of wide political disturbance as soon as the war is over, if not before. Moreover, the ambitions aroused by our pouring in of money as loans and as outright gifts must of necessity remain unfulfilled. There is no way of maintaining an artificially stimulated economy after the prime motive for it, the winning of the war, has come to an end. Nor even in the event of full employment in the United States will we provide an adequate cushioning for the transition from a war to a peace economy. The income of the governments will in all probability shrink to something like their former levels; the sources of national income will remain narrow as they were before; and the flow of easy, if not free money, perhaps even the flow of investment money, will come to an end.

This is said without undue pessimism. It must simply be remembered that there is no way, in the long run, of maintaining an economy above its natural level, and that charity—if the word be permitted—is not a healthy or a permanent basis for either economic or political stability. What Latin America needs, if either political or economic stability is to be achieved, is the growth of a numerous, independent, small landowning peasantry and the growth of a large and vigorous middle class. But the achievement of both of these essential objectives involves not only an investment of capital in Latin America but a continuity of public policy there that is probably not to be had in human affairs.

Chapter 16

The United States

THE American people have played a crucial role in winning the war. Without our intervention there could have been no V-days. Without our aid, the Allies would still be struggling desperately with their backs to the wall, if indeed they had not suffered crushing defeat on every front.

American effort, so necessary to winning the war, is no less essential to the gigantic task of winning the peace. The United States alone cannot create a new world order. But we can speed greatly or retard fatally the physical reconstruction and human rehabilitation of the devastated countries. And unless we play an active and constructive political role there can be no security for anyone and no promise of an enduring peace.

The United States, in short, is a world power in the fullest sense of the word. American strength, prestige, and influence are so great that Washington is inevitably a factor in every international equation. Our advice may not be asked, or it may not be heeded. But the attitude of the United States government will be carefully noted and evaluated on every international question, and our stand will affect in one way or another the policies of all other countries.

This is a heavy responsibility, and there is no certainty that we shall rise to meet it. We turned our back upon the Old World after the last war, and thereby contributed not a little to the conditions which produced the Second World War. Voices are raised today advocating either a passive or an armed isolationism that ignores the lessons of the past generation. Great states can use their power capriciously and arbitrarily. Or they can pursue a negative policy of sabotage and opposition. Or they can play an active and constructive political role in collaboration with other nations. But in our rapidly shrinking world of ever more deadly and longer range weapons, no people, least of all the United States, can escape the consequences of their own acts and policies.

The world-wide influence of the United States today springs from no single source. It stems in large degree from the demonstrated prowess of American arms—on land, upon the seas, and in the air. But that is by no means all. American influence springs also from our enormous economic productivity, and consequent ability to give or to withhold desperately needed aid for reconstruction. Food and machines are potent weapons in the battle for the peace. But ideas and ideals, too, are sources of influence. Under American leadership the nations and fragments of nations continuing the desperate up-hill struggle against the Axis were welded into the United Nations, a global coalition dedicated not only to winning military victory but also to framing a just peace and an enduring world order.

It will help us to grasp the realities of our situation today, and to judge the continued adequacy of time-tried American policies, if we take a brief look back over the road we have traveled during the past century and a half. The United States of 1790 consisted of a fringe of settlements strung along the Atlantic coast from Maine to Georgia. Except where a few larger rivers gave easy access to the interior, the country one hundred miles from tidewater was almost everywhere virtually unbroken forest.

The coal, iron, oil, and other resources which have made possible the phenomenal economic development of the United States were either undiscovered or largely inaccessible. Though politically independent and a recognized member of the family of nations, the United States was still an economic colony of Great Britain. British sea power, moreover, commanded American waters right up to the coast, and thereby controlled the main connecting links between the principal centers of population.

The situation along the land frontiers was scarcely better. The United States was surrounded on three sides by colonial territories of European powers. Almost nowhere did Americans have secure and unchallenged possession of their own land frontiers. On neither land nor sea was American power and prestige sufficient to command respect for the most obvious rights and claims against the greater powers of Europe.

Fortunately for the young republic, those early years were years of struggle and turmoil in Europe. First the French Revolution and then Napoleon's wars of conquest kept Europeans almost continuously occupied until 1815. That struggle left Europe exhausted and divided. England emerged supreme upon the oceans. But the British never gained ascendancy over the European continent. To forestall future threats from the mainland, British statecraft labored to keep Europe divided, a policy known as promoting the balance of power. But not even Britain enjoyed a completely free hand overseas, for the British had always to reckon with the possibility that the European powers would form a dangerous coalition against them. Thus was created a situation in which the Great Powers of the Old World more or less cancelled each other out as aggressive factors in the New World.

It was under such conditions that the strategy of American security took form. Our forbears asked nothing so much of Europe as to be left alone. Conversely, and to this end, they left Europe alone as much as possible. Hence the traditional American policies of neutrality toward European wars, non-intervention in the internal affairs of European countries, and no entangling alliances that would embroil the United States in the strife of the Old World.

Americans have generally taken it for granted that it was the wide oceans—so frequently mentioned by the Founding Fathers—that protected the United States. We can now perceive that it was not only the oceans but also the relatively stable and self-limiting balance of power in the Old World. Those conditions gave us a century and more of remarkable security at almost no cost to the United States.

Those conditions had vanished long before the outbreak of the Second World War. But only today are Americans beginning to appreciate either the nature or the implications of the change that has taken place. There is no longer a self-limiting balance of power in Europe. Europe itself is no longer the political dynamo of our world. Great Britain can no longer play its historic role of keeping the balance level and stable. The Soviet Union has emerged as the dominant power in Eurasia. Soviet policies are as much a question-mark as those of the United States.

In preceding chapters we have sketched these and other developments which present an over-all situation unlike anything that has confronted us before. Traditional American policies provide no ready-made formulae for coping with these new world conditions. Great as American strength indubitably is today, it still may be totally insufficient to give us security, without fundamental changes in our national strategy and foreign policy. Whether or not this is the case can be ascertained only by subjecting our own situation to an inquiry as searching as that which we have attempted with respect to other nations. Only thus can we evaluate our altered world position. Only thus can we judge the adequacy of American traditions of foreign policy, or chart a course with reasonable assurance of safety in the uncertain years to come.

This is no easy undertaking. Nothing is quite so difficult as to view one's own country objectively and dispassionately. It is like trying to make an impersonal appraisal of one's parents. We cannot easily stand back and look at the United States as others see us, or strike a balance of our national assets and liabilities, or evaluate the new relationships, dangers, and responsibilities thrust upon us by changing conditions at home and abroad.

But difficult as it may be, the task must not be shirked. Without a clear picture of our own strength, both in absolute and in relative terms, and of the limitations as well as opportunities implicit in our geographical position, it will be infinitely more difficult to avoid disastrous blunders in our relations with other powers. Without such knowledge brought continuously up-to-date, it will be impossible to frame sound military and diplomatic policies to supplement and strengthen the world organization which we hope to develop into a real bulwark of international security.

AMERICA AND THE AMERICANS—AS OTHERS SEE US

By D. W. Brogan

From Introduction to *The American Character*, by D. W. Brogan. Copyright 1944 by D. W. Brogan; Alfred Knopf, New York, 1944; reproduced by permission. The author, professor of political science at Cambridge University, is one of England's leading authorities on the culture and history of the American people.

In the late summer of 1936, I arrived in Kansas City (Missouri). When I tried to buy a ticket for St. Louis at the Union Station, I was interrogated in a friendly, American fashion by the ticket clerk. "You from Europe?" "Yes." "Well, don't go back—it's going to Hell." I was more than half convinced that he was right—although I was going back. A month or so before, I had lain on the shore in Somerset [in England] on a Sunday evening and had been aroused from day-dreaming by a noise in the air and a swirl of excitement around me. Above, magnificent, serene, and ominous was a Zeppelin, moving east. It was low and clearly seen; a day before, it had been in New York; by tomorrow's dawn it would be in Frankfort. The swastika was plainly visible as it moved on, over Glastonbury where, the legend runs, Joseph of Arimathea had brought the Holy Thorn and built the first Christian church in Britain. A shadow was crossing England: women on the beach looked at their children—with a faint and how inadequate perception of what was soon to befall Bristol where they came from. How remote it all seemed in the hot sun of western Missouri, how remote it was even from me, and how much more remote from the people of Midwest America, with fifteen hundred miles each way between them and the oceans, with the huge war memorial outside the station to remind the citizens of Kansas City of their first adventure overseas and to confirm their resolution that it would be the last.

I went a day or two later to see a friend of mine who lives in a small town in Illinois. We went together to the corner drugstore to get ice cream for supper. It was a scene familiar enough to me ... the Main Street of a small American town on a Saturday night in late summer.... There was over the street and over the town that indefinable American air of happiness and ease, at least for the young. There was that general friendliness and candor....

Looking at the people ... it was hard to remember the tension of English life, the worse tension of French life. Life, it is true, was not altogether easy and agreeable for these people. Those who had definitely put youth behind them showed signs of fatigue and worry.... All that region had been badly hit by very bad times, by crop failures, by bank failures. But there was still an impression of hope, of recovery....

There was no way in which the inevitable, deplorable, maddening impact of the outside world on Illinois and on the whole Mississippi Valley could be brought home to the dwellers therein. If men and women in England in 1938 could profess to believe in "peace in our time," why should not these happy Americans believe with far more plausibility in peace in their time—for them? ...

As the shadow over Europe grew longer and darker, as the darkness was made more terrifying by the whistling with which our leaders tried to keep up their courage and ours, as the chances of peace in Europe became more and more dependent on the temptations of easy victory for Germany, and those temptations more and more controlled by the possible reaction of the American people, the problem of the American temper became more urgent. It was largely a question of time: if the American people had been prepared in 1931 to do what they were prepared to do in 1939, if they had been as ready in 1939 as they were in 1941 for the dangers of the time! But it is an endless sequence of "ifs" that it is not very profitable to follow out. What is more profitable is to try to make plain how natural, how justifiable, how given by historical conditions was the tempo of American awakening, the slow acceptance of the fact that the shadow cast over Somerset was also cast over Illinois. It took the actual shadow, repeated again and again, to awaken Somerset; Illinois had to awaken with far less help from the eye and ear.

But it was not only Illinois. All over the United States there was the same life, conditioned by the same history, by an experience in which the outside world grew more and more remote, backward, barbarous, and—so it was thought—relatively weak. On the new concrete roads, new model cars made American nomadism the expression of American civilization.... Into the great inland nodal points the trains poured. ... But only a few Canadian trains in the north, only a few Mexican trains in the south, to recall the outside world, and doing it not much more effectually than an occasional Rolls-Royce, Duesenberg or Hispano-Suiza lost among the Lincolns, Packards, Buicks, Chevrolets,

Fords. The air was getting fuller of passenger planes; the airports more numerous and more splendid. And it was as natural, though as wrong, to think of the new technique as an American invention and practically an American monopoly, as to think of Colonel Lindbergh as the first man to fly the Atlantic. . . .

Our fate, the fate of civilization in Europe, the fate of constitutional freedom in America . . . were bound up with the defeat of a self-confident, energetic, efficient, and ruthless political and military system that denie[d] our premises and dislike[d] and despise[d] our aims. . . . This was the meaning of the shadow cast over England. But that shadow was not cast in such dramatic form over America. . . .

[The power of the United States] was so easy to underestimate, and each such underestimation made war more likely. It was easy for the Japanese to underestimate it . . . it would be easy to surprise the complacent, ill-informed, and unsuspecting Americans at Pearl Harbor in 1941. . . .

It was easy for the Germans to despise the people whom Herr von Papen in 1916 had described as "those idiotic Yankees." . . . I remembered a discussion in Paris in 1939 with a very eminent White Russian diplomat, a Baltic baron by origin, who told me that his friends in the German Embassy were not in the least interested in the power of the United States. "Whatever they do will be done too late. . . ." So spoke the experts of the Third Reich. I said that I did not believe this; that I knew America well, that to awaken the national pride and anger of the American people would be the most fatal mistake of the gamblers in charge of the destiny of Germany and the peace of Europe. . . .

I remembered, too, that when the British troops . . . marched out at Yorktown in 1781 to surrender to Washington and Rochambeau, their bands played *The World Turned Upside Down*. And as in the darkening months and years, I heard the apologists for the new Danegeld preach the policy of buying Hitler off—even, if absolutely necessary, with British property—I wondered whether they, with their subservience to the new enemy of all American political religion, really cared nothing for American good will or whether, like the Germans, they thought that it was a mere matter of sentiment, that there was time enough before the American giant awoke to see that he should awake, like Gulliver in Lilliput, bound hand and foot.

But many of them, English and German, did not even think that he was a giant, that the world had really been turned upside down at Yorktown, that it was time for even the smuggest Prussian expert or English politician to learn what it meant that the United States had grown to its present stature and to its present unity. . . .

A country has the kind of army its total ethos, its institutions, resources, habits of peaceful life, make possible to it. The American army is the army of a country which is law-respecting without being law-abiding. It is the army of a country which, having lavish natural wealth provided for it and lavish artificial wealth created by its own efforts, is extravagant and wasteful. It is the army of a country in which melodramatic pessimism is often on the surface but below it is the permanent optimism of a people that has licked a more formidable enemy than Germany or Japan, primitive North America. . . . It is the army of an untidy country which has neither the time, the temperament, nor the need for economy. It is the army of a country in which great economic power is often piled up for sudden use. . . . It is the army of a country of gamblers who are more or less phlegmatic in taking and calculating their losses, but who feel with all their instincts that they can never go wrong over a reasonable period of time in refusing to sell America short.

So the American way of war is bound to be like the American way of life. It is bound to be mechanized like the American farm and kitchen (the farms and kitchens of a lazy people who want washing machines and bulldozers to do the job for them). It is the army of a nation of colossal business enterprises, often wastefully run in detail, but winning by their mere scale and by their ability to wait until that scale tells. It is the army of a country where less attention is paid than in any other society to formal dignity, either of persons or of occupations, where results count, where being a good loser is not thought nearly so important as being a winner, good or bad. It is the country where you try anything once, *especially* if it has not been tried before. It is a country that naturally infuriates the Germans with their pedantry and their pathological conception of "honor." It is a country that irritates the English with their passion for surface fidelity to tradition and good form. It is the country of such gadget-minded originals as Franklin and Ford. It is a country whose navy, fighting its first great battles in a century and a half after it could boast of Paul Jones, recovered from a great initial disaster and taught the heirs of Togo with what speed the heirs of Decatur and Farragut could back out of their corners, fighting.

The Coral Sea, Midway, these are dates for the world to remember along with the new Thermopylae of the Marines at Wake Island or the new Bloody Angle of Tarawa. It is a country—and so an army—used to long periods of incubation of great railroads and great victories. It is the army of a people that took a long time to get from the Atlantic to the Pacific and that found the French and the Spaniards and the Russians before them. But they got there and stayed. The two hundred and fifty years from Virginia to California, like the four years from Washington to Richmond, must be remembered by us —and by the Germans. That General Washington, after six years of barely holding his own, combined with the French fleet to capture a British army as easily as taking a rabbit in a snare—that is to be remembered too, for it was a matter not of fighting but of careful timing, of logistics.

That typical western soldier and adventurer, Sam Houston, waiting patiently until the Mexicans had rushed on to deliver themselves into his hands at San Jacinto—that is to be remembered. It is not Custer, foolhardy and dramatic with his long hair and his beard who is the typical Indian fighter, but great soldiers like Sherman and Sheridan planning from St. Louis or Chicago the supplying of frontier posts, the concentration of adequate force. The Indian chiefs Joseph and Rain-in-the-Face were often artists in war at least on a level with Rommel. But to the Americans war is a business, not an art; they are not interested in moral victories, but in victory. No great corporation ever successfully excused itself on moral grounds to its stockholders for being in the red; the United States is a great, a very great, corporation whose stockholders expect (with all their history to justify the expectation) that it will be in the black. Other countries, less fortunate in position and resources, more burdened with feudal and gentlemanly traditions, richer in national reverence and discipline, can and must wage war in a very different spirit.

But look again at the cast-iron soldier of the Civil War memorial [in so many American towns and cities]. A few years before, he was a civilian in an overwhelmingly civil society; a few years later he was a civilian again in a society as civilian as ever, a society in which it was possible to live for many years without ever seeing a professional soldier at all.... Such a nation cannot "get there fustest with mostest." It must wait and plan till it can get there with mostest. This recipe has never yet failed, and Berlin and Tokyo realize[d], belatedly, that it [was] not going to fail this time—that in a war of machines it is the height of imprudence to have provoked the great makers and users of machines and, in a war of passions, to have awakened, slowly but more and more effectively, the passions of a people who hitherto have fought only one war with all their strength (and that a civil war), but who can be induced by their enemies, not by their friends, to devote to the task of making the world tolerable for the United States that tenacity, ingenuity, and power of rational calculations which decided between 1861 and 1865 that there should be a United States which would twice crush the hopes of a nation of military professionals, to whom war is an art and a science, to be lovingly cultivated in peace and practiced in war....

THE AMERICAN PEOPLE

By the Royal Institute of International Affairs

From *U.S.A.*, Information Notes No. 4. The Royal Institute of International Affairs, London, 1943; reproduced by permission.

The United States has been chiefly peopled from the Old World. The first settlers on the Atlantic seaboard were predominantly English, but they were followed by emigrants from Scandinavia and Germany as well as from all parts of the British Isles, and later on, between about 1890 and 1914, by people from eastern and southern Europe. The expanding territories and growing industrialization of the United States offered attractive opportunities for a better and freer life, and between 1820 and 1938, 38 million immigrants landed in the country, a number equivalent to the present population of England and Wales. It is not, therefore, surprising that of the present white population a good deal less than half claim British descent. It was not until 1921 that any serious legal restrictions were put on the inflow of new immigrants. Since then a quota system has allowed only about 150,000 people to come in every year and the majority of these have had to be from western Europe, including Germany.

The European population of America numbers about 118 millions. To these must be added some 13 million negroes, 351,000 American Indians, and about half a million other races, including Chinese and Japanese. These last have been mostly concentrated in the Pacific states, but large numbers of Japanese (who were nearly 139,000 in the 1930 census), on account of the special risks involved, have been moved into the interior since the outbreak of war with Japan. The total population of the country, according to the 1940 census, was over 131 millions.

It cannot be too strongly emphasized that America is proud of her cosmopolitan character, that almost all immigrants have been accepted as American citizens, and that to Americans it is this citizenship that matters, not racial origins.

Any list of well-known American names would be a witness of this successful assimilation. . . .

The only exception to this assimilation—apart from local prejudices against some outstanding national groups—are the negroes. . . .

MANPOWER COMPARISONS

By the Editors

As noted above, the 1940 census yielded a total U.S. population exceeding 131 millions. In size and age distribution, this population compared with those of the other Great Powers as follows:

Total Population

U.S.A.	131,669,000
U.S.S.R.	174,000,000
Germany	69,500,000
Great Britain	50,200,000
France	41,200,000

Population 15-44 years of age

U.S.A.	64,594,000
U.S.S.R.	82,100,000
Germany	33,160,000
Great Britain	23,570,000
France	18,200,000

From the studies of the Office of Population Research at Princeton University, it seems clear that Great Britain, France, Germany, and most other countries of Western and West-Central Europe have about reached—in some instances already passed—their peak of population growth. Much the same holds for the English-speaking populations of the British Commonwealth of Nations.

Most of Southern and Eastern Europe and the Soviet Union, on the contrary, are still in an earlier stage of demographic development. Their situation is characterized by high birth-rates, declining death-rates, and consequent rapid growth in total numbers of people. But for the war, the population of the Soviet Union alone might have exceeded 250 millions by 1970. Even with heavy war losses, the increase may still amount to 40-50 millions. That would give the Soviet Union a total population greater than the expected totals for England, France, Germany, and Italy combined.

Other areas, including China, India, Southeast Asia, large parts of Africa and of Latin America, represent a still earlier phase of demographic development. In these predominantly agrarian lands, birth-rates are still higher but death-rates also remain high, with increase in total numbers consequently slow. But these peoples have enormous capacity for growth as has been dramatically illustrated in India where slight improvement in the living standard, and resultant drop in the death-rate, has produced an alarming increase in total numbers.

How do these trends abroad compare with the population outlook in the United States? What stage in the demographic process have we reached? What may we anticipate in the way of military manpower and working population ten, fifteen, twenty-five, or more years hence?

PROSPECTS FOR FUTURE GROWTH

By P. M. Hauser and Conrad Taeuber

From "The Changing Population of the United States," by P. M. Hauser and Conrad Taeuber, in *The Annals of the American Academy of Political and Social Science,* January 1945. Copyright 1945 by The Academy of Political and Social Science, Philadelphia; reproduced by permission. P. M. Hauser is assistant director of the U.S. Bureau of the Census. Conrad Taeuber is an official in the Department of Agriculture.

In the course of a century and a half the United States has developed from a

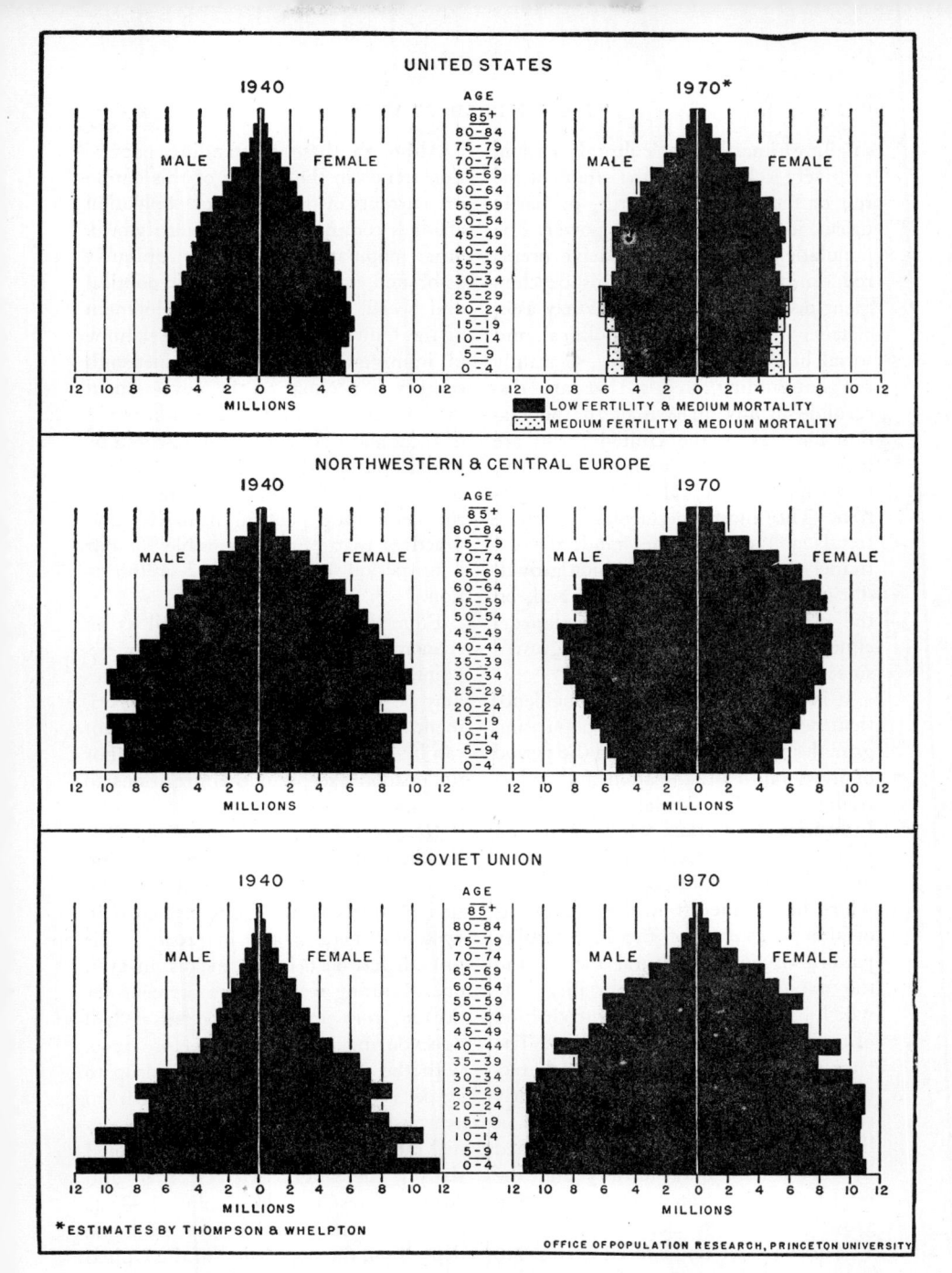

FIG. 42. Age and sex distribution of the populations of 1940 and of the projected populations of 1970, for the United States, northwestern and central Europe, and the Soviet Union (values for the United States from Thompson and Whelpton, *Estimates of Future Population of the United States, 1940-2000*, pp. 68-69 and 92-94; values for Europe and the Soviet Union from Notestein and Others, *The Future Population of Europe and the Soviet Union*, pp. 242-43, 312-13).

Reproduced from: Theodore W. Schultz, editor, *Food for the World* (Chicago, University of Chicago Press, 1945), p. 44.

small, primarily agricultural nation, relatively isolated from the affairs of the rest of the world, to a large, primarily urban, industrialized world power. The population changes which have occurred during the course of this development necessarily have been closely associated with the economic, political, and social history of the country. Certainly the outstanding trends that are discernible in any analysis of the population changes in the United States are intimately associated with the impact in this country of the Industrial Revolution. The most spectacular of these trends are, on the one hand, the extremely rapid rate of population growth during the nineteenth century and, on the other, the equally spectacular decline in the rate of population growth since the turn of the century.

It is more than historical coincidence that the period of most rapid population growth in this country is also the period of most rapid urbanization and industrialization. The initial stage of the Industrial Revolution, wherever its impact has been felt, has been characterized by a period of rapid population growth which has resulted from the joint effects of the persistence of the high-fertility pattern of an agricultural society and the rapidly declining mortality rate which has accompanied the introduction of modern sanitation and medicine. The later stages of industrialization, characterized by the presence of predominantly city populations and urban patterns of life, have inevitably been accompanied by rapidly declining fertility and the retardation of rates of population growth. These correlative phenomena, as evidenced in the United States, are part of the pattern of population trends in all of western civilization and may be regarded as integral characteristics of successive stages of industrialization.

Although these outstanding population trends in the history of this nation are currents in the stream of population changes common to the western world, other population trends are uniquely associated with peculiar historic political and social factors in the development of the United States. The large volume of immigration during the nineteenth century is peculiar to the development of the western frontier. The admixture of races and nationalities represented by the people of the United States is a unique phenomenon directly related to the democratic political principles and practices that were responsible for our long period of unrestricted immigration.

From a demographic, as well as an economic, political, and social, viewpoint, the history of the United States may be regarded as an exciting experiment. The elements of this experiment can be neither adequately described nor understood except in their relations to one another....

Growth of Total Population. One hundred and fifty years of census-taking have recorded the growth of the population of this country from 3,929,000 in 1790 to 131,669,000 in 1940. This growth has been by no means an even one. Running well over 30 per cent per decade from 1790 to 1880, as it had done during most decades before 1790, with the single exception of a drop to 23 per cent for the decade 1860 to 1870 as a result of the Civil War, the decennial rate of population increase declined sharply thereafter. Between 1930 and 1940, as a result of the combined effects of secular trend and severe economic depression, the population of the United States increased by only 7.2 per cent. This rate was less than half that shown in any previous decade and the absolute increase was smaller than any other since that of the decade of the Civil

War. Since 1940 the rate of population growth has turned upward and has averaged 1.2 per cent per year for the period April 1, 1940, to April 1, 1944, as compared with an average annual rate of population increase of 0.7 per cent for the preceding decade. This upturn in rate of population growth may be regarded as a temporary phenomenon resulting jointly from the period of boom prosperity which immediately preceded and followed the entrance of the United States into World War II and from the impetus given to marriage and fertility rates by the passage and administration of the Selective Service laws.

The effects of wartime demographic developments will be felt in the population for a long time to come. The exceptionally large number of births of recent years will make itself noticeable some fifteen to twenty years hence by a growth in the number of women entering childbearing age and the number of men entering the age groups which include the labor force and members of the armed forces. War losses, which are concentrated among men of military age, also will be reflected in the composition of the population for a long time. . . .

The slowing rate of population growth which was apparent before the war will probably continue after the war in all the western industrialized countries. On the whole, the trends of future population in the United States may be expected to be similar to those of other western countries, although actual population decline is less imminent; nor does it seem probable that in the United States the losses from the war will exceed the wartime increase in number of births. The fact that this country did not sustain heavy military losses in World War I means also that it does not have a problem like that of the "hollow age classes" in France, Germany, or England. In the United States the military losses of World War II will not be superimposed on a smaller age cohort because of a birth deficit during the First World War.

Although its effects cannot be fully evaluated at present, it appears probable that the deviations from trend lines produced by the war will be temporary. To a large extent, prospective trends are inherent in the present structure of the population. Vital rates may change from year to year, but the size and composition of the population at any given time are the composite effects of almost a century of births and deaths. With immigration and emigration at very low levels . . . every birth which occurs, on an average, means a unit in the population for approximately sixty years. The social, economic, and political conditions which prevail in the years immediately after the war obviously will have a decided effect upon the trends in fertility, and, to a lesser extent, upon the trends in mortality. Their effect upon currents of migration will be even more direct.

Projections of the future population of the United States made by Thompson and Whelpton based on assumptions of medium fertility and mortality, show a considerable decline in the rate of population growth from 1940 to 1985 and an actual decrease in the population of the United States after that date. By 1985, according to these projections, the country will have a total population of 161,385,000 persons—which by the year 2000 will have declined to 159,420,000 persons.

Components of Growth. The population of the country as a whole can grow only through net immigration and through natural increase, i.e. an excess of births over deaths. From the founding of this nation to approximately 1930, immigration constituted a fairly important source of population increment. From 1820 to 1850 the total was approximately two and a half million, with a similar number for each decade from 1850 to 1880. The number of immigrants swelled to five and a quarter million from 1880 to 1890, dropped in the following decade, and reached an all-time peak of almost 8.8 million from 1900 to 1910. Although total immigration remained at fairly high levels through 1930, constituting 5.7 million between 1910 and 1920 and 4.1 million between 1920 and 1930, it dropped rapidly after 1924 and further after 1930 as a result of the immigration quota laws and world-wide depression. Under present laws and practices immigration can no longer be regarded as a significant source of population increase in the United States.

Fertility. The rapid population increase in the United States during the nineteenth century, as has been indicated, resulted from a combination of high fertility, declining mortality, and immigration. As in the case of western civilization in general, however, the birth-rate of the United States has shown a consistent decline from the time of the earliest reliable records. For example, the birth-rate for the white population of the United States, which was estimated at 55 per 1,000 persons in 1800, had declined to 30 by 1900 and to about 18 by 1940. The birth-rate underwent a sharp decline during the depression of the 1930's and a relatively sharp rise during the period of boom prosperity immediately preceding and following the entrance of the United States into World War II.

The number of births since 1940 was large enough to have increased the present population by more than a million above the recent Thompson-Whelpton estimates (assuming medium fertility and medium mortality). The high level of the number of births is likely to be temporary, as to some extent it represents the last of the "catching up" of births which did not occur on account of the depression, and, to an even greater extent, an "advance" on births which under more normal conditions would have taken place somewhat later than they did. The fact that the major increase has been in first and second births suggests that there may be some reduction in birth rates later.

... The number of women of child-bearing age increased rapidly between 1940 and 1945, reflecting in large part the high level of births in the early 'twenties. The prospects are that there will be relative stability in the number of such women between 1945 and 1960, and that after 1960 there will be some increases which will reflect the increase in births of the early 1940's. Such a comparison, however, hides some internal changes which are of considerable significance. The prospective trends in numbers of women 20 to 29 years old, the age group which accounts for about 60 per cent of the births, do not indicate such stability. The number of women in this age group is expected to decline from 11.9 million in 1945 to 10.6 million by 1960. Such a projection involves no assumption about the course of fertility, for all the persons involved have already been born. After 1960 a temporary increase sufficient to raise the number above the level of 1945 for a few years may occur.

In addition to these considerations, two major social developments also lead to the expectation that fertility is more likely to fall below its present level than to remain there or to rise above it. The contribution of foreign-born women to the total birth-rate has been a major one in the past, for the fertility of the foreign-born in general exceeded that of the native-born. But the number of women of foreign birth in the younger childbearing ages is rapidly decreasing, with little prospect for replacement. Within this country the process of shifting population from rural areas in which fertility is high to urban areas in which fertility is low has been accelerated. In the past such a shift has usually been accompanied by a lowering of fertility among the groups affected, and it is likely that this result will follow from recent migrations. In fact, it may well be that the large-scale employment of women who have migrated from rural to urban areas may hasten the process of assimilation to urban behavior patterns in respect to fertility.

Mortality. Although only fragmentary data are available for the historical analysis of the death-rate in this country, it is clear that a huge reduction in mortality rates has been accomplished. For the state of Massachusetts, for example, the death rate was reduced from a high of 27.8 per thousand in 1789 to 11.9 in 1940, a reduction of 57.2 per cent. Most of the decline in mortality has been effected through decrease in the death-rate during the early part of life. Although the average length of life has increased considerably—for example, for white males in Massachusetts from 34.5 in 1789 to 59.3 in 1930—the life span of human beings has probably not changed much, if at all. Although large decreases in mortality of the type experienced during the last century are hardly to be expected in the decades which lie ahead, it is likely that death-rates will continue to decline. The decline will probably be greatest at the younger ages and smallest at the older ages.

Natural Increase. Throughout the history of the nation, natural increase—that is, the excess of births over deaths—has been more important by far than net immigration as a factor in population growth. The contribution of immigration to intercensal population increase was greatest in the decade 1880-1890 when it constituted 43 per cent of the total increase. For the first time in the history of the nation, it has been noted, all of the increase in population between 1930 and 1940 was the result of natural increase. Although projections show some decline in both fertility and mortality in the years which lie ahead, the former will decline more rapidly than the latter so that the rate of natural increase will also decline. Thus, it is estimated that the population of the United States will increase through natural increase by only 303,000 between 1980 and 1990, the last intercensal decade of this century which will show any natural increase (as compared with about 9,000,000 between 1930 and 1940). Between 1990 and 2000, according to these projections, there would be a natural decrease of almost 2,000,000.

Net Reproduction. A useful measure in summarizing the potential effects of the balance of current fertility and mortality rates is afforded by the net reproduction rate. This rate indicates the extent to which current age-specific fertility and mortality, if indefinitely projected, would result in population maintenance [thus, if the risks of death and the fertility of each age group remained unchanged, and if there was no migration, a rate of 150, for example, would yield an increase of 50 per cent per generation; a rate of 100 would yield a stationary population; a rate of 50, a decrease of one-half per generation; etc.]. The United States, for example, from 1905 to 1910 had a net reproduction rate of 134 which indicates that the age-specific fertility and mortality rates for that period, if continued indefinitely, would potentially result in an increase of the population at a rate of 34 per cent per generation (25 to 30 years). In contrast, from 1935 to 1940 the net reproduction rate of 98 indicates that the pattern of age-specific fertility and mortality rate for that period, if projected indefinitely, would result in the decline of the population at a rate of 2 per cent per generation. The net reproduction rate of the country as a whole has shown a consistent decline, and for the first time fell below replacement level in the period immediately preceding 1940. This reflects the effects of the depression of the 1930's as well as the long-time trend. The increase in birth-rates since 1940 has again placed the net reproduction rate of the country above the replacement level. It is doubtful, however, whether the net reproduction rate of the United States will for long remain above the level required for population maintenance.

Urban and Rural Growth. The growth and development of cities in the United States is one of the most striking population phenomena of all time. In 1790, of the twenty-four urban places in the United States, only two, New York and Philadelphia, had a population of 25,000 or more. At that time only 200,000 persons, or approximately 5 per cent of the total population, were living in urban areas. By 1920 there were 2,722 urban places in the United States containing a total of over 54 million inhabitants— more than half the population of the United States. By 1940, the 3,464 urban places in the United States comprised over 74 million people, which constituted 56.5 per cent of the total population of the country. Included in these urban places were 5 with populations of a million or more and 92 with populations of 100,000 or more.

Along with the rapid concentration of population in urban areas came a considerable shrinking in the proportion which the rural farm population constituted of the total population in the United States. In 1920 the rural farm population numbered 31 million and made up 29.7 per cent of the total population. By 1940 it had shrunk to a total of slightly over 30 million or 22.9 per cent of the population. By the end of 1944 the farm population had declined still further, to about 20 per cent of the national total. The rural nonfarm population changed from 20 million or 19.1 per cent of the population in 1920 to 27 million or 20.5 per cent in 1940.

The rate of population increase in urban areas has declined markedly since 1890. It reached an all-time low during the 1930's when, in contrast with preceding decades which witnessed rates of urban growth often six or more times as great as rates of rural growth, it barely exceeded the rural population increase (7.9 as compared with 6.4 per cent).

The interstate wartime movement of population has been accompanied by large-scale shifts of population from rural to urban areas. The movement of population from farms was larger than that recorded for any previous period of similar length. This movement, in large part, appears to represent an accentuation of former trends rather than a sharp break with the past. Under the circumstances, it is hardly to be expected that the post-war period will lead to a back-to-the-land movement of sufficient size to bring the farm population back to its 1940 level. Unless economic conditions are so unfavorable that migration from farms is drastically retarded or that large numbers of persons seek subsistence on the land, as they did immediately after 1929, it is probable that the number of persons living on farms in this country in the near future will be smaller than it has been in the recent past. The increases of agricultural productivity of the last four years, and the prospects for increased productivity in agriculture as soon as current restrictions on machinery and supplies are removed, leave little prospect that the goal of full employment will mean an increased population in agriculture. . . .

Age. As a concomitant of the declining birth-rate, the population of the United States, from decade to decade in the course of its development, has contained a larger proportion of older persons. The median age of the population in 1820 was approximately 16.7 years; by 1900 it was 22.9 years; by 1940, 29.0 years. The proportion of persons 65 years of age and over increased from 2.5 in 1840 to 6.8 per cent in 1940; whereas the proportion of persons under 20 years of age declined from 54.6 to 34.4 per cent. The changing age distribution of the population of the United States reflects the large declines in fertility and the increased average length of life.

The continued increase in the number of older persons can be projected with relative certainty, for it is unlikely that mortality will alter rapidly enough to affect appreciably the trends. According to the Thompson-Whelpton estimates the number of persons 65 and older will increase from 9 million in 1940 to 14 million by 1960, and to 18 million by 1980. The total population of working age, 20 to 64, is expected to increase from 77 million in 1940 to 90 million in 1960, and a larger proportion of those persons will be at the more advanced ages in 1960 than in 1940. The number of persons 45 to 64 years is expected to increase from 26 million in 1940 to 34 million by 1960, and to 40 million by 1975. In contrast, the number of persons 20 to 44 years of age is expected to increase only from 51 million in 1940 to 57 million in 1975. . . .

U.S. in Relation to World Population.
The prospect is that the population of the United States will have reached relative stability or actual decline before the end of this century. In that respect the situation in this country is similar to that of the other economically advanced industrial and urbanized nations, including Europe (except for the eastern and southern parts), Canada, Australia, New Zealand, and the white population of the Union of South Africa. Altogether, these nations include somewhat less than one-fifth of the world's population. Another fifth of the world's population is included in those parts of the world in which the transition to an industrial and urban economy, and therefore to a low-fertility pattern, has not gone so far. This group includes the Soviet Union, Japan, Eastern and Southern Europe, and parts of Latin America. Relative population stability or actual decline in these countries is likely to come somewhat later than in the other group, but developments to date suggest that such an occurrence is only a matter of time. In both groups of countries there are some in which wartime losses may be so great that in the present generation their populations will not exceed the 1939 level.

In striking contrast to these areas of the world are the great agrarian regions of Asia and Africa, where fertility rates have dropped less rapidly than mortality rates. Western penetration in these countries has meant relative political stability, the improvement of agricultural techniques, and minimum standards of epidemic control and famine relief. Diffusion of the standards and values that might limit fertility has been relatively slow, but it is reasonable to expect that as industrialization and urbanization do expand, these areas also will exhibit the slowing down of population growth which has characterized those parts of the world in which modern industrial development has proceeded farthest.

In the first hundred years of its development as an independent nation the United States underwent a remarkably rapid growth. This followed from its own high fertility and the population overflows of western European countries which were simultaneously experiencing high fertility for the same reason—the lag between the decline in mortality and fertility which accompanies the first impact of the Industrial Revolution.

During the first quarter of the twentieth century the United States became a world power and now represents the most powerful combination of population mass, industrial potential, and military might in Western and also in world history. In the years which lie ahead it is possible that the relative position of the United States from the standpoint of the demography of the world will become increasingly less important. Certainly the continuing rapid rate of increase of the already large population masses of the Orient will necessarily make the population of the United States a smaller and smaller proportion of the total population of the world. Whether this fact, together with the increasing industrialization of the rest of the world, will affect the position of the United States as a world power in international economic and political affairs is a matter for speculation that only the future can tell.

NATURE'S GIFTS TO THE UNITED STATES

By Derwent Whittlesey and J. K. Wright

From chap. 7 of *Geographical Foundations of National Power*. Army Service Forces Manual M-103-2. Government Printing Office, Washington, 1944. Dr. Whittlesey is professor of geography at Harvard University. Dr. Wright is director of the American Geographical Society.

Though not an island, the United States is, in effect, geographically the most isolated of the Great Powers. Wide oceans guard its shores against attack from Europe or Asia. Not since the War of 1812 has it been invaded from the sea. Recently, however, the degree of protection afforded by the sea has been progressively diminishing with the widening range and increasing speed of naval action and with the rise of air power.

The United States is virtually immune to invasion by land except in the improbable event that one or both of its neighbors, Canada or Mexico, were first to become the prey of an enemy from overseas—an event that the United States would make every effort to forestall. Canada and Mexico, because of the enormous disproportion in strength between either of them and the United States, cannot be considered potential threats to the United States. . . .

In mere extent of area the United States with its possessions stands far below both the British Empire and Soviet Russia. It is only three-fourths as large as the French or Chinese empires, and not much larger than Brazil. The "coreland" of each of these empires may be defined as the territory of relatively dense population on which the predominant people have established themselves. The whole continental United States, exclusive of Alaska, may reasonably be considered the nation's "coreland." This is very nearly equal in area to the coreland of Russia or China and is enormously larger than that of any of the other Great Powers. . . .

From the military point of view, large size and compact shape give the United States the advantage of great depth.

Every major climate of Europe, except that of the tundra belt of the far north, has a counterpart in the United States. To these the United States adds climates of types not represented in Europe, notably that of the deserts of the southwest interior and the continental climate of the east coast which, with its cool to cold winters and hot, humid summers, is comparable to the climate of coastal China. The early British and Irish settlers had to adapt themselves to environmental conditions that differed substantially from those of the home country, and it was not until the tide of settlement finally reached the northwest coast that a climate was found which essentially duplicates that of the British Isles. Subsequently, immigrants from Northern, Central, and Southern Europe could all settle, if they wished, in regions where the climate would remind them of the lands whence they came, and to some extent those who have made their homes in the rural districts have sought out such regions (e.g. Scandinavians in the northern Middle West, Germans somewhat farther south, Finns in New England, etc.).

Although much land in the United States, as in all large countries, is relatively unproductive and sparsely settled, no other Great Power has so generally favorable a natural environment. The position and range in latitude of the country are such as to assure an immense variety of crops, livestock, and forest products. China is the only other middle-latitude nation whose boundaries reach both farther north and farther south, but it is doubtful whether China is thereby more favored by its climate. Soviet Russia also covers a wider range of latitude, but as a whole lies so far north that its variety of agricultural products is more limited than that of the United States.

The Middle Western United States is one of three large regions on the earth that possess first-quality soil combined with a climate which makes for high yields, the others being southern Russia and Argentina. Only a few parts of the country are handicapped by really infertile soil. Nowhere, except on high mountains, do low temperatures preclude the raising of crops. Most of the nation's wastelands are deserts because of deficient rainfall rather than poor soil.

A comparison with other countries may be useful. Among the least fertile soils, largely unfarmed, are some similar in origin and character to those of the best part of Finland. Sandy soils on the Atlantic and Gulf coastal plains are about as productive as similar soils in Denmark and Germany, allowing for differences of climate. The more favorable soils of the South are at least as good as the best soils in India. California is much like Mediterranean Europe. The soils of New England and the Middle Atlantic States are similar to those of northwestern Europe. This basic reservoir of virgin fertility has unfortunately, in common with many other resources, suffered seriously under a system of wasteful exploitation which has looked to the gain of the moment, disregarding the fact that irreplaceable capital was thus being destroyed. Agricultural experts have declared that the very basis of the United States' civilization rests on 8 inches of topsoil. Erosion through improper farming methods and wholesale deforestation are estimated to have removed on the average, one-quarter of that thin layer. Present efforts are beginning to stop such waste.

The mineral wealth of the United

States is immense and varied. No other Great Power except perhaps Soviet Russia has nearly so great an abundance of basic mineral materials immediately available within its own borders. In the production of coal, the United States ranks first, with 25 to 30 per cent of the world total, closely followed by Germany, the United Kingdom, and Soviet Russia. In the production of petroleum, the United States leads by a wide margin, with more than half of the world total, followed by Russia. In the production of iron ore the United States shares first place with France, and in the production of copper it shares first place with Chile. In the future, the potential mineral wealth of Soviet Russia may prove comparable in richness, but at the present time much of this is undeveloped.

Thus the United States is, in almost every respect, well endowed with the products of field, forest, and subsoil. It could produce nearly all the crops and livestock needed for military purposes, and it has a generous share of most of the minerals that a modern state requires in large quantities. Nevertheless, our mineral deficiencies, both for peace and war, are such as to warrant concern. In the [late] war the large measure of sea and air control maintained by the United Nations has softened the impact of such deficiencies. With the sea lanes and most major oversea sources of supply open, our **military power potential is enormous**. . . .

MINERAL RESERVES

By C. K. Leith

From chaps. 3 and 10 of *World Minerals and World Peace*, by C. K. Leith *et al*. Copyright 1943 by The Brookings Institution, Washington; reproduced by permission. Dr. Leith is professor of geology at the University of Wisconsin.

DOMESTIC reserves of high-grade iron ore, natural gas, and petroleum, supplemented by hydroelectric power, are ample to meet demand for possibly a quarter of a century. Coal and beneficiated iron ore reserves will have a much longer life. These elements, as it is well known, constitute the foundation on which large-scale industry is built. Domestic production of copper, lead, and zinc is adequate except under war conditions, but reserves are in sight for only two or three decades. The country's resources of potash, phosphates, and artificial nitrates are sufficient to last for centuries, and thus ensure future ability to replace these elements in soils that would otherwise become impoverished from intensive use for food crops. The United States has the world's largest resources in sulphur. However, for certain minerals, such as long-fiber asbestos, dielectric mica, manganese, nickel, cobalt, chromium, diamonds, and quartz crystal, the country is dependent upon foreign sources. . . .

The glaring shortage of some of the key minerals of industry, brought to light during World War I, was soon forgotten, and once again the United States reverted to its former placid assurance that all necessary supplies could be secured through international trade.

A notable exception to this policy was the domestic development of potash. The methods pursued by the government in the mining, production, and in part the marketing of the potash obtained from the polyhalites of the Carlsbad district of New Mexico, have made the United States self-sufficient for this valuable salt. The government has also developed and kept control of the production of helium.

As a result of the trying experiences of World War I, Mr. [Bernard] Baruch, in his report of December 24, 1919, to the President, urged that steps be taken at once to accumulate adequate stockpiles of raw materials for future emergency. In the 20 years that followed, the same program was vigorously urged on Congress by many individuals and agencies, public and private, including the Secretaries of War and Navy, many members of Congress, the Bureau of Mines, the Planning Committee for Mineral Policy appointed by President Roosevelt, the American Institute of Mining and Metallurgical Engineers, the Mining and Metallurgical Society of America, and many others. It was not until 1938, however, that the first small appropriation was made by Congress. In fact, when our war effort seriously started in June 1940, less than 5 per cent of the materials then known to be needed had been accumulated. The percentage is far smaller when measured against the vastly expanded program which has been adopted since that time.

The long delay of Congress in starting this program, in spite of the patriotic efforts of some of its members, was due in part to apathy and lack of realization of the problem. In part, it must be said, it was due also to the belief in some quarters that the money should be spent in developing resources at home rather than in foreign purchases. In view of the remarkable record of the United States in developing minerals in the past, it is not surprising that many people should have expected this success to extend in time through the entire mineral field. This feeling was epitomized in the common saying that it does not pay to sell the United States short.

Because of the failure to prepare in advance it [became] necessary to allocate the limited supplies available, to restrict civilian consumption, to require the use of substitutes, to conserve by technological changes in manufacture and consumption, to develop at high cost all possible domestic sources of low-grade supplies, to devise new processes for the beneficiation and use of these supplies, and above all to use shipping badly needed for military purposes. All of these steps were anticipated and warned against, but to no avail. Our accumulation of the necessary stocks to fight a war started too late. While the aggregate weight of metal available to the United States . . . in the long run, greatly exceed[ed] the limited supplies accumulated by the Axis powers, we . . . lost the advantage of bringing our superior weight to bear at the outset.

INTEGRATION OF AMERICAN RESOURCES

By the National Resources Committee

From chap. 3 of *The Structure of the American Economy*. National Resources Committee, Government Printing Office, Washington, 1939.

The most concrete resources of the nation are its natural resources—soil and minerals, forests and streams. Equally concrete is the plant developed by men—the homes and factories, dams and powerhouses, machinery and equipment, farm improvements and irrigated areas—all the man-made physical improvements. These natural resources and man-made improvements provide the physical resources available for further production and contribute to the structure of the American economy. . . .

Of greater significance as a resource is the manpower of the nation. Without the skills and the activity of men and women, physical resources would be of no avail. Skilled farmers and workers, skilled craftsmen and technicians, skilled scientists, businessmen, politicians, artists, and homemakers—these and other productive workers constitute the nation's greatest resource. The characteristics of the available manpower make up an element in the structure of the whole economy.

In addition to the natural resources, plant, and manpower ... there are other types of resources which condition the process of production even though they are not themselves consumed. These resources are (1) the climate and topography which condition the physical environment of production, (2) the techniques of production, developed in the past, upon which current activity rests, and (3) the social institutions which provide the social framework without which organized production could not take place....

Natural Resources. As compared with other nations, the United States is richly supplied with cropland, forest, the basic mineral resources necessary for peacetime activity, and the strategic minerals upon which war industries depend. The soil and climate of the United States will permit the production of all of the major crops with the exception of such tropical products as rubber, tea, and coffee. Most of the industrially important minerals are available in the continental United States. Power is available in great quantities direct from the rivers and streams and generated from ample supplies of fuel. Since the country is waterbound on both the east and west, the resources of both oceans are available. Codfish of the East and salmon of the West as well as the other fisheries from oceans and lakes provide a significant food resource. In natural resources, the country is indeed rich....

Productive Plant. Of secondary importance for longer periods, but of great importance for shorter periods, is the productive plant which men have developed. In the course of the centuries during which the continent has been inhabited, productive instruments for making use of natural resources have been developed and now exist in the form of the buildings, equipment, and improvements. This productive plant includes that employed in all the branches of economic activity, in agriculture, mining, manufacturing, trade, construction, government, the service industries, and residential housing.

The total value of this plant in 1935 was something like 190 billion dollars....

The structural significance of the productive plant as a resource is primarily a short-run matter of location and of industrial mobility. Man-made plant differs from natural resources in not being fixed and located by nature. A new plant can be built; a new mineral deposit can only be found. Plant location thus does not constitute the same fixed element in the structure of the economy as does the location of natural resources. At the same time, existing plant, until it becomes obsolete or wears out, is like a fixed natural resource except to the extent that it can be dismantled and in part removed to a new location as some textile mills were moved from New England to the South. Thus, the national plant can be thought of as capable of a gradual change in location as particular buildings and equipment wear out or become obsolete and are replaced by new buildings and equipment in new locations, and as equipment is occasionally transferred from one region to another.

Existing plant represents an element of relative fixity in relation to type of industrial activity as well as of place. Many buildings and even some equipment may be put to various uses. But insofar as buildings and equipment are specialized, like a railway locomotive or a knitting frame, they give direction to activity until they are abandoned or replaced by plant designed for other uses.

The possible speed of this slow mobility of plant is suggested by the rate at which new plant and equipment is built. In the period since 1919 new plant was built at a rate to duplicate the value of the total existing plant in approximately 15 years. . . .

The secondary importance of the existing plant can be seen by comparing its value with the annual production of the country. In 1929 and again in 1937 the national production amounted to approximately 66 billions of 1935 dollars. Since the productive plant amounted in 1935 to approximately 190 billion dollars the plant is only equal to the value of approximately three years of production at the levels of those years. If residential housing and government plant be excepted the value of the total agricultural and industrial plant would be equal to less than 2 years' production at that level. If the whole waste of the depression due to idle men and idle machines could have been used to build agricultural and industrial plant, the existing plant could have been completely rebuilt. Thus, in comparison with annual production or with the wastes of depression, existing plant is not of dominant long-run importance. It is mainly important for the structure of the economy as its character and location condition the structure of production in the immediate future.

Manpower. Manpower is by far the most important resource of the nation and the resource likely to involve the largest waste. The millions of individual workers constitute the backbone of production, and their activity as skilled and unskilled workers, managers, artisans, farmers, teachers, doctors, or independent businessmen, provides the primary basis for the nation's standard of living. Correspondingly, if available workers are idle, production and level of living are lower than resources make possible. Manpower, potential work, is a perishable resource like waterpower. Ten or fifteen million idle workers combined with idle machines can mean a tremendous loss in potential national income. In addition, the failure to use available manpower reduces the effectiveness of future production as idleness breeds frustration and loss of skills. The magnitude of losses from waste of manpower throw the wastes in the exploitation of natural resources into insignificance.

Just what constitutes the nation's available manpower is a question which cannot be easily answered. Much of the productive activity of the country is carried on within the homes as the housewife prepares meals, keeps house, nurses children, launders clothes, and carries on the numerous home activities. Yet the available statistics are geared to throw light only on manpower available for gainful activity, i.e. activity aimed to bring in money income. From the point of view of the structure of the whole economy this part of the total manpower is undoubtedly the more significant in that the organizational structure concerns primarily the relations among these gainfully employed.

An approximate idea of the manpower available for gainful employment can be obtained from the census of occupations. As of April 1, 1930, the date of the most recent occupational census, 48,829,920 persons, or 39.8 per cent of the population reported themselves as "gainfully occupied." This figure includes not only wage and salaried workers but business and professional workers, farmers and unpaid family workers on farms. It includes people who were temporarily unemployed but does not include persons who were seeking employment but had not yet held a job. It probably includes some persons who had retired but might be induced to take gainful employment if conditions made such employment desirable. Very probably it includes many persons who were unwilling to report that they had no gainful occupation. The figures for gainfully occupied taken from the occupational census can only give an indication of the magnitude of the available manpower and its characteristics and should not be regarded as precise. . . .

Nonconsumable Resources. With these three resources which are consumed in the process of satisfying wants—natural resources, plant, and manpower—there must also be considered the three great resources which condition production without being consumed in the process—physical environment, technology and social institutions.

Physical Environment. Physical environment as a resource conditioning production requires little discussion. The varying and on the whole favorable climate of the United States is in a very real sense one of its richest resources, with temperatures ranging from those necessary for the growing of cotton and citrus fruit to those suitable for spring wheat and fur-bearing animals, and a rainfall ranging from desert dryness to the heavy rainfall of the Pacific Northwest and the Atlantic Coast. The topography of the country, too, is on the whole favorable. Open land without insurmountable mountain ranges, open sea fronts with plentiful harbors, great lakes, and navigable streams provide a setting for the productive activity of the country's 50 million workers.

Technology. The second great resource conditioning production is the existing technology—the knowledge of ways to apply manpower to physical resources for meeting human wants. Modern technology is the product of centuries of trial and error, of selection and adaptation. Each effective technique, whether physical or social is a tried and effective way of doing something, of acting to attain a given end, of getting from here to there. As such, it is a resource no less than the physical materials to which it is applied and the human skill and energy which apply it. Personal skill alone does not ensure productivity. Often unskilled use of the best technique is more productive than skilled use of an obsolete technique. Unskilled but intelligent use of a steam shovel can be more productive than the most skilled use of pick and shovel. Understanding of the best known way of doing things can make the difference between a high and a low level of living. The Indians on this continent had much the same natural resources as exist today and had great personal skills, but they did not have modern techniques.

By its very nature technology is a resource which cannot be measured. Whether a new technique is the result of the inventor's imagination or the recognition of a fortunate chance event, the time between the initial step and the adoption of a method as a common practice may be a matter of generations. At any given time, knowledge and skills, and their implementation in different fields, is at all stages from imagination of recognition to routine practice. It may be possible to trace for any particular technique the steps from the mind of the inventor or discoverer on. It is also possible to recognize, in the place held by science and the energy devoted to research, conditions favorable to the further development of techniques. But it is not possible to reduce to a common measure and express in meaningful terms the total technological resource of the country at a given time.

Yet modern technology is at the very heart of the basic economic problem of the day. Mass production, rapid transportation and communication, improved techniques of management, and mass financing are as characteristically modern as the automobile, the radio, and the talking movie. Both reflect modern techniques and typify modern production.

Social Institutions. Social institutions are a resource to which people are so accustomed that they seldom think of them in this light and often are unconscious even of their existence. Yet almost every productive act is conditioned by a complex of social institutions which have developed in the past. Without this complex of social institutions social living would be almost impossible.

In this discussion an attempt has been made to bring into focus the resources of the nation. We have ample natural resources with no significant limitation except that involving tropical products; extensive plant, but plant which could be rapidly replaced if occasion arose; a labor force of over 50 million persons with varied skills and aptitudes only partly employed [in normal times]; an equable climate; effective techniques of production; and a complex of social institutions which bind the whole population into a functioning economy. . . .

UNITED STATES NATURAL RESOURCES AND ECONOMIC DEVELOPMENT

By The Royal Institute of International Affairs

From *The U.S.A.*, Information Notes No. 4. The Royal Institute of International Affairs, London, 1943; reproduced by permission.

The United States has tremendous actual and potential economic strength. It is difficult to make a comparison of the strength of different nations, but if national income, or, in other words, the sum total of goods and services actually produced, is taken as a measure, the United States is by far the largest and richest economic unit in the world. In the period 1925-1934, which includes years both of world prosperity and depression, the average sum total of goods and services produced (if valued at the same prices for different nations) was far greater for the United States than for any other single country; three times as great as that for the United Kingdom, and slightly greater than for the whole of continental Europe. Further, if the national income is divided among all occupied persons, including wage earners, salaried workers, business and professional men, etc., and even unemployed, it can be shown that on an average they are the richest in the world. Although in certain classes there is considerable poverty and the years of depression brought much unemployment, the standard of living is in general higher than in any other country and the excess of income above that required for subsistence correspondingly greater. This means that America has a great potential economic reserve, for the resources normally devoted to the production of many luxuries can be released and transferred to meet exceptional demands as, for instance, war production.

The great wealth of the United

States was at first built up mainly on the production and export of vast quantities of basic agricultural products such as grains and cotton. Although the riches gained, together with the wealth of her mineral resources, led to immense industrial and commercial development within the country, so that agriculture now provides a much smaller proportion of total wealth, yet the fact that, in spite of the growth of population, the United States is still largely self-sufficient in food supplies and agricultural raw materials, adds greatly to her strength. While the United Kingdom has to import large quantities of foodstuffs and agricultural raw materials, the United States lacks little except such tropical products as coffee, tea, cane sugar, and rubber. Of certain agricultural products, including cotton, wheat, maize, tobacco, pork, and fruit, she normally has a considerable export surplus. Apart from pulp for paper-making, a most essential import, which she gets from Canada and Newfoundland, she is practically self-supporting in forestry products.

The known mineral resources of the United States are very great, and she possesses nearly all the more important minerals in large quantities. With only about 7 per cent of the world's population and area, she produced in 1937 the following proportions of world mineral supplies: over 60 per cent of petroleum, nearly 40 per cent of iron ore and copper, well over 30 per cent of coal, as well as very large supplies of lead, zinc, aluminum, sulphur, and potash. Before the war, her only important gaps in metals were: nickel (which she obtains from Canada), tin, mercury, and some of the steel alloys—manganese, chromium, antimony, and tungsten.

Although the American mines produce such a high proportion of world supplies, output is very largely consumed internally by the great domestic industries. Apart from having very large resources of coal and petroleum for fuel requirement, the United States uses, and she is the only country that does so extensively, natural gas (a by-product of petroleum), which is piped hundreds of miles to large urban industrial centers. As regards waterpower, in addition to the famous Niagara plant, within recent years many new dams have been constructed to tap the waterpower of the great rivers; such as the great Boulder Dam on the Colorado and the dams on the Tennessee and Columbia rivers.

The wide variety of United States resources inevitably diminishes the relative importance of imports as an item in the national income, as compared with smaller countries. Nevertheless that very success which has been attained in utilizing these resources itself makes foreign trade more important for the United States than a formal statistical statement might at first sight suggest. Some of the items which must be purchased from abroad are essential elements for a highly industrialized economy, and any serious decline in exports also tends to have repercussions extending far beyond the industry immediately affected.

The most significant fact about American manufacturing industry was its high productivity per head of persons employed. The number of persons employed before the war was only about twice the number in Great Britain, but total output was several times greater. For example, in coal-mining, steel, tin-plate, and flour production the American workman normally produced four times as much as the British. The chief reason for the superior efficiency is the greater amount of machinery and power which the American workman has at his disposal; he has more machines, more mechanical power than the average laborer in any other country. The horsepower [of mechanical energy] per worker before the war was about twice what it was in Great Britain.

The second factor in productivity, distinct from though not unrelated to the first, is the large scale of American production. The internal market of the United States is enormous. The federal government is entrusted with the regulation of inter-state commerce, and individual states are forbidden to impose tariffs on it, so that the whole combination of states together form the greatest free-trade unit in the world. This means that extensive division of labor is possible for each region and each state, and each plant can specialize in the production of goods which it is best suited to make, and commodities can be manufactured on mass-production scale with great economies in the use of machinery and mechanical power. The most striking example of the development of mass-production is the motor-car industry, in which between 1914 and 1929 production increased per man-hour between 200 and 300 per cent, but even in other industries there were increases of from 30 to 150 per cent. With the high standard of living the level of consumption is also high, and the United States consumes per head more of such goods as rolling-stock, motor cars, bathtubs, silk stockings, razor blades, etc., than any other economic unit in the world. The Americans actually own some 90 per cent of the world's bathtubs, and 75 per cent of the world's private motor cars; not less than one person in five owns a high-powered car.

Another factor responsible for the lead in productivity of American industry is continuous advance in technique. Expenditure, even before the war, on industrial research was about £50 million per annum, some forty times as great as the annual budget of all the colleges of the University of Oxford. Great technical advances have resulted, and spectacular accomplishments have been made in the use of by-products and the development of new industries.

Steel has for long been the giant of American industry and production. The capacity of the American steel industry is nearly as great as that of all the rest of the world. The construction industry did not, in peacetime, enjoy the same economies of large-scale production as some other industries, but it had already solved the problem of speed, and large factories and buildings can be completed within a few months after plans have been drawn.

Transport facilities in the United States are very well developed. The railways were subsidized in early times by grants and loans from the federal government, which has also spent huge sums on the improvement of through highways and on air transport. Great advantages are derived from the facilities available for the transport of heavy goods at cheap rates by waterways including the intercoastal routes between east and west through the Panama Canal. It is a striking fact that on the Great Lakes more tonnage passes through Sault Ste. Marie annually than through both the Panama and Suez Canals. By the waterways of the Mississippi, goods, including cotton, can be carried down to the southern coast at New Orleans.

Although the industrial war strength of a country is greatly dependent on the time available for preparation, in the long run war potential is very nearly related to general economic strength, in which the United States is so powerful. The difficulties of transferring from a peacetime to a maximum war economy are, however, very great, especially for a country like the United States that normally produces few armaments except military airplanes. Even though she is so well provided with basic raw materials, it was inevitable that shortages should occur owing to the phenomenal demands for war industries, and that skilled manpower should also be in short supply. The United States has nevertheless turned over to a very high level of war production with astonishing speed.

STEEL AS A YARDSTICK OF AMERICAN STRENGTH

By the Editors

STEEL is only one of the components of national strength. But in this machine age it is one of the crucial components. Steel is the basis of the automotive, railroad, and shipbuilding industries. Steel enters into the aircraft industry at innumerable points. Without abundant steel, we could never have licked the transportation—logistics—problem upon which our whole war effort depended. Steel also is a vital component of guns, shells, bombs, and countless other munitions. Steel production is not synonymous with military power. But without steel there can be no modern military power.

We have waged war on several distant and widely separated fronts at the end of supply lines thousands of miles long. We have steadily increased our cargo carrying marine in the face of staggering losses from enemy submarine and air attack. We have provided immense quantities of military equipment for our allies while meeting the astronomical requirements of our own highly mechanized land, sea, and air forces.

No other country today has a steel industry that could duplicate this achievement of the American steel industry. How was this achievement possible? Could it be repeated in the future? Answers to these questions are vital to an understanding of American strength today and in the years to come.

AMERICAN STEEL: TODAY AND TOMORROW

By the Editors of "Fortune"

From "Steel: Report on the War Years," in *Fortune*, May 1945. Copyright 1945 by Time Inc.; reproduced by permission.

No one can say when the war began for steel. But if, arbitrarily, the date be set at January 1, 1940, four months after Germany marched on Poland and five months before the fall of France, the American steel industry between then and [1945] produced 414,000,000 ingot tons of steel. That is more steel than was made in the preceding ten years, and about as much as was produced in the rest of the world by enemy and ally together during the war years.

The steel industry is remarkable both for its expansion and for its lack of expansion during the war years. The 400,000,000 tons, to use round numbers, could have been made in the open hearths, Bessemers, and electric furnaces that existed before the war. On January 1, 1940, the industry had a rated annual capacity of 81,619,000 tons. Multiply that by five and there it is, and in fact most of the 400,000,000 did come from American pre-war plant. Steel increased its output by tapping its traditional over-capacity. The steel industry with which the U.S. went to war was a pyramid that for half a century had been forced to outgrow a growing nation.

In the 1930's the nation's industrial growth was interrupted, but special circumstances combined . . . to add 9,000,000 tons of steel capacity even during this unprosperous decade. . . .

If some of the war steel was a dividend from the past misfortunes of the industry, more of it was the result of its greatest good fortune. That is the Lake Superior ore region, where the greatest good luck of all is the Mesabi Range. More steel might have been produced without more plant but it could not have been produced without more ore. More ore could not have been had from underground mines except at near-prohibitive costs in time, materials, and manpower. In the open pits of the Mesabi, it took only more power shovels, trucks, and conveyors, and longer hours—and twenty-two more ore carriers to ride the ore down the lakes. Eighty-five per cent of the iron ore for the 400,000,000 tons came from the Lake Superior iron ranges; of this, Mesabi alone supplied 75 per cent.

Expansion. Since the beginning of 1940 magnesium plant has been expanded almost ninety-fold. Aluminum capacity has been increased 600 per cent. Steel capacity has been increased only 17 per cent. Without any increase in capacity the U.S. could all but outproduce the world. But the increase— the 17 per cent—amounts to 14,000,000 ingot tons. Fourteen million tons of steel capacity is enough to make any country a major industrial power. It is twice as much plant as the Japanese Empire ever reported it had, and at least 2,000,000 tons more than it actually had. It is more than France had when the Germans crossed the Meuse. It is nearly as much steel as England had of its own to fight the war, and probably as much as Russia kept out of German hands. And it is nearly a third as much as Germany deemed necessary to subdue the Western world. . . .

Most of the new capacity was built by Big Steel [U.S. Steel] and the big companies that are called Little Steel. Most of it was scrambled—that is to say, it was built alongside older facilities, often where new open hearths or electric furnaces would balance up existing finishing capacity or new blast furnaces would serve existing steel capacity. The industry argued that only by building in this way could production be obtained quickly. To the scrambled expansion there have been two spectacular exceptions. One is $200 million Geneva Steel near Utah Lake, perhaps the finest steel mill in the world, fully integrated and owned by the U.S. government, though operated by U.S. Steel. The other is Kaiser's Fontana plant in the orchards outside of Los Angeles. . . .

Because of the scrambled pattern of expansion, war changed the geography of steel production but slightly. In 1939 almost exactly 40 per cent of the steel was made in Pittsburgh and Youngstown and the grimy valleys around and between. In 1944 the old steel towns made 37,000,000 of the 90,000,000 ingot tons produced. The Chicago steel mills, which means those of Gary, Indiana Harbor, South Chicago, and East Chicago, were second last year as they were in 1939; of the 90,000,000 total, they made 20,000,000. The eastern mills—primarily those of Bethlehem in eastern Pennsylvania and at Sparrows Point, Maryland—were a close third, with 18,000,000 tons. They were also third in 1939. The Detroit and Cleveland area (with 7,400,000 tons) was fourth as it was before. The South, which is primarily Birmingham, made 4,100,000 tons. Colorado Fuel & Iron, Columbia Steel, and the other western mills made 1,300,000 tons in 1939; Geneva and Fontana boosted the total to 3,600,000 tons last year. In no other area was the relative increase so great, and had the West Coast plants operated at capacity throughout the year, western production would have been 5,000,000 tons. That is a respectable steel industry but the West as a steel producer is still no Pittsburgh, no Gary.

Distribution. The 400,000,000 ingot tons of wartime steel made about 300,000,000 tons of finished steel in the five years beginning with 1940. . . .

More than 40,000,000 tons have gone into construction—into plane factories, shipyards, and into the new steel plants themselves. Construction demands reached a peak of 10,700,000 tons in 1942. In 1944 construction requirements dropped to 6,200,000 tons, little more than 1939.

Almost 40,000,000 tons have been used in shipbuilding to give the U.S. a merchant and tanker fleet of 46,000,000 deadweight tons and a Navy of 12,000,000 "lightship" displacement tons—each bigger than the merchant fleets and navies of all the rest of the world combined.

Exports have taken almost the same amount—a little less than 40,000,000 tons. . . . Just as the elder Pitt once supplied his continental allies with gold, the U.S. has supplied its allies with steel. Nearly all has gone on lend-lease to Britain and Russia, and the total does not include the ships, tanks, trucks, jeeps, and airplanes that have gone to allies as finished products.

The aircraft and automotive industries used a little over 30,000,000 tons, the aircraft industry, which used negligible quantities in 1940, used 7.5 per cent of the supply in 1944.

Railroads got 26,000,000 tons. Contrary to the popular impression that they had little steel, they obtained about 50 per cent more steel in 1944 than in 1940. The container industry, despite rationing, used 20,000,000 tons of steel, the farm-machinery industry 8,500,000 tons.

The above classifications . . . used more than two-thirds of all the finished steel produced during the five war years. What remained went for machine tools, oil, gas, and mining, for Big Inch and Little Big Inch [oil pipelines], for shell cases and bombs, and for all the thousands of other things, down to razor blades and bobby pins, that are made of steel. . . .

Mesabi. However else steel is changed by the war, there will remain one embarrassment of poverty and one of riches. The legacy of poverty will be in ore. The simple fact is that Mesabi's high-grade, easily mined ore is playing out and the unprecedented demands of war have hastened its exhaustion. About 1,000,000,000 tons of Mesabi's highgrade ore remain, but war has been using 85,000,000 tons a year. In 1942 E. W. Davis, who is director of the University of Minnesota Mines Experiment Station, reported to the War Production Board that, depending on the rate of wartime depletion, the highgrade ore would be gone between 1950 and 1954. Competent critics of Professor Davis' report believe that it underestimates the remaining ore supply. Gano Dunn, though never a man to expect the worst, told the Minnesota Resources Commission this year that the known "merchantable" ore in Minnesota would last at least for another sixteen years at the 1944 rate of production. One fact, however, is clear. After sixty years, . . . the end of Mesabi's rich and famous ore is in sight.

There is little chance of finding important new deposits of high-grade ore in the U.S. or even in North America. Steep Rock in Canada, an excellent deposit uncovered by draining a lake, is not greatly in excess of Canada's potential needs.

The alternative to Mesabi is not a shutdown. Ore can be imported, as it has been for Sparrows Point. Good though less plentiful domestic reserves remain, such as those of upstate New York. But Mesabi's real alternative is low-grade U.S. ore, of which there is an unlimited supply. The steel industry is already searching for methods of using low-grade ores at reasonable cost. About 40 per cent of the Lake Superior ores are already being processed to some extent before shipping. The Corporation, which owns 82 per cent of the best of the open-pit ore, plans as soon as the war is over to open a forty-man laboratory at Duluth to experiment with beneficiation of the ores that abound nearby. By refining them in part near the mine it hopes to avoid transporting useless slag. Meanwhile the question is being asked: should Mesabi be allowed to run out? In an emergency its high-grade, accessible ores would be invaluable. The Truman Committee `... recommended that what remains of Mesabi's best ores after the war be set aside as a national reserve. Some steelmen have urged that at least 300,000,000 tons, enough for three years at the present rate of production, be kept in the bank. After the war ends this decision cannot be delayed very long.

Future. Steel's embarrassment of riches will be in capacity. When the war ends there will be about as much steel capacity in the U.S. as in all the rest of the world, and about one-third more than in 1929. Probably 10 per cent of the end-of-war capacity will be retired as obsolete. More will remain than the industry expects to use. The Iron and Steel Institute, adding peak prewar demands by nineteen leading steel customers ... has concluded that the best demand ever would use only two-thirds of present production.

A little can be done to promote the use of steel but not much. After the war there will be far better steels; there may be colored, corrosion-proof steels that will make the use of paint on automobiles unnecessary. There has even been talk of steel stockings, enough talk anyway to impress a sceptical public with the fineness of some of the new stainless-steel wires. But in one sense the future of steel is clear:... If business is good, steel's business will be very, very good, and if business is bad, steel's business will be worse than most. In 1929 when the U.S. had a national income of $83 billion it produced 63,000,000 tons of steel ingots. In 1932 the national income was $40 billion and 15,000,000 tons were produced. With a high national income after the war ... nearly all the present steel capacity can be used. By the amount that national income falls short of prosperity levels, blast furnaces will be cold and open hearths will be down. Not forever, because the per capita use of steel in the U.S. rises on a long-term trend. In the very long run demand will catch up with almost any capacity. In the very long run, unfortunately, even steelmen are dead.

AMERICAN SCIENCE AND TECHNOLOGY

By the Editors

As repeatedly emphasized in these pages, a people's tools and skills, in short their technology, constitute one of the most important sources of their national strength and influence in the world. This is as true of peace as of war. It has always been so. But it is even more so today than formerly, because of the rapid changes that are taking place in weapons, communications, and other instrumentalities of our machine age.

We Americans were slow to grasp the idea that our national security, possibly our survival, might depend upon the quality as well as the quantity of our laboratories and of the scientists who man them. "It is only very recently," says Dr. Arthur H. Compton, the distinguished American physicist, "that the United States has taken a leading place in searching our nature's secrets. . . . While Europe was refining her science, we were applying our knowledge to the everyday jobs of making agricultural machinery, electric lights, and transcontinental railroads. We found those things worthwhile because they enabled more people to live better. During the last war [1917-18] we learned, however, that in spite of our great industrial strength, our European allies and enemies were ahead of us in devising new weapons. We found them leading us in almost all branches of fundamental science."

As a result of that sobering experience, a determined effort was made between wars to put American science into the front rank. "The great educational foundations," Dr. Compton continues, "established fellowships to encourage study and research. The universities [during the 1920's and 1930's] rapidly built up their departments of science. By the time the second war came we had become respected the world over for our work in science. In medicine and chemistry and physics and astronomy we trained thousands of capable young men and developed many recognized leaders. . . ." (From *Science*, March 2, 1945).

These achievements, however, should be viewed in proper perspective. They were possible in part because of the very large quantity of scientific and technical personnel turned out by our universities during the inter-war period. We owe much also to our British and Russian allies who held the lines while we mobilized on the scientific as well as on the military and industrial fronts. But in our gratification and pride in the achievements of American scientists, we should not forget that we approached the crisis with no prepared plan for mobilizing science in support of our armed forces.

According to the editors of *Fortune* magazine, "Germany, Japan, and, it now strongly appears, Soviet Russia were well prepared with close-knit technological high commands—commands in which technical men were brought to the fore and given their heads over all economic and industrial considerations to create total-war machines of striking power. . . . But for the United States and Britain the movement [could] still be described [in 1942] only as a forced evolution by progression from disaster to disaster" ("A Technological High Command," *Fortune*, April 1942).

"Before it is even possible to measure U.S. technology as a democratic weapon of total war," continues the same source, "it is necessary to understand the order and structure of the technological world.

"At the top of the order is pure science—the creative mind exploring for new knowledge to add to man's store. Below this, and the most vital link of all, is development engineering, which takes the germ emplanted by the pure scientist and attempts to build it into a functioning new process, engine, or product. Below this is applied science, working with accepted knowledge for practical, profit-making ends, and its outward visible form is modern industry. Below these are the ranks of skilled technicians, laboratory men, tool- and die-makers, and the like.

"The orthodox notion is that these are widely separated interests, working in separate compartments, with only the remotest connections between them. . . . In reality the above structure is an organic whole, of which the top two members are the brains, industry the body, and technical labor the skilled hands. It doesn't function properly any longer except as a whole. In the fiery test of modern war, failure to see it whole and in perspective is fatal."

The *Fortune* editors recount some of the disastrous blunders in the early stages of our war effort: the "baffling muddle in aeronautics . . . failure, except for manganese, to put sufficient stockpiles of strategic raw materials . . . failure to get any considerable or progressive conversion and pooling of the automobile industry and other industries to war production . . . the sudden discovery that the U.S. had almost no magnesium production . . . the long, dragging resistance to expansion of aluminum production . . . the failure, once the stockpile failure was recognized, to make all-out provision for other raw material sources—low-grade domestic-ore production in strategic metals and synthetic-rubber plants in rubber." Emphasizing that this is by no means an exhaustive list, the article continues: "In every case ample forewarnings are to be found in technical reports, recommendations, and proposals, and even in lay journals . . . back as far as one, two, or even five years" before 1942.

"The key to most of these blunders runs in a word through the whole structure of U.S. war technology. The word is 'advisory'—which means that the technical bodies cannot act until a problem is presented to them, have no responsibility except to make a report, and end by spreading all responsibility so thin that it almost disappears. Not even OSRD [Office of Scientific Research and Development, of which more later], which has the power to initiate research, can do more than present it to the military. The technical brains are almost completely advisory to something else. Between the technical data and the correct technical action something else intervenes. The ultimate decision for action or non-action in these essentially technological matters rested in the hands of men who were without the capacity or spirit to make the correct technical decisions. . . .

"The repetitious blunders are all blunders of *not* doing something—*not* converting plants, *not* building synthetic-rubber plants, *not* providing for long-range fighter planes. It was the endless battle of corporate research versus corporate finance, of engineer versus the military—and in these large national issues the cautious mind always won. The men and agencies and industries involved have long and even plausible rationalizations as to why things were not done. They were uneconomic, it is explained, or policies weren't clear, or the nation wasn't yet awake. But when a civilization begins to accumulate more reasons for not doing things than for doing them it is in a fair way to stagnation—even on a national income of $94.5 billion a year. Technology as a whole—science, development engineering, industry, and technical labor—is the driving force against the two great inertias that lose wars . . . the inertia of the military mind . . . [and] the inertia of industry's heavy investment in plant and equipment."

[The following selection describes how the United States government met the crucial problem of mobilizing science for total war and of overcoming the fatal "inertias that lose wars."]

SCIENCE AND TECHNOLOGY GO TO WAR

By G. W. Gray

From chaps. 2 and 3 of *Science at War*, by G. W. Gray. Copyright 1943 by G. W. Gray; Harper & Bros., New York; reproduced by permission. The writer is one of America's most trustworthy popular interpreters of science.

[IN 1916 the National Academy of Sciences, an organization dating from the Civil War of 1861-1865, offered the services of American science to the government in view of the war in Europe and the deepening crisis with Germany.]

President Wilson said yes to their offer. He agreed that it would be decidedly helpful if the scientific resources of the country—civilian, naval and military, educational and industrial, private institutions and governmental bureaus—were enlisted and welded into a team for national defense. It was in order to provide a working structure for this wartime undertaking that the academy organized the National Research Council.

. . . The council was not created as an independent body but rather as a branch of the academy—indeed as its operating agency, to which scientific men outside the academy's small membership could be appointed to serve for limited terms on desired investigations. The council thus provided a piece of machinery through which any qualified research man, young or old, could be called for service.

With the entire personnel of American science to draw upon, the National Research Council [operated] an extensive research program. It worked through a series of committees, each focused on a specialty of the natural sciences, the medical sciences and the engineering fields. There were projects in ship camouflage, in submarine warfare, in nitrogen fixation, explosives, gas warfare and other fields of chemistry, in ballistics and other problems of ordnance engineering. In this way a great many laboratory resources were brought into action.

President Wilson was highly pleased with the outcome. In 1918, several months before the armistice, he expressed a wish that the council be continued as a permanent arm of the academy, for service in peace as well as in war. The President issued an executive order to that effect, and the continuity of what had been organized as a temporary wartime agency was assured. Today more than fifty scientific and engineering societies are represented in the membership of the National Research Council, and their contributions through the years have been of inestimable value to the nation. . . .

The arsenals of the United States Army have fostered studies of guns, explosives, and other military equipment and supplies for over a century; and in so doing they have made important contributions to industrial practice. The idea of interchangeable manufacture was early applied to the production of rifles at the Springfield Armory in Massachusetts. Important advances in the hardening of steel, the centrifugal casting of gun barrels and other techniques of metal-working were made at the Watertown Arsenal, second oldest among the army ordnance institutions, also in Massachusetts. It was at Watertown, too, that the use of x-rays in the examination of large castings and welds was first applied on the extensive scale —a practice of safeguarding against hidden flaws that has become universal with heavy machine manufacturers. Other arsenals are Rock Island in Iowa, Watervliet in northern New York, Frankford in Pennsylvania, and Picatinny in New Jersey. The Edgewood Arsenal in Maryland is the Chemical Warfare Service's headquarters for research and testing. The Ordnance Department maintains a proving ground of several thousand acres at Aberdeen in Maryland, the center for its research in ballistics, and a Tank Arsenal in Detroit.

Laboratory investigations contributing to developments of both army and navy have been carried on by various outside scientific bureaus of the government, particularly the Bureau of Standards, the Bureau of Mines, the Weather Bureau, the Geological Survey, and the Coast and Geodetic Survey. For example, during and immediately following World War I the Navy Department maintained at the Bureau of Standards a group in radio research, and important advances in communication engineering were made here. The navy's function as timekeeper for the nation involved it early in the business of broadcasting time signals by wireless, and for some years its transmitter at Arlington was the most powerful in the hemisphere.

In 1923 the Navy Department ventured deeper into science by establishing a Naval Research Laboratory at Anacostia, on the banks of the Potomac, a few miles out of Washington. In creating it, Congress outlined the field of activities as "laboratory and research work on gun erosion, torpedo motive power, the gyroscope, submarine guns; protection against submarine, torpedo and mine attack; improvement in submarine attachments; improvement and development in submarine engines, storage batteries, and propulsion; airplanes and aircraft; improvements in radio installations." Not all of these subjects are under investigation at Anacostia. Many have been farmed out to other institutions, and in some instances more than one laboratory is tackling a highly complicated problem, but the list is an enlightening reminder of the sort of secrets that naval engineers have to think about. The use of radio waves for the detection of ships and aircraft is a technology that has been the subject of successful development at the Naval Research Laboratory for a number of years. Its work in this field antedated by several years the British development of radio-location. And so with underwater sound waves, and how to detect their slightest manifestation and use them to spot submarines—that too is a study in which the Naval Research Laboratory has specialized and produced results.

The National Advisory Committee for Aeronautics is a joint board of civilian and military technologists. Its success is credited in large measure to this joint form of organization, which was unique at the time it was constituted [in 1915]. There are fifteen committeemen: two from the U.S. Army, two from the U.S. Navy, two representing the Civil Aeronautics Authority, one each from the Bureau of Standards, the Weather Bureau and the Smithsonian Institution, with six members chosen from the ranks of aeronautical engineering and related sciences. Appointments are made by the President of the United States. The chairman is usually a civilian.

. . . [In 1939] its equipment for research was modern, and if not complete was more nearly so than that of any other laboratory in the land. Its relations with the aeronautical industry and with the army and navy were wholesome, stimulating and productive. Its relations with other research institutions were close and cooperative. Above all, it was a going concern capable of stepping up its research and developmental program almost overnight. And because of the preponderating weight of aviation in the new warfare which Europe was engaged in perpetrating, the committee became at once a key institution in the American movement for rearmament, preparedness and national defense.

One of the members of the National Advisory Committee for Aeronautics—its chairman in 1939 when the German dictator began his raid of Europe—was Vannevar Bush. Dr. Bush was also president of the Carnegie Institution of Washington, which is the parent body of several laboratories and other outposts of science. The Carnegie group includes such varied institutions as the Mount Wilson Observatory in California, the Geophysical Laboratory and the Department of Terrestrial Magnetism in Washington, the Embryological Laboratory in Baltimore, the Department of Genetics on Long Island, and the Nutrition Laboratory in Boston, with an archeological branch in Yucatan and magnetic observatories in Peru and Australia. From his administration of these research centers, so different in their methods and materials of study and yet so integrated within the central organization of the Carnegie Institution, Dr. Bush was well acquainted with what could be done through scientific research, and particularly through coordinated scientific research. His experience on the National Advisory Committee for Aeronautics had demonstrated what could be done in a single field of engineering that was highly strategic to national defense. And yet in other fields, equally critical and important to American preparedness for the inescapable war, so little was being done, and what was being done was so loosely organized.

As Bush talked with his friends in the laboratories he found that other men of science were concerned over this situation—deeply, anxiously concerned. Frank B. Jewett, president of the National Academy of Sciences, was one of these. But the academy could not take the initiative on any problem; it must await the call of the government, was restricted to a purely advisory service, and moreover had no funds for war research. The same restrictions applied to the academy's subsidiary body, the National Research Council. Three others who consulted with Bush and Jewett on the dangerous lack of integration between scientific resources and national emergency needs were James B. Conant, president of Harvard University; Karl T. Compton, president of Massachusetts Institute of Technology; and Richard C. Tolman, a dean of California Institute of Technology. . . . Bush and Jewett are engineers, Conant is a chemist, Compton and Tolman are physicists. These five men became the unofficial spearhead of American science in what was rapidly maturing as a world emergency. Soon their function was to be made official.

In June of 1940, as Hitler's war machine was racing westward across Holland and Belgium, President Roosevelt's Council of National Defense issued an order setting up the National Defense Research Committee and appointing these five scientists as members. In form the new committee was modeled after the National Advisory Committee for Aeronautics. There was one member from the army, Brigadier General G. V. Strong; one from the navy, Rear Admiral H. G. Bowen, and one from a government civilian bureau of science, Commissioner C. P. Coe of the Patent Office, in addition to Bush, Compton, Conant, Jewett and Tolman. The committee was allotted federal funds and authorized to undertake researches on "instruments and instrumentalities of warfare."

In 1941 the organization was broadened, though the essential pattern was not changed, by appointment of a coordinate Committee on Medical Research and the creation by Presidential decree of a new agency, the Office of Scientific Research and Development. This office was ordained as the top authority of American wartime science, embodying and integrating the two committees. President Roosevelt named Bush director of the new over-all agency, which immediately took its place in the alphabetical hierarchy of Washington as OSRD, and at the same time President Conant of Harvard and Dr. A. N. Richards of the University of Pennsylvania Medical School were appointed chairmen of the committees.

Through this office with its two operating committees a vast program in the natural and the medical sciences has been forwarded. Within Dr. Conant's National Defense Research Committee the scientific problems to be investigated were classified under four general headings, and four divisions corresponding to these were organized. Eventually, as the work expanded and problems in other fields developed in importance, it became necessary to reorganize, and toward the end of 1942 this was done by setting up eighteen divisions in place of the original four. Similarly, within Dr. Richards's Committee on Medical Research, various subdivisions on war medicine and surgery have been organized, utilizing previously existing committees of the National Research Council. In most instances the divisions within the two committees are broken down into still more specialized sections, and altogether more than 1,000 of the leading scientists and engineers of the country were enlisted within this departmentalized organization. They come from universities, industrial laboratories and professional practice, from large institutions and small, some from private laboratories, and they represent all parts of the nation. Many of these men serve without remuneration on a part-time basis; others are on the government payroll while on leave of absence from their home institutions. But in every case they were chosen for their individual qualifications, and serve as individuals.

Through these groups of experts every scientific technique or specialty that offers a prospect of contributing to the winning of the war has been canvassed. Those proposals which are accepted for laboratory investigation and development are organized as government research projects.

In a few fields of study special laboratories have been built to carry on the research. For example, the division concerned with problems of submarine warfare found it necessary to provide their investigators with subsurface experiment stations and to install highly specialized equipment. But such cases are exceptional, and for the most part the projects have been cared for by established institutions which are already equipped and manned for first-class scientific research.

The arrangement between these institutions and the government is on the basis of a no-profit-no-loss contract. The Office of Scientific Research and Development selects the university, college, institute, or industrial or private laboratory that is best prepared to undertake the particular problem designated for investigation. It then enters into a contract by which OSRD agrees to finance the research to its conclusion. At the end of 1942 the number of contracts in operation totaled more than 2,000 and employed between 6,000 and 7,000 scientists in 280 institutions.

In some instances, when the problem is the development of a novel type of weapon involving new techniques which require the combined efforts of many highly competent investigators, the project has been entrusted to a single institution instead of being divided among several. Usually the place chosen is the one that has the men and equipment that provide the best available nucleus for the research, and then workers from other institutions are assigned there to complete and round out the team. In one case of this kind, when a bold problem involving advanced studies of electronics was to be investigated, the top physicists, engineers and mathematicians of twenty-five laboratories scattered from coast to coast were brought together in one university. There they were organized as a closely knit group, under a young and dynamic leader, and for months they lived with their problem, worked at it and, it is fair to say, mastered it to a degree that twenty-five scattered independent research centers could hardly have attained in double or triple the time....

During its first twelve months, ending June 30, 1942, the Office of Scientific Research and Development spent $37,000,000. Its report to Congress showed that 100 devices, formulas and methods which have been developed through these government-supported studies were already in use by the army and navy. By that time the federal agencies had placed orders with industry for many hundreds of millions of dollars worth of equipment and materials which either did not exist or whose military value was unknown until the scientists mobilized their forces. This record is remarkable, as any industrial research director would agree. Ordinarily it takes at least three years, and usually five or more, from an idea in the laboratory to its use in industry. Under this intensive, highly compartmented but coordinated and adequately supported plan of attack, problems have been solved in a matter of months and, as one of the scientists put it, "results are taking form in copper and iron." By January 1943 the office was making expenditures at the rate of about $100,000,000 a year.

A fundamental reason that this new agency has been able to do what it is doing lies in its possession of power of initiative. The National Academy of Sciences and its National Research Council are by their charter advisory bodies and, as Dr. Jewett described them, are "in the position of a doctor waiting for patients." But the Office of Scientific Research and Development has both authority and funds. It can initiate research. After it has devised a new implement of war it can submit its results directly to the War and Navy Departments.

Another factor which has contributed to success is the policy of picking brilliant investigators in frontier fields of science and entrusting difficult problems to them. The use of nuclear physicists to investigate the application of radio to weapons is an example. These are the chaps, most of them young, who have been building cyclotrons and other novel electronic devices, who have been hurling subatomic projectiles through the vacuum, smashing atoms, transmuting the elements, discovering new isotopes, exploring the borderland where physics overlaps chemistry. Such work of necessity calls for new techniques, stimulates the imagination, and tends to eliminate the pedestrian thinker; so in these fields daring young men of science were to be found, and they have been put to work, and their labors have issued in new and powerful instruments of war. Physical chemists also are frontiersmen, and it is interesting to find some of the knotty problems of medical research being assigned to these borderland investigators.

Beyond its responsibility for organizing American science for war, the Office of Scientific Research and Development has a coordinating function. Its membership includes with civilian scientists representatives of the army and navy, and on questions of the use of scientific research in the war effort it speaks for the President who created it. Not only the top organization but each division of the National Defense Research Committee and the Committee on Medical Research has attached to it army and navy men as liaison officers. They tell of the needs and problems of the armed forces, join in the councils, sit around a table, talk it out; and the success of the war research program owes much to this close tie-in of civilian, army and navy scientists on the technical problems of weapons. In its original organization, however, the office had no part in councils on strategy.

In the spring of 1942, following the establishment of the Joint U.S. Chiefs of Staff, this situation was changed. The organization of the Joint U.S. Chiefs of Staff was itself revolutionary, for it provided a mechanism for issuing orders jointly by army and navy. One of the first acts of the new body was to appoint a Joint Committee on New Weapons and Equipment, assigning to it responsibility for recommending policies regarding new weapons of both army and navy. To this Joint Committee ... the chiefs of staff appointed an admiral, a general and a civilian, Dr. Bush; and they named Bush chairman of the committee.

Then, for the first time in United States military and naval history, a civilian scientist was brought into the war councils on strategy; not simply as a guest or a consultant, but as chairman, executive, leader. He is there, in the highest deliberations of the military and naval command, as the spokesman of American science.

PLANNING FOR THE FUTURE

By the Editors

In the Second World War, the United States had time to mobilize. We had time to expand the navy, to train a mass army, and to create a huge air force virtually from the ground up. We had time also to convert our industries and to organize our scientific and technical personnel. But the margin of safety was dangerously narrow, and nowhere did the decision hang more perilously in the balance than in our scientific laboratories.

This fact is sometimes overlooked in public discussion of post-war defense policy. We shall pay dearly if we neglect the military implications of the rapidly advancing front of science. A million men under arms, and millions more in a trained reserve, would be as helpless as the Polish army in 1939 unless adequately supported by creative and applied science and technology on a scale never before approached.

If past experience is any guide, it will probably be easier to secure appropriations for training men and for procuring impressive-looking tanks and planes, than for purchasing laboratory equipment and training scientists. This problem weighs heavily upon the minds of leading scientists and statesmen today.

THE PROBLEM OF SCIENTIFIC PERSONNEL

By Arthur H. Compton

From "Science and Our Nation's Future," by A. H. Compton. The following selection is from a radio address by the noted American physicist, delivered January 14, 1945, under the sponsorship of the United States Rubber Co., and printed in *Science*, March 2, 1945; reproduced by permission.

The international competition for leadership in science, though on a friendly basis, is nevertheless intense. I recall in 1927 commenting to the director of Germany's great National Institute of Physics and Chemistry with regard to the high quality of his scientific instruments. Though Germany was complaining then of her poverty, in our country no universities or government laboratories could afford such equipment. The reason, said Dr. Paschen, was not far to seek. The Reichstag was determined to give all possible support to German science. . . .

This was the spirit that has enabled our enemy to match step by step the combined technical developments of ourselves and our allies. It is true that when the Nazis came into power, the study of fundamental science was greatly curtailed and even the technical schools fell to roughly 25 per cent of their full enrollment as they were building up their armies just before 1939. Yet this did not go as far toward destroying their scientific strength as we have gone in weakening our own science in this war. Just as the war began, the Germans came to realize the danger to their future because of their failure to train enough scientific and technical men. They set aside an increased group of young men best qualified for science and barred them from entering the armed forces.

[Until the eve of final German collapse, these students continued] their training for careers in science and technology. The result is that the German war industries and research organizations [had] an indefinitely continuing supply of fully trained men.

Our national policy with regard to the training of scientific men has been precisely the reverse. We have gambled on a short war. Science professors and students alike have left the universities. All their effort is concentrated on devising and developing new and improved weapons. Because we were caught unprepared for a war in which scientific developments have become so vital, this has seemed to be the only possible procedure. Yet [in January 1945] practically no students over 18, except a few 4-F's, [were] studying science. . . .

It takes at least six years for a capable eighteen-year-old to train himself for effective scientific research. Even if we should start now to resume such training, it will thus be at least six years before a normal supply of young professionals will again be available to our laboratories. Can we afford to wait any longer?

This is a situation of national concern which needs to be carefully watched lest . . . we may find that we have gained a Pyrrhic victory, having lost so much of our technical strength that we shall be unable to carry on the great task of world leadership which we now see before us.

THE IMPACT OF CHANGING CONDITIONS

By Edward M. Earle

Adapted by the author from "American Security—Its Changing Conditions," by Edward M. Earle, in *The Annals of the American Academy of Political and Social Science,* November 1941. Copyright 1941 by the American Academy of Political and Social Science, Philadelphia; reproduced by permission. Dr. Earle is professor in the School of Economics and Politics at the Institute for Advanced Study, Princeton, New Jersey. He has served as special consultant to the commanding general of the Army Air Forces.

AMERICAN foreign policies over the past century and a half—indeed, over three hundred years—may be divided into three general categories:

1. Those concerned primarily (although by no means exclusively) with

overseas trade, commerce, and investment. In this group must be included the historic policy of the freedom of the seas, as well as the policy of the open door (in China and elsewhere). In its latest phase, however, freedom of the seas is concerned almost exclusively with military strategy, not, as heretofore, with the right to trade with belligerents in the ordinary way; certainly it has nothing to do with commonly accepted theories of "neutrality."

2. Those motivated primarily (but again not exclusively) by a deep-rooted American interest in the cause of freedom. If these policies have not always been clearly defined, and indeed have not always had official expression, they have nevertheless exerted a powerful influence at critical points in our history. Nor is this mere sentimentalism or ideology; it is rather evidence of the fact, as Mr. Hull has said time and again, that the United States has a stake in an ordered world.

3. Those concerned primarily with considerations of national security. These are the policies which are symbolized best by the Monroe Doctrine. But they go beyond that historic pronouncement. They include our attempts, before independence and after, to eliminate European powers from the continent of North America (Louisiana, Florida, Alaska, e.g.); to prevent the transfer of territory in this hemisphere from one non-American power to another; to maintain a navy adequate to secure the approaches to our shores; to secure to ourselves such outposts of defense (Hawaii, Puerto Rico, the Virgin Islands) as seem essential; to enter into appropriate arrangements with our American neighbors (the Havana Conference, the Ogdensburg Agreement, the Hyde Park Declaration) to give effect to hemispheric defense.

Of these several American policies, those which best stand the test of time and which enlist the strongest popular support are those motivated by a determination to assure to the United States the greatest practicable degree of military security. It is natural and proper that such should be the case, for there is no function of government more fundamental than the duty of defense of the nation and its interests. As Hamilton said in a famous passage in *The Federalist,* "Safety from external danger is the most powerful dictator of national conduct." Security involves more than defense. It is active, not passive; it demands foresight and initiative, so that national policy shall be more concerned with measures that prevent trouble than with those which salvage what one can from disaster. It is to the credit of American statesmanship that, from the first, it has been governed by considerations of this character. It has taken the long view.

Security is a state of affairs in which the nation's territorial domain, political independence, rights, and vital interests are free from substantial threat of aggression from abroad or from internal forces operating under foreign influence or control. Should aggression nevertheless materialize, it must then be under conditions most favorable to successful resistance. Security may arise either from the nation's own strength (actual, inherent, or potential), combined with the strength of its allies (existent or probable), or it may arise from the weakness or non-aggressive policies of others, or from conditions of regional or world-wide stability. It is of necessity a relative, not an absolute, thing. And it has important subjective aspects, as is indicated in the derivation of the word (*se,* without; *cura,* care, anxiety, apprehension). If the *belief* in security does not exist, its *substance* may be destroyed; hence the potentialities of the "strategy of terror" which has been so effective as a weapon of aggression. Fear or lack of confidence, justifiable or otherwise, may be used to justify "preventive" or punitive measures (such as Poincaré's policies toward Germany in the post-war years) or abject surrender of vital interests (as in the case of Blum's "nonintervention" in Spain and Daladier's abandonment of Czechoslovakia). On the other hand, overconfidence may result in a false sense of security—typified by the phenomenon of Chamberlainism in Great Britain or isolationism in the United States. . . .

The permanent desideratum of American policy should be the furthering by all available means of those conditions which will enable us to live our lives with reasonable freedom from care, anxiety, or apprehension. Certainly, such seems to have been the main objective of American statesmanship since its very inception. Throughout our history, or at least until the opening of the twentieth century, our sense of security has been based primarily upon the "precious advantage" (as Madison called it) of an almost unique geographical position. Furthermore, as a nation of continental proportions and seemingly boundless natural resources, we thought ourselves almost immune to economic pressures such as non-intercourse or blockade. There was on the North American continent no frontier in the European sense of the word; as Mr. Mackenzie King has put it, we have been fortunate both in our neighbors and our lack of neighbors. Hence, more than any other Great Power, we have based our national strategy less upon arms than upon the facts of geography and upon a diplomacy designed to assure a continuance of the advantages inherent in our situation.

To a marked degree, the security of the United States has been attributable to conditions for which we have not been altogether responsible, but of which we have been the principal beneficiaries. Our military and foreign policies have been formulated as a result of certain basic assumptions. In estimating the changing conditions of American security in a dynamic world, we are obliged to ask ourselves these questions: What have been these basic assumptions? To what extent are they now valid? If the conditions have been fundamentally altered to our disadvantage, with what imperatives are we now confronted?

As I see it, the premises of our national policy heretofore have been these:

1. The assumption of invulnerability. This was based not only upon our own geographical position and fabulous natural resources, but also upon the existence of a balance of power in Europe and the Far East, upon a British or Anglo-American control of the seas, and upon a relatively static military and naval technology which strengthened nations we considered peaceful and friendly as against those which we considered aggressive and hostile.

2. The assumption of a relatively stable international order. The nineteenth century (1815-1914) was hailed as a century of peace because of the absence of any world wars; there were wars, to be sure, but they were localized, and some wars' (including the American Civil War) seemed justifiable as promoting the ideals of nationalism and liberalism. Treaties were entered into with a deep sense of obligation. There was a common European cultural tradition and a general acceptance of standards of law and justice, founded upon the Greco-Roman-Christian heritage. There was an absence of world-wide revolutionary forces threatening the existence of the established order—

such revolutions as did occur (in China, Turkey, Japan, Russia in 1905, for example) were designed to bring reactionary governments into line with Western Europe and America. The Second International was evolutionary rather than revolutionary, and there were no subversive movements nurtured and financed by governments.

3. *The assumption of a relatively liberal economic system.* Mercantilism had been repudiated in favor of a welfare economy, marked by the "wonderful century" of expanding capitalism. Despite its marked advance, especially after 1890, protectionism was recognized as an evil the consequences of which were mitigated by the fact that it was outstripped by a rising standard of living. There were relatively free access to raw materials, a relatively free flow of goods and capital, and enough overseas immigration to relieve pressures and avoid grievances. It must be admitted, however, that this civilization contained the germs of its own destruction, to borrow the Marxian terminology.

4. *The assumption of progress.* Progressive democracy was taken for granted. So were pacifism, abolitionism, anti-militarism, and anti-imperialism. There was a belief in rational processes and in the power of enlightened public opinion. Although the functions of the state were being rapidly extended, they were circumscribed by the fundamental idea that the state existed for man, not man for the state. The dignity of the individual and the dignity of nationality were basic to any system of statecraft. The ideal was government by law rather than by men or arbitrary power.

. . . A word may appropriately be said about the role of changing military and naval technology. The invention and perfection of new weapons of war is not a subject to which, as a rule, laymen give much heed. Nevertheless, weapons may revolutionize the world in which we now live, as the invention of gunpowder was a powerful factor in the destruction of feudalism. Most of the inventions which affected the science of war during the century 1815 to 1914 operated to preserve rather than to upset the balance of power; furthermore, they were of a character to entrench Anglo-American control of the seas and, in the case of the machine gun, to strengthen the defense of those powers, like France, which the United States and Britain considered friendly. The mine, the torpedo, and the submarine in the First World War were insufficiently exploited by Germany (which, instead, tried unsuccessfully to outbuild Great Britain and the United States in capital ships). Military aviation, despite its marked progress, was still in its infancy when the bugles sounded the "cease fire" in November 1918. The tank, which neutralized and overcame the power of a static defense based upon the machine gun, was not introduced until late in the First World War, and, like the bombing plane, revealed its terrifying potentialities only as part of Hitler's Blitzkrieg.

The speed, range, and destructiveness of modern aircraft—particularly the bomber—have revolutionized warfare. In combination with the submarine, the airplane compels reexamination of all military postulates, especially those which relate to command of the seas. In view of the strides made in aviation during the past ten years, only a temerarious man would prophesy the effects of further developments upon the military position of the United States. . . .

In a highly integrated world, security is a complicated equation. A great industrial power like the United States, organized on a welfare economy for purposes of peace, finds itself at an enormous disadvantage in relation to another industrial power like Germany, which chooses a power economy for purposes of war. By our easy-going, *laissez faire* policies of the past twenty years we ... promoted the construction of modern manufacturing establishments for the aggressor nations, ... provided them with the materials of war (such as steel scrap, in which we now face an acute shortage), and ... placed at their disposal the unequaled inventive and managerial capacities of our motor and aircraft industries. ...

We have decided, by freely debated acts of Congress—not by mere Executive fiat—that the continued existence of China, Britain, and all other nations which resist the Axis, is a vital interest of the United States. And we have adopted a grand strategy based upon that decision. Our strategy is predicated on the sound military principle of defense in depth—that is to say, that we will support strongly our farthest outposts; that we will defend at all costs the second line, which is the high seas; that we will not permit the establishment of enemy bases along the third line in Latin America; and that, having done these things, we may rest assured that we shall not have to defend our own shores against an invader. ...

The strategy which we have now adopted is in the American tradition. It is essentially the same strategy that brought about the expulsion of the French from Canada and Louisiana, the Spaniards from Florida and the Caribbean, and the Russians from Alaska. It is guided by the same considerations as led to the pronouncement of the Monroe Doctrine and its firm entrenchment in our foreign policy. It is the strategy which explains most of our Caribbean policy, our possession of Hawaii, and our determination to be a naval power of first rank. To be sure, new occasions require new duties. But time seems only to confirm the old truths. Fundamental to every move we make on the complicated world checkerboard is the justified belief that keeping aggression out of the Americas involves keeping it off the high seas which wash our shores. And, as in 1917 and 1918, it means preserving the integrity of buffer states on the Atlantic seaboard and on the Asiatic mainland.

In the end, of course, security is incompatible with wars and rumors of wars. The very technological changes which have produced the Blitzkrieg can be made to work in the interest of security for all as well as security for each. To provide for such security, after victory, will be the supreme challenge of our time. It is indeed true that peace and safety are indivisible.

THE PROBLEM OF AMERICAN FOREIGN POLICY TODAY

By Walter Lippmann

From chap. 6 of *U.S. Foreign Policy, Shield of the Republic,* by Walter Lippmann. Copyright 1943 by Walter Lippmann; Little, Brown & Co., Boston; reproduced by permission.

The fundamental conception upon which the foreign policy of the United States must be formed [can be stated as follows:] Between the New World and the Old there is an ocean of sea and air. The two Americas are, in relation to the rest of the world, islands in this ocean.

They are also islands in respect to one another. For the Isthmus of Panama is not an effective land bridge.

Moreover, the greater part of the inhabited portion of South America, below the bulge of Brazil, is at present more easily accessible by sea, and in some respects by air, to and from Europe and Africa than it is to and from the arsenals and military depots of the United States.

FIG. 43. World Position of the United States, as it appears on an azimuthal equidistant projection centered on St. Louis, Mo.

From N. J. Spykman, *Geography of the Peace*. Copyright 1944 by Harcourt, Brace & Co., New York; reproduced by permission.

At the same time North America is more accessible to and from the British Isles, Western Europe, Russia, and Japan than it is accessible to and from South America, or China, or the South Pacific.

Thus, among the Great Powers, the nearest neighbors of the United States are Britain, Russia, and Japan. They are also, with the exception of Germany, the principal military powers of the modern world—that is to say the powers which are most capable in the present era of raising large fighting forces and of arming them with the most modern weapons.

The relations of Britain, Russia, Japan, and the United States—as foes, as allies, or as neutrals—has since about 1900 regulated, and will for the predictable future regulate, the issues of peace and war for the New World. Germany, the other principal military power, bears upon the New World as the enemy or as the ally of the other Great Powers who are our nearer neighbors. Thus in the First World War it was no longer possible for the United States to be neutral toward Germany when in 1917 she threatened, by conquering Britain, to become our nearest neighbor. In the Second World War, neutrality became impossible when in 1940 Germany, which was already the ally of Japan, was again threatening to become our nearest neighbor by conquering Britain. *Our* vital relations with Germany depend upon *her* relations with Britain, Russia, and Japan.

This is the system of power within which the United States is living. It is necessary to fix clearly in view these naked elements of our position in the world. For otherwise it is not likely that we can form a foreign policy in which we define lucidly our true interests, recognize the meaning of our commitments and the means of fulfilling them.

The defense of South America is, for example, a vital interest of the United States. But since South America contains no principal military power which can help greatly to ensure the defense, we must—as Monroe, Jefferson, and Madison realized—regard the defense of South America as a heavy commitment. It is a commitment which can be challenged only by one of the Great Powers of the Northern Hemisphere, and the fulfillment of our commitment depends upon whether, in our relations with the Great Powers, our friends outweigh our foes.

Our other relations are also controlled by the alignment of the Great Powers within the system. Thus it is theoretically possible for the United States alone to fulfill its obligation in the Philippines, or even its moral obligation to

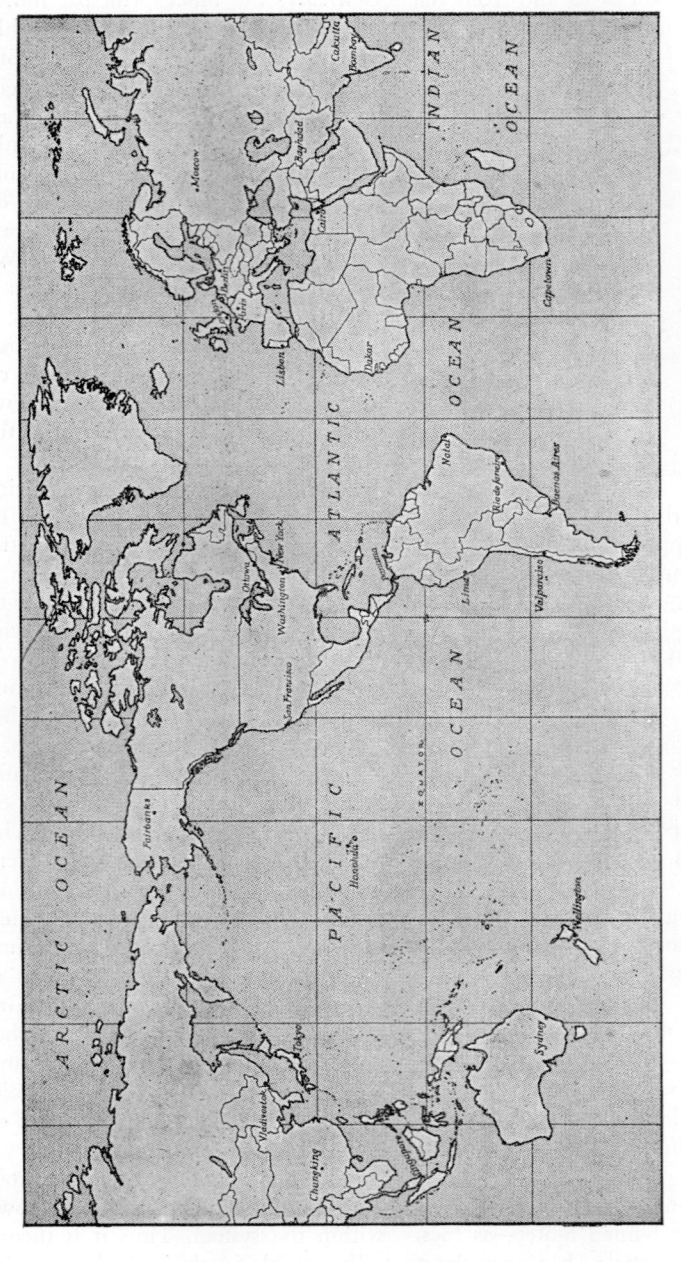

FIG. 44. World Position of the United States, as it appears on Miller's modified Mercator projection centered on the Western Hemisphere.

From N. J. Spykman, *Geography of the Peace*. Copyright 1944 by Harcourt, Brace & Co., New York; reproduced by permission.

ensure the integrity of China. But even theoretically an isolated victory over Japan is possible only if the United States is not engaged in a great war elsewhere and if Japan has no effective ally in her war with us. In fact, as the event has shown, a separate and isolated Japanese-American War is an impossibility. The course of war between Japan and the United States is regulated by the relationship among all the Great Powers.

The fact of the matter is that the principal military powers form a system in which they must all be at peace or all at war. This is not a new and recent development in human affairs brought about by the rapidity of modern communications. It has been the condition of American life since the European settlement of the New World. It is nothing but an illusion, fostered by the false reading of history, which has led so many to think that America has ever been able to stay out of any great war in which there was at stake the order of power in the oceans which surround the Americas. The people who live on this continent have from the beginning of their history been involved in the relations of war and peace among the Great Powers which face the same ocean.

The settlement in North America by men who spoke English and read the English Bible and adhered to the English common law did not begin until more than a century after the voyages of Columbus. The settlement began in fact in the generation which followed the triumph of British over Spanish sea power in 1588. Before that change in the order of power there was already a great Spanish Empire extending from Florida to Peru. But there were no English settlements until the Northern Atlantic Ocean highway had been opened to the colonists who planted themselves in Virginia and in Massachusetts Bay. Beginning in 1688 and ending in 1815 a series of great wars was fought between Britain and France. In all of them Americans participated, sometimes with the British and sometimes against them. They fought with the British in what Europeans call the War of the League of Augsburg (1688-1697), the War of the Spanish Succession (1701-1714), the War of the Austrian Succession (1740-1748), the Seven Years' War (1756-1763). The American phases of these wars are called King William's War, Queen Anne's War, King George's War, the French and Indian Wars. To be sure the Americans fought in these wars as colonists owing allegiance to the British crown. But that does not alter the fact that in the great wars in Europe there were at stake American affairs. Nor does it alter the fact that in severing the British connection the Americans sought allies in Europe, nor the fact that after the British connection had been severed Americans were immediately involved in all the great wars within the order of power. During the Napoleonic Era they waged the Quasi-War against France, and the War of 1812 against England. They formed the concert with Britain to resist the Holy Alliance. They have fought in both the German wars of the twentieth century.

There have been no other great wars which involved the order of power in our surrounding oceans. The Crimean, the Franco-Prussian, the Sino-Japanese, the Russo-Japanese, and the Balkan Wars did not, at the time they were fought, affect the order of power in which America moves. The supremacy of British sea power and Monroe's concert with it were not at issue in these wars, and from these wars America could and did remain aloof.

Therefore, though the nations which

have played a leading part in the order of power have changed in the course of three centuries, there has never been a time when the vital interests of America were not involved in that order. It has been merely an accident that for more than a hundred years after Monroe the order of power was so stable that Americans forgot that it existed. And in spite of our two great wars of the twentieth century it is still uncertain whether the nation has learned to appreciate the reality of its position among the Great Powers.

Yet it is not possible to be prepared for war or to make a lasting peace unless the nation is able to form a foreign policy based upon its true position in the order of power. . . .

This nation cannot, as Lincoln said, escape history. It can, however, at fearful cost misread its own history. It can imagine, until it is smitten by the hard realities of life, that by some special dispensation of Providence or some peculiarity of geography it can be a Great Power without being involved in the order of the Great Powers.

Yet though this illusion is passing, there remains the practical question of how in fact to form an American foreign policy which fits the realities of the American position. In answering it we cannot afford to deceive ourselves and, therefore, we must begin by recognizing the uncomfortable fact that our commitments in the outer world are tremendously extended and that our position for fulfilling them is extremely vulnerable.

We are committed to defend at the risk of war the lands and the waters around them extending from Alaska to the Philippines and Australia, from Greenland to Brazil to Patagonia. The area of these commitments is very nearly half the surface of the globe, and within this area we insist that no other Great Power may enlarge its existing dominion, that no new Great Power may establish itself.

The area of American defensive commitment is not quite 40 per cent of the land surface of the earth. But it contains a little less than 25 per cent of the population of the earth. The Old World contains 75 per cent of mankind living on 60 per cent of the land of this globe. Thus it is evident that the potential military strength of the Old World is enormously greater than that of the New World. When we look more closely at the facts of power the disparity is even greater. The only arsenal of the New World is in North America; and Canada, which provides an important part of it, is an independent state which has strong ties of interest and of tradition outside the area of our commitments. The Old World, on the other hand, comprises the military states of Britain, Russia, Germany, France Japan, Italy, and China—all of them arsenals or potential arsenals and each of them with a population used to war and the carrying of arms.

. . . The limits of our resources in men and materials are in sight. Yet the combat force we are able to develop is small in comparison with the combat power of the Old World. The total combat power that can be mobilized by Britain, Russia, Germany, Japan, China, France, Italy, Poland, the Central European and the Balkan countries is overwhelmingly superior to that which with the extremest exertion we could possibly mobilize.

These calculations may at first glance seem to some irrelevant because it must seem so unlikely that we should ever have to face the combined power of the Old World. Those who think this are already granting what I am attempting to demonstrate, namely that the New World cannot afford to be isolated against the combined forces of the Old World, and that it must, therefore, find in the Old World dependable friends. They should also remember that as a matter of historic fact this country's vital interests have been threatened by the combined power of the Old World. . . . Experience teaches us that the combination of the Old World against our commitments in the New World is not inconceivable, and wisdom requires that we should never ignore it.

The fact of our military inferiority as an isolated state becomes more portentous when we realize how vulnerable is our strategic position. We have to defend two-thirds of the surface of the globe from our continental base in North America. We are an island. South America is an island. The Philippines are islands. Australia is an island. Greenland is an island. All these islands lie in an immense oceanic lake of which the other Great Powers control the shores. Thus, if we are isolated and have no allies among the Great Powers, we have to defend most of the lake without any strategic support upon the mainland from which an attack would be launched. If we knew that the attack was being prepared, we would have no means of striking first to forestall it. We should have to let the combined forces of our enemies prepare themselves at their leisure, and strike when they were ready, and where they chose. This would present us with the dilemma of remaining in an advanced stage of mobilization, or of leaving our vast and scattered domain undefended against surprise attack. But even if we remained highly mobilized our military isolation would bind us to the static defensive. Thus our inferior power in resources and men would be profoundly aggravated by the fact that we would have to disperse our power. But our enemies, having the initiative, could concentrate according to their plans.

If this estimate of our real position seems at first to be incredible, let us remember that it seems incredible only because we have talked about our isolation but have never been so foolish or so unlucky as to be in fact isolated. We were extricated in 1823 from the threat of true isolation by the statesmanship of Canning and Monroe. Their construction lasted until 1917 when we averted the threat of true isolation by Wilson's intervention. In 1940 we were so near to true isolation that for a whole appallingly dangerous year the issue hung precariously upon the valor and skill of the people of Britain, and upon the historic campaign which President Roosevelt waged to arouse this country in time to its awful peril.

The security which Monroe had been able to achieve by diplomacy, Wilson and Roosevelt were unable to accomplish without engaging in war. But in all three instances the United States was faced with the problem of averting the threat of military isolation. The fact that Monroe averted it by diplomacy, and, indeed, by secret diplomacy, and that Wilson and Roosevelt averted it by joining an alliance which was already in the field, has prevented many Americans from perceiving the realities of our position. They do not believe that the consequences of isolation would be so fatal as they would in fact be because, thus far in our history, we have always in the nick of time found adequate allies.

But our luck might not hold. Our improvisations at the eleventh hour might the next time be too little and too late. Thus we must safeguard the future by founding our foreign policy on the undeniable necessity of forming dependable alliances in the Old World.

SOME QUESTIONS FOR THE FUTURE

By E. H. Carr

From chap. 7 of *Conditions of the Peace*, by E. H. Carr. Copyright 1942 by the Macmillan Co., New York; reproduced by permission. The author, for many years a member of the British diplomatic service, is professor of international politics at the University College of Wales.

ACTUALLY as well as potentially, the United States will almost certainly emerge from the war as the strongest world power.... Doubt exists not of the capacity of the United States to lead the world, but of their readiness to do so. There has hitherto been a marked reluctance on the part of Americans to admit that the position attained by them entails any responsibilities save, perhaps, those of a humanitarian order. Nor are the difficulties purely psychological. The spoken or unspoken assumption, which underlies many discussions of the subject on both sides of the Atlantic, that the United States are destined to play in the twentieth century the role of world leadership played by Great Britain in the nineteenth century is wholly uncritical and requires careful scrutiny.

When Great Britain rose to unchallenged world supremacy a century ago, she had a 300-year-old seafaring tradition, territories under her rule in every continent, an industry in the early stages of an unprecedented expansion, a low degree of self-sufficiency in terms of the requirements of modern civilization, a politically mature governing class, a rapidly increasing population and a static and weak landed interest. These inter-connected factors conditioned British development and the character of British power. Not one of them is present in the United States today. Here we have a vast continuous territory favored by an unusually high degree of self-sufficiency, a strong continental, isolationist and specifically anti-European tradition, a rigid constitution which impedes prompt action, a nearly stationary population, a powerful agricultural interest and an industry which, while still possessing an immense potential capacity for development, is already haunted by the same problems which everywhere confront modern industrialized society. These factors will clearly have an important bearing on the prospects and conditions of American world leadership. Will the desire persist to build up and maintain an overwhelmingly powerful navy, and to use it to police the world? Will there be a regular outflow of Americans ready and eager to play their part in developing and governing the backward regions of the world? Will the American Constitution be so modified, either in the letter or in its practical working, as to make it possible for the United States to have an active foreign policy? Will the United States offer an extensive market for the products of the rest of the world and thereby become a great center of international commerce? Will American financiers or the American government be content to become the bankers of the world, lending far and wide on a long- and short-term basis in order to keep the machinery of world finance running smoothly? Few people would confidently answer any of these questions—much less all of them —in the affirmative. Yet if they are not so answered, it becomes rash to speak of a twentieth century American leadership of the world comparable in character to nineteenth century British leadership.

Part V

Foundations of Peace and a New World Order

Chapter 17

The Terms of Peace

AMERICANS tended, in the Second World War as in the First, to separate the job of winning the war from the problem of framing a just and lasting peace. The tendency was to regard military victory as an end in itself, rather than a means to other ends. There was serious study and a great deal of public discussion of plans for setting up a new world organization to succeed the League of Nations. Americans generally gave less thought to redrawing boundaries, reconstitution of liberated countries, the future of dependent peoples, treatment and control of the enemy countries, special alliances within the United Nations, and other specific features of the emerging world situation. As a result of all this, the American people were not fully prepared in advance for the problems that were bound to arise just as soon as the dam gave way, and enemy resistance collapsed.

The surrender of the enemy states was bound to alter drastically the political relations of all the United Nations. The strongest bond of inter-Allied unity was broken. Coordinated effort against the common enemy tended to dissolve into rivalry and struggle over the fruits of victory. It took a high order of statesmanship to forge the victory coalition of the United Nations. It takes a still higher order of statesmanship to preserve that hard-won solidarity during the critical transition from war to peace, and in the years of reconstruction that lie ahead.

People approach the problem of peace-making from different angles, with different backgrounds of experience, with different feelings, prejudices, and preconceptions. There is the very human desire for retributive justice against a cruel and heartless foe. Some fear nothing so much as the loosening of social bonds and the freeing of explosive revolutionary forces in the wake of the war's devastation and chaos. Many despair of reeducating the peoples of Germany and Japan, and see no alternative but to occupy and rule those countries with an iron hand for years to come. Still others hold that the regeneration of Germany and Japan, and their readmission into the society of nations, is absolutely essential to the establishment of any enduring peace.

Lurking ever in the background is the looming question-mark of Anglo-Soviet-American relations. The terms of peace will set the pattern of future dealings not only with the defeated powers, but also among the victors as well. A resurgent Germany allied with Soviet Russia would almost certainly be regarded as a deadly menace to the Anglo-Saxon peoples. We might well feel much the same way with respect to any attempt to bring Japan into the post-war orbit of the Soviet Union, or to extend Soviet influence over China. The Russians can be expected, in turn, to view with deepest suspicion and alarm any moves on the part of the United States or Great Britain to turn against the Soviet Union the energies of the defeated nations.

German and Japanese statesmen and propagandists played constantly and skillfully on the latent distrust between the Soviet Union and the Western Allies. They knew full well that only a rupture of the Big Three could give them the opportunity to stage a political and military comeback and to resume their interrupted programs of aggressive imperialism.

Such possibilities make the problem of peace-making a matter of the utmost concern to every American. The American people walked out on the last peace settlement. We can scarcely afford to do so again. For in framing the terms of peace we are shaping our world of tomorrow. There are no easy or infallible answers to the questions confronting the United Nations in their dealings with each other and with the defeated peoples. The following selections state the issues, together with various and sometimes conflicting opinions on the terms of peace for Germany and Japan.

THE AMERICAN APPROACH TO PEACE-MAKING

By the Editors of
the "New York Times"

From "America's Responsibility," an editorial in the *New York Times*, December 17, 1944. Copyright 1944 by the New York Times Co.; reproduced by permission.

In the course of a dispatch to this newspaper explaining the political situation in Italy, Herbert L. Matthews, our correspondent at Rome, remarked that: "Britain, Russia, and other European nations see war as an instrument of politics, but for the United States it is something purely and narrowly military—to win the war and then go home."

Many Americans not only agree that such a difference in national attitude exists, but pride themselves on this difference. They talk as if it were merely selfish and calculating to fight a war for any reason beyond itself, and as if winning the war and then going home were the only altruistic and noble course for us to pursue.

But a little reflection will show how ill-considered such an attitude really is. Every war in which reasonable men participate is fought for a purpose. For America, as for England and Russia, the primary purpose of the present war was to remove a threat to its national survival. But once such a threat is removed, a rational people will use their victory to try to ensure, as far as possible, that the threat does not arise again. They will try to establish the conditions under which international prosperity, good-will and a lasting peace are possible. We have not spent $400 billion and sacrificed half a million casualties in order to have nothing to do with Europe. We did not participate in this war in order to wash our hands of the result. That is what we did the last time. The ultimate consequence was that we were forced to participate in a war incomparably more costly to us.

War is necessarily an instrument of political policy. But too many Americans think of "political policy" only in the bad sense. They associate it with schemes for spheres of influence, dubious military alliances, territorial aggrandizement, and with all sorts of Machiavellian intrigue. But if we do nothing, or merely proclaim our intention not to "interfere" in this, that, or the other local situation brought about directly or indirectly by our participation in the war, we shall in effect leave the actual framing of policy to others; and we shall be inconsistent if we later complain that the policy actually adopted is a harmful one from a world point of view or from that of our own national interests. The true alternative to narrow and shortsighted national policies is not no national policy at all, but far-sighted policies that look beyond immediate national interest to our larger interests as citizens of a single world.

But such policies are not to be achieved either by self-righteously announcing a "hands-off" policy in Europe or by repeating a few idealistic slogans. They can be put into effect only by specific decisions in specific situations. Our war and post-war policies will not be decided merely by what we do regarding the agreements reached at Dumbarton Oaks. They are actually being decided every day by what we do or fail to do, by what we say or fail to say, with regard to specific situations in Italy, Belgium, Greece, Yugoslavia, Poland, or a score of other points. But if in these specific situations we do nothing, if we fail to make our influence felt, if we keep publicly washing our hands of responsibility for what is being done in a situation which we helped to create, we merely leave a vacuum so far as American policy is concerned; and we shall hardly be entitled to complain if others rush in to fill that vacuum with policies that go counter to our own interests or to those of a durable peace.

1919 AND 1945

By the Editors

In November 1918, Germany surrendered to the Allies bringing the First World War to an end. In January 1919 representatives of the Allied powers met in Paris to draft terms of peace.

The problems confronting the victors of 1918 were not the same as those which we face today. But there are striking points of similarity as well as difference. It will help to understand the problems of today if we approach them via the victory of 1918. In this connection, one should mention once again Sir Halford Mackinder's little book, *Democratic Ideals and Reality*.

This book, it will be recalled, was written as a tract for the times. It was finished early in 1919 just as the peace conference was getting down to business. Mackinder presented both a broad interpretation of history and a specific plan for European peace. Selections embodying Mackinder's interpretation of history appear in an earlier chapter (see pp. 86*ff*. above). His views on European peace and reconstruction are equally arresting, if for no other reasons than because these views seemed so reasonable at the time, and because they found their way into the peace treaties and then proved so inadequate as a means of restraining Germany.

Mackinder foresaw the danger of German military recovery, accompanied by resumption of German expansion. He understood the frightening outlook for the oceanic powers if Germany should succeed in its second attempt to master Eastern Europe and the Eurasian Heartland. His scheme for keeping Germany in check was to build a tier of small independent states across Eastern Europe from the Baltic to the Black Sea. By this means Russia, then in the throes of revolution, was to be protected from Germany, and Germany was to be kept within bounds.

This solution harmonized admirably with President Wilson's principle of the right of every nationality to choose its own form of government. In the main this principle of self-determination, as it was called, was incorporated into the treaties of peace. The buffer states were set up across Eastern Europe. But they proved in the end to be a wholly illusory barrier to the resurgence of German power and aggression.

To some the failure of 1919 has been a source of discouragement and despair. One encounters widespread pessimism which doubts our ability to win the peace. People who hold such views believe that Germany and Japan will somehow wriggle out of the chains and that our children will have it all to do over again. This pessimism lurks constantly in the background of discussion of the terms of peace.

Is this pessimism justified? And what must be done differently this time to avoid the mistakes of last time?

These questions have been repeatedly asked in recent months. The three following selections represent some of the best thought on the European aspects of the problem. The authors are all internationally known figures. Harold Nicholson, author of "Five Lessons for the Peacemakers," attended the peace conference of 1919 as a member of the British delegation. Sumner Welles, author of *The Time For Decision*, served as Under-Secretary of State from 1937 to 1943. Arnold Wolfers, author of "The Outlook for Europe," is professor of international relations at Yale University.

LESSONS FROM THE LAST PEACE

By Harold Nicholson

From "Five Lessons for the Peacemakers," by Harold Nicholson, in the *New York Times Magazine*, April 8, 1945. Copyright 1945 by the New York Times Co.; reproduced by permission.

[With victory in Europe achieved] it is natural that men and women on both sides of the Atlantic should be asking themselves whether the ensuing peace settlement is likely to be more durable than that which followed upon the first

German war. What lessons can be learned from the mistakes or misfortunes of those who sought, after that gigantic upheaval, to lay the foundations of future repose? . . .

It may be said in general—and the point is important—that the Treaty of Versailles failed because it was never carried out. Had every article of that treaty been observed in its entirety we should in all certainty not have been at war today. The most important lesson to be learned, therefore, from the last peace settlement is that no treaty, however perfect may be its terms, is likely to be effective if those terms are subsequently allowed to lapse. The Treaty of Versailles contained many stipulations which, had they been maintained, would have rendered it impossible for Germany to embark upon a second war.

Thus, whatever safeguards we may conceive this time—and they are likely to be more precise and more compulsive than those devised in 1919—will, in their turn, prove unavailing if public opinion in the victorious countries allows their safeguards to be progressively relaxed.

The Germans, as well as the Japs, are adepts at what might be called the "artichoke method of diplomacy": a method which consists of disintegrating an agreed settlement by surreptitiously, and sometimes openly, detaching leaf after leaf. Each single leaf does not at the moment seem so vitally important as to justify the sacrifice of "improved relations," and vigilance is relaxed until the dire moment when it is discovered that nothing but the "choke" remains.

This lesson may seem so obvious that it needs no emphasis. We may all of us imagine that we shall be more wary and more vigilant next time. Yet it is customary after a long and dangerous war for the spirit of man to seek for repose, and for those who utter warnings and preach action to be disregarded. . . . I see no reason to believe that the inevitable reaction toward isolationism will be any less marked in my own country than it was in 1919. I should imagine that even in the United States there will be many who will feel that victory has been so complete and overwhelming that for a space of time, at least, America can well concentrate attention upon her own affairs.

The British, like the American people, are by nature deeply pacific; they dislike prolonged quarrels and prefer concord; when immediate danger has passed they dislike being reminded that danger may recur; and they are apt, and will always be apt, to relax into a mood of optimism and to devote their efforts to domestic rather than to external problems. It is this mood of unawareness which our enemies, as the memories of the war recede into the background, will endeavor to exploit.

This, then, is the first and fundamental lesson which we must learn from past experience—namely, that it is useless to frame a peace settlement unless in after years you see to it that its provisions are strictly observed.

There are, however, certain other lessons which can also be derived from our experiences during the years which followed upon 1919. As one who was present in Paris during the last peace negotiations and who has since devoted much study and some thought to the problem of peace-making, I may be allowed to suggest what, in fact, were the main errors of 1919 and to what extent these errors are likely or unlikely to repeat themselves next time.

In the first place, it should be realized that it is difficult, if not impossible, to make a quick peace after a long war. In 1919 the negotiators were confronted with two forms of pressure which in fact contradicted each other. On the one hand public opinion demanded a peace which would remove the possibility of a second war; on the other hand that opinion demanded early demobilization. If, therefore, a firm peace was to be enforced it was necessary to enforce it as quickly as possible and before the public slogan, "Get the boys home," became so insistent that all means of enforcement would evaporate.

It thus arose that many sections of the treaty were drafted without giving full consideration to the problems involved, and that the whole treaty was completed during a period when the passions of fear, anger, and resentment were still operative. There is little doubt that the settlements drafted by the Paris Conference would have been saner, and therefore more durable, had they been reached, not in 1919, but in 1922. One of the most damaging misfortunes of the Paris Conference was the acute time pressure under which we were obliged to conduct our labors.

This time it is probable that, owing to the circumstances, a longer delay will be inevitable. . . . Peace this time will come to us gradually, in successive phases, and over extending areas of pacified or occupied territory. This process will entail a cruel strain upon the patience of the Allied armies and people; but it will have this advantage, that it will enable peace also to be established gradually and, so to speak, upon the spot.

However great may have been the sectional differences which separated the Allied and Associated Powers at the time of the last peace conference, there was at least one central purpose which was common to all parties. That purpose was "security," or, in other words, the prevention of a second world war.

In regard to this central aim there was no divergence between the several governments; the divergence arose as to the means by which this central purpose should be secured and thereafter maintained. There occurred in this connection an acute difference of opinion between the idealists and the realists. The former, believing that man was fundamentally a pacific animal, contended that future wars could be eliminated by the removal of causes of discontent; the latter, holding that man was by nature a pugnacious animal, argued that the only means of controlling violence was to confront it with overwhelming physical force.

It is possible to assert that had either of these two opposing theories been applied in its entirety, then peace on earth would have been assured. The misfortune was that a compromise between these two opposites was attempted, with the result that the peace settlement finally agreed upon was sufficiently provocative to perpetuate resentment, and not sufficiently forceful to render that resentment ineffective.

We can hope that this time a wiser policy will prevail. Instead of allowing the compromise between force and conciliation to permeate the whole treaty, it is probable that security will be maintained in terms of power (or if you prefer it "physical guarantees"), whereas the minor penalties which rendered the Treaty of Versailles a nest of pinpricks will become less provocative.

It was this constant endeavor to compromise between idealism and realism which created the third misfortune of the Paris Conference—namely, that flavor of hypocrisy which did so much to discredit the whole settlement. Moral judgments intruded into treaties which should have been as stark and objective as a balance sheet; devices such as "mandates," "reparations" and "minority treaties" were introduced to cover the discrepancies between past pronouncements and present needs.

I am not saying that the mandatory system, as such, was a fraudulent expedient, since it contained many provisions and restrictions which were valuable in themselves. I am saying only that the phraseology of the treaties was couched in evangelical language which cast unnecessary discredit upon the settlement as a whole.

A fourth misfortune of the Paris Conference was the secret [inter-Allied] treaties which then existed and which, while impeding a settlement based upon sound principles, left behind them much rancor and many lasting disappointments.

A fifth error of the peacemakers of Paris was that they believed too readily in the uniform application of a single theory or formula. Those who, after the Napoleonic Wars, took part in the Congress of Vienna were convinced that by the universal application of the balance of power one could maintain that "just equilibrium" which was the foundation of peace. In Paris we were contemptuous of the solution favored by our predecessors at Vienna and were convinced that by applying the principle of "self-determination" we could remove all causes of future wars. We did not realize in time that this principle cannot be applied in its totality without violating the laws of economics and we were thus able only to apply our own principle in a piecemeal fashion, with the most unfortunate results. We ended by violating concurrently both the principle of nationality and the requirements of economics. . . .

A settlement therefore which aims at applying a single formula to diverse conditions will always be a transitory settlement; a lasting settlement can only be made by applying different formulas to different conditions and on the basis of a just balance between nationality, defensive necessities, security, and economic need.

Such were a few of the major errors and misfortunes which complicated and perhaps destroyed the last peace settlement. Some of them will not occur next time; some of them, while they will certainly be present, will be present in a different form; against some of them the negotiators may be warned by the lessons of past experience.

The causes of war are multiform and by removing only some of them one may intensify the virulence of the rest. It may, indeed, be beyond the capacity of the human brain accurately to diagnose all the causes of war or to devise their several antidotes. But one thing at least is certain—namely, that violence can only be restrained by physical strength. And that even the wisest treaty becomes but tissue paper unless those who framed it for their own safety remain united in their resolve to see that it is kept.

HOW TO END THE GERMAN MENACE

By Sumner Welles

From chap. 9 of *The Time for Decision,* by Sumner Welles. Copyright 1944 by Sumner Welles; published by Harper & Bros., New York; reproduced by permission.

Throughout the past one hundred years, whether the rallying point for German patriotism was the venerable figure of William I, Bismarck, the superficial and spectacular Wilhelm II, the Marshal President Hindenburg, or, in most recent times, Hitler himself, public opinion in this country has always been prone to take the figurehead as the reality. It has overlooked the fact that German policy during the past eighty years has been inspired and directed, not by the Chief of State, but by the German General Staff. It is this living, continuing, destructive force that must be extirpated if the German people are ever to make a constructive contribution to the stability of Europe, and if any organized international society is to be able to safeguard the security of free peoples in the years to come.

The German General Staff . . . has made detailed plans for a later renewal of its attempt to dominate the world. Measures have already been taken throughout the globe to facilitate the execution of these plans when the favorable moment arrives, whether that moment be ten years or two generations from now.

The General Staff itself is only one-half visible. Half the mechanism is secret and will so remain. The General Staff considers the Anglo-Saxon powers the only antagonists that will be permanently and inevitably opposed to it. It bases all its preparations upon the cynical assumption that the policies of the Anglo-Saxon nations will not long remain consistent. And, lastly, it is confident that the reasoning of Anglo-Saxon peoples is solely a posteriori, whereas it conceives of its own reasoning as being invariably a priori.

With this in mind, the German officers who are to prepare the way for the next war will be guided by the following assumptions. They have been told that the war which Germany forced upon the world in 1939 will be lost solely because the material resources of the German armies were insufficient; that although the German armies greatly excelled their adversaries in strategy, in tactics, and in audacity, their superior intelligence and bravery was finally outweighed by the superior industrial production of the United States, which her geographical isolation made possible. Therefore, in order to overcome this purely material handicap, the German General Staff must prepare for the new war by taking as its basis of operations the whole of Europe rather than Germany itself. All the industrial and scientific contacts and knowledge made available in the countries of Europe which Germany has occupied during the past four years must be turned to advantage.

To do this, the economic and political sections of the German General Staff have perfected the theory of "indirect complicity." . . . The theory of "indirect complicity" is simple in conception but extremely complicated in detail. According to the bland assertions of German officers captured in the present war, it will prove so incomprehensible to the Anglo-Saxon mind in its entirety that the idea will not be fully grasped.

The German reasoning is as follows: Experience has shown that a purely military occupation by no means results in the complete political and economic domination of a conquered country. Only through actual possession of the key industries and through direct accomplices in the political life of the occupied country can satisfactory control be exercised. If such foreign intervention becomes known to the public, it is bound to provoke a patriotic reaction difficult to overcome. If, however, it is undertaken secretly by indirect accomplices, preferably nationals of the country over whom a sure measure of control can be exercised, there can be constructed without any unfavorable public reaction a system which slowly, little by little, can impose itself upon the life of the entire country.

When, as in the case of occupied France, Germany is able by imperceptible degrees to reach a point where there remains little practical difference between secret domination and open and avowed domination, she can pass from one system to the other without danger of an open revolt.

In any modern war, the German military authorities maintain, a victory is possible only after indirect complicities have been created. But, they say, this arm devised by the German military brain can be successfully wielded in the economic and political fields only under military control, since only under military authority can it maneuver with the required rapidity.

Finally, according to the German belief, the employment of this weapon against the Anglo-Saxon powers will be made much easier by reason of the fact that Anglo-Saxons react primarily to accomplished facts and only rarely to abstract theories. Neither the British nor ourselves are regarded as capable of understanding "indirect complicity."

The agents of the German General Staff will believe fanatically that theirs is a "life mission," for the accomplishment of which they are responsible to no one save to their superior officers. They will endeavor to carry out this mission so long as there is breath in their bodies, no matter what upheavals or political changes may take place within Germany herself.

At first glance the theory of "indirect complicity" seems very simple and easy to deal with. It obviously implies the use by a foreign power for its own ends of the nationals of another power without their conscious knowledge. But it would be disastrous to dismiss the danger lightly because of a belief that we can readily construct the necessary legal safeguards, or that we can meet it solely by expanding our existing intelligence agencies.

The principal danger is that after the present war the people of the democracies, and particularly of the United States, will wish once more, as in 1920, to plunge themselves into the oblivion of "normalcy." We will be inclined to believe that because the war has ended with our victory there need be no continuing process to maintain the safety won at so huge a cost. We will be inclined to accept at its face value the propaganda which will once more emanate from German sources and, unfortunately, from many wholly sincere and patriotic American sources susceptible to the influence of German propaganda. The very nature of the German plan will, in peacetime, seem fantastic.

The German General Staff will seek to put its theory into practice in three principal ways: (a) It will try to create doubts among the people of each country as to the ability, integrity, wisdom, or loyalty of their leading statesmen; (b) in critical moments it will attempt to paralyze or to diminish the capacity for cool thinking by the people as a whole; and (c) it will search in each country for men who, through ambition, vanity, or personal interest, will be disposed to serve the causes which the German General Staff desires at that particular moment to further.

In order that these plans may be carried out without interruption and with complete efficiency, agents of the German General Staff have already been naturalized, usually in two successive countries, so that their future activities will be less suspect. The majority of them are being trained to appear as men of large commercial or financial interests, who will be able to dispose of considerable amounts of capital derived from the reserves which the German General Staff has already, during the past years, deposited under one guise or another in neutral countries. These agents will be fully trained to follow at least two entirely distinct pursuits. They will have a direct and active part in large-scale industrial or commercial enterprises.

In this way, each agent will be able to cultivate a circle of indirect and unknowing accomplices, nationals of the country where he is stationed, who can determine opinion, control industrial production and even influence the results of elections.

The German General Staff is convinced that over a period of years it can gain a controlling influence in labor unions, in the banking world, in chambers of commerce, and, through these channels, an indirect influence in the press. It believes that it can thus discourage the growth of industrial systems disadvantageous to Germany when Germany strikes again, and, when the right time comes, stimulate internal dissension sufficiently to destroy the morale of the people in those countries marked as victims.

The technique that the German General Staff has used in the occupied countries differs only in that it is simpler. Its inner workings are now becoming known. We are ready to recognize that "fifth column" activities contributed greatly to the speed of German military victories in 1940. We are too ready, however, to think of those activities as being carried on only by the Quislings and other direct accomplices. We are consequently too inclined to believe that that "can never happen here," because the American citizen, with rare exceptions, is not apt knowingly to become a traitor. The danger lies in our failure to recognize that the German General Staff looks for the weakest spot in the political structure of each country, and that in the Anglo-Saxon democracies the weakest point is not the direct accomplice, but the indirect accomplice.

The German high command had many indirect accomplices in the United States prior to Pearl Harbor. Some of them were American-born citizens who had gained high distinction in this country. For the most part they were wholly sincere; entirely patriotic according to their own lights. To this day the majority of them do not realize how they were being used, and what harm they did to our national interest....

In thinking about how to deal with the German menace in the future, it is necessary to take as a starting point the assumption that a practical world organization will be established at the close of the present war, and that it will have the power to enforce decisions believed by us to be expedient and wise.

Germany became a menace to the rest of the civilized world only after two major developments in her history. The first of these was that the German people came to believe in German militarism as the supreme glory of the race, a concept implanted and fostered by Clausewitz and his school, and in Pan-Germanism as an ideal which German militarism alone could achieve. The German General Staff became the agency for bringing about these objectives.

The second development was the centralization of authority over all the widely divergent peoples of the German race. The unification of the German peoples, first envisaged in 1848, actually begun in 1866, consistently furthered during the four decades of the Second Reich, and forced to its final completion by Hitler himself, has coincided with the rise of Germany as a threat to the rest of the world.

Neither development, however, could have proved a major danger without the other. With each successive stage in the centralization of authority, the power of the German General Staff was correspondingly increased. Without such centralization it could not have attained its position of supremacy in 1914. If Hitler had not abolished all the remaining barriers between the former German states, German militarism could never have carried out its policies so successfully in the years between 1933 and 1939, nor could it have obtained the complete control which it had acquired when the war finally began.

The unification of Germany, with the centralization of all power in Berlin, has made possible the building up of Germany's destructive power.

It has enabled a central government to stereotype the education of all German youth in order that it might voluntarily become the tool of Pan-Germanism.

It has destroyed the opportunity, and even the capacity, for individual thinking in German universities and schools, which might to some extent have operated as a counterweight to purely military influence.

It weakened the ability of Germans as individual citizens to think for themselves, and made possible that persistent official encroachment upon the liberty of the press and all other means of popular information which had its climax in the total control over all sources of information by the Nazis.

Finally, it has eliminated all the earlier countervailing balances to stark Pan-Germanism.

The power of religion, whether Catholic or Protestant, to influence the German people against Hitlerism was gravely weakened as soon as a centralized government was able to stamp out religious freedom. That a Bavarian government, for example, could never have accomplished in Bavaria. The different peoples within Germany had the chance to resist being dragged into military adventures and to withstand the contagion of mass hysteria only so long as they retained their autonomy, and remained primarily Bavarian, Saxon, or Hessian. Once these age-old safeguards had been broken down, the German peoples as a whole became a malleable instrument for the use of their overlords.

The abolition of local government, with the substitution of authoritarian rule from Berlin, destroyed the last vestiges of regional autonomy which had remained from the days of the Empire and of the Republic, and completed the obliteration of German individual liberty.

Centralization also stimulated the unhealthy growth of those vast financial, commercial, insurance, and shipping combines which have spread their tentacles throughout the world during the past two generations. They have proved one of the most effective agencies for the schemes of the military high command.

No world organization, however effective, will be able to combat the danger which will exist if after the war a centralized Germany continues to be subject to German militarism. The purely military controls imposed by the world organization will inevitably become weakened as time passes, as the ravages of the present war are partially effaced, and as the instinctive human desire to forget becomes intensified. When that day comes a centralized Germany will start another war of revenge, waged this time in the light of the experience gained by the German military commanders in the present war.

Many people will agree that German militarism must be crushed and are satisfied that the major military powers should take care of this as soon as Germany is occupied. They say, however, that there is no similar justification for destroying her present unification.

Many responsible Americans are already maintaining that any partition of the German peoples is inherently unjust and will prove unworkable. They insist that the major powers will be unwilling to enforce the partition at the time when the German people clamor to be reunited. And they are confident that enforcement will require a continuing military force of occupation which none of the major powers will be disposed to furnish. These are the main arguments against a partition of Germany.

First, the centripetal urge among the German people is so great and so persistent that any attempt on the part of a world organization to prevent German unity would soon result in a new form of eruption.

Second, partition would develop an inferiority complex similar to that which it is claimed the German people contracted as a result of the war guilt clause in the Versailles Treaty. Any such sense of inferiority, it is said, will prevent their ever becoming cooperative citizens in a new Europe.

Third, partition of Germany would mean the economic ruin of the people, with such unemployment and distress as to give rise to some dangerous form of Communism.

Fourth, any partition of Germany into separate units would be answered by concerted efforts at evasion, and, owing to their great organizing ability, the Germans would soon find satisfactory means to get around it and prepare for a new attempt at unification whenever the moment seems propitious.

I would be the last to underestimate the force of these arguments. My whole individual predisposition is in favor of the unity of the German people. It is only because of my conviction that German unity means a continuing threat to the peace of the entire world that I have reached the conclusion that partition is the only way of offsetting the German menace in the future.

The so-called centripetal urge on the part of the German people is far from being the powerful force that so many have claimed during the past twenty years. The vociferous demand for the reconstitution of the German Reich and the unification of all the German peoples has been largely stimulated by the German General Staff. It has provided Hitler with some of his most effective propaganda in consolidating his own regime. Certainly the unification of the German peoples is by no means a prerequisite for the happiness and prosperity of individual Germans. The several German nations were both happy and prosperous during the nineteenth century. Even under changed economic conditions this situation can be brought about in our time.

Those who favor the continued unification of Germany are inclined to overlook for how brief a period the German states have been governed by a central authority, and how bitterly many of the German peoples struggled against unification. . . .

The point made with regard to the creation of a national inferiority complex within Germany, if partition is undertaken, is undoubtedly true. But that complex, with all its unfortunate psychological effects, will exist in any event as a result of German defeat, whether Germany remains a centralized unit or is separated into several entities.

If the economic prospects of the German people were to be irreparably damaged by partition, the objections raised on this score would be conclusive. But there is no valid reason why they should be. In my opinion no greater safeguard can be devised against future German military aggression than measures that will afford every German equality of economic opportunity with the citizens of other European countries. He should be assured that he need not look ahead to the same dark and uncertain future that he faced in 1919. Such economic security can be obtained only if basic economic arrangements which ensure the eventual prosperity of the German people are taken into full account in any division of the present German Reich. Next to the military considerations, these appear to me to be the determining factors.

As for the final objection, there is of course not the slightest doubt that many Germans for one or two generations to come will make every effort to evade the results of partition and to pave the way for a renewed unity. The precise manner in which to deal with these attempts may only be determined in the light of future conditions. For some years they will have to be forcefully repressed by the future world organization. But the surest guarantee of permanence will lie in the kind of partition undertaken. It will be effective only if it proves practicable from the economic and political standpoints, and is based upon economic, political, and cultural considerations.

The possibility of a partition of Germany has undoubtedly received close study from many of the governments of the United Nations. A number of plans have been devised, varying from the reconstitution of the old German Federation, as it existed prior to 1848, to the inclusion within a federation of Western Europe, as an autonomous state, of the industrial regions west of the Rhine, leaving the remainder of Germany, except for slight frontier rectifications, much as it was prior to 1936.

Arguments can be advanced in favor of many such schemes. If one proceeds, however, upon the theory that Germany is to be divided solely to prevent her from again becoming a military menace, and that at the same time individual Germans must be given every opportunity to achieve economic security and ultimately to comprehend, and to enjoy, popular government, the following basis for partition is probably the one best calculated to procure these results.

Exclusive of East Prussia, Germany should be divided at the time of the armistice into the following three separate states, the boundaries being determined primarily by cultural, historic, and economic factors:

A new state of Southern Germany, comprising the former sovereign nations of Bavaria, Württemberg, Baden, and Hesse-Darmstadt, together with those regions which may roughly be defined as the Rhineland and the Saar. It will be noted that the populations which would be comprised within this division are predominantly Catholic.

A state consisting of the following old German subdivisions, together with the smaller subdivisions contiguous to them: Upper Hesse, Thuringia, Westphalia, Hanover, Oldenburg, Hamburg.

A state, omitting the enumeration of small contiguous political subdivisions, composed of Prussia (exclusive of East Prussia), Mecklenburg, and Saxony. It will be noted again that in the second and third states the populations are predominantly Protestant. In each one of these three new states the historical, as well as the religious and cultural, divisions which existed during the centuries prior to the creation of the Third Reich have been maintained.

. . . By this suggested division a complete economic balance, both agricultural and industrial, would be established within each of the three states, and the proportionate relationship within each state of the prime economic factors, such as agricultural and industrial production, and mineral resources, would be roughly equivalent to that in each of the two others. If, as I hope may prove to be the case, the end of the war sees the lowering of customs barriers within Europe, and the creation of customs unions, the new German states should be afforded free opportunity to take part in such customs unions.

The capacity for economic development in each one of the proposed states is almost unlimited. What would vanish would be the giant combines which could be used again as a means of military penetration in other countries. It cannot be claimed that the existence of these huge cartels was in any sense necessary to a healthy German national economy. . . .

Partition will do more than anything else to break the hold which German militarism has on the German people. But it is also certain that the plans of the militarists have taken this possibility fully into account, and that the General Staff, as such, will continue its activities for many years to come.

There is only one sure way by which this danger can be blotted out of existence. A wholly new spirit must be brought to life within the German people, and a totally new concept of what is worth living and striving for. But I fear it would be as softheaded as it would be softhearted for the United Nations to assume that such a change can be brought about during the lifetime of the present generation. For that reason all preventive measures which the victorious powers take to guard against German military activities in peacetime must be persistently enforced for many years.

The effective use by the German General Staff of indirect accomplices demands that the precise nature of their operations be kept secret. The best counteractive measure will be full ventilation through the press and radio of the United Nations of every detail of such activities as they are brought to light.

In order that such facts can be made known, their existence must be ascertained and verified. This requires efficient intelligence services. The precise nature of such services is a matter which can be determined only by each government. However, it can readily be seen that all governments must have far more definite knowledge than in the past of the origin of capital investments made from abroad, as well as of the individuals of foreign origin taking part in the industrial and financial life of the nation.

To many of us, when peace is restored, these precautions will seem fantastic and altogether unnecessary. But it would be foolhardy to forget what the past has so clearly proved. The only proof that such precautions are no longer necessary will lie in the ability of the Germans to convince the other peoples of the world that they have permanently discarded the gods they have been taught to serve by their own war lords.

After the First World War, when the Allied Nations were told that, with the establishment of the Weimar Republic, the freely expressed voice of the German people would now be heard, they tacitly accepted the truth of these assertions. I should be the first to deny that Fritz Ebert and his immediate associates were either insincere or undemocratic in their beliefs. But the events of the past twenty-five years have shown conclusively not only that the German people were not responsive to democracy, but also that the Allied governments did nothing to stimulate the growth of democracy within Germany.

We already hear many Germans, refugees in the United States, insisting that the way to assure Germany's good behavior in the future is to give the German people another opportunity to establish a true democracy within a unified Germany. More and more citizens of the western democracies, many of them advanced liberals, are publicly professing the same convictions.

One of the chief reasons why it is difficult for some close observers of recent German history to accept this view is the fact that when Germany is defeated this time conditions will be far less propitious for the creation of a real democracy than they were at the end of the First World War. Since Hitler gained control of the German Reich, the youth of Germany has been hopelessly corrupted. It would be an optimist indeed, no matter how deep his sympathy for the German people, who would have any hope that the younger generation will ever be able even to understand what democracy is. During their formative years the younger Germans have had no education other than that given them by the Nazi machine. They have been taught to believe in no ideals other than that of the master race and the inherent right of the Germanic peoples to dominate the world. They have watched with enthusiasm the consistent and effective efforts of their leaders to reduce the population and the future population of the peoples of the occupied countries. They have had inbred in them a total contempt for religion, and a brutal hatred for other races. These millions of Germans will be at the prime of life during the next two decades. They will be a controlling force within Germany. Theirs will be a force of fanaticism and of revenge.

The brutalities of Hitlerism have become a daily commonplace to all generations of present-day Germans. They have necessarily produced a coarsening of the national psychology which cannot be modified overnight solely by such a change in governmental structure as took place in 1919.

By the time the war is over, the Nazi regime will have succeeded not only in destroying the value of the savings and property of all classes in the occupied countries, but, through its domestic policies and the war requisitions, in obliterating all but real property within Germany itself. Everyone save the higher authorities in the Nazi machine will be destitute. The misery and starvation will be far greater than it was in 1918.

In all probability, the first stratagem of the German military command will be to stimulate throughout Germany the growth of Communism in its world-revolutionary form. Conditions will favor it. The establishment of Communistic governments of such a type is a foregone conclusion, provided the United Nations forces of occupation make no objection. Many well-intentioned liberal elements within the United Nations will hold that the creation of such governments is proof positive that the German people have seen the light and have at last set foot upon the road leading to popular self-government.

This would by no means necessarily be the case. The establishment within Germany of Communism of the Trotskyist, or world-revolutionary, type would give the German General Staff precisely the advantages it will seek. For, after the war is over, all the occupied countries of Europe and many countries in other parts of the world will be seething with social unrest as a result of economic prostration. A new German Communism, furthering the doctrines of world revolution and directed by the cold and ruthless brains of the German General Staff, would find in many parts of the world a situation made to order for the purpose of

Pan-Germanism. The kind of governments, therefore, that the German people are to be permitted to install must be decided by common agreement between the United Nations with full regard for the dangers which may arise from any hidden military schemes of the General Staff.

The United Nations must continue to occupy various regions of Germany for a considerable period after the war, under the supreme authority of the future world organization. The war criminals must first of all be tried and sentenced. The return to self-government must be gradual, commencing with the establishment of municipal administrations, after all Nazi officeholders have been eliminated. Furthermore, until the immediate distress of the post-war period within Germany has been relieved, and until the German people can once more put their industry and agriculture on something approaching a peacetime basis, it would be extremely inadvisable, as well as against their best interests, to hasten their resumption of self-government. Certainly Germany must be both socially and economically stable, even under an alien occupation, before the United Nations can safely permit other than local governments to be established.

Even then, certain safety measures will have to be enforced. There must be a system of controls, organized and carried out by the world organization, to make sure that German rearmament is impossible and that every store of arms and munitions remaining at the time of the armistice is delivered into the hands of the United Nations. There must this time be no such fatal inefficiency in this matter as existed in 1920. In the same manner and for the same purpose, controls must be imposed over German mining and heavy goods industries. The controls must likewise be exercised over German imports. Finally, if all Central European communications and sources of power development, including railroads, coastal and fluvial shipping, radio and telegraph, and electric power facilities, were to be internationalized, no development could prove of more practical value from a purely economic standpoint, as well as in preventing the German people from using these instruments for military purposes.

All the safeguards that have so far been considered are in a sense negative. They are preventive measures. What will in the last analysis be far more important are the constructive measures which may be taken to encourage the German people to become of their own initiative cooperative members of human society.

For as I see it, if the treatment accorded to the German people is to result in the strengthening of the foundations of world peace, such treatment must not be punitive. It should be the result of the adoption of a policy by the world organization which is remedial as well as precautionary. It should prepare the German people for true popular self-government when they have actually learned to value such a form of government as the one best calculated to assure their welfare.

The policy to be followed should be designed not to destroy Germany, but to construct out of Germany a safe and cooperative member of world society.

The start in this direction must be made from the first moment after Germany's defeat, even though it may be a long period before the German people can again be safely permitted to walk alone. But first it is essential to canvass the salutary forces within Germany which, if encouraged and strengthened, may provide the means of her salvation.

As I see them, there are, first of all,

the forces which will spring from a renewal of religious freedom. Among the few admirable figures who have appeared upon the German scene during the years of Hitlerism are those who have dared to speak in the name of the churches. The spiritual reformation which can result from freedom of religion in Germany may be very great.

Freedom of information, which is indispensable, also can become one of the great constructive forces in the creation of a new German national conscience. To a people deprived of the means of access to the truth during the past ten years, full freedom to learn the truth will come at first as a bitter shock. It may well become eventually a means of national regeneration.

The freedom from fear which will come through the establishment of an effective world organization and the freedom from want which will be assured by the establishment of a sane economic policy with regard to the German people will have their stabilizing effect upon the German mind.

Many German nationals now in exile because of their hatred of Nazism are disposed to work for the ultimate salvation of their people. The United Nations should give them every encouragement, as soon as the time is ripe, in order that their voices may be heard by their fellow countrymen.

Already the organization of "Free Germans" and the groups of well-intentioned, liberal-minded citizens of the United States who support the efforts of these organizations are moving rapidly to create a state of mind on the part of public opinion within this country which will hold that the fourth German Reich can be trusted, provided German "democrats" are aided in seizing and holding the reins of government. I would count myself a member of this body of opinion if I could believe that democracy could really determine the destinies of the German people within a foreseeable future. The basic point to remember is that democracy cannot be imposed upon any people. It can only exist in reality when it springs from the consciousness, and from the will, of a people. There is no proof which can be offered, worthy of credence, that the history of the German people during the past twenty-five years holds even a spark of promise that democracy would become a true, or a predominant, force within Germany so long as the tragically poisoned German youth of the Hitler years remain a majority of the German people.

If, after the years of trial have passed, and a new generation of Germans comes of age under conditions which make the new Germans conscious of what the word "liberty" really means, we may all hope democracy—true and not artificial—will prevail in every region of Germany. When such a time comes the German people should once more be afforded by the international organization as full an opportunity to determine freely their political destinies as any other people of the earth. But until that moment comes, even the most idealistic of the liberal groups within the United Nations should pause to remember the bloody pages of the history of the past decade.

The treatment accorded Germany by the United Nations when their victory is won should be neither Draconian nor vengeful. It should be formulated, however, in the light of the stark reality that Germany has twice within a quarter of a century brought war and devastation to mankind. The peoples of the world are obligated, to ensure their own survival and the survival of all those things which they hold most dear, to see to it that the German race cannot again so afflict humanity.

PREREQUISITES OF PEACE IN EUROPE

By Arnold Wolfers

From "The Outlook for Europe," by Arnold Wolfers, in the Yale Review, December 1944. Copyright 1944 by Yale University Press; reproduced by permission.

The group of countries which can be called strictly European today has become smaller than it once was; Europe has also lost to others the position of political preeminence which it held for many centuries. The turning point came not with this war but with the last. Russia veered away from Europe when in 1917 she became the Soviet Union; soon the Urals were the center of a newly developed Eurasian empire. England, too, ceased to be, properly speaking, a European power when the Dominions attained a position of equality with the mother country. Thereafter England formed part of a commonwealth that belonged not to Europe alone but to every continent. What was left of Europe after 1918, therefore, was hardly more than a ring of countries surrounding defeated Germany—a continent divided against itself.

The Nazis, in the course of this war, would have liked to make Germany appear as the champion and defender of Europe against danger threatening it from outside. This, however, meant adding insult to injury, since it was they who by sacrificing Europe's interests to the ambitions of the "master race" pulled the continent down to a point where recovery of even a measure of independence and prosperity will require almost superhuman efforts.

As the Nazi empire crumbled it almost looked as if Europe, lacking any strong voice in the high councils of the world, were to become a kind of glorified Balkans—a grouping of small or lesser powers living under the shadow of powerful neighbors. The pleasure which Europeans took in the early revival of France and in her proud and vigorous insistence on equality with the Great Powers may have been an indication of how much the people of Europe dreaded such a fate. But the Great Powers outside of Europe have no interest in saddling themselves with a "European question" more troublesome even, because of its potentialities, than the notorious "Eastern question," which for over a century haunted the members of the Concert of Europe. They must realize that a continent the size of Europe, with more than three hundred million people, composed of nations with seemingly indomitable energy and unconsumed spiritual resources, will either get back on its feet or become a menace to the peace of the world.

If the continent were united or were heading toward some kind of union, it could rely on its own ability to regain a satisfactory place for itself. But there is nothing to indicate that anything even remotely resembling a European union or federation is in the making. The fight against Nazism has not had the effect, which some may have expected, of arousing a sense of European solidarity strong enough to overcome the fervent nationalism of the time. On the contrary, the struggle against foreign oppression appears to have rallied all groups and classes more firmly around the national banner, leading even the Communists to employ nationalist slogans. It is hardly surprising that the liberated countries, in their eagerness to restore some measure of political and economic order, should prefer at the start to trust their former institutions and methods of procedure rather than embark on new and untried international ventures. As a result, Europe will come out of the war divided as before into a large number of states, each of them as eager as ever to guard its own characteristic features and loath to limit its sovereignty. While this lack of political unity may rob Europe of much of the influence it could otherwise hope to exercise, and may render difficult the execution of any plans for overall reconstruction of the continent, it enables each nation to set itself vigorously and enthusiastically to the task of putting its country back on the road to prosperity and progress. The results in the end may be better for an early recovery of the world, particularly since the countries of Europe differ enormously in their ways of life, their social structure, and their economic interests.

But while the multiplicity of independent countries may have its good sides, friction and conflict between them would be a matter of serious consequence. Unfortunately, a number of old and bitter feuds are likely to be carried over into the post-war era. Aside from the formidable German question, which overshadows all others, the territorial disputes between countries like Italy and Yugoslavia, Hungary and Rumania still seem far from solutions which would be satisfactory to all. The peace of Europe and the world may not be much endangered by quarrels of this kind between weak countries. It should be remembered that Hungary, as passionately "revisionist" as any country could be, hesitated to take up arms even after Germany had broken the peace in 1939. Cooperation in Europe would, nevertheless, be constantly hampered by the existence of such zones of friction and animosity.

No great gift of insight is needed to see that the end of hostilities in Europe cannot end the struggle with Germany which twice in a generation has turned the continent into a battlefield. For some time after her armies surrender, Germany, it is true, will be powerless and at the mercy of the victors. With Allied occupation and sweeping measures of disarmament coming on top of aerial destruction, demoralization, and possibly political disintegration, the Heartland of Europe will represent hardly more than a heavily controlled depressed area. And yet Germany will continue to be a source of European anxiety. Why should this be the case?

If the German problem were in the nature of a boundary dispute, it might have been hoped that wise statesmanship, possibly after a cooling-off period, would find a solution which would straighten out the main difficulties and pave the way for peaceful cooperation. But the real issue is of a different kind. It concerns German power and German intentions to wage war. Situated in the center of Europe, Germany with her sixty to seventy million inhabitants, with her skills and resources, can always—if given a chance to act as a unit and to mobilize her strength—overrun not merely each of her neighbors separately but all of them combined. More than that, experience in two successive wars has shown that for one of the major world powers to come in on the side of the victims of a German attack was not enough to stop her. Even a coalition which in the end comprised almost all the major powers was unable in these two wars to save Europe from temporary subjugation by the Germans. As to Germany's intentions, all one can say today is that she has surrounded herself by such an abyss of distrust that nothing she could do in the near future would convince her neighbors of her genuine desire for peace. Thus, for the time being at least, the non-German parts of Europe can base their hopes of security only upon guarantees of outside military assistance, on the one hand, and upon measures which will cripple and hold down German military power, on the other.

There is no way by which at the close of hostilities German power—if we mean by that her potential as well as her actual power—could be eliminated once and for all in the way Carthage was disposed of by the Romans. A nation of seventy million cannot be destroyed—at least not by means which the victors in this war would be ready to employ. Drastic settlements have been suggested, but they do not qualify as "Carthaginian." If, for instance, Germany were broken up into a number of separate states or were radically de-industrialized today, peace would still depend on whether she would be prevented from reuniting or rebuilding her industries at a later date. Outright annexation by Germany's neighbors of considerable parts of her territory might seem to guarantee a more lasting reduction of her power. But given the relative weakness of the countries concerned, they would still depend on outside assistance if they were not to live in fear of revolt inside the remaining parts of Germany and irredentist action among the populations separated from her, which such dismemberment might eventually provoke.

As long as it is impossible, therefore, to remove the German danger other than by tackling it from a power angle, the security of Europe and the world must rest on measures designed to prevent Germany from turning her potential power—which will continue strong—into actual striking power. This means a long period of continued watchfulness and readiness to enforce the terms imposed on Germany.

Countries which have suffered the hardships and inhumanities of German invasion and occupation—many of them twice in the course of this century—cannot feel happy at the prospect of once again having to rest their security on their ability and that of other people to keep Germany down wholly by force or by the threat of force. Experience after Versailles taught them that unilateral disarmament, international control, prohibition of Anschluss [unification with Austria] and the like, while successful in the beginning—and while there is least need—may well break down later. They cannot help remembering that when Germany seriously started to evade the terms of the Versailles Treaty and began to rearm, the non-European powers were not only unwilling to take action against her but had become hostile even to measures which Germany's neighbors might have undertaken if they had received at least moral support.

Here, then, lies the crux of the matter. The German problem will not have been solved at all, however harsh the immediate terms imposed on Germany may be, if after ten or fifteen years she were allowed again to prepare herself for war. But how can Europe be assured of the willingness of the great victors in the Second World War to enforce or even to permit enforcement of the terms, not only today but in a relatively distant future? Often time works in favor of the vanquished. His revolt against measures of discrimination tends to gain momentum as time goes on. The watchfulness and the readiness of the victors to use force, on the other hand, tend to decline, particularly when nations are involved that are relatively remote from the scene. No promises or commitments made in the heat of the war can quite dispel the misgivings which arise out of this situation.

Some have suggested as a way out that the harshest possible terms be imposed upon Germany now while British, Russian, and American hatred of the Germans is running high. Certainly the neighbors of Germany have a right to expect that the measures taken will not only destroy Germany's ability to attack for a long time to come but will make it extremely difficult and time-consuming for her, whatever the Allies may do later, to restore anything like the superiority she once possessed. In view, however, of the long-run considerations which need to be emphasized, it would be a mistake to believe that the victors could not err on the side of excessive harshness as they might on the side of excessive leniency. While harsher terms mean greater weakness of Germany in the early period, when there is obviously the least danger, they might increase the threat of war later. This is true for two reasons: the one is that they could turn more Germans into rabid "revisionists" ready to have their country risk war rather than abide by the *status quo;* the other, and more serious one, is that harsher terms are less likely to be enforced vigilantly over a long period. Whether people will continue after the first few post-war years to accept the risks and sacrifices involved in the enforcement of peace terms obviously depends not on whether they approve of them today but on whether at a later date when war passions have receded and the longing for normalcy is strong, they still regard them as both essential and expedient. Since this is likely to hold true particularly for this country and for Britain, spokesmen for the English-speaking world would render the neighbors of Germany a poor service if they failed to point out the wisdom of obtaining a peace which would afford the maximum security for Europe with the minimum danger that ten or twenty years from now its underwriters would weaken in holding Germany to its terms. The aim should be the sternest possible peace compatible with long-run enforcement.

As a matter of fact, views of this nature have recently been expressed in Europe. Some of the liberated people are apparently aware of the fact that the security of their countries cannot forever and alone depend on measures to keep Germany down. Despite their present hatred of the Reich and despite all they have suffered at the hands of their German oppressors, they know that the ultimate objective must be cooperation with a peaceful Germany and the entrance of such a Germany as an equal into the European family. This means that they must look forward eventually to changing not her power but her intentions.

It may seem preposterous at this moment to look forward to any such "conversion" of the German people—although other European nations in the course of their history have turned their backs on dreams of conquest and grandeur to become preoccupied solely with the defense of their country and the welfare of their people. In every case, military defeat has proved the most persuasive argument. Much depends, therefore, on whether a second crushing defeat, demonstrating as it will the new military might of Russia and the United States, will sufficiently impress the Germans with the hopelessness of their expansionist ambitions and whether the unity of the present Allied coalition will be maintained long enough to prove to the Germans that any new attack would be met with an even more overwhelming superiority. Millions of Germans were convinced before 1939 of the folly of another war though they were too few or too weak to enforce their conviction. The question for the future is whether after the war more millions—enough in number and power to turn their country's course firmly in the direction of peace —will reach the same conviction.

Neither fear of another defeat nor social and constitutional changes in Germany will suffice to bring this about. Unless the patriotic German can see ways of peace which will enable his country, if duly committed to those ways, at some future time to rise from its pariah position and regain its freedom, he will again support a policy of war. For this reason Germany's neighbors would do well to consider carefully the wisdom of annexing outright large stretches of German territory. Such territorial annexations are intended to be permanent. That puts them in a category by themselves. All other measures, however drastic, can be terminated at a later date. If their termination is made to depend on a sincere and convincing change of mind on the part of Germany, they even set a premium on "conversion" rather than bar forever the chances of a real pacification of Europe. . . .

However much Europe may yearn for the time when it will no longer be a powder keg or military camp, it will over a long period have to resign itself to the need of watching, controlling, and coercing Germany. The liberated countries will wish to take an active part in this task; but they cannot carry the risks and burden alone any more than they can recover their prosperity by relying on themselves alone. Relations with the major non-European powers are bound, therefore, to become matters of the utmost concern to them. There would be little to worry about in this respect if all that was desired was either a maximum of reliable assistance or, on the contrary, a minimum of outside interference. The dilemma arises from the fact that Europe needs both.

In speaking of the relations with each of the major non-European powers separately, attention must first be focused upon the effects on Europe of the spectacular ascendance of Soviet power. They cannot fail to be tremendous, particularly since Soviet might has expressed itself not merely in the victories of the Red Army over the "invincible" Wehrmacht but in a westward expansion of Soviet territory and influence. It is one thing for Russia and its present regime to cover distant lands east of Lake Peipus, the Pripet Marshes, and the Dniester River, but quite another thing for Russian controls, whether direct or indirect, to extend westward to the Oder, the Danube Basin, and the Mediterranean. When writing *Mein Kampf* twenty years ago Hitler could still imagine Russia to be a land of empty spaces and internal chaos tempting to a European conqueror and colonizer; today Europe as seen from Moscow must look, in contrast, like a crowded peninsula on the western fringes of Soviet Eurasia. Thus once again, as after the First World War, the most revolutionary change affecting Europe started in the East. If last time it took the form of a Communist revolution, it consists this time in a radical shift of the balance of power.

Already one can see in Europe the contrast if not the conflict between those who advocate a "Russian orientation" and those who dread the future Russian impact on the affairs of the continent. The cleavage between the two groups does not run strictly along ideological or class lines, although extremists in both camps may call each other "fellow travelers" and "pro-Fascist reactionaries," respectively. When President Beneš decided to align Czechoslovakia with the Soviet Union, he was thinking of the security of his country. This, it may be assumed, did not mean favoring Communism; Beneš may, indeed, have hoped that friendship with the Soviets would result in less

Russian interference. In the case of Marshal Tito, the hope that Russia might support drastic social reforms in Yugoslavia may have played an important role, but the old friendship between the two Slav countries also entered into the picture. Thus Communist sympathies, Pan-Slavism, political opportunism, and the quest for security against Germany tend to draw countries and groups into the Russian orbit. But against them are arrayed all those who fear either the expansionist drive of so overpowering a neighbor or continued world revolutionary tendencies in the Soviet regime. It is a fact that Europe, even if united, could do little without outside aid to stop Stalin if someday he decided to push his country's boundaries farther westward, and while the dissolution of the Third International may have allayed some fears, it cannot be overlooked that the Communist parties in countries like Italy, France, and Yugoslavia have all, as if by order, changed to new but identical slogans.

It will depend, in the first place, on Stalin whether in coming years these fears diminish and whether the feud between the two camps is prevented from reaching dangerous proportions. If the Soviet Union continues to limit its territorial claims to those put forth in the beginning, if neighboring countries friendly to it come to enjoy the independence which has been promised them, and if Stalin and the European Communist parties continue their support of genuinely democratic governments in the rest of Europe, much of the wind will be taken out of the sails of militant anti-Communism.

In the next few years, hardly less responsibility will rest with the leaders of public opinion in the opposite camp. Unreasoned and excessive suspicion of Russian intentions, particularly if coupled with an hysterical fear of social change, might easily push Europe into the abyss of civil war and thereby heighten the chances of another world conflagration. The United States and Britain can best assist Europe in its adjustment to the new situation which has developed in the East if, instead of pouring oil into the fire, they offer counsel of moderation and continue to cooperate closely with the Soviet Union —later within the framework of a world organization.

While Russia will necessarily stand first on the list of Europe's external worries, the United States, though for different reasons, may follow as a notable second. Few in Europe will question the fact that security and welfare for most of the continent have come close to being a function of American policies. Particularly for Western Europe, favorable agreements with this country in such matters as money, capital, and markets will far outweigh anything that might be achieved on any purely intra-European basis. Without continued active American interest in the peace of Europe, a sense of inescapable dependency on Russia might come to prevail with consequences in every field which can easily be imagined.

Yet the exponents of an "American orientation," of which there will be many even in Eastern Europe, will run up against many objections. They will be told in the first place that it is futile to rely on the United States for military protection. The part America has played in both the great European wars of this century and the amazing display of American military might would seem to offer a cogent counter-argument. But it will not be forgotten that on both occasions, years elapsed before the powerful American arm could reach across the ocean. There will be similar questioning about continued American economic assistance, particularly in the matter of markets. Finally, misgivings about American interference will also play a considerable role. There will be fear less of American foreign policy than of sudden shifts in this policy. There will be those who dread the overpowering economic might and influence of American big business, while others may be more perturbed at the idea of Europe being subjected to lofty but impracticable American schemes of betterment and reform.

As with Russia, Europe will, in any case, find itself plunged into a process of adjustment and rethinking in regard to the United States. The productive capacities of this country were highly esteemed even before the war; they have, however, far exceeded expectations. The ingenuity of the American fighting forces and supply services have come as a revelation, while the undreamed-of display of American might in the air has completely changed all former power calculations. All this may lead to a revaluation of America and its civilization. It will not make Europe, with its pride and cultural traditions, eager to be Americanized; but it seems certain that this country, though in competition with Russia, will exercise a vigorous and rejuvenating influence on practically every field of European activity.

In treating Europe's relations with Great Britain last I do not mean to imply that her influence on Europe is suffering an eclipse. It may even become stronger than it was before the war, while creating fewer difficulties than are found to exist in respect to the other major powers.

Whatever the present feelings toward Britain may be—and they appear in France and in Italy to be more friendly than one might have expected—there is reason to believe that in the course of time Britain and the Continent will be drawn closer together than they have been for a long time. The British may not cherish the idea of "returning" to Europe as a strictly European power; but planes, robot bombs, amphibious operations, as well as political considerations, are pulling them in that direction. Britain, if she wishes to rank as an equal with the United States and the Soviet Union, will need to have close allies and collaborators. It is doubtful whether the Dominions—small powers scattered around the globe and intent upon their independence—will prove able or willing to lend Britain the strength which she will be seeking. Statements which indicate a growing interest in Western and Southern Europe made recently by leading spokesmen for Britain are therefore not surprising. As a matter of fact, a very close community of interest exists between England and other countries of Europe which, having entered upon an era of retrenchment like herself, are going to be preoccupied with the defense of their homeland, their colonies, and their standard of living.

Not all of Europe will seek to align itself with Britain. Countries falling within the orbit of the Soviet Union will naturally be excluded, while the neutrals of this war, although keener than ever, one should expect, to retain Britain's traditional friendship and protection, may seek to remain aloof from any ties with a specific country. If a kind of Anglo-European grouping should come into existence, extending possibly to the economic as well as to the political sphere, it will require all the art of statesmanship, with which Britain fortunately is richly endowed, to prevent it from degenerating into an anti-Russian if not into an anti-American bloc.

This raises the question of Europe's

position in respect not to the individual great non-European powers but to the Big Three as a group—the acceptance of France as one of the great world powers, while contributing greatly to her position and prestige in Europe, will not change the fact that she and the rest of Europe will have to adjust themselves to the influence and leading role of the United States, Great Britain, and the Soviet Union. Here again European statesmen will find themselves torn between contradictory interests.

There are obvious advantages for Europe in the continuance of intimate collaboration between its great neighbors in the West and the East. Nothing could do more to remove the danger of another war in which Europe would be bound to be one of the main sufferers; nothing short of it could offer a guarantee of real security against Germany. If ever a rift should develop between the western democracies and the Soviet Union, every European country would feel the necessity of taking sides. Germany would not alone begin to pick the winner. Threatened by another conflagration and torn apart by rival neighbors, Europe would come to resemble the Balkans in their most tragic days or share the recent fate of Spain.

But while agreement among the leading powers offers the best chance for stability as well as for economic recovery, there is bound to be fear that such an overpowering alignment might lead to interference in European affairs if not to foreign domination. By proposing to set up a world organization for peace in which the smaller powers are to have some voice, the Great Powers have sought, among other things, to dispel such apprehension both in Europe and elsewhere. Whether they will succeed in doing so will depend on whether the weaker countries become convinced that the "sovereign equality" promised them is going to be more than an empty shell. It is not that the small powers are unwilling to accept the leadership of the big powers and to grant them the privileges without which they would be unable to assume the major responsibility for peace. Many European statesmen have given voice to this view. But the weaker powers will not, if one may judge from past experience, feel that they have obtained the necessary guarantees of their independence if participation of any kind in coercive action, in the form of actual co-belligerency, the passage of troops over their territory, or the use of their ports, is not left to their own decision. They need not, as a matter of fact, be unduly alarmed about their future role and status, since every one of the major powers will continue to be vitally interested in the confidence and wholehearted collaboration of a large number of smaller countries.

Europe would be facing a more serious danger if the exponents of exclusive influence zones should some day gain the upper hand. Carried to its extremes, such a policy would turn the small countries of Europe into mere satellites of Russia or Britain and might induce these two powers to divide Germany between them, possibly along the Elbe River. . . . It would not be surprising if the interest of the United States in Europe and in the peace of the world would be regarded by the peoples of Europe as the surest guarantee against any such development of closed and potentially hostile blocs.

If the major non-European powers continue to strive for a common peace policy, the danger of interference, by any one of them acting alone, in the domestic affairs of others will be much reduced. One might hope for definite commitments in this respect. But whether the Great Powers will find it possible or expedient to refrain from common intervention will depend less on their sense of self-restraint or their good intentions than on the conditions which come to prevail in Europe. If the Continent were to become the scene of civil war or anarchy, they could hardly abstain from taking a hand in what to them would be a matter of vital importance. Their intervention, however, would raise the specter not only of foreign domination over parts of Europe but also of a clash between the intervening powers. Thus Europe's responsibility for orderly internal conditions reaches beyond the continent. The outside world, including even the Soviet Union, may insist that prolonged and violent revolutionary action, however necessary some groups may believe it to be, shall be sacrificed on the altar of world peace.

As a matter of fact, the need for drastic "cleansing revolutions" seems questionable anyhow, at least as far as Western Europe is concerned. Despite what Marxists may say about a prevailing "crisis of capitalism" in all of Europe, conditions there before the war were by no means uniform or uniformly bad. It is well to note that every one of the revolutions and counter-revolutions which have shaken Europe in the course of this century occurred in the least "bourgeois" parts of the Continent where, as in Central and Eastern Europe or Spain, feudal traditions and institutions continued to be powerful. In the West, where democratic government and the middle classes were firmly entrenched, adjustment, both social and economic, to the changing needs and opinions of the time took place without serious upheaval and along the customary lines of compromise and reform. Whether that will continue to be the case under present conditions of misery and ruin, impassioned feeling, and factional strife remains to be seen.

The present swing toward the Left and toward some form of state socialism, observed in many parts of Europe, offers little basis for prediction. It looks as if the offensive remnants of feudalism in the East would be swept away without civil war. One would wish the same could be said of Spain. In the West a policy of nationalization, social reform, and increased government regulation will also, so it now seems, be carried out and accepted without fierce opposition. But the leaders of the Left cannot fail to take the persistent conservatism of the broad middle class and peasant masses into consideration. Even if these groups are less organized and articulate at the moment they, together with the upper classes, would constitute a formidable obstacle to any proletarian revolution and once aroused might threaten to bring a civil war to a Fascist rather than to a socialist conclusion. Fearing such an outcome, the great non-European powers have every interest in helping Europe weather the early postwar storms. It will not be easy to exercise the moderating influence necessary for this task without, unwittingly perhaps, crushing the promising spirit of regeneration and renovation which has been born out of the resistance to the Germans or without stiffening the backs of those new Metternichs whose only goal is the restoration, pure and simple, of a much discredited *status quo ante*. Yet this will not be impossible.

Whatever the outcome of the social struggle now in progress in many parts of Europe, the Old World will for many years face one of the gravest crises of its history. If the nations of Europe which were suffering from a deep malaise and despondency even before the war recover new hope and self-confidence, it will not be primarily because of any economic or political changes they may undertake but because these last years of suffering have revealed to them their own tenacity, spiritual resilience, and courage as well as a community of spirit transcending national boundaries. Prophets of doom have tried for many years to convince Europe that its civilization is spent. But it is worth remembering two things: first, that according to Spengler, who popularized this notion, democratic America and Bolshevik Russia were even more hopelessly infected by the germ of decadence than Europe; and, second, that both Spengler, the prophet of cultural collapse, and Marx, the prophet of revolution, were not speaking as pessimists but as experts in wishful thinking who could hardly wait to see the dawn of their Utopias.

The peoples of Europe, sobered by the horrors of war and revolution, may have grown weary of both the promises and the alarms of the extremists. If, unlike the Nazis, who reacted blindly and savagely against the West and the East, they strive constructively to blend the influences of both with their own rich and living cultural heritage, they will help to bridge the gulf which in thought and institutions separates their great neighbors and at the same time regain for themselves a place of honor at the side of other and rising centers of civilization.

PEACE TERMS FOR JAPAN

All discussion of peace terms for Japan starts with the Cairo Declaration. This is the statement issued jointly by President Roosevelt, Prime Minister Churchill, and General Chiang Kai-shek, on December 1, 1943, after their conference in the Near East. The text of the statement is as follows:

"The several military missions have agreed upon future military operations against Japan. The Three Great Allies expressed their resolve to bring unrelenting pressure against their brutal enemies by sea, land, and air. This pressure is already rising.

"The Three Great Allies are fighting this war to restrain and punish the aggression of Japan. They covet no gain for themselves and have no thought of territorial expansion. It is their purpose that Japan shall be stripped of all the islands in the Pacific which she has seized or occupied since the beginning of the First World War in 1914, and that all the territories Japan has stolen from the Chinese, such as Manchuria, Formosa, and the Pescadores, shall be restored to the Republic of China. Japan will also be expelled from all other territories which she has taken by violence and greed. The aforesaid three Great Powers, mindful of the enslavement of the people of Korea, are determined that in due course Korea shall become free and independent.

"With these objects in view the three Allies, in harmony with those of the United Nations at war with Japan, will continue to persevere in the serious and prolonged operations necessary to procure the unconditional surrender of Japan."

A BRITISH VIEW

By Sir George Sansom

From *Japan,* by Sir George Sansom. Oxford Pamphlets on World Affairs, No. 70. Oxford University Press, London, 1944; reproduced by permission. The author is a distinguished British diplomat with many years of service in Japan.

Once Japan is thoroughly defeated and, in accordance with the terms of the Cairo Declaration, deprived of all her overseas possessions and strategic holdings, her military and economic strength will be reduced to such a point that she cannot menace the security of the Pacific so long as the United Nations exercise reasonable vigilance. Indeed after defeat she may well find herself hard put to it to support her own population and concerned for a long period with plans to restore her own domestic economy rather than with hopes of revenge and conquest.

But of course it cannot be taken for granted that she will settle down to life as a respectable weak power. The question therefore arises whether, in addition to preventive measures, there is any policy which can safely be pursued by the United Nations calculated to persuade the Japanese people to abandon military ambitions. The answer to this question depends mainly upon the prospects of change in the nature of Japanese political institutions.

It is clear that the survival of the present oligarchic system would be dangerous and that some more popular form of government would lessen the risks of a revival of aggression. But we cannot assume that a democracy of Western type would be welcome to or workable by an Eastern people whose history is so unlike our own. We might, of course, as victorious powers impose upon a defeated Japan certain conditions as to the nature of her political institutions, but we could have little confidence in a system which the Japanese people had neither the will nor the experience to operate. Political reforms to be durable must represent a substantial and genuine public sentiment, and it is better to hope not for a counterfeit of Anglo-Saxon political practice but for a system growing and developing naturally from progressive elements already existing in Japan.

The prospects here are not entirely discouraging. There is no evidence of an organized underground movement, but there is a good deal in modern political history to show that there are latent forces opposed to autocratic rule and in favor of more liberal institutions. Between 1920 and 1930, democracy was in favor in Japan, partly no doubt because the democratic powers had been successful in war but also because of a genuine though perhaps not very deep-seated popular feeling. Successors of the party leaders who at that time strove to increase parliamentary authority may well emerge, and secure political reforms which would give Japan a system of responsible cabinet government. This would need certain amendments of the constitution, not very drastic in the circumstances; it would definitely curb the naval and military leaders, and it would probably leave the monarchy in a position of high prestige but stripped of mystical and legendary attributes. Since the parties would depend upon popular support, extensions of the suffrage might be expected and the public would before long have gained both political experience and political power which they would not readily abandon.

Such progress would certainly be modest, but it would be something naturally evolved from past experience and in that respect might be sounder than more striking and revolutionary changes. Revolutionary changes, however, are by no means improbable. Japan has never suffered defeat and there is no means of judging how she will react to national disaster. But it is reasonable to presume that in a time of great crisis many Japanese will begin to question assumptions upon which their national life has been based. Failure and humiliation are likely to discredit the military caste in particular and established authority in general and may create powerful forces of opposition. The army will no longer contain a majority of peasants, upon whose conservative habits the army leaders have relied, but will include all types of the urban population, which will have its own grievances. Economic depression including widespread unemployment and hunger in the towns, and possibly agrarian disturbances, will produce such suffering and discontent that the mass of the people will be disposed to listen to new teachings. Certainly they will find little consolation in the principles with which they have been for so long indoctrinated.

It is difficult to foresee what ideals will replace those which they abandon. Popular initiative is not to be expected, but there are grounds for thinking that a movement of revolt launched by dissident members of the governing class would find considerable popular support. It has been suggested that the shock of disillusionment might turn the minds of the Japanese people toward some version of Communism, because they will need a new militant faith to replace what they have lost and because they are already schooled to corporate life. It may be so. All one can say with confidence is that the form of government which they will adopt will depend not only upon the Japanese themselves but also upon the hopes and inducements held out to them by the victorious powers. Japan's most pressing problem will be that of feeding and employing 75 million people on her diminished resources. Relieved of the burden of armaments, the Japanese should have ample capacity to produce goods for their own civilian consumption. But for that purpose they will need to export in order to import the materials which they lack at home. Consequently their future depends upon their foreign trade. It will be for the victorious powers to devise a plan by which Japan can be ensured a livelihood but denied the power of aggression. Liberal government will not flourish in a country struggling for the very means of subsistence; and though it is true that the satisfaction of Japan's peaceful economic needs will not of itself check her ambitions, it may at least promote the growth of a new social and political order favorable to international collaboration. The United Nations will be in a position to influence the trend without prescribing the forms of political development in Japan, since they will hold the key to her survival. They can indicate to Japan that her prospects of being readmitted to international society will improve as she reforms her institutions. Among the specific changes which they may suggest are an extension of popular rights; a gradual improvement in the legal and personal status of women; the abolition of an oppressive police system; a considerable development of freedom of speech and freedom of religious belief; and a relaxation of state control of education.

These are reforms which could not be imposed against the will of a whole nation, but there is no good reason to think that they could not be welcome to a majority of the Japanese people. They would however be resisted by many reactionary groups and individuals, and therefore one of the dangers to be guarded against in dealing with Japan immediately after the war will be the appearance of autocratic leaders in liberal disguise. Such men will not cease to conspire until they are convinced that their country's defeat is irrevocable, that the United Nations will permanently stand by the Cairo Declaration. Unless this can be assumed, there is little use in considering what are desirable changes in the social and political structure of Japan, for so long as she sees possibilities of recovering power we cannot be sure that liberal institutions will restrain the expansive urge of her vigorous and numerous people.

AN AMERICAN VIEW

By T. A. Bisson

From "The Price of Peace for Japan," by T. A. Bisson, in *Pacific Affairs*, March 1944. Copyright 1944 by The Institute of Pacific Relations, New York; reproduced by permission. The author is associate editor of *Pacific Affairs*.

The peace with Japan will be a harsh one in many of its aspects, notably those affecting territories, disarmament, and possible reparations. When the costs and sacrifices of defeating Japan's ruthless aggression are placed in the reckoning, nothing less should be expected or desired. These terms of the peace will, in some cases, be setting right old wrongs that have endured for a generation or longer. They are also required to limit Japan's power to engage in a second adventure in aggression. . . .

[But revenge is not the ultimate objective.] Any such policy would be self-defeating. Sir George Sansom has rightly declared that the existence of "a nation of over 70 million desperate and frustrated people would ruin any plan designed to bring prosperity and peace to Asia." The principles enunciated by President Roosevelt for the German people must also be taken as applying to the Japanese people—they will be given "a normal chance to develop, in peace, as useful and respectable members" of the world community. . . .

[The achievement of such a peace] . . . makes serious demands on the United Nations, as well as on Japan. They must assist her to develop along peaceful lines on both the political and economic levels; they must assume direct responsibility for the type of political and social structure established in Japan after her defeat. . . . The enemy nations must be restored to health and then must be fitted into a constructive system of international collaboration.

It thus becomes evident that the harsher aspects of the peace settlement constitute merely the preliminary and not the most important stage. They represent nonetheless an indispensable foundation which must be carefully laid. It is essential, above all, that these punitive terms not be applied in such a fashion as to jeopardize the constructive ends in view. . . .

It may be taken for granted that the decision of the Cairo conference to strip Japan of her territorial acquisitions since 1895 will be enforced. . . . Before . . . 1895 Japan was a nation of some 40 million people living mainly on the 148,000 square miles of its home islands. . . . After the peace, she will have about 75 million Japanese, again living mainly on the restricted area of her home islands.

Along with this drastic change will go a series of strict disarmament provisions. . . . For a period of years, which will probably not be definitely fixed, Japan will be prohibited from maintaining a naval or military force of any kind. . . .

Thus far it may be assumed that little disagreement would exist. More extreme proposals call for the total abolition of Japanese industry and the return of that country to an agrarian subsistence economy. Since proposals of this kind would condemn possibly one-quarter of Japan's present 75 million people to death by starvation, it would seem the part of wisdom to discount and reject them. Extermination is not a rational solution of the problem. Persons advocating such methods are evading the real task which faces the

United Nations—the bringing into existence of a decent Japan which can cooperate with other nations in establishing an enlightened world community.

In one other aspect of Japanese disarmament, however, it might be advisable to impose even stricter conditions than are generally suggested. This affects the treatment of the Japanese officer class, military and naval, which has largely supplied the Hitlers and the Himmlers of Japan, the spearheads of Japan's totalitarianism. . . . The free circulation of this group of officers inside Japan during the immediate postwar years would seriously jeopardize all that we should hope to see develop there.

On reparations, there is likely to be considerable difference of opinion. It is only natural that the Chinese people, conscious of the devastation wrought in their country since 1937, should insist that full reparation be made for the injury suffered. Part of this reparation, at least, may be obtained in the recovered territories. The Chinese will inherit important and sizeable industrial installations in Manchuria and Formosa, unless extensive damage is caused there later on by bombing raids or a "scorched earth" policy. Particularly in Manchuria, with its coal and iron mines, blast furnaces, and rolling mills . . . China will obtain an increment of heavy industry of significant proportions. It might be well to transfer to China on reparation account all Japanese vested interests in Manchuria and Formosa, without regard to the present legal character of the titles; the same principle could also be applied, with a considerable degree of justice, in Korea. This type of action would be doubly advantageous. At one stroke it would settle the intractable issues clustering around Japanese "rights and interests" in these territories, mostly gained by force and chicanery, which helped to precipitate the Manchurian invasion in September 1931. Joined to restoration of Chinese sovereignty, it would give China full mastery in the regained territories. It would have the further advantage of telescoping reparations into a single well-defined act, thus avoiding the handicap to restoration of normal economic and psychological conditions which long-drawn-out reparations payments bring in their train.

Strong reasons can be mustered against the advisability of exacting further reparations of any considerable scope from Japan. Thrown back on the narrow limits of its home islands, Japan will be faced at best with an exceedingly onerous task of self-support. Extreme proposals calling for the transfer of the equipment of Japan's home industry to China or other Far Eastern countries have a dubious validity. Aside from their uneconomic character, such proposals are merely another way of insisting that Japan return to its agrarian economy of a century ago, previously noted as an irrational extermination policy. If the proposals seek merely the transfer of presently existing equipment, leaving Japan free to replace it, then one can be sure that Japan will replace it with new and better machinery within five or ten years.

Actually there is no valid reason for placing artificial barriers in the path of Japan's economic progress. With the security issue settled, it may be assumed that Japan's economic advance will be to the advantage and not to the detriment of all other Far Eastern countries. Disarmament and security provisions should be kept within their own proper sphere, where the terms already envisaged will leave Japan hopelessly weak for a long period of years. It is not advisable that reparations be used as an indirect means of disarmament by keeping the country weak through an enforced economic backwardness. This, too, is a method that dodges the central task of restoring the enemy country to political and social health and enabling it to play a constructive role in an expanding world economy. . . .

The problem of establishing peace thus runs much deeper than the mere handling of disarmament issues. Extension of disarmament into the factory, a necessity under modern conditions, still treats the symptoms, not the disease itself. The key issue in the degree of success attending the United Nations' dealings with a defeated Japan is not how well the country is disarmed but how greatly its outlook and motivation are changed. In the last analysis, what is required is a thorough recasting of Japan's political and social leadership. . . .

In this task, it will be necessary to have a clear understanding of the old Japan which we are seeking to transform. Who are the forces that have ruled Japan, making it the predatory, aggressive power that it is today? As in Germany they consist mainly of the large landlords, the big industrialists, and the army, with its ruthless fanaticism, its ideology of the master race, and spirit of aggressive conquest. . . .

In many respects [the militarists] perform the key function in directing the aggressive side of Japanese imperial expansion. . . . The Japanese militarists, without any formal organization, were the Nazi party of Japan for many years prior to 1940. They had their own means of appeal to the masses, through a host of chauvinist societies, and through inflammatory speeches and pamphlets circulating in hundreds of thousands of copies. They utilized Nazi methods of direct action, including assassination and overt uprisings. They held a decisive initiative in foreign policy through their assumed power of launching military operations in a foreign country on their own authority, irrespective of the policy of the Cabinet that happened to be in office at the time. . . .

The militarists came to wield this tremendous power mainly because the Constitution granted by the Emperor in 1889 accorded the army and navy leaders direct access to the Emperor and allowed them to exercise a political authority not possessed by the armed services of any other modern state. These powers enabled the Japanese militarists to arrogate the right of being the authorized interpreters of the Emperor's will and of the mission of the "divinely-empowered" Japanese race. On this basis, they developed an ideology thoroughly akin in spirit and purpose to the ideology of Hitlerism. Throughout the 'thirties they conducted an unrelenting campaign against all liberal attempts to define the Emperor's position in any way which would permit the evolution of a constitutional monarchy in Japan. . . . This fact should give pause to those persons who advocate maintenance of the Emperor as a "stabilizing force" in the Japanese political structure or who believe in the feasibility of establishing a liberal constitutional monarchy in Japan. . . .

It is not necessary, after victory, that there be carried to Japan a complete blueprint of reform which shall then be forced *in toto* upon the Japanese people. It is necessary that the United Nations' administrators be thoroughly familiar with the old forces that have been operating there and that they should set a course that will prevent these old forces from reasserting control, on the one hand, and will encourage those new forces that will be able to bring into being a different Japan. . . .

Agrarian reform, involving land redistribution and changes in the system of land tenure and rural credit, is a prerequisite to the establishment of social and economic health in Japan. Improved living conditions for the farmers will force higher wage standards for the industrial workers by removing that inexhaustible reservoir of cheap labor on which the *Zaibatsu* have waxed fat. The resultant increase in purchasing power by the mass of the population will expand Japan's home market and thus reduce the pressure to export; by the same token, the higher cost of labor will diminish the keen edge of Japanese competition which Western merchants have experienced to their distress. An economic margin for these domestic reforms will be provided by the abolition of armament expenditures which have hitherto absorbed such a large proportion of Japan's national income.

The outside world will have to undergird this development by providing Japan with the fullest access to raw materials and markets. Foreign trade will be Japan's "lifeline" after the war in a sense quantitatively so enhanced as almost to make a qualitative difference. Large amounts of raw materials formerly within Japan's "domestic" sphere, notably in Manchuria, Korea, and Formosa, will henceforth be in foreign countries. Much of these will be absorbed locally, and so entirely removed from Japan's economic orbit. Similarly, the former Japanese-controlled markets in these territories will henceforth be foreign markets. . . .

No one can predict the exact conditions which will exist in Japan at the end of the war. It is possible, but not at all certain, that a vast social revolutionary upheaval will occur, burning away in its fires much of the dross of old Japan. . . . If such conditions developed toward the end of the war, they would help to shorten its last stages. If they developed after defeat, they could perform many tasks which it would be less politic for us to impose in the peace terms. It would rather be the function of the United Nations to hold the ring while the issue is being settled by the Japanese, and then to seek immediate relations with the representatives of the new popular forces which had asserted their leadership. . . .

It is necessary to end this analysis on a note of warning. There is no certainty that we shall have the will, the patience, or the skill adequate to guide Japan along new and better paths of development. But we should be forewarned that, if the old forces are permitted to reestablish themselves in Japan, it will be impossible for us to hold them in leading strings or to prevent them from amassing the power to strike again, first for their independence from our controls and then for domination. . . . The old forces can be replaced; they cannot be restored to power and then permanently curbed. . . .

THE PROBLEM OF PEACE IN THE FAR EAST

By Sumner Welles

From chap. 7 of *The Time for Decision,* by Sumner Welles. Copyright 1944 by Sumner Welles; Harper & Brothers, N.Y.; reproduced by permission. The author was Assistant Secretary of State, 1933-1937, and Under Secretary, 1937-1943.

However completely the physical results of the Japanese attempt to dominate the Pacific and Asia may be obliterated, it must frankly be recognized that one psychological development—the growth of nationalism among the peoples of the Far East—has been greatly accelerated by their triumphs of 1942. It was not only the quick collapse of British resistance in Burma that struck eastern observers in that year, but also the apparently incredible rapidity of the surrender of the great British naval base at Singapore, and the general elimination of all western resistance to Japan. This nationalistic development is due in part to healthy and spontaneous growth, as represented by the birth of a greatly unified China and by the demands of the people of India during the past quarter of a century for the right of self-government. But it has likewise been stimulated by Japanese propaganda during the past five years or more, in all of which much emphasis has been laid upon the issue of "Asia for the Asiatics."

The inherent justice of that thesis, if divorced from the fact that it has been put forward to serve their own ends by a people who have shown the most cynical disregard for the rights of others, has necessarily made an appeal to all the peoples of the Far East. For that matter, it has appealed to many peoples in other parts of the world as well.

Moreover, during the years between 1920 and 1940 a period in the history of the Asiatic and Pacific peoples was in any event drawing to its close. The startling development of Japan as a world power, and the slower but nevertheless steady emergence of China as a full member of the family of nations, together with the growth of popular institutions among many other peoples of Asia, notably India, all combined to erase very swiftly indeed the fetish of white supremacy cultivated by the big colonial powers during the nineteenth century. The thesis of white supremacy could only exist so long as the white race actually proved to be supreme. The nature of the defeats suffered by the western nations in 1942 dealt the final blow to any concept of white superiority which still remained.

Another factor in the Asiatic situation, which we of the West must constantly bear in mind, is that, quite apart from the fact that we cannot logically expect any people to derive satisfaction from their domination by an alien power, the colonizing powers of Europe have only in a few instances used their authority with any regard for the rights or interests of the people over whom they have ruled. Resentments, as a result, are deeply rooted. They have their roots not only in the memory of early brutalities and shocking injustices, but also in such recent horrors as the massacre at Amritsar. They find their origin likewise in the very natural human reaction to the contemptuous treatment usually accorded a subject people. . . .

The British government, like the government of the Netherlands, has undoubtedly demonstrated a desire to deal justly with the people within the British Empire, and the spirit of devotion, of decency, and of self-abnegation shown by many thousands of British colonial administrators can only be admired. Yet only too many British representatives in the Far East have demonstrated that type of thinking which is so well exemplified in the words of a high British official in India at the outset of the present century when he expressed a conviction which he asserted "was shared by every Englishman in India, from the highest to the lowest . . . the conviction in every man that he belongs to a race whom God has destined to govern and subdue."

These words might well have been spoken in this present year of grace [1944] to the German people by Hitler, or by one of his Nazi associates. They assert the existence of a master race, and the right of that master race to "govern and subdue." We ourselves, the British people, and all free peoples are at the present moment fighting and dying in order to show the intrinsic falsity of any such philosophies as these.

It is hardly surprising, therefore, that as the peoples of Asia have become increasingly conscious of their own individual virtues, of their own national strength, and of their own national resources, any such doctrine as that should become more and more intolerable. If the assertion of these alleged rights has already proved to be so completely unbearable to peoples ruled by the most humane and the least tyrannical of the colonial powers, how far more unbearable it must have proved to peoples dominated by colonial nations mainly bent upon the exploitation of the subject populations.

Some nations, like China, have in the past been only partially subject to foreign domination; others, like the Philippines, have been voluntarily granted their freedom and independence. To the present-day enlightened leaders of such nations, the continued exercise of colonial jurisdiction over the peoples of Asia by European powers has become morally repellent. Also, they necessarily regard it as a source of future peril to the steady development of their free institutions and as a continuing danger to the peace and stability of Asia.

Upon the conclusion of the present war a radical readjustment of international relationships throughout Asia and the regions of the Pacific is indispensable if there is to be any hope at all of political stability, economic security, and peaceful progress. The situation is replete with highly explosive factors. The dynamics of the situation can be regulated, provided the major European and western powers make the radical readjustments which are necessary. If they do not, it is difficult to foresee any other prospect in the Far East than a century of chaos and general anarchy.

I believe that these new forces of nationalism can successfully be canalized into peaceful and constructive channels only if the powers of the world, in a future international organization, are willing to adopt the basic principle that no nation possesses the inherent and unlimited right to dominate alien peoples. They must recognize that the so-called colonial powers are obligated to prove to world public opinion, as represented by an international organization, that their administration over alien peoples is to the interest of the governed, and has for its chief objective the assumption of self-government by these peoples. Once that great principle is established, it will still be necessary to construct machinery capable of carrying it out.

An international trusteeship of the kind suggested must be first of all responsible to the political executive body established by the world organization. For reasons of efficient administration, under the over-all authority of this supreme executive agency, regional authorities should be set up with jurisdiction over certain stated areas of the world within which local administration of subject peoples is exercised by a colonial power. Finally, representatives of the regional authority should reside within each colonial area in order that the authority may have, in addition to such reports and information as the administering power may be required to present to it periodically, the impartial and objective reports of individuals responsible solely to the international trusteeship. . . .

The problems with which any organization such as I have outlined would immediately be faced in the Far East fall into four main categories.

First, the problem presented by the people of Korea. In the Declaration issued at Cairo by Roosevelt, Churchill, and Chiang Kai-shek, with which the Soviet Union must clearly have been in accord, it was stated that the powers concerned would see to it that, upon the defeat of Japan, Korea would regain its independence "in due course." These words "in due course" have created much disquiet among certain Korean patriots. It must be clear, however, that, after a ruthless domination and exploitation such as the Korean people have suffered at the hands of Japan during the past thirty-seven years, a certain period of time must necessarily elapse before the last vestiges of Japanese rule can be wiped out and the independent economy of the country can once more be set up. The Korean people will need sufficient time to strengthen the atrophied muscles of self-government. It is equally clear that some friendly hands must be available to render the assistance required until all of the mechanics of self-government can be supplied by the Korean people themselves.

Such assistance must be given, under the ultimate jurisdiction of the world organization, by powers directly concerned in the welfare of the independent Korea and in the successful stabilization of the Far Eastern situation. In this case it would appear logical that the governments called upon to participate should be China, the Soviet Union, and the United States.

The trusteeship would last until the Korean people demonstrated their ability to walk alone. Until such time the trustee countries, through local administrators who might well be nationals of other countries, would undertake the task of expediting the return of the Korean people to the responsibilities of self-government.

The second category would comprise those peoples of the Far East now under the control of a colonial power, but believed to be capable of enjoying autonomy in the immediate future. Within this category could come India.

There is no useful purpose to be served by debating whether or not the people of India are capable of self-government, since upon several occasions since the conclusion of the First World War, notably two years ago during the special mission to India by Sir Stafford Cripps, the British government has officially announced its intention of granting self-government to India. As recently as January 28, 1944, that most enlightened and liberal-minded of Indian Viceroys, Lord Halifax, publicly stated in the name of the British government:

"We hope that India, in what we believe to be her own highest interests, will wish to remain within the British Commonwealth. But if, after the war, her people can establish an agreed constitution and then desire to sever their partnership with us, we have undertaken not to overrule such decision.... If India cannot yet agree to move forward as a single whole, we are prepared to see her large component elements move forward separately. We recognize all the objections to a rupture of Indian unity, but we also believe that stability cannot be found through compulsion of the great minorities.... This attitude is in complete conformity with the principle of the Atlantic Charter."

Thus it is clear that, provided the people of India and the British government can reach an agreement as to the basis upon which an independent government of India can be established, a solution for this ever-increasingly intricate and dangerous problem can be found. Such a solution will not be made easier by intemperate outpourings from

Downing Street, nor by equally intemperate insistence by pundits in the United States that the way to solve the problem is for British authority to remove itself bag and baggage from India between dawn and night. Obviously the ideal method of solution is through direct negotiation between the British government and the representative leaders of India. It is a method which has already frequently been adopted. However, should these efforts continue to fail, the executive council of the international organization, through its agencies, should stand ready to assist in composing the difficulties which might still exist.

Neither die-hardism in England nor ultraliberalism in other countries, such as the United States, can change one salient fact, and that is that the people of India are determined to obtain self-government. A continuation of the present impasse after the war will seriously endanger the peace and stability of all of the Far East. The independent peoples of the Far East today, let alone those still under alien rule, not only view the aspirations of the Indian leaders with the utmost sympathy, but regard the disposition to be made of India after the war as the acid test of the intentions of the western powers as set forth in the Atlantic Charter.

Equally clearly within this category fall the Netherlands East Indies. But I am inclined to believe that this problem has probably been solved already. In 1942 the Netherlands government-in-exile announced its decision that upon the liberation of Holland a new federal constitution would be promulgated under which the peoples of the Netherlands East Indies would be guaranteed precisely the same constitutional rights of self-government and individual liberty as the people of the Netherlands themselves. If this pledge can be carried out, the peoples of the Netherlands East Indies will have ample means of determining their own destiny, and any question of international trusteeship in their case should not arise.

The third category would include the problems of Burma, Malaya, and French Indo-China. The peoples of these countries have all passed the first milestone along the road toward self-government; but they have not as yet reached a stage of development where they can successfully undertake the exercise of those rights. In such cases the world organization, operating through the supreme agency of the international trusteeship and the regional authorities to be created, must assert its right to hold the present administering powers responsible for the nature of their administration. This will ensure that every practical step is taken to accelerate the course of these countries toward independence. I would further propose that the regional authority in this instance be entrusted to the present colonial powers, namely, Great Britain and France, and that China, Australia, New Zealand, and the future republic of the Philippines likewise participate in such regional authority. It seems to me logical, and from many standpoints highly desirable, that the seat of the executive agency of the regional authority should be at Manila.

The fourth category would comprise those colonial peoples of the Southwestern Pacific who are still uncivilized and as yet clearly incapable of governing themselves. The aborigines of the islands of the South Pacific, such as the peoples of New Guinea, would be an example. As in the case of the peoples comprised within the third category, the supreme agency of the international trusteeship, through a regional authority, should exercise ultimate control over the local government of the administering power. This will ensure that the peoples governed are treated with humanity and justice, that their natural resources will be exploited primarily for their benefit rather than for the benefit of the administering power. It will also make certain that all possible steps will be taken for their physical and moral improvement and for their education, until such time as their descendants may demonstrate their ability to exercise autonomy.

In this brief survey of possible future dispositions in the Pacific, it is of course assumed that the promises made in the Declaration of Cairo will be carried out. There it was announced that the territory seized from China during past generations by Japan would be restored to the sovereign jurisdiction of the Republic of China, and that the Pacific islands over which Japan obtained jurisdiction as a mandatory upon the conclusion of the First World War would be utilized by the international organization primarily for purposes of international security.

Apart, therefore, from normal and continuing participation in Pacific affairs by the nations of North and South America and by the Soviet Union, the New Order in the Far East, far different from that envisaged by Japan, will comprise the republic of China, restored to the control of the territories of which it has been robbed; the Dominions of Australia and New Zealand; the independent states of the Philippine Republic and Korea; India, as a self-governing Dominion or as an independent nation; the Netherlands East Indies, as an autonomous and integral part of the kingdom of the Netherlands; and a diminished Japan, to be placed, for at least a period of years, under some form of rigid international control exercised through the world organization.

The statesmanship of the United States government and the essential wisdom of the American people in the field of foreign affairs will be tested as they have never been before when the time comes to decide on the policy to be followed in regard to a defeated Japan. The future of the American people will in great part depend upon the nature of these decisions....

There can be no question but that Japan must be deprived of her stolen territories. The Japanese criminals, high or low, who have been guilty of the hideous atrocities perpetrated upon our own nationals and upon those of other countries during these war years must be relentlessly punished. Japan must be disarmed, and prevented from rearming, under a continuing form of international control. But, as Ambassador Grew has wisely said with regard to this very problem, if steam is confined in a vessel from which there is no outlet, there will be an inevitable explosion. Neither sentimentality nor softness, therefore, inspires my considered conviction that one of the factors determining whether the United States will in the future be secure, and whether a lasting world organization can be created, will be the manner in which the Japanese people are handled.

The people of Japan have demonstrated their power and their ability, however evil the purpose to which these may have been applied. They have shown their willingness to subordinate themselves as human beings to what they conceive to be their national interest. They can exist and prosper at an incredibly low standard of living. They breed fast. They are governed more directly as a national unit by blind hate and by the spirit of revenge than any other major people of the earth. Those are facts which cannot be brushed aside.

There is not the shadow of a doubt that the Japanese military and naval high commands, submerged though they will be after Japan's defeat, will keep alive their organization, precisely as the German General Staff will endeavor to keep alive its organization, and plan for the eventual day of revenge. In making our peace decisions, as in shaping our long-range policy, these facts should be kept uppermost in mind.

In my opinion there is but one constructive approach to the problem. This involves three major objectives which should be pursued consistently, whether or not the majority of Americans are once more lulled into a false feeling of security. First, an unswerving determination to make every necessary contribution toward the existence of an effective world organization. Second, the continued disarmament of Japan. Third, the establishment by international agreement of liberal economic policies which will afford the Japanese people an outlet for their abilities and for their enterprise. That is the only course by which they can gradually improve their standard of living, without at the same time endangering the peace of the rest of the world.

PREREQUISITES OF PEACE IN THE FAR EAST

By David N. Rowe

From chap. 9 of *China Among the Powers*, by David N. Rowe. Copyright 1945 by Harcourt, Brace & Co., New York; reproduced by permission. The author is associate professor of international relations at Yale University, and a member of the Institute of International Studies at Yale, which sponsored the work resulting in this study.

To solve the problem of security in Asia and the Pacific it is necessary to decide first from what quarters there could possibly come threats to the peace in that region. When the war ends, there will be only three powers of first-rank military strength with territorial possessions in the area. These are Britain, Soviet Russia, and the United States. It will be impossible for these powers to achieve security *against* each other. Among them, security can only come from the preservation in time of peace of their present collaboration *with* each other. This collaboration must be expressed in concrete terms in relation to the solution of definite problems.

One of these problems is the preservation of China's security after the war. It is a simple recognition of fact to state that no solution of China's security problem can be achieved or successfully carried through unless all of the three super-powers, as well as China, are agreeable to it. . . .

[Even the best plan of] territorial settlement, however, would not of itself be sufficient to insure peace in the Far East. It must be supplemented by the effective and continued disarmament of Japan. . . .

It is, however, precisely because disarmament measures can so easily fail that fundamental reliance for security must be placed on the military readiness of the powers. Of special importance in this respect is [an adequate] system of [American] bases in the Pacific. . . .

In the final analysis, security against Japan can only be provided by an adequate system of military measures, operated by the Great Powers in the interest of a stable peace. In such operations, the Great Powers must inevitably be guided by their separate and collective interests, conceived in the light of their understanding of the general and specific interests of other members of world society.

Chapter 18

Security for the United States: How Can We Achieve It?

The United States alone among the greater powers has escaped bombing and devastation in the war. For a few months after the attack on Pearl Harbor, it seemed possible that our mainland cities too might feel the shattering impact of enemy bombs. But no raids occurred, and for the vast majority of Americans practice blackouts were the nearest physical approach to the realities of modern war.

As a result of this experience the traditional American illusion of security was never really shattered. Most Americans simply cannot imagine themselves huddling in underground shelters, fighting incendiary fires, picking in the charred ruins of their burned-out homes.

Another consequence of our remoteness from the battlefields is all but universal confidence in the ability of American arms—preferably with allies, but alone if necessary—to defend our shores against any and all enemies. The task of organizing to prevent more war lacks for the ordinary American the urgency which it has acquired for the less favored peoples of our world. We have yet to grasp the changing character of war, and the bearing of that upon our own future.

The American people have been repeatedly told by their scientists, political leaders, and military experts that recent advances in war technology have brought every country within range of annihilating attack. We have seen pictures of Hiroshima, leveled by a single atomic bomb. We are warned of still more frightful weapons that can wipe out mankind unless ways and means are found to harness these new engines of violence within a framework of law and order.

One fears lest these warnings go unheeded. As the war recedes into the background, it will be easy to forget what happened to Hiroshima and Nagasaki. It will be easy to assume that "it can't happen here."

But the danger is all too real. The problem of creating a new international order is no less urgent for the United States than for the more crowded peoples of the Old World. There can be no security in isolation, armed or unarmed. Either we shall have "one world," or we shall probably have none.

This problem of building a new world order is one of the most baffling ever confronted. Statesmen cannot start with a clean slate. They must take the world pretty much as they find it. At best we can hope for no more than step-by-step progress within the existing framework of the multi-state system.

By now it is perfectly clear that no world super-state will take form in our time. The war has not weakened the bonds of nationalism. The architects of the new world order have generally recognized this fact. The charter of the new world organization envisages a partnership of nations, not an international corporation.

Discussion of international organization in the United States, however, has sometimes revealed alarming lack of realism. Americans as a rule have great faith in charters, formulae, and gadgets. There seems to be widespread belief that disparities of strength between great and small states can be largely neutralized, that the superior power of the greater states can be effectively shackled, and security for all be thus assured, if only we can contrive the right formula for voting in the world security council, for setting up international police forces, for revising unjust treaties, etc.

Such questions are important. No realistic student of world affairs would think of denying that. But questions of organization and procedure can be dealt with effectively only in the light of still more basic issues.

A great deal will depend upon the spirit that pervades the statecraft of the greater nations. If suspicion and distrust dominate their relations, if their peoples regard each other as potential enemies, if tyranny and exploitation mar their relations with weaker peoples, no charter will work. If, on the other hand, mutual trust and confidence become increasingly the keynote of Great Power relations, and if the greater states honor self-imposed restraints in their dealings with the lesser powers and with dependent peoples, a long step forward will have been taken on the road to a just and enduring peace.

Much also will depend upon clear understanding of the fundamental changes now taking place in the distribution of power among nations. As repeatedly emphasized in this book, the war has altered the value of many cards in the international deck. No enduring world order can be built upon prewar assumptions regarding the power and relations of nations. We must start with the world as it is, not as it was. Given such knowledge, coupled with a spirit of accommodation, a spirit of live-and-let-live, we can tackle with some optimism the gigantic tasks of world reconstruction.

The readings brought together in this final chapter deal with various aspects of this highly controversial subject of world reorganization. The authorities represented do not always agree with each other. But their views all reflect keen awareness not only of the urgency of the problem but also of the necessity of fitting any plan for world security into the framework of our multi-state system.

OUR LAST CHANCE: THE CHALLENGE TO MANKIND

By Raymond B. Fosdick

From "Our Last Chance at San Francisco," by R. B. Fosdick, in the *New York Times Magazine,* April 22, 1945. Copyright 1945 by the New York Times Co.; reproduced by permission. Mr. Fosdick is president of the Rockefeller Foundation.

MODERN science has at last brought us face to face with a decision which we can no longer evade. Thanks to our chemists and physicists, war as a method of settling disputes between nations has become so monstrous in its destruction that it is now a vast canopy of death spread over a blackened and smoking world. Another war would be nothing less than global suicide, with no possible outcome except that described by H. G. Wells in his grim prophecy that man will "blunder down the slopes of failure to his ultimate extinction."

Science has resolved the slaughter of the human race almost to a mathematical formula. What is now missing from the equation will be filled in during the next few years in laboratories around the world. All that science needs is just a little more time. The next war, if it comes, will be a matter of switchboards and push-buttons, releasing annihilation on a scale which will make the destruction of the present war seem amateurish. No nation will be exempt; all will be involved in epidemic calamity.

This is not scarehead mongering, whipped up to frighten people into supporting a peace plan. It is the cold, bitter truth—a truth which, although their lips are sealed by the necessities of this war, our physical scientists and technologists admit without reservation. They are themselves frightened by the powers of carnage which they have created. They are even more frightened by the new powers which are almost within their reach. About these new powers they scarcely dare whisper, even among themselves. A physicist whose name is known around the world said to the writer recently: "It is as if we had uncorked a bottle from which some violent genie has escaped; we cannot get it back into the bottle again."

Thus at long last we come to the end of the road, face to face with our final chance. This time we cannot postpone the issue; we cannot complacently sit back and say that the matter of peace has to be left to the slow processes of evolution. Man has suddenly become the architect of his own fate, the molder of his own future, and there is an imminence about that future from which he cannot wriggle away. This time the stakes are life or death on a terrestrial scale. This time we roll the dice with destiny. . . .

CAN SCIENTIFIC RESEARCH BE CONTROLLED?

By George Fielding Eliot

From "Science and Foreign Policy," by G. F. Eliot, in *Foreign Affairs*, April 1945. Copyright 1945 by the Council on Foreign Relations, New York; reproduced by permission. Major Eliot is the well known military analyst of the *New York Herald Tribune* and the Columbia Broadcasting System.

If the collective intelligence of mankind is unequal to the task of preventing another war, [the robot bomb, the rocket, the jet-propelled airplane, and the atomic bomb, unleashed in the final phase of the Second World War] will be used in perfected form at the outset, perhaps with instantly decisive effect. . . .

In considering how to guard against a catastrophe which threatens the total destruction of the civilization built up painfully by mankind through the centuries, we must ask whether we have not reached the point where the discoveries of science must become the common property of all, for the use of all. Can we permit any more secrets if machines secretly produced threaten to destroy us all? Can there any longer be private research, in the old sense of the word, for military purposes or for the commercial processes which can serve those purposes? . . .

Let us now, in the light of these general considerations, examine one specific consideration introduced by the nature of modern warfare—the fact that states now strike at one another through the air. . . . [No longer can] the centers of industry, the internal transportation facilities, even the homes of the people . . . be protected by armies defending the frontiers or advancing from them into enemy territory. Similarly, it is no longer true that they can be protected by command of a sea which an enemy must cross in order to attack them.

Science, mobilized along with the other resources of a nation, has given to warfare a succession of new weapons which have steadily increased in range, speed, destructive power and terribleness. These new weapons for the most part move through the air, where no material barriers can be erected. They strike at the centers of national power, directly and without warning. In a few years' time it will be possible to aim such attacks from any point on the surface of the earth against any other point.

Means of defense will be developed, of course, against such weapons, partly through scientific research, partly by the device of putting dwellings, factories, and military installations underground. . . . If our plan is to depend upon counter-research to provide technical means of defense, the question of time is of prime importance. Those who contemplate aggression will be stimulated to develop some new means of offense against which no defense has yet been worked out. If they were to produce a weapon of overwhelming power, the results might be decisive before there was time to counteract it. The chances that an aggressor nation might come forward suddenly with such a weapon would obviously be much greater if the scientists of every country were working in watertight compartments, each clutching his own secrets tightly to his bosom.

Science in general may be said to move on parallel lines in various localities. . . . Rarely in peacetime is any new advance in science announced without the claim being made that the same goal has almost been attained elsewhere. If the labors of all scientists in all peace-loving states are pooled, the chance of a sudden surprise by a new "terror-weapon" will be greatly reduced.

Obviously the progress of scientific research and development in the use of such weapons, and in means of defense against them, is a most important factor in future military policy. It is perhaps *the* most important factor. The degree of perfection to which man's instruments of self-destruction have already been carried makes it vitally necessary that the use and even the possession of such instruments be restricted by law—that is, by common agreement. This is the inexorable force which is impelling the peoples of the world to seek safety in union.

But this approach toward union has not yet extinguished nationalism. Suspicion and uncertainty still exist between nations. The practical problem of how to control scientific research and development in the military field is, therefore, far from easy to solve. . . .

Shall there be a complete and continuous interchange of information on the progress of scientific research among the United Nations, without any reservations? An interchange of this sort, on an all-out and completely reciprocal basis, exists today between the United States and the nations of the British Commonwealth, through the media of the Combined Chiefs of Staff and other joint agencies. Can and will this sort of interchange be extended to include all the other members of the new international organization, and will it be continued when the immediate pressure of military necessity has relaxed?

We might as well frankly face the fact that the great question mark in this proposition is Soviet Russia. Up to the time of the . . . Crimea Conference our exchange of information of any kind with the Russians left a great deal to be desired. They told us very little, even about military operations, and they were not members of the Combined Chiefs of Staff or of any of the other combined technical agencies. Possibly political reasons . . . have accounted in part for the Russian attitude; but it certainly is true to say that the Russians have kept their western Allies at arm's length in matters even relating to the war against Germany.

The future of the international security organization depends in large part on whether the Russians can be persuaded that this "Chinese wall" with which they have surrounded their country, for reasons which have seemed to them good, need no longer be maintained. . . . If the new organization is to succeed, there must be complete confidence between partner and partner; and in no field is it of greater consequence than in that of military-scientific research and development. A secret armament race between the United States and Russia would keep the world in terror and would undermine the whole structure of world security which we are hoping to build. It seems almost certain to come unless each partner keeps the others fully informed as to the new weapons which its scientists are developing and as to defenses which they are devising against existing weapons.

It is hard to see how such confidence can be assured without freedom of communication, of travel, of press and radio, and of academic and scientific interchange. The mere statement of these conditions shows how long and difficult is the road that must be traveled. The journey will hardly be completed in a single stage. A step-by-step advance, on a strictly reciprocal basis, will perhaps prove to be the only method of progress. The political and social differences of years and the unfortunate mistrusts which they engendered will not be dissipated easily; but we may hope that the comradeship of arms, the winning of a common victory and the tremendous stake which both peoples have in the preservation of peace may all have an influence in bringing about an eventual solution....

... The problems seem plain, and so do the dangers. The problems must be solved and the dangers must be averted, for they menace every human being on this earth, and his children yet unborn. Science can contribute many more discoveries to our prosperity and wellbeing. But if collective intelligence cannot find ways to control the terrible instruments which individual minds have brought and will bring into being, the human race and all its works will be destroyed in blood and fire.

AMERICA AND THE PEACE: LAST TIME—AND THIS

By Gordon A. Craig

From "American Foreign Policy: Retrospect and Prospect," by Gordon A. Craig, chap. 1 of *The Second Chance, America and the Peace*, edited by J. B. Whitton. Copyright 1944 by Princeton University Press. Dr. Craig is assistant professor of history at Princeton University. He is now on leave for war service as an officer in the U.S. Marine Corps.

If the United States is to do its share in the task of forging an enduring peace after this war, we must avoid a repetition of the experience of 1919 and 1920. In the foreground of all thinking and planning of American foreign policy, therefore, there must be a clear understanding of the reasons for the American withdrawal from the international community after the last war. Only with that understanding will we be able to recognize the beginning of a similar post-war reaction and to take the necessary steps to avoid it.

LAST TIME

There can be little doubt that, during the last war, the majority of the American people supported the main tenets of the Wilson program, including that part which called for continued cooperation with other nations for the maintenance of peace. Then, as now, public opinion polls showed that a clear majority of the American people favored the acceptance of the Versailles Treaty and the League of Nations. Early in 1919, when the first attacks were launched against the League in the Senate, the "irreconcilables" themselves admitted that they represented a very small part of the people. Senator Lodge admitted later that "the vocal classes of the community, most of the clergymen, the preachers of sermons, a large element in the teaching force of the universities, a large proportion of the newspaper editors, and finally the men and women who were in the habit of writing and speaking for publication ... were friendly to the League as it stood and were advocating it." The Republican Senators who congratulated Senator Borah after his attack on the League on February 21, 1919 said:

"That was great; that was fine; we agree with you; but we got to have some sort of league; everybody is for it."

Despite this large measure of public support, however, the Versailles Settlement and the League were defeated. Why were they defeated? Most authorities agree that, in large part, the defeat was caused by the shrewd tactics of the Senate opponents of the settlement. Protected by the two-thirds rule, Senator Lodge and his colleagues employed all of the weapons in the constitutional armory to delay and amend the treaty. In the end they smothered the document with reservations which the President considered inadmissible, shifted the onus of responsibility onto his stubborn shoulders, and defeated the treaty out of hand.

Granted the truth of these facts, they are insufficient in themselves to explain what happened in 1919. To lay the full responsibility for the defeat of the treaty at the door of the Senate is to oversimplify, if not to falsify, the record. In a democracy it is the mass of the people which decides what will, in the last analysis, be done. If the American people had been united, and if they had desired the acceptance of the Versailles Settlement with sufficient intensity, they could have compelled the Senate to ratify it. Indeed, after the first defeat of the treaty in November 1919, public opinion was strong enough to force the Senate to reconsider its decision. When, however, the treaty was defeated for a second time, in March 1920, that volume of public support for the treaty had largely disappeared. And in November 1920—in a presidential election which Mr. Wilson himself considered a solemn referendum on the treaty—the American people gave 404 out of a possible 531 electoral votes to a man who had obliquely repudiated the Wilson interpretation of international collaboration by stating, in his speech accepting nomination, that it was not the duty of the United States to attempt "to purge the Old World of the accumulated ills of rivalry and greed." In the 1920 election the Democratic candidate clearly advocated acceptance of both treaty and League; the Republican candidate's position on internationalism was so equivocal as to be meaningless. Yet it was the Republican who got the votes. It is true, of course, that many of those who voted for Warren Gamaliel Harding may have done so in the belief that, after election, he would support a broad program of international collaboration. If so, they bore their disappointment with equanimity. Certainly there was remarkably little protest when, in his inaugural address, the new President said: "The administration which came into power in March 1921 definitely and decisively put aside all thoughts of entering the League of Nations. It doesn't propose to enter now by the side door, back door, or cellar door."

It seems clear, in short, that in the two years between the Armistice and the election of 1920 the American public itself had weakened in its desire for the kind of international program outlined by President Wilson during the war years. Lip service was still being paid to the idea of international collaboration, but the American public by 1920 had begun to desire other things more intensely. They now wanted "not heroics but healing, not nostrums but normalcy, not revolution but restoration"; and, if the attainment of those goals involved the repudiation of Wilson's program, they were now ready to allow such repudiation.

Three things contributed to this swing from Wilsonism to the isolationism of the Harding administration.

In the first place, the American people were weary of the war and the very thought of the war. Even before the fighting had stopped this feeling was general in the United States. Once the Armistice was signed, the American people wanted one thing above all else —namely, a quick liquidation of the war and a speedy realization of the benefits they had been led to expect would flow from the peace. As he sailed for Paris in December 1918, Wilson was profoundly disturbed by the popular temper. He is reported to have said to George Creel: "All of these expectations have in themselves the quality of terrible urgency. There must be no delay. It has always been so. People will endure their tyrants for years but they will tear their deliverers to pieces if a millennium is not created immediately. Yet you know and I know these ancient wrongs, these present unhappinesses, are not to be remedied in a day or with the wave of a hand."

The American people saw no reason why they should not be so remedied. Only a few realized that the organization of the peace might be both a difficult and a lengthy process. The majority seemed to believe that peace could be declared, much as war is declared, in a moment, and that immediately all troops would be demobilized and peaceful intercourse would be resumed among the nations. When the negotiations at Paris were continued for seven months, during which time American troops were kept in the field, there was widespread dissatisfaction in the United States. The cry "Bring the boys home" was loud enough to disturb the negotiators at Paris and was proof in itself of the fact that, when confronted with the sacrifices necessary to make international collaboration a workable ideal, the American people were not sure they approved of them.

When, after the long negotiations in Paris, the Senate insisted upon talking about the treaty from July 1919 until March 1920, the weariness of the general public tended to degenerate into boredom. By the end of 1920 the American people were heartily sick of the whole business. It is significant that in choosing a slogan for their campaign, the Republicans steered carefully away from any reference to the international problem and chose the cheerful but meaningless phrase: "Let us be done with wiggle and wobble."

Had the supporters of the League made a concerted attempt to convince the American public that membership in a world organization was essential for the protection of their own vital interests, war weariness and boredom might not have taken such a powerful hold upon the popular consciousness. Most of the arguments for the League were impregnated with the moral idealism which had been so effective in 1918 but which was now losing its force. Indeed, the second factor which weakened popular support for the international cause was the very real slump in idealism which set in in 1919.

Even before the Armistice was signed, the American people were beginning to react violently against the ideals which had sustained them in the dark days of the war. For this reaction the President himself was partly to blame. As Frank P. Chambers has said: "Wilson's high-sounding wartime watchwords dropped to a sudden chilly bathos when in October 1918, before the congressional elections, he appealed for the return of a Democratic majority, and at a stroke injected party politics into the entire post-war settlement. In such an atmosphere, the hard-headed matter-of-factness which always belonged to the American political character quickly leavened the old missionary zeal, symbolized by the Fourteen Points." The electorate responded to the President's appeal by returning a Republican majority, and for many loyal Republicans from that time on the arguments for international collaboration seemed merely examples of Democratic electioneering.

The slump in idealism continued when disgruntled newspaper reporters, barred from the sessions at the Peace Conference, began to send to American papers exaggerated accounts of the differences among the Allies at Paris. The American public was encouraged to believe, first, that the President was freely sacrificing all of his much advertised ideals and, second, that our former allies were engaged in a frenzied pursuit of private interest. The natural difficulties of multilateral negotiation were so distorted as to suggest that we could no longer trust our allies, and this feeling had its inevitable effect in the Senate debate on the treaty.

Moreover, the relaxation of war censorship soon produced in the United States the first of a great horde of "debunkers." Men like Sir Philip Gibbs proceeded to demolish all of the arguments formerly used to justify the fighting of the war—branding the Belgian atrocity stories as war myths and portraying the Allied leaders as incompetent or cynical gamblers with human life. Even more startling material was released to the public as the Russian, German and Austrian archives were forced open by revolution. "The secret negotiations, conversations, agreements and treaties by which the Entente Powers had planned to break Germany and divide the spoils of war according to the ancient rules were exposed to the public gaze. In all its naked horror the sordid and grimy diplomacy which had precipitated the bloody conflict was revealed; and, by way of supplement, memoirs, papers, treatises and articles on the background of the war began to flow from the presses." By the end of 1919 the belief that the war had been fought to end all war had begun to weaken and the public desire for continued collaboration with European nations was at very low ebb.

Finally, there can be little doubt that much of the earlier popular support of the League was based upon lack of understanding of the cost involved. During the war and the first months thereafter, when the ideal of international collaboration was a mere abstraction, it was easy to support the League. As it threatened to become an actuality, and as it became apparent that pursuing it would involve certain sacrifices on the part of the United States, many of the men who had cheered Wilson's Fourteen Points began to have misgivings. After Wilson's collapse, his supporters were without leadership, and there was no one capable of explaining to the doubtful, in terms which would convince them, that the necessary sacrifices were small in comparison with the advantages to be gained. As a result, many people changed their minds, confused by the arguments put forth by the Senate critics and by the Hearst press, fearful that entrance into the League might really mean the end of American independence, and worried because international collaboration, upon closer examination, seemed to violate American practice and tradition. Irritated already by the necessity of keeping American troops in Europe during the peace negotiations, these people proved readily susceptible to the argument that cooperation with other nations in any world system would involve the sending of American troops abroad at any time. The chaos into which the German defeat had plunged Central and Eastern Europe—the Spartacist uprising in Germany, the disorders which followed the Bela Kun regime in Hungary, the bitter fighting between Poland and her neighbors—seemed to prove that peace could be secured for America only by complete abstention from entanglements with that unhappy continent.

In his speech of April 9, 1944, Secretary Hull said: "Under our constitutional system the will of the American people in this field [i.e. foreign policy] is not effective unless it is united will. If we are divided we are ineffective." That is an apt summary of our experience in 1919 and 1920. At the end of the war, the majority of the American people favored the execution of the international program expounded by President Wilson in 1918. But they were not united in this desire long enough. Wearied by the war and irritated at the delay in liquidating it, suspicious of their former allies, distrustful of the slogans which had inspired them during the conflict and ignorant of the true necessity of continued sacrifice, the American people wavered uncertainly, and in the end not only allowed the Senate to have its way but gave their stamp of approval to Harding's policy of isolationism.

THIS TIME

The record of 1919-1920 has a profound relevance for our own time. In an article in the *New York Times* in December 1943, Senator Claude Pepper pointed out that, despite the fact that both Houses of Congress had voted overwhelmingly in favor of United States participation in a broad scheme of post-war international collaboration, there were still enough "irreconcilables" in public office to block the effective implementation of that vote. Addressing himself particularly to the situation in the Senate, Senator Pepper said: "In any task of statesmanship so large in import, so broad in the scope of interests involved, so burdened with almost endless ramifications [as the drafting of an effective peace settlement], the odds that one-third of the membership of the United States Senate present and voting will find one reason or another for opposing it are almost overwhelming." The Senator then appealed to the American people to exert sufficient pressure upon the Senate to prevent any repetition of the 1919 pattern.

In trying to avoid the dangers outlined by Senator Pepper, we dare not count too heavily upon such public pressure. It would be well to remember that, as the war approaches its end, American public opinion will be subject to the same disruptive forces which weakened it in 1919-1920.

In the first place, since the burden of the war effort has been heavier during this war than during the last, so will the accumulating weariness with the war be stronger. The eagerness with which American newspapers have given prominent space to any and all predictions as to "when the war will be over" has been in itself evidence of the growth of that feeling. This desire for the end of the war is quite natural; it may, however, become dangerous. For this war, already so different from previous world conflicts, may not come to an end in the traditional manner. As E. H. Carr has pointed out: "The end of the present war may not be so much a single event as a series of disintegrations—a gradual transformation of organized warfare into local fighting by armed bands. . . . It should not be assumed without question that an armistice at the end of the present war will be either possible or desirable. It would be still rasher to make the same assumption about a peace conference. In 1919 the conception prevailed of peace-making as a single historical event limited in time and place—the drafting and signing of a diplomatic instrument or series of instruments—which would settle the destinies of the world for half a century or for all time; and impatience was expressed that the performance of these necessary acts had not been completed within six months of the Armistice. After the present war it will be wise to recognize that peace-making is not an event, but a continuous process which must be pursued in many places, under varying conditions, by many different methods and over a prolonged period of time; and anyone who supposes that it will be complete within six years should be regarded with the utmost suspicion."

Mr. Carr's view of what lies ahead is possibly exaggerated, but it is probably closer to the truth than that held by the majority of the American people at the present time. Despite current optimism, the formal collapse of the governments leagued against us may not permit an appreciable relaxation of the present intense war effort. The task of negotiating peace settlements will certainly take longer than it did in 1919. And while we are in the twilight zone between peace and war, American troops will in all likelihood be forced to garrison large sections of the world. The American people have not yet become fully aware of these unpleasant facts. When they do become aware of them, there will be danger of the same kind of irritated reaction which swept the country in 1919.

It is still impossible to say whether, in addition to this danger, there will be anything like the slump of idealism which came in 1919. But one of the factors contributing to the slump of 1919 was a growing distrust of our allies, and to this we are not even today wholly immune.

In every coalition of sovereign powers it is natural that there should be frequent differences of opinion. The history of past wars of coalition shows that such differences become more acute as the allies become more certain of victory. Thus, the Grand Alliance against Napoleon threatened to fly to pieces after the great victory at Leipzig, and at the Vienna Congress there were moments when the allies seemed ready to engage each other in war. So, too, the differences between the Allied and Associated Powers of the last war were more serious in the months following the Armistice than they had ever been in the critical days of 1917.

As the United Nations move closer to victory it is possible that their differences, too, will multiply. There is no reason, however, that they should become irreconcilable. In 1814 the allies were able to compose their quarrels and to lay the basis for a peace which lasted for forty years. We should be able to do as well if, as Mr. Hull points out, we realize that "agreement can be achieved only by trying to understand the other fellow's point of view and by going as far as possible to meet it."

The danger is that the natural differences rising from negotiations among sovereign powers will be exaggerated or misinterpreted in such a way as to convince large sections of the American public that we are being cheated by our allies or to sow doubts as to the validity of such declarations of united purpose as those of Moscow and Teheran. The Anglo-American negotiations over postwar air routes caused one candidate for high national office to announce in 1944 that we "must not be cheated at the peace table," a statement which bears implications scarcely flattering to our allies. Repeated statements of this kind may well swell the tide of distrust and suspicion and weaken the sound basis of public confidence essential to collaboration in the interest of lasting peace.

Finally, as in 1919, the American public still favors international collaboration as an abstraction and has yet to view it in terms of actual cost. When the average citizen is confronted with the necessary cost, he may very well be both startled and dismayed. In the first place, as has been already mentioned, the winning of the peace may necessitate the presence of American troops on foreign soil for a considerable period after the war. This may entail continued military conscription, an unpleasant prospect even to the most ardent advocate of international collaboration. In the second place, it is already apparent that, if we wish to lay the basis for a working international order, the United States will have to play a major role in relief and rehabilitation projects after the war. Not until the victory is won will we be able to gauge the extent of this effort and its financial cost. The cost may well be so great, however, that a considerable strain will be placed upon the domestic economy of the United States—or, at least a strain great enough to compel us to continue and even extend some aspects of the present rationing program. Again, many authorities believe that, in order to avoid the resurgence of dangerous economic nationalism, we shall have to agree to the establishment of some international authority to supervise foreign investments, allocation of raw materials, and competition for world markets—in short, a system of controls scarcely compatible with our time-honored policy of unlimited free enterprise. All in all, the costs of permanent peace promise to be great, greater than most Americans realize at the present time; and it is this unawareness which may be our most fertile source of trouble.

The establishment of an ordered and peaceful world will depend to a large extent upon whether the American people's desire for such a world can withstand the pressure of the forces mentioned above. Impatience at the unavoidable difficulties which will delay the peacemaking process, failure to understand the differences which will rise among the Allies, and reluctance to pay the heavy costs of enduring peace may quite possibly confuse and divide the American people. If this happens, the ever-present enemies of true international collaboration may be able to repeat their performance of 1919 and block the effective implementation of the present declared policy of the nation. In such circumstances, we should be forced to abandon wholly or partially our present intentions and our present hopes.

The disruptive forces outlined above must be checked before they seriously weaken the nation's will to peace. They can be checked if the nation's leaders realize their potency and move swiftly against them. In this respect, two things should be done. In the first place, the government should repeatedly and emphatically stress the difficulties that lie ahead, the sacrifices necessary to overcome them and the real advantages that will accrue when they are overcome. In the second place—and this is even more important—it must convince the American people that national security for the United States will be attained only if we follow the line plotted at Moscow and Teheran, and that an attempt to retreat and follow an alternative policy would certainly be disastrous.

At Moscow and Teheran the United States indicated its determination to continue its working union with Great Britain, Russia and China after the war and to use this as the nucleus for a wider union of free peoples working in common to preserve peace. What are the possible alternatives?

The first alternative is a return to

isolationism. This would be the most likely result of a sudden public revulsion from internationalism. Isolationism has in the past appealed to large sections of the American public. It may very well become popular again, either because it appears less expensive than a policy of full-scale international collaboration or because it seems a healthy return to the basic traditions of the nation and to the policies of its founding fathers.

It should not be difficult, however, to prove to the American public that isolationism cannot work under modern conditions. Indeed, it is possible to show that it has never worked in the past. Certainly, if avoidance of war is the test of its validity, isolationism has been completely ineffective. We have fought in every world war from the eighteenth century to the present.

The golden age of isolationism, the age in which the isolationist tradition was developed, was the period stretching from 1815 to 1917. If the United States was ever immune to attack from abroad it was in that period. Yet that immunity was due not so much to the inherent values of a policy of isolationism as to the existence of a number of factors completely outside our control. A balance of power in Europe and the Far East, British control of the Atlantic sea lanes, and a relatively static military and naval technology were the basic conditions of our security in the nineteenth century. When those conditions threatened to break down in 1917, we went to war to restore them. When they broke down completely in 1941, we were denied even that freedom desired by our first President, the freedom to "choose peace or war, as our interest, guided by justice, shall counsel." In 1941, we had war thrust upon us.

These facts in themselves should be enough to discourage a return to isolationism, if isolationism means merely the refusal to make any political commitments or enter into any international agreements in the hope that this refusal will persuade the world to leave us alone. The world has insisted upon intruding on us in the past; there is no reason to suppose that it will refrain from doing so in the future.

The impracticability of complete isolationism has of late been admitted even by the most extreme advocates of a unilateral policy for the United States in the post-war period. Realizing that a purely negative policy will no longer maintain the nation's security, they now advocate a positive, realistic, hard-boiled policy—an armed isolationism which would be not so much a withdrawal from as a defiance of the rest of the world. They urge that the United States must take advantage of the temporary armed superiority which it will enjoy after this war to make its world position impregnable, and they claim that, having done so, it will be able to follow its own course without interference from other nations.

The benefits which would accrue from such a policy are by no means apparent; its disadvantages are only too manifest. In the last analysis, armed isolation means arming ourselves to the teeth and holding the rest of the world at bay, a task which staggers the imagination. Even if we assume that the United States can consistently outbuild its power competitors, the cost of maintaining such armed superiority would be prohibitive. In 1796, George Washington urged abstention from European affairs as the only means by which we could "avoid the necessity of those overgrown military establishments, which, under any form of government, are inauspicious to liberty, and which are to be regarded as particularly hostile to Republican Liberty." That argument has now been turned upon itself. If there is any hope of lowering the load of armaments after the war, it must be found in international political agreements. Armed isolation would doom the American people to a permanent war economy which could not fail to jeopardize social progress in this country.

Moreover, once we had embarked upon a policy of armed isolation, we would certainly drift slowly but surely in the direction of imperialism. This is implicit, for instance, in the statement which appeared in the *New York Daily News* in November 1942, declaring that the United States "should have an air force big enough and good enough for the defense of this continent, or, preferably, of this hemisphere; and a Navy of such size as the final lessons of this war may indicate we need to armor-plate this continent by sea." But what if our continental neighbors did not wish to be armor-plated by the United States? What if the Latin American nations, for instance, should be less amenable to the delights of isolationism than the United States? What if they should insist upon maintaining traditional—but in our eyes dangerous—contacts with the outside world? It is possible, indeed likely, that we should then feel called upon to revert to something like the Theodore Roosevelt interpretation of the Monroe Doctrine—insisting that each of the Latin American nations have a government sympathetic to ourselves, compliant with our desires, and, in the last analysis, subject to our veto. We have already had sad experience with the difficulties of enforcing such a policy; in all probability we should find them magnified tenfold after the war.

Let us, however, make two additional and highly unlikely assumptions: first, that by a series of economic miracles we were able to continue to maintain and increase our military establishment without serious domestic repercussions and, second, that by a series of diplomatic *coups* we were able to convince our continental neighbors to join us, as equals or subordinates, in a policy of armed isolation against the rest of the world. There is no reason to suppose that our position in the post-war world would even then be secure. As an American geographer has pointed out, the Western Hemisphere is surrounded by land masses which possess two and a half times the area and ten times the population of the Americas. "Even though at the present time the industrial productivity of the New World would almost balance that of the Old, the United States would still find herself irresistibly encircled by a superior force if she should ever be confronted" by a union of the other major powers. It should be clear, moreover, that if we insist upon withdrawing from the rest of the world and upon attempting to outbuild it in military strength, we shall be inviting just such a union. "We cannot," as Secretary Hull has pointed out, "move in and out of international cooperation and in and out of participation in the responsibilities of a member of the family of nations," without paying the cost of such a policy. The cost in this event might very well be joint economic, political and eventually even military action against us.

The course of isolationism offers us, therefore, only great sacrifices and no tangible benefits. The time has gone by when our oceans protected us against the world. The advance in military technology and the impending growth of polar air routes have seriously weakened our strategic position. For the United States to try to stand alone in the world today would be most hazardous, even if it were possible.

It is conceivable, of course, that the

United States could retreat from the high ideals announced at Moscow and Teheran without being forced to fall back on a strictly unilateral policy. For the past two years there has been in this country considerable discussion of an Anglo-American alliance in the post-war period; and the eagerness with which this policy has been embraced by public figures not especially noted for their international sympathies would seem to indicate that it might be supported not as a preliminary to a broader scheme of world order but as an alternative to it.

But, if we should base our policy entirely upon an Anglo-American alliance, how effective would this policy be in maintaining the national security? On the surface, many arguments would seem to support it. A formal union of the English-speaking peoples would be in every sense a union of natural allies. Great Britain and the United States have a common heritage of language and religion, of law and justice, of political and economic institutions. There has existed between them also, since the end of the last century, a tradition of common action which is being strengthened by their joint effort in the present war. Moreover, since the deep-seated desire of both peoples is for peace and security, there will in all probability be a fundamental identity in aim between the two powers.

In addition to this, the strength of an Anglo-American combination would be formidable. With roughly 90 per cent of the world's sea power and most of the world's important bases at their disposal, the two powers would control the sea lanes of the globe, and they could use that control, backed by the tremendous economic strength afforded by their joint resources, to defend their joint national interests.

Yet despite the obvious attractions of an Anglo-American alliance, it would surely defeat its own purposes. For, in the last analysis, this combination is unnecessary if there is to be a wider union of powers; and it is highly dangerous if it is taken as an alternative to such wider union.

The very unity of purpose which makes Great Britain and the United States natural allies makes it unnecessary for us to formalize our association by a bilateral pact. There is no reason to suppose that the mutual cooperation which has so much to do with winning the war will collapse with the coming of the peace; and unless there were danger of such a collapse, or of Great Britain joining a combination directed against us, it is hard to see what additional advantages we would derive from a formal treaty.

On the other hand, the dangers of an Anglo-American alliance, in the absence of wider undertakings, would be very great. Aside from the unpleasant historical truth that dual alliances have rarely, if ever, operated to the advantage of both parties, a post-war Anglo-American alliance would arouse the fear and suspicion of all other powers, great and small. To Soviet Russia it would almost certainly appear to be a combination inspired by distrust of Communism and one which might in the future attempt to do in a different way what the capitalist powers tried to do to Russia between 1918 and 1920. To China it would almost certainly appear to be a combination designed to protect and promote Anglo-American imperialism in the Far East. To the smaller powers it would appear as an objectionable attempt to impose upon them a strictly Anglo-Saxon conception of world order.

The most likely result of a formal Anglo-American alliance would be the formation of rival blocs and alliances, and the world would be involved once more in the kind of political, economic and military competition which has so often produced major wars. In such a world, the strength of the Anglo-American combination would afford no real assurance of peace. It is not inconceivable that that strength in itself would compel the other nations to join in a desperate assault upon the Anglo-Saxon powers. The prospect of such a war will scarcely be comforting to anyone disposed to strategical thinking. We need only remember how different the outcome of the present war might have been had the Nazi-Soviet pact remained in force, and had it enabled Germany, Russia and Japan to join forces against the two sea powers.

The deliberate choice of an Anglo-American alliance in preference to a wider union of nations would be a gratuitous insult to the other powers and an invitation to them to take adequate steps against us. It would usher in the kind of world aptly described by George Canning—a world of "every nation for itself and God help all of us"; and in this respect its results would not be markedly different from those involved in a return to isolationism. As in the case of isolationism also, it would bring to the American people no real and lasting security. Emerging from the long and trying struggle which was precipitated in 1941, the American people would find themselves once more living in a state of constant apprehension and confronting a future in which growing armaments and mounting taxes encroached increasingly upon the freedom for which they had fought.

"The true measure of nations," said Winston Churchill in 1919, "is what they can do when they are tired." As we move ahead to the transition period which will follow the cessation of hostilities, the American people will be tired, and it is likely that they will be appalled at the enormity of the task that awaits them. If they falter, and if they embrace unilateral or bilateral expedients in preference to a genuine policy of world association, the hopes with which they took up the war burden will be grievously disappointed. They will be far less likely to falter or retreat if they are told in convincing terms what the consequences of retreat from the goals set at Moscow and Teheran will be. For, as John Jay wrote in 1787: "It is not a new observation that the people of any country (if, like the Americans, intelligent and well informed) seldom adopt and steadily persevere for many years in an erroneous opinion respecting their interests."

THE NATURE OF A NEW WORLD ORDER

By Gerhart Niemeyer

From "World Order and the Great Powers," by Gerhart Niemeyer; chap. 2 of *The Second Chance, America and the Peace,* edited by J. B. Whitton. Princeton University Press, 1944. Dr. Niemeyer is a professor at Oglethorpe University, and was until recently a member of the faculty of Princeton University.

In discussing the problem of peace, many people invoke the analogy of the criminal and the policeman. Wars are compared with burglary, arson, and murder, and the prevention of war with the system of criminal justice which protects the individual citizen. On the whole, this analogy was the basis of the League of Nations. I believe it to be erroneous. If we wish to draw a comparison between the order within a nation and order among nations, war should be compared not with crime but with revolution. Grave civil strife is not avoided by police and courts, but through adjustments between classes by disposing of their differences and grievances before they lead to high emotional tension and open violence. Such a moment calls for the statesman, not the judge or sheriff; it is the statesman alone who, through foresight and political acumen, can prevent such a situation from arising, and thereby preserve domestic peace through continuous adjustment, compensation, conciliation and balance. Legal machinery helps to preserve the stability thus attained, but it does not in itself constitute the main condition of social peace.

The prevention of war, like the prevention of revolution within the state, does not depend on legal procedures, but on the art of adjustment. None of the great conflicts of modern times could have been settled by judicial process, even if backed by sanctions. Whatever success attended the war-prevention procedures of the League of Nations must be attributed largely to the political weight thrown into the scale by the Great Powers. The latter, however, did not always support the League when faced by its crucial tests. They tended to follow established national policies that led each nation in its own separate direction. The League machinery could scarcely have been otherwise devised but this only goes to show that the key to peace will be found not in machinery alone, however well planned, but primarily in the policies of powers capable of leadership. Any scheme which distracts attention from this basic truth should be suspect.

The most important field for policies designed to promote world peace lies in the settlement of differences among the Great Powers themselves. It is here, if anywhere, that the inadequacy of mere legal procedures becomes evident. What international organization could undertake to coerce Russia, the British Empire, or the United States in matters they deem of vital concern? Conflicts among them will be avoided not by some formal decision of law but by methods whose supreme objective is the maintenance of harmony and confidence. Through such methods, the Big Three would do much more than merely settle their own affairs. They would establish a pattern of international politics from which smaller nations would find no reason to deviate. Just as the rivalries of the Great Powers incite other nations to seek petty advantage, often providing the concrete occasion for open conflict, so a continuous practice of policies of confidence and community would exercise a beneficial influence on the policies of most of the smaller nations.

On the other hand, discontent is bound to arise here and there, and unreasonableness is always with us. But since judicial methods are not designed to deal with a problem until the conflict has become acute, joint political leadership of the Big Three would be more effective than any kind of legalized procedure in bringing about an adjustment before tension rises. Pressure and even force must of course be used if the leading nations are to implement their assumption of responsibility for world peace, but if there is the will to peace it should not be difficult to submit such cases to a council of world opinion before drastic action is taken or even seriously contemplated. Even so, the methods employed in the effort to preserve peace must be those of the statesman rather than those of the criminal court.

If the foregoing analysis is correct, we have the solution to a number of problems which plagued the League of Nations. The sharpest attack on this institution was the contention that its main object was to preserve a *status quo* which happened to suit the dominant powers. While it was frequently pointed out that the only reasonable alternative to war was to be found in methods of peaceful change, the League Covenant, largely a matter of legal rules and procedures, failed to face this problem adequately. This is understandable enough, for no system of law has ever made provision for peaceful change by other than political methods. Change takes place outside of contracts and established rules, and the law, far from encouraging change, inevitably emphasizes stability, routine, and precedent. The courts have no choice but to apply the law that already exists and that may be the very basis of the conflict. Neither the methods nor the standards of the law are flexible enough to meet a need for change. True, legislation is a method of change, but it is clearly not a legal but a political process, and its operation is not yet assured in international relations, as no legislative body exists able to decide whenever a demand for change arises, and endowed with commanding authority over courts and individuals. Thus, if we find that even in domestic society the nature of change is political, this must apply in even higher degree to international relations. In short, in the community of nations peaceful change can come not through law but only through the political leadership of the Great Powers acting jointly to preserve order.

A very delicate feature of peaceful change remains to be considered. Leadership must not be conceived as a monopoly for all time. Yet to discover a principle to govern the qualification for leadership would be most difficult, especially so since we have not even succeeded in setting up a standard for leadership in domestic government. A change in leadership, like any other change, must be determined by wisdom, skill, and a feeling for the fundamental common interest. It would not be possible, for example, to predict under just what conditions China could join the Big Three as an equal bearer of responsibility. Whether a state can exercise the functions of leadership depends on a number of factors—the size of its armed forces, its productive capacity and war potential, but also the absence of national fears and a willingness to renounce expansionist policies. Furthermore, it must be prepared to commit itself to an active policy even in remote regions. When and how such conditions of leadership will be fulfilled, it is impossible to foretell. The problem must be solved by political wisdom rather than by any fixed procedure. It should be our goal to provide for necessary changes in leadership before such changes are forced on us. We should endeavor to have the kind of farsightedness shown by the British ruling classes when they decided to institute reforms which spared them an experience like the French Revolution. This example proves that change of leadership depends primarily on the enlightenment of those in power.

If we are correct in our appraisal of the methods of peace, the responsibility for world order rests squarely on the shoulders of the Great Powers. The aims they have in mind, the policies they pursue, the methods and the spirit of their actions will contain the seeds of either world conflict or world harmony. The example which the Big Three, in their mutual relationships, set for the world will be of crucial importance. The art of politics is the realization of concord among different groups obliged to live together. The primary aim of the foreign policies of the Big Three must therefore be to live in harmony with each other, and their secondary aim to help other nations to do likewise. Respect for the nationhood of other peoples is the prime prerequisite of such policies. Moreover, the leaders of the Big Three should realize that national weakness is accompanied by extreme sensitiveness. Having nothing to fear for their own existence, they should be able to treat small nations with special consideration and understanding. If, by any sacrifices they may make to the recurrent fears of small nations, they can manage to restore international confidence, they will have solved the most difficult task of international statesmanship.

THE ROLE OF THE GREAT POWERS IN THE MAINTENANCE OF PEACE AND SECURITY

By Harold Sprout

From "The Role of the Great States," by Harold Sprout, in *World Organization—Economic, Political, and Social*. Proceedings of the Academy of Political Science, Vol. 21, No. 3, May 1945. Copyright 1945 by the Academy of Political Science, Columbia University, New York; reproduced by permission.

The foundation to which must be fitted any workable international charter is a society of sovereign states whose distinguishing characteristics include legal equality, practical inequality, cultural diversity, linguistic barriers and intense nationalism. Equal in law, no two are equal in fact. Some are leaders in science, technology and the arts. Others have barely emerged from the stone age. Some are towering giants in strength. Others are pygmies by comparison. Some covet with savage lust their neighbors' possessions. Others seek only to live and to let live. With few exceptions, the citizens of all states are fired with a nationalism which recognizes no loyalty higher than the national state.

Passing from the general to the specific, one salient feature of the emerging world situation is the progressive concentration of power in fewer hands. This trend seems to be the inescapable result of modern industrialism. Significant military power is rapidly becoming the virtual monopoly of a few great states. These states possess, or have reasonably secure access to, vast stores of mechanical energy, huge quantities of raw materials, immense and diversified industrial plant, and millions of farmers, industrial workers and soldiers, all welded together into a complex going concern.

Broadly speaking, the trend of modern technology is to make the strong stronger, while the weak grow relatively weaker. Not one of the lesser European powers has been able in this war to fight even a protracted delaying action. Not one could have won back its freedom alone and unaided. Weak states are more than ever under the shadow of powerful neighbors. No paper guarantee of the integrity of small nations, no declaration of the sovereign equality of all nations, can alter the irreversible trend toward greater inequality of strength between the Great Powers and the weak.

Fundamental changes are also taking place within the ranks of the Great Powers. Before the war seven states formed this group. Three of these—Italy, Germany and Japan—have been, or will be, reduced to military impotence by devastation, defeat and the terms of peace. Their eventual status cannot now be foretold. But it may be safely assumed that they will play no role whatever in the establishment and early development of a world security organization.

A fourth Great Power—France—also suffered military defeat, and went through four years of German occupation and pillage. A new France is rising from the ashes, and has already regained some voice in European councils. But there is little ground for hope that France can recover quickly, if ever, the position of leadership held as recently as the early 1930's. As a result of all these developments, Central and Western Europe is in danger of becoming a political vacuum, and politics, like nature, abhors a vacuum.

Of the original seven, there remain Great Britain, the Soviet Union and the United States, significantly designated the Big Three. To these is tentatively added an eighth—China—whose heroic defense and critically important geographical position has won for the Chinese a provisional status and a voice in Far Eastern affairs far in excess of the realities of their power today.

China today is not a Great Power. China is a big country, with a huge population, and considerable mineral resources. But the country has almost no industrial plant. It lacks a modern transportation system, and has yet to achieve an assured political unity and stability. The United States has long regarded a strong united China as a prerequisite of peace and order in the Far East. Chinese ability to achieve this status, in fact as well as in theory, will determine in large degree whether the Far East too is to become a political vacuum following the defeat of Japan.

Of the Big Three, the future position of Great Britain is the most uncertain. Britain, in the words of a leading London journal, *The Economist,* emerges from the war a "conditional Great Power." The conditions, according to *The Economist,* are three. The first is "that the British Commonwealth and Empire continue to act together as a unit." The second, "that the communications between them remain open." The third, that Britain does not incur the active hostility of the United States. If these conditions are met, Britain will still rank with the strongest.

Will they be met? With respect to conditions one and three, relating respectively to the Dominions and to the United States, the answer is probably "yes." But the future security of British sea communications is more doubtful. It would seem to depend upon still a fourth condition: that northwestern Europe does not again become the seat of a great military power hostile to Great Britain.

But Britain's role, it should be recognized, cannot be measured solely by a strategical yardstick. Britain has a rich heritage of leadership. London is still the capital of a vast and far-flung empire. British freedom of diplomatic maneuver may well be less than Russia's or our own. But British influence today still ranks with that of Moscow and Washington.

The Soviet Union and the United States seem destined to be the political giants of the post-war world. In several respects their situation is quite similar. Both occupy the heart of a continent. Both stand in a central position between the two great oceans, Atlantic and Pacific. Both are centrally located between Europe and the Far East. The American people have traditionally enjoyed an inherently strong defensive position derived from their geographical remoteness from other centers of great power. The Soviet peoples will enjoy a comparable detachment from powerful neighbors after the defeat of Germany and Japan.

The similarity of the Soviet and American positions extends to economic resources. Both nations possess within their own frontiers greater mineral wealth and greater diversity of raw materials than does any other politically unified area upon the globe. Each possesses one of the three richest food-growing regions, the third being in Argentina. Both have presumptively secure access to essential supplementary resources in adjoining or nearby friendly countries.

The United States has a long head start in economic development. The Soviet Union is further handicapped by the necessity of rebuilding huge areas laid waste by the German invaders. But the Russians were making prodigious strides before the war. They have accomplished miracles with a partially crippled industrial plant during the war. Few would venture to prophesy that the Soviet Union's larger, younger and more rapidly growing population may not overtake our industrial lead within two or three decades.

The emergence of the Soviet Union as the strongest, if not actually dominant, power in Eurasia is one of the most revolutionary developments of our time. This development affects most immediately the peoples of Europe and Asia. But it also changes fundamentally the distribution and balance of political forces throughout the world.

The argument thus far can be summarized somewhat as follows: The present war and a rapidly advancing technology have unstabilized all international relations. An unprecedented concentration of power is taking place. The number of really Great Powers is being drastically reduced to two, or at most three. The Soviet Union and the United States have become, and seem certain to remain for some time, far stronger than all others.

From this point it is but a step to the next proposition: that in the policies of the Soviet Union and of the United States, and in their mutual relations, lies the key to success or failure of all efforts to establish any workable organization for the enforcement of security and the preservation of peace.

This proposition in no way minimizes or belittles the role of Great Britain, or of France, China, or still other nations. The attitude of these states, especially Britain, is extremely important. But their combined strength and opportunities for leadership would be insufficient to preserve peace in the face of deteriorating relations between the Soviet Union and the United States.

Such a catastrophe could take shape in a number of ways. Any attempt on our part, alone or in concert with Britain, to mold the states of Europe into an anti-Soviet bloc would almost certainly precipitate a power struggle with the Kremlin. Conversely, Russian attempts to reach out into the oceanic realm would just as certainly provoke defensive measures on the part of the Anglo-Saxon peoples. Serious deterioration of Soviet-American relations would bring into play all the weapons in the ideological as well as the political and military arsenals. One of the first fruits of such a struggle would be extinction of hopes for a stable enduring peace.

Fortunately, the major trend seems to be in the opposite direction. There is no denying the evidences of Soviet distrust of Britain and America. It cannot be denied that such feelings are reciprocal. But all evidence seems to indicate that most Russians, like most Englishmen and Americans, desire nothing so much as a long period of uninterrupted peace. And there seems to be, in the main, a genuine determination on both sides to accommodate their different ways of life, to compromise conflicting interests, and to get on together in the critical years that lie ahead.

Strategical facts favor such an accommodation. The Soviet Union and the United States have no common land frontier. They have no historic quarrels, except the ideological differences growing out of the Russian Revolution. Their vital strategic interests conflict at very few points upon the globe. Geography makes Russia predominantly a land power, and puts serious obstacles in the way of her becoming a major sea power. The United States is first and foremost a great sea power, for geographical reasons equally compelling. Aviation reinforces the unique strategical opportunities of each, without seriously jeopardizing the security of the other.

It is impossible to overemphasize the supreme importance of a large area of accord and agreement among the Big Three—Russia, Britain and the United States. Without it no world security organization could function at all. If, however, these greatest powers can carry beyond victory the solidarity forged in the heat of battle, the chances of success for any security charter are immensely improved. Big Three solidarity is a *sine qua non* of an enduring peace. Of that there can be no doubt.

It is more difficult to ascertain the probable area of Great Power agreement as to the ways and means of enforcing peace and achieving security. It seems reasonably clear that none of the Great Powers is willing to put all its money upon any security organization however constituted. Each will retain its own military establishment and defenses intact, and it remains to be seen, for example, how much scientific and technical military information each will be willing to clear through an international staff committee.

It may be doubted whether any of the Great Powers—especially the Soviet Union, and probably also the United States and Great Britain—would ever ratify a security charter which did not give them the legal means of blocking coercive action deemed contrary to their vital interests. If this be so, it is futile even to speculate whether an international security organization could ever take coercive action against one of its strongest members. It is equally futile to speculate whether such action could be taken against a lesser state over the determined opposition of the strongest. Even assuming that voting arrangements made such action technically possible, any persistent attempt to proceed against the unyielding opposition of one of the Great Powers would probably wreck the organization at the very least, and might even lead to war.

It is doubtful, furthermore, if any security organization could function with one of the greatest powers absent. The absent power, especially if it were the Soviet Union, would almost certainly regard the organization as a menace to its own security, and could be expected to set about building up its own rival coalition to block it. The eventual outcome of such a struggle could be scarcely other than total war to the death.

The prewar example of the United States, outside but not hostile to the League of Nations, is sometimes cited. That example, it is submitted, is scarcely relevant as an indication of presumptive Soviet, or even British or American, policy under possible future circumstances. The prewar distribution of power was totally different. No one state represented a military potential and a relative power position comparable to that of either the Soviet Union or the United States today. With two such giants, it is probably all in or all out.

That the weaker nations bitterly resent giving these prerogatives to the

Great Powers is already evident. That they might combine to prevent the creation of an organization so constituted is conceivable.

The attitude of these lesser powers is easily understood. They feel increasingly insecure as a result of the developments sketched. They desperately want some guarantee against their towering neighbors. Their spokesmen also have the perfectly human desire to share in the psychic dividends derived from having a voice in the decisions of great international questions. That some of the lesser states will remain intransigent is possible. That few, if any of them, will acknowledge their real dilemma is altogether probable.

Their dilemma is a hard one. It is especially so for those small countries which have a high level of culture and a rich political tradition. By opposing an international charter which legalizes the *de facto* primacy of a few Great Powers, they would run the risk of getting no world organization at all. Yet the probable alternatives for them are worse. These are either the perpetuation of Great Power rule through such *ad hoc* and secret arrangements as have prevailed during wartime, or unregulated rivalry among the Great Powers.

Only time can tell how far any security organization can succeed in protecting the weak against the strong in our imperfect world. One suspects that much will depend upon the moral values which guide Great Power diplomacy, and upon the restraints which the Great Powers are willing to impose upon themselves. It was, in part, the repudiation of such moral values and restraints that made German rule in Europe and Japanese rule in the Far East so odious to the conquered peoples. Spokesmen for the principal United Nations have repeatedly denounced the tyranny of such rule. Of their intention to exercise their own power with restraint and moral responsibility, there seems to be no doubt. If they can put their relations with each other, and with the smaller and weaker peoples, upon a basis of mutual trust and confidence, the unprecedented power in the hands of the few can provide the foundation of an enduring peace with security, and with it a *sense* of security for all nations.

THE LEADERSHIP OF THE BIG THREE

By Gerhart Niemeyer

From "World Order and the Great Powers," by Gerhart Niemeyer; chap. 2 of *The Second Chance, America and the Peace,* edited by J. B. Whitton. Copyright 1944 by Princeton University Press. Dr. Niemeyer is a professor at Oglethorpe University, and was until recently a member of the Princeton faculty.

It lies in the very nature of things that the Big Three, in order to offer leadership to a war-weary world, must remain in close accord. This is no utopian goal; in fact, the stage is admirably set for such an understanding. The three powers are widely separated by geography, and their relations are not troubled by any very strong conflicts of interest. They will have emerged from a war fought jointly against tyranny and aggression, each having helped to save the others by tremendous sacrifice of life and material goods. Their peoples and leaders have a common dread and abhorrence of war. They share the background of a Christian civilization, with its emphasis on human welfare, its dynamic conception of history, and its promise of equality and freedom. But they still fear one another.

If the Great Powers are to lead the

world, these fears must be removed. Leadership is above all a matter of spiritual guidance. History shows again and again that strength of soul and a clear mental vision are the qualities which make leaders among men. It is not different with nations. The sheer weight of material power is indispensable as a condition, but it is scarcely the substance of leadership. To lead is to inspire trust, confidence, and loyalty, and thereby to elicit allegiance. It is no accident that kings of every epoch have considered generosity as their most essential virtue. For generosity, disinterestedness, courage, and foresight—these qualities cause soldiers to follow their captain as well as nations to follow a Great Power. Such qualities can grow only in those whose position has placed them beyond ordinary fears. Kings could afford to be generous because power and wealth were theirs. By the same standard, we lift judges and other persons of responsibility above the ordinary worries of men, assuring them office "during good behavior." Leadership that inspires confidence can be expected only from someone who has managed to be fearless.

The inequality between the Great Powers on the one hand and the rest of the world on the other contributes in many ways to the possibility of true leadership among the nations. Above all, it enables the Big Three to create a situation in which they may be free from fear—a situation of which no Great Power has been able to boast since the days of the Caesars. It is essential to world leadership as well as to world peace that such a situation be created. Therefore the foreign policies of the Great Powers should above all aim at this goal.

The causes of the mutual fears which still prevail are not easily defined. Britain's anxieties, formulated in 1943 by Marshal Smuts, are apparently inspired by her limited manpower and inadequate production, the lack on metropolitan soil of many vital raw materials, the insecurity of her communications and other factors which may leave her permanently weakened. But she withstood the full might of a Nazi-organized Europe, thereby proving that there is, both in her geographical position and in her spirit, a strength which renders her unconquerable. Despite this proof of might, her anxiety in the company of the two "adolescent giants," Russia and America, is easily understandable. But while these fears are comprehensible, policies inspired by fear alone cannot remedy the situation. Modern history knows of no example of a power whose attempt to compensate for declining strength by adding satellites and alliances did not end in complete disaster. Whether we take Germany, Italy, France in the inter-war period, Austria-Hungary, Turkey, or any other power frantically seeking to break the circle imposed on her by nature and history, we find that fear of insufficient strength is the worst possible counsel for such a nation's diplomacy. Moreover, Britain's position is determined not so much by what she has as by what she is—a center of world trade, world transportation, and world colonization; a bond among autonomous nations; a mediator between continents; a watchman at the nations' crossroads; a teacher of political wisdom and of social harmony. Britain has no reason to fear, for neither the world order nor the two other Great Powers can dispense with her cooperation and co-leadership. Britain is also the only one of the three Great Powers equally familiar with, and acceptable to, both European and extra-European areas. In this matter Russia has occasioned too much suspicion among her European neighbors to rival England,

and America's lack of interest in Europe is traditional. Given this situation, both Russia and America will require England's help whenever the affairs of Western Europe become of general concern.

Of the Big Three, Russia has the least ground for fear. Once Germany and Japan have been defeated, what power would dare attack her? Yet Russia is full of apprehensions, as her policies toward Poland, her alliance with Czechoslovakia, and her subtle intervention in Yugoslavia amply demonstrate. The causes of Russia's present fears can be traced back to the days of the civil war, when other powers—allies and enemies alike—attempted to injure her. Even after the close of that period, Russia was separated from the rest of the western world by France's policy of the *cordon sanitaire,* and by England's reluctance to have any political dealings with the Soviets—policies that were not unprovoked, especially during the period of Russia's double dealing via the Third Internationale. All this, however, lies in the past; the vital task today is to gain Russia's full confidence. The Russians have a keen appreciation of blunt sincerity, and a hearty contempt for "leftist sentimentality." We should, therefore, not pretend that we are their blood-brothers in political philosophy, or that we like their system. But if we wish to make our way into their hearts we must show a genuine concern for Russia's troubles, fears and problems, especially since we have done so much to create them. Looking at the problem through Russian eyes, we must realize that they have great difficulty in understanding the outside world with which they have had so little connection. We should therefore refuse to become alarmed when Moscow shows signs of continued anxiety and distrust. If we keep faith with Russia, the time will come when our words will be trusted because our deeds justify such trust, and she will begin to lose her suspicions.

Russia's collaboration in a concert of Great Powers is indispensable and cannot be replaced by that of any other comparable nation. . . . Russia is the connecting link between Europe and Asia. The swelling tide of Asiatic nationalism, plus the rapid growth of national strength among the peoples of the East, is bound to become one of the most difficult problems of international relations. While she cannot play the role expected of China in this matter, Russia is nevertheless the only power with historical and spiritual roots both in Europe and in Asia. Moreover, her unique policy toward her many nationalities constitutes a novel approach to one of the major problems of this region, a policy worthy of application on a universal level. If Russia is freed from her present burden of perpetual suspicion, the realism which she has often manifested in her international relations should have a refreshing influence in international councils. But before Russia can bring these contributions to full fruition, we must explore with her the entire map of potential conflicts, from Finland to the Persian Gulf. On the basis of specific agreements thus reached, we must then be ready to offer her general guarantees of military assistance. The diplomatic spadework needed here resembles the type of arrangements reached between England and France after Fashoda, and between Russia and England prior to the First World War. If, through such agreements, a general system of world order is assured, the smaller powers need not fear that sacrifice of their interests will be the price of a Big Three accord.

The anxieties of the United States are not much more firmly grounded than those of Russia. As a result of the war, the United States will be freed of her only rival in the Pacific. As for the rest of the world, the American combination of sea power, air power, manpower, and productive capacity surpasses anything any other nation can muster. In peace, she can outproduce any other single competitor in the world. In spite of this comfortable margin of strength, the United States is afraid of both England and Russia. This fear is unrealistic. To attack America would be, for Britain, suicide, and, for Russia, political folly and military madness. Thus America's distrust of the other powers is actuated more by emotion than by reason. Although we are economically stronger than Britain, we still fear the wiliness of the British trader. Russia is now far removed from Communism, and doctrinaire Communists actually berate Stalin for his betrayal of the Revolution. Nevertheless, Soviet Russia is still regarded in this country with fear and trembling, as the home of "Reds" and a danger to our most cherished traditions. This lingering suspicion may be inspired entirely by Russia's revolutionary past, but it may also spring from the strangeness of Asiatics. In the American distrust of un-American ways some remnants of frontier parochialism may still survive. Since such fears reflect more a subjective state of mind than objective facts, they cannot be completely overcôme by anything the other powers could do or promise. A rising awareness, on the part of Americans, of their country's gigantic material and moral strength will gradually eliminate such anxieties. There may be some concrete steps which would contribute to that end. But in the last analysis the problem of American fears can be solved only by Americans themselves.

In the effort toward a general accord of the Big Three, the crux of the matter is to arrive at a point where each would feel assured that neither of the others was seeking to weaken it. Such confidence having been created, each power should find it logical to renounce policies such as alliances or other arrangements with smaller nations designed to strengthen one power in relation to the other. Existing agreements of this kind should be allowed to lapse when the treaties expire, for the practice of seeking support among secondary nations, with the quarrels resulting therefrom, has more than once led to conflict and to war. The chief aim of Big Three diplomacy should be to create an atmosphere in which such secondary supports would become meaningless. Otherwise it would be vain to expect harmony among them or leadership from them for the world at large. Only when the policies of alliances and counter-alliances have been discarded can nations assume the statesmanship of the Big Three to be free from self-interest to an extent sufficient to justify their confidence in it. This does not rule out the possibility of spheres of influence. They are in fact inevitable. Spheres of influence, however, are vicious only when used as a link in a system of outright alliances and protectorates. Properly conceived, they can be as harmless as the administrative divisions within a nation.

A further result of the diplomatic deck-clearing among the Big Three should be the reduction of armaments. The example of both Britain and America has proved that great nations are strong not because of the arms they already possess but because of those that they can produce. The combination of raw materials, industrial machinery and organization, and educated and intelligent manpower is what makes for the ultimate military strength of a nation.

In view of this fact, the Big Three would profit greatly from a considerable reduction in armaments. In the first place, the national economy would be relieved of the immense burden of a great yearly output of arms. Each power could depend on a small, highly mechanized, military force continuously developing its methods and weapons. Such a force is essential to that self-assurance of the Big Three which, as we have already insisted, is the condition of their effective leadership. Contingents of these forces might be stationed at bases strategically distributed throughout the globe. With respect to war production, the provision for stockpiles of vital materials and the maintenance of a skeleton armaments industry should give the Big Three all the security they could desire. Furthermore, it might be advisable to prohibit the export from the big nations of any but small-caliber arms. All in all, such a reduction of armaments would have immeasurable psychological benefits, and would enhance rather than impair the capacity of the Big Three to cope with any situation that might arise. Even with a greatly reduced army, navy, and air force, the big nations would still enjoy an almost complete monopoly of military power.

If the Big Three should attain, and maintain, the position here outlined, they could establish a leadership which, properly exercised, would become the foremost instrument of a future world order. The power of the Big Three, however, would be founded on no constitution, no legal instrument. It could be ultimately effective, therefore, only so far as the policies of the Great Powers succeeded in evoking the confidence and assent of the other nations. The latter, even when weak, have many ways of resisting an unwanted hegemony. Thus the power of the Big Three would have the character not of government but of leadership, resting ultimately more on consent than on authority.

THE ROLE OF THE LESSER POWERS IN THE MAINTENANCE OF PEACE AND SECURITY

By Arnold Wolfers

From "The Role of the Small States," by Arnold Wolfers, in *World Organization—Economic, Political, and Social*. Proceedings of the Academy of Political Science, Vol. 21, No. 3, May 1945. Copyright 1945 by the Academy of Political Science, Columbia University, New York; reproduced by permission. Dr. Wolfers is professor of international relations at Yale University.

There need be no quarrel with those who emphasize that the maintenance of peace depends largely on the Great Powers and that a third world war can be prevented only if the relationship between the Big Three continues to be one of close collaboration and friendship. This does not mean, however, that the present war has suddenly changed the character of the world and concentrated all power and influence in the hands of the great nations. The small countries and what are now being called the "middle powers" not only continue to exist in large numbers but will, when peace returns, be found to carry considerable weight. If, in the present war, they have proved themselves to be militarily weak, this was almost equally true of them in the past. There is nothing new in the fact that weak countries cannot trust their own military power to prevent aggression by a great neighbor or to liberate themselves from their conquerors. To point to the liberation of many of them by the Allied armies in this war does not prove, therefore, that their role has become less significant than it was before. Already, as the war draws to a close, more attention is being given them. Their recent reemergence as a political factor goes back to American initiative.

When this country declared itself for a universal security organization, thereby setting aside the idea of a grand alliance composed exclusively of Great Powers, it was paying tribute to the role of the lesser nations. It also gave them political bargaining power, since their consent is needed if such an organization is to come into being. The purpose of the San Francisco Conference [was] no other than to get the smaller nations to agree to a plan of organization based on the proposals worked out by the Big Three or Big Four at Dumbarton Oaks. . . .

The United States has a traditional interest in the friendship of small powers. The Good Neighbor Policy need only be mentioned to remind one of the patient efforts made in the course of years to establish relations of mutual confidence with the American Republics. Britain is in the same position. Since the British Commonwealth is an alignment of Great Britain with lesser powers, the opinions of Canada, Australia or New Zealand must necessarily carry much weight with Britain. She could not, in fact, be counted among the three Great Powers if it were not because she can so readily rely on the support of the Dominions.

The Soviet Union appears least concerned about the small countries. Soviet spokesmen are taking the view that all power of decision should rest with the real victors of the war. They often speak with contempt of the sentimentalists who turn their attention to weak countries, many of which owe their continued existence to the Red armies. Soviet experience in the past offers some explanation for this attitude. The Soviet Union was isolated throughout most of her brief history; she has been able to count on little friendship from her lesser neighbors. Then, too, her system of government may permit her more readily to turn small neighboring countries into satellites who will follow any lead given by the Soviet Union. It would be surprising, however, if in the course of the coming peace era Russia would not come to realize how much her security and influence in the world depend on the confidence she can inspire and the voluntary collaboration she can obtain from the many lesser powers which surround her on almost all sides. . . .

The interests of the small powers in regard to an international security organization cannot be easily defined because these countries fall not into one but into at least two categories. One group consists of countries which, being extremely vulnerable to an attack by one of their great neighbors, are primarily concerned with guarantees against such an attack. If it should be found that the proposed organization cannot offer reliable protection against that particular country, the interest of these small countries in the organization is likely to dwindle.

The other group is composed of small states which, because of their geographical location, have little reason to fear an attack on their territory. They are afraid of becoming entangled in coercive or belligerent action as a result of which they might become a battlefield for others. Countries like Canada, Sweden or Turkey might fall into this category.

Notwithstanding these differences of interest and outlook, something of a common attitude toward the planned Security Organization seems to express itself in the utterances of spokesmen for the small powers. All seem to prefer an international security organization to a grand alliance of the Great Powers. One might ask oneself why they are so much interested in sharing the responsibility for peace. Is it a matter of sheer prestige, or of blind faith in the symbol of sovereign equality? The answer is no. The small countries have a vital interest in participating in the consultation and decision-making of the Great Powers. Friendly collaboration between the major powers, while being a prerequisite of peace, is also a dynamic process which might degenerate into "deals" at the expense of lesser powers; too often in the past has peace between the Great Powers been preserved in that fashion. One need not think of the extreme case of a partition of a small country, but rather of intervention in its internal affairs or other interference with its interests or rights. The presence of small countries on the Security Council, given the existing solidarity among the weaker countries, offers valuable safeguards against such a contingency. It would be regrettable if, for the sake of increasing these safeguards, the number of small countries represented on the Security Council should be increased to a point where the Council would lose its effectiveness or cease to be of interest to the major powers.

The small countries favor an international security organization for another reason which carries decisive weight with some of the European countries—they regard such an organization as the only means of assuring United States collaboration in the preservation of peace. Anything that will put an end to American isolationism is welcomed by them and may induce them to make considerable sacrifices. The reason for their fear of American isolationism is not hard to guess. Without the United States many of them cannot feel secure from another resurgence of Germany or of Japan; without participation by the United States the power of the Soviet Union could not be balanced by any grouping of countries.

It may seem shocking to speak of the balance of power in this connection. To most people in this country, the international organization appears desirable because it represents an alternative to the old and discredited balance of power. Paradoxically enough, in the weaker countries of Europe and Asia, the opposite view is being held; the international organization is being heralded as a means of creating a more balanced world, one in which the Soviet Union and the English-speaking countries, while taking a common interest in the preservation of peace, will carry approximately equal weight.

The small powers have accepted the idea of Great Power leadership within the new organization and appear willing to consent to considerable privileges for the leading powers. This indicates a remarkable break with traditional attitudes. Apparently the smaller countries have come to understand that the failure of the League of Nations was due largely to the fact that the big powers did not identify themselves with the organization and did not regard its interests as their own. This, by the way, is different from saying that they blame themselves or their equality of rights for the fall of the League; they have no reason to do so. No case is known in which a small power prevented the League from taking strong and effective action.

If the small powers have good reasons for favoring the establishment of a security organization and for being agreeable to some of the proposals worked out at Dumbarton Oaks, there are, nevertheless, other provisions in the Charter which arouse their opposition. . . .

Much attention has quite naturally been given in this connection to the proposed veto powers of the major countries. Their right—a right denied to the other members—to veto any coercive action, whether it be directed against themselves or against others, constitutes a far-reaching privilege and a break with the traditional legal equality of all sovereign states.

It is well to emphasize that the weaker countries will gain some advantages from this veto. Since it means that the organization can take no coercive action that is not agreeable to all of its great members, no small power will be committing itself to action which might displease one of its powerful neighbors. More specifically, membership in the organization will commit no country to take part in any war in which the great victors of this war would be fighting on opposite sides. This very substantially reduces the risks which small powers might otherwise incur.

But if this is an advantage to them, it is accompanied by serious disadvantages. The fact that coercive action is made to depend on the consent of all of the major powers greatly diminishes the protection which the organization can offer to weaker countries; it does not leave the organization with the "teeth" for which there has been so much demand.

Since the veto provisions weaken the coercive features of the organization, countries in fear of attack will prefer to rely on bilateral or multilateral alliances directed specifically against countries the intentions of which they fear. While they will not consider these special alignments incompatible with the over-all organization, they will want to make sure that the Security Organization does not take the teeth out of the special agreements. Thus France and other neighbors of Germany may wish to be authorized to take action for the prevention of German rearmament without having to wait for the consent of the Security Council. Similarly, some of the countries of South America may press for a kind of mandate to the American Republics, constituted as a regional group, empowering them to take coercive action in this hemisphere without having to wait for the consent of countries such as Great Britain or the Soviet Union.

While the Great Power veto is likely to draw much criticism because it so clearly indicates a differentiation between the rights of the big and the small powers, there are other provisions in the charter which may turn out to be of even graver concern to the small countries. These provisions deal not so much with what the Great Powers can do but with the role assigned to the lesser countries in coercive action undertaken by the organization. . . .

It might be well to remember the expectations of many people in this country when a new international security organization was first being proposed. It was assumed that all countries would give up an essential part of their sovereignty and leave it to a majority of a council to decide when they and others should take action against a country threatening or violating the peace. By the introduction of the veto power the major countries are being excluded from any such sacrifice of their sovereignty; their participation in coercive action will continue to depend on their own individual decision. It would have been surprising if any major power had accepted any other solution, but that makes it all the more imperative to find out where this leaves the smaller countries.

Of one thing there can be no doubt:

The majority of the Security Council, meaning in fact the Great Powers, will have the right to take any action, military or other, which it deems necessary for the purpose of maintaining or restoring peace and security. Furthermore, according to the charter, such action shall be regarded as being undertaken on behalf of the whole organization. This means that whenever the Great Powers agree to act together and succeed in obtaining the concurrence of one or two of the lesser powers on the Council, their action, whatever it be, shall be deemed to represent the interests of the whole community. The other members of the organization shall be required to put no obstacles in the way of such action and shall refrain from giving assistance to the opponent. This is a reasonable but nevertheless a far-reaching concession on the part of those nations which were either not represented on the Council or, while being represented, voted against the decision. The concession is greater because of the fact that the Security Council is not accountable to any assembly or parliament and because its most powerful members are not elected but hold their position on the mere grounds of superior power. Even so, little opposition has been voiced to this provision except that some of the "middle powers" wish to be represented on the Security Council in order to be able to influence its decisions.

. . . In most cases, a weak country will not refuse participation if all of the Great Powers urge it to join them. A coalition composed of all of the Great Powers operating against a lesser power should be able to give such convincing evidence of its strength that small powers would feel that they were incurring no undue risk if they permitted the use of their territory. However, there might be refusals as there have been in this war. The fact that Eire did not open her ports to Britain or the United States or that Turkish airfields were not made available to the air forces of the United Nations when the Germans were being driven out of the Balkans undeniably hampered the war effort of the United Nations; a similar attitude might again, in the case of action by the international organization, delay victory.

In view of the delays caused by neutral powers and in view of the fact that the belligerents are sacrificing the lives and property of their peoples to win the war, it is too much to ask that they be sympathetic to the neutrals who have remained on the sidelines. It should be remembered, however, that such neutrality may have been the lesser evil. If small countries neighboring on the aggressor find themselves exposed to early conquest—as they were from 1939 to 1941 and as they may well be again under an international organization, since it takes time to organize defensive measures—they may have no choice, except for national suicide, but to throw in their lot with the aggressor or to remain neutral. It is not logical to ask the weaker nations to incur the risk of irreparable damage and complete destruction while at the same time demanding privileges for the Great Powers on the ground that they will have to bear the brunt of the burden.

This does not mean that any effort should be spared to obtain from as many lesser powers as possible binding commitments which will obligate them to participate in coercive action undertaken by the Council. All member countries, presumably, will have to undertake not to give economic assistance to an opponent of the organization and to offer positive economic aid to the countries acting for the organization. Some smaller countries like Belgium or Czechoslovakia, urgently in need of guarantees of security, may be willing to promise participation without any reservation; others may wish to protect themselves by a clause permitting them to refuse active participation, such as the use of their territory, in cases where they would incur risks disproportionate to the services they could render. More can hardly be expected; it is questionable whether it would be wise to press for more at this time.

There are several reasons for this. In the first place, more radical provisions may prevent some of the lesser countries from joining the organization; in that case, they would retain a completely free hand. In the second place, it has never paid to commit nations to a course of action with which they do not wholeheartedly agree. In an emergency they will find reasons to evade their obligations, thereby reducing the reliability of all of the engagements. This means that the success of the organization should rest on the ability of the Great Powers to gain from other countries all the voluntary cooperation they need. Their privileges and their leadership will be far more secure if, instead of asking for a blank check, they rely on their ability to convince enough nations of the wisdom of their course. This country certainly would be paying an unduly high price if it were to forfeit the good will of the weaker powers for the sake of obtaining powers for the Council which would only provoke resentment and anxiety.

POWER AND RESPONSIBILITY IN A NEW WORLD ORDER

By Gerhart Niemeyer

From "World Order and the Great Powers," by Gerhart Niemeyer; chap. 2 of *The Second Chance, America and the Peace,* edited by J. B. Whitton. Princeton University Press, 1944.

If we rely on the power of great nations as an institution of world order, we must also think of such national power not as an end in itself, or even as a means to mere nationalistic purposes, but as an instrument toward universal ends which lie beyond political expediency. Moreover, since an instrumental view of power gave rise to the system of checks and balances in our system of national government, it is important to consider a similar limitation of international power.

One type of limitation resides in the very nature of the leadership of the three Great Powers. If they exercise this leadership together, they can lead only so far as they succeed in solving their own conflicts. Some may object that most triumvirates in history have ended in the triumph of one of the triumvirs as dictator. The analogy, however, is not well drawn. A co-ruler may be eliminated by murder, but a nation cannot be thus removed. In this matter it is significant that nations are geographically confined to a fixed location in which they fulfill functions of regional order. This circumstance prescribes both a territorial and a functional division of power among the leader nations, and this means that, so long as its inner strength persists, each of the Big Three will be indispensable, as a co-ruler, to the others.

However, unless their leadership is also visibly limited, for instance by institutions and principles embodying the common interest, the Big Three may still appear to other nations to resemble a gang organized to exploit the weak. As this impression would defeat any attempt to create a world order, the Big Three should find it expedient to carve out a wide niche in which the smaller powers can enjoy a share of authority over world affairs. . . . Yet we must recognize that there is little chance of balance between weak states on the one hand and those with formidable military and economic resources on the other. The problem among nations is very different from that which obtains among individuals who, as Thomas Hobbes rightly observed, are on the whole on an equal footing. Some individuals are stronger and more intelligent than others, but so far as the general picture is concerned these differences cancel out. This very fact makes democratic government feasible. Nations, however, are fundamentally unequal. They differ so widely in population, territory and resources that they cannot be reduced to an average representative type. Thus a number of smaller nations cannot be matched against the might of a Great Power. Some may suggest a federation of small powers as an answer to this problem. It is doubtful, however, whether this would be a solution. Any new federation would immediately lay claim to the title and position of a Great Power although its actual strength might not place it in this category. Such a claim would be bound to run the test of conflict and war, recommencing the vicious circle, all without any benefit to the members of the federation. Thus it is clear that in international relations many a mickle does not make a muckle. The small nations can find some ways of counterbalancing the Big Three, but only on secondary issues. This type of balance cannot, therefore, be counted on as an effective safety device.

Despite their fundamental weakness, the secondary and small nations occupy a position of vital importance in a world order based on Big Three leadership. With all their strength, the Great Powers would have great difficulty in preserving order in the presence of widespread dissatisfaction and opposition. . . .

A promising way of reconciling the small nations with Big Three leadership would be to reserve for them a substantial share of responsibility and international prestige. The new system should provide ample opportunities for smaller nations to prove their worth and win the respect of the world, thereby convincing them that their military weakness does not rob them of influence. The new international organization, which will have to be set up for other reasons as well, would be the most logical framework for such participation of the smaller countries. On the one hand, the secondary powers should, in this organization, be drawn continually into the council of the Big Three, sharing with the latter the responsibility for political decisions. This would be particularly feasible on the regional level. On the other hand, smaller nations should be given the leading role in most of the administrative agencies likely to be established within the international organization. It would seem wise to institutionalize a monopoly of the small powers in this field in the same way in which Switzerland, for example, has enjoyed the sole privilege of organizing and administering the International Red Cross. Not only should the seat of such agencies be in the smaller countries; their citizens might be given the exclusive right to executive positions in these institutions. There are many tasks for which the world might come to rely completely on the services of the smaller nations, as it will rely for its peace on the harmonious leadership of the Big Three.

It is most important of all, however, that the small nations should be convinced that they will receive fair treatment. The criteria of fairness in international relations have not been crystallized in the form of anything like legal rules. In the absence of judicial precedent, such standards are still, for the most part, in the realm of morals. . . . While the prevailing notions of international justice are still vague, however, an international organization might become a forum in which legal criteria governing the relationship between large and small powers could evolve. Such principles, possibly growing out of specific regional conditions, would be indispensable to any stable political order. For greater effectiveness, however, they should not be laid down a priori, but should be formulated only in the light of proved political experience.

There is another way to balance and limit the power of nations, one which is, in fact, more promising than the attempt to oppose small nations to Great Powers. This is the opposition of private individuals to governments. In international as well as in domestic politics the only real check on governments issues from individuals acting in private associations and with a view to non-political ends. Though a private individual is both a citizen and a "political animal," he also looks beyond politics and conceives ends and values which he deems at least as important as national interests. Thus he is capable of transcending the realm of political conflict and finding motives for union where governments must clash. In fact, such sense of world community as has developed during the last three hundred years did not spring from any affection of governments for one another but from the fact that individuals in the several countries held in common many values and interests which were conceived apart from power politics and which cut across national boundaries.

Moreover, individual man is the agent for the moral truths of mankind and therefore the ultimate guide for the policies of nations. It is thus imperative that the voice of the individual be heard above the noise of politics. The common interests of the world, above all, must be formulated by private individuals who can look beyond national interests. The values which individuals all over the world jointly recognize must be given expression as a guide for policies of governments.

This is the only fruitful way to approach the thorny problem of the limitation of sovereignty. If the state is a compact entity, founded on the fervent allegiance of its citizens, performing for them indispensable services and constituting the main frame of reference for their moral judgments, then state sovereignty can be limited only by war and subjugation. Sovereignty depends on what the power of national government means to the people living under it. The way to limit it is to loosen gradually the tight fabric of the state, by making the people look beyond it, by gradually extending and expanding the scope of community feeling, and, finally, by creating universal agencies capable of providing services that had previously been discharged by national governments alone. Sovereignty is not only a conception; it is likewise a real fact, which can be overcome only by making the wider-than-national community an equally real phenomenon in the experience of individuals.

SECURITY FOR THE UNITED STATES: HOW CAN WE ACHIEVE IT?

By Grayson Kirk

From "The Future Security of the United States," by Grayson Kirk, in *World Organization—Economic, Political, and Social*. Proceedings of the Academy of Political Science, Vol. 21, No. 3, May 1945. Copyright 1945 by the Academy of Political Science, Columbia University, New York; reproduced by permission. Dr. Kirk is professor of government at Columbia University.

The task of the statesman is never simple and it is never finished. In the complex field of foreign affairs the essence of good statesmanship lies in the ability to protect the fundamental and persistent interests of the state by adapting traditional policies to meet the ever-changing conditions of the external world. If a foreign minister adheres slavishly to tradition, his course is likely to be fully as disastrous as if he adopts alternatives of reckless improvisation. The middle course, which requires a constant reexamination of the forces of stability and change, and the shaping of policy to fit them, is the only one which can be counted on to preserve the vital interests of the state in its foreign relations.

These general observations apply with particular force to the problem of national security. No single interest of the state is more fundamental, for unless there can be as much safety against external danger as the best intelligence and the full mobilization of the resources of the state can provide, then the entire life of the state must be carried on precariously under the constant shadow of insecurity. In considering this problem of our future security, we must ask ourselves whether the circumstances which our past policy has been shaped to meet continue to exist, or, if not, what policy changes are needed in order to provide us in the future with the same security that we had—or thought we had—in the world of a generation ago.

At the outset, I should like to suggest that our post-war world will differ from the world we have known in the past in at least two important ways, both of which have important implications for our future security. The first of these requires little elaboration; it is merely the old and rather trite observation concerning the way in which modern technology has brought about a shrinkage of global distances. The vast reaches of the Atlantic and the Pacific are no longer so vast, and they no longer provide us with impressive natural barriers behind which we can tend our own garden in assured peace and safety. If you hesitate at all to accept this conclusion, I would merely invite your attention to the magnitude of our own military effort now being conducted on the far side of each of these two oceans. If the United States can put forth such a prodigious effort, and can strike with such lethal power at these great distances from our homeland, then there is no geographical or technological reason why we may not in the future be the victims of an equally deadly attack launched from Europe or Asia against this continent. If we can do this to others, we face the prospect that others with the same power potential can do as much to us. Clearly, therefore, we shall only court disaster if we continue to think of our oceans as invulnerable bastions. Such a Maginot Line psychology would be as fatal to us as it was to the France of five years ago.

No less important is the changing distribution of world power. The situation which obtained in the latter part of the nineteenth century—when British power was supreme upon the sea lanes of the world, and when there was a fairly satisfactory balancing of power on the European continent—was one which favored American security to an extent which we have seldom recognized. Actually, it was scarcely necessary for us to have a foreign policy at all. I know of no other great state which had such favorable circumstances for such a long period of time. Small wonder that we thought of diplomacy and power politics and alliances as sinister trappings of the Old World from whose toils we had fortunately escaped. Our analysis was wrong, but we suffered no ill effects from it.

Today almost every aspect of this old situation has disappeared or is fast moving over the horizon. The continent of Europe, once the stronghold of world power, bids fair in the future to be little more than an enlarged Balkan area of small and middle-sized states situated in between the great peripheral power centers of Britain and the Soviet Union. Even though France, once the strongest of the continental states, does regain a large measure of her prewar strength, she will not be a front-rank power in the post-war sense of that term. This conclusion is warranted because developments in the Soviet Union and the United States are tending to raise the level of front-rank, Great Power status far beyond anything which the power potential of France can hope to match. To a lesser extent this same conclusion may also apply to Britain, first because she will be greatly weakened by the long-time effects of this costly war, and second because British power is scattered throughout a global empire whereas that of Russia and the United States is to a far greater extent concentrated at home where it can be more safely and efficiently utilized as needed.

This prospective bipolarity of greatest world power has been anticipated for some time. Let me cite the testimony of one distinguished observer who said:

"There are, at the present time, two great nations in the world which seem to tend toward the same end, although they started from different points: I allude to the Russians and the Americans. Both of them have grown up unnoticed, and while the attention of mankind was directed elsewhere, they have suddenly assumed a most prominent place among the nations; and the world learned of their existence and their greatness at almost the same time.

"All other nations seem to have nearly reached their natural limits, and only to be charged with the maintenance of their power; but these are still in the act of growth; all the others are stopped, or continue to advance with extreme difficulty; these are proceeding with ease and with celerity along a path to which the human eye can assign no term. . . . The Anglo-American relies upon personal interest to accomplish his ends, and gives free scope to the unguided exertions and common sense of the citizens; the Russian centers all the authority of society in a single arm. . . . Their starting point is different, and their courses are not the same; yet each of them seems to be marked out by the will of Heaven to sway the destinies of half the globe."

It will interest you, I think, to know that these words, which have such a contemporary ring, were written by Alexis de Tocqueville in his famous *Democracy in America,* which was first published in January 1835.

There is a first general conclusion to be drawn from reflection upon the disappearance of old barriers and the changing location of the world's power centers. This is that there is no assurance to us of any national security through a policy of withdrawal from the political affairs of the world. The possession of great power implies the assumption of great responsibility. This is not a counsel of altruism; it is a sober calculation of our national interest. Let me return to this point a little later.

If, in view of these changing world conditions, we can derive only danger from a policy of studied indifference to happenings in Europe and Asia, then what are the proper elements of a new security policy which will give us in a planned way in the future the same security which we had without planning for it in the past? This is a large order, but if we fail to deal with it intelligently, our children may be the worse for it in the future.

From a strictly military point of view certain conclusions are clear. One is that, from now on, we shall need to have much greater military strength in being than we have generally had in the past. A corollary of diminishing global distances is the prospect that we may not, in the future, have enough time, after we have been challenged, to prepare ourselves for a great military effort. We have been fortunate in this respect in the last two wars, but we cannot assume that we will always be equally so in the future. If not, then not only would we be exposed to great danger quickly, but we would have the added disadvantage of being required to fight on American soil. Certainly, one of the important aspects of any security policy is that it should enable you, if you cannot always keep the peace, at least to spare your own country as far as possible from the ghastly ravages of modern combat operations.

Also, we shall need a greater military establishment because of our obligations under the prospective international security organization. Whatever its precise form, such an organization necessarily will lay a primary burden of responsibility upon the states of greatest strength. This means that Britain, the Soviet Union and the United States will have the major obligation of using their strength jointly in behalf of the organization to maintain peace throughout the world. Otherwise, any organization will be impotent. To be able to carry our own share of this responsibility, we shall need to have a substantial army, navy and air force ready for such threats to world peace as may arise.

The precise nature of the military establishment which these new circumstances will necessitate is not a matter on which a civilian like myself can speak with any degree of authority. The desirable goal, however, is obvious. We must be able to apply substantial force at points far removed from our own shores with a minimum of delay. This will place an initial dependence upon a powerful navy and air force. Whether a program of universal military training, such as is now contained in the proposal before Congress, is also a necessary component part of our needs is, I think, a matter for careful and extended discussion. On the basis of the best opinion available, we should try to determine whether this great departure from our past practice is likely to do as much for our security as a comparable investment of time and money in other forms of military preparation. In making such a momentous decision we must keep in mind the fact that we have a dual object. One is the need to prepare ourselves for our role in the international organization. The other is to be able to meet the requirements of our own national defense in case the organization fails to ensure the peaceful adjustment of our disputes with other

Great Powers. In any event, if I may speak parenthetically for a moment, the decision should turn solely on the contribution which we believe universal training would make to our security. We should not be greatly influenced by other alleged advantages, such as its presumed contribution to standards of national education, public health, and the like. These are, at best, incidental benefits which could be obtained far more efficiently by other means.

Our need to be able to apply force quickly on the other side of our ocean frontiers naturally raises the question of new naval and air bases. This is far from a simple matter. From a technical military point of view any layman can see an obvious advantage in a nexus of bases to serve as sources of matériel supply for the aerial and naval spearheads of our overseas forces, and as strong points for the protection of our supply routes from the factories and arsenals of this country. But these are not the only considerations involved. Equally important, perhaps, is the effect which such a step might have upon the attitudes of other countries toward the United States. While we have the greatest confidence in our own motives, and we could sincerely assure the world that this military expansion was purely defensive, would we be able to convince others that this was so? Would it, on the other hand, have a tendency to make others suspicious of us, and would it lead them to try to form security combinations against us? If so, then the technical gain might be more than offset by the loss in the conditions of political security. Both facets of the problem must be considered before policy decisions are made.

In many ways, the political aspects of our security program are at least as important as those of a military character. If I read correctly the lessons of our involvement in the last two great wars, they point to the conclusion that the people of this country have an almost instinctive feeling that our security would be jeopardized by too great a concentration of power in the hands of any one state on either the Atlantic rimland of Europe or the Pacific rimland of Asia. Other things being equal, this is a reasonable and a sound conclusion. But what are its implications for the future? Does this mean that, in the future as in the past, we shall refrain from taking any action, when we see such concentrations of power developing, until we are confronted with a problem which can be dealt with only by a prodigious military effort? Twice we have followed this policy of protecting ourselves by the hardest and most dangerous course possible. This is not by any stretch of the imagination an illustration of wise and far-sighted statesmanship. Our success is, rather, a tribute to our military skill, our immense potential, and to the fact that, in each case, we have had allies who could deal with the foe until we were able to mobilize our latent power.

But even though all this is true, we must not be premature in deciding that we must now reverse this traditional policy entirely. Even though we cannot, in all fairness to our own safety, disinterest ourselves in political developments in these vital areas abroad, precisely what is the policy alternative? How can we manifest this interest to an extent commensurate with our needs without assuming political responsibilities beyond those limits which most Americans would approve? The simple and traditional way to implement such an interest would be by the conclusion of alliances which would pledge our aid to those states whose continued existence we regard as vital to our own safety. But it is clear that most of our fellow citizens might feel that the dangers of military embroilment through such an alliance relationship would outweigh the security advantages which we would derive from it. Also, such a policy of political commitment would raise the same difficulties, which I mentioned a moment ago in connection with the matter of bases, namely, that other states might understandably regard such a step as an evidence of an American policy directed against their own security. Clearly, the obverse of such a step, that is, the interference of another Great Power in such a fashion in this hemisphere, would be so regarded by the great majority of American citizens. We have felt this way ever since the days of James Monroe, and we could scarcely object, in all good conscience, if others felt the same way about us.

Is there any way out of this dilemma? At the moment, I can see only two possibilities. We could abandon any interest in continental affairs in Europe and Asia, and could undertake to make ourselves militarily as strong as possible in this hemisphere and in the two oceans. By strengthening our traditional ties with Britain, we could maintain an outpost close to Europe (though the British are understandably averse to our tendency to regard them merely in this light), and by maintaining a strong position in the Philippines we could have an advance base near the Asiatic mainland. The real difficulty would be that this policy would only be a streamlined version of our traditional isolationism. It would not offer any effective guarantees against a repetition of our experiences in the recent past. Being stronger militarily, we might be willing to act at an earlier stage to deal with a developing threat, but this would require a degree of prescience which has not thus far been characteristic of any peace-loving democratic society. We must not blink at the fact that our people will refrain from a willingness to resort to force until the last possible alternative has been exhausted. It is a price which we pay for our democratic way of life.

The other alternative is, I believe, the only one which would enable us to exert an active and continuous interest in European and Asiatic affairs without exposing ourselves to the dangers suggested above. This is the exercise of such an interest through the instrumentality of a world-wide security organization. This participation would enable us, in concert with other powers, to deal at an early stage with situations with which we would not, in all probability, undertake to deal if we were acting alone. Moreover, our collaboration inside such an organization should go far to make possible the adjustment of our own difficulties with those other powers whose friendly collaboration with us we recognize to be of vital importance to our own security.

It is important, though, that we should view this organization in the proper perspective. We should not allow our aspirations for an enduring peace to lead us to believe that the mere establishment of such an organization will, in itself, constitute a sufficient guarantee for our future national security. The new instrument will not, and cannot, cope firmly and effectively with disputes among the greatest powers. It can facilitate the peaceful adjustment of these disputes, but it cannot coerce the parties into the acceptance of an unpalatable settlement. In other words, it will not bring us the millennium tomorrow. We may be able to start toward permanent peace through the Golden Gate of San Francisco, but we will still have a long course to follow before we achieve our goal. Only if we are both wiser and stronger than we have been in the past will we be able to assure for ourselves—and for others—that freedom from fear which all reasonable men desire.

SUBJECT INDEX

Africa, impact of war on, 461; geography of, 463ff.; map of, 464; role of in world politics, 465

Afro-Asian Realm, description of, 458ff.; historical significance of, 459ff.; America's interest in, 459ff.

Alaska, 616f.

American Realm, definition of, 604ff., 607ff.; U.S. interest in, 606f.; political geography of, 615ff., 620ff.; American "Mediterranean," 618ff., 626f.; N. and S. America, 628ff.; hemispheric cooperation, 634ff. *See also* Latin America.

Argentina, 622, 624f., 634. *See also* American Realm *and* Latin America.

Australia, American interest in, 462; geography of, 491f.; map of, 491; strategical situation of, 492ff.

balance of power, 6, 12ff., 23

Brazil, 622ff. *See also* American Realm *and* Latin America.

British Empire, structure of, 192ff.; map of, 193. *See* Great Britain.

Canada, geography of, 616f.

Chiang Kai-shek, 556f., 588f., 591ff.

China, geographic description of, 493f., 549ff.; historical background of, 551; population and manpower of, 112f., 548, 558ff.; American interest in, 461f., 546f.; American policy toward, 546ff.; as military power today, 553ff.; agricultural economy of, 563ff.; industrial raw materials of, 569ff.; problems of industrial development in, 575ff.; transport and communications in, 580ff.; political and social organization of, 586ff.; civil war in, 591ff.; course of war with Japan, 595ff.; outlook for Chinese development, 598ff.; future position of, 118f., 548f.

Czechoslovakia, in peace settlement, 376ff., 380ff.; dismemberment of, 363f.

Egypt, 269f. *See also* Mediterranean region *and* Middle East.

Europe, historical role of, 122f., 134, 140; importance of location of, 124ff.; map showing same, 125; geographical description of, 127ff., 129ff., map, 130; resources of, 131f.; population trends of, 109ff., 146; North Sea countries of, 132f.; Mediterranean region of, 133f.; Eastern, 134; economic development of before 1914, 134ff.; effect of First World War on, 140f.; between wars, 140ff.; map of political boundaries of between wars, 141; future role of, 123f., 140, 144f., 145ff.

Europe, Eastern and Southeastern, map of, 374; historical significance of, 373ff.; map of nationalities of, 375; in peace settlement of 1919, 377f., 380; interest of U.S. in, 378ff.

Far East, components of region, 486f.; map of, 488; historic isolation of, 487ff.; political geography of, 490ff.; Japanese conquests in, 459ff.; map of Japan and Eastern Asia. *See also* China, Japan, etc.

France, geography of, 213ff.; map of, 214; strategical position of, 217ff.; natural resources of, 220ff., 222f.; economic development of, 223ff.; communications in, 224f.; population and manpower, 109f., 225ff., chart, 227; French Empire, 228ff.; map of, 229; foreign policy of, 17; pre-war, 231ff., 233ff.; post-war, 261ff.; defeat of, 237ff., 249ff.; recovery of, 256ff.; American interests in, 211ff.; future position of, 117ff., 144, 256ff., 260ff., 750ff.

Germany, geographical description of, 320ff.; strategical position of, 314ff.; map, 317; American interest in, 311ff.; development of before 1914, 135f., 313f., 325ff., 329, 332ff.; map of raw materials and industrial areas of Rhine valley, 323; population trends in, 109ff., 135f., 327ff.; chart of, 227; growth of power and ambition of, 335ff.; life in before 1914, 339ff.; foreign policy of Second Reich, 337f.; defeat of in 1918, 341f.; statecraft under Republic, 342ff.; life in between wars, 347ff.; foreign policy under Hitler, 353ff.; origins of Third Reich, 356ff.; Nazi statecraft, 358ff.; Hitler's grand strategy, 361ff.; defeat of, 1945, 370ff.; future of, 118, 145, 370ff.; plans of for a third war, 698ff. *See also* peace, terms of.

Great Britain, nineteenth century economic primacy, 114f., 149, 156ff., 160ff., 162f.; geographical position of, 151ff., 153ff., 163ff.; map, 164, 166ff.; American interests respecting, 148ff.; map of physical foundations of industrial development, 159; sea power of, 163ff.; map, 164, 166ff., 173ff.; twentieth century position of, 171f., 183ff., 185ff.; relations of with U.S., 172f.; European land power vs. sea power of, 180ff.; foreign policy of, 17, 196ff.; place of Military in society of, 199ff.; importance of Mediterranean region to, 275ff.; future position of, 117ff., 145, 207ff., 750ff., 754ff., 762ff. *See also* British Empire.

SUBJECT INDEX

Great Powers, importance of solidarity of, 386ff.; role of in keeping peace, 750ff., 754ff., 762ff.; relations with lesser powers in new world order, 762ff.

India, geographical description of, 478ff.; people and culture of, 469ff., 481ff.; population trends of, 111, 471, 482; industry and agriculture of, 473f., 483ff.; communications, 485f.; political structure of, 481f.
Indian Ocean, map of with borderlands, 467; role of in world politics, 466ff.
international politics, nature of, 4ff.; cp with domestic politics, 9ff.
Iraq, 300f.
Iran, 302f.
Italy, geography of, 266ff.; map, 267; strategical situation of, 276, 277ff.; Fascist ambitions, 277ff.; future status of, 144f., 281f.

Japan, historical background of, 498ff.; geographical description of, 494f., 505ff.; map of, 506; American interest in, 495ff.; U.S. relations with, 496, 502; natural resources of, 509ff.; industrial development of, 514ff.; political organization of, 521ff., 524ff.; Japanese behavior, 532ff.; strategy and fruits of Japanese imperialism, 538ff. See also peace, terms of.

Latin America, attitude toward U.S., 607, 634ff.; geographical relation to U.S., 618; pattern of development of, 630ff.; relations of U.S. with, 634ff. See also American Realm.
League of Nations 7, 11, 747

maps and map-making, 64ff., 68ff.; projections illustrated, 69, 71, 74, 75, 76
Mediterranean region, historical importance of, 264ff.; American interest in, 264ff.; geography of, 266ff., 268ff.; map, 267; natural resources of, 270ff.; role in Great-Power politics, 273ff.; Fascist ambitions in, 277ff.; situation of Spain in, 282f.; Nazi strategy in, 367f. See also Italy, Spain, etc.
Middle East, historical importance of, 264ff.; American interests in, 264ff.; geography of, 288ff.; people of and changing cultural patterns, 290ff., 292ff.; strategical importance of, 288ff., 303ff.; oil as political factor in, 307ff.; as fulcrum of Moslem world, 308ff.; modern transport in, 305ff. See also Iran, Iraq, etc.

national power, elements of, 29ff.; population, 38ff., 106ff.; charts, 651; foodstuffs and raw materials, 40ff.; technology, 48ff.; ideology, 54ff.; political organization, 57ff.; geography, 63ff.
national power, nature of, 12, 28ff.; military, 31f.; economic, 32ff.; over opinion, 35ff.
national state system, 3ff., 6ff., 10, 24ff.
Near East, see Middle East.

Oceania, description of, 492f.; Chinese penetration in, 493

Palestine, 299f.
Panama Canal, 620ff., 636
peace, terms of, U.S. attitudes toward, 692ff.; lessons for from last peace, 695ff.; British attitudes toward, 696; suggested treatment of Germany, 698ff., 709ff.; Cairo declaration on, for Japan, 718ff.; British view of terms for Japan, 718ff.; American view of same, 721ff.; problem of, in Far East, 724ff., 730
Poland, 364, 377, 380ff.

Saudi Arabia, 301f., 461
Scott, John, on development of Soviet Middle East, 423
Spain, geography of, 266ff.; map, 267; strategical situation of, 282f.; Axis intervention in, 363; future of, 283ff., 287f.
Suez Canal, significance of, 273, 304ff., 459. See also Egypt, Great Britain, Mediterranean region.
Syria, 297ff.

technology, development of industrial and military technology, 48ff., 50ff., 81ff.
Treaty of Versailles, faults of, 696ff. See also peace, terms of.
Turkey, geography of, 266ff.; map, 267; historical role of, 294ff.; recent development of, 295ff.

United Nations organization, American interest in, 731ff.; role of Great Powers in, 749ff., 753ff.; role of small powers in, 757ff.; power and responsibility in, 762ff.
U.S.S.R., before 1914, 136f.; pre-war relations of U.S. with, 384ff.; interest of U.S. in Russian victory, 388ff.; geography of, 391ff., 397ff.; map of, 392; natural resources of, 396f., 399, 435ff., map, 435; agriculture of, 395f.; political geography of, 399f.; the peoples of, 403f.; space and terrain in Soviet defense, 400ff.; Russian revolution, 404ff.; population trends of, 110ff., 136, 146; preparation for war, 409ff., 412ff.; industrial expansion of, 408f., 411f., 412ff., 420ff., 425ff., 428ff., 437f.; in Soviet Middle East, 420ff., 428ff.; in Soviet Far East, 425ff.; migration of industry to Urals, 428ff.; Soviet

industry, present and future, 430ff., 432ff., 437f., 441ff.; state structure and organization of, 438ff.; aims and policies of, 441ff.; role of as Great Power, 386ff., 749ff., 753ff., 762ff.; future position of, 117ff., 389f., 439ff., 441ff., 749ff.

U.S.A., geography of, 616, 658ff., strategic situation of in American realm, 626f.; attitude of toward Latin American nations, 634ff.; historic policies of, 643ff.; present power position of, 627f., 642ff.; strategic situation of, 643ff., 658; the American people, 645ff.; population and manpower of, 146, 650ff.; comparative chart, 651; resources of, 660f., 661ff.; economic development of, 665ff.; steel as yardstick of strength of, 668ff.; science and technology in, 671ff., 674ff.; scientific personnel in, 679ff.; problem of American foreign policy today, 680ff., 684ff., 690, 731ff., 749ff., 765ff.; maps of world position of, 685, 686; problem of security for, 731ff., 746ff., 764ff.; dangers of uncontrolled science in, 733ff.; responsibility of as Great Power, 117ff., 749ff., 753ff., 762ff.; America and the peace, 692ff., 735ff.

Western Hemisphere, 604, 607ff. *See also* American Realm.

AUTHOR INDEX

ANTONINI, LUIGI, on future of Italy, 281-2
BADEAU, J. S., on Near and Middle East, 288-310
BAERWALD, FRIEDRICH, on future of Europe, 145-7
BASSECHES, NIKOLAUS, on Russian preparation for total war, 412-20
BECKER, CARL, on power politics, 19-23
BEMIS, S. F., on geography and progress in N. and S. America, 628-30
BIDAULT, GEORGE, on future French foreign policy, 261-3
BISSON, T. A., on Japanese political system, 521-4; on peace terms for Japan, 721-4
BOGARDUS, J. F., on Germany's central position, 314-15
BOGGS, S. W., on Africa, 463-5; on Western Hemisphere, 607-14
BRANDT, KARL, on foodstuffs and raw materials as elements of national power, 40-4
BROGAN, D. W., on vulnerability and strength of democracy, 61-2; on place of Military in British society, 199-207; on defeat of France, 249-56; on American character, 645-9
BROWN UNIVERSITY ECONOMISTS, on population as element of national power, 39
BUTLER, HAROLD, on Germany before 1914, 339-41; on Germany between wars, 346-56
CARR, E. H., on nature of political power, 31-8; on Britain's economic position, 185-92; on future U.S. policy, 690
CHAMBERLAIN, SIR AUSTEN, on British foreign policy, 197-9
CHAMBERLIN, W. H., on Russian revolution, 404-9
COMPTON, A. H., on problem of scientific personnel in U.S., 679-80
COT, PIERRE, on defeat of France, 237-48

CRAIG, GORDON, on America and the peace, 736-46
CRESSEY, G. B., on geography of U.S.S.R., 397-400; on peoples of U.S.S.R., 403-4; on geography of India, 478-81; on people and culture of India, 481-6; on geography of Japan, 507-11; on geography of China, 549-53; on outlook for Chinese development, 598-601
CROWE, SIR EYRE, on bases of British foreign policy, 196-7; on German political ambitions, 335-7
DUNAWAY, PHILIP, on geography of Japan, 505; on Japan's economic potential, 514
EARLE, E. M., on methods of Nazi statecraft, 358-61; on impact of changing conditions on American security, 680-4
ECKEL, E. C., quoted on Britain's industrial leadership, 156-60; on German technology and steel, 332-5
EDELMAN, MAURICE, on Soviet industrialization, 409-12
FORTUNE, EDITORS OF, on Spain, 283-8; on industry of Japan, 515-21; on rulers of Japan, 524-32; on steel industry in U.S., 668-71
ELIOT, GEORGE FIELDING, on science and foreign policy, 734-6
EMENY, BROOKS, on international politics, 5-8; on world geography, 78-80
FAWCETT, C. B., on Britain's geographical position, 153-5; on British Empire, 192-6
FINCH, V. C., and WHITBECK, R. H., on physiography of Europe, 129-34; on land of France and its uses, 220-1; on French mineral resources, 222-3; on geography of Mediterranean borderlands, 268-73; on German resources and industries, 320-7
FISCHER, JOHN, on India, 469-78

AUTHOR INDEX 773

FOSDICK, R. B., on urgency of world organization, 733-4
FOX, W. T. R., on international politics, 24-7; on emerging pattern of world politics, 114-19
GÉRAUD, ANDRÉ (Pertinax), on future of France, 260-1
GRAJDANZEV, A. J., on Japanese industrial expansion, 514-15
GRAY, G. W., on American science at war, 674-9
HARRISON, R. E., and STRAUS-HUPÉ, ROBERT, on maps and world politics, 64-8
HARTSHORNE, RICHARD, on Eastern Europe, 378-83
HAUSER, P. M. and TAEUBER, C., on population trends in U.S., 651-8
HELFFERICH, KARL, on German population trends before 1913, 328
HORST MENDERHAUSEN, on population as element of power, 38-9
HUDSON, G. F., and RAJCHMAN, MARTHE, on historic isolation of Far East, 487-90
HUNTINGTON, ELLSWORTH, and VAN VALKENBURG, SAMUEL, on historic dominance of Europe, 124-8; on natural resources of France, 220
JAMES, P. E., on culture patterns of Latin America, 630-4
KEYNES, J. M., on Europe before 1914, 134-40
KING-HALL, STEPHEN, on London as economic capital of the world, 162-3
KIRK, DUDLEY, on population and power in the post-war world, 106-14
KIRK, GRAYSON, on problem of security for U.S., 765-9
LAUTERBACH, A. T., on vulnerability and strength of democracy, 57-60
LEITH, C. K., on natural resources of U.S.S.R., 436-7; on mineral resources of U.S., 660-1
LESUEUR, LARRY, on Soviet wartime migration to Urals, 428-30
LIPPMANN, WALTER, on international politics, 16-19; on American foreign policy, 684-9
MACKINDER, SIR HALFORD J., theories of on world power, 83ff.; on sea power vs. land power, 86-100; theories of discussed by N. J. Spykman, 101ff.; on Britain's geographical position, 151-2; on growth of German manpower, 328; views of regarding peace terms of 1918 discussed, 695
MAILLAUD, PIERRE, on geography of France, 213-17; on French foreign policy, 231-3; on French manpower after First World War, 226
MEARS, HELEN, on Japanese behavior, 532-8
MICAUD, C. A., and STRAUS-HUPÉ, ROBERT, on future of France, 256-60

MONROE, ELIZABETH, on Fascist ambitions in Mediterranean, 279, 280
MOORE, HARRIET, on Soviet Far East, 425-8
MOWRER, E. A., and RAJCHMAN, MARTHE, on Indian Ocean in world politics, 466-8
NATIONAL RESOURCES COMMITTEE, on population problems, 38-9; on integration of American resources, 661-5
NEW YORK TIMES, on American approach to peace-making, 693-4
NICHOLSON, HAROLD, on lessons from the last peace, 695-8
NIEMEYER, GERHART, on new world order, 746-9, 753-7, 762-4
NOTESTEIN, F. W. et al., on French population trends, 226-8; on population trends in U.S.S.R., 434-5
PARES, SIR BERNARD, on Soviet Union, 391-7
POLITICAL AND ECONOMIC PLANNING, on Britain's world position today, 207-10
RAJCHMAN, MARTHE, see Mowrer, E. A. and see Hudson, G. F.
ROWE, D. N., on China's political and military position, 553-98; on prerequisites of peace in Far East, 730
ROYAL INSTITUTE OF INTERNATIONAL AFFAIRS, on American people, 649-50; on U.S. natural resources and economic development, 665-8
RUSSELL, BERTRAND, on power of ideas, 54-7
SANSOM, SIR GEORGE, on historical foundations of modern Japan, 498-504; on terms of peace for Japan, 718-21
SCHUMAN, F. L., on origins of Third Reich, 356-8
SIEGFRIED, ANDRÉ, on Europe between wars, 140-4; on world economic primacy of Victorian England, 160-2; on British reaction to changing economic position, 184
SIMONDS, F. H., on situation of Italy in Mediterranean, 277-8; on Germany's central position, 314
SMUTS, J. C., on future of Europe, 144-5
SPROUT, HAROLD, on role of Great Powers in keeping peace, 749-53
SPROUT, HAROLD and MARGARET, on British sea power in Victorian era, 163-6; on Capt. A. T. Mahan's interpretation of British sea power, 166-70; on Britain's changing position, 1890-1914, 171-2; on Anglo-American reorientation, 172-3; on Anglo-Japanese Alliance, 173; on British sea power in twentieth century, 173-80
SPYKMAN, N. J., on international politics, 8-15; on maps and map-making, 68-78; on political map of Eurasia, 101-6; on Africa's role in world politics, 465-6; on political

AUTHOR INDEX

geography of Far East, 490-4; on political geography of Americas, 615-28

STEIGER, A. J., on Soviet Middle East, 420-5

STRAUS-HUPÉ, ROBERT, see Harrison, R. E., and see Micaud, C. A.

STRESEMANN, GUSTAV, on German policies under the Republic, 343-6

SULZBERGER, C. L., on secret of Soviet strength, 432-3

TAEUBER, CONRAD, see Hauser, P. M.

TANNENBAUM, FRANK, on inter-American relations, 634-41

THOMSON, DAVID, on strategical position of France, 217

TREWARTHA, G. T., on Japanese population trends, 512-14

TURNER, RALPH, on technology and national power, 48-54

VAN VALKENBURG, SAMUEL, on defense frontiers of France, 217-20; on French food supply and defense, 221-2. See also Huntington, Ellsworth

WELLES, SUMNER, on Soviet aims and policies, 441-55; on peace terms for Germany, 698-708; on problem of peace in Far East, 724-30

WHITBECK, R. H., see Finch, V. C.

WHITTLESEY, DERWENT, on German science, technology and economics, 329-32; on German foreign policy under Second Reich, 337-8

WHITTLESEY, DERWENT, and WRIGHT, J. K., on economic development of France, 223-4; on French communications, 224-5; on French population and manpower, 225-6; on French Empire, 228-31; on unification of Germany, 313-14; on Germany's pre-war frontiers, 316-20; on space and terrain in defense of U.S.S.R., 400-3; on geography of U.S., 658-60

WILLKIE, WENDELL, on Soviet industry, 430-2

WOLFERS, ARNOLD, on French foreign policy, 1919-39, 233-7; on prerequisites of peace in Europe, 709-18; on role of lesser powers in world order, 757-62

WRIGHT, J. K., see Whittlesey, Derwent